THE LITERATURE
OF AMERICA   2

THE LITERATURE OF AMERICA 2

Irving Howe
Hunter College

Mark Schorer
University of California at Berkeley

Larzer Ziff
University of California at Berkeley

McGraw-Hill Book Company

*New York   St. Louis   San Francisco   Düsseldorf   Johannesburg
Kuala Lumpur   London   Mexico   Montreal   New Delhi
Panama   Rio de Janeiro   Singapore   Sydney   Toronto*

THE LITERATURE OF AMERICA 2

Library of Congress Catalog Card Number 75-149716

07-030572-2

1 2 3 4 5 6 7 8 9 0   M W M W   7 9 8 7 6 5 4 3 2 1

This book was set in Primer by Monotype Composition Company, Inc., and printed on permanent paper and bound by McGregor & Werner, Incorporated. The designer was Barbara Ellwood.
The editors were Cheryl Kupper, Robert Fry, and David Dunham.
Les Kaplan supervised production.

ACKNOWLEDGMENTS

HENRY ADAMS, Letters "To Charles Francis Adams, Jr.," "To John Gorham Palfrey," and "To William James" from *Letters of Henry Adams*, edited by Worthington Chauncy Ford. "American Ideals" from *History of the United States of America during the Administration of Thomas Jefferson.* Chapter 1, "Quincy," Chapter 17, "President Grant," Chapter 22, "Chicago," and Chapter 25, "The Dynamo and the Virgin," from *The Education of Henry Adams.* Copyright 1946 by Charles F. Adams. Reprinted by permission of Houghton Mifflin Company.

CONRAD AIKEN, "And in the Hanging Gardens," "The Wedding," "Tetélestai," and "Another Lycidas," from *Selected Poems* by Conrad Aiken. Copyright © 1961 by Conrad Aiken. Reprinted by permission of Oxford University Press, Inc.

JAMES AGEE, "Emma" from *Let Us Now Praise Famous Men* by James Agee. Copyright 1941 by James Agee and Walker Evans. Copyright © 1960 by Walker Evans. Reprinted by permission of the publisher, Houghton Mifflin Company.

EDWARD ALBEE, "The Zoo Story" by Edward Albee. Copyright © 1960 by Edward Albee. NOTICE: This play is the sole property of the author and is fully protected by copyright. It may not be acted by professionals or amateurs without written consent. Public readings and radio or television broadcasts are likewise forbidden. All inquiries concerning these rights should be addressed to the author's agent, The William Morris Agency, 1350 Avenue of the Americas, New York, New York.

SHERWOOD ANDERSON, "The Strength of God" and "The Teacher" from *Winesburg, Ohio*. Reprinted by permission of Harold Ober Associates Incorporated.

JAMES BALDWIN, "Notes of a Native Son" from *Notes of a Native Son* by James Baldwin. Reprinted by permission of the Beacon Press, copyright © 1955 by James Baldwin.

JOHN BARTH, "Lost in the Fun House," copyright © 1967 by The Atlantic Monthly Company, from *Lost in the Fun House* by John Barth. Reprinted by permission of Doubleday & Company, Inc.

DONALD BARTHELME, "Report." Reprinted with the permission of Farrar, Straus & Giroux, Inc., from *Unspeakable Practices, Unnatural Acts* by Donald Barthelme. Copyright © 1967 by Donald Barthelme.

SAUL BELLOW, "Looking for Mr. Green" from *Seize the Day* by Saul Bellow. Copyright 1951 by Saul Bellow. Reprinted by permission of The Viking Press, Inc.

JOHN BERRYMAN, "There sat down, once, a thing on Henry's heart" and "He lay in the middle of the world, and twitcht." Reprinted with the permission of Farrar, Straus & Giroux, Inc., from *77 Dream Songs* by John Berryman. Copyright © 1959, 1962, 1963, 1964 by John Berryman.

ELIZABETH BISHOP, "Little Exercise" from *Complete Poems* by Elizabeth Bishop. Copyright 1940, 1946, 1947, 1948, 1949, 1951, 1952, 1955 by Elizabeth Bishop. First appeared in *The New Yorker*. Reprinted by permission of Farrar, Straus & Giroux, Inc. "Sunday 4 a.m." from *Questions of Travel* by Elizabeth Bishop. Copyright © 1958 by Elizabeth Bishop. First published in *The New Yorker*.

RANDOLPH BOURNE, "Our Cultural Humility" from *History of a Literary Radical and Other Essays*, by Randolph Bourne. Copyright 1920 by B. W. Huebsch, Inc., 1948 by The Viking Press, Inc. Reprinted by permission of The Viking Press, Inc.

GWENDOLYN BROOKS, "The Ballad of Rudolph Reed" from *Selected Poems* by Gwendolyn Brooks. Copyright © 1960 by Gwendolyn Brooks Blakely. Reprinted by permission of Harper & Row, Publishers.

VAN WYCK BROOKS, " 'Highbrow' and 'Lowbrow' " from the book *Three Essays on America* by Van Wyck Brooks. Copyright, 1934, by E. P. Dutton & Co., Inc. Renewal, 1952, by Van Wyck Brooks. Reprinted by permission of the publishers.

JOHN CHEEVER, "The Swimmer" from *The Brigadier and the Golf Widow* by John Cheever. Copyright © 1964 by John Cheever. Reprinted by permission of Harper & Row, Publishers.

ELDRIDGE CLEAVER, from *Soul on Ice* by Eldridge Cleaver. Copyright © 1968 by Eldridge Cleaver. Used with permission of McGraw-Hill Book Company.

MALCOLM COWLEY, "The French Line Pier, 1921" and "Form and Matter" from *Exile's Return* by Malcolm Cowley. Copyright 1934, 1951, © 1962 by Malcolm Cowley. Reprinted by permission of The Viking Press, Inc.

HART CRANE, all poems from *Complete Poems and Selected Letters and Prose of Hart Crane* by Hart Crane. Permission by Liveright Publishers, New York. Copyright 1933, 1958, 1966 by Liveright Publishing Corp.

ROBERT CREELEY, "Jack's Blues" (copyright © 1960 Robert Creeley) and "The Rain" (copyright © 1962 Robert Creeley) are reprinted with the permission of Charles Scribner's Sons from *For Love* by Robert Creeley. "For No Clear Reason" is reprinted with the permission of Charles Scribner's Sons from *Words* by Robert Creeley. Copyright © 1967 Robert Creeley.

E. E. CUMMINGS, "All in green went my love riding," "in Just-," "o sweet spontaneous," "Buffalo Bill's," and "the Cambridge ladies who live in furnished souls" from *Poems 1923–1954* by E. E. Cummings. Copyright, 1923, 1951, by E. E. Cummings. All reprinted by permission of Harcourt, Brace & World, Inc. "POEM, OR BEAUTY HURTS MR. VINAL," "a man who had fallen among thieves," and "my sweet old etcetera" from *Poems 1923–1954* by E. E. Cummings. Copyright, 1926, by Horace Liveright; copyright, 1954, by E. E. Cummings. Reprinted by permission of Harcourt, Brace & World, Inc. "somewhere i have never travelled,gladly beyond" from *Poems 1923–1954* by E. E. Cummings. Copyright, 1931, 1959 by E. E. Cummings. Reprinted by permission of Harcourt, Brace & World, Inc. "as freedom is a breakfastfood," "anyone lived in a pretty how town," and "my father moved through dooms of love" from *Poems 1923–1954* by E. E. Cummings. Copyright, 1940, by E. E. Cummings; copyright, 1968, by Marion Morehouse Cummings. Reprinted by permission of Harcourt, Brace & World, Inc. "plato told," "pity this busy monster,manunkind," and "what if a much of a which of a wind" from *Poems 1923–1954* by E. E. Cummings. Copyright, 1944, by E. E. Cummings. Reprinted by permission of Harcourt, Brace & World, Inc.

JAMES DICKEY, "The War Wound," copyright © 1964 by James Dickey. "The War Wound" was first published in *The New Yorker*. "Dust," copyright © 1965 by James Dickey. Reprinted from *Buckdancer's Choice*, by James Dickey, by permission of Wesleyan University Press.

JOHN DOS PASSOS, "Playboy" and "Body of an American" from *Nineteen Nineteen*, second volume of USA trilogy, by John Dos Passos, 1932 and 1960, published by Houghton Mifflin Company. "Vag" from *The Big Money*, third volume of USA trilogy, by John Dos Passos, copyright by John Dos Passos 1936 and 1964, published by Houghton Mifflin Company.

RICHARD EBERHART, "The Groundhog" and "In a Hard Intellectual Light" from *Collected Poems: 1930–1960* by Richard Eberhart. © 1960 by Richard Eberhart. Reprinted by permission of Oxford University Press, Inc.

T. S. ELIOT, "The Love Song of J. Alfred Prufrock," "Sweeney Among the Nightingales," *The Waste Land*, and "Burnt Norton" from *Collected Poems 1909–1962* by T. S. Eliot. Copyright, 1936, by Harcourt, Brace & World, Inc.; copyright, © 1943, 1963, 1964, by T. S. Eliot. Reprinted by permission of the publishers.

RALPH ELLISON, "Out of the Hospital and Under the Bar" from *Soon, One Morning: New Writing by American Negroes, 1940–1962*, ed. Herbert Hill, 1963. Copyright © 1963 by Ralph Ellison. Reprinted by permission of William Morris Agency, Inc.

WILLIAM FAULKNER, "The Old People." Copyright 1940 and renewed 1968 by Estelle Faulkner and Jill Faulkner Summers. Copyright 1942 by William Faulkner. Reprinted from *Big Woods*, by William Faulkner, by permission of Random House, Inc.

F. SCOTT FITZGERALD, "Winter Dreams" (copyright 1922 Frances Scott Fitzgerald Lanahan; renewal copyright 1950) is reprinted with the permission of Charles Scribner's Sons from *All the Sad Young Men* by F. Scott Fitzgerald.

ROBERT FROST, "Mowing," "The Tuft of Flowers," "Reluctance," "The Pasture," "Mending Wall," "The Death of the Hired Man," "After Apple-Picking," "The Road Not Taken," "Birches," "Fire and Ice," "Dust and Snow," "Stopping by Woods on a Snowy Evening," "The Onset," "Spring Pools," "Tree at My Window," "The Investment," "Desert Places," "Design," "The Gift Outright," and "Directive" from *Complete Poems of Robert Frost*. Copyright 1916, 1923, 1928, 1930, 1934, 1939, 1947, © 1967 by Holt, Rinehart and Winston, Inc. Copyright 1936, 1942, 1944, 1951, © 1956, 1958, 1962 by Robert Frost. Copyright © 1964, 1967 by Lesley Frost Ballantine. Reprinted by permission of Holt, Rinehart and Winston, Inc. "The Draft Horse" from *In the Clearing* by Robert Frost. Copyright © 1962 by Robert Frost. Reprinted by permission of Holt, Rinehart and Winston, Inc.

ALLEN GINSBERG, "Howl" from *Howl and Other Poems* by Allen Ginsberg. Copyright © 1956, 1959 by Allen Ginsberg. Reprinted by permission of City Lights Books.

MICHAEL GOLD, "Wilder: Prophet of the Genteel Christ" from *Proletarian Literature in the United States*, copyright © 1935. Reprinted by permission of *International Publishers Co. Inc.*

ERNEST HEMINGWAY, "Big Two-hearted River" (Parts I and II) are reprinted
with the permission of Charles Scribner's Sons from *In Our Time* by
Ernest Hemingway. Copyright 1925 Charles Scribner's Sons; renewal
copyright, 1953 Ernest Hemingway.

RANDALL JARRELL, "The Death of the Ball Turret Gunner" and "The Orient
Express" from *Randall Jarrell: The Complete Poems,* copyright 1945, 1950
by Mrs. Randall Jarrell. Reprinted by permission of Farrar, Straus and
Giroux, Inc.

ROBINSON JEFFERS, "To the Stone-cutters," copyright 1924 and renewed 1952
by Robinson Jeffers. "Boats in a Fog," "Shine, Perishing Republic," "Joy,"
and "Science," copyright 1925 and renewed 1953 by Robinson Jeffers.
"Hurt Hawks," copyright 1928 and renewed 1956 by Robinson Jeffers.
"Fire on the Hills," copyright 1932 and renewed 1960 by Robinson Jeffers.
"Rock and Hawk," copyright 1934 and renewed 1962 by Donnan Jeffers
and Garth Jeffers. "The Purse-seine," copyright 1937 and renewed 1965 by
Donnan Jeffers and Garth Jeffers. Reprinted from *The Selected Poetry of
Robinson Jeffers* by permission of Random House, Inc.

SARAH ORNE JEWETT, The "Hiltons' Holiday," from *The Best Stories* of Sarah
Orne Jewett, published by Houghton Mifflin Company.

LEROI JONES, *Dutchman,* copyright © 1964 by LeRoi Jones. Reprinted by permission of The Sterling Lord Agency.

STANLEY KUNITZ, "Father and Son" and "The Daughters of the Horseleech"
from *Selected Poems: 1928–1958* by Stanley Kunitz, copyright © 1958, by
Stanley Kunitz. Reprinted by permission of Atlantic-Little, Brown and Co.

VACHEL LINDSAY, "General William Booth Enters into Heaven," copyright 1913
by The Macmillan Company. "The Congo," copyright 1914 by The Macmillan Company renewed 1942 by Elizabeth C. Lindsay. Reprinted with
permission of The Macmillan Company from *Collected Poems* by Vachel
Lindsay.

ROBERT LOWELL, "Grandparents," reprinted with the permission of Farrar,
Straus & Giroux from *Life Studies* by Robert Lowell, copyright © 1959 by
Robert Lowell. "For the Union Dead," reprinted with the permission of
Farrar, Straus & Giroux from *For the Union Dead* by Robert Lowell, copy-
right © 1960 by Robert Lowell.

CARSON MC CULLERS, "A Tree. A Rock. A Cloud." from *Ballad of a Sad Cafe*
by Carson McCullers. Copyright 1951, by Carson McCullers. Reprinted by
permission of the publisher, Houghton Mifflin Company.

NORMAN MAILER, "The White Negro." Reprinted by permission of G. P.
Putnam's Sons from *Advertisements For Myself* by Norman Mailer. Copyright © 1959 by Norman Mailer.

BERNARD MALAMUD, "Still Life." Reprinted with the permission of Farrar, Straus & Giroux, Inc., from *Idiots First* by Bernard Malamud, copyright © 1962 by Bernard Malamud.

H. L. MENCKEN, "The National Letters." Copyright 1920 by Alfred A. Knopf, Inc. and renewed 1948 by H. L. Mencken. Reprinted from *The Vintage Mencken*, gathered by Alistair Cooke, by permission of the publisher.

JAMES MERRILL, "The Country of a Thousand Years of Peace," copyright © 1958 by James Merrill. Reprinted from *The Country of a Thousand Years of Peace and Other Poems*, by James Merrill, by permission of Alfred A. Knopf, Inc. This poem first appeared in *The New Yorker*. "The Mad Scene," from *Nights and Days* by James Merrill. Copyright 1962, © 1966 by James Merrill. Reprinted by permission of Atheneum Publishers. This poem originally appeared in *Poetry*.

JOSEPHINE MILES, "Purchase of a Blue, Green, or Orange Ode" and "The Savages" from *Poems: 1930–1960* by Josephine Miles. Reprinted by permission of Indiana University Press.

MARIANNE MOORE, "To a Steam Roller," "The Fish," "Poetry," "Critics and Connoisseurs," "The Monkeys," and "Peter." Reprinted with permission of The Macmillan Company from *Selected Poems* by Marianne Moore. Copyright 1935 by Marianne Moore, renewed 1963 by Marianne Moore and T. S. Eliot. "What Are Years?" Copyright 1941 by Marianne Moore. Reprinted with permission of The Macmillan Company from *Collected Poems* by Marianne Moore. "Nevertheless," "The Mind is an Enchanting Thing," and "In Distrust of Merits." Copyright 1944 by Marianne Moore. Reprinted with permission of the Macmillan Company from *Collected Poems* by Marianne Moore. "Granite and Steel," copyright © 1966 by Marianne Moore. Originally appeared in *The New Yorker*. "W. S. Landor," copyright © 1964 by Marianne Moore. Originally appeared in *The New Yorker*. "Arthur Mitchell," all rights reserved. "Tell Me, Tell Me," copyright © 1960 by Marianne Moore. Originally appeared in *The New Yorker*. Reprinted by permission of The Viking Press, Inc.

LEWIS MUMFORD, "Envoi" from *The Golden Day: A Study in American Experience and Culture*, 1926, by Lewis Mumford. Dover Publications, Inc., New York. Reprinted through the permission of the publisher.

FLANNERY O'CONNOR, "Everything That Rises Must Converge." Reprinted with the permission of Farrar, Straus & Giroux, Inc., from *Everything That Rises Must Converge* by Flannery O'Connor, copyright © 1961, 1965 by the Estate of Mary Flannery O'Connor.

EUGENE O'NEILL, *Desire Under the Elms,* by Eugene O'Neill. Copyright 1924 and renewed 1952 by Eugene O'Neill. Reprinted from *Nine Plays By Eugene O'Neill* by permission of Random House, Inc. *Caution:* Profes-

sionals and amateurs are hereby warned that this play, being fully protected under the copyright laws of the United States of America, the
British Empire, including the Dominion of Canada, and all other countries of the copyright union, is subject to a royalty. All rights, including
professional, amateur, motion pictures, recitation, public reading, radio
broadcasting, and the rights of translation into foreign languages are
strictly reserved. In its present form this play is dedicated to the reading
public only. All inquiries should be addressed to Richard J. Madden, 522
Fifth Ave., New York City, N.Y.

SYLVIA PLATH, "Lady Lazarus" and "Daddy," copyright © 1963 by Ted
Hughes, from *Ariel* (1966) by Sylvia Plath. Reprinted by permission of
Harper & Row, Publishers.

KATHERINE ANNE PORTER, "The Downward Path to Wisdom" from *Collected
Stories*, 1965. Copyright 1939 by Katherine Anne Porter. Reprinted from
her volume *The Leaning Tower and Other Stories* by permission of Harcourt, Brace & World, Inc.

EZRA POUND, "Erat hora," "Portrait d'une femme," "A Virginal," "The Return,"
"Salutation," "A Pact," "The Rest," "In a Station of the Metro," and *Hugh
Selwyn Mauberley (Life and Contracts)* from Ezra Pound, *Personae*.
Copyright 1926, 1954 by Ezra Pound. Reprinted by permission of New
Directions Publishing Corporation. "Canto II" from Ezra Pound, *The
Cantos*. Copyright 1934, © 1956 by Ezra Pound. Reprinted by permission
of New Directions Publishing Corporation.

JOHN CROWE RANSOM, "Bells for John Whiteside's Daughter," "Here Lies a
Lady," and "Old Mansion," copyright 1924 by Alfred Knopf, Inc., and re-
newed 1952 by John Crowe Ransom. "Piazza Piece," "Blue Girls," "Dead
Boy," "Man without Sense of Direction," "Survey of Literature," "The
Equilibrists," copyright 1927 by Alfred A. Knopf, Inc. and renewed 1955
by John Crowe Ransom. "Painted Head," copyright 1934 by Alfred A.
Knopf, Inc., and renewed 1962 by John Crowe Ransom. Reprinted from
Selected Poems, by John Crowe Ransom, by permission of the publisher.

EDWIN ARLINGTON ROBINSON, "John Evereldown," "Richard Cory," "Zola,"
"George Crabbe," and "Credo" are reprinted with the permission of
Charles Scribner's Sons from *The Children of the Night* by Edwin Arlington Robinson (1897). "Miniver Cheevy" (copyright 1907 Charles Scribner's Sons; renewal copyright 1935) and "For a Dead Lady" (copyright
1910 Charles Scribner's Sons; renewal copyright 1938 Ruth Nivison) are
reprinted with the permission of Charles Scribner's Sons from *The Town
Down the River* by Edwin Arlington Robinson. "Cassandra," "Eros
Turannos," copyright 1916 by Edwin Arlington Robinson, renewed 1944
by Ruth Nivison. "Mr. Flood's Party," "Many Are Called," copyright 1921
by Edwin Arlington Robinson, renewed 1949 by Ruth Nivison. "The

Sheaves" and "New England," copyright 1925 by Edwin Arlington Robinson, renewed 1952 by Ruth Nivison and Barbara R. Holt. Reprinted with the permission of The Macmillan Company from *Collected Poems* by Edwin Arlington Robinson. "Isaac and Archibald," copyright 1915 by Edwin Arlington Robinson, renewed 1943 by Ruth Nivison.

THEODORE ROETHKE, "Frau Bauman, Frau Schmidt, and Frau Schwartze," copyright 1952 by Theodore Roethke (originally in *The New Yorker*); "Dolor," copyright 1943 by Modern Poetry Association, Inc.; "I Knew A Woman," copyright 1954 by Theodore Roethke, from *The Collected Poems of Theodore Roethke*. Reprinted by permission of Doubleday & Company, Inc.

CARL SANDBURG, "Chicago," "Fish Crier," and "I Am the People, the Mob," from *Chicago Poems* by Carl Sandburg. Copyright 1916 by Holt, Rinehart and Winston, Inc. Copyright 1944 by Carl Sandburg. "Cool Tombs" from *Cornhuskers* by Carl Sandburg. Copyright 1918 by Holt, Rinehart and Winston, Inc. Copyright 1946 by Carl Sandburg. Reprinted by permission of Holt, Rinehart and Winston, Inc. "Ossawatomie," "Losers," and "A.E.F." from *Smoke and Steel* by Carl Sandburg; copyright 1920 by Harcourt, Brace & World, Inc.; renewed 1948 by Carl Sandburg. Reprinted by permission of the publisher.

GEORGE SANTAYANA, "Materialism and Idealism in American Life" from *Character and Opinion in the United States*, published by Charles Scribner's Sons.

DELMORE SCHWARTZ, "In the Naked Bed, in Plato's Cave" by Delmore Schwartz, *Selected Poems: Summer Knowledge*. Copyright 1938 by New Directions. Reprinted by permission of New Directions Publishing Corporation. "Gold Morning, Sweet Prince," copyright 1943 by Harrison Blaine, Inc., from *Summer Knowledge*, by Delmore Schwartz. Reprinted by permission of Doubleday & Company, Inc.

ANNE SEXTON, "The Starry Night" from *All My Pretty Ones* by Anne Sexton. Copyright © 1961, 1962 by Anne Sexton. "Flee on Your Donkey" from *Live or Die*. Copyright © 1966 by Anne Sexton. Reprinted by permission of the publisher.

KARL SHAPIRO, "University," copyright 1940 and renewed 1968 by Karl Shapiro. "Lord, I Have Seen Too Much," copyright 1944 by Karl Shapiro. Reprinted from *Selected Poems*, by Karl Shapiro, by permission of Random House, Inc.

W. D. SNODGRASS, "The Operation," copyright © 1959 by W. D. Snodgrass. "The Campus on the Hill," copyright © 1958 by W. D. Snodgrass. Reprinted from *Heart's Needle*, by W. D. Snodgrass. Reprinted by permission of Alfred A. Knopf, Inc.

WALLACE STEVENS, "The Plot Against the Giant," "Domination of Black," "The Emperor of Ice-cream," "Disillusionment of Ten O'clock," "Sunday Morning," "Anecdote of the Jar," "Peter Quince at the Clavier," and "Thirteen Ways of Looking at a Blackbird," copyright 1923 and renewed 1951 by Wallace Stevens. "The Idea of Order at Key West" and "The Man with the Blue Guitar," copyright 1936 by Wallace Stevens and renewed 1964 by Elsie Stevens and Holly Stevens. "The Glass of Water" and "Of Modern Poetry," copyright 1942 by Wallace Stevens. Reprinted from *The Collected Poems of Wallace Stevens* by permission of Alfred A. Knopf, Inc.

ALLEN TATE, "Ode to the Confederate Dead" (copyright 1932 Charles Scribner's Sons; renewal copyright © 1960 Allen Tate) and "Winter Mask to the Memory of W. B. Yeats" (copyright 1945 Allen Tate) and "Mr. Pope" are reprinted with the permission of Charles Scribner's Sons from *Poems* (1960) by Allen Tate.

JEAN TOOMER, "Avey" from *Cane* by Jean Toomer. Permission of Liveright, Publishers, New York. Copyright R 1951 by Jean Toomer.

DAVID WAGONER, "Staying Alive," from *Staying Alive* by David Wagoner. Reprinted by permission of Indiana University Press.

GEORGE WALD, "A Generation in Search of a Future." Reprinted with the permission of George Wald.

ROBERT PENN WARREN, "Original Sin: A Short Story" and "Bearded Oaks," copyright 1942 by Robert Penn Warren. Reprinted from *Selected Poems: New and Old,* 1923–1966, by Robert Penn Warren, by permission of Random House, Inc.

EUDORA WELTY, "Livvie," copyright, 1942, by Eudora Welty. Reprinted from her volume *The Wide Net* by permission of Harcourt, Brace & World, Inc.

EDITH WHARTON, "The Other Two," from *The Descent of Man* by Edith Wharton (Charles Scribner's Sons, 1904).

RICHARD WILBUR, "Love Calls Us to the Things of This World" from *Things of This World,* © 1956, by Richard Wilbur. Reprinted by permission of Harcourt, Brace & World, Inc. "Shame," © 1961 by Richard Wilbur. Reprinted from his volume *Advice to a Prophet and Other Poems* by permission of Harcourt, Brace & World, Inc.

THORNTON WILDER, "The Skin of Our Teeth" in *Three Plays* by Thornton Wilder. Copyright, 1942 by Thornton Wilder. Reprinted by permission of Harper & Row, Publishers. *Caution! The Skin of Our Teeth* is the sole property of the author and is fully protected by copyright. It may not be acted by professionals or amateurs without formal permission and the payment of a royalty. All rights, including professional, amateur, stock, radio and television, broadcasting, motion picture, recitation, lecturing,

CONTENTS

PREFACE

For a preface to be helpful to the prospective reader, it should conform to the Latin root of the word, and say something "beforehand." Let this preface, then, be a guide to these books and not a repetition of what is so ably said in the critical introductions provided by the three editors.

Covering three and one-half centuries of American literature is an impossible task, as any instructor knows. Even in a three-semester course, the difficult choice to sacrifice fascinating but minor authors and many social and historical documents must be made. Wherever possible, the editors sought to confine their personal tastes and subjective judgments to general introductions and headnotes and to make objective choices among authors and selections. The emphasis, of course, was on major authors, most of them represented in depth, and on as many writers of lesser stature as space allowed. From the opening selection by John Smith to the last by George Wald, literary merit was the primary criterion of choice, relevance to the age and to intellectual history the second.

Volume One opens with Professor Ziff's introduction to the Colonial Period, a tightly knit evaluation of the first 200 years of America's writing. He represents these two centuries with a wide variety of genres: poetry, journals, history, letters, theological treatises, political essays, drama. Names such as Bradford, Byrd, Wigglesworth, Edwards, Taylor, and political writers such as Jefferson, Adams, Paine, and Madison are familiar to all students of the period. Others less frequently reprinted are Thomas Morton of Merrymount fame, the poets Samuel Danforth and Thomas Tillam, and the leading representative of New England Federalism, Fisher Ames. Mr. Ziff represents the Connecticut Wits by excerpting works by John Trumbull, Timothy Dwight, and Joel Barlow, and perhaps most important of all, he introduces the student to the first comedy written by an American, Royall Tyler's *The Contrast*.

Professor Howe's introduction to the first half of the nineteenth century culminates with the condescending question first raised by Sidney Smith in 1820: "An American literature?" Twenty-eight authors illustrate the richness of our early national period. The first group includes the New York writers: Irving, Cooper, Bryant, and Poe, as well as John James Audubon and Richard

Henry Dana. In addition to the familiar New England Brahmins, he includes poems by Jones Very and Frederick Goddard Tuckerman. The American Renaissance, which includes Emerson, Thoreau, Hawthorne, Melville, Whitman, and Dickinson, bulks the heaviest. Some may wonder why the last two writers do not appear in Volume Two, since Whitman was still writing in the 1890s and America did not see much of Emily Dickinson's poetry until that decade. Yet *Leaves of Grass* first appeared in 1855 and went through three new editions in the next twelve years, and Emily Dickinson accomplished over half of her work between 1859 and 1865, placing both poets in the company of our great mid-nineteenth-century writers.

Mr. Howe's final section gathers together a group of writers speaking of the Civil War. It includes fiction, poetry, and prose by Lincoln, Grant, Timrod, Bierce, and Stowe, of course, but also the memoirs of an ex-slave, Frederick Douglass, the fiction of John William DeForest, the diaries of Mary Boykin Chestnutt, and the recollections of Benjamin Shepard under the pseudonym of Francis Grierson.

Volume Two opens with an introduction to the Gilded Age and its attendant problems of "urbanism, industrialism, mass migration, political corruption, and terror against the freed black man," coupled with its tenacious dream of the frontier. The direct conflict between this "dream of paradise," portrayed in Cooper's Natty Bumppo and Mark Twain's Huck Finn as "anarchic yearning," and "fixed authority," with the "coarse actualities" of business and the growth of the cities, forms the substance of this section. Mr. Howe's final group of selections traces the change from vernacular to sophisticated art—from the myth of Davy Crockett to the regionalism of Longstreet and Jewett to the grim realism of Twain and Stephen Crane. Professor Schorer's first section bridges the two centuries with a series of critiques of our culture before World War I by Henry Adams, William James, George Santayana, and others. These two sections emphasize socio-historic concerns for the best of reasons. Except for a few novelists, the last forty years of the nineteenth century were devoid of major writers. The American theatre awaited the advent of a Eugene O'Neill, poetry the advent of a Frost and an Eliot.

Had Professor Schorer only to cope with O'Neill, Eliot, or any twenty other major figures, his problem would have been greatly simplified. As his introduction to the twentieth century clearly indicates, American letters after 1914 burgeoned; words like "ebullience" and "explosion" quite naturally describe the appearance of new writers and the achievements of men born in the closing years of the nineteenth century. Among three score important names in poetry alone, Mr. Schorer settled on a substantial representation of fifteen poets born before 1900, followed by a brilliant cross-section of "younger" poets, those who came to prominence in the forties and spanned the fifties as well as the new voices of the sixties. Fiction he treats in the same chronological fashion.

Our nation's array of playwrights was more difficult to sample. O'Neill's *Desire Under the Elms* serves to introduce what was called "experimental theatre" in the 1920s. Then Mr. Schorer moves from the social drama of the thirties to the Off-Broadway theatre of the sixties with Thornton Wilder's inventive *The Skin of Our Teeth* (1942) and two contemporary one-act plays considered shocking when first produced in New York, Edward Albee's *The Zoo Story* (1958) and LeRoi Jones's *Dutchman* (1964).

One final word. It would have been possible to impose a uniform approach on all this material, to ask the three editors to standardize their introductions and headnotes, but the publishers decided from the outset that personal opinions, even *very* personal opinions, bring life to literary anthologies. As a consequence, each section of these two volumes bears the stamp of individual taste. The academic impedimenta—footnotes, bibliographies, guides to sources—are regularized, of course, but beyond that we hope students and instructors alike will find the editorial matter a reflection not only of different ages in our country's literary history but also of differing critical judgments.

Richard M. Ludwig
Princeton, New Jersey

Introduction: 1860s to 1900

Among cultivated Americans in the years directly after the Civil War, a feeling gradually arose that the republic had lost its bearings. Few thoughtful persons could continue to believe that the country still lived by the earlier vision of a simple egalitarianism. A whole array of new problems made themselves felt—urbanism, industrialism, mass immigration, political corruption, terror directed against the freed black men. American society seemed to have turned in an unfamiliar and puzzling direction.

The literary effects were slow in coming, and in any case, the ten or fifteen years after the Civil War were not—in terms of published writing—exactly brilliant. Melville wrote his angular and anguished war poems during the years of the fighting, though by now he had scarcely an audience left. Whitman wrote his tender poems of wartime suffering and then subsided into relatively minor work. And in the next several decades some of the leading generals, like Grant and Sherman, published memoirs of the war that were remarkably vivid and well written. The first major novel about the war, however, did not appear until 1895, when a brilliant young writer named Stephen Crane published *The Red Badge of Courage*.

Though barren for literature, the years immediately following the Northern victory were marked by a tremendous economic expansion. "The Gilded Age," "the Age of the Robber Barons," "the Age of the Great Barbecue"—these are some of the unflattering designations that cultural historians have given to the 1870s and 1880s. During these years American society took on the major characteristics of industrial capitalism: a large-scale concentration of wealth and power in a few hands, the growth of enormous personal fortunes, the use of technology and science for industrial development, bitter clashes between corporations and newly organized workers.

Abraham Lincoln himself had foreseen these developments and the problems they would bring:

I see in the near future a crisis arising that unnerves me and causes me to tremble for the safety of my country. By a result of the war, corporations have been enthroned, and an era of corruption in high places will follow, and the money power of the country will endeavor to prolong its reign by working upon the prejudices of the people, until all wealth is aggregated in a few hands and the Republic is destroyed.

Economic and technological changes were amazingly rapid. Between 1865 and 1900 railroad mileage in the United States increased from thirty-five thousand to two hundred thousand. Built with the sweat of underpaid immigrant labor, and made possible by generous federal subsidies in the form of land grants, the railroads helped create a unified national economy. Between 1865 and 1878 United States internal investment in manufactures increased from 1½ billion dollars to 3 billion dollars. In 1864 the Bessemer process for the making of steel was introduced, and by 1879 the production of steel in the United States had reached 925,000 tons. Similar developments took place in the meat-packing industry—the spread of railroads, the invention of refrigeration—and in the production of oil. Clothes began to be mass- and machine-manufactured, cheaply and in bright colors. Within the major industries, the factory system—involving careful division of labor, the breakdown of work into relatively simple tasks, strict supervision of employees by foremen, and the rationalization of production in accordance with "scientific" precepts—became more and more prevalent. Together with these developments went the growth of a modern communications industry, first through the telegraph (1844) and then the telephone (1876). And even the countryside experienced a trend toward mechanization and concentration, with the family farm slowly being replaced by commercial agriculture requiring investments in mechanical equipment beyond the capacity of many small farmers.

A new class of millionaires arose—the Carnegies in steel, the Rockefellers in oil, the Fricks in coal. Some, later to be called the "Robber Barons," were unscrupulous speculators in stock manipulations. The number of millionaires increased from a mere handful in the early 1860s to more than 4,000 by the early 1890s. A sense of the business methods and morals of the period is suggested by the historian Allan Nevins in *The Emergence of Modern America*:

The most lurid light upon the rudimentary commercial morals of the period and the legal defenselessness of the public was that thrown by the great railway freebooters, whose operations were well launched before Grant took office. Daniel Drew, Jay Gould and Cornelius Vanderbilt, three New Yorkers, battled with an unscrupulousness previously unknown in American finance. All three men had risen from the humblest estate to positions of financial might. . . . Drew was born on a small farm in Putnam County, where he began life as a cattle drover; Gould, the son of a farmer in Delaware County, was successively a clerk in a country store, a surveyor and a tanner; while Vanderbilt, a native of Staten Island, had gained his first capital by running a ferry to Manhattan. Drew, now a very old man but as energetic and unscrupulous as ever, was no better than a sharper though he maintained a snuffling piety. Whenever he had been unusually fortunate in plucking trustful men, he salved his conscience by a grant to some philanthropic object; it was he who founded the Drew Theological Seminary in New Jersey with promised gifts totaling a million, most of which was never delivered. Gould was a coldhearted corruptionist who never hesitated to debauch a newspaper, prostitute a legislature or make city officials his pawns. As for Vanderbilt (called "the Commodore" from his success in building boats), he maintained an air of high respectability and public spirit, but he never forgot his pocket interests.

Vanderbilt's effort in the late sixties to wrest control of the Erie from Drew and Drew's associate, Gould, brought on a veritable battle of the giants in which all thought of public rights and all considerations of decency were lost. The "Commodore" played a lone hand. Drew not only relied heavily upon the cunning Gould, but enlisted also the extraordinary figure known as "Jim" Fisk. Fisk had begun his career as a peddler in Vermont, had been the manager of an itinerant circus and had finally made a profitable place for himself among the New York stock gamblers. He became distinguished as a fat, flashy, boastful voluptuary who kept a harem of mistresses, maintained a costly opera house, and lived a life of gilded luxury. This triumvirate not only outplayed Vanderbilt, but employed methods that shocked the whole nation as a revelation of business corruption run wild.

From Europe, especially the Slavic and east European countries, there came vast numbers of immigrants. They poured into the new industrial cities in the East and Midwest, ready to work hard for low wages in order to get a start in the New World. Inevitably, bitter and violent strikes broke out, such as the country had never seen before, and large-scale trade-union organization began, first in the craft-oriented Knights of Labor and then in the more inclusive American Federation of Labor.

Great cities, bursting with slums and corruption, sprang up. In 1860 only one-sixth of the American population lived in cities, but by 1900 the percentage had dramatically increased to one-third. In twenty years, between 1880 and 1900, the population of Chicago tripled, from half a million to a million and a half. All the blights of urban life with which Americans of our own time are only too familiar, began to make their appearance in these years: crime, juvenile delinquency, prostitution, oppression of the poor.

American society, even in the 1870s and 1880s, was not without its social critics, men who kept pointing, often vainly, to the growth of economic injustice and the lowered tone of public life. In addition to social reformers, the more aristocratic intellectuals, of whom Henry Adams was the most distinguished example, felt a growing despair over the quality of American society: its corruption, its vulgarity, its crass materialism, its indulgence in a fatuous and superficial "optimism," and its turn toward the pernicious doctrines of Social Darwinism, according to which human life is organized on an analogy to that of the jungle, and men inevitably find themselves caught up in a cutthroat struggle in which only the "fittest" (often the richest) survive.

In the far West, as the Indians were steadily beaten back and deprived of their rights, the land was being finally settled—the last stage of a great sweep of social migration. By 1890 the frontier was gone. The country had been completely, if sparsely, settled, and the hope for a new start in the West, by now a deeply ingrained part of American mythology, could no longer prompt thousands of Easterners to uproot themselves each year. Yet the frontier has remained a powerful force in our cultural life, growing all the stronger in our shared nostalgic fantasies (the Western movie, the cowboy hero) as it has ceased to be a practical solution to our problems in reality.

Meanwhile, after the brief period of Reconstruction, during which federal authority was directly exerted in the Southern states and the former slaves enjoyed a measure of political freedom, the South gradually reestablished a more subtle, though by no means benevolent, version of its old racial hierarchy. Terror was frequently used against the Negroes; relations were improved with the federal government (which by the late 1870s had abandoned whatever slight intention it had of helping the former slaves gain economic independence); and as a result, the remnants of the old plantation class, together with a new class of commercial parasites and predators, reconsolidated political power in the South. Between the end of the war and 1900, the Southern states enacted a series of Jim Crow laws enforcing segregation quite as rigidly as—and sometimes with greater brutality than—it had enforced slavery itself.

For American writers and intellectuals, indeed for all thoughtful Americans, this was a depressing time. They felt the values of the older Jeffersonian America slipping away and the values of the new industrial America proving brutish and corrupt. "Wherever men of cultivation looked," writes the historian Richard Hofstadter, "they found themselves facing hostile forces and an alien mentality." There emerged a "peculiarly American underground of frustrated aristocrats, a type of genteel reformer whose very existence dramatized the alienation of education and intellect from significant political and economic power." Somewhat later, after the turn of the century, this revulsion from the grossness of the new American ruling classes would be expressed with a witty fastidiousness in *The Education of Henry Adams*. More immediately, during the 1870s and 1880s, other writers responded with open disgust and silent dismay. Mark Twain publicly lashed out against the vulgarities of commercialism, frequently succumbed to them himself, and then ricocheted to a misanthropic pessimism. Melville shrank into virtual anonymity, quite forgotten by American readers and clearly not at ease in a world he had so uncannily anticipated in his book *The Confidence-Man.* Among our major writers only Walt Whitman, aging into the serenity of a native saint, tried directly to cope with the problem of American society. In his lengthy essay *Democratic Vistas* he remained stubbornly, even heroically, faithful to the democratic and egalitarian ideal.

Whitman lashed out in two directions, first against those intellectuals who had withdrawn into aristocratic notions of culture and looked down their noses at "the mob," and then against those who had succumbed to the corruptions of the marketplace. It was the latter who drew his main attention, for it was they who now seemed the more immediate and larger threat. "Everywhere in shop, street, church, theatre, barroom, official chair are pervading flippancy and vulgarity, low cunning, infidelity;" everywhere "the depraving influences of riches just as much as poverty, the absence of all high ideals of character." As against the sterile gentility of the Brahmins and the "optimistic" mindlessness of those who aligned themselves with the new industrial society, Whitman advanced a vision of "the People" as a source of strength and value, "the People" from whom there might yet come "a sublime and serious Religious Democracy." As against the cult of "individualism, which isolated" men from other men, he spoke for "adhesiveness or love, that fuses, ties and aggregates." As against the paleface writings of Boston and "the mean flat average" of the popular writers of the moment, he proposed a vigorous democratic culture in which men would cultivate independent tastes, reading would be "not a half-sleep but ... a gymnast's struggle," and the United States yet become "a nation of supple and athletic minds."

Moving these words still are; but the truth is that Whitman failed to answer the question of how and whether this vision could be realized—perhaps because no answer existed. A democratic culture in which men would be both equal and independent, fraternal and strong-minded—yes. But how could that culture flourish, how could it so much as survive, in a world ruled by money and brute force? The estrangement of the artist from commercial society which has become a commonplace of twentieth-century life, Whitman foresaw and disliked; but he had no solution for the problems that gave rise to this estrangement. His noble voice would echo through the following decades and inspire other critics of our culture, but the perplexities with which he grappled in *Democratic Vistas* he could not finally cope with. Nor, for that matter, has anyone else.

In the two decades that followed the Civil War, the major American writers went their own and often lonely ways. Emily Dickinson, living in Amherst and all but deaf to mundane American society, wrote her poems and kept the bulk of them in manuscript; Mark

Twain wrote his novels and stories; Herman Melville, the works of his old age, mostly short fiction; and Whitman, the occasional minor poems of his declining years. What was popular, and to some extent new, during these years was the work of several groups of regional writers who have since been lumped under the heading of "local color." In the South, the West, and New England the local-color writers sought to depict—sometimes to exploit for purposes of romantic sentimentalism—the distinctive traits of regional society and culture. (For further comments on local-color writers, see page 806.) The best of these writers, like Sarah Orne Jewett in New England, made their local observation into a foundation for a strong realism dealing with the life of common people. In the Midwest there arose a number of writers, limited in talent but serious and honest in intent, who wrote about farm and small-town life with an unprecedented astringency: Ed Howe in *The Story of a Country Town*, Joseph Kirkland in *Zury: The Meanest Man in Spring County*, Hamlin Garland in *Main Traveled Roads*. Grim and often depressing reports of disillusionment with farm and small-town life in the Midwest, such books tried primarily to dispel the genteel deceits of popular writing and the ingrained self-deceptions of popular mythology in late-nineteenth-century America. They focused on the moral parochialism, the psychic repressiveness, and the social injustices of agrarian America; they were concerned, above all, to tell a bitter truth about the meanness and deprivation of that part of American life which was most often romanticized; they expressed the desire of sensitive young men to break loose from their provincial origins and find some principle of humaneness with which to look back upon their younger years. Some of these books now seem more interesting as social reportage than as imaginative literature; but they had a distinct importance as pioneer efforts in the turn to realism which became the central fact about American writing during the 1880s and 1890s.

One literary historian, Bernard Bowron, has keenly described some of the forces in American culture which led serious writers to turn toward a socially critical and harshly worded realism:

Disenchantment is a great power for realism; and, as a somewhat younger generation of writers took the measure of rural America, they found less and less reason to idealize it. It had been all very well for Jefferson, in his remote world, to declare that "those who work in the earth are the chosen people of God . . . whose breasts He has made His peculiar deposit for substantial and genuine virtues." But Jefferson . . . had not lived to see the countryside put under bondage to the cities. In post Civil-War America . . . technology had shifted the political and cultural axis of our civilization. As the "Lord of the Soil" lost his potency as folk hero, the urban tycoon stepped in to take his place. The farmer was now only a hick, a hayseed; even his sons deserted him for the richer possibilities of city life. The westward movement was reversing itself. One response to this tremendous social fact was the nostalgia of the local color regionalists. A more significant one was the regionalism of disillusion. Men like Ed Howe, Hamlin Garland, Harold Frederic—thoroughly ambivalent about their own rural origins—tried to examine their regions in the light of the altered social perspective. . . .

Clearly, their disillusion with the agrarian myth struck very deep. It was not just a question of whether the American farmer was more or less prosperous and content than he was supposed to be. What was at issue, rather, was an entire way of life, now losing its power over the mind as the world of cities superseded it. . . .

It was the particular importance of the novelist William Dean Howells that he served as a cultural link between the older and the newer America. He was the friend of Mark Twain, the prose elegist of pastoral America, and the friend of Henry James, the novelist who would bridge the gap between New England innocence and European sophistication. Howells had grown up in agrarian Ohio and later remembered his youth with a fond nostalgia, but he wrote most of his realistic novels about the life of Americans in the cities. He depicted the gradual decline of old-fashioned, individualist businessmen when assaulted by unscrupulous operators, the violence of conflict between worker and employer, the ways in which life in the city came increasingly to resemble a jungle where ". . . the fierce struggle for survival, with the stronger life persisting . . . seemed . . . lawless, goodless." A benign and mild figure himself, closer in temperament to the simplicities he had left behind than to the bewildering problems he now felt obliged to confront, Howells embodied in his own career the transition of American literature from a realism of agrarian disillusion to a realism of urban dismay. (Further discussion of realism in American writing and the idea of literary realism itself can be found on pages 808–810.)

The century ends with Stephen Crane's harshly realistic *Maggie*, a novel about a tenement girl's fall into prostitution and suicide, intended, as Crane wrote, "to show that environment is a tremendous thing in the world and frequently shapes lives regardless. . . ." After *Maggie*, Crane went ahead to write *The Red Badge of Courage*, a great novel about men in the Civil War, which is realistic in temper but more artful in method than those techniques we usually associate with the term "realism."

Howells and Crane had made their contribution; Henry James would continue writing until the First World War; Theodore Dreiser would soon appear on the literary scene. The way lay clear for the beginning of twentieth-century American writing.

IV

Any literature as far-ranging as that of nineteenth-century America must clearly have a wide diversity of themes, preoccupations, techniques, and forms. Suppose, however, we ask ourselves by way of conclusion: Can we discover, at whatever risk of simplification, a major unifying theme or preoccupation in nineteenth-century American literature? Even to attempt this, we must put aside the new realistic writings of the 1880s and 1890s and concentrate instead on the work of those who wrote before the Civil War or whose careers span both the pre- and post-Civil War periods.

For many of our writers in the first half of the nineteenth century, and for some, like Mark Twain, in the second half, America as a collective experience signified the possibility of a new start for humanity, paradise regained. The wilderness and sometimes the frontier appeared to writers like Cooper and Twain (and in our own century, to a writer like Faulkner) as source and scene of mobility, freedom, innocence. Once society developed, it tended to hollow out these values. And not one or another form of society, not a better or worse society, but the very idea of society itself was regarded with skepticism and distaste.

This myth—it lies deeply imbedded in our fictions and legends—borrows credence from the hold of the frontier on our national life. A myth of space, it recalls a time when men could measure their independence by their physical distance from one another. It is a myth that records the secret voice of a society regretting its own existence.

Inescapably the settling of the wilderness was a violation. For a short time afterward a precarious balance could still be established between the natural and the social—a balance which might preserve a margin of paradise. But the pioneer equilibrium could not last for long, and soon the wilderness was gone. So, too, was the possibility of an independent and self-sustained life: paradise had been lost, again.

This on the level of myth—that is, those deepest attitudes, stories, and legends which, in their sum, animate a culture. But on the level of history, things are very different. The Founding Fathers of the United States were hard-headed and realistic men who set about creating a state that would protect their social interests while at the same time avoiding tyranny, both aristocratic and popular. As they went at the task of state-making, they grasped the need to reconcile a wide range of conflicting interests in a society which, precisely because it was a society, could yield only limited satisfactions.

They worked into the Constitution a series of balances, which to this very day inhibit both the direct expression of the popular will and the tendencies toward autocratic usurpation. It is a system which rests on the premise that the best way to ensure stable social conditions and provide adequate protection of human rights is through a politics of countervailing coalitions. In the *Federalist* papers James Madison stated the philosophical premise behind this system of government with classical precision:

> Ambition must be made to counteract ambition.... It may be a reflection on human nature that such devices should be necessary to control the abuses of government. But what is government itself but the greatest of all reflections on human nature? If men were angels, no government would be necessary.... In framing a government which is to be administered by men over men, the great difficulty lies in this: you must first enable the government to control the governed; and in the next place oblige it to control itself.

Now the question we encounter is this: Could the principles upon which the American government was founded and the expectations that had arisen with the beginning of American settlement be at all reconciled? Can one bring together the worldly realism of the *Federalist* papers with the edenic nostalgia expressed by so many nineteenth-century writers? That this conflict was a real one, and so regarded by the principle actors, may be seen in a caustic passage Hamilton wrote for the *Federalist* papers:

> Reflections of this kind [in behalf of a balance of power] may have trifling weight with men who hope to see realized in America the halcyon scenes of the poetic or fabulous age; but to those who believe we are likely to experience a common portion of the vicissitudes and calamities which have fallen to the lot of other nations ... etc., etc.

During the 1820s and 1830s, many Americans must have felt that a harmonious relation between institutions and desires was indeed possible. Soon enough, everything changed. With time, it became clear that America was trapped in a conflict between its guiding institutions (better though these might seem than any other within sight or memory) and its guiding myth (poignant as this would seem in its absolute unrealizability). And from this conflict there have followed enormous consequences.

Classical European literature often displays an extratemporal dimension—its urge to transcendence breaks past the cramped social horizons and crowded spaces of an old world, to create itself anew in the guise of an ideal future, a heavenly prospect sanctioned by Christianity and thereby removed from the paltriness of time. But at least until the idea of America takes hold of the European imagination there is, for Europeans, no place else to go. Locked into space, they can only transfer their hopes to a time beyond time. Their escape is vertical.

In nineteenth-century American literature the wish to break past the limits of the human condition manifests itself through images of space. Our characteristic fictions chart journeys not so much in order to get their heroes out of America but to transport the idea of America into a new and undefiled space. The urge to transcendence appears in our fictions as accounts of men who move away, past frontiers and borders, into the "territory" or out to sea, in order to preserve their images of possibility. For the enticements of space offer the hope—perhaps only a delusion—of a new beginning: so that, for a time, an individual hero can be seen as reenacting, within or beyond the society, the myth upon which the society rests but which it has not been able to fulfill. In America this new start is seen not so much in terms of an improvement or a reordering of the social structure, but as a leap wholly beyond the edge of society—a wistful ballet of transcendence.

Now many critics have noticed these elements in our literature, and have usefully discussed them in terms of an Adamic myth, a wish to return to innocence, a nostalgia for the purity we never had. Or they have seen in our writing a wish to escape the guilt brought on by the defilement of the countryside; to put down the burdens of success, family, and women; and to be done with the whole idea of society and sink back into a state of primal fraternity: blood brothers on the raft, the hunting ground, the lonely river—everyone (black, red, and white) in common friendliness.

Let us see what happens, however, if we accept this approach to nineteenth-century American literature and then somewhat shift its terms. Let us see what happens if we acknowledge the cogency of interpreting many of our major poems and fictions as releasing a hunger for a state of nature not yet soiled by history and commerce; if we further agree that troubled responses to sexuality and perhaps a wish to discard the threat of mature sexual life in behalf of a fellowship of innocents are involved in these poems and fictions; and if we then look at them in political terms.

It is a special kind of politics that is here at stake: not primarily the usual struggles for power among contending classes within a fixed society; nor the study of the mechanics of power as employed by a stable ruling class; nor even the dynamics of party maneuvering; but rather a politics concerned with the *idea* of society itself, a politics that dares consider—wonderful question—whether society is good and—still more wonderful—whether society is necessary. The paradox of it all is that a literature which on any manifest level is not really political at all, a literature which has little to tell us about the social surface and instead reaches for the psychic and metaphysical depths of man, should nevertheless be precisely the literature to raise the most fundamental problems in political theory: what is the rationale for society, the justification for the state?

And if we agree for a moment—as a limited perspective—so to regard nineteenth-century American literature, we discover running through it a strong if subterranean current of anarchism.

Not anarchism as the political movement known to nineteenth-century Europe: a movement with an established ideology and a spectrum of emphases ranging from populism to terrorism. That kind of thing has meant very little in the United States. We have in mind something else: anarchism as a social vision arising spontaneously and with the greatest urgency from the conditions of preindustrial American culture: anarchism as a bias of the American imagination in terms of its deepest, which is perhaps to say, its most frustrated yearnings.

Anarchism here signifies a vision of a human community beyond the calculation of good and evil; beyond the need for the state as an apparatus of law and suppression; beyond the yardsticks of moral measurement; beyond the need, in fact, for the constraints of authority. It envisages a community of autonomous persons, each secure in his own being and aware of his own mind. Anarchism here signifies a collective wish to refuse the contaminations of history, precisely at the point where the nation's history begins to seem oppressive and irreversible. The anarchist vision coursing through nineteenth-century American literature speaks for a wish to undo or unravel restrictions which violate the deepest myth of the very society which has felt the necessity of establishing these restrictions. What is novel here is the assumption that because of our blessed locale we could find space—a little beyond the border, further past the shore—in which to return, backward and free, to a stateless fraternity, so that the very culture created on the premise of mankind's second chance would, in failing that chance, yet allow its people a series of miniature recurrences.

The oppressive system of laws, what Melville would later call the "forms" in *Billy Budd*, gives way to the self-ordering discipline of persons in a fraternal relationship. While this relationship is seen as enabled by, and perhaps only possible within, the arena of an unsullied nature, it is not so much the thought of pastorale which excites our major nineteenth-century writers as it is a vision of human ease, brotherhood, and comradeship being fulfilled within the pastoral setting. And thereby the problem of authority, perhaps the most difficult that can be faced in political thought, is—at least on the imaginative plane—simply dissolved: which to some of us may seem a solution as inadequate as it is entrancing.

The dream of paradise is lodged deep in the imaginations of our nineteenth-century American writers, as in those of almost all sensitive
Americans of the time. Yet they live in a society Madison helped to
form, Jackson to reform, and the expansion of American business
to transform. The conviction that injustice and vulgarity grow
stronger during the nineteenth century is shared by many of our
writers—a conviction, finally, that an America is being created
which frustrates both the dream of a new Eden and the political
idea of a democracy resting upon sturdy, independent citizens.
Neither in practice nor thought can our writers find a way of dealing with this sense of disenchantment, if only because the country
with which they become disenchanted has itself been the object of
enormous expectations. In their bitterness with the social reality
and their tacit recognition that they cannot really affect its course,
American writers seek to get around or to "transcend" the intracta-
bility of what they encounter. Whatever they cannot change
head-on, they will now turn away from, clinging meanwhile to that
anarchic vision which seems all the more beautiful as it reaches
into the distance of lost possibilities. And thereby they create an
ideal place of the imagination—precarious, transient, unstained—
which speaks far more eloquently to the inner desires of our collective life than it can represent or cope with its coarse actualities.

Is this not a paradigm of *Huckleberry Finn,* as Mark Twain turned
from the torments of slavery and all it represents to the idyll of
Nigger Jim and Huck on the raft? If American literature in the
nineteenth century seldom succeeds in depicting with any complexity or directness the rough textures of social life, it nevertheless
has an enormous relevance to our moral life.

This vision first appears with imaginative strength in James Fenimore
Cooper's fiction. Like Hawthorne after him, Cooper was deeply
conservative in his thought, and some of his novels are meant to
defend privileges of the Upstate New York landowners. But together with this conscious bias there can be detected in Cooper's
fiction a yearning for a state of social comeliness which he saw
embodied in the life of the Indians and, more persuasively, in the
habits of his culture hero, Natty Bumppo.

Cooper's anarchist vision appears as a substratum of feeling, a cluster
of wistful images, picturesque set-pieces and mythic figures. It is a
vision that breaks past his pompous style, as if meant to shatter
his conservative opinions. In Cooper's fiction the Indian tribes are
never burdened with government, in the sense of a centralized
authority commanding force against its own citizens. Within the
tribe, the essential unit of social life is the family, in many respects
a more powerful unit than the tribe itself. Military service is voluntary, and when the braves go on the warpath, they act out of their

own free will. As Cooper portrays it—and historical accuracy need not concern us for a moment—the life of the Indians can be severely bound by tradition, rites, concepts of honor, and limitations of mind, but it is not subject to the institutional authority and the social regulations we associate with the state. With Natty Bumppo, the Deerslayer and Pathfinder, Cooper identifies more openly, for in Natty his conservative and anarchist impulses find a genuine harmony. Natty brings together a refined version of civilized decorum and the purity of natural man—indeed, it is precisely the unlikelihood of this mixture which makes him so poignant a figure. Propertyless as a matter of principle and self-governing through ascetic training, Natty is a monk of the woods living in a fraternal closeness with Chingachgook, his Indian companion, at ease with the natural world and apart from social crowding and hypocrisy. Natty is the American at once free from historical sophistication and primitivist degradation; he bears out D. H. Lawrence's remark that the Leatherstocking Tales are "a wish-fulfillment, a kind of yearning myth." In Natty self and society are at peace; or better yet, society becomes absorbed into self, in a truce of composure. Natty lives out the anarchist idyll of a life so beautifully attuned to its own inner needs and thereby so lucidly harmonious with the external world that there is need for neither rules nor restraints.

In *Huckleberry Finn* the anarchist motif reaches its greatest if least explicit embodiment. When Huck and Nigger Jim are alone on that indispensable raft (itself so wonderful a symbol of the isolation, purity, and helplessness upon which the anarchist vision rests), they set up a communal order transcending in value the charms of their personal friendliness. They create a community of equals, because a community goes beyond the mere *idea* of equality. The idea of equality is enforced by a state and requires that, unavoidable violations apart, fixed norms and regulations be imposed on persons of varying needs and powers. The community of equals is established by persons and involves a delicate adjustment, moment by moment, to the desires each perceives in the other.

The community of the raft is a community of friends, quietly competent at the tasks facing them: tasks of self-preservation and self-ordering. The impulse to freedom embodied in the escape of Huck and Nigger Jim is a freedom that cannot be confined to, or even adequately described in, social terms. It comes into spontaneous existence, and not as a matter of status obligation, or legal right. It exists as an active relationship, a shared capacity for sympathetic identification with the natural world, which is seen neither as inherently good nor inherently bad but as a resource which those with the proper sense of reverence can tap. Or it can be a sympathetic identification with other men, which is seen in the novel as something to be learned, so that the learning becomes a way of moving past mere learning and received morality. Huck's education is a kind of education, perhaps the only kind, that matters: an education of the emotions. And on the raft his emotions are freed because he knows that *they*—the people of the town, the figures of judgment, the men of authority, the agents of the state—are away. As every reader notices, Huck Finn does not reach a conceptual grasp of the problem of slavery: what, come to think of it, would be so remarkable in his decision to help Nigger Jim gain freedom if he, Huck, concluded that it was the right thing to do? As a decent American boy, he would then be under moral obligation to offer his help. What is remarkable about Huck's decision is that he makes it in violation of norms he accepts, so that it becomes a triumph of nature over culture, impulse over convention, anarchic fraternity over registered authority. It is, for Huck, a matter of *friendliness*. And in a state of friendliness, men—at least in nineteenth-century American fiction—do not need society. Yet, precisely because he does not understand practically the problem he has surmounted spiritually, Huck is also helpless before it: he may not need society, but society wants him.

As long as Huck and Nigger Jim can float upon that blessed raft there is no need for fixed measurements of right and wrong, good and evil. When Huck and Nigger Jim achieve their moments of fraternal union, we are transported to a kind of ecstasy, a muted rapture enabling them to rise beyond the calculations of morality. One is reminded of the Hasidic legend which has it that if you move upward step by step on the ladder of morality you will in the end break loose and float away into a buoying space.

Yet Twain was too shrewd a writer and too troubled a man to compose a mere idyll. The precarious community of friends established on the raft is threatened at almost every moment. It is invaded by alien figures, the Duke and the Dauphin, who are presented in terms of comedy but whose significance is steadily felt to be ominous. To the extent that Huck and Nigger Jim overcome them, and also fend off assaults from enemies both on the river and from the shore, it is partly as a triumph of their innocence, the innocence of friends, and partly as a triumph of shrewdness, Huck's shrewd social personality which upon need he quickly reestablishes.

Huck is a figure at once fixed and amorphous, recognizable and anonymous. On the raft he sheds his mask—perhaps one might even say, his skin—of personality; everything which a human being absorbs or introjects from his society. The more comfortable he feels, the less individual he seems; for he blends into a state of passive receptivity; he is no longer a demarcated character but a

current of experience. The self grows harmonious with its surroundings; it exists as awareness and caress rather than wariness and
will. Between Huck and Jim there develops an I-Thou relationship,
a sentience so keen that for a few moments the whole American
self-violation seems blotted out and we live in the rapture of idyll,
the America that might have been, the paradise of anarchy. On the
river Huck's personality is always in process of dissolution, for
there he can leave behind both anxiety and shrewdness and ease
himself into repose and contemplation. On the land Huck chooses
the masquerades of personality, or more accurately, he knows that
he must choose them. He adopts a variety of names, sometimes
passing himself off as Tom Sawyer, the commonplace American
boy, and sometimes as the less-than-beatific, riverside Huck Finn.
Even on land he is very fine, an admirable moral figure. But on the
raft he has no need for disguise, no burden of personality, no
strategy of shrewdness. In the community of friends, lawless and
stateless, there are story telling, amiable philosophizing about Sol-
lermun the King, eating, sleeping, and keeping loose.

It cannot last. For all the while Twain is making certain that we remember paradise consists of a few rickety boards nailed together;
that the raft contains a run-away slave worth a sizable number of
dollars; that violence and corruption threaten at every bend of the
shore; and that the paradisial journey is a drift southward, deeper
and deeper into the darkness of slavery. The anarchic enclave must
disintegrate under the pressure of the world, and perhaps, in the
end, contribute to conservative resignation. Before the world itself,
Huck and Nigger Jim are helpless. At one and the same time they
represent the power of transcendence, of rising above the crippling
grasp of society, and the pitiable vulnerability of a boy and a slave
who try to evade the authority of that society. Between these two
extremes is there not a causal relationship, one in which our most
splendid yearnings come out of our most utter impotence?

The clash between anarchic yearning and fixed authority leads both
to the marvellously open and spacious quality of nineteenth-century
American writing and to the choked misanthropy that so often
follows. For writers caught up with the utopian vision it is particularly hard, as they grow older, to find those modulated resolutions
that characterize the classical European writers. Our literature is
schizoid, flaring to ecstasy and falling into misanthropy, but rarely
passing at the middle level of social engagement and realism. The
American myth, of which the anarchic vision is one mode, exerts
too great a hold upon our nineteenth-century masters; and then,
as it shatters itself upon the shores of reality, there follows a disenchantment beyond bearing. Where the traditional treatment of
society in the English novel occurs in terms of class adjustments,

contained conflicts, even class revolutions—all within the shared assumption of the inescapability of social authority and visible power—the American imagination, at its deepest level, keeps calling into question the idea of society itself. And as the nation moves irrevocably into the modern world, what can that come to but absolute despair?

In no other Western culture of the past two centuries, to my knowledge, has so much attention been paid to and so many demands expressed for the "creation of values." When one comes to think of it, that is really extraordinary. The literatures of Europe either sustain traditional values or enlarge upon revolutionary values; but both are seen as inseparable from the social order in which the writer writes and the reader reads. In our culture we have made the unprecedented demand upon writers that they create values quite apart from either tradition or insurgency. What we have often meant by this is that they establish a realm of values apart from the setting of actual life, that they become priests of the possible in a world of shrinking possibilities. We ask them to discover, out of their desperate clarity, a vision which we can cherish and cherish perhaps in direct proportion to our knowledge that we will not—or cannot— live by it. The result is that every now and again we strike off a fiction of such transparent powers it sends the world into enchantment but also that we deny ourselves the possibilities of a hard realism in both our literature and our politics. Yet, within our literature, the anarchic impulse—together with the accompanying moral ultimatism and apolitical politics—remains enormously powerful, and even those who grow skeptical about its value must grant that it still has a notable imaginative thrust.

In our world, the vision of a society of true friends living in composed affability and fraternity is one that must bring the writer to a ferocious impasse. For when that always entrancing voice calls once more, "Come back to the raft ag'in, Huck honey," the reply of the age is, "You can't go home again."

An endless dialectic in our life and our literature, this clash between anarchy and authority. It courses through the work of many of our major nineteenth-century American writers—Cooper, Twain, Melville most of all—and its influence can be felt in many of our twentieth-century writers as well. Abstractly considered, this clash between the dream of anarchic bliss and the need commonly felt for social authority may be beyond resolution. But in the greatest of our writers it is embodied, dramatized, celebrated, and mourned with an urgency of desire which marks the distinctiveness of our culture and our literature.

FROM VERNACULAR TO SOPHISTICATED ART: TOWARD THE TWENTIETH CENTURY

From Vernacular to Sophisticated Art

In the two or three decades after the Civil War, a number of our greatest nineteenth-century writers continued with their work, often their best work. Some of them lived in circumstances of extreme isolation (Melville and Emily Dickinson, for example), others as public figures receiving enormous public approval (Whitman and Twain). Melville, a popular writer in the prewar years, now entered a phase of almost complete public obscurity, suffering neglect from both readers and critics, but quietly continuing to write works of poetry and fiction. Emily Dickinson, living in Amherst, Massachusetts, and seemingly deaf to the affairs of ordinary American society, wrote her poems during these years but insisted on keeping most of them out of public print. Mark Twain, the one American writer of the nineteenth century whom the ordinary reading public recognized as its cultural spokesman, composed his best work during these postwar years. And it was also in these decades that the young Henry James wrote a number of his sophisticated and artful novels. (Because James's literary career cuts across the nineteenth and twentieth centuries and reaches its fulfillment in the latter, his work is presented and discussed in the third volume of this anthology.)

Apart from these major figures, however, a whole series of new literary schools and impulses during the 1870s and 1880s began to appear: first, local-color writing, then the realistic novel, and after that, the beginnings of naturalist and impressionist fiction. The writings in this section illustrate some of these trends—though by its very nature the realistic novel cannot be adequately represented in an anthology.

It would be a mistake to suppose that the Civil War is some sort of Chinese wall completely separating the literature composed before it from that composed after it. In retrospect we can see that the Civil War did mark a major turning point for the people who lived through it, including many of the writers who appear in this section, but their lives do demonstrate a considerable amount of continuity. That is one reason this section covers writing which spans the war—from pre-Civil War humor playing with the manners and vocabulary of a regional culture (Longstreet) to post-Civil War fiction delicately investigating the details of a regional experience (Sarah Orne Jewett); from writings meant to record the common speech of an area faithfully or for purposes of comic exaggeration (Crockett, the early Twain) to writings tensed and complicated into a new American style (the later Twain, Stephen Crane).

In the introduction to the early nineteenth century one section discusses the importance of regionalism in nineteenth-century culture and literature. The point is made there that during the 1830s and 1840s, when American literary men were strongly preoccupied with the need to forge a national consciousness and create a distinctively American literature, regionalism was really the major force (or at least one major force) shaping the poetry and fiction of the time. After the Civil War, however, a curious twist takes place. As a result of the nationalistic sentiment created by the war, and also because of the growth of industrialism and the remarkable improvement in transportation and communications, the United States as a nation takes on a much more unified character than it had previously had, yet at the same time there flourishes a popular kind of writing, usually called "local color," that tries deliberately to exploit the distinctive traits and idiosyncracies of the slowly vanishing ways of regional life. Perhaps there is a causal connection here. Precisely as the country becomes more homogenous, precisely as the differences among the various regions begin to fade in importance and vividness, there occurs a strong outburst of popular nostalgia, quickly seized upon by many writers, for everything in the American past that is disappearing.

Is there a difference between regional and local-color writing? Some literary historians and critics have tried to draw a sharp distinction between the two, and as long as we remember that it is a convenience of analysis more than a reality of history, this line of distinction can be very useful. It runs something like this: Regional writing is authentic, often naïve in character, close to folk experience. As it emerges from that experience, it can exhibit the charm and shrewdness of life in preindustrial America, especially its varieties of humor. Often it employs precisely shaded regional dialects for effects of credibility and color—also, to get away from the formalities and stiffness of literary prose. Regional writers publish their work in books and magazines, which means they may earn money from doing so; but by and large they are not, or not mainly, concerned with a conscious *exploitation* of nostalgia for passing ways of life; they are not intent primarily on cooking up a confection of quaintness for middle-class urban audiences indulging their nostalgia in the safety of living rooms. Regional writers are often quite modest in their ambition, trying simply to capture the surface tones and colors of a limited arc of our national experience. But a few of them, precisely through the accuracy with which they do this, succeed in breaking through to larger ends. The particular detail can yield universal significance.

Local color, by contrast, is often seen as a kind of fiction which has become self-conscious, slick, and exploitative in regard to the region about which the writer tells his stories. He may know a great deal about the region; he may himself have emerged from it; but he now is writing with an eye toward the magazine public. The local colorist tries to make the life of the region picturesque, even if that means evading unpleasant details; he draws his picture with a glow of deceit, sometimes self-deceit; he inclines toward set formulas of narrative rather than truthful depictions of experience. These and other weaknesses of local-color writing are well described by Carlos Baker:

the curious pursuit of the unique, idiosyncratic, or grotesque in local character . . . a noticeable though not universal tendency to gloss over the uglier aspects of the human predicament; a reactionary glorification and sentimentalization of a wealthy and powerful plantation aristocracy . . . an equally deplorable tendency to overdo the "common man" motif . . . an attempt to petrify and monumentalize that which in all classes and castes was petering out through its own internal weakness or decadence . . . The predilection for dialect . . . in which authors played at amateur phonetics under the mistaken impression that the use of heavily apostrophized contractions, barbaric misspellings, and other desperate expedients would be useful to future linguistic historians, is distressing. . . .

Yet the analytic distinction between regional writing and local-color writing soon breaks down under the pressures of historical examination. Some regional writing at its best—like the exquisite cameo art of Sarah Orne Jewett and some of the more ambitious fiction of George Washington Cable—avoids the characteristic faults of local-color writing. But the truth is that regionalism always contains within itself the temptation of the quaint provincial and the expansive picturesque, while local color contains the possibility of transcending its own limitations and moving toward a modest and intimate realism. Bernard Bowron has made this point very well:

American realism owes a good deal to the literature of local color, ambivalently realistic though it was. In its pure form, best represented by Bret Harte's sentimental tales, it falsified experience unconscionably. Hearts of gold appear with monotonous regularity under the unlikeliest exteriors, to the moral uplift of a happy, tear-drenched audience. No deviation from the correct sentiments is allowed; a local milieu is exploited simply for its "exotic" qualities, which means that it is neither rendered fully nor organically related to the characters who move within it. Everything is innocent and meaningless. Still, even at the worst, this is not the whole story. Except for its Southern offshoot, which could not let go the myth of a "befo' de war" aristocracy, local-color fiction based itself on the important assumption that the proper material for literature was the life of common people. . . .

Moreover, though magazine editors of the seventies and eighties may have favored and promoted a sentimental pattern for the local-color story or novel, by no means all local colorists confined themselves strictly to such a pattern. From the beginning, serious writers sought out, or at least could not avoid, the play of environmental influences upon local character. This certainly holds true for Harriet Beecher Stowe, whose New England novels of the sixties set the stage for the local-color movement of the following decades. Beneath her tireless didacticism one discovers a durable core of realistic observation. *The Minister's Wooing, The Pearl of Orr's Island*, and especially *Old Town Folks* pay considerable attention to the details of New England domestic life, customs, and theology and to the geographical rather than the mere "landscape" qualities of the region. To the extent that Mrs. Stowe brings these elements to bear upon the shaping of character, her people appeal to a reader's sense of "the probable and ordinary course of man's experience."

The same—with all due allowance for romantic and sentimental excrescences—must be said for such later writers as Eggleston, Kirkland, Cable, Freeman, and Jewett. Their stories may have sold themselves to editors and readers as local color, but they were something more than that, something far more promising for realism; in them, region as exotic backdrop for an improbable didactic drama gives way to region as an actor and force *within* the drama of everyday life. Thus the local-color movement served to establish an audience for a more serious treatment of commonplace existence, and at the same time gave rise to an occasional piece of honest and persuasive regionalism.

About the term *realism* there has been endless discussion and dispute among literary historians and critics—indeed, among all readers of literature. It is a difficult and tricky term, yet we find that in discussing literature we really cannot do without it. We can banish the word but not the ideas surrounding it.

In the last two or so decades of the nineteenth century, realism in American literature signified at least the following elements:

A desire to represent in works of fiction the immediate, commonplace experience of ordinary Americans as it could be observed in a recognizable social locale and at a specific historical moment. Not legendary white whales, not ladies with scarlet letters on their bosoms, not mythical pathfinders in mythical Western prairies; but the kinds of people who might actually be found in a Midwestern small town, or in a Maine fishing village, or in an upstate New York city, men who worked on farms or ran little stores—these were now the favored characters for writers like William Dean Howells, Hamlin Garland, Ed Howe, Joseph Kirkland, Harold Frederic, and Sarah Orne Jewett.

A wish no longer to indulge in rosy self-idealization, and instead a readiness to show the drabness of life in a small town, the poverty of life in a large city. And this signified an intention not only to expose the faults and evils of society, but also to show the psychic and moral costs of those faults and evils.

A strong need to exorcise—to get out of their system— the small towns from which many American writers had come and which had traditionally been celebrated as the seat of American virtue and innocence. Now, instead, the new realistic novelists turned with wrath or bitterness, often with disillusionment, on the life of their origins. The same held true for those who came from rural America: their disenchantment proved a strong incentive toward realistic portraiture of what life had been like on the farm.

A new readiness to confront the sensual nature of human beings. No longer were such matters to be avoided or glossed over; instead, in the work of writers like Howe and Frederic, as to a lesser extent Howells, there was a frank recognition of the power of sexuality in human affairs and a strong interest in the ways that power could be made into a major motif in a work of fiction.

A new perspective upon American society, no longer seen as a homogeneous Jeffersonian community, but as a locale in which many of the class conflicts and ideological disputes of European society could more or less be found.

Realism, then, meant both a way of looking at human experience and a way of writing a work of fiction. Ian Watt offers an excellent brief description of the realistic novel:

[It works on] the premise, or primary convention, that the novel is a full and authentic report of human experience and is therefore under an obligation to satisfy its reader with such details of the story as the individuality of the actors concerned, the particulars of the times and places of their actions, details which are presented through a more largely referential use of language than is common in other literary forms.

These remarks are only the barest beginnings of an enormously complicated problem in the history and criticism of literature; and in regard to late-nineteenth-century American writing, they do no more than point toward new possibilities, gathering energies, and only partially realized hopes. A sustained discussion of the development of realistic fiction in the United States could not break off with the turn of the century for it is only at the beginning of the twentieth century, with the work of Theodore Dreiser and Edith Wharton, that the realistic novel comes into its own. Meanwhile, however, the realistic movement in fiction branches out into other directions: the complex psychological fictions of Henry James which contain elements not only of realism but of fable and of fantasy; the brilliant novels and stories of Stephen Crane, which move into the kinds of fiction commonly described as naturalism and impressionism. But perhaps the most useful hint is this: labels like realism, naturalism, impressionism, and the like, can help us to find common elements in the works of different writers; but finally, these labels should not to be taken too solemnly; they are like scaffolds—to be discarded once the building is up. What matters most is our relationship to, our sense of, our involvement with, a particular work of literature.

DAVY CROCKETT (1786–1836)

Half mortal, half myth, Davy Crockett was born in a log cabin. It could hardly have been otherwise.

Master hunter, Indian fighter, living emblem of the frontier, spinner of tall tales, homespun humorist, Davy Crockett grew up in Tennessee at a time when it was still part of the Far West. He wasted little time with "book-larnin'," because everything he needed to know he could find out in the woods and from the old trappers. He fought in the Creek War (1813 to 1814) under Andrew Jackson, and was then elected to the state legislature and twice to Congress (1827 to 1831, 1833 to 1835). Helping the Texans defend the Alamo, he died a hero.

Even during his lifetime Davy had become a figure of folklore, and with the shrewdness of such figures, he decided to cast far his wit and wisdom—as well as gain the material awards that might come from the casting—by issuing his autobiography in 1834, Narrative of the Life of David Crockett of West Tennessee. By then, hundreds of Davy Crockett stories had been spread by the richly imaginative liars who were making the hard life of early settlements a little more cheerful. Davy became a superman in coonskins, doing great feats of bravery and telling stories that expanded in repetition. When he died, Davy was already a figure somewhat larger than life, and after death he slipped happily into a paradise of legend.

FURTHER READING

Constance Rourke's biography *Davy Crockett* (1934) is superb. See also Richard Dorson's *Davy Crockett: American Comic Legend* (1939) and J. A. Shackford's *David Crockett: The Man and the Legend* (1955).

Narrative of the Life of David Crockett of West Tennessee (1834)

Chapter 5

I was living ten miles below Winchester when the Creek war commenced; and as military men are making so much fuss in the world at this time, I must give an account of the part I took in the defence of the country. If it should make me president, why I can't help it; such things will sometimes happen; and my pluck is, never "to seek, nor decline office."

It is true, I had a little rather not; but yet, if the government can't get on without taking another president from Tennessee, to finish the work of "retrenchment and reform," why, then, I reckon I must go in for it. But I must begin about the war, and leave the other matter for the people to begin on.

The Creek Indians had commenced their open hostilities by a most bloody butchery at Fort Mimms. There had been no war among us for so long, that but few, who were not too old to bear arms, knew any thing about the business. I, for one, had often thought about war, and had often heard it described; and I did verily believe in my own mind, that I couldn't fight in that way at all; but my after experience convinced me that this was all a notion. For when I heard of the mischief which was done at the fort, I instantly felt like going, and I had none of the dread of dying that I expected to feel. In a few days a general meeting of the militia was called for the purpose of raising volunteers; and when the day arrived for that meeting, my wife, who had heard me say I meant to go to the war, began to beg me not to turn out. She said she was a stranger in the parts where we lived, had no connexions living near her, and that she and our little children would be left in a lonesome and unhappy situation if I went away. It was mighty hard to go against such arguments as these; but my countrymen had been murdered, and I knew that the next thing would be, that the Indians would be scalping the women and the children all about there, if we didn't put a stop to it. I reasoned the case with her as well as I could, and told her, that if every man would wait till his wife got willing for him to go to war, there would be no fighting done, until we would all be killed in our own houses; that I was as able to go as any man in the world; and that I believed it was a duty I owed to my country. Whether she was satisfied with this reasoning or not, she did not tell me; but seeing I was bent on it, all she did was to cry a little, and turn about to her work. The truth is, my dander was up, and nothing but war could bring it right again. . . .

About eight hundred of the volunteers, and of that number I was one, were now sent back, crossing the Tennessee river, and on through Huntsville, so as to cross the river again at another place, and to get on the Indians in another direction. After we passed Huntsville, we struck on the river at the Muscle Shoals, and at a place on them called Melton's Bluff. This river is here about two miles wide, and a rough bottom; so much so, indeed, in many places, as to be dangerous; and in fording it this time, we left several of the horses belonging to our men, with their feet fast in the crevices of the rocks. The men, whose horses were thus left, went ahead on foot. We pushed on till we got to what was called the Black Warrior's town, which stood near the very spot where Tuscaloosa now stands, which is the seat of government for the state of Alabama.

This Indian town was a large one; but when we arrived we found the Indians had all left it. There was a large field of corn standing out, and a pretty good supply in some cribs. There was also a fine quantity of dried beans, which were very acceptable to us; and without delay we secured them as well as the corn, and then burned the town to ashes; after which we left the place. . . .

We then marched to a place, which we called Camp Wills; and here it was that Captain Cannon was promoted to a colonel, and Colonel Coffee to a general. We then marched to the Ten Islands, on the Coosa river, where we established a fort; and our spy companies were sent out. They soon made prisoners of Bob Catala and his warriors, and, in a few days afterwards, we heard of some Indians in a town about eight miles off. So we mounted our horses, and put out for that town, under the direction of two friendly Creeks we had taken for pilots. We had also a Cherokee colonel, Dick Brown, and some of his men with us. When we got near the town we divided; one of our pilots going with each division. And so we passed on each side of the town, keeping near to it, until our lines met on the far side. We then closed up at both ends, so as to surround it completely; and then we sent Captain Hammond's company of rangers to bring on the affray. He had advanced near the town, when the Indians saw him, and they raised the yell, and came running at him like so many red devils. The main army was now formed in a hollow square around the town, and they pursued Hammond till they came in reach of us. We then gave them a fire, and they returned it, and then ran back into their town. We began to close on the town by making our files closer and closer, and the Indians soon saw they were our property. So most of them wanted us to take them prisoners; and their squaws and all would run and take hold of any of us they could, and give themselves up. I saw seven squaws have hold of one man, which made me think of the Scriptures. So I hollered out the Scriptures was fulfilling; that there was seven women holding to one man's coat tail. But I believe it was a hunting-shirt all the time. We took them all prisoners that came out to us in this way; but I saw some warriors run into a house, until I counted forty-six of them. We pursued them until we got near the house, when we saw a squaw sitting in the door, and she placed her feet against the bow she had in her hand, and then took an arrow, and, raising her feet, she drew with all her might, and let fly at us, and she killed a man, whose name, I believe, was Moore. He was a lieutenant, and his death so enraged us all, that she was fired on, and had at least twenty balls blown through her. This was the first man I ever saw killed with a bow and arrow. We now shot them like dogs; and then set the house on fire, and burned it up with the forty-six warriors in it. I recollect seeing a boy who was shot down near the house. His arm and thigh was broken, and he was so near the burning house that the grease was stewing out of him. In this situation he was still trying to crawl along; but not a murmur escaped him, though he was only about twelve years old. So sullen is the Indian, when his dander is up, that he had sooner die than make a noise, or ask for quarters.

The number that we took prisoners, being added to the number we killed, amounted one hundred and eighty-six; though I don't remember the exact number of either. We had five of our men killed. We then returned to our camp, at which our fort was erected, and known by the name of Fort Strother. No provisions had yet reached us, and we had now been for several days on half rations. However we went back to our Indian town on the next day, when many of the carcasses of the Indians were still to be seen. They looked very awful, for the burning had not entirely consumed them, but given them a very terrible appearance, at least what remained of them. It was, somehow or other, found out that the house had a potatoe cellar under it, and an immediate examination was made, for we were all as hungry as wolves. We found a fine chance of potatoes in it, and hunger compelled us to eat them, though I had a little rather not; if I could have helped it, for the oil of the Indians we had burned up on the day before had run down on them, and they looked like they had been stewed with fat meat. We then again returned to the army, and remained there for several days almost starving, as all our beef was gone. We commenced eating the beef-hides, and continued to eat every scrap we could lay our hands on. . . .

I continued at home now, working my farm for two years, as the war finally closed soon after I quit the service. The battle at New Orleans had already been fought, and treaties were made with the Indians which put a stop to their hostilities.

But in this time, I met with the hardest trial which ever falls to the lot of man. Death, that cruel leveller of all distinctions,—to whom the prayers and tears of husbands, and of even helpless infancy, are addressed in vain,—entered my humble cottage, and tore from my children an affectionate good mother, and from me a tender and loving wife. . . .

There lived in the neighbourhood, a widow lady whose husband had been killed in the war. She had two children, a son and daughter, and both quite small, like my own. I began to think, that as we were both in the same situation, it might be that we could do something for each other; and I therefore began to hint a little around the matter, as we were once and a while together. She was a good industrious woman, and owned a snug little farm, and lived quite comfortable. I soon began to pay my respects to her in real good earnest; but I was as sly about it as a fox when he is going to rob a hen-roost. I found that my company wasn't at all disagreeable to her; and I thought I could treat her children with so much friendship as to make her a good stepmother to mine, and in this I wan't mistaken, as we soon bargained, and got married, and then went ahead. In a great deal of peace we raised our first crop of children, and they are all married and doing well. But we had a second crop together; and I shall notice them as I go along, as my wife and myself both had a hand in them, and they therefore belong to the history of my second marriage. . . .

The place on which I lived was sickly, and I was determined to leave it. I therefore set out the next fall to look at the country which had been purchased of the Chickasaw tribe of Indians. I went on to a place called Shoal Creek, about eighty miles from where I lived, and here again I got sick. I took the ague and fever, which I supposed was brought on me by camping out. I remained here for some time, as I was unable to go farther; and in that time, I became so well pleased with the country about there, that I resolved to settle in it. It was just only a little distance in the purchase, and no order had been established there; but I thought I could get along without order as well as any body else. And so I moved and settled myself down on the head of Shoal Creek. We remained here some two or three years, without any law at all; and so many bad characters began to flock in upon us, that we found it necessary to set up a sort of temporary government of our own. I don't mean that we made any president, and called him the "government," but we met and made what we called a corporation; and I reckon we called *it* wrong, for it wa'n't a bank, and hadn't any deposites; and now they call the bank a corporation. But be this as it may, we lived in the back-woods, and didn't profess to know much, and no doubt used many wrong words. But we met, and appointed magistrates and constables to keep order. We didn't fix any laws for them, tho': for we supposed they would know law enough, whoever they might be; and so we left it to themselves to fix the laws.

I was appointed one of the magistrates; and when a man owed a debt, and wouldn't pay it, I and my constable ordered our warrant, and then he would take the man, and bring him before me for trial. I would give judgment against him, and then an order of an execution would easily scare the debt out of him. If any one was charged with marking his neighbour's hogs, or with stealing any thing, which happened pretty often in those days,—I would have him taken, and if there was tolerable grounds for the charge, I would have him well whip'd and cleared. . . .

Next morning, being the first day of May, I went to some of the newspaper offices, read the news, and returned to take a ride with Colonel S. D. Jackson, in an elegant barouche. We drove up the city [New York] and took a view of the improvements and beautiful houses in the new part. By the time we returned down Broadway, it seemed to me that the city was flying before some awful calamity. "Why," said I, "colonel, what under heaven is the matter? Everybody appears to be pitching out their furniture, and packing it off." He laughed, and said this was the general "mooving day." Such a sight nobody ever saw, unless it was in this same city. It seemed a kind of frolic, as if they were changing houses just for fun. Every street was crowded with carts, drays, and people. So the world goes. It would take a good deal to get me out of my log house; but here, I understand, many persons "moove" every year.

Having alighted, and taken some refreshment, I asked Colonel Webb to go with me to the "Fivepoints," a noted place near the centre of the city. This is the place where Van Buren's warriors came from during the election, when the wild Irish, with their clubs and bludgeons, knocked down every one they could find that would not huzza for Jackson. However, I had a great curiosity to see them; and on we went, the major and me, and in the midst of that great city we came to a place where five streets all come together; and from this it takes the name of the "Five-points." The buildings are little, old, frame houses, and looked like some little country village. The houses all had cellars; and as that day was fashionable to moove, they were mooving too. The streets looked like a *clearing*, in my part of the world, as they were emptying and burning the straw out of their beds. It appeared as if the cellars was jam full of people; and such fidling and dancing nobody ever saw before in this world. I thought they were the true "heaven-borns." Black and white, white and black, all hug-em-snug together, happy as lords and ladies, sitting sometimes round in a ring, with a jug of liquor between them: and I do think I saw more drunk folks, men and women, that day, than I ever saw before. This is part of what is called by the Regency the "glorious sixth ward"—the regular Van Buren ground-floor. I thought I would rather risque myself in an Indian fight than venture among these creatures after night. I said to the colonel, "God deliver me from such constituents, or from a party supported by such. In my country, when you meet an Irishman, you find a first-rate gentleman; but these are worse than savages; they are too mean to swab hell's kitchen." He took me to the place where the election was held. It appeared to me that all the place round was made ground, and that there was more room in the houses under-ground than above; and I suppose there must have been a flood of rain during the election, which forced those rats out of their holes. There is more people stowed away together here than any place I ever saw. I heard a story, and it is asserted to be true, that about here, some years ago, a committee visited all the houses, to see how they were coming on. One house, that was four stories high, and four rooms on a floor, had sixteen families in it, and four in the garret, which was divided into four parts by a streak of charcoal. An old lady, that was spinning up there, was asked how they made out. She said, pretty well; and that they would be quiet enough if it was not for the old woman in the opposite corner, and she took boarders, and they often made a noise. I believe it is true. What a miserable place a city is for poor people: they are half starved, poorly clothed, and perished for fire. I sometimes wonder they don't clear out to a new country, where every skin hangs by its own tail; but I suppose they think an hour's indulgence in vice is sweet enough for the bitter of the rest.

AUGUSTUS BALDWIN LONGSTREET (1790–1870)

Born in Augusta, Georgia, Longstreet—like many upper-class Southern boys of his time—was sent North to Yale University for his higher education. In 1815 he was admitted to the Georgia bar, and in 1822 he became a judge. In 1839 he was chosen to be president of what is now Emory University; later he became president of the Universities of Mississippi (1848 to 1856) and of South Carolina (from 1858 to the Civil War.)

In his later, eminently respectable, years Longstreet was somewhat embarrassed by the humorous sketches he had written in the early 1830s. Originally published in Southern newspapers and journals, these sketches proved so popular that he collected them under the title of Georgia Scenes, Characters, Incidents etc. in the First Half Century of the Republic (1835). The older Longstreet need not have felt this book beneath his dignity, for it has assured him a modest place in American literary history.

Longstreet's sketches follow a pattern characteristic of much early American humor. The writer is obviously a well-educated man. Through hints of erudition, attitudes expressed by a phrase here and there, and above all a rather formal style, he makes it perfectly clear that he should not be confused with the country roughs he writes about. But some impulse toward realism gets the better of his vanity, and he employs the vernacular when he has his characters speak. The lively speech of the characters, if it does not become so faithful to local dialect as to be undecipherable, almost always proves more interesting than the writer's stuffy prose. In "The Horse Swap" this contrast of style is very noticeable, as is the contrast between the two horse traders, each of whom represents a tradition— wanton overstatement and sly understatement—in folk speech.

FURTHER READING

J. D. Wade's Augustus Baldwin Longstreet (1924) is a standard biography. Brief critical discussions can be found in Constance Rourke's American Humor (1931), Bernard De Voto's Mark Twain's America (1932), and Walter Blair's Native American Humor (1937).

FROM **Georgia Scenes** *(1835)*

The Horse Swap

During the session of the Superior Court in the village of ———,
about three weeks ago, when a number of people were collected in the
principal street of the village, I observed a young man riding up and
down the street, as I supposed, in a violent passion. He galloped this
way, then that, and then the other; spurred his horse to one group of
citizens, then to another; then dashed off at half-speed, as if fleeing from
danger; and, suddenly checking his horse, returned—first in a pace,
then in a trot, and then in a canter. While he was performing these
various evolutions he cursed, swore, whooped, screamed, and tossed
himself in every attitude which man could assume on horseback. In
short, he cavorted most magnanimously (a term which, in our tongue,
expresses all that I have described, and a little more), and seemed to
be setting all creation at defiance. As I like to see all that is passing, I
determined to take a position a little nearer to him, and to ascertain, if
possible, what it was that affected him so sensibly. Accordingly I approached a crowd before which he had stopped for a moment, and examined it with the strictest scrutiny. But I could see nothing in it that
seemed to have anything to do with the cavorter. Every man appeared
to be in good humor, and all minding their own business. Not one so
much as noticed the principal figure. Still he went on. After a semicolon
pause, which my appearance seemed to produce (for he eyed me closely
as I approached), he fetched a whoop, and swore that "he could out-
swap any live man, woman, or child that ever walked these hills, or that
ever straddled horseflesh since the days of old daddy Adam." "Stranger,"
said he to me, "did you ever see the *Yellow* Blossom from Jasper?"

"No," said I, "but I have often heard of him."

"I'm the boy," continued he; "perhaps a *leetle*, jist a *leetle* of the
best man at horse-swap that ever trod shoe-leather."

I began to feel my situation a little awkward, when I was relieved
by a man somewhat advanced in years, who stepped up and began to
survey the Yellow Blossom's horse with much apparent interest. This
drew the rider's attention, and he turned the conversation from me to
the stranger.

"Well, my old coon," said he, "do you want to swap *hosses?*"

"Why, I don't know," replied the stranger; "I believe I've got a beast
I'd trade with you for that one, if you like him."

"Well, fetch up your nag, my old cock; you're jist the lark I wanted
to get hold of. I am perhaps a *leetle*, jist a *leetle*, of the best man at a
horse swap that ever stole *cracklins* out of his mammy's fat gourd.
Where's your *hoss?*"

"I'll bring him presently; but I want to examine your horse a little."

"Oh, look at him," said the Blossom, alighting and hitting him a cut—"look at him! He's the best piece of *hoss*-flesh in the thirteen united universal worlds. There's no sort o' mistake in little Bullet. He can pick up miles on his feet, and fling 'em behind him as fast as the next man's *hoss*, I don't care where he comes from. And he can keep at it as long as the sun can shine without resting."

During this harangue little Bullet looked as if he understood it all, believed it, and was ready at any moment to verify it. He was a horse of goodly countenance, rather expressive of vigilance than fire; though an unnatural appearance of fierceness was thrown into it by the loss of his ears, which had been cropped pretty close to his head. Nature had done but little for Bullet's head and neck; but he managed, in a great measure, to hid their defects by bowing perpetually. He had obviously suffered severely for corn; but if his ribs and hip bones had not disclosed the fact, *he* never would have done it; for he was in all respects as cheerful and happy as if he commanded all the corn-cribs and fodder-stacks in Georgia. His height was about twelve hands; but as his shape partook somewhat of that of the giraffe, his haunches stood much lower. They were short, strait, peaked, and concave. Bullet's tail, however, made amends for all his defects. All that the artist could do to beautify it had been done; and all that horse could do to compliment the artist, Bullet did. His tail was nicked in superior style, and exhibited the line of beauty in so many directions that it could not fail to hit the most fastidious taste in some of them. From the root it dropped into a graceful festoon, then rose in a handsome curve, then resumed its first direction, and then mounted suddenly upward like a cypress knee to a perpendicular of about two and a half inches. The whole had a careless and be-witching inclination to the right. Bullet obviously knew where his beauty lay, and took all occasions to display it to the best advantage. If a stick cracked, or if any one moved suddenly about him, or coughed, or hawked, or spoke a little louder than common, up went Bullet's tail like lightning; and if the *going up* did not please, the *coming down* must of necessity, for it was as different from the other movement as was its direction. The first was a bold and rapid flight upward, usually to an angle of forty-five degrees. In this position he kept his interesting ap-pendage until he satisfied himself that nothing in particular was to be done; when he commenced dropping it by half inches, in second beats, then in triple time, then faster and shorter, and faster and shorter still, until it finally died away imperceptibly into its natural position. If I might compare sights to sounds, I should say its *settling* was more like the note of a locust than anything else in nature.

Either from native sprightliness of disposition, from uncontrollable activity, or from an unconquerable habit of removing flies by the stamp-ing of the feet, Bullet never stood still, but always kept up a gentle fly-scaring movement of his limbs, which was peculiarly interesting.

"I tell you, man," proceeded the Yellow Blossom, "he's the best live hoss that ever trod the grit of Georgia. Bob Smart knows the hoss. Come here, Bob, and mount this hoss, and show Bullet's motion." Here Bullet bristled up, and looked as if he had been hunting for Bob all day long, and had just found him. Bob sprang on his back. "Boo-oo-oo!" said Bob, with a fluttering noise of the lips, and away went Bullet as if in a quarter race, with all his beauties spread in handsome syle.

"Now fetch him back," said Blossom. Bullet turned and came in pretty much as he went out.

"Now trot him by." Bullet reduced his tail to *customary*, sidled to the right and left airily, and exhibited at least three varieties of trot in the short space of fifty yards.

"Make him pace!" Bob commenced twitching the bridle and kicking at the same time. These inconsistent movements obviously (and most naturally) disconcerted Bullet; for it was impossible for him to learn from them whether he was to proceed or stand still. He started to trot, and was told that wouldn't do. He attempted a canter, and was checked again. He stopped, and was urged to go on. Bullet now rushed into the wide field of experiment, and struck out a gait of his own that completely turned the tables upon his rider, and certainly deserved a patent. It seemed to have derived its elements from the jig, the minuet, and the cotillion. If it was not a pace, it certainly had *pace* in it, and no man would venture to call it anything else; so it passed off to the satisfaction of the owner.

"Walk him!" Bullet was now at home again, and he walked as if money were staked on him.

The stranger, whose name I afterwards learned was Peter Ketch, having examined Bullet to his heart's content, ordered his son Neddy to go and bring up Kit. Neddy soon appeared upon Kit, a well-formed sorrel of the middle size, and in good order. His *tout-ensemble* threw Bullet entirely in the shade, though a glance was sufficient to satisfy any one that Bullet had the decided advantage of him in point of intellect.

"Why, man," said Blossom, "do you bring such a hoss as that to trade for Bullet? Oh, I see, you've no notion of trading!"

"Ride him off, Neddy!" said Peter. Kit put off at a handsome lope.

"Trot him back!" Kit came in at a long sweeping trot, and stopped suddenly at the crowd.

"Well," said Blossom, "let me look at him; maybe he'll do to plough."

"Examine him," said Peter, taking hold the bridle close to the mouth; "he's nothing but a tacky. He ain't as *pretty* a horse as Bullet, I know, but he'll do. Start 'em together for a hundred and fifty *mile*, and if Kit ain't twenty mile ahead of him at the coming out, any man may take Kit for nothing. But he's a monstrous mean horse, gentlemen; any man may see that. He's the scariest horse, too, you ever saw. He won't do to hunt on, nohow. Stranger, will you let Neddy have your rifle to shoot off him? Lay the rifle between his ears, Neddy, and shoot at the blaze in that stump. Tell me when his head is high enough."

Ned fired and hit the blaze, and Kit did not move a hair's breadth.

"Neddy, take a couple of sticks, and beat on that hogs-head at Kit's tail."

Ned made a tremendous rattling, at which Bullet took fright, broke his bridle, and dashed off in grand style, and would have stopped all farther negotiations by going home in disgust, had not a traveller arrested him and brought him back; but Kit did not move.

"I tell you, gentlemen," continued Peter, "he's the scariest horse you ever saw. He ain't as gentle as Bullet, but he won't do any harm if you watch him. Shall I put him in a cart, gig, or wagon for you, stranger? He'll cut the same capers there he does here. He's a monstrous mean horse."

During all this time Blossom was examining him with the nicest scrutiny. Having examined his frame and limbs, he now looked at his eyes.

"He's got a curious look out of his eyes," said Blossom.

"Oh yes, sir," said Peter, "just as blind as a bat. Blind horses always have clear eyes. Make a motion at his eyes, if you please, sir."

Blossom did so, and Kit threw up his head rather as if something pricked him under the chin than as if fearing a blow. Blossom repeated the experiment, and Kit jerked back in considerable astonishment.

"Stone-blind, you see, gentlemen," proceeded Peter; "but he's just as good to travel of a dark night as if he had eyes."

"Blame my buttons," said Blossom, "if I like them eyes!"

"No," said Peter, "nor I neither. I'd rather have 'em made of diamonds; but they'll do—if they don't show as much white as Bullet's."

"Well," said Blossom, "make a pass at me."

"No," said Peter, "you made the banter, now make your pass."

"Well, I'm never afraid to price my hosses. You must give me twenty-five dollars boot."

"Oh, certainly; say fifty, and my saddle and bridle in. Here, Neddy, my son, take away daddy's horse."

"Well," said Blossom, "I've made my pass, now you make yours."

"I'm for short talk in a horse swap, and therefore always tell a gentleman at once what I mean to do. You must give me ten dollars."

Blossom swore absolutely, roundly, and profanely that he never would give boot.

"Well," said Peter, "I didn't care about trading; but you cut such high shines that I thought I'd like to back you out, and I've done it. Gentlemen, you see I've brought him to a back."

"Come, old man," said Blossom, "I've been joking with you. I begin to think you do want to trade; therefore, give me five dollars and take Bullet. I'd rather lose ten dollars any time than not make a trade, though I hate to fling away a good hoss."

"Well," said Peter, "I'll be as clever as you are. Just put the five dollars on Bullet's back, and hand him over; it's a trade."

Blossom swore again, as roundly as before, that he would not give boot; and, said he, "Bullet wouldn't hold five dollars on his back, no how. But, as I bantered you, if you say an even swap, here's at you."

"I told you," said Peter, "I'd be as clever as you; therefore, here goes two dollars more, just for trade sake. Give me three dollars, and it's a bargain."

Blossom repeated his former assertion; and here the parties stood for a long time, and the by-standers (for many were now collected) began to taunt both parties. After some time, however, it was pretty unanimously decided that the old man had backed Blossom out.

At length Blossom swore he "never should be backed out for three dollars after bantering a man"; and, accordingly, they closed the trade.

"Now," said Blossom, as he handed Peter the three dollars, "I'm a man that, when he makes a bad trade, makes the most of it until he can make a better. I'm for no rues and after-claps."

"That's just my way," said Peter; "I never goes to law to mend my bargains."

"Ah, you're the kind of boy I love to trade with. Here's your hoss, old man. Take the saddle and bridle off him, and I'll strip yours; but lift up the blanket easy from Bullet's back, for he's a mighty tender-backed hoss."

The old man removed the saddle, but the blanket stuck fast. He attempted to raise it, and Bullet bowed himself, switched his tail, danced a little, and gave signs of biting.

"Don't hurt him, old man," said Blossom, archly; "take it off easy. I am, perhaps, leetle of the best man at a horse-swap that ever catched a coon."

Peter continued to pull at the blanket more and more roughly, and Bullet became more and more *cavortish,* insomuch that, when the blanket came off, he had reached the *kicking* point in good earnest.

The removal of the blanket disclosed a sore on Bullet's back that seemed to have defied all medical skill. It measured six full inches in length and four in breadth, and had as many features as Bullet had motions. My heart sickened at the sight; and I felt that the brute who had been riding him in that situation deserved the halter.

The prevailing feeling, however, was that of mirth. The laugh became loud and general at the old man's expense, and rustic witticisms were liberally bestowed upon him and his late purchase. These Blossom continued to provoke by various remarks. He asked the old man "if he thought Bullet would let five dollars lie on his back." He declared most seriously that he had owned that horse three months, and had never discovered before that he had a sore back, "or he never should have thought of trading him," etc., etc.

The old man bore it all with the most philosophic composure. He evinced no astonishment at his late discovery, and made no replies. But his son Neddy had not disciplined his feelings quite so well. His eyes opened wider and wider from the first to the last pull of the blanket, and when the whole sore burst upon his view, astonishment and fright seemed to contend for the mastery of his countenance. As the blanket disappeared, he stuck his hands in his breeches pockets, heaved a deep sigh, and lapsed into a profound reverie, from which he was only roused by the cuts at his father. He bore them as long as he could; and, when he could contain himself no longer, he began, with a certain wildness of expression which gave a peculiar interest to what he uttered: "His back's mighty bad off; but dod drot my sould if he's put it to daddy as bad as he thinks he has, for old Kit's both blind and *deef*, I'll be dod drot if he eint!"

"The devil he is!" said Blossom.

"Yes, dod drot my soul if he *eint!*" You walk him, and see if he *eint*. His eyes don't look like it; but he's *jist as leve go agin the* house with you, or in a ditch, as anyhow. Now you go try him." The laugh was now turned on Blossom, and many rushed to test the fidelity of the little boy's report. A few experiments established its truth beyond controversy.

"Neddy," said the old man, "you oughtn't to try and make people discontented with their things. Stranger, don't mind what the little boy says. If you can only get Kit rid of them little failings you'll find him all sorts of a horse. You are a *leetle* the best man at a horse-swap that ever I got hold of but don't fool away Kit. Come, Neddy, my son, let's be moving; the stranger seems to be getting snappish."

KATE CHOPIN (1851–1904)

Born Katherine O'Flaherty in St. Louis of a French mother and Irish father, Kate Chopin married a New Orleans banker and, at the age of nineteen, went to live among the Acadians of Louisiana. One of the Chopin plantations had belonged to a New Englander notorious for brutality to his slaves, a man who had been the model for Simon Legree in Uncle Tom's Cabin. *Kate found herself stirred and horrified by this sense of past wrongs hanging over the place she had come to, and she used this setting in her first novel,* At Fault *(1890).*

The Chopin family spent much of its time in France, but Kate immersed herself in Louisiana customs and legends and produced some very fine short stories. After her husband's death in the early 1880s she returned to St. Louis and horrified the city by publishing in 1899 a novel, The Awakening, *which is notable for the frankness with which its sensuous heroine follows her desires.*

"Désirée's Baby" gives further evidence that Kate Chopin was free of many of the shibboleths of her age. This compactly plotted story portrays the miseries and deceits attendant on a racially segregated society, and especially those which follow from notions of racial superiority. Miss Chopin's materials will strike some readers as an anticipation, on a miniature scale, of William Faulkner's great novel Absalom, Absalom.

FURTHER READING

Daniel S. Rankin, *Kate Chopin and Her Creole Stories* (1932).

Désirée's Baby (1894)

As the day was pleasant, Madame Valmondé drove over to L'Abri to see Désirée and the baby.

It made her laugh to think of Désirée with a baby. Why, it seemed but yesterday that Désirée was little more than a baby herself; when Monsieur in riding through the gateway of Valmondé had found her lying asleep in the shadow of the big stone pillar.

The little one awoke in his arms and began to cry for "Dada." That was as much as she could do or say. Some people thought she might have strayed there of her own accord, for she was of the toddling age. The prevailing belief was that she had been purposely left by a party of Texans, whose canvas-covered wagon, late in the day, had crossed the ferry that Coton Maïs kept, just below the plantation. In time Madame Valmondé abandoned every speculation but the one that Désirée had been sent to her by a beneficent Providence to be the child of her affection, seeing that she was without child of the flesh. For the girl grew to be beautiful and gentle, affectionate and sincere,—the idol of Valmondé.

It was no wonder, when she stood one day against the stone pillar in whose shadow she had lain asleep, eighteen years before, that Armand Aubigny riding by and seeing her there, had fallen in love with her. That was the way all the Aubignys fell in love, as if struck by a pistol shot. The wonder was that he had not loved her before; for he had known her since his father brought him home from Paris, a boy of eight, after his mother died there. The passion that awoke in him that day, when he saw her at the gate, swept along like an avalanche, or like a prairie fire, or like anything that drives headlong over all obstacles.

Monsieur Valmondé grew practical and wanted things well considered: that is, the girl's obscure origin. Armand looked into her eyes and did not care. He was reminded that she was nameless. What did it matter about a name when he could give her one of the oldest and proudest in Louisiana? He ordered the *corbeille* from Paris, and contained himself with what patience he could until it arrived; then they were married.

Madame Valmondé had not seen Désirée and the baby for four weeks. When she reached L'Abri she shuddered at the first sight of it, as she always did. It was a sad looking place, which for many years had not known the gentle presence of a mistress, old Monsieur Aubigny having married and buried his wife in France, and she having loved her own land too well ever to leave it. The roof came down steep and black like a cowl, reaching out beyond the wide galleries that encircled the yellow stuccoed house. Big, solemn oaks grew close to it, and their thick-leaved, far-reaching branches shadowed it like a pall. Young Aubigny's rule was a strict one, too, and under it his negroes had forgotten how to be gay, as they had been during the old master's easy-going and indulgent lifetime.

The young mother was recovering slowly, and lay full length, in her soft white muslins and laces, upon a couch. The baby was beside her, upon her arm, where he had fallen asleep, at her breast. The yellow nurse woman sat beside a window fanning herself.

Madame Valmondé bent her portly figure over Désirée and kissed her, holding her an instant tenderly in her arms. Then she turned to the child.

"This is not the baby!" she exclaimed, in startled tones. French was the language spoken at Valmondé in those days.

"I knew you would be astonished," laughed Désirée, "at the way he has grown. The little *cochon de lait!* Look at his legs, mamma, and his hands and fingernails,—real finger-nails. Zandrine had to cut them this morning. Isn't it true, Zandrine?"

The woman bowed her turbaned head majestically, "Mais si, Madame."

"And the way he cries," went on Désirée, "is deafening. Armand heard him the other day as far away as La Blanche's cabin."

Madame Valmondé had never removed her eyes from the child. She lifted it and walked with it over to the window that was lightest. She scanned the baby narrowly, then looked as searchingly at Zandrine, whose face was turned to gaze across the fields.

"Yes, the child has grown, has changed;" said Madame Valmondé, slowly, as she replaced it beside its mother. "What does Armand say?"

Désirée's face became suffused with a glow that was happiness itself.

"Oh, Armand is the proudest father in the parish, I believe, chiefly because it is a boy, to bear his name; though he says not,—that he would have loved a girl as well. But I know it isn't true. I know he says that to please me. And mamma," she added, drawing Madame Valmondé's head down to her, and speaking in a whisper, "he hasn't punished one of them—not one of them—since baby is born. Even Négrillon, who pretended to have burnt his leg that he might rest from work —he only laughed, and said Négrillon was a great scamp. Oh, mamma, I'm so happy! it frightens me."

What Désirée said was true. Marriage, and later the birth of his son, had softened Armand Aubigny's imperious and exacting nature greatly. This was what made the gentle Désirée so happy, for she loved him desperately. When he frowned she trembled, but loved him. When he smiled, she asked no greater blessing of God. But Armand's dark, handsome face had not often been disfigured by frowns since the day he fell in love with her.

When the baby was about three months old, Désirée awoke one day to the conviction that there was something in the air menacing her peace. It was at first too subtle to grasp. It had only been a disquieting suggestion; an air of mystery among the blacks; unexpected visits from far-off neighbors who could hardly account for their coming. Then a strange, an awful change in her husband's manner, which she dared not ask him to explain. When he spoke to her, it was with averted eyes, from which the old love-light seemed to have gone out. He absented himself from home; and when there, avoided her presence and that of her child, without excuse. And the very spirit of Satan seemed suddenly to take hold of him in his dealings with the slaves. Désirée was miserable enough to die.

She sat in her room, one hot afternoon, in her *peignoir*, listlessly drawing through her fingers the strands of her long, silky brown hair that hung about her shoulders. The baby, half naked, lay asleep upon her own great mahogany bed, that was like a sumptuous throne, with its satin-lined half-canopy. One of La Blanche's little quadroon boys— half naked too—stood fanning the child slowly with a fan of peacock feathers. Désirées eyes had been fixed absently and sadly upon the baby, while she was striving to penetrate the threatening mist that she felt closing about her. She looked from her child to the boy who stood beside him, and back again; over and over. "Ah!" It was a cry that she could not help; which she was not conscious of having uttered. The blood turned like ice in her veins, and a clammy moisture gathered upon her face.

She tried to speak to the little quadroon boy; but no sound would come, at first. When he heard his name uttered, he looked up, and his mistress was pointing to the door. He laid aside the great, soft fan, and obediently stole away, over the polished floor, on his bare tiptoes.

She stayed motionless, with gaze riveted upon her child, and her face the picture of fright.

Presently her husband entered the room, and without noticing her, went to a table and began to search among some papers which covered it.

"Armand," she called to him, in a voice which must have stabbed him, if he was human. But he did not notice. "Armand," she said again. Then she rose and tottered towards him. "Armand," she panted once more, clutching his arm, "look at our child. What does it mean? tell me."

He coldly but gently loosened her fingers from about his arm and thrust the hand away from him. "Tell me what it means!" she cried despairingly.

"It means," he answered lightly, "that the child is not white; it means that you are not white."

A quick conception of all that this accusation meant for her nerved her with unwonted courage to deny it. "It is a lie; it is not true, I am white! Look at my hair, it is brown; and my eyes are gray, Armand, you know they are gray. And my skin is fair," seizing his wrist. "Look at my hand; whiter than yours, Armand," she laughed hysterically.

"As white as La Blanche's," he returned cruelly; and went away leaving her alone with their child.

When she could hold a pen in her hand, she sent a despairing letter to Madame Valmondé.

"My mother, they tell me I am not white. Armand has told me I am not white. For God's sake tell them it is not true. You must know it is not true. I shall die. I must die. I cannot be so unhappy, and live."

The answer that came was as brief:

"My own Désirée: Come home to Valmondé; back to your mother who loves you. Come with your child."

When the letter reached Désirée she went with it to her husband's study, and laid it open upon the desk before which he sat. She was like a stone image: silent, white, motionless after she placed it there.

In silence he ran his cold eyes over the written words. He said nothing. "Shall I go, Armand?" she asked in tones sharp with agonized suspense.

"Yes, go."

"Do you want me to go?"

"Yes, I want you to go."

He thought Almighty God had dealt cruelly and unjustly with him; and felt, somehow, that he was paying Him back in kind when he stabbed thus into his wife's soul. Moreover he no longer loved her, because of the unconscious injury she had brought upon his home and his name.

She turned away like one stunned by a blow, and walked slowly towards the door, hoping he would call her back.

"Good-by, Armand," she moaned.

He did not answer her. That was his last blow at fate.

Désirée went in search of her child. Zandrine was pacing the sombre gallery with it. She took the little one from the nurse's arms with no word of explanation, and descending the steps, walked away, under the live-oak branches.

It was an October afternoon; the sun was just sinking. Out in the still fields the negroes were picking cotton.

Désirée had not changed the thin white garment nor the slippers which she wore. Her hair was uncovered and the sun's rays brought a golden gleam from its brown meshes. She did not take the broad, beaten road which led to the far-off plantation of Valmondé. She walked across a deserted field, where the stubble bruised her tender feet, so delicately shod, and tore her thin gown to shreds.

She disappeared among the reeds and willows that grew thick along the banks of the deep, sluggish bayou; and she did not come back again.

Some weeks later there was a curious scene enacted at L'Abri. In the centre of the smoothly swept back yard was a great bonfire. Armand

Aubigny sat in the wide hallway that commanded a view of the spectacle; and it was he who dealt out to a half dozen negroes the material which kept this fire ablaze.

A graceful cradle of willow, with all its dainty furbishings, was laid upon the pyre, which had already been fed with the richness of a priceless *layette*. Then there were silk gowns, and velvet and satin ones added to these; laces, too, and embroideries; bonnets and gloves; for the *corbeille* had been of rare quality.

The last thing to go was a tiny bundle of letters; innocent little scribblings that Désirée had sent to him during the days of their espousal. There was the remnant of one back in the drawer from which he took them. But it was not Désirée's; it was part of an old letter from his mother to his father. He read it. She was thanking God for the blessing of her husband's love: —

"But, above all," she wrote, "night and day, I thank the good God for having so arranged our lives that our dear Armand will never know that his mother, who adores him, belongs to the race that is cursed with the brand of slavery."

SARAH ORNE JEWETT (1849–1909)

Born in South Berwick, Maine, Miss Jewett accompanied her father, a cultivated and humane country doctor, as he made the rounds of his patients' homes. For a writer who evokes the verities and surfaces of life along the Maine coast, this was an ideal preparation: she met a wide range of characters, and even while being charmed by their saltiness, she was persuaded of their humanity. As a girl Miss Jewett also read, and loved, Harriet Beecher Stowe's The Pearl of Orr's Island, *a fiction portraying Maine life, though with more concessions to the melodrama and self-indulgence of local color than Miss Jewett would ever allow.*

At the age of twenty Miss Jewett began to publish her stories, and in 1877, encouraged by William Dean Howells, she collected them in a volume called Deephaven. *Her finest book, from which "The Hiltons' Holiday" is taken, is* The Country of the Pointed Firs *(1896), a masterpiece in miniature.*

Miss Jewett wrote:

When I was perhaps fifteen, the first city boarders began to make their appearance near Berwick, and the way they misconstrued the country people and made game of their peculiarities fired me with indignation. I determined to teach the world that country people were not the awkward, ignorant set these people seemed to think. I wanted the world to know their grand, simple lives; and, as far as I had a mission, when I first began to write, I think that was it.

But Miss Jewett had more than a mission, she had a keen awareness of the problems of literary craft. She knew the special problems pertaining to her special kind of fiction: "It is difficult to report the great events of New England; expression is so slight, and those few words which escape us in moments of deep feeling look meager on the printed page."

The usual perspective of Miss Jewett's stories is retrospective. A sensitive observer, clearly a version of the author herself, looks back upon the decline of the once thriving Maine country; the past is recaptured through delicate cameos of character and incident that owe their success to the utmost purity of phrasing; the tone is nostalgic yet highly disciplined, at once tender, amused, and respectful. And while the narrator is clearly no longer quite at one with these people, she is also deeply involved with them and knows from the inside their speech, their customs, and their emotions. (It is interesting to compare Miss Jewett's stories with somewhat similar ones in the lovely little book Cranford, published in 1853, about a small and declining English town by the novelist Elizabeth Gaskell.)

If Miss Jewett's stories are occasionally wistful, they are rarely sentimental. She enjoys the Maine people, and rarely does she indulge in the habitual fault of local-color writing, which is to hold up provincial oddities to cosmopolitan inspection. She can be brisk about Maine faults and sharp about Maine limitations because she looks upon her characters as both special in cultural qualities and universal in human traits. And she is always in control, a craftsman choosing her words with New England frugality and scrupulousness.

It has been customary to speak of Miss Jewett's work as "minor," but it is time that this misapprehension came to an end. She precisely and faithfully rendered life in the small, with imaginative care. Why should we condescend with words like "minor"? Sarah Orne Jewett was one of the finest writers this country has had.

FURTHER READING

Willa Cather, the distinguished twentieth-century novelist, edited a two-volume edition, *The Best Stories of Sarah Orne Jewett* (1925). F. O. Matthiessen's *Sarah Orne Jewett* (1929) is an affectionate study.

The Hiltons' Holiday (1896)

1

There was a bright, full moon in the clear sky, and the sunset was still shining faintly in the west. Dark woods stood all about the old

Hilton farmhouse, save down the hill, westward, where lay the shadowy fields which John Hilton, and his father before him, had cleared and tilled with much toil,—the small fields to which they had given the industry and even affection of their honest lives.

John Hilton was sitting on the doorstep of his house. As he moved his head in and out of the shadows, turning now and then to speak to his wife, who sat just within the doorway, one could see his good face, rough and somewhat unkempt, as if he were indeed a creature of the shady woods and brown earth, instead of the noisy town. It was late in the long spring evening, and he had just come from the lower field as cheerful as a boy, proud of having finished the planting of his potatoes.

"I had to do my last row mostly by feelin'," he said to his wife. "I'm proper glad I pushed through, an' went back an' ended off after supper. 'T would have taken me a good part o' to-morrow mornin', an' broke my day."

"'T ain't no use for ye to work yourself all to pieces, John," answered the woman quickly. "I declare it does seem harder than ever that we couldn't have kep' our boy; he'd been comin' fourteen years old this fall, most a grown man, and he'd work right 'longside of ye now the whole time."

"'T was hard to lose him; I do seem to miss little John," said the father sadly. "I expect there was reasons why 't was best. I feel able an' smart to work; my father was a girt strong man, an' a monstrous worker afore me. 'T ain't that; but I was thinkin' by myself to-day what a sight o' company the boy would ha' been. You know, small's he was, how I could trust to leave him anywheres with the team, and how he'd beseech to go with me wherever I was goin'; always right in my tracks I used to tell 'em. Poor little John, for all he was so young he had a great deal o' judgment; he'd ha' made a likely man."

The mother sighed heavily as she sat within the shadow.

"But then there's the little girls, a sight o' help an' company," urged the father eagerly, as if it were wrong to dwell upon sorrow and loss. "Katy, she's most as good as a boy, except that she ain't very rugged. She's a real little farmer, she's helped me a sight this spring; an' you've got Susan Ellen, that makes a complete little housekeeper for ye as far as she's learnt. I don't see but we're better off than most folks, each on us having a work-mate."

"That's so, John," acknowledged Mrs. Hilton wistfully, beginning to rock steadily in her straight, splint-bottomed chair. It was always a good sign when she rocked.

"Where be the little girls so late?" asked their father. "'T is gettin' long past eight o'clock. I don't know when we've all set up so late, but it's so kind o' summer-like an' pleasant. Why, where be they gone?"

"I've told ye; only over to Becker's folks," answered the mother. "I don't see myself what keeps 'em so late; they beseeched me after supper till I let 'em go. They're all in a dazzle with the new teacher; she asked 'em to come over. They say she's unusual smart with 'rethmetic, but she has a kind of gorpen look to me. She's goin' to give Katy some pieces for her doll, but I told Katy she ought to be ashamed wantin' dolls' pieces, big as she's gettin' to be. I don't know's she ought, though; she ain't but nine this summer."

"Let her take her comfort," said the kind-hearted man. "Them things draws her to the teacher, an' makes them acquainted. Katy's shy with new folks, more so 'n Susan Ellen, who's of the business kind. Katy's shy-feelin' and wishful."

"I don't know but she is," agreed the mother slowly. "Ain't it sing'lar how well acquainted you be with that one, an' I with Susan Ellen? 'T was always so from the first. I'm doubtful sometimes our Katy ain't one that'll be like to get married—anyways not about here. She lives right with herself, but Susan Ellen ain't nothin' when she's alone, she's always after company; all the boys is waitin' on her a'ready. I ain't afraid but she'll take her pick when the time comes. I expect to see Susan Ellen well settled,—she feels grown up now,—but Katy don't care one mite 'bout none o' them things. She wants to be rovin' out o' doors. I do believe she'd stand an' hark to a bird the whole forenoon."

"Perhaps she'll grow up to be a teacher," suggested John Hilton. "She takes to her book more 'n the other one. I should like one on 'em to be a teacher same's my mother was. They're good girls as anybody's got."

"So they be," said the mother, with unusual gentleness, and the creak of her rocking-chair was heard, regular as the ticking of a clock. The night breeze stirred in the great woods, and the sound of a brook that went falling down the hillside grew louder and louder. Now and then one could hear the plaintive chirp of a bird. The moon glittered with whiteness like a winter moon, and shone upon the low-roofed house until its small window-panes gleamed like silver, and one could almost see the colors of a blooming bush of lilac that grew in a sheltered angle by the kitchen door. There was an incessant sound of frogs in the low-lands.

"Be you sound asleep, John?" asked the wife presently.

"I don't know but what I was a'most," said the tired man, starting a little. "I should laugh if I was to fall sound asleep right here on the step; 't is the bright night, I expect, makes my eyes feel heavy, an' 't is so peaceful. I was up an' dressed a little past four an' out to work. Well, well!" and he laughed sleepily and rubbed his eyes. "Where's the little girls? I'd better step along an' meet 'em."

"I wouldn't just yet; they'll get home all right, but 't is late for 'em certain. I don't want 'em keepin' Mis' Becker's folks up neither. There, le' 's wait a few minutes," urged Mrs. Hilton.

"I've be'n a-thinkin' all day I'd like to give the child'n some kind of a treat," said the father, wide awake now. "I hurried up my work 'cause I had it so in mind. They don't have the opportunities some do, an' I want 'em to know the world, an' not stay right here on the farm like a couple o'bushes."

"They're a sight better off not to be so full o' notions as some is," protested the mother suspiciously.

"Certain," answered the farmer; "but they're good, bright child'n, an' commencin' to take a sight o' notice. I want 'em to have all we can give 'em. I want 'em to see how other folks does things."

"Why, so do I,"—here the rocking-chair stopped ominously,—"but so long 's they're contented"—

"Contented ain't all in this world; hopper-toads may have that quality an' spend all their time a-blinkin'. I don't know's bein' contented is all there is to look for in a child. Ambition's somethin' to me."

"Now you've got your mind on to some plot or other." (The rocking-chair began to move again.) "Why can't you talk right out?"

"'T ain't nothin' special," answered the good man, a little ruffled; he was never prepared for his wife's mysterious powers of divination. "Well there, you do find things out the master! I only thought perhaps I'd take 'em to-morrow, an' go off somewhere if 't was a good day. I've been promisin' for a good while I'd take 'em to Topham Corners; they've never been there since they was very small."

"I believe you want a good time yourself. You ain't never got over bein' a boy." Mrs. Hilton seemed much amused. "There, go if you want to an' take 'em; they've got their summer hats an' new dresses. I don't know o' nothin' that stands in the way. I should sense it better if there was a circus or anythin' to go to. Why don't you wait an' let the girls pick 'em some strawberries or nice ros'berries, and then they could take an' sell 'em to the stores?"

John Hilton reflected deeply. "I should like to get me some good yellow-turnip seed to plant late. I ain't more 'n satisfied with what I've been gettin' o' late years o' Ira Speed. An I'm goin' to provide me with a good hoe; mine's gettin' wore out an' all shackly. I can't seem to fix it good."

"Them's excuses," observed Mrs. Hilton, with friendly tolerance. "You just cover up the hoe with somethin', if you get it—I would. Ira Speed's so jealous he'll remember it of you this twenty year, your goin' an' buyin' a new hoe o' anybody but him."

"I've always thought 't was a free country," said John Hilton soberly. "I don't want to vex Ira neither; he favors us all he can in trade. 'T is difficult for him to spare a cent, but he's as honest as daylight."

At this moment there was a sudden sound of young voices, and a pair of young figures came out from the shadow of the woods into the moonlighted open space. An old cock crowed loudly from his perch in the shed, as if he were a herald of royalty. The little girls were hand in hand, and a brisk young dog capered about them as they came.

"Wa'n't it dark gittin' home through the woods this time o' night?" asked the mother hastily, and not without reproach.

"I don't love to have you gone so late; mother an' me was timid about ye, and you've kep' Mis' Becker's folks up, I expect," said their father regretfully. "I don't want to have it said that my little girls ain't got good manners."

"The teacher had a party," chirped Susan Ellen, the elder of the two children. "Goin' home from school she asked the Grover boys, an' Mary an' Sarah Speed. An' Mis' Becker was real pleasant to us: she passed round some cake, an' handed us sap sugar on one of her best plates, an' we played games an' sung some pieces too. Mis' Becker thought we did real well. I can pick out most of a tune on the cabinet organ; teacher says she'll give me lessons."

"I want to know, dear!" exclaimed John Hilton.

"Yes, an' we played Copenhagen, an' took sides spellin', an' Katy beat everybody spellin' there was there."

Katy had not spoken; she was not so strong as her sister, and while Susan Ellen stood a step or two away addressing her eager little audience, Katy had seated herself close to her father on the doorstep. He put his arm around her shoulders, and drew her close to his side, where she stayed.

"Ain't you got nothin' to tell, daughter?" he asked, looking down fondly; and Katy gave a pleased little sigh for answer.

"Tell 'em what's goin' to be the last day o' school, and about our trimmin' the schoolhouse," she said; and Susan Ellen gave the programme in most spirited fashion.

"'T will be a great time," said the mother, when she had finished. "I don't see why folks wants to go trapesin' off to strange places when such things is happenin' right about 'em." But the children did not observe her mysterious air. "Come, you must step yourselves right to bed!"

They all went into the dark, warm house; the bright moon shone upon it steadily all night, and the lilac flowers were shaken by no breath of wind until the early dawn.

2

The Hiltons always waked early. So did their neighbors, the crows and song-sparrows and robins, the lightfooted foxes and squirrels in the woods. When John Hilton waked, before five o'clock, an hour later than usual because he had sat up so late, he opened the house door and came out into the yard, crossing the short green turf hurriedly as if the day were too far spent for any loitering. The magnitude of the plan for taking a whole day of pleasure confronted him seriously, but the weather was fair, and his wife, whose disapproval could not have been set aside, had accepted and even smiled upon the great project. It was inevitable now, that he and the children should go to Topham Corners. Mrs. Hilton had the pleasure of waking them, and telling the news.

In a few minutes they came frisking out to talk over the great plans. The cattle were already fed, and their father was milking. The only sign of high festivity was the wagon pulled out into the yard, with both seats put in as if it were Sunday; but Mr. Hilton still wore his every-day clothes, and Susan Ellen suffered instantly from disappointment.

"Ain't we goin', father?" she asked complainingly; but he nodded and smiled at her, even though the cow, impatient to get to pasture, kept whisking her rough tail across his face. He held his head down and spoke cheerfully, in spite of this vexation.

"Yes, sister, we're goin' certain', an' goin' to have a great time too." Susan Ellen thought that he seemed like a boy at that delightful moment, and felt new sympathy and pleasure at once. "You go an' help mother about breakfast an' them things; we want to get off quick 's we can. You coax mother now, both on ye, an' see if she won't go with us."

"She said she wouldn't be hired to," responded Susan Ellen. "She says it's goin' to be hot, an' she's laid out to go over an' see how her aunt Tamsen Brooks is this afternoon."

The father gave a little sigh; then he took heart again. The truth was that his wife made light of the contemplated pleasure, and, much as he usually valued her companionship and approval, he was sure that they should have a better time without her. It was impossible, however, not to feel guilty of disloyalty at the thought. Even though she might be completely unconscious of his best ideals, he only loved her and the ideals the more, and bent his energies to satisfying her indefinite expectations. His wife still kept much of that youthful beauty which Susan Ellen seemed likely to reproduce.

An hour later the best wagon was ready, and the great expedition set forth. The little dog sat apart, and barked as if it fell entirely upon him to voice the general excitement. Both seats were in the wagon, but the empty place testified to Mrs. Hilton's unyielding disposition. She had wondered why one broad seat would not do, but John Hilton meekly suggested that the wagon looked better with both. The little girls sat on the back seat dressed alike in their Sunday hats of straw with blue ribbons, and their little plaid shawls pinned neatly about their small shoulders. They wore gray thread gloves, and sat very straight. Susan Ellen was half a head the taller, but otherwise, from behind, they looked much alike. As for their father, he was in his Sunday best,—a plain black coat, and a winter hat of felt, which was heavy and rusty-looking for that warm early summer day. He had it in mind to buy a new straw hat at Topham, so that this with the turnip seed and the hoe made three important reasons for going.

"Remember an' lay off your shawls when you get there, an' carry them over your arms," said the mother, clucking like an excited hen to her chickens. "They'll do to keep the dust off your new dresses goin' an' comin'. An' when you eat your dinners don't get spots on you, an' don't point at folks as you ride by, an' stare, or they'll know you come from the country. An' John, you call into Cousin Ad'line Marlow's an' see how they all be, an' tell her I expect her over certain to stop awhile before hayin'. It always eases her phthisic to git up here on the highland, an I've got a new notion about doin' over her best-room carpet sence I see her that'll save rippin' one breadth. An' don't come home all wore out; an', John, don't you go an' buy me no kick-shaws to fetch home. I ain't a child, an' you ain't got no money to waste. I expect you'll go, like 's not, an' buy you some kind of a foolish boy's hat; do look an' see if it's reasonable good straw, an' won't splinter all off round the edge. An' you mind, John"—

"Yes, yes, hold on!" cried John impatiently; then he cast a last affectionate, reassuring look at her face, flushed with the hurry and responsibility of starting them off in proper shape. "I wish you was goin' too," he said, smiling. "I do so!" Then the old horse started, and they went out at the bars, and began the careful long descent of the hill. The young dog, tethered to the lilac-bush, was frantic with piteous appeals; the little girls piped their eager good-bys again and again, and their father turned many times to look back and wave his hand. As for their mother, she stood alone and watched them out of sight.

There was one place far out on the high-road where she could catch a last glimpse of the wagon, and she waited what seemed a very long time until it appeared and then was lost to sight again behind a low hill. "They're nothin' but a pack o' child'n together," she said aloud; and then felt lonelier than she expected. She even stooped and patted the unresigned little dog as she passed him, going into the house.

The occasion was so much more important than any one had foreseen that both the little girls were speechless. It seemed at first like going to church in new clothes, or to a funeral; they hardly knew how to behave at the beginning of a whole day of pleasure. They made grave bows at such persons of their acquaintance as happened to be straying in the road. Once or twice they stopped before a farmhouse, while their father talked an inconsiderately long time with some one about the crops and the weather, and even dwelt upon town business and the doings of the select-men, which might be talked of at any time. The explanations that he gave of their excursion seemed quite unnecessary. It was made entirely clear that he had a little business to do at Topham Corners, and thought he had better give the little girls a ride; they had been very steady at school, and he had finished planting, and could take the day as well as not. Soon, however, they all felt as if such an excursion were an every-day affair, and Susan Ellen began to ask eager questions, while Katy silently sat apart enjoying herself as she never had done before. She liked to see the strange houses, and the children who belonged to them; it was delightful to find flowers that she knew growing all along the road, no matter how far she went from home. Each small homestead looked its best and pleasantest, and shared the exquisite beauty that early summer made,—shared the luxury of greenness and floweriness that decked the rural world. There was an early peony or a late lilac in almost every dooryard.

It was seventeen miles to Topham. After a while they seemed very far from home, having left the hills far behind, and descended to a great level country with fewer tracts of woodland, and wider fields where the crops were much more forward. The houses were all painted, and the roads were smoother and wider. It had been so pleasant driving along that Katy dreaded going into the strange town when she first caught sight of it, though Susan Ellen kept asking with bold fretfulness if they were not almost there. They counted the steeples of four churches, and their father presently showed them the Topham Academy, where their grandmother once went to school, and told them that perhaps some day they would go there too. Katy's heart gave a strange leap; it was such a tremendous thing to think of, but instantly the suggestion was transformed for her into one of the certainties of life. She looked with solemn awe at the tall belfry, and the long rows of windows in the front of the academy, there where it stood high and white among the clustering trees. She hoped that they were going to drive by, but something forbade her taking the responsibility of saying so.

Soon the children found themselves among the crowded village houses. Their father turned to look at them with affectionate solicitude.

"Now sit up straight and appear pretty," he whispered to them. "We're among the best people now, an' I want folks to think well of you."

"I guess we're as good as they be," remarked Susan Ellen, looking at some innocent passers-by with dark suspicion, but Katy tried indeed to sit straight, and folded her hands prettily in her lap, and wished with all her heart to be pleasing for her father's sake. Just then an elderly woman saw the wagon and the sedate party it carried, and smiled so kindly that it seemed to Katy as if Topham Corners had welcomed and received them. She smiled back again as if this hospitable person were an old friend, and entirely forgot that the eyes of all Topham had been upon her.

"There, now we're coming to an elegant house that I want you to see; you'll never forget it," said John Hilton. "It's where Judge Masterson lives, the great lawyer; the handsomest house in the county, everybody says."

"Do you know him, father?" asked Susan Ellen.

"I do," answered John Hilton proudly. "Him and my mother went to school together in their young days, and were always called the two best scholars of their time. The judge called to see her once; he stopped to our house to see her when I was a boy. An' then, some years ago— you've heard me tell how I was on the jury, an' when he heard my name spoken he looked at me sharp, and asked if I wa'n't the son of Catharine Winn, an' spoke most beautiful of your grandmother, an' how well he remembered their young days together."

"I like to hear about that," said Katy.

"She had it pretty hard, I'm afraid, up on the old farm. She was keepin' school in our district when father married her—that's the main reason I backed 'em down when they wanted to tear the old schoolhouse all to pieces," confided John Hilton, turning eagerly. "They all say she lived longer up here on the hill than she could anywhere, but she never had her health. I wa'n't but a boy when she died. Father an' me lived alone afterward till the time your mother come; 't was a good while, too; I wa'n't married so young as some. 'T was lonesome, I tell you; father was plumb discouraged losin' of his wife, an' her long sickness an' all set him back, an' we'd work all day on the land an' never say a word. I s'pose 't is bein' so lonesome early in life that makes me so pleased to have some nice girls growin' up round me now."

There was a tone in her father's voice that drew Katy's heart toward him with new affection. She dimly understood, but Susan Ellen was less interested. They had often heard this story before, but to one child it was always new and to the other old. Susan Ellen was apt to think it tiresome to hear about her grandmother, who, being dead, was hardly worth talking about.

"There's Judge Masterson's place," said their father in an every-day manner, as they turned a corner, and came into full view of the beautiful old white house standing behind its green trees and terraces and lawns. The children had never imagined anything so stately and fine, and even Susan Ellen exclaimed with pleasure. At that moment they saw an old gentleman, who carried himself with great dignity, coming slowly down the wide box-bordered path toward the gate.

"There he is now, there's the judge!" whispered John Hilton excitedly, reining his horse quickly to the green roadside. "He's goin' downtown to his office; we can wait right here an' see him. I can't expect him to remember me; it's been a good many years. Now you are goin' to see the great Judge Masterson!"

There was a quiver of expectation in their hearts. The judge stopped at his gate, hesitating a moment before he lifted the latch, and glanced up the street at the country wagon with its two prim little girls on the back seat, and the eager man who drove. They seemed to be waiting for something; the old horse was nibbling at the fresh roadside grass. The Judge was used to being looked at with interest, and responded now with a smile as he came out to the sidewalk, and unexpectedly turned their way. Then he suddenly lifted his hat with grave politeness, and came directly toward them.

"Good-morning, Mr. Hilton," he said. "I am very glad to see you, sir;" and Mr. Hilton, the little girls' own father, took off his hat with equal courtesy, and bent forward to shake hands.

Susan Ellen cowered and wished herself away, but little Katy sat straighter than ever, with joy in her father's pride and pleasure shining in her pale, flower-like little face.

"These are your daughters, I am sure," said the old gentleman kindly, taking Susan Ellen's limp and reluctant hand; but when he looked at Katy, his face brightened. "How she recalls your mother!" he said with great feeling. "I am glad to see this dear child. You must come to see me with your father, my dear," he added, still looking at her. "Bring both the little girls, and let them run about the old garden; the cherries are just getting ripe," said Judge Masterson hospitably. "Perhaps you will have time to stop this afternoon as you go home?"

"I should call it a great pleasure if you would come and see us again some time. You may be driving our way, sir," said John Hilton.

"Not very often in these days," answered the old judge. "I thank you for the kind invitation. I should like to see the fine view again from your hill westward. Can I serve you in any way while you are in town? Good-by, my little friends!"

Then they parted, but not before Katy, the shy Katy, whose hand the judge still held unconsciously while he spoke, had reached forward as he said good-by, and lifted her face to kiss him. She could not have told why, except that she felt drawn to something in the serious, worn face. For the first time in her life the child had felt the charm of manners; perhaps she owned a kinship between that which made him what he was, and the spark of nobleness and purity in her own simple soul. She turned again and again to look back at him as they drove away.

"Now you have seen one of the first gentlemen in the country," said their father. "It was worth comin' twice as far"—but he did not say any more, nor turn as usual to look in the children's faces.

In the chief business street of Topham a great many country wagons like the Hiltons' were fastened to the posts, and there seemed to our holiday-makers to be a great deal of noise and excitement.

"Now I've got to do my errands, and we can let the horse rest and feed," said John Hilton. "I'll slip his headstall right off, an' put on his halter. I'm goin' to buy him a real good treat o' oats. First we'll go an' buy me my straw hat; I feel as if this one looked a little past to wear in Topham. We'll buy the things we want, an' then we'll walk all along the street, so you can look in the windows an' see the han'some things, same's your mother likes to. What was it mother told you about your shawls?"

"To take 'em off an' carry 'em over our arms," piped Susan Ellen, without comment, but in the interest of alighting and finding themselves afoot upon the pavement the shawls were forgotten. The children stood at the doorway of a shop while their father went inside, and they tried to see what the Topham shapes of bonnets were like, as their mother had advised them; but everything was exciting and confusing, and they could arrive at no decision. When Mr. Hilton came out with a hat in his hand to be seen in a better light, Katy whispered that she wished he would buy a shiny one like Judge Masterson's; but her father only smiled and shook his head, and said that they were plain folks, he and Katy. There were dry-goods for sale in the same shop, and a young clerk who was measuring linen kindly pulled off some pretty labels with gilded edges and gay pictures, and gave them to the little girls, to their exceeding joy. He may have had small sisters at home, this friendly lad, for he took pains to find two pretty blue boxes besides, and was rewarded by their beaming gratitude.

It was a famous day; they even became used to seeing so many people pass. The village was full of its morning activity, and Susan Ellen gained a new respect for her father, and an increased sense of her own consequence, because even in Topham several persons knew him and called him familiarly by name. The meeting with an old man who had once been a neighbor seemed to give Mr. Hilton the greatest pleasure. The old man called to them from a house doorway as they were passing, and they all went in. The children seated themselves wearily on the wooden step, but their father shook his old friend eagerly by the hand, and declared that he was delighted to see him so well and enjoying the fine weather.

"Oh, yes," said the old man, in a feeble, quavering voice, "I'm astonishin' well for my age. I don't complain, John, I don't complain."

They talked long together of people whom they had known in the past, and Katy, being a little tired, was glad to rest, and sat still with her hands folded, looking about the front yard. There were some kinds of flowers that she never had seen before.

"This is the one that looks like my mother," her father said, and touched Katy's shoulder to remind her to stand up and let herself be seen. "Judge Masterson saw the resemblance; we met him at his gate this morning."

"Yes, she certain does look like your mother, John," said the old man, looking pleasantly at Katy, who found that she liked him better than at first. "She does, certain; the best of young folks is, they remind us of the old ones. 'T is nateral to cling to life, folks say, but for me, I git impatient at time. Most everybody's gone now, an' I want to be goin'. 'T is somethin' before me, an' I want to have it over with. I want to be there 'long o' the rest o' the folks. I expect to last quite a while though; I may see ye couple o' times more, John."

John Hilton responded cheerfully, and the children were urged to pick some flowers. The old man awed them with his impatience to be gone. There was such a townful of people about him, and he seemed as lonely as if he were the last survivor of a former world. Until that moment they had felt as if everything were just beginning.

"Now I want to buy somethin' pretty for your mother," said Mr. Hilton, as they went soberly away down the street, the children keeping fast hold of his hands. "By now the old horse will have eat his dinner and had a good rest, so pretty soon we can jog along home. I'm goin' to take you round by the academy, and the old North Meetinghouse where Dr. Barstow used to preach. Can't you think o' somethin' that your mother'd want?" he asked suddenly, confronted by a man's difficulty of choice.

"She was talkin' about wantin' a new pepper-box, one day; the top o' the old one won't stay on," suggested Susan Ellen, with delightful readiness. "Can't we have some candy, father?"

"Yes, ma'am," said John Hilton, smiling and swinging her hand to and fro as they walked. "I feel as if some would be good myself. What's all this?" They were passing a photographer's doorway with its enticing array of portraits. "I do declare!" he exclaimed excitedly, "I'm goin' to have our pictures taken; 't will please your mother more 'n a little."

This was, perhaps, the greatest triumph of the day, except the delightful meeting with the judge; they sat in a row, with the father in the middle, and there was no doubt as to the excellence of the likeness. The best hats had to be taken off because they cast a shadow, but they were not missed, as their owners had feared. Both Susan Ellen and Katy looked their brightest and best; their eager young faces would forever shine there; the joy of the holiday was mirrored in the little picture. They did not know why their father was so pleased with it; they would not know until age had dowered them with the riches of association and remembrance.

Just at nightfall the Hiltons reached home again, tired out and happy. Katy had climbed over into the front seat beside her father, because that was always her place when they went to church on Sundays. It was a cool evening, there was a fresh sea wind that brought a light mist with it, and the sky was fast growing cloudy. Somehow the children looked different; it seemed to their mother as if they had grown older and taller since they went away in the morning, and as if they belonged to the town now as much as to the country. The greatness of their day's experience had left her far behind; the day had been silent and lonely without them, and she had had their supper ready, and been watching anxiously, ever since five o'clock. As for the children themselves they had little to say at first—they had eaten their luncheon early on the way to Topham. Susan Ellen was childishly cross, but Katy was pathetic and wan. They could hardly wait to show the picture, and their mother was as much pleased as everybody had expected.

"There, what did make you wear your shawls?" she exclaimed a moment afterward, reproachfully. "You ain't been an' wore 'em all day long? I wanted folks to see how pretty your new dresses was, if I did make 'em. Well, well! I wish more'n ever now I'd gone an' seen to ye!"

"An here's the pepper-box!" said Katy, in a pleased, unconscious tone.

"That really is what I call beautiful," said Mrs. Hilton, after a long and doubtful look. "Our other one was only tin. I never did look so high as a chiny one with flowers, but I can get us another any time for every day. That's a proper hat, as good as you could have got, John. Where's your new hoe?" she asked as he came toward her from the barn, smiling with satisfaction.

"I declare to Moses if I didn't forget all about it," meekly acknowledged the leader of the great excursion. "That an' my yellow-turnip seed, too; they went clean out o' my head, there was so many other things to think of. But 't ain't no sort o' matter; I can get a hoe just as well to Ira Speed's."

His wife could not help laughing. "You an' the little girls have had a great time. They was full o' wonder to me about everything, and I expect they'll talk about it for a week. I guess we was right about havin' 'em see somethin' more o' the world."

"Yes," answered John Hilton, with humility, "yes, we did have a beautiful day. I didn't expect so much. They looked as nice as anybody, and appeared so modest an' pretty. The little girls will remember it perhaps by an' by. I guess they won't never forget this day they had 'long o' father."

It was evening again, the frogs were piping in the lower meadows, and in the woods, higher up the great hill, a little owl began to hoot. The sea air, salt and heavy, was blowing in over the country at the end of the hot bright day. A lamp was lighted in the house, the happy children were talking together, and supper was waiting. The father and mother lingered for a moment outside and looked down over the shadowy fields; then they went in, without speaking. The great day was over, and they shut the door.

JOHN HAY (1838–1905)

Born in Pike County, Illinois, Hay graduated from Brown University, then practiced law in Springfield in an office next door to Lincoln's. When Lincoln was elected President, Hay went along as his assistant. After the war, he served as legation secretary in Paris, Vienna, and Madrid.

Returning to the United States, he joined the staff of the New York Tribune, *where some of his Pike County ballads were first published. Hay employed a strong and swinging ballad meter to tell the tales of Jim Bludso, a Mississippi steamboat captain, and other rough-and-tumble Midwestern characters. He also tried to simulate local dialects. Later, when he became United States Ambassador to Great Britain and then Secretary of State under McKinley and Theodore Roosevelt, Hay was embarrassed by the widespread popularity of these ballads, sometimes quoted to him even by literary figures in Europe.*

FURTHER READING

Tyler Dennett, *John Hay from Poetry to Politics* (1934).

Jim Bludso *(1899)*

Of the Prairie Belle

Wall, no! I can't tell whar he lives,
    Because he don't live, you see;
Leastways, he's got out of the habit
    Of livin' like you and me.
Whar have you been for the last three year
    That you have n't heard folks tell
How Jimmy Bludso passed in his checks
    The night of the Prairie Belle?

He were n't no saint,—them engineers
    Is all pretty much alike,—
One wife in Natchez-under-the-Hill   *10*
    And another one here, in Pike;
A keerless man in his talk was Jim,
    And an awkward hand in a row,
But he never flunked, and he never lied,—
    I reckon he never knowed how.

And this was all the religion he had,—
    To treat his engine well;
Never be passed on the river;
    To mind the pilot's bell;   *20*
And if ever the Prairie Belle took fire,—
    A thousand times he swore,
He'd hold her nozzle agin the bank
    Till the last soul got ashore.

All boats has their day on the Mississip,
    And her day come at last,—
The Movastar was a better boat,
    But the Belle she *would n't* be passed.
And so she come tearin' along that night—
    The oldest craft on the line—   *30*
With a nigger squat on her safety-valve,
    And her furnace crammed, rosin and pine.

The first bust out as she clared the bar,
    And burnt a hole in the night,
And quick as a flash she turned, and made
    For that willer-bank on the right.
There was runnin' and cursin', but Jim yelled out,
    Over all the infernal roar,
"I'll hold her nozzle agin the bank
    Till the last galoot's ashore."   *40*

Through the hot, black breath of the burnin' boat
    Jim Bludso's voice was heard,
And they all had trust in his cussedness,
    And knowed he would keep his word.
And, sure's you're born, they all got off
    Afore the smokestacks fell,—
And Bludso's ghost went up alone
    In the smoke of the Prairie Belle.

He were n't no saint,—but at jedgment
    I'd run my chance with Jim,   50
'Longside of some pious gentlemen
    That would n't shook hands with him.
He seen his duty, a dead-sure thing,—
    And went for it thar and then;
And Christ ain't a-going to be too hard
    On a man that died for men.

Little Breeches *(1899)*

I don't go much on religion,
    I never ain't had no show;
But I've got a middlin' tight grip, sir,
    On the handful o' things I know.
I don't pan out on the prophets
    And free-will, and that sort of thing,—
But I b'lieve in God and the angels,
    Ever sence one night last spring.

I come into town with some turnips,
    And my little Gabe come along,—   10
No four-year-old in the county
    Could beat him for pretty and strong,
Peart and chipper and sassy,
    Always ready to swear and fight,—
And I'd larnt him to chaw terbacker
    Jest to keep his milk-teeth white.

The snow come down like a blanket
    As I passed by Taggart's store;
I went in for a jug of molasses
    And left the team at the door.   20
They scared at something and started,—
    I heard one little squall,
And hell-to-split over the prairie
    Went team, Little Breeches, and all.

Hell-to-split over the prairie!
    I was almost froze with skeer;
But we rousted up some torches,
    And sarched for 'em far and near.
At last we struck hosses and wagon,
    Snowed under a soft white mound,   *30*
Upsot, dead beat,—but of little Gabe
    No hide nor hair was found.

And here all hope soured on me,
    Of my fellow-critter's aid,—
I jest flopped down on my marrow-bones,
    Crotch-deep in the snow, and prayed.
By this, the torches was played out,
    And me and Isrul Parr
Went off for some wood to a sheepfold
    That he said was somewhar thar.   *40*

We found it at last, and a little shed
    Where they shut up the lambs at night.
We looked in and seen them huddled thar,
    So warm and sleepy and white;
And thar sot Little Breeches and chirped,
    As peart as ever you see,
"I want a chaw of terbacker,
    And that's what's the matter of me."

How did he git thar? Angels.
    He could never have walked in that storm;   *50*
They jest scooped down and toted him
    To whar it was safe and warm.
And I think that saving a little child,
    And fotching him to his own,
Is a derned sight better business
    Than loafing around the Throne.

MARK TWAIN (1835–1910)

*In the life and work of a good many American writers there is a pattern
so recurrent it cannot be dismissed as merely accidental: the career
that begins with buoyant energy, full of pleasure and democratic
optimism, ends despairingly, full of bitterness and misanthropy.
Sometimes, as in Melville's Billy Budd, there is a culminating resolution: the old writer, weary of his earlier struggles and skepticisms,
comes to accept the world as it is; he makes his peace. But with a*

writer like Mark Twain, who in his best fiction is the master of the American idyll, the final vision of life is bleak, angry, unreconciled.

Samuel Clemens (Mark Twain was his pen name, adopted while working on a Nevada newspaper) was born in Florida, Missouri, then a frontier settlement of a few log cabins. When he was four years old, the family moved to Hannibal, Missouri, a river town boasting 500 souls and sharing in the prosperity of the Mississippi. For the next six or seven years the Clemens's lived in Hannibal, and it was from those years that Twain would draw his most precious memories. From them he would recall the melancholy and loneliness of the woods, the idleness of loafers on sleepy streets, the residual pieties of transplanted New Englanders trying to live right, the hustle and noise when boats would stop at the town wharf.

He was eleven when his father died, and to keep the family afloat he was apprenticed to a printer. Shortly afterward he began almost two years of personal wandering—and, it turned out, literary preparation. He was a printer in river towns (Keokuk, Iowa, St. Louis, and Cincinnati), as well as in New York, Philadelphia, and Washington. He learned to pilot a steamboat between St. Louis and New Orleans, a skill that enabled him to earn good money and of which he would always be extremely proud. During the Civil War he spent a few weeks in a Confederate unit, but he clearly had little enthusiasm for the South (he always spoke with horror of slavery) and less for soldiering. So he headed West, prospecting in Nevada and becoming a reporter for the Virginia City Territorial Enterprise.

By now Twain had been apprenticed to three trades—printing, piloting, and mining—and each would contribute something to his career as writer. In those days printers were often men of quasiliterary inclinations, from whom one could learn more than just how to set a line of type. Piloting was an occupation for men of independence, a craft and maybe an art, which Twain would later celebrate in one of his best books. The days he spent out West helped him too, for he got to know a wide range of native types, to say nothing of home-grown eccentrics, whom he would depict in his books. And the raw journalism of the West could teach a young man to compose with speed and economy.

In 1870 Twain married Olivia Langdon, a wealthy and genteel young lady from Elmira, New York. Over the decades Olivia has been given rough treatment by some of Twain's biographers and critics who have blamed her for censoring Twain's language, bringing him into a world of Eastern swells uncongenial to his talent and character, and in effect, taming his native genius. Twain's own conventional adoration of his wife—"I would quit wearing socks if she thought

them immoral"—contributed to this impression. Mostly, however,
these biographers and critics are wrong. Twain's language remained
firmly under his own command and he had quite as great a distaste
for the off-color phrase (at least in print) as did his wife. He himself
wanted to enter the company of the Eastern swells, both financial
and cultural—for if he was sometimes a caustic rebel against commercial standards, he could also be uncritically subservient to the
values of "success." It is not clear that being lionized in Boston really
hurt Twain as a writer, but if it did, Olivia is hardly to blame. And
as for taming him, he was in this respect the archetypal American
husband: he wanted, he demanded to be tamed. Instead of wondering whether his wife kept Twain from writing more great books
than he did, it might be profitable to wonder how, or whether, she
helped him write the great books that he did.

After their marriage the couple moved to Hartford in 1871 and, encouraged by the success of his early books, built an enormous and expensive house. There Twain lived—prosperous, happy, and productive—until the panic of 1893 caught him financially overextended.
Having invested heavily in a typesetting machine and in his own
printing firm, Twain faced ruin until a Standard Oil executive took
over and straightened out his affairs. By prolonged lecturing abroad,
Twain then earned enough to repay his creditors.

The final years were hard. One of his daughters suffered from epileptic
seizures, another died suddenly of spinal meningitis. Olivia died in
1904 after a long illness, and Twain, a dedicated family man, found
himself lonely and adrift. He was famous, he was comfortable, he
was honored (he went to Oxford for a degree and found pleasure in
the scarlet robes: "I like the degree well enough, but I'm crazy about
the clothes."). But he still had to face the common lot of weary
bones and failing powers. His last writings, many of them left in
fragmentary form, are explosions of wrath, sometimes merely of
irritation, against the stupidity of the human race; fierce denunciations of American imperialist policies at the turn of the century; and
exercises in a rather crude philosophical determinism not always
to be distinguished from cracker-barrel agnosticism.

Mark Twain's triumphant entry into our literature marks the cultural
emergence of a new area of American life, the midcontinental heart-
land. As a distinctive region, the Mississippi Valley represented
something sharply different from the Eastern seaboard. Its economy,
its social relationships, its geographic sense, its cultural tone, its
very use of the English language—all were more insular and
plebeian, rough and self-sufficient than those of the New England
or mid-Atlantic states. The mark of the pioneer was still visible, the
memory of the Indians still strong. And the literature that began to

be composed in this part of the country was naturally distinctive,
too. One of Twain's best critics, Bernard De Voto, has remarked:

It is absurd to speak of this as the first American literature that was independent of European influences, for our literature had obediently divorced
itself from Europe as soon as Emerson ordered it to. The humorous core
of Innocents Abroad was not independence of Europe, but indifference to
it. Thoreau and Emerson and Poe were detached from Europe but completely aware of being heirs to it, but here was a literature which had
grown up in disregard of Europe—which had looked inward toward the
Mississippi and not outward toward the Atlantic.

Twain's first book, Innocents Abroad (1869), is a humorous, sometimes
raucously slapstick, account of a travel journey undertaken by a
group of Americans innocently persuaded that no marvel of the
Old World can compare with the comforts of the New. Its irreverent,
even disdainful, tone toward European culture marks it as a book
no Bostonian or New Yorker could have written. Innocents Abroad
contains a wide streak of philistinism, reflecting a bit too accurately
the values of the region from which Twain derived, but there is also,
it must be admitted, a kind of relief to be gained from its happy-
go-lucky dismissal of Europe.

The work of the early Twain is marked above all by exuberance, the
energy and gaiety of a man who does not feel the weight of the past
heavy on his shoulders, who believes implicitly in the good nature
of himself, his characters, and his readers, and who, almost unawares, exudes the self-delight of a burgeoning young culture. Between Twain's early—and to a lesser extent, his late—work one can
detect several subliterary traditions:

The humor of the old Southwest (discussed in the General Introduction,
pages 14 to 15), which provided him with some of his basic materials and
techniques—the tall tale, the deadpan spinner of the tall tale whose glum
manner serves to accentuate the extravagance of what he is recounting,
the contrast between the accomplished prose the author is capable
of employing, and the picturesque dialect of his backwoods characters

The tradition of Western story telling, with its pleasure in physical experience,
its easy-going acceptance of rogues and worse, its mockery of the tenderfoot from back East, its friendly commerce with the natural world, and
its freedom from Eastern nail-biting moralism

The work of the professional humorists like Artemus Ward and Josh Billings,
skillful vaudevillians touring the lecture circuits and doing pieces for the
newspapers in which they would pose as semiliterates running a seven-
year war against traditional spelling, but still notable for their shrewd
common sense

Twain soon moved beyond these cultural sources. Roughing It (1872), a lively book about the old West, still employs the formulas of the popular humorists; Twain can clown with the best of them, and his account of a visit to a Mormon elder besieged by wives and noisy children is one of the funniest pieces ever written by an American. But he is also developing new resources, touches of ironic observation about the mores and manners of the West, passages of nostalgia for earlier pioneer days unsullied by money grubbing, and a prose style notable for its freshness and clarity.

Early in his career Twain became the darling of the American public, the kind of writer often called a "culture hero." By this we mean a writer who speaks both for and to an entire culture, articulating its deepest values and winning the adoration of its entire range of audiences. What Twain expressed in his earlier writing with both good nature and ironic sharpness was the notion, deeply grounded in American folklore, that in the West life was more "natural" and men more unspoiled than in the effete and "cultured" East. Westerners of course loved this, feeling that after all those decades of Boston tyranny, their day in American writing had finally come. Easterners liked it too, for it spoke to their nostalgia for a simpler— and did not simpler mean better?—America, no longer to be found along the Atlantic but movingly evoked in Twain's books.

Twain wrote a lot, and much of what he wrote is second rate or worse. He had uncertain critical faculties in regard to his own work, and to the end of his life he believed that his soupy book on Joan of Arc was his best. But in addition to a pleasing book like Roughing It and a distinguished near-miss like Puddn'head Wilson (1894), there are three volumes on which his claim to greatness finally rests.

The first is Old Times on the Mississippi (1875) a recollection of the pre-Civil War Mississippi Valley which De Voto has rightly called "a study in pure ecstacy." There are few books in American or any other literature which describe so well the state of human contentment with a job well done, which celebrate so finely the values of craft and work. And few books use the English language to such disciplined effect—here indeed is the beginning of the American style, colloquial but not scrappy, relaxed but not sprawling, vivid but not exhibitionist. It is a style that derives from but transcends speech: it has the directness and ease we like to associate with, though in fact are rarely present in, speech. Anyone who wants to learn to write English well could do no better than to study Old Times on the Mississippi.

The second is Tom Sawyer (1876), a boy's book but also an American masterpiece: the idyll of the average boy, geared to the nostalgia, fantasies, and decent limitations of the average man.

The third of Twain's major achievements is of course Huckleberry Finn
*(1884), by common consent one of the world's great books. Discussed
in the General Introduction (pages 37 to 39,* Huckleberry Finn
*is a novel at once transparent as clear water and endlessly complex
and subtle. It is an idyll of boyhood, a parable of fraternity breaking
past the social obsessions of the race, a deadly accurate portrait of
the society of the Mississippi, an account of a boy's initiation into
the entanglements of moral judgment, a stirring dream of a moment
of perfect freedom, and a moral fable about the conflict between
friendship and conscience, humane impulse and law. The painful
contrast between the arcadian promise of early American democracy
and the disappointments brought about by its phase of industrial
and financial power would haunt Twain through all his later years;
and in* Huckleberry Finn *this theme finds oblique but unforgettable
representation. It is above all a beautiful book, and no one has
written more attractively about its language than Richard Chase:*

> *The book makes a music of words which is beautifully sustained and modu-
> lated to the very end. The language is original and it has proved to be
> one of the most important discoveries—for it was discovered and adapted
> rather than being created out of the whole cloth—that have occurred in
> American literature. Hemingway's well-known pronouncement that "all
> modern American literature comes from one book by Mark Twain . . ."
> states a large truth. . . . Wherever we find, in writers such as Stephen
> Crane, Sherwood Anderson, Sinclair Lewis, Faulkner, or Hemingway him-
> self, a style that flows with the easy grace of colloquial speech and gets
> its directness and simplicity by leaving out subordinate words and clauses,
> we will be right in thinking that this is the language of Mark Twain. . . .
> The language of* Huckleberry Finn *is a kind of joyous exorcism of tradi-
> tional literary English, but this ritual act allies it irrevocably with what it
> exorcises. But it is also literary because, unlike ordinary spoken language,
> it is always conscious of the traditional English—notably of the Bible
> and Shakespeare—from which it is departing.*

*Of Twain's work in his late period, the period of determinism and de-
spair, "The Man Who Corrupted Hadleyburg" (1898) is an efficient
example. One should read such things with an awareness in mind
of how greatly the young Twain had once hoped, how joyously he
had expressed the ethos of early America. Only then can the bitterness of the late work be fully tasted.*

FURTHER READING

William M. Gibson and Henry Nash Smith edited the *Mark Twain-
Howells* letters in 1960. The single•best critical study is Henry Nash
Smith, *Mark Twain: The Development of a Writer* (1962); a fine
introduction is Bernard De Voto, *The Portable Mark Twain* (1946).

Also: Kenneth R. Andrew, *Nook Farm: Mark Twain's Hartford Years* (1950); Walter Blair, *Mark Twain and Huck Finn* (1960); Bernard De Voto, *Mark Twain at Work* (1942); DeLancey Ferguson, *Mark Twain: Man and Legend* (1943); Dixon Wecter, *Sam Clemens of Hannibal* (1952).

The Notorious Jumping Frog of Calaveras County *(1865)*

In compliance with the request of a friend of mine, who wrote me from the East, I called on good-natured, garrulous old Simon Wheeler, and inquired after my friend's friend, Leonidas W. Smiley, as requested to do, and I hereunto append the result. I have a lurking suspicion that *Leonidas* W. Smiley is a myth; that my friend never knew such a personage; and that he only conjectured that if I asked old Wheeler about him, it would remind him of his infamous *Jim* Smiley, and he would go to work and bore me to death with some exasperating reminiscence of him as long and as tedious as it should be useless to me. If that was the design, it succeeded.

I found Simon Wheeler dozing comfortably by the barroom stove of the dilapidated tavern in the decayed mining camp of Angel's, and I noticed that he was fat and bald-headed, and had an expression of winning gentleness and simplicity upon his tranquil countenance. He roused up, and gave me good day. I told him that a friend of mine had commissioned me to make some inquiries about a cherished companion of his boyhood named *Leonidas* W. Smiley—*Rev. Leonidas* W. Smiley, a young minister of the Gospel, who he had heard was at one time a resident of Angel's Camp. I added that if Mr. Wheeler could tell me anything about this Rev. Leonidas W. Smiley, I would feel under many obligations to him.

Simon Wheeler backed me into a corner and blockaded me there with his chair, and then sat down and reeled off the monotonous narrative which follows this paragraph. He never smiled, he never frowned, he never changed his voice from the gentle-flowing key to which he tuned his initial sentence, he never betrayed the slightest suspicion of enthusiasm; but all through the interminable narrative there ran a vein of impressive earnestness and sincerity, which showed me plainly that, so far from his imagining that there was anything ridiculous or funny about his story, he regarded it as a really important matter, and admired its two heroes as men of transcendent genius in *finesse*. I let him go on in his own way, and never interrupted him once.

"Rev. Leonidas W. H'm, Reverend Le—well, there was a feller here once by the name of *Jim* Smiley, in the winter of '49—or maybe it was the spring of '50—I don't recollect exactly, somehow, though what

makes me think it was one or the other is because I remember the big
flume warn't finished when he first come to the camp; but anyway, he
was the curiousest man about always betting on anything that turned
up you ever see, if he could get anybody to bet on the other side; and if
he couldn't he'd change sides. Any way that suited the other man would
suit *him*—any way just so's he got a bet, *he* was satisfied. But still he
was lucky, uncommon lucky; he most always come out winner. He was
always ready and laying for a chance; there couldn't be no solit'ry thing
mentioned but that feller'd offer to bet on it, and take ary side you please,
as I was just telling you. If there was a horse-race, you'd find him flush
or you'd find him busted at the end of it; if there was a dog-fight, he'd
bet on it; if there was a cat-fight, he'd bet on it; if there was a chicken-
fight, he'd bet on it; why, if there was two birds setting on a fence, he
would bet you which one would fly first; or if there was a camp-meeting,
he would be there reg'lar to bet on Parson Walker, which he judged to
be the best exhorter about here, and so he was too, and a good man.
If he even see a straddle-bug start to go anywheres, he would bet you
how long it would take him to get to—to wherever he was going to,
and if you took him up, he would foller that straddle-bug to Mexico but
what he would find out where he was bound for and how long he was
on the road. Lots of the boys here has seen that Smiley, and can tell
you about him. Why, it never made no difference to *him*—he'd bet on
any thing—the dangdest feller. Parson Walker's wife laid very sick once,
for a good while, and it seemed as if they warn't going to save her; but
one morning he come in, and Smiley up and asked him how she was,
and he said she was considerable better—thank the Lord for his inf'nite
mercy—and coming on so smart that with the blessing of Prov'dence
she'd get well yet; and Smiley, before he thought, says, 'Well, I'll resk
two-and-a-half she don't anyway.'

"Thish-yer Smiley had a mare—the boys called her the fifteen-
minute nag, but that was only in fun, you know, because of course she
was faster than that—and he used to win money on that horse, for all
she was so slow and always had the asthma, or the distemper, or the
consumption, or something of that kind. They used to give her two or
three hundred yards' start, and then pass her under way; but always at
the fag end of the race she'd get excited and desperate like, and come
cavorting and straddling up, and scattering her legs around limber,
sometimes in the air, and sometimes out to one side among the fences,
and kicking up m-o-r-e dust and raising m-o-r-e racket with her coughing
and sneezing and blowing her nose—and *always* fetch up at the stand
just about a neck ahead, as near as you could cipher it down.

"And he had a little small bull-pup, that to look at him you'd think
he warn't worth a cent but to set around and look ornery and lay for a
chance to steal something. But as soon as money was up on him he was
a different dog; his under-jaw'd begin to stick out like the fo'castle of a
steamboat, and his teeth would uncover and shine like the furnaces.

And a dog might tackle him and bully-rag him, and bite him, and throw him over his shoulder two or three times, and Andrew Jackson—which was the name of the pup—Andrew Jackson would never let on but what *he* was satisfied, and hadn't expected nothing else—and the bets being doubled and doubled on the other side all the time, till the money was all up; and then all of a sudden he would grab that other dog jest by the j'int of his hind leg and freeze to it—not chaw, you understand, but only just grip and hang on till they throwed up the sponge, if it was a year. Smiley always come out winner on that pup, till he harnessed a dog once that didn't have no hind legs, because they'd been sawed off in a circular saw, and when the thing had gone along far enough, and the money was all up, and he come to make a snatch for his pet holt, he see in a minute how he'd been imposed on, and how the other dog had him in the door, so to speak, and he 'peared surprised, and then he looked sorter discouraged-like, and didn't try no more to win the fight, and so he got shucked out bad. He give Smiley a look, as much as to say his heart was broke, and it was *his* fault, for putting up a dog that hadn't no hind legs for him to take holt of, which was his main dependence in a fight, and then he limped off a piece and laid down and died. It was a good pup, was that Andrew Jackson, and would have made a name for hisself if he'd lived, for the stuff was in him and he had genius—I know it, because he hadn't no opportunities to speak of, and it don't stand to reason that a dog could make such a fight as he could under them circumstances if he hadn't no talent. It always makes me feel sorry when I think of that last fight of his'n, and the way it turned out.

"Well, thish-yer Smiley had rat-tarriers, and chicken cocks, and tom-cats and all them kind of things, till you couldn't rest, and you couldn't fetch nothing for him to bet on but he'd match you. He ketched a frog one day, and took him home, and said he cal'lated to educate him; and so he never done nothing for three months but set in his back yard and learn that frog to jump. And you bet you he *did* learn him, too. He'd give him a little punch behind, and the next minute you'd see that frog whirling in the air like a doughnut—see him turn one summer-set, or maybe a couple, if he got a good start, and come down flat-footed and all right, like a cat. He got him up so in the matter of ketching flies, and kep' him in practice so constant, that he'd nail a fly every time as fur as he could see him. Smiley said all a frog wanted was education, and he could do 'most anything—and I believe him. Why, I've seen him set Dan'l Webster down here on this floor—Dan'l Webster was the name of the frog—and sing out, 'Flies, Dan'l, flies!' and quicker'n you could wink he'd spring straight up and snake a fly off'n the counter there, and flop down on the floor ag'in as solid as a gob of mud, and fall to scratching the side of his head with his hind foot as indifferent as if he hadn't no idea he'd been doin' any more'n any frog might do. You never see a frog so modest and straight-for'ard as he was, for all he was so gifted. And when it come to fair and square jumping on a dead level, he could get over more ground at one straddle than any animal of his breed you ever see. Jumping on a dead level was his strong suit, you understand; and when it come to that, Smiley would ante up money on him as long as he had a red. Smiley was monstrous proud of his frog, and well he might be, for fellers that had traveled and been everywheres all said he laid over any frog that ever *they* see.

"Well, Smiley kep' the beast in a little lattice box, and he used to fetch him downtown sometimes and lay for a bet. One day a feller—a stranger in the camp, he was—come acrost him with his box, and says:

"'What might it be that you've got in the box?'

"And Smiley says, sorter indifferent-like, 'It might be a parrot, or it might be a canary, maybe, but it ain't—it's only just a frog.'

"And the feller took it, and looked at it careful, and turned it round this way and that, and says, 'H'm—so 'tis. Well, what's *he* good for?'

"'Well,' Smiley says, easy and careless, 'he's good enough for *one* thing, I should judge—he can outjump any frog in Calaveras County.'

"The feller took the box again, and took another long, particular look, and give it back to Smiley, and says, very deliberate, 'Well,' he says, 'I don't see no p'ints about that frog that's any better'n any other frog.'

"'Maybe you don't,' Smiley says. 'Maybe you understand frogs and maybe you don't understand 'em; maybe you've had experience, and maybe you ain't only a amature, as it were. Anyways, I've got *my* opinion, and I'll resk forty dollars that he can outjump any frog in Calaveras County.'

"And the feller studied a minute, and then says, kinder sad-like, 'Well, I'm only a stranger here, and I ain't got no frog; but if I had a frog, I'd bet you.'

"And then Smiley says, 'That's all right—that's all right—if you'll hold my box a minute, I'll go and get you a frog.' And so the feller took the box, and put up his forty dollars along with Smiley's, and set down to wait.

"So he set there a good while thinking and thinking to himself, and then he got the frog out and prized his mouth open and took a teaspoon and filled him full of quail-shot—filled him pretty near up to his chin—and set him on the floor. Smiley he went to the swamp and slopped around in the mud for a long time, and finally he ketched a frog, and fetched him in, and give him to this feller, and says:

"'Now, if you're ready, set him alongside of Dan'l, with his fore paws just even with Dan'ls, and I'll give the word.' Then he says, 'One—two—three—*git!*' and him and the feller touched up the frogs from behind, and the new frog hopped off lively, but Dan'l give a heave, and hysted up his shoulders—so—like a Frenchman, but it warn't no use—he couldn't budge; he was planted as solid as a church, and he couldn't

no more stir than if he was anchored out. Smiley was a good deal surprised, and he was digusted too, but he didn't have no idea what the
matter was, of course.

"The feller took the money and started away; and when he was
going out at the door, he sorter jerked his thumb over his shoulder—
so—at Dan'l, and says again, very deliberate, 'Well,' he says, 'I don't see
no p'ints about that frog that's any better'n any other frog.'

"Smiley he stood scratching his head and looking down at Dan'l a
long time, and at last he says, 'I do wonder what in the nation that frog
throw'd off for—I wonder if there ain't something the matter with him—
he 'pears to look mighty baggy, somehow.' And he ketched Dan'l by the
nap of the neck, and hefted him, and says, 'Why blame my cats if he
don't weigh five pound!' and turned him upside down and he belched
out a double handful of shot. And then he see how it was, and he was
the maddest man—he set the frog down and took out after that feller,
but he never ketched him. And——"

[Here Simon Wheeler heard his name called from the front yard,
and got up to see what was wanted.] And turning to me as he moved
away, he said: "Just set where you are, stranger, and rest easy—I ain't
going to be gone a second."

But, by your leave, I did not think that a continuation of the history
of the enterprising vagabond *Jim* Smiley would be likely to afford me
much information concerning the Rev. *Leonidas* W. Smiley, and so I
started away.

At the door I met the sociable Wheeler returning, and he button-
holed me and recommenced:

"Well, thish-year Smiley had a yaller one-eyed cow that didn't have
no tail, only just a short stump like a bannanner, and——"

However, lacking both time and inclination, I did not wait to hear
about the afflicted cow, but took my leave.

FROM *Old Times on the Mississippi* (1875)[1]

The Boys' Ambition

When I was a boy, there was but one permanent ambition among
my comrades in our village[2] on the west bank of the Mississippi River.
That was, to be a steamboatman. We had transient ambitions of other
sorts, but they were only transient. When a circus came and went, it left
us all burning to become clowns; the first negro minstrel show that ever
came to our section left us all suffering to try that kind of life; now and
then we had a hope that, if we lived and were good, God would permit

[1] In 1875 Mark Twain published in *The Atlantic Monthly* a series of reminiscences
about "old Mississippi days of steamboating glory and grandeur as I saw them
[2] Hannibal, Missouri. *Au.*

us to be pirates. These ambitions faded out, each in its turn: but the
ambition to be a steamboatman always remained.

Once a day a cheap, gaudy packet arrived upward from St. Louis, and
another downward from Keokuk. Before these events, the day was glorious
with expectancy; after them, the day was a dead and empty thing. Not
only the boys, but the whole village, felt this. After all these years I can
picture that old time to myself now, just as it was then: the white town
drowsing in the sunshine of a summer's morning; the streets empty or
pretty nearly so; one or two clerks sitting in front of the Water Street
stores, with their splint-bottomed chairs tilted back against the wall, chins
on breasts, hats slouched over their faces, asleep—with shingle-shavings
enough around to show what broke them down; a sow and a litter of pigs
loafing along the sidewalk, doing a good business in watermelon rinds and
seeds; two or three lonely little freight piles scattered about the "levee;" a
pile of "skids" [3] on the slope of the stone-paved wharf, and the fragrant
town drunkard asleep in the shadow of them; two or three wood flats at
the head of the wharf, but nobody to listen to the peaceful lapping of the
wavelets against them; the great Mississippi, the majestic, the magnificent
Mississippi, rolling its mile-wide tide along, shining in the sun; the dense
forest away on the other side; the "point" above the town, and the
"point" below, bounding the river-glimpse and turning it into a sort of
sea, and withal a very still and brilliant and lonely one. Presently a film
of dark smoke appears above one of those remote "points;" instantly a
negro drayman, famous for his quick eye and prodigious voice, lifts up
the cry, "S-t-e-a-m-boat a-comin'!" and the scene changes! The town
drunkard stirs, the clerks wake up, a furious clatter of drays follows,
every house and store pours out a human contribution, and all in a
twinkling the dead town is alive and moving. Drays, carts, men, boys,
all go hurrying from many quarters to a common centre, the wharf.
Assembled there, the people fasten their eyes upon the coming boat as
upon a wonder they are seeing for the first time. And the boat *is*
rather a handsome sight, too. She is long and sharp and trim and pretty;
she has two tall fancy-topped chimneys, with a gilded device of some
kind swung between them; a fanciful pilot-house, all glass and "ginger-
bread," perched on top of the "texas" deck behind them; the paddle-

---

(during 5 years) *from the pilot house."* Eight years later he enlarged—and diluted—
the original work, publishing it as a book under the title *Life on the Mississippi*.
It is an all but universal critical judgment that the earlier work, *Old Times on the
Mississippi*, is superior, more compact, more coherent, more evocative.

What follows here is the bulk of *Old Times on the Mississippi*, minus only
some concluding pages which drop the narrative line and offer journalistic information about piloting.

[3] Wooden fenders hung over the side of a boat to protect it while taking cargo on
and off.

boxes are gorgeous with a picture or with gilded rays above the boat's name; the boiler deck, the hurricane deck, and the texas deck are fenced and ornamented with clean white railings; there is a flag gallantly flying from the jack-staff; the furnace doors are open and the fires glaring bravely; the upper decks are black with passengers; the captain stands by the big bell, calm, imposing, the envy of all; great volumes of the blackest smoke are rolling and tumbling out of the chimneys—a hus-banded grandeur created with a bit of pitch pine just before arriving at a town; the crew are grouped on the forecastle; the broad stage is run far out over the port bow, and an envied deck-hand stands picturesquely on the end of it with a coil of rope in his hand; the pent steam is scream-ing through the gauge-cocks; the captain lifts his hand, a bell rings, the wheels stop; then they turn back, churning the water to foam, and the steamer is at rest. Then such a scramble as there is to get aboard, and to get ashore, and to take in freight and to discharge freight, all at one and the same time; and such a yelling and cursing as the mates facili-tate it all with! Ten minutes later the steamer is under way again, with no flag on the jack-staff and no black smoke issuing from the chimneys. After ten more minutes the town is dead again, and the town drunkard asleep by the skids once more.

My father was a justice of the peace, and I supposed he possessed the power of life and death over all men and could hang anybody that offended him. This was distinction enough for me as a general thing; but the desire to be a steamboatman kept intruding, nevertheless. I first wanted to be a cabin-boy, so that I could come out with a white apron on and shake a table-cloth over the side, where all my old comrades could see me; later I thought I would rather be the deck-hand who stood on the end of the stage-plank with the coil of rope in his hand, because he was particularly conspicuous. But these were only day-dreams,—they were too heavenly to be contemplated as real possibilities. By and by one of our boys went away. He was not heard of for a long time. At last he turned up as apprentice engineer or "striker" on a steamboat. This thing shook the bottom out of all my Sunday-school teachings. That boy had been notoriously worldy, and I just the reverse; yet he was exalted to this eminence, and I left in obscurity and misery. There was nothing generous about this fellow in his greatness. He would always manage to have a dusty bolt to scrub while his boat tarried at our town, and he would sit on the inside guard and scrub it, where we all could see him and envy him and loathe him. And whenever his boat was laid up he would come home and swell around the town in his blackest and greasiest clothes, so that nobody could help remembering that he was a steamboatman; and he used all sorts of steamboat technicalities in his talk, as if he were so used to them that he forgot common people could not understand them. He would speak of the "labboard" side of a horse in an easy, natural way that would make one wish he was dead. And he was always talking about "St. Looey" like an old citizen; he would refer

casually to occasions when he was "coming down Fourth Street," or
when he was "passing by the Planter's House," or when there was a fire
and he took a turn on the brakes[4] of "the old Big Missouri;" and then
he would go on and lie about how many towns the size of ours were
burned down there that day. Two or three of the boys had long been
persons of consideration among us because they had been to St. Louis
once and had a vague general knowledge of its wonders, but the day of
their glory was over now. They lapsed into a humble silence, and learned
to disappear when the ruthless "cub"-engineer approached. This fellow
had money, too, and hair oil. Also an ignorant silver watch and a showy
brass watch-chain. He wore a leather belt and used no suspenders. If
ever a youth was cordially admired and hated by his comrades, this one
was. No girl could withstand his charms. He "cut out" every boy in the
village. When his boat blew up at last, it diffused a tranquil contentment
among us such as we had not known for months. But when he came
home the next week, alive, renowned, and appeared in church all battered up and bandaged, a shining hero, stared at and wondered over by
everybody, it seemed to us that the partiality of Providence for an unde-
serving reptile had reached a point where it was open to criticism.

This creature's career could produce but one result, and it speedily
followed. Boy after boy managed to get on the river. The minister's son
became an engineer. The doctor's and the postmaster's sons became
"mud clerks;" the wholesale liquor dealer's son became a barkeeper on
a boat; four sons of the chief merchant, and two sons of the county
judge, became pilots. Pilot was the grandest position of all. The pilot,
even in those days of trivial wages, had a princely salary—from a hundred and fifty to two hundred and fifty dollars a month, and no board
to pay. Two months of his wages would pay a preacher's salary for a
year. Now some of us were left disconsolate. We could not get on the
river—at least our parents would not let us.

So by and by I ran away. I said I would never come home again till
I was a pilot and could come in glory. But somehow I could not manage
it. I went meekly aboard a few of the boats that lay packed together like
sardines at the long St. Louis wharf, and very humbly inquired for the
pilots, but got only a cold shoulder and short words from mates and
clerks. I had to make the best of this sort of treatment for the time
being, but I had comforting day-dreams of a future when I should be a
great and honored pilot, with plenty of money, and could kill some of
these mates and clerks and pay for them.

I Want to Be a Cub-Pilot

Months afterward the hope within me struggled to a reluctant death,
and I found myself without an ambition. But I was ashamed to go home.

[4] The handles of a pump.

I was in Cincinnati, and I set to work to map out a new career. I had been reading about the recent exploration of the river Amazon by an expedition sent out by our government. It was said that the expedition, owing to difficulties, had not thoroughly explored a part of the country lying about the head-waters, some four thousand miles from the mouth of the river. It was only about fifteen hundred miles from Cincinnati to New Orleans, where I could doubtless get a ship. I had thirty dollars left; I would go and complete the exploration of the Amazon. This was all the thought I gave to the subject. I never was great in matters of detail. I packed my valise, and took passage on an ancient tub called the "Paul Jones," for New Orleans. For the sum of sixteen dollars I had the scarred and tarnished splendor of "her" main saloon principally to myself, for she was not a creature to attract the eye of wiser travelers.

When we presently got under way and went poking down the broad Ohio, I became a new being, and the subject of my own admiration. I was a traveller! A word never had tasted so good in my mouth before. I had an exultant sense of being bound for mysterious lands and distant climes which I never have felt in so uplifting a degree since. I was in such a glorified condition that all ignoble feelings departed out of me, and I was able to look down and pity the untravelled with a compassion that had hardly a trace of contempt in it. Still, when we stopped at villages and wood-yards, I could not help lolling carelessly upon the railings of the boiler deck to enjoy the envy of the country boys on the bank. If they did not seem to discover me, I presently sneezed to attract their attention, or moved to a position where they could not help seeing me. And as soon as I knew they saw me I gaped and stretched, and gave other signs of being mightily bored with travelling.

I kept my hat off all the time, and stayed where the wind and the sun could strike me, because I wanted to get the bronzed and weather-beaten look of an old traveller. Before the second day was half gone, I experienced a joy which filled me with the purest gratitude; for I saw that the skin had begun to blister and peel off my face and neck. I wished that the boys and girls at home could see me now.

We reached Louisville in time—at least the neighborhood of it. We stuck hard and fast on the rocks in the middle of the river, and lay there four days. I was now beginning to feel a strong sense of being a part of the boat's family, a sort of infant son to the captain and younger brother to the officers. There is no estimating the pride I took in this grandeur, or the affection that began to swell and grow in me for those people. I could not know how the lordly steamboatman scorns that sort of presumption in a mere landsman. I particularly longed to acquire the least trifle of notice from the big stormy mate, and I was on the alert for an opportunity to do him a service to that end. It came at last. The riotous powwow of setting a spar was going on down on the forecastle, and I went down there and stood around in the way—or mostly skipping out of it—till the mate suddenly roared a general order for somebody to bring him a capstan bar. I sprang to his side and said: "Tell me where it is—I 'll fetch it!"

If a rag-picker had offered to do a diplomatic service for the Emperor of Russia, the monarch could not have been more astounded than the mate was. He even stopped swearing. He stood and stared down at me. It took him ten seconds to scrape his disjointed remains together again. Then he said impressively: "Well, if this don't beat hell!" and turned to his work with the air of a man who had been confronted with a problem too abstruse for solution.

I crept away, and courted solitude for the rest of the day. I did not go to dinner; I stayed away from supper until everybody else had finished. I did not feel so much like a member of the boat's family now as before. However, my spirits returned, in instalments, as we pursued our way down the river. I was sorry I hated the mate so, because it was not in (young) human nature not to admire him. He was huge and muscular, his face was bearded and whiskered all over; he had a red woman and a blue woman tattooed on his right arm,—one on each side of a blue anchor with a red rope to it; and in the matter of profanity he was sublime. When he was getting out cargo at a landing, I was always where I could see and hear. He felt all the majesty of his great position, and made the world feel it, too. When he gave even the simplest order, he discharged it like a blast of lightning, and sent a long, reverberating peal of profanity thundering after it. I could not help contrasting the way in which the average landsman would give an order, with the mate's way of doing it. If the landsman should wish the gang-plank moved a foot farther forward, he would probably say: "James, or William, one of you push the plank forward, please;" but put the mate in his place, and he would roar out: "Here, now, start that gangplank for'ard! Lively, now! *What* 're you about! Snatch it! *snatch* it! There! there! Aft again! aft again! Don't you hear me? Dash it to dash! are you going to *sleep* over it! 'Vast heaving. 'Vast heaving, I tell you! Going to heave it clear astern? WHERE 're you going with the barrel! *for'ard* with it 'fore I make you swallow it, you dash-dash-dash-*dashed* split between a tired mud-turtle and a crippled hearse-horse!"

I wished I could talk like that.

When the soreness of my adventure with the mate had somewhat worn off, I began timidly to make up to the humblest official connected with the boat—the night watchman. He snubbed my advances at first, but I presently ventured to offer him a new chalk pipe, and that softened him. So he allowed me to sit with him by the big bell on the hurricane deck, and in time he melted into conversation. He could not well have helped it, I hung with such homage on his words and so plainly showed that I felt honored by his notice. He told me the names of dim capes and shadowy islands as we glided by them in the solemnity of the night, under the winking stars, and by and by got to talking about himself. He seemed over-sentimental for a man whose salary was six dollars a week—or rather he might have seemed so to an older person than I. But I drank in his words hungrily, and with a faith that might have moved mountains if it had been applied judiciously. What was it to me that he was soiled and seedy and fragrant with gin? What was it to me that his grammar was bad, his construction worse, and his profanity so void of art that it was an element of weakness rather than strength in his conversation? He was a wronged man, a man who had seen trouble, and that was enough for me. As he mellowed into his plaintive history his tears dripped upon the lantern in his lap, and I cried, too, from sympathy. He said he was the son of an English nobleman—either an earl or an alderman, he could not remember which, but believed he was both; his father, the nobleman, loved him, but his mother hated him from the cradle; and so while he was still a little boy he was sent to "one of them old, ancient colleges"—he couldn't remember which; and by and by his father died and his mother seized the property and "shook" him, as he phrased it. After his mother shook him, members of the nobility with whom he was acquainted used their influence to get him the position of "loblolly-boy in a ship;" and from that point my watchman threw off all trammels of date and locality and branched out into a narrative that bristled all along with incredible adventures; a narrative that was so reeking with bloodshed, and so crammed with hair-breadth escapes and the most engaging and unconscious personal villanies, that I sat speechless, enjoying, shuddering, wondering, worshipping.

It was a sore blight to find out afterwards that he was a low, vulgar, ignorant, sentimental, half-witted humbug, an untravelled native of the wilds of Illinois, who had absorbed wildcat literature and appropriated its marvels, until in time he had woven odds and ends of the mess into this yarn. and then gone on telling it to fledglings like me, until he had come to believe it himself.

A Cub-Pilot's Experience

What with lying on the rocks four days at Louisville, and some other delays, the poor old "Paul Jones" fooled away about two weeks in making the voyage from Cincinnati to New Orleans. This gave me a chance to get acquainted with one of the pilots, and he taught me how to steer the boat, and thus made the fascination of river life more potent than ever for me.

It also gave me a chance to get acquainted with a youth who had taken deck passage—more's the pity; for he easily borrowed six dollars of me on a promise to return to the boat and pay it back to me the day after we should arrive. But he probably died or forgot, for he never came. It was doubtless the former, since he had said his parents were wealthy, and he only travelled deck passage [5] because it was cooler.

---

[5] "Deck" passage—i.e., steerage passage. *Au.*

I soon discovered two things. One was that a vessel would not be likely to sail for the mouth of the Amazon under ten or twelve years; and the other was that the nine or ten dollars still left in my pocket would not suffice for so impossible an exploration as I had planned, even if I could afford to wait for a ship. Therefore it followed that I must contrive a new career. The "Paul Jones" was now bound for St. Louis. I planned a siege against my pilot, and at the end of three hard days he surrendered. He agreed to teach me the Mississippi River from New Orleans to St. Louis for five hundred dollars, payable out of the first wages I should receive after graduation. I entered upon the small enterprise of "learning" twelve or thirteen hundred miles of the great Mississippi River with the easy confidence of my time of life. If I had really known what I was about to require of my faculties, I should not have had the courage to begin. I supposed that all a pilot had to do was to keep his boat in the river, and I did not consider that that could be much of a trick, since it was so wide.

The boat backed out from New Orleans at four in the afternoon, and it was "our watch" until eight. Mr. Bixby, my chief, "straightened her up," plowed her along past the sterns of the other boats that lay at the Levee, and then said, "Here, take her; shave those steamships as close as you 'd peel an apple." I took the wheel, and my heart-beat fluttered up into the hundreds; for it seemed to me that we were about to scrape the side off every ship in the line, we were so close. I held my breath and began to claw the boat away from the danger; and I had my own opinion of the pilot who had known no better than to get us into such peril, but I was too wise to express it. In half a minute I had a wide margin of safety intervening between the "Paul Jones" and the ships; and within ten seconds more I was set aside in disgrace, and Mr. Bixby was going into danger again and flaying me alive with abuse of my cowardice. I was stung, but I was obliged to admire the easy confidence with which my chief loafed from side to side of his wheel, and trimmed the ships so closely that disaster seemed ceaselessly imminent. When he had cooled a little he told me that the easy water was close ashore and the current outside, and therefore we must hug the bank, up-stream, to get the bene-fit of the former, and stay well out, down-stream, to take advantage of the latter. In my own mind I resolved to be a down-stream pilot and leave the up-streaming to people dead to prudence.

Now and then Mr. Bixby called my attention to certain things. Said he, "This is Six-Mile Point." I assented. It was pleasant enough informa-tion, but I could not see the bearing of it. I was not conscious that it was a matter of any interest to me. Another time he said, "This is Nine-Mile Point." Later he said, "This is Twelve-Mile Point." They were all about level with the water's edge; they all looked about alike to me; they were monotonously unpicturesque. I hoped Mr. Bixby would change the sub-ject. But no; he would crowd up around a point, hugging the shore with affection, and then say: "The slack water ends here, abreast this bunch of China trees; now we cross over." So he crossed over. He gave me the wheel once or twice, but I had no luck. I either came near chipping the edge of a sugar-plantation, or I yawed too far from shore, and so dropped back into disgrace again and got abused.

The watch was ended at last, and we took supper and went to bed. At midnight the glare of a lantern shone in my eyes, and the night watchman said : —

"Come! turn out!"

And then he left. I could not understand this extraordinary procedure; so I presently gave up trying to, and dozed off to sleep. Pretty soon the watchman was back again, and this time he was gruff. I was annoyed. I said : —

"What do you want to come bothering around here in the middle of the night for? Now, as like as not, I 'll not get to sleep again to-night."

The watchman said : —

"Well, if this an't good, I 'm blest."

The "off-watch" was just turning in, and I heard some brutal laughter from them and such remarks as "Hello, watchman! an't the new cub turned out yet? He 's delicate, likely. Give him some sugar in a rag, and send for the chambermaid to sing rock-a-by-baby to him."

About this time Mr. Bixby appeared on the scene. Something like a minute later I was climbing the pilot-house steps with some of my clothes on and the rest in my arms. Mr. Bixby was close behind, commenting. Here was something fresh—this thing of getting up in the middle of the night to go to work. It was a detail in piloting that had never occurred to me at all. I knew that boats ran all night, but somehow I had never happened to reflect that somebody had to get up out of a warm bed to run them. I began to fear that piloting was not quite so romantic as I had imagined it was; there was something very real and work-like about this new phase of it.

It was a rather dingy night, although a fair number of stars were out. The big mate was at the wheel, and he had the old tub pointed at a star and was holding her straight up the middle of the river. The shores on either hand were not much more than half a mile apart, but they seemed wonderfully far away and ever so vague and indistinct. The mate said : —

"We've got to land at Jones's plantation, sir."

The vengeful spirit in me exulted. I said to myself, I wish you joy of your job, Mr. Bixby; you'll have a good time finding Mr. Jones's plantation such a night as this; and I hope you never *will* find it as long as you live.

Mr. Bixby said to the mate : —

"Upper end of the plantation, or the lower?"

"Upper."

"I can't do it. The stumps there are out of water at this stage. It's no great distance to the lower, and you 'll have to get along with that."

"All right, sir. If Jones don't like it, he'll have to lump it, I reckon."

And then the mate left. My exultation began to cool and my wonder to come up. Here was a man who not only proposed to find this plantation on such a night, but to find either end of it you preferred. I dreadfully wanted to ask a question, but I was carrying about as many short answers as my cargo-room would admit of, so I held my peace. All I desired to ask Mr. Bixby was the simple question whether he was ass enough to really imagine he was going to find that plantation on a night when all plantations were exactly alike and all of the same color. But I held in. I used to have fine inspirations of prudence in those days.

Mr. Bixby made for the shore and soon was scraping it, just the same as if it had been daylight. And not only that, but singing—

"Father in heaven, the day is declining," etc.

It seemed to me that I had put my life in the keeping of a peculiarly reckless outcast. Presently he turned on me and said:—

"What's the name of the first point above New Orleans?"

I was gratified to be able to answer promptly, and I did. I said I did n't know.

"Don't *know?*"

This manner jolted me. I was down at the foot again, in a moment. But I had to say just what I had said before.

"Well, you 're a smart one," said Mr. Bixby. "What 's the name of the *next* point?"

Once more I did n't know.

"Well, this beats anything. Tell me the name of *any* point or place I told you."

I studied a while and decided that I could n't.

"Look here! What do you start out from, above Twelve-Mile Point, to cross over?"

"I—I—don't know."

"You—you—don't know?" mimicking my drawling manner of speech. "What *do* you know?"

"I—I—nothing, for certain."

"By the great Caesar's ghost, I believe you! You 're the stupidest dunderhead I ever saw or heard of, so help me Moses! The idea of *you* being a pilot—*you!* Why, you don't know enough to pilot a cow down a lane."

Oh, but his wrath was up! He was a nervous man, and he shuffled from one side of his wheel to the other as if the floor was hot. He would boil awhile to himself, and then overflow and scald me again.

"Look here! What do you suppose I told you the names of those points for?"

I tremblingly considered a moment, and then the devil of temptation provoked me to say:—

"Well to—to—be entertaining, I thought."

This was a red rag to the bull. He raged and stormed so (he was crossing the river at the time) that I judged it made him blind, because he ran over the steering-oar of a trading-scow. Of course the traders sent up a volley of red-hot profanity. Never was a man so grateful as Mr. Bixby was: because he was brim ful, and here were subjects who would *talk back.* He threw open a window, thrust his head out, and such an irruption followed as I never had heard before. The fainter and farther away the scowmen's curses drifted, the higher Mr. Bixby lifted his voice and the weightier his adjectives grew. When he closed the window he was empty. You could have drawn a seine through his system and not caught curses enough to disturb your mother with. Presently he said to me in the gentlest way: —

"My boy, you must get a little memorandum-book; and every time I tell you a thing, put it down right away. There 's only one way to be a pilot, and that is to get this entire river by heart. You have to know it just like A B C."

That was a dismal revelation to me; for my memory was never loaded with anything but blank cartridges. However, I did not feel discouraged long. I judged that it was best to make some allowances, for doubtless Mr. Bixby was "stretching." Presently he pulled a rope and struck a few strokes on the big bell. The stars were all gone now, and the night was as black as ink. I could hear the wheels churn along the bank, but I was not entirely certain that I could see the shore. The voice of the invisible watchman called up from the hurricane deck: —

"What 's this, sir?"

"Jones's plantation."

I said to myself, I wish I might venture to offer a small bet that it is n't. But I did not chirp. I only waited to see. Mr. Bixby handled the engine bells, and in due time the boat's nose came to the land, a torch glowed from the forecastle, a man skipped ashore, a darky's voice on the bank said, "Gimme de k'yarpet-bag, Mars' Jones," and the next moment we were standing up the river again, all serene. I reflected deeply a while, and then said,—but not aloud,—Well, the finding of that plantation was the luckiest accident that ever happened; but it could n't happen again in a hundred years. And I fully believed it *was* an accident, too.

By the time we had gone seven or eight hundred miles up the river, I had learned to be a tolerably plucky upstream steersman, in daylight, and before we reached St. Louis I had made a trifle of progress in night-work, but only a trifle. I had a note-book that fairly bristled with the names of towns, "points," bars, islands, bends, reaches, etc.; but the information was to be found only in the note-book—none of it was in head. It made my heart ache to think I had only got half of the river set down; for as our watch was four hours off and four hours on, day and night, there was a long four-hour gap in my book for every time I had slept since the voyage began.

My chief was presently hired to go on a big New Orleans boat, and I packed my satchel and went with him. She was a grand affair. When I stood in her pilot-house I was so far above the water that I seemed perched on a mountain; and her decks stretched so far away, fore and aft, below me, that I wondered how I could ever have considered the little "Paul Jones" a large craft. There were other differences, too. The "Paul Jones's" pilot-house was a cheap, dingy, battered rattle-trap, cramped for room: but here was a sumptuous glass temple; room enough to have a dance in; showy red and gold window-curtains; an imposing sofa; leather cushions and a back to the high bench where visiting pilots sit, to spin yarns and "look at the river;" bright, fanciful "cuspadores," instead of a broad wooden box filled with sawdust; nice new oilcloth on the floor; a hospitable big stove for winter; a wheel as high as my head, costly with inlaid work; a wire tiller-rope; bright brass knobs for the bells; and a tidy, white-aproned, black "texas-tender," to bring up tarts and ices and coffee during mid-watch, day and night. Now this was "something like;" and so I began to take heart once more to believe that piloting was a romantic sort of occupation after all. The moment we were under way I began to prowl about the great steamer and fill myself with joy. She was as clean and as dainty as a drawing-room; when I looked down her long, gilded saloon, it was like gazing through a splendid tunnel; she had an oil-picture, by some gifted sign-painter, on every stateroom door; she glittered with no end of prism-fringed chandeliers; the clerk's office was elegant, the bar was marvel-lous, and the bar-keeper had been barbered and upholstered at incredible cost. The boiler deck (*i.e.*, the second story of the boat, so to speak), was as spacious as a church, it seemed to me; so with the forecastle; and there was no pitiful handful of deck-hands, firemen, and roust-abouts down there, but a whole battalion of men. The fires were fiercely glaring from a long row of furnaces, and over them were eight huge boilers! This was unutterable pomp. The mighty engines—but enough of this. I had never felt so fine before. And when I found that the regi-ment of natty servants respectfully "sir'd" me, my satisfaction was complete.

A Daring Deed

When I returned to the pilot-house St. Louis was gone, and I was lost. Here was a piece of river which was all down in my book, but I could make neither head nor tail of it: you understand, it was turned around. I had seen it when coming upstream, but I had never faced about to see how it looked when it was behind me. My heart broke again, for it was plain that I had got to learn this troublesome river *both ways*.

The pilot-house was full of pilots, going down to "look at the river." What is called the "upper river" (the two hundred miles between St.

Louis and Cairo, where the Ohio comes in) was low; and the Mississippi changes its channel so constantly that the pilots used to always find it necessary to run down to Cairo to take a fresh look, when their boats were to lie in port a week; that is, when the water was at a low stage. A deal of this "looking at the river" was done by poor fellows who seldom had a berth, and whose only hope of getting one lay in their being always freshly posted and therefore ready to drop into the shoes of some reputable pilot, for a single trip, on account of such pilot's sudden illness, or some other necessity. And a good many of them constantly ran up and down inspecting the river, not because they ever really hoped to get a berth, but because (they being guests of the boat) it was cheaper to "look at the river" than stay ashore and pay board. In time these fellows grew dainty in their tastes, and only infested boats that had an established reputation for setting good tables. All visiting pilots were useful, for they were always ready and willing, winter or summer, night or day, to go out in the yawl and help buoy the channel or assist the boat's pilot in any way they could. They were likewise welcome because all pilots are tireless talkers, when gathered together, and as they talk only about the river they are always understood and are always interesting. Your true pilot cares nothing about anything on earth but the river, and his pride in his occupation surpasses the pride of kings.

We had a fine company of these river inspectors along this trip. There were eight or ten; and there was abundance of room for them in our great pilot-house. Two or three of them wore polished silk hats, elaborate shirt-fronts, diamond breastpins, kid gloves, and patent-leather boots. They were choice in their English, and bore themselves with a dignity proper to men of solid means and prodigious reputation as pilot. The others were more or less loosely clad, and wore upon their heads tall felt cones that were suggestive of the days of the Commonwealth.

I was a cipher in this august company, and felt subdued, not to say torpid. I was not even of sufficient consequence to assist at the wheel when it was necessary to put the tiller hard down in a hurry; the guest that stood nearest did that when occasion required—and this was pretty much all the time, because of the crookedness of the channel and the scant water. I stood in a corner; and the talk I listened to took the hope all out of me. One visitor said to another: —

"Jim, how did you run Plum Point, coming up?"

"It was in the night, there, and I ran it the way one of the boys on the 'Diana' told me; started out about fifty yards above the wood pile on the false point, and held on the cabin under Plum Point till I raised the reef—quarter less twain—then straightened up for the middle bar till I got well abreast the old one-limbed cotton-wood in the mend, then got my stern on the cotton-wood and head on the low place above the point, and came through a-booming—nine and a half."

"Pretty square crossing, ain't it?"

"Yes, but the upper bar's working down fast."

Another pilot spoke up and said:—

"I had better water than that, and ran it lower down; started out from the false point—mark twain—raised the second reef abreast the big snag in the bend, and had quarter less twain."

One of the gorgeous ones remarked:—

"I don't want to find fault with your leadsmen, but that 's a good deal of water for Plum Point, it seems to me."

There was an approving nod all around as this quiet snub dropped on the boaster and "settled" him. And so they went on talk-talk-talking. Meantime, the thing that was running in my mind was, "Now, if my ears hear aright, I have not only to get the names of all the towns and islands and bends, and so on, by heart, but I must even get up a warm personal acquaintanceship with every old snag and one-limbed cotton-wood and obscure wood pile that ornaments the banks of this river for twelve hundred miles; and more than that, I must actually know where these things are in the dark, unless these guests are gifted with eyes that can pierce through two miles of solid blackness. I wish the piloting business was in Jericho and I had never thought of it."

At dusk Mr. Bixby tapped the big bell three times (the signal to land), and the captain emerged from his drawing-room in the forward end of the texas, and looked up inquiringly. Mr. Bixby said:—

"We will lay up here all night, captain."

"Very well, sir."

That was all. The boat came to shore and was tied up for the night. It seemed to me a fine thing that the pilot could do as he pleased, without asking so grand a captain's permission. I took my supper and went immediately to bed, discouraged by my day's observations and experiences. My late voyage's note-booking was but a confusion of meaningless names. It had tangled me all up in a knot every time I had looked at it in the daytime. I now hoped for respite in sleep; but no, it revelled all through my head till sunrise again, a frantic and tireless nightmare.

Next morning I felt pretty rusty and low-spirited. We went booming along, taking a good many chances, for we were anxious to "get out of the river" (as getting out to Cairo was called) before night should over-take us. But Mr. Bixby's partner, the other pilot, presently grounded the boat, and we lost so much time getting her off that it was plain the darkness would overtake us a good long way above the mouth. This was a great misfortune, especially to certain of our visiting pilots, whose boats would have to wait for their return, no matter how long that might be. It sobered the pilot-house talk a good deal. Coming up-stream, pilots did not mind low water or any kind of darkness; nothing stopped them but fog. But down-stream work was different; a boat was too nearly helpless, with a stiff current pushing behind her; so it was not customary to run down-stream at night in low water.

There seemed to be one small hope, however: if we could get through the intricate and dangerous Hat Island crossing before night, we could venture the rest, for we would have plainer sailing and better water. But it would be insanity to attempt Hat Island at night. So there was a deal of looking at watches all the rest of the day, and a constant ciphering upon the speed we were making; Hat Island was the eternal subject; sometimes hope was high and sometimes we were delayed in a bad crossing, and down it went again. For hours all hands lay under the burden of this suppressed excitement; it was even communicated to me, and I got to feeling so solicitous about Hat Island, and under such an awful pressure of responsibility, that I wished I might have five minutes on shore to draw a good, full, relieving breath, and start over again. We were standing no regular watches. Each of our pilots ran such portions of the river as he had run when coming up-stream, because of his greater familiarity with it; but both remained in the pilot-house constantly.

An hour before sunset Mr. Bixby took the wheel, and Mr. W—— stepped aside. For the next thirty minutes every man held his watch in his hand and was restless, silent, and uneasy. At last somebody said, with a doomful sigh,—

"Well yonder's Hat Island—and we can't make it."

All the watches closed with a snap, everybody sighed and muttered something about its being "too bad, too bad—ah, if we could *only* have got here half an hour sooner!" and the place was thick with the atmosphere of disappointment. Some started to go out, but loitered, hearing no bell-tap to land. The sun dipped behind the horizon, the boat went on. Inquiring looks passed from one guest to another; and one who had his hand on the door-knob and had turned it, waited, then presently took away his hand and let the knob turn back again. We bore steadily down the bend. More looks were exchanged, and nods of surprised admiration—but no words. Insensibly the men drew together behind Mr. Bixby, as the sky darkened and one or two dim stars came out. The dead silence and sense of waiting became oppressive. Mr. Bixby pulled the cord, and two deep, mellow notes from the big bell floated off on the night. Then a pause, and one more note was struck. The watchman's voice followed, from the hurricane-deck: —

"Labboard lead, there! Stabboard lead!"

The cries of the leadsmen began to rise out of the distance, and were gruffly repeated by the word-passers on the hurricane deck.

"M-a-r-k three! .... M-a-r-k three! .... Quarter-less-three! .... Half twain! .... Quarter twain! .... M-a-r-k twain! .... Quarter-less"—

Mr. Bixby pulled two bell-ropes, and was answered by faint jinglings far below in the engine room, and our speed slackened. The steam began to whistle through the gauge-cocks. The cries of the leadsmen went on—and it is a wierd sound, always, in the night. Every pilot in the lot was watching now, with fixed eyes, and talking under his breath. Nobody was calm and easy but Mr. Bixby. He would put his wheel down and stand on a spoke, and as the steamer swung into her (to me) utterly invisible marks—for we seemed to be in the midst of a wide and gloomy sea—he would meet and fasten her there. Out of the mumur of half-audible talk, one caught a coherent sentence now and then—such as:

"There; she's over the first reef all right!

After a pause, another subdued voice:—

"Her stern's coming down just *exactly* right, by *George!*"

"Now she's in the marks; over she goes!"

Somebody else muttered:—

"Oh, it was done beautiful—*beautiful!*"

Now the engines were stopped altogether, and we drifted with the current. Not that I could see the boat drift, for I could not, the stars being all gone by this time. This drifting was the dismalest work; it held one's heart still. Presently I discovered a blacker gloom than that which surrounded us. It was the head of the island. We were closing right down upon it. We entered its deeper shadow, and so imminent seemed the peril that I was likely to suffocate; and I had the strongest impulse to do *something*, anything, to save the vessel. But still Mr. Bixby stood by his wheel, silent, intent as a cat, and all the pilots stood shoulder to shoulder at his back.

She'll not make it!" somebody whispered.

The water grew shoaler and shoaler, by the leadsman's cries, till it was down to:—

"Eight-and-a-half! . . . . E-i-g-h-t feet! . . . . E-i-g-h-t feet! . . . . Seven-and"—

Mr. Bixby said warningly through his speaking-tube to the engineer:—

"Stand by, now!"

"Aye-aye, sir!"

"Seven-and-a-half! Seven feet! *Six* and"—

We touched bottom! Instantly Mr. Bixby set a lot of bells ringing, shouted through the tube, "*Now*, let her have it—every ounce you 've got!" then to his partner, "Put her hard down! snatch her! snatch her!" The boat rasped and ground her way through the sand, hung upon the apex of disaster a single tremendous instant, and then over she went! And such a shout as went up at Mr. Bixby's back never loosened the roof of a pilot-house before!

There was no more trouble after that. Mr. Bixby was a hero that night; and it was some little time, too, before his exploit ceased to be talked about by river men.

Fully to realize the marvellous precision required in laying the great steamer in her marks in that mirky waste of water, one should know that not only must she pick her intricate way through snags and blind reefs, and then shave the head of the island so closely as to brush the overhanging foliage with her stern, but at one place she must pass almost within arm's reach of a sunken and invisible wreck that would snatch the hull timbers from under her if she should strike it, and destroy a quarter of a million dollars' worth of steamboat and cargo in five minutes, and maybe a hundred and fifty human lives into the bargain.

The last remark I heard that night was a compliment to Mr. Bixby, uttered in soliloquy and with unction by one of our guests. He said:—

"By the Shadow of Death, but he's a lightning pilot!"

Perplexing Lessons

At the end of what seemed a tedious while, I had managed to pack my head full of islands, towns, bars, "points," and bends; and a curiously inanimate mass of lumber it was, too. However, inasmuch as I could shut my eyes and reel off a good long string of these names without leaving out more than ten miles of river in every fifty, I began to feel that I could make her skip those little gaps. But of course my complacency could hardly get start enough to lift my nose a trifle into the air, before Mr. Bixby would think of something to fetch it down again. One day he turned on me suddenly with this settler:—

"What is the shape of Walnut Bend?"

He might as well have asked me my grandmother's opinion of protoplasm. I reflected respectfully, and then said I did n't know it had any particular shape. My gunpowdery chief went off with a bang, of course, and then went on loading and firing until he was out of adjectives.

I had learned long ago that he only carried just so many rounds of ammunition, and was sure to subside into a very placable and even remorseful old smooth-bore as soon as they were all gone. That word "old" is merely affectionate; he was not more than thirty-four. I waited. By and by he said:—

"My boy, you 've got to know the *shape* of the river perfectly. It is all there is left to steer by on a very dark night. Everything else is blotted out and gone. But mind you, it has n't the same shape in the night that it has in the day-time."

"How on earth am I ever going to learn it, then?"

"How do you follow a hall at home in the dark? Because you know the shape of it. You can't see it."

"Do you mean to say that I 've got to know all the million trifling variations of shape in the banks of this interminable river as well as I know the shape of the front hall at home?"

"On my honor, you 've got to know them *better* than any man ever did know the shapes of the halls in his own house."

"I wish I was dead!"

"Now I don't want to discourage you, but"—

"Well, pile it on me; I might as well have it now as another time."

"You see, this has got to be learned; there is n't any getting around it. A clear starlight night throws such heavy shadows that, if you did n't know the shape of a shore perfectly, you would claw away from every bunch of timber, because you would take the black shadow of it for a solid cape; and you see you would be getting scared to death every fifteen minutes by the watch. You would be fifty yards from shore all the time when you ought to be within fifty feet of it. You can't see a snag in one of those shadows, but you know exactly where it is, and the shape of the river tells you when you are coming to it. Then there 's your pitch-dark night; the river is a very different shape on a pitch-dark night from what it is on a starlight night. All shores seem to be straight lines, then, and mighty dim ones, too; and you 'd *run* them for straight lines, only you know better. You boldly drive your boat right into what seems to be a solid, straight wall (you knowing very well that in reality there is a curve there), and that wall falls back and makes way for you. Then there 's your gray mist. You take a night when there 's one of these grisly, drizzly, gray mists, and then there is n't *any* particular shape to a shore. A gray mist would tangle the head of the oldest man that ever lived. Well, then different kinds of *moonlight* change the shape of the river in different ways. You see"—

"Oh, don't say any more, please! Have I got to learn the shape of the river according to all these five hundred thousand different ways? If I tried to carry all that cargo in my head it would make me stoop-shouldered."

"*No!* you only learn *the* shape of the river; and you learn it with such absolute certainty that you can always steer by the shape that 's *in your head*, and never mind the one that 's before your eyes."

"Very well, I 'll try it; but, after I have learned it, can I depend on it? Will it keep the same form and not go fooling around?"

Before Mr. Bixby could answer, Mr. W—— came in to take the watch, and he said,—

"Bixby, you 'll have to look out for President's Island, and all that country clear away up above the Old Hen and Chickens. The banks are caving and the shape of the shores changing like everything. Why, you would n't know the point above 40. You can go up inside the old sycamore snag, now." [6]

So that question was answered. Here were leagues of shore changing shape. My spirits were down in the mud again. Two things seemed pretty apparent to me. One was, that in order to be a pilot a man had got to learn more than any one man ought to be allowed to know; and the other was, that he must learn it all over again in a different way every twenty-four hours.

---

[6] It may not be necessary, but still it can do no harm to explain that "inside" means between the snag and the shore. *Au.*

That night we had the watch until twelve. Now it was an ancient river custom for the two pilots to chat a bit when the watch changed. While the relieving pilot put on his gloves and lit his cigar, his partner,[7] the retiring pilot, would say something like this: —

"I judge the upper bar is making down a little at Hale's Point; had quarter twain with the lower lead and mark twain [8] with the other."

"Yes, I thought it was making down a little, last trip. Meet any boats?"

"Met one abreast the head of 21, but she was away over hugging the bar, and I couldn't make her out entirely. I took her for the 'Sunny South'—had n't any skylight forward of the chimneys."

And so on. And as the relieving pilot took the wheel his partner [8] would mention that we were in such-and-such a bend, and say we were abreast of such-and-such a man's wood-yard or plantation. This was courtesy; I supposed it was *necessity*. But Mr. W—— came on watch full twelve minutes late on this particular night,—a tremendous breach of etiquette; in fact, it is the unpardonable sin among pilots. So Mr. Bixby gave him no greeting whatever, but simply surrendered the wheel and marched out of the pilot-house without a word. I was appalled; it was a villanous night for blackness, we were in a particularly wide and blind part of the river, where there was no shape or substance to anything, and it seemed incredible that Mr. Bixby should have left that poor fellow to kill the boat trying to find out where he was. But I resolved that I would stand by him any way. He should find that he was not wholly friendless. So I stood around, and waited to be asked where we were. But Mr. W—— plunged on serenely through the solid firmament of black cats that stood for an atmosphere, and never opened his mouth. Here is a proud devil, thought I; here is a limb of Satan that would rather send us all to destruction than put himself under obligations to me, because I am not yet one of the salt of the earth and privileged to snub captains and lord it over everything dead and alive in a steamboat. I presently climbed up on the bench; I did not think it was safe to go to sleep while this lunatic was on watch.

However, I must have gone to sleep in the course of time, because the next thing I was aware of was the fact that day was breaking, Mr. W—— gone, and Mr. Bixby at the wheel again. So it was four o'clock and all well—but me; I felt like a skinful of dry bones and all of them trying to ache at once.

Mr. Bixby asked me what I had stayed up there for. I confessed that it was to do Mr. W—— a benevolence,—tell him where he was. It took five minutes for the entire preposterousness of the thing to filter into Mr. Bixby's system, and then I judge it filled him nearly up to the

---

[7] "Partner" is technical for "the other pilot." *Au.*

[8] Two fathoms. Quarter twain is 2¼ fathoms, 13½ feet. Mark three is three fathoms. *Au.*

chin; because he paid me a compliment—and not much of a one either. He said,—

"Well, taking you by-and-large, you do seem to be more different kinds of an ass than any creature I ever saw before. What did you suppose he wanted to know for?"

I said I thought it might be a convenience to him.

"Convenience! D–nation! Did n't I tell you that a man's got to know the river in the night the same as he'd know his own front hall?"

"Well, I can follow the front hall in the dark if I know it *is* the front hall; but suppose you set me down in the middle of it in the dark and not tell me which hall it is; how am *I* to know?"

"Well, you've *got* to, on the river!"

"All right. Then I 'm glad I never said anything to Mr. W——"

"I should say so! Why, he'd have slammed you through the window and utterly ruined a hundred dollars' worth of windowsash and stuff."

I was glad this damage had been saved, for it would have made me unpopular with the owners. They always hated anybody who had the name of being careless, and injuring things.

I went to work now to learn the shape of the river; and of all the eluding and ungraspable objects that ever I tried to get mind or hands on, that was the chief. I would fasten my eyes upon a sharp, wooden point that projected far into the river some miles ahead of me, and go to laboriously photographing its shape upon my brain; and just as I was beginning to succeed to my satisfaction, we would draw up toward it and the exasperating thing would begin to melt away and fold back into the bank; If there had been a conspicuous dead tree standing upon the very point of the cape, I would find that tree inconspicuously merged into the general forest, and occupying the middle of a straight shore, when I got abreast of it! No prominent hill would stick to its shape long enough for me to make up my mind what its form really was, but it was as dissolving and changeful as if it had been a mountain of butter in the hottest corner of the tropics. Nothing ever had the same shape when I was coming down-stream that it had borne when I went up. I mentioned these little difficulties to Mr. Bixby. He said,—

"That 's the very main virtue of the thing. If the shapes did n't change every three seconds they would n't be of any use. Take this place where we are now, for instance. As long as that hill over yonder is only one hill, I can boom right along the way I 'm going; but the moment it splits at the top and forms a V, I know I 've got to scratch to starboard in a hurry, or I 'll bang this boat's brains out against a rock; and then the moment one of the prongs of the V swings behind the other, I 've got to waltz to larboard again, or I 'll have a misunderstanding with a snag that would snatch the keelson out of this steamboat as neatly as if it were a sliver in your hand. If that hill did n't change its shape on bad nights there would be an awful steamboat grave-yard around here inside of a year."

It was plain that I had got to learn the shape of the river in all the different ways that could be thought of,—upside down, wrong end first, inside out, fore-and-aft, and "thort-ships,"—and then know what to do on gray nights when it had n't any shape at all. So I set about it. In the course of time I began to get the best of this knotty lesson, and my self-complacency moved to the front once more. Mr. Bixby was all fixed, and ready to start it to the rear again. He opened on me after this fashion:—

"How much water did we have in the middle crossing at Hole-in-the-Wall, trip before last?"

I considered this an outrage. I said:—

"Every trip, down and up, the leadsmen are singing through that tangled place for three quarters of an hour on a stretch. How do you reckon I can remember such as mess as that?"

"My boy, you 've got to remember it. You 've got to remember the exact spot and the exact marks the boat lay in when we had the shoalest water, in every one of the five hundred shoal places between St. Louis and New Orleans; and you must n't get the shoal soundings and marks of one trip mixed up with the shoal soundings and marks of another, either, for they're not often twice alike. You must keep them separate."

When I came to myself again, I said,—

"When I get so that I can do that, I 'll be able to raise the dead, and then I won't have to pilot a steamboat to make a living. I want to retire from this business. I want a slush-bucket and a brush; I'm only fit for a roustabout. I have n't got brains enough to be a pilot; and if I had I would n't have strength enough to carry them around, unless I went on crutches."

"Now drop that! When I say I 'll learn [9] a man the river, I mean it. And you can depend on it, I 'll learn him or kill him."

Continued Perplexities

There was no use in arguing with a person like this. I promptly put such a strain on my memory that by and by even the shoal water and the countless crossing-marks began to stay with me. But the result was just the same. I never could more than get one knotty thing learned before another presented itself. Now I had often seen pilots gazing at the water and pretending to read it as if it were a book; but it was a book that told me nothing. A time came at last, however, when Mr. Bixby seemed to think me far enough advanced to bear a lesson on water-reading. So he began:—

"Do you see that long, slanting line on the face of the water? Now, that 's a reef. Moreover, it 's a bluff reef. There is a solid sandbar under

---

[9] "Teach" is not in the river vocabulary. *Au.*

it that is nearly as straight up and down as the side of a house. There is plenty of water close up to it, but mighty little on top of it. If you were to hit it you would knock the boat's brains out. Do you see where the line fringes out at the upper end and begins to fade away?"

"Yes, sir."

"Well, that is a low place; that is the head of the reef. You can climb over there, and not hurt anything. Cross over, now, and follow along close under the reef—easy water there—not much current."

I followed the reef along till I approached the fringed end. Then Mr. Bixby said,—

"Now get ready. Wait till I give the word. She won't want to mount the reef; a boat hates shoal water. Stand by—wait—*wait*—keep her well in hand. *Now* cramp her down! Snatch her! snatch her!"

He seized the other side of the wheel and helped to spin it around until it was hard down, and then we held it so. The boat resisted, and refused to answer for a while, and next she came surging to starboard, mounted the reef, and sent a long, angry ridge of water foaming away from her bows.

"Now watch her; watch her like a cat, or she 'll get away from you. When she fights strong and the tiller slips a little, in a jerky, greasy sort of way, let up on her a trifle; it is the way she tells you at night that the water is too shoal; but keep edging her up, little by little, toward the point. You are well up on the bar, now; there is a bar under every point, because the water that comes down around it forms an eddy and allows the sediment to sink. Do you see those fine lines on the face of the water that branch out like the ribs of a fan? Well, those are little reefs; you want to just miss the ends of them, but run them pretty close. Now look out—look out! Don't you crowd that slick, greasy-looking place; there ain't nine feet there; she won't stand it. She begins to smell it; look sharp, I tell you! Oh, blazes, there you go! Stop the starboard wheel! Quick! Ship up to back! Set her back!"

The engine bells jingled and the engines answered promptly, shooting white columns of steam far aloft out of the 'scape pipes, but it was too late. The boat had "smelt" the bar in good earnest; the foamy ridges that radiated from her bows suddenly disappeared, a great dead swell came rolling forward, and swept ahead of her, she careened far over to larboard, and went tearing away toward the other shore as if she were about scared to death. We were a good mile from where we ought to have been, when we finally got the upper hand of her again.

During the afternoon watch the next day, Mr. Bixby asked me if I knew how to run the next few miles. I said: —

"Go inside the first snag above the point, outside the next one, start out from the lower end of Higgins's wood-yard, make a square crossing, and"—

"That 's all right. I 'll be back before you close up on the next point."

But he was n't. He was still below when I rounded it and entered upon a piece of the river which I had some misgivings about. I did not know that he was hiding behind a chimney to see how I would perform. I went gayly along, getting prouder and prouder, for he had never left the boat in my sole charge such a length of time before. I even got to "setting" her and letting the wheel go, entirely, while I vaingloriously turned my back and inspected the stern marks and hummed a tune, a sort of easy indifference which I had prodigiously admired in Bixby and other great pilots. Once I inspected rather long, and when I faced to the front again my heart flew into my mouth so suddenly that if I had n't clapped my teeth together I should have lost it. One of those frightful bluff reefs was stretching its deadly length right across our bows! My head was gone in a moment; I did not know which end I stood on; I gasped and could not get my breath; I spun the wheel down with such rapidity that it wove itself together like a spider's web; the boat answered and turned square away from the reef, but the reef followed her! I fled, but still it followed still it kept—right across my bows! I never looked to see where I was going, I only fled. The awful crash was imminent. Why did n't that villain come? If I committed the crime of ringing a bell, I might get thrown overboard. But better that than kill the boat. So in blind desperation I started such a rattling "shivaree" down below as never had astounded an engineer in this world before, I fancy. Amidst the frenzy of the bells the engines began to back and fill in a furious way, and my reason forsook its throne— we were about to crash into the woods on the other side of the river. Just then Mr. Bixby stepped calmly into view on the hurricane deck. My soul went out to him in gratitude. My distress vanished; I would have felt safe on the brink of Niagara, with Mr. Bixby on the hurricane deck. He blandly and sweetly took his tooth-pick out of his mouth between his fingers, as if it were a cigar,—we were just in the act of climbing an overhanging big tree, and the passengers were scudding astern like rats,—and lifted up these commands to me ever so gently:—

"Stop the starboard. Stop the larboard. Set her back on both."

The boat hesitated, halted, pressed her nose among the boughs a critical instant, then reluctantly began to back away.

"Stop the larboard. Come ahead on it. Stop the starboard. Come ahead on it. Point her for the bar."

I sailed away as serenely as a summer's morning. Mr. Bixby came in and said, with mock simplicity,—

"When you have a hail, my boy, you ought to tap the big bell three times before you land, so that the engineers can get ready."

I blushed under the sarcasm, and said I had n't had any hail.

"Ah! Then it was for wood, I suppose. The officer of the watch will tell you when he wants to wood up."

I went on consuming, and said I was n't after wood.

"Indeed? Why, what could you want over here in the bend, then? Did you ever know of a boat following a bend up-stream at this stage of the river?"

"No, sir,—and *I* was n't trying to follow it. I was getting away from a bluff reef."

"No, it was n't a bluff reef; there is n't one within three miles of where you were."

"But I saw it. It was as bluff as that one yonder."

"Just about. Run over it!"

"Do you give it as an order?"

"Yes, Run over it!"

"If I don't, I wish I may die."

"All right; I am taking the responsibility."

I was just as anxious to kill the boat, now, as I had been to save it before. I impressed my orders upon my memory, to be used at the inquest, and made a straight break for the reef. As it disappeared under our bows I held my breath; but we slid over it like oil.

"Now, don't you see the difference? It was n't anything but a *wind* reef. The wind does that."

So I see. But it is exactly like a bluff reef. How am I ever going to tell them apart?"

"I can't tell you. It is an instinct. By and by you will just naturally *know* one from the other, but you never will be able to explain why or how you know them apart."

It turned out to be true. The face of the water, in time, became a wonderful book—a book that was a dead language to the uneducated passenger, but which told its mind to me without reserve, delivering its most cherished secrets as clearly as if it uttered them with a voice. And it was not a book to be read once and thrown aside, for it had a new story to tell every day. Throughout the long twelve hundred miles there was never a page that was void of interest, never one that you could leave unread without loss, never one that you would want to skip, thinking you could find higher enjoyment in some other thing. There never was so wonderful a book written by man; never one whose interest was so absorbing, so unflagging, so sparklingly renewed with every re-perusal. The passenger who could not read it was charmed with a peculiar sort of faint dimple on its surface (on the rare occasions when he did not overlook it altogether); but to the pilot that was an *italicized* passage; indeed, it was more than that, it was a legend of the largest capitals, with a string of shouting exclamation points at the end of it; for it meant that a wreck or a rock was buried there that could tear the life out of the strongest vessel that ever floated. It is the faintest and simplest expression the water ever makes, and the most hideous to a pilot's eye. In truth, the passenger who could not read this book saw nothing but all manner of pretty pictures in it, painted by the sun and shaded by the clouds, whereas to the trained eye these were not pictures at all, but the grimmest and most dead-earnest of reading-matter.

Now when I had mastered the language of this water and had come to know every trifling feature that bordered the great river as familiarly as I knew the letters of the alphabet, I had made a valuable acquisition.

But I had lost something, too. I had lost something which could never be restored to me while I lived. All the grace, the beauty, the poetry, had gone out of the majestic river! I still keep in mind a certain wonderful sunset which I witnessed when steamboating was new to me. A broad expanse of the river was turned to blood; in the middle distance the red hue brightened into gold, through which a solitary log came floating, black and conspicuous; in one place a long, slanting mark lay sparkling upon the water; in another the surface was broken by boiling, tumbling rings, that were as many-tinted as an opal; where the ruddy flush was faintest, was a smooth spot that was covered with graceful circles and radiating lines, ever so delicately traced; the shore on our left was densely wooded, and the sombre shadow that fell from this forest was broken in one place by a long ruffled trail that shone like silver; and high above the forest wall a clean-stemmed dead tree waved a single leafy bough that glowed like a flame in the unobstructed splendor that was flowing from the sun. There were graceful curves, reflected images, woody heights, soft distances; and over the whole scene, far and near, the dissolving lights drifted steadily, enriching it, every passing moment, with new marvels of coloring.

I stood like one bewitched. I drank it in, in a speechless rapture. The world was new to me, and I had never seen anything like this at home. But as I have said, a day came when I began to cease from noting the glories and the charms which the moon and the sun and the twilight wrought upon the river's face; another day came when I ceased altogether to note them. Then, if that sunset scene had been repeated, I should have looked upon it without rapture, and should have commented upon it, inwardly, after this fashion: This sun means that we are going to have wind to-morrow; that floating log means that the river is rising, small thanks to it; that slanting mark on the water refers to a bluff reef which is going to kill somebody's steamboat one of these nights, if it keeps on stretching out like that; those tumbling "boils" show a dissolving bar and a changing channel there; the lines and circles in the slick water over yonder are a warning that that troublesome place is shoaling up dangerously; that silver streak in the shadow of the forest is the "break" from a new snag, and he has located himself in the very best place he could have found to fish for steamboats; that tall dead tree, with a single living branch, is not going to last long, and then how is a body ever going to get through this blind place at night without the friendly old landmark?

No, the romance and beauty were all gone from the river. All the value any feature of it had for me now was the amount of usefulness it could furnish toward compassing the safe piloting of a steamboat. Since those days, I have pitied doctors from my heart. What does the lovely flush in a beauty's cheek mean to a doctor but a "break" that ripples above some deadly disease? Are not all her visible charms sown thick with what are to him the signs and symbols of hidden decay?

Does he ever see her beauty at all, or does n't he simply view her professionally, and comment upon her unwholesome condition all to himself? And does n't he sometimes wonder whether he has gained most or lost most by learning his trade?

Completing My Education

Whosoever has done me the courtesy to read my chapters which have preceded this may possibly wonder that I deal so minutely with piloting as a science. It was the prime purpose of those chapters; and I am not quite done yet. I wish to show, in the most patient and painstaking way, what a wonderful science it is. Ship channels are buoyed and lighted, and therefore it is a comparatively easy undertaking to learn to run them; clear-water rivers, with gravel bottoms, change their channels very gradually, and therefore one needs to learn them but once; but piloting becomes another matter when you apply it to vast streams like the Mississippi and the Missouri, whose alluvial banks cave and change constantly, whose snags are always hunting up new quarters, whose sand-bars are never at rest, whose channels are forever dodging and shirking, and whose obstructions must be confronted in all nights and all weathers without the aid of a single lighthouse or a single buoy; for there is neither light nor buoy to be found anywhere in all this three or four thousand miles of villainous river.[10] I feel justified in enlarging upon this great science for the reason that I feel sure no one has ever yet written a paragraph about it who had piloted a steamboat himself, and so had a practical knowledge of the subject. If the theme were hackneyed, I should be obliged to deal gently with the reader; but since it is wholly new, I have felt at liberty to take up a considerable degree of room with it.

When I had learned the name and position of every visible feature of the river; when I had so mastered its shape that I could shut my eyes and trace it from St. Louis to New Orleans; when I had learned to read the face of the water as one would cull the news from the morning paper; and finally, when I had trained my dull memory to treasure up an endless array of soundings and crossing-marks, and keep fast hold of them, I judged that my education was complete: so I got to tilting my cap to the side of my head, and wearing a toothpick in my mouth at the wheel. Mr. Bixby had his eye on these airs. One day he said,—

"What is the height of that bank yonder, at Burgess's?"

"How can I tell, sir? It is three quarters of a mile away."

"Very poor eye—very poor. Take the glass."

I took the glass and presently said,—

"I can't tell. I suppose that that bank is about a foot and a half high."

[10] True at the time referred to, not true now (1882). *Au.*

"Foot and a half! That's a six-foot bank. How high was the bank along here last trip?"

"I don't know; I never noticed."

"You did n't? Well, you must always do it hereafter."

"Why?"

"Because you 'll have to know a good many things that it tells you. For one thing, it tells you the stage of the river—tells you whether there 's more water or less in the river along here than there was last trip."

"The leads tell me that." I rather thought I had the advantage of him there.

"Yes, but suppose the leads lie? The bank would tell you so, and then you 'd stir those leadsmen up a bit. There was a ten-foot bank here last trip, and there is only a six-foot bank now. What does that signify?"

"That the river is four feet higher than it was last trip."

"Very good. Is the river rising or falling?"

"Rising."

"No it ain't."

"I guess I am right, sir. Yonder is some driftwood floating down the stream."

"A rise *starts* the drift-wood, but then it keeps on floating a while after the river is done rising. Now the bank will tell you about this. Wait till you come to a place where it shelves a little. Now here; do you see this narrow belt of fine sediment? That was deposited while the water was higher. You see the drift-wood begins to strand, too. The bank helps in other ways. Do you see that stump on the false point?"

"Ay, ay, sir."

"Well, the water is just up to the roots of it. You must make a note of that."

"Why?"

"Because that means that there 's seven feet in the chute of 103."

"But 103 is a long way up the river yet."

"That's where the benefit of the bank comes in. There is water enough in 103 *now*, yet there may not be by the time we get there, but the bank will keep us posted all along. You don't run close chutes on a falling river, up-stream, and there are precious few of them that you are allowed to run at all down-stream. There 's a law of the United States against it. The river may be rising by the time we get to 103, and in that case we 'll run it. We are drawing—how much?"

"Six feet aft,—six and a half forward."

"Well, you do seem to know something."

"But what I particularly want to know is, if I have got to keep up an everlasting measuring of the banks of this river, twelve hundred miles, month in and month out?"

"Of course!"

My emotions were too deep for words for a while. Presently I said,—

"And how about these chutes? Are there many of them?"

"I should say so. I fancy we shan't run any of the river this trip as you 've seen it run before—so to speak. If the river begins to rise again, we 'll go up behind bars that you 've always seen standing out of the river, high and dry like a roof of a house; we 'll cut across low places that you 've never noticed at all, right through the middle of bars that cover three hundred acres of river; we 'll creep through cracks where you 've always thought was solid land; we 'll dart through the woods and leave twenty-five miles of river off to one side; we 'll see the hind side of every island between New Orleans and Cairo."

"Then I 've got to go to work and learn just as much more river as I already know."

"Just about twice as much more, as near as you can come at it."

"Well, one lives to find out. I think I was a fool when I went into this business."

"Yes, that is true. And you are yet. But you 'll not be when you 've learned it."

"Ah, I never can learn it."

"I will see that you *do*."

By and by I ventured again: —

"Have I got to learn all this thing just as I know the rest of the river—shapes and all—and so I can run it at night?"

"Yes. And you 've got to have good fair marks from one end of the river to the other, that will help the bank tell you when there is water enough in each of these countless places—like that stump, you know. When the river first begins to rise, you can run half a dozen of the deepest of them; when it rises a foot more you can run another dozen; the next foot will add a couple of dozen, and so on: so you see you have to know your banks and marks to a dead moral certainty, and never get them mixed; for when you start through one of those cracks, there 's no backing out again, as there is in the big river; you 've got to go through, or stay there six months if you get caught on a falling river. There are about fifty of these cracks which you can't run at all except when the river is brim full and over the banks."

"This new lesson is a cheerful prospect."

"Cheerful enough. And mind what I 've just told you; when you start into one of those places you 've got to go through. They are too narrow to turn around in, too crooked to back out of, and the shoal water is always *up at the head;* never elsewhere. And the head of them is always likely to be filling up, little by little, so that the marks you reckon their depth by, this season, may not answer for next."

"Learn a new set, then, every year?"

"Exactly. Cramp her up to the bar! What are you standing up through the middle of the river for?"

The next few months showed me strange things. On the same day that we held the conversation above narrated, we met a great rise coming down the river. The whole vast face of the stream was black with drifting dead logs, broken boughs, and great trees that had caved in and been washed away. It required the nicest steering to pick one's way through this rushing raft, even in the day-time, when crossing from point to point; and at night the difficulty was mightily increased; every now and then a huge log, lying deep in the water, would suddenly appear right under our bows, coming head-on; no use to try to avoid it then; we could only stop the engines, and one wheel would walk over that log from one end to the other, keeping up a thundering racket and careening the boat in a way that was very uncomfortable to passengers. Now and then we would hit one of these sunken logs a rattling bang, dead in the center, with a full head of steam, and it would stun the boat as if she had hit a continent. Sometimes this log would lodge, and stay right across our nose, and back the Mississippi up before it; we would have to do a little crawfishing, then, to get away from the obstruction. We often hit *white* logs in the dark, for we could not see them till we were right on them, but a black log is a pretty distinct object at night. A white snag is an ugly customer when the daylight is gone.

Of course, on the great rise, down came a swarm of prodigious timber-rafts from the headwaters of the Mississippi, coal-barges from Pittsburgh, little trading scows from everywhere, and broadhorns from "Posey County," Indiana, freighted with "fruit and furniture"—the usual term for describing it, though in plain English the freight thus aggrandized was hoop-poles and pumpkins. Pilots bore a mortal hatred to these craft, and it was returned with usury. The law required all such helpless traders to keep a light burning, but it was a law that was often broken. All of a sudden, on a murky night, a light would hop up, right under our bows, almost, and an agonized voice, with the back-woods "whang" to it, would wail out:—

"Whar 'n the —— you goin' to! Cain 't you see nothin', you dash-dashed aig-suckin', sheep-stealin', one-eyed son of a stuffed monkey!"

Then for an instant, as we whistled by, the red glare from our fur-naces would reveal the scow and the form of the gesticulating orator, as if under a lightning-flash, and in that instant our firemen and deck-hands would send and receive a tempest of missiles and profanity, one of our wheels would walk off with the crashing fragments of a steering-oar, and down the dead blackness would shut again. And that flatboat-man would be sure to go into New Orleans and sue our boat, swearing stoutly that he had a light burning all the time, when in truth his gang had the lantern down below to sing and lie and drink and gamble by, and no watch on deck. Once, at night, in one of those forest-bordered crevices (behind an island) which steamboatmen intensely describe with the phrase "as dark as the inside of a cow," we should have eaten up a Posey County family, fruit, furniture, and all, but that they happened to be fiddling down below and we just caught the sound of the music in time to sheer off, doing no serious damage, unfortunately, but coming so near it that we had good hopes for a moment. These people brought up their lantern, then, of course; and as we backed and filled to get away, the precious family stood in the light of it—both sexes and various ages—and cursed us till everything turned blue. Once a coal-boatman sent a bullet through our pilot-house, when we borrowed a steering-oar of him in a very narrow place.

The River Rises

During this big rise these small-fry craft were an intolerable nuisance. We were running chute after chute,—a new world to me,—and if there was a particularly cramped place in a chute, we would be pretty sure to meet a broad-horn there; and if he failed to be there, we would find him in a still worse locality, namely, the head of the chute, on the shoal water. And then there would be no end of profane cordialities exchanged.

Sometimes, in the big river, when we would be feeling our way cautiously along through a fog, the deep hush would suddenly be broken by yells and a clamor of tin pans, and all in an instant a log raft would appear vaguely through the webby veil, close upon us; and then we did not wait to swap knives, but snatched our engine bells out by the roots and piled on all the steam we had, to scramble out of the way! One does n't hit a rock or a solid log raft with a steamboat when he can get excused.

You will hardly believe it, but many steamboat clerks always carried a large assortment of religious tracts with them in those old departed steamboating days. Indeed they did. Twenty times a day we would be cramping up around a bar, while a string of these small-fry rascals were drifting down into the head of the bend away above and beyond us a couple of miles. Now a skiff would dart away from one of them, and come fighting its laborious way across the desert of water. It would "ease all," in the shadow of our forecastle, and the panting oarsmen would shout, "Gimme a pa-a-per!" as the skiff drifted swiftly astern. The clerk would throw over a file of New Orleans journals. If these were picked up *without comment*, you might notice that now a dozen other skiffs had been drifting down upon us without saying anything. You understand, they had been waiting to see how No. 1 was going to fare. No. 1 making no comment, all the rest would bend to their oars and come on, now; and as fast as they came the clerk would heave over neat bundles of religious tracts, tied to shingles. The amount of hard swearing which twelve packages of religious literature will command when impartially divided up among twelve raftsmen's crews, who have pulled a heavy skiff two miles on a hot day to get them, is simply incredible.

As I have said, the big rise brought a new world under my vision. By the time the river was over its banks we had forsaken our old paths and were hourly climbing over bars that had stood ten feet out of water before; we were shaving stumpy shores, like that at the foot of Madrid Bend, which I had always seen avoided before; we were clattering through chutes like that of 82, where the opening at the foot was an unbroken wall of timber till our nose was almost at the very spot. Some of these chutes were utter solitudes. The dense, untouched forest overhung both banks of the crooked little crack, and one could believe that human creatures had never intruded there before. The swinging grape-vines, the grassy nooks and vistas glimpsed as we swept by, the flowering creepers waving their red blossoms from the tops of dead trunks, and all the spendthrift richness of the forest foliage, were wasted and thrown away there. The chutes were lovely places to steer in; they were deep, except at the head; the current was gentle; under the "points" the water was absolutely dead, and the invisible banks so bluff that where the tender willow thickets projected you could bury your boat's broadside in them as you tore along, and then you seemed fairly to fly.

Behind other islands we found wretched little farms, and wretcheder little log-cabins; there were crazy rail fences sticking a foot or two above the water, with one or two jeans-clad, chills-racked, yellow-faced male miserables roosting on the top-rail, elbows on knees, jaws in hands, grinding tobacco and discharging the result at floating chips through crevices left by lost teeth; while the rest of the family and the few farm-animals were huddled together in an empty wood-flat riding at her moorings close at hand. In this flatboat the family would have to cook and eat and sleep for a lesser or greater number of days (or possibly weeks), until the river should fall two or three feet and let them get back to their log-cabins and their chills again—chills being a merciful provision of an all-wise Providence to enable them to take exercise without exertion. And this sort of watery camping out was a thing which these people were rather liable to be treated to a couple of times a year: by the December rise out of the Ohio, and the June rise out of the Mississippi. And yet these were kindly dispensations, for they at least enabled the poor things to rise from the dead now and then, and look upon life when a steamboat went by. They appreciated the blessing, too, for they spread their mouths and eyes wide open and made the most of these occasions. Now what *could* these banished creatures find to do to keep from dying of the blues during the low-water season!

Once, in one of these lovely island chutes, we found our course completely bridged by a great fallen tree. This will serve to show how narrow some of the chutes were. The passengers had an hour's recreation in a virgin wilderness, while the boat-hands chopped the bridge away; for there was no such thing as turning back, you comprehend.

From Cairo to Baton Rouge, when the river is over its banks, you have no particular trouble in the night; for the thousand-mile wall of dense forest that guards the two banks all the way is only gapped with a farm or wood-yard opening at intervals, and so you can't "get out of the river" much easier than you could get out of a fenced lane; but from Baton Rouge to New Orleans it is a different matter. The river is more than a mile wide, and very deep—as much as two hundred feet, in places. Both banks, for a good deal over a hundred miles, are shorn of their timber and bordered by continuous sugar plantations, with only here and there a scattering sapling or row of ornamental China-trees. The timber is shorn off clear to the rear of the plantations, from two to four miles. When the first frost threatens to come, the planters snatch off their crops in a hurry. When they have finished grinding the cane, they form the refuse of the stalks (which they call *bagasse*) into great piles and set fire to them, though in other sugar countries the bagasse is used for fuel in the furnaces of the sugar mills. Now the piles of damp bagasse burn slowly, and smoke like Satan's own kitchen.

An embankment ten or fifteen feet high guards both banks of the mississippi all the way down that lower end of the river, and this embankment is set back from the edge of the shore from ten to perhaps a hundred feet, according to circumstances; say thirty or forty feet, as a general thing. Fill that whole region with an impenetrable gloom of smoke from a hundred miles of burning bagasse piles, when the river is over the banks, and turn a steamboat loose along there at midnight and see how she will feel. And see how you will feel, too! You find yourself away out in the midst of a vague dim sea that is shoreless, that fades out and loses itself in the murky distances; for you cannot discern the thin rib of embankment, and you are always imagining you see a straggling tree when you don't. The plantations themselves are transformed by the smoke, and look like a part of the sea. All through your watch you are tortured with the exquisite misery of uncertainty. You hope you are keeping in the river, but you do not know. All that you are sure about is that you are likely to be within six feet of the bank *and* destruction, when you think you are a good half-mile from shore. And you are sure, also, that if you chance suddenly to fetch up against the embankment and topple your chimneys overboard, you will have the small comfort of knowing that it is about what you were expecting to do. One of the great Vicksburg packets darted out into a sugar plantation one night, at such a time, and had to stay there a week. But there was no novelty about it; it had often been done before.

I thought I had finished this chapter, but I wish to add a curious thing, while it is in my mind. It is only relevant in that it is connected with piloting. There used to be an excellent pilot on the river, a Mr. X., who was a somnambulist. It was said that if his mind was troubled about a bad piece of river, he was pretty sure to get up and walk in his sleep and do strange things. He was once fellow-pilot for a trip or two with George Ealer, on a great New Orleans passenger packet. During a considerable part of the first trip George was uneasy, but got over it by and by, as X. seemed content to stay in his bed when asleep. Late one night the boat was approaching Helena, Arkansas; the water was low, and the crossing above the town in a very blind and tangled condition. X. had seen the crossing since Ealer had, and as the night was particularly drizzly, sullen, and dark, Ealer was considering whether he had not better have X. called to assist in running the place, when the door opened and X. walked in. Now on very dark nights, light is a deadly enemy to piloting; you are aware that if you stand in a lighted room, on such a night, you cannot see things in the street to any purpose; but if you put out the lights and stand in the gloom you can make out objects in the street pretty well. So, on very dark nights, pilots do not smoke; they allow no fire in the pilot-house stove, if there is a crack which can allow the least ray to escape; they order the furnaces to be curtained with huge tarpaulins and the sky-lights to be closely blinded. Then no light whatever issues from the boat. The undefinable shape that now entered the pilot-house had Mr. X.'s voice. This said,—

"Let me take her, George; I 've seen this place since you have, and it is so crooked that I reckon I can run it myself easier than I could tell you how to do it."

"It is kind of you, and I swear *I* am willing. I have n't got another drop of perspiration left in me. I have been spinning around and around the wheel like a squirrel. It is so dark I can't tell which way she is swinging till she is coming around like a whirligig."

So Ealer took a seat on the bench, panting and breathless. The black phantom assumed the wheel without saying anything, steadied the waltzing steamer with a turn or two, and then stood at ease, coaxing her a little to this side and then to that, as gently and as sweetly as if the time had been noonday. When Ealer observed this marvel of steering, he wished he had not confessed! He stared, and wondered, and finally said,—

"Well, I thought I knew how to steer a steamboat, but that was another mistake of mine."

X. said nothing, but went serenely on with his work. He rang for the leads; he rang to slow down the steam; he worked the boat carefully and neatly into invisible marks, then stood at the centre of the wheel and peered blandly out into the blackness, fore and aft, to verify his position; as the leads shoaled more and more, he stopped the engines entirely, and the dead silence and suspense of "drifting" followed; when the shoalest water was struck, he cracked on the steam, carried her handsomely over, and then began to work her warily into the next system of shoal marks; the same patient, heedful use of leads and engines followed, the boat slipped through without touching bottom, and entered upon the third and last intricacy of the crossing; imperceptibly she moved through the gloom, crept by inches into her marks, drifted tediously till the shoalest water was cried, and then, under a tremendous head of steam, went swinging over the reef and away into deep water and safety!

Ealer let his long-pent breath pour in a great relieving sigh, and said:—

"That 's the sweetest piece of piloting that was ever done on the Mississippi River! I would n't believe it could be done, if I had n't seen it."

There was no reply, and he added:—

"Just hold her five minutes longer, partner, and let me run down and get a cup of coffee."

A minute later Ealer was biting into a pie, down in the "texas," and comforting himself with coffee. Just then the night watchman happened in, and was about to happen out again, when he noticed Ealer and exclaimed,—

"Who is at the wheel, sir?"

"X."

"Dart for the pilot-house, quicker than lightning!"

The next moment both men were flying up the pilot-house companion-way, three steps at a jump! Nobody there! The great steamer was whistling down the middle of the river at her own sweet will! The watchman shot out of the place again; Ealer seized the wheel, set an engine back with power, and held his breath while the boat reluctantly swung away from a "towhead" which she was about to knock into the middle of the Gulf of Mexico!

By and by the watchman came back and said,—

"Did n't that lunatic tell you he was asleep, when he first came up here?"

"No."

"Well, he was. I found him walking along on top of the railings, just as unconcerned as another man would walk a pavement; and I put him to bed; now just this minute there he was again, away astern, going through that sort of tight-rope deviltry the same as before."

"Well, I think I 'll stay by next time he has one of those fits. But I hope he 'll have them often. You just ought to have seen him take this boat through Helena crossing. *I* never saw anything so gaudy before. And if he can do such gold-leaf, kid-glove, diamond-breastpin piloting when he is sound asleep, what *could n't* he do if he was dead!"

Sounding

When the river is very low, and one's steamboat is "drawing all the water" there is in the channel,—or a few inches more, as was often the case in the old times,—one must be painfully circumspect in his piloting. We used to have to "sound" a number of particularly bad places almost every trip when the river was at a very low stage.

Sounding is done in this way. The boat ties up at the shore, just above the shoal crossing; the pilot not on watch takes his "cub" or steersman and a picked crew of men (sometimes an officer also), and goes out in the yawl—provided the boat has not that rare and sump-

tuous luxury, a regularly devised "sounding-boat"—and proceeds to
hunt for the best water, the pilot on duty watching his movements
through a spy-glass, meantime, and in some instances assisting by signals of the boat's whistle, signifying "try higher up" or "try lower down;"
for the surface of the water, like an oil-painting, is more expressive and
intelligible when inspected from a little distance than very close at
hand. The whistle signals are seldom necessary, however, never, perhaps, except when the wind confuses the significant ripples upon the
water's surface. When the yawl has reached the shoal place, the speed
is slackened, the pilot begins to sound the depth with a pole ten or
twelve feet long, and the steersman at the tiller obeys the order to
"hold her up to starboard;" or "let her fall off to larboard;"[11] or "steady
—steady as you go."

When the measurements indicate that the yawl is approaching the
shoalest part of the reef, the command is given to "ease all!" Then the
men stop rowing and the yawl drifts with the current. The next order
is, "Stand by with the buoy!" The moment the shallowest point is
reached, the pilot delivers the order, "Let go the buoy!" and over she
goes. If the pilot is not satisfied, he sounds the place again; if he finds
better water higher up or lower down, he removes the buoy to that
place. Being finally satisfied, he gives the order, and all the men stand
their oars straight up in the air, in line; a blast from the boat's whistle
indicates that the signal has been seen; then the men "give way" on
their oars and lay the yawl alongside the buoy; the steamer comes
creeping carefully down, is pointed straight at the buoy, husbands her
power for the coming struggle, and presently, at the critical moment,
turns on all her steam and goes grinding and wallowing over the buoy
and the sand, and gains the deep water beyond. Or maybe she doesn't;
maybe she "strikes and swings." Then she has to while away several
hours (or days) sparring herself off.

Sometimes a buoy is not laid at all, but the yawl goes ahead, hunting the best water, and the steamer follows along in its wake. Often
there is a deal of fun and excitement about sounding, especially if it
is a glorious summer day, or a blustering night. But in winter the cold
and the peril take most of the fun out of it.

A buoy is nothing but a board four or five feet long, with one end
turned up; it is a reversed school-house bench, with one of the supports
left and the other removed. It is anchored on the shoalest part of the
reef by a rope with a heavy stone made fast to the end of it. But for
the resistance of the turned-up end of the reversed bench, the current
would pull the buoy under water. At night, a paper lantern with a
candle in it is fastened on top of the buoy, and this can be seen a mile
or more, a little glimmering spark in the waste of blackness.

---

[11] The term "'larboard" is never used at sea, now, to signify the left hand; but was
always used on the river in my time. *Au.*

Nothing delights a cub so much as an opportunity to go out sounding. There is such an air of adventure about it; often there is danger; it is so gaudy and man-of-war-like to sit up in the stern-sheets and steer a swift yawl; there is something fine about the exultant spring of the boat when an experienced old sailor crew throw their souls into the oars; it is lovely to see the white foam stream away from the bows; there is music in the rush of the water; it is deliciously exhilarating, in summer, to go speeding over the breezy expanses of the river when the world of wavelets is dancing in the sun. It is such grandeur, too, to the cub, to get a chance to give an order; for often the pilot will simply say, "Let her go about;" and leave the rest to the cub, who instantly cries, in his sternest tone of command, "Ease starboard! Strong on the larboard! Starboard give way! With a will, men!" The cub enjoys sounding for the further reason that the eyes of the passengers are watching all the yawl's movements with absorbing interest if the time be daylight; and if it be night he knows that those same wondering eyes are fastened upon the yawl's lantern as it glides out into the gloom and dims away in the remote distance.

One trip a pretty girl of sixteen spent her time in our pilot-house with her uncle and aunt, every day and all day long. I fell in love with her. So did Mr. Thornburg's cub, Tom G——. Tom and I had been bosom friends until this time; but now a coolness began to arise. I told the girl a good many of my river adventures, and made myself out a good deal of a hero; Tom tried to make himself appear to be a hero, too, and succeeded to some extent, but then he always had a way of embroidering. However, virtue is its own reward, so I was a barely perceptible trifle ahead in the contest. About this time something happened which promised handsomely for me: the pilots decided to sound the crossing at the head of 21. This would occur about nine or ten o'clock at night, when the passengers would be still up; it would be Mr. Thornburg's watch, therefore my chief would have to do the sounding. We had a perfect love of a sounding-boat—long, trim, graceful, and as fleet as a greyhound; her thwarts were cushioned; she carried twelve oarsmen; one of the mates was always sent in her to transmit orders to her crew, for ours was a steamer where no end of "style" was put on.

We tied up at the shore above 21, and got ready. It was a foul night, and the river was so wide, there, that a landsman's uneducated eye could discern no opposite shore through such a gloom. The passengers were alert and interested; everything was satisfactory. As I hurried through the engine-room, picturesquely gotten up in storm toggery, I met Tom, and could not forbear delivering myself of a mean speech:—

"Ain't you glad *you* don't have to go out sounding?"

Tom was passing on, but he quickly turned, and said,—

"Now just for that, you can go and get the sounding-pole yourself. I was going after it, but I 'd see you in Halifax, now, before I 'd do it."

"Who wants you to get it? *I* don't. It 's in the sounding-boat."

"It ain't, either. It 's been new-painted; and it 's been up on the ladies cabin guards two days, drying."

I flew back, and shortly arrived among the crowd of watching and wondering ladies just in time to hear the command:

"Give way, men!"

I looked over, and there was the gallant sounding-boat booming away, the unprincipled Tom presiding at the tiller, and my chief sitting by him with the sounding-pole which I had been sent on a fool's errand to fetch. Then that young girl said to me,—

"Oh, how awful to have to go out in that little boat on such a night! Do you think there is any danger?"

I would rather have been stabbed. I went off, full of venom, to help in the pilot-house. By and by the boat's lantern disappeared, and after an interval a wee spark glimmered upon the face of the water a mile away. Mr. Thornburg blew the whistle in acknowledgment, backed the steamer out, and made for it. We flew along for a while, then slackened steam and went cautiously gliding toward the spark. Presently Mr. Thornburg exclaimed,—

"Hello, the buoy-lantern's out!"

He stopped the engines. A moment or two later he said,—

"Why, there it is again!"

So he came ahead on the engines once more, and rang for the leads. Gradually the water shoaled up, and then began to deepen again! Mr. Thornburg muttered:—

"Well, I don't understand this. I believe that buoy has drifted off the reef. Seems to be a little too far to the left. No matter, it is safest to run over it, anyhow."

So, in that solid world of darkness we went creeping down on the light. Just as our bows were in the act of plowing over it, Mr. Thornburg seized the bell-ropes, rang a startling peal, and exclaimed,—

"My soul, it's the sounding-boat!"

A sudden chorus of wild alarms burst out far below—a pause—and then a sound of grinding and crashing followed. Mr. Thornburg exclaimed,—

"There! the paddle-wheel has ground the sounding-boat to lucifer matches! Run! See who is killed!"

I was on the main deck in the twinkling of an eye. My chief and the third mate and nearly all the men were safe. They had discovered their danger when it was too late to pull out of the way; then, when the great guards overshadowed them in a moment later, they were prepared and knew what to do; at my chief's order they sprang at the right instant, seized the guard, and were hauled aboard. The next moment the sounding-yawl swept aft to the wheel and was struck and splintered to atoms. Two of the men and the cub Tom, were missing—a fact which spread like wildfire over the boat. The passengers came flocking to the forward gangway, ladies and all, anxious-eyed, white-faced, and talked in awed voices of the dreadful thing. And often and again I heard them say, "Poor fellows! poor boy, poor boy!"

By this time the boat's yawl was manned and away, to search for the missing. Now a faint call was heard, off to the left. The yawl had disappeared in the other direction. Half the people rushed to one side to encourage the swimmer with their shouts; the other half rushed the other way to shriek to the yawl to turn about. By the callings, the swimmer was approaching, but some said the sound showed failing strength. The crowd massed themselves against the boiler-deck railings, leaning over and staring into the gloom; and every faint and fainter cry wrung from them such words as "Ah, poor fellow, poor fellow! is there *no* way to save him?"

But still the cries held out, and drew nearer, and presently the voice said pluckily,—

"I can make it! Stand by with a rope!"

What a rousing cheer they gave him! The chief mate took his stand in the glare of a torch-basket, a coil of rope in his hand, and his men grouped about him. The next moment the swimmer's face appeared in the circle of light, and in another one the owner of it was hauled aboard, limp and drenched, while cheer on cheer went up. It was that devil Tom.

The yawl crew searched everywhere, but found no sign of the two men. They probably failed to catch the guard, tumbled back, and were struck by the wheel and killed. Tom had never jumped for the guard at all, but had plunged head-first into the river and dived under the wheel. It was nothing; I could have done it easy enough, and I said so; but everybody went on just the same, making a wonderful to-do over that ass, as if he had done something great. That girl could n't seem to have enough of that pitiful "hero" the rest of the trip; but little I cared; I loathed her, any way.

The way we came to mistake the sounding-boat's lantern for the buoy-light was this. My chief said that after laying the buoy he fell away and watched it till it seemed to be secure; then he took up a position a hundred yards below it and a little to one side of the steamer's course, headed the sounding-boat up-stream, and waited. Having to wait some time, he and the officer got to talking; he looked up when he judged that the steamer was about on the reef; saw that the buoy was gone, but supposed that the steamer had already run over it; he went on with his talk; he noticed that the steamer was getting very close down to him, but that was the correct thing; it was her business to shave him closely, for convenience in taking him aboard; he was expecting to sheer off, until the last moment; then it flashed upon him that she was trying to run him down, mistaking his lantern for the buoy light; so he sang out, "Stand by to spring for the guard, men!" and the next instant the jump was made.

A Pilot's Needs

But I am wandering from what I was intending to do; that is, make plainer than perhaps appears in the previous chapters some of the peculiar requirements of the science of piloting. First of all, there is one faculty which a pilot must incessantly cultivate until he has brought it to absolute perfection. Nothing short of perfection will do. That faculty is memory. He cannot stop with merely thinking a thing is so and so; he must *know* it; for this is eminently one of the "exact" sciences. With what scorn a pilot was looked upon, in the old times, if he ever ventured to deal in that feeble phrase "I think," instead of the vigorous one "I know!" One cannot easily realize what a tremendous thing it is to know every trivial detail of twelve hundred miles of river and know it with absolute exactness. If you will take the longest street in New York, and travel up and down it, conning its features patiently until you know every house and window and lamp-post and big and little sign by heart, and know them so accurately that you can instantly name the one you are abreast of when you are set down at random in that street in the middle of an inky black night, you will then have a tolerable notion of the amount and the exactness of a pilot's knowledge who carries the Mississippi River in his head. And then if you will go on until you know every street crossing, the character, size, and position of the crossing-stones, and the varying depth of mud in each of these numberless places, you will have some idea of what the pilot must know in order to keep a Mississippi steamer out of trouble. Next, if you will take half of the signs in that long street, and *change their places* once a month, and still manage to know their new positions accurately on dark nights, and keep up with these repeated changes without making any mistakes, you will understand what is required of a pilot's peerless memory by the fickle Mississippi.

I think a pilot's memory is about the most wonderful thing in the world. To know the Old and New Testaments by heart, and be able to recite them glibly, forward or backward, or begin at random anywhere in the book and recite both ways and never trip or make a mistake, is no extravagant mass of knowledge, and no marvellous facility, compared to a pilot's massed knowledge of the Mississippi and his marvellous facility in the handling of it. I make this comparison deliberately, and believe I am not expanding the truth when I do it. Many will think my figure too strong, but pilots will not.

And how easily and comfortably the pilot's memory does its work; how placidly effortless is its way; how *unconsciously* it lays up its vast stores, hour by hour, day by day, and never loses or mislays a single valuable package of them all! Take an instance. Let a leadsman cry, "Half twain! half twain! half twain! half twain! half twain!" until it becomes as monotonous as the ticking of a clock; let conversation be going on all the time, and the pilot be doing his share of the talking, and no longer consciously listening to the leadsman; and in the midst

of this endless string of half twains let a single "quarter twain" be interjected, without emphasis, and then the half twain cry go on again, just
as before: two or three weeks later that pilot can describe with precision the boat's position in the river when that quarter twain was uttered,
and give you such a lot of head-marks, stern-marks, and side-marks to
guide you, that you ought to be able to take the boat there and put her
in that same spot again yourself! The cry of "quarter twain" did not
really take his mind from his talk, but his trained faculties instantly
photographed the bearings, noted the change of depth, and laid up the
important details for future reference without requiring any assistance
from *him* in the matter. If you were walking and talking with a friend,
and another friend at your side kept up a monotonous repetition of the
vowel sound A, for a couple of blocks, and then in the midst interjected
an R, thus A, A, A, A, A, R, A, A, A, etc., and gave the R no emphasis,
you would not be able to state, two or three weeks afterward, that the
R had been put in, nor be able to tell what objects you were passing at
the moment it was done. But you could if your memory had been
patiently and laboriously trained to do that sort of thing mechanically.

Give a man a tolerably fair memory to start with, and piloting will
develop it into a very colossus of capability. But *only in the matters it
is daily drilled in.* A time would come when the man's faculties could
not help noticing landmarks and soundings, and his memory could not
help holding on to them with the grip of a vice; but if you asked that
same man at noon what he had had for breakfast, it would be ten
chances to one that he could not tell you, Astonishing things can be
done with the human memory if you will devote it faithfully to one
particular line of business.

At the time that wages soared so high on the Missouri River, my
chief, Mr. Bixby, went up there and learned more than a thousand
miles of that stream with an ease and rapidity that were astonishing.
When he had seen each division *once* in the daytime and *once* at night,
his education was so nearly complete that he took out a "daylight"
license; a few trips later he took out a full license, and went to piloting
day and night,—and he ranked A 1, too.

Mr. Bixby placed me as steersman for a while under a pilot whose
feats of memory were a constant marvel to me. However, his memory
was born in him, I think, not built. For instance, somebody would mention a name. Instantly Mr. Brown would break in: —

"Oh, I knew *him*. Sallow-faced, red-headed fellow, with a little scar
on the side of his throat, like a splinter under the flesh. He was only in
the Southern trade six months. That was thirteen years ago. I made a
trip with him. There was five feet in the upper river then; the 'Henry
Blake' grounded at the foot of Tower Island drawing four and a half;
the 'George Elliott' unshipped her rudder on the wreck of the 'Sunflower' "—

"Why, the 'Sunflower' did n't sink until"—

"I know when she sunk; it was three years before that, on the 2d of December; Asa Hardy was captain of her, and his brother John was first clerk; and it was his first trip in her, too; Tom Jones told me these things a week afterward in New Orleans; he was first mate of the 'Sunflower.' Captain Hardy stuck a nail in his foot the 6th of July of the next year, and died of the lockjaw on the 15th. His brother John died two years after,—3d of March,—erysipelas. I never saw either of the Hardys,—they were Alleghany River men,—but people who knew them told me all these things. And they said Captain Hardy wore yarn socks winter and summer just the same, and his first wife's name was Jane Shook,—she was from New England,—and his second one died in a lunatic asylum. It was in the blood. She was from Lexington, Kentucky. Name was Horton before she was married."

And so on, by the hour, the man's tongue would go. He could *not* forget anything. It was simply impossible. The most trivial details remained as distinct and luminous in his head, after they had lain there for years, as the most memorable events. His was not simply a pilot's memory; its grasp was universal. If he were talking about a trifling letter he had received seven years before, he was pretty sure to deliver you the entire screed from memory. And then without observing that he was departing from the true line of his talk, he was more than likely to hurl in a long-drawn parenthetical biography of the writer of that letter; and you were lucky indeed, if he did not take up that writer's relatives, one by one, and give you their biographies, too.

Such a memory as that is a great misfortune. To it, all occurrences are of the same size. Its possessor cannot distinguish an interesting circumstance from an uninteresting one. As a talker, he is bound to clog his narrative with tiresome details and make himself an insufferable bore. Moreover, he cannot stick to his subject. He picks up every little grain of memory he discerns in his way, and so is led aside. Mr. Brown would start out with the honest intention of telling you a vastly funny anecdote about a dog. He would be "so full of laugh" that he could hardly begin; then his memory would start with the dog's breed and personal appearance; drift into a history of his owner; of his owner's family, with descriptions of weddings and burials that had occurred in it, together with recitals of congratulatory verses and obituary poetry provoked by the same; then this memory would recollect that one of these events occurred during the celebrated "hard winter" of such and such a year, and a minute description of that winter would follow, along with the names of people who were frozen to death, and statistics showing the high figures which pork and hay went up to. Pork and hay would suggest corn and fodder; corn and fodder would suggest cows and horses; cows and horses would suggest the circus and certain celebrated bareback rides; the transition from the circus to the menagerie was easy and natural; from the elephant to equatorial Africa was but a step; then of course the heathen savages would suggest religion; and at the end of three or four hours' tedious jaw, the watch would change, and Brown would go out of the pilot-house muttering extracts from sermons he had heard years before about the efficacy of prayer as a means of grace. And the original first mention would be all you had learned about that dog, after all this waiting and hungering.

A pilot must have a memory; but there are two higher qualities which he must also have. He must have good and quick judgment and decision, and a cool, calm courage that no peril can shake. Give a man the merest trifle of pluck to start with, and by the time he has become a pilot he cannot be unmanned by any danger a steamboat can get into; but one cannot quite say the same for judgment. Judgment is a matter of brains, and a man must *start* with a good stock of that article or he will never succeed as a pilot.

The growth of courage in the pilot-house is steady all the time, but it does not reach a high and satisfactory condition until some time after the young pilot has been "standing his own watch," alone and under the staggering weight of all the responsibilities connected with the position. When the apprentice has become pretty thoroughly acquainted with the river, he goes clattering along so fearlessly with his steamboat, night or day, that he presently begins to imagine that it is *his* courage that animates him; but the first time the pilot steps out and leaves him to his own devices he finds out it was the other man's. He discovers that the article has been left out of his own cargo altogether. The whole river is bristling with exigencies in a moment; he is not prepared for them; he does not know how to meet them; all his knowledge forsakes him; and within fifteen minutes he is as white as a sheet and scared almost to death. Therefore pilots wisely train these cubs by various strategic tricks to look danger in the face a little more calmly. A favorite way of theirs is to play a friendly swindle upon the candidate.

Mr. Bixby served me in this fashion once, and for years afterward I used to blush even in my sleep when I thought of it. I had become a good steersman; so good, indeed, that I had all the work to do on our watch, night and day; Mr. Bixby seldom made a suggestion to me; all he ever did was to take the wheel on particularly bad nights or in particularly bad crossings, land the boat when she needed to be landed, play gentleman of leisure nine tenths of the watch, and collect the wages. The lower river was about bank-full, and if anybody had questioned my ability to run any crossing between Cairo and New Orleans without help or instruction, I should have felt irreparably hurt. The idea of being afraid of any crossing in the lot, in the *day-time*, was a thing too preposterous for contemplation. Well, one matchless summer's day I was bowling down the bend above Island 66, brimful of self-conceit and carrying my nose as high as a giraffe's, when Mr. Bixby said,—

"I am going below a while. I suppose you know the next crossing?"

This was almost an affront. It was about the plainest and simplest crossing in the whole river. One could n't come to any harm, whether he ran it right or not; and as for depth, there never had been any bottom there. I knew all this, perfectly well.

"Know how to *run* it? Why, I can run it with my eyes shut."

"How much water is there in it?"

"Well, that is an old question. I could n't get bottom there with a church steeple."

"You think so, do you?"

The very tone of the question shook my confidence. That was what Mr. Bixby was expecting. He left, without saying anything more. I began to imagine all sorts of things. Mr. Bixby, unknown to me, of course, sent somebody down to the forecastle with some mysterious instructions to the leadsmen, another messenger was sent out to whisper among the officers, and then Mr. Bixby went into hiding behind a smoke-stack where he could observe results. Presently the captain stepped out on the hurricane deck; next the chief mate appeared; then a clerk. Every moment or two a straggler was added to my audience; and before I got to the head of the island I had fifteen or twenty people assembled down there under my nose. I began to wonder what the trouble was. As I started across, the captain glanced aloft at me and said, with a sham uneasiness in his voice,—

"Where is Mr. Bixby?"

"Gone below, sir."

But that did the business for me. My imagination began to construct dangers out of nothing, and they multiplied faster than I could keep the run of them. All at once I imagined I saw shoal water ahead! The wave of coward agony that surged through me then came near dislocating every joint in me. All my confidence in that crossing vanished. I seized the bell-rope; dropped it, ashamed; seized it again; dropped it once more; clutched it tremblingly once again, and pulled it so feebly that I could hardly hear the stroke myself. Captain and mate sang out instantly, and both together,—

"Starboard lead there! and quick about it!"

This was another shock. I began to climb the wheel like a squirrel; but I would hardly get the boat started to port before I would see new dangers on that side, and away I would spin to the other; only to find perils accumulating to starboard, and be crazy to get to port again. Then came the leadsman's sepulchral cry:—

"D-e-e-p four!"

Deep four in a bottomless crossing! The terror of it took my breath away.

"M-a-r-k three! ... M-a-r-k three! ... Quarter less three! ... Half twain!"

This was frightful! I seized the bell-ropes and stopped the engines.

"Quarter twain! Quarter twain! *Mark* twain!"

I was helpless. I did not know what in the world to do. I was quaking from head to foot, and I could have hung my hat on my eyes, they stuck out so far.

"Quarter *less* twain! Nine and a *half!*"

We were *drawing* nine! My hands were in a nerveless flutter. I could not ring a bell intelligibly with them. I flew to the speaking-tube and shouted to the engineer,—

"Oh, Ben, if you love me, *back* her! Quick, Ben! Oh, back the immortal *soul* out of her!"

I heard the door close gently. I looked around, and there stood Mr. Bixby, smiling a bland, sweet smile. Then the audience on the hurricane deck sent up a thundergust of humiliating laughter. I saw it all, now, and I felt meaner than the meanest man in human history. I laid in the lead, set the boat in her marks, came ahead on the engines, and said:—

"It was a fine trick to play on an orphan, *was n't* it? I suppose I 'll never hear the last of how I was ass enough to heave the lead at the head of 66."

"Well, no, you won't, maybe. In fact I hope you won't; for I want you to learn something by that experience. Did n't you *know* there was no bottom in that crossing?"

"Yes, sir, I did."

"Very well, then. You should n't have allowed me or anybody else to shake your confidence in that knowledge. Try to remember that. And another thing: when you get into a dangerous place, don't turn coward. That is n't going to help matters any."

It was a good enough lesson, but pretty hardly learned. Yet about the hardest part of it was that for months I so often had to hear a phrase which I had conceived a particular distaste for. It was, "Oh, Ben, if you love me, back her!"

Rank and Dignity of Piloting

In my preceding chapters I have tried, by going into the minutiæ of the science of piloting, to carry the reader step by step to a comprehension of what the science consists of; and at the same time I have tried to show him that it is a very curious and wonderful science, too, and very worthy of his attention. If I have seemed to love my subject, it is no surprising thing, for I loved the profession far better than any I have followed since, and I took a measureless pride in it. The reason is plain: a pilot, in those days, was the only unfettered and entirely independent human being that lived in the earth. Kings are but the hampered servants of parliament and the people; parliaments sit in chains forged by their constituency; the editor of a newspaper cannot be independent, but must work with one hand tied behind him by party and patrons, and be content to utter only half or two thirds of his mind; no clergyman is a free man and may speak the whole truth, regardless of his parish's opinions; writers of all kinds are manacled servants of the public. We write frankly and fearlessly, but then we "modify" before we print. In truth, every man and woman and child has a master, and worries and frets in servitude; but in the day I write of, the Mississippi pilot had *none*. The captain could stand upon the hurricane deck, in the pomp of a very brief authority, and give him five or six orders while the vessel backed into the stream, and then that skipper's reign was over. The moment that the boat was under way in the river, she was under the sole and unquestioned control of the pilot. He could do with her exactly as he pleased, run her when and whither he chose, and tie her up to the bank whenever his judgment said that that course was best. His movements were entirely free; he consulted no one, he received commands from nobody, he promptly resented even the merest suggestions. Indeed, the law of the United States forbade him to listen to commands or suggestions, rightly considering that the pilot necessarily knew better how to handle the boat than anybody could tell him. So here was the novelty of a king without a keeper, an absolute monarch who was absolute in sober truth and not by a fiction of words. I have seen a boy of eighteen taking a great steamer serenely into what seemed almost certain destruction, and the aged captain standing mutely by, filled with apprehension but powerless to interfere. His interference, in that particular instance, might have been an excellent thing, but to permit it would have been to establish a most pernicious precedent. It will easily be guessed, considering the pilot's boundless authority, that he was a great personage in the old steamboating days. He was treated with marked courtesy by the captain and with marked deference by all officers and servants; and this deferential spirit was quickly communicated to the passengers, too. I think pilots were about the only people I ever knew who failed to show, in some degree, embarrassment in the presence of travelling foreign princes. But then, people in one's own grade of life are not usually embarrassing objects.

By long habits, pilots came to put all their wishes in the form of commands. It "gravels" me, to this day, to put my will in the weak shape of a request, instead of launching it in the crisp language of an order.

In those old days, to load a steamboat at St. Louis, take her to New Orleans and back, and discharge cargo, consumed about twenty-five days, on an average. Seven or eight of these days the boat spent at the wharves of St. Louis and New Orleans, and every soul on board was hard at work, except the two pilots; *they* did nothing but play gentleman up town, and receive the same wages for it as if they had been on duty. The moment the boat touched the wharf at either city, they were ashore; and they were not likely to be seen again till the last bell was ringing and everything in readiness for another voyage.

When a captain got hold of a pilot of particularly high reputation, he took pains to keep him. When wages were four hundred dollars a month on the Upper Mississippi, I have known a captain to keep such a pilot in idleness, under full pay, three months at a time, while the river was frozen up. And one must remember that in those cheap times four hundred dollars was a salary of almost inconceivable splendor. Few men on shore got such pay as that, and when they did they were mightily looked up to. When pilots from either end of the river wandered into our small Missouri village, they were sought by the best and the fairest, and treated with exalted respect. Lying in port under wages was a thing which many pilots greatly enjoyed and appreciated; especially if they belonged in the Missouri River in the heyday of that trade (Kansas times[12]), and got nine hundred dollars a trip, which was equivalent to about eighteen hundred dollars a month. Here is a conversation of that day. A chap out of the Illinois River, with a little stern-wheel tub, accosts a couple of ornate and gilded Missouri River pilots:—

"Gentlemen, I 've got a pretty good trip for the up-country, and shall want you about a month. How much will it be?"

"Eighteen hundred dollars apiece."

"Heavens and earth! You take my boat, let me have your wages, and I 'll divide!"

I will remark, in passing, that Mississippi steamboatmen were important in landsmen's eyes (and in their own, too, in a degree) according to the dignity of the boat they were on. For instance, it was a proud thing to be of the crew of such stately craft as the "Aleck Scott" or the "Grand Turk." Negro firemen, deck hands, and barbers belonging to those boats were distinguished personages in their grade of life, and they were well aware of that fact, too. A stalwart darkey once gave offense at a negro ball in New Orleans by putting on a good many airs. Finally one of the managers bustled up to him and said,—

"Who *is* you, any way? Who *is* you? dat's what *I* wants to know!"

The offender was not disconcerted in the least, but swelled himself up and threw that into his voice which showed that he knew he was not putting on all those airs on a stinted capital.

"Who *is* I? Who *is* I? I let you know mighty quick who I is! I want you niggers to understan' dat I fires de middle do'[13] on de 'Aleck Scott!' "

That was sufficient.

The barber of the "Grand Turk" was a spruce young negro, who aired his importance with balmy complacency, and was greatly courted by the circle in which he moved. The young colored population of New Orleans were much given to flirting, at twilight, on the banquettes of the back streets. Somebody saw and heard something like the following, one evening, in one of those localities. A middle-aged negro woman projected her head through a broken pane and shouted (very willing that the neighbors should hear and envy), "You Mary Ann, come in de house dis minute! Stannin' out dah foolin' 'long wid dat low trash, an' heah's de barber off'n de 'Gran' Turk' wants to conwerse wid you!"

12 In the late 1850s there was a heavy migration into Kansas.
13 Door. *Au.*

My reference, a moment ago, to the fact that a pilot's peculiar official position placed him out of the reach of criticism or command, brings Stephen W—— naturally to my mind. He was a gifted pilot, a good fellow, a tireless talker, and had both wit and humor in him. He had a most irreverent independence, too, and was deliciously easy-going and comfortable in the presence of age, official dignity, and even the most august wealth. He always had work, he never saved a penny, he was a most persuasive borrower, he was in debt to every pilot on the river, and to the majority of the captains. He could throw a sort of splendor around a bit of harum-scarum, devil-may-care piloting, that made it almost fascinating—but not to everybody. He made a trip with good old Captain Y—— once, and was "relieved" from duty when the boat got to New Orleans. Somebody expressed surprise at the discharge. Captain Y—— shuddered at the mere mention of Stephen. Then his poor, thin old voice piped out something like this:

"Why, bless me! I would n't have such a wild creature on my boat for the world—not for the whole world! He swears, he sings, he whistles, he yells—I never saw such an Injun to yell. All times of the night—it never made any difference to him. He would just yell that way, not for anything in particular, but merely on account of a kind of devilish comfort he got out of it. I never could get into a sound sleep but he would fetch me out of bed, all in a cold sweat, with one of those dreadful war-whoops. A queer being,—very queer being; no respect for anything or anybody. Sometimes he called me 'Johnny.' And he kept a fiddle, and a cat. He played execrably. This seemed to distress the cat, and so the cat would howl. Nobody could sleep where that man—and his family—was. And reckless? There never was anything like it. Now you may believe it or not, but as sure as I am sitting here, he brought my boat a-tilting down through those awful snags at Chicot under a rattling head of steam, and the wind a-blowing like the very nation, at that! My officers will tell you so. They saw it. And, sir, while he was a-tearing right down through those snags, and I a-shaking in my shoes and praying, I wish I may never speak again if he didn't pucker up his mouth and go to *whistling!* Yes, sir; whistling 'Buffalo gals, can't you come out to-night, can't you come out to-night, can't you come out to-night;' and doing it as calmly as if we were attending a funeral and were n't related to the corpse. And when I remonstrated with him about it, he smiled down on me as if I was his child, and told me to run in the house and try to be good, and not be meddling with my superiors!" [14]

Once a pretty mean captain caught Stephen in New Orleans out of work and as usual out of money. He laid steady siege to Stephen, who was in a very "close place," and finally persuaded him to hire with him

---

[14] Considering a captain's ostentatious but hollow chieftainship, and a pilot's real authority, there was something impudently apt and happy about that way of phrasing it. *Au.*

at one hundred and twenty-five dollars per month, just half wages, the captain agreeing not to divulge the secret and so bring down the contempt of all the guild upon the poor fellow. But the boat was not more than a day out of New Orleans before Stephen discovered that the captain was boasting of his exploit, and that all the officers had been told. Shephen winced, but said nothing. About the middle of the afternoon the captain stepped out on the hurricane deck, cast his eye around, and looked a good deal surprised. He glanced inquiringly aloft at Stephen, but Stephen was whistling placidly, and attending to business. The captain stood around a while in evident discomfort, and once or twice seemed about to make a suggestion; but the etiquette of the river taught him to avoid that sort of rashness, and so he managed to hold his peace. He chafed and puzzled a few minutes longer, then retired to his apartments. But soon he was out again, and apparently more perplexed than ever. Presently he ventured to remark with deference,—

"Pretty good stage of the river now, ain't it, sir?"

"Well, I should say so! Bank-full *is* a pretty liberal stage."

"Seems to be a good deal of current here."

"Good deal don't describe it! It's worse than a mill-race."

"Is n't it easier in toward shore than it is out here in the middle?"

"Yes, I reckon it is; but a body can't be too careful with a steamboat. It's pretty safe out here; can't strike any bottom here, you can depend on that."

The captain departed, looking rueful enough. At this rate, he would probably die of old age before his boat got to St. Louis. Next day he appeared on deck and again found Stephen faithfully standing up the middle of the river, fighting the whole vast force of the Mississippi, and whistling the same placid tune. This thing was becoming serious. In by the shore was a slower boat clipping along in the easy water and gaining steadily; she began to make for an island chute; Stephen stuck to the middle of the river. Speech was *wrung* from the captain. He said,—

"Mr. W——., don't that chute cut off a good deal of distance?"

"I think it does, but I don't know."

"Don't know! Well, is n't there water enough in it now to go through?"

"I expect there is, but I am not certain."

"Upon my word this is odd! Why, those pilots on that boat yonder are going to try it. Do you mean to say that you don't know as much as they do?"

"*They!* Why, *they* are two-hundred-and-fifty-dollar pilots! But don't you be uneasy; I know as much as any man can afford to know for a hundred and twenty-five!"

The captain surrendered.

Five minutes later Stephen was bowling through the chute and showing the rival boat a two-hundred-and-fifty-dollar pair of heels.

The Man That Corrupted Hadleyburg (1898)

I

It was many years ago. Hadleyburg was the most honest and upright town in all the region around about. It had kept that reputation unsmirched during three generations, and was prouder of it than of any other of its possessions. It was so proud of it, and so anxious to insure its perpetuation, that it began to teach the principles of honest dealing to its babies in the cradle, and made the like teachings the staple of their culture thenceforward through all the years devoted to their education. Also, throughout the formative years temptations were kept out of the way of the young people, so that their honesty could have every chance to harden and solidify, and become a part of their very bone. The neighboring towns were jealous of this honorable supremacy, and affected to sneer at Hadleyburg's pride in it and call it vanity; but all the same they were obliged to acknowledge that Hadleyburg was in reality an incorruptible town; and if pressed they would also acknowledge that the mere fact that a young man hailed from Hadleyburg was all the recommendation he needed when he went forth from his natal town to seek for responsible employment.

But at last, in the drift of time, Hadleyburg had the ill luck to offend a passing stranger—possibly without knowing it, certainly without caring, for Hadleyburg was sufficient unto itself, and cared not a rap for strangers or their opinions. Still, it would have been well to make an exception in this one's case, for he was a bitter man and revengeful. All through his wanderings during a whole year he kept his injury in mind, and gave all his leisure moments to trying to invent a compensating satisfaction for it. He contrived many plans, and all of them were good, but none of them was quite sweeping enough; the poorest of them would hurt a great many individuals, but what he wanted was a plan which would comprehend the entire town, and not let so much as one person escape unhurt. At last he had a fortunate idea, and when it fell into his brain it lit up his whole head with an evil joy. He began to form a plan at once, saying to himself, "That is the thing to do—I will corrupt the town."

Six months later he went to Hadleyburg, and arrived in a buggy at the house of the old cashier of the bank about ten at night. He got a sack out of the buggy, shouldered it, and staggered with it through the cottage yard, and knocked at the door. A woman's voice said "Come in," and he entered, and set his sack behind the stove in the parlor, saying politely to the old lady who sat reading the *Missionary Herald* by the lamp:

"Pray keep your seat, madam, I will not disturb you. There—now it is pretty well concealed; one would hardly know it was there. Can I see your husband a moment, madam?"

No, he was gone to Brixton, and might not return before morning.

"Very well, madam, it is no matter. I merely wanted to leave that sack in his care, to be delivered to the rightful owner when he shall be found. I am a stranger; he does not know me; I am merely passing through the town tonight to discharge a matter which has been long in my mind. My errand is now completed, and I go pleased and a little proud, and you will never see me again. There is a paper attached to the sack which will explain everything. Good night, madam."

The old lady was afraid of the mysterious big stranger, and was glad to see him go. But her curiosity was roused, and she went straight to the sack and brought away the paper. It began as follows:

TO BE PUBLISHED; *or, the right man sought out by private inquiry—either will answer. This sack contains gold coin weighing a hundred and sixty pounds four ounces—*

"Mercy on us, and the door not locked!"

Mrs. Richards flew to it all in a tremble and locked it, then pulled down the window-shades and stood frightened, worried, and wondering if there was anything else she could do toward making herself and the money more safe. She listened awhile for burglars, then surrendered to curiosity and went back to the lamp and finished reading the paper:

I am a foreigner, and am presently going back to my own country, to remain there permanently. I am grateful to America for what I have received at her hands during my long stay under her flag; and to one of her citizens—a citizen of Hadleyburg—I am especially grateful for a great kindness done me a year or two ago. Two great kindnesses, in fact. I will explain. I was a gambler. I say I was. I was a ruined gambler. I arrived in this village at night, hungry and without a penny. I asked for help—in the dark; I was ashamed to beg in the light. I begged of the right man. He gave me twenty dollars— that is to say, he gave me life, as I considered it. He also gave me fortune; for out of that money I have made myself rich at the gaming-table. And finally, a remark which he made to me has remained with me to this day, and has at last conquered me; and in conquering has saved the remnant of my morals; I shall gamble no more. Now I have no idea who that man was, but I want him found, and I want him to have this money, to give away, throw away, or keep, as he pleases. It is merely my way of testifying my gratitude to him. If I could stay, I would find him myself; but no matter, he will be found. This is an honest town, an incorruptible town, and I know I can trust it without fear. This man can be identified by the remark which he made to me; I feel persuaded that he will remember it.

And now my plan is this: If you prefer to conduct the inquiry privately, do so. Tell the contents of this present writing to any one who is likely to be the right man. If he shall answer, 'I am the man; the remark I made was so-and-so,' apply the test—to wit: open the sack, and in it you will find a sealed envelope containing that remark. If the remark mentioned by the candidate tallies with it, give him the money, and ask no further questions, for he is certainly the right man.

But if you shall prefer a public inquiry, then publish this present writing in the local paper—with these insructions added, to wit: Thirty days from now, let the candidate appear at the town-hall at eight in the evening (Friday), and hand his remark, in a sealed envelope, to the Rev. Mr. Burgess (if he will be kind enough to act); and let Mr. Burgess there and then destroy the seals of the sack, open it, and see if the remark is correct; if correct, let the money be delivered, with my sincere gratitude, to my benefactor thus identified.

Mrs. Richards sat down, gently quivering with excitement, and was soon lost in thinkings—after this pattern: "What a strange thing it is! . . . And what a fortune for that kind man who set his bread afloat upon the waters! . . . If it had only been my husband that did it!—for we are so poor, so old and poor! . . ." Then, with a sigh—"But it was not my Edward; no, it was not he that gave a stranger twenty dollars. It is a pity, too; I see it now. . . ." Then, with a shudder—"But it is *gambler's* money! the wages of sin: we couldn't take it; we couldn't touch it. I don't like to be near it; it seems a defilement." She moved to a farther chair. . . . "I wish Edward would come and take it to the bank; a burglar might come at any moment; it is dreadful to be here all alone with it."

At eleven Mr. Richards arrived, and while his wife was saying, "I am *so* glad you've come!" he was saying, "I'm so tired—tired clear out; it is dreadful to be poor, and have to make these dismal journeys at my time of life. Always at the grind, grind, grind, on a salary—another man's slave, and he sitting at home in his slippers, rich and comfortable."

"I am so sorry for you, Edward, you know that; but be comforted: we have our livelihood; we have our good name—"

"Yes, Mary, and that is everything. Don't mind my talk—it's just a moment's irritation and doesn't mean anything. Kiss me—there, it's all gone now, and I am not complaining any more. What have you been getting? What's in the sack?"

Then his wife told him the great secret. It dazed him for a moment; then he said:

"It weighs a hundred and sixty pounds? Why, Mary, it's for-ty thousand dollars—think of it—a whole fortune! Not ten men in this village are worth that much. Give me the paper."

He skimmed through it and said:

"Isn't it an adventure! Why, it's a romance; it's like the impossible things one reads about in books, and never sees in life." He was well stirred up now; cheerful, even gleeful. He tapped his old wife on the cheek, and said, humorously, "Why, we're rich, Mary, rich; all we've got to do is to bury the money and burn the papers. If the gambler ever comes to inquire, we'll merely look coldly upon him and say: 'What is this nonsense you are talking? We have never heard of you and your sack of gold before'; and then he would look foolish, and—"

"And in the meantime, while you are running on with your jokes, the money is still here, and it is fast getting along toward burglar-time."

"True. Very well, what shall we do—make the inquiry private? No, not that; it would spoil the romance. The public method is better. Think what a noise it will make! And it will make all the other towns jealous; for no stranger would trust such a thing to any town but Hadleyburg, and they know it. It's a great card for us. I must get to the printing-office now, or I shall be too late."

"But stop—stop—don't leave me here alone with it, Edward!"

But he was gone. For only a little while, however. Not far from his own house he met the editor-proprietor of the paper, and gave him the document, and said, "Here is a good thing for you, Cox—put it in."

"It may be too late, Mr. Richards, but I'll see."

At home again he and his wife sat down to talk the charming mystery over; they were in no condition for sleep. The first question was, Who could the citizen have been who gave the stranger the twenty dollars? It seemed a simple one; both answered it in the same breath:

"Barclay Goodson."

"Yes," said Richards, "he could have done it, and it would have been like him, but there's not another in the town."

"Everybody will grant that, Edward—grant it privately, anyway. For six months, now, the village has been its own proper self once more—honest, narrow, self-righteous, and stingy."

"It is what he always called it, to the day of his death—said it right out publicly, too."

"Yes, and he was hated for it."

"Oh, of course; but he didn't care. I reckon he was the best-hated man among us, except the Reverend Burgess."

"Well, Burgess deserves it—he will never get another congregation here. Mean as the town is, it knows how to estimate *him*. Edward, doesn't it seem odd that the stranger should appoint Burgess to deliver the money?"

"Well, yes—it does. That is—that is—"

"Why so much that-*is*-ing? Would *you* select him?"

"Mary, maybe the stranger knows him better than this village does."

"Much *that* would help Burgess!"

The husband seemed perplexed for an answer; the wife kept a steady eye upon him, and waited. Finally Richards said, with the hesitancy of one who is making a statement which is likely to encounter doubt:

"Mary, Burgess is not a bad man."

His wife was certainly surprised.

"Nonsense!" she exclaimed.

"He is not a bad man. I know. The whole of his unpopularity had its foundation in that one thing—the thing that made so much noise."

"That 'one thing,' indeed! As if that 'one thing' wasn't enough, all by itself."

"Plenty. Plenty. Only he wasn't guilty of it."

"How you talk! Not guilty of it! Everybody knows he *was* guilty."

"Mary, I give you my word—he was innocent."

"I can't believe it, and I don't. How do you know?"

"It is a confession. I am ashamed, but I will make it. I was the only man who knew he was innocent. I could have saved him, and—and—well, you know how the town was wrought up—I hadn't the pluck to do it. It would have turned everybody against me. I felt mean, ever so mean; but I didn't dare; I hadn't the manliness to face that."

Mary looked troubled, and for a while was silent. Then she said, stammeringly:

"I—I don't think it would have done for you to—to—One mustn't—er—public opinion—one has to be so careful—so—" It was a difficult road, and she got mired; but after a little she got started again. "It was a great pity, but—Why, we couldn't afford it, Edward—we couldn't indeed. Oh, I wouldn't have had you do it for anything!"

"It would have lost us the good will of so many people, Mary; and then—and then—"

"What troubles me now is, what *he* thinks of us, Edward."

"He? *He* doesn't suspect that I could have saved him."

"Oh," exclaimed the wife, in a tone of relief, "I am glad of that! As long as he doesn't know that you could have saved him, he—he—well, that makes it a great deal better. Why, I might have known he didn't know, because he is always trying to be friendly with us, as little encouragement as we give him. More than once people have twitted me with it. There's the Wilsons, and the Wilcoxes, and the Harknesses, they take a mean pleasure in saying, '*Your friend* Burgess,' because they know it pesters me. I wish he wouldn't persist in liking us so; I can't think why he keeps it up."

"I can explain it. It's another confession. When the thing was new and hot, and the town made a plan to ride him on a rail, my conscience hurt me so that I couldn't stand it, and I went privately and gave him notice, and he got out of the town and staid out till it was safe to come back."

"Edward! If the town had found it out—"

"*Don't!* It scares me yet, to think of it. I repented of it the minute it was done; and I was even afraid to tell you, lest your face might betray it to somebody. I didn't sleep any that night, for worrying. But after a few days I saw that no one was going to suspect me, and after that I got to feeling glad I did it, And I feel glad yet, Mary—glad through and through."

"So do I, now, for it would have been a dreadful way to treat him. Yes, I'm glad; for really you did owe him that, you know. But, Edward, suppose it should come out yet, some day!"

"It won't."

"Why?"

"Because everybody thinks it was Goodson."

"Of course they would!"

"Certainly. And of course *he* didn't care. They persuaded poor old Sawlsberry to go and charge it on him, and he went blustering over there and did it. Goodson looked him over, like as if he was hunting for a place on him that he could despise the most, then he says, 'So you are the Committee of Inquiry, are you?' Sawlsberry said that was about what he was. 'Hm. Do they require particulars, or do you reckon a kind of a *general* answer will do?' 'If they require particulars, I will come back, Mr. Goodson; I will take the general answer first.' 'Very well, then, tell them to go to hell—I reckon that's general enough. And I'll give you some advice, Sawlsberry; when you come back for the particulars, fetch a basket to carry the relics of yourself home in.' "

"Just like Goodson; it's got all the marks. He had only one vanity: he thought he could give advice better than any other person."

"It settled the business, and saved us, Mary. The subject was dropped."

"Bless you, I'm not doubting *that*."

Then they took up the gold-sack mystery again, with strong interest. Soon the conversation began to suffer breaks—interruptions caused by absorbed thinkings. The breaks grew more and more frequent. At last Richards lost himself wholly in thought. He sat long, gazing vacantly at the floor, and by and by he began to punctuate his thoughts with little nervous movements of his hands that seemed to indicate vexation. Meantime his wife too had relapsed into a thoughtful silence, and her movements were beginning to show a troubled discomfort. Finally Richards got up and strode aimlessly about the room, plowing his hands through his hair, much as a somnambulist might do who was having a bad dream. Then he seemed to arrive at a definite purpose; and without a word he put on his hat and passed quickly out of the house. His wife sat brooding, with a drawn face, and did not seem to be aware that she was alone. Now and then she murmured, "Lead us not into t— ... but—but—we are so poor, so poor! ... Lead us not into ... Ah, who would be hurt by it?—and no one would ever know. ... Lead us ..." The voice died out in mumblings. After a little she glanced up and muttered in a half-frightened, half-glad way:

"He is gone! But, oh dear, he may be too late—too late. ... Maybe not—maybe there is still time." She rose and stood thinking, nervously clasping and unclasping her hands. A slight shudder shook her frame, and she said, out of a dry throat, "God forgive me—it's awful to think such things—but ... Lord, how we are made—how strangely we are made!"

She turned the light low, and slipped stealthily over and kneeled down by the sack and felt of its ridgy sides with her hands, and fondled them lovingly; and there was a gloating light in her poor old eyes. She fell into fits of absence; and came half out of them at times to mutter, "If we had only waited!—oh, if we had only waited a little, and not been in such a hurry!"

Meantime Cox had gone home from his office and told his wife all about the strange thing that had happened, and they had talked it over eagerly, and guessed that the late Goodson was the only man in the town who could have helped a suffering stranger with so noble a sum as twenty dollars. Then there was a pause, and the two became thoughtful and silent. And by and by nervous and fidgety. At last the wife said, as if to herself:

"Nobody knows this secret but the Richardses ... and us ... nobody."

The husband came out of his thinkings with a slight start, and gazed wistfully at his wife, whose face was become very pale; then he hestitatingly rose, and glanced furtively at his hat, then at his wife—a sort of mute inquiry. Mrs. Cox swallowed once or twice, with her hand at her throat, then in place of speech she nodded her head. In a moment she was alone, and mumbling to herself.

And now Richards and Cox were hurrying through the deserted streets, from opposite directions. They met, panting, at the foot of the printing-office stairs; by the night light there they read each other's face. Cox whispered:

"Nobody knows about this but us?"

The whispered answer was,

"Not a soul—on honor, not a soul!"

"If it isn't too late to—"

The men were starting up-stairs; at this moment they were overtaken by a boy, and Cox asked:

"Is that you, Johnny?"

"Yes, sir."

"You needn't ship the early mail—nor *any* mail; wait till I tell you."

"It's already gone, sir."

"*Gone?*" It had the sound of an unspeakable disappointment in it.

"Yes, sir. Time-table for Brixton and all the towns beyond changed to-day, sir—had to get the papers in twenty minutes earlier than common. I had to rush; if I had been two minutes later—"

The men turned and walked slowly away, not waiting to hear the rest. Neither of them spoke during ten minutes; then Cox said, in a vexed tone:

"What possessed you to be in such a hurry, *I* can't make out."

The answer was humble enough:

"I see it now, but somehow I never thought, you know, until it was too late. But the next time—

"Next time be hanged! It won't come in a thousand years."

Then the friends separated without a good night, and dragged themselves home with the gait of mortally stricken men. At their homes their wives sprang up with an eager "Well?"—then saw the answer with their eyes and sank down sorrowing, without waiting for it to come in words. In both houses a discussion followed of a heated sort—

a new thing; there had been discussions before, but not heated ones, not ungentle ones. The discussions to-night were a sort of seeming plagiarisms of each other. Mrs. Richards said,

"If you had only waited, Edward—if you had only stopped to think; but no, you must run straight to the printing-office and spread it all over the world."

"It *said* publish it."

"That is nothing; it also said do it privately, if you liked. There, now—is that true, or not?

"Why, yes—yes, it is true; but when I thought what a stir it would make, and what a compliment it was to Hadleyburg that a stranger should trust it so—"

"Oh, certainly, I know all that; but if you had only stopped to think, you would have seen that you *couldn't* find the right man, because he is in his grave, and hasn't left chick nor child nor relation behind him; and as long as the money went to somebody that awfully needed it, and nobody would be hurt by it, and—and—"

She broke down, crying. Her husband tried to think of some comforting thing to say, and presently came out with this:

"But after all, Mary, it must be for the best—it *must* be; we know that. And we must remember that it was so ordered—"

"Ordered! Oh, everything's *ordered*, when a person has to find some way out when he has been stupid. Just the same, it was *ordered* that the money should come to us in this special way, and it was you that must take it on yourself to go meddling with the designs of Providence—and who gave you the right? It was wicked, that is what it was—just blasphemous presumption, and no more becoming to a meek and humble professor of—"

"But, Mary, you know how we have been trained all our lives long, like the whole village, till it is absolutely second nature to us to stop not a single moment to think when there's an honest thing to be done—"

"Oh, I know it, I know it—it's been one everlasting training and training and training in honesty—honesty shielded, from the very cradle, against every possible temptation, and so it's *artificial* honesty, and weak as water when temptation comes, as we have seen this night. God knows I never had shade nor shadow of a doubt of my petrified and indestructible honesty until now—and now, under the very first big and real temptation, I—Edward, it is my belief that this town's honesty is as rotten as mine is; as rotten as yours is. It is a mean town, a hard, stingy town, and hasn't a virtue in the world but this honesty it is so celebrated for and so conceited about; and so help me, I do believe that if ever the day comes that its honesty falls under great temptation, its grand reputation will go to ruin like a house of cards. There, now, I've made confession, and I feel better; I am a humbug, and I've been one all my life, without knowing it. Let no man call me honest again—I will not have it."

"I—well, Mary, I feel a good deal as you do; I certainly do. It seems strange, too, so strange. I never could have believed it—never."

A long silence followed; both were sunk in thought. At last the wife looked up and said:

"I know what you are thinking, Edward."

Richards had the embarrassed look of a person who is caught.

"I am ashamed to confess it, Mary, but—"

"It's no matter, Edward, I was thinking the same question myself."

"I hope so. State it."

"You were thinking, if a body could only guess out *what the remark was* that Goodson made to the stranger."

"It's perfectly true. I feel guilty and ashamed. And you?"

"I'm past it. Let us make a pallet here; we've got to stand watch till the bank vault opens in the morning and admits the sack. . . . Oh dear, oh dear—if we hadn't made the mistake!"

The pallet was made, and Mary said:

"The open sesame—what could it have been? I do wonder what that remark could have been? But come; we will get to bed now."

"And sleep?"

"No: think."

"Yes, think."

By this time the Coxes too had completed their spat and their reconciliation, and were turning in—to think, to think, and toss, and fret, and worry over what the remark could possibly have been which Goodson made to the stranded derelict; that golden remark; that remark worth forty thousand dollars, cash.

The reason that the village telegraph-office was open later than usual that night was this: The foreman of Cox's paper was the local representative of the Associated Press. One might say its honorary representative, for it wasn't four times a year that he could furnish thirty words that would be accepted. But this time it was different. His despatch stating what he had caught got an instant answer:

Send the whole thing—all the details—twelve hundred words.

A colossal order! The foreman filled the bill; and he was the proudest man in the State. By breakfast-time the next morning the name of Hadleyburg the Incorruptible was on every lip in America, from Montreal to the Gulf, from the glaciers of Alaska to the orange-groves of Florida; and millions and millions of people were discussing the stranger and his money-sack, and wondering if the right man would be found, and hoping some more news about the matter would come soon—right away.

II

Hadleyburg village woke up world-celebrated—astonished—happy—vain. Vain beyond imagination. Its nineteen principal citizens and their wives went about shaking hands with each other, and beaming, and smiling, and congratulating, and saying *this* thing adds a new word to the dictionary—*Hadleyburg,* synonym for *incorruptible*—destined to live in dictionaries forever! And the minor and unimportant citizens and their wives went around acting in much the same way. Everybody ran to the bank to see the gold-sack; and before noon grieved and envious crowds began to flock in from Brixton and all neighboring towns; and that afternoon and next day reporters began to arrive from everywhere to verify the sack and its history and write the whole thing up anew, and make dashing free-hand pictures of the sack, and of Richards's house, and the bank, and the Presbyterian church, and the Baptist church, and the public square, and the town-hall where the test would be applied and the money delivered; and damnable portraits of the Richardses, and Pinkerton the banker, and Cox, and the foreman, and Reverend Burgess, and the postmaster—and even of Jack Halliday, who was the loafing, good-natured, no-account, irreverent fisherman, hunter, boys' friend, stray-dogs' friend, typical "Sam Lawson" of the town. The little, mean, smirking, oily Pinkerton showed the sack to all comers, and rubbed his sleek palms together pleasantly, and enlarged upon the town's fine old reputation for honesty and upon this wonderful indorsement of it, and hoped and believed that the example would now spread far and wide over the American world, and be epoch-making in the matter of moral regeneration. And so on, and so on.

By the end of a week things had quieted down again; the wild intoxication of pride and joy had sobered to a soft, sweet, silent delight—a sort of deep, nameless, unutterable content. All faces bore a look of peaceful, holy happiness.

Then a change came. It was a gradual change: so gradual that its beginnings were hardly noticed; maybe were not noticed at all, except by Jack Halliday, who always noticed everything; and always made fun of it, too, no matter what it was. He began to throw out chaffing remarks about people not looking quite so happy as they did a day or two ago; and next he claimed that the new aspect was deepening to positive sadness; next, that it was taking on a sick look; and finally he said that everybody was become so moody, thoughtful, and absent-minded that he could rob the meanest man in town of a cent out of the bottom of his breeches pocket and not disturb his revery.

At this stage—or at about this stage—a saying like this was dropped at bedtime—with a sigh, usually—by the head of each of the nineteen principal households: "Ah, what *could* have been the remark that Goodson made?"

And straightway—with a shudder—came this, from the man's wife: "Oh, *don't!* What horrible thing are you mulling in your mind? Put it away from you, for God's sake!"

But that question was wrung from those men again the next night—and got the same retort. But weaker.

And the third night the men uttered the question yet again—with anguish, and absently. This time—and the following night—the wives fidgeted feebly, and tried to say something. But didn't.

And the night after that they found their tongues and responded—longingly:

"Oh, if we *could* only guess!"

Halliday's comments grew daily more and more sparklingly disagreeable and disparaging. He went diligently about, laughing at the town, individually and in mass. But his laugh was the only one left in the village: it fell upon a hollow and mournful vacancy and emptiness. Not even a smile was findable anywhere. Halliday carried a cigar-box around on a tripod, playing that it was a camera, and halted all passers and aimed the thing and said, "Ready!—now look pleasant, please," but not even this capital joke could surprise the dreary faces into any softening.

So three weeks passed—one week was left. It was Saturday evening—after supper. Instead of the aforetime Saturday-evening flutter and bustle and shopping and larking, the streets were empty and desolate. Richards and his old wife sat apart in their little parlor—miserable and thinking. This was become their evening habit now: the lifelong habit which had preceded it, of reading, knitting, and contented chat, or receiving or paying neighborly calls, was dead and gone and forgotten, ages ago—two or three weeks ago; nobody talked now, nobody read, nobody visited—the whole village sat at home, sighing, worrying, silent. Trying to guess out that remark.

The postman left a letter. Richards glanced listlessly at the superscription and the postmark—unfamiliar, both—and tossed the letter on the table and resumed his might-have-beens and his hopeless dull miseries where he had left them off. Two or three hours later his wife got wearily up and was going away to bed without a good night—custom now—but she stopped near the letter and eyed it awhile with a dead interest, then broke it open, and began to skim it over. Richards, sitting there with his chair tilted back against the wall and his chin between his knees, heard something fall. It was his wife. He sprang to her side, but she cried out:

"Leave me alone, I am too happy. Read the letter—read it!"

He did. He devoured it, his brain reeling. The letter was from a distant state, and it said:

I am a stranger to you, but no matter: I have somehting to tell. I have just arrived home from Mexico, and learned about that episode. Of course you do not know who made that remark, but I know, and I am the only person living who does know. It was GOODSON. *I knew him well, many years ago. I passed through your village that very night, and was his guest till the midnight train came along. I overheard him make that remark to the stranger in the dark—it was in Hale Alley. He and I talked of it the rest of the way home, and while smoking in his house. He mentioned many of your villagers in the course of* *his talk—most of them in a very uncomplimentary way, but two or three favorably; among these latter yourself. I say "favorably"—nothing stronger. I remember his saying he did not actually* LIKE *any person in the town—not one; but that you—I* THINK *he said you—am almost sure—had done him a very great service once, possibly without knowing the full value of it, and he wished he had a fortune, he would leave it to you when he died, and a curse apiece for the rest of the citizens. Now, then, if it was you that did him that service, you are his legitimate heir, and entitled to the sack of gold. I know that I can trust to your honor and honesty, for in a citizen of Hadleyburg these virtues are an unfailing inheritance, and so I am going to reveal to you the remark, well satisfied that if you are not the right man you will seek and find the right one and see that poor Goodson's debt of gratitude for the service referred to is paid. This is the remark:* "YOU ARE FAR FROM BEING A BAD MAN: GO, AND REFORM."*

Howard L. Stephenson.

"Oh, Edward, the money is ours, and I am so grateful, *oh*, so grateful—kiss me, dear, it's forever since we kissed—and we needed it so—the money—and now you are free of Pinkerton and his bank, and nobody's slave any more; it seems to me I could fly for joy."

It was a happy half-hour that the couple spent there on the settee caressing each other; it was the old days come again—days that had begun with their courtship and lasted without a break till the stranger brought the deadly money. By and by the wife said:

"Oh, Edward, how lucky it was you did him that grand service, poor Goodson! I never liked him, but I love him now. And it was fine and beautiful of you never to mention it or brag about it." Then, with a touch of reproach, "But you ought to have told *me*, Edward, you ought to have told your wife, you know."

"Well, I—er—well, Mary, you see—"

"Now stop hemming and hawing, and tell me about it, Edward. I always loved you, and now I'm proud of you. Everybody believes there was only one good generous soul in this village, and now it turns out that you—Edward, why don't you tell me?"

"Well—er—er—Why, Mary, I can't!"

"You *can't*? *Why* can't you?"

"You see, he—well, he—he made me promise I wouldn't."

The wife looked him over, and said, very slowly:

"Made—you—promise? Edward, what do you tell me that for?"

"Mary, do you think I would lie?"

She was troubled and silent for a moment, then she laid her hand within his and said:

"No . . . no. We have wandered far enough from our bearings—God spare us that! In all your life you have never uttered a lie. But now—now that the foundations of things seem to be crumbling from under us, we—we—" She lost her voice for a moment, then said, brokenly, "Lead us not into temptation. . . . I think you made the promise, Edward.

Let it rest so. Let us keep away from that ground. Now—that is all gone by; let us be happy again; it is no time for clouds."

Edward found it something of an effort to comply, for his mind kept wandering—trying to remember what the service was that he had done Goodson.

The couple lay awake the most of the night, Mary happy and busy, Edward busy but not so happy. Mary was planning what she would do with the money. Edward was trying to recall that service. At first his conscience was sore on account of the lie he had told Mary—if it was a lie. After much reflection—suppose it *was* a lie? What then? Was it such a great matter? Aren't we always *acting* lies? Then why not *tell* them? Look at Mary—look what she had done. While he was hurrying off on his honest errand, what was she doing? Lamenting because the papers hadn't been destroyed and the money kept! Is theft better than lying?

That point lost its sting—the lie dropped into the background and left comfort behind it. The next point came to the front: *Had* he rendered that service? Well, here was Goodson's own evidence as reported in Stephenson's letter; there could be no better evidence than that— it was even *proof* that he had rendered it. Of course. So that point was settled.... No, not quite. He recalled with a wince that this unknown Mr. Stephenson was just a trifle unsure as to whether the performer of it was Richards or some other—and, oh dear, he had put Richards on his honor! He must himself decide whither that money must go— and Mr. Stephenson was not doubting that if he was the wrong man he would go honorably and find the right one. Oh, it was odious to put a man in such a situation—ah, why couldn't Stephenson have left out that doubt! What did he want to intrude that for?

Further reflection. How did it happen that *Richards's* name remained in Stephenson's mind as indicating the right man, and not some other man's name? That looked good. Yes, that looked very good. In fact, it went on looking better and better, straight along—until by and by it grew into positive *proof*. And then Richards put the matter at once out of his mind, for he had a private instinct that a proof once established is better left so.

He was feeling reasonably comfortable now, but there was still one other detail that kept pushing itself on his notice: of course he had done that service—that was settled; but what *was* that service? He must recall it—he would not go to sleep till he had recalled it; it would make his peace of mind perfect. And so he thought and thought. He thought of a dozen things—possible services, even probable services— but none of them seemed adequate, none of them seemed large enough, none of them seemed worth the money—worth the fortune Goodson had wished he could leave in his will. And besides, he couldn't remember having done them, anyway. Now, then—now, then—what *kind* of a service would it be that would make a man so inordinately grateful? Ah—the saving of his soul! That must be it. Yes, he could remember, now, how he once set himself the task of converting Goodson, and labored at it as much as—he was going to say three months; but upon closer examination it shrunk to a month, then to a week, then to a day, then to nothing. Yes, he remembered now, and with unwelcome vividness, that Goodson had told him to go to thunder and mind his own business—*he* wasn't hankering to follow Hadleyburg to heaven!

So that solution was a failure—he hadn't saved Goodson's soul. Richards was discouraged. Then after a little came another idea: had he saved Goodson's property? No, that wouldn't do—he hadn't any. His life? That is it! Of course. Why, he might have thought of it before. This time he was on the right track, sure. His imagination-mill was hard at work in a minute, now.

Thereafter during a stretch of two exhausting hours he was busy saving Goodson's life. He saved it in all kinds of difficult and perilous ways. In every case he got it saved satisfactorily up to a certain point; then, just as he was beginning to get well persuaded that it had really happened, a troublesome detail would turn up which made the whole thing impossible. As in the matter of drowning, for instance. In that case he had swum out and tugged Goodson ashore in an unconscious state with a great crowd looking on and applauding, but when he had got it all thought out and was just beginning to remember all about it, a whole swarm of disqualifying details arrived on the ground: the town would have known of the circumstance, Mary would have known of it, it would glare like a limelight in his own memory instead of being an inconspicuous service which he had possibly rendered "without knowing its full value." And at this point he remembered that he couldn't swim, anyway.

Ah—*there* was a point which he had been overlooking from the start: it had to be a service which he had rendered "possibly without knowing the full value of it." Why, really, that ought to be an easy hunt—much easier than those others. And sure enough, by and by he found it. Goodson, years and years ago, came near marrying a very sweet and pretty girl, named Nancy Hewitt, but in some way or other the match had been broken off; the girl died, Goodson remained a bachelor, and by and by became a soured one and a frank despiser of the human species. Soon after the girl's death the village found out, or thought it had found out, that she carried a spoonful of negro blood in her veins. Richards worked at these details a good while, and in the end he thought he remembered things concerning them which must have gotten mislaid in his memory through long neglect. He seemed to dimly remember that it was *he* that found out about the negro blood; that it was he that told the village; that the village told Goodson where they got it; that he thus saved Goodson from marrying the tainted girl; that he had done him this great service "without knowing the full value of it," in fact without knowing that he *was* doing it; but that Goodson knew the value of it, and what a narrow escape he had had, and so went to his grave grateful to his benefactor and wishing he had a fortune to leave him. It was all clear and simple now, and the more he went over it the more luminous and certain it grew; and at last, when he nestled to sleep satisfied and happy, he remembered the whole thing just as if it had been yesterday. In fact, he dimly remembered Goodson's *telling* him his gratitude once. Meantime Mary had spent six thousand dollars on a new house for herself and a pair of slippers for her pastor, and then had fallen peacefully to rest.

That same Saturday evening the postman had delivered a letter to each of the other principal citizens—nineteen letters in all. No two of the envelopes were alike, and no two of the superscriptions were in the same hand, but the letters inside were just like each other in every detail but one. They were exact copies of the letters received by Richards—handwriting and all—and were all signed by Stephenson, but in place of Richards's name each receiver's own name appeared.

All night long eighteen principal citizens did what their caste-brother Richards was doing at the same time—they put in their energies trying to remember what notable service it was that they had unconsciously done Barclay Goodson. In no case was it a holiday job; still they succeeded.

And while they were at this work, which was difficult, their wives put in the night spending the money, which was easy. During that one night the nineteen wives spent an average of seven thousand dollars each out of the forty thousand in the sack—a hundred and thirty-three thousand altogether.

Next day there was a surprise for Jack Halliday. He noticed that the faces of the nineteen chief citizens and their wives bore that expression of peaceful and holy happiness again. He could not understand it, neither was he able to invent any remarks about it that could damage it or disturb it. And so it was his turn to be dissatisfied with life. His private guesses at the reasons for the happiness failed in all instances, upon examination. When he met Mrs. Wilcox and noticed the placid ecstasy in her face, he said to himself, "Her cat has had kittens"—and went and asked the cook: it was not so; the cook had detected the happiness, but did not know the cause. When Halliday found the duplicate ecstasy in the face of "Shadbelly" Billson (village nickname), he was sure some neighbor of Billson's had broken his leg, but inquiry showed that this had not happened. The subdued ecstasy in Gregory Yates's face could mean but one thing—he was a mother-in-law short: it was another mistake. "And Pinkerton—Pinkerton—he has collected ten cents that he thought he was going to lose." And so on, and so on. In some cases the guesses had to remain in doubt, in the others they proved distinct errors. In the end Halliday said to himself, "Anyway it foots up that there's nineteen Hadleyburg families temporarily in heaven: I don't know how it happened; I only know Providence is off duty to-day."

An architect and builder from the next state had lately ventured to set up a small business in this unpromising village, and his sign had now been hanging out a week. Not a customer yet; he was a discouraged man, and sorry he had come. But his weather changed suddenly now. First one and then another chief citizen's wife said to him privately:

"Come to my house Monday week—but say nothing about it for the present. We think of building."

He got eleven invitations that day. That night he wrote his daughter and broke off her match with her student. He said she could marry a mile higher than that.

Pinkerton the banker and two or three other well-to-do men planned country-seats—but waited. That kind don't count their chickens until they are hatched.

The Wilsons devised a grand new thing—a fancy-dress ball. They made no actual promises, but told all their acquaintanceship in confidence that they were thinking the matter over and thought they should give it—"and if we do, you will be invited, of course." People were surprised, and said, one to another, "Why, they are crazy, those poor Wilsons, they can't afford it." Several among the nineteen said privately to their husbands, "It is a good idea: we will keep still till their cheap thing is over, then *we* will give one that will make it sick."

The days drifted along, and the bill of future squanderings rose higher and higher, wilder and wilder, more and more foolish and reckless. It began to look as if every member of the nineteen would not only spend his whole forty thousand dollars before receiving-day, but be actually in debt by the time he got the money. In some cases light-headed people did not stop with planning to spend, they really spent—on credit. They bought land, mortgages, farms, speculative stocks, fine clothes, horses, and various other things, paid down the bonus, and made themselves liable for the rest—at ten days. Presently the sober second thought came, and Halliday noticed that a ghastly anxiety was beginning to show up in a good many faces. Again he was puzzled, and didn't know what to make of it. "The Wilcox kittens aren't dead, for they weren't born; nobody's broken a leg; there's no shrinkage in mother-in-laws; *nothing* has happened—it is an unsolvable mystery."

There was another puzzled man, too—the Rev. Mr. Burgess. For days, wherever he went, people seemed to follow him or to be watching out for him; and if he ever found himself in a retired spot, a member of the nineteen would be sure to appear, thrust an envelope privately into his hand, whisper "To be opened at the town-hall Friday evening," then vanish away like a guilty thing. He was expecting that there might be one claimant for the sack—doubtful, however, Goodson being dead—but it never occurred to him that all this crowd might be claimants. When the great Friday came at last, he found that he had nineteen envelopes.

III

The town hall had never looked finer. The platform at the end of it was backed by a showy draping of flags; at intervals along the walls were festoons of flags; the gallery fronts were clothed in flags; the supporting columns were swathed in flags; all this was to impress the stranger, for he would be there in considerable force, and in a large degree he would be connected with the press. The house was full. The 412 fixed seats were occupied; also the 68 extra chairs which had been packed into the aisles; the steps of the platform were occupied; some distinguished strangers were given seats on the platform; at the horseshoe of tables which fenced the front and sides of the platform sat a strong force of special correspondents who had come from everywhere. It was the best-dressed house the town had ever produced. There were some tolerably expensive toilets there, and in several cases the ladies who wore them had the look of being unfamiliar with that kind of clothes. At least the town thought they had that look, but the notion could have arisen from the town's knowledge of the fact that these ladies had never inhabited such clothes before.

The gold-sack stood on a little table at the front of the platform where all the house could see it. The bulk of the house gazed at it with a burning interest, a mouth-watering interest, a wistful and pathetic interest; a minority of nineteen couples gazed at it tenderly, lovingly, proprietarily, and the male half of this minority kept saying over to themselves the moving little impromptu speeches of thankfulness for the audience's applause and congratulations which they were presently going to get up and deliver. Every now and then one of these got a piece of paper out of his vest pocket and privately glanced at it to refresh his memory.

Of course there was a buzz of conversation going on—there always is; but at last when the Rev. Mr. Burgess rose and laid his hand on the sack he could hear his microbes gnaw, the place was so still. He related the curious history of the sack, then went on to speak in warm terms of Hadleyburg's old and well-earned reputation for spotless honesty, and of the town's just pride in this reputation. He said that this reputation was a treasure of priceless value; that under Providence its value had now become inestimably enhanced, for the recent episode had spread this fame far and wide, and thus had focused the eyes of the American world upon this village, and made its name for all time, as he hoped and believed, a synonym for commercial incorruptibility. [*Applause.*] "And who is to be the guardian of this noble treasure—the community as a whole? Not! The responsibility is individual, not communal. From this day forth each and every one of you is in his own person its special guardian, and individually responsible that no harm shall come to it. Do you—does each of you—accept this great trust? [*Tumultuous assent.*] Then all is well. Transmit it to your children and to your children's children. To-day your purity is beyond reproach—see to it that it shall remain so. To-day there is not a person in your community who could be beguiled to touch a penny not his own—see to it that you abide in this grace. ["*We will! we will!*"] This is not the place to make comparisons between ourselves and other communities—some of them ungracious toward us; they have their ways, we have ours; let us be content. [*Applause.*] I am done. Under my hand, my friends, rests a stranger's eloquent recognition of what we are; through him the world will always henceforth know what we are. We do not know who he is, but in your name I utter your gratitude, and ask you to raise your voices in indorsement."

The house rose in a body and made the walls quake with the thunders of its thankfulness for the space of a long minute. Then it sat down, and Mr. Burgess took an envelope out of his pocket. The house held its breath while he slit the envelope open and took from it a slip of paper. He read its contents—slowly and impressively—the audience listening with tranced attention to this magic document, each of whose words stood for an ingot of gold:

"*'The remark which I made to the distressed stranger was this: "You are very far from being a bad man: go, and reform."'*" Then he continued:

"We shall know in a moment now whether the remark here quoted corresponds with the one concealed in the sack; and if that shall prove to be so—and it undoubtedly will—this sack of gold belongs to a fellow-citizen who will henceforth stand before the nation as the symbol of the special virtue which has made our town famous throughout the land—Mr. Billson!"

The house had gotten itself all ready to burst into the proper tornado of applause; but instead of doing it, it seemed stricken with a paralysis; there was a deep hush for a moment or two, then a wave of whispered murmurs swept the place—of about this tenor: "*Billson!* oh, come, this is *too* thin! Twenty dollars to a stranger—or *anybody—Billson!* tell it to the marines!" And now at this point the house caught its breath all of a sudden in a new access of astonishment, for it discovered that whereas in one part of the hall Deacon Billson was standing up with his head meekly bowed, in another part of it Lawyer Wilson was doing the same. There was a wondering silence now for a while.

Everybody was puzzled, and nineteen couples were surprised and indignant.

Billson and Wilson turned and stared at each other. Billson asked, bitingly:

"Why do *you* rise, Mr. Wilson?"

"Because I have a right to. Perhaps you will be good enough to explain to the house why *you* rise?"

"With great pleasure. Because I wrote that paper.

"It is an impudent falsity! I wrote it myself."

It was Burgess's turn to be paralyzed. He stood looking vacantly at first one of the men and then the other, and did not seem to know what to do. The house was stupefied. Lawyer Wilson spoke up, now, and said,

"I ask the Chair to read the name signed to that paper."

That brought the Chair to itself, and it read out the name:

" 'John Wharton *Billson*.' "

"There!" shouted Billson, "what have you got to say for yourself, now? And what kind of apology are you going to make to me and to this insulted house for the imposture which you have attempted to play here?"

"No apologies are due, sir; and as for the rest of it, I publicly charge you with pilfering my note from Mr. Burgess and substituting a copy of it signed with your own name. There is no other way by which you could have gotten hold of the test-remark; I alone, of living men, possessed the secret of its wording."

There was likely to be a scandalous state of things if this went on; everybody noticed with distress that the short-hand scribes were scribbling like mad; many people were crying "Chair, Chair! Order! order!" Burgess rapped with his gavel, and said:

"Let us not forget the proprieties due. There has evidently been a mistake somewhere, but surely that is all. If Mr. Wilson gave me an envelope—and I remember now that he did—I still have it."

He took one out of his pocket, opened it, glanced at it, looked surprised and worried, and stood silent a few moments. Then he waved his hand in a wandering and mechanical way, and made an effort or two to say something, then gave it up, despondently. Several voices cried out:

"Read it! read it! What is it?"

So he began in a dazed and sleep-walker fashion:

" '*The remark which I made to the unhappy stranger was this:* "*You are far from being a bad man.* [The house gazed at him, marveling.] *Go, and reform.*' " [*Murmurs:* "Amazing! what can this mean?"] This one," said the Chair, "is signed Thurlow G. Wilson."

"There!" cried Wilson. "I reckon that settles it! I knew perfectly well my note was purloined."

"Purloined!" retorted Billson, "I'll let you know that neither you nor any man of your kidney must venture to—"

The Chair. "Order, gentlemen, order! Take your seats, both of you, please."

They obeyed, shaking their heads and grumbling angrily. The house was profoundly puzzled; it did not know what to do with this curious emergency. Presently Thompson got up. Thompson was the hatter. He would have liked to be a Nineteener; but such was not for him: his stock of hats was not considerable enough for the position. He said:

"Mr. Chairman, if I may be permitted to make a suggestion, can both of these gentlemen be right? I put it to you, sir, can both have happened to say the very same words to the stranger? It seems to me—"

The tanner got up and interrupted him. The tanner was a disgruntled man; he believed himself entitled to be a Nineteener, but he couldn't get recognition. It made him a little unpleasant in his ways and speech. Said he:

"Sho, *that's* not the point! *That* could happen—twice in a hundred years—but not the other thing. *Neither* of them gave the twenty dollars!

[*A ripple of applause.*]

Billson. "I did!"

Wilson. "I did!"

Then each accused the other of pilfering.

The Chair. "Order! Sit down, if you please—both of you. Neither of the notes has been out of my possession at any moment."

A Voice. "Good—that settles *that!*"

The Tanner. "Mr. Chairman, one thing is now plain: one of these men has been eavesdropping under the other one's bed, and filching family secrets. If it is not unparliamentary to suggest it, I will remark that both are equal to it. [*The Chair.* "Order! order!"] I withdraw the remark, sir, and will confine myself to suggesting that *if* one of them has overheard the other reveal the test-remark to his wife, we shall catch him now."

A Voice. "How?"

The Tanner. "Easily. The two have not quoted the remark in exactly the same words. You would have noticed that, if there hadn't been a considerable stretch of time and an exciting quarrel inserted between the two readings."

A Voice. "Name the difference."

The Tanner. "The word *very* is in Billson's note, and not in the other."

Many Voices. "That's so—he's right!"

The Tanner. "And so, if the Chair will examine the test-remark in the sack, we shall know which of these two frauds—[*The Chair.* "Order!"]—which of these two adventurers—[*The Chair.* "Order! order!"]—which of these two gentlemen—[*laughter and applause*]—is entitled to wear the belt as being the first dishonest blatherskite ever bred in this town—which he has dishonored, and which will be a sultry place for him from now out!" [*Vigorous applause.*]

Many Voices. "Open it!—open the sack!"

Mr. Burgess made a slit in the sack, slid his hand in and brought out an envelope. In it were a couple of folded notes. He said:

"One of these is marked, 'Not to be examined until all written communications which have been addressed to the Chair—if any—shall have been read. The other is marked 'The Test.' Allow me. It is worded —to wit:

" 'I do not require that the first half of the remark which was made to me by my benefactor shall be quoted with exactness, for it was not striking, and could be forgotten; but its closing fifteen words are quite striking, and I think easily rememberable; unless *these* shall be accurately reproduced, let the applicant be regarded as an impostor. My benefactor began by saying he seldom gave advice to any one, but that it always bore the hall-mark of high value when he did give it. Then he said this—and it has never faded from my memory: *"You are far from being a bad man—"'"*

Fifty Voices. "That settles it—the money's Wilson's! Wilson! Wilson! Speech! Speech!"

People jumped up and crowded around Wilson, wringing his hand and congratulating fervently—meantime the Chair was hammering with the gavel and shouting:

"Order, gentlemen! Order! Order! Let me finish reading, please." When quiet was restored, the reading was resumed—as follows:

*"'"Go, and reform—or, mark my words—some day, for your sins, you will die and go to hell or Hadleyburg—*TRY AND MAKE IT THE FORMER."'"

A ghastly silence followed. First an angry cloud began to settle darkly upon the faces of the citizenship; after a pause the cloud began to rise, and a tickled expression tried to take its place; tried so hard that it was only kept under with great and painful difficulty; the reporters, the Brixtonites, and other strangers bent their heads down and shielded their faces with their hands, and managed to hold in by main strength and heroic courtesy. At this most inopportune time burst upon the stillness the roar of a solitary voice—Jack Halliday's:

"That's got the hall-mark on it!"

Then the house let go, strangers and all. Even Mr. Burgess's gravity broke down presently, then the audience considered itself officially absolved from all restraint, and it made the most of its privilege. It was a good long laugh, and a tempestuously whole-hearted one, but it ceased at last—long enough for Mr. Burgess to try to resume, and for the people to get their eyes partially wiped; then it broke out again; and afterward yet again; then at last Burgess was able to get out these serious words:

It is useless to try to disguise the fact—we find ourselves in the presence of a matter of grave import. It involves the honor of your town, it strikes at the town's good name. The difference of a single word between the test-remarks offered by Mr. Wilson and Mr. Billson was itself a serious thing, since it indicated that one or the other of these gentlemen had committed a theft—"

The two men were sitting limp, nerveless, crushed; but at these words both were electrified into movement, and started to get up—

"Sit down!" said the Chair, sharply, and they obeyed. "That, as I have said, was a serious thing. And it was—but for only one of them. But the matter has become graver; for the honor of *both* is now in formidable peril. Shall I go even further, and say in inextricable peril? *Both* left out the crucial fifteen words." He paused. During several moments he allowed the pervading stillness to gather and deepen its impressive effects, then added: "There would seem to be but one way whereby this could happen. I ask these gentlemen—Was there *collusion?—agreement?*"

A low murmur sifted through the house; its import was, "He's got them both."

Billson was not used to emergencies; he sat in a helpless collapse. But Wilson was a lawyer. He struggled to his feet, pale and worried, and said:

"I ask the indulgence of the house while I explain this most painful matter. I am sorry to say what I am about to say, since it must inflict irreparable injury upon Mr. Billson, whom I have always esteemed and respected until now, and in whose invulnerability to temptation I entirely believed—as did you all. But for the preservation of my own honor I must speak—and with frankness. I confess with shame—and I now beseech your pardon for it—that I said to the ruined stranger all of the words contained in the test-remark, including the disparaging fifteen. [*Sensation.*] When the late publication was made I recalled them, and I resolved to claim the sack of coin, for by every right I was entitled to it. Now I will ask you to consider this point, and weigh it well: that stranger's gratitude to me that night knew no bounds; he said himself that he could find no words for it that were adequate, and that if he should ever be able he would repay me a thousandfold. Now, then, I ask you this: Could I expect—could I believe—could I even remotely imagine—that, feeling as he did, he would do so ungrateful a thing as to add those quite unnecessary fifteen words to his test?—set a trap for me?—expose me as a slanderer of my own town before my own people assembled in a public hall? It was preposterous; it was impossible. His test would contain only the kindly opening clause of my remark. Of that I had no shadow of doubt. You would have thought as I did. You would not have expected a base betrayal from one whom you had befriended and against whom you had committed no offense. And so, with perfect confidence, perfect trust, I wrote on a piece of paper the opening words—ending with 'Go, and reform,'—and signed it. When I was about to put it in an envelope I was called into my back office, and without thinking I left the paper lying open on my desk." He stopped, turned his head slowly toward Billson, waited a moment, then added: "I ask you to note this: when I returned, a little later, Mr. Billson was retiring by my street door." [*Sensation.*]

In a moment Billson was on his feet and shouting:

"It's a lie! It's an infamous lie!"

The Chair. "Be seated, sir! Mr. Wilson has the floor."

Billson's friends pulled him into his seat and quieted him, and Wilson went on:

"Those are the simple facts. My note was now lying in a different place on the table from where I had left it. I noticed that, but attached no importance to it, thinking a draught had blown it there. That Mr.

Billson would read a private paper was a thing which could not occur to me; he was an honorable man, and he would be above that. If you will allow me to say it, I think his extra word *'very'* stands explained; it is attributable to a defect of memory. I was the only man in the world who could furnish here any detail of the test-remark—by *honorable* means. I have finished."

There is nothing in the world like a persuasive speech to fuddle the mental apparatus and upset the convictions and debauch the emotions of an audience not practised in the tricks and delusions of oratory. Wilson sat down victorious. The house submerged him in tides of approving applause; friends swarmed to him and shook him by the hand and congratulated him, and Billson was shouted down and not allowed to say a word. The Chair hammered and hammered with its gavel, and kept shouting:

"But let us proceed, gentlemen, let us proceed!"

At last there was a measurable degree of quiet, and the hatter said:

"But what is there to proceed with, sir, but to deliver the money?"

Voices. "That's it! That's it! Come forward, Wilson!"

The Hatter. "I move three cheers for Mr. Wilson, Symbol of the special virtue which—"

The cheers burst forth before he could finish; and in the midst of them—and in the midst of the clamor of the gavel also—some enthusiasts mounted Wilson on a big friend's shoulder and were going to fetch him in triumph to the platform. The Chair's voice now rose above the noise—

"Order! To your places! You forget that there is still a document to be read." When quiet had been restored he took up the document, and was going to read it, but laid it down again saying, "I forgot; this is not to be read until all written communications received by me have first been read." He took an envelope out of his pocket, removed its inclosure, glanced at it—seemed astonished—held it out and gazed at it—stared at it.

Twenty or thirty voices cried out:

"What is it? Read it! read it!"

And he did—slowly, and wondering:

"'The remark which I made to the stranger—[*Voices.* "Hello! how's this?"]—was this: "You are far from being a bad man. [*Voices.* "Great Scott!"] Go, and reform."' [*Voice.* "Oh, saw my leg off!"] Signed by Mr. Pinkerton, the banker."

The pandemonium of delight which turned itself loose now was of a sort to make the judicious weep. Those whose withers were unwrung laughed till the tears ran down; the reporters, in throes of laughter, set down disordered pot-hooks which would never in the world be decipherable; and a sleeping dog jumped up, scared out of its wits, and barked itself crazy at the turmoil. All manner of cries were scattered through the din: "We're getting rich—*two* Symbols of Incorruptibility!—without counting Billson!" "*Three!*—count Shadbelly in—we can't have too many!" "All right—Billson's elected!" "Alas, poor Wilson—victim of *two* thieves!"

A Powerful Voice. "Silence! The Chair's fished up something more out of its pocket."

Voices. "Hurrah! Is it something fresh? Read it! read! read!"

The Chair [*reading*]. " 'The remark which I made,' etc.: ' "You are far from being a bad man. Go," ' etc. Signed 'Gregory Yates.' "

Tornado of Voices. "Four Symbols!" " 'Rah for Yates!" "Fish again!"

The house was in a roaring humor now, and ready to get all the fun out of the occasion that might be in it. Several Nineteeners, looking pale and distressed, got up and began to work their way toward the aisles, but a score of shouts went up:

"The doors, the doors—close the doors; no Incorruptible shall leave this place! Sit down, everybody!"

The mandate was obeyed.

"Fish again! Read! read!"

The Chair fished again, and once more the familiar words began to fall from its lips—" 'You are far from being a bad man.' "

"Name! name! What's his name?"

" 'L. Ingoldsby Sargent.' "

"Five elected! Pile up the Symbols! Go on, go on!"

" 'You are far from being a bad—' "

"Name! name!"

" 'Nicholas Whitworth.' "

"Hooray! hooray! it's a symbolical day!"

Somebody wailed in, and began to sing this rhyme (leaving out "it's") to the lovely "Mikado" tune of "When a man's afraid, a beautiful maid—"; the audience joined in, with joy; then, just in time, somebody contributed another line—

And don't this you forget—

The house roared it out. A third line was at once furnished—

Corruptibles far from Hadleyburg are—

The house roared that one too. As the last note died, Jack Halliday's voice rose high and clear, freighted with a final line—

But the Symbols are here, you bet!

That was sung, with booming enthusiasm. Then the happy house started in at the beginning and sang the four lines through twice, with immense swing and dash, and finished up with a crashing three-times-three and a tiger for "Hadleyburg the Incorruptible and all Symbols of it which we shall find worthy to receive the hall-mark to-night."

Then the shouting at the Chair began again, all over the place:

"Go on! go on! Read! read some more! Read all you've got!"

"That's it—go on! We are winning eternal celebrity!"

A dozen men got up now and began to protest. They said that this farce was the work of some abandoned joker, and was an insult to the whole community. Without a doubt these signatures were all forgeries—

"Sit down! sit down! Shut up! You are confessing. We'll find *your* names in the lot."

"Mr. Chairman, how many of those envelopes have you got?"

The Chair counted.

"Together with those that have been already examined, there are nineteen."

A storm of derisive applause broke out.

"Perhaps they all contain the secret. I move that you open them all and read every signature that is attached to a note of that sort—and read also the first eight words of the note."

"Second the motion!"

It was put and carried—uproariously. Then poor old Richards got up, and his wife rose and stood at his side. Her head was bent down, so that none might see that she was crying. Her husband gave her his arm, and so supporting her, he began to speak in a quavering voice:

"My friends, you have known us two—Mary and me—all our lives, and I think you have liked us and respected us—"

The Chair interrupted him:

"Allow me. It is quite true—that which you are saying, Mr. Richards: this town *does* know you two; it *does* like you; it *does* respect you; more—it honors you and *loves* you—"

Halliday's voice rang out:

"That's the hall-marked truth, too! If the Chair is right, let the house speak up and say it. Rise! Now, then—hip! hip! hip!—all together!"

The house rose in mass, faced toward the old couple eagerly, filled the air with a snow-storm of waving handkerchiefs, and delivered the cheers with all its affectionate heart.

The Chair then continued:

"What I was going to say is this: We know your good heart, Mr. Richards, but this is not a time for the exercise of charity toward offenders. [*Shouts of "Right! right!"*] I see your generous purpose in your face, but I cannot allow you to plead for these men—"

"But I was going to—"

"Please take your seat, Mr. Richards. We must examine the rest of these notes—simple fairness to the men who have already been exposed requires this. As soon as that has been done—I give you my word for this—you shall be heard."

Many Voices. "Right!—the Chair is right—no interruption can be permitted at this stage! Go on!—the names! the names!—according to the terms of the motion!"

The old couple sat reluctantly down, and the husband whispered to the wife, "It is pitifully hard to have to wait; the shame will be greater than ever when they find we were only going to plead for *ourselves*."

Straightway the jollity broke loose again with the reading of the names.

" 'You are far from being a bad man—' Signature, 'Robert J. Titmarsh.'

" 'You are far from being a bad man—' Signature, 'Eliphalet Weeks.'

" 'You are far from being a bad man—' Signature, 'Oscar B. Wilder.' "

At this point the house lit upon the idea of taking the eight words out of the Chairman's hands. He was not unthankful for that. Thenceforward he held up each note in its turn, and waited. The house droned out the eight words in a massed and measured and musical deep volume of sound (with a daringly close resemblance to a well-known church chant)—" 'You are f-a-r from being a b-a-a-a-d man.' " Then the Chair said, "Signature, 'Archibald Willcox.' " And so on, and so on, name after name, and everybody had an increasingly and gloriously good time except the wretched Nineteen. Now and then, when a particularly shining name was called, the house made the Chair wait while it chanted the whole of the test-remark from the beginning to the closing words, "And go to hell or Hadleyburg—try and make it the for-or-m-e-r!" and in these special cases they added a grand and agonized and imposing "A-a-a-a-*men!*"

The list dwindled, dwindled, dwindled, poor old Richards keeping tally of the count, wincing when a name resembling his own was pronounced, and waiting in miserable suspense for the time to come when it would be his humiliating privilege to rise with Mary and finish his plea, which he was intending to word thus: ". . . for until now we have never done any wrong thing, but have gone our humble way unreproached. We are very poor, we are old, and have no chick nor child to help us; we were sorely tempted, and we fell. It was my purpose when I got up before to make confession and beg that my name might not be read out in this public place, for it seemed to us that we could not bear it; but I was prevented. It was just; it was our place to suffer with the rest. It has been hard for us. It is the first time we have ever heard our name fall from any one's lips—sullied. Be merciful—for the sake of the better days; make our shame as light to bear as in your charity you can." At this point in his revery Mary nudged him, perceiving that his mind was absent. The house was chanting, "You are f-a-r," etc.

"Be ready," Mary whispered. "Your name comes now; he has read eighteen."

The chant ended.

"Next! next! next!" came volleying from all over the house.

Burgess put his hand into his pocket. The old couple, trembling, began to rise. Burgess fumbled a moment, then said,

"I find I have read them all."

Faint with joy and surprise, the couple sank into their seats, and Mary whispered:

"Oh, bless God, we are saved!—he has lost ours—I wouldn't give this for a hundred of those sacks!"

The house burst out with its "Mikado" travesty, and sang it three times with ever-increasing enthusiasm, rising to its feet when it reached for the third time the closing line—

But the Symbols are here, you bet!

and finishing up with cheers and a tiger for "Hadleyburg purity and our eighteen immortal representatives of it."

Then Wingate, the saddler, got up and proposed cheers "for the cleanest man in town, the one solitary important citizen in it who didn't try to steal that money—Edward Richards."

They were given with great and moving heartiness; then somebody proposed that Richards be elected sole guardian and Symbol of the now Sacred Hadleyburg Tradition, with power and right to stand up and look the whole sarcastic world in the face.

Passed, by acclamation; then they sang the "Mikado" again, and ended it with:

And there's *one* Symbol left, you bet!

There was a pause; then—

A Voice. "Now, then who's to get the sack?"

The Tanner (with bitter sarcasm). "That's easy. The money has to be divided among the eighteen Incorruptibles. They gave the suffering stranger twenty dollars apiece—and that remark—each in his turn—it took twenty-two minutes for the procession to move past. Staked the stranger—total contribution, $360. All they want is just the loan back—and interest—forty thousand dollars altogether."

Many Voices [derisively]. "That's it! Divvy! divvy! Be kind to the poor—don't keep them waiting!"

The Chair. "Order! I now offer the stranger's remaining document. It says: 'If no claimant shall appear [*grand chorus of groans*] I desire that you open the sack and count out the money to the principal citizens of your town, they to take it in trust [*cries of "Oh! Oh! Oh!"*], and use it in such ways as to them shall seem best for the propagation and preservation of your community's noble reputation for incorruptible honesty [*more cries*]—a reputation to which their names and their efforts will add a new and far-reaching luster.' [*Enthusiastic outburst of sarcastic applause.*] That seems to be all. No—here is a postscript:

" 'P. S.—CITIZENS OF HADLEYBURG: There *is* no test-remark—nobody made one. [*Great sensation.*] There wasn't any pauper stranger, nor any twenty-dollar contribution, nor any accompanying benediction and compliment—these are all inventions. [*General buzz and hum of astonishment and delight.*] Allow me to tell my story—it will take but a word or two. I passed through your town at a certain time, and received a deep offense which I had not earned. Any other man would have been content to kill one or two of you and call it square, but to me that would have been a trivial revenge, and inadequate; for the dead do not *suffer*. Besides, I could not kill you all—and, anyway, made as I am, even that would not have satisfied me. I wanted to damage every man in the place, and every woman—and not in their bodies or in their estate, but in their vanity—the place where feeble and foolish people are most vulnerable. So I disguised myself and came back and studied you. You were easy game. You had an old and lofty reputation for honesty, and naturally you were proud of it—it was your treasure of treasures, the very apple of your eye. As soon as I found out that you carefully and vigilantly kept yourselves and your children *out of temptation,* I knew how to proceed. Why, you simple creatures, the weakest of all weak things is a virtue which has not been tested in the fire. I laid a plan, and gathered a list of names. My project was to corrupt Hadleyburg the Incorruptible. My idea was to make liars and thieves of nearly half a hundred smirchless men and women who had never in their lives uttered a lie or stolen a penny. I was afraid of Goodson. He was neither born nor reared in Hadleyburg. I was afraid that if I started to operate my scheme by getting my letter laid before you, you would say to yourselves, "Goodson is the only man among us who would give away twenty dollars to a poor devil"—and then you might not bite at my bait. But Heaven took Goodson; then I knew I was safe, and I set my trap and baited it. It may be that I shall not catch all the men to whom I mailed the pretended test secret, but I shall catch the most of them, if I know Hadleyburg nature. [*Voices.* "Right—he got every last one of them."] I believe they will even steal ostensible *gamble*-money, rather than miss, poor, tempted, and mistrained fellows. I am hoping to eternally and everlastingly squelch your vanity and give Hadleyburg a new renown—one that will *stick*—and spread far. If I have succeeded, open the sack and summon the Committee on Propagation and Preservation of the Hadleyburg Reputation.' "

A *Cyclone of Voices.* "Open it! Open it! The Eighteen to the front! Committee on Propagation of the Tradition! Forward—the Incorruptibles!"

The Chair ripped the sack wide, and gathered up a handful of bright, broad, yellow coins, shook them together, then examined them—

"Friends, they are only gilded disks of lead!"

There was a crashing outbreak of delight over this news, and when the noise had subsided, the tanner called out:

"By right of apparent seniority in this business, Mr. Wilson is Chairman of the Committee on Propagation of the Tradition. I suggest that he step forward on behalf of his pals, and receive in trust the money."

A *Hundred Voices.* "Wilson! Wilson! Wilson! Speech! Speech!"

Wilson [*in a voice trembling with anger*]. "You will allow me to say, and without apologies for my language, *damn* the money!"

A Voice. "Oh, and him a Baptist!"

A Voice. "Seventeen Symbols left! Step up, gentlemen, and assume your trust!"

There was a pause—no response.

The Saddler. "Mr. Chairman, we've got *one* clean man left, anyway, out of the late aristocracy; and he needs money, and deserves it. I move that you appoint Jack Halliday to get up there and auction off that sack of gilt twenty-dollar pieces, and give the result to the right man—the man whom Hadleyburg delights to honor—Edward Richards."

This was received with great enthusiasm, the dog taking a hand again; the saddler started the bids at a dollar, the Brixton folk and Barnum's representative fought hard for it, the people cheered every jump that the bids made, the excitement climbed moment by moment higher and higher, the bidders got on their mettle and grew steadily more and more daring, more and more determined, the jumps went from a dollar up to five, then to ten, then to twenty, then fifty, then to a hundred, then—

At the beginning of the auction Richards whispered in distress to his wife: "O Mary, can we allow it? It—it—you see, it is an honor-reward, a testimonial to purity of character, and—and—can we allow it? Hadn't I better get up and—O Mary, what ought we to do?—what do you think we—[*Halliday's voice.* "Fifteen I'm bid!—fifteen for the sack!—twenty!—ah, thanks!—thirty—thanks again! Thirty, thirty, thirty!—do I hear forty?—forty it is! Keep the ball rolling, gentlemen, keep it rolling!—fifty! thanks, noble Roman! going at fifty, fifty, fifty!—seventy!—ninety!—splendid!— a hundred!—pile it up, pile it up!—hundred and twenty—forty!—just in time!—hundred and fifty!—*TWO hundred!—superb! Do I hear two h— thanks!—two hundred and fifty!—*"]

"It is another temptation, Edward—I'm all in a tremble—but, oh, we've escaped *one* temptation, and that ought to warn us to— [*"Six did I hear?—thanks!—six-fifty, six-f—*SEVEN hundred!*"*] And yet, Edward, when you think—nobody susp— [*"Eight hundred dollars!—hurrah!— make it nine!—Mr. Parsons, did I hear you say—thanks—nine!—this noble sack of virgin lead going at only nine hundred dollars, gilding and all—come! do I hear—a thousand!—gratefully yours!—did some one say eleven?—a sack which is going to be the most celebrated in the whole Uni—*"] O Edward" (beginning to sob), "we are *so* poor!—but— but—do as you think best—do as you think best."

Edward fell—that is, he sat still; sat with a conscience which was not satisfied, but which was overpowered by circumstances.

Meantime a stranger, who looked like an amateur detective gotten up as an impossible English earl, had been watching the evening's proceedings with manifest interest, and with a contented expression in his face; and he had been privately commenting to himself. He was now soliloquizing somewhat like this: "None of the Eighteen are bidding; that is not satisfactory; I must change that—the dramatic unities require it; they must buy the sack they tried to steal; they must pay a heavy price, too—some of them are rich. And another thing, when I make a mistake in Hadleyburg nature the man that puts that error upon me is entitled to a high honorarium, and some one must pay it. This poor old Richards has brought my judgment to shame; he is an honest man:—I don't understand it, but I acknowledge it. Yes, he saw my deuces *and* with a straight flush, and by rights the pot is his. And it shall be a jackpot, too, if I can manage it. He disappointed me, but let that pass."

He was watching the bidding. At a thousand, the market broke; the prices tumbled swiftly. He waited—and still watched. One competitor dropped out; then another, and another. He put in a bid or two, now. When the bids had sunk to ten dollars, he added a five; some one raised him a three; he waited a moment, then flung in a fifty-dollar jump, and the sack was his—at $1,282. The house broke out in cheers—then stopped; for he was on his feet, and had lifted his hand. He began to speak.

"I desire to say a word, and ask a favor. I am a speculator in rarities, and I have dealings with persons interested in numismatics all over the world. I can make a profit on this purchase, just as it stands; but there is a way, if I can get your approval, whereby I can make every one of these leaden twenty-dollar pieces worth its face in gold, and perhaps more. Grant me that approval, and I will give part of my gains to your Mr. Richards, whose invulnerable probity you have so justly and so cordially recognized tonight; his share shall be ten thousand dollars, and I will hand him the money to-morrow. [*Great applause from the house.* But the "invulnerable probity" made the Richardses blush prettily; however, it went for modesty, and did no harm.] If you will pass my proposition by a good majority—I would like a two-thirds vote—I will regard that as the town's consent, and that is all I ask. Rarities are always helped by any device which will rouse curiosity and compel remark. Now if I may have your permission to stamp upon the faces of each of these ostensible coins the names of the eighteen gentlemen who—"

Nine-tenths of the audience were on their feet in a moment—dog and all—and the proposition was carried with a whirlwind of approving applause and laughter.

They sat down, and all the Symbols except "Dr." Clay Harkness got up, violently protesting against the proposed outrage, and threatening to—

"I beg you not to threaten me," said the stranger, calmly. "I know my legal rights, and am not accustomed to being frightened at bluster." [*Applause.*] He sat down. "Dr." Harkness saw an opportunity here. He was one of the two very rich men of the place, and Pinkerton was the other. Harkness was proprietor of a mint; that is to say, a popular patent medicine. He was running for the legislature on one ticket, and Pinkerton on the other. It was a close race and a hot one, and getting hotter every day. Both had strong appetites for money; each had bought a great tract of land, with a purpose; there was going to be a new railway, and each wanted to be in the legislature and help locate the route to his own advantage; a single vote might make the decision, and with it two or three fortunes. The stake was large, and Harkness was a daring speculator. He was sitting close to the stranger. He leaned over while one or another of the other Symbols was entertaining the house with protests and appeals, and asked, in a whisper:

"What is your price for the sack?"

"Forty thousand dollars."

"I'll give you twenty."

"No."

"Twenty-five."

"No."

"Say thirty."

"The price is forty thousand dollars; not a penny less."

"All right, I'll give it. I will come to the hotel at ten in the morning. I don't want it known: will see you privately."

"Very good." Then the stranger got up and said to the house:

"I find it late. The speeches of these gentlemen are not without merit, not without interest, not without grace; yet if I may be excused I will take my leave. I thank you for the great favor which you have shown me in granting my petition. I ask the Chair to keep the sack for me until to-morrow, and to hand these three five-hundred-dollar notes to Mr. Richards." They were passed up to the Chair. "At nine I will call for the sack, and at eleven will deliver the rest of the ten thousand to Mr. Richards in person, at his home. Good night."

Then he slipped out, and left the audience making a vast noise, which was composed of a mixture of cheers, the "Mikado" song, dog-disapproval, and the chant, "You are f-a-r from being a b-a-a-d man—a-a-a-a-men!"

IV

At home the Richardses had to endure congratulations and compliments until midnight. Then they were left to themselves. They looked a little sad, and they sat silent and thinking. Finally Mary sighed and said,

"Do you think we are to blame, Edward—*much* to blame?" and her eyes wandered to the accusing triplet of big bank-notes lying on the table, where the congratulators had been gloating over them and reverently fingering them. Edward did not answer at once; then he brought out a sigh and said, hesitatingly:

"We—we couldn't help it, Mary. It—well, it was ordered. *All* things are."

Mary glanced up and looked at him steadily, but he didn't return the look. Presently she said:

"I thought congratulations and praises always tasted good. But—it seems to me, now—Edward?"

"Well?"

"Are you going to stay in the bank?"

"N-no."

"Resign?"

"In the morning—by note."

"It does seem best."

Richards bowed his head in his hands and muttered:

"Before, I was not afraid to let oceans of people's money pour through my hands, but—Mary, I am so tired, so tired—"

"We will go to bed."

At nine in the morning the stranger called for the sack and took it to the hotel in a cab. At ten Harkness had a talk with him privately. The stranger asked for and got five checks on a metropolitan bank—drawn to "Bearer"—four for $1,500 each, and one for $34,000. He put one of the former in his pocketbook, and the remainder, representing $38,500, he put in an envelope, and with these he added a note, which he wrote after Harkness was gone. At eleven he called at the Richards house and knocked. Mrs. Richards peeped through the shutters, then went and received the envelope, and the stranger disappeared without a word. She came back flushed and a little unsteady on her legs, and gasped out:

"I am sure I recognized him! Last night it seemed to me that maybe I had seen him somewhere before."

"He is the man that brought the sack here?"

"I am almost sure of it."

"Then he is the ostensible Stephenson, too, and sold every important citizen in this town with his bogus secret. Now if he has sent checks instead of money, we are sold, too, after we thought we had escaped. I was beginning to feel fairly comfortable once more, after my night's rest, but the look of that envelope makes me sick. It isn't fat enough; $8,500 in even the largest bank-notes makes more bulk than that."

"Edward, why do you object to checks?"

"Checks signed by Stephenson! I am resigned to take the $8,500 if it could come in bank-notes—for it does seem that it was so ordered, Mary—but I have never had much courage, and I have not the pluck to try to market a check signed with that disastrous name. It would be a trap. That man tried to catch me; we escaped somehow or other; and now he is trying a new way. If it is checks—"

"Oh, Edward, it is *too* bad!" and she held up the checks and began to cry.

"Put them in the fire! quick! we mustn't be tempted. It is a trick to make the world laugh at *us*, along with the rest, and—Give them to *me*, since you can't do it!" He snatched them and tried to hold his grip till he could get to the stove; but he was human, he was a cashier, and he stopped a moment to make sure of the signature. Then he came near to fainting.

"Fan me, Mary, fan me! They are the same as gold!"

"Oh, how lovely, Edward! Why?"

"Signed by Harkness. What can the mystery of that be, Mary?"

"Edward, do you think—"

"Look here—look at this! Fifteen—fifteen—fifteen—thirty-four. Thirty-eight thousand five hundred! Mary, the sack isn't worth twelve dollars, and Harkness—apparently—has paid about par for it."

"And does it all come to us, do you think—instead of the ten thousand?"

"Why, it looks like it. And the checks are made to 'Bearer,' too."

"Is that good, Edward? What is it for?"

"A hint to collect them at some distant bank, I reckon. Perhaps Harkness doesn't want the matter known. What is that—a note?"

"Yes. It was with the checks."

It was in the "Stephenson" handwriting, but there was no signature. It said:

I am a disappointed man. Your honesty is beyond the reach of temptation. I had a different idea about it, but I wronged you in that, and I beg pardon, and do its sincerely. I honor you—and that is sincere too. This town is not worthy to kiss the hem of your garment. Dear sir, I made a square bet with myself that there were nineteen debauchable men in your self-righteous community. I have lost. Take the whole pot, you are entitled to it.

Richards drew a deep sigh, and said:

"It seems written with fire—it burns so. Mary—I am miserable again."

"I, too. Ah, dear, I wish—"

"To think, Mary—he *believes* in me."

"Oh, don't, Edward—I can't bear it."

"If those beautiful words were deserved, Mary—and God knows I believed I deserved them once—I think I could give the forty thousand dollars for them. And I would put that paper away, as representing more than gold and jewels, and keep it always. But now— We could not live in the shadow of its accusing presence, Mary."

He put it in the fire.

A messenger arrived and delivered an envelope.

Richards took from it a note and read it; it was from Burgess.

You saved me, in a difficult time. I saved you last night. It was at cost of a lie, but I made the sacrifice freely, and out of a grateful heart. None in this village knows so well as I know how brave and good and noble you are. At bottom you cannot respect me, knowing as you do of that matter of which I am accused, and by the general voice condemned; but I beg that you will at least believe that I am a grateful man; it will help me to bear my burden.

                                                    [Signed]   *"Burgess."*

"Saved, once more. And on such terms!" He put the note in the fire. "I—I wish I were dead, Mary, I wish I were out of it all."

"Oh, these are bitter, bitter days, Edward. The stabs, through their very generosity, are so deep—and they come so fast!"

Three days before the election each of two thousand voters suddenly found himself in possession of a prized memento—one of the renowned bogus double-eagles. Around one of its faces was stamped these words: "THE REMARK I MADE TO THE POOR STRANGER WAS—" Around the other face was stamped these: "GO, AND REFORM. [SIGNED] PINKERTON." Thus the entire remaining refuse of the renowned joke was emptied upon a single head, and with calamitous effect. It revived the recent vast laugh and concentrated it upon Pinkerton; and Harkness's election was a walkover.

Within twenty-four hours after the Richardses had received their checks their consciences were quieting down, discouraged; the old couple were learning to reconcile themselves to the sin which they had committed. But they were to learn, now, that a sin takes on new and real terrors when there seems a chance that it is going to be found out. This gives it a fresh and most substantial and important aspect. At church the morning sermon was of the usual pattern; it was the same old things said in the same old way; they had heard them a thousand times and found them innocuous, next to meaningless, and easy to sleep under; but now it was different: the sermon seemed to bristle with accusations; it seemed aimed straight and specially at people who were concealing deadly sins. After church they got away from the mob of congratulators as soon as they could, and hurried homeward, chilled to the bone at they did not know what—vague, shadowy, indefinite fears. And by chance they caught a glimpse of Mr. Burgess as he turned a corner. He paid no attention their nod of recognition! He hadn't seen it; but they did not know that. What could his conduct mean? It might mean—it might mean—oh, a dozen dreadful things. Was it possible that he knew that Richards could have cleared him of guilt in that bygone time, and had been silently waiting for a chance to even up accounts? At home, in their distress they got to imagining that their servant might have been in the next room listening when Richards revealed the secret to his wife that he knew of Burgess's innocence; next, Richards began to imagine that he had heard the swish of a gown in there at that time; next, he was sure he *had* heard it. They would call Sarah in, on a pretext, and watch her face: if she had been betraying them to Mr. Burgess, it would show in her manner. They asked her some questions—questions which were so random and incoherent and seemingly purposeless that the girl felt sure that the old people's minds had been affected by their sudden good fortune; the sharp and watchful gaze which they bent upon her frightened her, and that completed the business. She blushed, she became nervous and confused, and to the old people these were plain signs of guilt—guilt of some fearful sort or other—without doubt she was a spy and a traitor. When they were alone

again they began to piece many unrelated things together and get horrible results out of the combination. When things had got about to the
worst, Richards was delivered of a sudden gasp, and his wife asked:

"Oh, what is it?—what is it?"

"The note—Burgess's note! Its language was sarcastic, I see it now."
He quoted: "'At bottom you cannot respect me, *knowing,* as you do, of
that matter of which I am accused'—oh, it is perfectly plain, now, God
help me! He knows that I know! You see the ingenuity of the phrasing.
It was a trap—and like a fool, I walked into it. And Mary—?"

"Oh, it is dreadful—I know what you are going to say—he didn't
return your transcript of the pretended test-remark."

"No—kept it to destroy us with. Mary, he has exposed us to some
already. I know it—I know it well. I saw it in a dozen faces after
church. Ah, he wouldn't answer our nod of recognition—*he* knew what
he had been doing!"

In the night the doctor was called. The news went around in the
morning that the old couple were rather seriously ill—prostrated by the
exhausting excitement growing out of their great windfall, the congratulations, and the late hours, the doctor said. The town was sincerely
distressed; for these old people were about all it had left to be proud of,
now.

Two days later the news was worse. The old couple were delirious,
and were doing strange things. By witness of the nurses, Richards had
exhibited checks—for $8,500? No—for an amazing sum—$38,500!
What could be the explanation of this gigantic piece of luck?

The following day the nurses had more news—and wonderful. They
had concluded to hide the checks, lest harm come to them; but when
they searched they were gone from under the patient's pillow—vanished away. The patient said:

"Let the pillow alone; what do you want?"

"We thought it best that the checks—"

"You will never see them again—they are destroyed. They came
from Satan. I saw the hell-brand on them, and I knew they were sent
to betray me to sin." Then he fell to gabbling strange and dreadful
things which were not clearly understandable, and which the doctor
admonished them to keep to themselves.

Richards was right; the checks were never seen again.

A nurse must have talked in her sleep, for within two days the
forbidden gabblings were the property of the town; and they were of a
surprising sort. They seemed to indicate that Richards had been a
claimant for the sack himself, and that Burgess had concealed that fact
and then maliciously betrayed it.

Burgess was taxed with this and stoutly denied it. And he said it
was not fair to attach weight to the chatter of a sick old man who was
out of his mind. Still, suspicion was in the air, and there was much
talk.

After a day or two it was reported that Mrs. Richards's delirious
deliveries were getting to be duplicates of her husband's. Suspicion

flamed up into conviction, now, and the town's pride in the purity of its one undiscredited important citizen began to dim down and flicker toward extinction.

Six days passed, then came more news. The old couple were dying. Richards's mind cleared in his latest hour, and he sent for Burgess. Burgess said:

"Let the room be cleared. I think he wishes to say something in privacy."

"No!" said Richards: "I want witnesses. I want you all to hear my confession, so that I may die a man, and not a dog. I was clean—artificially—like the rest; and like the rest I fell when temptation came. I signed a lie, and claimed the miserable sack. Mr. Burgess remembered that I had done him a service, and in gratitude (and ignorance) he suppressed my claim and saved me. You know the thing that was charged against Burgess years ago. My testimony, and mine alone, could have cleared him, and I was a coward, and left him to suffer disgrace—"

"No—no—Mr. Richards, you—"

"My servant betrayed my secret to him—"

"No one has betrayed anything to me—"

—"and then he did a natural and justifiable thing, he repented of the saving kindness which he had done me, and he *exposed* me—as I deserved—"

"Never!—I make oath—"

"Out of my heart I forgive him."

Burgess's impassioned protestations fell upon deaf ears; the dying man passed away without knowing that once more he had done poor Burgess a wrong. The old wife died that night.

The last of the sacred Nineteen had fallen a prey to the fiendish sack; the town was stripped of the last rag of its ancient glory. Its mourning was not showy, but it was deep.

By act of the Legislature—upon prayer and petition—Hadleyburg was allowed to change its name to (never mind what—I will not give it away), and leave one word out of the motto that for many generations had graced the town's official seal.

It is an honest town once more, and the man will have to rise early that catches it napping again.

WILLIAM DEAN HOWELLS (1837–1920)

For many years William Dean Howells was the central figure—which is not to say the greatest writer—in the literary life of the United States. A man of wide cultural and humane sympathies, Howells helped introduce a new realism into late-nineteenth-century American writing both through his own fiction and as a champion of the European masters who were then being translated into English.

The son of a newspaperman, Howells was born in Ohio and lived there for most of his boyhood, moving from town to town as his father changed jobs. While still a youth he went to work on the Columbus paper, Ohio State Journal, *and by the time he was twenty-three he had published two books (one, a campaign biography of Lincoln) and some poems in the* Atlantic Monthly. *In 1860 he took a journey to Boston which marked his entry into the literary world of the East, and at a famous dinner attended by Holmes and Lowell, there occurred what Holmes would describe as "the apostolic succession . . . the laying on of hands."*

Largely as the result of the Lincoln book, Howells was appointed United States consul in Venice; a series of travel letters from there, republished as Venetian Life *(1866), enhanced his reputation, and by the time he was thirty-five, he was editor of the* Atlantic. *While maintaining his cordial relations with the Brahmins of Boston, he also encouraged such writers as Henry James, Mark Twain, and Sarah Orne Jewett. He would, in fact, be a life-long friend of both James and Twain, symbolically centered between these great figures at the opposite poles of our culture. During this period Howells began to evolve his theories of realistic fiction and to portray the "poor Real Life, which I love" in such novels as* Their Wedding Journey *(1872),* A Modern Instance *(1882),* The Rise of Silas Lapham *(1885), and* A Hazard of New Fortunes *(1890). Howells explained his literary views:*

I feel more and more persuaded that we have only to study American life with the naked eye in order to find it infinitely various and entertaining. The trouble has always been that we have looked at it through somebody else's confounded literary telescope. I find it hard work myself to trust my eyes, and I catch myself feeling for the telescope, but I hope to do without it, altogether, by and by.

Toward the end of the century Howells began to write literary and social criticism that reflected his deepening humanitarian interests and his turn, influenced by a reading of Tolstoy, toward a mild form of socialism. Meanwhile he kept lending his warm-hearted support to new writers such as Crane, Garland, and Frank Norris.

Howells's reputation has rested mainly on his realistic social novels. Their realism depends on an intimate knowledge of the surface details—the manners, speech, dress, appearances—of late-nineteenth-century American life. No other American novelist has known so well, or written with such a mixture of sympathy and ironic distance, about the life of the American middle class. Howells was one of the first Americans to write novels in the way nineteenth-century English and Continental writers did—that is, to write works of fiction dealing with commonplace social life, set in familiar places and populated with recognizable characters. Yet Howells's realism, though always earnest, was rarely whole-hearted; there were aspects of life from which he flinched, even though his honesty as a writer forced him to approach them. His realism was inhibited by a native prudishness and by a failure to cope with those drives in human existence which cannot be understood, let alone contained, by goodwill and common sense.

Those of Howells's novels dealing with social problems—the decline of the small businessman, the conflict between labor and employer—are now likely to seem a little tepid. They lack fire, dramatic concentration, boldness of imagination. They are attenuated by the very gentility which Howells in his conscious mind wanted to leave behind—at least, leave behind in part. By contrast, some of Howells's less ambitious novels, mostly his novels of social comedy, are notable for a quiet shrewdness of observation and now seem livelier. Such works as Indian Summer *(1886),* The Landlord at Lion's Head *(1897), and* The Vacation of the Kelwyns *(1910) retain their point and sparkle. Howells's books of reminiscence have also stood the test of time:* A Boy's Town *(1890) is a classic portrait of small-town American life in the mid-nineteenth century, and* My Mark Twain *(1910) is a lovely summoning of things past.*

Howells, like Cooper, is a writer who does not lend himself to anthologizing, for his best effects are secured in his books as a whole. The selections from his nonfiction that appear below should yield a glimpse of his talents as critic and memorialist, while "Editha," a story with a shade more tartness than one usually finds in Howells's novels, shows his capacity for evoking certain modes of feminine psychology.

FURTHER READING

Edwin Cady, *The Road to Realism* (1956) and *The Realist at War* (1958), a two-volume work tracing Howells's career; Everett Carter, *Howells and the Age of Realism* (1954).

FROM *The Smiling Aspects*
of American Life (1886)[1]

... While *The Crime and the Punishment*[2] may be read with the
deepest sympathy and interest, and may enforce with unique power the
lessons which it teaches, it is to be praised only in its place, and its
message is to be received with allowances by readers exterior to the
social and political circumstances in which it was conceived. It used to
be one of the disadvantages of the practice of romance in America,
which Hawthorne more or less whimsically lamented, that there were
so few shadows and inequalities in our broad level of prosperity; and
it is one of the reflections suggested by Dostoïevsky's book that whoever
struck a note so profoundly tragic in American fiction would do a false
and mistaken thing—as false and as mistaken in its way as dealing in
American fiction with certain nudities which the Latin peoples seem to
find edifying. Whatever their deserts, very few American novelists have
been led out to be shot, or finally exiled to the rigors of a winter at
Duluth; one might make Herr Most[3] the hero of a labor-question
romance with perfect impunity; and in a land where journeyman
carpenters and plumbers strike for four dollars a day the sum of hunger
and cold is certainly very small, and the wrong from class to class is
almost inappreciable. We invite our novelists, therefore, to concern
themselves with the more smiling aspects of life, which are the more
American, and to seek the universal in the individual rather than the
social interests. It is worth while, even at the risk of being called commonplace, to be true to our well-to-do actualities; the very passions
themselves seem to be softened and modified by conditions which cannot be said to wrong any one, to cramp endeavor, or to cross lawful
desire. Sin and suffering and shame there must always be in the world,
we suppose, but we believe that in this new world of ours it is mainly
from one to another one, and oftener still from one to one's self. We have
death too in America, and a great deal of disagreeable and painful disease, which the multiplicity of our patent medicines does not seem to
cure; but this is tragedy that comes in the very nature of things, and
is not peculiarly American, as the large, cheerful average of health and
success and happy life is. It will not do to boast, but it is well to be
true to the facts, and to see that, apart from these purely mortal
troubles, the race here enjoys conditions in which most of the ills that
have darkened its annals may be averted by honest work and unselfish
behavior.

[1] First published in *Harper's Magazine*, 1886, this essay, slightly modified, was reprinted by Howells in his book *Criticism and Fiction* (1891).
[2] The novel by Fyodor Dostœvsky (1821–1881).
[3] Johann Most (1846–1906), anarchist leader who spent his later years in the
United States.

It is only now and then, when some dark shadow of our shameful past appears, that we can believe there ever was a tragic element in our prosperity. Even then, when we read such an artlessly impressive sketch as Mrs. Sarah Bradford [4] writes of Harriet Tubman [5]—once famous as the Moses of her people—the self-freed bondwoman who led three hundred of her brethren out of slavery, and with a price set upon her head, risked her life and liberty nineteen times in this cause; even then it affects us like a tale

Of old, unhappy, far-off things,
And battles long ago,

and nothing within the date of actual history. We cannot realize that most of the men and women now living were once commanded by the law of the land to turn and hunt such fugitives back into slavery, and to deliver such an outlaw as Harriet over to her owner; that those who abetted such outlaws were sometimes mulcted to the last dollar of their substance in fines. We can hardly imagine such things now for the purposes of fiction; all troubles that now hurt and threaten us are as crumpled rose leaves in our couch. But we may nevertheless read Dostoïevsky, and especially our novelists may read him, to advantage, for in spite of his terrible picture of a soul's agony he is hopeful and wholesome, and teaches in every page patience, merciful judgment, humble helpfulness, and that brotherly responsibility, that duty of man to man, from which not even the Americans are emancipated.

FROM *My Mark Twain* (1910)

At the time of our first meeting, which must have been well toward the winter, Clemens (as I must call him instead of Mark Twain, which seemed always somehow to mask him from my personal sense) was wearing a sealskin coat, with the fur out, in the satisfaction of a caprice, or the love of strong effect which he was apt to indulge through life. I do not know what droll comment was in Fields's mind with respect to this garment, but probably he felt that here was an original who was not to be brought to any Bostonian book in the judgment of his vivid qualities. With his crest of dense red hair, and the wide sweep of his flaming mustache, Clemens was not discordantly clothed in that sealskin coat, which afterward, in spite of his own warmth in it, sent the cold chills through me when I once accompanied it down Broadway, and shared the immense publicity it won him. He had always a relish for personal effect, which expressed itself in the white suit of complete serge which he wore in his last years, and in the Oxford gown which he put on for every possible occasion, and said he would like to wear all the time. That was not vanity in him, but a keen feeling for costume which the severity of our modern tailoring forbids men, though it flatters women to every excess in it; yet he also enjoyed the shock, the offence, the pang which it gave the sensibilities of others. . . .

To the period of Clemens's residence in Fifth Avenue belongs his efflorescence in white serge. He was always rather aggressively indifferent about dress, and at a very early date in our acquaintance Aldrich and I attempted his reform by clubbing to buy him a cravat. But he would not put away his stiff little black bow, and until he imagined the suit of white serge, he wore always a suit of black serge, truly deplorable in the cut of the sagging frock. After his measure had once been taken he refused to make his clothes the occasion of personal interviews with his tailor; he sent the stuff by the kind elderly woman who had been in the service of the family from the earliest days of his marriage, and accepted the result without criticism. But the white serge was an inspiration which few men would have had the courage to act upon. The first time I saw him wear it was at the authors' hearing before the Congressional Committee on Copyright in Washington. Nothing could have been more dramatic than the gesture with which he flung off his long loose overcoat, and stood forth in white from his feet to the crown of his silvery head. It was a magnificent *coup,* and he dearly loved a *coup;* but the magnificent speech which he made, tearing to shreds the venerable farrago of nonsense about non-property in ideas which had formed the basis of all copyright legislation, made you forget even his spectacularity.

It is well known how proud he was of his Oxford gown, not merely because it symbolized the honor in which he was held by the highest literary body in the world, but because it was so rich and so beautiful. The red and the lavender of the cloth flattered his eyes as the silken black of the same degree of Doctor of Letters, given him years before at Yale, could not do. His frank, defiant happiness in it, mixed with a due sense of burlesque, was something that those lacking his poet-soul could never imagine; they accounted it vain, weak; but that would not have mattered to him if he had known it. In his London sojourn he had formed the top-hat habit, and for a while he lounged splendidly up and down Fifth Avenue in that society emblem; but he seemed to tire of it, and to return kindly to the soft hat of his Southwestern tradition. . . .

Once when I came on from Cambridge he followed me to my room to see that the water was not frozen in my bath, or something of the kind, for it was very cold weather, and then hospitably lingered. Not to lose time in banalities I began at once from the thread of thought in my mind. "I wonder why we hate the past so," and he responded from the depths of his own consciousness, "It's so damned humiliating," which is what any man would say of his past if he were honest; but honest men are few when it comes to themselves. Clemens was one of the few, and the first of them among all the people I have known. I have known, I suppose, men as truthful, but not so promptly, so absolutely, so positively, so almost aggressively truthful. He could lie, of course, and did to save others from grief or harm; he was not stupidly truthful; but his first impulse was to say out the thing and everything that was in him. To those who can understand it will not be contradictory of his sense of humiliation from the past, that he was not ashamed for anything he ever did to the point of wishing to hide it. He could be, and he was, bitterly sorry for his errors, which he had enough of in his life, but he was not ashamed in that mean way. What he had done he owned to, good, bad, or indifferent, and if it was bad he was rather amused than troubled as to the effect in your mind. He would not obtrude the fact upon you, but if it were in the way of personal history he would not dream of withholding it, far less of hiding it.

He was the readiest of men to allow an error if he were found in it. . . .

Fully half our meetings were at my house in Cambridge, where he made himself as much at home as in Hartford. He would come ostensibly to stay at the Parker House, in Boston, and take a room, where he would light the gas and leave it burning, after dressing, while he drove out to Cambridge and stayed two or three days with us. Once, I suppose it was after a lecture, he came in evening dress and passed twenty-four hours with us in that guise, wearing an overcoat to hide it when we went for a walk. Sometimes he wore the slippers which he preferred to shoes at home, and if it was muddy, as it was wont to be in Cambridge, he would put a pair of rubbers over them for our rambles. He like the lawlessness and our delight in allowing it, and he rejoiced in the confession of his hostess, after we had once almost worn ourselves out in our pleasure with the intense talk, with the stories and the laughing, that his coming almost killed her, but it was worth it.

In those days he was troubled with sleeplessness, or, rather, with reluctant sleepiness, and he had various specifics for promoting it. At first it had been champagne just before going to bed, and we provided that, but later he appeared from Boston with four bottles of lager-beer under his arms; lager-beer, he said now, was the only thing to make you go to sleep, and we provided that. Still later, on a visit I paid him at Hartford, I learned that hot Scotch was the only soporific worth considering, and Scotch whiskey duly found its place on our sideboard. One day, very long afterward, I asked him if he were still taking hot Scotch to make him sleep. He said he was not taking anything. For a while he had found going to bed on the bath-room floor a soporific; then one night he went to rest in his own bed at ten o'clock, and had gone promptly to sleep without anything. He had done the like with the like effect ever since. Of course, it amused him; there were few experiences, of life, grave or gay, which did not amuse him, even when they wronged him.

He came on to Cambridge in April, 1875, to go with me to the centennial ceremonies at Concord in celebration of the battle of the Minute Men with the British troops a hundred years before. We both

had special invitations, including passage from Boston; but I said, Why
bother to go into Boston when we could just as well take the train for
Concord at the Cambridge station? He equally decided that it would be
absurd; so we breakfasted deliberately, and then walked to the station,
reasoning of many things as usual. When the train stopped, we found
it packed inside and out. People stood dense on the platforms of the
cars; to our startled eyes they seemed to project from the windows, and
unless memory betrays me they lay strewn upon the roofs like brake-
men slain at the post of duty. Whether this was really so or not, it is
certain that the train presented an impenetrable front even to our
imagination, and we left it to go its way without the slightest effort to
board. We remounted the fame-worn steps of Porter's Station, and
began exploring North Cambridge for some means of transportation
overland to Concord, for we were that far on the road by which the
British went and came on the day of the battle. The liverymen whom
we appealed to received us, some with compassion, some with derision,
but in either mood convinced us that we could not have hired a cat
to attempt our conveyance, must less a horse, or vehicle of any description. It was a raw, windy day, very unlike the exceptionally hot April
day when the routed redcoats, pursued by the Colonials, fled panting
back to Boston, with "their tongues hanging out like dogs," but we could
not take due comfort in the vision of their discomfiture; we could
almost envy them, for they had at least got to Concord. A swift procession of coaches, carriages, and buggies, all going to Concord, passed
us, inert and helpless, on the sidewalk in the peculiarly cold mud of
North Cambridge. We began to wonder if we might not stop one of
them and bribe it to take us, but we had not the courage to try, and
Clemens seized the opportunity to begin suffering with an acute indiges-
tion, which gave his humor a very dismal cast. I felt keenly the shame
of defeat, and the guilt of responsibility for our failure, and when a
gay party of students came toward us on the top of a tally-ho, luxuriously empty inside, we felt that our chance had come, and our last
chance. He said that if I would stop them and tell them who I was they
would gladly, perhaps proudly, give us passage; I contended that if with
his far vaster renown he would approach them, our success would be
assured. While we stood, lost in this "contest of civilities," the coach
passed us, with gay notes blown from the horns of the students, and
then Clemens started in pursuit, encouraged with shouts from the
merry party who could not imagine who was trying to run them down,
to a rivalry in speed. The unequal match could end only in one way,
and I am glad I cannot recall what he said when he came back to me.
Since then I have often wondered at the grief which would have wrung
those blithe young hearts if they could have known that they might
have had the company of Mark Twain to Concord that day and did not.

We hung about, unavailingly, in the bitter wind a while longer, and
then slowly, very slowly, made our way home. We wished to pass as

much time as possible, in order to give probability to the deceit we intended to practise, for we could not bear to own ourselves baffled in our boasted wisdom of taking the train at Porter's Station, and had agreed to say that we had been to Concord and got back. Even after coming home to my house, we felt that our statement would be wanting in verisimilitude without further delay, and we crept quietly into my library, and made up a roaring fire on the hearth, and thawed ourselves out in the heat of it before we regained our courage for the undertaking. With all these precautions we failed, for when our statement was imparted to the proposed victim she instantly pronounced it unreliable, and we were left with it on our hands intact. I think the humor of this situation was finally a greater pleasure to Clemens than an actual visit to Concord would have been; only a few weeks before his death he laughed our defeat over with one of my family in Bermuda, and exulted in our prompt detection.

Editha (1905)

The air was thick with the war feeling, like the electricity of a storm which has not yet burst. Editha sat looking out into the hot spring afternoon, with her lips parted, and panting with the intensity of the question whether she could let him go. She had decided that she could not let him stay, when she saw him at the end of the still leafless avenue, making slowly up towards the house, with his head down and his figure relaxed. She ran impatiently out on the veranda, to the edge of the steps, and imperatively demanded greater haste of him with her will before she called aloud to him: "George!"

He had quickened his pace in mystical response to her mystical urgence, before he could have heard her; now he looked up and answered, "Well?"

"Oh, how united we are!" she exulted, and then she swooped down the steps to him. "What is it?" she cried.

"It's war," he said, and he pulled her up to him and kissed her.

She kissed him back intensely, but irrelevantly, as to their passion, and uttered from deep in her throat. "How glorious!"

"It's war," he repeated, without consenting to her sense of it; and she did not know just what to think at first. She never knew what to think of him; that made his mystery, his charm. All through their courtship, which was contemporaneous with the growth of the war feeling, she had been puzzled by his want of seriousness about it. He seemed to despise it even more than he abhorred it. She could have understood his abhorring any sort of bloodshed; that would have been a survival of his old life when he thought he would be a minister, and before he changed and took up the law. But making light of a cause so high and noble seemed to show a want of earnestness at the core of his being. Not but that she felt herself able to cope with a congenital defect of that sort, and make his love for her save him from himself. Now perhaps the miracle was already wrought in him. In the presence of the tremendous fact that he announced, all triviality seemed to have gone out of him; she began to feel that. He sank down on the top step, and wiped his forehead with his handkerchief, while she poured out upon him her question of the origin and authenticity of his news.

All the while, in her duplex emotioning, she was aware that now at the very beginning she must put a guard upon herself against urging him, by any word or act, to take the part that her whole soul willed him to take, for the completion of her ideal of him. He was very nearly perfect as he was, and he must be allowed to perfect himself. But he was peculiar, and he might very well be reasoned out of his peculiarity. Before her reasoning went her emotioning: her nature pulling upon his nature, her womanhood upon his manhood, without her knowing the means she was using to the end she was willing. She had always supposed that the man who won her would have done something to win her; she did not know what, but something. George Gearson had simply asked her for her love, on the way home from a concert, and she gave her love to him, without, as it were, thinking. But now, it flashed upon her, if he could do something worthy to *have* won her—be a hero, *her* hero—it would be even better than if he had done it before asking her; it would be grander. Besides, she had believed in the war from the beginning.

"But don't you see, dearest," she said, "that it wouldn't have come to this if it hadn't been in the order of Providence? And I call any war glorious that is for the liberation of people who have been struggling for years against the cruelest oppression. Don't you think so, too?"

"I suppose so," he returned, languidly. "But war! Is it glorious to break the peace of the world?"

"That ignoble peace! It was no peace at all, with that crime and shame at our very gates." She was conscious of parroting the current phrases of the newspapers, but it was no time to pick and choose her words. She must sacrifice anything to the high ideal she had for him, and after a good deal of rapid argument she ended with the climax: "But now it doesn't matter about the how or why. Since the war has come, all that is gone. There are no two sides any more. There is nothing now but our country."

He sat with his eyes closed and his head leant back against the veranda, and he remarked, with a vague smile, as if musing aloud, "Our country—right or wrong."

"Yes, right or wrong!" she returned, fervidly. "I'll go and get you some lemonade." She rose rustling, and whisked away; when she came back with two tall glasses of clouded liquid on a tray, and the ice clucking in them, he still sat as she had left him, and she said, as if there had been no interruption: "But there is no question of wrong in this case. I call it a sacred war. A war for liberty and humanity, if ever there was one. And I know you will see it just as I do, yet."

He took half the lemonade at a gulp, and he answered as he set the glass down: "I know you always have the highest ideal. When I differ from you I ought to doubt myself."

A generous sob rose in Editha's throat for the humility of a man, so very nearly perfect, who was willing to put himself below her.

Besides, she felt, more subliminally, that he was never so near slipping through her fingers as when he took that meek way.

"You shall not say that! Only, for once I happen to be right." She seized his hand in her two hands, and poured her soul from her eyes into his. "Don't you think so?" she entreated him.

He released his hand and drank the rest of his lemonade, and she added, "Have mine, too," but he shook his head in answering, "I've no business to think so, unless I act so, too."

Her heart stopped a beat before it pulsed on with leaps that she felt in her neck. She had noticed that strange thing in men: they seemed to feel bound to do what they believed, and not think a thing was finished when they said it, as girls did. She knew what was in his mind, but she pretended not, and she said, "Oh, I am not sure," and then faltered.

He went on as if to himself, without apparently heeding her: "There's only one way of proving one's faith in a thing like this."

She could not say that she understood, but she did understand.

He went on again. "If I believed you—if I felt as you do about this war—Do you wish me to feel as you do?"

Now she was really not sure; so she said: "George, I don't know what you mean."

He seemed to muse away from her as before. "There is a sort of fascination in it. I suppose that at the bottom of his heart every man would like at times to have his courage tested, to see how he would act."

"How can you talk in that ghastly way?"

"It *is* rather morbid. Still, that's what it comes to, unless you're swept away by ambition or driven by conviction. I haven't the conviction or the ambition, and the other thing is what it comes to with me. I ought to have been a preacher, after all; then I couldn't have asked it of myself, as I must, now I'm a lawyer. And you believe it's a holy war, Editha?" he suddenly addressed her. "Oh, I know you do! But you wish me to believe so, too?"

She hardly knew whether he was mocking or not, in the ironical way he always had with her plainer mind. But the only thing was to be outspoken with him.

"George, I wish you to believe whatever you think is true, at any and every cost. If I've tried to talk you into anything, I take it all back."

"Oh, I know that, Editha. I know how sincere you are, and how—I wish I had your undoubting spirit! I'll think it over; I'd like to believe as you do. But I don't, now; I don't, indeed. It isn't this war alone; though this seems peculiarly wanton and needless; but it's every war— so stupid; it makes me sick. Why shouldn't this thing have been settled reasonably?"

"Because," she said, very throatily again, "God meant it to be war."

"You think it was God? Yes, I suppose that is what people will say."

"Do you suppose it would have been war if God hadn't meant it?"

"I don't know. Sometimes it seems as if God had put this world into men's keeping to work it as they pleased."

"Now, George, this is blasphemy."

"Well, I won't blaspheme. I'll try to believe in your pocket Providence," he said, and then he rose to go.

"Why don't you stay to dinner?" Dinner at Balcom's Works was at one o'clock.

"I'll come back to supper, if you'll let me. Perhaps I shall bring you a convert."

"Well, you may come back, on that condition."

"All right. If I don't come, you'll understand."

He went away without kissing her, and she felt it a suspension of their engagement. It all interested her intensely; she was undergoing a tremendous experience, and she was being equal to it. While she stood looking after him, her mother came out through one of the long windows onto the veranda, with a catlike softness and vagueness.

"Why didn't he stay to dinner?"

"Because—because—war has been declared," Editha pronounced, without turning.

Her mother said, "Oh, my!" and then said nothing more until she had sat down in one of the large Shaker chairs and rocked herself for some time. Then she closed whatever tacit passage of thought there had been in her mind with the spoken words: "Well, I hope *he* won't go."

"And *I* hope he *will*," the girl said, and confronted her mother with a stormy exaltation that would have frightened any creature less unimpressionable than a cat.

Her mother rocked herself again for an interval of cogitation. What she arrived at in speech was: "Well, I guess you've done a wicked thing, Editha Balcom."

The girl said, as she passed indoors through the same window her mother had come out by: "I haven't done anything—yet."

In her room, she put together all her letters and gifts from Gearson, down to the withered petals of the first flower he had offered, with that timidity of his veiled in that irony of his. In the heart of the packet she enshrined her engagement ring which she had restored to the pretty box he had brought it her in. Then she sat down, if not calmly yet strongly, and wrote:

GEORGE:—I understood when you left me. But I think we had better emphasize your meaning that if we cannot be one in everything we had better be one in nothing. So I am sending these things for your keeping till you have made up your mind.

I shall always love you, and therefore I shall never marry any one else. But the man I marry must love his country first of all, and be able to say to me, "I Could not love thee, dear, so much,
Loved I not honor more."
There is no honor above America with me. In this great hour there is no other honor.

Your heart will make my words clear to you. I had never expected to say so much, but it has come upon me that I must say the utmost. EDITHA.

She thought she had worded her letter well, worded it in a way that could not be bettered; all had been implied and nothing expressed.

She had it ready to send with the packet she had tied with red, white, and blue ribbon, when it occurred to her that she was not just to him, that she was not giving him a fair chance. He had said he would go and think it over, and she was not waiting. She was pushing, threatening, compelling. That was not a woman's part. She must leave him free, free, free. She could not accept for her country or herself a forced sacrifice.

In writing her letter she had satisfied the impulse from which it sprang; she could well afford to wait till he had thought it over. She put the packet and the letter by, and rested serene in the consciousness of having done what was laid upon her by her love itself to do, and yet used patience, mercy, justice.

She had her reward. Gearson did not come to tea, but she had given him till morning, when, late at night there came up from the village the sound of a fife and drum, with a tumult of voices, in shouting, singing, and laughing. The noise drew nearer and nearer; it reached the street end of the avenue; there it silenced itself, and one voice, the voice she knew best, rose over the silence. It fell; the air was filled with cheers; the fife and drum struck up, with the shouting, singing, and laughing again, but now retreating; and a single figure came hurrying up the avenue.

She ran down to meet her lover and clung to him. He was very gay, and he put his arm around her with a boisterous laugh. "Well, you must call me Captain now; or Cap, if you prefer; that's what the boys call me. Yes, we've had a meeting at the town-hall, and everybody has volunteered; and they selected me for captain, and I'm going to the war, the big war, the glorious war, the holy war ordained by the pocket Providence that blesses butchery. Come along; let's tell the whole family about it. Call them from their downy beds, father, mother, Aunt Hitty, and all the folks!"

But when they mounted the veranda steps he did not wait for a larger audience; he poured the story out upon Editha alone.

"There was a lot of speaking, and then some of the fools set up a shout for me. It was all going one way, and I thought it would be a good joke to sprinkle a little cold water on them. But you can't do that with a crowd that adores you. The first thing I knew I was sprinkling hell-fire on them. 'Cry havoc, and let slip the dogs of war.' That was the style. Now that it had come to the fight, there were no two parties; there was one country, and the thing was to fight to a finish as quick as possible. I suggested volunteering then and there, and I wrote my name first of all on the roster. Then they elected me—that's all. I wish I had some ice-water."

She left him walking up and down the veranda, while she ran for the ice-pitcher and a goblet, and when she came back he was still walking up and down, shouting the story he had told her to her father and mother, who had come out more sketchily dressed than they commonly were by day. He drank goblet after goblet of the ice-water without noticing who was giving it, and kept on talking, and laughing through his talk wildly. "It's astonishing," he said, "how well the worse reason looks when you try to make it appear the better. Why, I believe I was the first convert to the war in that crowd tonight! I never thought I should like to kill a man; but now I shouldn't care; and the smokeless powder lets you see the man drop that you kill. It's all for the country! What a thing it is to have a country that *can't* be wrong, but if it is, is right, anyway!"

Editha had a great, vital thought, an inspiration. She set down the ice-pitcher on the veranda floor, and ran up-stairs and got the letter she had written him. When at last he noisily bade her father and mother, "Well, good-night. I forgot I woke you up; I sha'n't want any sleep myself," she followed him down the avenue to the gate. There, after the whirling words that seemed to fly away from her thoughts and refuse to serve them, she made a last effort to solemnize the moment that seemed so crazy, and pressed the letter she had written upon him.

"What's this?" he said. "Want me to mail it?"

"No, no. It's for you. I wrote it after you went this morning. Keep it—keep it—and read it sometime—" She thought, and then her inspiration came: "Read it if ever you doubt what you've done, or fear that I regret your having done it. Read it after you've started."

They strained each other in embraces that seemed as ineffective as their words, and he kissed her face with quick, hot breaths that were so unlike him, that made her feel as if she had lost her old lover and found a stranger in his place. The stranger said: "What a gorgeous flower you are, with your red hair, and your blue eyes that look black now, and your face with the color painted out by the white moonshine! Let me hold you under the chin, to see whether I love blood, you tiger-lily!" Then he laughed Gearson's laugh, and released her, scared and giddy. Within her wilfulness she had been frightened by a sense of subtler force in him, and mystically mastered as she had never been before.

She ran all the way back to the house, and mounted the steps panting. Her mother and father were talking of the great affair. Her mother said: "Wa'n't Mr. Gearson in rather of an excited state of mind? Didn't you think he acted curious?"

"Well, not for a man who'd just been elected captain and had set 'em up for the whole of Company A," her father chuckled back.

"What in the world do you mean, Mr. Balcom? Oh! There's Editha!" She offered to follow the girl indoors.

"Don't come mother!" Editha called, vanishing.

Mrs. Balcom remained to reproach her husband. "I don't see much of anything to laugh at."

"Well, it's catching. Caught it from Gearson. I guess it won't be much of a war, and I guess Gearson don't think so, either. The other fellows will back down as soon as they see we mean it. I wouldn't lose any sleep over it. I'm going back to bed, myself."

Gearson came again next afternoon, looking pale and rather sick, but quite himself, even to his languid irony. "I guess I'd better tell you, Editha, that I consecrated myself to your god of battles last night by pouring too many libations to him down my own throat. But I'm all right now. One has to carry off the excitement, somehow."

"Promise me," she commanded, "that you'll never touch it again!"

"What! Not let the cannikin clink? Not let the soldier drink? Well, I promise."

"You don't belong to yourself now; you don't even belong to *me*. You belong to your country, and you have a sacred charge to keep yourself strong and well for your country's sake. I have been thinking, thinking all night and all day long."

"You look as if you had been crying a little, too," he said, with his queer smile.

"That's all past. I've been thinking, and worshipping *you*. Don't you suppose I know all that you've been through, to come to this? I've followed you every step from your old theories and opinions."

"Well, you've had a long row to hoe."

"And I know you've done this from the highest motives—"

"Oh, there won't be much pettifogging to do till this cruel war is—"

"And you haven't simply done it for my sake. I couldn't respect you if you had."

"Well, then we'll say I haven't. A man that hasn't got his own respect intact wants the respect of all the other people he can corner. But we won't go into that. I'm in for the thing now, and we've got to face our future. My idea is that this isn't going to be a very protracted struggle; we shall just scare the enemy to death before it comes to a fight at all. But we must provide for contingencies, Editha. If anything happens to me—"

"Oh, George!" She clung to him, sobbing.

"I don't want you to feel foolishly bound to my memory. I should hate that, wherever I happened to be."

"I am yours, for time and eternity—time and eternity." She liked the words; they satisfied her famine for phrases.

"Well, say eternity; that's all right; but time's another thing; and I'm talking about time. But there is something! My mother! If anything happens—"

She winced, and he laughed. "You're not the bold soldier-girl of yesterday!" Then he sobered. "If anything happens, I want you to help my mother out. She won't like my doing this thing. She brought me up to think war a fool thing as well as a bad thing. My father was in the Civil War; all through it; lost his arm in it." She thrilled with the sense of the arm round her; what if that should be lost? He laughed as if divining her: "Oh, it doesn't run in the family, as far as I know!" Then he added, gravely: "He came home with misgivings about war, and they grew on him. I guess he and mother agreed between them that I was to be brought up in his final mind about it; but that was before my time. I only knew him from my mother's report of him and his opinions; I don't know whether they were hers first; but they were hers last. This will be a blow to her. I shall have to write and tell her—"

He stopped, and she asked: "Would you like me to write, too, George?"

"I don't believe that would do. No, I'll do the writing. She'll understand a little if I say that I thought the way to minimize it was to make war on the largest possible scale at once—that I felt I must have been helping on the war somehow if I hadn't helped keep it from coming, and I knew I hadn't; when it came, I had no right to stay out of it."

Whether his sophistries satisfied him or not, they satisfied her. She clung to his breast, and whispered, with closed eyes and quivering lips: "Yes, yes, yes!"

"But if anything should happen, you might go to her and see what you could do for her. You know? It's rather far off; she can't leave her chair—"

"Oh, I'll go, if it's the ends of the earth! But nothing will happen! Nothing *can*! I—"

She felt herself lifted with his rising, and Gearson was saying, with his arm still round her, to her father: "Well, we're off at once, Mr. Balcom. We're to be formally accepted at the capital, and then bunched up with the rest somehow, and sent into camp somewhere, and got to the front as soon as possible. We all want to be in the van, of course; we're the first company to report to the Governor. I came to tell Editha, but I hadn't got round to it."

She saw him again for a moment at the capital, in the station, just before the train started southward with his regiment. He looked well, in his uniform, and very soldierly, but somehow girlish, too, with his clean-shaven face and slim figure. The manly eyes and the strong voice satisfied her, and his preoccupation with some unexpected details of duty flattered her. Other girls were weeping and bemoaning themselves, but she felt a sort of noble distinction in the abstraction, the almost unconsciousness, with which they parted. Only at the last moment he said: "Don't forget my mother. It mayn't be such a walk-over as I supposed," and he laughed at the notion.

He waved his hand to her as the train moved off—she knew it among a score of hands that were waved to other girls from the platform of the car, for it held a letter which she knew was hers. Then he went inside the car to read it, doubtless, and she did not see him again. But she felt safe for him through the strength of what she called her love. What she called her God, always speaking the name in a deep voice and with the implication of a mutual understanding, would watch over him and keep him and bring him back to her. If with an empty sleeve, then he should have three arms instead of two, for both of hers should be his for life. She did not see, though, why she should always be thinking of the arm his father had lost.

There were not many letters from him, but they were such as she could have wished, and she put her whole strength into making hers such as she imagined he could have wished, glorifying and supporting him. She wrote to his mother glorifying him as their hero, but the brief answer she got was merely to the effect that Mrs. Gearson was not well enough to write herself, and thanking her for her letter by the hand of some one who called herself, "Yrs truly, Mrs. W. J. Andrews."

Editha determined not to be hurt, but to write again quite as if the answer had been all she expected. Before it seemed as if she could have written, there came news of the first skirmish, and in the list of the killed, which was telegraphed as a trifling loss on our side, was Gearson's name. There was a frantic time of trying to make out that it might be, must be, some other Gearson; but the name and the company and the regiment and the State were too definitely given.

Then there was a lapse into depths out of which it seemed as if she never could rise again; then a lift into clouds far above all grief, black clouds, that blotted out the sun, but where she soared with him, with George—George! She had the fever that she expected of herself, but she did not die in it; she was not even delirious, and it did not last long. When she was well enough to leave her bed, her one thought was of George's mother, of his strangely worded wish that she should go to her and see what she could do for her. In the exaltation of the duty laid upon her—it buoyed her up instead of burdening her—she rapidly recovered.

Her father went with her on the long railroad journey from northern New York to western Iowa; he had business out at Davenport, and he said he could just as well go then as any other time; and he went with her to the little country town where George's mother lived in a little

house on the edge of the illimitable cornfields, under trees pushed to a
top of the rolling prairie. George's father had settled there after the
Civil War, as so many other old soldiers had done; but they were Eastern people, and Editha fancied touches of the East in the June rose
overhanging the front door, and the garden with early summer flowers
stretching from the gate of the paling fence.

It was very low inside the house, and so dim, with the closed blinds,
that they could scarcely see one another: Editha tall and black in her
crapes which filled the air with the smell of their dyes; her father standing decorously apart with his hat on his forearm, as at funerals; a
woman rested in a deep arm-chair, and the woman who had let the
strangers in stood behind the chair.

The seated woman turned her head round and up, and asked the
woman behind her chair: "*Who* did you say?"

Editha, if she had done what she expected of herself, would have
gone down on her knees at the feet of the seated figure and said, "I am
George's Editha," for answer.

But instead of her own voice she heard that other woman's voice,
saying: "Well, I don't know as I *did* get the name just right. I guess I'll
have to make a little more light in here," and she went and pushed two
of the shutters ajar.

Then Editha's father said, in his public will-now-address-a-few-re-
marks tone: "My name is Balcom, ma'am—Junius H. Balcom, of
Balcom's Works, New York; my daughter—"

"Oh!" the seated woman broke in, with a powerful voice, the voice
that always surprised Editha from Gearson's slender frame. "Let me see
you. Stand round where the light can strike on your face," and Editha
dumbly obeyed. "So, you're Editha Balcom," she sighed.

"Yes," Editha said, more like a culprit than a comforter.

"What did you come for?" Mrs. Gearson asked.

Editha's face quivered and her knees shook. "I came—because—
because George—" She could go no further.

"Yes," the mother said, "he told me he had asked you to come if he
got killed. You didn't expect that, I suppose, when you sent him."

"I would rather have died myself than done it!" Editha said, with
more truth in her deep voice than she ordinarily found in it. "I tried
to leave him free—"

"Yes, that letter of yours, that came back with his other things, left
him free."

Editha saw now where George's irony came from.

"It was not to be read before—unless—until— I told him so," she
faltered.

"Of course, he wouldn't read a letter of yours, under the circumstances, till he thought you wanted him to. Been sick?" the woman
abruptly demanded.

"Very sick," Editha said, with self-pity.

"Daughter's life," her father interposed, "was almost despaired of, at one time."

Mrs. Gearson gave him no heed. "I suppose you would have been glad to die, such a brave person as you! I don't believe *he* was glad to die. He was always a timid boy, that way; he was afraid of a good many things; but if he was afraid he did what he made up his mind to. I suppose he made up his mind to go, but I knew what it cost him by what it cost me when I heard of it. I had been through *one* war before. When you sent him you didn't expect he would get killed."

The voice seemed to compassionate Editha, and it was time. "No," she huskily murmured.

"No, girls don't; women don't, when they give their men up to their country. They think they'll come marching back, somehow, just as gay as they went, or if it's an empty sleeve, or even an empty pantaloon, it's all the more glory, and they're so much the prouder of them, poor things!"

The tears began to run down Editha's face; she had not wept till then; but it was now such a relief to be understood that the tears came.

"No, you didn't expect him to get killed," Mrs. Gearson repeated, in a voice which was startlingly like George's again. "You just expected him to kill some one else, some of those foreigners, that weren't there because they had any say about it, but because they had to be there, poor wretches—conscripts, or whatever they call 'em. You thought it would be all right for my George, *your* George, to kill the sons of those miserable mothers and the husbands of those girls that you would never see the faces of." The woman lifted her powerful voice in a psalmlike note. "I thank my God he didn't live to do it! I thank my God they killed him first, and that he ain't livin' with their blood on his hands!" She dropped her eyes, which she had raised with her voice, and glared at Editha. "What you got that black on for?" She lifted herself by her powerful arms so high that her helpless body seemed to hang limp its full length. "Take it off, take it off, before I tear it from your back!"

The lady who was passing the summer near Balcom's Works was sketching Editha's beauty, which lent itself wonderfully to the effects of a colorist. It had come to that confidence which is rather apt to grow between artist and sitter, and Editha had told her everything.

"To think of your having such a tragedy in your life!" the lady said. She added: I suppose there are people who feel that way about war. But when you consider the good this war has done—how much it has done for the country! I can't understand such people, for my part. And when you had come all the way out there to console her—got up out of a sick-bed! Well!"

"I think," Editha said, magnanimously, "she wasn't quite in her right mind; and so did papa."

"Yes," the lady said, looking at Editha's lips in nature and then at her lips in art, and giving an empirical touch to them in the picture. "But how dreadful of her! How perfectly—excuse me—how *vulgar!*"

A light broke upon Editha in the darkness which she felt had been without a gleam of brightness for weeks and months. The mystery that had bewildered her was solved by the word; and from that moment she rose from grovelling in shame and self-pity, and began to live again in the ideal.

STEPHEN CRANE (1871–1900)

That genius—so Henry James is reported to have murmured after hearing the news of Stephen Crane's death. It is a phrase of recognition that seems to occur spontaneously to people when they first experience the shock of his fiction. For almost all readers, including those who dislike or are unnerved by it, feel that in his novels and stories, sometimes in his poems, there resides that mysterious quality—inspiration, power, technical mastery—we call "genius." Crane did not live long enough to leave behind him a large body of major writing, but in his brilliant novel The Red Badge of Courage (1895) *and in half a dozen or so stories (including the three in this anthology), he showed himself a writer of the first rank, as well as a precursor of the literary modernism that would flower in the twentieth century.*

Stephen Crane was the fourteenth child of a Methodist minister, Jonathan Townley Crane. Though in his mature life Crane would reject both the dogmas and solaces of religion, preferring instead to struggle with a view of the universe as determined by laws both unknowable and hostile, the heritage of Methodism nevertheless shows itself in his writings. His stories are laced with religious imagery and allusion; he sometimes rebels openly and sardonically against the watery comforts of late-nineteenth-century religiosity; and at a still deeper level he returns to a sense of those ineradicable cruelties and perversities in the human psyche which has an oblique kinship with the Christian doctrine of Original Sin.

In 1879 the Crane family settled in Port Jervis, New York, after moving from one New Jersey town to another. Two years later the father died, and in a short while Stephen was contributing to the family income by doing legwork for the news agency run in Asbury Park, New Jersey, by his brother Townley. His formal education was sparse: he spent a semester at Lafayette College and another at Syracuse. His literary culture was thin, and it would remain so till the end of his career. Deciding that "humanity was a more interest-

ing study" than the college curriculum, he quit school to become a full-time reporter for his brother's agency. But that job like the agency itself, quickly came to an end, when Crane wrote a caustic report of a workingmen's parade in Asbury Park, a resort town frequented by the wealthy. Good citizens were shocked at his social sacrilege and newspaper editors apologized to their readers. Townley's agency was finished.

Here is a sentence from Crane's report which shows the beginnings of his terse, ironic, even cruel style: "The bona fide Asbury Parker is a man to whom a dollar, when held close to his eye, often shuts out any impression he may have that other people possess rights." A twenty-one-year-old novice who could turn out that kind of sentence wasn't likely to remain an ordinary reporter for long.

He didn't. Crane moved to New York City and became a free-lance writer, experiencing poverty for a time and starting what he would call his "artistic education on the Bowery." In 1892—after publishers had refused it—he put out his first novel, Maggie, A Girl of the Streets. *Uneven in quality but strikingly powerful in parts, this naturalistic novel brought friendly reviews from William Dean Howells and Hamlin Garland. A forerunner of the harsh portraits of slum life that would later be composed by writers like Theodore Dreiser and James T. Farrell,* Maggie, *said Crane, was meant*

to show that environment is a tremendous thing in the world and frequently shapes lives regardless. If one proves that theory, one makes room in Heaven for all sorts of souls (notably an occasional street girl) who are not confidently expected to be there by many excellent people. . . .

In 1895 came The Red Badge of Courage, *one of the finest novels ever written by an American. Though Crane himself had never "smelled even the powder of battle," this story of a young soldier facing his first test under fire in the Civil War pulsates with the atmosphere of the battlefield. Crane's imagination, which allowed him to enter the tangle of fears experienced by his young soldier, served him better than the experience of many other writers. "A psychological portrait of fear," as Crane called it,* The Red Badge of Courage *depicts the initiation of a youth into terror, and then that fortitude of will and solidarity of men by means of which terror can be confronted. It is also a work radically original both in method and language, one of the first American ventures into literary impressionism. Upon its appearance, Crane achieved immediate and deserved international fame.*

Fame brought problems. Young as he was, Crane could see

the majestic forces which are arrayed against man's true success—not the world—the world is silly, changeable, any of its decisions can be re-

*versed—but man's own colossal impulses more strong than chains, and I
perceived that the fight was not going to be with the world but with
myself.*

In his few remaining years Crane traveled a great deal as a newspaper
correspondent. He went to the West and to Mexico, he endured
shipwreck off the Florida coast, he covered wars in Greece and
Cuba, he became the friend in England of the great writers Henry
James and Joseph Conrad. He lived recklessly, he wasted his
energies and talents. To fulfill his role as journalist, he underwent
constant ordeals and dangers—perhaps also to fulfill his image of
what a writer should be, a writer who lives on the brink of danger
and personally encounters all the sensations of life. Wherever he
went, he saw violence. And violence, he felt, was the outer sign of
an inner condition; violence was the condition of man. Crane wore
himself out, though not before entering domesticity of a sort. In
1896 he met Cora Taylor, a Jacksonville madam with not merely
a heart of gold but a headful of brains, who cared for him after his
shipwreck, followed him to wars in Europe, and lived as his com-
mon-law wife.

Exhausted from overwork and exposure, Crane succumbed in 1899 to
the final stages of tuberculosis. In the spring of 1900 Cora arranged
for him to take a rest cure in the Black Forest in Germany, but a
week after their arrival he died. Crane's life, like his best work,
was brief, violent and brilliant; it seemed to follow the nineteenth-
century pattern of romantic excess and self-destruction, but together with these there was a tough discipline and a hard, ironic
spirit. He was never a shattered butterfly.

In speaking about his novels we have used the literary terms naturalism
and impressionism. By their very nature these cannot be entirely
precise, yet they can be useful, if only in illuminating certain qualities Crane's work shared with other late-nineteenth-century writers.
Naturalism is an extreme version of realism, often associated with
the French novelist Émile Zola. Zola believed he was composing
his novels on scientific principles, according to laws of natural inheritance and social determinism. Most naturalistic novelists have
since been inclined to write about men and women, usually those
of the lower classes sunk in poverty and degradation, as helpless
agents and victims of forces beyond their control. Sometimes these
forces are seen as inherent in the very nature of existence, sometimes as conditioned by an oppressive social system; the first view
leads to resignation, the second to radicalism. In their effort to
show how human life is shaped and misshaped—then broken—by
these external forces, naturalistic novelists often use a method of
accumulation, patiently piling on detail after detail to create the

impression that the story they tell has an internal and inexorable logic. Now, to some extent, Maggie follows the naturalistic pattern, especially in Crane's use of the slum setting and his bias toward social determinism; but in his literary methods Crane is quite far from the naturalists, since usually he is fiercely selective rather than coldly accumulative, nervously rapid rather than ploddingly slow.

The term impressionism *makes more sense in describing Crane's work. Ford Madox Ford, himself a distinguished novelist, has said about impressionism:*

> We saw that Life did not narrate, but made impressions on our brains. We in turn, if we wished to produce on you an effect of life, must not narrate but render . . . impressions.

The same idea has been developed by an Italian critic, Sergio Perosa, with greater detail:

> the basic canons of impressionistic writing [are] the apprehension of life through the play of perceptions, the significant montage of sense impressions, the reproduction of chromatic touches by colorful and precise notations, the reduction of elaborate syntax to the correlation of sentences, which leads to a sketchy, and at the same time evocative, kind of writing.

But even when useful, such critical categories as naturalism and impressionism do not yet tell us what is distinctive about a writer's work; they only help us approach it. All of Crane's important fiction is a fiction of extreme situations. It portrays men at the point where civilized norms begin to break down and the structure of human character buckles under the thrust of primitive drives. The norms of civilization are tested—perhaps, suggests Crane, they can really be tested only—by experiences in which all the energies and emotions swirling beneath civilized life are mobilized.

Men are thrust into situations of danger. Being men, they cannot avoid the sensations of fear and sometimes panic. They discover, when forced to confront such terrors in common, that they can now reach a kind of brotherhood. But this brotherhood is likely to be maintained only for a moment, at the peak of danger, when it seems too frightful to be alone. And even then, it is viewed by Crane with strong ironic qualifications, for once the threat comes to an end, either because it has been met successfully or has engulfed its victims, men revert to their "normal" condition of vanity, self-deceit and loneliness. Only at the edge of fear can they discover the color of their souls. Only then can they know the distance, large or small, between the codes of behavior by which they would like to live and the inner natures with which they must live. Toward

*these men—as Crane's best critic, John Berryman, has remarked—
Crane is both ally and enemy: he burrows into their consciousness,
he shares their ordeals, he becomes one of them, yet he also stands
apart at a cold distance, sardonically watching their pitiful efforts
to maintain their dignity, excuse their failures, and regain their
pomposity. A contemporary of Stephen Crane, the critic Edward
Garnett, had already observed these qualities in his work, praising*

his wonderful insight into and mastery of the primary passions, and his
irony deriding the swelling emotions of the self. . . . It is the perfect fusion
of these two forces of passion and irony that creates Crane's spiritual background, and raises his work, at its finest, into the higher zone of man's
tragic conflict with the universe.

*Crane's stories of initiation and test vary, of course, from one another
and in the degree to which they follow the pattern described above.
"The Open Boat" comes the closest to conforming to the pattern of
an elemental testing of untried men under circumstances which
both reveal and disintegrate their characters. "The Blue Hotel" presents a major and brilliant variation: the Swede brings to the action
his own preconceived panic, a result of excessive imagination and
weak nerves, and through the uncontainable workings of this panic
he provokes a situation in which the threat he had feared now
materializes and the doom he had expected overwhelms him. "The
Bride Comes to Yellow Sky" represents a charmingly comic variant:
a dangerous confrontation builds up, but the social circumstances
and rituals to which the actors are accustomed have changed, and
as a result they no longer know how to act out their conflict—the
Old West is no longer the Old West, the sheriff will no longer have
to play dangerous games with Scratchy, and everyone can go home
relieved.*

*What interests Crane in these stories is not so much the internal history
of human character nor the familiar external social relations of
the ordinary world. What interests him is the response to extreme
crisis, the possibility that Ernest Hemingway would later call "grace
under pressure"—or the absence of grace under pressure. John
Berryman lists some of the literary consequences:*

Crane's stories are as unlike earlier stories as his poems are unlike earlier
poems. He threw away, thoughtfully, plot; outlawed juggling and arrangement of material (Poe, Bierce, O'Henry); excluded the whole usual mechanism of society; banished equally sex (Maupassant) and romantic love
(Chekhov—unknown to him); decided not to develop his characters; decided not to have any conflicts between them as characters; resolved not
to have any characters at all in the usual sense; simplified everything that
remained and, watching intently, tenderly, and hopelessly, blew Fate
through it—saying with inconceivable rapidity and an air of immense
deliberation what he saw.

*Inevitably, the kind of story Crane wrote had to be brief, cutting away
the history and background of crisis in order to focus on crisis
itself. Inevitably, the tone had to be tense, violent, seemingly barbaric. And inevitably, the language had to be stripped of the oro-
tundness, decorations, and qualifications of earlier American prose.
It had to be a language that would come at the reader like a blow,
ferocious in its primary impact, violent in its imagery, venturing
all kinds of unexpected mixtures of impression, and shocking the
reader into a fresh apprehension of the strangeness of the world.
In* The Red Badge of Courage *the columns of troops are "like two
serpents crawling out of the cavern of the night." The red sun is
"pasted in the sky like a wafer." When its central character runs
from the battle, "There was the law, he said. Nature had given him
a sign. The squirrel, immediately upon recognizing danger, had
taken to his legs without ado." And examine, for an effect of power
and surprise, the opening sentence of "The Open Boat."*

FURTHER READING

Crane's letters have been edited by R. W. Stallman and Lilian Gilkes,
Stephen Crane: Letters (1960). An early vivid but not always reli-
able biography is Thomas Beer, *Shephen Crane: A Study in American Letters* (1923). The best critical biography is John Berryman,
Stephen Crane (1950). The poetry is studied in Daniel Hoffman,
The Poetry of Stephen Crane (1957). An excellent early criticism
is H. G. Wells, "Stephen Crane from an English Standpoint," reprinted in Edmund Wilson, *The Shock of Recognition.*

The Open Boat *(1897)*[1]

*A Tale Intended to be after the Fact: Being the Experience of Four Men
from the Sunk Steamer "Commodore"*

I

None of them knew the color of the sky. Their eyes glanced level,
and were fastened upon the waves that swept toward them. These waves
were of the hue of slate, save for the tops, which were of foaming

[1] Crane sailed as a correspondent on the *Commodore*, an American steamer, which
on January 1, 1897, left Jacksonville, Florida, with munitions and men for Cuban
rebels. That night the steamer sank; there were suspicions of sabotage. With four
others, Crane got back to Daytona Beach in a ten-foot dinghy. In June, 1897, he
published his fictional account, *The Open Boat*, in *Scribner's Magazine*.

white, and all of the men knew the colors of the sea. The horizon narrowed and widened, and dipped and rose, and at all times its edge was jagged with waves that seemed thrust up in points like rocks.

Many a man ought to have a bathtub larger than the boat which here rode upon the sea. These waves were most wrongfully and barbarously abrupt and tall, and each froth-top was a problem in small-boat navigation.

The cook squatted in the bottom, and looked with both eyes at the six inches of gunwale which separated him from the ocean. His sleeves were rolled over his fat forearms, and the two flaps of his unbuttoned vest dangled as he bent to bail out the boat. Often he said, "Gawd! that was a narrow clip." As he remarked it he invariably gazed eastward over the broken sea.

The oiler, steering with one of the two oars in the boat, sometimes raised himself suddenly to keep clear of water that swirled in over the stern. It was a thin little oar, and it seemed often ready to snap.

The correspondent, pulling at the other oar, watched the waves and wondered why he was there.

The injured captain, lying in the bow, was at this time buried in that profound dejection and indifference which comes, temporarily at least, to even the bravest and most enduring when, willy-nilly, the firm fails, the army loses, the ship goes down. The mind of the master of a vessel is rooted deep in the timbers of her, though he command for a day or a decade; and this captain had on him the stern impression of a scene in the grays of dawn of seven turned faces, and later a stump of a topmast with a white ball on it, that slashed to and fro at the waves, went low and lower, and down. Thereafter there was something strange in his voice. Although steady, it was deep with mourning, and of a quality beyond oration or tears.

"Keep 'er a little more south, Billie," said he.

"A little more south, sir," said the oiler in the stern.

A seat in this boat was not unlike a seat upon a bucking broncho, and, by the same token, a broncho is not much smaller. The craft pranced and reared and plunged like an animal. As each wave came, and she rose for it, she seemed like a horse making at a fence outrageously high. The manner of her scramble over these walls of water is a mystic thing, and, moreover, at the top of them were ordinarily these problems in white water, the foam racing down from the summit of each wave requiring a new leap, and a leap from the air. Then, after scornfully bumping a crest, she would slide and race and splash down a long incline, and arrive bobbing and nodding in front of the next menace.

A singular disadvantage of the sea lies in the fact that, after successfully surmounting one wave, you discover that there is another behind it just as important and just as nervously anxious to do something effective in the way of swamping boats. In a ten-foot dinghy one can get an idea of the resources of the sea in the line of waves that is not probable to the average experience, which is never at sea in a dinghy. As each slaty wall of water approached, it shut all else from the view of the men in the boat, and it was not difficult to imagine that this particular wave was the final outburst of the ocean, the last effort of the grim water. There was a terrible grace in the move of the waves, and they came in silence, save for the snarling of the crests.

In the wan light the faces of the men must have been gray. Their eyes must have glinted in strange ways as they gazed steadily astern. Viewed from a balcony, the whole thing would, doubtless, have been weirdly picturesque. But the men in the boat had no time to see it, and if they had had leisure, there were other things to occupy their minds. The sun swung steadily up the sky, and they knew it was broad day because the color of the sea changed from slate to emerald-green streaked with amber lights, and the foam was like tumbling snow. The process of the breaking day was unknown to them. They were aware only of this effect upon the color of the waves that rolled toward them.

In disjointed sentences the cook and the correspondent argued as to the difference between a life-saving station and a house of refuge. The cook had said: "There's a house of refuge just north of the Mosquito Inlet Light, and as soon as they see us they'll come off in their boat and pick us up."

"As soon as who see us?" said the correspondent.

"The crew," said the cook.

"Houses of refuge don't have crews," said the correspondent. "As I understand them, they are only places where clothes and grub are stored for the benefit of shipwrecked people. They don't carry crews."

"Oh, yes, they do," said the cook.

"No, they don't," said the correspondent.

"Well, we're not there yet, anyhow," said the oiler in the stern.

"Well," said the cook, "perhaps it's not a house of refuge that I'm thinking of as being near Mosquito Inlet Light; perhaps it's a life-saving station."

"We're not there yet," said the oiler in the stern.

II

As the boat bounced from the top of each wave the wind tore through the hair of the hatless men, and as the craft plopped her stern down again the spray slashed past them. The crest of each of these waves was a hill, from the top of which the men surveyed for a moment a broad, tumultuous expanse, shining and wind-riven. It was probably splendid, it was probably glorious, this play of the free sea, wild with lights of emerald and white and amber.

"Bully good thing it's an on-shore wind," said the cook. "If not, where would we be? Wouldn't have a show."

"That's right," said the correspondent.

The busy oiler nodded his assent.

Then the captain, in the bow, chuckled in a way that expressed humor, contempt, tragedy, all in one. "Do you think we've got much of a show now, boys?" said he.

Whereupon the three were silent, save for a trifle of hemming and hawing. To express any particular optimism at this time they felt to be childish and stupid, but they all doubtless possessed this sense of the situation in their minds. A young man thinks doggedly at such times. On the other hand, the ethics of their condition was decidedly against any open suggestion of hopelessness. So they were silent.

"Oh, well," said the captain, soothing his children, "we'll get ashore all right."

But there was that in his tone which made them think; so the oiler quoth, "Yes! if this wind holds."

The cook was bailing. "Yes! if we don't catch hell in the surf."

Canton-flannel gulls flew near and far. Sometimes they sat down on the sea, near patches of brown seaweed that rolled over the waves with a movement like carpets on a line in a gale. The birds sat comfortably in groups, and they were envied by some in the dinghy, for the wrath of the sea was no more to them than it was to a covey of prairie chickens a thousand miles inland. Often they came very close and stared at the men with black, bead-like eyes. At these times they were uncanny and sinister in their unblinking scrutiny, and the men hooted angrily at them, telling them to be gone. One came, and evidently decided to alight on the top of the captain's head. The bird flew parallel to the boat and did not circle, but made short sidelong jumps in the air in chicken fashion. His black eyes were wistfully fixed upon the captain's head. "Ugly brute," said the oiler to the bird. "You look as if you were made with a jackknife." The cook and the correspondent swore darkly at the creature. The captain naturally wished to knock it away with the end of the heavy painter, but he did not dare do it, because anything resembling an emphatic gesture would have capsized this freighted boat; and so, with his open hand, the captain gently and carefully waved the gull away. After it had been discouraged from the pursuit the captain breathed easier on account of his hair, and others breathed easier because the bird struck their minds at this time as being somehow gruesome and ominous.

In the meantime the oiler and the correspondent rowed; and also they rowed. They sat together in the same seat, and each rowed an oar. Then the oiler took both oars; then the correspondent took both oars, then the oiler; then the correspondent. They rowed and they rowed. The very ticklish part of the business was when the time came for the reclining one in the stern to take his turn at the oars. By the very last star of truth, it is easier to steal eggs from under a hen than it was to change seats in the dinghy. First the man in the stern slid his hand along the thwart and moved with care, as if he were of Sèvres. Then the man in the rowing-seat slid his hand along the other thwart. It was all done with the most extraordinary care. As the two sidled past each other, the whole party kept watchful eyes on the coming wave, and the captain cried: "Look out, now! Steady, there!"

The brown mats of seaweed that appeared from time to time were like islands, bits of earth. They were travelling, apparently, neither one way nor the other. They were, to all intents, stationary. They informed the men in the boat that it was making progress slowly toward the land.

The captain, rearing cautiously in the bow after the dinghy soared on a great swell, said that he had seen the lighthouse at Mosquito Inlet. Presently the cook remarked that he had seen it. The correspondent was at the oars then, and for some reason he too wished to look at the lighthouse; but his back was toward the far shore, and the waves were important, and for some time he could not seize an opportunity to turn his head. But at last there came a wave more gentle than the others, and when at the crest of it he swifty scoured the western horizon.

"See it?" said the captain.

"No," said the correspondent, slowly; "I didn't see anything."

"Look again," said the captain. He pointed. "It's exactly in that direction."

At the top of another wave the correspondent did as he was bid, and this time his eyes chanced on a small, still thing on the edge of the swaying horizon. It was precisely like the point of a pin. It took an anxious eye to find a lighthouse so tiny.

"Think we'll make it, Captain?"

"If this wind holds and the boat don't swamp, we can't do much else," said the captain.

The little boat, lifted by each towering sea and splashed viciously by the crests, made progress that in the absence of seaweed was not apparent to those in her. She seemed just a wee thing wallowing, miraculously top up, at the mercy of five oceans. Occasionally a great spread of water, like white flames, swarmed into her.

"Bail her, cook," said the captain, serenely.

"All right, Captain," said the cheerful cook.

III

It would be difficult to describe the subtle brotherhood of men that was here established on the seas. No one said that it was so. No one mentioned it. But it dwelt in the boat, and each man felt it warm him. They were a captain, an oiler, a cook, and a correspondent, and they were friends—friends in a more curiously iron-bound degree than may be common. The hurt captain, lying against the water jar in the bow, spoke always in a low voice and calmly; but he could never command a more ready and swiftly obedient crew than the motley three of the dinghy. It was more than a mere recognition of what was best for the common safety. There was surely in it a quality that was personal and heartfelt. And after this devotion to the commander of the boat, there was this comradeship, that the correspondent, for instance, who had been taught to be cynical of men, knew even at the time was the best experience of his life. But no one said that it was so. No one mentioned it.

"I wish we had a sail," remarked the captain. "We might try my overcoat on the end of an oar, and give you two boys a chance to rest." So the cook and the correspondent held the mast and spread wide the overcoat; the oiler steered; and the little boat made good way with her new rig. Sometimes the oiler had to scull sharply to keep a sea from breaking into the boat, but otherwise sailing was a success.

Meanwhile the lighthouse had been growing slowly larger. It had now almost assumed color, and appeared like a little gray shadow on the sky. The man at the oars could not be prevented from turning his head rather often to try for a glimpse of this little gray shadow.

At last, from the top of each wave, the men in the tossing boat could see land. Even as the lighthouse was an upright shadow on the sky, this land seemed but a long black shadow on the sea. It certainly was thinner than paper. "We must be about opposite New Smyrna," said the cook, who had coasted this shore often in schooners. "Captain, by the way, I believe they abandoned that life-saving station there about a year ago."

"Did they?" said the captain.

The wind slowly died away. The cook and the correspondent were not now obliged to slave in order to hold high the oar, but the waves continued their old impetuous swooping at the dinghy, and the little craft, no longer under way, struggled woundily over them. The oiler or the correspondent took the oars again.

Shipwrecks are *apropos* of nothing. If men could only train for them and have them occur when the men had reached pink condition, there would be less drowning at sea. Of the four in the dinghy none had slept any time worth mentioning for two days and two nights previous to embarking in the dinghy, and in the excitement of clambering about the deck of a foundering ship they had also forgotten to eat heartily.

For these reasons, and for others, neither the oiler nor the correspondent was fond of rowing at this time. The correspondent wondered ingenuously how in the name of all that was sane could there be people who thought it amusing to row a boat. It was not an amusement; it was a diabolical punishment, and even a genius of mental aberrations could never conclude that it was anything but a horror to the muscles and a crime against the back. He mentioned to the boat in general how the amusement of rowing struck him, and the weary-faced oiler smiled in full sympathy. Previously to the foundering, by the way, the oiler had worked double watch in the engine-room of the ship.

"Take here easy now boys," said the captain. "Don't spend your-selves. If we have to run a surf you'll need all your strength, because we'll sure have to swim for it. Take your time."

Slowly the land arose from the sea. From a black line it became a line of black and a line of white—trees and sand. Finally the captain said that he could make out a house on the shore. "That's the house of refuge, sure," said the cook. "They'll see us before long, and come out after us."

The distant lighthouse reared high. "The keeper ought to be able to make us out now, if he's looking through a glass," said the captain. "He'll notify the life-saving people."

"None of those other boats could have got ashore to give word of the wreck," said the oiler, in a low voice, "else the life boat would be out hunting us."

Slowly and beautifully the land loomed out of the sea. The wind came again. It had veered from the northeast to the southeast. Finally a new sound struck the ears of the men in the boat. It was the low thunder of the surf on the shore. "We'll never be able to make the lighthouse now," said the captain. "Swing her head a little more north, Billie."

"A little more north, sir," said the oiler.

Whereupon the little boat turned her nose once more down the wind, and all but the oarsman watched the shore grow. Under the influ-ence of this expansion doubt and direful apprehension were leaving the minds of the men. The management of the boat was still most absorb-ing, but it could not prevent a quiet cheerfulness. In an hour, perhaps, they would be ashore.

Their backbones had become thoroughly used to balancing in the boat, and they now rode this wild colt of a dinghy like circus men. The correspondent thought that he had been drenched to the skin, but hap-pening to feel in the top of his coat, he found therein eight cigars. Four of them were soaked with sea water; four were perfectly scatheless. After a search, somebody produced three dry matches; thereupon the four waifs rode in their little boat and, with an assurance of an impend-ing rescue shining in their eyes, puffed at the big cigars, and judged well and ill of all men. Everybody took a drink of water.

IV

"Cook," remarked the captain, "there don't seem to be any signs of life about your house of refuge."

"No," replied the cook. "Funny they don't see us!"

A broad stretch of lowly coast lay before the eyes of the men. It was of low dunes topped with dark vegetation. The roar of the surf was plain, and sometimes they could see the white lip of a wave as it spun up the beach. A tiny house was blocked out black upon the sky. South-ward, the slim lighthouse lifted its little gray length.

Tide, wind, and waves were swinging the dinghy northward. "Funny they don't see us," said the men.

The surf's roar was here dulled, but its tone was nevertheless thunderous and mighty. As the boat swam over the great rollers the men sat listening to this roar. "We'll swamp sure," said everybody.

It is fair to say here that there was not a life-saving station within twenty miles in either direction; but the men did not know this fact, and in consequence they made dark and opprobrious remarks concerning the eyesight of the nation's life savers. Four scowling men sat in the dinghy and surpassed records in the invention of epithets.

"Funny they don't see us."

The light-heartedness of a former time had completely faded. To their sharpened minds it was easy to conjure pictures of all kinds of incompetency and blindness and, indeed, cowardice. There was the shore of the populous land, and it was bitter and bitter to them that from it came no sign.

"Well," said the captain, ultimately, "I suppose we'll have to make a try for ourselves. If we stay out here too long, we'll none of us have strength left to swim after the boat swamps."

And so the oiler, who was at the oars, turned the boat straight for the shore. There was a sudden tightening of muscles. There was some thinking.

"If we don't all get ashore," said the captain—"If we don't all get ashore, I suppose you fellows know where to send news of my finish?"

They then briefly exchanged some addresses and admonitions. As for the reflections of the men, there was a great deal of rage in them. Perchance they might be formulated thus: "If I am going to be drowned—if I am going to be drowned—if I am going to be drowned, why, in the name of the seven mad gods who rule the sea, was I allowed to come thus far and contemplate sand and trees? Was I brought here merely to have my nose dragged away as I was about to nibble the sacred cheese of life? It is preposterous! If this old ninny woman, Fate, cannot do better than this, she should be deprived of the management of men's fortunes. She is an old hen who knows not her intention. If she has decided to drown me, why did she not do it in the beginning and save me all this trouble? The whole affair is absurd.... But no; she cannot mean to drown me. She dare not drown me. She cannot drown me. Not after all this work!" Afterward the man might have had an impulse to shake his fist at the clouds. "Just you drown me, now, and then hear what I call you!"

The billows that came at this time were more formidable. They seemed always just about to break and roll over the little boat in a turmoil of foam. There was a preparatory and long growl in the speech of them. No mind unused to the sea would have concluded that the dinghy could ascend these sheer heights in time. The shore was still afar. The oiler was a wily surfman. "Boys," he said swifty, "she won't live three minutes more, and we're too far out to swim. Shall I take her to sea again, Captain?"

"Yes; go ahead!" said the captain.

This oiler, by a series of quick miracles and fast and steady oarsmanship, turned the boat in the middle of the surf and took her safely to sea again.

There was a considerable silence as the boat bumped over the furrowed sea to deeper water. Then somebody in gloom spoke: "Well, anyhow, they must have seen us from the shore by now."

The gulls went in slanting flight up the wind toward the gray, desolate east. A squall, marked by dingy clouds and clouds brick-red, like smoke from a burning building, appeared from the southeast.

"What do you think of those life-saving people? Ain't they peaches?"

"Funny they haven't seen us."

"Maybe they think we're out here for sport! Maybe they think we're fishin'. Maybe they think we're damned fools."

It was a long afternoon. A changed tide tried to force them southward, but wind and wave said northward. Far ahead, where coast-line, sea, and sky formed their mighty angle, there were little dots which seemed to indicate a city on the shore.

"St. Augustine?"

The captain shook his head. "Too near Mosquito Inlet."

And the oiler rowed, and then the correspondent rowed; then the oiler rowed. It was a weary business. The human back can become the seat of more aches and pains than are registered in books for the composite anatomy of a regiment. It is a limited area, but it can become the theater of innumerable muscular conflicts, tangles, wrenches, knots, and other comforts.

"Did you ever like to row, Billie?" asked the correspondent.

"No," said the oiler; "hang it!"

When one exchanged the rowing-seat for a place in the bottom of the boat, he suffered a bodily depression that caused him to be careless of everything save an obligation to wiggle one finger. There was cold sea water swashing to and fro in the boat, and he lay in it. His head, pillowed on a thwart, was within an inch of the swirl of a wave crest, and sometimes a particularly obstreperous sea came inboard and drenched him once more. But these matters did not annoy him. It is almost certain that if the boat had capsized he would have tumbled comfortably out upon the ocean as if he felt sure that it was a great, soft mattress.

"Look! There's a man on the shore!"

"Where?"

"There! See 'im? See 'im?"

"Yes, sure! He's walking along."

"Now he's stopped. Look! He's facing us!"

"He's waving at us!"

"So he is! By thunder!"

"Ah, now we're all right! Now we're all right! There'll be a boat out here for us in half an hour."

"He's going on. He's running. He's going up to that house there."

The remote beach seemed lower than the sea, and it required a searching glance to discern the little black figure. The captain saw a floating stick, and they rowed to it. A bath towel was by some weird chance in the boat, and, tying this on the stick, the captain waved it. The oarsman did not dare turn his head, so he was obliged to ask questions.

"What's he doing now?"

"He's standing still again. He's looking, I think. . . . There he goes again—toward the house. . . . Now he's stopped again."

"Is he waving at us?"

"No, not now; he was though."

"Look! There comes another man!"

"He's running."

"Look at him go, would you!"

"Why, he's on a bicycle. Now he's met the other man. They're both waving at us. Look!"

"There comes something up the beach."

"What the devil is that thing?"

"Why, it looks like a boat."

"Why, certainly, it's a boat."

"No; it's on wheels."

"Yes, so it is. Well, that must be the life boat. They drag them along shore on a wagon."

"That's the life boat, sure."

"No, by —— , it's—it's an omnibus."

"I tell you it's a life boat."

"It is not! It's an omnibus. I can see it plain. See? One of these big hotel omnibuses."

"By thunder, you're right. It's an omnibus, sure as fate. What do you suppose they are doing with an omnibus? Maybe they are going around collecting the life crew, hey?"

"That's it, likely. Look! There's a fellow waving a little black flag. He's standing on the steps of the omnibus. There come those other two fellows. Now they're all talking together. Look at the fellow with the flag. Maybe he ain't waving it!"

"That ain't a flag, is it? That's his coat. Why, certainly, that's his coat."

"So it is; it's his coat. He's taken it off and is waving it around his head. But would you look at him swing it!"

"Oh, say, there isn't any life-saving station there. That's just a winter-resort hotel omnibus that has brought over some of the boarders to see us drown."

"What's that idiot with the coat mean? What's he signalling, anyhow?"

"It looks as if he were trying to tell us to go north. There must be a life-saving station up there."

"No; he thinks we're fishing. Just giving us a merry hand. See? Ah, there, Willie!"

"Well, I wish I could make something out of those signals. What do you suppose he means?"

"He don't mean anything; he's just playing."

"Well, if he'd just signal us to try the surf again, or to go to sea and wait, or go north, or south, or go to hell, there would be some reason in it. But look at him! He just stands there and keeps his coat revolving like a wheel. The ass!"

"There come more people."

"Now there's quite a mob. Look! Isn't that a boat?"

"Where? Oh, I see where you mean. No, that's no boat."

"That fellow is still waving his coat."

"He must think we like to see him do that. Why don't he quit it? It don't mean anything."

"I don't know. I think he is trying to make us go north. It must be that there's a life-saving station there somewhere."

"Say, he ain't tired yet. Look at 'im wave!"

"Wonder how long he can keep that up. He's been revolving his coat ever since he caught sight of us. He's an idiot. Why aren't they getting men to bring a boat out? A fishing boat—one of those big yawls—could come out here all right. Why don't he do something?"

"Oh, it's all right now."

"They'll have a boat out here for us in less than no time, now that they've seen us."

A faint yellow tone came into the sky over the low land. The shadows on the sea slowly deepened. The wind bore coldness with it, and the men began to shiver.

"Holy smoke!" said one, allowing his voice to express his impious mood, "if we keep on monkeying out here! If we've got to flounder out here all night!"

"Oh, we'll never have to say here all night! Don't you worry. They've seen us now, and it won't be long before they'll come chasing out after us."

The shore grew dusky. The man waving a coat blended gradually into this gloom, and it swallowed in the same manner the omnibus and the group of people. The spray, when it dashed uproariously over the side, made the voyagers shrink and swear like men who were being branded.

"I'd like to catch the chump who waved the coat. I feel like soaking him one, just for luck."

"Why? What did he do?"

"Oh, nothing, but then he seemed so damned cheerful."

In the meantime the oiler rowed, and then the correspondent rowed, and then the oiler rowed. Gray-faced and bowed forward, they mechanically, turn by turn, plied the leaden oars. The form of the lighthouse had vanished from the southern horizon, but finally a pale star appeared, just lifting from the sea. The streaked saffron in the west passed before the all-merging darkness, and the sea to the east was black. The land had vanished, and was expressed only by the low and drear thunder of the surf.

"If I am going to be drowned—if I am going to be drowned—If I am going to be drowned, why, in the name of the seven mad gods who rule the sea, was I allowed to come thus far and contemplate sand and trees? Was I brought here merely to have my nose dragged away as I was about to nibble the sacred cheese of life?"

The patient captain, drooped over the water jar, was sometimes obliged to speak to the oarsman.

"Keep her head up! Keep her head up!"

"Keep her head up, sir." The voices were weary and low.

This was surely a quiet evening. All save the oarsman lay heavily and listlessly in the boat's bottom. As for him, his eyes were just capable of noting the tall black waves that swept forward in a most sinister silence, save for an occasional subdued growl of a crest.

The cook's head was on a thwart, and he looked without interest at the water under his nose. He was deep in other scenes. Finally he spoke. "Billie," he murmured dreamfully, "what kind of pie do you like best?"

V

"Pie!" said the oiler and the correspondent, agitatedly. "Don't talk about those things, blast you!"

"Well," said the cook, "I was just thinking about ham sandwiches, and—"

A night on the sea in an open boat is a long night. As darkness settled finally, the shine of the light, lifting from the sea in the south, changed to full gold. On the northern horizon a new light appeared, a small bluish gleam on the edge of the waters. These two lights were the furniture of the world. Otherwise there was nothing but waves.

Two men huddled in the stern, and distances were so magnificent in the dinghy that the rower was enabled to keep his feet partly warm by thrusting them under his companions. Their legs indeed extended far under the rowing-seat until they touched the feet of the captain forward. Sometimes, despite the efforts of the tired oarsman, a wave came piling into the boat, an icy wave of the night, and the chilling water soaked them anew. They would twist their bodies for a moment and groan, and sleep the dead sleep once more, while the water in the boat gurgled about them as the craft rocked.

The plan of the oiler and the correspondent was for one to row until he lost the ability, and then arouse the other from his sea-water couch in the bottom of the boat.

The oiler plied the oars until his head drooped forward and the overpowering sleep blinded him; and he rowed yet afterward. Then he touched a man in the bottom of the boat, and called his name. "Will you spell me for a little while?" he said meekly.

"Sure, Billie," said the correspondent, awaking and dragging himself to a sitting position. They exchanged places carefully, and the oiler, cuddling down in the sea water at the cook's side, seemed to go to sleep instantly.

The particular violence of the sea had ceased. The waves came without snarling. The obligation of the man at the oars was to keep the boat headed so that the tilt of the rollers would not capsize her, and to preserve her from filling when the crests rushed past. The black waves were silent and hard to be seen in the darkness. Often one was almost upon the boat before the oarsman was aware.

In a low voice the correspondent addressed the captain. He was not sure that the captain was awake, although this iron man seemed to be always awake. "Captain, shall I keep her making for that light north, sir?"

The same steady voice answered him. "Yes. Keep it about two points off the port bow."

The cook had tied a life belt around himself in order to get even the warmth which this clumsy cork contrivance could donate, and he seemed almost stove-like when a rower, whose teeth invariably chattered wildly as soon as he ceased his labor, dropped down to sleep.

The correspondent, as he rowed, looked down at the two men sleeping underfoot. The cook's arm was around the oiler's shoulders, and, with their fragmentary clothing and haggard faces, they were the babes of the sea—a grotesque rendering of the old babes in the wood.

Later he must have grown stupid at his work, for suddenly there was a growling of water, and a crest came with a roar and a swash into the boat, and it was a wonder that it did not set the cook afloat in his life belt. The cook continued to sleep, but the oiler sat up, blinking his eyes and shaking with the new cold.

"Oh, I'm awful sorry, Billie," said the correspondent, contritely.

"That's all right, old boy," said the oiler, and lay down again and was asleep.

Presently it seemed that even the captain dozed, and the correspondent thought that he was the one man afloat on all the oceans. The wind had a voice as it came over the waves, and it was sadder than the end.

There was a long, loud swishing astern of the boat, and a gleaming trail of phosphorescence, like blue flame, was furrowed on the black waters. It might have been made by a monstrous knife.

Then there came a stillness, while the correspondent breathed with open mouth and looked at the sea.

Suddenly there was another swish and another long flash of bluish light, and this time it was alongside the boat, and might almost have been reached with an oar. The correspondent saw an enormous fin speed like a shadow through the water, hurling the crystalline spray and leaving the long glowing trail.

The correspondent looked over his shoulder at the captain. His face was hidden, and he seemed to be asleep. He looked at the babes of the sea. They certainly were asleep. So, being bereft of sympathy, he leaned a little way to one side and swore softly into the sea.

But the thing did not then leave the vicinity of the boat. Ahead or astern, on one side or the other, at intervals long or short, fled the long sparkling streak, and there was to be heard the *whiroo* of the dark fin. The speed and power of the thing was greatly to be admired. It cut the water like a gigantic and keen projectile.

The presence of this biding thing did not affect the man with the same horror that it would if he had been a picnicker. He simply looked at the sea dully and swore in an undertone.

Nevertheless, it is true that he did not wish to be alone with the thing. He wished one of his companions to awake by chance and keep him company with it. But the captain hung motionless over the water jar, and the oiler and the cook in the bottom of the boat were plunged in slumber.

VI

"If I am going to be drowned—if I am going to be drowned—if I am going to be drowned, why, in the name of the seven mad gods who rule the sea, was I allowed to come thus far and contemplate sand and trees?"

During this dismal night, it may be remarked that a man would conclude that it was really the intention of the seven mad gods to drown him, despite the abominable injustice of it. For it was certainly an abominable injustice to drown a man who had worked so hard, so hard. The man felt it would be a crime most unnatural. Other people had drowned at sea since galleys swarmed with painted sails, but still—

When it occurs to a man that nature does not regard him as important, and that she feels she would not maim the universe by disposing of him, he at first wishes to throw bricks at the temple, and he hates deeply the fact that there are no bricks and no temples. Any visible expression of nature would surely be pelleted with his jeers.

Then, if there be no tangible thing to hoot, he feels, perhaps, the desire to confront a personification and indulge in pleas, bowed to one knee, and with hands supplicant, saying, "Yes, but I love myself."

A high cold star on a winter's night is the word he feels that she says to him. Thereafter he knows the pathos of his situation.

The men in the dinghy had not discussed these matters, but each had, no doubt, reflected upon them in silence and according to his mind. there was seldom any expression upon their faces save the general one of complete weariness. Speech was devoted to the business of the boat.

To chime the notes of his emotion, a verse mysteriously entered the correspondent's head. He had even forgotten that he had forgotten this verse, but it suddenly was in his mind.

A soldier of the Legion lay dying in Algiers;
There was lack of woman's nursing, there was dearth of woman's tears;
But a comrade stood beside him, and he took the comrade's hand,
And he said, "I never more shall see my own, my native land."

In his childhood the correspondent had been made acquainted with the fact that a soldier of the Legion lay dying in Algiers, but he had never regarded it as important. Myriads of his school-fellows had informed him of the soldier's plight, but the dinning had naturally ended by making him perfectly indifferent. He had never considered it his affair that a soldier of the Legion lay dying in Algiers, nor had it appeared to him as a matter for sorrow. It was less to him than breaking a pencil's point.

Now, however, it quaintly came to him as a human, living thing. It was no longer merely a picture of a few throes in the breast of a poet, meanwhile drinking tea and warming his feet at the grate; it was an actuality—stern, mournful, and fine.

The correspondent plainly saw the soldier. He lay on the sand with his feet out straight and still. While his pale left hand was upon his chest in an attempt to thwart the going of his life, the blood came between his fingers. In the far Algerian distance, a city of low square forms was set against a sky that was faint with the last sunset hues. The correspondent, plying the oars and dreaming of the slow and slower movements of the lips of the soldier, was moved by a profound and perfectly impersonal comprehension. He was sorry for the soldier of the Legion who lay dying in Algiers.

The thing which had followed the boat and waited had evidently grown bored at the delay. There was no longer to be heard the slash of the cutwater, and there was no longer the flame of the long trail. The light in the north still glimmered, but it was apparently no nearer to the boat. Sometimes the boom of the surf rang in the correspondent's ears, and he turned the craft seaward then and rowed harder. Southward, some one had evidently built a watch fire on the beach. It was too low and too far to be seen, but it made a shimmering, roseate reflection upon the bluff back of it, and this could be discerned from the boat. The wind came stronger, and sometimes a wave suddenly raged out like a mountain cat, and there was to be seen the sheen and sparkle of a broken crest.

The captain, in the bow, moved on his water jar and sat erect. "Pretty long night," he observed to the correspondent. He looked at the shore. "Those life-saving people take their time."

"Did you see that shark playing around?"

"Yes, I saw him. He was a big fellow, all right."

"Wish I had known you were awake."

Later the correspondent spoke into the bottom of the boat. "Billie!" There was a slow and gradual disentanglement. "Billie, will you spell me?"

"Sure," said the oiler.

As soon as the correspondent touched the cold, comfortable sea water in the bottom of the boat and had huddled close to the cook's life belt he was deep in sleep, despite the fact that his teeth played all the popular airs. This sleep was so good to him that it was but a moment before he heard a voice call his name in a tone that demonstrated the last stages of exhaustion. "Will you spell me?"

"Sure, Billie."

The light in the north had mysteriously vanished, but the correspondent took his course from the wide-awake captain.

Later in the night they took the boat farther out to sea, and the captain directed the cook to take one oar at the stern and keep the boat facing the seas. He was to call out if he should hear the thunder of the surf. This plan enabled the oiler and the correspondent to get respite together. "We'll give those boys a chance to get into shape again," said the captain. They curled down and, after a few preliminary chatterings and trembles, slept once more the dead sleep. Neither knew they had bequeathed to the cook the company of another shark, or perhaps the same shark.

As the boat caroused on the waves, spray occasionally bumped over the side and gave them a fresh soaking, but this had no power to break their repose. The ominous slash of the wind and the water affected them as it would have affected mummies.

"Boys," said the cook, with the notes of every reluctance in his voice, "She's drifted in pretty close. I guess one of you had better take her to sea again." The correspondent, aroused, heard the crash of the toppled crests.

As he was rowing, the captain gave him some whiskey and water, and this steadied the chills out of him. "If I ever get ashore and anybody shows me even a photograph of an oar—"

At last there was a short conversation.

"Billie! . . . Billie, will you spell me?"

"Sure," said the oiler.

VII

When the correspondent again opened his eyes, the sea and the sky were each of the gray hue of the dawning. Later, carmine and gold was painted upon the waters. The morning appeared finally, in its splendor, with a sky of pure blue, and the sunlight flamed on the tips of the waves.

On the distant dunes were set many little black cottages, and a tall white windmill reared above them. No man, nor dog, nor bicycle appeared on the beach. The cottages might have formed a deserted village.

The voyagers scanned the shore. A conference was held in the boat. "Well," said the captain, "if no help is coming, we might better try a run through the surf right away. If we stay out here much longer we will be too weak to do anything for ourselves at all." The others silently acquiesced in this reasoning. The boat was headed for the beach. The correspondent wondered if none ever ascended the tall wind-tower, and if then they never looked seaward. This tower was a giant, standing with its back to the plight of the ants. It represented in a degree, to the correspondent, the serenity of nature amid the struggles of the individual—nature in the wind, and nature in the vision of men. She did not seem cruel to him then, nor beneficent, nor treacherous, nor wise. But she was indifferent, flatly indifferent. It is, perhaps, plausible that a man in this situation, impressed with the unconcern of the universe, should see the innumerable flaws of his life and have them taste wickedly in his mind, and wish for another chance. A distinction between right and wrong seems absurdly clear to him, then, in this new ignorance of the grave-edge, and he understands that if he were given another opportunity he would mend his conduct and his words, and be better and brighter during an introduction or at a tea.

"Now, boys," said the captain, "she is going to swamp sure. All we can do is to work her in as far as possible, and then when she swamps, pile out and scramble for the beach. Keep cool now, and don't jump until she swamps sure."

The oiler took the oars. Over his shoulders he scanned the surf. "Captain," he said, "I think I'd better bring her about and keep her head-on to the seas, and back her in."

"All right, Billie," said the captain. "Back her in." The oiler swung the boat then, and, seated in the stern, the cook and the correspondent were obliged to look over their shoulders to contemplate the lonely and indifferent shore.

The monstrous inshore rollers heaved the boat high until the men were again enabled to see the white sheets of water scudding up the slanted beach. "We won't get in very close," said the captain. Each time a man could wrest his attention from the roller, he turned his glance towards the shore, and in the expression of the eyes during this contemplation there was a singular quality. The correspondent, observing the others, knew that they were not afraid, but the full meaning of their glances was shrouded.

As for himself, he was too tired to grapple fundamentally with the fact. He tried to coerce his mind into thinking of it, but the mind was dominated at this time by the muscles, and the muscles said they did not care. It merely occurred to him that if he should drown it would be a shame.

There were no hurried words, no pallor, no plain agitation. The men simply looked at the shore. "Now, remember to get well clear of the boat when you jump," said the captain.

Seaward the crest of a roller suddenly fell with a thunderous crash, and the long white comber came roaring down upon the boat.

"Steady now," said the captain. The men were silent. They turned their eyes from the shore to the comber and waited. The boat slid up the incline, leaped at the furious top, bounced over it, and swung down the long back of the wave. Some water had been shipped, and the cook bailed it out.

But the next crest crashed also. The tumbling, boiling flood of white water caught the boat and whirled it almost perpendicular. Water swarmed in from all sides. The correspondent had his hands on the gunwale at this time, and when the water entered at that place he swiftly withdrew his fingers, as if he objected to wetting them.

The little boat, drunken with this weight of water, reeled and snuggled deeper into the sea.

"Bail her out, cook! Bail her out!" said the captain.

"All right, Captain," said the cook.

"Now, boys, the next one will do for us sure," said the oiler. "Mind to jump clear of the boat."

The third wave moved forward, huge, furious, implacable. It fairly swallowed the dinghy, and almost simultaneously the men tumbled into the sea. A piece of life belt had lain in the bottom of the boat, and as the correspondent went overboard he held this to his chest with his left hand.

The January water was icy, and he reflected immediately that it was colder than he had expected to find it off the coast of Florida. This appeared to his dazed mind as a fact important enough to be noted at the time. The coldness of the water was sad; it was tragic. This fact was somehow mixed and confused with his opinion of his own situation so that it seemed almost a proper reason for tears. The water was cold.

When he came to the surface he was conscious of little but the noisy water. Afterward he saw his companions in the sea. The oiler was ahead in the race. He was swimming strongly and rapidly. Off to the correspondent's left, the cook's great white and corked back bulged out of the water; and in the rear the captain was hanging with one good hand to the keel of the overturned dinghy.

There is a certain immovable quality to a shore, and the correspondent wondered at it amid the confusion of the sea.

It seemed also very attractive; but the correspondent knew that it was a long journey, and he paddled leisurely. The piece of life preserver lay under him, and sometimes he whirled down the incline of a wave as if he were on a hand-sled.

But finally he arrived at a place in the sea where the travel was beset with difficulty. He did not pause swimming to inquire what manner of current had caught him, but there his progress ceased. The shore was set before him like a bit of scenery on a stage, and he looked at it, and understood with his eyes each detail of it.

As the cook passed, much farther to the left, the captain was calling to him, "Turn over on your back, cook! Turn over on your back and use the oar."

"All right, sir." The cook turned on his back, and, paddling with an oar, went ahead as if he were a canoe.

Presently the boat also passed to the left of the correspondent, with the captain clinging with one hand to the keel. He would have appeared like a man raising himself to look over a board fence if it were not for the extraordinary gymnastics of the boat. The correspondent marvelled that the captain could still hold to it.

They passed on nearer to shore—the oiler, the cook, the captain— and following them went the water jar, bouncing gaily over the seas.

The correspondent remained in the grip of this strange new enemy, a current. The shore, with its white slope of sand and its green bluff, topped with little silent cottages, was spread like a picture before him. It was very near to him then, but he was impressed as one who, in a gallery, looks at a scene from Britanny or Algiers.

He thought: "I am going to drown? Can it be possible? Can it be possible? Can it be possible?" Perhaps an individual must consider his own death to be the final phenomenon of nature.

But later a wave perhaps whirled him out of this small deadly current, for he found suddenly that he could again make progress towards the shore. Later still he was aware that the captain, clinging with one hand to the keel of the dinghy, had his face turned away from the shore and towards him and was calling his name. "Come to the boat! Come to the boat!"

In his struggle to reach the captain and the boat, he reflected that when one gets properly wearied drowning must really be a comfortable arrangement—a cessation of hostilities accompanied by a large degree of relief; and he was glad of it, for the main thing in his mind for some moments had been horror of the temporary agony; he did not wish to be hurt.

Presently he saw a man running along the shore. He was undressing with most remarkable speed. Coat, trousers, shirt, everything flew magically off him.

"Come to the boat!" called the captain.

"All right, Captain." As the correspondent paddled, he saw the captain let himself down to bottom and leave the boat. Then the correspondent performed his one little marvel of the voyage. A large wave caught him and flung him with ease and supreme speed completely over the boat and far beyond it. It struck him even then as an event in gymnastics and a true miracle of the sea. An overturned boat in the surf is not a plaything to a swimming man.

The correspondent arrived in water that reached only to his waist, but his condition did not enable him to stand for more than a moment. Each wave knocked him into a heap, and the undertow pulled at him.

Then he saw the man who had been running and undressing, and undressing and running, come bounding into the water. He dragged ashore the cook, and then waded toward the captain; but the captain waved him away and sent him to the correspondent. He was naked— naked as a tree in winter; but a halo was about his head, and he shone like a saint. He gave a strong pull, and a long drag, and a bully heave at the correspondent's hand. The correspondent, schooled in the minor formulae, said, "Thanks, old man." But suddenly the man cried, "What's that?" He pointed a swift finger. The correspondent said, "Go."

In the shallows, face downward, lay the oiler. His forehead touched sand that was periodically, between each wave, clear of the sea.

The correspondent did not know all that transpired afterward. When he achieved safe ground he fell, striking the sand with each particular part of his body. It was as if he had dropped from a roof, but the thud was grateful to him.

It seems that instantly the beach was populated with men with blankets, clothes, and flasks, and women with coffee pots and all the remedies sacred to their minds. The welcome of the land to the men from the sea was warm and generous; but a still and dripping shape was carried slowly up the beach, and the land's welcome for it could only be the different and sinister hospitality of the grave.

When it came night, the white waves paced to and fro in the moonlight, and the wind brought the sound of the great sea's voice to the men on the shore, and they felt that they could then be interpreters.

The Blue Hotel (1898)

I

The Palace Hotel at Fort Romper was painted a light blue, a shade that is on the legs of a kind of heron, causing the bird to declare its position against any background. The Palace Hotel, then, was always screaming and howling in a way that made the dazzling winter landscape of Nebraska seem only a gray swampish hush. It stood alone on the prairie, and when the snow was falling the town two hundred yards away was not visible. But when the traveller alighted at the railway station he was obliged to pass the Palace Hotel before he could come upon the company of low clapboard houses which composed Fort Romper, and it was not to be thought that any traveller could pass the Palace Hotel without looking at it. Pat Scully, the proprietor, had proved himself a master of strategy when he chose his paints. It is true that on clear days, when the great transcontinental expresses, long lines of swaying Pullmans, swept through Fort Romper, passengers were overcome at the sight, and the cult that knows the brown-reds and the subdivisions of the dark greens of the East expressed shame, pity, horror, in a laugh. But to the citizens of this prairie town and to the people who would naturally stop there, Pat Scully had performed a feat. With this opulence and splendor, these creeds, classes, egotisms, that streamed through Romper on the rails day after day, they had no color in common.

As if the displayed delights of such a blue hotel were not sufficiently enticing, it was Scully's habit to go every morning and evening to meet the leisurely trains that stopped at Romper and work his seductions upon any man that he might see wavering, gripsack in hand.

One morning, when a snow-crusted engine dragged its long string of freight cars and its one passenger coach to the station, Scully performed the marvel of catching three men. One was a shaky and quick-eyed Swede, with a great shining cheap valise; one was a tall bronzed cowboy, who was on his way to a ranch near the Dakota line; one was a little silent man from the East, who didn't look it, and didn't announce it. Scully practically made them prisoners. He was so nimble and merry and kindly that each probably felt it would be the height of brutality to try to escape. They trudged off over the creaking board sidewalks in the wake of the eager little Irishman. He wore a heavy fur cap squeezed tightly down on his head. It caused his two red ears to stick out stiffly, as if they were made of tin.

At last, Scully, elaborately, with boisterous hospitality, conducted them through the portals of the blue hotel. The room which they entered was small. It seemed to be merely a proper temple for an enormous stove, which, in the center, was humming with godlike violence. At various points on its surface the iron had become luminous and glowed yellow from the heat. Beside the stove Scully's son Johnnie was playing High-Five with an old farmer who had whiskers both gray and sandy. They were quarrelling. Frequently the old farmer turned his face towards a box of sawdust—colored brown from tobacco juice—that was behind the stove, and spat with an air of great impatience and irritation. With a loud flourish of words Scully destroyed the game of cards, and bustled his son upstairs with part of the baggage of new guests. He himself conducted them to three basins of the coldest water in the world. The cowboy and the Easterner burnished themselves fiery red with this water, until it seemed to be some kind of a metal polish. The Swede, however, merely dipped his fingers gingerly and with trepidation. It was notable that throughout this series of small ceremonies the three travellers were made to feel that Scully was very benevolent. He was conferring great favors upon them. He handed the towel from one another with an air of philanthropic impulse.

Afterward they went to the first room, and, sitting about the stove, listened to Scully's officious clamor at his daughters, who were preparing the midday meal. They reflected in the silence of experienced men who tread carefully amid new people. Nevertheless, the old farmer, stationary, invincible in his chair near the warmest part of the stove, turned his face from the sawdust box frequently and addressed a glowing commonplace to the strangers. Usually he was answered in short but adequate sentences by either the cowboy or the Easterner. The Swede said nothing. He seemed to be occupied in making furtive estimates of each man in the room. One might have thought that he had the sense of silly suspicion which comes to guilt. He resembled a badly frightened man.

Later, at dinner, he spoke a little, addressing his conversation entirely to Scully. He volunteered that he had come from New York, where for ten years he had worked as a tailor. These facts seemed to strike Scully as fascinating, and afterward he volunteered that he had lived at Romper for fourteen years. The Swede asked about the crops and the price of labor. He seemed barely to listen to Scully's extended replies. His eyes continued to rove from man to man.

Finally, with a laugh and a wink, he said that some of these Western communities were very dangerous; and after his statement he straightened his legs under the table, tilted his head, and laughed again, loudly. It was plain that the demonstration had no meaning to the others. They looked at him wondering and in silence.

II

As the men trooped heavily back into the front room, the two little windows presented views of a turmoiling sea of snow. The huge arms of the wind were making attempts—mighty, circular, futile—to embrace the flakes as they sped. A gate-post like a still man with a blanched face stood aghast amid this profligate fury. In a hearty voice Scully announced the presence of a blizzard. The guests of the blue hotel, lighting their pipes, assented with grunts of lazy masculine contentment. No island of the sea could be exempt in the degree of this little room with its humming stove. Johnnie, son of Scully, in a tone which defined his opinion of his ability as a card player, challenged the old farmer of both gray and sandy whiskers to a game of High-Five. The farmer agreed with a contemptuous and bitter scoff. They sat close to the stove, and squared their knees under a wide board. The cowboy and the Easterner watched the game with interest. The Swede remained near the window, aloof, but with a countenance that showed signs of an inexplicable excitement.

The play of Johnnie and the gray-beard was suddenly ended by another quarrel. The old man arose while casting a look of heated scorn at his adversary. He slowly buttoned his coat, and then stalked with fabulous dignity from the room. In the discreet silence of all the other men the Swede laughed. His laughter rang somehow childish. Men by this time had begun to look at him askance, as if they wished to inquire what ailed him.

A new game was formed jocosely. The cowboy volunteered to become the partner of Johnnie, and they all then turned to ask the Swede to throw in his lot with the little Easterner. He asked some questions about the game, and, learning that it wore many names, and that he had played it when it was under an alias, he accepted the invitation. He strode towards the men nervously, as if he expected to be assaulted. Finally, seated, he gazed from face to face and laughed shrilly. This laugh was so strange that the Easterner looked up quickly, the cowboy sat intent and with his mouth open, and Johnnie paused, holding the cards with still fingers.

Afterward there was a short silence. Then Johnnie said, "Well, let's get at it. Come on now!" They pulled their chairs forward until their knees were bunched under the board. They began to play, and their interest in the game caused the others to forget the manner of the Swede.

The cowboy was a board-whacker. Each time that he held superior cards he whanged them, one by one, with exceeding force, down upon the improvised table, and took the tricks with a glowing air of prowess and pride that sent thrills of indignation into the hearts of his opponents. A game with a board-whacker in it is sure to become intense. The countenances of the Easterner and the Swede were miserable whenever the cowboy thundered down his aces and kings, while Johnnie, his eyes gleaming with joy, chuckled and chuckled.

Because of the absorbing play none considered the strange ways of the Swede. They paid strict heed to the game. Finally, during a lull caused by a new deal, the Swede suddenly addressed Johnnie: "I suppose there have been a good many men killed in this room." The jaws of the others dropped and they looked at him.

"What in hell are you talking about?" said Johnnie.

The Swede laughed again his blatant laugh, full of a kind of false courage and defiance. "Oh, you know what I mean all right," he answered.

"I'm a liar if I do!" Johnnie protested. The card game was halted, and the men stared at the Swede. Johnnie evidently felt that as the son of the proprietor he should make a direct inquiry. "Now, what might you be drivin' at, mister?" he asked. The Swede winked at him. It was a wink full of cunning. His fingers shook on the edge of the board. "Oh, maybe you think I have been to nowheres. Maybe you think I'm a tenderfoot?"

"I don't know nothin' about you," answered Johnnie, "and I don't give a damn where you've been. All I got to say is that I don't know what you're driving at. There hain't never been nobody killed in this room."

The cowboy, who had been steadily gazing at the Swede, then spoke: "What's wrong with you, mister?"

Apparently it seemed to the Swede that he was formidably menaced. He shivered and turned white near the corners of his mouth. He sent an appealing glance in the direction of the little Easterner. During these moments he did not forget to wear his air of advanced pot-valor. "They say they don't know what I mean," he remarked mockingly to the Easterner.

The latter answered after prolonged and cautious reflection. "I don't understand you," he said, impassively.

The Swede made a movement then which announced that he thought he had encountered treachery from the only quarter where he had expected sympathy, if not help. "Oh, I see you are all against me. I see—"

The cowboy was in a state of deep stupefaction. "Say," he cried, as he tumbled the deck violently down upon the board "—say, what are you gittin' at, hey?"

The Swede sprang up with the celerity of a man escaping from a snake on the floor. "I don't want to fight!" he shouted. "I don't want to fight!"

The cowboy stretched his long legs indolently and deliberately. His hands were in his pockets. He spat into the sawdust box. "Well, who the hell thought you did?" he inquired.

The Swede backed rapidly toward a corner of the room. His hands were out protectingly in front of his chest, but he was making an obvious struggle to control his fright. "Gentlemen," he quavered, "I suppose I am going to be killed before I can leave this house! I suppose I am going to be killed before I can leave this house!" In his eyes was the dying-swan look. Through the windows could be seen the snow turning blue in the shadow of dusk. The wind tore at the house and some loose thing beat regularly against the clapboards like a spirit tapping.

A door opened, and Scully himself entered. He paused in surprise as he noted the tragic attitude of the Swede. Then he said, "What's the matter here?"

The Swede answered him swiftly and eagerly: "These men are going to kill me."

"Kill you!" ejaculated Scully. "Kill you! What are you talkin'?"

The Swede made the gesture of a martyr.

Scully wheeled sternly upon his son. "What is this, Johnnie?"

The lad had grown sullen. "Damned if I know," he answered. "I can't make no sense to it." He began to shuffle the cards, fluttering them together with an angry snap. "He says a good many men have been killed in this room, or something like that. And he says he's goin' to be killed here too. I don't know what ails him. He's crazy, I shouldn't wonder."

Scully then looked for explanation to the cowboy, but the cowboy simply shrugged his shoulders.

"Kill you?" said Scully again to the Swede. "Kill you? Man, you're off your nut."

"Oh, I know," burst out the Swede. "I know what will happen. Yes, I'm crazy—yes. Yes, of course, I'm crazy—yes. But I know one thing—" There was a sort of sweat of misery and terror upon his face. "I know I won't get out of here alive."

The cowboy drew a deep breath, as if his mind was passing into the last stages of dissolution. "Well, I'm doggoned," he whispered to himself.

Scully wheeled suddenly and faced his son. "You've been troublin' this man!"

Johnnie's voice was loud with its burden of grievance. "Why, good Gawd, I ain't done nothin' to 'im."

The Swede broke in. "Gentlemen, do not disturb yourselves. I will leave this house. I will go away, because"—he accused them dramatically with his glance—"because I do not want to be killed."

Scully was furious with his son. "Will you tell me what is the matter, you young divil? What's the matter, anyhow? Speak out!"

"Blame it!" cried Johnnie in despair, "don't I tell you I don't know? He—he says we want to kill him, and that's all I know. I can't tell what ails him."

The Swede continued to repeat: "Never mind, Mr. Scully; never mind. I will leave this house. I will go away, because I do not wish to be killed. Yes, of course, I am crazy—yes. But I know one thing! I will go away. I will leave this house. Never mind, Mr. Scully; never mind. I will go away."

"You will not go 'way," said Scully. "You will not go 'way until I hear the reason of this business. If anybody has troubled you I will take care of him. This is my house. You are under my roof, and I will not allow any peaceable man to be troubled here." He cast a terrible eye upon Johnnie, the cowboy, and the Easterner.

"Never mind, Mr. Scully; never mind. I will go away. I do not wish to be killed." The Swede moved towards the door which opened upon the stairs. It was evidently his intention to go at once for his baggage.

"No, no," shouted Scully peremptorily; but the white-faced man slid by him and disappeared. "Now," said Scully severely, "what does this mane?"

Johnnie and the cowboy cried together: "Why, we didn't do nothin' to 'im!"

Scully's eyes were cold. "No," he said, "you didn't?"

Johnnie swore a deep oath. "Why, this is the wildest loon I ever see. We didn't do nothin' at all. We were jest sittin' here playin' cards, and he—"

The father suddenly spoke to the Easterner. "Mr. Blanc," he asked, "what has these boys been doin'?"

The Easterner reflected again. "I didn't see anything wrong at all," he said at last slowly.

Scully began to howl. "But what does it mane?" He stared ferociously at his son. "I have a mind to lather you for this, me boy."

Johnnie was frantic. "Well, what have I done?" he bawled at his father.

III

"I think you are tongue-tied," said Scully finally to his son, the cowboy, and the Easterner; and at the end of this scornful sentence he left the room.

Upstairs the Swede was swiftly fastening the straps of his great valise. Once his back happened to be half turned towards the door, and, hearing a noise there, he wheeled and sprang up, uttering a loud cry. Scully's wrinkled visage showed grimly in the light of the small lamp he carried. This yellow effulgence, streaming upward, colored only his prominent features, and left his eyes, for instance, in mysterious shadow. He resembled a murderer.

"Man! man!" he exclaimed, "have you gone daffy?"

"Oh, no! Oh, no!" rejoined the other. "There are people in this world who know pretty nearly as much as you do—understand?"

For a moment they stood gazing at each other. Upon the Swede's deathly pale cheeks were two spots brightly crimson and sharply edged, as if they had been carefully painted. Scully placed the light on the table and sat himself on the edge of the bed. He spoke ruminatively. "By cracky, I never heard of such a thing in my life. It's a complete muddle. I can't, for the soul of me, think how you ever got this idea into your head." Presently he lifted his eyes and asked: "And did you sure think they were going to kill you?"

The Swede scanned the old man as if he wished to see into his mind. "I did," he said at last. He obviously suspected that this answer might precipitate an outbreak. As he pulled on a strap his whole arm shook, the elbow wavering like a bit of paper.

Scully banged his hand impressively on the footboard of the bed. "Why, man, we're goin' to have a line of ilictric street cars in this town next spring."

"'A line of electric street cars,'" repeated the Swede, stupidly.

"And," said Scully, "there's a new railroad goin' to be built down from Broken Arm to here. Not to mintion the four churches and the smashin' big brick schoolhouse. Then there's the big factory, too. Why, in two years Romper'll be a met-tro-*pol*-is."

Having finished the preparation of his baggage, the Swede straightened himself. "Mr. Scully," he said, with sudden hardihood, "how much do I owe you?"

"You don't owe me anythin'," said the old man, angrily.

"Yes, I do," retorted the Swede. He took seventy-five cents from his pocket and tendered it to Scully; but the latter snapped his fingers in disdainful refusal. However, it happened that they both stood gazing in a strange fashion at three silver pieces on the Swede's open palm.

"I'll not take your money," said Scully at last. "Not after what's been goin' on here." Then a plan seemed to strike him. "Here," he cried, picking up his lamp and moving towards the door. "Here! Come with me a minute."

"No," said the Swede, in overwhelming alarm.

"Yes," urged the old man. "Come on! I want you to come and see a picter—just across the hall—in my room."

The Swede must have concluded that his hour was come. His jaw dropped and his teeth showed like a dead man's. He ultimately followed Scully across the corridor, but he had the step of one hung in chains.

Scully flashed the light high on the wall of his own chamber. There was revealed a ridiculous photograph of a little girl. She was leaning against a balustrade of gorgeous decoration, and the formidable bang to her hair was prominent. The figure was as graceful as an upright sled-stake, and, withal, it was of the hue of lead. "There," said Scully, tenderly, "that's the picter of my little girl that died. Her name was Carrie. She had the purtiest hair you ever saw! I was that fond of her, she—"

Turning then, he saw that the Swede was not contemplating the picture at all, but, instead, was keeping keen watch on the gloom in the rear.

"Look, man!" cried Scully, heartily. "That's the picter of my little gal that died. Her name was Carrie. And then here's the picter of my oldest boy, Michael. He's a lawyer in Lincoln, an' doin' well. I gave that boy a grand eddication, and I'm glad for it now. He's a fine boy. Look at 'im now. Ain't he bold as blazes, him there in Lincoln, an honored an' respicted gintleman! An honored and respicted gintleman," concluded Scully with a flourish. And, so saying, he smote the Swede jovially on the back.

The Swede faintly smiled.

"Now," said the old man, "there's only one more thing." He dropped suddenly to the floor and thrust his head beneath the bed. The Swede could hear his muffled voice. "I'd keep it under me piller if it wasn't for that boy Johnnie. Then there's the old woman—Where is it now? I never put it twice in the same place. Ah, now come out with you!"

Presently he backed clumsily from under the bed, dragging with him an old coat rolled into a bundle. "I've fetched him," he muttered. Kneeling on the floor, he unrolled the coat and extracted from its heart a large yellow-brown whiskey bottle.

His first manœuver was to hold the bottle up to the light. Reassured, apparently, that nobody had been tampering with it, he thrust it with a generous movement towards the Swede.

The weak-kneed Swede was about to eagerly clutch this element of strength, but he suddenly jerked his hand away and cast a look of horror upon Scully.

"Drink," said the old man affectionately. He had risen to his feet, and now stood facing the Swede.

There was a silence. Then again Scully said: "Drink!"

The Swede laughed wildly. He grabbed the bottle, put it to his mouth; and as his lips curled absurdly around the opening and his throat worked, he kept his glance, burning with hatred, upon the old man's face.

IV

After the departure of Scully the three men, with the card board still upon their knees, preserved for a long time an astounded silence. Then Johnnie said: "That's the doddangedest Swede I ever see."

"He ain't no Swede," said the cowboy, scornfully.

"Well, what is he then?" cried Johnnie. "What is he then?"

"It's my opinion," replied the cowboy deliberately, "he's some kind of a Dutchman." It was a venerable custom of the country to entitle as Swedes all light-haired men who spoke with a heavy tongue. In consequence the idea of the cowboy was not without its daring. "Yes, sir," he repeated. "It's my opinion this feller is some kind of a Dutchman."

"Well, he says he's a Swede, anyhow," muttered Johnnie, sulkily. He turned to the Easterner: "What do you think, Mr. Blanc?"

"Oh, I don't know," replied the Easterner.

"Well, what do you think makes him act that way?" asked the cowboy.

"Why, he's frightened." The Easterner knocked his pipe against a rim of the stove. "He's clear frightened out of his boots."

"What at?" cried Johnnie and the cowboy together.

The Easterner reflected over his answer.

"What at?" cried the others again.

"Oh, I don't know, but it seems to me this man has been reading dime novels, and he thinks he's right out in the middle of it—the shootin' and stabbin' and all."

"But," said the cowboy, deeply scandalized, "this ain't Wyoming, ner none of them places. This is Nebrasker."

"Yes," added Johnnie, "an' why don't he wait till he gits *out West*?"

The travelled Easterner laughed. "It isn't different there even—not in these days. But he thinks he's right in the middle of hell."

Johnnie and the cowboy mused long.

"It's awful funny," remarked Johnnie at last.

"Yes," said the cowboy. "This is a queer game. I hope we don't git snowed in, because then we'd have to stand this here man bein' around with us all the time. That wouldn't be no good."

"I wish pop would throw him out," said Johnnie.

Presently they heard a loud stamping on the stairs, accompanied by ringing jokes in the voice of old Scully, and laughter, evidently from the Swede. The men around the stove stared vacantly at each other. "Gosh!" said the cowboy. The door flew open, and old Scully, flushed and anecdotal, came into the room. He was jabbering at the Swede, who followed him, laughing bravely. It was the entry of two roisterers from a banquet hall.

"Come now," said Scully sharply to the three seated men, "move up and give us a chance at the stove." The cowboy and the Easterner obediently sidled their chairs to make room for the newcomers. Johnnie, however, simply arranged himself in a more indolent attitude, and then remained motionless.

"Come! Git over, there," said Scully.

"Plenty of room on the other side of the stove," said Johnnie.

"Do you think we want to sit in the draught?" roared the father.

But the Swede here interposed with a grandeur of confidence. "No, no. Let the boy sit where he likes," he cried in a bullying voice to the father.

"All right! All right!" said Scully, deferentially. The cowboy and the Easterner exchanged glances of wonder.

The five chairs were formed in a crescent about one side of the stove. The Swede began to talk; he talked arrogantly, profanely, angrily. Johnnie, the cowboy, and the Easterner maintained a morose silence, while old Scully appeared to be receptive and eager, breaking in constantly with sympathetic ejaculations.

Finally the Swede announced that he was thristy. He moved in his chair, and said that he would go for a drink of water.

"I'll git it for you," cried Scully at once.

"No," said the Swede, contemptuously. "I'll get it for myself." He arose and stalked with the air of on owner off into the executive parts of the hotel.

As soon as the Swede was out of hearing Scully sprang to his feet and whispered intensely to the others: "Upstairs he thought I was tryin' to poison 'im."

"Say," said Johnnie, "this makes me sick. Why don't you throw 'im out in the snow?"

"Why, he's all right now," declared Scully. "It was only that he was from the East, and he thought this was a tough place. That's all. He's all right now."

The cowboy looked with admiration upon the Easterner. "You were straight," he said. "You were on to that there Dutchman."

"Well," said Johnnie to his father, "he may be all right now, but I don't see it. Other time he was scared, but now he's too fresh."

Scully's speech was always a combination of Irish brogue and idiom, Western twang and idiom, and scraps of curiously formal diction taken from the story-books and newspapers. He now hurled a strange mass of language at the head of his son. "What do I keep? What do I keep? What do I keep?" he demanded, in a voice of thunder. He slapped his knee impressively, to indicate that he himself was going to make reply, and that all should heed. "I keep a hotel," he shouted. "A hotel, do you mind? A guest under my roof has sacred privileges. He is to be intimidated by none. Not one word shall he hear that would prijudice him in favor of goin' away. I'll not have it. There's no place in this here town where they can say they iver took in a guest of mine because he was afraid to stay here." He wheeled suddenly upon the cowboy and the Easterner. "Am I right?"

"Yes, Mr. Scully," said the cowboy, "I think you're right."

"Yes, Mr. Scully," said the Easterner, "I think you're right."

V

At six-o'clock supper, the Swede fizzed like a fire-wheel. He sometimes seemed on the point of bursting into riotous song, and in all his madness he was encouraged by old Scully. The Easterner was encased in reserve; the cowboy sat in wide-mouthed amazement, forgetting to eat, while Johnnie wrathily demolished great plates of food. The daughters of the house, when they were obliged to replenish the biscuits, approached as warily as Indians, and, having succeeded in their purpose, fled with ill-concealed trepidation. The Swede domineered the whole feast, and he gave it the appearance of a cruel bacchanal. He seemed to have grown suddenly taller; he gazed, brutally disdainful, into every face. His voice rang through the room. Once when he jabbed out harpoon-fashion with his fork to pinion a biscuit, the weapon nearly impaled the hand of the Easterner, which had been stretched quietly out for the same biscuit.

After supper, as the men filed towards the other room, the Swede smote Scully ruthlessly on the shoulder. "Well, old boy, that was a good, square meal." Johnnie looked hopefully at his father; he knew that shoulder was tender from an old fall; and, indeed, it appeared for a moment as if Scully was going to flame out over the matter, but in the end he smiled a sickly smile and remained silent. The others understood from his manner that he was admitting his responsibility for the Swede's new viewpoint.

Johnnie, however, addressed his parent in an aside. "Why don't you license somebody to kick you downstairs?" Scully scowled darkly by way of reply.

When they were gathered about the stove, the Swede insisted on another game of High-Five. Scully gently deprecated the plan at first, but the Swede turned a wolfish glare upon him. The old man subsided, and the Swede canvassed the others. In his tone there was always a great threat. The cowboy and the Easterner both remarked indifferently that they would play. Scully said that he would presently have to go to meet the 6:58 train, and so the Swede turned menacingly upon Johnnie. For a moment their glances crossed like blades, and then Johnnie smiled and said, "Yes, I'll play."

They formed a square, with the little board on their knees. The Easterner and the Swede were again partners. As the play went on, it was noticeable that the cowboy was not board-whacking as usual. Meanwhile, Scully, near the lamp, had put on his spectacles and, with an appearance curiously like an old priest, was reading a newspaper. In time he went out to meet the 6:58 train, and, despite his precautions, a gust of polar wind whirled into the room as he opened the door. Besides scattering the cards, it chilled the players to the marrow. The Swede cursed frightfully. When Scully returned, his entrance disturbed a cosy and friendly scene. The Swede again cursed. But presently they were once more intent, their heads bent forward and their hands moving swiftly. The Swede had adopted the fashion of board-whacking.

Scully took up his paper and for a long time remained immersed in matters which were extraordinarily remote from him. The lamp burned badly, and once he stopped to adjust the wick. The newspaper, as he turned from page to page, rustled with a slow and comfortable sound. Then suddenly he heard three terrible words: "You are cheatin'!"

Such scenes often prove that there can be little of dramatic import in environment. Any room can present a tragic front; any room can be comic. This little den was now hideous as a torture-chamber. The new faces of the men themselves had changed it upon the instant. The Swede held a huge fist in front of Johnnie's face, while the latter looked steadily over it into the blazing orbs of his accuser. The Easterner had grown pallid; the cowboy's jaw had dropped in that expression of bovine amazement which was one of his important mannerisms. After the three words, the first sound in the room was made by Scully's paper as it floated forgotten to his feet. His spectacles had also fallen from his nose, but by a clutch he had saved them in air. His hand, grasping the spectacle, now remained poised awkwardly and near his shoulder. He stared at the card-players.

Probably the silence was while a second elapsed. Then, if the floor had been suddenly twiched out from under the men they could not have moved quicker. The five had projected themselves headlong towards a common point. It happened that Johnnie, in rising to hurl himself upon the Swede, had stumbled slightly because of his curiously instinctive care for the cards and the board. The loss of the moment allowed time for the arrival of Scully, and also allowed the cowboy time to give the Swede a great push which sent him staggering back. The men found tongue together, and hoarse shouts of rage, appeal, or fear burst from every throat. The cowboy pushed and jostled feverishly at the Swede, and the Easterner and Scully clung wildly to Johnnie; but through the smoky air, above the swaying bodies of the peace-controllers, the eyes of the two warriors ever sought each other in glances of challenge that were at once hot and steely.

Of course the board had been overturned, and now the whole company of cards was scattered over the floor, where the boots of the men trampled the fat and painted kings and queens as they gazed with their silly eyes at the war that was waging above them.

Scully's voice was dominating the yells. "Stop now! Stop, I say! Stop, now—"

Johnnie, as he struggled to burst through the rank formed by Scully and the Easterner, was crying, "Well, he says I cheated! He says I cheated! I won't allow no man to say I cheated! If he says I cheated, he's a —— ——!"

The cowboy was telling the Swede, "Quit, now! Quit, d'ye hear—"

The screams of the Swede never ceased: "He did cheat! I saw him! I saw him—"

As for the Easterner, he was importuning in a voice that was not heeded: "Wait a moment, can't you? Oh, wait a moment. What's the good of a fight over a game of cards? Wait a moment—"

In this tumult no complete sentences were clear. "Cheat"—"Quit"—"He says"—these fragments pierced the uproar and rang out sharply. It was remarkable that, whereas Scully undoubtedly made the most noise, he was the least heard of any of the riotous band.

Then suddenly there was a great cessation. It was as if each man had paused for breath; and although the room was still lighted with the anger of men, it could be seen that there was no danger of immediate conflict, and at once Johnnie, shouldering his way forward, almost succeeded in confronting the Swede, "What did you say I cheated for? What did you say I cheated for? I don't cheat, and I won't let no man say I do?"

The Swede said, "I saw you! I saw you!"

"Well," cried Johnnie, "I'll fight any man what says I cheat!"

"No, you won't," said the cowboy. "Not here."

"Ah, be still, can't you?" said Scully, coming between them.

The quiet was sufficient to allow the Easterner's voice to be heard. He was repeating, "Oh, wait a moment, can't you? What's the good of a fight over a game of cards? Wait a moment!"

Johnnie, his red face appearing above his father's shoulder, hailed the Swede again. "Did you say I cheated?"

The Swede showed his teeth. "Yes."

"Then," said Johnnie, "we must fight."

"Yes, fight," roared the Swede. He was like a demoniac. "Yes, fight! I'll show you what kind of a man I am! I'll show you who you want to fight! Maybe you think I can't fight! Maybe you think I can't! I'll show you, you skin, you card-sharp! Yes, you cheated! You cheated!"

"Well, let's go at it, then, mister," said Johnnie, coolly.

The cowboy's brow was beaded with sweat from his efforts in intercepting all sorts of raids. He turned in despair to Scully. "What are you goin' to do now?"

A change had come over the Celtic visage of the old man. He now seemed all eagerness; his eyes glowed.

"We'll let them fight," he answered, stalwartly. "I can't put up with it any longer. I've stood this damned Swede till I'm sick. We'll let them fight."

VI

The men prepared to go out-of-doors. The Easterner was so nervous that he had great difficulty in getting his arms into the sleeves of his new leather coat. As the cowboy drew his fur cap down over his ears his hands trembled. In fact, Johnnie and old Scully were the only ones who displayed no agitation. These preliminaries were conducted without words.

Scully threw open the door. "Well, come on," he said. Instantly a terrific wind caused the flame of the lamp to struggle at its wick, while a puff of black smoke sprang from the chimney-top. The stove was in midcurrent of the blast, and its voice swelled to equal the roar of the storm. Some of the scarred and bedabbled cards were caught up from the floor and dashed helplessly against the farther wall. The men lowered their heads and plunged into the tempest as into a sea.

No snow was falling, but great whirls and clouds of flakes, swept up from the ground by the frantic winds, were streaming southward with the speed of bullets. The land was blue with the sheen of bullets. The covered land was blue with the sheen of an unearthly satin, and there was no other hue save where, at the low, black railway station—which seemed incredibly distant—one light gleamed like a tiny jewel. As the men floundered into a thigh-deep drift, it was known that the Swede was bawling out something. Scully went to him, put a hand on his shoulder, and projected an ear. "What's that you say?" he shouted.

"I say," bawled the Swede again, "I won't stand much show against this gang. I know you'll all pitch on me."

Scully smote him reproachfully on the arm. "Tut, man!" he yelled. The wind tore the words from Scully's lips and scattered them far alee.

"You are all a gang of—" boomed the Swede, but the storm also seized the remainder of this sentence.

Immediately turning their backs upon the wind, the men had swung around a corner to the sheltered side of the hotel. It was the function of the little house to preserve here, amid this great devastation of snow, an irregular V-shape of heavily encrusted grass, which crackled beneath the feet. One could imagine the great drifts piled against the windward side. When the party reached the comparative peace of this spot it was found that the Swede was still bellowing.

"Oh, I know what kind of a thing this is! I know you'll all pitch on me. I can't lick you all!"

Scully turned upon him panther-fashion. "You'll not have to whip all of us. You'll have to whip my son Johnnie. An' the man what troubles you durin' that time will have me to deal with."

The arrangements were swiftly made. The two men faced each other, obedient to the harsh commands of Scully, whose face, in the subtly luminous gloom, could be seen set in the austere impersonal lines that are pictured on the countenances of the Roman veterans. The Easterner's teeth were chattering, and he was hopping up and down like a mechanical toy. The cowboy stood rock-like.

The contestants had not stripped off any clothing. Each was in his ordinary attire. Their fists were up, and they eyed each other in a calm that had the elements of leonine cruelty in it.

During this pause, the Easterner's mind, like a film, took lasting impressions of three men—the iron-nerved master of the ceremony; the Swede, pale, motionless, terrible; and Johnnie, serene yet ferocious, brutish yet heroic. The entire prelude had in it a tragedy greater than the tragedy of action, and this aspect was accentuated by the long, mellow cry of the blizzard, as it sped the tumbling and wailing flakes into the black abyss of the south.

"Now!" said Scully.

The two combatants leaped forward and crashed together like bullocks. There was heard the cushioned sound of blows, and of a curse squeezing out from between the tight teeth of one.

As for the spectators, the Easterner's pent-up breath exploded from him with a pop of relief, absolute relief from the tension of the preliminaries. The cowboy bounded into the air with a yowl. Scully was immovable as from supreme amazement and fear at the fury of the fight which he himself had permitted and arranged.

For a time the encounter in the darkness was such a perplexity of flying arms that it presented no more detail than would a swiftly revolving wheel. Occasionally a face, as if illumined by a flash of light, would shine out, ghastly and marked with pink spots. A moment later, the men might have been known as shadows, if it were not for the involuntary utterance of oaths that came from them in whispers.

Suddenly a holocaust of warlike desire caught the cowboy, and he bolted forward with the speed of a broncho. "Go it. Johnnie! go it! Kill him! Kill him!"

Scully confronted him. "Kape back," he said; and by his glance the cowboy could tell that this man was Johnnie's father.

To the Easterner there was a monotony of unchangeable fighting that was an abomination. This confused mingling was eternal to his sense, which was concentrated in a longing for the end, the priceless end. Once the fighters lurched near him, and as he scrambled hastily backward he heard them breathe like men on the rack.

"Kill him, Johnnie! Kill him! Kill him! Kill him!" The cowboy's face was contorted like one of those agony masks in museums.

"Keep still," said Scully, icily.

Then there was a sudden loud grunt, incomplete, cut short, and Johnnie's body swung away from the Swede and fell with sickening heaviness to the grass. The cowboy was barely in time to prevent the mad Swede from flinging himself upon his prone adversary. "No, you don't," said the cowboy, interposing an arm. "Wait a second."

Scully was at his son's side. "Johnnie! Johnnie, me boy!" His voice had a quality of melancholy tenderness. "Johnnie! Can you go on with it?" He looked anxiously down into the bloody, pulpy face of his son.

There was a moment of silence, and then Johnnie answered in his ordinary voice, "Yes, I—it—yes."

Assisted by his father he struggled to his feet. "Wait a bit now till you git your wind," said the old man.

A few paces away the cowboy was lecturing the Swede. "No, you don't! Wait a second!"

The Easterner was plucking at Scully's sleeve. "Oh, this is enough," he pleaded. "This is enough! Let it go as it stands. This is enough!

"Bill," said Scully, "git out of the road." The cowboy stepped aside. "Now." The combatants were actuated by a new caution as they advanced towards collision. They glared at each other, and then the Swede aimed a lightning blow that carried with it his entire weight. Johnnie was evidently half stupid from weakness, but he miraculously dodged, and his fist sent the over-balanced Swede sprawling.

The cowboy, Scully, and the Easterner burst into a cheer that was like a chorus of triumphant soldiery, but before its conclusion the Swede had scuffled agilely to his feet and come in berserk abandon at his foe. There was another perplexity of flying arms, and Johnnie's body again swung away and fell, even as a bundle might fall from a roof. The Swede instantly staggered to a little wind-waved tree and leaned upon it, breathing like an engine, while his savage and flame-lit eyes roamed from face to face as the men bent over Johnnie. There was a splendor of isolation in his situation at this time which the Easterner felt once when, lifting his eyes from the man on the ground, he beheld that mysterious and lonely figure, waiting.

"Are you any good yet, Johnnie?" asked Scully in a broken voice.

The son gasped and opened his eyes languidly. After a moment he answered, "No—I ain't—any good—any—more." Then, from shame and bodily ill, he began to weep, the tears furrowing down through the blood-stains on his face. "He was too—too—too heavy for me."

Scully straightened and addressed the waiting figure. "Stranger," he said, evenly, "it's all up with our side." Then his voice changed into that vibrant huskiness which is commonly the tone of the most simple and deadly announcements. "Johnnie is whipped."

Without replying, the victor moved off on the route to the front door of the hotel.

The cowboy was formulating new and unspellable blasphemies. The Easterner was startled to find that they were out in a wind that seemed to come direct from the shadowed arctic floes. He heard again the wail of the snow as it was flung to its grave in the south. He knew now that all this time the cold had been sinking into him deeper and deeper, and he wondered that he had not perished. He felt indifferent to the condition of the vanquished man.

"Johnnie, can you walk?" asked Scully.

"Did I hurt—hurt him any?" asked the son.

"Can you walk, boy? Can you walk?"

Johnnie's voice was suddenly strong. There was a robust impatience in it. "I asked you whether I hurt him any!"

"Yes, yes, Johnnie," answered the cowboy, consolingly; "he's hurt a good deal."

They raised him from the ground, and as soon as he was on his feet he went tottering off, rebuffing all attempts at assistance. When the party rounded the corner they were fairly blinded by the pelting of the snow. It burned their faces like fire. The cowboy carried Johnnie through the drift to the door. As they entered, some cards again rose from the floor and beat against the wall.

The Easterner rushed to the stove. He was so profoundly chilled that he almost dared to embrace the glowing iron. The Swede was not in the room. Johnnie sank into a chair and, folding his arms on his knees, buried his face in them. Scully, warming one foot and then the other at a rim of the stove, muttered to himself with Celtic mournfulness. The cowboy had removed his fur cap, and with a dazed and rueful air he was running one hand through his tousled locks. From overhead they could hear the creaking of boards, as the Swede tramped here and there in his room.

The sad quiet was broken by the sudden flinging open of a door that led toward the kitchen. It was instantly followed by an inrush of women. They precipitated themselves upon Johnnie amid a chorus of lamentation. Before they carried their prey off to the kitchen, there to be bathed and harangued with that mixture of sympathy and abuse which is a feat of their sex, the mother straightened herself and fixed old Scully with an eye of stern reproach. "Shame be upon you, Patrick Scully!" she cried. "Your own son, too. Shame be upon you!"

"There, now! Be quiet, now!" said the old man, weakly.

"Shame be upon you, Patrick Scully!" The girls, rallying to this slogan, sniffled disdainfully in the direction of those trembling accomplices, the cowboy and the Easterner. Presently they bore Johnnie away, and left the three men to dismal reflection.

VII

"I'd like to fight this here Dutchman myself," said the cowboy, breaking a long silence.

Scully wagged his head sadly. "No, that wouldn't do. It wouldn't be right. It wouldn't be right."

"Well, why wouldn't it?" argued the cowboy. "I don't see no harm in it."

"No," answered Scully, with mournful heroism. "It wouldn't be right. It was Johnnie's fight, and now we mustn't whip the man just because he whipped Johnnie."

"Yes, that's true enough," said the cowboy; "but—he better not get fresh with me, because I couldn't stand no more of it."

"You'll not say a word to him," commanded Scully, and even then they heard the tread of the Swede on the stairs. His entrance was made theatric. He swept the door back with a bang and swaggered to the middle of the room. No one looked at him. "Well," he cried, insolently, at Scully, "I s'pose you'll tell me now how much I owe you?"

The old man remained stolid, "You don't owe me nothin'."

"Huh!" said the Swede, "huh! Don't owe 'im nuthin'."

The cowboy addressed the Swede. "Stranger, I don't see how you come to be so gay around here."

Old Scully was instantly alert. "Stop!" he shouted, holding his hand forth, fingers upward. "Bill, you shut up!"

The cowboy spat carelessly into the sawdust box. "I didn't say a word, did I?" he asked.

"Mr. Scully," called the Swede, "how much do I owe you?" It was seen that he was attired for departure, and that he had his valise in his hand.

"You don't owe me nothin'," repeated Scully in the same imperturbable way.

"Huh!" said the Swede. "I guess you're right. I guess if it was any way at all, you'd owe me somethin'. That's what I guess." He turned to the cowboy. "Kill him! Kill him! Kill him!'" he mimicked, and then guffawed victoriously. "'Kill him!'" He was convulsed with ironical humor.

But he might have been jeering the dead. The three men were immovable and silent, staring with glassy eyes at the stove.

The Swede opened the door and passed into the storm, giving one dirisive glance backward at the still group.

As soon as the door was closed, Scully and the cowboy leaped to their feet and began to curse. They tramped to and fro, waving their arms and smashing into the air their fists. "Oh, but that was a hard minute!" wailed Scully. "That was a hard minute! Him there leerin' and scoffin'! One bang at his nose was worth forty dollars to me that minute! How did you stand it, Bill?"

"How did I stand it?" cried the cowboy in a quivering voice. "How did I stand it? Oh!"

The old man burst into sudden brogue. "I'd loike to take that Swade," he wailed, "and hould 'im down on a shtone flure and bate 'im to a jelly wid a shtick!"

The cowboy groaned in sympathy. "I'd like to git him by the neck and ha-ammer him"—he brought his hand down on a chair with a noise like a pistol-shot—"hammer that there Dutchman until he couldn't tell himself from a dead coyote!"

"I'd bate 'im until he—"

"I'd show *him* some things—"

And then together they raised a yearning, fanatic cry—"Oh-o-oh! if we only could—"

"Yes!"

"Yes!"

"And then I'd—"

"O-o-oh!"

VIII

The Swede, tightly gripping his valise, tacked across the face of the storm as if he carried sails. He was following a line of little naked, gasping trees which, he knew, must mark the way of the road. His face, fresh from the pounding of Johnnie's fists, felt more pleasure than pain in the wind and the driving snow. A number of square shapes loomed upon him finally, and he knew them as the houses of the main body of the town. He found a street and made travel along it, leaning heavily upon the wind whenever, at a corner, a terrific blast caught him.

He might have been in a deserted village. We picture the world as thick with conquering and elate humanity, but here, with the bugles of the tempest pealing, it was hard to imagine a peopled earth. One viewed the existence of man then as a marvel, and conceded a glamor of wonder to these lice which were caused to cling to a whirling, fire-smote, ice-locked, disease-stricken, space-lost bulb. The conceit of man was explained by this storm to be the very engine of life. One was a coxcomb not to die in it. However, the Swede found a saloon.

In front of it an indomitable red light was burning, and the snowflakes were made blood-color as they flew through the circumscribed territory of the lamp's shining. The Swede pushed open the door of the saloon and entered. A sanded expanse was before him, and at the end of it four men sat about a table drinking. Down one side of the room extended a radiant bar, and its guardian was leaning upon his elbows listening to the talk of the men at the table. The Swede dropped his valise upon the floor and, smiling fraternally upon the barkeeper, said, "Gimme some whiskey, will you?" The man placed a bottle, a whiskey-glass, and a glass of ice-thick water upon the bar. The Swede poured himself an abnormal portion of whiskey and drank it in three gulps. "Pretty bad night," remarked the bartender, indifferently. He was making the pretension of blindness which is usually a distinction of his class; but it could have been seen that he was furtively studying the half-erased blood stains on the face of the Swede, "Bad night," he said again.

"Oh, it's good enough for me," replied the Swede, hardily, as he poured himself some more whiskey. The barkeeper took his coin and manœvered it through its reception by the highly nickelled cash-machine. A bell rang; a card labelled "20 cts." had appeared.

"No," continued the Swede, "this isn't too bad weather. It's good enough for me."

"So?" murmured the barkeeper, languidly.

The copious drams made the Swede's eyes swim, and he breathed a trifle heavier. "Yes, I like this weather. It suits me." It was apparently his design to impart a deep significance to these words.

"So?" murmured the bartender again. He turned to gaze dreamily at the scroll-like birds and bird-like scrolls which had been drawn with soap upon the mirrors in back of the bar.

"Well, I guess I'll take another drink," said the Swede, presently. "Have something?"

"No, thanks; I'm not drinkin'," answered the bartender. Afterward he asked, "How did you hurt your face?"

The Swede immediately began to boast loudly. "Why, in a fight. I thumped the soul out of a man down here at Scully's hotel."

The interest of the four men at the table was at last aroused.

"Who was it?" said one.

"Johnnie Scully," blustered the Swede. "Son of the man what runs it. He will be pretty near dead for some weeks, I can tell you. I made a nice thing of him. I did. He couldn't get up. They carried him in the house. Have a drink?"

Instantly the men in some subtle way encased themselves in reserve. "No, thanks," said one. The group was of curious formation. Two were prominent local business men; one was the district attorney; and one was a professional gambler of the kind known as "square." But a scrutiny of the group would not have enabled an observer to pick the gambler from the men of more reputable pursuits. He was, in fact, a man so delicate in manner, when among people of fair class, and so judicious in his choice of victims, that in the strictly masculine part of the town's life he had come to be explicitly trusted and admired. People called him a thoroughbred. The fear and contempt with which his craft was regarded were undoubtedly the reason why his quiet dignity shone conspicuous above the quiet dignity of men who might be merely hatters, billiard-markers, or grocery-clerks. Beyond an occasional unwary traveller who came by rail, this gambler was supposed to prey solely upon reckless and senile farmers, who, when flush with good crops, drove into town in all the pride and confidence of an absolutely invulnerable stupidity. Hearing at times in circuitous fashion of the despoilment of such a farmer, the important men of Romper invariably laughed in contempt of the victim, and if they thought of the wolf at all, it was with a kind of pride at the knowledge that he would never dare think of attacking their wisdom and courage. Besides, it was popular that this gambler had a real wife and two real children in a neat cottage in a suburb, where he led an exemplary home life; and when any one even suggested a discrepancy in his character, the crowd immediately vociferated descriptions of this virtuous family circle. Then men who led exemplary home lives, and men who did not lead exemplary home lives, all subsided in a bunch, remarking that there was nothing more to be said.

However, when a restriction was placed upon him—as, for instance, when a strong clique of members of the new Pollywog Club refused to permit him, even as a spectator, to appear in the rooms of the organization—the candor and gentleness with which he accepted the judgment disarmed many of his foes and made his friends more desperately partisan. He invariably distinguished between himself and a respectable Romper man so quickly and frankly that his manner actually appeared to be a continual broadcast compliment.

And one must not forget to declare the fundamental fact of his entire position in Romper. It is irrefutable that in all affairs outside his business, in all matters that occur eternally and commonly between man and man, this thieving card-player was so generous, so just, so moral, that, in a contest, he could have put to flight the consciences of nine-tenths of the citizens of Romper.

And so it happened that he was seated in this saloon with the two prominent local merchants and the district attorney.

The Swede continued to drink raw whiskey, meanwhile babbling at the barkeeper and trying to induce him to indulge in potations. "Come on. Have a drink. Come on. What—no? Well, have a little one, then. By gawd, I've whipped a man to-night, and I want to celebrate. I whipped him good, too. Gentlemen," the Swede cried to the men at the table. "have a drink?"

"Ssh!" said the barkeeper.

The group at the table, although furtively attentive, had been pretending to be deep in talk, but now a man lifted his eyes towards the Swede and said, shortly, "Thanks. We don't want any more."

At this reply the Swede ruffled out his chest like a rooster. "Well," he exploded, "It seems I can't get anybody to drink with me in this town. Seems so, don't it? Well!"

"Ssh!" said the barkeeper.

"Say," snarled the Swede, "don't you try to shut me up. I won't have it. I'm a gentleman, and I want people to drink with me. And I want 'em to drink with me now. *Now*—do you understand?" He rapped the bar with his knuckles.

Years of experience had calloused the bartender. He merely grew sulky. "I hear you," he answered.

"Well," cried the Swede, "listen hard then. See those men over there? Well, they're going to drink with me, and don't you forget it. Now you watch."

"Hi!" yelled the barkeeper, "this won't do!"

"Why won't it?" demanded the Swede. He stalked over to the table, and by chance laid his hand upon the shoulder of the gambler. "How about this?" he asked wrathfully. "I asked you to drink with me."

The gambler simply twisted his head and spoke over his shoulder. "My friend, I don't know you."

"Oh, hell!" answered the Swede, "come and have a drink."

"Now, my boy," advised the gambler, kindly, "take your hand off my shoulder and go 'way and mind your own business." He was a little, slim man, and it seemed strange to hear him use this tone of heroic patronage to the burly Swede. The other men at the table said nothing.

"What! You won't drink with me, you little dude? I'll make you, then! I'll make you!" The Swede had grasped the gambler frenziedly at the throat, and was dragging him from his chair. The other men sprang up. The barkeeper dashed around the corner of his bar. There was a great tumult, and then was seen a long blade in the hand of the gambler. It shot forward, and a human body, this citadel of virtue, wisdom, power, was pierced as easily as if it had been a melon. The Swede fell with a cry of supreme astonishment.

The prominent merchants and the district attorney must have at once tumbled out of the place backward. The bartender found himself hanging limply to the arm of a chair and gazing into the eyes of a murderer.

"Henry," said latter, as he wiped his knife on one of the towels that hung beneath the bar rail, "you tell 'em where to find me. I'll be home, waiting for 'em." Then he vanished. A moment afterward the barkeeper was in the street dinning through the storm for help and, moreover, companionship.

The corpse of the Swede, alone in the saloon, had its eyes fixed upon a dreadful legend that dwelt atop of the cash-machine: "This registers the amount of your purchase."

IX

Months later, the cowboy was frying pork over the stove of a little ranch near the Dakota line, when there was a quick thud of hoofs outside, and presently the Easterner entered with the letters and the papers.

"Well," said the Easterner at once, "the chap that killed the Swede has got three years. Wasn't much, was it?"

"He has? Three years?" The cowboy poised his pan of pork, while he ruminated upon the news. "Three years. That ain't much."

"No. It was light sentence," replied the Easterner as he unbuckled his spurs. "Seems there was a good deal of sympathy for him in Romper."

"If the bartender had been any good," observed the cowboy, thoughtfully, "he would have gone in and cracked that there Dutchman on the head with a bottle in the beginnin' of it and stopped all this here murderin'."

"Yes, a thousand things might have happened," said the Easterner, tartly.

The cowboy returned his pan of pork to the fire, but his philosophy continued. "It's funny, ain't it? If he hadn't said Johnnie was cheatin' he'd be alive this minute. He was an awful fool. Game played for fun, too. Not for money. I believe he was crazy."

"I feel sorry for that gambler," said the Easterner.

"Oh, so do I," said the cowboy. "He don't deserve none of it for killin' who he did."

"The Swede might not have been killed if everything had been square."

"Might not have been killed?" exclaimed the cowboy. "Everythin' square? Why, when he said that Johnnie was cheatin' and acted like such a jackass? And then in the saloon he fairly walked up to git hurt?" With these arguments the cowboy browbeat the Easterner and reduced him to rage.

"You're a fool!" cried the Easterner, viciously. "You're a bigger jackass than the Swede by a million majority. Now let me tell you one thing. Let me tell you something. Listen! Johnnie *was* cheating!"

" 'Johnnie,' " said the cowboy, blankly. There was a minute of silence, and then he said, robustly, "Why, no. The game was only for fun."

"Fun or not," said the Easterner, "Johnnie was cheating. I saw him. I know it. I saw him. And I refused to stand up and be a man. I let the Swede fight it out alone. And you—you were simply puffing around the place and wanting to fight. And then old Scully himself! We are all in it! This poor gambler isn't even a noun. He is a kind of an adverb. Every sin is the result of a collaboration. We, five of us, have collaborated in the murder of this Swede. Usually there are from a dozen to forty women really involved in every murder, but in this case it seems to be only five men—you, I, Johnnie, old Scully; and that fool of an unfortunate gambler came merely as a culmination, the apex of a human movement, and gets all the punishment."

The cowboy, injured and rebellious, cried out blindly into this fog of mysterious theory: "Well, I didn't do anythin', did I?"

The Bride Comes to Yellow Sky (*1898*)

I

The great Pullman was whirling onward with such dignity of motion that a glance from the window seemed simply to prove that the plains of Texas were pouring eastward. Vast flats of green grass, dull-hued spaces of mesquit and cactus, little groups of frame houses, woods of light and tender trees, all were sweeping into the east, sweeping over the horizon, a precipice.

A newly married pair had boarded this coach at San Antonio. The man's face was reddened from many days in the wind and sun, and a direct result of his new black clothes was that his brick-colored hands were constantly performing in a most conscious fashion. From time to time he looked down respectfully at his attire. He sat with a hand on each knee, like a man waiting in a barber's shop. The glances he devoted to other passengers were furtive and shy.

The bride was not pretty, nor was she very young. She wore a dress of blue cashmere, with small reservations of velvet here and there, and with steel buttons abounding. She continually twisted her head to regard her puff sleeves, very stiff, straight, and high. They embarrassed her. It was quite apparent that she had cooked, and that she expected to cook, dutifully. The blushes caused by the careless scrutiny of some passengers as she had entered the car were strange to see upon this plain, under-class countenance, which was drawn in placid, almost emotionless lines.

They were evidently very happy. "Ever been in a parlor-car before?" he asked, smiling with delight.

"No," she answered; "I never was. It's fine, ain't it?"

"Great! And then after a while we'll go forward to the diner, and get a big lay-out. Finest meal in the world. Charge a dollar."

"Oh, do they?" cried the bride. "Charge a dollar? Why, that's too much—for us—ain't it, Jack?"

"Not this trip, anyhow," he answered bravely. "We're going to go the whole thing."

Later he explained to her about the trains. "You see, it's a thousand miles from one end of Texas to the other; and this train runs right across it, and never stops but for four times." He had the pride of an owner. He pointed out to her the dazzling fittings of the coach; and in truth her eyes opened wider as she contemplated the sea-green figured velvet, the shining brass, silver, and glass, the wood that gleamed as darkly brilliant as the surface of a pool of oil. At one end a bronze figure sturdily held a support for a separated chamber, and at convenient places on the ceiling were frescoes in olive and silver.

To the minds of the pair, their surroundings reflected the glory of their marriage that morning in San Antonio; this was the environment of their new estate; and the man's face in particular beamed with an elation that made him appear ridiculous to the negro porter. This individual at times surveyed them from afar with an amused and superior grin. On other occasions he bullied them with skill in ways that did not make it exactly plain to them that they were being bullied. He subtly used all the manners of the most unconquerable kind of snobbery. He oppressed them; but of this oppression they had small knowledge, and they speedily forgot that infrequently a number of travellers covered them with stares of derisive enjoyment. Historically there was supposed to be something infinitely humorous in their situation.

"We are due in Yellow Sky at 3:42," he said, looking tenderly into her eyes.

"Oh, are we?" she said, as if she had not been aware of it. To evince surprise at her husband's statement was part of her wifely amiability. She took from a pocket a little silver watch; and as she held it before her, and stared at it with a frown of attention, the new husband's face shone.

"I bought it in San Anton' from a friend of mine," he told her gleefully.

"It's seventeen minutes past twelve," she said, looking up at him with a kind of shy and clumsy coquetry. A passenger, noting this play, grew excessively sardonic, and winked at himself in one of the numerous mirrors.

At last they went to the dining-car. Two rows of negro waiters, in glowing white suits, surveyed their entrance with the interest, and also the equanimity, of men who had been forewarned. The pair fell to the lot of a waiter who happened to feel pleasure in steering them through their meal. He viewed them with the manner of a fatherly pilot, his countenance radiant with benevolence. The patronage, entwined with the ordinary deference, was not plain to them. And yet, as they returned to their coach, they showed in their faces a sense of escape.

To the left, miles down a long purple slope, was a little ribbon of mist where moved the keening Rio Grande. The train was approaching it at an angle, and the apex was Yellow Sky. Presently it was apparent that, as the distance from Yellow Sky grew shorter, the husband became commensurately restless. His brick-red hands were more insistent in their prominence. Occasionally he was even rather absent-minded and far-away when the bride leaned forward and addressed him.

As a matter of truth, Jack Potter was beginning to find the shadow of a deed weigh upon him like a leaden slab. He, the town marshal of Yellow Sky, a man known, liked, and feared in his corner, a prominent person, had gone to San Antonio to meet a girl he believed he loved, and there, after the usual prayers, had actually induced her to marry him, without consulting Yellow Sky for any part of the transaction. He was now bringing his bride before an innocent and unsuspecting community.

Of course people in Yellow Sky married as it pleased them, in accordance with a general custom; but such was Potter's thought of his duty to his friends, or of their idea of his duty, or of an unspoken form which does not control men in these matters, that he felt he was heinous. He had committed an extraordinary crime. Face to face with this girl in San Antonio, and spurred by his sharp impulse, he had gone headlong over all the social hedges. At San Antonio he was like a man hidden in the dark. A knife to sever any friendly duty, any form, was easy to his hand in that remote city. But the hour of Yellow Sky—the hour of daylight—was approaching.

He knew full well that his marriage was an important thing to his town. It could only be exceeded by the burning of the new hotel. His friends could not forgive him. Frequently he had reflected on the advisability of telling them by telegraph, but a new cowardice had been upon him. He feared to do it. And now the train was hurrying him toward a scene of amazement, glee, and reproach. He glanced out of the window at the line of haze swinging slowly in toward the train.

Yellow Sky had a kind of brass band, which played painfully, to the delight of the populace. He laughed without heart as he thought of it. If the citizens could dream of his prospective arrival with his bride, they would parade the band at the station and escort them, amid cheers and laughing congratulations, to his adobe home.

He resolved that he would use all the devices of speed and plainscraft in making the journey from the station to his house. Once within that safe citadel, he could issue some sort of vocal bulletin, and then not go among the citizens until they had time to wear off a little of their enthusiasm.

The bride looked anxiously at him. "What's worrying you, Jack?"

He laughed again. "I'm not worrying, girl; I'm only thinking of Yellow Sky."

She flushed in comprehension.

A sense of mutual guilt invaded their minds and developed a finer tenderness. They looked at each other with eyes softly aglow. But Potter often laughed the same nervous laugh; the flush upon the bride's face seemed quite permanent.

The traitor to the feelings of Yellow Sky narrowly watched the speeding landscape. "We're nearly there," he said.

Presently the porter came and announced the proximity of Potter's home. He held a brush in his hand, and, with all his airy superiority gone, he brushed Potter's new clothes as the latter slowly turned this way and that way. Potter fumbled out a coin and gave it to the porter, as he had seen others do. It was a heavy and muscle-bound business, as that of a man shoeing his first horse.

The porter took their bag, and as the train began to slow they moved forward to the hooded platform of the car. Presently the two engines and their long string of coaches rushed into the station of Yellow Sky.

"They have to take water here," said Potter, from a constricted throat and in mournful cadence, as one announcing death. Before the train stopped his eye had swept the length of the platform, and he was glad and astonished to see there was none upon it but the station-agent, who, with a slightly hurried and anxious air, was walking toward the water-tanks. When the train had halted, the porter alighted first, and placed in position a little temporary step.

"Come on, girl," said Potter, hoarsely. As he helped her down they each laughed on a false note. He took the bag from the negro, and bade his wife cling to his arm. As they slunk rapidly away, his hang-dog glance perceived that they were unloading the two trunks, and also that the station agent, far ahead near the baggage car, had turned and was running towards him, making gestures. He laughed, and groaned as he laughed, when he noted the first effect of his marital bliss upon Yellow Sky. He gripped his wife's arm firmly to his side, and they fled. Behind them the porter stood, chuckling fatuously.

II

The California express on the Southern Railway was due at Yellow Sky in twenty-one minutes. There were six men at the bar of the Weary Gentleman Saloon. One was a drummer who talked a great deal and rapidly; three were Texans who did not care to talk at that time; and two were Mexican sheep-herders, who did not talk as a general practice in the Weary Gentleman Saloon. The barkeeper's dog lay on the board walk that crossed in front of the door. His head was on his paws, and he glanced drowsily here and there with the constant vigilance of a dog that is kicked on occasion. Across the sandy street were some vivid green grass-plots, so wonderful in appearance, amid the sands that burned near them in a blazing sun, that they caused a doubt in the mind. They exactly resembled the grass mats used to represent lawns on the stage. At the cooler end of the railway station, a man without a coat sat in a tilted chair and smoked his pipe. The fresh-cut bank of the Rio Grande circled near the town, and there could be seen beyond it a great plum-colored plain of mesquit.

Save for the busy drummer and his companions in the saloon, Yellow Sky was dozing. The newcomer leaned gracefully upon the bar, and recited many tales with the confidence of a bard who has come upon a new field.

"—and at the moment that the old man fell downstairs with the bureau in his arms, the old woman was coming up with two scuttles of coal, and of course—"

The drummer's tale was interrupted by a young man who suddenly appeared in the open door. He cried: "Scratchy Wilson's drunk, and has turned loose with both hands." The two Mexicans at once set down their glasses and faded out of the rear entrance of the saloon.

The drummer, innocent and jocular, answered: "All right, old man. S'pose he has? Come in and have a drink, anyhow."

But the information had made such an obvious cleft in every skull in the room that the drummer was obliged to see its importance. All had become instantly solemn. "Say," said he, mystified, "what is this?" His three companions made the introductory gesture of eloquent speech; but the young man at the door forestalled them.

"It means, my friend," he answered, as he came into the saloon, "that for the next two hours this town won't be a health resort."

The barkeeper went to the door, and locked and barred it; reaching out of the window, he pulled in heavy wooden shutters, and barred them. Immediately a solemn, chapel-like gloom was upon the place. The drummer was looking from one to another.

"But say," he cried, "what is this anyhow? You don't mean there is going to be a gun-fight?"

"Don't know whether there'll be a fight or not," answered one man, grimly; "but there'll be some shootin'—some good shootin'."

The young man who had warned them waved his hand. "Oh, there'll be a fight fast enough, if any one wants it. Anybody can get a fight out there in the street. There's a fight just waiting."

The drummer seemed to be swayed between the interest of a foreigner and a perception of personal danger.

"What did you say his name was?" he asked.

"Scratchy Wilson," they answered in chorus.

"And will he kill anybody? What are you going to do? Does this happen often? Does he rampage around like this once a week or so? Can he break in that door?"

"No; he can't break down that door," replied the barkeeper. "He's tried it three times. But when he comes you'd better lay down on the floor, stranger. He's dead sure to shoot at it, and a bullet may come through."

Thereafter the drummer kept a strict eye upon the door. The time had not yet been called for him to hug the floor, but, as a minor precaution, he sidled near to the wall. "Will he kill anybody?" he said again.

The men laughed low and scornfully at the question.

"He's out to shoot, and he's out for trouble. Don't see any good in experimentin' with him."

"But what do you do in a case like this? What do you do?"

A man responded: "Why, he and Jack Potter—"

"But," in chorus the other men interrupted, "Jack Potter's in San Anton'."

"Well, who is he? What's he got to do with it?"

"Oh, he's the town marshal. He goes out and fights Scratchy when he gets on one of these tears."

"Wow!" said the drummer, mopping his brow. "Nice job he's got."

The voices had toned away to mere whisperings. The drummer wished to ask further questions, which were born of an increasing anxiety and bewilderment; but when he attempted them, the men merely looked at him in irritation and motioned him to remain silent. A tense waiting hush was upon them. In the deep shadows of the room their eyes shone as they listened for sounds from the street. One man made three gestures at the barkeeper; and the latter moving like a ghost, handed him a glass and a bottle. The man poured a full glass of whiskey, and set down the bottle noiselessly. He gulped the whiskey in a swallow, and turned again toward the door in immovable silence. The drummer saw that the barkeeper, without a sound, had taken a Winchester from beneath the bar. Later he saw this individual beckoning to him, so he tiptoed across the room.

"You better come with me back of the bar."

"No, thanks," said the drummer, perspiring; "I'd rather be where I can make a break for the back door."

Whereupon the man of bottles made a kindly but peremptory gesture. The drummer obeyed it, and, finding himself seated on a box with his head below the level of the bar, balm was laid upon his soul at sight of various zinc and copper fittings that bore a resemblance to armor-plate. The barkeeper took a seat comfortably upon an adjacent box.

"You see," he whispered, "this here Scratchy Wilson is a wonder with a gun—a perfect wonder; and when he goes on the war-trail, we hunt our holes—naturally. He's about the last one of the old gang that used to hang out along the river here. He's a terror when he's drunk. When he's sober he's all right—kind of simple—wouldn't hurt a fly— nicest fellow in town. But when he's drunk—whoo!"

There were periods of stillness. "I wish Jack Potter was back from San Anton'," said the barkeeper. "He shot Wilson up once—in the leg— and he would sail in and pull out the kinks in this thing."

Presently they heard from a distance the sound of a shot, followed by three wild yowls. It instantly removed a bond from the men in the darkened saloon. There was a shuffling of feet. They looked at each other. "Here he comes," they said.

III

A man in a maroon-colored flannel shirt, which had been purchased for purposes of decoration, and made principally by some Jewish women on the East Side of New York, rounded a corner and walked into the middle of the main street of Yellow Sky. In either hand the man held a long, heavy, blue-black revolver. Often he yelled, and these cries rang through a semblance of a deserted village, shrilly flying over the roofs in a volume that seemed to have no relation to the ordinary vocal strength of a man. It was as if the surrounding stillness formed the arch of a tomb over him. These cries of ferocious challenge rang against walls of silence. And his boots had red tops with gilded imprints, of the kind beloved in winter by little sledding boys on the hillsides of New England.

The man's face flamed in a rage begot of whiskey. His eyes, rolling, and yet keen for ambush, hunted the still doorways and windows. He walked with the creeping movement of the midnight cat. As it occurred to him, he roared menacing information. The long revolvers in his hands were as easy as straws; they were moved with an electric swiftness. The little fingers of each hand played sometimes in a musician's way. Plain from the low collar of the shirt, the cords of his neck straightened and sank, straightened and sank as passion moved him. The only sounds were his terrible invitations. The calm adobes preserved their demeanor at the passing of this small thing in the middle of the street.

There was no offer of fight—no offer of fight. The man called to the sky. There were no attractions. He bellowed and fumed and swayed his revolvers here and everywhere.

The dog of the barkeeper of the Weary Gentleman Saloon had not appreciated the advance of events. He yet lay dozing in front of his master's door. At sight of the dog, the man paused and raised his revolver humorously. At sight of the man, the dog sprang up and walked diagonally away, with a sullen head, and growling. The man yelled, and the dog broke into a gallop. As it was about to enter an alley, there was a loud noise, a whistling, and something spat the ground directly before it. The dog screamed, and, wheeling in terror, galloped headlong in a new direction. Again there was a noise, a whistling, and sand was kicked viciously before it. Fear-stricken, the dog turned and flurried like an animal in a pen. The man stood laughing, his weapons at his hips.

Ultimately the man was attracted by the closed door of the Weary Gentleman Saloon. He went to it and, hammering with a revolver, demanded drink.

The door remaining imperturbable, he picked a bit of paper from the walk, and nailed it to the framework with a knife. He then turned his back contemptuously upon this popular resort, and, walking to the opposite side of the street and spinning there on his heel quickly and lithely, fired at the bit of paper. He missed it by a half-inch. He swore at himself, and went away. Later he comfortably fusilladed the windows of his most intimate friend. The man was playing with this town; it was a toy for him.

But still there was no offer of fight. The name of Jack Potter, his ancient antagonist, entered his mind, and he concluded that it would be a glad thing if he should go to Potter's house, and by bombardment induce him to come out and fight. He moved in the direction of his desire, chanting Apache scalp-music.

When he arrived at it, Potter's house presented the same still front as had the other adobes. Taking up a strategic position, the man howled a challenge. But this house regarded him as might a great stone god. It gave no sign. After a decent wait, the man howled further challenges, mingling with them wonderful epithets.

Presently there came the spectacle of a man churning himself into deepest rage over the immobility of a house. He fumed at it as the winter wind attacks a prairie cabin in the North. To the distance there should have gone the sound of a tumult like the fighting of two hundred Mexicans. As necessity bade him, he paused for breath or to reload his revolvers.

IV

Potter and his bride walked sheepishly and with speed. Sometimes they laughed together shamefacedly and low.

"Next corner, dear," he said finally.

They put forth the efforts of a pair walking bowed against a strong wind. Potter was about to raise a finger to point the first appearance of the new home when, as they circled the corner, they came face to face with a man in a maroon-colored shirt, who was feverishly pushing cartridges into a large revolver. Upon the instant the man dropped his revolver to the ground, and, like lightning, whipped another from its holster. The second weapon was aimed at the bridegroom's chest.

There was a silence. Potter's mouth seemed to be merely a grave for his tongue. He exhibited an instinct to at once loosen his arm from the woman's grip, and he dropped the bag to the sand. As for the bride, her face had gone as yellow as old cloth. She was a slave to hideous rites, gazing at the apparitional snake.

The two men faced each other at a distance of three paces. He of the revolver smiled with a new and quiet ferocity.

"Tried to sneak up on me," he said. "Tried to sneak up on me!" His eyes grew more baleful. As Potter made a slight movement, the man thrust his revolver venomously forward. "No; don't you do it, Jack Potter. Don't you move a finger toward a gun just yet. Don't you move an eyelash. The time has come for me to settle with you, and I'm goin' to do it my own way, and loaf along with no interferin'. So if you don't want a gun bent on you, just mind what I tell you."

Potter looked at his enemy. "I ain't got a gun on me, Scratchy." he said. "Honest, I ain't." He was stiffening and steadying, but yet somewhere at the back of his mind a vision of the Pullman floated: the sea-green figured velvet, the shining brass, silver, and glass, the wood that gleamed as darkly brilliant as the surface of a pool of oil—all the glory of the marriage, the environment of the new estate. "You know I fight when it comes to fighting, Scratchy Wilson; but I ain't got a gun on me. You'll have to do all the shootin' yourself."

His enemy's face went livid. He stepped forward, and lashed his weapon to and fro before Potter's chest. "Don't you tell me you ain't got no gun on you, you whelp. Don't tell me no lie like that. There ain't a man in Texas ever seen you without no gun. Don't take me for no kid." His eyes blazed with light, and his throat worked like a pump.

"I ain't takin' you for no kid," answered Potter. His heels had not moved an inch backward. "I'm takin' you for a —— fool. I tell you I ain't got a gun, and I ain't. If you're goin' to shoot me up, you better begin now; you'll never get a chance like this again."

So much enforced reasoning had told on Wilson's rage; he was calmer. "If you ain't got a gun, why ain't you got a gun?" he sneered. "Been to Sunday school?"

"I ain't got a gun because I've just come from San Anton' with my wife. I'm married," said Potter. "And if I'd thought there was going to be any galoots like you prowling around when I brought my wife home, I'd had a gun, and don't you forget it."

"Married!" said Scratchy, not at all comprehending.

"Yes, married. I'm married," said Potter, distinctly.

"Married?" said Scratchy. Seemingly for the first time, he saw the drooping, drowning woman at the other man's side. "No!" he said. He was like a creature allowed a glimpse of another world. He moved a pace backward, and his arm, with the revolver, dropped to his side. "Is this the lady?" he asked.

"Yes; this is the lady," answered Potter.

There was another period of silence.

"Well," said Wilson at last, slowly, "I s'pose it's all off now."

"It's all off if you say so, Scratchy. You know I didn't make the trouble." Potter lifted his valise.

"Well, I 'low it's off, Jack," said Wilson. He was looking at the ground. "Married!" He was not a student of chivalry; it was merely that in the presence of this foreign condition he was a simple child of the earlier plains. He picked up his starboard revolver, and, placing both weapons in their holsters, he went away. His feet made funnel-shaped tracks in the heavy sand.

Black Riders Came from the Sea (1895)

Black riders came from the sea.
There was clang and clang of spear and shield,
And clash and clash of hoof and heel,
Wild shouts and the wave of hair
In the rush upon the wind:
Thus the ride of Sin.

In the Desert *(1895?)*

In the desert
I saw a creature, naked, bestial,
Who, squatting upon the ground,
Held his heart in his hands,
And ate of it.
I said, "Is it good, friend?"
"It is bitter—bitter," he answered;
"But I like it
Because it is bitter,
And because it is my heart."   10

War Is Kind *(1899)*

Do not weep, maiden, for war is kind.
Because your lover threw wild hands toward the sky
And the affrighted steed ran on alone,
Do not weep.
War is kind.

Hoarse, booming drums of the regiment,
Little souls who thirst for fight,
These men were born to drill and die.
The unexplained glory flies above them,
Great is the battle-god, great, and his kingdom—   10
A field where a thousand corpses lie.

Do not weep, babe, for war is kind.
Because your father tumbled in the yellow trenches,
Raged at his breast, gulped and died,
Do not weep.
War is kind.

Swift blazing flag of the regiment,
Eagle with crest of red and gold,
These men were born to drill and die.
Point for them the virtue of slaughter,   20
Make plain to them the excellence of killing
And a field where a thousand corpses lie.
Mother whose heart hung humble as a button
On the bright splendid shroud of your son,
Do not weep.
War is kind.

A Man Said to the Universe *(1899)*

A man said to the universe:
"Sir, I exist!"
"However," replied the universe,
"The fact has not created in me
A sense of obligation."

A Man Adrift on a Slim Spar *(POSTHUMOUS)*

A man adrift on a slim spar
A horizon smaller than the rim of a bottle.
Tented waves rearing lashy dark points
The near whine of froth in circles.
    God is cold.

The incessant raise and swing of the sea
And the growl after growl of crest
The sinkings, green, seething, endless
The upheaval half-completed.
    God is cold.   *10*

The seas are in the hollow of Thy Hand;
Oceans may be turned to a spray
Raising down through the stars
Because of a gesture of pity toward a babe.
Oceans may become gray ashes
Die with a long moan and roar
Amid the tumult of the fishes
And the cries of the ships,
Because The Hand beckons the mice.

A horizon smaller than a doomed assassin's cap, *20*
Inky, surging tumults
A reeling, drunken sky and no sky
A pale hand sliding from a polished spar.
    God is cold.

The puff of a coat imprisoning air:
A face kissing the water-death
A weary slow sway of a lost hand
And the sea, the moving sea, the sea.
    God is cold.

Introduction to the Twentieth Century

In the last decade of the last century and in the first of this, a series of startling declarations of one kind or another suggested that many latent forces in American life were gathering together for the explosion of the twentieth century and, with that, an extraordinary cultural resurgence and insurgence. And if the first ten or twelve years of the new century seemed a time of apathy in literature, that was appearance only, for it was, in effect, gathering itself together for its own explosion. Should one list some of these "declarations," one might well wish to begin with Frederick Jackson Turner's classic paper of 1893, "The Significance of the Frontier in American History," which not only analyzed the relation between the pioneering effort and a necessary development of American individualism, but also announced the closing of the frontier. If the gigantic enterprise of exploring and staking out the vast areas of wilderness and plains, mountains and deserts, that stretched across the continent was completed, and so swiftly, another enterprise—call it a counterenterprise—was already well under way: fantastic capitalist expansion and urbanization. In 1894, when Hamlin Garland published *Crumbling Idols,* our first major assertion of literary naturalism, he provided a sanction not only for his own "veritist" accounts of the bleak brutalities of the post-pioneer experience in rural America, but also for the treatment of the harsher brutalities—the extremities of luxury and poverty—of urban life in such fiction as Stephen Crane's *Maggie: A Girl of the Streets* of the year before and, still to come, Theodore Dreiser's *Sister Carrie.*

Literary naturalism as it developed in the United States (as opposed to that of France, for example, with its much more systematic underpinning in science and philosophy) is only a logical part of a whole complex of ideas and events that came along with the general influence of post-Darwinian attitudes. It clearly relates to the thought of William James, whose positivist individualism found expression in four major works of these years: *The Principles of Psychology* (1890), *The Will to Believe* (1897), *The Varieties of Religious Experience* (1902), and *Pragmatism* (1907). It relates no less to the educational theories of James's pupil, the "instrumentalist" John Dewey—those influential ideas about the individual's adaptation to his environment that found expression in such works as *The School and Society* (1897). Again, it clearly connects with a new realism in economic theory as found, for example, in Thorstein Veblen's *The Theory of the Leisure Class* (1899); in sociology as found in William Graham Sumner's *Folkways* (1907); in political science as found in James Allen Smith's *The Spirit of American Government*, (1907), the work that was presently to provide Charles A. Beard with a thesis for what then seemed daring, his *Economic Interpretation of the Constitution* (1913). While not in itself a reformist, let alone a revolutionary, movement, naturalism yet has its clear connections with the socialism of such a writer as Jack London and with the Populism of and before the Progressive era of Theodore Roosevelt. These latter moods found their chief literary expression (and it was not very literary, in the strict sense) in the work of the muck-rakers, most notably, perhaps, in Lincoln Steffens's exposures of corruption in *The Shame of the Cities* (1904) and in Gustavus Myer's *The History of the Great American Fortunes* (1910). In critical theory itself, literary naturalism took a more rigorous form than Garland's in the essays that made up Frank Norris's *The Responsibilities of the Novelist* (1903), and it was, of course, part and parcel of that whole new age of technological and materialistic power elegiacally announced by Henry Adams in his *Education* in 1907.

With all this ferment, this pervasive impulse in so many areas of interest to see the human and the social facts as they really are and, if possible, to set them right, how could the first decade of the century have been merely apathetic in literature? The 1890s had seen the radical fiction of Hamlin Garland, Harold Frederic, Stephen Crane, and Frank Norris, but by the early 1900s these men were either dead or soon to die or, in the first instance, much softened in attitude. The vitality of old New England was certainly exhausted, but the genteel tradition still had its grip on large areas of taste. If, for example, Theodore Dreiser could publish his extraordinarily truthful *Sister Carrie* in 1900, his publishers, on second thought, could also suppress the book and deny it circulation—so shocking its author into novelistic silence for more than ten years. Two great poets, Edwin Arlington Robinson and Robert Frost, were writing in New England, but the first had so small an audience that his publications had to be privately subsidized, and the second was so discouraged by the lack of attention paid to him that in 1912 he removed himself to England for three years. There was no drama that could be taken seriously as art. William Dean Howells was still writing fiction, but he was an old and weary gentleman, and the force of his best novels of the 1880s and 1890s had long drained away. Henry James was to publish his three greatest novels in the first decade of the century, but his audience had become increasingly select as his fiction became more and more subtle. Edith Wharton, his pupil, was just getting under way in these years (the year 1905 saw, to be sure, one of her finest novels, *The House of Mirth*), and so with

Willa Cather, who, in that decade, published only a volume of un-distinguished verse and another of fine but then little-known short stories.

Yet these were some of the lights that flickered, however sparsely, on that nervous terrain that marked the difference between our gawky adolescence in the Gilded Age and our not entirely certain maturity in the opening years of the age of new technology, new commerce, new money, new wars, new poverty, new agony, and finally, new and nearly intolerable anxieties. With a whole new world, not only of human activity but also of human conceptions—of Darwin, of course, but also of Marx, Freud, and Einstein—just opening up, it is hardly surprising that older spirits fell mute and that younger ones, for the moment at least, stood gaping.

Then suddenly everything changed, and the change was marked by the appearance of a series of new periodicals, each in its way fresh and daring, each established to give a platform to the fresh and daring. In 1912, in Chicago, Harriet Monroe founded *Poetry: A Magazine of Verse*. In New York, the same year saw the beginnings of *The Masses* (later *New Masses*), with which one associates such names as Max Eastman, Jack Reed, Floyd Dell. In Chicago again, Margaret A. Anderson established *The Little Review* in 1914. And although *Smart Set* had been published since 1908, it was in 1914, when H. L. Mencken and George Jean Nathan became its editors, that it became a voice of the new literary times, a voice that, ten years later, they were to turn into a kind of national institution in the pages of *The American Mercury*. It was 1914, too, that saw the founding of the *New Republic*, that "weekly journal of opinion" that from its start gave space to such major critics as Randolph Bourne and Van Wyck Brooks and was edited, significantly, by Herbert Croly, who in 1909 had published *The Promise of American Life*, an optimistic survey of democratic prospects in a drastically changing society. *The Seven Arts*, with Waldo Frank as one of its editors, appeared in 1916. And if its pacifist program was to kill it in late 1917, its place was taken in the following year when the *Dial*, for many years a conservative periodical, moved to New York from Chicago and opened its pages to the new and the experimental, to become the most distinguished literary periodical in the United States and hold that place for the entire decade of the 1920s.

Throughout those two decades many noncommercial magazines came and went, not a few of them published abroad; most were dedicated to experiment in general—some to special *isms* in writing, a number to regional expression and sectional interests. This was the era of all those little magazines "that died to make verse free."

It was Harriet Monroe, in Chicago, who initiated this exciting literary hum and buzz, and Chicago indeed, for a brief time, was the base of the "little renaissance." Native bards like Carl Sandburg and Vachel Lindsay were introduced to an audience in *Poetry*, and to that audience they seemed to be boldly shattering all the gentle metrical control of sentiment that had been attenuating American poetry since Whitman. Another native spirit, although of a different order, was also published in *Poetry* and found his audience: Robert Frost, who had achieved his own idiom with the publication of his second volume, *North of Boston*, presently returned to the United States to become a kind of permanent dean of acceptable poetry, reading his work at last on the facade of the Capitol itself, on a great public occasion, in the impossible blast of a brilliant winter blizzard. (No one in 1914 could have predicted this remarkable television spectacle of 1961, yet we must remind ourselves that an earlier President, Theodore Roosevelt, had befriended another major poet, E. A. Robinson, who now, in the second decade, likewise found a following at last.)

Although Harriet Monroe became the champion of such regional iconoclasts, she had no interest in producing a merely regional magazine. In the first issue she introduced the work of Ezra Pound (who was to achieve his own very different kind of public repute three decades later). In the second issue of *Poetry*, Pound was named its "foreign correspondent," and it was chiefly through his efforts in England and presently on the Continent that *Poetry* became the organ of the international avant-garde and European modernism. He probably knew that he was making literary history in October of 1914 when he submitted the first famous poem by T. S. Eliot, "The Love Song of J. Alfred Prufrock." In a now well-known letter he described Eliot as "the only American I know of who has made what I call adequate preparation for writing. He has actually trained himself *and* modernized himself *on his own*"; and as for "Prufrock," it was "the most interesting contribution I've had from an American."

With Eliot, Harriet Monroe was now also publishing such other difficult young poets as William Carlos Williams, Wallace Stevens, Marianne Moore, and presently, Hart Crane. Thus there was a double strain in the "new poetry": the work of the regional poets who were experimental to a point but not particularly difficult, and that of the poets of the avant-garde whose unfamiliar techniques first made them seem difficult indeed. These advanced poets, when not associated with Europe like Pound and Eliot, were closer to New York than to Chicago, and indeed, at just about the time that *Poetry* began in Chicago, "bohemianism" as represented by Greenwich Village in lower Manhattan was beginning to flourish as the concentrated center of expression for all the "new freedoms."

Anarchism, socialism, and Marxism; woman suffrage and birth control and "free love"; vegetarianism and New Thought; psychoanalysis and pacifism; the rights of labor; the new poetry, the new theater, the new painting, the new photography; the new fashion of Dostoevsky and Tolstoi, of Nietzsche and Bergson, of Shaw and Wells; the new music of Schönberg, Bartók, Stravinsky—all this and much more poured into that mélange of enthusiasms for which the Village provided the container. The year 1913 saw the famous Armory Show, which introduced a whole generation of American intellectuals to the new painting from abroad—impressionism, fauvism, cubism, futurism, expressionism. In 1915, Diaghilev's great Ballet Russe came to New York for the first time, with its striking stage designs by some of the new painters and its choreography set to scores by the new composers. It was all part of the impact of modern Europe on an America that was no longer quite provincial.

In the summers there was a kind of Village hegira to Provincetown, Massachusetts, on Cape Cod; and there, in 1915, the Provincetown Players offered their first theatrical productions in a fish house on a wharf. In the winter, the efforts of the Wharf Theater continued with new, experimental plays performed in a barn on McDougall Street in the Village. In revolt against the stultifying conventions of the Broadway theater and the commercial theater in general, the company produced many new and exciting plays; following its example, little theaters sprang up all over the United States. But its greatest service to the drama was the encouragement it gave to the finest American dramatist of this century, Eugene O'Neill, all of whose early plays were presented by this company. It was in 1915, too, that the Washington Square Players opened their first season. With a wider repertory than that of the Provincetown Players, including works by many fine European playwrights, they nevertheless also encouraged new efforts from young Americans, and when they reorganized as the Theater Guild and moved onto Broadway in 1918, not only had the American theater been established as a living, imaginative achievement, but the theater in general had been revolutionized. An entire genre had been emancipated from the stupid and choking conventions of many theatrical generations.

Emancipation was, of course, the rallying cry of the whole decade; emancipation from all those stifling restrictions on manners, artistic no less than social, which were generally regarded as the inheritance of our Puritan past, but emancipation, too, from those newer, middle-class standards—politically conservative, socially restrictive, aesthetically philistine—which an increasingly commercialized culture encouraged and solidified. The period saw, too, a certain relaxation of old racial prejudices and repressions; for the first time a considerable group of Negro writers came to public attention with such concentration that they were associated as a literary movement referred to then as the "Harlem Renaissance." Emancipation was a spirit that continued into the next decade, but with a new admixture of cynicism and "sophistication," as well as with a new despair, until nearly its end. That such a mood should have encouraged much that was merely frivolous and even silly is not surprising; and that much work that was only trivial was taken quite seriously is no more so. If the frothy novels of Joseph Hergesheimer, James Branch Cabell, and Carl Van Vechten were once treated as works of art, we must remind ourselves that the hardly less flighty first novel of a real artist, F. Scott Fitzgerald, was treated similarly in 1920. We must remind ourselves, too, that all this was a kind of counterpoint to the dreary solemnities and corruptions of the Harding-Coolidge years, to the activities of John S. Sumner and the Society for the Suppression of Vice, to the folly of the Prohibition era, and to the alarming proliferation of organized crime and violence. In counterpoint, too, was the increasingly influential voice of H. L. Mencken, who, in the pages of *The American Mercury*, could lampoon all this activity together with the general inanities of the "booboisie" in direct satire, or, less directly, in his defense of such writers as the novelist Theodore Dreiser.

What, then, of fiction? To answer that question we must return to the Middle West and the second decade. Dreiser, who was brought up in grim circumstances in Indiana, had chosen Chicago as the setting for the first half of his novel *Sister Carrie*, which he managed to reissue to considerable acclaim in 1912, a year after he had published a second novel about adultery, *Jennie Gerhardt*. In Chicago in the years immediately following, Sherwood Anderson worked at and finally published his first two rather faulty novels and, in 1919, his one great work of fiction, *Winesburg, Ohio*, interlocking sketches about the sick dreams and frustrations of small-town life in the Midwest, some of which were first published by Margaret Anderson in *The Little Review*. In the same years, Willa Cather, some of whose first stories had also dealt with small-town frustrations, looked back to her native Nebraska and produced two fine novels of the frontier, *O Pioneers!* (1913) and *My Ántonia* (1918). In the meantime, writing from Europe, Edith Wharton published *Ethan Frome* (1911), *The Custom of the Country* (1913), and *The Age of Innocence* (1920)—all stories having to do in one way or another with the sacrifice of ideals and human hope to social rigidities or vulgarizations. The satiric gift fleetingly evident in these early books, and quite prominent in *The Custom of the Country*, was cultivated by a younger novelist, Sinclair Lewis. In 1920, after five earlier and quite unremarkable novels, he published *Main Street*, an extraordinary success, the most vigorous denunciation that our literature contains of the constrictive prejudices and conventionality of life in the American hinterland. Significantly, it was published just as the national census showed that we had passed from an agrarian into an urban economy.

We had also passed into a postwar world. It may be wondered how all this ebullience could have found its expression in precisely those darkest European years, when all the lights were going out. "It is the glory of the present age," said Randolph Bourne less than a year before the shot at Sarajevo, "that in it one can be young." The fact is that the First World War did not cast a pall over the United States. For a long time it seemed distant, Europe's war, not ours. At home we were living in the years of President Wilson's New Freedom. We entered the war late and for a relatively brief time, and since it was a war to "make the world safe for Democracy," we could enter it with a certain exultation. Young men, young aspiring writers like John Dos Passos, Ernest Hemingway, and E. E. Cummings, were eager to get into that great adventure and in their impatience did not wait for the mobilization of American troops, but got into it by joining various medical services. For most of them it *was* an adventure—even for Hemingway, who suffered a wound from which, in a profound sense, his imagination was never to recover. The final victory was the climax to all earlier acts of emancipation. In his introduction to a 1969 reprint (incidentally, the first correct and unexpurgated text) of his book about the war experience, *One Man's Initiation: 1917* (1920), Dos Passos could write, "The more I saw of that war, though I must admit I desperately enjoyed the travel and adventure after the dullness of four college years, the more I felt it was futile and senseless. . . . What was war like? We wanted to see with our own eyes. We flocked into the volunteer services. I respected the conscientious objectors, and occasionally felt I should take that course myself, but hell, I wanted to see the show . . . "; but he could also, in the text itself, more than fifty years before, let one of his characters, after the satisfaction of a French meal, exclaim to the hero, "After the war, Howe, ole man, let's riot all over Europe; I'm getting a taste for this sort of livin'." It was only after President Wilson's defeat at Versailles in 1919 that such boyish ebullience turned into the new bitterness. Ezra Pound, in his long poem *Hugh Selwyn Mauberley*, wrote later of returning soldiers:

came home, home to a lie,
home to many deceits,
home to old lies and new infamy;
usury age-old and age-thick
and liars in public places.

And that bitterness, it developed, was directed at reigning American values, rather than at the state of the world, even as we came out of that war as the most powerful nation on earth.

The older novelists whom we have named continued to write very much along the lines that they had already set for themselves: Dreiser in his stolid naturalism, Edith Wharton in her more stylish gloom, and so on. Sherwood Anderson and Sinclair Lewis, even at their most critical, continued to base their criticism on an expectation that American democracy could yet fulfill its promises. But the younger novelists, those who had come into their maturity during the war years and many of whom now fled from the United States for residence in Europe, had no such expectations.

This new alienation was in no sense a negative thing from the point of view of art. It gave these writers, and their contemporaries among poets no less, a thrilling new awareness in the life of sensation and an acute sense that the value of life is in the act of living itself. These are probably the prime elements in all fine and vital art. The new alienation had, besides, an extraordinary purifying effect aesthetically: it gave these younger writers an intense devotion to art and its technical resources such as our literature had not seen since, at least, Henry James—and he, perhaps, was deficient in that other quality, the sharp sensuous response to experience that was theirs. The result was that Katherine Anne Porter, F. Scott Fitzgerald, John Dos Passos, William Faulkner, and Ernest Hemingway, at their best, gave us fiction that astonished the world and that stands firmly with our finest.

The new poetry came to its climax in 1922 with the publication of Eliot's *The Waste Land,* and that poem was itself a climax in the use of literary allusion and mythical substructure, techniques with which Eliot had all along been experimenting in his shorter poems. Robinson and Frost and the other older poets, like the older novelists, continued pretty much in their own course, but no younger poet came up who did not have to take Eliot's achievement into account. This continued to be the fact for many years, even after Eliot himself had moved into that new style of the thirties and forties that was to characterize his grave religious meditations, the *Four Quartets.* On the stage, O'Neill continued his experiments (as he did to the end of his writing life), trying out many ways by which he might *internalize* the drama, and following his example, many worthy if less spectacularly talented men tried out others. The result was that, at least until the Second World War, the commercial theater continued to give its audiences exciting aesthetic fare in relative abundance.

The year 1929 provided the first of two great crises in the American imaginative life of this century (the second came in 1945, when we dropped the first atomic bomb). With the stock-market crash of October and the following years of deep economic depression, the entire mood of literature necessarily changed. Many writers now made political commitments: most moved to the Left, some into the Communist Party, almost everyone at least influenced by what was regarded as Marxist criticism; a few, particularly those associated with the short-lived movement called the New Humanism, moved to the Right. After the developing novel of sensibility of the late 1920s, there was now a resurgence of Dreiserian naturalism (with an added political bias), perhaps most notably in the novels of James T. Farrell and, less insistently, in those of John Steinbeck. A prevailing mood of militant despair affected not only fiction but poetry as well and especially, perhaps, drama, most movingly in the plays of Clifford Odets. The efforts of Franklin D. Roosevelt's New Deal (after 1933) to alleviate the situation—the Works Progress Administration specifically assisted unemployed writers and artists, and the Eighteenth Amendment was repealed—introduced some little hope; but the simultaneous rise and aggressive success of Adolf Hitler in Germany (following over a decade of fascist supremacy in Italy) more than countered such hope in tragic dismay. It was not until 1936, in Spain, when General Francisco Franco and his insurgent cohorts, with the assistance of Germany and Italy, overturned a legally constituted Socialist government, that many American writers were united in sympathy with many European writers in what has been called "the Last Great Cause." In the United States, the Spanish war resulted in at least one remarkable work of literature, Hemingway's longest novel, *For Whom the Bell Tolls* (1940). But by then the Spanish Republicans had lost their war, and Europe was in flames in a much larger one after Hitler's invasion of Poland in September of 1939. Now the bells were truly tolling, and no longer only for those millions of Jews who had been systematically murdered at the order of the funny-looking madman from a place called Braunau, near Munich.

The twentieth century had exploded in a very different way from that first spirited and hopeful revolt of 1910 to 1916. That was to get us into life; this was sheerest, maddest, massive death. If the first explosion was metaphorical, this one was all too devastatingly literal. This time—even though we again hesitated to become involved in a conflict that many Americans regarded as a local dispute between European countries until the assault on Pearl Harbor forced our hand in 1941—our literature *did* suffer.

The war years saw the publication of first books by impressive new writers, of course—in fiction (Richard Wright, Eudora Welty, Carson McCullers, John Cheever, Saul Bellow) and in poetry (Theodore

Roethke, John Berryman, Randall Jarrell, Robert Lowell, Elizabeth Bishop); and these are very bright names, even though, probably, not those of giants. However that may be, a process began, not of disintegration, certainly, but of what one might call fragmentation, of a diffusion of literary effort so wide and so various that it becomes nearly impossible to generalize. This process seems to have continued over the years right into the present.

If the end of the war was an exhilarating occasion for some—Ernest Hemingway, for example, with his famous (and foolish) "liberation" of the Ritz in Paris—most of us, when we think of that country in those years, are likely to remember Cartier-Bresson's extraordinary photograph of grieving faces when Paris fell. Certainly the destruction of Hiroshima and Nagasaki in 1945 was a numbing experience for the bulk of mankind and perhaps particularly for creative men. W. B. Yeats once said that the artist "loves above all life at peace with itself," and this is only natural, since his function is the creation of harmonies. How can this function be expected to thrive in a world in which technology has been brought to the point where the instant mechanical extinction of millions is momentarily possible? We have indeed arrived at that desperate point announced by Freud in 1930 at the end of *Civilization and Its Discontents:* "Men have gained control over the forces of nature to such an extent that with their help they would have no difficulty in exterminating one another to the last man. They know this, and hence comes a large part of their current unrest, their unhappiness and their mood of anxiety." If one day must be named, it was August 6, 1945, that swept us into Auden's Age of Anxiety. The resilience of the creative imagination is nowhere better demonstrated than in the fact that it should have continued to manifest itself at all after that day, in whatever state of diffusion.

Some tendencies can of course be discerned. Most obvious almost certainly is the swift deterioration of the commercial theater and the compensatory development of the "off-Broadway" theaters in New York and their equivalents in every major city. These have made possible a new surge of experiment both in the structure and the production of plays and the appearance of a good number of impressive new playwrights who, in turn, have had a stimulating influence on the commercial theater, to which a number of them are now welcome. If they have a single predecessor, it is probably Thornton Wilder in *The Skin of Our Teeth* (1942), a play that, interestingly enough, achieved great success on Broadway in the dark depths of wartime.

In fiction, there was again a brief reassertion of naturalism, notably in the novels of Richard Wright and in Norman Mailer's *The Naked and the Dead* (1948), perhaps the only important novel to have come out of World War II. But the techniques of naturalism can very readily transform themselves into the service of the hallucinatory and the surreal, as in at least three of the four novels of Nathanael West, in Ralph Ellison's *Invisible Man* (1952), and in Saul Bellow's *Henderson the Rain King* (1959); and this, indeed, is the trend that most of the fiction of our gifted male writers has taken, including the work of the earlier naturalist, Norman Mailer, in such a macabre fantasy as *Why Are We in Vietnam?* (1967). In our gifted female writers, Eudora Welty, Carson McCullers, Flannery O'Connor, perhaps under the influence of Katherine Anne Porter, the turn has been rather to a heightened lyricism and a new extension of the fiction of sensibility, often—certainly in the work of Carson McCullers—achieving the same kind of dreamlike world, dark with dread and brooding love. Accompanying both developments is the increasingly frequent appearance (in an unheroic world) of the antihero—the clown, the cripple, the fugitive, the fumbler, the deranged. In a world where social forms and sanctions have largely lost their meaning or their relevance to the sense of one's existence, the posed question, implicit or explicit, is almost always that of one's self, the sometimes frenetic search for it, and the often desperate struggle to hang on to it. In this later fiction, unlike much of the fiction of the twenties, the individual may accept the world in which he finds himself, but he must almost necessarily remain isolated within it if he is to exist at all.

Wars follow upon wars. After the great war came the trouble with a divided Korea and, after that, the protracted and shameful horror of Vietnam, with which we are still trying to live. Out of war, the poets produced a few beautiful cries of pain and anger and dismay (Randall Jarrell's famous "Death of the Ball Turret Gunner" is an example), but on the whole, these wars have not lent themselves to direct expression in poetry. The influence is more oblique. In general, the later poetry has developed in much the way of the later fiction, and indeed, the two genres have moved closer together than they have ever been, until it sometimes seems as if one is about to disappear into the other.

On the whole, this later poetry is "easier" than the work of the poets of the earlier generation, or at least it is more direct, less densely allusive, frequently a poetry of statement, often, to be sure, of enigmatic statement. It moves in a wide arc of extremities. At one end we have the cool, controlled, rather meditative poems of Richard Eberhart, Stanley Kunitz, Richard Wilbur, and others; generally these are metrically even, often rimed, objective. Then we have the more nervous, more personal, and more expansive work of Theodore Roethke and the "confessional" mode brought into vogue by Robert

Lowell. Beyond that is the incantatory hymn of denunciation, rage, spleen, praise of Allen Ginsberg, the poem of urban violence and crummy wreckage. Then there is the poetry of hallucination and dream, composed and even rather tranquil in James Merrill; highly distraught, agitated, jittery in the sonnets of John Berryman. Finally, in the work of Anne Sexton and Sylvia Plath, we have poems of despairing madness and death, as painful in their very texture as exposed nerves or broken bones. And we take a step (for mankind?) into the last third of the twentieth century, having walked on and dumped our technological junk upon the face of the once mysterious moon.

CRITICS OF THE CULTURE: BEFORE WORLD WAR I

HENRY ADAMS (1838–1918)

As a young man Henry Adams dreamed of "a national set of young men like ourselves or better, to start new influences not only in politics, but in literature, in law, in society, and throughout the whole social organization of the country—a national school of our own generation." In part he was expressing here that ideal of disinterested public service which had inspired the best of the Bostonians during the nineteenth century and had found its most brilliant embodiment in the history of his own family. Adams's great-grandfather, John, had been a founding father of the republic and second President of the United States; his grandfather, John Quincy, had also been a President of the United States; his father, Charles Francis, had served in the crucial post of United States Ambassador to England during the Civil War; and other relatives had occupied prominent places in the government of their country. Henry Adams thus grew up in a milieu where public office, public power, and public influence were taken for granted. If one can speak of an American aristocracy or patriciate resting upon wealth and cultivation, patriotism and intelligence, then the Adams family stood at its very center.

Yet together with this tradition the family shared in the experience of another, one that began with the defeat of grandfather John Quincy Adams by Andrew Jackson in 1828. This second tradition, still a minor one, was that of responding to the growing democratization and urbanization of American society by an act of withdrawal, sometimes hard to distinguish from Brahmin snobbishness but always founded in the Adams's sense of moral principle. With the years, it would prove to be the special fate of Henry Adams that he would be the most extreme representative of this impulse to withdraw.

As a boy Henry Adams had been reared in the most simulating and cultivated of circumstances. A brilliant student at Harvard, already displaying his formidable powers for assimilating quantities of knowledge, he began, after his graduation in 1858, a career as both world traveler and world scholar, continuing his researches in Germany, Switzerland, France, and Italy. He also began to write regularly for leading American periodicals, though in a letter to his brother Charles he growled in a style that anticipates his later attitudes: "I will not go down into the rough-and-tumble, nor mix with the crowd, nor write anonymously. . . . You like the strife of the world. I detest and despise it. . . . You like roughness and strength; I like taste and dexterity."

After a number of his muckraking pieces made advancement under the Grant administration seem unlikely, Adams abandoned journalism and became a professor of history at Harvard. He was, by all ac-

counts, a superb teacher, employing a version of the Socratic method in his lectures and training his students to use original documents in his seminars. Meanwhile, in 1872, he had married Marian Hooper, an attractive and intelligent woman, and when the Adams's moved to Washington in 1877, their house became a center of social and intellectual life.

It is roughly at this point that his major achievements as historian and writer begin. There were two novels, Democracy *(1880), a biting if somewhat thin depiction of jungle politics in Washington, and* Esther *(1884), a sensitive if also thin depiction of intellectual and private life among cultivated Americans. In 1879 Adams had published a distinguished biography of Albert Gallatin, Jefferson's Secretary of the Treasury, whom Adams saw as a prototype of the selfless and high-minded public servant undone by the degradation of democratic society. And in 1882 he issued a life of John Randolph, whom Adams saw as the prototype of the selfless and high-minded public servant undone by weaknesses of character. Adams grew increasingly dubious about the democratic experiment which his own family had done so much to promote: he wrote a friend in 1885 that he was "struck by the remarkable way in which politics deteriorates the moral tone of everyone who mixes in them."*

Adams's greatest historical work, a masterpiece of its kind, is the History of the United States of America during the Administrations of Jefferson and Madison *(1889 to 1891), which brought him fame and approval. It is a work in which his emotions are deeply committed, since it deals with a period of our national history he most admired and felt not yet fatally corrupted; it is a work, as well, in which he develops on a full scale his talents for narrative excitement and character portraiture, without, however, imposing those insistently pessimistic theories that would later shape—and as some critics believe, misshape—his views of history.*

Despite these enormous achievements and the acclaim they brought him, Adams felt, or kept publicly saying that he felt, more and more a stranger in his native land. He denied himself the pleasures of success, he withdrew from the applause of all but a tiny circle of cultivated friends. In 1885 his wife took her life, and this catastrophe shattered him emotionally, persuading him that he was a failure not only publicly but privately. Adams became a wanderer across the continents, a man of great intellectual power and personal force but without social or national roots. Traveling in Europe, he found himself increasingly drawn to the medieval period, in which he saw a harmony and comeliness of life, above all a unity of values and belief, that was sadly absent from all subsequent centuries. In 1904 he published Mont-Saint-Michel and Chartres, *an historical tour de force in which he painted a glowing picture of the way medieval man, through his worship of the Virgin Mary, achieved a moral and psychic integration containing "the highest idea of himself as a unit in a unified universe." Since that high point of civilization, roughly in the eleventh century, the life of Western man had crumbled—Adams thought—into chaos, uncertainty, disbelief, and multiplicity: man no longer knew who he was, why he lived, nor what impulsions led him to act. The great myth of the Virgin had been replaced by the lifeless energy of the Dynamo.*

With this sense of a catastrophic relativization of values, Adams was to live for the rest of his life. The actuality of his experience, as a spry and greatly honored intellectual figure, was not nearly so grim as he would make it out; there was in Adams a tendency to self-dramatization that cannot always be distinguished from self-pity. But that he agonized over his predicament is not to be denied, even if seen as the predicament of a cultural persona at least as much as that of an actual person: this son of the Boston great who felt repelled by American public life, this intellectual who grew increasingly alienated from the course of history, this amateur philosopher who could find no moral purpose or meaning in the universe and now concluded that there was a steady running-down of energies in human affairs that soon would lead to an atomic apocalypse.

In 1907 Adams privately printed his autobiography, The Education of Henry Adams, in its way as remarkable a book as his History. The Education, which was not made available to the general public until his death in 1918, is a classical record of the self-torment—but also, it should be noticed, the self-mockery—of a romantic sensibility. Writing about himself in the third person, Adams tries to see himself not only as a cultural prototype but also as a slightly preposterous fellow: the mixture of self-importance and self-deprecation is fluid, changing from section to section, and not always easy to measure precisely.

The earliest and best parts of the Education deal with Adams's childhood in Quincy, Massachusetts, and these pages offer an incomparable evocation of life in early republican America, at least that life as it was experienced by the New England patriciate. Adams's years as secretary to his father when the latter was Ambassador to England during the Civil War are treated caustically. And the sections on the Grant administration and the Chicago Exposition, each crucial to the transformation of American civilization that Adams meant indirectly to portray in his autobiography, are fine examples of Adams's abilities as social satirist and historical analyst. Throughout the Education there are passages of reflection, sometimes introspection, in which Adams assays his own role as representative intellectual, a figure of failure and futility, unable to affect the course of events. Perhaps the dominant social motif in the book is

Adams's profound disillusionment with the United States in the years after the Civil War. The hopes that had once been held for a Jeffersonian democracy, preindustrial and without extreme differences in wealth and power, now lay shattered; and instead, as Adams saw it, the country had entered a degeneration symbolized by such names as Gould and Fisk, Vanderbilt and Rockefeller.

Like many intellectuals to come after him, Adams also felt himself homeless on a larger, more "cosmic," scale. In a world deprived of God and the unifying dignities of religion, a world that science could measure and to some extent control but not make any the more intelligible or bearable, Adams wondered where men would now find the values by which to live—indeed, whether they would now care to look for them. Everything seemed to have crumbled into multiplicity and relativism; there were no objective criteria for judgment. Society was headed for an ice age of materialism, or a crackup of warfare. All that remained for men of conscience and perception was to keep a clear vision, to insist upon standards of excellence, to defend the lonely bulwarks of truth. It was a posture at once heroic and peevish, and for many younger writers soured by the betrayals of the First World War Adams naturally came to seem a culture hero, a model of clear-sightedness in a false world.

Whatever one may feel about Adams's final views, there can hardly be any doubt that in the Education he composed a book of the first order. Gripping in its account of intellectual drama, rich with portraits of notable times and men, enormously complex in its circling of the narrator's self, the book is one of the major texts in the history of modern intellectual life.

FURTHER READING

Ernest Samuels's The Young Henry Adams (1948) and his Henry Adams: The Middle Years (1958) compose the first two volumes of a three-volume standard biography; the last volume is in progress. Four volumes of Adams's letters have been edited by Worthington C. Ford (1920, 1930, 1938). J. C. Levenson's The Mind and Art of Henry Adams (1957) is a good critical study.

FROM **History of the United States of America during the Administration of Thomas Jefferson** *(1889 to 1891)*[1]

Volume 1, Chapter 6   American Ideals

Nearly every foreign traveller who visited the United States during these early years, carried away an impression sober if not sad. A thousand miles of desolate and dreary forest, broken here and there by settlements; along the sea-coast a few flourishing towns devoted to commerce; no arts, a provincial literature, a cancerous disease of negro slavery, and differences of political theory fortified within geographical lines—what could be hoped for such a country except to repeat the story of violence and brutality which the world already knew by heart, until repetition for thousands of years had wearied and sickened mankind? Ages must probably pass before the interior could be thoroughly settled; even Jefferson, usually a sanguine man, talked of a thousand years with acquiescence, and in his first Inaugural Address, at a time when the Mississippi River formed the Western boundary, spoke of the country as having "room enough for our descendants to the hundredth and thousandth generation." No prudent person dared to act on the certainty that when settled, one government could comprehend the whole; and when the day of separation should arrive, and America should have her Prussia, Austria, and Italy, as she already had her England, France, and Spain, what else could follow but a return to the old conditions of local jealousies, wars, and corruption which had made a slaughter-house of Europe?

The mass of Americans were sanguine and self-confident, partly by temperament, but partly also by reason of ignorance; for they knew little of the difficulties which surrounded a complex society. The Duc de Liancourt,[2] like many critics, was struck by this trait. Among other instances, he met with one in the person of a Pennsylvania miller, Thomas Lea, "a sound American patriot, persuading himself that nothing good is done, and that no one has any brains, except in America; that the wit, the imagination, the genius of Europe are already in decrepitude"; and the duke added: "This error is to be found in almost all Americans,—legislators, administrators, as well as millers, and is less innocent there." In the year 1796 the House of Representatives debated

---

1 Adams's nine-volume work was published in the years between 1889 and 1891. In his great work Adams was one of the first American historians to attempt an historical work along "scientific" principles, though this chapter is actually an example of Adams's powers as a literary artist.

2 Francois Alexandre Frédéric de la Rochefoucauld-Liancourt (1747–1827), a French royalist who, after the abolition of the monarch in 1792, spent some time in the United States.

whether to insert in the Reply to the President's Speech a passing remark that the nation was "the freest and most enlightened in the
world,"—a nation as yet in swaddling-clothes, which had neither literature, arts, sciences, nor history; nor even enough nationality to be sure
that it was a nation. The moment was peculiarly ill-chosen for such a
claim, because Europe was on the verge of an outburst of genius. Goethe
and Schiller, Mozart and Haydn, Kant and Fichte, Cavendish and
Herschel were making way for Walter Scott, Wordsworth, and Shelley,
Heine and Balzac, Beethoven and Hegel, Oersted and Cuvier, great
physicists, biologists, geologists, chemists, mathematicians, meta-
physicians, and historians by the score. Turner was painting his earliest
landscapes, and Watt completing his latest steam-engine; Napoleon was
taking command of the French armies, and Nelson of the English fleets;
investigators, reformers, scholars, and philosophers swarmed, and the
influence of enlightenment, even amid universal war, was working with
an energy such as the world had never before conceived. The idea that
Europe was in her decrepitude proved only ignorance and want of
enlightenment, if not of freedom, on the part of Americans, who could
only excuse their error by pleading that notwithstanding these objections, in matters which for the moment most concerned themselves
Europe was a full century behind America. If they were right in thinking that the next necessity of human progress was to lift the average
man upon an intellectual and social level with the most favored, they
stood at least three generations nearer than Europe to their common
goal. The destinies of the United States were certainly staked, without
reserve or escape, on the soundness of this doubtful and even improbable principle, ignoring or overthrowing the institutions of church,
aristocracy, family, army, and political intervention, which long experience had shown to be needed for the safety of society. Europe might be
right in thinking that without such safeguards society must come to an
end; but even Europeans must concede that there was a chance, if no
greater than one in a thousand, that America might, at least for a time,
succeed. If this stake of temporal and eternal welfare stood on the
winning card; if man actually should become more virtuous and enlightened, by mere process of growth, without church or paternal authority;
if the average human being could accustom himself to reason with the
logical processes of Descartes and Newton!—what then?

Then, no one could deny that the United States would win a stake
such as defied mathematics. With all the advantages of science and
capital, Europe must be slower than America to reach the common goal.
American society might be both sober and sad, but except for negro
slavery it was sound and healthy in every part, Stripped for the hardest
work, every muscle firm and elastic, every ounce of brain ready for use,
and not a trace of superfluous flesh on his nervous and supple body, the
American stood in the world a new order of man. From Maine to Florida,
society was in this respect the same, and was so organized as to use its
human forces with more economy than could be approached by any

society of the world elsewhere. Not only were artificial barriers carefully removed, but every influence that could appeal to ordinary ambition was applied. No brain or appetite active enough to be conscious of stimulants could fail to answer the intense incentive. Few human beings, however sluggish, could long resist the temptation to acquire power; and the elements of power were to be had in America almost for the asking. Reversing the old-world system, the American stimulant increased in energy as it reached the lowest and most ignorant class, dragging and whirling them upward as in the blast of a furnace. The penniless and homeless Scotch or Irish immigrant was caught and consumed by it; for every stroke of the axe and the hoe made him a capitalist, and made gentlemen of his children. Wealth was the strongest agent for moving the mass of mankind; but political power was hardly less tempting to the more intelligent and better-educated swarms of American-born citizens, and the instinct of activity, once created, seemed heritable and permanent in the race.

Compared with this lithe young figure, Europe was actually in decrepitude. Mere class distinctions, the *patois* or dialect of the peasantry, the fixity of residence, the local costumes and habits marking a history that lost itself in the renewal of identical generations, raised from birth barriers which paralyzed half the population. Upon this mass of inert matter rested the Church and the State, holding down activity of thought. Endless wars withdrew many hundred thousand men from production, and changed them into agents of waste; huge debts, the evidence of past wars and bad government, created interests to support the system and fix its burdens on the laboring class; courts, with habits of extravagance that shamed common-sense, helped to consume private economics. All this might have been borne; but behind this stood aristocracies, sucking their nourishment from industry, producing nothing themselves, employing little or no active capital or intelligent labor, but pressing on the energies and ambition of society with the weight of an incubus. Picturesque and entertaining as these social anomalies were, they were better fitted for the theatre or for a museum of historical costumes than for an active workshop preparing to compete with such machinery as America would soon command. From an economical point of view, they were as incongruous as would have been the appearance of a mediæval knight in helmet and armor, with battle-axe and shield, to run the machinery of Arkwright's cotton-mill; but besides their bad economy they also tended to prevent the rest of society from gaining a knowledge of its own capacities. In Europe, the conservative habit of mind was fortified behind power. During nearly a century Voltaire himself—the friend of kings, the wit and poet, historian and philosopher of his age—had carried on, in daily terror, in exile and excommunication, a protest against an intellectual despotism contemptible even to its own supporters. Hardly was Voltaire dead, when Priestley,[3] as great a

---

[3] Joseph Priestley (1733–1804), English scientist.

man if not so great a wit, trying to do for England what Voltaire tried to do for France, was mobbed by the people of Birmingham and driven to America. Where Voltaire and Priestley failed, common men could not struggle; the weight of society stifled their thought. In America the balance between conservative and liberal forces was close; but in Europe conservatism held the physical power of government. In Boston a young Buckminster[4] might be checked for a time by his father's prayers or commands in entering the path that led toward freer thought; but youth beckoned him on, and every reward that society could offer was dangled before his eyes. In London or Paris, Rome, Madrid, or Vienna, he must have sacrificed the worldly prospects of his life.

Granting that the American people were about to risk their future on a new experiment, they naturally wished to throw aside all burdens of which they could rid themselves. Believing that in the long run interest, not violence, would rule the world, and that the United States must depend for safety and success on the interests they could create, they were tempted to look upon war and preparations for war as the worst of blunders; for they were sure that every dollar capitalized in industry was a means of overthrowing their enemies more effective than a thousand dollars spent on frigates or standing armies. The success of the American system was, from this point of view, a question of economy. If they could relieve themselves from debts, taxes, armies, and government interference with industry, they must succeed in outstripping Europe in economy of production; and Americans were even then partly aware that if their machine were not so weakened by these economics as to break down in the working, it must of necessity break down every rival. If their theory was sound, when the day of competition should arrive, Europe might choose between American and Chinese institutions, but there would be no middle path; she might become a confederated democracy, or a wreck.

Whether these ideas were sound or weak, they seemed self-evident to those Northern democrats who, like Albert Gallatin, were comparatively free from slave-owning theories, and understood the practical forces of society. If Gallatin wished to reduce the interference of government to a minimum, and cut down expenditures to nothing, he aimed not so much at saving money as at using it with the most certain effect. The revolution of 1800 was in his eyes chiefly political, because it was social; but as a revolution of society, he and his friends hoped to make it the most radical that had occurred since the downfall of the Roman empire. Their ideas were not yet cleared by experience, and were confused by many contradictory prejudices, but wanted neither breadth nor shrewdness.

Many apparent inconsistencies grew from this undeveloped form of American thought, and gave rise to great confusion in the different

---

[4] Joseph Buckminster (1784–1812), a prominent liberal Unitarian clergyman in New England.

estimates of American character that were made both at home and abroad.

That Americans should not be liked was natural; but that they should not be understood was more significant by far. After the downfall of the French republic they had no right to expect a kind word from Europe, and during the next twenty years they rarely received one. The liberal movement of Europe was cowed, and no one dared express democratic sympathies until the Napoleonic tempest had passed. With this attitude Americans had no right to find fault, for Europe cared less to injure them than to protect herself. Nevertheless, observant readers could not but feel surprised that none of the numerous Europeans who then wrote or spoke about America seemed to study the subject seriously. The ordinary traveller was apt to be little more reflective than a bee or an ant, but some of these critics possessed powers far from ordinary; yet Talleyrand alone showed that had he but seen America a few years later than he did, he might have suggested some sufficient reason for apparent contradictions that perplexed him in the national character. The other travellers—great and small, from the Duc de Liancourt to Basil Hall,[5] a long and suggestive list—were equally perplexed. They agreed in observing the contradictions, but all, including Talleyrand, saw only sordid motives. Talleyrand expressed extreme astonishment at the apathy of Americans in the face of religious sectarians; but he explained it by assuming that the American ardor of the moment was absorbed in money-making. The explanation was evidently insufficient, for the Americans were capable of feeling and showing excitement, even to their great pecuniary injury, as they frequently proved; but in the foreigner's range of observation, love of money was the most conspicuous and most common trait of American character. "There is, perhaps, no civilized country in the world," wrote Félix de Beaujour,[6] soon after 1800, "where there is less generosity in the souls, and in the heads fewer of those illusions which make the charm or the consolation of life. Man here weighs everything, calculates everything, and sacrifices everything to his interest." An Englishman named Fearon,[7] in 1818, expressed the same idea with more distinctness: "In going to America, I would say generally, the emigrant must expect to find, not an economical or cleanly people; not a social or generous people; not a people of enlarged ideas; not a people of liberal opinions, or toward whom you can express your thoughts free as air; not a people friendly to the advocates of liberty in Europe; not a people who understand liberty from investigation and principle; not a people who comprehend the meaning of the words 'honor' and 'generosity.'" Such quotations might be multiplied almost without limit. Rapacity was the accepted explanation of American

---

[5] Basil Hall (1788–1844), British travel writer.

[6] Félix de Beaujour (1765–1836), French consul general to the United States in 1804, who wrote *Sketch of the United States* (1814).

[7] Henry Fearon (1770–1825), author of *Sketches of America* (1818).

peculiarities; yet every traveller was troubled by inconsistencies that required explanations of a different kind. "It is not in order to hoard that the Americans are rapacious," observed Liancourt as early as 1796. The extravagance, or what economical Europeans thought extravagance, with which American women were allowed and encouraged to spend money, was as notorious in 1790 as a century later; the recklessness with which Americans often risked their money, and the liberality with which they used it, were marked even then, in comparison with the ordinary European habit. Europeans saw such contradictions, but made no attempt to reconcile them. No foreigner of that day—neither poet, painter, nor philosopher—could detect in American life anything higher than vulgarity; for it was something beyond the range of their experience, which education and culture had not framed a formula to express. Moore[8] came to Washington, and found there no loftier inspiration than any Federalist rhymester of Dennie's[9] school.

Take Christians, Mohawks, democrats and all,
From the rude wigwam to the Congress hall,—
From man the savage, whether slaved or free,
To man the civilized, less tame than he:
'T is one dull chaos, one unfertile strife
Betwixt half-polished and half-barbarous life;
Where every ill the ancient world can brew
Is mixed with every grossness of the new;
Where all corrupts, though little can entice,
And nothing's known of luxury but vice.

Moore's two small volumes of Epistles, printed in 1807, contained much more so-called poetry of the same tone,— poetry more polished and less respectable than that of Barlow and Dwight[10]; while, as though to prove that the Old World knew what grossness was, he embalmed in his lines the slanders which the Scotch libeller Callender invented against Jefferson: —

The weary statesman for repose hath fled
From halls of council to his negro's shed;
Where, blest, he woos some black Aspasia's grace,
And dreams of freedom in his slave's embrace.

To leave no doubt of his meaning, he explained in a footnote that his allusion was to the President of the United States; and yet even Moore, trifler and butterfly as he was, must have seen, if he would, that between

[8] Thomas Moore (1779–1852), Irish poet.
[9] Joseph Dennie (1768–1812), American writer of Federalist sympathies.
[10] Joel Barlow (1754–1812) and Timothy Dwight (1752–1817), American poets and public men, leaders of the literary group known as "the Connecticut wits."

the morals of politics and society in America and those then prevailing in Europe, there was no room for comparison,—there was room only for contrast.

Moore was but an echo of fashionable England in his day. He seldom affected moral sublimity; and had he in his wanderings met a race of embodied angels, he would have sung of them or to them in the slightly erotic notes which were so well received in the society he loved to frequent and flatter. His remarks upon American character betrayed more temper than truth; but even in this respect he expressed only the common feelings of Europeans, which was echoed by the Federalist society of the United States. Englishmen especially indulged in unbounded invective against the sordid character of American society, and in shaping their national policy on this contempt they carried their theory into practice with so much energy as to produce its own refutation. To their astonishment and anger, a day came when the Americans, in defiance of self-interest and in contradiction of all the qualities ascribed to them, insisted on declaring war; and readers of this narrative will be surprised at the cry of incredulity, not unmixed with terror, with which Englishmen started to their feet when they woke from their delusion on seeing what they had been taught to call the meteor flag of England, which had burned terrific at Copenhagen and Trafalgar, suddenly waver and fall on the bloody deck of the "Guerriere." Fearon and Beaujour, with a score of other contemporary critics, could see neither generosity, economy, honor, nor ideas of any kind in the American breast; yet the obstinate repetition of these denials itself betrayed a lurking fear of the social forces whose strength they were candid enough to record. What was it that, as they complained, turned the European peasant into a new man within half an hour after landing at New York? Englishmen were never at a loss to understand the poetry of more prosaic emotions. Neither they nor any of their kindred failed in later times to feel the "large excitement" of the country boy, whose "spirit leaped within him to be gone before him," when the lights of London first flared in the distance; yet none seemed ever to feel the larger excitement of the American immigrant. Among the Englishmen who criticized the United States was one greater than Moore,—one who thought himself at home only in the stern beauty of a moral presence. Of all poets, living or dead, Wordsworth felt most keenly what he called the still, sad music of humanity; yet the highest conception he could create of America was not more poetical than that of any Cumberland beggar he might have met in his morning walk: —

Long-wished-for sight, the Western World appeared;
And when the ship was moored, I leaped ashore
Indignantly,—resolved to be a man,
Who, having o'er the past no power, would live
No longer in subjection to the past,

With abject mind—from a tyrannic lord
Inviting penance, fruitlessly endured.
So, like a fugitive whose feet have cleared
Some boundary which his followers may not cross
In prosecution of their deadly chase,
Respiring, I looked round. How bright the sun,
The breeze how soft! Can anything produced
In the Old World compare, thought I, for power
And majesty, with this tremendous stream
Sprung from the desert? And behold a city
Fresh, youthful, and aspiring! . . .
                              Sooth to say,
On nearer view, a motley spectacle
Appeared, of high pretensions—unreproved
But by the obstreperous voice of higher still;
Big passions strutting on a petty stage,
Which a detached spectator may regard
Not unamused. But ridicule demands
Quick change of objects; and to laugh alone,
. . . in the very centre of the crowd
To keep the secret a poignant scorn,
                              . . . is least fit
For the gross spirit of mankind.[11]

Thus Wordsworth, although then at his prime, indulging in what sounded like a boast that he alone had felt the sense sublime of something interfused, whose dwelling is the light of setting suns, and the round ocean, and the living air, and the blue sky, and in the mind of man,— even he, whose moods the heavy and the weary weight of all this unintelligible world was lightened by his deeper sympathies with nature and the soul, could do no better, when he stood in the face of American democracy, than "keep the secret of a poignant scorn."

Possibly the view of Wordsworth and Moore, of Weld, Dennie, and Dickens was right. The American democrat possessed little art of expression, and did not watch his own emotions with a view of uttering them either in prose or verse; he never told more of himself than the world might have assumed without listening to him. Only with diffidence could history attribute to such a class of men a wider range of thought or feeling than they themselves cared to proclaim. Yet the difficulty of denying or even ignoring the wider range was still greater, for no one questioned the force or the scope of an emotion which caused the poorest peasant in Europe to see what was invisible to poet and philosopher,—the dim outline of a mountain-summit across the ocean, rising high above the mist and mud of American democracy. As though to call

[11] These lines come from William Wordsworth's *The Excursion*, III, 870.

attention to some such difficulty, European and American critics, while affirming that Americans were a race without illusions or enlarged ideas, declared in the same breath that Jefferson was a visionary whose theories would cause the heavens to fall upon them. Year after year, with endless iteration, in every accent of contempt, rage, and despair, they repeated this charge against Jefferson. Every foreigner and Federalist agreed that he was a man of illusions, dangerous to society and unbounded in power of evil; but if this view of his character was right, the same visionary qualities seemed also to be a national trait, for every one admitted that Jefferson's opinions, in one form or another, were shared by a majority of the American people.

Illustrations might be carried much further, and might be drawn from every social class and from every period in national history. Of all presidents, Abraham Lincoln has been considered the most typical representative of American society, chiefly because his mind, with all its practical qualities, also inclined, in certain directions, to idealism. Lincoln was born in 1809, the moment when American character stood in lowest esteem. Ralph Waldo Emerson, a more distinct idealist, was born in 1803. William Ellery Channing, another idealist, was born in 1780. Men like John Fitch, Oliver Evans, Robert Fulton, Joel Barlow, John Stevens, and Eli Whitney were all classed among visionaries. The whole society of Quakers belonged in the same category. The records of the popular religious sects abounded in examples of idealism and illusion to such an extent that the masses seemed hardly to find comfort or hope in any authority, however old or well established. In religion as in politics, Americans seemed to require a system which gave play to their imagination and their hopes.

Some misunderstanding must always take place when the observer is at cross-purposes with the society he describes. Wordsworth might have convinced himself by a moment's thought that no country could act on the imagination as America acted upon the instincts of the ignorant and poor, without some quality that deserved better treatment than poignant scorn; but perhaps this was only one among innumerable cases in which the unconscious poet breathed an atmosphere which the self-conscious poet could not penetrate. With equal reason he might have taken the opposite view,—that the hard, practical, money-getting American democrat, who had neither generosity nor honor nor imagination, and who inhabited cold shades where fancy sickened and where genius died, was in truth living in a world of dream, and acting a drama more instinct with poetry than all the avatars of the East, walking in gardens of emerald and rubies, in ambition already ruling the world and guiding Nature with a kinder and wiser hand than had ever yet been felt in human history. From this point his critics never approached him,—they stopped at a stone's throw; and at the moment when they declared that the man's mind had no illusions, they added that he was a knave or a lunatic. Even on his practical and sordid side, the American might easily have been represented as a victim to illusion. If the Englishman had lived as the American speculator did,—in the future,—the hyperbole of enthusiasm would have seemed less monstrous. "Look at my wealth!" cried the American to his foreign visitor. "See these solid mountains of salt and iron, of lead, copper, silver, and gold! See these magnificent cities scattered broadcast to the Pacific! See my cornfields rustling and waving in the summer breeze from ocean to ocean, so far that the sun itself is not high enough to mark where the distant mountains bound by golden seas! Look at this continent of mine, fairest of created worlds, as she lies turning up to the sun's never-failing caress her broad and exuberant breasts, overflowing with milk for her hundred million children! See how she glows with youth, health, and love!" Perhaps it was not altogether unnatural that the foreigner, on being asked to see what needed centuries to produce, should have looked about him with bewilderment and indignation. "Gold! cities! cornfields! continents! Nothing of the sort! I see nothing but tremendous wastes, where sickly men and women are dying of home-sickness or are scalped by savages! mountain-ranges a thousand miles long, with no means of getting to them, and nothing in them when you get there! swamps and forests choked with their own rotten ruins! nor hope of better for a thousand years! Your story as a fraud, and you are a liar and swindler!"

Met in this spirit, the American, half perplexed and half defiant, retaliated by calling his antagonist a fool, and by mimicking his heavy tricks of manner. For himself he cared little, but his dream was his whole existence. The men who denounced him admitted that they left him in his forest-swamp quaking with fever, but clinging in the delirium of death to the illusions of his dazzled brain. No class of men could be required to support their convictions with a steadier faith, or pay more devotedly with their persons for the mistakes of their judgment. Whether imagination or greed led them to describe more than actually existed, they still saw no more than any inventor or discoverer must have seen in order to give him the energy of success. They said to the rich as to the poor, "Come and share our limitless riches! Come and help us bring to light these unimaginable stores of wealth and power!" The poor came, and from them were seldom heard complaints of deception or delusion. Within a moment, by the mere contact of a moral atmosphere, they saw the gold and jewels, the summer cornfields and the glowing continent. The rich for a long time stood aloof,—they were timid and narrow-minded; but this was not all,—between them and the American democrat was a gulf.

The charge that Americans were too fond of money to win the confidence of Europeans was a curious inconsistency; yet this was a common belief. If the American deluded himself and led others to their death by baseless speculations; if he buried those he loved in a gloomy forest where they quaked and died while he persisted in seeing there a splendid, healthy, and well-built city,—no one could deny that he sacrificed wife and child to his greed for gain, that the dollar was his god, and a sordid avarice his demon. Yet had this been the whole truth, no European capitalist would have hesitated to make money out of his grave; for, avarice against avarice, no more sordid or meaner type existed in America than could be shown on every 'Change in Europe. With much more reason Americans might have suspected that in America Englishmen found everywhere a silent influence, which they found nowhere in Europe, and which had nothing to do with avarice or with the dollar, but, on the contrary, seemed likely at any moment to sacrifice the dollar in a cause and for an object so illusory that most Englishmen could not endure to hear it discussed. European travellers who passed through America noticed that everywhere, in the White House at Washington and in log-cabins beyond the Alleghanies, except for a few Federalists, every American, from Jefferson and Gallatin down to the poorest squatter, seemed to nourish an idea that he was doing what he could to overthrow the tyranny which the past had fastened on the human mind. Nothing was easier than to laugh at the ludicrous expressions of this simple-minded conviction, or to cry out against its coarseness, or grow angry with its prejudices; to see its nobler side, to feel the beatings of a heart underneath the sordid surface of a gross humanity, was not so easy. Europeans seemed seldom or never conscious that the sentiment could possess a noble side, but found only matter for complaint in the remark that every American democrat believed himself to be working for the overthrow of tyranny, aristocracy, hereditary privilege, and priesthood, wherever they existed. Even where the American did not openly proclaim this conviction in words, he carried so dense an atmosphere of the sentiment with him in his daily life as to give respectable Europeans an uneasy sense of remoteness.

Of all historical problems, the nature of a national character is the most difficult and the most important. Readers will be troubled, at almost every chapter of the coming narrative, by the want of some formula to explain what share the popular imagination bore in the system pursued by government. The acts of the American people during the administrations of Jefferson and Madison were judged at the time by no other test. According as bystanders believed American character to be hard, sordid, and free from illusion, they were severe and even harsh in judgment. This rule guided the governments of England and France. Federalists in the United States, knowing more of the circumstances, often attributed to the democratic instinct a visionary quality which they regarded as sentimentality, and charged with many bad consequences. If their view was correct, history could occupy itself to no better purpose than in ascertaining the nature and force of the quality which was charged with results so serious; but nothing was more elusive than the spirit of American democracy. Jefferson, the literary representative of the class, spoke chiefly for Virginians, and dreaded so greatly his own reputation as a visionary that he seldom or never uttered his whole thought. Gallatin and Madison were still more cautious. The press in no country could give shape to a mental condition so shadowy. The people themselves, although millions in number, could not have expressed their finer instincts had they tried, and might not have recognized them if expressed by others.

In the early days of colonization, every new settlement represented an idea and proclaimed a mission. Virginia was founded by a great, liberal movement aiming at the spread of English liberty and empire. The Pilgrims of Plymouth, the Puritans of Boston, the Quakers of Pennsylvania, all avowed a moral purpose, and began by making institutions that consciously reflected a moral idea. No such character belonged to the colonization of 1800. From Lake Erie to Florida, in long, unbroken line, pioneers were at work, cutting into the forests with the energy of so many beavers, and with no more express moral purpose than the beavers they drove away. The civilization they carried with them was rarely illumined by an idea; they sought room for no new truth, and aimed neither at creating, like the Puritans, a government of saints, nor, like the Quakers, one of love and peace; they left such experiments behind them, and wrestled only with the hardest problems of frontier life. No wonder that foreign observers, and even the educated, well-to-do Americans of the sea-coast, could seldom see anything to admire in the ignorance and brutality of frontiersmen, and should declare that virtue and wisdom no longer guided the United States! What they saw was not encouraging. To a new society, ignorant and semi-barbarous, a mass of demagogues insisted on applying every stimulant that could inflame its worst appetites, while at the same instant taking away every influence that had hitherto helped to restrain its passions. Greed for wealth, lust for power, yearning for the blank void of savage freedom such as Indians and wolves delighted in,—these were the fires that flamed under the caldron of American society, in which, as conservatives believed, the old, well-proven, conservative crust of religion, government, family, and even common respect for age, education, and experience was rapidly melting away, and was indeed already broken into fragments, swept about by the seething mass of scum ever rising in greater quantities to the surface.

Against this Federalist and conservative view of democratic tendencies, democrats protested in a thousand forms, but never in any mode of expression which satisfied them all, or explained their whole character. Probably Jefferson came nearest to the mark, for he represented the hopes of science as well as the prejudices of Virginia; but Jefferson's writings may be searched from beginning to end without revealing the whole measure of the man, far less of the movement. Here and there in his letters a suggestion was thrown out, as though by chance, revealing larger hopes,—as in 1815, at a moment of despondency, he wrote: "I fear from the experience of the last twenty-five years that morals do not of necessity advance hand in hand with the sciences." In 1800, in the flush of triumph, he believed that his task in the world was to establish a democratic republic, with the sciences for an intellectual field, and physical and moral advancement keeping pace with their advance. Without an excessive introduction of more recent ideas, he might be imagined to define democratic progress, in the somewhat affected precision of his French philosophy: "Progress is either physical or intellectual. If we can bring it about that men are on the average an inch taller in the next generation than in this; if they are an inch larger round the chest; if their brain is an ounce or two heavier, and their life a year or two longer,—that is progress. If fifty years hence the average man shall invariably argue from two ascertained premises where he now jumps to a conclusion from a single supposed revelation,—that is progress! I expect it to be made here, under our democratic stimulants, on a great scale, until every man is potentially an athlete in body and an Aristotle in mind." To this doctrine the New Englander [John Adams] replied, "What will you do for moral progress?" Every possible answer to this question opened a chasm. No doubt Jefferson held the faith that men would improve morally with their physical and intellectual growth; but he had no idea of any moral improvement other than that which came by nature. He could not tolerate a priesthood, a state church, or revealed religion. Conservatives, who could tolerate no society without such pillars of order, were, from their point of view, right in answering, "Give us rather the worst despotism of Europe,—there our souls at least may have a chance of salvation!" To their minds vice and virtue were not relative, but fixed terms. The Church was a divine institution. How could a ship hope to reach port when the crew threw overboard sails, spars, and compass, unshipped their rudder, and all the long day thought only of eating and drinking. Nay, even should the new experiment succeed in a wordly sense, what was a man profited if he gained the whole world, and lost his own soul? The Lord God was a jealous God, and visited the sins of the parents upon the children; but what worse sin could be conceived than for a whole nation to join their chief in chanting the strange hymn with which Jefferson, a new false prophet, was deceiving and betraying his people: "It does me no injury for my neighbor to say there are twenty Gods or no God!"

On this ground conservatism took its stand, as it had hitherto done with success in every similar emergency in the world's history, and fixing its eyes on moral standards of its own, refused to deal with the subject as further open to argument. The two parties stood facing opposite ways, and could see no common ground of contact.

Yet even then one part of the American social system was proving itself to be rich in results. The average American was more intelligent than the average European, and was becoming every year still more active-minded as the new movement of society caught him up and swept him through a life of more varied experiences. On all sides the national mind responded to its stimulants. Deficient as the American was in the machinery of higher instruction; remote, poor; unable by any exertion to acquire the training, the capital, or even the elementary textbooks he needed for a fair development of his natural powers,—his native energy and ambition already responded to the spur applied to them. Some of his triumphs were famous throughout the world; for Benjamin Franklin had raised high the reputation of American printers, and the actual President of the United States, who signed with Franklin the treaty of peace with Great Britain, was the son of a small farmer, and had himself kept a school in his youth. In both these cases social recognition followed success; but the later triumphs of the American mind were becoming more and more popular. John Fitch was not only one of the poorest, but one of the least-educated Yankees who ever made a name; he could never spell with tolerable correctness, and his life ended as it began,—in the lowest social obscurity. Eli Whitney was better educated than Fitch, but had neither wealth, social influence, nor patron to back his ingenuity. In the year 1800 Eli Terry, another Connecticut Yankee of the same class, took into his employ two young men to help him make wooden clocks, and this was the capital on which the greatest clock-manufactory in the world began its operations. In 1797 Asa Whittemore, a Massachusetts Yankee, invented a machine to make cards for carding wool, which "operated as if it had a soul," and became the foundation for a hundred subsequent patents. In 1790 Jacob Perkins, of Newbury-port, invented a machine capable of cutting and turning out two hundred thousand nails a day; and then invented a process for transferring engraving from a very small steel cylinder to copper, which revolutionized cotton-printing. The British traveller Weld, passing through Wilmington, stopped, as Liancourt had done before him, to see the great flour-mills on the Brandywine. "The improvements," he said, "which have been made in the machinery of the flour-mills in America are very great. The chief of these consist in a new application of the screw, and the introduction of what are called elevators, the idea of which was evidently borrowed from the chain-pump." This was the invention of Oliver Evans, a native of Delaware, whose parents were in very humble life, but who was himself, in spite of every disadvantage, an inventive genius of the first order. Robert Fulton, who in 1800 was in Paris with Joel Barlow, sprang from the same source in Pennsylvania. John Stevens, a native of New York, belonged to a more favored class, but followed the same impulses. All these men were the outcome of typical American society, and all their inventions transmuted the democratic instinct into a practical and tangible shape. Who would undertake to say that there was a limit to the fecundity of this teeming source? Who that saw only the narrow, practical, money-getting nature of these devices could venture to assert that as they wrought their end and raised the standard of millions, they would not also raise the creative power of those millions to a higher plane? If the priests and barons who set their names to Magna Charta had been told that in a few centuries every swine-herd and cobbler's apprentice would write and read with an ease such as few kings could then command, and reason with better logic than any university could then practise, the priest and baron would have been more incredulous than any man who was told in 1800 that within another five centuries the ploughboy would go a-field whistling a sonata of Beethoven, and figure out in quarternions the relation of his furrows. The American democrat knew so little of art that among his popular illusions he could not then nourish artistic ambition; but leaders like Jefferson, Gallatin, and Barlow might without extravagance count upon a coming time when diffused ease and education should bring the masses into familiar contact with higher forms of human achievement, and their vast creative power, turned toward a nobler culture, might rise to the level of that democratic genius which found expression in the Parthenon; might revel in the delights of a new Buonarotti and a richer Titan; might create for five hundred million people the America of thought and art which alone could satisfy their omnivorous ambition.

Whether the illusions, so often affirmed and so often denied to the American people, took such forms or not, there were in effect the problems that lay before American society: Could it transmute its social power into the higher forms of thought? Could it provide for the moral and intellectual needs of mankind? Could it take permanent political shape? Could it give new life to religion and art? Could it create and maintain in the mass of mankind those habits of mind which had hitherto belonged to men of science alone? Could it physically develop the convolutions of the human brain? Could it produce, or was it compatible with the differentiation of a higher variety of the human race? Nothing less than this was necessary for its complete success.

FROM **The Education of Henry Adams** (1907)

Chapter 1 *Quincy (1838–1848)*

Under the shadow of Boston State House, turning its back on the house of John Hancock, the little passage called Hancock Avenue runs, or ran, from Beacon Street, skirting the State House grounds, to Mount Vernon Street, on the summit of Beacon Hill; and there, in the third house below Mount Vernon Place, February 16, 1838, a child was born, and christened later by his uncle, the minister of the First Church after the tenets of Boston Unitarianism, as Henry Brooks Adams.

Had he been born in Jerusalem under the shadow of the Temple and circumcised in the Synagogue by his uncle the high priest, under the name of Israel Cohen, he would scarcely have been more distinctly branded, and not much more heavily handicapped in the races of the coming century, in running for such stakes as the century was to offer;

but, on the other hand, the ordinary traveller, who does not enter the field of racing, finds advantage in being, so to speak, ticketed through life, with the safeguards of an old, established traffic. Safeguards are often irksome, but sometimes convenient, and if one needs them at all, one is apt to need them badly. A hundred years earlier, such safeguards as his would have secured any young man's success; and although in 1838 their value was not very great compared with what they would have had in 1738, yet the mere accident of starting a twentieth-century career from a nest of associations so colonial—to troglodytic—as the First Church, the Boston State House, Beacon Hill, John Hancock and John Adams, Mount Vernon Street and Quincy, all crowding on ten pounds of unconscious babyhood, was so queer as to offer a subject of curious speculation to the baby long after he had witnessed the solution. What could become of such a child of the seventeenth and eighteenth centuries, when he should wake up to find himself required to play the game of the twentieth? Had he been consulted, would he have cared to play the game at all, holding such cards as he held, and suspecting that the game was to be one of which neither he nor any one else back to the beginning of time knew the rules or the risks or the stakes? He was not consulted and was not responsible, but had he been taken into the confidence of his parents, he would certainly have told them to change nothing as far as concerned him. He would have been astounded by his own luck. Probably no child, born in the year, held better cards than he. Whether life was an honest game of chance, or whether the cards were marked and forced, he could not refuse to play his excellent hand. He could never make the usual plea of irresponsibility. He accepted the situation as though he had been a party to it, and under the same circumstances would do it again, the more readily for knowing the exact values. To his life as a whole he was a consenting, contracting party and partner from the moment he was born to the moment he died. Only with that understanding—as a consciously assenting member in full partnership with the society of his age—had his education an interest to himself or to others.

As it happened, he never got to the point of playing the game at all; he lost himself in the study of it, watching the errors of the players; but this is the only interest in the story, which otherwise has no moral and little incident. A story of education—seventy years of it—the practical value remains to the end in doubt, like other values about which men have disputed since the birth of Cain and Abel; but the practical value of the universe has never been stated in dollars. Although every one cannot be a Gargantua-Napoleon-Bismarck and walk off with the great bells of Notre Dame, every one must bear his own universe, and most persons are moderately interested in learning how their neighbors have managed to carry theirs.

This problem of education, started in 1838, went on for three years, while the baby grew, like other babies, unconsciously, as a vegetable, the outside world working as it never had worked before, to get his new universe ready for him. Often in old age he puzzled over the question whether, on the doctrine of chances, he was at liberty to accept himself or his world as an accident. No such accident had ever happened before in human experience. For him, alone, the old universe was thrown into the ash heap and a new one created. He and his eighteenth-century, troglodytic Boston were suddenly cut apart—separated forever—in act if not in sentiment, by the opening of the Boston and Albany Railroad; the appearance of the first Cunard steamers in the bay; and the telegraphic messages which carried from Baltimore to Washington the news that Henry Clay and James K. Polk were nominated for the Presidency. This was in May, 1844; he was six years old; his new world was ready for use, and only fragments of the old met his eyes.

Of all this that was being done to complicate his education, he knew only the color of yellow. He first found himself sitting on a yellow kitchen floor in strong sunlight. He was three years old when he took this earliest step in education; a lesson of color. The second followed soon; a lesson of taste. On December 3, 1841, he developed scarlet fever. For several days he was as good as dead, reviving only under the careful nursing of his family. When he began to recover strength, about January 1, 1842, his hunger must have been stronger than any other pleasure or pain, for while in after life he retained not the faintest recollection of his illness, he remembered quite clearly his aunt entering the sick-room bearing in her hand a saucer with a baked apple.

The order of impressions retained by memory might naturally be that of color and taste, although one would rather suppose that the sense of pain would be first to educate. In fact, the third recollection of the child was that of discomfort. The moment he could be removed, he was bundled up in blankets and carried from the little house in Hancock Avenue to a larger one which his parents were to occupy for the rest of their lives in the neighboring Mount Vernon Street. The season was midwinter, January 10, 1842, and he never forgot his acute distress for want of air under his blankets, or the noises of moving furniture.

As a means of variation from a normal type, sickness in childhood ought to have a certain value not to be classed under any fitness or unfitness of natural selection; and especially scarlet fever affected boys seriously, both physically and in character, though they might through life puzzle themselves to decide whether it had fitted or unfitted them for success; but this fever of Henry Adams took greater and greater importance in his eyes, from the point of view of education, the longer he lived. At first, the effect was physical. He fell behind his brothers two or three inches in height, and proportionally in bone and weight. His character and processes of mind seemed to share in this fining-down process of scale. He was not good in a fight, and his nerves were more delicate than boys' nerves ought to be. He exaggerated these weaknesses as he grew older. The habit of doubt; of distrusting his own judgment and of totally rejecting the judgment of the world; the tendency to regard every question as open; the hesitation to act except as a choice of evils; the shirking of responsibility; the love of line, form, quality; the horror of ennui; the passion for companionship and the antipathy to society—all these are well-known qualities of New England character in no way peculiar to individuals but in this instance they seemed to be stimulated by the fever, and Henry Adams could never make up his mind whether, on the whole, the change of character was morbid or healthy, good or bad for his purpose. His brothers were the type; he was the variation.

As far as the boy knew, the sickness did not affect him at all, and he grew up in excellent health, bodily and mental, taking life as it was given; accepting its local standards without a difficulty, and enjoying much of it as keenly as any other boy of his age. He seemed to himself quite normal, and his companions seemed always to think him so. Whatever was peculiar about him was education, not character, and came to him, directly and indirectly, as the result of that eighteenth-century inheritance which he took with his name.

The atmosphere of education in which he lived was colonial, revolutionary, almost Cromwellian, as though he were steeped, from his greatest grandmother's birth, in the odor of political crime. Resistance to something was the law of New England nature; the boy looked out on the world with the instinct of resistance; for numberless generations his predecessors had viewed the world chiefly as a thing to be reformed, filled with evil forces to be abolished, and they saw no reason to suppose that they had wholly succeeded in the abolition; the duty was unchanged. That duty implied not only resistance to evil, but hatred of it. Boys naturally look on all force as an enemy, and generally find it so, but the New Englander, whether boy or man, in his long struggle with stingy or hostile universe, had learned also to love the pleasure of hating; his joys were few.

Politics, as a practice, whatever its professions, had always been the systematic organization of hatreds, and Massachusetts politics had been as harsh as the climate. The chief charm of New England was harshness of contrasts and extremes of sensibility—a cold that froze the blood, and a heat that boiled it—so that the pleasure of hating—one's self if no better victim offered—was not its rarest amusement; but the charm was a true and natural child of the soil, not a cultivated weed of the ancients. The violence of the contrast was real and made the strongest motive of education. The double exterior nature gave life its relative values. Winter and summer, cold and heat, town and country, force and freedom, marked two modes of life and thought, balanced like lobes of the brain. Town was winter confinement, school, rule, discipline; straight, gloomy streets, piled with six feet of snow in the middle; frosts that made the snow sing under wheels or runners; thaws when the streets became dangerous to cross; society of uncles, aunts, and cousins who

expected children to behave themselves, and who were not always gratified; above all else, winter represented the desire to escape and go free.
Town was restraint, law, unity. Country, only seven miles away, was
liberty, diversity, outlawry, the endless delight of mere sense impressions given by nature for nothing, and breathed by boys without knowing it.

Boys are wild animals, rich in the treasures of sense, but the New
England boy had a wider range of emotions than boys of more equable
climates. He felt his nature crudely, as it was meant. To the boy Henry
Adams, summer was drunken. Among senses, smell was the strongest—
smell of hot pine-woods and sweet-fern in the scorching summer noon;
of new-mown hay; of ploughed earth; of box hedges; of peaches, lilacs,
syringas; of stables, barns, cow-yards; of salt water and low tide on the
marshes; nothing came amiss. Next to smell came taste, and the children knew the taste of everything they saw or touched, from pennyroyal
and flagroot to the shell of a pignut and the letters of a spelling-book—
the taste of A-B, AB, suddenly revived on the boy's tongue sixty years
afterwards. Light, line, and color as sensual pleasures, came later and
were as crude as the rest. The New England light is glare, and the
atmosphere harshens color. The boy was a full man before he ever knew
what was meant by atmosphere; his idea of pleasure in light was the
blaze of a New England sun. His idea of color was a peony, with the
dew of early morning on its petals. The intense blue of the sea, as he
saw it a mile or two away, from the Quincy hills; the cumuli in a June
afternoon sky; the strong reds and greens and purples of colored prints
and children's picture-books, as the American colors then ran; these
were ideals. The opposites or antipathies, were the cold grays of November evenings, and the thick, muddy thaws of Boston winter. With such
standards, the Bostonian could not but develop a double nature. Life
was a double thing. After a January blizzard, the boy who could look
with pleasure into the violent snow-glare of the cold white sunshine,
with its intense light and shade, scarcely knew what was meant by tone.
He could reach it only by education.

Winter and summer, then, were two hostile lives, and bred two
separate natures. Winter was always the effort to live; summer was
tropical license. Whether the children rolled in the grass, or waded in
the brook, or swam in the salt ocean, or sailed in the bay, or fished for
smelts in the creeks, or netted minnows in the salt-marshes, or took to
the pine-woods and the granite quarries, or chased muskrats and hunted
snapping-turtles in the swamps, or mushrooms or nuts on the autumn
hills, summer and country were always sensual living, while winter was
always compulsory learning. Summer was the multiplicity of nature;
winter was school.

The bearing of the two seasons on the education of Henry Adams
was no fancy; it was the most decisive force he ever knew; it ran
through life, and made the division between its perplexing, warring,

irreconcilable problems, irreducible opposites, with growing emphasis to the last year of study. From earliest childhood the boy was accustomed to feel that, for him, life was double. Winter and summer, town and country, law and liberty, were hostile, and the man who pretended they were not, was in his eyes a schoolmaster—that is, a man employed to tell lies to little boys. Though Quincy was but two hours' walk from Beacon Hill, it belonged in a different world. For two hundred years, every Adams, from father to son, had lived within sight of State Street,[1] and sometimes had lived in it, yet none had ever taken kindly to the town, or been taken kindly by it. The boy inherited his double nature. He knew as yet nothing about his great-grandfather, who had died a dozen years before his own birth: he took for granted that any great-grandfather of his must have always been good, and his enemies wicked; but he divined his great-grandfather's character from his own. Never for a moment did he connect the two ideas of Boston and John Adams; they were separate and antagonistic; the idea of John Adams went with Quincy. He knew his grandfather John Quincy Adams only as an old man of seventy-five or eighty who was friendly and gentle with him, but except that he heard his grandfather always called "the President," and his grandmother "the Madam," he had no reason to suppose that his Adams grandfather differed in character from his Brooks grandfather who was equally kind and benevolent. He like the Adams side best, but for no other reason than that it reminded him of the country, the summer, and the absence of restraint. Yet he felt also that Quincy was in a way inferior to Boston, and that socially Boston looked down on Quincy. The reason was clear enough even to a five-year old child. Quincy had no Boston style. Little enough style had either; a simpler manner of life and thought could hardly exist, short of cave-dwelling. The flint-and-steel with which his grandfather Adams used to light his own fires in the early morning was still on the mantel-piece of his study. The idea of a livery or even a dress for servants or of an evening toilette, was next to blasphemy. Bathrooms, water-supplies, lighting, heating, and the whole array of domestic comforts, were unknown at Quincy. Boston had already a bathroom, a water-supply, a furnace, and gas. The superiority of Boston was evident, but a child liked it no better for that.

The magnificence of his grandfather Brooks's house in Pearl Street or South Street has long ago disappeared, but perhaps his country house at Medford may still remain to show what impressed the mind of a boy in 1845 with the idea of city splendor. The President's place at Quincy was the larger and older and far the more interesting of the two; but a boy felt at once its inferiority in fashion. It showed plainly enough its want of wealth. It smacked of colonial age, but not of Boston style or plush curtains. To the end of his life he never quite overcame the prejudice thus drawn in with his childish breath. He never could compel

---

[1] The financial district of Boston.

himself to care for nineteenth-century style. He was never able to adopt it, any more than his father or grandfather or great-grandfather had done. Not that he felt it as particularly hostile, for he reconciled himself to much that was worse; but because, for some remote reason, he was born an eighteenth-century child. The old house at Quincy was eighteenth century. What style it had was in its Queen Anne mahogany panels and its Louis Seize chairs and sofas. The panels belonged to an old colonial Vassall who built the house; the furniture had been brought back from Paris in 1789 or 1801 or 1817, along with porcelain and books and much else of old diplomatic remnants; and neither of the two eighteenth-century styles—neither English Queen Anne nor French Louis Seize—was comfortable for a boy, or for any one else. The dark mahogany had been painted white to suit daily life in winter gloom. Nothing seemed to favor, for a child's objects, the older forms. On the contrary, most boys, as well as grown-up people, preferred the new, with good reason, and the child felt himself distinctly at a disadvantage for the taste.

Nor had personal preference any share in his bias. The Brooks grandfather was as amiable and as sympathetic as the Adams grandfather. Both were born in 1767, and both died in 1848. Both were kind to children, and both belonged rather to the eighteenth than to the nineteenth centuries. The child knew no difference between them except that one was associated with winter and the other with summer; one with Boston, the other with Quincy. Even with Medford, the association was hardly easier. Once as a very young boy he was taken to pass a few days with his grandfather Brooks under charge of his aunt, but became so violently homesick that within twenty-four hours he was brought back in disgrace. Yet he could not remember ever being seriously homesick again.

The attachment to Quincy was not altogether sentimental or wholly sympathetic. Quincy was not a bed of thornless roses. Even there the curse of Cain set its mark. There as elsewhere a cruel universe combined to crush a child. As though three or four vigorous brothers and sisters, with the best will, were not enough to crush any child, every one else conspired towards an education which he hated. From cradle to grave this problem of running order through chaos, direction through space, discipline through freedom, unity through multiplicity, has always been, and must always be, the task of education, as it is the moral of religion, philosophy, science, art, politics, and economy; but a boy's will is his life, and he dies when it is broken, as the colt dies in harness, taking a new nature in becoming tame. Rarely has the boy felt kindly towards his tamers. Between him and his master has always been war. Henry Adams never knew a boy of his generation to like a master, and the task of remaining on friendly terms with one's own family, in such a relation, was never easy.

All the more singular it seemed afterwards to him that his first serious contact with the President should have been a struggle of will, in which the old man almost necessarily defeated the boy, but instead of leaving, as usual in such defeats, a lifelong sting, left rather an impression of as fair treatment as could be expected from a natural enemy. The boy met seldom with such restraint. He could not have been much more than six years old at the time—seven at the utmost—and his mother had taken him to Quincy for a long stay with the President during the summer. What became of the rest of the family he quite forgot; but he distinctly remembered standing at the house door one summer morning in a passionate outburst of rebellion against going to school. Naturally his mother was the immediate victim of his rage; that is what mothers are for, and boys also; but in this case the boy had his mother at unfair disadvantage, for she was a guest, and had no means of enforcing obedience. Henry showed a certain tactical ability by refusing to start, and he met all efforts at compulsion by successful, though too vehement protest. He was in fair way to win, and was holding his own, with sufficient energy, at the bottom of the long staircase which led up to the door of the President's library, when the door opened, and the old man slowly came down. Putting on his hat, he took the boy's hand without a word, and walked with him, paralyzed by awe, up the road to the town. After the first moments of consternation at this interference in a domestic dispute, the boy reflected that an old gentleman close on eighty would never trouble himself to walk near a mile on a hot summer morning over a shadeless road to take a boy to school, and that it would be strange if a lad imbued with the passion of freedom could not find a corner to dodge around, somewhere before reaching the school door. Then and always, the boy insisted that this reasoning justified his apparent submission; but the old man did not stop, and the boy saw all his strategical points turned, one after another, until he found himself seated inside the school, and obviously the centre of curious if not malevolent criticism. Not till then did the President release his hand and depart.

The point was that this act, contrary to the inalienable rights of boys, and nullifying the social compact, ought to have made him dislike his grandfather for life. He could not recall that it had this effect even for a moment. With a certain maturity of mind, the child must have recognized that the President, though a tool of tyranny, had done his disreputable work with a certain intelligence. He had shown no temper, no irritation, no personal feeling, and had made no display of force. Above all, he had held his tongue. During their long walk he had said nothing; he had uttered no syllable of revolting cant about the duty of obedience and the wickedness of resistance to law; he had shown no concern in the matter; hardly even a consciousness of the boy's existence. Probably his mind at that moment was actually troubling itself little about his grandson's iniquities, and much about the iniquities of President Polk, but the boy could scarcely at that age feel the whole satisfaction of thinking that President Polk was to be the vicarious victim of his own sins, and he gave his grandfather credit for intelligent silence. For this forbearance he felt instinctive respect. He admitted force as a form of right; he admitted even temper, under protest; but the seeds of a moral education would at that moment have fallen on the stoniest soil in Quincy, which is, as every one knows, the stoniest glacial and tidal drift known in any Puritan land.

Neither party to this momentary disagreement can have felt rancor, for during these three or four summers the old President's relations with the boy were friendly and almost intimate. Whether his older brothers and sisters were still more favored he failed to remember, but he was himself admitted to a sort of familiarity which, when in his turn he had reached old age, rather shocked him, for it must have sometimes tried the President's patience. He hung about the library; handled the books; deranged the papers; ransacked the drawers; searched the old purses and pocket-books for foreign coins; drew the sword-cane; snapped the travelling-pistols; upset everything in the corners, and penetrated the President's dressing-closet where a row of tumblers, inverted on the shelf, covered caterpillars which were supposed to become moths or butterflies, but never did. The Madam bore with fortitude the loss of the tumblers which her husband purloined for these hatcheries; but she made protest when he carried off her best cut-glass bowls to plant with acorns or peachstones that he might see the roots grow, but which, she said, he commonly forgot like the caterpillars.

At that time the President rode the hobby of tree-culture, and some fine old trees should still remain to witness it, unless they have been improved off the ground; but his was a restless mind, and although he took his hobbies seriously and would have been annoyed had his grandchild asked whether he was bored like an English duke, he probably cared more for the processes than for the results, so that his grandson was saddened by the sight and smell of peaches and pears, the best of their kind, which he brought up from the garden to rot on his shelves for seed. With the inherited virtues of his Puritan ancestors, the little boy Henry conscientiously brought up to him in his study the finest peaches he found in the garden, and ate only the less perfect. Naturally he ate more by way of compensation, but the act showed that he bore no grudge. As for his grandfather, it is even possible that he may have felt a certain self-reproach for his temporary rôle of schoolmaster—seeing that his own career did not offer proof of the worldly advantages of docile obedience—for there still exists somewhere a little volume of critically edited Nursery Rhymes with the boy's name in full written in the President's trembling hand on the fly-leaf. Of course there was also the Bible, given to each child at birth, with the proper inscription in the President's hand on the fly-leaf; while their grandfather Brooks supplied the silver mugs.

So many Bibles and silver mugs had to be supplied, that a new house, or cottage, was built to hold them. It was "on the hill," five minutes' walk above "the old house," with a far view eastward over Quincy Bay, and northward over Boston. Till his twelfth year, the child passed his summers there, and his pleasures of childhood mostly centered in it. Of education he had as yet little to complain. Country schools were not very serious. Nothing stuck to the mind except home impressions, and the sharpest were those of kindred children; but as influences that warped a mind, none compared with the mere effect of the back of the President's bald head, as he sat in his pew on Sundays, in line with that of President Quincy, who, though some ten years younger, seemed to children about the same age. Before railways entered the New England town, every parish church showed half-a-dozen of these leading citizens, with gray hair, who sat on the main aisle in the best pews, and had sat there, or in some equivalent dignity, since the time of St. Augustine, if not since the glacial epoch. It was unusual for boys to sit behind a President grandfather, and to read over his head the tablet in memory of a President great-grandfather, who had "pledged his life, his fortune, and his sacred honor" to secure the independence of his country and so forth; but boys naturally supposed, without much reasoning, that other boys had the equivalent of President grandfathers, and that churches would always go on, with the bald-headed leading citizens on the main aisle, and Presidents or their equivalents on the walls. The Irish gardener once said to the child: "You'll be thinkin' you'll be President too!" The casualty of the remark made so strong an impression on his mind that he never forgot it. He could not remember ever to have thought on the subject; to him, that there should be a doubt of his being President was a new idea. What had been would continue to be. He doubted neither about Presidents nor about Churches, and no one suggested at that time a doubt whether a system of society which had lasted since Adam would outlast one Adams more.

The Madam was a little more remote than the President, but more decorative. She stayed much in her own room with the Dutch tiles, looking out on her garden with the box walks, and seemed a fragile creature to a boy who sometimes brought her a note or a message, and took distinct pleasure in looking at her delicate face under what seemed to him very becoming caps. He liked her refined figure; her gentle voice and manner; her vague effect of not belonging there, but to Washington or to Europe, like her furniture, and writing-desk with little glass doors above and little eighteenth-century volumes in old binding, labelled "Peregrine Pickle" or "Tom Jones" or "Hannah More." Try as she might, the Madam could never be Bostonian, and it was her cross in life, but to the boy it was her charm. Even at that age, he felt drawn to it. The Madam's life had been in truth far from Boston. She was born in London in 1775, daughter of Joshua Johnson, an American merchant, brother of Governor Thomas Johnson of Maryland; and Catherine Nuth, of an English family in London. Driven from England by the Revolutionary

War, Joshua Johnson took his family to Nantes, where they remained till the peace. The girl Louisa Catherine was nearly ten years old when brought back to London, and her sense of nationality must have been confused; but the influence of the Johnsons and the services of Joshua obtained for him from President Washington the appointment of Consul in London on the organization of the Government in 1790. In 1794 President Washington appointed John Quincy Adams Minister to The Hague. He was twenty-seven years old when he returned to London, and found the Consul's house a very agreeable haunt. Louisa was then twenty.

At that time, and long afterwards, the Consul's house, far more than the Minister's, was the centre of contact for travelling Americans, either official or other. The Legation was a shifting point, between 1785 and 1815; but the Consulate, far down in the City, near the Tower, was convenient and inviting; so inviting that it proved fatal to young Adams. Louisa was charming, like a Romney portrait, but among her many charms that of being a New England woman was not one. The defect was serious. Her future mother-in-law, Abigail, a famous New England woman whose authority over her turbulent husband, the second President, was hardly so great as that which she exercised over her son, the sixth to be, was troubled by the fear that Louisa might not be made of stuff stern enough, or brought up in conditions severe enough, to suit a New England climate, or to make an efficient wife for her paragon son, and Abigail was right on that point, as on most others where sound judgment was involved; but sound judgment is sometimes a source of weakness rather than of force, and John Quincy already had reason to think that his mother held sound judgments on the subject of daughters-in-law which human nature, since the fall of Eve, made Adams helpless to realize. Being three thousand miles away from his mother, and equally far in love, he married Louisa in London, July 26, 1797, and took her to Berlin to be the head of the United States Legation. During three or four exciting years, the young bride lived in Berlin; whether she was happy or not, whether she was content or not, whether she was socially successful or not, her descendants did not surely know; but in any case she could by no chance have become educated there for a life in Quincy or Boston. In 1801 the overthrow of the Federalist Party[2] drove her and her husband to America, and she became at last a member of the Quincy household, but by that time her children needed all her attention, and she remained there with occasional winters in Boston and Washington, till 1809. Her husband was made Senator in 1803, and in 1809 was appointed Minister to Russia. She went with him to St. Petersburg, taking her baby, Charles Francis, born in 1807; but broken-hearted at having to leave her two older boys behind. The life at St. Petersburg was hardly gay for her; they were far too poor to shine in that extravagant

---

[2] This refers to the election of Thomas Jefferson to the Presidency.

society; but she survived it, though her little girl baby did not, and in the winter of 1814–15, alone with the boy of seven years old, crossed Europe from St. Petersburg to Paris, in her travelling-carriage, passing through the armies, and reaching Paris in the *Cent Jours* [3] after Napoleon's return from Elba. Her husband next went to England as Minister, and she was for two years at the Court of the Regent. In 1817 her husband came home to be Secretary of State, and she lived for eight years in F Street, doing her work of entertainer for President Monroe's administration. Next she lived four miserable years in the White House. When that chapter was closed in 1829, she had earned the right to be tired and delicate, but she still had fifteen years to serve as wife of a Member of the House, after her husband went back to Congress in 1833. Then it was that the little Henry, her grandson, first remembered her, from 1843 to 1848, sitting in her panelled room, at breakfast, with her heavy silver teapot and sugar-bowl and cream-jug, which still exist somewhere as an heirloom of the modern safety-vault. By that time she was seventy years old or more, and thoroughly weary of being beaten about a stormy world. To the boy she seemed singularly peaceful, a vision of silver gray, presiding over her old President and her Queen Anne mahogany; an exotic, like her Sèvres china; an object of deference to every one, and of great affection to her son Charles; but hardly more Bostonian than she had been fifty years before, on her wedding-day, in the shadow of the Tower of London.

Such a figure was even less fitted than that of her old husband, the President, to impress on a boy's mind, the standards of the coming century. She was Louis Seize, like the furniture. The boy knew nothing of her interior life, which had been, as the venerable Abigail, long since at peace, foresaw, one of severe stress and little pure satisfaction. He never dreamed that from her might come some of those doubts and self-questionings, those hesitations, those rebellions against law and discipline, which marked more than one of her descendants; but he might even then have felt some vague instinctive suspicion that he was to inherit from her the seeds of the primal sin, the fall from grace, the curse of Abel, that he was not of pure New England stock, but half exotic. As a child of Quincy he was not a true Bostonian, but even as a child of Quincy he inherited a quarter taint of Maryland blood. Charles Francis, half Marylander by birth, had hardly seen Boston till he was ten years old, when his parents left him there at school in 1817, and he never forgot the experience. He was to be nearly as old as his mother had been in 1845, before he quite accepted Boston, or Boston quite accepted him.

A boy who began his education in these surroundings, with physical strength inferior to that of his brothers, and with a certain delicacy of

[3] Hundred days, refers to Napoleon's restoration to power, ending with his destruction at Waterloo.

mind and bone, ought rightly to have felt at home in the eighteenth
century and should, in proper self-respect, have rebelled against the
standards of the nineteenth. The atmosphere of his first ten years must
have been very like that of his grandfather at the same age, from 1767
till 1776, barring the battle of Bunker Hill, and even as late as 1846,
the battle of Bunker Hill remained actual. The tone of Boston society
was colonial. The true Bostonian always knelt in self-abasement before
the majesty of English standards; far from concealing it as a weakness,
he was proud of it as his strength. The eighteenth century ruled society
long after 1850. Perhaps the boy began to shake it off rather earlier
than most of his mates.

Indeed this prehistoric stage of education ended rather abruptly with
his tenth year. One winter morning he was conscious of a certain confusion in the house in Mount Vernon Street, and gathered, from such
words as he could catch, that the President, who happened to be then
staying there, on his way to Washington, had fallen and hurt himself.
Then he heard the word paralysis. After that day he came to associate
the word with the figure of his grandfather, in a tall-backed, invalid
armchair, on one side of the spare bedroom fireplace, and one of his old
friends, Dr. Parkman or P. P. F. Degrand, on the other side, both dozing.

The end of this first, or ancestral and Revolutionary, chapter came
on February 21, 1848—and the month of February brought life and
death as a family habit—when the eighteenth century, as an actual and
living companion, vanished. If the scene on the floor of the House,
when the old President fell, struck the still simple-minded American
public with a sensation unusually dramatic, its effect on a ten-year-old
boy, whose boy-life was fading away with the life of his grandfather,
could not be slight. One had to pay for Revolutionary patriots; grandfathers and grandmothers; Presidents; diplomats; Queen Anne mahogany and Louis Seize chairs, as well as for Stuart portraits. Such things
warp young life. Americans commonly believed that they ruined it, and
perhaps the practical common-sense of the American mind judged right.
Many a boy might be ruined by much less than the emotions of the
funeral service in the Quincy church, with its surroundings of national
respect and family pride. By another dramatic chance it happened that
the clergyman of the parish, Dr. Lunt, was an unusual pulpit orator,
the ideal of a somewhat austere intellectual type, such as the school of
Buckminster and Channing inherited from the old Congregational
clergy. His extraordinarily refined appearance, his dignity of manner,
his deeply cadenced voice, his remarkable English and his fine appreciation, gave to the funeral service a character that left an overwhelming impression on the boy's mind. He was to see many great functions—
funerals and festivals—in after-life, till his only thought was to see no
more, but he never again witnessed anything nearly so impressive to
him as the last services at Quincy over the body of one President and the
ashes of another.

The effect of the Quincy service was deepened by the official ceremony which afterwards took place in Faneuil Hall[4]; when the boy was
taken to hear his uncle, Edward Everett, deliver a Eulogy. Like all Mr.
Everett's orations, it was an admirable piece of oratory, such as only an
admirable orator and scholar could create; too good for a ten-year-old
boy to appreciate at its value; but already the boy knew that the dead
President could not be in it, and had even learned why he would have
been out of place there; for knowledge was beginning to come fast. The
shadow of the War of 1812 still hung over State Street; the shadow of
the Civil War to come had already begun to darken Faneuil Hall. No
rhetoric could have reconciled Mr. Everett's audience to his subject. How
could he say there, to an assemblage of Bostonians in the heart of
mercantile Boston, that the only distinctive mark of all the Adamses,
since old Sam Adams's father a hundred and fifty years before, had
been their inherited quarrel with State Street, which had again and
again broken out into riot, bloodshed, personal feuds, foreign and civil
war, wholesale banishments and confiscations, until the history of
Florence was hardly more turbulent than that of Boston? How could he
whisper the word Hartford Convention[5] before the men who had made
it? What would have been said had he suggested the chance of Seces-
sion and Civil War?

Thus already, at ten years old, the boy found himself standing face
to face with a dilemma that might have puzzled an early Christian.
What was he?—where was he going? Even then he felt that something
was wrong, but he concluded that it must be Boston. Quincy had always
been right, for Quincy represented a moral principle—the principle of
resistance to Boston. His Adams ancestors must have been right, since
they were always hostile to State Street. If State Street was wrong,
Quincy must be right! Turn the dilemma as he pleased, he still came
back on the eighteenth century and the law of Resistance; of Truth; of
Duty, and of Freedom. He was a ten-year-old priest and politician. He
could under no circumstances have guessed what the next fifty years
had in store, and no one could teach him; but sometimes, in his old age,
he wondered—and could never decide—whether the most clear and
certain knowledge would have helped him. Supposing he had seen a
New York stock-list of 1900, and had studied the statistics of railways,
telegraphs, coal, and steel—would he have quitted his eighteenth-
century, his ancestral prejudices, his abstract ideals, his semi-clerical
training, and the rest, in order to perform an expiatory pilgrimage to
State Street, and ask for the fatted calf of his grandfather Brooks and
a clerkship in the Suffolk Bank?

[4] Meeting place for American revolutionaries in Boston, known as "cradle of
liberty."
[5] A secret meeting of Federalists in 1814, opposing war with England.

Sixty years afterwards he was still unable to make up his mind. Each course had its advantages, but the material advantages, looking back, seemed to lie wholly in State Street.

Chapter 17   President Grant (1869)

. . . At least four-fifths of the American people—Adams among the rest—had united in the election of General Grant to the Presidency,[6] and probably had been more or less affected in their choice by the parallel they felt between Grant and Washington. Nothing could be more obvious. Grant represented order. He was a great soldier, and the soldier always represented order. He might be as partisan as he pleased, but a general who had organized and commanded half a million or a million men in the field, must know how to administer. Even Washington, who was, in education and experience, a mere cave-dweller, had known how to organize a government, and had found Jeffersons and Hamiltons to organize his departments. The task of bringing the Government back to regular practices, and of restoring moral and mechanical order to administration, was not very difficult; it was ready to do it itself, with a little encouragement. No doubt the confusion, especially in the old slave States and in the currency, was considerable, but the general disposition was good, and every one had echoed the famous phrase: "Let us have peace."

Adams was young and easily deceived, in spite of his diplomatic adventures, but even at twice his age he could not see that this reliance on Grant was unreasonable. Had Grant been a Congressman one would have been on one's guard, for one knew the type. One never expected from a Congressman more than good intentions and public spirit. Newspaper-men as a rule had no great respect for the lower House; Senators had less; and Cabinet officers had none at all. Indeed, one day when Adams was pleading with a Cabinet officer for patience and tact in dealing with Representatives, the Secretary impatiently broke out: "You can't use tact with a Congressman! A Congressman is a hog! You must take a stick and hit him on the snout!" Adams knew far too little, compared with the Secretary, to contradict him, though he thought the phrase somewhat harsh and even as applied to the average Congressman of 1869—he saw little or nothing of later ones—but he knew a shorter way of silencing criticism. He had but to ask: "If a Congressman is a hog, what is a Senator?" This innocent question, put in a candid spirit, petrified any executive officer that ever sat a week in his office. Even Adams admitted that Senators passed belief. The comic side of their egotism partly disguised its extravagance, but faction had gone so far under Andrew Johnson that at times the whole Senate seemed to

[6] In 1868.

catch hysterics of nervous bucking without apparent reason. Great leaders, like Sumner [7] and Conkling,[8] could not be burlesqued; they were more grotesque than ridicule could make them; even Grant, who rarely sparkled in epigram, became witty on their account; but their egotism and factiousness were no laughing matter. They did permanent and terrible mischief, as Garfield [9] and Blaine,[10] and even McKinley [11] and John Hay,[12] were to feel. The most troublesome task of a reform President was that of bringing the Senate back to decency.

Therefore no one, and Henry Adams less than most, felt hope that any President chosen from the ranks of politics or politicians would raise the character of government; and by instinct if not by reason, all the world united on Grant. The Senate understood what the world expected, and waited in silence for a struggle with Grant more serious than that with Andrew Johnson. Newspaper-men were alive with eagerness to support the President against the Senate. The newspaper-man is, more than most men, a double personality; and his person feels best satisfied in its double instincts when writing in one sense and thinking in another. All newspaper-men, whatever they wrote, felt alike about the Senate. Adams floated with the stream. He was eager to join in the fight which he foresaw as sooner or later inevitable. He meant to support the executive in attacking the Senate and taking away its two-thirds vote and power of confirmation, nor did he much care how it should be done, for he thought it safer to effect the revolution in 1870 than to wait till 1920.

With this thought in mind, he went to the Capitol to hear the names announced which should reveal the carefully guarded secret of Grant's Cabinet. To the end of his life, he wondered at the suddenness of the revolution which actually, within five minutes, changed his intended future into an absurdity so laughable as to make him ashamed of it. He was to hear a long list of Cabinet announcements not much weaker or more futile than that of Grant, and none of them made him blush, while Grant's nominations had the singular effect of making the hearer ashamed, not so much of Grant, as of himself. He had made another total misconception of life—another inconceivable false start. Yet, unlikely as it seemed, he had missed his motive narrowly, and his intention had been more than sound, for the Senators made no secret of saying with senatorial frankness that Grant's nominations betrayed his

[7] Charles Sumner (1811–1874), United States Senator from Massachusetts.

[8] Roscoe Conkling (1829–1888), United States Senator from New York.

[9] James Garfield (1831–1881), twentieth President of the United States, assassinated four months after his inauguration.

[10] James Blaine (1830–1893), United States political leader.

[11] William McKinley (1843–1902), twenty-fifth President of the United States (1897–1901).

[12] John Hay (1838–1905), Secretary of State under McKinley.

intent as plainly as they betrayed his incompetence. A great soldier might be a baby politician.

Adams left the Capitol, much in the same misty mental condition that he recalled as marking his railway journey to London on May 13, 1861; he felt in himself what Gladstone [13] bewailed so sadly, "the incapacity of viewing things all round." He knew, without absolutely saying it, that Grant had cut short the life which Adams had laid out for himself in the future. After such a miscarriage, no thought of effectual reform could revive for at least one generation, and he had no fancy for ineffectual politics. What course could he sail next? He had tried so many, and society had barred them all! For the moment, he saw no hope but in following the stream on which he had launched himself. The new Cabinet, as individuals, were not hostile. Subsequently Grant made changes in the list which were mostly welcome to a Bostonian— or should have been—although fatal to Adams. The name of Hamilton Fish, as Secretary of State, suggested extreme conservatism and probable deference to Sumner. The name of George S. Boutwell, as Secretary of the Treasury, suggested only a somewhat lugubrious joke; Mr. Boutwell could be described only as the opposite of Mr. McCulloch, and meant inertia; or, in plain words, total extinction for any one resembling Henry Adams. On the other hand, the name of Jacob D. Cox, as Secretary of the Interior, suggested help and comfort; while that of Judge Hoar, as Attorney-General, promised friendship. On the whole, the personal outlook, merely for literary purposes, seemed fairly cheerful, and the political outook, though hazy, still depended on Grant himself. No one doubted that Grant's intention had been one of reform; that his aim had been to place his administration above politics; and until he should actually drive his supporters away, one might hope to support him. One's little lantern must therefore be turned on Grant. One seemed to know him so well, and really knew so little.

By chance it happened that Adam Badeau [14] took the lower suite of rooms at Dohna's, and, as it was convenient to have one table, the two men dined together and became intimate. Badeau was exceedingly social, though not in appearance imposing. He was stout; his face was red, and his habits were regularly irregular; but he was very intelligent, a good newspaper-man, and an excellent military historian. His life of Grant was no ordinary book. Unlike most newspaper-men, he was a friendly critic of Grant, as suited an officer who had been on the General's staff. As a rule, the newspaper correspondents in Washington were unfriendly, and the lobby sceptical. From that side one heard tales that made one's hair stand on end, and the old West Point army officers were no more flattering. All described him as vicious, narrow, dull, and vindictive. Badeau, who had come to Washington for a consulate which

[13] William Gladstone (1809–1898), British statesman.
[14] Adam Badeau (1831–1895), a close friend of Adams.

was slow to reach him, resorted more or less to whiskey for encouragement, and became irritable, besides being loquacious. He talked much about Grant, and showed a certain artistic feeling for analysis of character, as a true literary critic would naturally do. Loyal to Grant, and still more so to Mrs. Grant, who acted as his patroness, he said nothing, even when far gone, that was offensive about either, but he held that no one except himself and Rawlins understood the General. To him, Grant appeared as an intermittent energy, immensely powerful when awake, but passive and plastic in repose. He said that neither he nor the rest of the staff knew why Grant succeeded; they believed in him because of his success. For stretches of time, his mind seemed torpid. Rawlins and the others would systematically talk their ideas into it, for weeks, not directly, but by discussion among themselves, in his presence. In the end, he would announce the idea as his own, without seeming conscious of the discussion; and would give the orders to carry it out with all the energy that belonged to his nature. They could never measure his character or be sure when he would act. They could never follow a mental process in his thought. They were not sure that he did think.

In all this, Adams took deep interest, for although he was not, like Badeau, waiting for Mrs. Grant's power of suggestion to act on the General's mind in order to germinate in a consulate or a legation, his portrait gallery of great men was becoming large, and it amused him to add an authentic likeness of the greatest general the world had seen since Napoleon. Badeau's analysis was rather delicate; infinitely superior to that of Sam Ward [15] or Charles Nordhoff.[16]

Badeau took Adams to the White House one evening and introduced him to the President and Mrs. Grant. First and last, he saw a dozen Presidents at the White House, and the most famous were by no means the most agreeable, but he found Grant the most curious object of study among them all. About no one did opinions differ so widely. Adams had no opinion, or occasion to make one. A single word with Grant satisfied him that, for his own good, the fewer words he risked, the better. Thus far in life he had met with but one man of the same intellectual or unintellectual type—Garibaldi.[17] Of the two, Garibaldi seemed to him a trifle the more intellectual, but, in both, the intellect counted for nothing; only the energy counted. The type was pre-intellectual, archaic, and would have seemed so even to the cave-dwellers. Adam, according to legend, was such a man.

In time one came to recognize the type in other men, with differences and variations, as normal; men whose energies were the greater, the less they wasted on thought; men who sprang from the soil to power;

15 Sam Ward (1814–1884), an American author.
16 Charles Nordhoff (1830–1901), an American author.
17 Giuseppi Garibaldi (1807–1882), Italian nationalist revolutionary.

apt to be distrustful of themselves and of others; shy; jealous; sometimes vindictive; more or less dull in outward appearance; always needing stimulants; but for whom action was the highest stimulant—the instinct of fight. Such men were forces of nature, energies of the prime, like the *Pteraspis*,[18] but they made short work of scholars. They had commanded thousands of such and saw no more in them than in others. The fact was certain; it crushed argument and intellect at once.

Adams did not feel Grant as a hostile force; like Badeau he saw only an uncertain one. When in action he was superb and safe to follow; only when torpid he was dangerous. To deal with him one must stand near, like Rawlins, and practice more or less sympathetic habits. Simpleminded beyond the experience of Wall Street or State Street, he resorted, like most men of the same intellectual calibre, to commonplaces when at a loss for expression: "Let us have peace!" or, "The best way to treat a bad law is to execute it"; or a score of such reversible sentences generally to be gauged by their sententiousness; but sometimes he made one doubt his good faith; as when he seriously remarked to a particularly bright young woman that Venice would be a fine city if it were drained. In Mark Twain, this suggestion would have taken rank among his best witticisms; in Grant it was a measure of simplicity not singular. Robert E. Lee betrayed the same intellectual commonplace, in a Virginian form, not to the same degree, but quite distinctly enough for one who knew the American. What worried Adams was not the commonplace; it was, as usual, his own education. Grant fretted and irritated him, like the *Terebratula*,[19] as a defiance of first principles. He had no right to exist. He should have been extinct for ages. The idea that, as society grew older, it grew one-sided, upset evolution, and made of education a fraud. That, two thousand years after Alexander the Great and Julius Cæsar, a man like Grant should be called—and should actually and truly be—the highest product of the most advanced evolution, made evolution ludicrous. One must be as commonplace as Grant's own commonplaces to maintain such an absurdity. The progress of evolution from President Washington to President Grant, was alone evidence enough to upset Darwin.

Chapter 22   Chicago (1893)

... By the time he got back to Washington on September 19, the storm having partly blown over, life had taken on a new face, and one so interesting that he set off to Chicago to study the Exposition again, and stayed there a fortnight absorbed in it. He found matter of study to fill a hundred years, and his education spread over chaos. Indeed, it seemed to him as though, this year, education went mad. The silver question, thorny as it was, fell into relations as simple as words of one

[18] A fossil form of fish, the most ancient known.
[19] A bivalved mollusk that attaches itself to rocks, etc.

syllable, compared with the problems of credit and exchange that came to complicate it; and when one sought rest at Chicago, educational game started like rabbits from every building, and ran out of sight among thousands of its kind before one could mark its burrow. The Exposition itself defied philosophy. One might find fault till the last gate closed, one could still explain nothing that needed explanation. As a scenic display, Paris had never approached it, but the inconceivable scenic display consisted in its being there at all—more surprising, as it was, than anything else on the continent, Niagara Falls, the Yellowstone Geysers, and the whole railway system thrown in, since these were all natural products in their place; while, since Noah's Ark, no such Babel of loose and ill-joined, such vague and ill-defined and unrelated thoughts and half-thoughts and experimental outcries as the Exposition, had ever ruffled the surface of the Lakes.

The first astonishment became greater every day. That the Exposition should be a natural growth and product of the Northwest offered a step in evolution to startle Darwin; but that it should be anything else seemed an idea more startling still; and even granting it were not—admitting it to be a sort of industrial, speculative growth and product of the Beaux Arts [20] artistically induced to pass the summer on the shore of Lake Michigan—could it be made to seem at home there? Was the American made to seem at home in it? Honestly, he had the air of enjoying it as though it were all his own; he felt it was good; he was proud of it; for the most part, he acted as though he had passed his life in landscape gardening and architectural decoration. If he had not done it himself, he had known how to get it done to suit him, as he knew how to get his wives and daughters dressed at Worth's or Paquin's. Perhaps he could not do it again; the next time he would want to do it himself and would show his own faults; but for the moment he seemed to have leaped directly from Corinth and Syracuse and Venice, over the heads of London and New York, to impose classical standards on plastic Chicago. Critics had no trouble in criticising the classicism, but all trading cities had always shown traders' taste, and, to the stern purist of religious faith, no art was thinner than Venetian Gothic. All traders' taste smelt of bric-à-brac; Chicago tried at least to give her taste a look of unity.

One sat down to ponder on the steps beneath Richard Hunt's [21] dome almost as deeply as on the steps of Ara Cœli,[22] and much to the same purpose. Here was a breach of continuity—a rupture in historical sequence! Was it real, or only apparent? One's personal universe hung on the answer, for, if the rupture was real and the new American world could take this sharp and conscious twist towards ideals, one's personal

[20] The main and conservative art academy of Paris.
[21] Richard Hunt (1827–1895), American architect, designed main building at Chicago Fair of 1893.
[22] An ancient church in Rome which Adams especially liked.

friends would come in, at last, as winners in the great American chariot-race for fame. If the people of the Northwest actually knew what was good when they saw it, they would some day talk about Hunt and Richardson,[23] La Farge[24] and St. Gaudens,[25] Burnham[26] and McKim,[27] and Stanford White[28] when their politicians and millionaires were otherwise forgotten. The artists and architects who had done the work offered little encouragement to hope it; they talked freely enough, but not in terms that one cared to quote; and to them the Northwest refused to look artistic. They talked as though they worked only for themselves; as though art, to the Western people, was a stage decoration; a diamond shirt-stud; a paper collar; but possibly the architects of Pæstum and Girgenti had talked in the same way, and the Greek had said the same thing of Semitic Carthage two thousand years ago.

Jostled by these hopes and doubts, one turned to the exhibits for help, and found it. The industrial schools tried to teach so much and so quickly that the instruction ran to waste. Some millions of other people felt the same helplessness, but few of them were seeking education, and to them helplessness seemed natural and normal, for they had grown up in the habit of thinking a steam-engine or a dynamo as natural as the sun, and expected to understand one as little as the other. For the historian alone the Exposition made a serious effort. Historical exhibits were common, but they never went far enough; none were thoroughly worked out. One of the best was that of the Cunard steamers, but still a student hungry for results found himself obliged to waste a pencil and several sheets of paper trying to calculate exactly when, according to the given increase of power, tonnage, and speed, the growth of the ocean steamer would reach its limits. His figures brought him, he thought, to the year 1927; another generation to spare before force, space, and time should meet. The ocean steamer ran the surest line of triangulation into the future, because it was the nearest of man's products to a unity; railroads taught less because they seemed already finished except for mere increase in number; explosives taught most, but needed a tribe of chemists, physicists, and mathematicians to explain; the dynamo taught least because it had barely reached infancy, and, if its progress was to be constant at the rate of the last ten years, it would result in infinite costly energy within a generation. One lingered long among the dynamos, for they were new, and they gave to history a new phase. Men of science could never understand the ignorance and naïveté of the historian, who, when he came suddenly on a new power, asked naturally what it was; did it pull or did it push? Was it a screw or

[23] Henry Richardson (1838–1886), American architect.
[24] John La Farge (1835–1910), American artist, much admired by Adams.
[25] Augustus St. Gaudens (1848–1907), American sculptor.
[26] Daniel Burnham (1846–1912), leading architect of Chicago World's Fair.
[27] Charles McKim (1847–1909), architect of Boston Public Library.
[28] Stanford White (1853–1906), a leading American architect.

thrust? Did it flow or vibrate? Was it a wire or a mathematical line? And a score of such questions to which he expected answers and was astonished to get none.

Education ran riot at Chicago, at least for retarded minds which had never faced in concrete form so many matters of which they were ignorant. Men who knew nothing whatever—who had never run a steam-engine, the simplest of forces—who had never put their hands on a lever—had never touched an electric battery—never talked through a telephone, and had not the shadow of a notion what amount of force was meant by a *watt* or an *ampère* or an *erg*, or any other term of measurement introduced within a hundred years—had no choice but to sit down on the steps and brood as they had never brooded on the benches of Harvard College, either as student or professor, aghast at what they had said and done in all these years, and still more ashamed of the childlike ignorance and babbling futility of the society that let them say and do it. The historical mind can think only in historical processes, and probably this was the first time since historians existed, that any of them had sat down helpless before a mechanical sequence. Before a metaphysical or a theological or a political sequence, most historians had felt helpless, but the single clue to which they had hitherto trusted was the unity of natural force.

Did he himself quite know what he meant? Certainly not! If he had known enough to state his problem, his education would have been complete at once. Chicago asked in 1893 for the first time the question whether the American people knew where they were driving. Adams answered, for one, that he did not know, but would try to find out. On reflecting sufficiently deeply, under the shadow of Richard Hunt's architecture, he decided that the American people probably knew no more than he did; but that they might still be driving or drifting unconsciously to some point in thought, as their solar system was said to be drifting towards some point in space; and that, possibly, if relations enough could be observed, this point might be fixed. Chicago was the first expression of American thought as a unity. . . .

Chapter 25   *The Dynamo and the Virgin (1900)*

Until the Great Exposition of 1900 [29] closed its doors in November, Adams haunted it, aching to absorb knowledge, and helpless to find it. He would have liked to know how much of it could have been grasped by the best-informed man in the world. While he was thus meditating chaos, Langley [30] came by, and showed it to him. At Langley's behest,

[29] In Paris.

[30] Samuel Langley (1834–1906), astronomer, inventor of instrument for measuring solar heat, flew first model airplane in 1896.

the Exhibition dropped its superfluous rags and stripped itself to the skin. For Langley knew what to study, and why, and how; while Adams might as well have stood outside in the night, staring at the Milky Way. Yet Langley said nothing new, and taught nothing that one might not have learned from Lord Bacon, three hundred years before; but though one should have known the "Advancement of Science" as well as one knew the "Comedy of Errors," the literary knowledge counted for nothing until some teacher should show how to apply it. Bacon took a vast deal of trouble in teaching King James I and his subjects, American or other, towards the year 1620, that true science was the development or economy of forces; yet an elderly American in 1900 knew neither the formula nor the forces; or even so much as to say to himself that his historical business in the Exposition concerned only the economies or developments of force since 1893, when he began the study at Chicago.

Nothing in education is so astonishing as the amount of ignorance it accumulates in the form of inert facts. Adams had looked at most of the accumulations of art in the storehouses called Art Museums; yet he did not know how to look at the art exhibits of 1900. He had studied Karl Marx and his doctrines of history with profound attention, yet he could not apply them at Paris. Langley, with the ease of a great master of experiment, threw out of the field every exhibit that did not reveal a new application of force, and naturally threw out, to begin with, almost the whole art exhibit. Equally, he ignored almost the whole industrial exhibit. He led his pupil directly to the forces. His chief interest was in new motors to make his airship feasible, and he taught Adams the astonishing complexities of the new Daimler [31] motor, and of the automobile, which, since 1893, had become a nightmare at a hundred kilometres an hour, almost as destructive as the electric tram which was only ten years older; and threatening to become as terrible as the locomotive steam-engine itself, which was almost exactly Adams's own age.

Then he showed his scholar the great hall of dynamos, and explained how little he knew about electricity or force of any kind, even of his own special sun, which spouted heat in inconceivable volume, but which, as far as he knew, might spout less or more, at any time, for all the certainty he felt in it. To him, the dynamo itself was but an ingenious channel for conveying somewhere the heat latent in a few tons of poor coal hidden in a dirty engine-house carefully kept out of sight; but to Adams the dynamo became a symbol of infinity. As he grew accustomed to the great gallery of machines, he began to feel the forty-foot dynamos as a moral force, much as the early Christians felt the Cross. The planet itself seemed less impressive, in its old-fashioned, deliberate, annual or daily revolution, than this huge wheel, revolving within arm's-length at some vertiginous speed, and barely murmuring—scarcely humming an audible warning to stand a hair's-breadth further for respect of

[31] Gottlieb Daimler (1834–1900), pioneer inventor of the automobile.

power—while it would not wake the baby lying close against its frame. Before the end, one began to pray for it; inherited instinct taught the natural expression of man before silent and infinite force. Among the thousand symbols of ultimate energy, the dynamo was not so human as some, but it was the most expressive.

Yet the dynamo, next to the steam-engine, was the most familiar of exhibits. For Adams's objects its value lay chiefly in its occult mechanism. Between the dynamo in the gallery of machines and the engine-house outside, the break of continuity amounted to abysmal fracture for a historian's objects. No more relation could he discover between the steam and the electric current than between the Cross and the cathedral. The forces were interchangeable if not reversible, but he could see only an absolute *fiat* in electricity as in faith. Langley could not help him. Indeed, Langley seemed to be worried by the same trouble, for he constantly repeated that the new forces were anarchical, and specially that he was not responsible for the new rays, that were little short of parricidal in their wicked spirit towards science. His own rays, with which he had doubled the solar spectrum, were altogether harmless and beneficent; but Radium [32] denied its God—or, what was to Langley the same thing, denied the truths of his Science. The force was wholly new.

A historian who asked only to learn enough to be as futile as Langley or Kelvin,[33] made rapid progress under this teaching, and mixed himself up in the tangle of ideas until he achieved a sort of Paradise of ignorance vastly consoling to his fatigued senses. He wrapped himself in vibrations and rays which were new, and he would have hugged Marconi and Branly had he met them, as he hugged the dynamo; while he lost his arithmetic in trying to figure out the equation between the discoveries and economies of force. The economies, like the discoveries, were absolute, supersensual, occult; incapable of expression in horse-power. What mathematical equivalent could he suggest as the value of a Branly [34] coherer? Frozen air, or the electric furnace, had some scale of measurement, no doubt, if somebody could invent a thermometer adequate to the purpose; but X-rays had played no part whatever in man's consciousness, and the atom itself had figured only as a fiction of thought. In these seven years man had translated himself into a new universe which had no common scale of measurement with the old. He had entered a supersensual world, in which he could measure nothing except by chance collisions of movements imperceptible to his senses, perhaps even imperceptible to his instruments, but perceptible to each other, and so to some known ray at the end of the scale. Langley seemed prepared for anything, even for an indeterminable number of universes interfused—physics stark mad in metaphysics.

[32] Recently discovered, in 1898, by Mme. Curie.
[33] Lord Kelvin (1824–1907), pioneer in thermodynamics.
[34] Edouard Branley (1846–1940), French scientist who invented an instrument for detecting radio waves.

Historians undertake to arrange sequences,—called stories, or histories—assuming in silence a relation of cause and effect. These assumptions, hidden in the depths of dusty libraries, have been astounding, but commonly unconscious and childlike; so much so, that if any captious critic were to drag them to light, historians would probably reply, with one voice, that they had never supposed themselves required to know what they were talking about. Adams, for one, had toiled in vain to find out what he meant. He had even published a dozen volumes of American history for no other purpose than to satisfy himself whether, by the severest process of stating, with the least possible comment, such facts as seemed sure, in such order as seemed rigorously consequent, he could fix for a familiar moment a necessity sequence of human movement. The result had satisfied him as little as at Harvard College. Where he saw sequence, other men saw something quite different, and no one saw the same unit of measure. He cared little about his experiments and less about his statesmen, who seemed to him quite as ignorant as himself and as a rule, no more honest; but he insisted on a relation of sequence, and if he could not reach it by one method, he would try as many methods as science knew. Satisfied that the sequence of men led to nothing and that the sequence of their society could lead no further, while the mere sequence of time was artificial, and the sequence of thought was chaos, he turned at last to the sequence of force; and thus it happened that, after ten years' pursuit, he found himself lying in the Gallery of Machines at the Great Exposition of 1900, his historical neck broken by the sudden irruption of forces totally new.

Since no one else showed much concern, an elderly person without other cares had no need to betray alarm. The year 1900 was not the first to upset schoolmasters. Copernicus and Galileo had broken many professorial necks about 1600; Columbus had stood the world on its head towards 1500; but the nearest approach to the revolution of 1900 was that of 310, when Constantine [35] set up the Cross. The rays that Langley disowned, as well as those which he fathered, were occult, supersensual, irrational; they were what, in terms of medieval science, were called immediate modes of the divine substance.

The historian was thus reduced to his last resources. Clearly if he was bound to reduce all these forces to a common value, this common value could have no measure but that of their attraction on his own mind. He must treat them as they had been felt; as convertible, reversible, interchangeable attractions on thought. He made up his mind to venture it; he would risk translating rays into faith. Such a reversible process would vastly amuse a chemist, but the chemist could not deny that he, or some of his fellow physicists, could feel the force of both. When Adams was a boy in Boston, the best chemist in the place had probably never heard of Venus except by way of scandal, or of the Virgin except as idolatry;

[35] Constantine I (c. 280–337), reported to have seen a cross in the sky indicating victory for him in battle.

neither had he heard of dynamos or automobiles or radium; yet his mind was ready to feel the force of all, though the rays were unborn and the women were dead.

Here opened another totally new education, which promised to be by far the most hazardous of all. The knife-edge along which he must crawl, like Sir Lancelot in the twelfth century, divided two kingdoms of force which had nothing in common but attraction. They were as different as a magnet is from gravitation, supposing one knew what a magnet was, or gravitation, or love. The force of the Virgin was still felt at Lourdes, and seemed to be as potent as X-rays but in America neither Venus nor Virgin ever had value as a force—at most as sentiment. No American had ever truly been afraid of either.

This problem in dynamics gravely perplexed an American historian. The Woman had once been supreme; in France she still seemed potent, not merely as a sentiment, but as a force. Why was she unknown in America? For evidently America was ashamed of her, and she was ashamed of herself, otherwise they would not have strewn fig-leaves so profusely all over her. When she was a true force, she was ignorant of fig-leaves, but the monthly-magazine-made American female had not a feature that would have been recognized by Adam. The trait was notorious, and often humorous, but any one brought up among Puritans knew that sex was a sin. In any previous age, sex was strength. Neither art nor beauty was needed. Every one, even among Puritans, knew that neither Diana of the Ephesians nor any of the Oriental goddesses was worshipped for her beauty. She was goddess because of her force; she was the animated dynamo; she was reproduction—the greatest and most mysterious of all energies; all she needed was to be fecund. Singularly enough, not one of Adams's many schools of education had ever drawn his attention to the opening lines of Lucretius, though they were perhaps the finest in all Latin literature, where the poet invoked Venus exactly as Dante invoked the Virgin:—

Quae quoniam rerum naturam sola gubernas.[36]

The Venus of Epicurean philosophy survived in the Virgin of the Schools:—

Donna, sei tanto grande, e tanto vali,
Che qual vuol grazia, e a te non ricorre,
Sua disianza vuol volar senz' ali.[37]

All this was to American thought as though it had never existed. The true American knew something of the facts, but nothing of the feelings; he read the letter, but he never felt the law. Before this historical chasm,

[36] "Since thou art, above all, sole mistress of the nature of things, . . ." (from *de Rerum Natura*).

[37] "Lady, thou art so great in all things/That he who wishes grace and seeks thee not/His desires fly upwards without wings" (from *The Divine Comedy*).

a mind like that of Adams felt itself helpless; he turned from the Virgin to the Dynamo as though he were a Branly coherer. On one side, at the Louvre and at Chartres, as he knew by the record of work actually done and still before his eyes, was the highest energy ever known to man, the creator of four-fifths of his noblest art, exercising vastly more attraction over the human mind than all the steam-engines and dynamos ever dreamed of; and yet this energy was unknown to the American mind. An American Virgin would never dare command; an American Venus would never dare exist.

The question, which to any plain American of the nineteenth century seemed as remote as it did to Adams, drew him almost violently to study, once it was posed; and on this point Langleys were as useless as though they were Herbert Spencers[38] or dynamos. The idea survived only as art. There one turned as naturally as though the artist were himself a woman. Adams began to ponder, asking himself whether he knew of any American artist who had ever insisted on the power of sex, as every classic had always done; but he could think only of Walt Whitman; Bret Harte, as far as the magazines would let him venture; and one or two painters, for the flesh-tones. All the rest had used sex for sentiment, never for force; to them, Eve was a tender flower, and Herodias an unfeminine horror. American art, like the American language and American education, was as far as possible sexless. Society regarded this victory over sex as its greatest triumph, and the historian readily admitted it, since the moral issue, for the moment, did not concern one who was studying the relations of unmoral force. He cared nothing for the sex of the dynamo until he could measure its energy.

Vaguely seeking a clue, he wandered through the art exhibit, and, in his stroll, stopped almost every day before St. Gaudens's General Sherman, which had been given the central post of honor. St. Gaudens himself was in Paris, putting on the work his usual interminable last touches, and listening to the usual contradictory suggestions of brother sculptors. Of all the American artists who gave to American art whatever life it breathed in the seventies, St. Gaudens was perhaps the most sympathetic, but certainly the most inarticulate. General Grant or Don Cameron had scarcely less instinct of rhetoric than he. All the others— the Hunts, Richardson, John La Farge, Stanford White—were exuberant; only St. Gaudens could never discuss or dilate on an emotion, or suggest artistic arguments for giving to his work the forms that he felt. He never laid down the law, or affected the despot, or became brutalized like Whistler by the brutalities of his world. He required no incense; he was no egoist; his simplicity of thought was excessive; he could not imitate, or give any form but his own to the creations of his hand. No one felt more strongly than he the strength of other men, but the idea that they could affect him never stirred an image in his mind.

---

[38] Herbert Spencer (1820–1903), British philosopher and sociologist.

This summer his health was poor and his spirits were low. For such a temper, Adams was not the best companion, since his own gaiety was not *folle;* [39] but he risked going now and then to the studio on Mont Parnasse to draw him out for a stroll in the Bois de Boulogne, or dinner as pleased his moods, and in return St. Gaudens sometimes let Adams go about in his company.

Once St. Gaudens took him down to Amiens, with a party of Frenchmen, to see the cathedral. Not until they found themselves actually studying the sculpture of the western portal, did it dawn on Adams's mind that, for his purposes, St. Gaudens on that spot had more interest to him than the cathedral itself. Great men before great monuments express great truths, provided they are not taken too solemnly. Adams never tired of quoting the supreme phrase of his idol Gibbon, before the Gothic cathedrals; "I darted a contemptuous look on the stately monuments of superstition." Even in the footnotes of his history Gibbon had never inserted a bit of humor more human than this, and one would have paid largely for a photograph of the fat little historian, on the background of Notre Dame of Amiens, trying to persuade his readers—perhaps himself—that he was darting a contemptuous look on the stately monument, for which he felt in fact the respect which every man of his vast study and active mind always feels before objects worthy of it; but besides the humor, one felt also the relation. Gibbon ignored the Virgin, because in 1789 religious monuments were out of fashion. In 1900 his remark sounded fresh and simple as the green fields to ears that had heard a hundred years of other remarks, mostly no more fresh and certainly less simple. Without malice, one might find it more instructive than a whole lecture of Ruskin. One sees what one brings, and at that moment Gibbon brought the French Revolution. Ruskin brought reaction against the Revolution. St. Gaudens had passed beyond all. He liked the stately monuments much more than he liked Gibbon or Ruskin; he loved their dignity; their unity; their scale; their lines; their lights and shadows; their decorative sculpture; but he was even less conscious than they of the force that created it all—the Virgin, the Woman—by whose genius "the stately monuments of superstition" were built, through which she was expressed. He would have seen more meaning in Isis [40] with the cow's horns, at Edfoo, who expressed the same thought. The art remained, but the energy was lost even upon the artist.

Yet in mind and person St. Gaudens was a survival of the 1500; he bore the stamp of the Renaissance, and should have carried an image of the Virgin round his neck, or stuck in his hat, like Louis XI. In mere time he was a lost soul that had strayed by chance into the twentieth century, and forgotten where it came from. He writhed and cursed at his ignorance, much as Adams did at his own, but in the opposite sense. St. Gaudens was a child of Benvenuto Cellini, smothered in an Ameri-

[39] Wild.
[40] Egyptian fertility goddess.

can cradle. Adams was a quintessence of Boston, devoured by curiosity to think like Benvenuto. St. Gaudens's art was starved from birth, and Adams's instinct was blighted from babyhood. Each had but half of a nature, and when they came together before the Virgin of Amiens they ought both to have felt in her the force that made them one; but it was not so. To Adams she became more than ever a channel of force; to St. Gaudens she remained as before a channel of taste.

For a symbol of power, St. Gaudens instinctively preferred the horse, as was plain in his horse and Victory of the Sherman monument. Doubtless Sherman also felt it so. The attitude was so American that, for at least forty years, Adams had never realized that any other could be in sound taste. How many years had he taken to admit a notion of what Michael Angelo and Rubens were driving at? He could not say; but he knew that only since 1895 had he begun to feel the Virgin or Venus as force, and not everywhere even so. At Chartres—perhaps at Lourdes—possibly at Cnidos [41] if one could still find there the divinely naked Aphrodite of Praxiteles—but otherwise one must look for force to the goddesses of Indian mythology. The idea died out long ago in the German and English stock. St. Gaudens at Amiens was hardly less sensitive to the force of the female energy than Matthew Arnold at the Grande Chartreuse. [42] Neither of them felt goddesses as power—only as reflected emotion, human expression, beauty, purity, taste, scarcely even as sympathy. They felt a railway train as power; yet they, and all other artists, constantly complained that the power embodied in a railway train could never be embodied in art. All the steam in the world could not, like the Virgin, build Chartres.

Yet in mechanics, whatever the mechanicians might think, both energies acted as interchangeable forces on man, and by action on man all known force may be measured. Indeed, few men of science measured force in any other way. After once admitting that a straight line was the shortest distance between two points, no serious mathematician cared to deny anything that suited his convenience, and rejected no symbol, unproved or unproveable, that helped him to accomplish work. The symbol was force, as a compass-needle or a triangle was force, as the mechanist might prove by losing it, and nothing could be gained by ignoring their value. Symbol or energy, the Virgin had acted as the greatest force the Western world ever felt, and had drawn man's activities to herself more strongly than any other power, natural or supernatural, had ever done; the historian's business was to follow the track of the energy; to find where it came from and where it went to; its complex source and shifting channels; its values, equivalents, conversions. It

[41] Shrine to Aphrodite in Asia Minor.
[42] An old Carthusian monastery near Grenoble, France. Adams invokes the name of Matthew Arnold because Arnold had written a poem, "Stanzas from the Grand Chartreuse" which Adams liked to quote, especially the famous lines: "Wandering between two worlds, one dead/The other powerless to be born."

could scarcely be more complex than radium; it could hardly be deflected, diverted, polarized, absorbed more perplexingly than other radiant matter. Adams knew nothing about any of them, but as a mathematical problem of influence on human progress, though all were occult,
all reacted on his mind, and he rather inclined to think the Virgin
easiest to handle.

The pursuit turned out to be long and tortuous, leading at last into the
vast forests of scholastic science. From Zeno to Descartes, hand in hand
with Thomas Aquinas, Montaigne, and Pascal, one stumbled as stupidly as
though one were still a German student of 1860. Only with the instinct of
despair could one force one's self into this old thicket of ignorance after
having been repulsed at a score of entrances more promising and more
popular. Thus far, no path had led anywhere, unless perhaps to an exceedingly modest living. Forty-five years of study had proved to be quite
futile for the pursuit of power; one controlled no more force in 1900
than in 1850, although the amount of force controlled by society had
enormously increased. The secret of education still hid itself somewhere
behind ignorance, and one fumbled over it as feebly as ever. In such
labyrinths, the staff is a force almost more necessary than the legs; the
pen becomes a sort of blind-man's dog, to keep him from falling into the
gutters. The pen works for itself, and acts like a hand, modelling the
plastic material over and over again to the form that suits it best. The
form is never arbitrary, but is a sort of growth like crystallization, as
any artist knows too well; for often the pencil or pen runs into side-paths
and shapelessness, loses its relations, stops or is bogged. Then it has to
return on its trail, and recover, if it can, its line of force. The result of
a year's work depends more on what is struck out than on what is left
in; on the sequence of the main lines of thought, than on their play or
variety. Compelled once more to lean heavily on this support, Adams
covered more thousands of pages with figures as formal as though they
were algebra, laboriously striking out, altering, burning, experimenting,
until the year had expired, the Exposition had long been closed, and
winter drawing to its end before he sailed from Cherbourg, on January 19, 1901 for home.

WILLIAM JAMES (1842–1910)

William James, a year older than his brother Henry, was the son of a wealthy upper New York State man who rejected his family's rigid Calvinism, became interested in Swedenborgianism, and published a half dozen impenetrable books on theological and other subjects. The boys were brought up in Europe and Newport, and the example of their father's prose to the contrary, the older was to become our most brilliant stylist in philosophy, the younger our most brilliant stylist in fiction—each brilliant in quite his own fashion. More than that, William James became one of the most lucid, outgoing, engaging, and beloved men in the history of American thought, in spite of the fact that he suffered from a variety of plaguing nervous ailments. He revered the humanly normal in all its individuated distinctiveness: the family, friends, human energies and freedom, and of course—but without a touch of arrogance—greatness.

One thinks of him somehow as the best American, if one thinks at all in such generalizing terms. He had a hard time making up his mind about what he should be, a state of indecision that surely marks one of our more attractive traits. First he thought that he would be a painter, but then he took an M.D. at the Harvard Medical School (and never practiced medicine); he lectured on physiology at Harvard, and then found Harvard willing to let him move on into his continuing interests, psychology and then philosophy. What is great about him, of course, is that each of these interests made the next one more perceptive. And this lesson, of accumulated various experience, is the lesson of William James's life for us.

His career at Harvard went on until 1907, but, traveling and lecturing extensively and teaching at other universities, including Berkeley, Edinburgh, and Oxford, he became a figure of international renown.

James was first of all a positivist, that is, one who declines to speculate on absolutes or ultimate causes and is concerned with the positive phenomena of factual existence. The position becomes clear in his first great work, The Principles of Psychology *(1890), in which he rejected the usual antithesis between mind and body and argued that mind is the function by which the human organism adjusts itself to its environment. He was, next, the great exponent of pragmatism, a view which argues that ideas have meaning only in terms of their consequences in the world of feeling and action, that ideas, including ideas about the supernatural, are "true" in the degree to which they satisfy the person who holds them. Life is the laboratory in which ideas are tested. This view is made evident in* The Will to Believe *(1897) and* The Varieties of Religious Experience *(1902), and it is systematically enunciated in* Pragmatism *(1907). It leads easily enough to the third position that we can ascribe to him, pluralism. The universe itself is open and never finished and is so rich and varied in its meanings for each individual that no one dogma or absolute can be usefully insisted upon; each man is morally free to determine his own destiny. The metaphysics of this position he worked out in his late lectures,* A Pluralistic Universe *(1909).*

As he disliked dogma, so he disliked tyranny, and he could not tolerate the thought of war. Yet he recognized aggression in the nature of man and believed it to be a basic and valuable ingredient that could be directed to the finest ends. This is the burden of his famous essay, "The Moral Equivalent of War," a statement published in the year of his death and a charming farewell.

FURTHER READING

Ralph Barton Perry's important two-volume work, *The Thought and Character of William James* (1935) was reprinted in 1962. The definitive biographical study is by Gay Wilson Allen, *William James: A Biography* (1967). Edward C. Moore combines biography and criticism in *William James* (1965), as does Lloyd Morris in *William James: The Message of a Modern Mind* (1951). John J. McDermott is the editor of a recent collection, *The Writings of William James* (1967).

The Moral Equivalent of War (1910)

The war against war is going to be no holiday excursion or camping party. The military feelings are too deeply grounded to abdicate their place among our ideals until better substitutes are offered than the glory and shame that come to nations as well as to individuals from the ups and downs of politics and the vicissitudes of trade. There is something highly paradoxical in the modern man's relation to war. Ask all our millions, north and south, whether they would vote now (were such a thing possible) to have our war for the Union expunged from history, and the record of a peaceful transition to the present time substituted for that of its marches and battles, and probably hardly a handful of eccentrics would say yes. Those ancestors, those efforts, those memories and legends, are the most ideal part of what we now own together, a sacred spiritual possession worth more than all the blood poured out. Yet ask those same people whether they would be willing in cold blood to start another civil war now to gain another similar possession, and not one man or woman would vote for the proposition. In modern eyes, precious though wars may be, they must not be waged solely for the sake of the ideal harvest. Only when forced upon one, only when an enemy's injustice leaves us no alternative, is a war now thought permissible.

It was not thus in ancient times. The earlier men were hunting men, and to hunt a neighboring tribe, kill the males, loot the village and possess the females, was the most profitable, as well as the most exciting, way of living. Thus were the more martial tribes selected, and in chiefs and peoples a pure pugnacity and love of glory came to mingle with the more fundamental appetite for plunder.

Modern war is so expensive that we feel trade to be a better avenue to plunder; but modern man inherits all the innate pugnacity and all the love of glory of his ancestors. Showing war's irrationality and horror is of no effect upon him. The horrors make the fascination. War is the *strong* life; it is life *in extremis;* war-taxes are the only ones men never hesitate to pay, as the budgets of all nations show us.

History is a bath of blood. The Iliad is one long recital of how Diomedes and Ajax, Sarpedon and Hector *killed*. No detail of the wounds they made is spared us, and the Greek mind fed upon the story. Greek history is a panorama of jingoism and imperialism—war for war's sake, all the citizens being warriors. It is horrible reading, because of the irrationality of it all—save for the purpose of making "history"—and the history is that of the utter ruin of a civilization in intellectual respects perhaps the highest the earth has ever seen.

Those wars were purely piratical. Pride, gold, women, slaves, excitement, were their only motives. In the Peloponnesian war for example, the Athenians ask the inhabitants of Melos (the island where the "Venus of Milo" was found), hitherto neutral, to own their lordship. The envoys meet, and hold a debate which Thucydides gives in full, and which, for sweet reasonableness of form, would have satisfied Matthew Arnold. "The powerful exact what they can," said the Athenians, "and the weak grant what they must." When the Meleans say that sooner than be slaves they will appeal to the gods, the Athenians reply: "Of the gods we believe and of men we know that, by a law of their nature, wherever they can rule they will. This law was not made by us, and we are not the first to have acted upon it; we did but inherit it, and we know that you and all mankind, if you were as strong as we are, would do as we do. So much for the gods; we have told you why we expect to stand as high in their good opinion as you." Well, the Meleans still refused, and their town was taken. "The Athenians," Thucydides quietly says, "thereupon put to death all of who were of military age and made slaves of the women and children. They then colonized the island, sending thither five hundred settlers of their own."

Alexander's career was piracy pure and simple, nothing but an orgy of power and plunder, made romantic by the character of the hero. There was no rational principle in it, and the moment he died his generals and governors attacked one another. The cruelty of those times is incredible. When Rome finally conquered Greece, Paulus Æmilius was told by the Roman Senate to reward his soldiers for their toil by "giving" them the old kingdom of Epirus. They sacked seventy cities and carried off a hundred and fifty thousand inhabitants as slaves. How many they killed I know not; but in Etolia they killed all the senators, five hundred and fifty in number. Brutus was "the noblest Roman of them all," but to reanimate his soldiers on the eve of Philippi he similarly promises to give them the cities of Sparta and Thessalonica to ravage, if they win the fight.

Such was the gory nurse that trained societies to cohesiveness. We inherit the warlike type; and for most of the capacities of heroism that the human race is full of we have to thank this cruel history. Dead men tell no tales, and if there were any tribes of other type than this they have left no survivors. Our ancestors have bred pugnacity into our bone and marrow, and thousands of years of peace won't breed it out of us. The popular imagination fairly fattens on the thought of wars. Let public opinion once reach a certain fighting pitch, and no ruler can withstand it. In the Boer war both governments began with bluff but couldn't stay there, the military tension was too much for them. In 1898 our people had read the word "war" in letters three inches high for three months in every newspaper. The pliant politician McKinley [1] was swept away by their eagerness, and our squalid war with Spain became a necessity.

At the present day, civilized opinion is a curious mental mixture. The military instincts and ideals are as strong as ever, but are confronted by reflective criticisms which sorely curb their ancient freedom. Innumerable writers are showing up the bestial side of military service. Pure loot and mastery seem no longer morally avowable motives, and pretexts must be found for attributing them solely to the enemy. England and we, our army and navy authorities repeat without ceasing, arm solely for "peace," Germany and Japan it is who are bent on loot and glory. "Peace" in military mouths to-day is a synonym for "war expected." The word has become a pure provocative, and no government wishing peace sincerely should allow it ever to be printed in a newspaper. Every up-to-date dictionary should say that "peace" and "war" mean the same thing, now *in posse*,[2] now *in actu*.[3] It may even reasonably be said that the intensely sharp competitive *preparation* for war by the nations *is the real war*, permanent, unceasing; and that the battles are only a sort of public verification of the mastery gained during the "peace" interval.

It is plain that on this subject civilized man has developed a sort of double personality. If we take European nations, no legitimate interest of any one of them would seem to justify the tremendous destructions which a war to compass it would necessarily entail. It would seem as though common sense and reason ought to find a way to reach agreement in every conflict of honest interests. I myself think it our bounden duty to believe in such international rationality as possible. But, as

[1] William McKinley (1843–1901), President of the United States from 1897 to 1901. The Spanish-American War took place in 1898.
[2] In potential.
[3] In actuality.

things stand, I see how desperately hard it is to bring the peace-party and the war-party together, and I believe that the difficulty is due to certain deficiencies in the program of pacificism which set the militarist imagination strongly, and to a certain extent justifiably, against it. In the whole discussion both sides are on imaginative and sentimental ground. It is but one utopia against another, and everything one says must be abstract and hypothetical. Subject to this criticism and caution, I will try to characterize in abstract strokes the opposite imaginative forces, and point out what to my own very fallible mind seems the best utopian hypothesis, the most promising line of conciliation.

In my remarks, pacificist though I am, I will refuse to speak of the bestial side of the war-*régime* (already done justice to by many writers) and consider only the higher aspects of militaristic sentiment. Patriotism no one thinks discreditable; nor does any one deny that war is the romance of history. But inordinate ambitions are the soul of every patriotism, and the possibility of violent death the soul of all romance. The militarily patriotic and romantic-minded everywhere, and especially the professional military class, refuse to admit for a moment that war may be a transitory phenomenon in social evolution. The notion of a sheep's paradise like that revolts, they say, our higher imagination. Where then would be the steeps of life? If war had ever stopped, we should have to re-invent it, on this view, to redeem life from flat degeneration.

Reflective apologists for war at the present day all take it religiously. It is a sort of sacrament. Its profits are to the vanquished as well as to the victor; and quite apart from any question of profit, it is an absolute good, we are told, for it is human nature at its highest dynamic. Its "horrors" are a cheap price to pay for rescue from the only alternative supposed, of a world of clerks and teachers, of co-education and zoophily, of "consumer's leagues" and "associated charities," of industrialism unlimited, and femininism unabashed. No scorn, no hardness, no valor any more! Fie upon such a cattleyard of a planet!

So far as the central essence of this feeling goes, no healthy minded person, it seems to me, can help to some degree partaking of it. Militarism is the great preserver of our ideals of hardihood, and human life with no use for hardihood would be contemptible. Without risks or prizes for the darer, history would be insipid indeed; and there is a type of military character which every one feels that the race should never cease to breed, for every one is sensitive to its superiority. The duty is incumbent on mankind, of keeping military characters in stock—of keeping them, if not for use, then as ends in themselves and as pure pieces of perfection,—so that Roosevelt's[4] weaklings and molly-coddles may not end by making everything else disappear from the face of nature.

---

[4] Theodore Roosevelt (1858–1919), President of the United States from 1901 to 1909.

This natural sort of feeling forms, I think, the innermost soul of army-writings. Without any exception known to me, militarist authors take a highly mystical view of their subject, and regard war as a biological or sociological necessity, uncontrolled by ordinary psychological checks and motives. When the time of development is ripe the war must come, reason or no reason, for the justifications pleaded are invariably fictitious. War is, in short, a permanent human *obligation*. General Homer Lea, in his recent book "The Valor of Ignorance," plants himself squarely on this ground. Readiness for war is for him the essence of nationality, and ability in it the supreme measure of the health of nations.

Nations, General Lea says, are never stationary—they must necessarily expand or shrink, according to their vitality or decrepitude. Japan now is culminating; and by the fatal law in question it is impossible that her statesmen should not long since have entered, with extraordinary foresight, upon a vast policy of conquest—the game in which the first moves were her wars with China and Russia and her treaty with England, and of which the final objective is the capture of the Philippines, the Hawaiian Islands, Alaska, and the whole of our Coast west of the Sierra Passes. This will give Japan what her ineluctable vocation as a state absolutely forces her to claim, the possession of the entire Pacific Ocean; and to oppose these deep designs we Americans have, according to our author, nothing but our conceit, our ignorance, our commercialism, our corruption, and our feminism. General Lea makes a minute technical comparison of the military strength which we at present could oppose to the strength of Japan, and concludes that the islands, Alaska, Oregon, and Southern California, would fall almost without resistance, that San Francisco must surrender in a fortnight to a Japanese investment, that in three or four months the war would be over, and our republic, unable to regain what it had heedlessly neglected to protect sufficiently, would then "disintegrate," until perhaps some Cæsar should arise to weld us again into a nation.

A dismal forecast indeed! Yet not unplausible, if the mentality of Japan's statesmen be of the Cæsarian type of which history shows so many examples, and which is all that General Lea seems able to imagine. But there is no reason to think that women can no longer be the mothers of Napoleonic or Alexandrian characters; and if these come in Japan and find their opportunity, just such surprises as "The Valor of Ignorance" paints may lurk in ambush for us. Ignorant as we still are of innermost recesses of Japanese mentality, we may be foolhardy to disregard such possibilities.

Other militarists are more complex and more moral in their considerations. The "Philosophie des Krieges," by S. R. Steinmetz[5] is a

---

[5] Sebald Rudolf Steinmetz (1862–1940), German-educated Dutch professor and sociologist.

good example. War, according to this author, is an ordeal instituted by God, who weighs the nations in its balance. It is the essential form of the State, and the only function in which peoples can employ all their powers at once and convergently. No victory is possible save as the resultant of a totality of virtues, no defeat for which some vice or weakness is not responsible. Fidelity, cohesiveness, tenacity, heroism, conscience, education, inventiveness, economy, wealth, physical health and vigor—there isn't a moral or intellectual point of superiority that doesn't tell, when God holds his assizes and hurls the peoples upon one another. *Die Weltgeschichte ist das Weltgericht,*[6] and Dr. Steinmetz does not believe that in the long run chance and luck play any part in apportioning the issues.

The virtues that prevail, it must be noted, are virtues anyhow, superiorities that count in peaceful as well as in military competition; but the strain on them, being infinitely intenser in the latter case, makes war infinitely more searching as a trial. No ordeal is comparable to its winnowings. Its dread hammer is the welder of men into cohesive states, and nowhere but in such states can human nature adequately develop its capacity. The only alternative is "degeneration."

Dr. Steinmetz is a conscientious thinker, and his book, short as it is, takes much into account. Its upshot can, it seems to me, be summed up in Simon Patten's word, that mankind was nursed in pain and fear, and that the transition to a "pleasure-economy" may be fatal to a being wielding no powers of defence against its disintegrative influences. If we speak of the *fear of emancipation from the fear-régime,* we put the whole situation into a single phrase; fear regarding ourselves now taking the place of the ancient fear of the enemy.

Turn the fear over as I will in my mind, it all seems to lead back to two unwillingnesses of the imagination, one æsthetic, and the other moral; unwillingness, first to envisage a future in which army-life, with its many elements of charm, shall be forever impossible, and in which the destinies of peoples shall nevermore be decided quickly, thrillingly, and tragically, by force, but only gradually and insipidly by "evolution"; and, secondly, unwillingness to see the supreme theatre of human strenuousness closed, and the splendid military aptitudes of men doomed to keep always in a state of latency and never show themselves in action. These insistent unwillingnesses, no less than other æsthetic and ethical insistencies, have, it seems to me, to be listened to and respected. One cannot meet them effectively by mere counter-insistency on war's expensiveness and horror. The horror makes the thrill; and when the question is of getting the extremest and supremest out of human nature, talk of expense sounds ignominious. The weakness of so much merely negative criticism is evident—pacificism makes no converts from the military party. The military party denies neither the bestiality nor the

6 "World-history is the last judgment."

horror, nor the expense; it only says that these things tell but half the story. It only says that war is *worth* them; that, taking human nature as a whole, its wars are its best protection against its weaker and more cowardly self, and that mankind cannot *afford* to adopt a peace-economy.

Pacificists ought to enter more deeply into the æsthetical and ethical point of view of their opponents. Do that first in any controversy, says J. J. Chapman,[7] *then move the point*, and your opponent will follow. So long as anti-militarists propose no substitute for war's disciplinary function, no *moral equivalent* of war, analogous, as one might say, to the mechanical equivalent of heat, so long they fail to realize the full inwardness of the situation. And as a rule they do fail. The duties, penalties, and sanctions pictured in the utopias they paint are all too weak and tame to touch the military-minded. Tolstoi's pacificism is the only exception to this rule, for it is profoundly pessimistic as regards all this world's values, and makes the fear of the Lord furnish the moral spur provided elsewhere by the fear of the enemy. But our socialistic peace-advocates all believe absolutely in this world's values; and instead of the fear of the Lord and the fear of the enemy, the only fear they reckon with is the fear of poverty if one be lazy. This weakness pervades all the socialistic literature with which I am acquainted. Even in Lowes Dickinson's [8] exquisite dialogue,[9] high wages and short hours are the only forces invoked for overcoming man's distaste for repulsive kinds of labor. Meanwhile men at large still live as they always have lived, under a pain-and-fear economy—for those of us who live in an ease-economy are but an island in the stormy ocean—and the whole atmosphere of present-day utopian literature tastes mawkish and dishwatery to people who still keep a sense for life's more bitter flavors. It suggests, in truth, ubiquitous inferiority.

Inferiority is always with us, and merciless scorn of it is the keynote of the military temper. "Dogs, would you live forever?" shouted Frederick the Great. "Yes," say our utopians, "let us live forever, and raise our level gradually." The best thing about our "inferiors" to-day is that they are as tough as nails, and physically and morally almost as insensitive. Utopianism would see them soft and squeamish, while militarism would keep their callousness, but transfigure it into a meritorious characteristic, needed by "the service," and redeemed by that from the suspicion of inferiority. All the qualities of a man acquire dignity when he knows that the service of the collectivity that owns him needs them. If proud of the collectivity, his own pride rises in proportion. No collectivity is like an army for nourishing such pride; but it has to be confessed that the only sentiment which the image of pacific cosmopolitan industrialism is capable of arousing in countless worthy breasts is

[7] John J. Chapman (1862–1933), American man of letters.
[8] Goldsworthy Lowes Dickinson (1862–1932), English historian and philosopher.
[9] "Justice and Liberty," N.Y., 1909. *Au.*

shame at the idea of belonging to *such* a collectivity. It is obvious that
the United States of America as they exist to-day impress a mind like
General Lea's as so much human blubber. Where is the sharpness and
precipitousness, the contempt for life, whether one's own, or another's?
Where is the savage "yes" and "no," the unconditional duty? Where is
the conscription? Where is the blood-tax? Where is anything that one
feels honored by belonging to?

Having said thus much in preparation, I will now confess my own
utopia. I devoutly believe in the reign of peace and in the gradual advent
of some sort of a socialistic equilibrium. The fatalistic view of the war-
function is to me nonsense, for I know that war-making is due to definite motives and subject to prudential checks and reasonable criticisms,
just like any other form of enterprise. And when whole nations are the
armies, and the science of destruction vies in intellectual refinement
with the sciences of production, I see that war becomes absurd and impossible from its own monstrosity. Extravagant ambitions will have to
be replaced by reasonable claims, and nations must make common
cause against them. I see no reason why all this should not apply to
yellow as well as to white countries, and I look forward to a future
when acts of war shall be formally outlawed as between civilized
peoples.

All these beliefs of mine put me squarely into the anti-militarist
party. But I do not believe that peace either ought to be or will be permanent on this globe, unless the states pacifically organized preserve
some of the old elements of army-discipline. A permanently successful
peace-economy cannot be a simple pleasure-economy. In the more or
less socialistic future towards which mankind seems drifting we must
still subject ourselves collectively to those severities which answer to
our real position upon this only partly hospitable globe. We must make
new energies and hardihoods continue the manliness to which the
military mind so faithfully clings. Martial virtues must be the enduring
cement; intrepidity, contempt of softness, surrender of private interest,
obedience to command, must still remain the rock upon which states
are built—unless, indeed, we wish for dangerous reactions against
commonwealths fit only for contempt, and liable to invite attack whenever a centre of crystallization for military-minded enterprise gets
formed anywhere in their neighborhood.

The war-party is assuredly right in affirming and reaffirming that
the martial virtues, although originally gained by the race through war,
are absolute and permanent human goods. Patriotic pride and ambition
in their military form are, after all, only specifications of a more general
competitive passion. They are its first form, but that is no reason for
supposing them to be its last form. Men now are proud of belonging to
a conquering nation, and without a murmur they lay down their persons and their wealth, if by so doing they may fend off subjection. But
who can be sure that *other aspects of one's country* may not, with time
and education and suggestion enough, come to be regarded with simi-

larly effective feelings of pride and shame? Why should men not some
day feel that it is worth a blood-tax to belong to a collectivity superior
in *any* ideal respect? Why should they not blush with indignant shame
if the community that owns them is vile in any way whatsoever? Individuals, daily more numerous, now feel this civic passion. It is only a
question of blowing on the spark till the whole population gets incandescent, and on the ruins of the old morals of military honor, a stable
system of morals of civic honor builds itself up. What the whole community comes to believe in grasps the individual as in a vise. The war-
function has grasped us so far; but constructive interests may some day
seem no less imperative, and impose on the individual a hardly lighter
burden.

Let me illustrate my idea more concretely. There is nothing to make
one indignant in the mere fact that life is hard, that men should toil
and suffer pain. The planetary conditions once for all are such, and we
can stand it. But that so many men, by mere accidents of birth and
opportunity, should have a life of *nothing else* but toil and pain and
hardness and inferiority imposed upon them, should have *no* vacation,
while others natively no more deserving never get any taste of this
campaigning life at all,—*this* is capable of arousing indignation in reflective minds. It may end by seeming shameful to all of us that some
of us have nothing but campaigning, and others nothing but unmanly
ease. If now—and this is my idea—there were, instead of military conscription a conscription of the whole youthful population to form for a
certain number of years a part of the army enlisted against *Nature,* the
injustice would tend to be evened out, and numerous other goods to the
commonwealth would follow. The military ideals of hardihood and discipline would be wrought into the growing fibre of the people; no one
would remain blind as the luxurious classes now are blind, to man's
relations to the globe he lives on, and to the permanently sour and hard
foundations of his higher life. To coal and iron mines, to freight trains,
to fishing fleets in December, to dishwashing, clothes-washing, and
window-washing, to road-building and tunnel-making, to foundries and
stoke-holes, and to the frames of skyscrapers, would our gilded youths
be drafted off, according to their choice, to get the childishness knocked
out of them, and to come back into society with healthier sympathies
and soberer ideas. They would have paid their blood-tax, done their own
part in the immemorial human warfare against nature; they would
tread the earth more proudly, the women would value them more
highly, they would be better fathers and teachers of the following generation.

Such a conscription, with the state of public opinion that would
have required it, and the many moral fruits it would bear, would preserve in the midst of a pacific civilization the manly virtues which the
military party is so afraid of seeing disappear in peace. We should get
toughness without callousness, authority with as little criminal cruelty

as possible, and painful work done cheerily because the duty is temporary, and threatens not, as now, to degrade the whole remainder of one's life. I spoke of the "moral equivalent" of war. So far, war has been the only force that can discipline a whole community, and until an equivalent discipline is organized, I believe that war must have its way. But I have no serious doubt that the ordinary prides and shames of social man, once developed to a certain intensity, are capable of organizing such a moral equivalent as I have sketched, or some other just as effective for preserving manliness of type. It is but a question of time, of skilful propagandism, and of opinion-making men seizing historic opportunities.

The martial type of character can be bred without war. Strenuous honor and disinterestedness abound elsewhere. Priests and medical men are in a fashion educated to it, and we should all feel some degree of it imperative if we were conscious of our work as an obligatory service to the state. We should be *owned,* as soldiers are by the army, and our pride would rise accordingly. We could be poor, then, without humiliation, as army officers now are. The only thing needed henceforward is to inflame the civic temper as past history has inflamed the military temper. H. G. Wells, as usual, sees the center of the situation. "In many ways," he says, "military organization is the most peaceful of activities. When the contemporary man steps from the street, of clamorous insincere advertisement, push, adulteration, underselling and intermittent employment into the barrack-yard, he steps on to a higher social plane, into an atmosphere of service and cooperation and of infinitely more honorable emulations. Here at least men are not flung out of employment to degenerate because there is no immediate work for them to do. They are fed and drilled and trained for better services. Here at least a man is supposed to win promotion by self-forgetfulness and not by self-seeking. And beside the feeble and irregular endowment of research by commercialism, its little short-sighted snatches at profit by innovation and scientific economy, see how remarkable is the steady and rapid development of method and appliances in naval and military affairs! Nothing is more striking than to compare the progress of civil conveniences which has been left almost entirely to the trader, to the progress in military apparatus during the last few decades. The house-appliances of to-day for example, are little better than they were fifty years ago. A house of to-day is still almost as ill-ventilated, badly heated by wasteful fires, clumsily arranged and furnished as the house of 1858. Houses a couple of hundred years old are still satisfactory places of residence, so little have our standards risen. But the rifle or battleship of fifty years ago was beyond all comparison inferior to those we possess; in power, in speed, in convenience alike. No one has a use now for such superannuated things."[10]

[10] "First and Last Things," 1908, p. 215. *Au.*

Wells adds[11] that he thinks that the conceptions of order and discipline, the tradition of service and devotion, of physical fitness, unstinted exertion, and universal responsibility, which universal military duty is now teaching European nations, will remain a permanent acquisition, when the last ammunition has been used in the fireworks that celebrate the final peace. I believe as he does. It would be simply preposterous if the only force that could work ideals of honor and standards of efficiency into English or American natures should be the fear of being killed by the Germans or the Japanese. Great indeed is Fear; but it is not, as our military enthusiasts believe and try to make us believe, the only stimulus known for awakening the higher ranges of men's spiritual energy. The amount of alteration in public opinion which my utopia postulates is vastly less than the difference between the mentality of those black warriors who pursued Stanley's party on the Congo with their cannibal war-cry of "Meat! Meat!" and that of the "general-staff" of any civilized nation. History has seen the latter interval bridged over: the former one can be bridged over much more easily.

GEORGE SANTAYANA (1863–1952)

When his Spanish parents christened him in Madrid, where he was born, they named him Jorge Ruiz de Santayana y Borrais, but since he was brought to the United States at the age of nine and remained here for forty years, the English form of his name is the one he accepted and the one by which we know him.

He was graduated from Harvard College and, after some study in Germany and England, returned to take a Ph.D. at Harvard in 1886, whereupon he was appointed to the department of philosophy and continued in that connection until 1912, when he returned to Europe for his remaining forty years. He lived in France and England and finally in Italy, where he died in a nursing home to which, late in life, he had withdrawn, a fragile but still active ancient, attended by nuns.

Aesthetician, moral philosopher, literary critic, essayist, cultural analyst, poet, novelist, and autobiographer, Santayana produced a body of writing as remarkable in its scope as it is prodigious in quantity. The poetry came early and is of no great consequence; the single novel came relatively late and had the widest audience. This book, The Last Puritan (1935), *with a New England intellectual ascetic as hero, looks back to Santayana's Boston experience and his immersion in the "genteel tradition," a phrase that Santayana coined in*

[11] "First and Last Things," 1908, p. 226. *Au.*

1911 and which we have used ever since to characterize the dying end of New England literary culture. It was Santayana, too, who characterized "genteel American poetry" in a single sentence:

It was a simple, sweet, humane, Protestant literature, grandmotherly in that sedate spectacled wonder with which it gazed at this terrible world and said how beautiful and how interesting it all was.

The sentence suggests what a witty writer Santayana was, and the wit pervades all his work.

His philosophical work is elegantly written in a cadenced prose sometimes suggestive of that of Walter Pater. The early books are the best. The Sense of Beauty (1896), The Life of Reason (1905–1906), and Three Philosophical Poets (1910), all of which came directly out of his teaching experience, have a lucidity and congenial humanity that give his rational naturalism connection with everyday life. But Santayana, curiously, hated teaching (he professed), although he was an extremely effective teacher, and he chafed throughout his New England years. To his colleague, William James, he wrote:

You tax me several times with impertinence and superior airs. I wonder if you realize the years of suppressed irritation which I have passed in the midst of an unintelligible, sanctimonious and often disingenuous Protestantism, which is thoroughly alien and repulsive to me. . . .

This experience found its literary expression not only in his novel, but in a number of other books about the United States, all casting back to his life before 1912: Opinion in America *(1918),* Character and Opinion in the United States *(1920), and* The Genteel Tradition at Bay *(1931). The second, which centers on the conflict of materialism and idealism in American life, has continuing relevance and in its judgments is much more just than one might expect as it is much more perceptive than those of most later European commentators upon life in the United States.*

With his withdrawal from the academic life and increasingly from life itself, Santayana's philosophical work became more and more abstract and disembodied. But at the very end, the three volumes of his autobiography, Persons and Places *(1944, 1945, 1953), return him vividly to the real world, and we are reminded that Santayana all his life insisted that intelligence is "the highest form of vitality."*

FURTHER READING

Daniel Cory has edited *The Letters of Santayana* (1955) and followed that with a portrait with letters, *Santayana: The Later Years* (1963). Important critical studies include Richard Butler, *The Mind* of *Santayana* (1956); Irving Singer, *Santayana's Aesthetics: A Critical Introduction* (1957); and Jerome Ashmore, *Santayana, Art, and Aesthetics* (1966).

Materialism and Idealism in American Life *(1920)*

The language and traditions common to England and America are like other family bonds: they draw kindred together at the greater crises in life, but they also occasion at times a little friction and fault-finding. The groundwork of the two societies is so similar, that each nation, feeling almost at home with the other, and almost able to understand its speech, may instinctively resent what hinders it from feeling at home altogether. Differences will tend to seem anomalies that have slipped in by mistake and through somebody's fault. Each will judge the other by his own standards, not feeling, as in the presence of complete foreigners, that he must make an effort of imagination and put himself in another man's shoes.

In matters of morals, manners, and art, the danger of comparisons is not merely that they may prove invidious, by ranging qualities in an order of merit which might wound somebody's vanity; the danger is rather that comparisons may distort comprehension, because in truth good qualities are all different in kind, and free lives are different in spirit. Comparison is the expedient of those who cannot reach the heart of the things compared; and no philosophy is more external and egotistical than that which places the essence of a thing in its relation to something else. In reality, at the centre of every natural being there is something individual and incommensurable, a seed with its native impulses and aspirations, shaping themselves as best they can in their given environment. Variation is a consequence of freedom, and the slight but radical diversity of souls in turn makes freedom requisite. Instead of instituting in his mind any comparisons between the United States and other nations, I would accordingly urge the reader to forget himself and, in so far as such a thing may be possible for him or for me, to transport himself ideally with me into the outer circumstances of American life, the better to feel its inner temper, and to see how inevitably the American shapes his feelings and judgements, honestly reporting all things as they appear from his new and unobstructed station.

I speak of the American in the singular, as if there were not millions of them, north and south, east and west, of both sexes, of all ages, and of various races, professions, and religions. Of course the one American I speak of is mythical; but to speak in parables is inevitable in such a subject, and it is perhaps as well to do so frankly. There is a sort of poetic ineptitude in all human discourse when it tries to deal with natural and existing things. Practical men may not notice it, but in fact human discourse is intrinsically addressed not to natural existing things but to ideal essences, poetic or logical terms which thought may define and play with. When fortune or necessity diverts our attention from this congenial ideal sport to crude facts and pressing issues, we turn our frail poetic ideas into symbols for those terrible irruptive things. In that paper money of our own stamping, the legal tender of the mind, we are obliged to reckon all the movements and values of the world. The universal American I speak of is one of these symbols; and I should be still speaking in symbols and creating moral units and a false simplicity, if I spoke of classes pedantically subdivided, or individuals ideally integrated and defined. As it happens, the symbolic American can be made largely adequate to the facts; because, if there are immense differences between individual Americans—for some Americans are black—yet there is a great uniformity in their environment, customs, temper, and thoughts. They have all been uprooted from their several soils and ancestries and plunged together into one vortex, whirling irresistibly in a space otherwise quite empty. To be an American is of itself almost a moral condition, an education, and a career. Hence a single ideal figment can cover a large part of what each American is in his character, and almost the whole of what most Americans are in their social outlook and political judgements.

The discovery of the new world exercised a sort of selection among the inhabitants of Europe. All the colonists, except the negroes, were voluntary exiles. The fortunate, the deeply rooted, and the lazy remained at home; the wilder instincts or dissatisfaction of others tempted them beyond the horizon. The American is accordingly the most adventurous, or the descendant of the most adventurous, of Europeans. It is in his blood to be socially a radical, though perhaps not intellectually. What has existed in the past, especially in the remote past, seems to him not only not authoritative, but irrelevant, inferior, and outworn. He finds it rather a sorry waste of time to think about the past at all. But his enthusiasm for the future is profound; he can conceive of no more decisive way of recommending an opinion or a practice than to say that it is what everybody is coming to adopt. This expectation of what he approves, or approval of what he expects, makes up his optimism. It is the necessary faith of the pioneer.

Such a temperament is, of course, not maintained in the nation merely by inheritance. Inheritance notoriously tends to restore the average of a race, and plays incidentally many a trick of atavism. What maintains this temperament and makes it national is social contagion or pressure—something immensely strong in democracies. The luckless American who is born a conservative, or who is drawn to poetic subtlety, pious retreats, or gay passions, nevertheless has the categorical excellence of work, growth, enterprise, reform, and pros-

perity dinned into his ears: every door is open in this direction and
shut in the other; so that he either folds up his heart and withers in a
corner—in remote places you sometimes find such a solitary gaunt
idealist—or else he flies to Oxford or Florence or Montmartre to save
his soul—or perhaps not to save it.

The optimism of the pioneer is not limited to his view of himself
and his own future: it starts from that; but feeling assured, safe,
and cheery within, he looks with smiling and most kindly eyes on
everything and everybody about him. Individualism, roughness, and
self-trust are supposed to go with selfishness and a cold heart; but I
suspect that is a prejudice. It is rather dependence, insecurity, and
mutual jostling that poison our placid gregarious brotherhood; and
fanciful passionate demands upon people's affections, when they are
disappointed, as they soon must be, breed ill-will and a final meanness.
The milk of human kindness is less apt to turn sour if the vessel that
holds it stands steady, cool, and separate, and is not too often un-
corked. In his affections the American is seldom passionate, often
deep, and always kindly. If it were given me to look into the depths
of a man's heart, and I did not find goodwill at the bottom, I should
say without any hesitation, You are not an American. But as the
American is an individualist his good-will is not officious. His instinct
is to think well of everybody, and to wish everybody well, but in a
spirit of rough comradeship, expecting every man to stand on his own
legs and to be helpful in his turn. When he has given his neighbour a
chance he thinks he has done enough for him; but he feels it is an
absolute duty to do that. It will take some hammering to drive a
coddling socialism into America.

As self-trust may pass into self-sufficiency, so optimism, kindness,
and goodwill may grow into a habit of doting on everything. To the
good American many subjects are sacred: sex is sacred, women are
sacred, children are sacred, business is sacred, America is sacred,
Masonic lodges and college clubs are sacred. This feeling grows out
of the good opinion he wishes to have of these things, and serves to
maintain it. If he did not regard all these things as sacred he might
come to doubt sometimes if they were wholly good. Of this kind, too,
is the idealism of single ladies in reduced circumstances who can see
the soul of beauty in ugly things, and are perfectly happy because
their old dog has such pathetic eyes, their minister is so eloquent, their
garden with its three sun-flowers is so pleasant, their dead friends were
so devoted, and their distant relations are so rich.

Consider now the great emptiness of America: not merely the
primitive physical emptiness, surviving in some regions, and the continental spacing of the chief natural features, but also the moral emptiness of a settlement where men and even houses are easily moved
about, and no one, almost, lives where he was born or believes what
he has been taught. Not that the American has jettisoned these im-

pedimenta in anger; they have simply slipped from him as he moves. Great empty spaces bring a sort of freedom to both soul and body. You may pitch your tent where you will; or if ever you decide to build anything, it can be in a style of your own devising. You have room, fresh materials, few models, and no critics. You trust your own experience, not only because you must, but because you find you may do so safely and prosperously; the forces that determine fortune are not yet too complicated for one man to explore. Your detachable condition makes you lavish with money and cheerfully experimental; you lose little if you lose all, since you remain completely yourself. At the same time your absolute initiative gives you practice in coping with novel situations, and in being original; it teaches you shrewd management. Your life and mind will become dry and direct, with few decorative flourishes. In your works everything will be stark and pragmatic; you will not understand why anybody should make those little sacrifices to instinct or custom which we call grace. The fine arts will seem to you academic luxuries, fit to amuse the ladies, like Greek and Sanskirt; for while you will perfectly appreciate generosity in men's purposes, you will not admit that the execution of these purposes can be anything but business. Unfortunately the essence of the fine arts is that the execution should be generous too, and delightful in itself; therefore the fine arts will suffer, not so much in their express professional pursuit—for then they become practical tasks and a kind of business—as in that diffused charm which qualifies all human action when men are artists by nature. Elaboration, which is something to accomplish, will be preferred to simplicity, which is something to rest in; manners will suffer somewhat; speech will suffer horribly. For the American the urgency of his novel attack upon matter, his zeal in gathering its fruits, precludes meanderings in primrose paths; devices must be short cuts, and symbols must be mere symbols. If his wife wants luxuries, of course she may have them; and if he has vices, that can be provided for too; but they must all be set down under those headings in his ledgers.

At the same time, the American is imaginative; for where life is intense, imagination is intense also. Were he not imaginative he would not live so much in the future. But his imagination is practical, and the future it forecasts is immediate; it works with the clearest and least ambiguous terms known to his experience, in terms of number, measure, contrivance, economy, and speed. He is an idealist working on matter. Understanding as he does the material potentialities of things, he is successful in invention, conservative in reform, and quick in emergencies. All his life he jumps into the train after it has started and jumps out before it has stopped; and he never once gets left behind, or breaks a leg. There is an enthusiasm in his sympathetic handling of material forces which goes far to cancel the illiberal character which it might otherwise assume. The good workman hardly distinguishes his artistic intention from the potency in himself and in things which is about to realise that intention. Accordingly his ideals fall into the form of premonitions and prophecies; and his studious prophecies often come true. So do the happy workmanlike ideals of the American. When a poor boy, perhaps, he dreams of an education, and presently he gets an education, or at least a degree; he dreams of growing rich, and he grows rich—only more slowly and modestly, perhaps, than he expected; he dreams of marrying his Rebecca and, even if he marries a Leah[1] instead, he ultimately finds in Leah his Rebecca after all. He dreams of helping to carry on and to accelerate the movement of a vast, seething, progressive society, and he actually does so. Ideals clinging so close to nature are almost sure of fulfilment; the American beams with a certain self-confidence and sense of mastery; he feels that God and nature are working with him.

Idealism in the American accordingly goes hand in hand with present contentment and with foresight of what the future very likely will actually bring. He is not a revolutionist; he believes he is already on the right track and moving towards an excellent destiny. In revolutionists, on the contrary, idealism is founded on dissatisfaction and expresses it. What exists seems to them an absurd jumble of irrational accidents and bad habits, and they want the future to be based on reason and to be the pellucid embodiment of all their maxims. All their zeal is for something radically different from the actual and (if they only knew it) from the possible; it is ideally simple, and they love it and believe in it because their nature craves it. They think life would be set free by the destruction of all its organs. They are therefore extreme idealists in the region of hope, but not at all, as poets and artists are, in the region of perception and memory. In the atmosphere of civilised life they miss all the refraction and all the fragrance; so that in their conception of actual things they are apt to be crude realists; and their ignorance and inexperience of the moral world, unless it comes of ill-luck, indicates their incapacity for education. Now incapacity for education, when united with great inner vitality, is one root of idealism. It is what condemns us all, in the region of sense, to substitute perpetually what we are capable of imagining for what things may be in themselves; it is what condemns us, wherever it extends, to think *a priori;* it is what keeps us bravely and incorrigibly pursuing what we call the good—that is, what would fulfil the demands of our nature— however little provision the fates may have made for it. But the want of insight on the part of revolutionists touching the past and the present infects in an important particular their idealism about the future;

---

[1] In Genesis, 29:15–31, Jacob wishes to marry Rachel (*not* Rebecca, who is his mother) and serves seven years at her father's house. But he first must wed Leah, whom he does not love, and only after seven more years of service can he claim Rachel.

it renders their dreams of the future unrealisable. For in human
beings—this may not be true of other animals, more perfectly pre-
formed—experience is necessary to pertinent and concrete thinking;
even our primitive instincts are blind until they stumble upon some
occasion that solicits them; and they can be much transformed or
deranged by their first partial satisfactions. Therefore a man who does
not idealise his experience, but idealises *a priori*, is incapable of true
phophecy; when he dreams he raves, and the more he criticises the
less he helps. American idealism, on the contrary, is nothing if not
helpful, nothing if not pertinent to practicable transformations; and
when the American frets, it is because whatever is useless and impertinent, be it idealism or inertia, irritates him; for it frustrates the good
results which he sees might so easily have been obtained.

The American is wonderfully alive; and his vitality, not having
often found a suitable outlet, makes him appear agitated on the surface; he is always letting off an unnecessarily loud blast of incidental
steam. Yet his vitality is not superficial; it is inwardly prompted, and
as sensitive and quick as a magnetic needle. He is inquisitive, and
ready with an answer to any question that he may put to himself of
his own accord; but if you try to pour instruction into him, on matters
that do not touch his own spontaneous life, he shows the most extraordinary powers of resistance and oblivescence; so that he often is
remarkably expert in some directions and surprisingly obtuse in others.
He seems to bear lightly the sorrowful burden of human knowledge.
In a word, he is young.

What sense is there in this feeling, which we all have, that the
American is young? His country is blessed with as many elderly
people as any other, and his descent from Adam, or from the Darwin-
ian rival of Adam, cannot be shorter than that of his European
cousins. Nor are his ideas always very fresh. Trite and rigid bits of
morality and religion, with much seemly and antique political lore,
remain axiomatic in him, as in the mind of a child; he may carry all
this about with an unquestioning familiarity which does not comport
understanding. To keep traditional sentiments in this way insulated and
uncriticised is itself a sign of youth. A good young man is naturally
conservative and loyal on all those subjects which his experience has
not brought to a test; advanced opinions on politics, marriage, or literature are comparatively rare in America; they are left for the ladies
to discuss, and usually to condemn, while the men get on with their
work. In spite of what is old-fashioned in his more general ideas, the
American is unmistakably young; and this, I should say, for two
reasons: one, that he is chiefly occupied with his immediate environment, and the other, that his reactions upon it are inwardly prompted,
spontaneous, and full of vivacity and self-trust. His views are not yet
lengthened; his will is not yet broken or transformed. The present
moment, however, in this, as in other things, may mark a great change

in him; he is perhaps now reaching his majority, and all I say may hardly apply to-day, and may not apply at all to-morrow. I speak of him as I have known him; and whatever moral strength may accrue to him later, I am not sorry to have known him in his youth. The charm of youth, even when it is a little boisterous, lies in nearness to the impulses of nature, in a quicker and more obvious obedience to that pure, seminal principle which, having formed the body and its organs, always directs their movements, unless it is forced by vice or necessity to make them crooked, or to suspend them. Even under the inevitable crust of age the soul remains young, and, wherever it is able to break through, sprouts into something green and tender. We are all as young at heart as the most youthful American, but the seed in his case has fallen upon virgin soil, where it may spring up more bravely and with less respect for the giants of the wood. Peoples seem older when their perennial natural youth is encumbered with more possessions and prepossessions, and they are mindful of the many things they have lost or missed. The American is not mindful of them.

In America there is a tacit optimistic assumption about existence, to the effect that the more existence the better. The soulless critic might urge that quantity is only a physical category, implying no excellence, but at best an abundance of opportunities both for good and for evil. Yet the young soul, being curious and hungry, views existence *a priori* under the form of the good; its instinct to live implies a faith that most things it can become or see or do will be worth while. Respect for quantity is accordingly something more than the childish joy and wonder at bigness; it is the fisherman's joy in a big haul, the good uses of which he can take for granted. Such optimism is amiable. Nature cannot afford that we should begin by being too calculating or wise, and she encourages us by the pleasure she attaches to our functions in advance of their fruits, and often in excess of them; as the angler enjoys catching his fish more than eating it, and often, waiting patiently for the fish to bite, misses his own supper. The pioneer must devote himself to preparations; he must work for the future, and it is healthy and dutiful of him to love his work for its own sake. At the same time, unless reference to an ultimate purpose is at least virtual in all his activities, he runs the danger of becoming a living automaton, vain and ignominious in its mechanical constancy. Idealism about work can hide an intense materialism about life. Man, if he is a rational being, cannot live by bread alone nor be a labourer merely; he must eat and work in view of an ideal harmony which overarches all his days, and which is realised in the way they hang together, or in some ideal issue which they have in common. Otherwise, though his technical philosophy may call itself idealism, he is a materialist in morals; he esteems things, and esteems himself, for mechanical uses and energies. Even sensualists, artists, and pleasure-lovers are wiser than that, for though their idealism may be desultory or corrupt, they attain something ideal, and prize things only for their living effects, moral though perhaps fugitive. Sensation, when we do not take it as a signal for action, but arrest and peruse what it positively brings before us, reveals something ideal—a colour, shape, or sound; and to dwell on these presences, with no thought of their material significance, is an æsthetic or dreamful idealism. To pass from this idealism to the knowledge of matter is a great intellectual advance, and goes with dominion over the world; for in the practical arts the mind is adjusted to a larger object, with more depth and potentiality in it; which is what makes people feel that the material world is real, as they call it, and that the ideal world is not. Certainly the material world is real; for the philosophers who deny the existence of matter are like the critics who deny the existence of Homer. If there was never any Homer, there must have been a lot of other poets no less Homeric than he; and if matter does not exist, a combination of other things exists which is just as material. But the intense reality of the material world would not prevent it from being a dreary waste in our eyes, or even an abyss of horror, if it brought forth no spiritual fruits. In fact, it does bring forth spiritual fruits, for otherwise we should not be here to find fault with it, and to set up our ideals over against it. Nature is material, but not materialistic; it issues in life, and breeds all sorts of warm passions and idle beauties. And just as sympathy with the mechanical travail and turmoil of nature, apart from its spiritual fruits, is moral materialism, so the continual perception and love of these fruits is moral idealism—happiness in the presence of immaterial objects and harmonies, such as we envisage in affection, speculation, religion, and all the forms of the beautiful.

The circumstances of his life hitherto have necessarily driven the American into moral materialism; for in his dealings with material things he can hardly stop to enjoy their sensible aspects, which are ideal, nor proceed at once to their ultimate uses, which are ideal too. He is practical as against the poet, and worldly as against the clear philosopher or the saint. The most striking expression of this materialism is usually supposed to be his love of the almighty dollar; but that is a foreign and unintelligent view. The American talks about money, because that is the symbol and measure he has at hand for success, intelligence, and power; but as to money itself he makes, loses, spends, and gives it away with a very light heart. To my mind the most striking expression of his materialism is his singular preoccupation with quantity. If, for instance, you visit Niagara Falls, you may expect to hear how many cubic feet or metric tons of water are precipitated per second over the cataract; how many cities and towns (with the number of their inhabitants) derive light and motive power from it; and the annual value of the further industries that might very well be carried on by the same means, without visibly depleting the world's greatest wonder or injuring the tourist trade. That is what I confidently ex-

pected to hear on arriving at the adjoining town of Buffalo; but I
was deceived. The first thing I heard instead was that there are more
miles of asphalt pavement in Buffalo than in any city in the world. Nor
is this insistence on quantity confined to men of business. The President of Harvard College, seeing me once by chance soon after the
beginning of a term, inquired how my classes were getting on; and
when I replied that I thought they were getting on well, that my men
seemed to be keen and intelligent, he stopped me as if I was about to
waste his time. "I meant," said he, "*what is the number* of students in
your classes."

Here I think we may perceive that this love of quantity often has
a silent partner, which is diffidence as to quality. The democratic
conscience recoils before anything that savours of privilege; and lest it
should concede an unmerited privilege to any pursuit or person, it
reduces all things as far as possible to the common denominator of
quantity. Numbers cannot lie: but if it came to comparing the ideal
beauties of philosophy with those of Anglo-Saxon, who should decide?
All studies are good—why else have universities?—but those must be
most encouraged which attract the greatest number of students. Hence
the President's question. Democratic faith, in its diffidence about quality, throws the reins of education upon the pupil's neck, as Don
Quixote threw the reins on the neck of Rocinante, and bids his divine
instinct choose its own way.

The American has never yet had to face the trials of Job. Great
crises, like the Civil War, he has known how to surmount victoriously;
and now that he has surmounted a second great crisis victoriously, it is
possible that he may relapse, as he did in the other case, into an
apparently complete absorption in material enterprise and prosperity.
But if serious and irremediable tribulation ever overtook him, what
would his attitude be? It is then that we should be able to discover
whether materialism or idealism lies at the base of his character. Meantime his working mind is not without its holiday. He spreads humour
pretty thick and even over the surface of conversation, and humour
is one form of moral emancipation. He loves landscape, he loves mankind, and he loves knowledge; and in music at least he finds an art
which he unfeignedly enjoys. In music and landscape, in humour and
kindness, he touches the ideal more truly, perhaps, than in his ponderous academic idealisms and busy religions; for it is astonishing how
much even religion in America (can it possibly be so in England?)
is a matter of meetings, building-funds, schools, charities, clubs, and
picnics. To be poor in order to be simple, to produce less in order that
the product may be more choice and beautiful, and may leave us less
burdened with unnecessary duties and useless possessions—that is an
ideal not articulate in the American mind; yet here and there I seem to
have heard a sigh after it, a groan at the perpetual incubus of business
and shrill society. Significant witness to such aspirations is borne by

those new forms of popular religion, not mere variations on tradition, which have sprung up from the soil—revivalism, spiritualism, Christian Science, the New Thought.[2] Whether or no we can tap, through these or other channels, some cosmic or inner energy not hitherto at the disposal of man (and there is nothing incredible in that), we certainly may try to remove friction and waste in the mere process of living; we may relax morbid strains, loosen suppressed instincts, iron out the creases of the soul, discipline ourselves into simplicity, sweetness, and peace. These religious movements are efforts toward such physiological economy and hygiene; and while they are thoroughly plebeian, with no great lights, and no idea of raising men from the most vulgar and humdrum worldly existence, yet they see the possibility of physical and moral health on that common plane, and pursue it. That is true morality. The dignities of various types of life or mind, like the gifts of various animals, are relative. The snob adores one type only, and the creatures supposed by him to illustrate it perfectly; or envies and hates them, which is just as snobbish. Veritable lovers of life, on the contrary, like Saint Francis or like Dickens, know that in every tenement of clay, with no matter what endowment or station, happiness and perfection are possible to the soul. There must be no brow-beating, with shouts of work or progress or revolution, any more than with threats of hell-fire. What does it profit a man to free the whole world if his soul is not free? Moral freedom is not an artificial condition, because the ideal is the mother tongue of both the heart and the senses. All that is requisite is that we should pause in living to enjoy life, and should lift up our hearts to things that are pure goods in themselves, so that once to have found and loved them, whatever else may betide, may remain a happiness that nothing can sully. This natural idealism does not imply that we are immaterial, but only that we are animate and truly alive. When the senses are sharp, as they are in the American, they are already half liberated, already a joy in themselves; and when the heart is warm, like his, and eager to be just, its ideal destiny can hardly be doubtful. It will not be always merely pumping and working; time and its own pulses will lend it wings.

RANDOLPH [SILLIMAN] BOURNE (1886–1918)

This man, ugly as sin through accidents of birth, only 5 feet tall because of a deformed back (he never appeared in public without being encased in a large black cape), with practically no chin and with a distorted ear that repelled anyone who had to look at it— this man now seems to be one of the most attractive and important

[2] A doctrine advocating that the power of ideas can change and control physical and mental circumstances.

people who lived in that remote time before and during the First World War; he is perhaps, of them all, the one who one most intensely wishes could have lived longer.

He was born in a respectable middle-class community—Bloomfield, New Jersey—into a family with a Calvinistic tradition. When his father failed in business, that kind of Calvinism attributed his failure to moral deficiency, and he was asked to leave. The boy's uncle on his mother's side took over the household and refused to send him to college. It was only in 1909, at the age of twenty-three, that Randolph Bourne became a freshman at Columbia on his own initiative and with a scholarship. Some of his professors at once recognized his qualities of mind, and it was at this time that he himself felt he had begun to live. A Columbia dean, no less, encouraged the young Bourne to write a reply to a stuffy attack on the "younger generation" that had appeared in The Atlantic Monthly; the result was Randolph Bourne's first appearance in commercial print in 1911, a defense of the young.

His first book, a collection of essays that he had contributed to The Columbia Monthly and the Atlantic, was called Youth and Life (1913), and it established his tone and his pitch in the tone of those insurgent times. He announced, to the horror of many then, what has since come to be called the "generation gap." Nothing has changed much, one is forced to conclude, as one listens to the young Bourne's protests against his elders, his certainty that ". . . the stupidities and cruelties of their management of the world fill youth with an intolerant rage."

After his graduation from Columbia in 1913, a scholarship enabled Bourne to travel in Europe for two years. One of the several essays that resulted from this journey was "Our Cultural Humility," in which he implored American writers and American artists in general to reassert their native rather than their chameleonlike character. This essay implies the program that he made explicit in his essay of 1916, "Trans-National America": the United States will have no culture at all until it both accepts and learns to treasure all the differences in the immigrant cultural strains that have poured and are still pouring into it.

Returning to the United States, Bourne continued an editorial association with the New Republic that had been established earlier, wrote many pieces for that journal, and having been deeply influenced as a Columbia student by John Dewey, published two books on education, which he saw as the only gateway to a decent democratic society. This interest was deflected by the war in Europe and the probability of American participation, and Bourne became the major spokesman for antiwar radicals. He lost and relinquished friends, *including John Dewey, but not his eloquence. Ironically, he died in the epidemic of influenza that the end of the war brought to the United States.*

His late pieces were collected by his friends after his death—by James Oppenheim in Untimely Papers *(1919) and by Van Wyck Brooks in* The History of a Literary Radical and Other Essays *(1920).*

FURTHER READING

The best biography, by John Adam Moreau, is *Randolph Bourne: Legend and Reality* (1966). Louis Filler's *Randolph Bourne* (1943) is a documented critical study. A useful anthology, *The World of Randolph Bourne* (1965), was edited by Lillian Schlissel.

Our Cultural Humility (1912)

It was Matthew Arnold, read and reverenced by the generation immediately preceding our own, who set to our eyes a definition and a goal of culture which has become the common property of all our world. To know the best that had been thought and said, to appreciate the master-works which the previous civilizations had produced, to put our minds and appreciations in contact with the great of all ages,— here was a clear ideal which dissolved the mists in which the vaguenesses of culture had been lost. And it was an ideal that appealed with peculiar force to Americans. For it was a democratic ideal; every one who had the energy and perseverance could reasonably expect to acquire by taking thought that orientation of soul to which Arnold gave the magic name of culture. And it was a quantitative ideal; culture was a matter of acquisition—with appreciation and prayerfulness perhaps, but still a matter of adding little by little to one's store until one should have a vision of that radiant limit, when one knew all the best that had been thought and said and pictured in the world.

I do not know in just what way the British public responded to Arnold's eloquence; if the prophetic wrath of Ruskin failed to stir them, it is not probable that they were moved by the persuasiveness of Arnold. But I do know that, coming at a time when America was producing rapidly an enormous number of people who were "comfortably off," as the phrase goes, and who were sufficiently awake to feel their limitations, with the broader horizons of Europe just opening on the view, the new doctrine had the most decisive effect on our succeeding spiritual history. The "land-of-liberty" American of the era of Dickens still exists in the British weeklies and in observations of America by callow young journalists, but as a living species he has long been extinct. His place has been taken by a person whose pride is measured not by the greatness of the "land of the free," but by his own orientation in Europe.

Already in the nineties, our college professors and our artists were beginning to require the seal of a European training to justify their existence. We appropriated the German system of education. Our millionaires began the collecting of pictures and the endowment of museums with foreign works of art. We began the exportation of school-teachers for a summer tour of Europe. American art and music colonies sprang up in Paris and Berlin and Munich. The movement became a rush. That mystical premonition of Europe, which Henry James tells us he had from his earliest boyhood, became the common property of the talented young American, who felt a certain starvation in his own land, and longed for the fleshpots of European culture. But the bourgeoisie soon followed the artistic and the semi-artistic, and Europe became so much the fashion that it is now almost a test of respectability to have traveled at least once abroad.

Underlying all this vivacious emigration, there was of course a real if vague thirst for "culture," and, in strict accord with Arnold's definition, the idea that somehow culture could be imbibed, that from the contact with the treasures of Europe there would be rubbed off on us a little of that grace which had made the art. So for those who could not travel abroad, our millionaires transported, in almost terrifying bulk and at staggering cost, samples of everything that the foreign galleries had to show. We were to acquire culture at any cost, and we had no doubt that we had discovered the royal road to it. We followed it, at any rate, with eye single to the goal. The naturally sensitive, who really found in the European literature and arts some sort of spiritual nourishment, set the pace, and the crowd followed at their heels.

This cultural humility of ours astonished and still astonishes Europe. In England, where "culture" is taken very frivolously, the bated breath of the American, when he speaks of Shakespeare or Tennyson or Browning, is always cause for amusement. And the Frenchman is always a little puzzled at the crowds who attend lectures in Paris on "How to See Europe Intelligently," or are taken in vast parties through the Louvre. The European objects a little to being so constantly regarded as the keeper of a huge museum. If you speak to him of culture, you find him frankly more interested in contemporaneous literature and art and music than in his worthies of the olden time, more interested in discriminating the good of today than in accepting the classics. If he is a cultivated person, he is much more interested usually in quarreling about a living dog than in reverencing a dead lion. If he is a French *lettré*,[1] for instance, he will be producing a book on the psychology of some living writer, while the Anglo-Saxon

---

[1] "Man of letters."

will be writing another on Shakespeare. His whole attitude towards the things of culture, be it noted, is one of daily appreciation and intimacy, not that attitude of reverence with which we Americans approach alien art, and which penalizes cutural heresy among us.

The European may be enthusiastic, polemic, radiant, concerning his culture; he is never humble. And he is, above all, never humble before the culture of another country. The Frenchman will hear nothing but French music, read nothing but French literature, and prefers his own art to that of any other nation. He can hardly understand our almost pathetic eagerness to learn of the culture of other nations, our humility of worship in the presence of art that in no sense represents the expression of any of our ideals and motivating forces.

To a genuinely patriotic American this cultural humility of ours is somewhat humiliating. In response to this eager inexhaustible interest in Europe, where is Europe's interest in us? Europe is to us the land of history, of mellow tradition, of the arts and graces of life, of the best that has been said and thought in the world. To Europe we are the land of crude racial chaos, of skyscrapers and bluff, of millionaires and "bosses." A French philosopher visits us, and we are all eagerness to get from him an orientation in all that is moving in the world of thought across the seas. But does he ask about our philosophy, does he seek an orientation in the American thought of the day? Not at all. Our humility has kept us from forcing it upon his attention, and it scarcely exists for him. Our advertising genius, so powerful and universal where soap and biscuits are concerned, wilts and languishes before the task of trumpeting our intellectual and spiritual products before the world. Yet there can be little doubt which is the more intrinsically worth advertising. But our humility causes us to be taken at our own face value, and for all this patient fixity of gaze upon Europe, we get little reward except to be ignored, or to have our interest somewhat contemptuously dismissed as parasitic.

And with justice! For our very goal and ideal of culture has made us parasites. Our method has been exactly wrong. For the truth is that the definition of culture, which we have accepted with such devastating enthusiasm, is a definition emanating from that very barbarism from which its author recoiled in such horror. If it were not that all our attitude showed that we had adopted a quite different standard, it would be the merest platitude to say that culture is not an acquired familiarity with things outside, but an inner and constantly operating taste, a fresh and responsive power of discrimination, and the insistent judging of everything that comes to our minds and senses. It is clear that such a sensitive taste cannot be acquired by torturing our appreciations into conformity with the judgments of others, no matter how "authoritative" those judgments may be. Such a method means a hypnotization of judgment, not a true development of soul.

At the back of Arnold's definition is, of course, the implication that if we have only learned to appreciate the "best," we shall have been trained thus to discriminate generally, that our appreciation of Shakespeare will somehow spill over into admiration of the incomparable art of Mr. G. Lowes Dickinson. This is, of course, exactly to reverse the psychological process. A true appreciation of the remote and the magnificent is acquired only after the judgement has learned to discriminate with accuracy and taste between the good and bad, the sincere and the false, of the familiar and contemporaneous art and writing of every day. To set up an alien standard of the classics is merely to give our lazy taste a resting-point, and to prevent forever any genuine culture.

This virus of the "best" rages throughout all our Anglo-Saxon campaign for culture. Is it not a notorious fact that our professors of English literature make no attempt to judge the work produced since the death of the last consecrated saint of the literary canon,—Robert Louis Stevenson? In strict accordance with Arnold's doctrine, they are waiting for the judgment upon our contemporaries which they call the test of time, that is, an authoritative objective judgement, upon which they can unquestioningly rely. Surely it seems as if the principle of authority, having been ousted from religion and politics, had found a strong refuge in the sphere of culture. This tyranny of the "best" objectifies all our taste. It is a "best" that is always outside of our native reactions to the freshness and sincerities of life, a "best" to which our spontaneities must be disciplined. By fixing our eyes humbly on the ages that are past, and on foreign countries, we effectually protect ourselves from that inner taste which is the only sincere "culture."

Our cultural humility before the civilizations of Europe, then, is the chief obstacle which prevents us from producing any true indigenous culture of our own. I am far from saying, of course, that it is not necessary for our arts to be fertilized by the civilizations of other nations past and present. The culture of Europe has arisen only from such an extensive cross-fertilization in the past. But we have passed through that period of learning, and it is time for us now to set up our individual standards. We are already "heir of all the ages" through our English ancestry, and our last half-century of European idolatry has done for us all that can be expected. But, with our eyes fixed on Europe, we continue to strangle whatever native genius springs up. Is it not a tragedy that the American artist feels the imperative need of foreign approval before he can be assured of his attainment? Through our inability or unwillingness to judge him, through our cultural humility, through our insistence on the objective standard, we drive him to depend on a foreign clientèle, to live even in foreign countries, where taste is more confident of itself and does not require the label, to be assured of the worth of what it appreciates.

The only remedy for this deplorable situation is the cultivation of a new American nationalism. We need that keen introspection into the beauties and vitalities and sincerities of our own life and ideals that characterizes the French. The French culture is animated by principles and tastes which are as old as art itself. There are "classics," not in the English and Arnoldian sense of a consecrated canon, dissent from which is heresy, but in the sense that each successive generation, putting them to the test, finds them redolent of those qualities which are characteristically French, and so preserves them as a precious heritage. This cultural chauvinism is the most harmless of patriotisms; indeed it is absolutely necessary for a true life of civilization. And it can hardly be too intense, or too exaggerated. Such an international art exhibition as was held recently in New York, with the frankly avowed purpose of showing American artists how bad they were in comparison with the modern French, represents an appalling degradation of attitude which would be quite impossible in any other country. Such groveling humility can only have the effect of making us feeble imitators, instead of making us assert, with all the power at our command, the genius and individuality which we already possess in quantity, if we would only see it.

In the contemporary talent that Europe is exhibiting, or even in the genius of the last half-century, one will go far to find greater poets than our Walt Whitman, philosophers than William James, essayists than Emerson and Thoreau, composers than MacDowell, sculptors than Saint-Gaudens. In any other country such names would be focuses to which interest and enthusiasms would converge, symbols of a national spirit about which judgments and tastes would revolve. For none of them could have been born in another country than our own. If some of them had their training abroad, it was still the indigenous America that their works expressed,—the American ideals and qualities, our pulsating democracy, the vigor and daring of our pioneer spirit, our sense of *camaraderie*, our dynamism, the big-heartedness of our scenery, our hospitality to all the world. In the music of MacDowell, the poetry of Whitman, the philosophy of James, I recognize a national spirit, "l'esprit américain," as superbly clear and gripping as anything the culture of Europe has to offer us, and immensely more stimulating, because of the very body and soul of to-day's interest and aspirations.

To come to an intense self-consciousness of these qualities, to feel them in the work of these masters, and to search for them everywhere among the lesser artists and thinkers who are trying to express the soul of this hot chaos of America,— this will be the attainment of culture for us. Not to look on ravished while our marvelous millionaires fill our museums with "old masters," armor, and porcelains, but to turn our eyes upon our own art for a time, shut ourselves in with our own genius, and cultivate with an intense and partial pride what we have already achieved against the obstacles of our cultural humility. Only thus shall we conserve the American spirit and saturate the next generation with those qualities which are our strength. Only thus can we take our rightful place among the cultures of the world, to which we are entitled if we would but recognize it. We shall never be able to perpetuate our ideals except in the form of art and literature; the world will never understand our spirit except in terms of art. When shall we learn that "culture," like the kingdom of heaven, lies within us, in the heart of our national soul, and not in foreign galleries and books? When shall we learn to be proud? For only pride is creative.

VAN WYCK BROOKS (1886–1963)

The interior lives of most human beings, including distinguished ones, do not ordinarily present themselves with a structure that is fictional or dramatic. That of Van Wyck Brooks almost does. It is like Virginia Woolf's novel, To the Lighthouse. *There are two parts, sharply anti-thetical, and an interlude between them called "Time Passes." Or it is like Eliot's* Murder in the Cathedral: *again, two acts, perfectly balanced, separated not by a long sermon, as in Eliot's play, but by the purgatorial nightmare of a nervous breakdown. If convictions about literature could somehow be objectified as representations of psychic states, and so in turn become material for literature, this life could be written as a novel or a play.*

He had everything, it would seem: born into a wealthy Plainfield, New Jersey, family that knew and enjoyed Europe, admitted to Harvard College, a success there, widely traveled while still young, he enjoyed a soaring reputation as the most perceptive critic of American life and letters in the years from 1910 to 1925. The basis of that criticism is enunciated in his first book, The Wine of the Puritans *(1909), and summarized in the opening chapter, " 'Highbrow' and 'Lowbrow,' " of* America's Coming-of-Age *(1915); it is developed and orchestrated in the books that followed:* Letters and Leadership *(1918),* The Ordeal of Mark Twain *(1920),* The Pilgrimage of Henry James *(1925),* The Literary Life in America *(1927),* Emerson and Others *(1927), and still more.*

Editorially involved as he was in such avant-garde publications as The Seven Arts, The Freeman, *and* The American Caravan, *Brooks was a literary radical and a socialist. Early enamored of the high civilization and the gracious daily rituals of life in Europe, he had yet decided that his place was in the United States, whether in New York, California, or Connecticut. In these places, chiefly, he worked out his judgment.*

The Puritan tradition in America had split our life into an antithetical duality: the transcendental strain developed into a watered idealism, academicism, gentility, the "highbrow" character without relation to actualities; the physical pressures of Puritan life developed into our rampant commercialism, materialism, business-mindedness, the "lowbrow" character that made the actualities. A true culture, which should have found its dynamic place somewhere between these two, was a void. For artists the situation was impossible: if, like Mark Twain, one compromised and settled for the second, one was fractured by guilt and near madness; if, like Henry James, one deracinated oneself on behalf of the first, one became tragically remote from reality and isolated oneself in a more and more tenuous and finally meaningless technical virtuosity. It was Brooks's aim to bridge this gulf, and he decided that the figure who could point the way was Emerson, whose Life *he published in 1932. In the meantime, however, the strain of the cultural split (and who knows what other strains?) became unendurable for Brooks himself, and from 1925 until nearly 1932, he lived in a state of complete and desperate collapse.*

Recovering, he reversed himself. Now he took the view of the "lowbrow," and the critical estimate of his own work was reversed as well: where before he had been revered, he was now pitied, patronized, and despised. For he had decided that he had been wrong about the United States; our traditions did indeed contain a brilliant and dynamic "useable past" (his phrase). Beginning with The Flowering of New England *(1936) and continuing through the four other volumes that comprise* Makers and Finders, *a literary history of the United States, he tried through a curious and indiscriminating anecdotal impressionism to define it in full. His earlier radicalism washed away; he deplored and despised all the best in modern writing, especially Eliot and the "Elioteers"; and he himself ended up as the archetype of the "middlebrow."*

The profound pathos, like the prejudices of this extraordinary career, is made plain in a series of reminiscences, memoirs, and autobiographies of the 1940s and 1950s.

FURTHER READING

Van Wyck Brooks's *An Autobiography* (three volumes in one, 1965); Gladys Brooks's *If Strangers Meet: A Memory* (1967); and *Van Wyck Brooks: The Early Years* (1968), a selection of his writing, edited by Claire Sprague. *The Van Wyck Brooks-Lewis Mumford Letters: The Record of a Literary Friendship, 1921–1963* (1970), edited by Robert E. Spiller, is moving and revealing.

"Highbrow" and "Lowbrow" (1915)

The middle of humanity thou never knewest,
but the extremity of both ends.
Timon of Athens

I

At the time when he was trying to release humanity from the cross of gold on which, as he said, it was crucified, the apostle of Free Silver [1]—representing a point of view that might have been called American—announced that the opinion of all the professors in the United States would not affect his opinions in the least. There was a dilemma!—if one chose to see it. For on the one hand stood a body of supposed experts in economic theory, on the other a man whose profession it was to change and reform economic practice—the one knowing, the other doing; and not only were they at swords' points but an openly avowed and cynical contempt of theory in relation to practical matters was a principal element in the popularity of a popular hero. But was Bryan himself to blame for this? To know anything of the economic theory which is taught in American universities—in many cases compulsorily taught—is to confess that blame is not the right word. For this economic theory is at the least equally cynical. It revolves round and round in its tree-top dream of the economic man; and no matter how much the wind blows, political economy never comes down. Incompatibility, mutual contempt between theory and practice, is in the very nature of the case.

One might extend the illustration to literature, merely substituting one professor for another and putting any typical best-selling novelist in the place of Bryan. It is a peculiar twist in the academic mind to suppose that a writer belongs to literature only when he is dead; living he is, vaguely, something else; and a habitual remoteness from the creative mood has made American professors quite peculiarly academic. "Literature," as distinguished from excellent writing, is, in the American universities, a thing felt to have been done; and, while for all one knows it may continue to be done, the quality in it which makes it literature only comes out, like the quality in wines, with age.

Now I suppose that most of the American novelists in our day are university men; they have learned to regard literature as an august compound of Browning, Ben Jonson and Hesiod; and consequently, when they begin to write, it is in a spirit of real humility that they set themselves to the composition of richly rewarded trash. I am sure of this: it is modesty that lies behind the "best-seller"; and there is an

[1] William Jennings Bryan (1860–1925), American politician.

aspect in which the spectacle of writers regarding themselves as humble tradesfolk has a certain charm. But the conception of literature as something, so to speak, high and dry gives to the craft of authorship in America a latitude like that of morality in Catholic countries: so long as the heavenly virtues are upheld mundane virtues may shift as they will. In a word, writers are relieved of responsibility, and, while their ethical conscience remains quite sound, they absolve themselves from any artistic conscience whatsoever. And the worst of it is that precisely these writers of irredeemable trash are often the bright, vigorous, intuitive souls who *could* make literature out of American life. Has it ever been considered how great a knowledge of men, what psychological gifts of the first order their incomparable achievement of popularity implies?

These two attitudes of mind have been phrased once for all in our vernacular as "Highbrow" and "Lowbrow." I have proposed these terms to a Russian, an Englishman and a German, asking each in turn whether in his country there was anything to correspond with the conceptions implied in them. In each case they have been returned to me as quite American, authentically our own, and, I should add, highly suggestive.

What side of American life is not touched by this antithesis? What explanation of American life is more central or more illuminating? In everything one finds this frank acceptance of twin values which are not expected to have anything in common: on the one hand, a quite unclouded, quite unhypocritical assumption of transcendent theory ("high ideals"), on the other a simultaneous acceptance of catchpenny realities. Between university ethics and business ethics, between American culture and American humour, between Good Government and Tammany, between academic pedantry and pavement slang, there is no community, no genial middle ground.

The very accent of the words "Highbrow" and "Lowbrow" implies an instinctive perception that this is a very unsatisfactory state of affairs. For both are used in a derogatory sense. The "Highbrow" is the superior person whose virtue is admitted but felt to be an inept unpalatable virtue; while the "Lowbrow" is a good fellow one readily takes to, but with a certain scorn for him and all his works. And what is true of them as personal types is true of what they stand for. They are equally undesirable, and they are incompatible; but they divide American life between them.

II

They always have divided American life between them; and to understand them one has to go back to the beginning of things—for without doubt the Puritan theocracy is the all-influential fact in the history of the American mind. It was the Puritan conception of the Deity as not alone all-determining but precisely responsible for the practical affairs of the race, as constituting, in fact, the State itself, which precluded in advance any central bond, any responsibility, any common feeling in American affairs and which justified the unlimited centrifugal expediency that has always marked American life. And the same instinct that made against centrality in government made against centrality in thought, against common standards of any kind. The eternal issues the Puritans felt so keenly, the practical issues they experienced so monotonously threw almost no light on one another; there was no middle ground between to mitigate, combine or harmonize them.

So it is that from the beginning we find two main currents in the American mind running side by side but rarely mingling—a current of overtones and a current of undertones—and both equally unsocial: on the one hand, the transcendental current, originating in the piety of the Puritans, becoming a philosophy in Jonathan Edwards, passing through Emerson, producing the fastidious refinement and aloofness of the chief American writers, and resulting in the final unreality of most contemporary American culture; and on the other hand the current of catchpenny opportunism, originating in the practical shifts of Puritan life, becoming a philosophy in Franklin, passing through the American humorists, and resulting in the atmosphere of our contemporary business life.

Thus the literature of the seventeenth century in America is composed in equal parts, one may fairly say, of piety and advertisement; and the revered chronicles of New England had the double effect of proving how many pilgrim souls had been elected to salvation and of populating with hopeful immigrants a land where heaven had proved so indulgent.

For three generations the prevailing American character was compact in one type, the man of action who was also the man of God. Not until the eighteenth century did the rift appear and with it the essential distinction between "Highbrow" and "Lowbrow." It appeared in the two philosophers, Jonathan Edwards and Benjamin Franklin, who shared the eighteenth century between them. In their singular purity of type and in the apparent incompatibility of their aims they determined the American character as a racial fact, and after them the Revolution became inevitable. Channing,[2] Lincoln, Emerson, Whitman, Grant, Webster, Garrison,[3] Edison, Rockefeller, Mrs. Eddy,[4] Woodrow Wilson are all, in one way or another, permutations and combinations of these two grand progenitors of the American mind.

Strange that at the very outset two men should have arisen so aptly side by side and fixed the poles of our national life! For no one has ever

[2] William Ellery Channing (1780–1842), American writer and clergyman.

[3] William Lloyd Garrison (1805–1879), leader in the abolitionist movement.

[4] Mrs. Mary Baker Eddy (1821–1910), founder of the Christian Science Church.

more fully than Jonathan Edwards displayed the infinite inflexibility of the upper levels of the American mind, nor has anyone displayed more fully than Franklin the infinite flexibility of its lower levels.

The intellect of Jonathan Edwards was like the Matterhorn; steep, icy and pinnacled. At its base were green slopes and singing valleys filled with little tender wild-flowers—for he was the most lovable of men; but as soon as the ground began to rise in good earnest all this verdurous life came to an abrupt end: not one green or living thing could subsist in that frozen soil, on those pale heights. It was the solitude of logic that led him to see in destiny only a wrathful tyrant and a viper's trail in the mischievous ways of little boys and girls.

I confess to an old-time and so to speak aboriginal affection for this man, so gently solicitous to make up in his daily walk and conversation for the ferocious impulsions of that brain of his. He was even the most romantic of men, as I thought once, and I well remember that immense old musty book of his theology, covered with mildew, with its desert of tiny print, which I carried out with me into the fields and read, in the intervals of bird's-nesting, under the hedgerows and along the borders of the wood: the sun fell for the first time on those clammy old pages and the pallid thoughts that lay in them, and the field-sparrows all about were twittering in a language which, to tell the truth, was no more unintelligible to me. But everything that springs from solitude shines by a light of its own, and Manfred among the Alps was not more lonely than this rapt scholar in his parsonage among the Indians.

There are, however, solitudes and solitudes. Great poets and fruitful thinkers live apart themselves, perhaps, but they have society and the ways of men in their blood. They recollect in tranquility, as it were, gestate, live again, and reveal the last significance of active generations rich in human stuff, in experience, in emotion, in common reason. Nothing like this existed in the background of Jonathan Edwards, no profound and complex race-life. Intellect in him, isolated and not responsible to the other faculties, went on its way unchecked; and he was able to spin his inept sublimities by subtracting from his mind every trace of experience, every touch of human nature as it really was among his innocent countryfolk.

Notoriously, of course, our great Dr. Franklin simplified existence in precisely the opposite way; for the opposite of unmitigated theory is unmitigated practicality. Who can deny that in *Poor Richard* the "Lowbrow" point of view for the first time took definite shape, stayed itself with axioms, and found a sanction in the idea of "policy"? It emerges there full-fledged, in its classical form, a two-dimensional wisdom, a wisdom shorn of overtones, the most accommodating wisdom in the world.

Were ever two views of life more incompatible than these? What indeed could Poor Richard have in common with an Angry God? And what could Bryan have in common with political economy?

III

"Our people," said Emerson, "have their intellectual culture from one country and their duties from another." In how many spheres that phrase can be applied! Desiccated culture at one end and stark utility at the other have created a deadlock in the American mind, and all our life drifts chaotically between the two extremes. Consider, for example, our use of the English language. Literary English in England is naturally a living speech, which occupies the middle of the field and expresses the flesh and blood of an evolving race. Literary English with us is a tradition, just as Anglo-Saxon law with us is a tradition. They persist not as the normal expressions of a race, the essential fibre of which is permanently Anglo-Saxon, but through prestige and precedent and the will and habit of a dominating class largely out of touch with a national fabric unconsciously taking form "out of school." No wonder that our literary style is "pure," that our literary tradition, our tradition especially in oratory and political prose, retains the spirit of the eighteenth century. But at what a cost! At the cost of expressing a popular life that bubbles with energy and spreads and grows and slips away ever more and more from the control of tested ideas, a popular life "with the lid off," which demands an intellectual outlet and finds one in slang, journalism and unmannerly fiction.

After seventy years Carlyle's well-known appeal to Emerson still applies to the spirit of American culture: "For the rest, I have to object still (what you will call objecting against the Law of Nature) that we find you a speaker indeed, but as it were a *Soliloquizer* on the eternal mountain-tops only, in vast solitudes where men and their affairs lie all hushed in a very dim remoteness; and only *the man* and the stars and the earth are visible—whom, so fine a fellow seems he, we could perpetually punch into, and say, 'Why won't you come and help us then? We have terrible need of one man like you down among us! It is cold and vacant up there; nothing paintable but rainbows and emotions; come down and you shall do life-pictures, passions, facts. . . .' "

And what a comment on the same utterance that at this very moment an amiable New Englander should have been painting in Parson Wilbur and Hosea Biglow,[5] respectively, unconscious of any tragic symbolism of things to come, the unbridgeable chasm between literate and illiterate America! Morally, no doubt, in Jaalam, they understood one another and got along very well, as Yankees will. But in Chicago?

IV

To pass now from the social to the personal question, since the question is at bottom a personal one, let us figure to ourselves how this

---

[5] Two characters from the *Biglow Papers*, satirical poems by James Russell Lowell. Parson Wilbur is the purported "editor" of the letters of farmer Hosea Biglow.

divergence comes about and how it is that our educational system, instead of creating what President Eliot [6] called a "serviceable fellowship" between theory and practice, tends to set them apart and to confirm us all either in the one extreme or in the other.

Let us figure to ourselves a typical American who has grown up, as an American typically does grow up, in a sort of orgy of lofty examples, moralized poems, national anthems and baccalaureate sermons, until he is charged with all manner of ideal purities, ideal honorabilities, ideal femininities, flag-wavings and skyscrapings of every sort—until he comes to feel in himself the hovering presence of all manner of fine potentialities, remote, vaporous and evanescent as a rainbow. All this time, it may fairly be said, he has not been taught to associate himself personally with ends even much lower than these. He has not been taught that life is a legitimate progress toward spiritual or intellectual ends at all. His instincts of acquisition, pleasure, enterprise and desire have in no way been linked and connected with disinterested ends; he has had it embedded in his mind that the getting of a living is not a necessity incidental to some higher and more disinterested end, but that it is the prime and central end. And, as a corollary of this, he has been encouraged to assume that the world is a stamping-ground for his every untrained, greedy and aggressive impulse, that, in short, society is fair prey for what he can get out of it.

Let us imagine that, having grown up in this way, he is sent to college. And here, in order to keep the case a typical one, we shall have to exercise a little discrimination in the choice of a university.

It will not be Harvard, because the ideal of Harvard, as I shall point out, is not a typically modern American ideal. Nor will it be one of the modern utilitarian universities, which have no ideal at all. It will be any one of the others; and when I say this I mean that each of the others is in one way or another a development of the old country college; its ideal, its experience, its tradition spring out of and lead one back to that. Now, among these old colleges Harvard might have been figured as an ever-developing, ever-liberalizing catholicism, of which they were all sectarian offshoots, established on a principle of progressive theological fragmentation, each one defending an orthodoxy its predecessors had outworn or violently setting up in defence of some private orthodoxy of its own. They founded themselves each on a remote dogma or system of dogmas, as their central and sufficient basis, and all their wheels turned in relation to the central theological dynamo. In a sense, this was true also of Harvard, but with a marked difference. For the theologians who founded Harvard were men of action as well. In the seventeenth century, a New England minister was also a politician, and the education of ministers for which Harvard was mainly established implied an education for public affairs as well, and educa-

---

[6] Charles William Eliot (1834–1926), American educator, president of Harvard from 1860 to 1909.

tion for society. Thus at the outset the founders of Harvard drove in
the wedge of secularism: Harvard had, from the beginning, a sort of
national basis, at least among New Englanders, and its dogmatic
structure consequently reflected, and shifted with, and accommodated
itself to, the currents of national thought. Remaining in touch with
society, it educated to a certain extent, relatively to an extraordinary
extent, the social function of its students; and it is thus no accident
that for many years so large a proportion of the political, the literary
and the scientific life of America sprang from it. But in the eighteenth
century the conditions under which Harvard was established had ceased
to prevail. The minister was no longer a man of affairs—he was a stark
theologian, and often of a type which the majority of his flock had
outgrown. Yale, Princeton and virtually all the other typically American
colleges were founded by men of this type. Jonathan Edwards may
figure for them all, the motive which led him to become the president
of Princeton being precisely that his New England flock could no
longer see the anger of God eye to eye with him. Already in his time
the fathers and mothers of young America had submitted to the
charms of *Poor Richard's Almanac;* but they seem to have believed that
an Angry God might still be a good influence over young America himself.

To return now to our typical case, let us imagine that he makes a
typical choice and goes to a typical university. Having arrived there,
will he be confronted with an Angry God, or any sort of direct theological dogma? By no means. But there will have remained in the air
a certain fragrance and vibration, as if an ideal had passed that way
and not stayed, there will be intangible whispers and seductions, there
will be a certain faint, rarefied, remote, but curiously pervasive and
insistent influence—like the sound of an Æolian harp or the recollection of Plato in some uncouth slum; there will be memories and
portraits of many an old metaphysician, white, unearthly, fragile. It
will all seem very much as if, the significance of these remote dogmas
having evaporated, only the remoteness, in a way, had remained.

One would have to be very insensitive not to feel the quite unbal-
ancing charm of this quality—so different from its comparatively
robust Oxford parallel—in the old New England colleges, as in
Princeton, Yale and the other universities which have developed out
of them; but one cannot help feeling also, I think, something vaguely
Circean [7] in it. And in fact, given the preliminary method of bringing-
up which I have sketched, what will be its effect in the case we are
considering? Suddenly confronted during four years with just this
remote influence of ideals, out of which the intellectual structure has
evaporated and which never possessed a social structure, will he not
find them too vague, too intangible, too unprepared-for to be incor-

[7] The enchantress Circe turned Odysseus' companions into swine by means of a
magic potion.

porated into his nature? Certainly ideals of this kind, in this way
presented, in this way prepared for, cannot enrich life, because they are
wanting in all the elements of personal contact. Wholly dream-like and
vaporous, they end by breeding nothing but cynicism and chagrin; and,
in becoming permanently catalogued in the mind as impracticable, they
lead to a feeling that all ideas are unreal.

Indeed, there is nothing so tragic and so ominous as the familiar
saying that college is the happiest time of one's life. Yet perhaps a
majority of college men think of their college life in this way. They
deliberately put their Golden Age behind them—and, as things are,
they know it is behind them. But consider what a comment this is on
the American university itself—a place, one would almost say, where
ideals are cherished precisely because they are ineffectual, because
they are ineptly and mournfully beautiful, because they make one
cynical, because they make life progressively uninteresting, because,
in effect, they are illusions and frauds and charming lies. There, surely,
is the last and the most impenetrable stronghold of Puritanism, refined
to the last degree of intangibility, which persists in making the world
a world inevitably sordid, basely practical, as if its definition of the
ideal were that which has no connection with the world!

Thus far with our typical university man. He has been consistently
educated in twin values that are incompatible. The theoretical atmosphere in which he has lived is one that bears no relation to society,
the practical atmosphere in which he has lived bears no relation to
ideals. Theory has become for him permanently a world in itself, an
end in itself; practice has become simply a world of dollars.

Now supposing he is interested in economics, three paths are open
to him: either he can give himself once for all to economics, or he can
go the way of all flesh, i.e., into business, or he can hesitate between
the two, becoming an economist for the time being and eventually
going into business.

It is just here, at the moment of choice, that the want of ballast in
his education becomes manifest. There is nothing for him but to lurch
violently to the one extreme or to the other; and this he does, according as intellect or the sense of action preponderates in his nature. If he
is preponderantly intellectual he adopts the first course; that is to say,
he dedicates himself to the service of a type of economic theory that
bears no relation to this wicked world at all, leaving all the good people
who are managing the economic practice of society (and, for the want
of him, chiefly muddling it)—leaving all these good people to talk
nonsense in the wilderness. If he is preponderantly a man of action,
he adopts the second course; that is to say, he dedicates himself to the
service of a private end which knows nothing of theory, which is most
cynically contemptuous of ideals, flatulent or other, and which is
precisely as indifferent to the economic life of society as the professor
of economics himself.

Well, good riddance to both of them, one might be inclined to say, except that on second thought the professor and the business man between them hold in their hands so great a part of human destiny. It is the third case that is really interesting and really tragic. For just so far as our typical student is a normal man, just so far as he shares the twin elements of intellect and activity in equal parts, just so far will he be on the fence. The probability is that in this case he will become a professor for as long as he can stand it and then burst into business and become a first-rate millionaire as quickly as possible. The sense of action in him will rebel against the sense of theory, and finding in theory no basis for action, no relation to action, will press him into a fresh life where the theoretical side of his nature will at least be of some slight use in furthering his own aggrandizement, and that alone.

V

Naturally the question of economics is only typical. Any branch of human activity that is represented by professors—and which is not?—would serve equally well. Human nature itself in America exists on two irreconcilable planes, the plane of stark intellectuality and the plane of stark business; and in the back of its mind lies heaven knows what world of poetry, hidden away, too inaccessible, too intangible, too unreal in fact ever to be brought into the open, or to serve, as the poetry of life should serve, in harnessing thought and action together, turning life into a disinterested adventure.

Whichever way one argues, from the individual to society or from society to the individual, the result is the same. Just as the American attitude towards the State has been the attitude of an oratorical and vague patriotism which has not based itself on a concrete interest in public affairs; just as, in consequence of this, the "invisible government" of business has swept in and taken possession of the field and become the actual government under which we live, overgrowing and supplanting the government we recognize: so also in the case of the individual. The cherishing of ideals that are simply unmapped regions to which nobody has the least intention of building roads, the baccalaureate sermons that are no just, organic comment on the educational system that precedes them—precisely these themselves strengthen the forces from below; the invisible government of self-interest, built up carefully from the beginning by maxim and example, fills the vacuum a disinterested purpose ought to have occupied.

Thirty or forty years ago, it would have been generally assumed that the only hope for American society lay in somehow lifting the "Lowbrow" elements to the level of the "Highbrow" elements. But the realism of contemporary thought makes it plain that the mere idealism of university ethics, the loftiness of what is called culture, the purity

of so-called Good Government, left to themselves, produce a glassy
inflexible priggishness on the upper levels that paralyzes life. It is
equally plain that the lower levels have a certain humanity, flexibility,
tangibility which are indispensable in any programme: that Tammany
has quite as much to teach Good Government as Good Government
has to teach Tammany, that slang has quite as much in store for
culture as culture has for slang—that the universities, while emphatically not becoming more "practical," must base their disinterestedness on human, moral, social, artistic and personal needs, impulses and
experience.

But society cannot become humane of itself; and it is for this
reason that the movements of reform are so external and so superficial. The will-to-reform springs from a conviction *ex post facto*. It
suggests the frame of mind of business men who retire at sixty and
collect pictures. Nothing so exemplifies it as the spectacle of Andrew
Carnegie spending three-quarters of his life in providing steel for
battleships and the last quarter of it in trying to abolish war. He himself
surely was not conscious of any inward revolution; plainly with him
as with others the will to create disorder, or what amounts to this,
and the will to reform it sprang from the same inner condition of
mind. The impetus of reform is evidently derived from the hope that a
sufficient number of reformers can be trained and brought into the field
to match the forces of business—the one group cancelling the other
group. The ideal of reform, in short, is the attainment of zero.

Nothing is more absurd than to attack business as such. But the
motives and circumstances of business vary from age to age, and there
is a world of difference between industry conceived as a social process
and trade conceived as a private end. A familiar distinction between
the nineteenth and twentieth centuries is that the problem of civilization is no longer the problem of want but the problem of surplus.
Roughly speaking, the hereditary American class—the prevailing class,
I mean—is faced with the problem not of making money but of spending it; the prevailing American class is in a position of relative, but
relatively great, economic freedom, and under these conditions it is
plain that in them economic self-assertion ("enterprise") has become
to a large extent a vicious anachronism. But force of habit, the sheer
impetus and ground-swell of an antiquated pioneering spirit, finds them
with no means of personal outlet except, on the one hand, a continued
economic self-assertion and on the other a reckless overflow of surplus
wealth that takes the form of doing what everybody else does, and
doing it as much more so as possible.

Because it was for so long the law of the tribe, economic self-
assertion still remains to most Americans a sort of moral obligation,
while self-fulfillment still looks like a pretty word for selfishness. Yet
self-fulfillment through science, or literature, or mechanics, or industry
itself—the working out of one's own personality, one's own inventive-

ness through forms of activity that are directly social, as all these activities are directly social, gives a man, through his very sociality, through the feeling he has that, as a good workman, he is coöperating with all other good workmen, a life-interest apart from his rewards. And as this principle is diffused and understood, the incentive is withdrawn from economic self-assertion, a relative competence being notoriously satisfying to the man whose prime end is the fulfilling of his own creative instincts; and the wealth of the world is already socialized.

One cannot have personality, one cannot have the expressions of personality so long as the end of society is an impersonal end like the accumulation of money. For the individual whose personal end varies too greatly from the end of the mass of men about him suffers acutely and becomes abnormal; indeed, he actually cannot accomplish anything healthily fine at all. The best and most disinterested individual can only express the better intuitions and desires of his age and place; there must be some sympathetic touch between him and some visible or invisible host about him, since the mind is a flower that has an organic connection with the soil from which it springs.

The only serious approach to society is the personal approach, and the quickening realism of contemporary social thought is at bottom simply a restatement for the mass of commercialized men, and in relation to issues that directly concern men as a whole, of those personal instincts that have been the essence of art, religion, literature— the essence of personality itself—since the beginning of things. It will remain of the least importance to patch up politics, to become infected with social consciousness, or to do any of the other easy popular contemporary things unless, in some way, personality can be made to release itself on a middle plane between vaporous idealism and self-interested practicality; unless, in short, self-fulfillment as an ideal can be substituted for self-assertion as an ideal. On the economic plane, this implies socialism; on every other plane it implies something which a majority of Americans in our day certainly do not possess—an object in living.

VI

It is perhaps just as well that Cervantes lived and died in Spain three hundred years ago. Had he been born an American of the twentieth century he might have found the task of satire an all too overwhelming one. Yet his fable, which has its personal bearing in all men always, has in America a social bearing that is perhaps unique. Don Quixote is the eternal "Highbrow" under a polite name, just as Sancho Panza is the eternal "Lowbrow"; and if the adorable Dulcinea is not a vision of the night and a daily goal in the mind of our professors, then there is no money in Wall Street. One admits the charm of both extremes, the one so fantastically above, the other so fantastically below the level of right reason; to have any kind of relish for muddled humanity is necessarily to feel the charm of both extremes. But where is all that is real, where is personality and all its works, if it is not essentially somewhere, somehow, in some not very vague way, between?

EARLIER
POETRY

Earlier Poetry (poets born before 1900)

The "new poets" had one thing in common, the vow to *make it new*—an admonition that they took as their banner more than twenty years before Ezra Pound used the phrase as the title of a book. They meant that they would try to say what they felt, not what they should feel; what they saw, not what they were expected to see. There was a turning away from nineteenth-century conventions in poetry, from a poetry that was inclined to talk about emotions (diluting them in the process), to a poetry of things and situations that gave rise to emotions in the first place (undiluted and direct). This change involved a revolution in poetic language: tired and generalizing rhetoric was rejected for precise, defining terms, for common speech when that was wanted, and for literary allusiveness when that was wanted. Through this new, complex medium the poet would say what his subject (object) exactly was, in order to invoke his true feeling about it. The one injunction: make it new; that is, make it real!

Except for this overriding impulse, the new poets were, as one would hope true poets always have been and will be, very different from one another. Still, some were more like some than they were like others. As we have said, ". . . there was a double strain in the 'new poetry': the work of the regional poets who were experimental to a point but not particularly difficult, and that of the poets of the avant-garde whose unfamiliar techniques first made them seem difficult indeed." There were subtler and important differences within each of the two groups, but this is certainly the basic distinction.

Of the regional poets, two, Carl Sandburg and Vachel Lindsay, who at first appeared to be technically very radical, were, in fact, what might be called "public" poets, and their innovations were so broad as to attract rather than to bewilder a large audience. Like orators, they were given too much to mere rhetorical effects to produce a poetry of genuine intensity or distinction of feeling. The result is that they now seem quite old-fashioned, however therapeutic their initial appearance may have been. Wanting to communicate their sense of the vitality and strength of American life, they were, as has been said, "yea-sayers" who had not "earned the right to say yea by having suffered in saying nay."

Of the other four poets in this selection whom we can call regional—always reminding ourselves that they are more than merely regional—E. A. Robinson, until recently the most neglected, may prove finally to be the most rewarding, although technically he was the most traditional. With his roots clearly fixed in the nineteenth

century, he yet comes to an increasing number of readers as one of
the most disturbing poets in the twentieth. His sense of himself
was that he must create a new poetry with the materials of wreckage:

But still my dream was to command
  New life into that shrunken clay.
  I tried it. And you scan to-day,
With uncommiserating glee,
  The songs of one who strove to play
The broken flutes of Arcady.

Using those "broken flutes" of traditional verse, he became the
great poet of failure and disaster brought on by illusions, lies, and
self-deception. Writing at his best in short narrative forms, he told
his tragic stories with a comic grace, just as he combined in his style
a rich, romantic eloquence with a prevailingly dry, even laconic,
"down East" vernacular. A witty poet of understatement, he did not
intercede on behalf of his characters, nor did he rule against them.
His profound pessimism was in some ways like that of his English
contemporary, Thomas Hardy; it was unlike Hardy's in that his
sense of the fallibility of all final judgement did not exclude his
own.

Beside him, that other New England poet, Robert Frost, seems sometimes all too ready to play the sage. A man of firm, even rigid, opinions, he was, in his verse, fortunately, no dogmatist. Indeed, his
wisdom lay in the constant balancing of alternatives: if there are
many poems of loneliness and dread, of uncertainty and isolation, of
discontinuity and a malign design in things ("What but design of
darkness to appall?"), there are also poems of love and faith, of
bravery, of hope for continuity and order ("If design govern in a
thing so small"). Most important, the opposing moods can come
together within single poems, where they are complements rather
than oppositions, to say, in effect, "If this is true to the human reality, so, no less, is this." The very act of creatively *balancing* both
elements, the good and the bad, can make of a poem what Frost
called it, "a momentary stay against confusion." Still, it can be
argued—and has been—that the grounds on which Frost presented
his human reality were not sufficiently ample or complex to provide
a true test. Frost deliberately excluded from his poetic universe
everything that we think of as modern—the urban, the industrial,
the technocratic. His is the pastoral, if not the necessarily kind,
world of New England farm and field and woods, and in this world
the individual is almost always alone in a natural, but not a social,
communion, let alone conflict. The individual isolation is, of course,
the basic element of Frost's view of the human condition, and trying to test that condition in purity, rather than in contingency and
multiplicity, is conceivably to put it to its severest test. This, he

would have been the first to argue, is the only test that can have meaning for the kind of stoic that he was.

If there is a certain aesthetic frugality, even parsimony, about Frost, an unwillingness to *give*, it no doubt is appropriate enough to that spirit of rural New England apart from which it is nearly impossible to see him. Putting beside him such a different figure as John Crowe Ransom, one can make nearly the same generalization: the very texture of his poems derives from the regional culture with which he is associated. Indeed, it may be asked whether Ransom would have become a poet at all if he had not first been a Southerner. This is the justification for grouping him with regional poets with whom he has so little else in common, for, except in a very few poems, his *subjects* were not regional, but his style was entirely so. In this he is markedly different from such younger Southern poets as his friends Allen Tate and Robert Penn Warren. Ransom's is a highly personal style that is marked by its elegance, even its artificiality, a strange vocabulary in part archaic, a frankly aristocratic bias in the rhetoric, a general air of courtliness, and the utilization of his literary culture as inherent in his whole culture, not an imposition upon it, an external instrument by means of which to understand it. This use of his culture separates him from most of the poets of the avant-garde group and relates him back to Frost, whose youthfully acquired knowledge of the Latin poets sinks unannounced, though not so prevalently, into the texture of his own metrics. These qualities add up to only part of a part of the South, and a part that perhaps no longer exists; but it was Ransom's, and he felt free to let it serve him intimately, gravely, and consistently, if sparingly, without profligacy: he wishes to preserve only forty-four short poems.

Of Robinson Jeffers, the poet of a wildly beautiful and then still uncorrupted California coast, the last of this group of poets, it should be said that he is the most difficult to represent through a selection of his shorter poems. His most impressive work was in long narrative poems of rapt and morbid violence, crashing crescendos. Yet his shorter poems serve to indicate, at least, that of all these individualists, Jeffers was the archindividualist, the least given to any concern with current views or social grace, antihumanist, nihilist, the most alone and far beyond loneliness, the poet whose preference is for rocks and grass and hawks over men, "the animals Christ was rumored to have died for," the father who advised his sons to "be in nothing so moderate as in love of man."

About Ezra Pound, the literary history of the second and third decades of this century can be secure in naming him the major catalyst in breadth of influence; what it cannot yet do is attempt to measure the depth of his own poetic achievement. If the literary criticism of T. S. Eliot was presently to prove more influential, Pound's personal

influence on poets and poetry in those two decades was much the
more pervasive and dramatic. He knew everyone; he helped, lectured, hectored, and corrected everyone (including Yeats and Eliot);
and he developed at least fifty-seven varieties of aesthetic, economic,
social, and finally, political cures. Whether or not his mind was at
some period entirely deranged, who is to say? But in our easier use
of a synonym, he was certainly always mad. Mad, at least, for a new
life in poetry, and with this impulse, he threw himself from the
beginning of his career into one enthusiasm after another and became in effect the public relations man for each. None, probably,
was more important for him and for other poets than the movement
called *imagism*, not in the narrow sense that it produced a number
of poets, a few of them interesting, who wrote a certain kind of
short poem in free verse, but in its total implications and effects.

The movement came about in England largely through the doctrines of
T. E. Hulme, who was impatient with the lingering influences of
romanticism, its softness, its vagueness, its rambling silliness; he
wanted a tough, fibrous poetry, "dry" and "hard," to use his own
terms. From Hulme, Pound derived the imagist principles, which
he communicated in turn to such other disseminators as Harriet
Monroe and Amy Lowell. "An 'Image,'" Pound wrote in *Poetry* in
1913, "is that which presents an intellectual and emotional complex
in an instant of time." Expanded, this somewhat opaque definition
means that poetry must be concrete, exact in observation, terse, dry,
hard, without generalizing comment; it must use ordinary speech
and ordinary subject matter; and its rhythm must be true to the
experience it recreates rather than to any imposed metrical or rime
pattern. While Pound was to lose interest presently in imagism as a
movement, these general principles did much to form his own style
and, amplified by other enthusiasms, continued in large part to
mould his effort. They were a corrective to the excesses of his first
influences—the Provencal singers, Robert Browning, the poets of
the English "decadence"—and they found supplements in his study
of Chinese poetry, of the Japanese short forms, the *tanka* and the
haiku, and of the Noh play. They apparently led him, too, to a new
"insistence upon clarity and precision, upon the prose tradition,"
and this insistence may well have been instrumental in what became the considerable invasion of the ideal of excellent prose into
the character of modern poetry.

The first twenty years of Pound's own rather miscellaneous career as a
poet came to a climax in the many parts of the long *Hugh Selwyn
Mauberley*, his farewell to London in 1919, a poem that not only
reviews much of his earlier achievement but also looks forward to
many of the techniques (notably the analogical use of myth and
history and the refractions of his own reading) that he would employ in the interminable and very uneven *Cantos* which were effec-

tively to usurp the rest of his life as a poet. Doing this, *Mauberley* also gives us his view of the London literary scene as he had known it and his reasons for departing from it. In France, and later in Italy, he would continue to make his influence felt on the work of others, but perhaps never again with the kind of force that it exerted in the second decade.

His service to T. S. Eliot, particularly in compressing the original version of *The Waste Land* into the amazing poem that readers have known since 1922, is an established fact of literary history (the recent discovery of Eliot's original with Pound's alterations put the final documentary seal on this curious transaction). But Eliot had, of course, been writing poetry before he met Pound and had already acknowledged in his work his major influences, the English metaphysical poets and the Elizabethan dramatists, the French symbolists, particularly Jules LaForgue, and Dante; and through his use of these influences (and others drawn from such areas as anthropology and comparative religion), the techniques of analogical allusion, association, and juxtaposition that *The Waste Land* was to make famous as the "mythical method." That T. E. Hulme's principles and Pound's dissemination of them played their part in helping Eliot focus his own aims and great middle style is hardly to be questioned, but it is probable that Eliot would have developed pretty much as he did with or without Pound. The religious aspiration that Eliot probably felt from the beginning, and which was finally to thrust him beyond the complexities that characterize his middle style into the relaxed lucidities of the final style, would have found no sanction at all in Pound's example.

A poet just two years older than Pound, William Carlos Williams, who had known him from his student days and whose imagination always operated happily and stubbornly within the phenomena of the natural world, reflected more directly the tenets of Pound's imagist program. Abandoning his first efforts at emulating Keats and Whitman, he began a lifelong battle against all poetry that utilized meter or rime or any other technical devices that put themselves between the reader and a direct experience of the poet's observation. Eliot seemed to Williams the complete antithesis of everything that he sought in verse, and with the success of *The Waste Land*, he announced that his ambitions for poetry had been set back twenty years. He wrote countless poems that can stand as the most successful products of imagist principles, although he himself early lost patience with the movement on the grounds that its use of free verse produced only invertebrate statements. He preferred for himself the term *objectivist*. Concerned always with particulars, never with generalities, he sought a "measure" (his term) based immediately on the beat of speech that would also give to experience objective existence, or structure. His motto might well be found in his own statement, "No ideas but in things." "Things," however, have no reality until language gives it to them, and when he came to write his long poem, *Paterson*, he was really only dramatizing, against the screen of rather loosely mytholigized local history, his lifetime quest for that "redeeming language" that would give its actuality to the actual.

E. E. Cummings, whom Williams once hailed as "Robinson Crusoe at the moment when he first saw the print of a naked human foot in the sand," was no less concerned than Williams and Pound with the renovation of language, but in a rather special and more eccentric way. A superb lyric poet whose love poems have much in common with the early work of Ezra Pound, he marked his difference from the beginning through typographical tricks and a fracturing of syntactical conventions that were apparently intended to shock the reader's eye into making his ear attend. Irrepressibly youthful, many of his poems are frankly high jinks, yet interestingly enough he was a master of that most conventional of forms, the sonnet. His variety of mood is extraordinary, ranging as it does from sheer burlesque and undisguised eroticism to the stately, the courtly, the deeply elegiac. If there is a single theme to which this poet over and over returns, it is that most serious of all themes, the transcendence of self through love, which is also to say the discovery of self in love.

Among Cummings's admirers is Marianne Moore, who, while always speaking in her own uniquely personal voice, is almost never concerned with the self, as Cummings so persistently was. Hers is probably the most objective poetry that we have had in this century, and its ancestor was, again, imagism. Its first principles are a nearly scientific exactness of observation and precision of statement. Its language is that of cultivated speech that does not hesitate to absorb into itself words drawn from science, business, statistics, and other such unpoetic areas. Taking the syllable rather than the foot as its measure, its cadences are those of prose, albeit prose intensely concentrated. Often unrimed, when it does rime, it does so almost undetectedly, without any musical urgency or clamor. It goes far beyond imagism in its bold sweep of generalizations, but these are always founded on particularities, and in these she has something of a penchant for the exotic, even the fantastic. It is further different in its innovative habit, begun in 1915, of incorporating quotations from the works of others but never with any break in the integrity of its own rhythms. Ironic, humorous, mingling a shy modesty with a kind of admonitory hauteur, it is marvelously controlled and, above all, elegant.

In elegance she stands beside Wallace Stevens, who was the great stylistic dandy among the new poets. An early friend of hers and of Williams, he too responded to the imagist call. Like Marianne

Moore, his observations were attracted by the bizarre, even the outré; unlike her, whose poems combined the particular with the generalizing, his tended to fall into two kinds, one the bizarrely imagistic, the other the sparely discursive. Like Eliot, he was deeply influenced by certain nineteenth-century French poets, but from them he learned not so much the techniques of the evocation of subjective states as he did a certain vinous sparkle of style (he liked to talk about the "gaiety" of poetic language) and a kind of masquelike artifice. Like Frost, he was much concerned with the balancing, indeed, the interaction of opposites, of alternatives, but Stevens's were not so much ethical as aesthetic, and from these arise his central and pervasive theme no less than his poetic method: chaos and order, "fact and miracle," reality and imagination, life and art. The finest life resides in the highest art.

Conrad Aiken is a much more various poet than either Marianne Moore or Wallace Stevens and is correspondingly more difficult to characterize. It may be for this reason, among others, that he has never attracted quite the kind of following that all the other poets we have talked about have enjoyed. This is the readers' loss, for Aiken was an innovator who brought to poetry elements that go far beyond language. In his poetic speech, indeed, he was much more content than these others to utilize the traditional vocabulary of romantic poetry. But he was the first American poet explicitly to introduce into his work the insights of Freudian and post-Freudian psychology, and the first, therefore, who many decades ago made a central concern of the now familiar concept of identity, as opposed to personality. He was the first American poet, too, to found his structures on musical analogies, writing his "symphonies" long before Eliot was to produce his "quartets." His poetic style, cultivating the sinuosities of music, is luxuriant and decorative in a way that marks him off from most of his contemporaries, with their ideal of a leaner style, although some of them before their end may have learned from him. Finally, he is different from most of them in that he is committed to a creed of liberal and humane relativism, and his poems do not suppress this commitment.

Hart Crane, who died young, necessarily left a smaller and more homogeneous body of poems. His early work was influenced by some of the same poets who had influenced Aiken, notably Swinburne and Wilde, but presently his chief mentors became first Pound and then Eliot. But when he was still very young, twenty-one or twenty-two, he had established his own idiom and was pursuing his own vision. We use the word *vision* thoughtfully, because Crane's was above all a visionary poetry. He aspired to the mystical experience of final unity, and on one occasion, at least, he thought that he had had it. Under a dentist's anesthetic, he wrote to a friend, ". . . my mind spiraled to a kind of seventh heaven of consciousness and egoistic

dance among the seven spheres—and something like an objective
voice kept saying to me—'You have the higher consciousness—you
have the higher consciousness. This is something that very few
have. This is what is called genius'. . . . I felt the two worlds. And at
once . . . I have known moments in eternity." The incantatory techniques of his shorter poems tried to reproduce this condition, and
the controlling symbol (and its corollaries) of his major effort, *The
Bridge,* tried to will it. This poem, essentially a lyric but pushed into
what Crane thought were epic proportions, is not successful as an
entirety, but it is vividly remarkable throughout, one of the great
fractured monuments of our literature. As Crane's life was: in that,
too, through jazz music, alcohol, sexual ecstasy, violence, and
horror, he tried to induce the "vision" of ultimate peace. Like Arthur
Rimbaud in France, he hoped to push his imagination into uncharted realms through a derangement of the senses. He was, with
Edgar Allan Poe, the only other *poète maudit* that American literature has put forth. All the younger ones who aspire to that status
seem to be imitators only, like most of the converts to Catholicism
following upon Eliot: more fashion than fate, more concept than
character.

Allen Tate, a friend of Crane's and an early enthusiast for Eliot, became, well along in his life, a convert to Catholicism, and the observation that we have just made about religious conversion is in no
way applicable to him. Indeed, his one subject has been described
as "simply what is left of Christendom, that western knowledge of
ourselves which is our identity. He may be classed as a religious
writer, and that from the very beginning." Impatient with the limitations of his Southern culture, he very early accustomed himself to
the international style; but almost at the same time, he reasserted
his local allegiance. The result in his verse is impressive, and catholic in a larger sense than he avows. His poems—of which there are
all too few—are, in a way, "cold," a quality almost inevitably following on his classic notions of aesthetic control, but if one is willing
to read them deeply, one finds oneself in agreement with Tate's
youthful disciple, Robert Lowell, who said that ". . . all of them,
even the slightest, are terribly personal. Out of splutter and shambling comes a killing eloquence. Perhaps, this is the resonance of
desperation, or rather the formal resonance of desperation." The
very control that characterizes his poems tells us that he has suffered, that he was *there.* With his fine, moderating intelligence, he
also became one of our best critics, and it is perhaps he who, in
one of his essays, defined, in the largest way, the whole effort of
these poets: ". . . poetry does not explain our experience. . . . It is
the art of apprehending and concentrating our experience in the
mysterious limitations of form."

EDWIN ARLINGTON ROBINSON (1869–1935)

Until he was a year old, he had no first name, and he so disliked the name finally chosen for him, that he always signed himself with his initials. He was born in Head Tide, Maine, but when still an infant, his family moved to Gardiner, Maine, the "Tilbury Town" of his poems. He began to write verse when he was eleven years old, and later he was to find friends in Gardiner who could help him with it, notably Dr. Alanson Tucker Schumann, a physician and versifier himself, and Laura E. Richards, the daughter of Julia Ward Howe, who wrote "The Battle Hymn of the Republic." Robinson went to Harvard, but his career there was interrupted after two years by the death of his father and the dissipation of the family fortune under the mismanagement of one of his brothers. He returned to Gardiner and lived there through the disintegration of his family; one disaster followed another, until the protracted death of his mother in 1896, when he left the town forever.

In that year he published his first volume of poems, The Torrent and the Night Before, *and in the next year, his second,* The Children of the Night. *These books contained the earliest Tilbury poems and announced his dark, sardonic view of things, but they were largely unnoticed. He was living a hand-to-mouth existence in New York City, taking such jobs as came his way, wretchedly poor and drawn to alcohol. After the publication of* Captain Craig *in 1902, Theodore Roosevelt became impressed by his work and found him a position as clerk in the New York Customs House, which he held until 1910. In that year he published* The Town Down the River.

The MacDowell Colony in Peterborough, New Hampshire, rescued him, and he was to spend most of the rest of his life under its patronage. His best work was in the short lyric and the relatively short narrative poem, but in 1914 and 1915 he published two plays of no consequence, and he even tried his hand at fiction (and probably wisely destroyed this material). Distinguished volumes of short poems continued to appear: The Man Against the Sky *(1916),* The Three Taverns *(1920),* Avon's Harvest *(1921), and the last,* Dionysus in Doubt *(1925). They attracted no wide interest. Ironically enough, Robinson, who was himself rather taciturn and certainly withdrawn and thin-lipped, was always tempted by longer forms, in which he inevitably became garrulous, speculating on large and windy transcendental abstractions.* Merlin *(1917) was the first of three volumes about the Arthurian legends in which these qualities became apparent, and while the splendid short poems were largely ignored, the third volume,* Tristam, *won him public recognition at last with the Pulitzer Prize in 1927. He was nearly sixty. The imaginative effort of his remaining years went almost entirely into similar works*

*of diffused speculation on ultimate mysteries which he might better
have left unpursued. He could never cast off his Puritan heritage
(Anne Bradstreet, the first American poet, was one of his ancestors),
and he was plagued by glimmering questions about eternal and
supernatural possibilities.*

*He impresses upon us the difference between poetry and philosophy.
He was influenced by the thought of William James, whose refusal
to shut out such possibilities as the supernatural makes for great intellectual richness. In Robinson, a poet, it makes for wordy mawkishness.*

*Robinson was at his complex and moving best when he asked the least
of life, nothing at all. And then, we can now see, he was great.*

FURTHER READING

For biography, see Hermann Hagedorn, *Edwin Arlington Robinson*
(1938); Emery Neff, *Edwin Arlington Robinson* (1948); and Chard
Powers Smith, *Where the Lights Falls: A Portrait of Edwin Arlington
Robinson* (1965). For criticism, see Yvor Winters, *Edwin Arlington
Robinson* (1946); Ellsworth S. Barnard, *Edwin Arlington Robinson:
A Critical Study* (1952); and Louis Coxe, *Edwin Arlington Robin-
son: The Life of Poetry* (1969).

FROM **The Children of the Night** *(1897)*

John Evereldown

"Where are you going to-night, to-night,—
    Where are you going, John Evereldown?
There's never the sign of a star in sight,
    Nor a lamp that's nearer than Tilbury Town.
Why do you stare as a dead man might?
Where are you pointing away from the light?
And where are you going to-night, to-night,—
    Where are you going, John Evereldown?"

"Right through the forest, where none can see,
    There's where I'm going, to Tilbury Town.   10
The men are asleep,—or awake, may be,—
    But the women are calling John Evereldown.
Ever and ever they call for me,
And while they call can a man be free?
So right through the forest, where none can see,
    There's where I'm going, to Tilbury Town."

"But why are you going so late, so late,—
    Why are you going, John Evereldown?
Though the road be smoothed and the way be straight,
    There are two long leagues to Tilbury Town.   20
Come in by the fire, old man, and wait!
Why do you chatter out there by the gate?
And why are you going so late, so late,—
    Why are you going, John Evereldown?"

"I follow the women wherever they call,—
    That's why I'm going to Tilbury Town.
God knows if I pray to be done with it all,
    But God is no friend to John Evereldown.
So the clouds may come and the rain may fall,
The shadows may creep and the dead men crawl,—   30
But I follow the women wherever they call,
    And that's why I'm going to Tilbury Town."

Richard Cory

Whenever Richard Cory went down town,
We people on the pavement looked at him:
He was a gentleman from sole to crown,
Clean favored, and imperially slim.

And he was always quietly arrayed,
And he was always human when he talked;
But still he fluttered pulses when he said,
"Good-morning," and he glittered when he walked.

And he was rich—yes, richer than a king—
And admirably schooled in every grace: 10
In fine, we thought that he was everything
To make us wish that we were in his place.

So on we worked, and waited for the light,
And went without the meat, and cursed the bread;
And Richard Cory, one calm summer night,
Went home and put a bullet through his head.

Zola [1]

Because he puts the compromising chart
Of hell before your eyes, you are afraid;
Because he counts the price that you have paid
For innocence, and counts it from the start,
You loathe him. But he sees the human heart
Of God meanwhile, and in His hand was weighed
Your squeamish and emasculate crusade
Against the grim dominion of his art.

Never until we conquer the uncouth
Connivings of our shamed indifference   10
(We call it Christian faith) are we to scan
The racked and shrieking hideousness of Truth
To find, in hate's polluted self-defence
Throbbing, the pulse, the divine heart of man.

George Crabbe [1]

Give him the darkest inch your shelf allows,
Hide him in lonely garrets, if you will,—
But his hard, human pulse is throbbing still
With the sure strength that fearless truth endows.
In spite of all fine science disavows,
Of his plain excellence and stubborn skill
There yet remains what fashion cannot kill,
Though years have thinned the laurel from his brows.

Whether or not we read him, we can feel
From time to time the vigor of his name   10
Against us like a finger for the shame
And emptiness of what our souls reveal
In books that are as altars where we kneel
To consecrate the flicker, not the flame.

[1] Emile Zola (1840–1902), French novelist.

[1] British poet (1754–1832).

Credo

I cannot find my way: there is no star
In all the shrouded heavens anywhere;
And there is not a whisper in the air
Of any living voice but one so far
That I can hear it only as a bar
Of lost, imperial music, played when fair
And angel fingers wove, and unaware,
Dead leaves to garlands where no roses are.

No, there is not a glimmer, nor a call,
For one that welcomes, welcomes when he fears,   10
The black and awful chaos of the night;
For through it all—above, beyond it all—
I know the far-sent message of the years,
I feel the coming glory of the Light.

FROM *Captain Craig: A Book of Poems* (1902)

Isaac and Archibald

(To Mrs. Henry Richards)

Isaac and Archibald were two old men.
I knew them, and I may have laughed at them
A little; but I must have honored them
For they were old, and they were good to me.

I do not think of either of them now,
Without remembering, infallibly,
A journey that I made one afternoon
With Isaac to find out what Archibald
Was doing with his oats. It was high time
Those oats were cut, said Isaac; and he feared   10
That Archibald—well, he could never feel
Quite sure of Archibald. Accordingly
The good old man invited me—that is,
Permitted me—to go along with him;
And I, with a small boy's adhesiveness
To competent old age, got up and went.
I do not know that I cared overmuch
For Archibald's or anybody's oats,
But Archibald was quite another thing,
And Isaac yet another; and the world   20

Was wide, and there was gladness everywhere.
We walked together down the River Road
With all the warmth and wonder of the land
Around us, and the wayside flash of leaves,—
And Isaac said the day was glorious;
But somewhere at the end of the first mile
I found that I was figuring to find
How long those ancient legs of his would keep
The pace that he had set for them. The sun
Was hot, and I was ready to sweat blood;   30
But Isaac, for aught I could make of him,
Was cool to his hat-band. So I said then
With a dry gasp of affable despair,
Something about the scorching days we have
In August without knowing it sometimes;
But Isaac said the day was like a dream,
And praised the Lord, and talked about the breeze,
I made a fair confession of the breeze,
And crowded casually on his thought
The nearness of a profitable nook   40
That I could see. First I was half inclined
To caution him that he was growing old,
But something that was not compassion soon
Made plain the folly of all subterfuge.
Isaac was old, but not so old as that.

So I proposed, without an overture,
That we be seated in the shade a while,
And Isaac made no murmur. Soon the talk
Was turned on Archibald, and I began
To feel some premonitions of a kind   50
That only childhood knows; for the old man
Had looked at me and clutched me with his eye,
And asked if I had ever noticed things.
I told him that I could not think of them,
And I knew then, by the frown that left his face
Unsatisfied, that I had injured him.
"My good young friend," he said, "you cannot feel
What I have seen so long. You have the eyes—
Oh, yes—but you have not the other things:
The sight within that never will deceive,   60
You do not know—you have no right to know;
The twilight warning of experience,
The singular idea of loneliness,—
These are not yours. But they have long been mine.
And they have shown me now for seven years
That Archibald is changing. It is not

So much that he should come to his last hand,
And leave the game, and go the old way down;
But I have known him in and out so long,
And I have seen so much of good in him   70
That other men have shared and have not seen,
And I have gone so far through thick and thin,
Through cold and fire with him, that now it brings
To this old heart of mine an ache that you
Have not yet lived enough to know about.
But even unto you, and your boy's faith,
Your freedom, and your untried confidence,
A time will come to find out what it means
To know that you are losing what was yours,
To know that you are being left behind;   80
And then the long contempt of innocence—
God bless you, boy!—don't think the worse of it
Because an old man chatters in the shade—
Will all be like a story you have read
In childhood and remembered for the pictures.
And when the best friend of your life goes down,
When first you know in him the slackening
That comes, and coming always tells the end,—
Now in a common word that would have passed
Uncaught from any other lips than his,   90
Now in some trivial act of every day,
Done as he might have done it all along
But for a twinging little difference
That nips you like a squirrel's teeth—oh, yes,
Then you will understand it well enough.
But oftener it comes in other ways;
It comes without your knowing when it comes;
You know that he is changing, and you know
That he is going—just as I know now
That Archibald is going, and that I   100
Am staying. . . . Look at me, my boy,
And when the time shall come for you to see
That I must follow after him, try then
To think of me, to bring me back again,
Just as I was to-day. Think of the place
Where we are sitting now, and think of me—
Think of old Isaac as you knew him then,
When you set out with him in August once
To see old Archibald."—The words come back
Almost as Isaac must have uttered them,   110
And there comes with them a dry memory
Of something in my throat that would not move.

If you had asked me then to tell just why
I made so much of Isaac and the things
He said, I should have gone far for an answer;
For I knew it was not sorrow that I felt,
Whatever I may have wished it, or tried then
To make myself believe. My mouth was full
Of words, and they would have been comforting
To Isaac, spite of my twelve years, I think;   120
But there was not in me the willingness
To speak them out. Therefore I watched the ground;
And I was wondering what made the Lord
Create a thing so nervous as an ant,
When Isaac, with commendable unrest,
Ordained that we should take the road again—
For it was yet three miles to Archibald's,
And one to the first pump. I felt relieved
All over when the old man told me that;
I felt that he had stilled a fear of mine   130
That those extremities of heat and cold
Which he had long gone through with Archibald
Had made the man impervious to both;
But Isaac had a desert somewhere in him,
And at the pump he thanked God for all things
That He had put on earth for men to drink,
And he drank well,—so well that I proposed
That we go slowly lest I learn too soon
The bitterness of being left behind,
And all those other things. That was a joke   140
To Isaac, and it pleased him very much;
And that pleased me—for I was twelve years old.

At the end of an hour's walking after that
The cottage of old Archibald appeared.
Little and white and high on a smooth round hill
It stood, with hackmatacks and apple-trees
Before it, and a big barn-roof beyond;
And over the place—trees, houses, fields and all—
Hovered an air of still simplicity
And a fragrance of old summers—the old style   150
That lives the while it passes. I dare say
That I was lightly conscious of all this
When Isaac, of a sudden, stopped himself,
And for the long first quarter of a minute
Gazed with incredulous eyes, forgetful quite
Of breezes and of me and of all else
Under the scorching sun but a smooth-cut field,

Faint yellow in the distance. I was young,
But there were a few things that I could see,
And this was one of them.—"Well, well!" said he;   *160*
And "Archibald will be surprised, I think,"
Said I. But all my childhood subtlety
Was lost on Isaac, for he strode along
Like something out of Homer—powerful
And awful on the wayside, so I thought.
Also I thought how good it was to be
So near the end of my short-legged endeavor
To keep the pace with Isaac for five miles.

Hardly had we turned in from the main road
When Archibald, with one hand on his back   *170*
And the other clutching his huge-headed cane,
Came limping down to meet us.—"Well! well! well!"
Said he; and then he looked at my red face,
All streaked with dust and sweat, and shook my hand,
And said it must have been a right smart walk
That we had had that day from Tilbury Town.—
"Magnificent," said Isaac; and he told
About the beautiful west wind there was
Which cooled and clarified the atmosphere.
"You must have made it with your legs, I guess,"   *180*
Said Archibald; and Isaac humored him
With one of those infrequent smiles of his
Which he kept in reserve, apparently,
For Archibald alone. "But why," said he,
"Should Providence have cider in the world
If not for such an afternoon as this?"
And Archibald, with a soft light in his eyes,
Replied that if he chose to go down cellar,
There he would find eight barrels—one of which
Was newly tapped, he said, and to his taste   *190*
An honor to the fruit. Isaac approved
Most heartily of that, and guided us
Forthwith, as if his venerable feet
Were measuring the turf in his own door-yard,
Straight to the open rollway. Down we went,
Out of the fiery sunshine to the gloom,
Grateful and half sepulchral, where we found
The barrels, like eight potent sentinels,
Close ranged along the wall. From one of them
A bright pine spile stuck out alluringly,   *200*
And on the black flat stone, just under it,
Glimmered a late-spilled proof that Archibald

Had spoken from unfeigned experience.
There was a fluted antique water-glass
Close by, and in it, prisoned, or at rest,
There was a cricket, of the brown soft sort
That feeds on darkness. Isaac turned him out,
And touched him with his thumb to make him jump,
And then composedly pulled out the plug
With such a practised hand that scarce a drop   210
Did even touch his fingers. Then he drank
And smacked his lips with a slow patronage
And looked along the line of barrels there
With a pride that may have been forgetfulness
That they were Archibald's and not his own.
"I never twist a spigot nowadays,"
He said, and raised the glass up to the light,
"But I thank God for orchards." And that glass
Was filled repeatedly for the same hand
Before I thought it worth while to discern   220
Again that I was young, and that old age,
With all his woes, had some advantages.
"Now, Archibald," said Isaac, when we stood
Outside again, "I have it in my mind
That I shall take a sort of little walk—
To stretch my legs and see what you are doing.
You stay and rest your back and tell the boy
A story: Tell him all about the time
In Stafford's cabin forty years ago,
When four of us were snowed up for ten days   230
With only one dried haddock. Tell him all
About it, and be wary of your back.
Now I will go along."—I looked up then
At Archibald, and as I looked I saw
Just how his nostrils widened once or twice
And then grew narrow. I can hear to-day
The way the old man chuckled to himself—
Not wholesomely, not wholly to convince
Another of his mirth,—as I can hear
The lonely sigh that followed.—But at length   240
He said: "The orchard now's the place for us;
We may find something like an apple there,
And we shall have the shade, at any rate."
So there we went and there we laid ourselves
Where the sun could not reach us; and I champed
A dozen of worm-blighted astrakhans
While Archibald said nothing—merely told
The tale of Stafford's cabin, which was good,

Though "master chilly"—after his own phrase—
Even for a day like that. But other thoughts   250
Were moving in his mind, imperative,
And writhing to be spoken: I could see
The glimmer of them in a glance or two,
Cautious, or else unconscious, that he gave
Over his shoulder: . . . "Stafford and the rest—
But that's an old song now, and Archibald
And Isaac are old men. Remember, boy,
That we are old. Whatever we have gained,
Or lost, or thrown away, we are old men.
You look before you and we look behind,   260
And we are playing life out in the shadow—
But that's not all of it. The sunshine lights
A good road yet before us if we look,
And we are doing that when least we know it;
For both of us are children of the sun,
Like you, and like the weed there at your feet.
The shadow calls us, and it frightens us—
We think; but there's a light behind the stars
And we old fellows who have dared to live,
We see it—and we see the other things,   270
The other things . . . Yes, I have seen it come
These eight years, and these ten years, and I know
Now that it cannot be for very long
That Isaac will be Isaac. You have seen—
Young as you are, you must have seen the strange
Uncomfortable habit of the man?
He'll take my nerves and tie them in a knot
Sometimes, and that's not Isaac. I know that—
And I know what it is: I get it here
A little, in my knees, and Isaac—here."   280
The old man shook his head regretfully
And laid his knuckles three times on his forehead.
"That's what it is: Isaac is not quite right.
You see it, but you don't know what it means:
The thousand little differences—no,
You do not know them, and it's well you don't;
You'll know them soon enough—God bless you, boy!—
You'll know them, but not all of them—not all.
So think of them as little as you can:
There's nothing in them for you, or for me—   290
But I am old and I must think of them;
I'm in the shadow, but I don't forget
The light, my boy,—the light behind the stars.
Remember that: remember that I said it;

And when the time that you think far away
Shall come for you to say it—say it, boy;
Let there be no confusion or distrust
In you, no snarling of a life half lived,
Nor any cursing over broken things
That your complaint has been the ruin of.   *300*
Live to see clearly and the light will come
To you, and as you need it.—But there, there,
I'm going it again, as Isaac says,
And I'll stop now before you go to sleep.—
Only be sure that you growl cautiously,
And always where the shadow may not reach you."

Never shall I forget, long as I live,
The quaint thin crack in Archibald's voice,
The lonely twinkle in his little eyes,
Or the way it made me feel to be with with him.   *310*
I know I lay and looked for a long time
Down through the orchard and across the road,
Across the river and the sun-scorched hills
That ceased in a blue forest, where the world
Ceased with it. Now and then my fancy caught
A flying glimpse of a good life beyond—
Something of ships and sunlight, streets and singing?
Troy falling, and the ages coming back,
And ages coming forward: Archibald
And Isaac were good fellows in old clothes,   *320*
And Agamemnon was a friend of mine;
Ulysses coming home again to shoot
With bows and feathered arrows made another,
And all was as it should be. I was young.

So I lay dreaming of what things I would,
Calm and incorrigibly satisfied
With apples and romance and ignorance,
And the still smoke from Archibald's clay pipe
There was a stillness over everything,
As if the spirit of heat had laid its hand   *330*
Upon the world and hushed it; and I felt
Within the mightiness of the white sun
That smote the land around us and wrought out
A fragrance from the trees, a vital warmth
And fullness for the time that was to come,
And a glory for the world beyond the forest.
The present and the future and the past,
Isaac and Archibald, the burning bush,
The Trojans and the walls of Jericho,

Were beautifully fused; and all went well 340
Till Archibald began to fret for Isaac
And said it was a master day for sunstroke.
That was enough to make a mummy smile,
I thought; and I remained hilarious,
In face of all precedence and respect,
Till Isaac (who had come to us unheard)
Found he had no tobacco, looked at me
Peculiarly, and asked of Archibald
What ailed the boy to make him chirrup so.
From that he told us what a blessed world 350
The Lord had given us.—"But, Archibald,"
He added, with a sweet severity
That made me think of peach-skins and goose-flesh,
"I'm half afraid you cut those oats of yours
A day or two before they were well set."
"They were set well enough," said Archibald,—
And I remarked the process of his nose
Before the words came out. "But never mind
Your neighbor's oats: you stay here in the shade
And rest yourself while I go find the cards. 360
We'll have a little game of seven-up
And let the boy keep count."—"We'll have the game,
Assuredly," said Isaac; "and I think
That I will have a drop of cider, also."

They marched away together towards the house
And left me to my childish ruminations
Upon the ways of men. I followed them
Down cellar with my fancy, and then left them
For a fairer vision of all things at once
That was anon to be destroyed again 370
By the sound of voices and of heavy feet—
One of the sounds of life that I remember,
Though I forget so many that rang first
As if they were thrown down to me from Sinai.

So I remember, even to this day,
Just how they sounded, how they placed themselves,
And how the game went on while I made marks
And crossed them out, and meanwhile made some Trojans
Likewise I made Ulysses, after Isaac,
And a little after Flaxman.[1] Archibald 380

[1] John Flaxman (1755–1826), English sculptor among whose best-known works were designs for Homer, familiar as illustrations of the *Iliad* and *Odyssey* in the nineteenth century.

Was injured when he found himself left out,
But he had no heroics, and I said so:
I told him that his white beard was too long
And too straight down to be like things in Homer.
"Quite so," said Isaac.—"Low," said Archibald;
And he threw down a deuce with a deep grin
That showed his yellow teeth and made me happy.
So they played on till a bell rang from the door,
And Archibald said, "Supper."—After that
The old men smoked while I sat watching them   390
And wondered with all comfort what might come
To me, and what might never come to me;
And when the time came for the long walk home
With Isaac in the twilight, I could see
The forest and the sunset and the sky-line,
No matter where it was that I was looking:
The flame beyond the boundary, the music,
The foam and the white ships, and two old men
Were things that would not leave me.—And that night
There came to me a dream—a shining one,   400
With two old angels in it. They had wings,
And they were sitting where a silver light
Suffused them, face to face. The wings of one
Began to palpitate as I approached,
But I was yet unseen when a dry voice
Cried thinly, with unpatronizing triumph,
"I've got you, Isaac; high, low, jack, and the game."

Isaac and Archibald have gone their way
To the silence of the loved and well-forgotten.
I knew them, and I may have laughed at them;   410
But there's a laughing that has honor in it,
And I have no regret for light words now.
Rather I think sometimes they may have made
Their sport of me;—but they would not do that,
They were too old for that. They were old men,
And I may laugh at them because I knew them.

FROM **The Town Down the River** *(1910)*

Miniver Cheevy

Miniver Cheevy, child of scorn,
    Grew lean while he assailed the seasons;
He wept that he was ever born,
    And he had reasons.

Miniver loved the days of old
    When swords were bright and steeds were prancing;
The vision of a warrior bold
    Would set him dancing.

Miniver sighed for what he was not,
    And dreamed, and rested from his labors;   10
He dreamed of Thebes and Camelot,
    And Priam's neighbors.

Miniver mourned the ripe renown
    That made so many a name so fragrant;
He mourned Romance, now on the town,
    And Art, a vagrant.

Miniver loved the Medici,
    Albeit he had never seen one;
He would have sinned incessantly
    Could he have been one.   20

Miniver cursed the commonplace
    And eyed a khaki suit with loathing;
He missed the mediæval grace
    Of iron clothing.

Miniver scorned the gold he sought,
    But sore annoyed was he without it;
Miniver thought, and thought, and thought,
    And thought about it.

Miniver Cheevy, born too late,
    Scratched his head and kept on thinking;   30
Miniver coughed, and called it fate,
    And kept on drinking.

For a Dead Lady

No more with overflowing light
Shall fill the eyes that now are faded,
Nor shall another's fringe with night
Their woman-hidden world as they did.
No more shall quiver down the days
The flowing wonder of her ways,
Whereof no language may requite
The shifting and the many-shaded.

The grace, divine, definitive,
Clings only as a faint forestalling;   10
The laugh that love could not forgive
Is hushed, and answers to no calling;
The forehead and the little ears
Have gone where Saturn [1] keeps the years;
The breast where roses could not live
Has done with rising and with falling.

The beauty, shattered by the laws
That have creation in their keeping,
No longer trembles at applause,
Or over children that are sleeping;   20
And we who delve in beauty's lore
Know all that we have known before
Of what inexorable cause
Makes Time so vicious in his reaping.

FROM **The Man Against the Sky** *(1916)*

Cassandra [1]

I heard one who said: "Verily,
    What word have I for children here?
Your Dollar is your only Word,
    The wrath of it your only fear.

"You build it altars tall enough
    To make you see, but you are blind;
You cannot leave it long enough
    To look before you or behind.

---

[1] Saturn, or Cronus, in Greek mythology, is often associated with time.

[1] The daughter of Priam, king of Troy, and Hecuba, Cassandra was a prophetess whose warnings were fated to be disbelieved.

"When Reason beckons you to pause,
    You laugh and say that you know best;   *10*
But what it is you know, you keep
    As dark as ingots in a chest.

"You laugh and answer, 'We are young;
    O leave us now, and let us grow.'—
Not asking how much more of this
    Will Time endure or Fate bestow.

"Because a few complacent years
    Have made your peril of your pride,
Think you that you are to go on
    Forever pampered and untried?   *20*

"What lost eclipse of history,
    What bivouac of the marching stars,
Has given the sign for you to see
    Millenniums and last great wars?

"What unrecorded overthrow
    Of all the world has ever known,
Or ever been, has made itself
    So plain to you, and you alone?

"Your Dollar, Dove and Eagle make
    A Trinity that even you   *30*
Rate higher than you rate yourselves;
    It pays, it flatters, and it's new.

"And though your very flesh and blood
    Be what your Eagle eats and drinks,
You'll praise him for the best of birds,
    Not knowing what the Eagle thinks.

"The power is yours, but not the sight;
    You see not upon what you tread;
You have the ages for your guide,
    But not the wisdom to be led.   *40*

"Think you to tread forever down
    The merciless old verities?
And are you never to have eyes
    To see the world for what it is?

"Are you to pay for what you have
    With all you are?"—No other word
We caught, but with a laughing crowd
    Moved on. None heeded, and few heard.

Eros Turannos [1]

She fears him, and will always ask
    What fated her to choose him;
She meets in his engaging mask
    All reasons to refuse him;
But what she meets and what she fears
Are less than are the downward years,
Drawn slowly to the foamless weirs
    Of age, were she to lose him.

Between a blurred sagacity
    That once had power to sound him,   *10*
And Love, that will not let him be
    The Judas that she found him,
Her pride assuages her almost,
As if it were alone the cost.—
He sees that he will not be lost,
    And waits and looks around him.

A sense of ocean and old trees
    Envelopes and allures him;
Tradition, touching all he sees,
    Beguiles and reassures him;   *20*
And all her doubts of what he says
Are dimmed with what she knows of days—
Till even prejudice delays
    And fades, and she secures him.

The falling leaf inaugurates
    The reign of her confusion;
The pounding wave reverberates
    The dirge of her illusion;
And home, where passion lived and died,
Becomes a place where she can hide,   *30*
While all the town and harbor side
    Vibrate with her seclusion.

We tell you, tapping on our brows,
    The story as it should be,—
As if the story of a house
    Were told, or ever could be;
We'll have no kindly veil between
Her visions and those we have seen,—
As if we guessed what hers have been,
    Or what they are or would be.   *40*

[1] King Love.

Meanwhile we do no harm; for they
    That with a god have striven,
Not hearing much of what we say,
    Take what the god has given;
Though like waves breaking it may be
Or like a changed familiar tree,
Or like a stairway to the sea
    Where down the blind are driven.

FROM **Avon's Harvest** (1921)

Mr. Flood's Party

Old Eben Flood, climbing alone one night
Over the hill between the town below
And the forsaken upland hermitage
That held as much as he should ever know
On earth again of home, paused warily.
The road was his with not a native near;
And Eben, having leisure, said aloud.
For no man else in Tilbury Town to hear:

"Well, Mr. Flood, we have the harvest moon
Again, and we may not have many more;   10
The bird is on the wing, the poet says,
And you and I have said it here before.
Drink to the bird." He raised up to the light
The jug that he had gone so far to fill,
And answered huskily: "Well, Mr. Flood,
Since you propose it, I believe I will."

Alone, as if enduring to the end
A valiant armor of scarred hopes outworn,
He stood there in the middle of the road
Like Roland's [1] ghost winding a silent horn.   20
Below him, in the town among the trees,
Where friends of other days had honored him,
A phantom salutation of the dead
Rang thinly till old Eben's eyes were dim.

---

[1] Legendary hero of the anonymous French medieval poem *Chanson de Roland.*
While fighting under Charlemagne, Roland is betrayed and surrounded by the
enemy. He sounds his horn for help, and his temples burst with the effort.

Then, as a mother lays her sleeping child
Down tenderly, fearing it may awake,
He set the jug down slowly at his feet
With trembling care, knowing that most things break;
And only when assured that on firm earth
It stood, as the uncertain lives of men   30
Assuredly did not, he paced away,
And with his hand extended paused again:

"Well, Mr. Flood, we have not met like this
In a long time; and many a change has come
To both of us, I fear, since last it was
We had a drop together. Welcome home!"
Convivially returning with himself,
Again he raised the jug up to the light;
And with an acquiescent quaver said:
"Well, Mr. Flood, if you insist, I might.   40

"Only a very little, Mr. Flood—
For auld lang syne. No more, sir; that will do."
So, for the time, apparently it did,
And Eben evidently thought so too;
For soon amid the silver loneliness
Of night he lifted up his voice and sang,
Secure, with only two moons listening,
Until the whole harmonious landscape rang—

"For auld lang syne." The weary throat gave out,
The last word wavered, and the song was done.   50
He raised again the jug regretfully
And shook his head, and was again alone.
There was not much that was ahead of him,
And there was nothing in the town below—
Where strangers would have shut the many doors
That many friends had opened long ago.

Many Are Called

The Lord Apollo,[1] who has never died,
Still holds alone his immemorial reign,
Supreme in an impregnable domain
That with his magic he has fortified;
And though melodious multitudes have tried

---

[1] Mythological Greek god of light, healing, music, poetry, prophecy.

In ecstasy, in anguish, and in vain,
With invocation sacred and profane
To lure him, even the loudest are outside.

Only at unconjectured intervals,
By will of him on whom no man may gaze,   *10*
By word of him whose law no man has read,
A questing light may rift the sullen walls,
To cling where mostly its infrequent rays
Fall golden on the patience of the dead.

FROM ***Dionysus in Doubt*** *(1925)*

The Sheaves

Where long the shadows of the wind had rolled,
Green wheat was yielding to the change assigned;
And as by some vast magic undivined
The world was turning slowly into gold.
Like nothing that was ever bought or sold
It waited there, the body and the mind;
And with a mighty meaning of a kind
That tells the more the more it is not told.

So in a land where all days are not fair,
Fair days went on till on another day   *10*
A thousand golden sheaves were lying there,
Shining and still, but not for long to stay—
As if a thousand girls with golden hair
Might rise from where they slept and go away.

New England

Here where the wind is always north-north-east
And children learn to walk on frozen toes,
Wonder begets an envy of all those
Who boil elsewhere with such a lyric yeast
Of love that you will hear them at a feast
Where demons would appeal for some repose,
Still clamoring where the chalice overflows
And crying wildest who have drunk the least.

Passion is here a soilure of the wits
We're told, and Love a cross for them to bear;   *10*

Joy shivers in the corner where she knits
And Conscience always has the rocking-chair,
Cheerful as when she tortured into fits
The first cat that was ever killed by Care.

ROBERT [LEE] FROST (1874–1963)

*Robert Frost has had so much greatness thrust upon him (which, to be
sure, he felt was only his due) that one is tempted to qualify a bit.
This mild and meditative sage was not at all the kindly presiding
presence that he chose to present himself publicly as being. His
poems created an image that he was happy to exploit, and in this he
is like Ernest Hemingway, who had the same human weakness
although aspiring to a different image. These men have never been
compared, probably because they were so different in temperament;
but there is an interesting similarity in the way that they saw themselves—gruff and stoic spirits, alone and "enduring" near the snowy
wood or on the edge of the treacherous swamp where real self-
knowledge might be tested. They were alike, too, socially: often
petty, spiteful, jealous, and mad for approval. Both won that approval from a very large audience. What may ultimately prove the
limitation of both is the absence in the work itself of some humane
quality that is central to great art. Their private lives seem to suggest this imaginative deficiency, even as those lives, in their time,
concealed it.*

*Robert Frost's parents were New Englanders who had moved to Cali-
fornia, and he was born in San Francisco. When he was eleven years
old he went, with his mother and his father's corpse, to New England, where his mother found work as a grammar school teacher in
Salem, New Hampshire, and the boy began to familiarize himself
with the stony landscape that was to become the setting of almost
everything he wrote.*

*After abortive attempts for an education at Dartmouth and later Har-
vard, he continued his earlier efforts to earn his living in any way
that he could—working in a mill, on a newspaper, with a shoe-
maker, as a teacher, as a farmer. He published his first poem in
1894 and married in the next year. Neither teaching nor farming
worked out, and the poems he was publishing attracted almost no
one. In 1912 he broke with it all, sold his farm, and removed himself and wife and four children to England. There he met Ezra
Pound, who, characteristically, advised, supervised, and helped at
once to advance Frost's poetry. Frost also became the friend of a
number of the Georgian poets whose work his own poems more*

nearly resembled than they did those of such an American experi-mentalist as Pound. In England he published his first volume, A Boy's Will (1913)—Longfellow gave him the title—and in the next year, his book of dramatic dialogs, North of Boston. These books attracted attention, and when Frost brought his family back to the United States in 1915, he found that he had a kind of fame. After that, publicly, at least, it was all like skiing down an easy slope into the domestic warmth of fireside affection. Happy fiction! Privately, it was more nearly a gruesome, ego-driven, destructive mania.

The rest is folklore. He became the most successful nonfarming farmer in the history of American literature—and the great near-deity that aspiring poets might hope to meet at the Breadloaf Writers' Confer-ence in the summers or after public readings on a thousand college campuses. Except for two rather strange dialogs of the 1940s, A Masque of Reason (1945) and A Masque of Mercy (1947), he made no attempt to extend the understated lyric style, at once laconic and taut, that he had initially mastered. Book followed book as the growing body of poems were collected and recollected. Honor fol-lowed honor: the Pulitzer Prize four times, countless academic de-grees, any academic appointment that he cared to consider, and finally, in the year before his death, official recognition of an almost unprecedented sort from the White House, when he was asked to read a poem at the inauguration of President John F. Kennedy.

He was a much better poet than is suggested by the public repute that he sought, his pose of reticent and simple rustic philosopher to the contrary. Some of his works will certainly survive, once they are freed from the overtones of folk wisdom in which he chose to im-mure himself. At their center is a hard core of absolute, crystalline aesthetic integrity.

FURTHER READING

The first volume of the authorized biography by Lawrence Thompson appeared in 1966: *Robert Frost: The Early Years, 1874–1915;* the second, *The Years of Triumph, 1915–1938,* in 1970. Briefer biog-raphies are by Sidney Cox, *Swinger of Birches* (1957), and Elizabeth Sargeant, *Robert Frost: The Trial by Existence* (1960). Among many critical studies, these are vital: Reginald Cook, *The Dimensions of Robert Frost* (1959); John Lynen, *The Pastoral Art of Robert Frost* (1960); Reuben Brower, *The Poetry of Robert Frost: Constellations of Intention* (1963); and Radcliffe Squires, *The Major Themes of Robert Frost* (1963).

FROM **A Boy's Will** *(1913)*

Mowing

There was never a sound beside the wood but one,
And that was my long scythe whispering to the ground.
What was it it whispered? I knew not well myself;
Perhaps it was something about the heat of the sun,
Something, perhaps, about the lack of sound—
And that was why it whispered and did not speak.
It was no dream of the gift of idle hours,
Or easy gold at the hand of fay or elf:
Anything more than the truth would have seemed too weak
To the earnest love that laid the swale in rows,   10
Not without feeble-pointed spikes of flowers
(Pale orchises), and scared a bright green snake.
The fact is the sweetest dream that labor knows.
My long scythe whispered and left the hay to make.

The Tuft of Flowers

I went to turn the grass once after one
Who mowed it in the dew before the sun.

The dew was gone that made his blade so keen
Before I came to view the leveled scene.

I looked for him behind an isle of trees;
I listened for his whetstone on the breeze.

But he had gone his way, the grass all mown,
And I must be, as he had been,—alone,

'As all must be,' I said within my heart,
'Whether they work together or apart.'   10

But as I said it, swift there passed me by
On noiseless wing a bewildered butterfly,

Seeking with memories grown dim o'er night
Some resting flower of yesterday's delight.

And once I marked his flight go round and round,
As where some flower lay withering on the ground.

And then he flew as far as eye could see,
And then on tremulous wing came back to me.

I thought of questions that have no reply,
And would have turned to toss the grass to dry; 20

But he turned first, and led my eye to look
At a tall tuft of flowers beside a brook,

A leaping tongue of bloom the scythe had spared
Beside a reedy brook the scythe had bared.

The mower in the dew had loved them thus,
By leaving them to flourish, not for us,

Nor yet to draw one thought of ours to him,
But from sheer morning gladness at the brim.

The butterfly and I had lit upon,
Nevertheless, a message from the dawn, 30

That made me hear the wakening birds around,
And hear his long scythe whispering to the ground,

And feel a spirit kindred to my own;
So that henceforth I worked no more alone;

But glad with him, I worked as with his aid,
And weary, sought at noon with him the shade;

And dreaming, as it were, held brotherly speech
With one whose thought I had not hoped to reach.

'Men work together,' I told him from the heart,
'Whether they work together or apart.' 40

Reluctance

Out through the fields and the woods
    And over the walls I have wended;
I have climbed the hills of view
    And looked at the world, and descended;
I have come by the highway home,
    And lo, it is ended.

The leaves are all dead on the ground,
    Save those that the oak is keeping
To ravel them one by one
    And let them go scraping and creeping 10
Out over the crusted snow,
    When others are sleeping.

And the dead leaves lie huddled and still,
      No longer blown hither and thither;
The last lone aster is gone;
      The flowers of the witch-hazel wither;
The heart is still aching to seek,
      But the feet question 'Whither?'

Ah, when to the heart of man
      Was it ever less than a treason   20
To go with the drift of things,
      To yield with a grace to reason,
And bow and accept the end
      Of a love or a season?

FROM **North of Boston** *(1914)*

The Pasture

I'm going out to clean the pasture spring;
I'll only stop to rake the leaves away
(And wait to watch the water clear, I may)
I sha'n't be gone long.—You come too.

I'm going out to fetch the little calf
That's standing by the mother. It's so young
It totters when she licks it with her tongue.
I sha'n't be gone long.—You come too.

Mending Wall

Something there is that doesn't love a wall,
That sends the frozen-ground-swell under it,
And spills the upper boulders in the sun;
And makes gaps even two can pass abreast.
The work of hunters is another thing:
I have come after them and made repair
Where they have left not one stone on a stone,
But they would have the rabbit out of hiding,
To please the yelping dogs. The gaps I mean,
No one has seen them made or heard them made,   10
But at spring mending-time we find them there.
I let my neighbor know beyond the hill;
And on a day we meet to walk the line

And set the wall between us once again.
We keep the wall between us as we go.
To each the boulders that have fallen to each.
And some are loaves and some so nearly balls
We have to use a spell to make them balance:
'Stay where you are until our backs are turned!'
We wear our fingers rough with handling them.   20
Oh, just another kind of outdoor game,
One on a side. It comes to little more:
There where it is we do not need the wall:
He is all pine and I am apple orchard.
My apple trees will never get across
And eat the cones under his pines, I tell him.
He only says, 'Good fences make good neighbors.'
Spring is the mischief in me, and I wonder
If I could put a notion in his head:
'*Why* do they make good neighbors? Isn't it   30
Where there are cows? But here there are no cows.
Before I built a wall I'd ask to know
What I was walling in or walling out,
And to whom I was like to give offense.
Something there is that doesn't love a wall,
That wants it down.' I could say 'Elves' to him,
But it's not elves exactly, and I'd rather
He said it for himself. I see him there
Bringing a stone grasped firmly by the top
In each hand, like an old-stone savage armed.   40
He moves in darkness as it seems to me,
Not of woods only and the shade of trees.
He will not go behind his father's saying,
And he likes having thought of it so well
He says again, 'Good fences make good neighbors.'

The Death of the Hired Man

Mary sat musing on the lamp-flame at the table
Waiting for Warren. When she heard his step,
She ran on tip-toe down the darkened passage
To meet him in the doorway with the news
And put him on his guard. 'Silas is back.'
She pushed him outward with her through the door
And shut it after her. 'Be kind,' she said.
She took the market things from Warren's arms
And set them on the porch, then drew him down
To sit beside her on the wooden steps.   10

'When was I ever anything but kind to him?
But I'll not have the fellow back,' he said.
'I told him so last haying, didn't I?
If he left then, I said, that ended it.
What good is he? Who else will harbor him
At his age for the little he can do?
What help he is there's no depending on.
Off he goes always when I need him most.
He thinks he ought to earn a little pay,
Enough at least to buy tobacco with,   20
So he won't have to beg and be beholden.
"All right," I say, "I can't afford to pay
Any fixed wages, though I wish I could."
"Someone else can." "Then someone else will have to."
I shouldn't mind his bettering himself
If that was what it was. You can be certain,
When he begins like that, there's someone at him
Trying to coax him off with pocket-money,—
In haying time, when any help is scarce.
In winter he comes back to us. I'm done.'   30

'Sh! not so loud: he'll hear you,' Mary said.

'I want him to: he'll have to soon or late.'

'He's worn out. He's asleep beside the stove.
When I came up from Rowe's I found him here,
Huddled against the barn-door fast asleep,
A miserable sight, and frightening, too—
You needn't smile—I didn't recognize him—
I wasn't looking for him—and he's changed.
Wait till you see.'

              'Where did you say he'd been?'   40

'He didn't say. I dragged him to the house,
And gave him tea and tried to make him smoke.
I tried to make him talk about his travels.
Nothing would do: he just kept nodding off.'

'What did he say? Did he say anything?'

'But little.'

         'Anything? Mary, confess
He said he'd come to ditch the meadow for me.'

'Warren!'

         'But did he? I just want to know.'   50

'Of course he did. What would you have him say?
Surely you wouldn't grudge the poor old man

Some humble way to save his self-respect.
He added, if you really care to know,
He meant to clear the upper pasture, too.
That sounds like something you have heard before?
Warren, I wish you could have heard the way
He jumbled everything. I stopped to look
Two or three times—he made me feel so queer—
To see if he was talking in his sleep.   60
He ran on Harold Wilson—you remember—
The boy you had in haying four years since.
He's finished school, and teaching in his college.
Silas declares you'll have to get him back.
He says they two will make a team for work:
Between them they will lay this farm as smooth!
The way he mixed that in with other things.
He thinks young Wilson a likely lad, though daft
On education—you know how they fought
All through July under the blazing sun,   70
Silas up on the cart to build the load,
Harold along beside to pitch it on.'

'Yes, I took care to keep well out of earshot.'

'Well, those days trouble Silas like a dream.
You wouldn't think they would. How some things linger!
Harold's young college boy's assurance piqued him.
After so many years he still keeps finding
Good arguments he sees he might have used.
I sympathize. I know just how it feels
To think of the right thing to say too late.   80
Harold's associated in his mind with Latin.
He asked me what I thought of Harold's saying
He studied Latin like the violin
Because he liked it—that an argument!
He said he couldn't make the boy believe
He could find water with a hazel prong—
Which showed how much good school had ever done him.
He wanted to go over that. But most of all
He thinks if he could have another chance
To teach him how to build a load of hay—'   90

'I know, that's Silas' one accomplishment.
He bundles every forkful in its place,
And tags and numbers it for future reference,
So he can find and easily dislodge it
In the unloading. Silas does that well.
He takes it out in bunches like big birds' nests.

You never see him standing on the hay
He's trying to lift, straining to lift himself.'

'He thinks if he could teach him that, he'd be
Some good perhaps to someone in the world.   *100*
He hates to see a boy the fool of books.
Poor Silas, so concerned for other folk,
And nothing to look backward to with pride,
And nothing to look forward to with hope,
So now and never any different.'

Part of a moon was falling down the west,
Dragging the whole sky with it to the hills.
Its light poured softly in her lap. She saw it
And spread her apron to it. She put out her hand
Among the harp-like morning-glory strings,   *110*
Taut with the dew from garden bed to eaves,
As if she played unheard some tenderness
That wrought on him beside her in the night.
'Warren,' she said, 'he has come home to die:
You needn't be afraid he'll leave you this time.'

'Home,' he mocked gently.

                  'Yes, what else but home?

It all depends on what you mean by home.
Of course he's nothing to us, any more
Than was the hound that came a stranger to us   *120*
Out of the woods, worn out upon the trail.'

'Home is the place where, when you have to go there,
They have to take you in.'

                   'I should have called it
Something you somehow haven't to deserve.'

Warren leaned out and took a step or two,
Picked up a little stick, and brought it back
And broke it in his hand and tossed it by.
'Silas has better claim on us you think
Than on his brother? Thirteen little miles   *130*
As the road winds would bring him to his door.
Silas has walked that far no doubt today.
Why doesn't he go there? His brother's rich,
A somebody—director in the bank.'

'He never told us that.'
                   'We know it though.'

'I think his brother ought to help, of course.
I'll see to that if there is need. He ought of right
To take him in, and might be willing to—
He may be better than appearances.   *140*
But have some pity on Silas. Do you think
If he had any pride in claiming kin
Or anything he looked for from his brother,
He'd keep so still about him all this time?'

'I wonder what's between them.'

                       'I can tell you.
Silas is what he is—we wouldn't mind him—
But just the kind that kinsfolk can't abide.
He never did a thing so very bad.
He don't know why he isn't quite as good   *150*
As anybody. Worthless though he is,
He won't be made ashamed to please his brother.'

'I can't think Si ever hurt anyone.'

'No, but he hurt my heart the way he lay
And rolled his old head on that sharp-edged chair-back.
He wouldn't let me put him on the lounge.
You must go in and see what you can do.
I made the bed up for him there tonight.
You'll be surprised at him—how much he's broken.
His working days are done; I'm sure of it.'   *160*

'I'd not be in a hurry to say that.'

'I haven't been. Go, look, see for yourself.
But, Warren, please remember how it is:
He's come to help you ditch the meadow.
He has a plan. You mustn't laugh at him.
He may not speak of it, and then he may.
I'll sit and see if that small sailing cloud
Will hit or miss the moon.'

                    It hit the moon.
Then there were three there, making a dim row,   *170*
The moon, the little silver cloud, and she.

Warren returned—too soon, it seemed to her,
Slipped to her side, caught up her hand and waited.

'Warren?' she questioned.

               'Dead,' was all he answered.

After Apple-Picking

My long two-pointed ladder's sticking through a tree
Toward heaven still,
And there's a barrel that I didn't fill
Beside it, and there may be two or three
Apples I didn't pick upon some bough.
But I am done with apple-picking now.
Essence of winter sleep is on the night,
The scent of apples: I am drowsing off.
I cannot rub the strangeness from my sight
I got from looking through a pane of glass   10
I skimmed this morning from the drinking trough
And held against the world of hoary grass.
It melted, and I let it fall and break.
But I was well
Upon my way to sleep before it fell,
And I could tell
What form my dreaming was about to take.
Magnified apples appear and disappear,
Stem end and blossom end,
And every fleck of russet showing clear.   20
My instep arch not only keeps the ache,
It keeps the pressure of a ladder-round.
I feel the ladder sway as the boughs bend.
And I keep hearing from the cellar bin
The rumbling sound
Of load on load of apples coming in.
For I have had too much
Of apple-picking: I am overtired
Of the great harvest I myself desired.
There were ten thousand thousand fruit to touch,   30
Cherish in hand, lift down, and not let fall.
For all
That struck the earth,
No matter if not bruised or spiked with stubble,
Went surely to the cider-apple heap
As of no worth.
One can see what will trouble
This sleep of mine, whatever sleep it is.
Were he not gone,
The woodchuck could say whether it's like his   40
Long sleep, as I describe its coming on,
Or just some human sleep.

FROM **Mountain Interval** *(1916)*

The Road Not Taken

Two roads diverged in a yellow wood,
And sorry I could not travel both
And be one traveler, long I stood
And looked down one as far as I could
To where it bent in the undergrowth;

Then took the other, as just as fair,
And having perhaps the better claim,
Because it was grassy and wanted wear;
Though as for that the passing there
Had worn them really about the same,   *10*

And both that morning equally lay
In leaves no step had trodden black.
Oh, I kept the first for another day!
Yet knowing how way leads on to way,
I doubted if I should ever come back.

I shall be telling this with a sigh
Somewhere ages and ages hence:
Two roads diverged in a wood, and I—
I took the one less traveled by,
And that has made all the difference.   *20*

Birches

When I see birches bend to left and right
Across the lines of straighter darker trees,
I like to think some boy's been swinging them.
But swinging doesn't bend them down to stay
As ice-storms do. Often you must have seen them
Loaded with ice a sunny winter morning
After a rain. They click upon themselves
As the breeze rises, and turn many-colored
As the stir cracks and crazes their enamel.
Soon the sun's warmth makes them shed crystal shells   *10*
Shattering and avalanching on the snow-crust—
Such heaps of broken glass to sweep away
You'd think the inner dome of heaven had fallen.
They are dragged to the whithered bracken by the load,

And they seem not to break; though once they are bowed
So low for long, they never right themselves:
You may see their trunks arching in the woods
Years afterwards, trailing their leaves on the ground
Like girls on hands and knees that throw their hair
Before them over their heads to dry in the sun.   20
But I was going to say when Truth broke in
With all her matter-of-fact about the ice-storm
I should prefer to have some boy bend them
As he went out and in to fetch the cows—
Some boy too far from town to learn baseball,
Whose only play was what he found himself,
Summer or winter, and could play alone.
One by one he subdued his father's trees
By riding them down over and over again
Until he took the stiffness out of them,   30
And not one but hung limp, not one was left
For him to conquer. He learned all there was
To learn about not launching out too soon
And so not carrying the tree away
Clear to the ground. He always kept his poise
To the top branches, climbing carefully
With the same pains you use to fill a cup
Up to the brim, and even above the brim.
Then he flung outward, feet first, with a swish,
Kicking his way down through the air to the ground. 40
So was I once myself a swinger of birches.
And so I dream of going back to be.
It's when I'm weary of considerations,
And life is too much like a pathless wood
Where your face burns and tickles with the cobwebs
Broken across it, and one eye is weeping
From a twig's having lashed across it open.
I'd like to get away from earth awhile
And then come back to it and begin over.
May no fate willfully misunderstand me   50
And half grant what I wish and snatch me away
Not to return. Earth's the right place for love:
I don't know where it's likely to go better.
I'd like to go by climbing a birch tree,
And climb black branches up a snow-white trunk
Toward heaven, till the tree could bear no more,
But dipped its top and set me down again.
That would be good both going and coming back.
One could do worse than be a swinger of birches.

FROM *New Hampshire: A Poem
with Notes and Grace Notes* (1923)

Fire and Ice

Some say the world will end in fire,
Some say in ice.
From what I've tasted of desire
I hold with those who favor fire.
But if it had to perish twice,
I think I know enough of hate
To say that for destruction ice
Is also great
And would suffice.

Dust of Snow

The way a crow
Shook down on me
The dust of snow
From a hemlock tree

Has given my heart
A change of mood
And saved some part
Of a day I had rued.

Stopping by Woods on a Snowy Evening

Whose woods these are I think I know.
His house is in the village though;
He will not see me stopping here
To watch his woods fill up with snow.

My little horse must think it queer
To stop without a farmhouse near
Between the woods and frozen lake
The darkest evening of the year.

He gives his harness bells a shake
To ask if there is some mistake.   10
The only other sound's the sweep
Of easy wind and downy flake.

The woods are lovely, dark and deep,
But I have promises to keep,
And miles to go before I sleep,
And miles to go before I sleep.

The Onset

Always the same, when on a fated night
At last the gathered snow lets down as white
As may be in dark woods, and with a song
It shall not make again all winter long
Of hissing on the yet uncovered ground,
I almost stumble looking up and round,
As one who overtaken by the end
Gives up his errand, and lets death descend
Upon him where he is, with nothing done
To evil, no important triumph won,   10
More than if life had never been begun.

Yet all the precedent is on my side:
I know that winter death has never tried
The earth but it has failed: the snow may heap
In long storms an undrifted four feet deep
As measured against maple, birch, and oak,
It cannot check the peeper's silver croak;
And I shall see the snow all go down hill
In water of a slender April rill
That flashes tail through last year's withered brake   20
And dead weeds, like a disappearing snake.
Nothing will be left white but here a birch,
And there a clump of houses with a church.

FROM **West-running Brook** *(1928)*

Spring Pools

These pools that, though in forests, still reflect
The total sky almost without defect,
And like the flowers beside them, chill and shiver,
Will like the flowers beside them soon be gone,
And yet not out by any brook or river,
But up by roots to bring dark foliage on.

The trees that have it in their pent-up buds
To darken nature and be summer woods—
Let them think twice before they use their powers
To blot out and drink up and sweep away   *10*
These flowery waters and these watery flowers
From snow that melted only yesterday.

Tree at My Window

Tree at my window, window tree,
My sash is lowered when night comes on;
But let there never be cutain drawn.
Between you and me.

Vague dream-head lifted out of the ground,
And thing next most diffuse to cloud,
Not all your light tongues talking aloud
Could be profound.

But, tree, I have seen you taken and tossed,
And if you have seen me when I slept,   *10*
You have seen me when I was taken and swept
And all but lost.

That day she put our heads together,
Fate had her imagination about her,
Your head so much concerned with outer,
Mine with inner, weather.

The Investment

Over back where they speak of life as staying
('You couldn't call it living, for it ain't'),
There was an old, old house renewed with paint,
And in it a piano loudly playing.

Out in the plowed ground in the cold a digger,
Among unearthed potatoes standing still,
Was counting winter dinners, one a hill,
With half an ear to the piano's vigor.

All that piano and new paint back there,
Was it some money suddenly come into?   *10*

Or some extravagance young love had been to?
Or old love on an impulse not to care—

Not to sink under being man and wife,
But get some color and music out of life?

FROM **A Further Range** *(1936)*

Desert Places

Snow falling and night falling fast, oh, fast
In a field I looked into going past,
And the ground almost covered smooth in snow,
But a few weeds and stubble showing last.

The woods around it have it—it is theirs.
All animals are smothered in their lairs.
I am too absent-spirited to count;
The loneliness includes me unawares.

And lonely as it is that loneliness
Will be more lonely ere it will be less—   10
A blanker whiteness of benighted snow
With no expression, nothing to express.

They cannot scare me with their empty spaces
Between stars—on stars where no human race is.
I have it in me so much nearer home
To scare myself with my own desert places.

Design

I found a dimpled spider, fat and white,
On a white heal-all, holding up a moth
Like a white piece of rigid satin cloth—
Assorted characters of death and blight
Mixed ready to begin the morning right,
Like the ingredients of a witches' broth—
A snow-drop spider, a flower like a froth,
And dead wings carried like a paper kite.

What had that flower to do with being white,
The wayside blue and innocent heal-all?   10

What brought the kindred spider to that height,
Then steered the white moth thither in the night?
What but design of darkness to appall?—
If design govern in a thing so small.

FROM **A Witness Tree** (1942)

The Gift Outright

The land was ours before we were the land's.
She was our land more than a hundred years
Before we were her people. She was ours
In Massachusetts, in Virginia,
But we were England's, still colonials,
Possessing what we still were unpossessed by,
Possessed by what we now no more possessed.
Something we were withholding made us weak
Until we found out that it was ourselves
We were withholding from our land of living,   10
And forthwith found salvation in surrender.
Such as we were we gave ourselves outright
(The deed of gift was many deeds of war)
To the land vaguely realizing westward,
But still unstoried, artless, unenhanced,
Such as she was, such as she would become.

FROM **Steeple Bush** (1947)

Directive

Back out of all this now too much for us,
Back in a time made simple by the loss
Of detail, burned, dissolved, and broken off
Like graveyard marble sculpture in the weather,
There is a house that is no more a house
Upon a farm that is no more a farm
And in a town that is no more a town.
The road there, if you'll let a guide direct you
Who only has at heart your getting lost,
May seem as if it should have been a quarry—   10
Great monolithic knees the former town

Long since gave up pretense of keeping covered.
And there's a story in a book about it:
Besides the wear of iron wagon wheels
The ledges show lines ruled southeast northwest,
The chisel work of an enormous Glacier
That braced his feet against the Arctic Pole.
You must not mind a certain coolness from him
Still said to haunt this side of Panther Mountain.
Nor need you mind the serial ordeal   20
Of being watched from forty cellar holes
As if by eye pairs out of forty firkins.
As for the woods' excitement over you
That sends light rustle rushes to their leaves,
Charge that to upstart inexperience.
Where were they all not twenty years ago?
They think too much of having shaded out
A few old pecker-fretted apple trees.
Make yourself up a cheering song of how
Someone's road home from work this once was,   30
Who may be just ahead of you on foot
Or creaking with a buggy load of grain.
The height of the adventure is the height
Of country where two village cultures faded
Into each other. Both of them are lost.
And if you're lost enough to find yourself
By now, pull in your ladder road behind you
And put a sign up CLOSED to all but me.
Then make yourself at home. The only field
Now left's no bigger than a harness gall.   40
First there's the children's house of make believe,
Some shattered dishes underneath a pine,
The playthings in the playhouse of the children.
Weep for what little things could make them glad.
Then for the house that is no more a house,
But only a belilaced cellar hole,
Now slowly closing like a dent in dough.
This was no playhouse but a house in earnest.
Your destination and your destiny's
A brook that was the water of the house,   50
Cold as a spring as yet so near its source,
Too lofty and original to rage.
(We know the valley streams that when aroused
Will leave their tatters hung on barb and thorn.)
I have kept hidden in the instep arch
Of an old cedar at the waterside

A broken drinking goblet like the Grail [1]
Under a spell so the wrong ones can't find it,
So can't get saved, as Saint Mark says they mustn't.
(I stole the goblet from the children's playhouse.)   60
Here are your waters and your watering place.
Drink and be whole again beyond confusion.

FROM **In the Clearing** (1962)

The Draft Horse

With a lantern that wouldn't burn
In too frail a buggy we drove
Behind too heavy a horse
Through a pitch-dark limitless grove.

And a man came out of the trees
And took our horse by the head
And reaching back to his ribs
Deliberately stabbed him dead.

The ponderous beast went down
With a crack of a broken shaft.   10
And the night drew through the trees
In one long invidious draft.

The most unquestioning pair
That ever accepted fate
And the least disposed to ascribe
Any more than we had to to hate,

We assumed that the man himself
Or someone he had to obey
Wanted us to get down
And walk the rest of the way.   20

[1] The cup or chalice from which, according to legend, Jesus drank at the Last
Supper and in which Joseph of Arimathea placed the last drops of Jesus' blood
after the Crucifixion.

CARL [AUGUST] SANDBURG (1878–1967)

The son of poor and illiterate Swedish immigrants, Carl Sandburg was born in Galesburg, Illinois. At seventeen he took to the road as a hobo and itinerant worker who picked up any odd job that offered itself. At twenty he enlisted and served in the Army during the Spanish-American War, and from Puerto Rico he wrote letters which were published in the Galesburg Evening Mail as war correspondence—his first published works. In Galesburg again, he attended Lombard College for four years but did not bother to take a degree; rather, he took to the road once more. Finally, in Milwaukee, he became a journalist, working on a number of newspapers; he also became an active Socialist and for two years served as secretary to the Socialist mayor of the city. From Milwaukee he went to Chicago. At thirty, he married a fellow Socialist, the sister of Edward Steichen, the great photographer.

He had published a small pamphlet of his poems in 1904, but it was not until 1914, when Poetry published a group of his Chicago poems and awarded him its Levinson Prize, that he crashed into the consciousness of the American poetry audience. His bold colloquialism and free forms, his vigorous native impressionism, and his outcry against social injustice immediately marked him as the leader of the writers of the Chicago "renaissance," and when he published Chicago Poems (1916), that leadership was established. The volumes that followed—Cornhuskers (1918), Smoke and Steel (1920), Slabs of the Sunburnt West (1922)—did not extend his style, but they consolidated his reputation as a great poet of the people and brought him a large popular audience.

But these poems came too easily. He could toss them off on the backs of envelopes while waiting to keep an appointment. Such relaxed composition leads to garrulity, and in later volumes such as Good Morning, America (1928) and The People, Yes (1936), he yielded not only to this impulse but also to another, the sentimental and banal. Whitman's vision of a United States in which common men everywhere were united by the bonds of a mistily creative comradeship no longer seemed very suited to the social facts.

In his later years he became a troubadour—craggy faced, roughly dressed, his guitar slung from his shoulder—and tramped across America singing his own poems and folk songs that he had collected to sometimes vast audiences in which not a few listeners found his sweet baritone moving them to tears. He published many of these tunes in American Songbag (1927). At the same time that he was collecting these songs he was also collecting every possible scrap of information about the life of Abraham Lincoln, his great hero, and *after fifteen years of writing, he produced the six-volume life of Lincoln which won him the Pulitzer Prize in 1939. (In 1950, his* Complete Poems *brought that award to him again.) At the time of publication many critics—the dramatist of Lincoln's life, Robert E. Sherwood, for example—thought it the greatest biography ever produced in America; today more sober critics regard it as a sentimental myth which, for all its substantial fact, is really only an extension of Sandburg's own temperament. Much of his other prose —Remembrance Rock (1948), a kind of poetic novel about the "American dream," and the autobiography of his early years,* Always the Young Strangers *(1953), would seem to support the latter judgment. He was singing about an America that never was and never would be.*

FURTHER READING

The primary source of biographical information is Sandburg's own reminiscence, *Always the Young Strangers* (1953). Additional information can be found in Harry Golden, *Carl Sandburg* (1961); Hazel Durnell, *The America of Carl Sandburg* (1965); and Joseph Haas and Gene Lovitz, *Carl Sandburg: A Pictorial Biography* (1967). For critical estimates see Richard Crowder, *Carl Sandburg* (1964); Karl Detzer, *Carl Sandburg: A Study in Personality and Background* (1941); and Michael Yatron, *America's Literary Revolt* (1959). Herbert Mitgang edited *The Letters of Carl Sandburg* (1968).

FROM **Chicago Poems** *(1916)*

Chicago

Hog Butcher for the World,
Tool Maker, Stacker of Wheat,
Player with Railroads and the Nation's Freight Handler;
Stormy, husky, brawling,
City of the Big Shoulders:

They tell me you are wicked and I believe them, for I have seen your
painted women under the gas lamps luring the farm boys.
And they tell me you are crooked and I answer: Yes, it is true I have
seen the gunman kill and go free to kill again.
And they tell me you are brutal and my reply is: On the faces of
women and children I have seen the marks of wanton hunger.
And having answered so I turn once more to those who sneer at this
my city, and I give them back the sneer and say to them:

Come and show me another city with lifted head singing so proud to be
     alive and coarse and strong and cunning.   10
Flinging magnetic curses amid the toil of piling job on job, here is a
     tall bold slugger set vivid against the little soft cities;
Fierce as a dog with tongue lapping for action, cunning as a savage
     pitted against the wilderness,
         Bareheaded,
         Shoveling,
         Wrecking,
         Planning,
         Building, breaking, rebuilding,
Under the smoke, dust all over his mouth, laughing with white teeth,
Under the terrible burden of destiny laughing as a young man laughs,
Laughing even as an ignorant fighter laughs who has never lost a battle,   20
Bragging and laughing that under his wrist is the pulse, and under his
     ribs the heart of the people,
         Laughing!
Laughing the stormy, husky, brawling laughter of Youth, half-naked,
     sweating, proud to be Hog Butcher, Tool Maker, Stacker of Wheat,
     Player with Railroads and Freight Handler to the Nation.

Fish Crier

I know a Jew fish crier down on Maxwell Street, with a voice like a
     north wind blowing over corn stubble in January.
He dangles herring before prospective customers evincing a joy identi-
     cal with that of Pavlova dancing.
His face is that of a man terribly glad to be selling fish, terribly glad
     that God made fish, and customers to whom he may call his wares
     from a pushcart.

I Am the People, the Mob

I am the people—the mob—the crowd—the mass.
Do you know that all the great work of the world is done through me?
I am the workingman, the inventor, the maker of the world's food and
     clothes.
I am the audience that witnesses history. The Napoleons come from
     me and the Lincolns. They die. And then I send forth more
     Napoleons and Lincolns.
I am the seed ground. I am a prairie that will stand for much plowing.
     Terrible storms pass over me. I forget. The best of me is sucked

out and wasted. I forget. Everything but Death comes to me and
makes me work and give up what I have. And I forget.
Sometimes I growl, shake myself and spatter a few red drops for
history to remember. Then—I forget.
When I, the People, learn to remember, when I, the People, use the
lessons of yesterday and no longer forget who robbed me last year,
who played me for a fool—then there will be no speaker in all the
world say the name: "The People," with any fleck of a sneer in
his voice or any far-off smile of derision.
The mob—the crowd—the mass—will arrive then.

FROM **Cornhuskers** *(1918)*

Cool Tombs

When Abraham Lincoln was shoveled into the tombs, he forgot the
copperheads and the assassin . . . in the dust, in the cool tombs.

And Ulysses Grant lost all thought of con men and Wall Street, cash
and collateral turned ashes . . . in the dust, in the cool tombs.

Pocahontas' body, lovely as a poplar, sweet as a red haw in November
or a pawpaw in May, did she wonder? does she remember? . . . in
the dust, in the cool tombs?

Take any streetful of people buying clothes and groceries, cheering a
hero or throwing confetti and blowing tin horns . . . tell me if the
lovers are losers . . . tell me if any get more than the lovers . . . in
the dust . . . in the cool tombs.

FROM **Smoke and Steel** *(1920)*

Osawatomie [1]

I don't know how he came,
shambling, dark, and strong.

He stood in the city and told men:
My people are fools, my people are young and strong, my people must
learn, my people are terrible workers and fighters.

[1] A town in Kansas where the abolitionist leader and rebel John Brown (1800–
1859), celebrated as "Brown of Osawatomie," lived. He later occupied the armory
at Harper's Ferry, Virginia, and was captured and hanged.

Always he kept on asking: Where did that blood come from?
> They said: You for the fool killer,
>   you for the booby hatch
>   and a necktie party.

They hauled him into jail.
They sneered at him and spit on him,   *10*
And he wrecked their jails,
Singing, "God damn your jails,"
And when he was most in jail
Crummy among the crazy in the dark
Then he was most of all out of jail
Shambling, dark, and strong,
Always asking: Where did that blood come from?
> They laid hands on him
> And the fool killers had a laugh
> And the necktie party was a go, by God.   *20*
They laid hands on him and he was a goner.
> They hammered him to pieces and he stood up.
They buried him and he walked out of the grave, by God,
> Asking again: Where did that blood come from?

Losers

If I should pass the tomb of Jonah
I would stop there and sit for a while;
Because I was swallowed one time deep in the dark
And came out alive after all.

If I pass the burial spot of Nero
I shall say to the wind, "Well, well!"—
I who have fiddled in a world on fire,
I who have done so many stunts not worth doing.

I am looking for the grave of Sinbad too.
I want to shake his ghost-hand and say,   *10*
"Neither of us died very early, did we?"

And the last sleeping-place of Nebuchadnezzar [1]—
When I arrive there I shall tell the wind:
"You ate grass; I have eaten crow—
Who is better off now or next year?"

[1] Nebuchadnezzar (c. 604–561 B.C.), King of Babylonia and conqueror of Jerusalem.
In Daniel 4:25–34 he is driven out of human society and made to eat grass like an
animal to inculcate the lesson of God's supreme power over earthly rulers.

Jack Cade,[2] John Brown, Jesse James,[3]
There too I could sit down and stop for a while.
I think I could tell their headstones:
"God, let me remember all good losers."

I could ask people to throw ashes on their heads   20
In the name of that sergeant at Belleau Woods,[4]
Walking into the drumfires, calling his men,
"Come on, you . . . Do you want to live forever?"

A.E.F.[1]

There will be a rusty gun on the wall, sweetheart,
The rifle grooves curling with flakes of rust.
A spider will make a silver string nest in the
    darkest, warmest corner of it.
The trigger and the range-finder, they too will be rusty.
And no hands will polish the gun, and it will hang on the wall.
Forefingers and thumbs will point absently and casually toward it.
It will be spoken among half-forgotten, wished-to-be-forgotten things.
They will tell the spider: Go on, you're doing good work.

[NICHOLAS] VACHEL LINDSAY (1879–1931)

Vachel Lindsay was born in Springfield, Illinois, to parents who were
    devout Campbellites (Disciples of Christ), and the evangelical, mil-
    lenarial element in Campbellite theology became the impetus of his
    verse. He thought of himself as an evangelist and a teacher rather
    than as a poet. Indeed, at first he did not plan to be a poet. He left
    Hiram College after three years to study art in Chicago and New
    York, and it was only when no one would buy his drawings and he
    could find no other means of livelihood that he decided to be a poet.
    But a poet of a special kind: he would become a beggar who bartered

---

2 Jack Cade (?–1450), the leader of an English rebellion during the reign of
Henry VI.
3 Jesse James (1847–1882), the American bank and railroad robber who became a
folk hero in balladry.
4 Site of a World War I battle, fought to maintain Allied positions in France. The
sergeant was one Dan Daly, a United States Marine, who is reputed to have
shouted, "Come on, you sons of bitches, do you want to live forever?"

---

1 American Expeditionary Force(s), i.e., U.S. armies in Europe during World War I.

*poems for food and lodging. For a number of years he tramped
across the United States, giving away his little pamphlets,* The Tree
of Laughing Bells *(1905) and* Rhymes to be Traded for Bread
(1912), and living on handouts.

*In the winters, when he could not tramp, he gave public lectures, often
under the auspices of the YMCA or the Anti-Saloon League. His
subject matter was based on the Campbellite vision of the world as
the scene of a vast struggle between good and evil forces, with the
promise of Jesus' imminent arrival to assist the good in routing the
evil. To this doctrine, he added his "Gospel of Beauty"—and this
was the title of his most frequent lecture—a belief that every town
in America could be transformed into a nearly celestial splendor if
only a prophet would appear in each to persuade adults that all children were potential artists and craftsmen. From this notion came,
too, much of Lindsay's incomprehensible "visionary" poetry.*

He was briefly deflected from his eccentricity in 1913, when Poetry
*published his poem "General William Booth Enters into Heaven."
In that year he published a poetry collection under the same title,
and in the next year,* The Congo and Other Poems.

*Harriet Monroe believed that she had discovered a new genre, the chant,
and Lindsay began to appear in public reciting these and other
poems, interrupting the recital with parentheses from the Gospel of
Beauty. For a time he was immensely popular. He called these performances "the higher vaudeville," and, with eyes closed and head
thrown back, he would thunder and whisper and gesticulate and
chant to a strong and peculiar beat into which he threw jazz syn-
copations and the spasmodic shouts of evangelical revival meetings.*
The Chinese Nightingale and Other Poems *(1917) increased his
repertory, and his performances went on for years. He thought that
by inducing his listeners to respond to his rantings, he was preparing them for the transformed life; but while he loved the audience's
enthusiasm, he came, out of the sheer repetition, to loathe his
performances.*

*He had, it need perhaps not be said, no power of intellect, hence no
power of self-criticism, and most of the remainder of his work is only
sodden and wordy. He died in despair; his biographer and old
hometown friend, Edgar Lee Masters, said that it was death by
poison. Altogether, he is one of the sad and curious sports of our
native culture.*

FURTHER READING

An "interpretive biography of Vachel Lindsay and Springfield, Illinois,"
is Mark Harris's *City of Discontent* (1952). The fullest factual

account of Lindsay's life is Eleanor Ruggles, *The West-going Heart*
(1959); the most intimate is still Edgar Lee Masters, *Vachel Lindsay:
A Poet in America* (1935).

FROM *General William Booth Enters
into Heaven and Other Poems* (1913)

General William Booth
Enters into Heaven [1]

*(To be sung to the tune of "The Blood of the Lamb" with indicated
    instrument)*

I
(Bass drum beaten loudly.)
Booth led boldly with his big bass drum—
(Are you washed in the blood of the Lamb?)
The Saints smiled gravely and they said: "He's come."
(Are you washed in the blood of the Lamb?)
Walking lepers followed, rank on rank,
Lurching bravos from the ditches dank,
Drabs from the alleyways and drug fiends pale—
Minds still passion-ridden, soul-powers frail:—
Vermin-eaten saints with moldy breath,
Unwashed legions with the ways of Death—   *10*
(Are you washed in the blood of the Lamb?)

  (Banjos.)
Every slum had sent its half-a-score
The round world over. (Booth had groaned for more.)
Every banner that the wide world flies
Bloomed with glory and transcendent dyes.
Big-voiced lasses made their banjos bang,
Tranced, fanatical they shrieked and sang:—
"Are you washed in the blood of the Lamb?"
Hallelujah! It was queer to see
Bull-necked convicts with that land make free.   *20*
Loons with trumpets blowed a blare, blare, blare
On, on upward thro' the golden air!
(Are you washed in the blood of the Lamb?)

[1] William Booth (1829–1912) was an English clergyman and founder of the
Salvation Army. His son, also named William (1856–1929), was a general of the
Salvation Army. This poem is about the father.

II

(Bass drum slower and softer.)
Booth died blind and still by faith he trod,
Eyes still dazzled by the ways of God.
Booth led boldly, and he looked the chief
Eagle countenance in sharp relief,
Beard a-flying, air of high command
Unabated in that holy land.

(Sweet flute music.)
Jesus came from out the court-house door,   30
Stretched his hands above the passing poor.
Booth saw not, but led his queer ones there
Round and round the mighty court-house square.
Then, in an instant all that blear review
Marched on spotless, clad in raiment new.
The lame were straightened, withered limbs uncurled
And blind eyes opened on a new, sweet world.

(Bass drum louder.)
Drabs and vixens in a flash made whole!
Gone was the weasel-head, the snout, the jowl!
Sages and sibyls now, and athletes clean,   40
Rulers of empires, and of forests green!

(Grand chorus of all instruments. Tambourines to the foreground.)
The hosts were sandalled, and their wings were fire!
(Are you washed in the blood of the Lamb?)
But their noise played havoc with the angel-choir.
(Are you washed in the blood of the Lamb?)
Oh, shout Salvation! It was good to see
Kings and Princes by the Lamb set free.
The banjos rattled and the tambourines
Jing-jing-jingled in the hands of Queens.

(Reverently sung, no instruments.)
And when Booth halted by the curb for prayer   50
He saw his Master thro' the flag-filled air.
Christ came gently with a robe and crown
For Booth the soldier, while the throng knelt down.
He saw King Jesus. They were face to face,
And he knelt a-weeping in that holy place.
Are you washed in the blood of the Lamb?

FROM *The Congo and Other Poems* *(1914)*

The Congo
A Study of the Negro Race [1]

(Being a memorial to Ray Eldred, a Disciple missionary of the Congo River)

I

THEIR BASIC SAVAGERY

Fat black bucks in a wine-barrel room,
Barrel-house kings, with feet unstable,
Sagged and reeled and pounded on the table,   *A deep rolling bass.*
Pounded on the table,
Beat an empty barrel with the handle of a broom,
Hard as they were able,
Boom, boom, BOOM,
With a silk umbrella and the handle of a broom,
Boomlay, boomlay, boomlay, BOOM.
THEN I had religion, THEN I had vision.   10
I could not turn from their revel in derision.
THEN I SAW THE CONGO, CREEPING THROUGH THE BLACK,   *More deliberate.*
CUTTING THROUGH THE FOREST WITH A GOLDEN TRACK.   *Solemnly chanted.*
Then along that riverbank
A thousand miles
Tattooed cannibals danced in files;
Then I heard the boom of the blood-lust song
And a thigh-bone beating on a tin-pan gong.   *A rapidly piling climax of speed and racket.*
And "BLOOD" screamed the whistles and the fifes of the
    warriors,
"BLOOD" screamed the skull-faced, lean witch-doctors,   20
"Whirl ye the deadly voo-doo rattle,
Harry the uplands,
Steal all the cattle,
Rattle-rattle, rattle-rattle,
Bing.

[1] This poem, particularly the third section, was suggested by an allusion in a sermon by my pastor, F. W. Burnham, to the heroic life and death of Ray Eldred. Eldred was a missionary of the Disciples of Christ who perished while swimming a treacherous branch of the Congo. See *A Master Builder on the Congo*, by Andrew F. Henesey, published by Fleming H. Revell. *Au.*

Boomlay, boomlay, boomlay, Boom,"
A roaring, epic, rag-time tune   *With a philo-*
From the mouth of the Congo   *sophic pause.*
To the Mountains of the Moon.
Death is an Elephant,   30
Torch-eyed and horrible,   *Shrilly and*
Foam-flanked and terrible.   *with a heavily*
                                                            accented metre.
Boom, steal the pygmies,
Boom, kill the Arabs,
Boom, kill the white men,
Hoo, Hoo, Hoo.
Listen to the yell of Leopold's [2] ghost   *Like the wind*
Burning in Hell for his hand-maimed host.   *in the chimney.*
Hear how the demons chuckle and yell
Cutting his hands off, down in Hell.   40
Listen to the creepy proclamation,
Blown through the lairs of the forest-nation,
Blown past the white-ants' hill of clay,
Blown past the marsh where the butterflies play: —
"Be careful what you do,
Or Mumbo-Jumbo, God of the Congo,   *All the "o"*
                                                            sounds very
And all of the other   *golden. Heavy*
Gods of the Congo,   *accents very*
                                                            heavy. Light
Mumbo-Jumbo will hoo-doo you,   *accents very*
Mumbo-Jumbo will hoo-doo you,   *light. Last line*
Mumbo-Jumbo will hoo-doo you."   *whispered.*

II

THEIR IRREPRESSIBLE HIGH SPIRITS

Wild crap-shooters with a whoop and a call   *Rather shrill*
Danced the juba in their gambling hall   *and high.*
And laughed fit to kill, and shook the town,
And guyed the policemen and laughed them down   55
With a boomlay, boomlay, boomlay, Boom,
THEN I SAW THE CONGO, CREEPING THROUGH THE BLACK,   *Read exactly as*
CUTTING THROUGH THE FOREST WITH A GOLDEN TRACK.   *in first section.*
A negro fairyland swung into view,   *Lay emphasis*
                                                            on the delicate
A minstrel river   *ideas. Keep as*
Where dreams come true.   *light-footed as*
                                                            possible.
The ebony palace soared on high
Through the blossoming trees to the evening sky.

[2] Leopold II (1865–1909), King of Belgium.

The inlaid porches and casements shone
With gold and ivory and elephant-bone.   65
And the black crowd laughed till their sides were sore
At the baboon butler in the agate door,
And the well-know tunes of the parrot band
That trilled on the bushes of that magic land.

A troupe of skull-faced witch-men came   *With*
Through the agate doorway in suits of flame,   *pomposity.*
Yea, long-tailed coats with a gold-leaf crust
And hats that were covered with diamond-dust.
And the crowd in the court gave a whoop and a call
And danced the juba from wall to wall.   75
But the witch-men suddenly stilled the throng   *With a great*
With a stern cold glare, and a stern old song: —   *deliberation*
                                                           and ghostliness.
"Mumbo-Jumbo will hoo-doo you." . . .
Just then from the doorway, as fat as shotes,   *With over-*
Came the cake-walk princes in the long red coats,   *whelming as-*
                                                           surance, good
Canes with a brilliant lacquer shine,   *cheer, and*
And tall silk hats that were red as wine.   *pomp.*
And they pranced with their butterfly partners there,   *With growing*
Coal-black maidens with pearls in their hair,   *speed and*
                                                           sharply marked
Knee-skirts trimmed with the jassamine sweet,   *dance-rhythm.*
And bells on their ankles and little black-feet.   85
And the couples railed at the chant and the frown
Of the witch-men lean, and laughed them down.
(Oh, rare was the revel, and well worth while
That made those glowering witch-men smile.)   90

The cake-walk royalty then began
To walk for a cake that was tall as a man
To the tune of "Boomlay, boomlay, Boom,"
While the witch-men laughed, with a sinister air,   *With a touch*
And sang with the scalawags prancing there: —   *of negro dia-*
                                                           lect, and
"Walk with care, walk with care,   *as rapidly as*
Or Mumbo-Jumbo, God of the Congo,   *possible toward*
                                                           the end.
And all of the other Gods of the Congo,
Mumbo-Jumbo will hoo-doo you.
Beware, beware, walk with care,   100
Boomlay, boomlay, boomlay, boom.
Boomlay, boomlay, boomlay, boom.
Boomlay, boomlay, boomlay, boom.
Boomlay boomlay, boomlay,
Boom."
(Oh, rare was the revel, and well worth while   *Slow philo-*
That made those glowering witch-men smile.)   *sophic calm.*

III

THE HOPE OF THEIR RELIGION

A good old negro in the slums of the town
Preached at a sister for her velvet gown.
Howled at a brother for his low-down ways,
His prowling, guzzling, sneak-thief days.
Beat on the Bible till he wore it out
Starting the jubilee revival shout.
And some had visions, as they stood on chairs,
And sang of Jacob, and the golden stairs,[3]
And they all repented, a thousand strong
From their stupor and savagery and sin and wrong
And slammed with their hymn books till they shook the room
With "glory, glory, glory,"
And "Boom, boom, Boom."
THEN I SAW THE CONGO, CREEPING THROUGH THE BLACK,
CUTTING THROUGH THE JUNGLE WITH A GOLDEN TRACK.
And the gray sky opened like a new-rent veil
And showed the Apostles with their coats of mail.
In bright white steele they were seated round
And their fire-eyes watched where the Congo wound.
And the twelve Apostles, from their thrones on high
Thrilled all the forest with their heavenly cry: —
"Mumbo-Jumbo will die in the jungle;
Never again will he hoo-doo you,
Never again will he hoo-doo you."

Then along that river, a thousand miles
The vine-snared trees fell down in files.
Pioneer angels cleared the way
For a Congo paradise, for babes at play,
For sacred capitals, for temples clean.
Gone were the skull-faced witch-men lean.
There, where the wild ghost-gods had wailed
A million boats of the angels sailed
With oars of silver, and prows of blue
And silken pennants that the sun shone through.
'Twas a land transfigured, 'twas a new creation.
Oh, a singing wind swept the negro nation
And on through the backwoods clearing, flew: —

Heavy bass. With a literal imitation of camp-meeting racket, and trance.

115

Exactly as in the first section. Begin with terror and power, end with joy.

125

Sung to the tune of "Hark, ten thousand harps and voices."
With growing deliberation and joy.

135

In a rather high key—as delicately as possible.

---

[3] In Genesis, 28:12, Jacob dreams that he sees a ladder set on the earth and reaching to heaven, which angels are ascending and descending.

"Mumbo-Jumbo is dead in the jungle.
Never again will he hoo-doo you.
Never again will he hoo-doo you.

*To the tune of
"Hark, ten
thousand harps
and voices."*

Redeemed were the forests, the beasts and the men,
And only the vulture dared again
By the far, lone mountains of the moon
To cry, in the silence, the Congo tune: —
Mumbo-Jumbo will hoo-doo you,
"Mumbo-Jumbo will hoo-doo you.
Mumbo . . . Jumbo . . . will . . . hoo-doo . . . you."

150

*Dying down
into a pene-
trating,
terrified
whisper.*

WALLACE STEVENS (1879–1955)

*In the decade between Stevens's birth and Eliot's (1888), most of the
now established great modern American poets were born: Williams,
Pound, Jeffers, Marianne Moore, and Ransom; Aiken, Cummings,
Crane, and Tate came along immediately after. Such surprising
confluences are not uncommon in literary history, which has no
way of accounting for them. American literature had seen them,
although not in such numbers, at least twice before: those fifteen
years that saw the birth of Emerson, Hawthorne, (Longfellow and
Whittier, if one wishes to include them), Poe, Jones Very, Thoreau,
Melville, and Whitman; and those seven years, two decades later,
that brought on Emily Dickinson, Samuel Clemens, William Dean
Howells, Henry Adams, and William and Henry James. Some poets
of the most recent group may finally fall from the pantheon, but all
present indications are that Wallace Stevens is secure there.*

*He was born in Reading, Pennsylvania, and spent three years at Har-
vard, which he left without a degree; then he attended the New
York Law School and was admitted to the bar in 1904. For more
than ten years he practiced law in New York City and mingled more
intimately with other poets and artists than he was ever to bother
to do again.*

*In the first years of the experimental theater, he attempted plays in
verse. In 1916* Poetry *published and gave a prize to his play called*
Three Travelers Watch a Sunrise, *and its success with some readers
involved in little-theater work led him to write two more,* Carlos
Among the Candles *and* Bowl, Cat and Broomstick. *All three had
brief productions of sorts, and the first two appeared in print (never
collected by Stevens himself), but the third was published only
recently. (The text of this play is available now, and the whole set
of circumstances is described in* The Quarterly Review of Literature,

*16, 1–2, 1969). These strange experiments in drama announce in
fact the earliest and the abiding interests of Stevens, the nondra-
matic poet.*

*As everyone has known for years, after his brief period as a New York
lawyer by day and Villager by night, Stevens moved to Connecticut
into a quiet steady life as legal adviser to the Hartford Accident and
Indemnity Company, of which, in 1934, he became vice-president,
and with which he stayed until his death. He had two lives, insurance and poetry, and was never disturbed by the difference. But
in his art, it made all the difference: in a profound sense the very
difference became his theme, life and beauty, and all the elegant
modulations of that basic antithesis that his work explored.*

His first book of poems, Harmonium *(1923), appeared when he was
already forty-four years old, and it did not arouse much interest; but
with his next volumes,* Ideas of Order *(1935) and* The Man with the
Blue Guitar *(1937), and later,* Transport to Summer *(1947), he began to attract that select and discriminating and highly devoted
audience that was to be his, the elite for which he wrote. With
these volumes and others came, too, certain public recognition in
prizes and honorary degrees.*

*His style from the beginning is characterized by its theatrical elegance,
its pose of dandyism, its wit and outré gaiety, and the odd accent of
the foreign. When many poets were making a program of bringing
poetry directly out of the vernacular and the rhythms of common
speech, Stevens chose to be as refined and artificial as suited his
imaginative needs.*

Natives of poverty, children of malheur,
The gaiety of language is our seigneur.

*Opposites—appearance and reality, fact and imagination, actuality and
art—these, but these in their* reciprocity, *were his thematic interests; and above all, he was concerned with how art makes order out
of the actual, how imagination gives form to fact: the object and the
observer, and how each modifies the other.*

*Stevens, we have said, wrote two kinds of poems, lyrics and meditations,
but the lyrics are seldom personal in the usual sense, and the meditations are hardly philosophical. Although Stevens's titles seem to
indicate a metaphysical base—"Ideas of Order," for example, or
"Notes Toward a Supreme Fiction"—it is a mistake to try to read
him as though he were a poet of ideas. It is a complex verbal music,
intertwining a few and often repeated themes with subtle variations,
that we must try to hear. One should not try too hard; the ear should
have a chance to do the work. Above all, one should not turn to
Stevens's own critical prose (collected in* The Necessary Angel,*

*1951) for help, because, witty and entertaining as much of this is,
it also is without logical coherence, shot through with inconsistencies, and planted with little booby traps for the solemn and unwary.*

Stevens's Collected Poems *were published in the year before his death,
and shortly after appeared* Opus Posthumous *(1957), which brings
together some of his plays, poems rejected or not previously collected
by him, and some miscellaneous prose.*

FURTHER READING

There is no biography. The primary source of biographical information
is *Letters of Wallace Stevens* (1966), edited by the poet's daughter,
Holly Stevens. Critical studies are numerous and increasing in
number. Frank Kermode's *Wallace Stevens* (1960) is a brief but
perceptive survey. Joseph Riddel's *The Clairvoyant Eye: The Poetry
and Poetics of Wallace Stevens* (1966) is intended "primarily as
readings, individually and chronologically, of Stevens's poems."
Robert Buttel's *Wallace Stevens: The Making of Harmonium*
(1967) discusses the poet's early work in detail. Important general
studies include Frank Doggett, *Stevens's Poetry of Thought* (1966);
James Baird, *The Dome and the Rock: Structure in the Poetry of
Wallace Stevens* (1968); Henry W. Wells, *Introduction to Wallace
Stevens* (1964); and Daniel Fuchs, *The Comic Spirit of Wallace
Stevens* (1963). R. H. Pearce and J. H. Miller have edited *The
Act of the Mind: Essays on the Poetry of Wallace Stevens* (1966), a
miscellaneous collection. The most recent and perhaps most helpful
explication is Helen Vendler's *On Extended Wings: Wallace Stevens'
Longer Poems* (1970).

FROM *Harmonium* *(1923, 1931)*

The Plot Against the Giant

FIRST GIRL

When this yokel comes maundering,
Whetting his hacker,[1]
I shall run before him,
Diffusing the civilest odors
Out of geraniums and unsmelled flowers.
It will check him.

---

[1] A tool for making incisions on trees.

SECOND GIRL

I shall run before him,
Arching cloths besprinkled with colors
As small as fish-eggs.
The threads   *10*
Will abash him.

THIRD GIRL

Oh, la . . . le pauvre! [2]
I shall run before him,
With a curious puffing.
He will bend his ear then.
I shall whisper
Heavenly labials in a world of gutturals.
It will undo him.

Domination of Black

At night, by the fire,
The colors of the bushes
And of the fallen leaves,
Repeating themselves,
Turned in the room,
Like the leaves themselves
Turning in the wind.
Yes: but the color of the heavy hemlocks
Came striding.
And I remembered the cry of the peacocks.   *10*

The colors of their tails
Were like the leaves themselves
Turning in the wind,
In the twilight wind.
They swept over the room,
Just as they flew from the boughs of the hemlocks
Down to the ground.
I heard them cry—the peacocks.
Was it a cry against the twilight
Or against the leaves themselves   *20*
Turning in the wind,

[2] "The poor man."

Turning as the flames
Turned in the fire,
Turning as the tails of the peacocks
Turned in the loud fire,
Loud as the hemlocks
Full of the cry of the peacocks?
Or was it a cry against the hemlocks?

Out of the window,
I saw how the planets gathered   30
Like the leaves themselves
Turning in the wind.
I saw how the night came,
Came striding like the color of the heavy hemlocks
I felt afraid.
And I remembered the cry of the peacocks.

The Emperor of Ice-cream

Call the roller of big cigars,
The muscular one, and bid him whip
In kitchen cups concupiscent curds.
Let the wenches dawdle in such dress
As they are used to wear, and let the boys
Bring flowers in last month's newspapers.
Let be be finale of seem.
The only emperor is the emperor of ice-cream.

Take from the dresser of deal,[1]
Lacking the three glass knobs, that sheet   10
On which she embroidered fantails [2] once
And spread it so as to cover her face.
If her horny feet protrude, they come
To show how cold she is, and dumb.
Let the lamp affix its beam.
The only emperor is the emperor of ice-cream.

[1] Fir or pine wood.
[2] A breed of pigeons with fanlike tails.

Disillusionment of Ten O'clock

The houses are haunted
By white night-gowns.
None are green,
Or purple with green rings,
Or green with yellow rings,
Or yellow with blue rings.
None of them are strange,
With socks of lace
And beaded ceintures.[1]
People are not going   10
To dream of baboons and periwinkles.[2]
Only, here and there, an old sailor,
Drunk and asleep in his boots,
Catches tigers
In red weather.

Sunday Morning

I

Complacencies of the peignoir, and late
Coffee and oranges in a sunny chair,
And the green freedom of a cockatoo
Upon a rug mingle to dissipate
The holy hush of ancient sacrifice.
She dreams a little, and she feels the dark
Encroachment of that old catastrophe,
As a calm darkens among water-lights.
The pungent oranges and bright, green wings
Seem things in some procession of the dead,   10
Winding across wide water, without sound.
The day is like wide water, without sound,
Stilled for the passing of her dreaming feet
Over the seas, to silent Palestine,
Dominion of the blood and sepulchre.

II

Why should she give her bounty to the dead?
What is divinity if it can come

[1] Belts.
[2] Sea snails; also evergreen plants with blue flowers.

Only in silent shadows and in dreams?
Shall she not find in comforts of the sun,
In pungent fruit and bright, green wings, or else   20
In any balm or beauty of the earth,
Things to be cherished like the thought of heaven?
Divinity must live within herself:
Passions of rain, or moods in falling snow;
Grievings in loneliness, or unsubdued
Elations when the forest blooms; gusty
Emotions on wet roads on autumn nights;
All pleasures and all pains, remembering
The bough of summer and the winter branch.
These are the measures destined for her soul.   30

III

Jove in the clouds had his inhuman birth.
No mother suckled him, no sweet land gave
Large-mannered motions to his mythy mind
He moved among us, as a muttering king,
Magnificent, would move among his hinds,
Until our blood, commingling, virginal,
With heaven, brought such requital to desire
The very hinds discerned it, in a star.
Shall our blood fail? Or shall it come to be
The blood of paradise? And shall the earth   40
Seem all of paradise that we shall know?
The sky will be much friendlier then than now,
A part of labor and a part of pain,
And next in glory to enduring love,
Not this dividing and indifferent blue.

IV

She says, "I am content when wakened birds,
Before they fly, test the reality
Of misty fields, by their sweet questionings;
But when the birds are gone, and their warm fields
Return no more, where, then, is paradise?"   50
There is not any haunt of prophecy,
Nor any old chimera of the grave,
Neither the golden underground, nor isle
Melodious, where spirits gat them home,
Nor visionary south, nor cloudy palm
Remote on heaven's hill, that has endured
As April's green endures; or will endure

Like her remembrance of awakened birds,
Or her desire for June and evening, tipped
By the consummation of the swallow's wings.   *60*

V

She says, "But in contentment I still feel
The need of some imperishable bliss."
Death is the mother of beauty; hence from her,
Alone, shall come fulfilment to our dreams
And our desires. Although she strews the leaves
Of sure obliteration on our paths,
The path sick sorrow took, the many paths
Where triumph rang its brassy phrase, or love
Whispered a little out of tenderness,
She makes the willow shiver in the sun   *70*
For maidens who were wont to sit and gaze
Upon the grass, relinquished to their feet.
She causes boys to pile new plums and pears
On disregarded plate. The maidens taste
And stray impassioned in the littering leaves.

VI

Is there no change of death in paradise?
Does ripe fruit never fall? Or do the boughs
Hang always heavy in that perfect sky,
Unchanging, yet so like our perishing earth,
With rivers like our own that seek for seas   *80*
They never find, the same receding shores
That never touch with inarticulate pang?
Why set the pear upon those river-banks
Or spice the shores with odors of the plum?
Alas, that they should wear our colors there,
The silken weavings of our afternoons,
And pick the strings of our insipid lutes!
Death is the mother of beauty, mystical,
Within whose burning bosom we devise
Our earthly mothers waiting, sleeplessly.   *90*

VII

Supple and turbulent, a ring of men
Shall chant in orgy on a summer morn
Their boisterous devotion to the sun,
Not as a god, but as a god might be,

Naked among them, like a savage source.
Their chant shall be a chant of paradise,
Out of their blood, returning to the sky;
And in their chant shall enter, voice by voice,
The windy lake wherein their lord delights,
The trees, like serafim,[1] and echoing hills,   *100*
That choir among themselves long afterward.
They shall know well the heavenly fellowship
Of men that perish and of summer morn.
And whence they came and whither they shall go
The dew upon their feet shall manifest.

VIII

She hears, upon that water without sound,
A voice that cries, "The tomb in Palestine
Is not the porch of spirits lingering.
It is the grave of Jesus, where he lay."
We live in an old chaos of the sun,   *110*
Or old dependency of day and night,
Or island solitude, unsponsored, free,
Of that wide water, inescapable.
Deer walk upon our mountains, and the quail
Whistle about us their spontaneous cries;
Sweet berries ripen in the wilderness;
And, in the isolation of the sky,
At evening, casual flocks of pigeons make
Ambiguous undulations as they sink,
Downward to darkness, on extended wings.   *120*

Anecdote of the Jar

I placed a jar in Tennessee,
And round it was, upon a hill.
It made the slovenly wilderness
Surround that hill.

The wilderness rose up to it,
And sprawled around, no longer wild.
The jar was round upon the ground
And tall and of a port in air.

[1] Celestial beings (seraphim).

It took dominion everywhere.
The jar was gray and bare.   *10*
It did not give of bird or bush,
Like nothing else in Tennessee.

Peter Quince at the Clavier [1]

I

Just as my fingers on these keys
Make music, so the selfsame sounds
On my spirit make a music, too.

Music is feeling, then, not sound;
And thus it is that what I feel,
Here in this room, desiring you,

Thinking of your blue-shadowed silk,
Is music. It is like the strain
Waked in the elders by Susanna.[2]

Of a green evening, clear and warm,   *10*
She bathed in her still garden, while
The red-eyed elders watching, felt

The bases of their beings throb
In witching chords, and their thin blood
Pulse pizzicati of Hosanna.

II

In the green water, clear and warm,
Susanna lay.
She searched
The touch of springs,
And found   *20*
Concealed imaginings.
She sighed,
For so much melody.

[1] Peter Quince is the carpenter in Shakespeare's *A Midsummer Night's Dream* who
directs the play of *Pyramus and Thisbe.*
[2] According to an apocryphal Old Testament story, two elders spied on the young
and beautiful Susanna in her bath. Susanna, faithful to her husband, spurned the
advances of the elders, who then accused her of attempting to seduce them. The
prophet Daniel saved Susanna from execution.

Upon the bank, she stood
In the cool
Of spent emotions.
She felt, among the leaves,
The dew
Of old devotions.

She walked upon the grass,   30
Still quavering.
The winds were like her maids,
On timid feet,
Fetching her woven scarves,
Yet wavering.

A breath upon her hand
Muted the night.
She turned—
A cymbal crashed,
And roaring horns.   40

III

Soon, with a noise like tambourines,
Came her attendant Byzantines.

They wondered why Susanna cried
Against the elders by her side;

And as they whispered, the refrain
Was like a willow swept by rain.

Anon, their lamps' uplifted flame
Revealed Susanna and her shame.

And then, the simpering Byzantines
Fled, with a noise like tambourines.   50

IV

Beauty is momentary in the mind—
The fitful tracing of a portal;
But in the flesh it is immortal.

The body dies; the body's beauty lives.
So evenings die, in their green going,
A wave, interminably flowing.
So gardens die, their meek breath scenting
The cowl of winter, done repenting.
So maidens die, to the auroral
Celebration of a maiden's choral.   60

Susanna's music touched the bawdy strings
Of those white elders; but, escaping,
Left only Death's ironic scraping.
Now, in its immortality, it plays
On the clear viol of her memory,
And makes a constant sacrament of praise.

Thirteen Ways of Looking at a Blackbird

I

Among twenty snowy mountains,
The only moving thing
Was the eye of the blackbird.

II

I was of three minds,
Like a tree
In which there are three blackbirds.

III

The blackbird whirled in the autumn winds.
It was a small part of the pantomime.

IV

A man and a woman
Are one.   10
A man and a woman and a blackbird
Are one.

V

I do not know which to prefer,
The beauty of inflections
Or the beauty of innuendoes,
The blackbird whistling
Or just after.

VI

Icicles filled the long window
With barbaric glass.

The shadow of the blackbird   20
Crossed it, to and fro.
The mood
Traced in the shadow
An indecipherable cause.

VII
O thin men of Haddam,[1]
Why do you imagine golden birds?
Do you not see how the blackbird
Walks around the feet
Of the women about you?

VIII
I know noble accents   30
And lucid, inescapable rhythms;
But I know, too,
That the blackbird is involved
In what I know.

IX
When the blackbird flew out of sight,
It marked the edge
Of one of many circles.

X
At the sight of blackbirds
Flying in a green light,
Even the bawds of euphony   40
Would cry out sharply.

XI
He rode over Connecticut
In a glass coach.
Once, a fear pierced him,
In that he mistook
The shadow of his equipage [2]
For blackbirds.

[1] A town in Connecticut near Hartford.
[2] Carriage.

XII

The river is moving.
The blackbird must be flying.

XIII

It was evening all afternoon.   *50*
It was snowing
And it was going to snow.
The blackbird sat
In the cedar-limbs.

FROM **Ideas of Order** *(1935)*

The Idea of Order at Key West

She sang beyond the genius of the sea.
The water never formed to mind or voice,
Like a body wholly body, fluttering
Its empty sleeves; and yet its mimic motion
Made constant cry, caused constantly a cry,
That was not ours although we understood,
Inhuman, of the veritable ocean.

The sea was not a mask. No more was she.
The song and water were not medleyed sound
Even if what she sang was what she heard,   *10*
Since what she sang was uttered word by word.
It may be that in all her phrases stirred
The grinding water and the gasping wind;
But it was she and not the sea we heard.

For she was the maker of the song she sang.
The ever-hooded, tragic-gestured sea
Was merely a place by which she walked to sing.
Whose spirit is this? we said, because we knew
It was the spirit that we sought and knew
That we should ask this often as she sang.   *20*

If it was only the dark voice of the sea
That rose, or even colored by many waves;
If it was only the outer voice of sky
And cloud, of the sunken coral water-walled,
However clear, it would have been deep air,
The heaving speech of air, a summer sound
Repeated in a summer without end

And sound alone. But it was more than that,
More even than her voice, and ours, among
The meaningless plungings of water and the wind,   30
Theatrical distances, bronze shadows heaped
On high horizons, mountainous atmospheres
Of sky and sea.

      It was her voice that made
The sky acutest at its vanishing.
She measured to the hour its solitude.
She was the single artificer of the world
In which she sang. And when she sang, the sea,
Whatever self it had, became the self
That was her song, for she was the maker. Then we,   40
As we beheld her striding there alone,
Knew that there never was a world for her
Except the one she sang and, singing, made.

Ramon Fernandez,[1] tell me, if you know,
Why, when the singing ended and we turned
Toward the town, tell why the glassy lights,
The lights in the fishing boats at anchor there,
As the night descended, tilting in the air,
Mastered the night and portioned out the sea,
Fixing emblazoned zones and fiery poles,   50
Arranging, deepening, enchanting night.

Oh! Blessed rage for order, pale Ramon,
The maker's rage to order words of the sea,
Words of the fragrant portals, dimly-starred,
And of ourselves and of our origins,
In ghostlier demarcations, keener sounds.

FROM **The Man with the Blue Guitar** (1937)*

I

The man bent over his guitar,
A shearsman of sorts. The day was green.

They said, "You have a blue guitar,
You do not play things as they are."

---

[1] Ramon Fernandez (1894–1944), French philosopher and critic. Stevens says that he picked "two every day names" at random, which accidentally turned out to be an "actual name." (In Friar and Brinnin, *Modern Poetry*, 1951, p. 538.)

* In its entirety this poem contains thirty-three sections.

The man replied, "Things as they are
Are changed upon the blue guitar."

And they said then, "But play, you must,
A tune beyond us, yet ourselves,

A tune upon the blue guitar
Of things exactly as they are."   10

II

I cannot bring a world quite round,
Although I patch it as I can.

I sing a hero's head, large eye
And bearded bronze, but not a man,

Although I patch him as I can
And reach through him almost to man.

If to serenade almost to man
Is to miss, by that, things as they are,

Say that it is the serenade
Of a man that plays a blue guitar.   20

III

Ah, but to play man number one,
To drive the dagger in his heart,

To lay his brain upon the board
And pick the acrid colors out,

To nail his thought across the door,
Its wings spread wide to rain and snow,

To strike his living hi and ho,
To tick it, tock it, turn it true,

To bang it from a savage blue,
Jangling the metal of the strings . . .   30

IV

So that's life, then: things as they are?
It picks its way on the blue guitar.

A million people on one string?
And all their manner in the thing,

And all their manner, right and wrong,
And all their manner, weak and strong?

The feelings crazily, craftily call,
Like a buzzing of flies in autumn air,

And that's life, then: Things as they are,
This buzzing of the blue guitar.   *40*

V

Do not speak to us of the greatness of poetry,
Of the torches wisping in the underground,

Of the structure of vaults upon a point of light.
There are no shadows in our sun,

Day is desire and night is sleep.
There are no shadows anywhere.

The earth, for us, is flat and bare.
There are no shadows. Poetry

Exceeding music must take the place
Of empty heaven and its hymns,   *50*

Ourselves in poetry must take their place,
Even in the chattering of your guitar.

VI

A tune beyond us as we are,
Yet nothing changed by the blue guitar;

Ourselves in the tune as if in space,
Yet nothing changed, except the place

Of things as they are and only the place
As you play them, on the blue guitar,

Placed, so, beyond the compass of change,
Perceived in a final atmosphere;   *60*

For a moment final, in the way
The thinking of art seems final when

The thinking of god is smoky dew.
The tune is space. The blue guitar

Becomes the place of things as they are,
A composing of senses of the guitar.

VII

It is the sun that shares our works.
The moon shares nothing. It is a sea.

When shall I come to say of the sun,
It is a sea; it shares nothing;   70

The sun no longer shares our works
And the earth is alive with creeping men,

Mechanical beetles never quite warm?
And shall I then stand in the sun, as now

I stand in the moon, and call it good,
The immaculate, the merciful good,

Detached from us, from things as they are?
Not to be part of the sun? To stand

Remote and call it merciful?
The strings are cold on the blue guitar.   80

VIII

The vivid, florid, turgid sky,
The drenching thunder rolling by,

The morning deluged still by night,
The clouds tumultuously bright

And the feeling heavy in cold chords
Struggling toward impassioned choirs,

Crying among the clouds, enraged
By gold antagonists in air—

I know my lazy, leaden twang
Is like the reason in a storm;   90

And yet it brings the storm to bear.
I twang it out and leave it there.

FROM **Parts of a World** (1942)

The Glass of Water

That the glass would melt in heat,
That the water would freeze in cold,
Shows that this object is merely a state,
One of many, between two poles. So,
In the metaphysical, there are these poles.

Here in the centre stands the glass. Light
Is the lion that comes down to drink. There
And in that state, the glass is a pool.
Ruddy are his eyes and ruddy are his claws
When light comes down to wet his frothy jaws   10

And in the water winding weeds move round.
And there and in another state—the refractions,
The *metaphysica*, the plastic parts of poems
Crash in the mind—But, fat Jocundus,[1] worrying
About what stands here in the centre, not the glass,

But in the centre of our lives, this time, this day,
It is a state, this spring among the politicians
Playing cards. In a village of the indigenes,
One would have still to discover. Among the dogs and dung,
One would continue to contend with one's ideas.   20

Of Modern Poetry

The poem of the mind in the act of finding
What will suffice. It has not always had
To find: the scene was set; it repeated what
Was in the script.
                    Then the theatre was changed
To something else. Its past was a souvenir.

It has to be living, to learn the speech of the place.
It has to face the men of the time and to meet
The women of the time. It has to think about war
And it has to find what will suffice. It has   10
To construct a new stage. It has to be on that stage

1 Latin adjective or noun meaning "jolly."

And, like an insatiable actor,   slowly   and
With meditation, speak words that in the ear,
In the delicatest ear of the mind,   repeat,
Exactly, that which it wants to hear, at the sound
Of which, an invisible audience listens,
Not to the play, but to itself, expressed
In an emotion as of two people, as of two
Emotions becoming one. The actor is
A metaphysician in the dark, twanging   20
An instrument, twanging a wiry string that gives
Sounds passing through sudden rightnesses, wholly
Containing the mind, below which it cannot descend,
Beyond which it has no will to rise.
                                        It must
Be the finding of a satisfaction, and may
Be of a man skating, a woman dancing, a woman
Combing. The poem of the act of the mind.

WILLIAM CARLOS WILLIAMS (1883–1963)

*Williams is a more stable figure than many in a generation of poets
notable for its restlessness and rootlessness. This is in part because
he always had another profession—medicine; and it is also probably
in part because he never had any great inclination to move about.
". . . too much dynamite inside for me to want to go wandering about
wasting time traveling," he said. "What the hell is there to see, anyway, compared with what's on the inside? I never saw anything outside equal to what I was going through in my innards."*

*He was born in Rutherford, New Jersey, and that was always his home.
There was some early travel, to be sure. He had his preparatory
schooling in Geneva and Paris, and then, after completing it at the
Horace Mann School in New York and after taking his M.D. at the
University of Pennsylvania, he did graduate work in pediatrics at the
University of Leipzig. Returning to Rutherford, he set up his practice as a pediatrician, his clients chiefly the families of industrial
workers in the area, and he continued that profession until his
retirement late in life. In 1912 he married Florence Herman and
they had two sons; again, remarkably enough in this poetic generation, his marriage lasted until his death, and "Flossie" figures in his
poems.*

*As a student at Pennsylvania he came to know Ezra Pound and H. D.
(Hilda Doolittle, later Mrs. Richard Aldington, one of the few imagist
poets who can still be read with some interest), and during his*

Leipzig time in Europe, he renewed his acquaintance with Pound, who introduced him to the literary life of prewar London.

Many of Williams's earliest poems are quite a lot like Pound's earliest poems. They are stylishly verbal, rather lacy, lazily romantic, full of classical allusions; some are even scannable in the later despised iambic line—all this quite evident in the first volume, Poems *(1909), published at his own expense, and still evident in his second,* The Tempers *(1913). By then he was also coming into his own stride: no more Keats, lushly archaic; no more Whitman, generalizing about freedom; instead, the poem direct, the poem of immediacy, each poem to decree its own speechlike rhythms. This resolution was the result not only of his later meetings with Pound, in his imagist years, but of Williams's own temperament. The poet's task, as he came to see it, is "not to talk in vague categories but to write particularly, as a physician works, upon the thing before him, in the particular to discover the universal."*

It is not important that Williams rejected the term imagism *and decided to write under another,* objectivism; *or that, toward the end of his life, he extended his style into longer, looser forms (as in poems like "The Desert Music" and the five books of* Paterson *produced between 1946 and 1958). The fact is that he wrote the best imagist poetry, for almost all of his career, and made imagism mean something in actual achievement by thrusting its rather narrow, theoretical "program" into the living stuff of his own life in its constant involvement in the world.*

Thus volume followed volume, and with the poetry came a good deal of distinguished prose: several volumes of impressionistic essays (In the American Grain *of 1925 is one of the most remarkable of modern prose works in English), some plays, four volumes of short stories, four novels, an autobiography, and very late in his life, a memoir of his mother.*

Another sign of what we have been calling his stability is the fact that once Williams had achieved his characteristic poetic style, it did not change significantly (although his many explosive statements about his aims might suggest that it was changing all the time) until that rather late shift, when he tried to write his epic. Some poets—Stevens, Moore, Cummings—have not aspired to that grandeur. Williams's long poem, Paterson *(mixed with a good deal of prose), taking as its framework the history of a town on the Passaic River, and centering in a half-mythical, half-autobiographical hero, has much in it that is imaginatively splendid, but, like Hart Crane's* The Bridge, *it is a fragmentary work, broken-backed, with no self-decreed formal limits; it could go on forever. The epic apparently is not for us now. One wonders why he tried, after all those beautifully*

sharp shorter poems that so accurately put us into the heart of the
thing that he was immediately seeing and feeling.

FURTHER READING

In lieu of a biography, see William Carlos Williams's *Autobiography*
(1951) and *The Selected Letters of William Carlos Williams*
(1957), edited by John C. Thirlwall. The first full-length study is
Vivienne Koch's *William Carlos Williams* (1950). John Malcolm
Brinnin's *William Carlos Williams* (1963) is a brief pamphlet, but
extremely useful. Recent larger studies include Linda W. Wagner,
The Poems of William Carlos Williams (1964); Alan Ostrom, *The
Poetic World of William Carlos Williams* (1966); and James Gui-
mond, *The Art of William Carlos Williams* (1968). J. Hillis Miller
has edited *William Carlos Williams: A Collection of Critical Essays*
(1966), and M. L. Rosenthal, *The William Carlos Williams Reader*
(1966). For the final poem in this selection, see especially, Sherman
Paul, *The Music of Survival* (1969). The most recent critical study.
is James E. Breslin's *William Carlos Williams: An American Artist*
(1970).

FROM **A Book of Poems:**
Al Que Quiere *(1917)*

Tract

I will teach you my townspeople
how to perform a funeral—
for you have it over a troop
of artists—
unless one should scour the world—
you have the ground sense necessary.

See! the hearse leads.
I begin with a design for a hearse.
For Christ's sake not black—
nor white either—and not polished!   10
Let it be weathered—like a farm wagon—
with gilt wheels (this could be
applied fresh at small expense)
or no wheels at all:
a rough dray to drag over the ground.

Knock the glass out!
My God—glass, my townspeople!
For what purpose? Is it for the dead
to look out or for us to see
how well he is housed or to see   20
the flowers or the lack of them—
or what?
To keep the rain and snow from him?
He will have a heavier rain soon:
pebbles and dirt and what not.
Let there be no glass—
and no upholstery phew!
and no little brass rollers
and small easy wheels on the bottom—
my townspeople what are you thinking of?   30

A rough plain hearse then
with gilt wheels and no top at all.
On this the coffin lies
by its own weight.

          No wreaths please—
especially no hot house flowers.
Some common memento is better,
something he prized and is known by:
his old clothes—a few books perhaps—
God knows what! You realize   40
how we are about these things
my townspeople—
something will be found—anything
even flowers if he had come to that.
So much for the hearse.

For heaven's sake though see to the driver!
Take off the silk hat! In fact
that's no place at all for him—
up there unceremoniously
dragging our friend out to his own dignity!   50
Bring him down—bring him down!
Low and inconspicuous! I'd not have him ride
on the wagon at all—damn him—
the undertaker's understrapper!
Let him hold the reins
and walk at the side
and inconspicuously too!

Then briefly as to yourselves:
Walk behind—as they do in France,
seventh class, or if you ride   60
Hell take curtains! Go with some show
of inconvenience; sit openly—
to the weather as to grief.
Or do you think you can shut grief in?
What—from us? We who have perhaps
nothing to lose? Share with us
share with us—it will be money
in your pockets.
                    Go now
I think you are ready.   70

Smell!

Oh strong ridged and deeply hollowed
nose of mine! what will you not be smelling?
What tactless asses we are, you and I, boney nose,
always indiscriminate, always unashamed,
and now it is the souring flowers of the bedraggled
poplars: a festering pulp on the wet earth
beneath them. With what deep thirst
we quicken our desires
to that rank odor of a passing springtime!
Can you not be decent? Can you not reserve your ardors
for something less unlovely? What girl will care   10
for us, do you think, if we continue in these ways?
Must you taste everything? Must you know everything?
Must you have a part in everything?

FROM **Sour Grapes** (1921)

Her body is not so white as
anemone petals nor so smooth—nor
so remote a thing. It is a field
of the wild carrot taking
the field by force; the grass
does not raise above it.
Here is no question of whiteness,
white as can be, with a purple mole
at the center of each flower.
Each flower is a hand's span   10
of her whiteness. Wherever
his hand has lain there is

a tiny purple blemish. Each part
is a blossom under his touch
to which the fibres of her being
stem one by one, each to its end,
until the whole field is a
white desire, empty, a single stem,
a cluster, flower by flower,
a pious wish to whiteness gone over—   20
or nothing.

FROM **Spring and All** *(1923)*

Spring and All

By the road to the contagious hospital
under the surge of the blue
mottled clouds driven from the
northeast—a cold wind. Beyond, the
waste of broad, muddy fields
brown with dried weeds, standing and fallen

patches of standing water
the scattering of tall trees

All along the road the reddish
purplish, forked, upstanding, twiggy   10
stuff of bushes and small trees
with dead, brown leaves under them
leafless vines—

Lifeless in appearance, sluggish
dazed spring approaches—

They enter the new world naked,
cold, uncertain of all
save that they enter. All about them
the cold, familiar wind—

Now the grass, tomorrow   20
the stiff curl of wildcarrot leaf

One by one objects are defined—
It quickens: clarity, outline of leaf

But now the stark dignity of
entrance—Still, the profound change
has come upon them: rooted they
grip down and begin to awaken

The Red Wheelbarrow

so much depends
upon

a red wheel
barrow

glazed with rain
water

beside the white
chickens

At the Ball Game

The crowd at the ball game
is moved uniformly

by a spirit of uselessness
which delights them—

all the exciting detail
of the chase

and the escape, the error
the flash of genius—

all to no end save beauty
the eternal—   10

So in detail they, the crowd,
are beautiful

for this
to be warned against

saluted and defied—
It is alive, venomous

it smiles grimly
its words cut—

The flashy female with her
mother, gets it—   20

The Jew gets it straight—it
is deadly, terrifying—

It is the Inquisition, the
Revolution

It is beauty itself
that lives

day by day in them
idly—

This is
the power of their faces   *30*

It is summer, it is the solstice
the crowd is

cheering, the crowd is laughing
in detail

permanently, seriously
without thought

FROM *Collected Poems, 1921–1931* *(1934)*

Portrait of a Lady

Your thighs are appletrees
whose blossoms touch the sky.
Which sky? The sky
where Watteau hung a lady's
slipper. Your knees
are a southern breeze—or
a gust of snow. Agh! what
sort of man was Fragonard?
—as if that answered
anything. Ah, yes—below   *10*
the knees, since the tune
drops that way, it is
one of those white summer days,
the tall grass of your ankles
flickers upon the shore—
Which shore?—
the sand clings to my lips—
Which shore?
Agh, petals maybe. How
should I know?   *20*
Which shore? Which shore?
I said petals from an appletree.

FROM **An Early Martyr
and Other Poems** (1935)

The Yachts

contend in a sea which the land partly encloses
shielding them from the too heavy blows
of an ungoverned ocean which when it chooses

tortures the biggest hulls, the best man knows
to pit against its beatings, and sinks them pitilessly.
Mothlike in mists, scintillant in the minute

brilliance of cloudless days, with broad bellying sails
they glide to the wind tossing green water
from their sharp prows while over them the crew crawls

ant like, solicitously grooming them, releasing,   *10*
making fast as they turn, lean far over and having
caught the wind again, side by side, head for the mark.

In a well guarded arena of open water surrounded by
lesser and greater craft which, sycophant, lumbering
and flittering follow them, they appear youthful, rare

as the light of a happy eye, live with the grace
of all that in the mind is feckless, free and
naturally to be desired. Now the sea which holds them

is moody, lapping their glossy sides, as if feeling
for some slightest flaw but fails completely.   *20*
Today no race. Then the wind comes again. The yachts

move, jockeying for a start, the signal is set and they
are off. Now the waves strike at them but they are too
well made, they slip through, though they take in canvas.

Arms with hands grasping seek to clutch at the prows.
Bodies thrown recklessly in the way are cut aside.
It is a sea of faces about them in agony, in despair

until the horror of the race dawns staggering the mind,
the whole sea become an entanglement of watery bodies
lost to the world bearing what they cannot hold. Broken,   *30*

beaten, desolate, reaching from the dead to be taken up
they cry out, failing, failing! their cries rising
in waves still as the skillful yachts pass over.

The Catholic Bells

Tho' I'm no Catholic
I listen hard when the bells
in the yellow-brick tower
of their new church

ring down the leaves
ring in the frost upon them
and the death of the flowers
ring out the grackle

toward the south, the sky
darkened by them, ring in   10
the new baby of Mr. and Mrs.
Krantz which cannot

for the fat of its cheeks
open well its eyes, ring out
the parrot under its hood
jealous of the child

ring in Sunday morning
and old age which adds as it
takes away. Let them ring
only ring! over the oil   20

painting of a young priest
on the church wall advertising
last week's Novena to St.
Anthony, ring for the lame

young man in black with
gaunt cheeks and wearing a
Derby hat, who is hurrying
to 11 o'clock Mass (the

grapes still hanging to
the vines along the nearby   30
Concordia Halle like broken
teeth in the head of an

old man) Let them ring
for the eyes and ring for
the hands and ring for
the children of my friend

who no longer hears
them ring but with a smile
and in a low voice speaks
of the decisions of her   40

daughter and the proposals
and betrayals of her
husband's friends. O bells
ring for the ringing!

the beginning and the end
of the ringing! Ring ring
ring ring ring ring ring!
Catholic bells—!

FROM ***The Desert Music*** *(1954)*

To a Dog Injured in the Street

It is myself,
           not the poor beast lying there
                yelping with pain
that brings me to myself with a start—
           as at the explosion
                of a bomb, a bomb that has laid
all the world waste.
           I can do nothing
                but sing about it
and so I am assuaged   10
           from my pain.

A drowsy numbness drowns my sense
           as if of hemlock
                I had drunk. I think
of the poetry
           of René Char
                and all he must have seen
and suffered
           that has brought him
                to speak only of   20
sedgy rivers,
           of daffodils and tulips
                whose roots they water,
even to the free-flowing river
           that laves the rootlets
                of those sweet-scented flowers
that people the
           milky
                way.

I remember Norma   30
            our English setter of my childhood
                        her silky ears
and expressive eyes.
            She had a litter
                        of pups one night
in our pantry and I kicked
            one of them
                        thinking, in my alarm,
that they
            were biting her breasts   40
                        to destroy her.

I remember also
            a dead rabbit
                        lying harmlessly
on the outspread palm
            of a hunter's hand.
                        As I stood by
watching
            he took a hunting knife
                        and with a laugh   50
thrust it
            up into the animal's private parts.
                        I almost fainted.

Why should I think of that now?
            The cries of a dying dog
                        are to be blotted out
as best I can.
            René Char
                        you are a poet who believes
in the power of beauty   60
            to right all wrongs.
                        I believe it also.
With invention and courage
            we shall surpass
                        the pitiful dumb beasts,
let all men believe it,
            as you have taught me also
                        to believe it.

The Desert Music

—the dance begins: to end about a form
propped motionless—on the bridge
between Juárez and El Paso—unrecognizable
in the semi-dark

          Wait!

The others waited while you inspected it,
on the very walk itself

         Is it alive?

              —neither a head,
legs nor arms!   10

      It isn't a sack of rags someone
has abandoned here   .   torpid against
the flange of the supporting girder   .   ?

        an inhuman shapelessness,
knees hugged tight up into the belly

     Egg-shaped!

          What a place to sleep!
on the International Boundary. Where else,
interjurisdictional, not to be disturbed?

How shall we get said what must be said?   20

Only the poem.

Only the counted poem, to an exact measure:
to imitate, not to copy nature, not
to copy nature

NOT, prostrate, to copy nature
          but a dance! to dance
two and two with him—
        sequestered there asleep,
          right end up!

   A music   30
supersedes his composure, hallooing to us
across a great distance   .   .

         wakens the dance
who blows upon his benumbed fingers!

        Only the poem
only the made poem, to get said what must

be said, not to copy nature, sticks
in our throats   .

The law? The law gives us nothing
but a corpse, wrapped in a dirty mantle.   40
The law is based on murder and confinement,
long delayed,
but this, following the insensate music,
is based on the dance:

                              an agony of self-realization
bound into a whole
by that which surrounds us   .

                         I cannot escape

I cannot vomit it up

Only the poem!   50

Only the made poem, the verb calls it
                              into being.

                    —it looks too small for a man.
A woman. Or a very shriveled old man.
Maybe dead. They probably inspect the place
and will cart it away later   .

                         Heave it into the river.
A good thing.

Leaving California to return east, the fertile desert,
                    (were it to get water)   60
surrounded us, a music of survival, subdued, distant, half
                    heard; we were engulfed
by it as in the early evening, seeing the wind lift
                    and drive the sand, we
passed Yuma. All night long, heading for El Paso to
                    meet our friend,[1]
we slept fitfully. Thinking of Paris, I waked to the tick
                    of the rails. The
jagged desert   .

                              —to tell   70
         what subsequently I saw and what heard

                         —to place myself (in
my nature) beside nature

[1] Robert McAlmon (1895–1956), former expatriate in Paris who, with Williams,
edited the little magazine, *Contact*, in the early twenties. At the time of this poem,
broken in health, he was working for his brothers in El Paso.

                              —to imitate
nature (for to copy nature would be a
      shameful thing)

                        I lay myself down:

The Old Market's ² a good place to begin:
Let's cut through here—
                          tequila's only   *80*
a nickel a slug in these side streets.

Keep out though. Oh, it's all right at
this time of day but I saw H. terribly
beaten up in one of those joints. He
asked for it. I thought he was going to
be killed. I do
my drinking on the main drag   .

                      That's the bull ring
Oh, said Floss,³ after she got used to the
change of light   .   *90*
                    What color! Isn't it
wonderful!

            —paper flowers *(para los santos)* ⁴
baked red-clay utensils, daubed
with blue, silverware,
dried peppers, onions, print goods, children's
clothing   .   the place deserted all but
for a few Indians squatted in the
booths, unnoticing (don't you think it)
as though they slept there   .   *100*

            There's a second tier. Do you
want to go up?

        What makes Texans so tall?
We saw a woman this morning in a mink cape
six feet if she was an inch. What a woman!

Probably a Broadway figure.

—tell you what else we saw: about a million
sparrows screaming their heads off
in the trees of that small park where
the buses stop, sanctuary,   *110*

² In Jaurez.
³ Mrs. Williams.
⁴ "For the saints."

I suppose,
from the wind driving the sand in that way
about the city   .

                    Texas rain they call it

—and those two alligators in the fountain   .

There were four

           I saw only two

                   They were looking
right at you all the time   .

Penny please! Give me penny please, mister.   120

            Don't give them anything.

                    instinctively
one has already drawn one's naked
wrist away from those obscene fingers
as in the mind a vague apprehension speaks
and the music rouses   .

                Let's get in here.
          a music! cut off as
the bar door closes behind us.

          We've got   130
another half hour.

         —returned to the street,
the pressure moves from booth to booth along
the curb. Opposite, no less insistent
the better stores are wide open. Come in
and look around. You don't have to buy: hats,
riding boots, blankets   .

        Look at the way,
slung from her neck with a shawl, that young
Indian woman carries her baby!   140

         —a stream of Spanish,
as she brushes by, intense, wide-
eyed in eager talk with her boy husband

—three half-grown girls, one of them eating a
pomegranate. Laughing.
         and the serious tourist,
man and wife, middle-aged, middle-western,

their arms loaded with loot, whispering
together—still looking for bargains   .
                              and the aniline   *150*
red and green candy at the little booth
tended by the old Indian woman.
              Do you suppose anyone actually
buys—and eats the stuff?

My feet are beginning to ache me.

                        We still got a few minutes.
Let's try here. They had the mayor
up last month for taking $3000 a week from
the whorehouses of the city. Not much left
for the girls. There's a show on.   *160*

                        Only a few tables
occupied. A conventional orchestra—this
place livens up later—playing the usual local
jing-a-jing—a boy and girl team, she
                        confidential with someone
off stage. Laughing: just finishing the act.

So we drink until the next turn—a strip tease.

Do you mean it? Wow! Look at her.

                        You'd have to be
pretty drunk to get any kick out of that.   *170*

She's no Mexican. Some worn-out trouper from
the States. Look at those breasts

              There is a fascination
              seeing her shake
              the beaded sequins from
              a string about her hips

              She gyrates but it's
              not what you think,
              one does not laugh
              to watch her belly.   *180*

              One is moved but not
              at the dull show. The
              guitarist yawns. She
              cannot even sing. She

              has about her painted
              hardihood a screen

of pretty doves which
flutter their wings.

Her cold eyes perfunc-
torily moan but do not   *190*
smile. Yet they bill
and coo by grace of
a certain candor. She

is heavy on her feet.
That's good. She
bends forward leaning
on the table of the
balding man sitting
upright, alone, so that
everything hangs for-   *200*
ward.
        What the hell
are you grinning
to yourself about? Not
at *her*?
        The music!
I like her. She fits

the music   .

Why don't these Indians get over this nauseating
prattle about their souls and their loves and sing   *210*
us something else for a change?

This place is rank
with it. She
at least knows she's
part of another tune,
knows her customers,
has the same
opinion of them as I
have. That gives her
one up   .   one up   *220*
following the lying
music   .

There is another music. The bright-colored candy
of her nakedness lifts her unexpectedly
to partake of its tune   .

                        Andromeda of those rocks,
the virgin of her mind   .   those unearthly
greens and reds

                     in her mockery of virtue
she becomes unaccountably virtuous .   230
                    though she in no
way pretends it .

Let's get out of this.

                    In the street it hit
me in the face as we started to walk again. Or
am I merely playing the poet? Do I merely invent
it out of whole cloth? I thought .

        What in the form of an old whore in
        a cheap Mexican joint in Juárez, her bare
        can waggling crazily can be   240
        so refreshing to me, raise to my ear
        so sweet a tune, built of such slime?

        Here we are. They'll be along any minute.[5]
        The bar is at the right of the entrance,
        a few tables opposite which you have to pass
        to get to the dining room, beyond.

        A foursome, two oversize Americans, no
        longer young, got up as cowboys,
        hats and all, are drunk and carrying on
        with their gals, drunk also,   250

        especially one inciting her man, the
        biggest, *Yip ee!* to dance in
        the narrow space, oblivious to everything
        —she is insatiable and he is trying

        stumblingly to keep up with her.
        Give it the gun, pardner! *Yip ee!* We
        pushed by them to our table, seven
        of us. Seated about the room

        were quiet family groups, some with
        children, eating. Rather a better   260
        class than you notice
        on the streets. So here we are. You

        can see through into the kitchen
        where one of the cooks, his shirt sleeves
        rolled up, an apron over
        the well-pressed pants of a street

---

[5] McAlmon's brothers and their wives.

suit, black hair neatly parted,
a tall
good-looking man, is working
absorbed, before a chopping block   270

Old fashioneds all around?

                    So this is William
Carlos Williams, the poet   .

                    Floss and I had half consumed
our quartered hearts of lettuce before
we noticed the others hadn't touched theirs   .
You seem quite normal. Can you tell me? Why
does one want to write a poem?

            Because it's there to be written.

Oh. A matter of inspiration then?   280

                            Of necessity.

Oh. But what sets it off?

            I am that he whose brains
            are scattered
                    aimlessly

                            —and so,
the hour done, the quail eaten, we were on
our way back to El Paso.

                    Good night. Good
night and thank you   . No. Thank you. We're   290
going to walk.

—and so, on the naked wrist, we feel again
those insistent fingers   .

                    Penny please, mister.
Penny please. Give me penny.

                    Here! now go away.

—but the music, the music has reawakened
as we leave the busier parts of the street
and come again to the bridge in the semi-dark,
pay our fee and begin again to cross   .   300
seeing the lights along the mountain back of El
Paso and pause to watch the boys calling out
to us to throw more coins to them standing
in the shallow water   .   so that's

where the incentive lay, with the annoyance
of those surprising fingers.

                    So you're a poet?
a good thing to be got rid of—half drunk,
a free dinner under your belt, even though you
get typhoid—and to have met people you   310
can at least talk to   .

             relief from that changeless, endless
inescapable and insistent music.

             What else, Latins, do you yourselves
seek but relief!
with the expressionless ding dong you dish up
to us of your souls and your loves, which
we swallow. Spaniards! (though these are mostly
Indians who chase the white bastards
through the streets on their Independence Day   320
and try to kill them)   .

                 What's that?

Oh, come on.

           But what's THAT?

                  the music! the
music! as when Casals struck
and held a deep cello tone
and I am speechless   .

                 There it sat
in the projecting angle of the bridge flange   330
as I stood aghast and looked at it—
in the half-light: shapeless or rather returned
to its original shape, armless, legless,
headless, packed like the pit of a fruit into
that obscure corner—or
a fish to swim against the stream—or
a child in the womb prepared to imitate life,
warding its life against
a birth of awful promise. The music
guards it, a mucus, a film that surrounds it,   340
a benumbing ink that stains the
sea of our minds—to hold us off—shed
of a shape close as it can get to no shape,
a music! a protecting music   .

I *am* a poet! I
am. I am. I am a poet, I reaffirmed, ashamed

Now the music volleys through as in
a lonely moment I hear it. Now it is all
about me. The dance! The verb detaches itself
seeking to become articulate   350
        And I could not help thinking
        of the wonders of the brain that
        hears that music and of our
        skill sometimes to record it.

EZRA [WESTON LOOMIS] POUND (1885–   )

*It is hard to believe that this one, the true original, the really extrava-
gant one, the most ceaselessly active, the one who suffered most
outrageously, should be the one who is still alive. He is not, one
gathers, exactly kicking up his heels in Venice, where he now lives,
and by the time these words are in print we may very well have
read that he is dead. But even that will be almost as hard to believe
as it is that he is not: his staying powers, like his saying powers, are
immense.*

*He was born in Hailey, Idaho, but was brought up in Pennsylvania,
where he was a student at the university before transferring to
Hamilton College, from which he was graduated. Returning to the
University of Pennsylvania on a small academic appointment, he
took an M.A. and then held a teaching position at Wabash College
for four months when, not because of any scholarly inadequacy but
because of his impatience with academic procedures, he was dismissed. In 1908 he went to Italy and there published his first book
of poems,* A Lume Spento.

*From 1908 to 1920 he lived in London, and from 1920 to 1924 in Paris.
In both cities he was a pivotal center of literary activity and worked
ceaselessly to bring American and European writers together in a
community of modernism. From 1924 until the end of the Second
World War he lived in Rapallo, Italy; and while his influence on
others did not cease, it began to decline, although he continued to be
heard from in one publication or another until 1960.*

*From the beginning his work showed the impact of extraordinarily
eclectic reading and unsystematic scholarship in many fields, which
finally became like a ton of luggage, a back-breaking burden upon
it. His main literary influences were certain nineteenth-century Eng-*

lish and French poets, medieval literature, Provençal singers and troubadours, the Greek and Latin classics, Chinese and Japanese lyric and dramatic forms, and Egyptian writing. His early work, intense and compressed and highly disciplined, even while freely experimental, showed a controlled and enriching use of many of these influences.

His production was unceasing. The major early volumes of poetry are Personae *and* Exultations *(1909),* Provença *(1910),* Canzoni *(1911),* Ripostes *(1912),* Lustra *(1916),* Quia Pauper Amavi *(1919), and* Hugh Selwyn Mauberley *(Life and Contacts) (1920). The poems in this last work probably mark the climax of his life as a poet. But in* Quia Pauper Amavi *he had published the first three cantos of what would prove to be a nearly interminable work that went on for years. The published number is now 109. Some critics hold that Pound's major poetry is contained in this storehouse, but it is unlikely that anyone would argue that the whole makes a sustained or even readable work at all points. What the* Cantos *are about is nearly impossible to say, unless one settles for the description of William Van O'Connor: ". . . they are about Pound's reactions to his own reading [of literature], of various economists and political leaders, and Pound's own literary recollections. . . ."*

Scattered throughout the publications of original poetry were many translations from various languages and a good deal of prose writing on literary, artistic, cultural, historical, and cranky economic subjects. His Literary Essays *were collected with an introduction by T. S. Eliot in 1954. Among the most telling prose titles are* Jefferson and/or Mussolini *(1935) and* Impact: Essays on Ignorance and the Decline of American Civilization *(1960).*

On December 7, 1941, Pound began to broadcast over the Italian state radio on behalf of fascism. He delivered 125 such propaganda pieces for which he was paid $17 each; all were violent and increasingly incoherent attacks on capitalism, the Western Allies, and the Jews. With the end of the war, Pound was arrested by the United States government on a charge of treason and for a time was imprisoned in an open cage at Pisa. There he wrote his Pisan Cantos *(1948). In 1946 he was returned to Washington where he was examined and declared "of unsound mind"; as a consequence, he was not brought to trial but became a prisoner in St. Elizabeth's Hospital near Washington until 1958, when the charges against him were dropped and he returned to Italy.*

While he was at St. Elizabeth's, many of his literary friends rallied to his cause. William Carlos Williams, an old friend, was one who frequently visited him. Williams described him as he then was: "His reddish hair, beard and moustaches have been permitted to grow wildly at random—the long hairs framing his unchanged

*features half-ludicrously, half-frighteningly, to resemble the face of
the beast in Cocteau's well-known film." In 1949, the judges for the
Bollingen–Library of Congress Award of $1000 for the best poetry
by an American citizen published in the previous year—T. S. Eliot,
W. H. Auden, Allen Tate, Robert Penn Warren, and Katherine Anne
Porter—announced* The Pisan Cantos *as the winner. The controversy that followed was probably the noisiest in our literary history.
The Library of Congress withdrew its sponsorship of the Bollingen
prizes, and Yale University took over that function. In 1952 William
Carlos Williams was unable to occupy the office of the Consultant
in Poetry to the Library of Congress because of congressional at-
tacks on his politics, which meant his long-time association with
Ezra Pound.*

FURTHER READING

The chief biographical study is Noel Stock, *The Life of Ezra Pound*
(1970), but see also Charles Norman, *Ezra Pound* (1960, revised
1969); Patricia Hutchins, *Ezra Pound's Kensington* (1965); Michael
Reck, *Ezra Pound: A Close-up* (1967); and D. D. Paige's edition of
The Letters of Ezra Pound, 1907–1941 (1950). The major critical
study is Hugh Kenner, *The Poetry of Ezra Pound* (1951). Other important volumes include M. L. Rosenthal, *A Primer of Ezra Pound*
(1960); G. S. Frazer, *Ezra Pound* (1960); Donald Davie, *Ezra Pound:
Poet as Sculptor* (1963); Noel Stock, *Poet in Exile: Ezra Pound*
(1964); and Hugh Witemeyer, *The Poetry of Ezra Pound: Forms and
Renewal, 1908–20* (1969). John J. Espey, in *Ezra Pound's Mauberley: A Study*, provides a thorough treatment of one of Pound's major
poems. Walter Sutton edited *Ezra Pound: A Collection of Critical
Essays* (1963).

FROM **Canzoni** *(1911)*

Erat hora [1]

"Thank you, whatever comes." And then she turned
And, as the ray of sun on hanging flowers
Fades when the wind hath lifted them aside,
Went swiftly from me. Nay, whatever comes
One hour was sunlit and the most high gods
May not make boast of any better thing
Than to have watched that hour as it passed.

---

[1] "There was an hour."

FROM **Ripostes** (1912)

Portrait d'une femme [1]

Your mind and you are our Sargasso Sea,
London has swept about you this score years
And bright ships left you this or that in fee:
Ideas, old gossip, oddments of all things,
Strange spars of knowledge and dimmed wares of price.
Great minds have sought you—lacking someone else.
You have been second always. Tragical?
No. You preferred it to the usual thing:
One dull man, dulling and uxorious,
One average mind—with one thought less, each year.   10
Oh, you are patient, I have seen you sit
Hours, where something might have floated up.
And now you pay one. Yes, you richly pay.
You are a person of some interest, one comes to you
And takes strange gain away:
Trophies fished up; some curious suggestion;
Fact that leads nowhere; and a tale or two,
Pregnant with mandrakes, or with something else
That might prove useful and yet never proves,
That never fits a corner or shows use,   20
Or finds its hour upon the loom of days:
The tarnished, gaudy, wonderful old work;
Idols and ambergris and rare inlays,
These are your riches, your great store; and yet
For all this sea-hoard of deciduous things,
Strange woods half sodden, and new brighter stuff:
In the slow float of differing light and deep,
No! there is nothing! In the whole and all,
Nothing that's quite your own.
                    Yet this is you.   30

A Virginal [1]

No, no! Go from me. I have left her lately.
I will not spoil my sheath with lesser brightness,
For my surrounding air hath a new lightness;
Slight are her arms, yet they have bound me straitly

---

[1] "Portrait of a lady."

[1] A rectangular spinet having only one wire to a note, popular in the sixteenth and seventeenth centuries.

And left me cloaked as with a gauze of æther;
As with sweet leaves; as with subtle clearness.
Oh, I have picked up magic in her nearness
To sheathe me half in half the things that sheathe her.
No, no! Go from me. I have still the flavour,
Soft as spring wind that's come from birchen bowers.   *10*
Green come the shoots, aye April in the branches,
As winter's wound with her sleight hand she staunches,
Hath of the trees a likeness of the savour:
As white their bark, so white this lady's hours.[2]

The Return

See, they return; ah, see the tentative
Movements, and the slow feet,
The trouble in the pace and the uncertain
Wavering!

See, they return, one, and by one,
With fear, as half-awakened;
As if the snow should hesitate
And murmur in the wind,
         and half turn back;
These were the "Wing'd-with-Awe,"   *10*
         Inviolable.

Gods of the winged shoe!
With them the silver hounds,
         sniffing the trace of air!

Haie! Haie!
    These were the swift to harry;
These the keen-scented;
These were the souls of blood.

Slow on the leash,
         pallid the leash-men!   *20*

[2] In the sense of a time or office for daily liturgical devotion.

FROM *Lustra* *(1916)*

Salutation

O generation of the thoroughly smug
    and thoroughly uncomfortable,
I have seen fishermen picnicking in the sun,
I have seen them with untidy families,
I have seen their smiles full of teeth
    and heard ungainly laughter.
And I am happier than you are,
And they were happier than I am;
And the fish swim in the lake
    and do not even own clothing.   10

A Pact

I make a pact with you, Walt Whitman—
I have detested you long enough.
I come to you as a grown child
Who has had a pig-headed father;
I am old enough now to make friends.
It was you that broke the new wood,
Now is a time for carving.
We have one sap and one root—
Let there be commerce between us.

The Rest

O helpless few in my country,
O remnant enslaved!

Artists broken against her,
A-stray, lost in the villages,
Mistrusted, spoken-against,

Lovers of beauty, starved,
Thwarted with systems,
Helpless against the control;

You who can not wear yourselves out
By persisting to successes,   10
You who can only speak,
Who can not steel yourselves into reiteration;

You of the finer sense,
Broken against false knowledge,
You who can know at first hand,
Hated, shut in, mistrusted:

Take thought:
I have weathered the storm,
I have beaten out my exile.

In a Station of the Metro

The apparition of these faces in the crowd;
Petals on a wet, black bough.

Hugh Selwyn Mauberley
(Life and Contacts) (1920)*
"Vocat aestus in umbram"†

I

E. P. Ode pour l'election de son sepulchre [1]

For three years, out of key with his time,
He strove to resuscitate the dead art
Of poetry; to maintain "the sublime"
In the old sense. Wrong from the start—

No, hardly, but seeing he had been born
In a half savage country, out of date;
Bent resolutely on wringing lilies from the acorn;
Capaneus [2]; trout for factitious bait;

Ἴδμεν γαρ τοι πανθ', οσ ενι Τροιη [3]
Caught in the unstopped ear;   *10*
Giving the rocks small lee-way
The chopped seas held him, therefore, that year.

* This poem, in eighteen sections, ends on page 191.

† "The summer calls us into the shade," from Ecologue IV by Marcus Aurelieus Olympius Nemesianus, a Carthaginian of the third century A.D.

[1] "Ezra Pound: Ode for the Election of his Sepulcher," allusion to Ronsard's "De l'election de son sepulchre" written in 1550, *Odes*, Book IV.

[2] Who marched on Thebes against Zeus's wishes, and was killed by a thunderbolt.

[3] *Odyssey*, 12, 189: "For we all know the many things that in broad Troy [the Greeks and the Trojans suffered at the will of the gods]," sung by the Sirens to Odysseus' "unstopped ear."

His true Penelope [4] was Flaubert,[5]
He fished by obstinate isles;
Observed the elegance of Circe's hair
Rather than the mottoes on sun-dials.

Unaffected by "the march of events,"
He passed from men's memory in *l'an trentiesme*
De son eage; [6] the case presents
No adjunct to the Muses' diadem.   20

II

The age demanded an image
Of its accelerated grimace,
Something for the modern stage,
Not, at any rate, an Attic grace;

Not, not certainly, the obscure reveries
Of the inward gaze;
Better mendacities
Than the classics in paraphrase!

The "age demanded" chiefly a mould in plaster,
Made with no loss of time,   10
A prose kinema, not, not assuredly, alabaster
Or the "sculpture" of rhyme.

III

The tea-rose tea-gown, etc.
Supplants the mousseline of Cos,[1]
The pianola "replaces"
Sappho's barbitos.[2]

Christ follows Dionysus,
Phallic and ambrosial

[4] Odysseus' loving wife who patiently awaits his return.
[5] Gustave Flaubert (1821–1880), the French novelist who emphasized meticulous phrasing and structure.
[6] "The thirtieth year of his age," adapted from Villon's *Grand Testament*, line 1: "En l'an de mon trentiesme de mon eage."

---

[1] Muslin from the Greek island cf Cos.
[2] The lyre of the Greek lyric poet.

Made way for macerations; [3]
Caliban casts out Ariel. [4]

All things are a flowing,
Sage Heracleitus [5] says;   *10*
But a tawdry cheapness
Shall outlast our days.

Even the Christian beauty
Defects—after Samothrace; [6]
We see το καλον [7]
Decreed in the market place.

Faun's [8] flesh is not to us,
Nor the saint's vision.
We have the press for wafer;
Franchise for circumcision.   *20*

All men, in law, are equals.
Free of Pisistratus, [9]
We choose a knave or an eunuch
To rule over us.

O bright Apollo,
τιν' ανδρα, τιν' ηρωα, τινα θεον, [10]
What god, man, or hero
Shall I place a tin wreath upon!

IV

These fought in any case,
and some believing,
        pro domo, [1] in any case . . .

[3] Breaking up or wasting away.
[4] The animal and the spiritual dramatizations of man in Shakespeare's *The Tempest*.
[5] Greek philosopher who believed that all things are in constant motion.
[6] Island where the statue "Winged Victory" was discovered.
[7] "The beautiful."
[8] Roman satyrs or rural deities represented as men with the ears, horns, tails, and hind legs of a goat.
[9] Tyrant of Athens (560–527 B.C.).
[10] "What man, what hero, what god [shall we extol]?" (From Pindar's "Second Olympian Ode.")

[1] "For home."

Some quick to arm,
some for adventure,
some from fear of weakness,
some from fear of censure,
some for love of slaughter, in imagination,
learning later . . .
some in fear, learning love of slaughter;   *10*

Died some, pro patria,
                    non "dulce" non "et decor" [2] . . .
walked eye-deep in hell
believing in old men's lies, then unbelieving
came home, home to a lie,
home to many deceits,
home to old lies and new infamy;
usury age-old and age-thick
and liars in public places.

Daring as never before, wastage as never before.   *20*
Young blood and high blood,
fair cheeks, and fine bodies;

fortitude as never before

frankness as never before,
disillusions as never told in the old days,
hysterias, trench confessions,
laughter out of dead bellies.

V

There died a myriad,
And of the best, among them,
For an old bitch gone in the teeth,
For a botched civilization,

Charm, smiling at the good mouth,
Quick eyes gone under earth's lid,

For two gross of broken statues,
For a few thousand battered books.

[2] "For country,/not 'sweet' nor 'and proper,'" allusion to Horace's famous line
"Dulce et decorum est pro patria mori" ("It is sweet and proper to die for one's
country"), *Odes*, 3, 2, 13.

Yeux glauques [1]

Gladstone [2] was still respected,
When John Ruskin produced
"King's Treasuries" [3]; Swinburne
And Rossetti still abused.

Fœtid Buchanan [4] lifted up his voice
When that faun's head of hers [5]
Became a pastime for
Painters and adulterers.

The Burne-Jones [6] cartons
Have preserved her eyes;   10
Still, at the Tate,[7] they teach
Cophetua [8] to rhapsodize;

Thin like brook-water,
With a vacant gaze.
The English Rubaiyat [9] was still-born
In those days.

The thin, clear gaze, the same
Still darts out faun-like from the half-ruin'd face,
Questing and passive....
"Ah, poor Jenny's [10] case" . . .   20

Bewildered that a world
Shows no surprise
At her last maquero's [11]
Adulteries.

[1] "Deep-green eyes," from the title of Théophile Gautier's poem, "Caerulei Oculi,"
probably refers to Elizabeth Siddal's eyes as described by Dante Gabriel Rossetti.
[2] William Gladstone (1809–1898), British statesman and prime minister.
[3] Ruskin's first essay in *Sesame and Lilies* (1865).
[4] Robert Williams Buchanan (1841–1901), who attacked Swinburne and Rossetti in
1871 in an essay entitled "The Fleshly School of Poetry."
[5] Refers to Elizabeth Siddal, a popular model married to Rossetti.
[6] Edward Burne-Jones (1833–1898), British painter and designer.
[7] A gallery in London.
[8] "King Cophetua and the Beggar Maid," a painting done by Burne-Jones in 1884
which hangs at the Tate.
[9] Edward Fitzgerald's translation of Omar Khayyám's poem in 1859.
[10] The name of a loose woman in a Rossetti poem of that title.
[11] Pimp's.

"Siena mi fe'; disfecemi Maremma" [1]

Among the pickled fœtuses and bottled bones,
Engaged in perfecting the catalogue,
I found the last scion of the
Senatorial families of Strasbourg, Monsieur Verog.[2]

For two hours he talked of Gallifet; [3]
Of Dowson [4]; of the Rhymers' Club; [5]
Told me how Johnson (Lionel) [6] died
By falling from a high stool in a pub . . .

But showed no trace of alcohol
At the autopsy, privately performed—   10
Tissue preserved—the pure mind
Arose toward Newman [7] as the whiskey warmed.

Dowson found harlots cheaper than hotels;
Headlam [8] for uplift; Image [9] impartially imbued
With raptures for Bacchus, Terpsichore [10] and the Church.
So spoke the author of "The Dorian Mood,"

M. Verog, out of step with the decade,
Detached from his contemporaries,
Neglected by the young,
Because of these reveries.   20

Brennbaum [1]

The sky-like limpid eyes,
The circular infant's face,
The stiffness from spats to collar
Never relaxing into grace;

1 Dante, *Purgatorio*, 5, 135: "Siena made me; Maremma undid me," spoken by a
woman from Siena who was killed in Maremma, Tuscany.
2 Victor Gustave Plarr (1863–1929), author of a book of poems entitled *In the
Dorian Mood* (1896), a friend of Lionel Johnson and Ernest Dowson.
3 A French military leader.
4 Ernest Dowson (1867–1900), British poet.
5 Literary club to which Dowson and Johnson belonged.
6 Lionel Johnson (1867–1902), British poet.
7 John Henry Cardinal Newman (1801–1890), famous convert to the Church of
Rome and a leader of the Oxford Movement.
8 Rev. Stewart Headlam, a member of the Rhymers' Club.
9 Selwyn Image, British editor and a friend of Dowson and Johnson.
10 Greek muse of dance and choral singing.

1 Probably Sir Max Beerbohm (1872–1956), British author and caricaturist.

The heavy memories of Horeb, Sinai and the forty years,[2]
Showed only when the daylight fell
Level across the face
Of Brennbaum "The Impeccable."

Mr. Nixon [1]

In the cream gilded cabin of his steam yacht
Mr. Nixon advised me kindly, to advance with fewer
Dangers of delay. "Consider
      "Carefully the reviewer.

"I was as poor as you are;
"When I began I got, of course,
"Advance on royalties, fifty at first," said Mr. Nixon,
"Follow me, and take a column,
"Even if you have to work free.

"Butter reviewers. From fifty to three hundred   10
"I rose in eighteen months;
"The hardest nut I had to crack
"Was Dr. Dundas.

"I never mentioned a man but with the view
"Of selling my own works.
"The tip's a good one, as for literature
"It gives no man a sinecure.

"And no one knows, at sight, a masterpiece.
"And give up verse, my boy,
"There's nothing in it."   20

Likewise a friend of Bloughram's [2] once advised me:
Don't kick against the pricks,
Accept opinion. The "Nineties" tried your game
And died, there's nothing in it.

[2] Areas where Moses wandered for forty years.

---

[1] Arnold Bennett (1867–1931), British novelist, is the likely model here.
[2] Bishop Blougram, a character in Browning's "Bishop Blougram's Apology."

X

Beneath the sagging roof
The stylist has taken shelter,[1]
Unpaid, uncelebrated,
At last from the world's welter

Nature receives him;
With a placid and uneducated mistress
He exercises his talents
And the soil meets his distress.

The haven from sophistications and contentions
Leaks through its thatch;   10
He offers succulent cooking;
The door has a creaking latch.

XI

"Conservatrix of Milésien" [1]
Habits of mind and feeling,
Possibly. But in Ealing [2]
With the most bank-clerkly of Englishmen?

No, "Milésian" is an exaggeration.
No instinct has survived in her
Older than those her grandmother
Told her would fit her station.

XII

"Daphne with her thighs in bark
Stretches toward me her leafy hands," [1]—
Subjectively. In the stuffed-satin drawing-room
I await The Lady Valentine's commands,

[1] Probably refers to British novelist Ford Madox Ford (1873–1939).

[1] Allusion to De Goncourt's line: "Femmes, conservatrices des traditions milésien-
nes" ("Women, conservers of Milesian traditions").
[2] A suburb of London.

[1] The nymph Daphne was changed into a laurel tree to escape the amorous pursuit
of Apollo. The entire quotation is from Gautier's poem, "Le château du souvenir."

Knowing my coat has never been
Of precisely the fashion
To stimulate, in her,
A durable passion;

Doubtful, somewhat, of the value
Of well-gowned approbation   10
Of literary effort,
But never of The Lady Valentine's vocation:

Poetry, her border of ideas,
The edge, uncertain, but a means of blending
With other strata
Where the lower and higher have ending;

A hook to catch the Lady Jane's attention,
A modulation toward the theatre,
Also, in the case of revolution,
A possible friend and comforter.   20

Conduct, on the other hand, the soul
"Which the highest cultures have nourished"
To Fleet St. where
Dr. Johnson [2] flourished;

Beside this thoroughfare
The sale of half-hose has
Long since superseded the cultivation
Of Pierian roses. [3]

Envoi

Go, dumb-born book, [1]
Tell her that sang me once that song of Lawes:
Hadst thou but song
As thou hast subjects known,
Then were there cause in thee that should condone

[2] Samuel Johnson (1709–1784), English lexicographer and writer. Fleet Street was
the center of London publishing.

[3] Pieria is a coastal region in Macedonia, the legendary birthplace of Orpheus and
the Muses. A Sappho poem refers to "the roses of Pieria" as a metonym for literary
cultivation.

[1] Adapted from Edmund Waller (1606–1687), "Go, Lovely Rose," a poem to which
Henry Lawes (1596–1662), English songwriter, composed the music.

Even my faults that heavy upon me lie,
And build her glories their longevity.

Tell her that sheds
Such treasure in the air,
Recking naught else but that her graces give   *10*
Life to the moment,
I would bid them live
As roses might, in magic amber laid,
Red overwrought with orange and all made
One substance and one colour
Braving time.

Tell her that goes
With song upon her lips
But sings not out the song, nor knows
The maker of it, some other mouth,   *20*
May be as fair as hers,
Might, in new ages, gain her worshippers,
When our two dusts with Waller's shall be laid,
Siftings on siftings in oblivion,
Till change hath broken down
All things save Beauty alone.

Mauberley

"*Vacuos exercet aera morsus.*" [1]

I
Turned from the "eau-forte
Par Jaquemart" [2]
To the strait head
Of Messalina: [3]

"His true Penelope
Was Flaubert,"

[1] "He bites emptily at the air," adapted from Ovid, *Metamorphoses*, 7, 786, where "vanos" ("in vain") appears instead of "vacuos." Ovid tells the lengend of Cephalus, whose dog, Laelaps, chased the monster that was terrorizing Thebes. Both Laelaps and the monster turn to stone and are thus fixed in eternal positions of pursuer and pursued.

[2] "Etching by" (Jules) Jaquemart (1837–1880), French painter and etcher.

[3] (Valeria) Messalina (d. A.D. 8) wife of emperor Claudius. Mauberley "turned from" etching to engraving, representing different poetic techniques.

And his tool
The engraver's.

Firmness,
Not the full smile,   *10*
His art, but an art
In profile;

Colourless
Pier Francesca,[4]
Pisanello [5] lacking the skill
To forge Achaia.[6]

II

Qu'est ce qu'ils savent de l'amour, et qu'est ce qu'ils peuvent comprendre?

  S'ils ne comprennent pas la poésie, s'ils ne sentent pas la musique, qu'est ce qu'ils peuvent comprendre de cette passion en comparaison avec laquelle la rose est grossière et le parfum des violettes un tonnerre?

Caid Ali[1]

For three years, diabolus in the scale,[2]
He drank ambrosia,
All passes, ANANGKE [3] prevails,
Came end, at last, to that Arcadia.

He had moved amid her phantasmagoria,
Amid her galaxies,
NUKTIS 'AGALMA [4]

Drifted . . . drifted precipitate,
Asking time to be rid of . . .

[4] Piero della Francesca (1418–1492), Italian painter.
[5] Alternate name for Vittore Pisano (1397–1455), the Italian painter and medalist who made many medals of Greek subjects (hence "forge Achaia").
[6] A district of Greece.

---

[1] "What do they know about love, and what can they understand?
  "If they do not understand poetry, if they do not feel music, what can they understand of that passion compared to which the rose is gross and the perfume of violets a thunderbolt?" "Caid Ali" is a psuedonym for Pound.
[2] Devil in the scale, a musical term.
[3] Greek for "fate."
[4] Greek for "the ornament of night." *Nuktis* is probably Pound's mistake and should read *Nuktos*.

Of his bewilderment; to designate   *10*
His new found orchid. . . .

To be certain . . . certain . . .
(Amid ærial flowers) . . . time for arrangements—
Drifted on
To the final estrangement;

Unable in the supervening blankness
To sift TO AGATHON [5] from the chaff
Until he found his sieve . . .
Ultimately, his seismograph:

—Given that is his "fundamental passion,"   *20*
This urge to convey the relation
Of eye-lid and cheek-bone
By verbal manifestations;

To present the series
Of curious heads in medallion—

He had passed, inconscient, full gaze,
The wide-banded irides [6]
And botticellian sprays implied
In their diastasis [7];

Which anæthesis,[8] noted a year late,   *30*
And weighed, revealed his great affect,
(Orchid), mandate
Of Eros, a retrospect.

             .   .   .

Mouths biting empty air,
The still stone dogs,[9]
Caught in metamorphosis, were
Left him as epilogues.

[5] Greek for "the Good."
[6] Plural for the flower iris, and for the iris of the eye ("full gaze").
[7] Means both "expansion" and "wide-banded."
[8] A misprint for "anaesthesis," insensibility.
[9] Refers to Cephalus's dog, Laelaps. See "Mauberley," page 185, note 1.

"The Age Demanded"

For this agility chance found
Him of all men, unfit
As the red-beaked steeds of
The Cytheræan [1] for a chain bit.

The glow of porcelain
Brought no reforming sense
To his perception
Of the social inconsequence.

Thus, if her colour
Came against his gaze,   10
Tempered as if
It were through a perfect glaze

He made no immediate application
Of this to relation of the state
To the individual, the month was more temperate
Because this beauty had been.

    The coral isle, the lion-coloured sand
    Burst in upon the porcelain revery:
    Impetuous troubling
    Of his imagery.   20

Mildness, amid the neo-Nietzschean clatter,
His sense of graduations,
Quite out of place amid
Resistance to current exacerbations,

Invitation, mere invitation to perceptivity
Gradually led him to the isolation
Which these presents place
Under a more tolerant, perhaps, examination.

By constant elimination
The manifest universe   30
Yielded an armour
Against utter consternation,

A Minoan [2] undulation,
Seen, we admit, amid ambrosial circumstances

---

[1] Aphrodite, whose chariot was drawn by swans and doves ("red-beaked steeds").
[2] Pertaining to the ancient Cretan civilization (3000–1100 B.C.).

Strengthened him against
The discouraging doctrine of chances,

And his desire for survival,
Faint in the most strenuous moods,
Became an Olympian *apathein* [3]
In the presence of selected perceptions.   40

A pale gold, in the aforesaid pattern,
The unexpected palms
Destroying, certainly, the artist's urge,
Left him delighted with the imaginary
Audition of the phantasmal sea-surge,

Incapable of the least utterance or composition,
Emendation, conservation of the "better tradition,"
Refinement of medium, elimination of superfluities,
August attraction or concentration.

Nothing, in brief, but maudlin confession,   50
Irresponse to human aggression,
Amid the precipitation, down-float
Of insubstantial manna,
Lifting the faint susurrus
Of his subjective hosannah.

Ultimate affronts to
Human redundancies;

Non-esteem of self-styled "his betters"
Leading, as he well knew,
To his final   60
Exclusion from the world of letters.

IV

Scattered Moluccas [1]
Not knowing, day to day,
The first day's end, in the next noon;
The placid water
Unbroken by the Simoon; [2]

Thick foliage
Placid beneath warm suns,

---

[3] Olympian: imposing, aloof; "*apathein*": Greek for apathy.

[1] Another name for the Molukka Islands, spice islands in the Malay Archipelago.

[2] Alternate spelling for "simoom," a hot wind in North Africa and the Middle East.

Tawn fore-shores
Washed in the cobalt of oblivions;

Or through dawn-mist   *10*
The grey and rose
Of the juridical
Flamingoes;

A consciousness disjunct,
Being but this overblotted
Series
Of intermittences;

Coracle [3] of Pacific voyages,
The unforecasted beach;
Then on an oar   *20*
Read this:

"I was
And I no more exist;
Here drifted
An hedonist."

Medallion

Luini [1] in porcelain!
The grand piano
Utters a profane
Protest with her clear soprano.

The sleek head emerges
From the gold-yellow frock
As Anadyomene [2] in the opening
Pages of Reinach.[3]

Honey-red, closing the face-oval,
A basket-work of braids which seem as if they were
Spun in King Minos' [4] hall
From metal, or intractable amber;

3 A broad boat common in Wales and West England.

---

1 Bernardino Luini (1475–1532), Italian painter.

2 Aphrodite.

3 Salomon Reinach (1858–1932), French scholar who published books on art.

4 King of Crete, who, in Greek mythology, became a judge in the lower world after his death.

The face-oval beneath the glaze,
Bright in its suave bounding-line, as,
Beneath half-watt rays,
The eyes turn topaz.

FROM **A Draft of XVI Cantos** *(1925)*

II

Hang it all, Robert Browning,
    there can be but the one "Sordello." [1]
But Sordello, and my Sordello?
Lo Sordels si fo di Mantovana. [2]
So-shu [3] churned in the sea.
Seal sports in the spray-whited circles of cliff-wash,
Sleek head, daughter of Lir, [4]
    eyes of Picasso
Under black fur-hood, lithe daughter of Ocean;
And the wave runs in the beach-groove: 10
"Eleanor, ἐλέναυς and ἑγέπτολις!" [5]
    And poor old Homer blind, blind, as a bat,
Ear, ear for the sea-surge, murmur of old men's voices:
"Let her go back to the ships,
Back among Grecian faces, lest evil come on our own,
Evil and further evil, and a curse cursed on our children,
Moves, yes she moves like a goddess
And has the face of a god
    and the voice of Schoeney's [6] daughters,
And doom goes with her in walking,

[1] British poet, Robert Browning (1812–1889), wrote a poem entitled "Sordello," inspired by the Italian Renaissance poet of that name.
[2] "Sordello was from around Mantua." This statement is in Provencal, the language in which Sordello wrote.
[3] In another poem ("Ancient Wisdom, Rather Cosmic") by Pound, So-shu appears as a philosopher. "So-shu" is the Japanese transliteration for Chuang Tzŭ, Chinese thinker and disciple of Taoism.
[4] A variation of a Celtic word meaning the "sea," ofter personified as a deity.
[5] "Eleanor, destroyer of ships and destroyer of cities!" Eleanor refers to Eleanor of Aquitaine, who is conflated with Helen of Troy. The Greek description is adapted from Aeschylus's characterization of Helen in *Agamemnon*. Homer's "murmur" about Helen is from *The Iliad*, 3, 139–160.
[6] "Schoeney's (Schoenius) daughter" refers to Atalanta, whose beauty caused the tragedy of the Calydonian boar hunt in which Meleager died.

Let her go back to the ships,   20
    back among Grecian voices."
And by the beach-run, Tyro,[7]
    Twisted arms of the sea-god,
Lithe sinews of water, gripping her, cross-hold,
And the blue-gray glass of the wave tents them,
Glare azure of water, cold-welter, close cover.
Quiet sun-tawny sand-stretch,
The gulls broad out their wings,
    nipping between the splay feathers;
Snipe come for their bath,   30
    bend out their wing-joints,
Spread wet wings to the sun-film,
And by Scios,[8]
    to left of the Naxos [9] passage,
Naviform [10] rock overgrown,
    algæ cling to its edge,
There is a wine-red glow in the shallows,
    a tin flash in the sun-dazzle.

The ship landed in Scios,
    men wanting spring-water,   40
And by the rock-pool a young boy loggy with vine-must,[11]
    "To Naxos? Yes, we'll take you to Naxos,
Cum' along lad." "Not that way!"
"Aye, that way is Naxos."
    And I said: "It's a straight ship."
And an ex-convict [12] out of Italy
    knocked me into the fore-stays,
(He was wanted for manslaughter in Tuscany)
    And the whole twenty against me,

[7] Tyro was Poseidon's mistress, and the "sea-god" possessed her on the beach while waves hid them from sight.

[8] Scios (Chios) is a Greek island.

[9] Naxos is a Greek island where Bacchus was a favored god.

[10] "Shaped like a ship."

[11] The "young boy" is the god of wine and revelry, Bacchus. The subsequent lines refer to the story of Bacchus and King Pentheus as told by Ovid (*Metamorphoses*, 3, 511–733), and also Euripides (*The Bacchae*). In Ovid's version Tiresias, the Theban prophet, warns King Pentheus that a "new god shall come" (Bacchus), and unless the King submits to the rites of Bacchus he will be killed by his own family. Pentheus disregards Tiresias' warning and orders Bacchus to be brought to him in chains. But Pentheus's servants return, instead, with one of Bacchus' worshippers, Acoetes. Acoetes recounts the tale of his meeting with Bacchus in a fishing boat ("The ship landed. . . .").

[12] The "ex-convict" is Lycabas, one of Acoetes' fishermen.

Mad for a little slave money.   50
  And they took her out of Scios
And off her course . . .
  And the boy came to, again, with the racket,
And looked out over the bows,
  and to eastward, and to the Naxos passage.
God-sleight then, god-sleight:
  Ship stock fast in sea-swirl,
Ivy upon the oars, King Pentheus,
  grapes with no seed but sea-foam,
Ivy in scupper-hole.   60
Aye, I, Acœtes,[11] stood there,
  and the god stood by me,
Water cutting under the keel,
Sea-break from stern forrads,
  wake running off from the bow,
And where was gunwale, there now was vine-trunk,
And tenthril where cordage had been,
  grape-leaves on the rowlocks,
Heavy vine on the oarshafts,
And, out of nothing, a breathing,   70
  hot breath on my ankles,
Beasts like shadows in glass,
  a furred tail upon nothingness.
Lynx-purr, and heathery smell of beasts,
  where tar smell had been,
Sniff and pad-foot of beasts,
  eye-glitter out of black air.
The sky overshot, dry, with no tempest,
Sniff and pad-foot of beasts,
  fur brushing my knee-skin,   80
Rustle of airy sheaths,
  dry forms in the *æther*.[13]
And the ship like a keel in ship-yard,
  slung like an ox in smith's sling,
Ribs stuck fast in the ways,
  grape-cluster over pin-rack,
  void air taking pelt.
Lifeless air become sinewed,
  feline leisure of panthers,
Leopards sniffing the grape shoots by scupper-hole,   90
Crouched panthers by fore-hatch,
And the sea blue-deep about us,
  green-ruddy in shadows,

[13] "Air."

And Lyæus [14]: "From now, Acœtes, my altars,
Fearing no bondage,
    fearing no cat of the wood,
Safe with my lynxes,
    feeding grapes to my leopards,
Olibanum [15] is my incense,
    the vines grow in my homage."   *100*

The back-swell now smooth in the rudder-chains,
Black snout of a porpoise
    where Lycabs [12] had been,
Fish-scales on the oarsmen.
    And I worship.
I have seen what I have seen.
    When they brought the boy I said:
"He has a god in him,
    though I do not know which god."
And they kicked me into the fore-stays.   *110*
I have seen what I have seen:
    Medon's [16] face like the face of a dory,
Arms shrunk into fins. And you, Pentheus,
Had as well listen to Tiresias,[17] and to Cadmus,[18]
    or your luck will go out of you.
Fish-scales over groin muscles,
    lynx-purr amid sea . . .
And of a later year,
    pale in the wine-red algæ,
If you will lean over the rock,   *120*
    coral face under wave-tinge,
Rose-paleness under water-shift,
    Ileuthyeria, fair Dafne [19] of sea-bords,
The swimmer's arms turned to branches,
Who will say in what year,
    fleeing what band of tritons,[20]

14 An adjective describing Bacchus as "the one who lightens burdens."
15 "Frankincense."
16 Bacchus changes the treacherous fishermen of the ship into animals. Medon, one of the men, is metamorphosed into a "dory" (sea fish).
17 Acoetes reminds Pentheus of the blind soothsayer's warning.
18 Cadmus was Pentheus's grandfather, who had cautioned Pentheus to recognize the cult of Bacchus.
19 Ileuthyeria and Dafne are nymphs, whom Pound associates with coral seen through water and branches.
20 Originally, Triton was the son of the sea god Poseidon and lived at the bottom of the sea. Later legends use the plural to describe sea creatures that are half man, half fish.

The smooth brows, seen, and half seen,
    now ivory stillness.
And So-shu churned in the sea, So-shu also,
    using the long moon for a churn-stick . . .   *130*
Lithe turning of water,
    sinews of Poseidon,[21]
Black azure and hyaline,
    glass wave over Tyro,
Close cover, unstillness,
    bright welter of wave-cords,
Then quiet water,
    quiet in the buff sands,
Sea-fowl stretching wing-joints,
    splashing in rock-hollows and sand-hollows   *140*
In the wave-runs by the half-dune;
Glass-glint of wave in the tide-rips against sunlight,
    pallor of Hesperus,[22]
Grey peak of the wave,
    wave, colour of grape's pulp,

Olive grey in the near,
    far, smoke grey of the rock-slide,
Salmon-pink wings of the fish-hawk
    cast grey shadows in water,
The tower like a one-eyed great goose   *150*
    cranes up out of the olive-grove,

And we have heard the fauns chiding Proteus [23]
    in the smell of hay under the olive-trees,
And the frogs singing against the fauns
    in the half-light.
And . . .

[21] Greek god of the sea (cf. Neptune).
[22] The evening star, Venus.
[23] The sea god capable of assuming various shapes.

[JOHN] ROBINSON JEFFERS (1887–1962)

Robinson Jeffers was born in Pittsburgh but was early taken to Europe, where he was educated by tutors and in private schools. Later he attended the University of Pittsburgh but was graduated from Occidental College in California. For a time he studied medicine at the University of Southern California and, after an interim at the University of Zurich, he took up forestry at the University of Wash-

ington. He was hunting for some tolerable activity by which he could live while writing poetry, his chief interest. After his marriage in 1913 (from which came twin sons), he was about to move to England, where he hoped to live by writing alone, when an uncle left him a legacy that made him independent. It was then that, with his own hands, he built the stone house and tower on the Big Sur, below Carmel on the California coast, which made of him a kind of legendary figure. He was not exactly a hermit, but he wanted no more than the few good friends he had, and his wife served as a buffer between him and a sometimes intrusive world, which he despised. He had been an athlete in his college days, and he was always physically active. Tall, rugged, with a bronzed face, high cheekbones and arched nose, he looked like a strange and noble Indian.

His first two volumes, Flagons and Apples *(1912) and* Californians *(1916) have no great distinction, but in* Tamar and Other Poems *(1924) he found the manner that was to mark him and his chief forms: short declamatory lyrics, usually taking off from rugged natural scenes or symbols (the hawk and the stone, untrammeled spirit and abiding earth, were his favorites), and long narrative poems written in heavily cadenced blank verse and often centering in sexual violence. The narrative poems were sometimes adaptations of older fictions, Biblical stories or Greek Myths.*

The chief volumes that followed were Roan Stallion, Tamar and Other Poems *(1925),* The Women at Point Sur *(1927),* Cawdor and Other Poems *(1928),* Dear Judas and Other Poems *(1929),* Descent to the Dead *(1931),* Thurso's Landing and Other Poems *(1932),* Give Your Heart to the Hawks *(1933),* Solstice *(1935), and* Such Counsels You Gave to Me *(1937). His* Selected Poetry *was published in 1938. There is no complete poems.*

In 1946 Jeffers found a wide audience through his adaptation of Euripides' play, Medea. *He had already retold the story in "Solstice," but it was probably the extraordinary performance of Judith Anderson, rather than the play itself, that ·compelled the great response. This, like other adaptations from the Greeks that Jeffers made, is melodramatic rather than tragic, a challenge to the nerves rather than to the heart or the intelligence.*

Jeffers called himself an "Inhumanist," and throughout his work, long and short, the nihilistic view is constant. The final volumes, The Double Axe *(1948),* Hungerfield and Other Poems *(1954), and* The Beginning and the End *(1963), show a faltering power but no softening of view. He believed that the human race was impossibly ingrown and dying, and eager to see the process hastened, he thought that war and other historic catastrophes were all to the*

*good. He held this view with such a fierce intensity that his was
always a perilous path on a cliff, and often enough he tumbled
from far-seeing grandeur into the morass of the merely grandiose.*

FURTHER READING

The chief source of biographical information is *The Selected Letters of
Robinson Jeffers* (1968), edited by Ann N. Ridgeway. The chief
critical study is Radcliffe Squires, *The Loyalties of Robinson Jeffers*
(1956). Further criticism can be found in Frederick I. Carpenter,
Robinson Jeffers (1962), and M. C. Monjian, *Robinson Jeffers:
A Study in Inhumanism* (1958).

FROM *Tamar and Other Poems* (1924)

To the Stone-cutters

Stone-cutters fighting time with marble, you foredefeated
Challengers of oblivion
Eat cynical earnings, knowing rock splits, records fall down,
The square-limbed Roman letters
Scale in the thaws, wear in the rain. The poet as well
Builds his monument mockingly;
For man will be blotted out, the blithe earth die, the brave sun
Die blind and blacken to the heart:
Yet stones have stood for a thousand years, and pained thoughts found
The honey of peace in old poems.   *10*

FROM *Roan Stallion, Tamar and Other Poems* (1925)

Boats in a Fog

Sports and gallantries, the stage, the arts, the antics of dancers,
The exuberant voices of music,
Have charm for children but lack nobility; it is bitter earnestness
That makes beauty; the mind
Knows, grown adult

             A sudden fog-drift muffled the ocean,
A throbbing of engines moved in it,
At length, a stone's throw out, between the rocks and the vapor,
One by one moved shadows

Out of the mystery, shadows, fishing-boats, trailing each other   *10*
Following the cliff for guidance,
Holding a difficult path between the peril of the sea-fog
And the foam on the shore granite.
One by one, trailing their leader, six crept by me,
Out of the vapor and into it,
The throb of their engines subdued by the fog, patient and cautious,
Coasting all round the peninsula
Back to the buoys in Monterey harbor. A flight of pelicans
Is nothing lovelier to look at;
The flight of the planets is nothing nobler; all the arts lose virtue   *20*
Against the essential reality
Of creatures going about their business among the equally
Earnest elements of nature.

Shine, Perishing Republic

While this America settles in the mould of its vulgarity, heavily
    thickening to empire,
And protest, only a bubble in the molten mass, pops and sighs out,
    and the mass hardens,

I sadly smiling remember that the flower fades to make fruit, the fruit
    rots to make earth.
Out of the mother; and through the spring exultances, ripeness and
    decadence; and home to the mother.

You making haste haste on decay: not blameworthy; life is good, be it
    stubbornly long or suddenly
A mortal splendor: meteors are not needed less than mountains:
    shine, perishing republic.

But for my children, I would have them keep their distance from the
    thickening center; corruption
Never has been compulsory, when the cities lie at the monster's
    feet there are left the mountains.

And boys, be in nothing so moderate as in love of man, a clever
    servant, insufferable master.
There is the trap that catches noblest spirits, that caught—they say—
    God, when he walked on earth.   *10*

Joy

Though joy is better than sorrow joy is not great;
Peace is great, strength is great.
Not for joy the stars burn, not for joy the vulture
Spreads her gray sails on the air
Over the mountain; not for joy the worn mountain
Stands, while years like water
Trench his long sides. "I am neither mountain nor bird
Nor star; and I seek joy."
The weakness of your breed: yet at length quietness
Will cover those wistful eyes.   *10*

Science

Man, introverted man, having crossed
In passage and but a little when the nature of things this latter century
Has begot giants; but being taken up
Like a maniac with self-love and inward conflicts cannot manage his
    hybrids.
Being used to deal with edgeless dreams,
Now he's bred knives on nature turns them also inward: they have
    thirsty points though.
His mind forebodes his own destruction;
Actæon who saw the goddess naked among leaves and his hounds
    tore him.[1]
A little knowledge, a pebble from the shingle,
A drop from the oceans: who would have dreamed this infinitely little
    too much?   *10*

[1] See Ovid's *Metamorphoses*, 3, 140ff: Actæon beheld Diana bathing naked, and
the goddess punished him by transforming him into a stag which she had torn to
pieces by his own hunting dogs.

FROM *Cawdor and Other Poems* (1928)

Hurt Hawks

I

The broken pillar of the wing jags from the clotted shoulder,
The wing trails like a banner in defeat,
No more to use the sky forever but live with famine
And pain a few days: cat nor coyote
Will shorten the week of waiting for death, there is game without
    talons.
He stands under the oak-bush and waits
The lame feet of salvation; at night he remembers freedom
And flies in a dream, the dawns ruin it.
He is strong and pain is worse to the strong, incapacity is worse.
The curs of the day come and torment him
At distance, no one but death the redeemer will humble that head,
The intrepid readiness, the terrible eyes.
The wild God of the world is sometimes merciful to those
That ask mercy, not often to the arrogant.
You do not know him, you communal people, or you have forgotten him;
Intemperate and savage, the hawk remembers him;
Beautiful and wild, the hawks, and men that are dying, remember him.

II

I'd sooner, except the penalties, kill a man than a hawk; but the great
    redtail
Had nothing left but unable misery
From the bone too shattered for mending, the wing that trailed under
    his talons when he moved.
We had fed him six weeks, I gave him freedom,
He wandered over the foreland hill and returned in the evening, asking
    for death,
Not like a beggar, still eyed with the old
Implacable arrogance. I gave him the lead gift in the twilight.
    What fell was relaxed,
Owl-downy, soft feminine feathers; but what
Soared: the fierce rush: the night-herons by the flooded river cried fear
    at its rising
Before it was quite unsheathed from reality.

FROM **Thurso's Landing** *(1932)*

Fire on the Hills

The deer were bounding like blown leaves
Under the smoke in front of the roaring wave of the brush-fire;
I thought of the smaller lives that were caught.
Beauty is not always lovely; the fire was beautiful, the terror
Of the deer was beautiful; and when I returned
Down the black slopes after the fire had gone by, an eagle
Was perched on the jag of a burnt pine,
Insolent and gorged, cloaked in the folded storms of his shoulders.
He had come from far off for the good hunting
With fire for his beater to drive the game; the sky was merciless   10
Blue, and the hills merciless black,
The sombre-feathered great bird sleepily merciless between them.
I thought, painfully, but the whole mind,
The destruction that brings an eagle from heaven is better than mercy.

FROM **Solstice and Other Poems** *(1935)*

Rock and Hawk

Here is a symbol in which
Many high tragic thoughts
Watch their own eyes.

This gray rock, standing tall
On the headland, where the seawind
Lets no tree grow,

Earthquake-proved, and signatured
By ages of storms: on its peak
A falcon has perched.

I think, here is your emblem   10
To hang in the future sky;
Not the cross, not the hive,

But this; bright power, dark peace;
Fierce consciousness joined with final
Disinterestedness;

Life with calm death; the falcon's
Realist eyes and act
Married to the massive

Mysticism of stone,
Which failure cannot cast down   20
Nor success make proud.

FROM *Such Councils You Gave to Me
and Other Poems* (1937)

The Purse-seine [1]

Our sardine fishermen work at night in the dark of the moon; daylight
  or moonlight
They could not tell where to spread the net, unable to see the
  phosphorescence of the shoals of fish.
They work northward from Monterey, coasting Santa Cruz; off New
  Year's Point or off Pigeon Point.
The look-out man will see some lakes of milk-color light on the sea's
  night-purple; he points, and the helmsman
Turns the dark prow, the motorboat circles the gleaming shoal and
  drifts out her seine-net. They close the circle
And purse the bottom of the net, then with great labor haul it in.

                                        I cannot tell you
How beautiful the scene is, and a little terrible, then, when the crowded
  fish
Know they are caught, and wildly beat from one wall to the other of
  their closing destiny the phosphorescent
Water to a pool of flame, each beautiful slender body sheeted with
  flame, like a live rocket
A comet's tail wake of clear yellow flame; while outside the narrowing   10
Floats and cordage of the net great sea-lions come up to watch, sighing
  in the dark; the vast walls of night
Stand erect to the stars.

                        Lately I was looking from a night mountain-top
On a wide city, the colored splendor, galaxies of light: how could I
  help but recall the seine-net
Gathering the luminous fish? I cannot tell you how beautiful the city
  appeared, and a little terrible.
I thought, We have geared the machines and locked all together into
  interdependence; we have built the great cities; now
There is no escape. We have gathered vast populations incapable of free
  survival, insulated

1 A fishing net whose ends are drawn together.

From the strong earth, each person in himself helpless, on all dependent. The circle is closed, and the net
Is being hauled in. They hardly feel the cords drawing, yet they shine
  already. The inevitable mass-disasters
Will not come in our time nor in our children's, but we and our
  children   20
Must watch the net draw narrower, government take all powers—or
  revolution, and the new government
Take more than all, add to kept bodies kept souls—or anarchy, the
  mass-disasters.

                          These things are Progress;
Do you marvel our verse is troubled or frowning, while it keeps
  its reason? Or it lets go, lets the mood flow
In the manner of the recent young men into mere hysteria, splintered
  gleams, crackled laughter. But they are quite wrong.
There is no reason for amazement: surely one always knew that cultures
  decay, and life's end is death.

MARIANNE [CRAIG] MOORE (1887–   )

*Marianne Moore was born within a year of T. S. Eliot, and both were
  born in St. Louis, Missouri—she the grand-daughter of a clergyman,
  he the grandson of another—but they did not meet for many years.
  When she was seven, her family moved to Carlisle, Pennsylvania,
  where she attended the Metzger Institute before enrolling at Bryn
  Mawr, from which she was graduated in 1909. She went to Carlisle
  Commercial College for a year, and for four years she taught commercial subjects—stenography, typing, bookkeeping, and so on—at
  the United States Industrial Indian School in Carlisle. A visit to
  New York in 1916 persuaded her that that was where she wished to
  live, but she did not move there until 1921, when, for four years,
  she worked in the New York Public Library. She lived in Greenwich
  Village until 1929 and then moved to Brooklyn. Recently, after the
  Dodgers, a baseball team whose fortunes she had passionately followed for years, moved to Los Angeles, she moved back to Manhattan, but perhaps not for that reason. In the years between she
  had won nearly every pennant that patrons of poetry in the United
  States can offer.*

*She had been writing poetry since she was an undergraduate and, still
  in her youth, was a friend of poets—H. D., William Carlos Williams,
  Ezra Pound, and, once in the Village, of many more. But their poetry
  had no particular influence upon hers, nor did the poetry of others,*

ancient or modern. Her influence came, rather, from the great English prose writers (whom she can quote extensively)—Bacon, Browne, Burke, Johnson, James in his essays. The influence is evident in her turning to syllabic rather than accentual verse (but she says that she does not count her syllables, they simply come that way, even as the shape of one stanza often repeats itself beautifully and precisely in the next and the next); in her using rime in the most delicate and apparently random way, and in some of her poems she prefers to think of it not as rime but as echo; in her conceiving not the line but the stanza (like the paragraph) as the rhythmical unit; and in the fact that many of her poems read, indeed, like splendid verse essays which can yet employ the bold discontinuities of association and the leaps in logic that poetry does but expository prose does not permit. There is a further connection with prose. In college she found her courses in biology" . . . exhilarating. I thought, in fact, of studying medicine. Precision, economy of statement, logic employed to ends that are disinterested, drawing and identifying, liberate—at least have some bearing on—the imagination, it seems to me." She sees no radical disjunction between the scientist and the poet.

She published her first poems in 1915, in The Egoist (London), Poetry, and Others. In 1921, two of her friends, H. D. and Bryher (Mrs. Robert McAlmon), published her first book, Poems, in England, without consulting her. In 1923 when she published a little pamphlet of poems called Marriage, T. S. Eliot wrote: "I can only think of five contemporary poets—English, Irish, French and German—whose works excite me as much or more than Miss Moore's." Her first real collection, Observations (1924), won the Dial Prize and gave her the reputation of being the best woman poet then alive—a reputation that remains unchallenged today, when she is well past eighty years old.

She became the editor of the Dial in 1926 and remained so until it ceased publication in 1929, and she made it the great magazine that it was. Hart Crane complained bitterly (in his letters to friends) about the way she chopped up "The Wine Menagerie" before she published it under a different title from his own, but such imperious editing was not entirely characteristic of her policies or personality, whose first characteristic is, probably, the recognition of and respect for integrity in persons and things as well as in poems This is also the first characteristic of her poetry as it presents a strange, essentialized world.

Her Selected Poems (1935) carried an introduction by Eliot. A number of volumes followed before her Collected Poems (1951), and then

still more separate volumes before the Complete Poems *(1967). She
has also published many essays on writers who interest her, in*
Predilections *(1955), and a translation of* The Fables of La Fontaine
(1954).

Her poems tend to begin, she says, when *"A felicitous phrase springs to
mind—a word or two, say—simultaneous usually with some thought
or object of equal attraction."* ("The mind is an enchanting thing,"
she said, was a phrase tossed off by her mother—and became that
poem). She then works by her own method of mosaic, fitting things
together—often phrases she has overheard or read in some unlikely
context and retained—until presently they settle into a poem:
enameled, patterned, flowing into the plastic fixity of form.

A favorite poem with many of her readers is "In Distrust of Merits,"
but she has taken occasion to say that she does not think this is a
poem at all. (She resists reading it, when it is inevitably asked for; but
she will do so under duress, rather throwing it off with vocal
shrugs.) Why is it not a poem? "It's just a burst of feeling. It's emotion recorded. . . . They are statements that I believe with all my
heart, but I think that a poem should have a form, a sound, like
a symphony. And that poem is prose. It all comes down to morality."
But then, she has said of the whole body of her work that it is called
poetry only because we have no other word for it. "I, too, dislike
it. . . ."

FURTHER READING

No biography of Marianne Moore exists. Critical evaluations can be
found in B. F. Engel, *Marianne Moore* (1963), and Jean Garrigue's
pamphlet, *Marianne Moore* (1965). A. Kingsley Weatherhead's *The
Edge of the Image: Marianne Moore, William Carlos Williams, and
Some Other Poets* (1967) places her in the context of the "New
Poetry" and the imagists. *A Marianne Moore Reader* (1961) includes both prose and verse chosen by the author.

FROM **Poems** *(1921)*

To a Steam Roller

The illustration
is nothing to you without the application.
   You lack half wit. You crush all the particles down
     into close conformity, and then walk back and forth on them.

Sparkling chips of rock
are crushed down to the level of the parent block.
   Were not 'impersonal judgment in æsthetic
     matters, a metaphysical impossibility,' you

might fairly achieve
it. As for butterflies, I can hardly conceive   10
   of one's attending upon you, but to question
     the congruence of the complement is vain, if it exists.

The Fish

wade
through black jade.
   Of the crow-blue mussel-shells, one keeps
   adjusting the ash-heaps;
     opening and shutting itself like

an
injured fan.
   The barnacles which encrust the side
   of the wave, cannot hide
     there for the submerged shafts of the   10

sun,
split like spun
   glass, move themselves with spotlight swiftness
   into the crevices—
     in and out, illuminating

the
turquoise sea
   of bodies. The water drives a wedge
   of iron through the iron edge
     of the cliff; whereupon the stars,   20

pink
rice-grains, ink

        bespattered jelly-fish, crabs like green
    lilies, and submarine
            toadstools, slide each on the other.
All
external
        marks of abuse are present on this
    defiant edifice—
            all the physical features of   30
ac-
cident—lack
        of cornice, dynamite grooves, burns, and
    hatchet strokes, these things stand
            out on it; the chasm-side is
dead.
Repeated
        evidence has proved that it can live
    on what cannot revive
            its youth. The sea grows old in it.   40

Poetry

I, too, dislike it: there are things that are important beyond all this
                fiddle.
    Reading it, however, with a perfect contempt for it, one discovers in
    it after all, a place for the genuine.
            Hands that can grasp, eyes
        that can dilate, hair that can rise
            if it must, these things are important not because a

high-sounding interpretation can be put upon them but because they are
    useful. When they become so derivative as to become unintelligible,
    the same thing may be said for all of us, that we
            do not admire what   10
        we cannot understand: the bat
            holding on upside down or in quest of something to

eat, elephants pushing, a wild horse taking a roll, a tireless wolf under
    a tree, the immovable critic twitching his skin like a horse that feels
                a flea, the base-
    ball fan, the statistician—
            nor is it valid
                to discriminate against 'business documents and

school books'[1]; all these phenomena are important. One must make a
    distinction
      however: when dragged into prominence by half poets, the result is
        not poetry,
    nor till the poets among us can be   20
      'literalists of
      the imagination'[2]—above
        insolence and triviality and can present
for inspection, imaginary gardens with real toads in them, shall we have
    it. In the meantime, if you demand on the one hand,
    the raw material of poetry in
      all its rawness and
      that which is on the other hand
        genuine, then you are interested in poetry.

FROM **Selected Poems** *(1935)*

Critics and Connoisseurs

There is a great amount of poetry in unconscious
    fastidiousness. Certain Ming[1]
      products, imperial floor-coverings of coach-
wheel yellow, are well enough in their way but I have seen
        something
    that I like better—a
      mere childish attempt to make an imperfectly ballasted
      animal stand up,
      similar determination to make a pup
      eat his meat from the plate.

I remember a swan under the willows in Oxford,
    with flamingo-coloured, maple-
      leaflike feet. It reconnoitred like a battle-   10
ship. Disbelief and conscious fastidiousness were the staple
    ingredients in its
      disinclination to move. Finally its hardihood was not
      proof against its

[1] Marianne Moore's notes direct the reader to a quotation from *The Diaries of Leo Tolstoy* (Dutton, 1917, p. 94): "Or else poetry is everything with the exception of business documents and school books."

[2] Miss Moore cites Yeats's essay on William Blake in *Ideas of Good and Evil* (Bullen, 1903, p. 182): ". . . he was a too literal realist of imagination."

---

[1] Chinese dynasty (1368–1644) in which art in particular flourished.

proclivity to more fully appraise such bits
of food as the stream

bore counter to it; it made away with which I gave it
to eat. I have seen this swan and
I have seen you; I have seen ambition without
understanding in a variety of forms. Happening to stand   20
by an ant-hill, I have
seen a fastidious ant carrying a stick north, south, east,
west, till it turned on
itself, struck out from the flower-bed into the lawn,
and returned to the point

from which it had started. Then abandoning the stick as
useless and overtaxing its
jaws with a particle of whitewash—pill-like but
heavy, it again went through the same course of procedure.
What is
there in being able   30
to say that one has dominated the stream in an attitude
of self-defence;
in proving that one has had the experience
of carrying a stick?

The Monkeys

winked too much and were afraid of snakes. The zebras, supreme in
their abnormality; the elephants with their fog-coloured skin
and strictly practical appendages
were there, the small cats; and the parrakeet—
trivial and humdrum on examination, destroying
bark and portions of the food it could not eat.

I recall their magnificence, now not more magnificent
than it is dim. It is difficult to recall the ornament,
speech, and precise manner of what one might
call the minor acquaintances twenty   10
years back; but I shall not forget him—that Gilgamesh [1]
among
the hairy carnivora—that cat with the

wedge-shaped, slate-gray marks on its forelegs and the resolute tail,
astringently remarking, 'They have imposed on us with their pale
half-fledged protestations, trembling about

[1] Hero of an early Babylonian epic.

    in inarticulate frenzy, saying
        it is not for us to understand art; finding it
    all so difficult, examining the thing

as if it were inconceivably arcanic, as symmet-
rically frigid as if it had been carved out of chrysoprase   20
    or marble—strict with tension, malignant
        in its power over us and deeper
            than the sea when it proffers flattery in exchange for hemp,
            rye, flax, horses, platinum, timber, and fur.'

Peter

Strong and slippery, built for the midnight grass-party confronted by
        four cats,
    he sleeps his time away—the detached first claw on the foreleg,
        which corresponds
to the thumb, retracted to its tip; the small tuft of fronds
    or katydid legs above each eye, still numbering the units in
        each group;
            the shadbones regularly set about the mouth, to droop or
            rise

in unison like the porcupine's quills—motionless. He lets himself be
        flat-
    tened out by gravity, as it were a piece of seaweed tamed and
        weakened by
exposure to the sun; compelled when extended, to lie
    stationary. Sleep is the result of his delusion that one must
        do as
            well as one can for oneself; sleep—epitome of what is to   10

him as to the average person, the end of life. Demonstrate on him how
    the lady caught the dangerous southern snake, placing a forked
        stick on either
side of its innocuous neck; one need not try to stir
    him up; his prune-shaped head and alligator eyes are not a
        party to the
            joke. Lifted and handled, he may be dangled like an eel or
            set

up on the forearm like a mouse; his eyes bisected by pupils of a pin's
    width, are flickeringly exhibited, then covered up. May be? I should
        say
    might have been; when he has been got the better of in a
        dream—as in a fight with nature or with cats—we all know it.

Profound sleep is
not with him a fixed illusion. Springing about with froglike
ac-   20
curacy, emitting jerky cries when taken in the hand, he is himself
again; to sit caged by the rungs of a domestic chair would be
unprofit-
able—human. What is the good of hypocrisy? It
is permissible to choose one's employment, to abandon the
wire nail, the
roly-poly, when it shows signs of being no longer a pleasure, to score the adjacent magazine with a double line of strokes. He
can
talk, but insolently says nothing. What of it? When one is frank,
one's very
presence is a compliment. It is clear that he can see
the virtue of naturalness, that he is one of those who do not
regard
the published fact as a surrender. As for the disposition   30
invariably to affront, an animal with claws wants to have to use
them; that eel-like extension of trunk into tail is not an accident.
To
leap, to lengthen out, divide the air—to purloin, to pursue.
To tell the hen: fly over the fence, go in the wrong way in
your perturba-
tion—this is life; to do less would be nothing but dis-
honesty.

FROM **What Are Years?** *(1941)*

What Are Years?

What is our innocence,
what is our guilt? All are
naked, none is safe. And whence
is courage: the unanswered question,
the resolute doubt,—
dumbly calling, deafly listening—that
in misfortune, even death,
encourages others
and in its defeat, stirs

the soul to be strong? He   10
sees deep and is glad, who
accedes to mortality

and in his imprisonment, rises
upon himself as
the sea in a chasm, struggling to be
free and unable to be,
      in its surrendering
      finds its continuing.

   So he who strongly feels,
behaves. The very bird,   20
      grown taller as he sings, steels
his form straight up. Though he is captive,
his mighty singing
says, satisfaction is a lowly
thing, how pure a thing is joy.
      This is mortality,
      this is eternity.

FROM **Nevertheless** (1944)

Nevertheless

you've seen a strawberry
    that's had a struggle; yet
    was, where the fragments met,

a hedgehog or a star-
    fish for the multitude
    of seeds. What better food

than apple-seeds—the fruit
    within the fruit—locked in
    like counter-curved twin

hazel-nuts? Frost that kills   10
    the little rubber-plant-
    leaves of *kok-saghyz*-stalks, can't

harm the roots; they still grow
    in frozen ground. Once where
    there was a prickly-pear-

leaf clinging to barbed wire,
    a root shot down to grow
    in earth two feet below;

as carrots form mandrakes
    or a ram's-horn root some-   20
    times. Victory won't come

to me unless I go
    to it; a grape-tendril
    ties a knot in knots till

knotted thirty times,—so
    the bound twig that's under-
    gone and over-gone, can't stir.

The weak overcomes its
    menace, the strong over-
    comes itself. What is there   30

like fortitude! What sap
    went through that little thread
    to make the cherry red!

The Mind Is an Enchanting Thing

is an enchanted thing
    like the glaze on a
katydid-wing
        subdivided by sun
        till the nettings are legion.
Like Gieseking [1] playing Scarlatti; [2]

like the apteryx-awl
    as a beak, or the
kiwi's [3] rain-shawl
        of haired feathers, the mind   10
        feeling its way as though blind,
walks along with its eyes on the ground.

It has memory's ear
    that can hear without
having to hear.
        Like the gyroscope's fall,
        truly unequivocal
because trued by regnant certainty,

it is a power of
        strong enchantment. It   20
is like the dove-

[1] Walter Gieseking (1895–1956), German pianist.

[2] Alessandro Scarlatti (1659–1725), Italian composer.

[3] The apteryx is a nearly extinct New Zealand bird with undeveloped wings; it is also called the kiwi.

neck animated by
        sun; it is memory's eye;
it's conscientious inconsistency.

It tears off the veil; tears
        the temptation, the
mist the heart wears,
                from its eyes,—if the heart
                has a face; it takes apart
dejection. It's fire in the dove-neck's   *30*

iridescence; in the
        inconsistencies
of Scarlatti.
                Unconfusion submits
                its confusion to proof; it's
not a Herod's oath ⁴ that cannot change.

In Distrust of Merits

Strengthened to live, strengthened to die for
        medals and position victories?
They're fighting, fighting, fighting the blind
        man who thinks he sees,—
who cannot see that the enslaver is
enslaved; the hater, harmed. O shining O
                firm star, O tumultuous
                ocean lashed till small things go
                as they will, the mountainous
                wave makes us who look, know   *10*

depth. Lost at sea before they fought! O
        star of David,¹ star of Bethlehem,²
O black imperial lion
        of the Lord—emblem
of a risen world—be joined at last, be
joined. There is hate's crown beneath which all is
                death; there's love's without which none

⁴ In Matthew, 14:3–11, Herod promised Salome anything if she would dance; he could not retract his word when her wish proved to be for the head of John the Baptist.

---

¹ A hexagram used as a symbol of Judaism.
² In Matthew, 2:1ff, the wise men were guided to the newborn Jesus by a star.

    is king; the blessed deeds bless
   the halo. As contagion
    of sickness makes sickness,   *20*

contagion of trust can make trust. They're
  fighting in deserts and caves, one by
one, in battalions and squadrons;
   they're fighting that I
may yet recover from the disease, My
Self; some have it lightly, some will die. "Man's
    wolf to man" and we devour
     ourselves. The enemy could not
    have made a greater breach in our
    defenses. One pilot-   *30*

ing a blind man can escape him, but
  Job disheartened by false comfort [3] knew
that nothing can be so defeating
   as a blind man who
can see. O alive who are dead, who are
proud not to see, O small dust of the earth
    that walks so arrogantly,
     trust begets power and faith is
    an affectionate thing. We
    vow, we make this promise   *40*

to the fighting—it's a promise—"We'll
  never hate black, white, red, yellow, Jew,
Gentile, Untouchable." We are
  not competent to
make our vows. With set jaw they are fighting,
fighting, fighting,—some we love whom we know,
   some we love but know not—that
    hearts may feel and not be numb.
   It cures me; or am I what
   I can't believe in? Some   *50*

in snow, some on crags, some in quicksands,
  little by little, much by much, they
are fighting fighting fighting that where
  there was death there may
be life. "When a man is prey to anger,
he is moved by outside things; when he holds
   his ground in patience patience
    patience, that is action or
   beauty," the soldier's defense

---

[3] See the Old Testament Book of Job *passim* for an account of the conduct of his three friends.

and hardest armor for   60
the fight. The world's an orphans' home. Shall
    we never have peace without sorrow?
without pleas of the dying for
    help that won't come? O
quiet form upon the dust, I cannot
look and yet I must. If these great patient
        dyings—all these agonies
            and woundbearings and bloodshed—
        can teach us how to live, these
            dyings were not wasted.   70

Hate-hardened heart, O heart of iron,
    iron is iron till it is rust.
There never was a war that was
    not inward; I must
fight till I have conquered in myself what
causes war, but I would not believe it.
        I inwardly did nothing.
            O Iscariotlike crime!
        Beauty is everlasting
            and dust is for a time.   80

FROM *Tell Me, Tell Me* (1966)

Granite and Steel [1]

Enfranchising cable, silvered by the sea,
    of woven wire, grayed by the mist,
    and Liberty [2] dominate the Bay—
    her feet as one on shattered chains,
    once whole links wrought by Tyranny.

Caged Circe of steel and stone,
    her parent German ingenuity.
    "O catenary curve" from tower to pier,[3]
    implacable enemy of the mind's deformity,

[1] The title comes from line 5 of the final section of Hart Crane's *The Bridge*. (See pages 305 to 307.)

[2] The Statue of Liberty, in New York harbor, a gift of the French government in 1886.

[3] The author's notes to this poem, explaining "Caged Circe" and "O catenary curve," refer the reader to Alan Trachtenberg's *Brooklyn Bridge: Fact and Symbol* (New York: 1965). The first reference is to a young newspaper reporter who in the 1870s found himself paralyzed with fright in one of the towers of the Brooklyn Bridge; the second is to a particular feat of engineering in the bridge's construction.

of man's uncompunctious greed,   10
his crass love of crass priority,
    just recently
obstructing acquiescent feet
about to step ashore when darkness fell [4]
    without a cause,
as if probity had not joined our cities
    in the sea.

"O path amid the stars
crossed by the seagull's wing!"
"O radiance that doth inherit me!" [5]   20
—affirming inter-acting harmony!

Untried expedient, untried; then tried;
sublime elliptic two-fold egg—
way out; way in; romantic passageway
first seen by the eye of the mind,
then by the eye. O steel! O stone!
Climactic ornament, double rainbow,
as if inverted by French perspicacity,
    John Roebling's [6] monument,
    German tenacity's also;   30
    composite span—an actuality.

W. S. Landor [1]

There
is someone I can bear—
    "a master of indignation . . .
meant for a soldier
    converted to letters," who could

---

[4] This apparently refers to the electric power failure in greater New York that darkened and immobilized the city for nearly twelve hours in 1966.

[5] These quotations are variations on motifs found in the opening and closing sections of Hart Crane's *The Bridge*.

[6] John Roebling (1806–1869), German-American engineer who designed the Brooklyn Bridge.

---

[1] Walter Savage Landor (1775–1864), English poet and prose writer. The author's notes send the reader to Havelock Ellis's introduction to Landor's *Imaginary Conversations* (Everyman's, 1933) where the sources of her quotations appear: the first on page *xxiii*, the second on *xx*, the third and fourth on *xxiii* (the last Ellis quotes from Landor himself—Diogenes to Plato). As is her usual habit, rather than quoting exactly, Miss Moore paraphrases in these borrowings.

throw
a man through the window,
      yet, "tender toward plants," say, "Good God,
the violets!" (below).
      "Accomplished in every   10

style
and tint"—considering meanwhile
      infinity and eternity,
he could only say, "I'll
      talk about them when I understand them."

Arthur Mitchell [1]

Slim dragonfly
too rapid for the eye
      to cage—
contagious gem of virtuosity—
make visible, mentality.
Your jewels of mobility

      reveal
            and veil
                  a peacock-tail.

Tell Me, Tell Me

      where might there be a refuge for me
            from egocentricity
and its propensity to bisect,
mis-state, misunderstand
            and obliterate continuity?
            Why, oh why, one ventures to ask, set
flatness on some cindery pinnacle
as if on Lord Nelson's revolving diamond rosette?

      It appeared: gem, burnished rarity
            and peak of delicacy—   10

[1] Black soloist with the New York City Ballet. Miss Moore here comments on his
performance as Puck in Balanchine's "A Midsummer Night's Dream" (1964).

in contrast with grievance touched off on
any ground—the absorbing
    geometry of a fantasy:
        a James, Miss Potter, Chinese
"passion for the particular," of a
tired man who yet, at dusk,
        cut a masterpiece of cerise—

    for no tailor-and-cutter jury—
    only a few mice to see,
who "breathed inconsistency and drank   20
contradiction," [1] dazzled
    not by the sun but by "shadowy
        possibility." (I'm referring
to Henry James and Beatrix Potter's Tailor.) [2]
I vow, rescued tailor
    of Gloucester, I am going

    to flee; by engineering strategy—
    the viper's traffic-knot—flee
to metaphysical newmown hay,
honeysuckle, or woods fragrance.   30
    Might one say or imply T.S.V.P. [3]—
        Taisez-vous? "Please" does not make sense
to a refugee from verbal ferocity; I am
perplexed. Even so, "deference";
        yes, deference may be my defense.

A *précis*?
    In this told-backward biography
    of how the cat's mice when set free
by the tailor of Gloucester, finished
the Lord Mayor's cerise coat—   40
    the tailor's tale ended captivity
    in two senses. Besides having told
of a coat which made the tailor's fortune,
it rescued a reader
    from being driven mad by a scold.

[1] "The literal played in our education as small a part as it perhaps ever played
in any and we wholesomely breathed inconsistency and ate and drank contradictions." Henry James's *Autobiography* (*A Small Boy and Others*, *Notes of a Son and
Brother*, *The Middle Years*), edited by F. W. Dupee (New York: Criterion, 1958).
[2] Beatrix Potter (1866–1943), English author and illustrator of children's books,
notably the Peter Rabbit series, but also *The Tailor of Gloucester*.
[3] Stands for the French, *taisez-vous s'il vous plait* ("please shut up!").

Marianne Moore's comment made after a public reading of this poem—it appears on page 5 of the volume *Tell Me, Tell Me* (1966)—may be helpful:

A Burning Desire to Be Explicit

Always, in whatever I wrote—prose or verse—I have had a burning desire to be explicit; beset always, however carefully I had written, by the charge of obscurity. Having entered Bryn Mawr with intensive zeal to write, I examined, for comment, the margin of a paper with which I had taken a great deal of trouble and found, "I presume you had an idea if one could find out what it is."

Again—recently! In a reading of my verse for a women's club, I included these lines from "Tell me, tell me":

I vow, rescued tailor
        of Gloucester, I am going

    to flee: by engineering strategy—
    the viper's traffic-knot—flee
to metaphysical newmown hay,
honeysuckle or woods fragrance. . . .

After the program, a strikingly well-dressed member of the audience, with equally positive manner, inquired, "*What* is metaphysical newmown hay?"

I said, "Oh, something like a sudden whiff of fragrance in contrast with the doggedly continuous opposition to spontaneous conversation that had gone before."

"Then why don't you *say* so?" the impressive lady rejoined.

JOHN CROWE RANSOM (1888–   )

John Crowe Ransom has been the central figure in two major movements in the literary history of this century. The first derives from the situation of his birth and upbringing. He was born in Pulaski, Tennessee, and he was educated at Vanderbilt University. After several years at Oxford as a Rhodes Scholar, he returned to Vanderbilt as a member of the department of English, and except for the period of his service in the First World War, remained there until 1937.

While on the faculty at Vanderbilt, he was one of the seven founders of the magazine The Fugitive, *a focus for the then burgeoning Southern "renaissance" as well as for agrarianism. This movement held the view that if the South was to survive and its fine traditions were to be sustained, it must turn away from an industrial to a "distributist" agrarian economy. On behalf of this view the group published two symposia, to each of which Ransom contributed an important essay,* I'll Take My Stand *(1930) and* Who Owns America? *(1936).*

In 1937 Ransom was invited to Kenyon College as the Carnegie Professor of Poetry. There, as editor of Kenyon Review *and one of the founders of the* Kenyon School of English *(later the School of Letters at Indiana University), he became the chief spokesman of the New Criticism. This is the "school," insofar as it is one, that dedicates itself to the structural and textural qualities of an individual literary work rather than to its historical, sociological, ideological, or biographical implications, or to the traditional form of literary history. The movement influenced graduate students for many years and has had a profound effect, probably both good and bad, on the teaching of literature in the United States and, later, in England.*

Ransom's influence made itself felt not only through his teaching and lecturing but through his published criticism, which is assembled in three volumes: God without Thunder: An Unorthodox Defense of Orthodoxy *(1930), an extended comment on science as destructive of God and ultimate values;* The World's Body *(1938), presenting the argument that scientific technology has not achieved the substance that is characteristic of literature; and* The New Criticism *(1941), in which he makes his famous call for what he named an "ontological" criticism.*

His own poetry—witty, grave, civilized, absolutely controlled, beautifully poised—was never profuse, and he has reduced it ruthlessly to the small body that he is willing to see preserved in Selected Poems *(1945) and* Poems and Essays *(1955). The first of his books of poems,* Poems about God *(1919), he has eliminated entirely, and he has not been willing to retain as much from* Chills and Fever *(1924) and* Two Gentlemen in Bonds *(1927) as many of his admirers would like to have. He has not added many poems since 1927. There is something characteristic and admirable, as well as moving, in the pitiless way that he measures his own production, being above all a humane and gentle man.*

FURTHER READING

A recent evaluation of Ransom's major poems is Robert Buffington, *The Equilibrists: A Study of John Crowe Ransom's Poems, 1916–1963* (1967). See also John L. Stewart, *John Crowe Ransom* (1962); Louise Cowan, *The Fugitive Group: A Literary History* (1959); and Karl F. Knight, *The Poetry of John Crowe Ransom* (1964). Thomas Daniel Young edited *John Crowe Ransom: Critical Essays and a Bibliography* (1968).

FROM *Chills and Fevers* (1924)

Bells for John Whiteside's Daughter

There was such speed in her little body,
And such lightness in her footfall,
It is no wonder her brown study
Astonishes us all.

Her wars were bruited in our high window.
We looked among orchard trees and beyond
Where she took arms against her shadow,
Or harried unto the pond

The lazy geese, like a snow cloud
Dripping their snow on the green grass,   10
Tricking and stopping, sleepy and proud,
Who cried in goose, Alas,

For the tireless heart within the little
Lady with rod that made them rise
From their noon apple-dreams and scuttle
Goose-fashion under the skies!

But now go the bells, and we are ready,
In one house we are sternly stopped
To say we are vexed at her brown study,
Lying so primly propped.   20

Here Lies a Lady

Here lies a lady of beauty and high degree.
Of chills and fever she died, of fever and chills,
The delight of her husband, her aunt, an infant of three,
And of medicos marveling sweetly on her ills.

For either she burned, and her confident eyes would blaze,
And her fingers fly in a manner to puzzle their heads—
What was she making? Why, nothing; she sat in a maze
Of old scraps of laces, snipped into curious shreds—

Or this would pass, and the light of her fire decline
Till she lay discouraged and cold, like a thin stalk white and blown,   10
And would not open her eyes, to kisses, to wine;
The sixth of these states was her last; the cold settled down.

Sweet ladies, long may ye bloom, and toughly I hope ye may thole,[1]
But was she not lucky? In flowers and lace and mourning,
In love and great honor we bade God rest her soul
After six little spaces of chill, and six of burning.

Old Mansion

As an intruder I trudged with careful innocence
To mask in decency a meddlesome stare,
Passing the old house often on its eminence,
Exhaling my foreign weed on its weighted air.

Here age seemed newly imaged for the historian
After his monstrous chateaux on the Loire,
A beauty not for depicting by old vulgarian
Reiterations which gentle readers abhor.

Each time of seeing I absorbed some other feature
Of a house whose annals in no wise could be brief   10
Nor ignoble; for it expired as sweetly as Nature,
With her tinge of oxidation on autumn leaf.

It was a Southern manor. One need hardly imagine
Towers, white monoliths, or even ivied walls;
But sufficient state if its peacock *was* a pigeon;
Where no courts kept, but grave rites and funerals.

Indeed, not distant, possibly not external
To the property, were tombstones, where the catafalque
Had carried their dead; and projected a note too charnel
But for the honeysuckle on its intricate stalk.   20

Stability was the character of its rectangle
Whose line was seen in part and guessed in part
Through trees. Decay was the tone of old brick and shingle.
Green blinds dragging frightened the watchful heart

To assert, "Your mansion, long and richly inhabited,
Its exits and entrances suiting the children of men,
Will not for ever be thus, O man, exhibited,
And one had best hurry to enter it if one can."

And at last, with my happier angel's own temerity,
Did I clang their brazen knocker against the door,   30

---

[1] Endure.

To beg their dole of a look, in simple charity,
Or crumbs of legend dropping from their great store.

But it came to nothing—and may so gross denial
Which has been deplored with a beating of the breast
Never shorten the tired historian, loyal
To acknowledge defeat and discover a new quest—

The old mistress was ill, and sent my dismissal
By one even more wrappered and lean and dark
Than that wrapped concierge and imperturbable vassal
Who bids you begone from her master's Gothic park.   40

Emphatically, the old house crumbled; the ruins
Would litter, as already the leaves, this petted sward;
And no annalist went in to the lords or the peons;
The antiquary would finger the bits of shard.

But on retreating I saw myself in the token,
How loving from my foreign weed the feather curled
On the languid air; and I went with courage shaken
To dip, alas, into some unseemlier world.

FROM *Two Gentlemen in Bonds* (1927)

Piazza Piece

—I am a gentleman in a dustcoat trying
To make you hear. Your ears are soft and small
And listen to an old man not at all,
They want the young men's whispering and sighing.
But see the roses on your trellis dying
And hear the spectral singing of the moon;
For I must have my lovely lady soon,
I am a gentleman in a dustcoat trying.

—I am a lady young in beauty waiting
Until my truelove comes, and then we kiss.   10
But what grey man among the vines is this
Whose words are dry and faint as in a dream?
Back from my trellis, Sir, before I scream!
I am a lady young in beauty waiting.

Blue Girls

Twirling your blue skirts, travelling the sward
Under the towers of your seminary,
Go listen to your teachers old and contrary
Without believing a word.

Tie the white fillets then about your hair
And think no more of what will come to pass
Than bluebirds that go walking on the grass
And chattering on the air.

Practise your beauty, blue girls, before it fail;
And I will cry with my loud lips and publish   10
Beauty which all our power shall never establish,
It is so frail.

For I could tell you a story which is true;
I know a lady with a terrible tongue,
Blear eyes fallen from blue,
All her perfections tarnished—yet it is not long
Since she was lovlier than any of you.

Dead Boy

The little cousin is dead, by foul subtraction,
A green bough from Virginia's aged tree,
And none of the county kin like the transaction,
Nor some of the world of outer dark, like me.

A boy not beautiful, nor good, nor clever,
A black cloud full of storms too hot for keeping,
A sword beneath his mother's heart—yet never
Woman bewept her babe as this is weeping.

A pig with a pasty face, so I had said,
Squealing for cookies, kinned by poor pretense   10
With a noble house. But the little man quite dead,
I see the forbears' antique lineaments.

The elder men have strode by the box of death
To the wide flag porch, and muttering low send round
The bruit of the day. O friendly waste of breath!
Their hearts are hurt with a deep dynastic wound.

He was pale and little, the foolish neighbors say;
The first-fruits, saith the Preacher, the Lord hath taken;
But this was the old tree's late branch wrenched away,
Grieving the sapless limbs, the shorn and shaken.   20

Man without Sense of Direction

Tell this to ladies: how a hero man
Assail a thick and scandalous giant
Who casts true shadow in the sun,
And die, but play no truant.

This is more horrible: that the darling egg
Of the chosen people hatch a creature
Of noblest mind and powerful leg
Who cannot fathom nor perform his nature.

The larks' tongues are never stilled
Where the pale spread straw of sunlight lies.   10
Then what invidious gods have willed
Him to be seized so otherwise?

Birds of the field and beasts of the stable
Are swollen with rapture and make uncouth
Demonstration of joy, which is a babble
Offending the ear of the fervorless youth.

Love—is it the cause? the proud shamed spirit?
Love has slain some whom it possessed,
But his was requited beyond his merit
And won him in bridal the loveliest.   20

Yet scarcely he issues from the warm chamber,
Flushed with her passion, when cold as dead
Once more he walks where waves past number
Of sorrow buffet his curse-hung head.

Whether by street, or in field full of honey,
Attended by clouds of the creatures of air
Or shouldering the city's companioning many,
His doom is on him; and how can he care

For the shapes that would fiddle upon his senses,
Wings and faces and mists that move,   30
Words, sunlight, the blue air which rinses
The pure pale head which he must love?

And he writhes like an antique man of bronze
That is beaten by furies visible,
Yet he is punished not knowing his sins
And for his innocence walks in hell.

He flails his arms, he moves his lips:
"Rage have I none, cause, time, nor country—
Yet I have traveled land and ships
And knelt my seasons in the chantry."   40

So he stands muttering; and rushes
Back to the tender thing in his charge
With clamoring tongue and taste of ashes
And a small passion to feign large.

But let his cold lips be her omen,
She shall not kiss that harried one
To peace, as men are served by women
Who comfort them in darkness and in sun.

Survey of Literature

In all the good Greek of Plato
I lack my roastbeef and potato.

A better man was Aristotle,
Pulling steady on the bottle.

I dip my hat to Chaucer,
Swilling soup from his saucer,

And to Master Shakespeare
Who wrote big on small beer.

The abstemious Wordsworth
Subsisted on a curd's-worth,   10

But a slick one was Tennyson,
Putting gravy on his venison.

What these men had to eat and drink
Is what we say and what we think.

The influence of Milton
Came wry out of Stilton.[1]

Sing a song for Percy Shelley,
Drowned in pale lemon jelly,

And for precious John Keats,
Dripping blood of pickled beets.   20

Then there was poor Willie Blake,
He foundered on sweet cake.

God have mercy on the sinner
Who must write with no dinner,

[1] Stilton cheese.

No gravy and no grub,
No pewter and no pub,

No belly and no bowels,
Only consonants and vowels.

The Equilibrists

Full of her long white arms and milky skin
He had a thousand times remembered sin.
Alone in the press of people traveled he,
Minding her jacinth, and myrrh, and ivory.

Mouth he remembered: the quaint orifice
From which came heat that flamed upcn the kiss,
Till cold words came down spiral from the head.
Grey doves from the officious tower illsped.

Body: it was a white field ready for love,
On her body's field, with the gaunt tower above,   10
The lilies grew, beseeching him to take,
If he would pluck and wear them, bruise and break.

Eyes talking: Never mind the cruel words,
Embrace my flowers, but not embrace the swords.
But what they said, the doves came straightway flying
And unsaid: Honor, Honor, they came crying.

Importunate her doves. Too pure, too wise,
Clambering on his shoulder, saying, Arise,
Leave me now, and never let us meet,
Eternal distance now command thy feet.   20

Predicament indeed, which thus discovers
Honor among thieves, Honor between lovers.
O such a little word is Honor, they feel!
But the grey word is between them cold as steel.

At length I saw these lovers fully were come
Into their torture of equilibrium;
Dreadfully had forsworn each other, and yet
They were bound each to each, and they did not forget.

And rigid as two painful stars, and twirled
About the clustered night their prison world,   30
They burned with fierce love always to come near,
But honor beat them back and kept them clear.

Ah, the strict lovers, they are ruined now!
I cried in anger. But with puddled brow
Devising for those gibbeted and brave
Came I descanting: Man, what would you have?

For spin your period out, and draw your breath,
A kinder saeculum [1] begins with Death.
Would you ascend to Heaven and bodiless dwell?
Or take your bodies honorless to Hell?   40

In Heaven you have heard no marriage is,
No white flesh tinder to your lecheries,
Your male and female tissue sweetly shaped
Sublimed away, and furious blood escaped.

Great lovers lie in Hell, the stubborn ones
Infatuate of the flesh upon the bones;
Stuprate; [2] they rend each other when they kiss,
The pieces kiss again, no end to this.

But still I watched them spinning, orbited nice.
Their flames were not more radiant than their ice.   50
I dug in the quiet earth and wrought the tomb
And made these lines to memorize their doom: —

EPITAPH

Equilibrists lie here; stranger, tread light;
Close, but untouching in each other's sight;
Mouldered the lips and ashy the tall skull.
Let them lie perilous and beautiful.

FROM **Selected Poems** (1945)

Painted Head

By dark severance the apparition head
Smiles from the air a capital on no
Column or a Platonic perhaps head
On a canvas sky depending from nothing;

Stirs up an old illusion of grandeur
By tickling the instinct of heads to be

[1] Age, era.
[2] To have sexual intercourse.

Absolute and to try decapitation
And to play truant from the body bush;

But too happy and beautiful for those sorts
Of head (homekeeping heads are happiest)   *10*
Discovers maybe thirty unwidowed years
Of not dishonoring the faithful stem;

Is nameless and has authored for the evil
Historian headhunters neither book
Nor state and is therefore distinct from tart
Heads with crowns and guilty gallery heads;

So that the extravagant device of art
Unhousing by abstraction this once head
Was capital irony by a loving hand
That knew the no treason of a head like this;   *20*

Makes repentance in an unlovely head
For having vinegarly traduced the flesh
Till, the hurt flesh recusing, the hard egg
Is shrunken to its own deathlike surface;

And an image thus. The body bears the head
(So hardly one they terribly are two)
Feeds and obeys and unto please what end?
Not to the glory of tyrant head but to

The increase of body. Beauty is of body.
The flesh contouring shallowly on a head   *30*
Is a rock-garden needing body's love
And best bodiness to colorify

The big blue birds sitting and sea-shell flats
And caves, and on the iron acropolis
To spread the hyacinthine hair and rear
The olive garden for the nightingales.

T[HOMAS] S[TEARNS] ELIOT (1888–1965)

*T. S. Eliot was born into one of the most distinguished families in the
United States, but, paradoxically, in the very heart of the "national
vulgarity," St. Louis, Missouri. His whole life can be viewed as a
movement backward through his own inheritance to a nobler time
and place, and this, again paradoxically, as he developed into one
of the foremost figures in twentieth-century modernism.*

*The first step back was easy enough. It was easy to get back to New
England: one had only to be enrolled in the Milton Academy outside*

*Boston and then go on to Harvard College, where one's own ances-
tors had been presiding spirits—among others, Charles Eliot Norton,
the great nineteenth-century professor of fine art, and Charles William Eliot, president of the college for forty years who completely
reformed it. And there one could begin to be a poet.*

*From 1907 to 1910 he contributed poems to the undergraduate literary
magazine,* The Harvard Advocate, *and became its editor. Before that
he had made the important discovery of Arthur Symons's* The Sym-
bolist Movement in Literature, *which introduced him to such French
poets as Baudelaire and Mallarmé and, above all, Jules Laforgue,
whom the young poet frankly imitated. But it was imitation that
worked with other influences, especially those of the late-Eliza-
bethan dramatists and the English metaphysical poets, to help him
forge his own surprising early style.*

*After a year's study at the Sorbonne he returned to Harvard to work for
a Ph.D.; and while he completed his doctoral dissertation on the
philosophy of F. H. Bradley at Merton College, Oxford, he did not
trouble to return to Cambridge or to take the degree. Instead, he
married in London and found work first as a teacher, then as a
banker, then as the editor of* The Egoist, *and finally as an editor in
the publishing firm of Faber and Faber, of which he ultimately
became a director.*

*At the same time he wrote poems, reviews, and essays, and he had
published his first two volumes,* Prufrock and Other Observations
(1917) and Poems *(1920). These poems, read at one level, can be
seen to be a rather systematic inspection of that New England
society to which he had briefly returned. There were three layers:
the top, his own effete class; the world of business and vulgar commerce; and the realm of "apeneck" Sweeney, of crime and the
slums. What did that spectacle offer to a searching spirit? Turning
to Europe in* The Waste Land *(1922), he discovered the same layers
—the pointlessly refined, the crass, the merely gross—and the end
of the poem points further back. The poems that followed trace the
path inevitably to* Ash Wednesday *(1930), the great poem of conversion. In 1927 Eliot had renounced his American citizenship and
become a British subject. In 1928 he announced that he was "an
Anglo-Catholic in religion, a classicist in literature, and a royalist
in politics."*

For some years he had been editing the influential periodical, The Criterion, *and publishing there and elsewhere his remarkable critical
essays. Many of these had to do with the idea of literary tradition in
general, but they were concerned especially with dramatic tradition.
And from 1935, with* Murder in the Cathedral, *to 1958, with* The
Elder Statesman, *Eliot's chief creative concern was to discover a*

form and a line that would make poetic drama once more viable on the stage. The theme of these plays, either explicit or implicit, was the salvation of the human soul in a faithless world, a world sordid and violent and suffering from an enormous ennui, or death of spirit.

The final poems, the Four *Quartets (1935–1943), are the meditative and lyrical counterparts of the plays. Here all his familiar themes are woven together in an always beautiful, often melancholy, but finally serene music of hints and glimpses: the isolation and alienation of the individual, problems of language and communication, despair of this world and the sense of another, memory and desire, time and eternity, the need for belief and the difficulty of clinging to it, and the tentatively expressed but ultimate assertion that "all shall be well."*

From The Waste Land *on, Eliot's was the major voice in poetry and criticism written in English. Although he had many detractors, his authority was recognized and honored by many more. In 1948 he was awarded the Nobel Prize in literature, but somehow that honor was only an incident. By then the achievement of his own work was established as an enduring monument that not only marked his place in the literary age but marked the changes in it that he had brought about.*

FURTHER READING

Herbert Howarth's *Notes on Some Figures Behind T. S. Eliot* (1964) is the best source for biographical information. The best critical studies are: F. O. Matthiessen, *The Achievement of T. S. Eliot* (1935; revised in 1947 and, by C. L. Barber, in 1958); Kristian Smidt, *Poetry and Belief in the Work of T. S. Eliot* (1949, revised 1961); Elizabeth Drew, *T. S. Eliot: The Design of His Poetry* (1949); Helen Gardner, *The Art of T. S. Eliot* (1950); D. E. S. Maxwell, *The Poetry of T. S. Eliot* (1952); and also Hugh Kenner, *The Invisible Poet: T. S. Eliot* (1959). For critical estimates of Eliot's plays see David E. Jones, *The Plays of T. S. Eliot* (1960), and Carol H. Smith, *T. S. Eliot's Dramatic Theory and Practise* (1963). Northrop Frye's *T. S. Eliot* (1963) is a valuable but highly condensed survey. George Williamson, *A Reader's Guide to T. S. Eliot* (1953), and Grover Smith Jr., *T. S. Eliot's Poetry and Plays: A Study in Sources and Meaning* (1956), are invaluable reference volumes and guides to Eliot's allusions and sources. Two collections of short critical studies of the poet are *T. S. Eliot: A Selected Critique* (1948), edited by Leonard Unger, and *T. S. Eliot* (1962), edited by Hugh Kenner.

FROM *Prufrock and Other Observations* (1917)

The Love Song of J. Alfred Prufrock

S'io credesse che mia risposta fosse
A persona che mai tornasse al mondo,
Questa fiamma staria senza piu scosse.
Ma perciocche giammai di questo fondo
Non torno vivo alcun, s'i'odo il vero,
Senza tema d'infamia ti rispondo.[1]

Let us go then, you and I,
When the evening is spread out against the sky
Like a patient etherised upon a table;
Let us go, through certain half-deserted streets,
The muttering retreats
Of restless nights in one-night cheap hotels
And sawdust restaurants with oyster-shells:
Streets that follow like a tedious argument
Of insidious intent
To lead you to an overwhelming question . . .   10
Oh, do not ask, "What is it?"
Let us go and make our visit.

    In the room the women come and go
Talking of Michelangelo.

    The yellow fog that rubs its back upon the window-panes,
The yellow smoke that rubs its muzzle on the window-panes
Licked its tongue into the corners of the evening,
Lingered upon the pools that stand in drains,
Let fall upon its back the soot that falls from chimneys,
Slipped by the terrace, made a sudden leap,   20
And seeing that it was a soft October night,
Curled once about the house, and fell asleep.

    And indeed there will be time
For the yellow smoke that slides along the street,
Rubbing its back upon the window-panes;
There will be time, there will be time
To prepare a face to meet the faces that you meet;
There will be time to murder and create,

[1] Dante, *Inferno*, 27, 61–66: Guido da Montefeltro's reply to Dante's question about why he is damned: "If I thought that my answer were to one who could ever return to the world, this flame would shake no more; but since none ever returns alive from this depth, if what I hear is true, I answer you without fear of infamy."

And time for all the works and days ² of hands
That lift and drop a question on your plate;   30
Time for you and time for me,
And time yet for a hundred indecisions,
And for a hundred visions and revisions,
Before the taking of a toast and tea.

    In the room the women come and go
Talking of Michelangelo.

    And indeed there will be time
To wonder, "Do I dare?" and, "Do I dare?"
Time to turn back and descend the stair,
With a bald spot in the middle of my hair—   40
[They will say: "How his hair is growing thin!"]
My morning coat, my collar mounting firmly to the chin,
My necktie rich and modest, but asserted by a simple pin—
[They will say: "But how his arms and legs are thin!"]
Do I dare
Disturb the universe?
In a minute there is time
For decisions and revisions which a minute will reverse.

    For I have known them all already, known them all: —
Have know the evenings, mornings, afternoons,   50
I have measured out my life with coffee spoons;
I know the voices dying with a dying fall
Beneath the music from a farther room.
    So how should I presume?

    And I have known the eyes already, known them all—
The eyes that fix you in a formulated phrase,
And when I am formulated, sprawling on a pin,
When I am pinned and wriggling on the wall,
Then how should I begin
To spit out all the butt-ends of my days and ways?   60
    And how should I presume?

    And I have known the arms already, known them all—
Arms that are braceleted and white and bare
[But in the lamplight, downed with light brown hair!]
Is it perfume from a dress
That makes me so digress?
Arms that lie along a table, or wrap about a shawl.

² See Hesiod's *Works and Days*, an encomium on agricultural labor written in the eighth century B.C.

And should I then presume?
And how should I begin?

.   .   .

Shall I say, I have gone at dusk through narrow streets   70
And watched the smoke that rises from the pipes
Of lonely men in shirt-sleeves, leaning out of windows? . . .

    I should have been a pair of ragged claws
Scuttling across the floors of silent seas.

.   .   .

And the afternoon, the evening, sleeps so peacefully!
Smoothed by long fingers,
Asleep . . . tired . . . or it malingers,
Stretched on the floor, here beside you and me.
Should I, after tea and cakes and ices,
Have the strength to force the moment to its crisis?   80
But though I have wept and fasted, wept and prayed,
Though I have seen my head [grown slightly bald] brought in upon a
    platter,[3]
I am no prophet—and here's no great matter;
I have seen the moment of my greatness flicker,
And I have seen the eternal Footman hold my coat, and snicker,
And in short, I was afraid.

    And would it have been worth it, after all,
After the cups, the marmalade, the tea,
Among the porcelain, among some talk of you and me,
Would it have been worth while,   90
To have bitten off the matter with a smile,
To have squeezed the universe into a ball
To roll it toward some overwhelming question,
To say: "I am Lazarus,[4] come from the dead,
Come back to tell you all, I shall tell you all"—
If one, settling a pillow by her head,
    Should say: "That is not what I meant at all.
    That is not it, at all."

    And would it have been worth it, after all,
Would it have been worth while,   100
After the sunsets and the dooryards and the sprinkled streets,
After the novels, after the teacups, after the skirts that trail along
    the floor—

[3] In Matthew, 14:1–11, the head of John the Baptist was brought to Herod on a
platter.
[4] In John, 11:1–44, Lazarus was raised from the dead by Jesus.

And this, and so much more?—
It is impossible to say just what I mean!
But as if a magic lantern threw the nerves in patterns on a screen:
Would it have been worth while
If one, settling a pillow or throwing off a shawl,
And turning toward the window, should say:
    "That is not it at all,
    That is not what I meant, at all."   *110*

.   .   .

No! I am not Prince Hamlet, nor was meant to be;
Am an attendant lord, one that will do
To swell a progress, start a scene or two,
Advise the prince; no doubt, an easy tool,
Deferential, glad to be of use,
Politic, cautious, and meticulous;
Full of high sentence, but a bit obtuse;
At times, indeed, almost ridiculous—
Almost, at times, the Fool.

    I grow old . . . I grow old . . .   *120*
I shall wear the bottoms of my trousers rolled.

    Shall I part my hair behind? Do I dare to eat a peach?
I shall wear white flannel trousers, and walk upon the beach.
I have heard the mermaids singing, each to each.

    I do not think that they will sing to me.

    I have seen them riding seaward on the waves
Combing the white hair of the waves blown back
When the wind blows the water white and black.

    We have lingered in the chambers of the sea
By sea-girls wreathed with seaweed red and brown   *130*
Till human voices wake us, and we drown.

Sweeney among the Nightingales [1]

ὤμοι, πέπληγμαι καιρίαν πληγὴν ἔσω. [2]

Apeneck Sweeney spreads his knees
Letting his arms hang down to laugh,
The zebra stripes along his jaw
Swelling to maculate [3] giraffe.

The circles of the stormy moon
Slide westward toward the River Plate, [4]
Death and the Raven drift above
And Sweeney guards the hornèd gate. [5]

Gloomy Orion and the Dog
Are veiled; and hushed the shrunken seas;   10
The person in the Spanish cape
Tries to sit on Sweeney's knees

Slips and pulls the table cloth
Overturns a coffee-cup,
Reorganized upon the floor
She yawns and draws a stocking up;

The silent man in mocha brown
Sprawls at the window-sill and gapes;
The waiter brings in oranges
Bananas figs and hothouse grapes;   20

The silent vertebrate in brown
Contracts and concentrates, withdraws;
Rachel *née* Rabinovitch
Tears at the grapes with murderous paws;

She and the lady in the cape
Are suspect, thought to be in league;
Therefore the man with heavy eyes
Declines the gambit, shows fatigue,

---

[1] In Greek legend Philomela, after being raped and having her tongue cut out to prevent her from accusing her ravisher, is turned into a nightingale and sings of her suffering.

[2] "Alas, I am struck a mortal blow within," from Aeschylus's play *Agamemnon*, line 1343, spoken by King Agamemnon as he is stabbed by his faithless wife Clytemnestra.

[3] Stained.

[4] In South America.

[5] The gate of Hades, which permits visions and dreams to emerge.

Leaves the room and reappears
Outside the window, leaning in,   *30*
Branches of wistaria
Circumscribe a golden grin;

The host with someone indistinct
Converses at the door apart,
The nightingales are singing near
The Convent of the Sacred Heart,

And sang within the bloody wood
When Agamemnon cried aloud,[6]
And let their liquid siftings fall
To stain the stiff dishonoured shroud.   *40*

The Waste Land *(1922)* *

Nam Sibyllam quidem Cumis ego ipse oculis meis vidi in ampulla pendere,
et cum illi pueri dicerent: Σίβυλλα τί θέλεις; respondebat illa: άποθανεῖν θέλω.[1]

For Ezra Pound
il miglior fabbro.[2]

I   THE BURIAL OF THE DEAD

April is the cruellest month, breeding
Lilacs out of the dead land, mixing
Memory and desire, stirring
Dull roots with spring rain.
Winter kept us warm, covering
Earth in forgetful snow, feeding
A little life with dried tubers.

[6] A conflation of Philomela's singing in "the bloody wood," where she was raped,
with Agamemnon's death cry in his bath as he was murdered.

---

* The editor's notes are supplementary to Eliot's own notes at the end of the poem,
expanding or translating when necessary.
1 "For once I myself saw with my own eyes the Sybil at Cumae hanging in a cage,
and when the boys said to her, 'Sybil, what do you want?' she replied, 'I want to
die.'" (Petronius, *Satyricon*, 48.) The Sybil of Cumae (along with Tiresias and
Madame Sosostris) is a prophet. The Cumaean Sybil was given immortality, but
she neglected to ask for eternal youth. Aeneas consulted her before descending into
Hades—i.e., you are about to enter hell.
2 "The best craftsman" (*Purgatorio*, 26, 117), originally referred to Arnaut Daniel.
Eliot uses the phrase to acknowledge Ezra Pound's help with *The Waste Land*.

Summer surprised us, coming over the Starnbergersee [3]
With a shower of rain; we stopped in the colonnade,
And went on in sunlight, into the Hofgarten,[4]   10
And drank coffee, and talked for an hour.
Bin gar keine Russin, stamm' aus Litauen, echt deutsch.[5]
And when we were children, staying at the archduke's,
My cousin's, he took me out on a sled,
And I was frightened. He said, Marie,
Marie, hold on tight. And down we went.
In the mountains, there you feel free.
I read, much of the night, and go south in the winter.

    What are the roots that clutch, what branches grow
Out of this stony rubbish? Son of man,[6]   20
You cannot say, or guess, for you know only
A heap of broken images, where the sun beats,
And the dead tree gives no shelter, the cricket no relief,[7]
And the dry stone no sound of water. Only
There is shadow under this red rock,[8]
(Come in under the shadow of this red rock),
And I will show you something different from either
Your shadow at morning striding behind you
Or your shadow at evening rising to meet you;
I will show you fear in a handful of dust.   30

        Frisch weht der Wind
        Der Heimat zu
        Mein Irisch Kind,
        Wo weilest du? [9]

"You gave me hyacinths first a year ago;
"They called me the hyacinth girl."
—Yet when we came back, late, from the Hyacinth garden,
Your arms full, and your hair wet, I could not
Speak, and my eyes failed, I was neither
Living nor dead, and I knew nothing,   40

---

[3] A lake in the vicinity of Munich.
[4] A park in Munich.
[5] "I am not at all Russian; come from Lithuania, truly German."
[6] God's words to Ezekiel: "Son of man, stand upon thy feet."
[7] A description of the miseries of growing old in Ecclesiastes: ". . . the grasshopper shall be a burden, and desire shall fail."
[8] Probably an allusion to Isaiah, 32:2, where the "righteous king" is described as "rivers of water in a dry place, as the shadow of a great rock in a weary land"; also, the Church (see Eliot's *The Rock*).
[9] "Fresh blows the wind to the home-country; my Irish child, where do you wait?" a sailor's call to a girl who has been abandoned (Wagner's *Tristan and Isolde,* tragedy of adultery).

Looking into the heart of light, the silence.
Oed' und leer das Meer.[10]

    Madame Sosostris,[11] famous clairvoyante,
Had a bad cold, nevertheless
Is known to be the wisest woman in Europe,
With a wicked pack of cards.[12] Here, said she,
Is your card, the drowned Phoenician Sailor,
(Those are pearls that were his eyes.[13] Look!)
Here is Belladonna,[14] the Lady of the Rocks,
The lady of situations,   50
Here is the man with three staves, and here the Wheel,[15]
And here is the one-eyed merchant,[16] and this card,
Which is blank, is something he carries on his back,
Which I am forbidden to see. I do not find
The Hanged Man.[17] Fear death by water.
I see crowds of people, walking round in a ring.
Thank you. If you see dear Mrs. Equitone,
Tell her I bring the horoscope myself:
One must be so careful these days.

    Unreal City,[18]   60
Under the brown fog of a winter dawn,

[10] "Waste and empty the sea," reports the shepherd to the dying Tristan who is awaiting Isolde's arrival.
[11] Perhaps suggested by Aldous Huxley's "Sesostris," a fake fortune teller in *Chrome Yellow* (1921).
[12] The Tarot deck, whose suits are the constituents of the symbols of the Grail quest: the lance, the cup, the sword, and the dish.
[13] Ariel's song about the supposed drowning and transformation of Alonso in Shakespeare's *The Tempest*, 1, 2, 398.
[14] "Beautiful lady," but also a poison and an eye cosmetic which produces a brilliant, glassy effect. Belladonna may suggest the Madonna, associated with "the Rocks" which represent the shelter of the Church; in herself, she represents as well the spiritual dryness of modern love.
[15] Eliot says in his note that he "arbitrarily" associates the man with the three staves with the Fisher King, who, in Jessie Weston's book, is the symbol of life and regeneration. The Wheel symbolizes the cycle of fortune as well as of the seasons.
[16] Associated with the "drowned Phoenician sailor," especially in part 4. According to Jessie Weston, Phoenician merchants were the purveyors of fertility rites. The merchant is "one-eyed" because the card shows him in profile. His burden may be the evils of the world or the secrets of fertility.
[17] The Hanged Man in the Tarot pack is represented by a figure hanging from a cross.
[18] Adapted from Baudelaire's poem "Les sept vieillards" ("The Seven Aged Men"): "Swarming city, city full of dreams,/Where the specter in broad daylight accosts the passerby."

A crowd flowed over London Bridge, so many,
I had not thought death had undone so many.[19]
Sighs, short and infrequent, were exhaled,[20]
And each man fixed his eyes before his feet.
Flowed up the hill and down King William Street,
To where Saint Mary Woolnoth [21] kept the hours
With a dead sound on the final stroke of nine.
There I saw one I knew, and stopped him, crying: "Stetson! [22]
"You who were with me in the ships at Mylae! [23]   70
"That corpse you planted last year in your garden,
"Has it begun to sprout? Will it bloom this year?
"Or has the sudden frost disturbed its bed?
"Oh keep the Dog far hence, that's friend to men,
"Or with his nails he'll dig it up again! [24]
"You! hypocrite lecteur!—mon semblable,—mon frère!" [25]

II   A GAME OF CHESS [26]

The Chair she sat in, like a burnished throne,
Glowed on the marble,[27] where the glass
Held up by standards wrought with fruited vines
From which a golden Cupidon peeped out   80
(Another hid his eyes behind his wing)

[19] Cf. *Inferno*, 3, 55–57. *Au*. The poet comments on the souls ". . . who were never really alive": "Such a long train of people/That I would have never believed/That death had undone so many."

[20] Cf. *Inferno*, 4, 25–27. *Au*. Dante observes the sighs of souls who lived before Christ, and who will never behold God: "Here, as far as I could ascertain by listening/There was no lamentation except sighs/Which made the eternal air vibrate."

[21] A church in London.

[22] Symbolically, an average man.

[23] A battle of the First Punic War (260 B.C.).

[24] Adapted from Webster's *White Devil*. *Au*. "But keep the wolf far hence, that's foe to man/For with his nails he'll dig them up again." Also suggests the rites of fertility and regeneration, since the Dog Star marked the seasonal overflow of the Nile.

[25] See Baudelaire's poem "To the Reader": "Hypocrite reader!—My double—my brother!" The poem claims that man's greatest sin is boredom.

[26] The title of this section alludes to Thomas Middleton's play *Women Beware Women*, 2, 2 (c. 1626), and to a scene in which a woman is seduced while her mother-in-law is involved in a game of chess. Middleton also wrote a play entitled *A Game at Chess*.

[27] A distortion of Enobarbus' well-known speech about Cleopatra in Shakespeare's *Antony and Cleopatra*, 2, 2, 196: "The barge she sat in, like a burnish'd throne,/Burn'd on the water."

Doubled the flames of sevenbranched candelabra
Reflecting light upon the table as
The glitter of her jewels rose to meet it,
From satin cases poured in rich profusion;
In vials of ivory and coloured glass
Unstoppered, lurked her strange synthetic perfumes,
Unguent, powdered, or liquid—troubled, confused
And drowned the sense in odours; stirred by the air
That freshened from the window, these ascended   90
In fattening the prolonged candle-flames,
Flung their smoke into the laquearia,[28]
Stirring the pattern on the coffered ceiling.
Huge sea-wood fed with copper
Burned green and orange, framed by the coloured stone,
In which sad light a carvèd dolphin swam.
Above the antique mantel was displayed
As though a window gave upon the sylvan scene [29]
The change of Philomel, by the barbarous king
So rudely forced; [30] yet there the nightingale   100
Filled all the desert with inviolable voice
And still she cried, and still the world pursues,
"Jug Jug" [31] to dirty ears.
And other withered stumps of time
Were told upon the walls; staring forms
Leaned out, leaning, hushing the room enclosed.
Footsteps shuffled on the stair.
Under the firelight, under the brush, her hair
Spread out in fiery points
Glowed into words, then would be savagely still.   110

    "My nerves are bad to-night. Yes, bad. Stay with me.
"Speak to me. Why do you never speak. Speak.
    "What are you thinking of? What thinking? What?
"I never know what you are thinking. Think."

    I think we are in rats' alley
Where the dead men lost their bones.

    "What is that noise?"
        The wind under the door.[32]

[28] From Virgil's "laquearia aureis," the "gold paneled ceiling" in Dido's palace, mentioned in the description of the banquet Dido gave for Aeneas.
[29] The initial description of Paradise as seen through the eyes of Satan in Milton's *Paradise Lost.*
[30] Refers to Ovid's description of the rape of Philomela by "the barbarous king" who was her brother-in-law, Tereus.
[31] Traditional Renaissance way of representing the sound of the nightingale.
[32] Cf. John Webster's play *The Devil's Law Case,* 3, 2, 162.

"What is that noise now? What is the wind doing?"
    Nothing again nothing.   *120*

    "Do
"You know nothing? Do you see nothing? Do you remember
"Nothing?"

    I remember
Those are pearls that were his eyes.
"Are you alive, or not? Is there nothing in your head?"
    But
O O O O that Shakespeherian Rag—
It's so elegant
So intelligent   *130*
"What shall I do now? What shall I do?"
"I shall rush out as I am, and walk the street
"With my hair down, so. What shall we do to-morrow?
"What shall we ever do?"
    The hot water at ten.
And if it rains, a closed car at four.
And we shall play a game of chess,
Pressing lidless eyes and waiting for a knock upon the door.

    When Lil's husband got demobbed,[33] I said—
I didn't mince my words, I said to her myself,   *140*
HURRY UP PLEASE ITS TIME [34]
Now Albert's coming back, make yourself a bit smart.
He'll want to know what you done with that money he gave you
To get yourself some teeth. He did, I was there.
You have them all out, Lil, and get a nice set,
He said, I swear, I can't bear to look at you.
And no more can't I, I said, and think of poor Albert,
He's been in the army four years, he wants a good time,
And if you don't give it him, there's others will, I said.
Oh is there, she said. Something o' that, I said.   *150*
Then I'll know who to thank, she said, and give me a straight look.
HURRY UP PLEASE ITS TIME
If you don't like it you can get on with it, I said.
Others can pick and choose if you can't.

But if Albert makes off, it won't be for lack of telling.
You ought to be ashamed, I said, to look so antique.
(And her only thirty-one.)
I can't help it, she said, pulling a long face,
It's them pills I took, to bring it off, she said.

---

[33] Demobilized.
[34] An English bartender's traditional way of announcing that the bar is closing.

(She's had five already, and nearly died of young George.)   *160*
The chemist ³⁵ said it would be all right, but I've never been the
    same.
You are a proper fool, I said.
Well, if Albert won't leave you alone, there it is, I said,
What you get married for if you don't want children?
HURRY UP PLEASE ITS TIME
Well, that Sunday Albert was home, they had a hot gammon,³⁶
And they asked me in to dinner, to get the beauty of it hot—
HURRY UP PLEASE ITS TIME
HURRY UP PLEASE ITS TIME
Goonight Bill. Goonight Lou. Goonight May. Goonight.   *170*
Ta ta. Goonight. Goonight.
Good night, ladies, good night, sweet ladies, good night, good
    night.³⁷

III   THE FIRE SERMON ³⁸

The river's ³⁹ tent is broken: the last fingers of leaf
Clutch and sink into the wet bank. The wind
Crosses the brown land, unheard. The nymphs are departed.
Sweet Thames, run softly, till I end my song.⁴⁰
The river bears no empty bottles, sandwich papers,
Silk handkerchiefs, cardboard boxes, cigarette ends
Or other testimony of summer nights. The nymphs are departed.
And their friends, the loitering heirs of city directors;   *180*
Departed, have left no addresses.
By the waters of Leman I sat down and wept ⁴¹ . . .
Sweet Thames, run softly till I end my song,
Sweet Thames, run softly, for I speak not loud or long.
But at my back in a cold blast I hear ⁴²
The rattle of the bones, and chuckle spread from ear to ear.
A rat crept softly through the vegetation

---

³⁵ Pharmacist.
³⁶ Bacon.
³⁷ Cf. Ophelia's farewell in Shakespeare's *Hamlet*, 4, 5, 72.
³⁸ Originally a Buddhist sermon attacking degenerate sexual passions.
³⁹ The Thames.
⁴⁰ The refrain of Edmund Spenser's "Prothalamion," a hymn to marriage. The
"departed nymphs" also alludes to Spenser's poem.
⁴¹ Leman refers to Lake Geneva, where part of Eliot's poem was written. "Leman"
is also a synonym for paramour. The line alludes to the lament of the wandering
Hebrew for Palestine in Psalm 137:1: "By the rivers of Babylon, there we sat down,
yea, we wept, when we remembered Zion."
⁴² Adapted from Andrew Marvell's "To His Coy Mistress," with the lines "But at
my back I always hear/Time's wingèd chariot hurrying near." (Also see line 196.)

Dragging its slimy belly on the bank
While I was fishing in the dull canal
On a winter evening round behind the gashouse   190
Musing upon the king my brother's wreck [43]
And on the king my father's death before him.
White bodies naked on the low damp ground
And bones cast in a little low dry garret,
Rattled by the rat's foot only, year to year.
But at my back from time to time I hear
The sound of horns and motors, which shall bring
Sweeney to Mrs. Porter in the spring.[44]
O the moon shone bright on Mrs. Porter
And on her daughter   200
They wash their feet in soda water
Et O ces voix d'enfants, chantant dans la coupole! [45]

    Twit twit twit
Jug jug jug jug jug jug
So rudely forc'd
Tereu [46]

    Unreal City
Under the brown fog of a winter noon
Mr. Eugenides, the Smyrna [47] merchant
Unshaven, with a pocket full of currants   210
C.i.f. London: documents as sight,
Asked me in demotic [48] French
To luncheon at the Cannon Street Hotel [49]
Followed by a weekend at the Metropole.[50]

    At the violet hour, when the eyes and back
Turn upward from the desk, when the human engine waits

[43] Cf. *The Tempest*, 1, 2. Au. Refers to lines 389 to 391, spoken by Ferdinand: "Sitting on a bank,/Weeping again the king my father's wreck/This music crept by me upon the waters,. . . ."

[44] Eliot adapts John Day's (1574–1640) poem about Actaeon; while hunting, he observed Diana, the goddess of chastity, bathing naked. For his offense, Actaeon was changed into a stag and hunted down by his own dogs.

[45] "And O those voices of children singing in the chapel!" In Verlaine's poem *Parsifal*, the hero restrains his sexual desires to maintain the requisite purity of the Grail quester.

[46] The nightingale ("jug"), Philomela ("So rudely forc'd"), and Tereus ("Tereu") are invoked again.

[47] Turkish port where Syrian and Phoenician merchants traded.

[48] Colloquial.

[49] A hotel in London.

[50] A resort hotel in Brighton.

Like a taxi throbbing waiting,
I Tiresias,[51] though blind, throbbing between two lives,
Old man with wrinkled female breasts, can see
At the violet hour, the evening hour that strives   220
Homeward, and brings the sailor home from sea,[52]
The typist home at teatime, clears her breakfast, lights
Her stove, and lays out food in tins.
Out of the window perilously spread
Her drying combinations touched by the sun's last rays,
On the divan are piled (at night her bed)
Stockings, slippers, camisoles, and stays.
I Tiresias, old man with wrinkled dugs
Perceived the scene, and foretold the rest—
I too awaited the expected guest.   230
He, the young man carbuncular, arrives,
A small house agent's clerk, with one bold stare,
One of the low on whom assurance sits
As a silk hat on a Bradford [53] millionaire.
The time is now propitious, as he guesses,
The meal is ended, she is bored and tired,
Endeavours to engage her in caresses
Which still are unreproved, if undesired.
Flushed and decided, he assaults at once;

[51] Tiresias is the blind prophet in Sophocles' *Oedipus Rex* who reveals why the gods made Thebes into a wasteland. The passage quoted in Eliot's notes from Ovid's *Metamorphoses*, 3, 322ff, is translated by the Loeb Classical Library as: "It chanced that Jove (as the story goes), while warmed with wine, put care aside and bandied good-humored jests with Juno in an idle hour. 'I maintain,' said he, 'that your pleasure in love is greater than that which we [men] enjoy.' She held the opposite view. And so they decided to ask the judgement of the wise Tiresias. He knew both sides of love. For once, with a blow of his staff, he had outraged two huge serpents mating in the green forest; and, wonderful to relate, from man he was changed into a woman, and in that form spent seven years. In the eighth year he saw the same serpents again and said: 'Since in striking you there is such magic power as to change the nature of the giver of the blow, now I will strike you once again.' So saying, he struck the serpents, and his former state was restored, and he became as he had been born. He therefore, being asked to arbitrate the playful dispute of the gods, took sides with Jove. Saturnia [Juno] they say, grieved more deeply than she should and than issue warranted, and condemned the arbitrator to perpetual blindness. But the Almighty Father (for no god may undo what another god has done) in return for his loss of sight gave Tiresias the power to know the future, lightening the penalty by the honor."

[52] Sappho's poem, to which Eliot alludes, addresses the evening star, which guides all men homeward.

[53] A manufacturing town in England.

Exploring hands encounter no defence;   240
His vanity requires no response,
And makes a welcome of indifference.
(And I Tiresias have foresuffered all
Enacted on this same divan or bed;
I who have sat by Thebes below the wall
And walked among the lowest of the dead.)
Bestows one final patronising kiss,
And gropes his way, finding the stairs unlit . . .

   She turns and looks a moment in the glass,
Hardly aware of her departed lover;   250
Her brain allows one half-formed thought to pass:
"Well now that's done: and I'm glad it's over."
When lovely woman stoops to folly and
Paces about her room again, alone,
She smoothes her hair with automatic hand,
And puts a record on the gramophone.[54]

   "This music crept by me upon the waters" [55]
And along the Strand, up Queen Victoria Street.
O City city, I can sometimes hear
Beside a public bar in Lower Thames Street,   260
The pleasant whining of a mandoline
And a clatter and a chatter from within
Where fishmen lounge at noon: where the walls
Of Magnus Martyr hold
Inexplicable splendour of Ionian white and gold.

      The river sweats [56]
   Oil and tar
   The barges drift
   With the turning tide
   Red sails   270
   Wide
   To leeward, swing on the heavy spar.
   The barges wash

[54] Adapted from the lines sung by Olivia in the novel, *The Vicar of Wakefield*, by
Oliver Goldsmith (1728–1774): "When lovely woman stoops to folly/And finds too
late that men betray/What charm can soothe her melancholy,/What art can wash
her guilt away?/The only art her guilt to cover,/To hide her shame from every
eye,/To give repentance to her lover/And wring his bosom—is to die."
[55] Ferdinand's description of Ariel's music in *The Tempest*.
[56] Eliot's "Thames-daughters" are an ironic contrast to the "Rhine-daughters" of
Wagner's *Die Götterdämmerung*. The Rhine-daughters grieve for the loss of their
gold and the consequent ruin of the river.

Drifting logs
Down Greenwich reach
Past the Isle of Dogs.[57]
     Weialala leia
     Wallala leialala [58]

     Elizabeth and Leicester [59]
Beating oars   280
The stern was formed
A gilded shell
Red and gold
The brisk swell
Rippled both shores
Southwest wind
Carried down stream
The peal of bells
White towers
     Weialala leia   290
     Wallala leialala

    "Trams and dusty trees.
Highbury bore me. Richmond and Kew
Undid me.[60] By Richmond I raised my knees
Supine on the floor of a narrow canoe."

    "My feet are at Moorgate,[61] and my heart
Under my feet. After the event
He wept. He promised 'a new start.'
I made no comment. What should I resent?"

    "On Margate Sands.[62]   300
I can connect
Nothing with nothing.
The broken fingernails of dirty hands.
My people humble people who expect
Nothing."
     la la

[57] A peninsula on the Thames.
[58] Cf. Wagner's *Das Rheingold*.
[59] Refers to the love of Queen Elizabeth and Sir Robert Dudley, the Earl of Leicester.
[60] Alludes to the fate of La Pia of Siena who was murdered by her husband in Maremma: "Siena made me, Maremma undid me." Highbury, Richmond, and Kew are sections of London.
[61] A section of London.
[62] A seaside resort in Kent.

    To Carthage then I came [63]

    Burning burning burning burning [64]
O Lord Thou pluckest me out
O Lord Thou pluckest   310

burning

IV   DEATH BY WATER [65]

Phlebas the Phoenician, a fortnight dead,
Forgot the cry of gulls, and the deep sea swell
And the profit and loss.
        A current under sea
Picked his bones in whispers. As he rose and fell
He passed the stages of his age and youth
Entering the whirlpool.
        Gentile or Jew
O you who turn the wheel and look to windward,   320
Consider Phlebas, who was once handsome and tall as you.

V   WHAT THE THUNDER SAID [66]

After the torchlight red on sweaty faces
After the frosty silence in the gardens
After the agony in stony places
The shouting and the crying
Prison and palace and reverberation
Of thunder of spring over distant mountains
He who was living is now dead [67]
We who were living are now dying
With a little patience   330

    Here is no water but only rock
Rock and no water and the sandy road

[63] This section of Augustine's *Confessions*, at the beginning of book 3, describes
Augustine's lustful feelings subsuming his love of God.
[64] The Buddhist Fire Sermon to which Eliot refers in his note asserts that the
things of this world are all "on fire" because they depend on impressions of the
eye. See also the Sermon on the Mount, *Matthew*, 5ff.
[65] A sacrificial drowning of the kind Jessie Weston describes, where the ritual
drowning of the head of Adonis is a prelude to his resurrection.
[66] A conflation of the figure of Christ and the drowned fertility god.
[67] The myth of the Fisher King merges with Christ's Passion and Christ's trial. The
period depicts the despair and spiritual dryness before resurrection.

The road winding above among the mountains
Which are mountains of rock without water
If there were water we should stop and drink
Amongst the rock one cannot stop or think
Sweat is dry and feet are in the sand
If there were only water amongst the rock
Dead mountain mouth of carious teeth that cannot spit
Here one can neither stand nor lie nor sit   340
There is not even silence in the mountains
But dry sterile thunder without rain
There is not even solitude in the mountains
But red sullen faces sneer and snarl
From doors of mudcracked houses
       If there were water
   And no rock
   If there were rock
   And also water
   And water   350
   A spring
   A pool among the rock
   If there were the sound of water only
   Not the cicada [68]
   And dry grass singing
   But sound of water over a rock
   Where the hermit-thrush sings in the pine trees
   Drip drop drip drop drop drop drop
   But there is no water

   Who is the third who walks always beside you? [69]   360
When I count, there are only you and I together
But when I look ahead up the white road
There is always another one walking beside you
Gliding wrapt in a brown mantle, hooded
I do not know whether a man or a woman
—But who is that on the other side of you?

   What is that sound high in the air
Murmur of maternal lamentation
Who are those hooded hordes swarming
Over endless plains, stumbling in cracked earth   370
Ringed by the flat horizon only
What is the city over the mountains

---

[68] Perhaps refers to Ecclesiastes: ". . . the grasshopper shall be a burden, and desire
shall fail."
[69] Cf. the journey to Emmaus, when Jesus walks beside his followers, unknown to
them (Luke 24:13ff).

Cracks and reforms and bursts in the violet air
Falling towers
Jerusalem Athens Alexandria
Vienna London
Unreal

    A woman drew her long black hair out tight
And fiddled whisper music on those strings
And bats with baby faces in the violet light   380
Whistled, and beat their wings
And crawled head downward down a blackened wall
And upside down in air were towers
Tolling reminiscent bells, that kept the hours
And voices singing out of empty cisterns and exhausted wells.

    In this decayed hole among the mountains
In the faint moonlight, the grass is singing
Over the tumbled graves, about the chapel
There is the empty chapel,[70] only the wind's home.
It has no windows, and the door swings,   390
Dry bones can harm no one.
Only a cock stood on the rooftree
Co co rico co co rico [71]
In a flash of lightning. Then a damp gust
Bringing rain

    Ganga [72] was sunken, and the limp leaves
Waited for rain, while the black clouds
Gathered far distant, over Himavant.[73]
The jungle crouched, humped in silence.
Then spoke the thunder   400
DA
Datta: what have we given? [74]
My friend, blood shaking my heart
The awful daring of a moment's surrender

---

[70] Refers to the Chapel Perilous, in which the adventurous knight is tested for faith and humility. The emptiness of the chapel is part of the trial.

[71] The cock's crowing, as in *Hamlet*, 1, 1, 57ff, indicates that evil spirits are returning to the depths; more specifically, perhaps, the reference is to the cock's cry announcing dawn and resurrection in Jesus' prediction of His betrayal (see Matt. 26:34 and Mark 14:30).

[72] The sacred river Ganges.

[73] A Himalayan mountain peak.

[74] The fable to which Eliot's note refers, tells of the answer which the father of gods, men, and demons gave to his creations. The answer was *Da*, which the three groups respectively interpreted as *Datta* (give), *Dayadhvam* (sympathize), and *Damyata* (control). This is "what the thunder [the divine creator] said."

Which an age of prudence can never retract
By this, and this only, we have existed
Which is not to be found in our obituaries
Or in memories draped by the beneficent spider
Or under seals broken by the lean solicitor
In our empty rooms   410
Da
Dayadhvam: I have heard the key [75]
Turn in the door once and turn once only
We think of the key, each in his prison
Thinking of the key, each confirms a prison
Only at nightfall, aethereal rumors
Revive for a moment a broken Coriolanus [76]
Da
Damyata: The boat responded   420
Gaily, to the hand expert with sail and oar
The sea was calm, your heart would have responded
Gaily, when invited, beating obedient
To controlling hands

      I sat upon the shore
Fishing, with the arid plain behind me
Shall I at least set my lands in order?
London Bridge is falling down falling down falling down
Poi s'ascose nel foco che gli affina [77]
Quando fiam uti chelidon [78]—O swallow swallow [79]   430
Le Prince d'Aquitaine à la tour abolie [80]

[75] Eliot's reference to the *Inferno* is to the section where Ugolino, traitor to his city, remembers hearing the turn of the key which imprisoned him in the tower where he and his children starved to death: "And I heard beneath the door of the dreadful tower being locked up."

[76] Coriolanus also betrayed his city (see Shakespeare's tragedy of that name).

[77] The speaker is Arnaut Daniel, great troubadour: " 'Now I pray you, by the virtue that leads you to the summit of these stairs, at times be mindful of my pain.' Then he hid himself in the fire that refines them."

[78] "When will I be like the swallow," from an early medieval poem, anonymous, "The Vigil of Venus," which has as its refrain, in Allen Tate's translation, the line: "Tomorrow may loveless, may lover tomorrow make love." The advent of spring and the promise of renewal suggests to the poet the myth of Philomela, Tereus, and Procne.

[79] Swinburne's poem, *Itylus*, is suggested by these words. We are reminded, too, of the bird of consolation that traditionally is said to have hovered over the Cross.

[80] "The Prince of Aquitaine came to the ruined tower." The Tower Struck by Lightning is the most sinister card in the Tarot pack, but the Tower is associated too with that Castle Perilous to which the questing knight must battle his way to demand of the lance and the cup, the male and female principles, their true meaning.

These fragments I have shored against my ruins
Why then Ile fit you. Hieronymo's mad againe.[81]
Datta. Dayadhvam. Damyata.
            Shantih shantih shantih

The Poet's Notes on "The Waste Land"

Not only the title, but the plan and a good deal of the incidental symbolism
of the poem were suggested by Miss Jessie L. Weston's book on the Grail
legend: *From Ritual to Romance* (Cambridge). Indeed, so deeply am I indebted, Miss Weston's book will elucidate the difficulties of the poem much
better than my notes can do; and I recommend it (apart from the great
interest of the book itself) to any who think such elucidation of the poem
worth the trouble. To another work of anthropolgy I am indebted in general,
one which has influenced our generation profoundly; I mean *The Golden
Bough;* I have used especially the two volumes *Adonis, Attis, Osiris.* Anyone
who is acquainted with these works will immediately recognise in the poem
certain references to vegetation ceremonies.

I   THE BURIAL OF THE DEAD

Line 20. Cf. Ezekiel II, i.

23. Cf. Ecclesiastes XII, v.

31. V. Tristan und Isolde, I, verses 5–8.

42. Id. III, verse 24.

46. I am not familiar with the exact constitution of the Tarot pack of
cards, from which I have obviously departed to suit my own convenience.
The Hanged Man, a member of the traditional pack, fits my purpose in two
ways: because he is associated in my mind with the Hanged God of Frazer,
and because I associate him with the hooded figure in the passage of the
disciples to Emmaus in Part V. The Phoenician Sailor and the Merchant
appear later; also the "crowds of people," and Death by Water is executed in
Part IV. The Man with Three Staves (an authentic member of the Tarot
pack) I associate, quite arbitrarily, with the Fisher King himself.

60. Cf. Baudelaire:

"Fourmillante cité, cité pleine de rêves,
"Où le spectre en plein jour raccroche le passant."

63. Cf. Inferno III, 55–57:

                        "si lunga tratta
di gente, ch'io non avrei mai creduto
    che morte tanta n'avesse disfatta."

64. Cf. Inferno IV, 25–27:

---

[81] "Hieronymo's mad againe" is the subtitle of Thomas Kyd's revenge tragedy
(1592–1594) in which Hieronymo's response to being asked to write a play, "Why
then, I'll fit you" (4, 1, 67) embodies the cunning of the betrayed father who
revenges his son's murder through the play he arranges. "Fit" means accommodate.

"Quivi, secondo che per ascoltare,
"non avea pianto, ma' che di sospiri,
"che l'aura eterna facevan tremare."
>68. A phenomenon which I have often noticed.
>74. Cf. the Dirge in Webster's *White Devil*.
>76. V. Baudelaire, Preface to *Fleurs du Mal*.

II A GAME OF CHESS

>77. Cf. *Antony and Cleopatra*, II, ii, 1. 190.
>92. Laquearia. V. *Aeneid*, I, 726:

dependent lychni laquearibus aureis incensi, et noctem flammi funalia
vincunt.
>98. Sylvan scene. V. Milton, *Paradise Lost*, IV, 140.
>99. V. Ovid, *Metamorphoses*, VI, Philomela.
>100. Cf. Part III, l. 204.
>115. Cf. Part III, l. 195.
>118. Cf. Webster: "Is the wind in that door still?"
>126. Cf. Part I, l. 37, 48.
>138. Cf. the game of chess in Middleton's *Women beware Women*.

III THE FIRE SERMON

>176. V. Spenser, *Prothalamion*.
>192. Cf. *The Tempest*, I, ii.
>196. Cf. Marvell, *To His Coy Mistress*.
>197. Cf. Day, *Parliament of Bees*:

"When of the sudden, listening, you shall hear,
"A noise of horns and hunting, which shall bring
"Actaeon to Diana in the spring,
"Where all shall see her naked skin . . ."
>199. I do not know the origin of the ballad from which these lines are taken: it was reported to me from Sydney, Australia.
>202. V. Verlaine, *Parsifal*.
>210. The currants were quoted at a price "carriage and insurance free to London"; and the Bill of Lading etc. were to be handed to the buyer upon payment of the sight draft.
>218. Tiresias, although a mere spectator and not indeed a "character," is yet the most important personage in the poem, uniting all the rest. Just as the one-eyed merchant, seller of currants, melts into the Phoenician Sailor, and the latter is not wholly distinct from Ferdinand Prince of Naples, so all the women are one woman, and the two sexes meet in Tiresias. What Tiresias *sees*, in fact, is the substance of the poem. The whole passage from Ovid is of great anthropological interest:

'. . . Cum Iunone iocos et maior vestra profecto est
Quam, quæ contingit maribus,' dixisse, 'voluptas.'
Illa negat; placuit quæ sit sententia docti

Quaerere Tiresiæ: venus huic erat utraque nota.
Nam duo magnorum viridi cœuntia silva
Corpora serpentum baculi violaverat ictu
Deque viro factus, mirabile, femina septem
Egerat autumnos; octavo rursus eosdem
Vidit et 'est vestræ si tanta potentia plagæ,'
Dixit 'ut auctoris sortem in contraria mutet,
Nunc quoque vos feriam!' percussis anguibus isdem
Forma prior rediit genetivaque venit imago.
Arbiter hic igitur sumptus de lite iocosa
Dicta Iovis firmat; gravius Saturnia iusto
Nec pro materia fertur doluisse suique
Iudicis æterna damnavit lumina nocte,
At pater omnipotens (neque enim licet inrita cuiquam
Facta dei fecisse deo) pro lumine adempto
Scire futura dedit pœnamque levavit honore.

221. This may not appear as exact as Sappho's lines, but I had in mind the "longshore" or "dory" fisherman, who returns at nightfall.

253. V. Goldsmith, the song in *The Vicar of Wakefield*.

257. V. *The Tempest*, as above.

264. The interior of St. Magnus Martyr is to my mind one of the finest among Wren's interiors. See *The Proposed Demolition of Nineteen City Churches*: (P. S. King & Son, Ltd.).

266. The Song of the (three) Thames-daughters begins here. From line 292 to 306 inclusive they speak in turn. V. *Götterdämmerung*, III, i: the Rhine-daughters.

279. V. Froude, *Elizabeth*, Vol. I, ch. iv, letter of De Quadra to Philip of Spain:
"In the afternoon we were in a barge, watching the games on the river. (The queen) was alone with Lord Robert and myself on the poop, when they began to talk nonsense, and went so far that Lord Robert at last said, as I was on the spot there was no reason why they should not be married if the queen pleased."

293. Cf. *Purgatorio*, V, 133:
"Ricorditi di me, che son la Pia;
"Siena mi fe', disfecemi Maremma."

307. V. St. Augustine's *Confessions*: "to Carthage then I came, where a cauldron of unholy loves sang all about mine ears."

308. The complete text of the Buddha's Fire Sermon (which corresponds in importance to the Sermon on the Mount) from which these words are taken, will be found translated in the late Henry Clarke Warren's *Buddhism in Translation* (Harvard Oriental Series). Mr. Warren was one of the great pioneers of Buddhist studies in the Occident.

309. From St. Augustine's *Confessions* again. The collocation of these two representatives of eastern and western asceticism, as the culmination of this part of the poem, is not an accident.

V   WHAT THE THUNDER SAID

In the first part of Part V three themes are employed: the journey to Emmaus, the approach to the Chapel Perilous (see Miss Weston's book) and the present decay of eastern Europe.

357. This is *Turdus aonalaschkæ pallasii*, the hermit-thrush which I have heard in Quebec Province. Chapman says (*Handbook of Birds of Eastern North America*) "it is most at home in secluded woodland and thickety retreats. . . . Its notes are not remarkable for variety or volume, but in purity and sweetness of tone and exquisite modulation they are unequalled." Its "water-dripping song" is justly celebrated.

360. The following lines were stimulated by the account of one of the Antarctic expeditions (I forget which, but I think one of Shackleton's): it was related that the party of explorers, at the extremity of their strength, had the constant delusion that there was *one more member* than could actually be counted.

367–77. Cf. Hermann Hesse, *Blick ins Chaos*: "Schon ist halb Europa, schon ist zumindest der halbe Osten Europas auf dem Wege zum Chaos, fährt betrunken im heiligem Wahn am Abgrund entlang und singt dazu, singt betrunken und hymnisch wie Dmitri Karamasoff sang. Ueber diese Lieder lacht der Bürger beleidigt, der Heilige und Seher hört sie mit Tränen."

402. "Datta, dayadhvam, damyata" (Give, sympathise, control). The fable of the meaning of the Thunder is found in the *Brihadaranyaka—Upanishad*, 5, 1. A translation is found in Deussen's *Sechzig Upanishads des Veda*, p. 489.

408. Cf. Webster, *The White Devil*, V, vi:

> ". . . they'll remarry

Ere the worm pierce your winding-sheet, ere the spider
Make a thin curtain for your epitaphs."

412. Cf. *Inferno*, XXXIII, 46:

"ed io sentii chiavar l'uscio di sotto
all'orribile torre."

Also F. H. Bradley, *Appearance and Reality*, p. 346.

"My external sensations are no less private to myself than are my thoughts or my feelings. In either case my experience falls within my own circle, a circle closed on the outside; and, with all its elements alike, every sphere is opaque to the others which surround it. . . . In brief, regarded as an existence which appears in a soul, the whole world for each is peculiar and private to that soul."

425. V. Weston: *From Ritual to Romance*; chapter on the Fisher King.

428. V. *Purgatorio*, XXVI, 148.

" 'Ara vos prec per aquella valor
'que vos guida al som de l'escalina,
'sovegna vos a temps de ma dolor.'
Poi s'ascose nel foco che gli affina."

429. V. *Pervigilium Veneris*. Cf. Philomela in Parts II and III.
430. V. Gerard de Nerval, Sonnet *El Desdichado*.
432. V. Kyd's *Spanish Tragedy*.
434. Shantih. Repeated as here, a formal ending to an Upanishad. "The Peace which passeth understanding" is our equivalent to this word.

FROM *Four Quartets* (1943)

Burnt Norton [1]

τοῦ λόγου δ'ἐόντος ξυνοῦ ζώουσιν οἱ πολλοί
ὡς ἰδίαν ἔχοντες φρόνησιν.
                              I. p. 77 Fr. 2.

ὁδὸς ἄνω κάτω μία καὶ ὡυτή.
                              I. p. 89. Fr. 60.

Diels: *Die Fragmente der Vorsokratiker* (Herakleitos).[2]

I

Time present and time past
Are both perhaps present in time future,
And time future contained in time past.[3]
If all time is eternally present
All time is unredeemable.[4]
What might have been is an abstraction
Remaining a perpetual possibility
Only in a world of speculation.
What might have been and what has been
Point to one end, which is always present.   10
Footfalls echo in the memory
Down the passage which we did not take
Towards the door we never opened
Into the rose-garden.[5] My words echo

[1] The name of a country house in Gloucestershire, which Eliot visited in 1934, built on the site of an earlier house destroyed by fire in the seventeenth century.
[2] "Even though the word is the common property of all, most people live as if they had a private perception." (I. p. 77. Fr. 2.) "The way up and the way down are one and the same." (I. p. 89. Fr. 60.) These quotations from Heraclitus, the pre-Socratic philosopher (fl. c. 500 B.C.), are taken from H. Diel's text (1934).
[3] Cf. Ecclesiastes, 3:15: "That which is, already has been; that which has to be, already has been; and God seeks what has been driven away."
[4] Cf. Colossians, 4:5, and Ephesians, 5:14–16, on "redeeming the time."
[5] The rose garden is often represented in the Renaissance as a symbol of spiritual purity and as the dwelling place of the Virgin Mary.

Thus, in your mind.
         But to what purpose
Disturbing the dust on a bowl of rose-leaves
I do not know.
         Other echoes
Inhabit the garden. Shall we follow?
Quick, said the bird, find them, find them,
Round the corner. Through the first gate,
Into our first world, shall we follow
The deception of the thrush? Into our first world.
There they were, dignified, invisible,
Moving without pressure, over the dead leaves,
In the autumn heat, through the vibrant air,
And the bird called, in response to
The unheard music [6] hidden in the shrubbery,
And the unseen eyebeam crossed, for the roses
Had the look of flowers that are looked at.
There they were as our guests, accepted and accepting.
So we moved, and they, in a formal pattern,
Along the empty alley, into the box circle,
To look down into the drained pool.
Dry the pool, dry concrete, brown edged,
And the pool was filled with water out of sunlight,
And the lotos rose, quietly, quietly,
The surface glittered out of heart of light, [7]
And they were behind us, reflected in the pool.
Then a cloud passed, and the pool was empty.
Go, said the bird, for the leaves were full of children,
Hidden excitedly, containing laughter.
Go, go, go, said the bird: human kind
Cannot bear very much reality.
Time past and time future
What might have been and what has been
Point to one end, which is always present.

II

Garlic and sapphires in the mud
Clot the bedded axle-tree. [8]

---

[6] Possible allusion to Keats's "Ode to the Grecian Urn": "Heard melodies are sweet, but those unheard/Are sweeter, ..."

[7] Cf. *Paradiso*, 12, 28–9: ". . . from the heart of one of the new lights then came a voice."

[8] Eliot has written that these lines were suggested by Mallarmé's poem "M'introduire dans ton historie" ("To introduce myself into your story"). The line reads, "Tonnerre et rubis aux moyeux," ("Thunder and rubies at the center of the axles,").

The trilling wire in the blood
Sings below inveterate scars
And reconciles forgotten wars.
The dance along the artery
The circulation of the lymph
Are figured in the drift of stars
Ascend to summer in the tree
We move above the moving tree
In light upon the figured leaf
And hear upon the sodden floor   60
Below, the boarhound and the boar
Pursue their pattern as before
But reconciled among the stars.

  At the still point of the turning world. Neither flesh nor fleshless
Neither from nor towards; at the still point, there the dance is,
But neither arrest nor movement. And do not call it fixity,
Where past and future are gathered. Neither movement from nor
  towards,
Neither ascent nor decline. Except for the point, the still point,
There would be no dance, and there is only the dance.
I can only say, *there* we have been: but I cannot say where.   70
And I cannot say, how long, for that is to place it in time.

  The inner freedom from the practical desire,
The release from action and suffering, release from the inner
And the outer compulsion, yet surrounded
By a grace of sense, a white light still and moving,
Erhebung [9] without motion, concentration
Without elimination, both a new world
And the old made explicit, understood
In the completion of its partial ecstasy,
The resolution of its partial horror.   80
Yet the enchainment of past and future
Woven in the weakness of the changing body,
Protects mankind from heaven and damnation
Which flesh cannot endure.
   Time past and time future
Allow but a little consciousness.
To be conscious is not to be in time
But only in time can the moment in the rose-garden,
The moment in the arbour where the rain beat,
The moment in the draughty church at smokefall   90
Be remembered; involved wth past and future.
Only through time time is conquered.

[9] "Rising," or "exaltation."

III

Here is a place of disaffection
Time before and time after
In a dim light: neither daylight
Investing form with lucid stillness
Turning shadow into transient beauty
With slow rotation suggesting permanence
Nor darkness to purify the soul
Emptying the sensual with deprivation   *100*
Cleansing affection from the temporal.
Neither plenitude nor vacancy. Only a flicker
Over the strained time-ridden faces
Distracted from distraction by distraction
Filled with fancies and empty of meaning
Tumid apathy with no concentration
Men and bits of paper, whirled by the cold wind
That blows before and after time,
Wind in and out of unwholesome lungs
Time before and time after.   *110*
Eructation [10] of unhealthy souls
Into the faded air, the torpid
Driven on the wind that sweeps the gloomy hills of London,
Hampstead and Clerkenwell, Campden and Putney,
Highgate, Primrose and Ludgate. Not here
Not here the darkness, in this twittering world.

Descend lower, descend only
Into the world of perpetual solitude,
World not world, but that which is not world,
Internal darkness, deprivation   *120*
And destitution of all property,
Desiccation of the world of sense,
Evacuation of the world of fancy,
Inoperancy of the world of spirit;
This is the one way, and the other
Is the same, not in movement
But abstention from movement; while the world moves
In appetency, on its metalled ways
Of time past and time future.

IV

Time and the bell have buried the day,   *130*
The black cloud carries the sun away.

---

[10] "Belching forth."

Will the sunflower turn to us, will the clematis [11]
Stray down, bend to us; tendril and spray
Clutch and cling?
Chill
Fingers of yew [12] be curled
Down on us? After the kingfisher's wing
Has answered light to light, and is silent, the light is still
At the still point of the turning world.

V

Words move, music moves   140
Only in time; but that which is only living
Can only die. Words, after speech, reach
Into the silence. Only by the form, the pattern,
Can words or music reach
The stillness, as a Chinese jar still
Moves perpetually in its stillness.
Not the stillness of the violin, while the note lasts,
Not that only, but the co-existence,
Or say that the end precedes the beginning,
And the end and the beginning were always there   150
Before the beginning and after the end.
And all is always now. Words strain,
Crack and sometimes break, under the burden,
Under the tension, slip, slide, perish,
Decay with imprecision, will not stay in place,
Will not stay still. Shrieking voices
Scolding, mocking, or merely chattering,
Always assail them. The Word in the desert
Is most attacked by voices of temptation,
The crying shadow in the funeral dance,   160
The loud lament of the disconsolate chimera. [13]

The detail of the pattern is movement,
As in the figure of the ten stairs. [14]
Desire itself is movement
Not in itself desirable;
Love is itself unmoving,

[11] A vine or herb having three leaflets; also called the Virgin's Bower.
[12] Symbolic of death, mourning, and immortality.
[13] A female monster in Greek mythology having a lion's head, a goat's body, and
a serpent's tail; also any illusion or fabrication of the mind.
[14] Cf. St. John of the Cross' description of the Ten Degrees of the Mystical Ladder
of Divine Love.

Only the cause and end of movement,
Timeless, and undesiring
Except in the aspect of time
Caught in the form of limitation
Between un-being and being.
Sudden in a shaft of sunlight
Even while the dust moves
There rises the hidden laughter
Of children in the foliage
Quick now, here, now, always—
Ridiculous the waste sad time
Stretching before and after.

170

CONRAD [POTTER] AIKEN (1889–   )

*Although his parents were of old New England stock, Conrad Aiken
was born in Savannah, Georgia, the first of three sons of a handsome mother and a gifted but unsteady father, a physician. In
1900, after a violent domestic tragedy—the father killed his wife
and then himself—the boy was taken to New Bedford, Massachusetts, to be brought up by a wealthy great-aunt. After his schooling
at Middlesex, in Concord, he entered Harvard, where he wrote
much verse, published frequently in the undergraduate periodicals,
and became class poet. As a senior he was put on probation for
having cut classes for ten days while he devoted himself to a
poetic adaptation of a French short story; in protest, he resigned
from the college and went to Italy. On his return, he married, traveled for a year, and then, on a small legacy, settled in Cambridge to
a life of letters. But he was to have three children and to be married
two more times, and his economic circumstances were by no means
always easy in the following years.*

*After the publication of two eclectically derivative volumes in 1914 and
1916, Aiken published two further volumes,* The Jig of Forslin: A
Symphony *(1916) and* Nocturne of Remembered Spring *(1917). In
the first, the Prufrock-like theme suggests the influence of Eliot,
but it should be observed that formally, as Aiken's first "symphony,"
it anticipates Eliot. In a savage and anonymous review of the second,
Aiken himself recognized the Eliot influence, a powerful force that
he always had to resist. (In his autobiography of 1952,* Ushant: An
Essay, *Eliot figures prominently as "the Tsetse.") It is possible, and
has been so suggested, that in* The House of Dust: A Symphony
(1920), Aiken in turn provided some suggestions for The Waste
Land, *still two years off. That he had his own voice, his own vision,*

and his own complex music was made clear in The Charnel Rose; Senlin: A Biography; and Other Poems *(1918).*

The First World War was over then. When Aiken had been summoned for service, he refused on the grounds that he was engaged in an essential industry, poetry. He was probably the only American poet who was ever excused from military service on those grounds.

No element of "industry" was evident in the continuing stream of his poetry, although its very profusion might suggest as much: Punch: The Immortal Liar, Documents in His History *(1921),* The Pilgrimage of Festus *(1923),* Priapus and the Pool and Other Poems *(1925),* Prelude *(1929). His* Selected Poems *of 1929 won the Pulitzer Prize, his first considerable public recognition.*

His poetry made increasingly clear his constant interest in psychoanalysis and the problem of identity. And when he turned to the writing of fiction in the 1920s, partly for reasons of economic necessity, this interest became in effect the substructure of his work, highly imaginative and characterized by its constant modulation of themes drawn from the psychically macabre. He published many short stories which were gathered together in three volumes, Bring! Bring! and Other Stories *(1925),* Costumes by Eros *(1928), and* Among the Lost People *(1934). These have been reassembled twice in single volumes of 1950 and 1960. He published, too, five novels, the second and third of which are extraordinary:* Blue Voyage *(1927), in which first appears the autobiographical character called Demarest who was (under the initial D.) to be the narrator of the autobiography,* Ushant; Great Circle *(1933);* King Coffin *(1935);* A Heart for the Gods of Mexico *(1939); and* Conversation: Or, Pilgrim's Progress *(1940).* Great Circle *so interested Sigmund Freud that he offered to analyze the novelist, and while a friend of Aiken's was prepared to pay the fee, Aiken declined, later somewhat to his regret.*

Aiken's other prose is chiefly literary criticism, much of which was written at the suggestion of Marianne Moore when she was editing the Dial. *Such of it as Aiken is interested in retaining was collected in* A Reviewer's ABC *in 1958. Even more neglected than most of his work, this criticism is impressive in its brisk independence, its refusal to be either pedantic or self-serving, its freedom from cultish malice, and its perceptiveness. (It was Aiken, for example, who first was willing to remark publicly about the often pretentious incoherence of Ezra Pound—who, in* Ushant, *appears as "Rabbi Ben Ezra.")*

For much of the 1930s, until the outbreak of the Second World War, Aiken lived at Rye, Sussex, where he and his wife conducted an informal school of writing and painting, limited to six students. For a time, he continued that enterprise at South Dennis, Cape Cod. More recently, he has lived in Brewster, Massachusetts, occasionally in an apartment in New York, and in Savannah, Georgia.

Since the Selected Poems, *twelve more volumes have appeared, including some of the most impressive; these can be found in the* Collected Poems *(1953). Now there are five more volumes, long and short, not including a* Selected Poems *of 1961. The latest word is that a new volume of his stories will be published in England, selected and with an introduction by William Burroughs, the author of* The Naked Lunch. *It is possible and devoutly to be wished that an even freer generation than his own will embark at last on some of those mind-expanding trips that Conrad Aiken offered over many years, but for which he found few takers.*

FURTHER READING

The only full-length critical study of Aiken is by Jay Martin, *Conrad Aiken: A Life of His Art* (1962). Frederick J. Hoffman, *Conrad Aiken* (1962), is a brief pamphlet.

FROM *Priapus and the Pool and Other Poems* (1925)

And in the Hanging Gardens

And in the hanging gardens there is rain
From midnight until one, striking the leaves
And bells of flowers, and stroking boles of planes,
And drawing slow arpeggios over pools,
And stretching strings of sound from eaves to ferns.
The princess reads. The knave of diamonds sleeps.
The king is drunk, and flings a golden goblet
Down from the turret window (curtained with rain)
Into the lilacs.

    And at one o'clock   10
The vulcan under the garden wakes and beats
The gong upon his anvil. Then the rain
Ceases, but gently ceases, dripping still,
And sound of falling water fills the dark
As leaves grow bold and upright, and as eaves
Part with water. The princess turns the page
Beside the candle, and between two braids
Of golden hair. And reads: 'From there I went

Northward a journey of four days, and came
To a wild village in the hills, where none   20
Was living save the vulture and the rat,
And one old man, who laughed, but could not speak.
The roofs were fallen in; the well grown over
With weed; and it was there my father died.
Then eight days further, bearing slightly west,
The cold wind blowing sand against our faces,
The food tasting of sand. And as we stood
By the dry rock that marks the highest point
My brother said: "Not too late is it yet
To turn, remembering home." And we were silent   30
Thinking of home.' The princess shuts her eyes
And feels the tears forming beneath her eyelids
And opens them, and tears fall on the page.
The knave of diamonds in the darkened room
Throws off his covers, sleeps, and snores again.
The king goes slowly down the turret stairs
To find the goblet.

    And at two o'clock
The vulcan in his smithy underground
Under the hanging gardens, where the drip   40
Of rain among the clematis and ivy
Still falls from sipping flower to purple flower,
Smites twice his anvil, and the murmur comes
Among the roots and vines. The princess reads:
'As I am sick, and cannot write you more,
Nor have not long to live, I give this letter
To him, my brother, who will bear it south
And tell you how I died. Ask how it was,
There in the northern desert, where the grass
Was withered, and the horses, all but one,   50
Perished' . . . The princess drops her golden head
Upon the page between her two white arms
And golden braids. The knave of diamonds wakes
And at his window in the darkened room
Watches the lilacs tossing, where the king
Seeks for the goblet.

    And at three o'clock
The moon inflames the lilac heads, and thrice
The vulcan, in his root-bound smithy, clangs
His anvil; and the sounds creep softly up   60
Among the vines and walls. The moon is round,
Round as a shield above the turret top.
The princess blows her candle out, and weeps

In the pale room, where scent of lilac comes,
Weeping, with hands across her eyelids, thinking
Of withered grass, withered by sandy wind.
The knave of diamonds, in his darkened room,
Holds in his hands a key, and softly steps
Along the corridor, and slides the key
Into the door that guards her. Meanwhile, slowly,   70
The king, with raindrops on his beard and hands,
And dripping sleeves, climbs up the turret stairs,
Holding the goblet upright in one hand;
And pauses on the midmost step, to taste
One drop of wine, wherewith wild rain has mixed.

The Wedding

At noon, Tithonus,[1] withered by his singing,
Climbing the oatstalk with his hairy legs,
Met grey Arachne, poisoned and shrunk down
By her own beauty; pride had shrivelled both.
In the white web—where seven flies hung wrapped—
She heard his footsteps; hurried to him; bound him;
Enshrouded him in silk; then poisoned him.
Twice shrieked Tithonus, feebly; then was still.
Arachne loved him. Did he love Arachne?
She watched him with red eyes, venomous sparks,   10
And the furred claws outspread . . . 'O sweet Tithonus!
Darling! Be kind, and sing that song again!
Are you much poisoned? sleeping? do you dream?
Shake the bright web again with that deep fiddling!
Darling Tithonus!'

    And Tithonus, weakly
Moving one hairy shin against the other
Within the silken sack, contrived to fiddle

---

[1] Tithonus, as mentioned by Ovid in *The Metamorphoses*, was a mortal for whom
Aurora obtained the gift of immortality. But, since the goddess of dawn had forgotten to request eternal youth as well for him, he shriveled with age and was
eventually turned into a grasshopper. The mortal woman Arachne, whose story is
recounted by Ovid, proudly claimed that her weaving was superior to the goddess
Minerva's. In the ensuing contest both did equally exquisite work, and Minerva, in
her jealousy, destroyed Arachne's work. When Arachne hanged herself in fury and
humiliation, Minerva relented and changed her into a spider with a talent for
weaving. This poem conflates these two metamorphoses.

A little tune, half-hearted: 'Shrewd Arachne!
Whom pride in beauty withered to this shape   20
As pride in singing shrivelled me to mine—
Unwrap me, let me go—and let me limp,
With what poor strength your venom leaves me, down
This oatstalk, and away.'

    Arachne, angry,
Stung him again, twirling him with rough paws,
The red eyes keen. 'What! You would dare to leave me?
Unkind Tithonus! Sooner I'll kill and eat you
Than let you go. But sing that tune again—
So plaintive was it!'   30

    And Tithonus faintly
Moved the poor fiddles, which were growing cold,
And sang: 'Arachne, goddess envied of gods,
Beauty's eclipse eclipsed by angry beauty,
Have pity, do not ask the withered heart
To sing too long for you! My strength goes out,
Too late we meet for love. O be content
With friendship, which the noon sun once may kindle
To give one flash of passion, like a dewdrop,
Before it goes! . . . Be reasonable,—Arachne!'   40

Arachne heard the song grow weaker, dwindle
To first a rustle, and then half a rustle,
And last a tick, so small no ear could hear it
Save hers, a spider's ear. And her small heart,
(Rusted away, like his, to a pinch of dust,)
Gleamed once, like his, and died. She clasped him tightly
And sunk her fangs in him. Tithonus dead,
She slept awhile, her last sensation gone;
Woke from the nap, forgetting him; and ate him.

Tetélestai [1]

I

How shall we praise the magnificence of the dead,
The great man humbled, the haughty brought to dust?
Is there a horn we should not blow as proudly
For the meanest of us all, who creeps his days,
Guarding his heart from blows, to die obscurely?
I am no king, have laid no kingdoms waste,
Taken no princes captive, led no triumphs,
Of weeping women through long walls of trumpets;
Say rather, I am no one, or an atom;
Say rather, two great gods, in a vault of starlight,   10
Play ponderingly at chess, and at the game's end
One of the pieces, shaken, falls to the floor
And runs to the darkest corner; and that piece
Forgotten there, left motionless, is I . . .
Say that I have no name, no gifts, no power,
Am only one of millions, mostly silent;
One who came with eyes and hands and a heart,
Looked on beauty, and loved it, and then left it.
Say that the fates of time and space obscured me,
Led me a thousand ways to pain, bemused me,   20
Wrapped me in ugliness; and like great spiders
Dispatched me at their leisure . . . Well, what then?
Should I not hear; as I lie down in dust,
The horns of glory blowing above my burial?

II

Morning and evening opened and closed above me:
Houses were built above me; trees let fall
Yellowing leaves upon me, hands of ghosts;
Rain has showered its arrows of silver upon me
Seeking my heart; winds have roared and tossed me;
Music in long blue waves of sound has borne me   30
A helpless weed to shores of unthought silence;
Time, above me, within me, crashed its gongs
Of terrible warning, sifting the dust of death;
And here I lie. Blow now your horns of glory

[1] "To have been finished;" from John 19:30: "When Jesus therefore had received
the vinegar, he said, It is finished; and he bowed his head, and gave up the
ghost."

Harshly over my flesh, you trees, you waters!
You stars and suns, Canopus, Deneb, Rigel,[2]
Let me, as I lie down, here in this dust,
Hear far off, your whispered salutation!
Roar now above my decaying flesh, you winds,
Whirl out your earth-scents over this body, tell me   40
Of ferns and stagnant pools, wild roses, hillsides!
Anoint me, rain, let crash your silver arrows
On this hard flesh! I am the one who named you,
I lived in you, and now I die in you.
I your son, your daughter, treader of music,
Lie broken, conquered . . . Let me not fall in silence.

III

I, the restless one; the circler of circles;
Herdsman and roper of stars, who could not capture
The secret of self; I who was tyrant to weaklings,
Striker of children; destroyer of women; corrupter   50
Of innocent dreamers, and laughter at beauty; I,
Too easily brought to tears and weakness by music,
Baffled and broken by love, the helpless beholder
Of the war in my heart of desire with desire, the struggle
Of hatred with love, terror with hunger; I
Who laughed without knowing the cause of my laughter, who grew
Without wishing to grow, a servant to my own body;
Loved without reason the laughter and flesh of a woman,
Enduring such torments to find her! I who at last
Grow weaker, struggle more feebly, relent in my purpose,   60
Choose for my triumph an easier end, look backward
At earlier conquests; or, caught in the web, cry out
In a sudden and empty despair, 'Tetélestai!'
Pity me, now! I, who was arrogant, beg you!
Tell me, as I lie down, that I was courageous.
Blow horns of victory now, as I reel and am vanquished.
Shatter the sky with trumpets above my grave.

IV

. . . Look! this flesh how it crumbles to dust and is blown!
These bones, how they grind in the granite of frost and are nothing!
This skull, how it yawns for a flicker of time in the darkness,   70

[2] Canopus is a star in the constellation Carina; Deneb is a star in the constellation Cyngnus; Rigel is a star in the constellation Orion.

Yet laughs not and sees not! It is crushed by a hammer of sunlight,
And the hands are destroyed . . . Press down through the leaves of the
   jasmine,
Dig through the interlaced roots—nevermore will you find me;
I was no better than dust, yet you cannot replace me . . .
Take the soft dust in your hand—does it stir: does it sing?
Has it lips and a heart? Does it open its eyes to the sun?
Does it run, does it dream, does it burn with a secret, or tremble
In terror of death? Or ache with tremendous decisions? . . .
Listen! . . . It says: 'I lean by the river. The willows
Are yellowed with bud. White clouds roar up from the south   80
And darken the ripples; but they cannot darken my heart,
Nor the face like a star in my heart . . . Rain falls on the water
And pelts it, and rings it with silver. The willow trees glisten,
The sparrows chirp under the eaves; but the face in my heart
Is a secret of music . . . I wait in the rain and am silent.'
Listen again! . . . It says: 'I have worked, I am tired,
The pencil dulls in my hand: I see through the window
Walls upon walls of windows with faces behind them,
Smoke floating up to the sky, an ascension of sea-gulls.
I am tired. I have struggled in vain, my decision was fruitless,   90
Why then do I wait? with darkness, so easy, at hand! . . .
But tomorrow, perhaps . . . I will wait and endure till tomorrow!' . . .
Or again: 'It is dark. The decision is made. I am vanquished
By terror of life. The walls mount slowly about me
In coldness. I had not the courage. I was forsaken.
I cried out, was answered by silence . . . Tetélestai! . . .'

V

Hear how it babbles!—Blow the dust out of your hand,
With its voices and visions, tread on it, forget it, turn homeward
With dreams in your brain . . . This, then, is the humble, the name-
   less,—
The lover, the husband and father, the struggler with shadows,   100
The one who went down under shoutings of chaos, the weakling
Who cried his 'forsaken!' like Christ on the darkening hilltop! . . .
This, then, is the one who implores, as he dwindles to silence,
A fanfare of glory . . . And which of us dares to deny him?

FROM **Selected Poems** *(1961)*

Another Lycidas [1]

I

Yet once more in the empty room review
the photomatic photo on the table
which years have faded but from which
still behind owlish glasses stubborn eyes
under an ancient hatbrim fix your own.
    Which nevertheless are his
since it is at a camera that he gazes
there in the railway station, his own image
rounded in a lens in a curtained cubicle
while outside, along an echoing concourse,   *10*
passengers hurry for trains and trains depart
    and overhead
the silent clock the electric clock
    sans tick *sans* tock
who after two martinis waits   *20*
with quivering hands pricks off another second
advancing for his life a last October.
    Yet once more view
the silent face whose fierce regard for you
follows you like a conscience: stubborn, sober,
and thus kills time till the opening of the gates.
What train it is he waits for we well know.
Leaving behind the evening suburbs it will go
south to the Islands and the pinewood Cape
where he was born, and grew, and knew
as if it were a legend learned by heart
each name each house each village, that ancient land
familiar to him as his face, the land
whence came with the ancestral name
inheritance of those steadfast eyes, the hand   *30*
salt-stung salt-harsh that for his forebears threw
the barbed harpoon or turned the wheel to windward
and kept it by the compass true.

II

Bequeathing us this gimcrack photo
as he himself would say *pictore ignoto* [2]

---

[1] "Lycidas," John Milton's pastoral elegy (1637) written in memory of a schoolmate who drowned.
[2] "Painter unknown."

for contemplation now that he is dead
bequeathing it by accident and not intent
yet speaking to us still and of that day:
what else would he have said or what else say?
  The massive head   40
and proud mustachios are not in his regard
and it is not at these he stares
who midway in his life no longer cares
(nel mezzo del cammin di nostra vita) [3]
for vanity of self: what there he sees
and with his vision frees
beyond the Islands and the ancestral seas
and the hall bedroom the humble furnished room
in which he lived until he died:
  beyond all these   50
is what he sees he has himself become
and, with him, us: and further still
what, out of yeoman courage, country skill,
the ploughshare patience, the seafarer's will,
has come, as for the sailor homeward bound,
a change of course.
  Profound:
and yet not so, since simple must to complex grow.
And he who as a boy trapped muskrats in the creek
or through snow-stippled poverty-grass 60
tramped to the ringing pond to fish through ice
or rolled the barrel in, to salt the pork,
or sawed and split the pine and oak
in the pale sweetgrass by the cedar swamp
under a harvest moon that rose again
to silhouette the weathervane
above the meetinghouse: and who would say
year after year when he returned
the 'frost is on the punkin',' or 'I know
clam chowders on the backs of kitchen stoves 70
that have been there for nigh a hundred years':
  or in the slate-cold churchyard,
where now unmarked he lies, point out the stone
on which appear these words alone:
'The Chinese woman, name unknown': then tell
her story, and a hundred others, which each house
bespoke for him along a mile of elm-tree-shaded road:
  he who from this had grown
and all this wood-lot lore had known
and never had forgotten, nevertheless 80

[3] "In the middle of the journey of our life" (the opening line of Dante's *Inferno*).

with this rich knowledge also took
to Buenos Aires Cadiz and the rest
    and Harvard too
his boyhood's book, the scholar's book,
the book that was his life. This was to be
his change of course. What his forefathers learned
of wisdom, courage, skill, on land or sea,
rounding the whalespout horn, or in a summer's 'tempest,'
or 'burning off' in spring or sanding down a bog
or making the strict entries in a log   *90*
beneath the swinging lamp, in a clear script
the latitude and longitude: this now would change
and the sea-change reverse. Chapter and verse
replace the log, and ripened scholarship
the island packet and the blue-water ship.

III

Humility was in that furnished room
as in the furnished room that was his mind.
The glass of sharpened pencils on the table
the pencil-sharpener on the windowsill
a row of well-worn books upon a bench   *100*
some Spanish and some French
the page-proofs spread out to be worked upon
a few whodunits and a lexicon
    in a top drawer
a flask of bourbon or the full-ripened corn
for those who *might* be to the manner born
    behind a curtain
the neatly folded clothes on hangers hung
an old guitar somewhat unstrung
and in its leather case upon the shelf   *110*
the top hat now no longer worn
    tarnished for certain
but much used in more prosperous days.
    An 'aluminum' kettle
sat in the corner behind his chair, for tea,
    beside it a red apple.
And the tea-leaves went down the W.C.

    Evening, by the Esplanade.[4]

---

[4] This and the following lines mention many Boston places, bars, restaurants, a famous burlesque house, and some people (Walter Piston, 1894–   , the Harvard composer; John [Brooks] Wheelwright, 1897–1940, Boston poet) familiar to the poet and his subject.

Sunset brindles the bridge, the evening star
pierces the cirrus over Chestnut Hill   120
    and we are still
asking the twilight question. Where shall it be:
tonight, tonight again, where shall it be?
    Down 'Mulberry' Street
beckon the streetlights, and our feet
    through rain or snow or sleet
once more in unison to eastward turn
not to Priapus Garden or to view
what the 'poast' says is 'plaid' today
    but if burlesque be on   130
to the Old Howard, or the Tam or Nip
the Oyster House or Silver Dollar Bar
then to the Athens, there once more to meet
with Piston's whole-tone wit or Wheelwright's neat
while martinis flow and clams are sweet
and he himself our morning star
until Apollo's taxi ploughs the dawn.

    Who would not mourn
for such a Lycidas? He did not know
himself to sing or build the lofty rhyme [5]   140
or so he would himself have said: and yet
this was not true: for in him grew
the poet's vision like a tree of light
    and leaves of light
were in him as the gift of tongues
    and he was of those few
who, as he heard, reshaped the Word,
and made the poem or the music true:
and he was generous with what he knew.
    Lightly, lightly, November,   150
the third unknown by him, with sunshot gale
from the Great Cove or Follins Pond bring home
the hawk and heron: while we remember
    the untold wealth he took
into the grave with him, the open book
that lies beneath the grass
of all he knew and was:
    composed by him
with calligraphic hand and curious eye
the pencil point unhurried, fine,   160
unfolding still its classic line

[5] Adapted from Milton's "Lycidas," 10–11: "Who would not sing for Lycidas? he
knew/Himself to sing, and build the lofty rhyme."

and waiting still for us to see:
and, at the end, the signet signature, 'G.B.' [6]

Death's but a progress, or so Whitehead [7] says.
The infant dies to childhood the child to boy
the boy to youth the youth to man.
    Try as we can
if we should think to try or makeshift make
    we cannot take
one age into another. Life is a span   170
which like the bridge the link not knowing link
comes to an end in earth as it began.
    We cannot think
end and beginning all at once but only
in the broken beam of light recall
the instant prism in a recession of successions.
And it is only we, the living, who can see
in such another instant of successions
    the span of such a man.

E[DWARD] E[STLIN] CUMMINGS (1894–1962)

*Always known as E. E. Cummings, it is said that he became the lower-
cased e e cummings, presented on his title pages for so long,
through the typographical inadequacy of the press of one of the
small printers who published some of his early poems, and that he
liked it that way—no capital letters, no punctuation, only that
clear, uninsistent and unstopped purity: e e cummings*

*The conceit is charming, with its suggestion of endlessness, infinity.
And perhaps poets born in old, stolid Cambridge, Massachusetts,
late in the last century felt a particular need to assert that kind of
freedom.*

*Edward Estlin was the son of the Reverend Edward Cummings, a
Congregationalist minister and for a time a teacher of English at
Harvard. The younger Cummings had his college education there
and left Cambridge in 1916 to become an ambulance driver in
France, where he was arrested on a technical charge and imprisoned
for a time. This experience became the material that went into his
novellike work of 1922,* The Enormous Room.

---

[6] Gordon Bassett, the subject of this elegy, the poet's lifelong friend, to whom he
dedicated his autobiography, *Ushant* (1952).

[7] Alfred North Whitehead (1861–1947), British philosopher and mathematician,
long a professor at Harvard.

*He returned to New York, then spent several years in France studying
painting, and, after 1924, lived most of the time in New York.
He took himself seriously as a painter and occasionally exhibited,
but his paintings, interestingly enough, are quite conventional in
one postimpressionist style or another. On the other hand, his poetry
from the beginning had seemed as unconventional as the titles that
he gave to his books.*

*Tulips and Chimneys (1923), as a title, does not seem very different
from Robinson Jeffer's Flagons and Apples of eleven years earlier,
but then began the parade of Cummings's shock-intended titles:
& (1925), XLI Poems (1925), is 5 (1926), ViVa (1931), no thanks
(1935), 1/20 (1936), 50 Poems (1940), XAIPE (1950). Collected at
various stages under more conventional titles, the whole body of
this poetry is available in Poems: 1923–1954 (1954). Two further
volumes appeared before and immediately after Cummings's death,
95 Poems (1958) and 73 Poems (1963).*

*The titles of his other works are no less interesting: him (1927), a play,
or as he called it, a "phantasmagoria," in twenty-one scenes that
was produced by the Provincetown Players in 1928; one book that
has no title at all and therefore can only be dated (1930); Eimi
(1933), a diarylike and highly critical account of travels in the
U.S.S.R.; Tom (1935), the libretto for a satirical ballet based on
Uncle Tom's Cabin; CIOPW (1931), an acronym, if it is, meaning
graphic works in charcoal, ink, oil, pencil, and watercolor; Santa
Claus (1946), a morality play presumably not intended for performance; and i: six nonlectures (1953), the Charles Eliot Norton
Lectures delivered at Harvard in the year before.*

*He probably expended more energy than was necessary on blasting the
conventions of typography and the conventional means of communication in general. One knows well enough, from the very substance
of his poems, why he did it. He could not tolerate a society that
more and more tried to deaden and then control the responses of its
members through the slogans and clichés of public relations and
advertising, through the media of mass communication that no
longer respected either language or the individual human being,
and through the stereotypes to which a prevailing commercialism
was reducing human feeling and human relations to some kind of
canned and plastic-packaged product: the world of Marshall Mac-
Luhan, long before that gentleman had made a name for himself
through those very processes. Beneath Cummings's apparently show-
off techniques is a warm lyric poet as well as a chilling ironist who
tries to tell us that we do not have to become the robots the media
want to make of us. Love is still possible (love is imperative) in spite
of all the slick corrupters of it. Kindness and warmth and art and a*

*living language—all these still exist; but even these are more and
more forced into a bristling, militant posture by the opposition. The
typewriter explodes in mingled exasperation and laughter.*

FURTHER READING

The authorized critical biography is by Charles Norman, *The Magic
Maker: E. E. Cummings* (1958, revised 1965). For more biographical information, see *Selected Letters of E. E. Cummings* (1969),
edited by F. W. Dupee and George Stade. Norman Friedman has
written two critical studies, *E. E. Cummings: The Art of His Poetry*
(1960), and *E. E. Cummings: The Growth of a Writer* (1964).
Also of critical interest are Robert E. Wegner, *The Poetry and Prose
of E. E. Cummings* (1965), and Barry Marks, *E. E. Cummings*
(1964).

FROM **Tulips and Chimneys** (1923)

All in green went my love riding

All in green went my love riding
on a great horse of gold
into the silver dawn.

four lean hounds crouched low and smiling
the merry deer ran before.

Fleeter be they than dappled dreams
the swift sweet deer
the red rare deer.

Four red roebuck at a white water
the cruel bugle sang before.   10

Horn at hip went my love riding
riding the echo down
into the silver dawn.

four lean hounds crouched low and smiling
the level meadows ran before.

Softer be they than slippered sleep
the lean lithe deer
the fleet flown deer.

Four fleet does at a gold valley
the famished arrow sang before.   20

Bow at belt went my love riding
riding the mountain down
into the silver dawn.

four lean hounds crouched low and smiling
the sheer peaks ran before.

Paler be they than daunting death
the sleek slim deer
the tall tense deer.

Four tall stags at a green mountain
the lucky hunter sang before.   30

All in green went my love riding
on a great horse of gold
into the silver dawn.

four lean hounds crouched low and smiling
my heart fell dead before.

in Just-

in Just-
spring   when the world is mud-
luscious the little
lame balloonman

whistles   far   and wee

and eddieandbill come
running from marbles and
piracies and it's
spring

when the world is puddle-wonderful   10

the queer
old balloonman whistles
far   and   wee
and bettyandisbel come dancing

from hop-scotch and jump-rope and

it's
spring
and
    the

        goat-footed   20

balloonMan   whistles
far
and
wee

O sweet spontaneous

O sweet spontaneous
earth how often have
the
doting

     fingers of
prurient philosophers pinched
and
poked

thee
, has the naughty thumb   10
of science prodded
thy

    beauty   . how
often have religions taken
thee upon their scraggy knees
squeezing and

buffeting thee that thou mightest conceive
gods
    (but
true   20

to the incomparable
couch of death thy
rhythmic
lover

    thou answerest

them only with

        spring)

Buffalo Bill's

Buffalo Bill's
defunct
     who used to
     ride a watersmooth-silver
               stallion
and break onetwothreefourfive pigeonsjustlikethat
                               Jesus

he was a handsome man
               and what i want to know is
how do you like your blueeyed boy   *10*
Mister Death

the Cambridge ladies
who live in furnished souls

the Cambridge ladies who live in furnished souls
are unbeautiful and have comfortable minds
(also, with the church's protestant blessings
daughters, unscented shapeless spirited)
they believe in Christ and Longfellow, both dead,
are invariably interested in so many things—
at the present writing one still finds
delighted fingers knitting for the is it Poles?
perhaps. While permanent faces coyly bandy
scandal of Mrs. N and Professor D   *10*
. . . . the Cambridge ladies do not care, above
Cambridge if sometimes in its box of
sky lavender and cornerless, the
moon rattles like a fragment of angry candy

FROM **is 5** *(1926)*

POEM, OR BEAUTY HURTS MR. VINAL

take it from me kiddo
believe me
my country, 'tis of

you, land of the Cluett
Shirt Boston Garter and Spearmint
Girl With The Wrigley Eyes(of you

land of the Arrow Ide
and Earl &
Wilson
Collars)of you i   *10*
sing: land of Abraham Lincoln and Lydia E. Pinkham,[1]
land above all of Just Add Hot Water And Serve—
from every B.V.D.

let freedom ring

amen. i do however protest, anent the un
-spontaneous and otherwise scented merde which
greets one(Everywhere Why)as divine poesy per
that and this radically defunct periodical. i would

suggest that certain ideas gestures
rhymes, like Gillette Razor Blades   *20*
having been used and reused
to the mystical moment of dullness emphatically are
Not To Be Resharpened. (Case in point

if we are to believe these gently O sweetly
melancholy trillers amid the thrillers
these crepuscular violinists among my and your
skyscrapers—Helen & Cleopatra were Just Too Lovely,
The Snail's On The Thorn enter Morn and God's
In His andsoforth [2]

do you get me?)according   *30*
to such supposedly indigenous
throstles Art is O World O Life
a formula:example, Turn Your Shirttails Into
Drawers and If It Isn't An Eastman It Isn't A
Kodak therefore my friends let
us now sing each and all fortissimo A-
mer
i

ca, I
love,   *40*
You. And there're a
hun-dred-mil-lion-oth-ers, like
all of you successfully if
delicately gelded(or spaded)
gentlemen(and ladies)—pretty

[1] Famous for nineteenth-century patent medicines for women.
[2] Cf. Pippa's song in Robert Browning's drama *Pippa Passes* (1841), scene 1.

littleliverpill-
hearted-Nujolneeding-There's-A-Reason
americans(who tensetendoned and with
upward vacant eyes, painfully
perpetually crouched, quivering, upon the   50
sternly allotted sandpile
—how silently
emit a tiny violetflavoured nuisance:Odor?

ono.[3]
comes out like a ribbon lies flat on the brush

a man who had fallen among thieves

a man who had fallen among thieves
lay by the roadside on his back
dressed in fifteenthrate ideas
wearing a round jeer for a hat

fate per a somewhat more then less
emancipated evening
had in return for consciousness
endowed him with a changeless grin

whereon a dozen staunch and leal
citizens did graze at pause   10
then fired by hypercivic zeal
sought newer pastures or because

swaddled with a frozen brook
of pinkest vomit out of eyes
which noticed nobody he looked
as if he did not care to rise

one hand did nothing on the vest
its wideflung friend clenched weakly dirt
while the mute trouserfly confessed
a button solemnly inert.   20

Brushing from whom the stiffened puke
i put him all into my arms
and staggered banged with terror through
a million billion trillion stars

[3] Odorono, one of the earliest and most widely advertised of deodorants.

my sweet old etcetera

my sweet old etcetera
aunt lucy during the recent

war could and what
is more did tell you just
what everybody was fighting

for,
my sister
isabel created hundreds
(and
hundreds)of socks not to   10
mention shirts fleaproof earwarmers

etcetera wristers etcetera, my
mother hoped that

i would die etcetera
bravely of course my father used
to become hoarse talking about how it was
a privilege and if only he
could meanwhile my

self etcetera lay quietly
in the deep mud et   20

cetera
(dreaming,
et
  cetera, of
Your smile
eyes knees and of your Etcetera)

FROM **ViVa** *(1931)*

somewhere i have never travelled,gladly beyond

somewhere i have never travelled,gladly beyond
any experience,your eyes have their silence:
in your most frail gesture are things which enclose me,
or which i cannot touch because they are too near

your slightest look easily will unclose me
though i have closed myself as fingers,

you open always petal by petal myself as Spring opens
(touching skilfully,mysteriously)her first rose

or if your wish be to close me,i and
my life will shut very beautifully,suddenly,
as when the heart of this flower imagines
the snow carefully everywhere descending;

nothing which we are to perceive in this world equals
the power of your intense fragility:whose texture
compels me with the colour of its countries,
rendering death and forever with each breathing

(i do not know what it is about you that closes
and opens;only something in me understands
the voice of your eyes is deeper than all roses)
nobody,not even the rain,has such small hands

FROM **50 Poems** *(1940)*

as freedom is a breakfastfood

as freedom is a breakfastfood
or truth can live with right and wrong
or molehills are from mountains made
—long enough and just so long
will being pay the rent of seem
and genius please the talentgang
and water most encourage flame

as hatracks into peachtrees grow
or hopes dance best on bald men's hair
and every finger is a toe
and any courage is a fear
—long enough and just so long
will the impure think all things pure
and hornets wail by children stung

or as the seeing are the blind
and robins never welcome spring
nor flatfolk prove their world is round
nor dingsters die at break of dong
and common's rare and millstones float
—long enough and just so long
tomorrow will not be too late

worms are the words but joy's the voice
down shall go which and up come who
breasts will be breasts thighs will be thighs
deeds cannot dream what dreams can do
—time is a tree(this life one leaf)
but love is the sky and i am for you
just so long and long enough

anyone lived in a pretty how town

anyone lived in a pretty how town
(with up so floating many bells down)
spring summer autumn winter
he sang his didn't he danced his did.

Women and men(both little and small)
cared for anyone not at all
they sowed their isn't they reaped their same
sun moon stars rain

children guessed(but only a few
and down they forgot as up they grew   10
autumn winter spring summer)
that noone loved him more by more

when by now and tree by leaf
she laughed his joy she cried his grief
bird by snow and stir by still
anyone's any was all to her

someones married their everyones
laughed their cryings and did their dance
(sleep wake hope and then)they
said their nevers they slept their dream   20

stars rain sun moon
(and only the snow can begin to explain
how children are apt to forget to remember
with up so floating many bells down)

one day anyone died I guess
(and noone stooped to kiss his face)
busy folk buried them side by side
little by little and was by was

all by all and deep by deep
and more by more they dream their sleep   30

noone and anyone earth by april
wish by spirit and if by yes.

Women and men(both dong and ding)
summer autumn winter spring
reaped their sowing and went their came
sun moon stars rain

my father moved through dooms of love

my father moved through dooms of love
through sames of am through haves of give,
singing each morning out of each night
my father moved through depths of height

this motionless forgetful where
turned at his glance to shining here;
that if(so timid air is firm)
under his eyes would stir and squirm

newly as from unburied which
floats the first who,his april touch
drove sleeping selves to swarm their fates
woke dreamers to their ghostly roots

and should some why completely weep
my father's fingers brought her sleep:
vainly no smallest voice might cry
for he could feel the mountains grow.

Lifting the valleys of the sea
my father moved through griefs of joy;
praising a forehead called the moon
singing desire into begin

joy was his song and joy so pure
a heart of star by him could steer
and pure so now and now so yes
the wrists of twilight would rejoice

keen as midsummer's keen beyond
conceiving mind of sun will stand,
so strictly(over utmost him
so hugely)stood my father's dream

his flesh was flesh his blood was blood:
no hungry man but wished him food;

10

20

30

no cripple wouldn't creep one mile
uphill to only see him smile.

Scorning the pomp of must and shall
my father moved through dooms of feel;
his anger was as right as rain
his pity was as green as grain

septembering arms of year extend
less humbly wealth to foe and friend
than he to foolish and to wise
offered immeasurable is   *40*

proudly and(by octobering flame
beckoned)as earth will downward climb,
so naked for immortal work
his shoulders marched against the dark

his sorrow was as true as bread:
no liar looked him in the head;
if every friend became his foe
he'd laugh and build a world with snow.

My father moved through theys of we,
singing each new leaf out of each tree   *50*
(and every child was sure that spring
danced when she heard my father sing)

then let men kill which cannot share,
let blood and flesh be mud and mire,
scheming imagine,passion willed,
freedom a drug that's bought and sold

giving to steal and cruel kind,
a heart to fear,to doubt a mind,
to differ a disease of same,
conform the pinnacle of am   *60*

though dull were all we taste as bright,
bitter all utterly things sweet,
maggoty minus and dumb death
all we inherit,all bequeath

and nothing quite so least as truth
—i say though hate were why men breathe—
because my father lived his soul
love is the whole and more than all

FROM **1** $\times$ **1** *(1944)*

plato told

plato told

him:he couldn't
believe it(jesus

told him;he
wouldn't believe
it)lao

tsze
certainly told
him,and general
(yes   10

mam)
sherman;
and even
(believe it
or

not)you
told him:i told
him;we told him
(he didn't believe it, no

sir)it took   20
a nipponized bit of
the old sixth

avenue
el;in the top of his head:to tell

him

pity this busy monster,manunkind,

pity this busy monster,manunkind,

not. Progress is a comfortable disease:
your victim(death and life safely beyond)

plays with the bigness of his littleness
—electrons deify one razorblade
into a mountainrange;lenses extend

unwish through curving wherewhen till unwish
returns on its unself.

A world of made

is not a world of born—pity poor flesh   *10*

and trees,poor stars and stones,but never this
fine specimen of hypermagical

ultraomnipotence. We doctors know

a hopeless case if—listen:there's a hell
of a good universe next door;let's go

what if a much of a which of a wind

what if a much of a which of a wind
gives the truth to summer's lie;
bloodies with dizzying leaves the sun
and yanks immortal stars awry?
Blow king to beggar and queen to seem
(blow friend to fiend:blow space to time)
—when skies are hanged and oceans drowned,
the single secret will still be man

what if a keen of a lean wind flays
screaming hills with sleet and snow: *10*
strangles valleys by ropes of thing
and stifles forests in white ago?
Blow hope to terror;blow seeing to blind
(blow pity to envy and soul to mind)
—whose hearts are mountains,roots are trees,
it's they shall cry hello to the spring

what if a dawn of a doom of a dream
bites this universe in two,
peels forever out of his grave
and sprinkles nowhere with me and you?   *20*
Blow soon to never and never to twice
(blow life to isn't:blow death to was)
—all nothing's only our hugest home;
the most who die,the more we live

[HAROLD] HART CRANE (1899–1932)

Hart Crane was one of those unfortunate human beings whose childhood and youth became the battleground for the disastrous conflicts of his parents' marriage. A consultant could have advised them that the effect in him would be an even greater disaster: it took the form of an aggressive and reckless homosexuality in a time when society was somewhat less indulgent of that condition than it is today.

He was born in Ohio, and after several moves his parents settled in Cleveland, where his father, a man of many successful enterprises, became the owner of a large candy manufacturing business. The marriage was characterized by endless quarrels, separations, and temporary reconciliations. The situation was classic: the mother, a Christian Scientist with a certain theatrical talent, dominated the boy and turned him against his father; the father, concerned only with his business affairs and physical satisfactions, in turn had no affection for the boy, who bewildered him. The parents were divorced at last, and at seventeen Hart Crane dropped out of high school and went alone to New York.

He had been writing verses since he was thirteen or fourteen, and one had even found publication in an obscure quarter. Now he was determined to launch out on the life of a poet. His work began to appear regularly in a periodical called The Pagan, *and at the end of 1917 one poem appeared in* The Little Review. *But he also felt compelled to earn a living, and for the next six or seven years he shunted back and forth between New York and Ohio in a miscellany of jobs, chiefly in advertising but also in humiliatingly menial chores for his father. At the same time he managed through his published work to establish himself as a young poet of promise, at least, and perhaps of genius. Often he was unemployed for weeks and months, but at the end of December, 1925, he was rescued from the uncertainties of this mode of life through the generous patronage of Otto Kahn, the famous philanthropist and banker.*

The next two years were of extraordinary creative activity and development. He wrote most of the poems that were to make up his first book, White Buildings (1926), *and, having conceived the grand scheme for* The Bridge *even earlier, he now finished much of its early drafts. He also established warm and creative friendships with many of the most gifted young men of the time—Waldo Frank, Gorham Munson, Allen Tate, Malcolm Cowley, Eugene O'Neill, Matthew Josephson, to name only a few of them—and many darker, destructive relationships, fugitive and anonymous.*

In 1926, too, he spent a long time at his mother's plantation on the Isle of Pines, and there he not only worked on The Bridge, but he wrote most of the poems that, after his death, were to appear under the title Key West: An Island Sheaf. The two years that followed maintained little of this creative surge: they were years of increasingly frenzied desperation, sexual and alcoholic dissipation, and anguished laceration both of self and others. It was only in late 1928, when he broke away for Europe, that his creative life improved again. In Paris, Harry and Caresse Crosby encouraged him to complete The Bridge (many parts of which, having already appeared in periodicals, had aroused a good deal of anticipation for the whole), and that work was to be published both at their Black Sun Press in Paris and by Liveright in New York in 1930.

In 1931 Crane was awarded a Guggenheim Fellowship that took him to Mexico, where he hoped to find the materials for another "epic," this one to be based on Mexican history. He entertained some hope that Peggy Baird, the first wife of Malcolm Cowley and his companion for much of the time there, could rescue his morale, could even rehabilitate him both in a general moral and a specific sexual sense, and there were plans for marriage. But he could not bring himself to write, except for one superb poem, "The Broken Tower." On the passage back to the United States in April of 1932, he leaped from the stern of the ship and drowned.

Whether this tangled life of self-torture is a tragedy depends upon one's definition; that it was one of the saddest losses in our literature is certain.

FURTHER READING

The most recent biography is John Unterecker, Voyager: A Life of Hart Crane (1969). Two older critical and still vital biographies are Philip Horton, Hart Crane (1937, 1957), and Brom Weber, Hart Crane (1948). Full-length critical studies are R. W. B. Lewis, The Poetry of Hart Crane (1967), and Herbert A. Leibowitz, Hart Crane (1968). Briefer introductions are Samuel Hazo, Hart Crane (1963); Vincent G. Quinn, Hart Crane (1963); and Monroe K. Spears, Hart Crane (1965). Brom Weber edited Letters of Hart Crane, 1916–1932 (1952).

FROM **White Buildings** (1926)

Praise for an Urn

In Memoriam: Ernest Nelson[1]

It was a kind and northern face
That mingled in such exile guise
The everlasting eyes of Pierrot
And, of Gargantua, the laughter.

His thoughts, delivered to me
From the white coverlet and pillow,
I see now, were inheritances—
Delicate riders of the storm.

The slant moon on the slanting hill
Once moved us toward presentiments   10
Of what the dead keep, living still,
And such assessments of the soul

As, perched in the crematory lobby,
The insistent clock commented on,
Touching as well upon our praise
Of glories proper to the time.

Still, having in mind gold hair,
I cannot see that broken brow
And miss the dry sound of bees
Stretching across a lucid space.   20

Scatter these well-meant idioms
Into the smoky spring that fills
The suburbs, where they will be lost.
They are no trophies of the sun.

Chaplinesque

We make our meek adjustments,
Contended with such random consolations
As the wind deposits
In slithered and too ample pockets.

[1] A poet and painter, older than Crane; a good friend whose art disintegrated under the pressures of poverty, he died in 1922.

For we can still love the world, who find
A famished kitten on the step, and know
Recesses for it from the fury of the street,
Or warm torn elbow coverts.

We will sidestep, and to the final smirk
Dally the doom of that inevitable thumb   *10*
That slowly chafes its puckered index toward us,
Facing the dull squint with what innocence
And what surprise!

And yet these fine collapses are not lies
More than the pirouettes of any pliant cane;
Our obsequies are, in a way, no enterprise.
We can evade you, and all else but the heart:
What blame to us if the heart live on.

The game enforces smirks; but we have seen
The moon in lonely alleys make   *20*
A grail of laughter of an empty ash can,
And through all sound of gaiety and quest
Have heard a kitten in the wilderness.

Repose of Rivers

The willows carried a slow sound,
A sarabande the wind mowed on the mead.
I could never remember
That seething, steady leveling of the marshes
Till age had brought me to the sea.

Flags, weeds. And remembrance of steep alcoves
Where cypresses shared the noon's
Tyranny; they drew me into hades almost.
And mammoth turtles climbing sulphur dreams
Yielded, while sun-silt rippled them   *10*
Asunder . . .

How much I would have bartered! the black gorge
And all the singular nestings in the hills
Where beavers learn stitch and tooth.
The pond I entered once and quickly fled—
I remember now its singing willow rim.

And finally, in that memory all things nurse;
After the city that I finally passed

With scalding unguents spread and smoking darts
The monsoon cut across the delta   20
At gulf gates . . . There, beyond the dykes

I heard wind flaking sapphire, like this summer,
And willows could not hold more steady sound.

The Wine Menagerie

Invariably when wine redeems the sight,
Narrowing the mustard scansions of the eyes,
A leopard ranging always in the brow
Asserts a vision in the slumbering gaze.

Then glozening decanters that reflect the street
Wear me in crescents on their bellies. Slow
Applause flows into liquid cynosures:
—I am conscripted to their shadows' glow.

Against the imitation onyx wainscoting
(Painted emulsion of snow, eggs, yarn, coal, manure)   10
Regard the forceps of the smile that takes her.
Percussive sweat is spreading to his hair. Mallets,
Her eyes, unmake an instant of the world . . .

What is it in this heap the serpent pries—
Whose skin, facsimile of time, unskeins
Octagon, sapphire transepts round the eyes;
—From whom some whispered carillon assures
Speed to the arrow into feathered skies?

Sharp to the window-pane guile drags a face,
And as the alcove of her jealousy recedes   20
An urchin who has left the snow
Nudges a cannister across the bar
While August meadows somewhere clasp his brow.

Each chamber, transept, coins some squint,
Remorseless line, minting their separate wills—
Poor streaked bodies wreathing up and out,
Unwitting the stigma that each turn repeals:
Between black tusks the roses shine!

New thresholds, new anatomies! Wine talons
Build freedom up about me and distill   30
This competence—to travel in a tear
Sparkling alone, within another's will.

Until my blood dreams a receptive smile
Wherein new purities are snared; where chimes
Before some flame of gaunt repose a shell
Tolled once, perhaps, by every tongue in hell.
—Anguished, the wit that cries out of me:

"Alas,—these frozen billows of your skill!
Invent new dominoes of love and bile . . .
Ruddy, the tooth implicit of the world   40
Has followed you. Though in the end you know
And count some dim inheritance of sand,
How much yet meets the treason of the snow.

"Rise from the dates and crumbs. And walk away,
Stepping over Holofernes' shins—
Beyond the wall, whose severed head floats by
With Baptist John's. Their whispering begins.

"—And fold your exile on your back again;
Petrushka's ¹ valentine pivots on its pin."

At Melville's Tomb

Often beneath the wave, wide from this ledge
The dice of drowned men's bones he saw bequeath
An embassy. Their numbers as he watched,
Beat on the dusty shore and were obscured.

And wrecks passed without sound of bells,
The calyx of death's bounty giving back
A scattered chapter, livid hieroglyph,
The portent wound in corridors of shells.

Then in the circuit calm of one vast coil,
Its lashings charmed and malice reconciled,   10
Frosted eyes there were that lifted altars;
And silent answers crept across the stars.

Compass, quadrant and sextant contrive
No farther tides . . . High in the azure steeps
Monody shall not wake the mariner.
This fabulous shadow only the sea keeps.

¹ The clown-puppet with a human heart, unrequitedly in love, in the ballet of that
name by Stravinsky and Fokine (1911), possibly telescoped with the smelly valet
who likes to drink in Gogol's *Dead Souls* (1842).

Voyages

I

Above the fresh ruffles of the surf
Bright striped urchins flay each other with sand.
They have contrived a conquest for shell shucks,
And their fingers crumble fragments of baked weed
Gaily digging and scattering.

And in answer to their treble interjections
The sun beats lightning on the waves,
The waves fold thunder on the sand;
And could they hear me I would tell them:

O brilliant kids, frisk with your dog,   10
Fondle your shells and sticks, bleached
By time and the elements; but there is a line
You must not cross nor ever trust beyond it
Spry cordage of your bodies to caresses
Too lichen-faithful from too wide a breast.
The bottom of the sea is cruel.

II

And yet this great wink of eternity,
Of rimless floods, unfettered leewardings,
Samite sheeted and processioned where
Her undinal vast belly moonward bends,   20
Laughing the wrapt inflections of our love;

Take this Sea, whose diapason knells
On scrolls of silver snowy sentences,
The sceptred terror of whose sessions rends
As her demeanors motion well or ill,
All but the pieties of lovers' hands.

And onward, as bells off San Salvador
Salute the crocus lustres of the stars,
In these poinsettia meadows of her tides,—
Adagios of islands, O my Prodigal,   30
Complete the dark confessions her veins spell.

Mark how her turning shoulders wind the hours,
And hasten while her penniless rich palms
Pass superscription of bent foam and wave,—
Hasten, while they are true,—sleep, death, desire,
Close round one instant in one floating flower.

Bind us in time, O Seasons clear, and awe.
O minstrel galleons of Carib fire,

Bequeath us to no earthly shore until
Is answered in the vortex of our grave   40
The seal's wide spindrift gaze toward paradise.

FROM ***The Bridge*** *(1930)*

TO BROOKLYN BRIDGE

How many dawns, chill from his rippling rest
The seagull's wings shall dip and pivot him,
Shedding white rings of tumult, building high
Over the chained bay waters Liberty—

Then, with inviolate curve, forsake our eyes
As apparitional as sails that cross
Some page of figures to be filed away;
—Till elevators drop us from our day . . .

I think of cinemas, panoramic sleights
With multitudes bent toward some flashing scene   10
Never disclosed, but hastened to again,
Foretold to other eyes on the same screen;

And Thee, across the harbor, silver-paced
As though the sun took step of thee, yet left
Some motion ever unspent in thy stride,—
Implicitly thy freedom staying thee!

Out of some subway scuttle, cell or loft
A bedlamite speeds to thy parapets,
Tilting there momently, shrill shirt ballooning,
A jest falls from the speechless caravan.   20

Down Wall, from girder into street noon leaks,
A rip-tooth of the sky's acetylene;
All afternoon the cloud-flown derricks turn . . .
Thy cables breathe the North Atlantic still.

And obscure as that heaven of the Jews,
Thy guerdon . . . Accolade thou dost bestow
Of anonymity time cannot raise:
Vibrant reprieve and pardon thou dost show.

O harp and altar, of the fury fused,
(How could mere toil align thy choiring strings!)   30
Terrific threshold of the prophet's pledge,
Prayer of pariah, and the lover's cry,—

Again the traffic lights that skim thy swift
Unfractioned idiom, immaculate sigh of stars,

Beading thy path—condense eternity:
And we have seen night lifted in thine arms.

Under thy shadow by the piers I waited;
Only in darkness is thy shadow clear.
The City's fiery parcels all undone,
Already snow submerges an iron year . . .   40

O Sleepless as the river under thee,
Vaulting the sea, the prairies' dreaming sod,
Unto us lowliest sometime sweep, descend
And of the curveship lend a myth to God.

THE HARBOR DAWN

Insistently through sleep—a tide of voices—
They meet you listening midway in your dream,   *400 years and*
The long, tired sounds, fog-insulated noises: *more . . . or is*
                                                      it from the
Gongs in white surplices, beshrouded wails,   *soundless*
Far strum of fog horns . . . signals dispersed in veils. *shore of sleep*
                                                      that time

And then a truck will lumber past the wharves   50
As winch engines begin throbbing on some deck;
Or a drunken stevedore's howl and thud below
Comes echoing alley-upward through dim snow.

And if they take your sleep away sometimes
They give it back again. Soft sleeves of sound
Attend the darkling harbor, the pillowed bay;
Somewhere out there in blankness steam

Spills into steam, and wanders, washed away
—Flurried by keen fifings, eddied
Among distant chiming buoys—adrift. The sky,   60
Cool feathery fold, suspends, distills
This wavering slumber. . . . Slowly—
Immemorially the window, the half-covered chair,
Ask nothing but this sheath of pallid air.

And you beside me, blessed now while sirens   *recalls you*
Sing to us, stealthily weave us into day—   *to your love,*
                                                     there in a
Serenely now, before day claims our eyes   *waking*
Your cool arms murmurously about me lay.   *dream to*
                                                     merge your
                                                     seed

While myriad snowy hands are clustering at the panes—   70

    your hands within my hands are deeds;
    my tongue upon your throat—singing
    Arms close; eyes wide, undoubtful
      dark

drink the dawn—
a forest shudders in your hair!

The window goes blond slowly. Frostily clears.
From Cyclopean towers across Manhattan waters   *—with whom?*
—Two—three bright window-eyes aglitter, disk
The sun, released—aloft with cold gulls hither.   79

The fog leans one last moment on the sill.   *Who is the*
Under the mistletoe of dreams, a star—   *woman with*
    us in the
As though to join us at some distant hill—   *dawn? . . .*
Turns in the waking west and goes to sleep.   *whose is the*
    flesh our feet
    have moved
    upon?

THE RIVER

Stick your patent name on a signboard
brother—all over—going west—young man   *. . . and past*
    the din and
Tintex—Japalac—Certain-teed Overalls ads   *slogans of*
and lands sakes! under the new playbill ripped   *the year—*
in the guaranteed corner—see Bert Williams what?
Minstrels when you steal a chicken just
save me the wing for if it isn't   90
Erie it ain't for miles around a
Mazda—and the telegraphic night coming on Thomas

a Ediford—and whistling down the tracks
a headlight rushing with the sound—can you
imagine—while an EXPRESS makes time like
SCIENCE—COMMERCE and the HOLYGHOST
RADIO ROARS IN EVERY HOME WE HAVE THE NORTHPOLE
WALLSTREET AND VIRGINBIRTH WITHOUT STONES OR
WIRES OR EVEN RUNning brooks connecting ears
and no more sermons windows flashing roar   100
Breathtaking—as you like it . . . eh?

        So the 20th Century—so
whizzed the Limited—roared by and left
three men, still hungry on the tracks, ploddingly
watching the tail lights wizen and converge, slipping gimleted and neatly out of sight.

The last bear, shot drinking in the Dakotas
Loped under wires that span the mountain stream.
Keen instruments, strung to a vast precision   109
Bind town to town and dream to ticking dream.
    to those
But some men take their liquor slow—and count   *whose*
—Though they'll confess no rosary nor clue—   *addresses are*
The river's minute by the far brook's year.   *never near*

Under a world of whistles, wires and steam
Caboose-like they go ruminating through
Ohio, Indiana—blind baggage—
To Cheyenne tagging . . . Maybe Kalamazoo.

Time's rendings, time's blendings they construe
As final reckonings of fire and snow;
Strange bird-wit, like the elemental gist   120
Of unwalled winds they offer, singing low
My Old Kentucky Home and *Casey Jones*,
Some Sunny Day. I heard a road-gang chanting so.
And afterwards, who had a colt's eyes—one said,
"Jesus! Oh I remember watermelon days!" And sped
High in a cloud of merriment, recalled
"—And when my Aunt Sally Simpson smiled," he drawled—
"It was almost Lousiana, long ago."

"There's no place like Booneville though, Buddy,"
One said, excising a last burr from his vest,   130
"—For early trouting." Then peering in the can,
"—But I kept on the tracks." Possessed, resigned,
He trod the fire down pensively and grinned,
Spreading dry shingles of a beard. . . .

                              Behind
My father's cannery works I used to see
Rail-squatters ranged in nomad raillery,
The ancient men—wifeless or runaway
Hobo-trekkers that forever search
An empire wilderness of freight and rails.   140
Each seemed a child, like me, on a loose perch,
Holding to childhood like some termless play.
John, Jake or Charley, hopping the slow freight
—Memphis to Tallahassee—riding the rods,
Blind fists of nothing, humpty-dumpty clods.

Yet they touch something like a key perhaps.
From pole to pole across the hills, the states
—They know a body under the wide rain;
Youngsters with eyes like fjords, old reprobates
With racetrack jargon,—dotting immensity   150
They lurk across her, knowing her yonder breast
Snow-silvered, sumac-stained or smoky blue—
Is past the valley-sleepers, south or west.
—As I have trod the rumorous midnights, too,

And past the circuit of the lamp's thin flame
(O Nights that brought me to her body bare!)

Have dreamed beyond the print that bound her name
Trains sounding the long blizzards out—I heard
Wail into distances I knew were hers.
Papooses crying on the wind's long mane   *160*
Screamed redskin dynasties that fled the brain,
—Dead echoes! But I knew her body there,
Time like a serpent down her shoulder, dark,
And space, an eaglet's wing, laid on her hair.

Under the Ozarks, domed by Iron Mountain,
The old gods of the rain lie wrapped in pools
Where eyeless fish curvet a sunken fountain   *nor the*
And re-descend with corn from querulous crows.   *myths of her*
                                                     fathers . . .
Such pilferings make up their timeless eatage,
Propitiate them for their timber torn   *170*
By iron, iron—always the iron dealt cleavage!
They doze now, below axe and powder horn.

And Pullman breakfasters glide glistening steel
From tunnel into field—iron strides the dew—
Straddles the hill, a dance of wheel on wheel.
You have a half-hour's wait at Siskiyou,
Or stay the night and take the next train through.
Southward, near Cairo passing, you can see
The Ohio merging,—borne down Tennessee;
And if it's summer and the sun's in dusk   *180*
Maybe the breeze will lift the River's musk
—As though the waters breathed that you might know
Memphis Johnny, Steamboat Bill, Missouri Joe.
Oh, lean from the window, if the train slows down,
As though you touched hands with some ancient clown,
—A little while gaze absently below.
And hum *Deep River* with them while they go.

Yes, turn again and sniff once more—look see,
O Sheriff, Brakeman and Authority—
Hitch up your pants and crunch another quid,
For you, too, feed the River timelessly.   *190*
And few evade full measure of their fate;
Always they smile out eerily what they seem.
I could believe he joked at heaven's gate—
Dan Midland—jolted from the cold brake-beam.

Down, down—born pioneers in time's despite,
Grimed tributaries to an ancient flow—
They win no frontier by their wayward plight,
But drift in stillness, as from Jordan's brow.

You will not hear it as the sea; even stone   200
Is not more hushed by gravity . . . But slow,
As loth to take more tribute—sliding prone
Like one whose eyes were buried long ago

The River, spreading, flows—and spends your dream.
What are you, lost within this tideless spell?
You are your father's father, and the stream—
A liquid theme that floating niggers swell.

Damp tonnage and alluvial march of days—
Nights turbid, vascular with silted shale   210
And roots surrendered down of moraine clays:
The Mississippi drinks the farthest dale.

O quarrying passion, undertowed sunlight!
The basalt surface drags a jungle grace
Ochreous and lynx-barred in lengthening might;
Patience! and you shall reach the biding place!

Over De Soto's bones the freighted floors
Throb past the City storied of three thrones.
Down two more turns the Mississippi pours
(Anon tall ironsides up from salt lagoons)

And flows within itself, heaps itself free.   220
All fades but one thin skyline 'round . . . Ahead
No embrace opens but the stinging sea;
The River lifts itself from its long bed,

Poised wholly on its dream, a mustard glow
Tortured with history, its one will—flow!
—The Passion spreads in wide tongues, choked and slow,
Meeting the Gulf, hosannas silently below.

THE DANCE

The swift red flesh, a winter king—
Who squired the glacier woman down the sky?
She ran the neighing canyons all the spring;
She spouted arms; she rose with maize—to die.

And in the autumn drouth, whose burnished hands
With mineral wariness found out the stone
Where prayers, forgotten, streamed the mesa sands?
He holds the twilight's dim, perpetual throne.

Mythical brows we saw retiring—loth,
Disturbed and destined, into denser green.

Then you shall see her truly—your blood remembering its first invasion of her secrecy, its first encounters with her kin, her chieftain lover . . . his shade that haunts the lakes and hills

Greeting they sped us, on the arrow's oath:
Now lie incorrigibly what years between . . .

There was a bed of leaves, and broken play;   240
There was a veil upon you, Pocahontas, bride—
O Princess whose brown lap was virgin May;
And bridal flanks and eyes hid tawny pride.

I left the village for dogwood. By the canoe
Tugging below the mill-race, I could see
Your hair's keen crescent running, and the blue
First moth of evening take wing stealthily.

What laughing chains the water wove and threw!
I learned to catch the trout's moon whisper; I
Drifted how many hours I never knew,   250
But, watching, saw that fleet young crescent die,—

And one star, swinging, take its place, alone,
Cupped in the larches of the mountain pass—
Until, immortally, it bled into the dawn.
I left my sleek boat nibbling margin grass . . .

I took the portage climb, then chose
A further valley-shed; I could not stop.
Feet nozzled wat'ry webs of upper flows;
One white veil gusted from the very top.

O Appalachian Spring! I gained the ledge;   260
Steep, inaccessible smile that eastward bends
And northward reaches in that violet wedge
Of Adirondacks!—wisped of azure wands,

Over how many bluffs, tarns, streams I sped!
—And knew myself within some boding shade:—
Grey tepees tufting the blue knolls ahead,
Smoke swirling through the yellow chestnut glade . . .

A distant cloud, a thunder-bud—it grew,
The blanket of the skies: the padded foot
Within,—I heard it; 'til its rhythm drew,   270
—Siphoned the black pool from the heart's hot root!

A cyclone threshes in the turbine crest,
Swooping in eagle feathers down your back;
Know, Maquokeeta,[1] greeting; know death's best;
—Fall, Sachem,[2] strictly as the tamarack!

[1] A mythical Indian figure, the supposed lover of Pocahontas.
[2] A term for an Indian chieftain.

A birch kneels. All her whistling fingers fly.
The oak grove circles in a crash of leaves;
The long moan of a dance is in the sky.
Dance, Maquokeeta: Pocahontas grieves . . .

And every tendon scurries toward the twangs   280
Of lightning deltaed down your saber hair.
Now snaps the flint in every tooth; red fangs
And splay tongues thinly busy the blue air . . .

Dance, Maquokeeta! snake that lives before,
That casts his pelt, and lives beyond! Sprout, horn!
Spark, tooth! Medicine-man, relent, restore—
Lie to us,—dance us back the tribal morn!

Spears and assemblies: black drums thrusting on—
O yelling battlements,—I, too, was liege
To rainbows currying each pulsant bone: 290
Surpassed the circumstance, danced out the siege!

And buzzard-circleted, screamed from the stake;
I could not pick the arrows from my side.
Wrapped in that fire, I saw more escorts wake—
Flickering, sprint up the hill groins like a tide.

I heard the hush of lava wrestling your arms,
And stag teeth foam about the raven throat;
Flame cataracts of heaven in seething swarms
Fed down your anklets to the sunset's moat.

O, like the lizard in the furious noon,   300
That drops his legs and colors in the sun,
—And laughs, pure serpent, Time itself, and moon
Of his own fate, I saw thy change begun!

And saw thee dive to kiss that destiny
Like one white meteor, sacrosanct and blent
At last with all that's consummate and free
There, where the first and last gods keep thy tent.

Thewed of the levin, thunder-shod and lean,
Lo, through what infinite seasons dost thou gaze—
Across what bivouacs of thin angered slain,   310
And see'st thy bride immortal in the maize!

Totem and fire-gall, slumbering pyramid—
Though other calendars now stack the sky,
Thy freedom is her largesse, Prince, and hid
On paths thou knewest best to claim her by.

High unto Labrador the sun strikes free
Her speechless dream of snow, and stirred again,
She is the torrent and the singing tree;
And she is virgin to the last of men . . .

West, west and south! winds over Cumberland   320
And winds across the llano grass resume
Her hair's warm sibilance. Her breasts are fanned
O stream by slope and vineyard—into bloom!

And when the caribou slant down for salt
Do arrows thirst and leap? Do antlers shine
Alert, star-triggered in the listening vault
Of dusk?—And are her perfect brows to thine?

We danced, O Brave, we danced beyond their farms
In cobalt desert closures made our vows . . .
Now is the strong prayer folded in thine arms,   330
The serpent with the eagle in the boughs.

ATLANTIS

*Music is then the knowledge of that which
relates to love in harmony and system.*

                                        Plato [3]

Through the bound cable strands, the arching path
Upward, veering with light, the flight of strings,—
Taut miles of shuttling moonlight syncopate
The whispered rush, telepathy of wires.
Up the index of night, granite and steel—
Transparent meshes—fleckless the gleaming staves—
Sibylline voices flicker, waveringly stream
As though a god were issue of the strings. . . .

And through that cordage, threading with its call   340
One arc synoptic of all tides below—
Their labyrinthine mouths of history
Pouring reply as though all ships at sea
Complighted in one vibrant breath made cry,—
"Make thy love sure—to weave whose song we ply!"
—From black embankments, moveless soundings hailed,
So seven oceans answer from their dream.

And on, obliquely up bright carrier bars
New octaves trestle the twin monoliths

[3] From the *Symposium*, in the translation of P. B. Shelley.

Beyond whose frosted capes the moon bequeaths   *350*
Two worlds of sleep (O arching strands of song!)—
Onward and up the crystal-flooded aisle
White tempest nets file upward, upward ring
With silver terraces the humming spars,
The loft of vision, palladium helm of stars.

Sheerly the eyes, like seagulls stung with rime—
Slit and propelled by glistening fins of light—
Pick biting way up towering looms that press
Sidelong with flight of blade on tendon blade
—Tomorrows into yesteryear—and link   *360*
What cipher-script of time no traveller reads
But who, through smoking pyres of love and death,
Searches the timeless laugh of mythic spears.

Like hails, farewells—up planet-sequined heights
Some trillion whispering hammers glimmer Tyre:
Serenely, sharply up the long anvil cry
Of inchling æons silence rivets Troy.
And you, aloft there—Jason! hesting Shout!
Still wrapping harness to the swarming air!
Silvery the rushing wake, surpassing call,   *370*
Beams yelling Æolus! splintered in the straits!

From gulfs unfolding, terrible of drums,
Tall Vision-of-the-Voyage, tensely spare—
Bridge, lifting night to cycloramic crest
Of deepest day—O Choir, translating time
Into what multitudinous Verb the suns
And synergy of waters ever fuse, recast
In myriad syllables,—Psalm of Cathay!
O Love, thy white, pervasive Paradigm . . . !

We left the haven hanging in the night—   *380*
Sheened harbor lanterns backward fled the keel.
Pacific here at time's end, bearing corn,—
Eyes stammer through the pangs of dust and steel.
And still the circular, indubitable frieze
Of heaven's meditation, yoking wave
To kneeling wave, one song devoutly binds—
The vernal strophe chimes from deathless strings!

O Thou steeled Cognizance whose leap commits
The agile precincts of the lark's return;
Within whose lariat sweep encinctured sing   *390*
In single chrysalis the many twain,—
Of stars Thou art the stitch and stallion glow

And like an organ, Thou, with sound of doom—
Sight, sound and flesh Thou leadest from time's realm
As love strikes clear direction for the helm.

Swift peal of secular light, intrinsic Myth
Whose fell unshadow is death's utter wound,—
O River-throated—iridescently upborne
Through the bright drench and fabric of our veins;
With white escarpments swinging into light,   400
Sustained in tears the cities are endowed
And justified conclamant [4] with ripe fields
Revolving through their harvests in sweet torment.

Forever Deity's glittering Pledge, O Thou
Whose canticle fresh chemistry assigns
To rapt inception and beatitude,—
Always through blinding cables, to our joy,
Of thy white seizure springs the prophecy:
Always through spiring cordage, pyramids
Of silver sequel, Deity's young name   410
Kinetic of white choiring wings . . . ascends.

Migrations that must needs void memory,
Inventions that cobblestone the heart,—
Unspeakable Thou Bridge to Thee, O Love.
Thy pardon for this history, whitest Flower,
O Answerer of all,—Anemone,—
Now while thy petals spend the suns about us, hold—
(O Thou whose radiance doth inherit me)
Atlantis,—hold thy floating singer late!

So to thine Everpresence, beyond time,   420
Like spears ensanguined of one tolling star
That bleeds infinity—the orphic strings,
Sidereal phalanxes, leap and converge:
—One Song, one Bridge of Fire! Is it Cathay,
Now pity steeps the grass and rainbows ring
The serpent with the eagle in the leaves . . . ?
Whispers antiphonal in azure swing.

[4] A calling out together.

FROM **Key West: An Island Sheaf** (1933)

Royal Palm

For Grace Hart Crane

Green rustlings, more than regal charities
Drift coolly from that tower of whispered light.
Amid the noontide's blazed asperities
I watched the sun's most gracious anchorite

Climb up as by communings, year on year
Uneaten of the earth or aught earth holds,
And the grey trunk, that's elephantine, rear
Its frondings sighing in ætherial folds.

Forever fruitless, and beyond that yield
Of sweat the jungle presses with hot love   10
And tendril till our deathward breath is sealed—
It grazes the horizons, launched above

Mortality—ascending emerald-bright,
A fountain at salute, a crown in view—
Unshackled, casual of its azured height
As though it soared suchwise through heaven too.

To Emily Dickinson

You who desired so much—in vain to ask—
Yet fed your hunger like an endless task,
Dared dignify the labor, bless the quest—
Achieved that stillness ultimately best,

Being, of all, least sought for: Emily, hear!
O sweet, dead Silencer, most suddenly clear
When singing that Eternity possessed
And plundered momently in every breast;

—Truly no flower yet withers in your hand,
The harvest you descried and understand   10
Needs more than wit to gather, love to bind.
Some reconcilement of remotest mind—

Leaves Ormus rubyless, and Ophir chill.
Else tears heap all within one clay-cold hill.

The Broken Tower

The bell-rope that gathers God at dawn
Dispatches me as though I dropped down the knell
Of a spent day—to wander the cathedral lawn
From pit to crucifix, feet chill on steps from hell.

Have you not heard, have you not seen that corps
Of shadows in the tower, whose shoulders sway
Antiphonal carillons launched before
The stars are caught and hived in the sun's ray?

The bells, I say, the bells break down their tower;
And swing I know not where. Their tongues engrave   10
Membrane through marrow, my long-scattered score
Of broken intervals. . . . And I, their sexton slave!

Oval encyclicals in canyons heaping
The impasse high with choir. Banked voices slain!
Pagodas, campaniles with reveilles outleaping—
O terraced echoes prostrate on the plain! . . .

And so it was I entered the broken world
To trace the visionary company of love, its voice
An instant in the wind (I know not whither hurled)
But not for long to hold each desperate choice.   20

My word I poured. But was it cognate, scored
Of that tribunal monarch of the air
Whose thigh embronzes earth, strikes crystal Word
In wounds pledged once to hope—cleft to despair?

The steep encroachments of my blood left me
No answer (could blood hold such a lofty tower
As flings the question true?)—or is it she
Whose sweet mortality stirs latent power?—

And through whose pulse I hear, counting the strokes
My veins recall and add, revived and sure   30
The angelus of wars my chest evokes:
What I hold healed, original now, and pure . . .

And builds, within, a tower that is not stone
(Not stone can jacket heaven)—but slip
Of pebbles—visible wings of silence sown
In azure circles, widening as they dip

The matrix of the heart, lift down the eye
That shrines the quiet lake and swells a tower . . .
The commodious, tall decorum of that sky
Unseals her earth, and lifts love in its shower.   40

[*JOHN ORLEY*] *ALLEN TATE (1899–   )*

A *number of young enthusiasts, writing about Allen Tate, have suggested that he had a double advantage in having been born and brought up in Kentucky, a border state, which gave him a basic allegiance to the South but also some capacity of forgiveness for the North. The thesis is limited. While he has certainly been concerned with the South and has lived most of his life in the North, his literary and intellectual interests have always transcended such regional divisions for a concern with the international community of letters and ideas.*

As *a boy he attended various schools, but the total time given to formal education, including the university, was twelve years. He was graduated from Vanderbilt University in 1923, where the teacher who most impressed him was a young assistant professor of English, John Crowe Ransom. Through him, Tate became the first undergraduate to join the group of writers who established* The Fugitive, *a periodical intended as a platform for Southern talent and for the expression of ideas about the South, specifically, ideas directed toward the development of an agrarian culture. It was this interest that led the group, Tate and eleven other Southerners, to publish* I'll Take My Stand: The South and the Agrarian Tradition *(1930); and, six years later, a similar work,* Who Owns America? A New Declaration of Independence, *edited by Tate and Herbert Agar; and two biographies of famous Southerners,* Stonewall Jackson: The Good Soldier *(1928) and* Jefferson Davis: His Rise and Fall *(1929).*

But *even as an undergraduate, as far as his poetry went, Tate looked far beyond the South, notably to W. B. Yeats and, presently, to T. S. Eliot, to whose work Hart Crane introduced him in 1922. After holding a brief teaching job in West Virginia, Tate left the South for New York in 1924. There he met Caroline Gordon, the novelist who in that year became his wife, and they left the city for Patterson, New York, where they rented eight rooms, two of which they turned over to Hart Crane. It was probably here that Tate began his best-known poem, the "Ode to the Confederate Dead," on which he continued to work for the next ten years. His first volume of poems,* Mr. Pope and Other Poems *(1928), brought him a Guggenheim Fellowship which enabled him to go to Paris where the Tates became familiar figures in expatriate artistic circles.*

On *his return, he began a sporadic teaching career at Southwestern at Memphis, and he then held positions at a number of universities, including North Carolina, Columbia, Princeton, Chicago, Minnesota.*

His *first volume of poems was followed by* Three Poems *(1930), which contained the first published version of the "Ode,"* Poems: 1928–

1931 *(1932), and* The Mediterranean and Other Poems *(1936). His* Selected Poems *(1937) was followed by three shorter volumes, with everything he wished to retain collected in* Poems: 1922–1957 *and then again in* Poems *(1960).*

His poems, beautifully and intricately wrought as they are, have probably not been as influential as his conversation, his public lectures, and his critical prose. He is the author of a number of fine short stories and of one novel, The Fathers *(1938), which has continued over the years to find new audiences. His first volume of criticism,* Reactionary Essays on Poetry and Ideas *(1936), was followed by four further volumes, with a selection from all of them in* The Man of Letters in the Modern World *(1955), a full gathering in* Collected Essays *(1959), and finally in* Essays of Four Decades *(1968). His sixtieth birthday was honored by the "Homage to Allen Tate" issue of* The Sewanee Review, *the periodical which he himself had edited from 1944 to 1946.*

Like John Crowe Ransom, his influence has been concentrated in two spheres, Southern agrarianism and New Criticism. But his criticism, like his poetry, esecially after his conversion to Roman Catholicism in 1950, cannot be easily typed; indeed, since 1950, both the style of his poetry and the range of his intellectual interests have undergone an interesting and unusual development.

FURTHER READING

Critical studies are George Hemphill, *Allen Tate* (1963); Roger K. Meiners, *The Last Alternatives: A Study of the Works of Allen Tate* (1963); and Ferman Bishop, *Allen Tate* (1967). See also John M. Bradbury, *The Fugitives: A Critical Account* (1958), and "Homage to Allen Tate: Essays, Notes, and Verses in Honor of His Sixtieth Birthday," in *The Sewanee Review* (1959).

FROM **Mr. Pope and Other Poems** *(1928)*

Mr. Pope

When Alexander Pope strolled in the city
Strict was the glint of pearl and gold sedans.
Ladies leaned out more out of fear than pity
For Pope's tight back was rather a goat's than man's:

Often one thinks the urn should have more bones
Than skeletons provide for speedy dust,

The urn gets hollow, cobwebs brittle as stones
Weave to the funeral shell a frivolous rust.

And he who dribbled couplets like a snake
Coiled to a lithe precision in the sun   *10*
Is missing. The jar is empty; you may break
It only to find that Mr. Pope is gone.

What requisitions of a verity
Prompted the wit and rage between his teeth
One cannot say. Around a crooked tree
A moral climbs whose name should be a wreath.

FROM **Selected Poems** (*1937*)

Ode to the Confederate Dead

Row after row with strict impunity
The headstones yield their names to the element,
The wind whirrs without recollection;
In the riven troughs the splayed leaves
Pile up, of nature the casual sacrament
To the seasonal eternity of death;
Then driven by the fierce scrutiny
Of heaven to their election in the vast breath,
They sough the rumor of mortality.

Autumn is desolation in the plot   *10*
Of a thousand acres where these memories grow
From the inexhaustible bodies that are not
Dead, but feed the grass row after rich row.
Think of the autumns that have come and gone!—
Ambitious November with the humors of the year,
With a particular zeal for every slab,
Staining the uncomfortable angels that rot
On the slabs, a wing chipped here, an arm there:
The brute curiosity of an angel's stare
Turns you, like them, to stone,   *20*
Transforms the heaving air
Till plunged to a heavier world below
You shift your sea-space blindly
Heaving, turning like the blind crab.

    Dazed by the wind, only the wind
    The leaves flying, plunge

You know who have waited by the wall
The twilight certainty of an animal,
Those midnight restitutions of the blood
You know—the immitigable pines, the smoky frieze   30
Of the sky, the sudden call: you know the rage,
The cold pool left by the mounting flood,
Of muted Zeno and Parmenides.[1]
You who have waited for the angry resolution
Of those desires that should be yours tomorrow,
You know the unimportant shrift of death
And praise the vision
And praise the arrogant circumstance
Of those who fall
Rank upon rank, hurried beyond decision—   40
Here by the sagging gate, stopped by the wall.

    Seeing, seeing only the leaves
    Flying, plunge and expire

Turn your eyes to the immoderate past,
Turn to the inscrutable infantry rising
Demons out of the earth—they will not last.
Stonewall, Stonewall,[2] and the sunken fields of hemp,
Shiloh, Antietam, Malvern Hill, Bull Run.
Lost in that orient of the thick-and-fast
You will curse the setting sun.   50

    Cursing only the leaves crying
    Like an old man in a storm

You hear the shout, the crazy hemlocks point
With troubled fingers to the silence which
Smothers you, a mummy, in time.

                The hound bitch
Toothless and dying, in a musty cellar
Hears the wind only.

           Now that the salt of their blood
Stiffens the saltier oblivion of the sea,   60
Seals the malignant purity of the flood,
What shall we who count our days and bow
Our heads with a commemorial woe
In the ribboned coats of grim felicity,

---

[1] Greek philosophers of the fifth century B.C.

[2] Stonewall Jackson (1824–1863), officer of the Confederate Army, who conducted
a brilliant command in the battles of the Seven Days (as listed by Tate). He died
in the midst of battle by unintentional shots from his own soldiers.

What shall we say of the bones, unclean,
Whose verdurous anonymity will grow?
The ragged arms, the ragged heads and eyes
Lost in these acres of the ínsane green?
The gray lean spiders come, they come and go;
In a tangle of willows without light   70
The singular screech-owl's tight
Invisible lyric seeds the mind
With the furious murmur of their chivalry.

    We shall say only the leaves
    Flying, plunge and expire

We shall say only the leaves whispering
In the improbable mist of nightfall
That flies on multiple wing;
Night is the beginning and the end
And in between the ends of distraction   80
Waits mute speculation, the patient curse
That stones the eyes, or like the jaguar leaps
For his own image in a jungle pool, his victim.
What shall we say who have knowledge
Carried to the heart? Shall we take the act
To the grave? Shall we, more hopeful, set up the grave
In the house? The ravenous grave?

                     Leave now
The shut gate and the decomposing wall:
The gentle serpent, green in the mulberry bush,   90
Riots with his tongue through the hush—
Sentinel of the grave who counts us all!

FROM **Poems, 1920–1945: A Selection** (1947)

Winter Mask

To the memory of W. B. Yeats

   I
Towards nightfall when the wind
Tries the eaves and casements
(A winter wind of the mind
Long gathering its will)
I lay the mind's contents

Bare, as upon a table,
And ask, in a time of war,
Whether there is still
To a mind frivolously dull
Anything worth living for.   10

II

If I am meek and dull
And a poor sacrifice
Of perverse will to cull
The act from the attempt,
Just look into damned eyes
And give the returning glare;
For the damned like it, the more
Damnation is exempt
From what would save its heir
With a thing worth living for.   20

III

The poisoned rat in the wall
Cuts through the wall like a knife,
Then blind, drying, and small
And driven to cold water,
Dies of the water of life:
Both damned in eternal ice,
The traitor become the boor
Who had led his friend to slaughter,
Now bites his head—not nice,
The food that he lives for.   30

IV

I supposed two scenes of hell,
Two human bestiaries,
Might uncommonly well
Convey the doom I thought;
But lest the horror freeze
The gentler estimation
I go to the sylvan door
Where nature has been bought
In rational proration
As a thing worth living for.   40

V

Should the buyer have been beware? [1]
It is an uneven trade
For man has wet his hair
Under the winter weather
With only fog for shade:
His mouth a bracketed hole
Picked by the crows that bore
Nature to their hanged brother,
Who rattles against the bole
The thing that he lived for.   50

VI

I asked the master Yeats
Whose great style could not tell
Why it is man hates
His own salvatiòn,
Prefers the way to hell,
And finds his last safety
In the self-made curse that bore
Him towards damnatiòn:
The drowned undrowned by the sea,
The sea worth living for.   60

[1] Alludes to the Latin warning *caveat emptor* ("buyer beware").

EARLIER DRAMA

The history of the American stage before 1915 records not one play that would be worth producing now and almost none that are worth reading. Within the next twenty-five years, an extraordinary repertory of plays of probably permanent theatrical and literary vitality had come into existence. If one date must be named as the beginning of this remarkable florescence, many lovers of the theater would point to that midsummer night in 1916 when Eugene O'Neill's first one-act play, *Bound East for Cardiff*, was presented on a small Provincetown wharf. It is an unvarnished presentation of sailors in the crowded forecastle of a freighter, talking as sailors talk; one man dies, dreaming of farmlands that now he will never see. Totally unpretentious, it had the poetry of truth—and was unlike anything that might be seen on Broadway, where, with a few exceptions, only absurd melodrama, flimsy farce, and sentimental romance had for decades been available. From the humbly moving beginning and break with all this made by O'Neill, the new theater would grow, and O'Neill himself would develop into the creative giant of that whole time.

His development was, roughly, from a period of early realistic plays with poetic overtones, to a period of both extensive and intensive experimentation in symbolic techniques, production methods, and acting styles, to a return to a realism much enriched by the imaginative experience of that experimentation. He began by exploring the liberating possibilities of the short one-acter and went on to write, in *Strange Interlude* and *Mourning Becomes Electra*, the longest plays in our stage history. His knowledge of the European stage enabled him to introduce expressionistic and other Continental modes into his treatment of American subject matter, and with these, a rich new strain of subjectivity and correlative dramatic tensions. His reading in the major European thinkers—Darwin, Marx, Nietzsche, Freud, Jung among others—brought into his native materials an intellectual dimension and a psychological thrust that the theater before him had not known. Yet his themes (except in the instance of his single comedy, *Ah, Wilderness!*) were almost always rooted in what was a nearly compulsive sense of the doom of dreams, of the torture and the terror to which the human psyche is subject. He brought the American drama as near to the truly and the fully tragic as modern life, necessarily subject to the restraining impositions of science, will apparently permit.

If Eugene O'Neill was the great example for other playwrights, one must not overlook the altering conditions of the stage itself as contributing to their efforts. The widespread growth of little-theater groups throughout the United States made the interest in fresh dramatic talent and experimentation a national, rather than a local, phenomenon. And the practice, beginning in 1915, of the Washington Square Players, the group that would evolve into the Theatre Guild, of bringing European plays—from those of August Strindberg of fifty years before to those of Bernard Shaw, immediately contemporary—before the American public, opened the national to the international theater. The grip of the old monopoly on Broadway houses and on houses in major cities across the country was at least loosened if not broken, and room was made for a whole generation of new actors to animate the new plays and new production methods to sharpen the focus of their dramatic intentions.

In the 1930s (the years of the Depression here, of the advance of totalitarianism in Europe, and of the threat of war throughout the world), a new spirit of organizational militancy came into the American drama. Early in the decade, the Group Theatre was formed to study and foster the stage methods made famous by the Moscow Art Theatre. The year 1935 saw the founding of the Federal Theater Project, a nationwide network organized by the government's Works Progress Administration to give employment to actors, musicians, technicians. This unique venture in our history put together a repertory of classic and modern, established and original plays of a scope never achieved before by any theatrical group. The Theater Union was organized in New York with the specific purpose of encouraging a new proletarian drama of social protest, and Orson Welles's Mercury Theater was set up to encourage a people's theater which would compete with the films in ticket prices. In 1937, five distinguished dramatists banded together in the Playwrights' Company in a determined effort to improve contract arrangements with producers, and again, to lower admission prices.

Under these altering circumstances of the stage, many individual talents were to flourish in those two decades and a half: Maxwell Anderson, Philip Barry, Elmer Rice, S. N. Behrman, Sidney Howard, Thornton Wilder, Robert E. Sherwood, Lillian Hellman, William Saroyan, Clifford Odets—these are the names of the brightest stars in the startling galaxy. Such a list hardly serves to indicate the individual achievement of these dramatists, but if we remind ourselves that each of these names is associated not only with one but with two or three or four fine plays, it should at least suggest the breadth of our dramatic development in those twenty-five years before the Second World War.

EUGENE [GLADSTONE] O'NEILL (1888–1953)

O'Neill was born in a hotel room in the theater district of New York. His father was James O'Neill, a well-known actor whose fame rested chiefly on his performance as the Count of Monte Christo in a play adapted from Dumas' novel with which the elder O'Neill's company endlessly toured. His mother was a drug addict, and his older actor-brother, while still young, became an alcoholic and led a generally dissolute life, into which he early introduced Eugene. This was a considerably disturbed family. Both parents were devout Roman Catholics, and such early education as the young Gene had was in Catholic boarding schools. At the end of one year he was suspended from Princeton for a youthful indiscretion, and he went to work in a mail-order firm. In 1909 he was secretly married and had a son in the following year, but this marriage was dissolved in 1912. In the meantime he had gone to Honduras, hunting for gold; but he contracted malaria there and returned to New York to join his father's company as an actor and assistant manager. Tiring of that, he abruptly shipped as a seaman to Buenos Aires. He was at sea for a year, with many carousals in many ports, including New York, where he frequented a bar called "Jimmy-the-Priest's," which he later made memorable in his plays Anna Christie and The Iceman Cometh. Briefly rejoining his father's company, he followed his parents to their summer home in New London in 1911 and went to work on a local newspaper. But his health had been injured by his life, and in 1912, suffering from tuberculosis, he was put in a sanatarium for six months.

It was a crucial period: he did an enormous amount of reading and took stock of himself. When he emerged, his disease arrested, he began to write eight one-act plays and two longer ones. Deciding that he needed technical training, he entered George Pierce Baker's "47 Workshop" at Harvard in 1914, and then, at the perfect moment, he settled into Greenwich Village.

The Provincetown Players produced ten of his short plays within three years; at the end of that time, in 1920, his first full-length play, Beyond the Horizon, appeared, and the Pulitzer Prize announced, in effect, the arrival of America's leading dramatist. (He was to win the Pulitzer three more times, once posthumously, and, of course, the Nobel in 1936.) From 1923 to 1927 he was associated with a second theatrical venture, the Greenwich Village Theatre, which, like the Provincetown, achieved its greatest distinction in productions of two O'Neill plays, All God's Chillun Got Wings and Desire Under the Elms, both of 1924. In the meantime, of the many plays that he wrote and presented, Anna Christie (1921) was probably the most durable.

In 1918 he was married for a second time; that marriage resulted in two children, Shane and Oona, and ended in divorce in 1929, when he married an actress named Carlotta Monterey. He had long left New York, first for Ridgefield, Connecticut, and then for France, then one of the Sea Islands off Georgia, then California, and finally Boston.

His early manner, that naturalistic presentation of drifters and yearners and the dispossessed—even with its poetic overtones—did not satisfy him, and he began to experiment with the symbolic techniques of expressionism in such plays as The Emperor Jones *and* The Hairy Ape. *In his compulsion to write tragedy, he began to call on classic or Biblical themes and historic subjects; even such a naturalistic effort as* Desire Under the Elms *is a free adaptation of the Theseus-Hippolytus-Phaedra legend. His first use of masks was in an adaptation of Coleridge's poem,* The Ancient Mariner *(1924), but his restless experiments were made both earlier and later, and sometimes they were mistaken.* The Fountain *(1925),* Lazarus Laughed *(1927), and* Marco Millions *(1928) are all very interesting, but the first, at least, is both a literary and a theatrical disaster.*

His ambition was both to extend the range of the theater and to intensify its effects. Strange Interlude *(1928), a drama in nine acts (the curtain rises in the afternoon and falls late at night, after an intermission for dinner), and* Mourning Becomes Electra *(1931), a trilogy, are the chief examples of a great but perhaps also overweening intention: fantastically long plays, they attempted, through what now seems a thin understanding of Freudian psychology, to make explicit those psychological involutions that the dramatic form might better be content to imply.*

In the 1930s, while he continued to write plays that were produced with great success—notably his sweet comedy, Ah, Wilderness! *(1933)—he retired into his most ambitious project, a cycle of nine plays with the general title,* A Tale of Possessors Self-Dispossessed, *the history of a family from 1777 to 1932. After his death, two plays from this cycle were produced—* A Touch of the Poet *(1957) and* More Stately Mansions *(1964). The two new plays produced before his death were* The Iceman Cometh, *written in 1939 but opening in 1946, a tragedy about the inevitability of death, and* A Moon for the Misbegotten, *written in 1946 and withdrawn during its out-of-town tryout in 1947.*

For some years before his death of bronchial pneumonia, he had contracted Parkinson's disease, a form of palsy that prevented any writing. His oldest son, Eugene O'Neill, Jr., an able Greek scholar, teacher, and writer, had committed suicide in 1950. O'Neill had refused to see his daughter after her marriage to Charles Chaplin, and in his will he eliminated both her and her brother, Shane, from any inheritance.

One of his last efforts, presented after his death, looks back at his life when he was a young man: Long Day's Journey into Night. *It is perfectly direct; written in an even more purely naturalistic manner than his earliest plays, it is a marvelous play that reveals a family committed to disaster. Perhaps he never wrote a tragedy—his language, at least, was not adequate to that exalted mood—but he lived one.*

FURTHER READING

The most ambitious biography to date is Arthur and Barbara Gelb, *O'Neill* (1962); Doris Alexander has begun her biography with *The Tempering of Eugene O'Neill* (1962); likewise, Louis Sheaffer, with *O'Neill: Son and Playwright* (1968). Members of the O'Neill family have also written biographical studies: Croswell Bowen and Shane O'Neill, *Curse of the Misbegotten: A Tale of the House of O'Neill* (1959); and Agnes Boulton, *Part of a Long Story* (1958). Important critical studies are Edwin A. Engel, *The Haunted Heroes of Eugene O'Neill* (1953); Doris V. Falk, *Eugene O'Neill and the Tragic Tension* (1958); John Raleigh, *The Plays of Eugene O'Neill* (1965); and Tumo Tiusanen, *O'Neill's Scenic Images* (1968). Brief general surveys are John Gassner, *Eugene O'Neill* (1965), and Frederic I. Carpenter, *Eugene O'Neill* (1964). Oscar Cargill and N. B. Fagin edited *O'Neill and His Plays: Four Decades of Criticism* (1961); a companion volume is Jordon Y. Miller, *Playwright's Progress: O'Neill and the Critics* (1965).

Desire Under the Elms (1924)

CHARACTERS

Ephraim Cabot
Simeon ⎤
Peter ⎟ *His sons*
Eben ⎦
Abbie Putnam
*Young Girl, Two Farmers, The Fiddler, A Sheriff, and other folk from
the neighboring farms*

The action of the entire play takes place in, and immediately outside of, the Cabot farmhouse in New England, in the year 1850. The
south end of the house faces front to a stone wall with a wooden gate
at center opening on a country road. The house is in good condition
but in need of paint. Its walls are a sickly grayish, the green of the
shutters faded. Two enormous elms are on each side of the house. They
bend their trailing branches down over the roof. They appear to protect
and at the same time subdue. There is a sinister maternity in their
aspect, a crushing, jealous absorption. They have developed from their
intimate contact with the life of man in the house an appalling
humaneness. They brood oppressively over the house. They are like
exhausted women resting their sagging breasts and hands and hair
on its roof, and when it rains their tears trickle down monotonously
and rot on the shingles.

There is a path running from the gate around the right corner of
the house to the front door. A narrow porch is on this side. The end
wall facing us has two windows in its upper story, two larger ones on
the floor below. The two upper are those of the father's bedroom and
that of the brothers. On the left, ground floor, is the kitchen—on the
right, the parlor, the shades of which are always drawn down.

PART ONE—SCENE ONE

*Exterior of the Farmhouse. It is sunset of a day at the beginning of
summer in the year 1850. There is no wind and everything is still. The
sky above the roof is suffused with deep colors, the green of the elms
glows, but the house is in shadow, seeming pale and washed out by
contrast.*

A door opens and EBEN CABOT *comes to the end of the porch and
stands looking down the road to the right. He has a large bell in his
hand and this he swings mechanically, awakening a deafening clangor.*

*Then he puts his hands on his hips and stares up at the sky. He sighs
with a puzzled awe and blurts out with halting appreciation.*

EBEN. God! Purty! (*His eyes fall and he stares about him frowningly. He is twenty-five, tall and sinewy. His face is well-formed, good-
looking, but its expression is resentful and defensive. His defiant, dark
eyes remind one of a wild animal's in captivity. Each day is a cage in
which he finds himself trapped but inwardly unsubdued. There is a
fierce repressed vitality about him. He has black hair, mustache, a thin
curly trace of beard. He is dressed in rough farm clothes.*

*He spits on the ground with intense disgust, turns and goes back
into the house.*

SIMEON *and* PETER *come in from their work in the fields. They are
tall men, much older than their half-brother* [SIMEON *is thirty-nine and*
PETER *thirty-seven], built on a squarer, simpler model, fleshier in body,
more bovine and homelier in face, shrewder and more practical. Their
shoulders stoop a bit from years of farm work. They clump heavily
along in their clumsy thick-soled boots caked with earth. Their clothes,
their faces, hands, bare arms and throats are earth-stained. They smell
of earth. They stand together for a moment in front of the house and,
as if with the one impulse, stare dumbly up at the sky, leaning on their
hoes. Their faces have a compressed, unresigned expression. As they
look upward, this softens*).

SIMEON. (*grudgingly*) Purty.

PETER. Ay-eh.

SIMEON. (*suddenly*) Eighteen year ago.

PETER. What?

SIMEON. Jenn. My woman. She died.

PETER. I'd fergot.

SIMEON. I rec'lect—now an' agin. Makes it lonesome. She'd hair
long's a hoss' tail—an' yaller like gold!

PETER. Waal—she's gone. (*This with indifferent finality—then
after a pause*) They's gold in the West, Sim.

SIMEON. (*still under the influence of sunset—vaguely*) In the sky?

PETER. Waal—in a manner o' speakin'—thar's the promise. (*Growing excited*) Gold in the sky—in the West—Golden Gate—Californi-a!
—Goldest West!—fields o' gold!

SIMEON. (*excited in his turn*) Fortunes layin' just atop o' the
ground waitin' t' be picked! Solomon's mines, they says! (*For a moment
they continue looking up at the sky—then their eyes drop*).

PETER. (*with sardonic bitterness*) Here—it's stones atop o' the
ground—stones atop o' stones—makin' stone walls—year atop o' year
—him 'n' yew 'n' me 'n' then Eben—makin' stone walls fur him to
fence us in!

SIMEON. We've wuked. Give our strength. Give our years. Plowed
'em under in the ground,—(*he stamps rebelliously*)—rottin'—makin'

soil for his crops! (*A pause*) Waal—the farm pays good for here-abouts.

PETER. If we plowed in Californi-a, they'd be lumps o' gold in the furrow!

SIMEON. Californi-a's t'other side o' earth, a'most. We got t' calc'late—

PETER. (*after a pause*) 'Twould be hard fur me, too, to give up what we've 'arned here by our sweat. (*A pause.* EBEN *sticks his head out of the dining-room window, listening*).

SIMEON. Ay-eh. (*A pause*) Mebbe—he'll die soon.

PETER. (*doubtfully*) Mebbe.

SIMEON. Mebbe—fur all we knows—he's dead now.

PETER. Ye'd need proof.

SIMEON. He's been gone two months—with no word.

PETER. Left us in the fields an evenin' like this. Hitched up an' druv off into the West. That's plum onnateral. He hain't never been off this farm 'ceptin' t' the village in thirty year or more, not since he married Eben's maw. (*A pause. Shrewdly*) I calc'late we might git him declared crazy by the court.

SIMEON. He skinned em' too slick. He got the best o' all on 'em. They'd never b'lieve him crazy. (*A pause*) We got t' wait—till he's under ground.

EBEN. (*with a sardonic chuckle*) Honor thy father! (*They turn, startled, and stare at him. He grins, then scowls*) I pray he's died. (*They stare at him. He continues matter-of-factly*) Supper's ready.

SIMEON *and* PETER. (*together*) Ay-eh.

EBEN. (*gazing up at the sky*) Sun's downin' purty.

SIMEON *and* PETER. (*together*) Ay-eh. They's gold in the West.

EBEN. Ay-eh. (*Pointing*) Yonder atop o' the hill pasture, ye mean?

SIMEON *and* PETER. (*together*) In Californi-a!

EBEN. Hunh? (*Stares at them indifferently for a second, then drawls*) Waal—supper's gittin' cold. (*He turns back into kitchen*).

SIMEON. (*startled—smacks his lips*) I air hungry!

PETER. (*sniffing*) I smells bacon!

SIMEON. (*with hungry appreciation*) Bacon's good!

PETER. (*in same tone*) Bacon's bacon! (*They turn, shouldering each other, their bodies bumping and rubbing together as they hurry clumsily to their food, like two friendly oxen toward their evening meal. They disappear around the right corner of house and can be heard entering the door*).

CURTAIN

SCENE TWO

The color fades from the sky. Twilight begins. The interior of the kitchen is now visible. A pine table is at center, a cookstove in the right rear corner, four rough wooden chairs, a tallow candle on the table. In the middle of the rear wall is fastened a big advertizing poster with a ship in full sail and the word "California" in big letters. Kitchen utensils hang from nails. Everything is neat and in order but the atmosphere is of a men's camp kitchen rather than that of a home.

Places for three are laid. EBEN *takes boiled potatoes and bacon from the stove and puts them on the table, also a loaf of bread and a crock of water.* SIMEON *and* PETER *shoulder in, slump down in their chairs without a word.* EBEN *joins them. The three eat in silence for a moment, the two elder as naturally unrestrained as beasts of the field,* EBEN *picking at his food without appetite, glancing at them with a tolerant dislike.*

SIMEON. (*suddenly turns to* EBEN) Looky here! Ye'd oughtn't t' said that, Eben.

PETER. 'Twa'n't righteous.

EBEN. What?

SIMEON. Ye prayed he'd died.

EBEN. Waal—don't yew pray it? (*A pause*).

PETER. He's our Paw.

EBEN. (*violently*) Not mine!

SIMEON. (*dryly*) Ye'd not let no one else say that about yer Maw! Ha! (*He gives one abrupt sardonic guffaw.* PETER *grins*).

EBEN. (*very pale*) I meant—I hain't his'n—I hain't like him—he hain't me!

PETER. (*dryly*) Wait till ye've growed his age!

EBEN. (*intensely*) I'm Maw—every drop o' blood! (*A pause. They stare at him with indifferent curiosity*).

PETER. (*reminiscently*) She was good t' Sim 'n' me. A good Step-maw's scurse.

SIMEON. She was good t' everyone.

EBEN. (*greatly moved, gets to his feet and makes an awkward bow to each of them—stammering*) I be thankful t' ye. I'm her—her heir. (*He sits down in confusion*).

PETER. (*after a pause—judicially*) She was good even t' him.

EBEN. (*fiercely*) An' fur thanks he killed her!

SIMEON. (*after a pause*) No one never kills nobody. It's allus somethin'. That's the murderer.

EBEN. Didn't he slave Maw t' death?

PETER. He's slaved himself t' death. He's slaved Sim 'n' me 'n' yew t' death—on'y none o' us hain't died—yit.

SIMEON. It's somethin'—drivin' him—t' drive us!

EBEN. (*vengefully*) Waal—I hold him t' jedgment! (*Then scornfully*) Somethin'! What's somethin'?

SIMEON. Dunno.

EBEN. (*sardonically*) What's drivin' yew to Californi-a, mebbe? (*They look at him in surprise*) Oh, I've heerd ye! (*Then, after a pause*) But ye'll never go t' the gold fields!

PETER. (*assertively*) Mebbe!

EBEN. Whar'll ye git the money?

PETER. We kin walk. It's an a'mighty ways—Californi-a—but if yew was t' put all the steps we've walked on this farm end t' end we'd be in the moon!

EBEN. The Injuns'll skulp ye on the plains.

SIMEON. (*with grim humor*) We'll mebbe make 'em pay a hair fur a hair!

EBEN. (*decisively*) But t'aint that. Ye won't never go because ye'll wait here fur yer share o' the farm, thinkin' allus he'll die soon.

SIMEON. (*after a pause*) We've a right.

PETER. Two-thirds belongs t'us.

EBEN. (*jumping to his feet*) Ye've no right! She wa'n't yewr Maw! It was her farm! Didn't he steal it from her? She's dead. It's my farm.

SIMEON. (*sardonically*) Tell that t' Paw—when he comes! I'll bet ye a dollar he'll laugh—fur once in his life. Ha! (*He laughs himself in one single mirthless bark*).

PETER. (*amused in turn, echoes his brother*) Ha!

SIMEON. (*after a pause*) What've ye got held agin us, Eben? Year after year it's skulked in yer eye—somethin'.

PETER. Ay-eh.

EBEN. Ay-eh. They's somethin'. (*Suddenly exploding*) Why didn't ye never stand between him 'n' my Maw when he was slavin' her to her grave—t' pay her back fur the kindness she done t' yew? (*There is a long pause. They stare at him in surprise*).

SIMEON. Waal—the stock'd got t' be watered.

PETER. 'R they was woodin' t' do.

SIMEON. 'R plowin'.

PETER. 'R hayin'.

SIMEON. 'R spreadin' manure.

PETER. 'R weedin'.

SIMEON. 'R prunin'.

PETER. 'R milkin'.

EBEN. (*breaking in harshly*) An' makin' walls—stone atop o' stone —makin' walls till yer heart's a stone ye heft up out o' the way o' growth onto a stone wall t' wall in yer heart!

SIMEON. (*matter-of-factly*) We never had no time t' meddle.

PETER. (*to* EBEN) Yew was fifteen afore yer Maw died—an' big fur yer age. Why didn't ye never do nothin'?

EBEN. (*harshly*) They was chores t' do, wa'n't they? (*A pause—then slowly*) It was on'y arter she died I come to think o' it. Me cookin'—doin' her work—that made me know her, suffer her sufferin'—she'd come back t' help—come back t' bile potatoes—come back t' fry bacon—come back t' bake biscuits—come back all cramped up t' shake the fire, an' carry ashes, her eyes weepin' an' bloody with smoke an' cinders same's they used t' be. She still comes back—stands by the stove thar in the evenin'—she can't find it nateral sleepin' an' restin' in peace. She can't git used t' bein' free—even in her grave.

SIMEON. She never complained none.

EBEN. She'd got too tired. She'd got too used t' bein' too tired. That was what he done. (*With vengeful passion*) An' sooner'r later, I'll meddle. I'll say the thin's I didn't say then t' him! I'll yell 'em at the top o' my lungs. I'll see t' it my Maw gits some rest an' sleep in her grave! (*He sits down again, relapsing into a brooding silence. They look at him with a queer indifferent curiosity*).

PETER. (*after a pause*) Whar in tarnation d'ye s'pose he went, Sim?

SIMEON. Dunno. He druv off in the buggy, all spick an' span, with the mare all breshed an' shiny, druv off clackin' his tongue an' wavin' his whip. I remember it right well. I was finishin' plowin', it was spring an' May an' sunset, an' gold in the West, an' he druv off into it. I yells "Whar ye goin', Paw?" an' he hauls up by the stone wall a jiffy. His old snake's eyes was glitterin' in the sun like he'd been drinkin' a jugful an' he says with a mule's grin: "Don't ye run away till I come back!"

PETER. Wonder if he knowed we was wantin' fur Californi-a?

SIMEON. Mebbe. I didn't say nothin' and he says, lookin' kinder queer an' sick: "I been hearin' the hens cluckin' an' the roosters crowin' all the durn day. I been listenin' t' the cows lowin' an' everythin' else kickin' up till I can't stand it no more. It's spring an' I'm feelin' damned," he says. "Damned like an old bare hickory tree fit on'y fur burnin'," he says. An' then I calc'late I must've looked a mite hopeful, fur he adds real spry and vicious: "But don't git no fool idee I'm dead. I've sworn t' live a hundred an' I'll do it, if on'y t' spite yer sinful greed! An' now I'm ridin' out t' learn God's message t' me in the spring, like the prophets done. An' yew git back t' yer plowin'," he says. An' he druv off singin' a hymn. I thought he was drunk—'r I'd stopped him goin'.

EBEN. (*scornfully*) No, ye wouldn't! Ye're scared o' him. He's stronger—inside—than both o' ye put together!

PETER. (*sardonically*) An' yew—be yew Samson?

EBEN. I'm gittin' stronger. I kin feel it growin' in me—growin' an' growin'—till it'll bust out—! (*He gets up and puts on his coat and a hat. They watch him, gradually breaking into grins.* EBEN *avoids their eyes sheepishly*) I'm goin' out fur a spell—up the road.

PETER. T' the village?

SIMEON. T' see Minnie?

EBEN. (*defiantly*) Ay-eh!

PETER. (*jeeringly*) The Scarlet Woman!

SIMEON. Lust—that's what's growin' in ye!

EBEN. Waal—she's purty!

PETER. She's been purty fur twenty year!

SIMEON. A new coat o' paint'll make a heifer out of forty.

EBEN. She hain't forty!

PETER. If she hain't she's teeterin' on the edge.

EBEN. (*desperately*) What d'yew know—

PETER. All they is . . . Sim knew her—an' then me arter—

SIMEON. An' Paw kin tell yew somethin' too! He was fust!

EBEN. D'ya mean t' say he . . . ?

SIMEON. (*with a grin*) Ay-eh! We air his heirs in everythin'!

EBEN. (*intensely*) That's more to it! That grows on it! It'll bust soon! (*Then violently*) I'll go smash my fist in her face! (*He pulls open the door in rear violently*).

SIMEON. (*with a wink at* PETER—*drawingly*) Mebbe—but the night's wa'm—purty—by the time ye git thar mebbe ye'll kiss her instead!

PETER. Sart'n he will! (*They both roar with coarse laughter.* EBEN *rushes out and slams the door—then the outside front door—comes around the corner of the house and stands still by the gate, staring up at the sky.*)

SIMEON. (*looking after him*) Like his Paw.

PETER. Dead spit an' image!

SIMEON. Dog'll eat dog!

PETER. Ay-eh. (*Pause. With yearning*) Mebbe a year from now we'll be in Californi-a.

SIMEON. Ay-eh. (*A pause. Both yawn*) Let's git t'bed. (*He blows out the candle. They go out door in rear.* EBEN *stretches his arms up to the sky—rebelliously*).

EBEN. Waal—thar's a star, an' somewhar's they's him, an' here's me, an' thar's Min up the road—in the same night. What if I does kiss her? She's like t'night, she's soft 'n' wa'm, her eyes kin wink like a star, her mouth's wa'm, her arms're wa'm, she smells like a wa'm plowed field, she's purty . . . Ay-eh! By God A'mighty she's purty, an' I don't give a damn how many sins she's sinned afore mine or who she's sinned 'em with, my sin's as purty as any one on 'em! (*He strides off down the road to the left*).

SCENE THREE

It is the pitch darkness just before dawn. EBEN *comes in from the left and goes around to the porch, feeling his way, chuckling bitterly and cursing half-aloud to himself.*

EBEN. The cussed old miser! (*He can be heard going in the front door. There is a pause as he goes upstairs, then a loud knock on the bedroom door of the brothers*) Wake up!

SIMEON. (*startedly*) Who's thar?

EBEN. (*pushing open the door and coming in, a lighted candle in his hand. The bedroom of the brothers is revealed. Its ceiling is the sloping roof. They can stand upright only close to the center dividing wall of the upstairs.* SIMEON *and* PETER *are in a double bed, front.* EBEN's *cot is to the rear.* EBEN *has a mixture of silly grin and vicious scowl on his face*) I be!

PETER. (*angrily*) What in hell's-fire . . . ?

EBEN. I got news fur ye! Ha! (*He gives one abrupt sardonic guffaw*).

SIMEON. (*angrily*) Couldn't ye hold it 'til we'd got our sleep?

EBEN. It's nigh sunup. (*Then explosively*) He's gone an' married agen!

SIMEON *and* PETER. (*explosively*) Paw?

EBEN. Got himself hitched to a female 'bout thirty-five—an' purty, they says . . .

SIMEON. (*aghast*) It's a durn lie!

PETER. Who says?

SIMEON. They been stringin' ye!

EBEN. Think I'm a dunce, do ye? The hull village says. The preacher from New Dover, he brung the news—told it t'our preacher —New Dover, that's whar the old loon got himself hitched—that's whar the woman lived—

PETER. (*no longer doubting—stunned*) Waal . . . !

SIMEON. (*the same*) Waal . . . !

EBEN. (*sitting down on a bed—with vicious hatred*) Ain't he a devil out o' hell? It's jest t' spite us—the damned old mule!

PETER. (*after a pause*) Everythin'll go t' her now.

SIMEON. Ay-eh. (*A pause—dully*) Waal—if it's done—

PETER. It's done us. (*Pause—then persuasively*) They's gold in the fields o' Californi-a, Sim. No good a-stayin' here now.

SIMEON. Jest what I was a-thinkin'. (*Then with decision*) S'well fust's last! Let's light out and git this mornin'.

PETER. Suits me.

EBEN. Ye must like walkin'.

SIMEON. (*sardonically*) If ye'd grow wings on us we'd fly thar!

EBEN. Ye'd like ridin' better—on a boat, wouldn't ye? (*Fumbles in his pocket and takes out a crumpled sheet of foolscap*) Waal, if ye sign this ye kin ride on a boat. I've had it writ out an' ready in case ye'd ever go. It says fur three hundred dollars t' each ye agree yewr shares o' the farm is sold t' me. (*They look suspiciously at the paper. A pause*).

SIMEON. (*wonderingly*) But if he's hitched agen—

PETER. An' whar'd yew git that sum o' money, anyways?

EBEN. (*cunningly*) I know whar it's hid. I been waitin'—Maw told me. She knew whar it lay fur years, but she was waitin' . . . It's her'n— the money he hoarded from her farm an' hid from Maw. It's my money by rights now.

PETER. Whar's it hid?

EBEN. (*cunningly*) Whar yew won't never find it without me. Maw spied on him—'r she'd never knowed. (*A pause. They look at him suspiciously, and he at them*) Waal, is it fa'r trade?

SIMEON. Dunno.

PETER. Dunno.

SIMEON. (*looking at window*) Sky's grayin'.

PETER. Ye better start the fire, Eben.

SIMEON. An' fix some vittles.

EBEN. Ay-eh. (*Then with a forced jocular heartiness*) I'll git ye a good one. If ye're startin' t' hoof it t' Californi-a ye'll need somethin' that'll stick t' yer ribs. (*He turns to the door, adding meaningly*) But ye kin ride on a boat if ye'll swap. (*He stops at the door and pauses. They stare at him*).

SIMEON. (*suspiciously*) Whar was ye all night?

EBEN. (*defiantly*) Up t' Min's. (*Then slowly*) Walkin' thar, fust I felt 's if I'd kiss her; then I got a-thinkin' o' what ye'd said o' him an' her an' I says, I'll bust her nose fur that! Then I got t' the village an' heerd the news an' I got madder'n hell an' run all the way t' Min's not knowin' what I'd do— (*He pauses—then sheepishly but more defiantly*) Waal—when I seen her, I didn't hit her—nor I didn't kiss her nuther—I begun t' beller like a calf an' cuss at the same time, I was so durn mad—an' she got scared—an' I jest grabbed holt an' tuk her! (*Proudly*) Yes, sirree! I tuk her. She may've been his'n—an' your'n, too—but she's mine now!

SIMEON. (*dryly*) In love, air yew?

EBEN. (*with lofty scorn*) Love! I don't take no stock in sech slop!

PETER. (*winking at* SIMEON) Mebbe Eben's aimin' t' marry, too.

SIMEON. Min'd make a true faithful he'pmeet! (*They snicker*).

EBEN. What do I care fur her—'ceptin' she's round an' wa'm? The p'int is she was his'n—an' now she b'longs t' me! (*He goes to the door—then turns—rebelliously*) An' Min hain't sech a bad un. They's worse'n Min in the world, I'll bet ye! Wait'll we see this cow the Old Man's hitched t'! She'll beat Min, I got a notion! (*He starts to go out*).

SIMEON. (*suddenly*) Mebbe ye'll try t' make her your'n, too?

PETER. Ha! (*He gives a sardonic laugh of relish at this idea*).

EBEN. (*spitting with disgust*) Her—here—sleepin' with him—stealin' my Maw's farm! I'd as soon pet a skunk 'r kiss a snake! (*He goes out. The two stare after him suspiciously. A pause. They listen to his steps receding*).

PETER. He's startin' the fire.

SIMEON. I'd like t' ride t' Californi-a—but—

PETER. Min might o' put some scheme in his head.

SIMEON. Mebbe it's all a lie 'bout Paw marryin'. We'd best wait an' see the bride.

PETER. An' don't sign nothin' till we does!

SIMEON. Nor till we've tested it's good money! (*Then with a grin*) But if Paw's hitched we'd be sellin' Eben somethin' we'd never git nohow!

PETER. We'll wait an' see. (*Then with sudden vindictive anger*) An' till he comes, let's yew 'n' me not wuk a lick, let Eben tend to thin's if he's a mind t', let's us jest sleep an' eat an' drink likker, an' let the hull damned farm go t' blazes!

SIMEON. (*excitedly*) By God, we've 'arned a rest! We'll play rich fur a change. I hain't a-going to stir outa bed till breakfast's ready.

PETER. An' on the table!

SIMEON. (*after a pause—thoughtfully*) What d'ye calc'late she'll be like—our new Maw? Like Eben thinks?

PETER. More'n' likely.

SIMEON. (*vindictively*) Waal—I hope she's a she-devil that'll make him wish he was dead an' livin' in the pit o' hell fur comfort!

PETER. (*fervently*) Amen!

SIMEON. (*imitating his father's voice*) I'm ridin' out t' learn God's message t' me in the spring like the prophets done," he says. I'll bet right then an' thar he knew plumb well he was goin' whorin', the stinkin' old hypocrite!

SCENE FOUR

Same as Scene Two—shows the interior of the kitchen with a lighted candle on table. It is gray dawn outside. SIMEON and PETER are just finishing their breakfast. EBEN sits before his plate of untouched food, brooding frowningly.

PETER. (*glancing at him rather irritably*) Lookin' glum don't help none.

SIMEON. (*sarcastically*) Sorrowin' over his lust o' the flesh!

PETER. (*with a grin*) Was she yer fust?

EBEN. (*angrily*) None o' yer business. (*A pause*) I was thinkin' o' him. I got a notion he's gittin' near—I kin feel him comin' on like yew kin feel malaria chill afore it takes ye.

PETER. It's too early yet.

SIMEON. Dunno. He'd like t' catch us nappin'—jest t' have somethin' t' hoss us 'round over.

PETER. (*mechanically gets to his feet.* SIMEON *does the same*) Waal—let's git t' wuk. (*They both plod mechanically toward the door before they realize. Then they stop short*).

SIMEON. (*grinning*) Ye're a cussed fool, Pete—and I be wuss! Let him see we hain't wukin'! We don't give a durn!

PETER. (*as they go back to the table*) Not a damned durn! It'll serve t' show him we're done with him. (*They sit down again.* EBEN *stares from one to the other with surprise*).

SIMEON. (*grins at him*) We're aimin' t' start bein' lilies o' the field.

PETER. Nary a toil 'r spin 'r lick o' wuk do we put in!

SIMEON. Ye're sole owner—till he comes—that's what ye wanted. Wall, ye got t' be sole hand, too.

PETER. The cows air bellerin'. Ye better hustle at the milkin'.

EBEN. (*with excited joy*) Ye mean ye'll sign the paper?

SIMEON. (*dryly*) Mebbe.

PETER. Mebbe.

SIMEON. We're considerin'. (*Peremptorily*) Ye better git t' wuk.

EBEN. (*with queer excitement*) It's Maw's farm agen! It's my farm! Them's my cows! I'll milk my durn fingers off fur cows o' mine! (*He goes out door in rear, they stare after him indifferently*).

SIMEON. Like his Paw.

PETER. Dead spit 'n' image!

SIMEON. Waal—let dog eat dog! (EBEN *comes out of front door and around the corner of the house. The sky is beginning to grow flushed with sunrise.* EBEN *stops by the gate and stares around him with glowing, possessive eyes. He takes in the whole farm with his embracing glance of desire*).

EBEN. It's purty! It's damned purty! It's mine! (*He suddenly throws his head back boldly and glares with hard, defiant eyes at the sky*) Mine, d'ye hear? Mine! (*He turns and walks quickly off left, rear, toward the barn. The two brothers light their pipes*).

SIMEON. (*putting his muddy boots up on the table, tilting back his chair, and puffing defiantly*) Waal—this air solid comfort—fur once.

PETER. Ay-eh. (*He follows suit. A pause. Unconsciously they both sigh*).

SIMEON. (*suddenly*) He never was much o' a hand at milkin', Eben wa'n't.

PETER. (*with a snort*) His hands air like hoofs! (*A pause*).

SIMEON. Reach down the jug thar! Let's take a swaller. I'm feelin' kind o' low.

PETER. Good idee! (*He does so—gets two glasses—they pour out drinks of whisky*) Here's t' the gold in Californi-a!

SIMEON. An' luck t' find it! (*They drink—puff resolutely—sigh—take their feet down from the table*).

PETER. Likker don't pear t' sot right.

SIMEON. We hain't used t' it this early. (*A pause. They become very restless*).

PETER. Gittin' close in this kitchen.

SIMEON. (*with immense relief*) Let's git a breath o' air. (*They arise briskly and go out rear—appear around house and stop by the gate. They stare up at the sky with a numbed appreciation*).

PETER. Purty!

SIMEON. Ay-eh. Gold's t' the East now.

PETER. Sun's startin' with us fur the Golden West.

SIMEON. (*staring around the farm, his compressed face tightened, unable to conceal his emotion*) Waal—it's our last mornin'—mebbe.

PETER. (*the same*) Ay-eh.

SIMEON. (*stamps his foot on the earth and addresses it desperately*) Waal—ye've thirty year o' me buried in ye—spread out over ye—blood an' bone an' sweat—rotted away—fertilizin' ye—richin' yer soul—prime manure, by God, that's what I been t' ye!

PETER. Ay-eh! An' me!

SIMEON. An' yew, Peter. (*he sighs—then spits*) Waal—no use'n cryin' over spilt milk.

PETER. They's gold in the West—an' freedom, mebbe. We been slaves t' stone walls here.

SIMEON. (*defiantly*) We hain't nobody's slaves from this out—nor no thin's slaves nuther. (*A pause—restlessly*) Speakin' o' milk, wonder how Eben's managin'?

PETER. I s'pose he's managin'.

SIMEON. Mebbe we'd ought t' help—this once.

PETER. Mebbe. The cows knows us.

SIMEON. An' likes us. They don't know him much.

PETER. An' the hosses, an' pigs, an' chickens. They don't know him much.

SIMEON. They knows us like brothers—an' likes us! (*Proudly*). Hain't we raised 'em t' be fust-rate, number one prize stock?

PETER. We hain't—not no more.

SIMEON. (*dully*) I was fergittin'. (*Then resignedly*) Waal, let's go help Eben a spell an' git waked up.

PETER. Suits me. (*They are starting off down left, rear, for the barn when Eben appears from there hurrying toward them, his face excited*).

EBEN. (*breathlessly*) Waal—har they be! The old mule an' the bride! I seen 'em from the barn down below at the turnin'.

PETER. How could ye tell that far?

EBEN. Hain't I as far-sight ah he's near-sight? Don't I know the
mare 'n' buggy, an' two people settin' in it? Who else . . . ? An' I tell
ye I kin feel 'em a-comin', too! (*He squirms as if he had the itch*).

PETER. (*beginning to be angry*) Waal—let him do his own unhitchin'!

SIMEON. (*angry in his turn*) Let's hustle in an' git our bundles an'
be a-goin' as he's a-comin'. I don't want never t' step inside the door
agen arter he's back. (*They both start back around the corner of the
house.* EBEN *follows them*).

EBEN. (*anxiously*) Will ye sign it afore ye go?

PETER. Let's see the color o' the old skinflint's money an' we'll sign.
(*They disappear left. The two brothers clump upstairs to get their
bundles.* EBEN *appears in the kitchen, runs to window, peers out,
comes back and pulls up a strip of flooring in under stove, takes out
a canvas bag and puts it on table, then sets the floorboard back in
place. The two brothers appear a moment after. They carry old carpet
bags*).

EBEN. (*puts his hand on bag guardingly*) Have ye signed?

SIMEON. (*shows paper in his hand*) Ay-eh. (*Greedily*) Be that the
money?

EBEN. (*opens bag and pours out pile of twenty-dollar gold pieces*)
Twenty-dollar pieces—thirty on 'em. Count 'em (*Peter does so, arranging them in stacks of five, biting one or two to test them*).

PETER. Six hundred. (*He puts them in bag and puts it inside his
shirt carefully*).

SIMEON. (*handing paper to* EBEN) Har ye be.

EBEN. (*after a glance, folds it carefully and hides it under his shirt
—gratefully*) Thank yew.

PETER. Thank yew fur the ride.

SIMEON. We'll send ye a lump o' gold fur Christmas. (*A pause.*
EBEN *stares at them and they at him*).

PETER. (*awkwardly*) Waal—we're a-goin'.

SIMEON. Comin' out t' the yard?

EBEN. No I'm waitin' in here a spell. (*Another silence. The brothers
edge awkwardly to door in rear—then turn and stand*).

SIMEON. Waal—good-by.

PETER. Good-by.

EBEN. Good-by. (*They go out. He sits down at the table, faces the
stove and pulls out the paper. He looks from it to the stove. His face,
lighted up by the shaft of sunlight from the window, has an expression
of trance. His lips move. The two brothers come out to the gate*).

PETER. (*looking off toward barn*) Thar he be—unhitchin'.

SIMEON. (*with a chuckle*) I'll bet ye he's riled!

PETER. An' thar she be.

SIMEON. Let's wait 'n' see what our new Maw looks like.

PETER. (*with a grin*) An' give him our partin' cuss!

SIMEON. (*grinning*) I feel like raisin' fun. I feel light in my head an' feet.

PETER. Me, too. I feel like laffin' till I'd split up the middle.

SIMEON. Reckon it's the likker?

PETER. No. My feet feel itchin' t' walk an' walk—an' jump high over thin's—an'. . . .

SIMEON. Dance? (*A pause*).

PETER. (*puzzled*) It's plumb onnateral.

SIMEON. (*a light coming over his face*) I calc'late it's 'cause school's out. It's holiday. Fur once we're free!

PETER. (*dazedly*) Free?

SIMEON. The halter's broke—the harness is busted—the fence bars is down—the stone walls air crumblin' an' tumblin'! We'll be kickin' up an' tearin' away down the road!

PETER. (*drawing a deep breath—oratorically*) Anybody that wants this stinkin' old rock-pile of a farm kin hev it. T'ain't our'n, no sirree!

SIMEON. (*takes the gate off its hinges and puts it under his arm*) We harby 'bolishes shet gates, an' open gates, an' all gates, by thunder!

PETER. We'll take it with us fur luck an' let er' sail free down some river.

SIMEON. (*as a sound of voices comes from left, rear*) Har they comes! (*The two brothers congeal into two stiff, grim-visaged statues.* EPHRIAM CABOT *and* ABBIE PUTNAM *come in.* CABOT *is seventy-five, tall and gaunt, with great, wiry, concentrated power, but stoop-shouldered from toil. His face is as hard as if it were hewn out of a boulder, yet there is a weakness in it, a petty pride in its own narrow strength. His eyes are small, close together, and extremely near-sighted, blinking continually in the effort to focus on objects, their stare having a straining, ingrowing quality. He is dressed in his dismal black Sunday suit.* ABBIE *is thirty-five, buxom, full of vitality. Her round face is pretty but marred by its rather gross sensuality. There is strength and obstinacy in her jaw, a hard determination in her eyes, and about her whole personality the same unsettled, untamed, desperate quality which is so apparent in* EBEN).

CABOT. (*as they enter—a queer strangled emotion in his dry cracking voice*) Har we be t' hum, Abbie.

ABBIE. (*with lust for the word*) Hum! (*Her eyes gloating on the house without seeming to see the two stiff figures at the gate*) It's purty—purty! I can't b'lieve it's r'ally mine.

CABOT. (*sharply*) Yewr'n? Mine! (*He stares at her penetratingly. She stares back. He adds relentingly*) Our'n—mebbe! It was lonesome too long. I was growin' old in the spring. A hum's got t' hev a woman.

ABBIE. (*her voice taking possession*) A woman's got t' hev a hum!

CABOT. (*nodding uncertainly*) Ay-eh. (*Then irritably*) Whar be they? Ain't thar nobody about—'r wukin'—r' nothin'?

ABBIE. (*sees the brothers. She returns their stare of cold appraising contempt with interest—slowly*) Thar's two men loafin' at the gate an' starin' at me like a couple o' strayed hogs.

CABOT. (*straining his eyes*) I kin see 'em—but I can't make out. . . .

SIMEON. It's Simeon.

PETER. It's Peter.

CABOT. (*exploding*) Why hain't ye wukin'?

SIMEON. (*dryly*) We're waitin' t' welcome ye hum—yew an' the bride!

CABOT. (*confusedly*) Huh? Waal—this be yer new Maw, boys. (*She stares at them and they at her*).

SIMEON. (*turns away and spits contemptuously*) I see her!

PETER. (*spits also*) An' I see her!

ABBIE. (*with the conqueror's conscious superiority*) I'll go in an' look at *my* house. (*She goes slowly around to porch*).

SIMEON. (*with a snort*) *Her* house!

PETER. (*calls after her*) Ye'll find Eben inside. Ye better not tell him it's *yewr* house.

ABBIE. (*mouthing the name*) Eben. (*Then quietly*) I'll tell Eben.

CABOT. (*with a contemptuous sneer*) Ye needn't heed Eben. Eben's a dumb fool—like his Maw—soft an' simple!

SIMEON. (*with his sardonic burst of laughter*) Ha! Eben's a chip o' yew—spit 'n' image—hard 'n' bitter's a hickory tree! Dog'll eat dog. He'll eat ye yet, old man!

CABOT. (*commandingly*) Ye git t' wuk!

SIMEON. (*as* ABBIE *disappears in house—winks at* PETER *and says tauntingly*) So that thar's our new Maw, be it? Whar in hell did ye dig her up? (*He and* PETER *laugh*).

PETER. Ha! Ye'd better turn her in the pen with the other sows. (*They laugh uproariously, slapping their thighs*).

CABOT. (*so amazed at their effrontery that he stutters in confusion*) Simeon! Peter! What's come over ye? Air ye drunk?

SIMEON. We're free, old man—free o' yew an' the hull damned farm! (*They grow more and more hilarious and excited*).

PETER. An' we're startin' out fur the gold fields o' Californi-a!

SIMEON. Ye kin take this place an' burn it!

PETER. An' bury it—fur all we cares!

SIMEON. We're free, old man! (*He cuts a caper*).

PETER. Free! (*He gives a kick in the air*).

SIMEON. (*in a frenzy*) Whoop!

PETER. Whoop! (*They do an absurd Indian war dance about the old man who is petrified between rage and the fear that they are insane*).

SIMEON. We're free as Injuns! Lucky we don't skulp ye!

PETER. An' burn yer barn an' kill the stock!

SIMEON. An' rape yer new woman! Whoop! (*He and* PETER *stop their dance, holding their sides, rocking with wild laughter*).

CABOT. (*edging away*) Lust fur gold—fur the sinful, easy gold o' Californi-a! It's made ye mad!

SIMEON. (*tauntingly*) Wouldn't ye like us to send ye back some sinful gold, ye old sinner?

PETER. They's gold besides what's in Californi-a! (*He retreats back beyond the vision of the old man and takes the bag of money and flaunts it in the air above his head, laughing*).

SIMEON. And sinfuller, too!

PETER. We'll be voyagin' on the sea! Whoop! (*He leaps up and down*).

SIMEON. Livin' free! Whoop! (*He leaps in turn*).

CABOT. (*suddenly roaring with rage*) My cuss on ye!

SIMEON. Take our'n in trade fur it! Whoop!

CABOT. I'll hev ye both chained up in the asylum!

PETER. Ye old skinflint! Good-by!

SIMEON. Ye old blood sucker! Good-by!

CABOT. Go afore I . . . !

PETER. Whoop! (*He picks a stone from the road.* SIMEON *does the same*).

SIMEON. Maw'll be in the parlor.

PETER. Ay-eh! One! Two!

CABOT. (*frightened*) What air ye . . . ?

PETER. Three! (*They both throw, the stones hitting the parlor window with a crash of glass, tearing the shade*).

SIMEON. Whoop!

PETER. Whoop!

CABOT. (*in a fury now, rushing toward them*) If I kin lay hands on ye—I'll break yer bones fur ye! (*But they beat a capering retreat before him,* SIMEON *with the gate still under his arm.* CABOT *comes back, panting with impotent rage. Their voices as they go off take up the song of the gold-seekers to the old tune of "Oh Susannah!"*)

"I jumped aboard the Liza ship,
  And traveled on the sea,
  And every time I thought of home
  I wished it wasn't me!
  Oh! Californi-a,
  That's the land fur me!
  I'm off to Californi-a!
  With my wash bowl on my knee."

(*In the meantime, the window of the upper bedroom on right is raised and* ABBIE *sticks her head out. She looks down at* CABOT—*with a sigh of relief*).

ABBIE. Waal—that's the last o' them two, hain't it? (*He doesn't answer. Then in possessive tones*) This here's a nice bedroom, Ephraim. It's a r'al nice bed. Is it my room, Ephraim?

CABOT. (*grimly—without looking up*) Our'n! (*She cannot control a grimace of aversion and pulls back her head slowly and shuts the window. A sudden horrible thought seems to enter* CABOT's *head*) They been up to somethin'! Mebbe—mebbe they've pizened the stock—'r somethin'! (*He almost runs off down toward the barn. A moment later the kitchen door is slowly pushed open and* ABBIE *enters. For a moment she stands looking at* EBEN. *He does not notice her at first. Her eyes take him in penetratingly with a calculating appraisal of his strength as against hers. But under this her desire is dimly awakened by his youth and good looks. Suddenly he becomes conscious of her presence and looks up. Their eyes meet. He leaps to his feet, glowering at her speechlessly*).

ABBIE. (*in her most seductive tones which she uses all through this scene*) Be you—Eben! I'm Abbie— (*She laughs*) I mean, I'm yer new Maw.

EBEN. (*viciously*) No, damn ye!

ABBIE. (*as if she hadn't heard—with a queer smile*) Yer Paw's spoke a lot o' yew. . . .

EBEN. Ha!

ABBIE. Ye mustn't mind him. He's an old man. (*A long pause. They stare at each other*) I don't want t' pretend playin' Maw t' ye, Eben. (*Admiringly*) Ye're too big an' too strong fur that. I want t' be frens with ye. Mebbe with me fur a fren ye'd find ye'd like livin' here better. I kin make it easy fur ye with him, mebbe. (*With a scornful sense of power*) I calc'late I kin git him t' do most anythin' fur me.

EBEN. (*with bitter scorn*) Ha! (*They stare again,* EBEN *obscurely moved, physically attracted to her—in forced stilted tones*) Yew kin go t' the devil!

ABBIE. (*calmly*) If cussin' me does ye good, cuss all ye've a mind t'. I'm all prepared t' have ye agin me—at fust. I don't blame ye nuther. I'd feel the same at any stranger comin' t' take my Maw's place. (*He shudders. She is watching him carefully*) Yew must've cared a lot fur yewr Maw, didn't ye? My Maw died afore I'd growed. I don't remember her none. (*A pause*) But yew won't hate me long, Eben. I'm not the wust in the world—an' yew an' me've got a lot in common. I kin tell that by lookin' at ye. Waal—I've had a hard life, too—oceans o' trouble an' nuthin' but wuk fur reward. I was a orphan early an' had t' wuk fur others in other folk's hums. Then I married an' he turned out a drunken spreer an' so he had to wuk fur others an' me too agen in other folks' hums, an' the baby died, an' my husband got sick an' died too, an' I was glad sayin' now I'm free fur once, on'y I diskivered right away all I was free fur was t' wuk agen in other folks' hum, doin' other folks' wuk till I'd most give up hope o' ever doin' my own wuk in my own hum, an' then your Paw come. . . . (*Cabot appears returning from the barn. He comes to the gate and looks down the road the brothers have gone. A faint strain of their retreating voices is heard: "Oh, Californi-a! That's the place for me." He stands glowering, his fist clenched, his face grim with rage*).

EBEN. (*fighting his growing attraction and sympathy—harshly*) An' bought yew—like a harlot! (*She is stung and flushes angrily. She has been sincerely moved by the recital of her troubles. He adds furiously*) An' the price he's payin' ye—this farm—was my Maw's, damn ye!—an' mine now!

ABBIE. (*with a cool laugh of confidence*) Yewr'n? We'll see 'bout that! (*Then strongly*) Waal—what if I did need a hum? What else'd I marry an old man like him fur?

EBEN. (*maliciously*) I'll tell him ye said that!

ABBIE. (*smiling*) I'll say ye're lyin' a-purpose—an' he'll drive ye off the place!

EBEN. Ye devil!

ABBIE. (*defying him*) This be my farm—this be my hum—this be my kitchen—!

EBEN. (*furiously, as if he were going to attack her*) Shut up, damn ye!

ABBIE. (*walks up to him—a queer coarse expression of desire in her face and body—slowly*) An' upstairs—that be my bedroom—an' my bed! (*He stares into her eyes, terribly confused and torn. She adds softly*) I hain't bad nor mean—'ceptin' fur an enemy—but I got t' fight fur what's due me out o' life, if I ever 'spect t' git it. (*Then putting her hand on his arm—seductively*) Let's yew 'n' me be frens, Eben.

EBEN. (*stupidly—as if hypnotized*) Ay-eh. (*Then furiously flinging off her arm*) No, ye durned old witch! I hate ye! (*He rushes out the door*).

ABBIE. (*looks after him smiling satisfiedly—then half to herself, mouthing the word*) Eben's nice. (*She looks at the table, proudly*) I'll wash up *my* dishes now. (EBEN *appears outside, slamming the door behind him. He comes around corner, stops on seeing his father, and stands staring at him with hate*).

CABOT. (*raising his arms to heaven in the fury he can no longer control*) Lord God o' Hosts, smite the undutiful sons with Thy wust cuss!

EBEN. (*breaking in violently*) Yew 'n' yewr God! Allus cussin' folks—allus naggin' 'em!

CABOT. (*oblivious to him—summoningly*) God o' the old! God o' the lonesome!

EBEN. (*mockingly*) Naggin' His sheep t' sin! T' hell with yewr God! (CABOT *turns. He and* EBEN *glower at each other*).

CABOT. (*harshly*) So it's yew. I might've knowed it. (*Shaking his finger threateningly at him*) Blasphemin' fool! (*Then quickly*) Why hain't ye t' wuk?

EBEN. Why hain't yew? They've went. I can't wuk it all alone.

CABOT. (*contemptuously*) Nor noways! I'm wuth ten o' ye yit, old's I be! Ye'll never be more'n half a man! (*Then, matter-of-factly*) Waal —let's git t' the barn. (*They go. A last faint note of the "Californi-a" song is heard from the distance.* ABBIE *is washing her dishes*).

CURTAIN

PART TWO—SCENE ONE

The exterior of the farmhouse, as in Part One—a hot Sunday afternoon two months later. ABBIE, *dressed in her best, is discovered sitting in a rocker at the end of the porch. She rocks listlessly, enervated by the heat, staring in front of her with bored, half-closed eyes.*

EBEN *sticks his head out of his bedroom window. He looks around furtively and tries to see—or hear—if anyone is on the porch, but although he has been careful to make no noise,* ABBIE *has sensed his movement. She stops rocking, her face grows animated and eager, she waits attentively.* EBEN *seems to feel her presence, he scowls back his thoughts of her and spits with exaggerated disdain—then withdraws back into the room.* ABBIE *waits, holding her breath as she listens with passionate eagerness for every sound within the house.*

EBEN *comes out. Their eyes meet. His falter, he is confused, he turns away and slams the door resentfully. At this gesture,* ABBIE *laughs tantalizingly, amused but at the same time piqued and irritated. He scowls, strides off the porch to the path and starts to walk past her to the road with a grand swagger of ignoring her existence. He is dressed in his store suit, spruced up, his face shines from soap and water.* ABBIE *leans forward on her chair, her eyes hard and angry now, and, as he passes her, gives a sneering, taunting chuckle.*

EBEN. (*stung—turns on her furiously*) What air yew cacklin' bout?
ABBIE. (*triumphant*) Yew!
EBEN. What about me?
ABBIE. Ye look all slicked up like a prize bull.
EBEN. (*with a sneer*) Waal—ye hain't so durned purty yerself, be ye? (*They stare into each other's eyes, his held by hers in spite of himself, hers glowingly possessive. Their physical attraction becomes a palpable force quivering in the hot air*).
ABBIE. (*softly*) Ye don't mean that, Eben. Ye may think ye mean it, mebbe, but ye don't. Ye can't. It's agin nature, Eben. Ye been fightin' yer nature ever since the day I come—tryin' t' tell yerself I hain't purty t'ye. (*She laughs a low humid laugh without taking her eyes from his. A pause—her body squirms desirously—she mumurs languorously*) Hain't the sun strong an' hot? Ye kin feel it burnin' into the earth—Nature—makin' thin's grow—bigger 'n' bigger—burnin'

inside ye—makin' ye want t' grow—into somethin' else—till ye're jined with it—an' it's your'n—but it owns ye, too—an' makes ye grow bigger—like a tree—like them elums— (*She laughs again softly, holding his eyes. He takes a step toward her, compelled against his will*) Nature'll beat ye, Eben. Ye might's well own up t' it fust 's last.

EBEN. (*trying to break from her spell—confusedly*) If Paw'd hear ye goin' on.... (*Resentfully*) But ye've made such a damned idjit out o' the old devil...! (ABBIE *laughs*).

ABBIE. Waal—hain't it easier fur yew with him changed softer?

EBEN. (*defiantly*) No. I'm fightin' him—fightin' yew—fightin' fur Maw's rights t' her hum! (*This breaks her spell for him. He glowers at her*) An' I'm onto ye. Ye hain't foolin' me a mite. Ye're aimin' t' swaller up everythin' an' make it your'n. Waal, you'll find I'm a heap sight bigger hunk nor yew kin chew! (*He turns from her with a sneer*).

ABBIE. (*trying to regain her ascendancy—seductively.*) Eben!

EBEN. Leave me be! (*He starts to walk away*).

ABBIE. (*more commandingly*) Eben!

EBEN. (*stops—resentfully*) What d'ye want?

ABBIE. (*trying to conceal a growing excitement*) Whar air ye goin'?

EBEN. (*with malicious nonchalance*) Oh—up the road a spell.

ABBIE. T' the village?

EBEN. (*airily*) Mebbe.

ABBIE. (*excitedly*) T' see that Min, I s'pose?

EBEN. Mebbe.

ABBIE. (*weakly*) What d'ye want t' waste time on her fur?

EBEN. (*revenging himself now—grinning at her*) Ye can't beat Nature, didn't ye say? (*He laughs and again starts to walk away*).

ABBIE. (*bursting out*) An ugly old hake!

EBEN. (*with a tantalizing sneer*) She's purtier'n yew be!

ABBIE. That every wuthless drunk in the country has....

EBEN. (*tauntingly*) Mebbe—but she's better'n yew. She owns up fa'r 'n' squar' t' her doin's.

ABBIE. (*furiously*) Don't ye dare compare....

EBEN. She don't go sneakin' an' stealin'—what's mine.

ABBIE. (*savagely seizing on his weak point*) Your'n? Yew mean—my farm?

EBEN. I mean the farm yew sold yerself fur like any other old whore—my farm!

ABBIE. (*stung—fiercely*) Ye'll never live t' see the day when even a stinkin' weed on it 'll belong t' ye! (*Then in a scream*) Git out o' my sight! Go on t' yer slut—disgracin' yer Paw 'n' me! I'll git yer Paw t' horsewhip ye off the place if I want t'! Ye're only livin' here 'cause I tolerate ye! Git along! I hate the sight o' ye! (*She stops, panting and glaring at him*).

EBEN. (*returning her glance in kind*) An' I hate the sight o' yew! (*He turns and strides off up the road. She follows his retreating figure*

with concentrated hate. Old CABOT *appears coming up from the barn.
The hard, grim expression of his face has changed. He seems in some
queer way softened, mellowed. His eyes have taken on a strange, incongruous dream quality. Yet there is no hint of physical weakness
about him—rather he looks more robust and younger.* ABBIE *sees him
and turns away quickly with unconcealed aversion. He comes slowly up
to her).*

CABOT. (*mildly*) War yew an' Eben quarrelin' agen?

ABBIE. (*shortly*) No.

CABOT. Ye was talkin' a'mighty loud. (*He sits down on the edge
of porch*).

ABBIE. (*snappishly*) If ye heerd us they hain't no need askin'
questions.

CABOT. I didn't hear what ye said.

ABBIE. (*relieved*) Waal—it wa'n't nothin' t' speak on.

CABOT. (*after a pause*) Eben's queer.

ABBIE. (*bitterly*) He's the dead spit 'n' image o' yew!

CABOT. (*queerly interested*) D'ye think so, Abbie? (*After a pause,
ruminatingly*) Me 'n' Eben's allus fit 'n' fit. I never could b'ar him
noways. He's so thunderin' soft—like his Maw.

ABBIE. (*scornfully*) Ay-eh! 'Bout as soft as yew be!

CABOT. (*as if he hadn't heard*) Mebbe I been too hard on him.

ABBIE. (*jeeringly*) Waal—ye're gittin' soft now—soft as slop!
That's what Eben was sayin'.

CABOT. (*his face instantly grim and ominous*) Eben was sayin?
Waal, he'd best not do nothin' t' try me 'r he'll soon diskiver.... (*A
pause. She keeps her face turned away. His gradually softens. He stares
up at the sky*) Purty, hain't it?

ABBIE. (*crossly*) I don't see nothin' purty.

CABOT. The sky. Feels like a wa'm field up thar.

ABBIE. (*sarcastically*) Air yew aimin' t' buy up over the farm too?
(*She snickers contemptuously*).

CABOT. (*strangely*) I'd like t' own my place up thar. (*A pause*)
I'm gittin' old, Abbie. I'm gittin' ripe on the bough. (*A pause. She stares
at him mystified. He goes on*) It's allus lonesome cold in the house—
even when it's bilin' hot outside. Hain't yew noticed?

ABBIE. No.

CABOT. It's wa'm down t' the barn—nice smellin' an' warm—with
the cows. (*A pause*) Cows is queer.

ABBIE. Like yew?

CABOT. Like Eben. (*A pause*) I'm gittin' t' feel resigned t' Eben—
jest as I got t' feel 'bout his Maw. I'm gittin' t' learn to b'ar his softness—jest like her'n. I calc'late I c'd a'most take t' him—if he wa'n't
sech a dumb fool! (*A pause*) I s'pose it's old age a-creepin' in my bones.

ABBIE. (*indifferently*) Waal—ye hain't dead yet.

CABOT. (*roused*) No, I hain't, yew bet—not by a hell of a sight—

I'm sound 'n' tough as hickory! (*Then moodily*) But arter three score and ten the Lord warns ye t' prepare. (*A pause*) That's why Eben's come in my head. Now that his cussed sinful brothers is gone their path t' hell, they's no one left but Eben.

ABBIE. (*resentfully*) They's me, hain't they? (*Agitatedly*) What's all this sudden likin' ye've tuk to Eben? Why don't ye say nothin' 'bout me? Hain't I yer lawful wife?

CABOT. (*simply*) Ay-eh. Ye be. (*A pause—he stares at her desirously—his eyes grow avid—then with a sudden movement he seizes her hands and squeezes them, declaiming in a queer camp meeting preacher's tempo*) Yew air my Rose o' Sharon! Behold, yew air fair; yer eyes air doves; yer lips air like scarlet; yer two breasts air like two fawns; year navel be like a round goblet; yer belly be like a heap o' wheat.[1] . . . (*He covers her hand with kisses. She does not seem to notice. She stares before her with hard angry eyes*).

ABBIE. (*jerking her hands away—harshly*) So ye're plannin' t' leave the farm t' Eben, air ye?

CABOT. (*dazedly*) Leave . . . ? (*Then with resentful obstinacy*) I hain't a-givin' it t' no one!

ABBIE. (*remorselessly*) Ye can't take it with ye.

CABOT. (*thinks a moment—then reluctantly*) No, I calc'late not. (*After a pause—with a strange passion*) But if I could, I would, by the Etarnal! 'R if I could, in my dyin' hour, I'd set it afire an' watch it burn—this house an' every ear o' corn an' every tree down t' the last blade o' hay! I'd sit an' know it was all a-dying with me an' no one else'd ever own what was mine, what I'd made out o' nothin' with my own sweat 'n' blood! (*A pause—then he adds with a queer affection*) 'Ceptin' the cows. Them I'd turn free.

ABBIE. (*harshly*) An' me?

CABOT. (*with a queer smile*) Ye'd be turned free, too.

ABBIE. (*furiously*) So that's the thanks I git fur marryin' ye—t' have ye change kind to Eben who hates ye, an' talk o' turnin' me out in the road.

CABOT. (*hastily*) Abbie! Ye know I wa'n't. . . .

ABBIE (*vengefully*) Just let me tell ye a thing or two 'bout Eben! Whar's he gone? T' see that harlot, Min! I tried fur t' stop him. Disgracin' yew an' me—on the Sabbath, too!

CABOT. (*rather guiltily*) He's a sinner—nateral-born. It's lust eatin' his heart.

ABBIE (*enraged beyond endurance—wildly vindictive*) An' his lust fur me! Kin ye find excuses fur that?

CABOT. (*stares at her—after a dead pause*) Lust—fur yew?

ABBIE. (*defiantly*) He was tryin' t' make love t' me—when ye heerd us quarrelin'.

---

[1] Cf. the Song of Solomon in the Old Testament.

CABOT. (*stares at her—then a terrible expression of rage comes over his face—he springs to his feet shaking all over*) By the A'mighty God—I'll end him!

ABBIE. (*frightened now for Eben*) No! Don't ye!

CABOT. (*violently*) I'll git the shotgun an' blow his soft brains t' the top o' them elums!

ABBIE. (*throwing her arms around him*) No, Ephraim!

CABOT. (*pushing her away violently*) I will, by God!

ABBIE. (*in a quieting tone*) Listen, Ephraim. 'Twa'n't nothin' bad—on'y a boy's foolin'—'twa'n't meant serious—jest jokin' an' teasin'. . . .

CABOT. Then why did ye say—lust?

ABBIE. It must hev sounded wusser'n I meant. An' I was mad at thinkin'—ye'd leave him the farm.

CABOT. (*quieter but still grim and cruel*) Waal then, I'll horsewhip him off the place if that much'll confent ye.

ABBIE. (*reaching out and taking his hand*) No. Don't think o' me! Ye mustn't drive him off. 'Tain't sensible. Who'll ye get to help ye on the farm? They's no one hereabouts.

CABOT. (*considers this—then nodding his appreciation*) Ye got a head on ye. (*Then irritably*) Waal, let him stay. (*He sits down on the edge of the porch. She sits beside him. He murmurs contemptuously*) I oughtn't t' git riled so—at that 'ere fool calf. (*A pause*) But har's the p'int. What son o' mine'll keep on here t' the farm—when the Lord does call me? Simeon an' Peter air gone t' hell—an' Eben's follerin' 'em.

ABBIE. They's me.

CABOT. Ye're on'y a woman.

ABBIE. I'm yer wife.

CABOT. That hain't me. A son is me—my blood—mine. Mine ought t' git mine. An' then it's still mine—even though I be six foot under. D'ye see?

ABBIE. (*giving him a look of hatred*) Ay-eh. I see. (*She becomes very thoughtful, her face growing shrewd, her eyes studying* CABOT *craftily*).

CABOT. I'm gittin' old—ripe on the bough. (*Then with a sudden forced reassurance*) Not but what I hain't a hard nut t' crack even yet—an' fur many a year t' come! By the Etarnal, I kin break most o' the young fellers' backs at any kind o' work any day o' the year!

ABBIE. (*suddenly*) Mebbe the Lord'll give *us* a son.

CABOT. (*turns and stares at her eagerly*) Ye mean—a son—t' me 'n' yew?

ABBIE. (*with a cajoling smile*) Ye're a strong man yet, hain't ye? 'Tain't noways impossible, be it? We know that. Why d'ye stare so? Hain't ye never thought o' that afore? I been thinkin' o' it all along. Ay-eh—an' I been prayin' it'd happen, too.

CABOT. (*his face growing full of joyous pride and a sort of religious ecstasy*) Ye been prayin', Abbie?—fur a son?—t' us?

ABBIE. Ay-eh. (*With a grim resolution*) I want a son now.

CABOT. (*excitedly clutching both of her hands in his*) It'd be the blessin' o' God, Abbie—the blessin' o' God A'mighty on me—in my old age—in my lonesomeness! They hain't nothin' I wouldn't do fur ye then, Abbie. Ye'd hev on'y t' ask it—anythin' ye'd a mind t'!

ABBIE. (*interrupting*) Would ye will the farm t' me then—t' me an' it . . . ?

CABOT. (*vehemently*) I'd do anythin' ye axed, I tell ye! I swar it! May I be everlastin' damned t' hell if I wouldn't (*He sinks to his knees pulling her down with him. He trembles all over with the fervor of his hopes*) Pray t' the Lord agen, Abbie. It's the Sabbath! I'll jine ye! Two prayers air better nor one. "An' God hearkened unto Rachel"! An' God hearkened unto Abbie! Pray, Abbie! Pray fur him to hearken! (*He bows his head, mumbling. She pretends to do likewise but gives him a side glance of scorn and triumph*).

SCENE TWO

About eight in the evening. The interior of the two bedrooms on the top floor is shown. EBEN *is sitting on the side of his bed in the room on the left. On account of the heat he has taken off everything but his undershirt and pants. His feet are bare. He faces front, brooding moodily, his chin propped on his hands, a desperate expression on his face.*

In the other room CABOT *and* ABBIE *are sitting side by side on the edge of their bed, an old four-poster with feather mattress. He is in his night shirt, she in her nightdress. He is still in the queer, excited mood into which the notion of a son has thrown him. Both rooms are lighted dimly and flickeringly by tallow candles.*

CABOT. The farm needs a son.

ABBIE. I need a son.

CABOT. Ay-eh. Sometimes ye air the farm an' sometimes the farm be yew. That's why I clove t' ye in my lonesomeness. (*A pause. He pounds his knee with his fist.*) Me an' the farm has got t' beget a son!

ABBIE. Ye'd best go t' sleep. Ye're gittin' thin's all mixed.

CABOT. (*with an impatient gesture*) No, I hain't. My mind's clear's a well. Ye don't know me, that's it. (*He stares hopelessly at the floor*).

ABBIE. (*indifferently*) Mebbe. (*In the next room* EBEN *gets up and paces up and down distractedly.* ABBIE *hears him. Her eyes fasten on the intervening wall with concentrated attention.* EBEN *stops and stares. Their hot glances seem to meet through the wall. Unconsciously he stretches out his arms for her and she half rises. Then aware, he mutters a curse at himself and flings himself face downward on the bed, his clenched fists above his head, his face buried in the pillow.* ABBIE *relaxes with a faint sigh but her eyes remain fixed on the wall; she listens with all her attention for some movement from* EBEN).

CABOT. (*suddenly raises his head and looks at her—scornfully*) Will ye ever know me—'r will any man 'r woman? (*Shaking his head*) No. I calc'late 't wa'n't t' be. (*He turns away.* ABBIE *looks at the wall. Then, evidently unable to keep silent about his thoughts, without looking at his wife, he puts out his hand and clutches her knee. She starts violently, looks at him, sees he is not watching her, concentrates on the wall and pays no attention to what he says*) Listen, Abbie. When I come here fifty odd year ago—I was jest twenty an' the strongest an' hardest ye ever seen—ten times as strong an' fifty times as hard as Eben. Waal—this place was nothin' but fields o' stones. Folks laughed when I tuk it. They couldn't know what I knowed. When ye kin make corn sprout out o' stones, God's livin' in yew! They wa'n't strong enuf fur that! They reckoned God was easy. They laughed. They don't laugh no more. Some died hereabouts. Some went West an' died. They're all under ground—fur follerin' arter an easy God. God hain't easy. (*He shakes his head slowly*) An' I growed hard. Folks kept allus sayin' he's a hard man like 'twas sinful t' be hard, so's at last I said back at 'em: Waal then, by thunder, ye'll git me hard an' see how ye like it! (*Then suddenly*) But I give in t' weakness once. 'Twas arter I'd been here two year. I got weak—despairful—they was so many stones. They was a party leavin', givin' up, goin' West. I jined 'em. We tracked on 'n' on. We come t' broad medders, plains whar the soil was black an' rich as gold. Nary a stone. Easy. Ye'd on'y to plow an' sow an' then set an' smoke yer pipe an' watch thin's grow. I could o' been a rich man—but somethin' in me fit me an' fit me—the voice o' God sayin': "This hain't wuth nothin' t' Me. Git ye back t' hum!" I got afeerd o' that voice an' I lit out back t' hum here, leavin' my claim an' crops t' whoever'd a mind t' take 'em. Ay-eh. I actoolly give up what was rightful mine! God's hard, not easy! God's in the stones! Build my church on a rock—out o' stones an' I'll be in them! That's what He meant t' Peter! (*He sighs heavily—a pause*) Stones. I picked 'em up an' piled 'em into walls. Ye kin read the years o' my life in them walls, every day a hefted stone, climbin' over the hills up and down, fencin' in the fields that was mine, whar I'd made thin's grow out o' nothin'—like the will o' God, like the servant o' His hand. It wa'n't easy. It was hard an' He made me hard fur it. (*He pauses*) All the time I kept gittin' lonesomer. I tuk a wife. She bore Simeon an' Peter. She was a good woman. She wuked hard. We was married twenty year. She never knowed me. She helped but she never knowed what she was helpin'. I was allus lonesome. She died. After that it wa'n't so lonesome fur a spell. (*A pause*) I lost count o' the years. I had no time t' fool away countin' 'em. Sim an' Peter helped. The farm growed. It was all mine! When I thought o' that I didn't feel lonesome. (*A pause*) But ye can't hitch yer mind t' one thin' day an' night. I tuk another wife—Eben's Maw. Her folks was contestin' me at law over my deeds t' the farm—my farm! That's why Eben keeps a-talkin' his fool talk o' this bein' his Maw's farm. She bore Eben. She was purty—but soft. She tried t' be hard. She couldn't. She never knowed me nor nothin'. It was lonesomer 'n hell with her. After a matter o' sixteen odd years, she died. (*A pause*) I lived with the boys. They hated me 'cause I was hard. I hated them 'cause they was soft. They coveted the farm without knowin' what it meant. It made me bitter 'n wormwood. It aged me—them coveting what I'd made fur mine. Then this spring the call come—the voice o' God cryin' in my wilderness, in my lonesomeness—t' go out an' seek an' find! (*Turning to her with strange passion*) I sought ye an' I found ye! Yew air my Rose o' Sharon! Yer eyes air like.... (*She has turned a blank face, resentful eyes to his. He stares at her for a moment—then harshly*) Air ye any the wiser fur all I've told ye?

ABBIE. (*confusedly*) Mebbe.

CABOT. (*pushing her away from him—angrily*) Ye don't know nothin'—nor never will. If ye don't hev a son t' redeem ye.... (*This is a tone of cold threat*).

ABBIE. (*resentfully*) I've prayed, hain't I?

CABOT. (*bitterly*) Pray agen—fur understandin'!

ABBIE. (*a veiled threat in her tone*) Ye'll have a son out o' me, I promise ye.

CABOT. How kin ye promise?

ABBIE. I got second-sight mebbe. I kin foretell. (*She gives a queer smile*).

CABOT. I believe ye have. Ye give me the chills sometimes. (*He shivers*) It's cold in this house. It's oneasy. They's thin's pokin' about in the dark—in the corners. (*He pulls on his trousers, tucking in his night shirt, and pulls on his boots*).

ABBIE. (*surprised*) Whar air ye goin'?

CABOT. (*queerly*) Down whar it's restful—whar it's warm—down t' the barn. (*Bitterly*) I kin talk t' the cows. They know. They know the farm an' me. They'll give me peace. (*He turns to go out the door*).

ABBIE. (*a bit frightenedly*) Air ye ailin' tonight, Ephraim?

CABOT. Growin'. Growin' ripe on the bough. (*He turns and goes, his boots clumping down the stairs. EBEN sits up with a start, listening. ABBIE is conscious of his movement and stares at the wall. CABOT comes out of the house around the corner and stands by the gate, blinking at the sky. He stretches up his hands in a tortured gesture*) God A'mighty, call from the dark! (*He listens as if expecting an answer. Then his arms drop, he shakes his head and plods off toward the barn.*

EBEN *and* ABBIE *stare at each other through the wall.* EBEN *sighs heavily and* ABBIE *echoes it. Both become terribly nervous, uneasy. Finally* ABBIE *gets up and listens, her ear to the wall. He acts as if he saw every move she was making, he becomes resolutely still. She seems driven into a decision—goes out the door in rear determinedly. His eyes follow her. Then as the door of his room is opened softly, he turns away, waits in an attitude of strained fixity.* ABBIE *stands for a second staring at him, her eyes burning with desire. Then with a little cry she runs over and throws her arms about his neck, she pulls his head back and covers his mouth with kisses. At first, he submits dumbly; then he puts his arms about her neck and returns her kisses, but finally, suddenly aware of his hatred, he hurls her away from him, springing to his feet. They stand speechless and breathless, panting like two animals).*

ABBIE. (*at last—painfully*) Ye shouldn't, Eben—ye shouldn't—I'd make ye happy!

EBEN. (*harshly*) I don't want t' be happy—from yew!

ABBIE. (*helplessly*) Ye do, Eben! Ye do! Why d'ye lie?

EBEN. (*viciously*) I don't take t'ye, I tell ye! I hate the sight o' ye!

ABBIE. (*with an uncertain troubled laugh*) Waal, I kissed ye anyways—an' ye kissed back—yer lips was burnin'—ye can't lie 'bout that! (*Intensely*) If ye don't care, why did ye kiss me back—why was yer lips burning'?

EBEN. (*wiping his mouth*). It was like pizen on 'em. (*Then tauntingly*) When I kissed ye back, mebbe I thought 'twas someone else.

ABBIE. (*wildly*) Min?

EBEN. Mebbe.

ABBIE. (*torturedly*) Did ye go t' see her? Did ye r'ally go? I thought ye mightn't. Is that why ye throwed me off jest now?

EBEN. (*sneeringly*) What if it be?

ABBIE. (*raging*) Then ye're a dog, Eben Cabot!

EBEN. (*threateningly*) Ye can't talk that way t' me!

ABBIE. (*with a shrill laugh*) Can't I? Did ye think I was in love with ye—a weak thin' like yew? Not much! I on'y wanted ye fur a purpose o' my own—an' I'll hev ye fur it yet 'cause I'm stronger'n yew be!

EBEN. (*resentfully*) I knowed well it was on'y part o' yer plan t' swaller everythin'!

ABBIE. (*tauntingly*) Mebbe!

EBEN. (*furious*) Git out o' my room!

ABBIE. This air my room an' ye're on'y hired help!

EBEN. (*threateningly*) Git out afore I murder ye!

ABBIE. (*quite confident now*) I hain't a mite afeerd. Ye want me, don't ye? Yes, ye do! An' yer Paw's son'll never kill what he wants! Look at yer eyes! They's lust fur me in 'em, burnin' 'em up! Look at yer lips now! They're tremblin' an' longin' t' kiss me, an' yer teeth t' bite! (*He is watching her now with a horrible fascination. She laughs a crazy triumphant laugh*) I'm a-goin' t' make all o' this hum my hum! They's one room hain't mine yet, but it's a-goin' t' be tonight. I'm a-goin' down now an' light up! (*She makes him a mocking bow*) Won't ye come courtin' me in the best parlor, Mister Cabot?

 EBEN. (*staring at her—horribly confused—dully*) Don't ye dare! It hain't been opened since Maw died an' was laid out thar! Don't ye ...! (*But her eyes are fixed on his so burningly that his will seems to wither before hers. He stands swaying toward her helplessly*).

ABBIE. (*holding his eyes and putting all her will into her words as she backs out the door*) I'll expect ye afore long, Eben.

EBEN. (*stares after her for a while, walking toward the door. A light appears in the parlor window. He murmurs*) In the parlor? (*This seems to arouse connotations for he comes back and puts on his white shirt, collar, half ties the tie mechanically, puts on coat, takes his hat, stands barefooted looking about him in bewilderment, mutters wonderingly*) Maw! Whar air yew? (*Then goes slowly toward the door in rear*).

SCENE THREE

A few minutes later. The interior of the parlor is shown. A grim, repressed room like a tomb in which the family has been interred alive. ABBIE *sits on the edge of the horsechair sofa. She has lighted all the candles and the room is revealed in all its preserved ugliness. A change has come over the woman. She looks awed and frightened now, ready to run away.*

The door is opened and EBEN *appears. His face wears an expression of obsessed confusion. He stands staring at her, his arms hanging disjointedly from his shoulders, his feet bare, his hat in his hand.*

ABBIE. (*after a pause—with a nervous, formal politeness*) Won't ye set?

EBEN. (*dully*) Ay-eh. (*Mechanically he places his hat carefully on the floor near the door and sits stiffly beside her on the edge of the sofa. A pause. They both remain rigid, looking straight ahead with eyes full of fear*).

ABBIE. When I fust come in—in the dark—they seemed somethin' here.

EBEN. (*simply*) Maw.

ABBIE. I kin still feel—somethin'. . . .

EBEN. It's Maw.

ABBIE. At fust I was feered o' it. I wanted t' yell an' run. Now—since yew come—seems like it's growin' soft an' kind t' me. (*Addressing the air—queerly*) Thank yew.

EBEN. Maw allus loved me.

ABBIE. Mebbe it knows I love yew, too. Mebbe that makes it kind t' me.

EBEN. (*dully*) I dunno. I should think she'd hate ye.

ABBIE. (*with certainty*) No. I kin feel it don't—not no more.

EBEN. Hate ye fur stealin' her place—here in her hum—settin' in her parlor whar she was laid—(*He suddenly stops, staring stupidly before him*).

ABBIE. What is it, Eben?

EBEN. (*in a whisper*) Seems like Maw didn't want me t' remind ye.

ABBIE. (*excitedly*) I knowed, Eben! It's kind t' me! It don't b'ar me no grudges fur what I never knowed an' couldn't help!

EBEN. Maw b'ars him a grudge.

ABBIE. Waal, so does all o' us.

EBEN. Ay-eh. (*With passion*) I does, by God!

ABBIE. (*taking one of his hands in hers and patting it*) Thar! Don't git riled thinkin' o' him. Think o' yer Maw who's kind t' us. Tell me about yer Maw, Eben.

EBEN. They hain't nothin' much. She was kind. She was good.

ABBIE. (*putting one arm over his shoulder. He does not seem to notice—passionately*) I'll be kind an' good t' ye!

EBEN. Sometimes she used t' sing fur me.

ABBIE. I'll sing fur ye!

EBEN. This was her hum. This was her farm.

ABBIE. This is my hum! This is my farm!

EBEN. He married her t' steal 'em. She was soft an' easy. He couldn't 'preciate her.

ABBIE. He can't 'preciate me!

EBEN. He murdered her with his hardness.

ABBIE. He's murderin' me!

EBEN. She died. (*A pause*) Sometimes she used to sing fur me. (*He bursts into a fit of sobbing*).

ABBIE. (*both her arms around him—with wild passion*) I'll sing fur ye! I'll die fur ye! (*In spite of her overwhelming desire for him, there is a sincere maternal love in her manner and voice—a horribly frank mixture of lust and mother love*) Don't cry, Eben! I'll take yer Maw's place! I'll be everythin' she was t' ye! Let me kiss ye, Eben! (*She pulls his head around. He makes a bewildered pretense of resistance. She is tender*) Don't be afeered! I'll kiss ye pure, Eben—same 's if I was a Maw t' ye—an' ye kin kiss me back 's if yew was my son—my boy—sayin' good-night t' me! Kiss me, Eben. (*They kiss in restrained fashion. Then suddenly wild passion overcomes her. She kisses him lustfully again and again and he flings his arms about her and returns her kisses. Suddenly, as in the bedroom, he frees himself from her violently and springs to his feet. He is trembling all over, in a strange state of terror. ABBIE strains her arms toward him with fierce pleading*) Don't ye leave me, Eben! Can't ye see it hain't enuf—lovin' ye like a

Maw—can't ye see it's got t' be that an' more—much more—a hundred times more—fur me t' be happy—fur yew t' be happy?

EBEN. (*to the presence he feels in the room*) Maw! Maw! What d'ye want? What air ye tellin' me?

ABBIE. She's tellin' ye t' love me. She knows I love ye an' I'll be good t' ye. Can't ye feel it? Don't ye know? She's tellin' ye t' love me, Eben!

EBEN. Ay-eh. I feel—mebbe she—but—I can't figger out—why—when ye've stole her place—here in her hum—in the parlor whar she was—

ABBIE. (*fiercely*) She knows I love ye!

EBEN. (*his face suddenly lighting up with a fierce, triumphant grin*) I see it! I sees why. It's her vengeance on him—so's she kin rest quiet in her grave!

ABBIE. (*wildly*) Vengeance o' God on the hull o' us! What d'we give a durn? I love ye, Eben! God knows I love ye! (*She stretches out her arms for him*).

EBEN. (*throws himself on his knees beside the sofa and grabs her in his arms—releasing all his pent-up passion*) An' I love yew, Abbie!— now I kin say it! I been dyin' fur want o' ye—every hour since ye come! I love ye! (*Their lips meet in a fierce, bruising kiss*).

SCENE FOUR

Exterior of the farmhouse. It is just dawn. The front door at right is opened and EBEN *comes out and walks around to the gate. He is dressed in his working clothes. He seems changed. His face wears a bold and confident expression, he is grinning to himself with evident satisfaction. As he gets near the gate, the window of the parlor is heard opening and the shutters are flung back and* ABBIE *sticks her head out. Her hair tumbles over her shoulders in disarray, her face is flushed, she looks at* EBEN *with tender, languorous eyes and calls softly*).

ABBIE. Eben. (*As he turns—playfully*) Jest one more kiss afore ye go. I'm goin' to miss ye fearful all day.

EBEN. An' me yew, ye kin bet! (*He goes to her. They kiss several times. He draws away, laughingly*) Thar. That's enuf, hain't it? Ye won't hev none left fur next time.

ABBIE. I got a million o' 'em left fur yew! (*Then a bit anxiously*) D'ye r'ally love me, Eben?

EBEN. (*emphatically*) I like ye better'n any gal I ever knowed! That's gospel!

ABBIE. Likin' hain't lovin'.

EBEN. Waal then—I love ye. Now air yew satisfied?

ABBIE. Ay-eh, I be. (*She smiles at him adoringly*).

EBEN. I better git t' the barn. The old critter's liable t' suspicion an' come sneakin' up.

ABBIE. (*with a confident laugh*) Let him! I kin allus pull the wool over his eyes. I'm goin' t' leave the shutters open and let in the sun 'n' air. This room's been dead long enuf. Now it's goin' t' be my room!

EBEN. (*frowning*) Ay-eh.

ABBIE. (*hastily*) I meant—our room.

EBEN. Ay-eh.

ABBIE. We made it our'n last night, didn't we? We give it life— our lovin' did. (*A pause*).

EBEN. (*with a strange look*) Maw's gone back t' her grave. She kin sleep now.

ABBIE. May she rest in peace! (*Then tenderly rebuking*) Ye oughtn't t' talk o' sad thin's—this mornin'.

EBEN. It jest come up in my mind o' itself.

ABBIE. Don't let it. (*He doesn't answer. She yawns*) Waal, I'm a-goin' t' steal a wink o' sleep. I'll tell the Old Man I hain't feelin' pert. Let him git his own vittles.

EBEN. I see him comin' from the barn. Ye better look smart an' git upstairs.

ABBIE. Ay-eh. Good-by. Don't ferget me. (*She throws him a kiss. He grins—then squares his shoulders and awaits his father confidently.* CABOT *walks slowly up from the left, staring up at the sky with a vague face*).

EBEN. (*jovially*) Mornin', Paw. Star-gazin' in daylight?

CABOT. Purty, hain't it?

EBEN. (*looking around him possessively*) It's a durned purty farm.

CABOT. I mean the sky.

EBEN. (*grinning*) How d'ye know? Them eyes o' your'n can't see that fur. (*This tickles his humor and he slaps his thigh and laughs*) Ho-ho! That's a good un!

CABOT. (*grimly sarcastic*) Ye're feelin' right chipper, hain't ye? Whar'd ye steal the likker?

EBEN. (*good-naturedly*) 'Tain't likker. Jest life. (*Suddenly holding out his hand—soberly*) Yew 'n' me is quits. Let's shake hands.

CABOT. (*suspiciously*) What's come over ye?

EBEN. Then don't. Mebbe it's jest as well. (*A moment's pause*) What's come over me? (*Queerly*) Didn't ye feel her passin'—goin' back t' her grave?

CABOT. (*dully*) Who?

EBEN. Maw. She kin rest now an' sleep content. She's quits with ye.

CABOT. (*confusedly*) I rested. I slept good—down with the cows. They know how t' sleep. They're teachin' me.

EBEN. (*suddenly jovial again*) Good fur the cows! Waal—ye better git t' work.

CABOT. (*grimly amused*) Air yew bossin' me, ye calf?

EBEN. (*beginning to laugh*) Ay-eh! I'm bossin' yew! Ha-ha-ha!
See how ye like it! Ha-ha-ha! I'm the prize rooster o' this roost.
Ha-ha-ha! (*He goes off toward the barn laughing*).

CABOT. (*looks after him with scornful pity*) Soft-headed. Like his
Maw. Dead spit 'n' image. No hope in him! (*He spits with contemptuous disgust*) A born fool! (*Then matter-of-factly*) Waal—I'm gittin'
peckish. (*He goes toward door*).

CURTAIN

PART THREE—SCENE ONE

*A night in late spring the following year. The kitchen and the two
bedrooms upstairs are shown. The two bedrooms are dimly lighted by
a tallow candle in each.* EBEN *is sitting on the side of the bed in his
room, his chin propped on his fists, his face a study of the struggle he
is making to understand his conflicting emotions. The noisy laughter
and music from below where a kitchen dance is in progress annoy
and distract him. He scowls at the floor.*

In the next room a cradle stands beside the double bed.

*In the kitchen all is festivity. The stove has been taken down to
give more room to the dancers. The chairs, with wooden benches added,
have been pushed back against the walls. On these are seated squeezed
in tight against one another, farmers and their wives and their young
folks of both sexes from the neighboring farms. They are all chattering
and laughing loudly. They evidently have some secret joke in common.
There is no end of winking, of nudging, of meaning nods of the head
toward* CABOT *who, in a state of extreme hilarious excitement increased
by the amount he has drunk, is standing near the rear door where
there is a small keg of whisky and serving drinks to all the men. In
the left corner, front, dividing the attention with her husband,* ABBIE
*is sitting in a rocking chair, a shawl wrapped about her shoulders.
She is very pale, her face is thin and drawn, her eyes are fixed anxiously
on the open door in rear as if waiting for someone.*

*The musician is tuning up his fiddle, seated in the far right corner.
He is a lanky young fellow with a long, weak face. His pale eyes blink
incessantly and he grins about him slyly with a greedy malice.*

ABBIE. (*suddenly turning to a young girl on her right*) Whar's
Eben?

YOUNG GIRL. (*eying her scornfully*) I dunno, Mrs. Cabot. I hain't
seen Eben in ages. (*Meaningly*) Seems like he's spent most o' his time
t' hum since yew come.

ABBIE. (*vaguely*) I tuk his Maw's place.

YOUNG GIRL. Ay-eh. So I've heerd. (*She turns away to retail this bit of gossip to her mother sitting next to her.* ABBIE *turns to her left to a big stoutish middle-aged man whose flushed face and starting eyes show the amount of "likker" he has consumed*).

ABBIE. Ye hain't seen Eben, hev ye?

MAN. No, I hain't. (*Then he adds with a wink*) If yew hain't who would?

ABBIE. He's the best dancer in the county. He'd ought t' come an' dance.

MAN. (*with a wink*) Mebbe he's doin' the dutiful an' walkin' the kid t' sleep. It's a boy, hain't it?

ABBIE. (*nodding vaguely*) Ay-eh—born two weeks back—purty's a picter.

MAN. They all is—t' their Maws. (*Then in a whisper, with a nudge and a leer*) Listen, Abbie—if ye ever git tired o' Eben, remember me! Don't fergit now! (*He looks at her uncomprehending face for a second—then grunts disgustedly*) Waal—guess I'll likker agin. (*He goes over and joins* CABOT *who is arguing noisily with an old farmer over cows. They all drink*).

ABBIE. (*this time appealing to nobody in particular*) Wonder what Eben's a-doin'? (*Her remark is repeated down the line with many a guffaw and titter until it reaches the fiddler. He fastens his blinking eyes on* ABBIE).

FIDDLER. (*raising his voice*) Bet I kin tell ye, Abbie, what Eben's doin'! He's down t' the church offerin' up prayers o' thanksgivin'. (*They all titter expectantly*).

A MAN. What fur? (*Another titter*).

FIDDLER. 'Cause unto him a—(*He hesitates just long enough*) brother is born! (*A roar of laughter. They all look from* ABBIE *to* CABOT. *She is oblivious, staring at the door.* CABOT, *although he hasn't heard the words, is irritated by the laughter and steps forward, glaring about him. There is an immediate silence*).

CABOT. What're ye all bleatin' about—like a flock o' goats? Why don't ye dance, damn ye? I axed ye here t' dance—t' eat, drink an' be merry—an' thar ye set cacklin' like a lot o' wet hens with the pip! Ye've swilled my likker an' guzzled my vittles like hogs, hain't ye? Then dance fur me, can't ye? That's fa'r an' squar', hain't it? (*A grumble of resentment goes around but they are all evidently in too much awe of him to express it openly*).

FIDDLER. (*slyly*) We're waitin' fur Eben. (*A suppressed laugh*).

CABOT. (*with a fierce exultation*) T'hell with Eben! Eben's done fur now! I got a new son! (*His mood switching with drunken suddenness*) But ye needn't t' laugh at Eben, none o' ye! He's my blood, if he be a dumb fool. He's better nor any o' yew! He kin do a day's work a'most up t' what I kin—an' that'd put any o' yew pore critters t' shame!

FIDDLER. An' he kin do a good night's work, too! (*A roar of laughter*).

CABOT. Laugh, ye damn fools! Ye're right jist the same, Fiddler. He kin work day an' night too, like I kin, if need be!

OLD FARMER. (*from behind the keg where he is weaving drunkenly back and forth—with great simplicity*) They hain't many t' touch ye, Ephraim—a son at seventy-six. That's a hard man fur ye! I be on'y sixty-eight an' I couldn't do it. (*A roar of laughter in which* CABOT *joins uproariously*).

CABOT. (*slapping him on the back*) I'm sorry fur ye, Hi. I'd never suspicion sech weakness from a boy like yew!

OLD FARMER. An' I never reckoned yew had in it ye nuther, Ephraim. (*There is another laugh*).

CABOT. (*suddenly grim*) I got a lot in me—a hell of a lot—folks don't know on. (*Turning to the fiddler*) Fiddle 'er up, durn ye! Give 'em somethin' t' dance t'! What air ye, an ornament? Hain't this a celebration? Then grease yer elbow an' go it!

FIDDLER. (*seizes a drink which the* OLD FARMER *holds out to him and downs it*) Here goes! (*He starts to fiddle "Lady of the Lake." Four young fellows and four girls form in two lines and dance a square dance. The* FIDDLER *shouts directions for the different movements, keeping his words in the rhythm of the music and interspersing them with jocular personal remarks to the dancers themselves. The people seated along the walls stamp their feet and clap their hands in unison.* CABOT *is especially active in this respect. Only* ABBIE *remains apathetic, staring at the door as if she were alone in a silent room*).

FIDDLER. Swing your partner t' the right! That's it, Jim! Give her a b'ar hug! Her Maw hain't lookin'. (*Laughter*) Change partners! That suits ye, don't it, Essie, now ye got Reub afore ye? Look at her redden up, will ye? Waal, life is short an' so's love, as the feller says. (*Laughter*).

CABOT. (*excitedly, stamping his foot*) Go it, boys! Go it, gals!

FIDDLER. (*with a wink at the others*) Ye're the spryest seventy-six ever I sees, Ephraim! Now if ye'd on'y good eye-sight . . . ! (*Suppressed laughter. He gives* CABOT *no chance to retort but roars*) Promenade! Ye're walkin' like a bride down the aisle, Sarah! Waal, while they's life they's allus hope, I've heerd tell. Swing your partner to the left! Gosh A'mighty, look at Johnny Cook high-steppin'! They hain't goin' t'be much strength left fur howin' in the corn lot t'morrow. (*Laughter*).

CABOT. Go it! Go it! (*Then suddenly, unable to restrain himself any longer, he prances into the midst of the dancers, scattering them, waving his arms about wildly*) Ye're all hoofs! Git out o' my road! Give me room! I'll show ye dancin'. Ye're all too soft! (*He pushes them roughly away. They crowd back toward the walls, muttering, looking at him resentfully*).

FIDDLER. (*jeeringly*) Go it, Ephraim! Go it! (*He starts "Pop, Goes

*the Weasel," increasing the tempo with every verse until at the end
he is fiddling crazily as fast as he can go*).

CABOT. (*starts to dance, which he does very well and with tremendous vigor. Then he begins to improvise, cuts incredibly grotesque
capers, leaping up and cracking his heels together, prancing around
in a circle with body bent in an Indian war dance, then suddenly
straightening up and kicking as high as he can with both legs. He is
like a monkey on a string. And all the while he intersperses his antics
with shouts and derisive comments*) Whoop! Here's dancin' fur ye!
Whoop! See that! Seventy-six, if I'm a day! Hard as iron yet! Beatin'
the young 'uns like I allus done! Look at me! I'd invite ye t' dance on
my hundredth birthday on'y ye'll all be dead by then. Ye're a sickly
generation! Yer hearts air pink, not red! Yer veins is full o' mud an'
water! I be the on'y man in the county! Whoop! See that! I'm a Injun!
I've killed Injuns in the West afore ye was born—an' skulped 'em too!
They's a arrer wound on my backside I c'd show ye! The hull tribe
chased me. I outrun 'em all—with the arrer stuck in me! An' I tuk
vengeance on 'em. Ten eyes fur an eye, that was my motter! Whoop!
Look at me! I kin kick the ceilin' off the room! Whoop!

FIDDLER. (*stops playing—exhaustedly*) God A'mighty, I got enuf.
Ye got the devil's strength in ye.

CABOT. (*delightedly*) Did I beat yew, too? Wa'al, ye played smart.
Hev a swig. (*He pours whisky for himself and* FIDDLER. *They drink.
The others watch* CABOT *silently with cold, hostile eyes. There is a
dead pause. The* FIDDLER *rests.* CABOT *leans against the keg, panting,
glaring around him confusedly. In the room above,* EBEN *gets to his
feet and tiptoes out the door in rear, appearing a moment later in the
other bedroom. He moves silently, even frightenedly, toward the cradle
and stands there looking down at the baby. His face is as vague as his
reactions are confused, but there is a trace of tenderness, of interested
discovery. At the same moment that he reaches the cradle,* ABBIE *seems
to sense something. She gets up weakly and goes to* CABOT).

ABBIE. I'm goin' up t' the baby.

CABOT. (*with real solicitation*) Air ye able fur the stairs! D'ye want
me t' help ye, Abbie?

ABBIE. No. I'm able. I'll be down agen soon.

CABOT. Don't ye git wore out! He needs ye, remember—our son
does! (*He grins affectionately, patting her on the back. She shrinks
from his touch*).

ABBIE. (*dully*) Don't—tech me. I'm goin'—up (*She goes.* CABOT
looks after her. A whisper goes around the room. CABOT *turns. It ceases.
He wipes his forehead streaming with sweat. He is breathing pant-
ingly*).

CABOT. I'm a-goin' out t' git fresh air. I'm feelin' a mite dizzy.
Fiddle up thar! Dance, all o' ye! Here's likker fur them as wants it.
Enjoy yerselves. I'll be back. (*He goes, closing the door behind him*).

FIDDLER. (*sarcastically*) Don't hurry none on our account! (*A suppressed laugh. He imitates* ABBIE) Whar's Eben? (*More laughter*).

A WOMAN. (*loudly*) What's happened in this house is plain as the nose on yer face! (ABBIE *appears in the doorway upstairs and stands looking in surprise and adoration at* EBEN *who does not see her*).

A MAN. Ssshh! He's li'ble t' be listenin' at the door. That'd be like him. (*Their voices die to an intensive whispering. Their faces are concentrated on this gossip. A noise as of dead leaves in the wind comes from the room.* CABOT *has come out from the porch and stands by the gate, leaning on it, staring at the sky blinkingly.* ABBIE *comes across the room silently.* EBEN *does not notice her until quite near*).

EBEN. (*starting*) Abbie!

ABBIE. Ssshh! (*She throws her arms around him. They kiss—then bend over the cradle together*) Ain't he purty?—dead spit 'n' image o' yew!

EBEN. (*pleased*) Air he? I can't tell none.

ABBIE. E-zactly like!

EBEN. (*frowningly*) I don't like this. I don't like lettin' on what's mine's his'n. I been doin' that all my life. I'm gittin' t' the end o' b'arin' it!

ABBIE. (*putting her finger on his lips*) We're doin' the best we kin. We got t' wait. Somethin's bound t' happen. (*She puts her arms around him*) I got t' go back.

EBEN. I'm goin' out. I can't b'ar it with the fiddle playin' an' the laughin'.

ABBIE. Don't git feelin' low. I love ye, Eben. Kiss me. (*He kisses her. They remain in each other's arms*).

CABOT. (*at the gate, confusedly*) Even the music can't drive it out—somethin'. Ye kin feel it droppin' off the elums, climbin' up the roof, sneakin' down the chimney, pokin' in the corners! They's no peace in houses, they's no rest livin' with folks. Somethin's always livin' with ye. (*With a deep sigh*) I'll go t' the barn an' rest a spell. (*He goes wearily toward the barn*).

FIDDLER. (*tuning up*) Let's celebrate the old skunk gittin' fooled! We kin have some fun now he's went. (*He starts to fiddle "Turkey in the Straw." There is real merriment now. The young folks get up to dance*).

SCENE TWO

*A half hour later—Exterior—*EBEN *is standing by the gate looking up at the sky, an expression of dumb pain bewildered by itself on his face.* CABOT *appears, returning from the barn, walking wearily, his eyes on the ground. He sees* EBEN *and his whole mood immediately changes. He becomes excited, a cruel, triumphant grin comes to his lips, he* *strides up and slaps* EBEN *on the back. From within comes the whining of the fiddle and the noise of stamping feet and laughing voices.*

CABOT. So har ye be!

EBEN. (*startled, stares at him with hatred for a moment—then dully*) Ay-eh.

CABOT. (*surveying him jeeringly*) Why hain't ye been in t' dance? They was all axin' fur ye.

EBEN. Let 'em ax!

CABOT. They's a hull passel o' purty gals.

EBEN. T' hell with 'em!

CABOT. Ye'd ought t' be marryin' one o' 'em soon.

EBEN. I hain't marryin' no one.

CABOT. Ye might 'arn a share o' a farm that way.

EBEN. (*with a sneer*) Like yew did, ye mean? I hain't that kind.

CABOT. (*stung*) Ye lie! 'Twas yer Maw's folks aimed t' steal my farm from me.

EBEN. Other folks don't say so. (*After a pause—defiantly*) An' I got a farm anyways!

CABOT. (*derisively*) Whar?

EBEN. (*stamps a foot on the ground*) Har!

CABOT. (*throws his head back and laughs coarsely*) Ho-ho! Ye hev, hev ye? Waal, that's a good un!

EBEN. (*controlling himself—grimly*) Ye'll see!

CABOT. (*stares at him suspiciously, trying to make him out—a pause—then with scornful confidence*) Ay-eh. I'll see. So'll ye. It's ye that's blind—blind as a mole underground. (EBEN *suddenly laughs, one short sardonic bark: "Ha." A pause.* CABOT *peers at him with renewed suspicion*) Whar air ye hawin' 'bout? (EBEN *turns away without answering.* CABOT *grows angry*) God A'mighty, yew air a dumb dunce! They's nothin' in that thick skull o' your'n but noise—like a empty keg it be! (EBEN *doesn't seem to hear.* CABOT's *rage grows*) Yewr farm! God A'mighty! If ye wa'n't a born donkey ye'd know ye'll never own stick nor stone on it, specially now arter him bein' born. It's his'n, I tell ye—his'n arter I die—but I'll live a hundred jest t' fool ye all—an' he'll be growed then—yewr age a'most (EBEN *laughs again his sardonic "Ha." This drives* CABOT *into a fury*) Ha? Ye think ye kin git 'round that someways, do ye? Waal, it'll be her'n, too—Abbie's—ye won't git 'round her—she knows yer tricks—she'll be too much fur ye—she wants the farm her'n—she was afeerd o' ye—she told me ye was sneakin' 'round tryin' t' make love t' her t' git her on yer side . . . ye . . . ye mad fool, ye! (*He raises his clenched fists threateningly*).

EBEN. (*is confronting him, choking with rage*) Ye lie, ye old skunk! Abbie never said no sech thing!

CABOT. (*suddenly triumphant when he sees how shaken* EBEN *is*) She did. An' I says, I'll blow his brains t' the top o' them elums—an' she says no, that hain't sense, who'll ye git t'help ye on the farm in his place—an' then she says yew'n me ought t' have a son—I know we kin, she says—an' I says, if we do, ye kin have anythin' I've got ye've a mind t'. An' she says, I wants Eben cut off so's this farm'll be mine when ye die! (*With terrible gloating*) An' that's what's happened, hain't it? An' the farm's her'n! An' the dust o' the road—that's you'rn! Ha! Now who's hawin'?

EBEN. (*has been listening, petrified with grief and rage—suddenly laughs wildly and brokenly*) Ha-ha-ha! So that's her sneakin' game—all along!—like I suspicioned at fust—t' swaller it all—an' me, too . . . ! (*Madly*) I'll murder her! (*He springs toward the porch but* CABOT *is quicker and gets in between*).

CABOT. No' ye don't!

EBEN. Git out o' my road! (*He tries to throw* CABOT *aside. They grapple in what becomes immediately a murderous struggle. The old man's concentrated strength is too much for* EBEN. CABOT *gets one hand on his throat and presses him back across the stone wall. At the same moment,* ABBIE *comes out on the porch. With a stifled cry she runs toward them*).

ABBIE. Eben! Ephraim! (*She tugs at the hand on* EBEN's *throat*) Let go, Ephraim! Ye're chokin' him!

CABOT. (*removes his hand and flings* EBEN *sideways full length on the grass, gasping and choking. With a cry,* ABBIE *kneels beside him, trying to take his head on her lap, but he pushes her away.* CABOT *stands looking down with fierce triumph*) Ye needn't t've fret, Abbie, I wa'n't aimin' t' kill him. He hain't wuth hangin' fur—not by a hell of a sight! (*More and more triumphantly*) Seventy-six an' him not thirty yit—an' look whar he be fur thinkin' his Paw was easy! No, by God, I hain't easy! An' him upstairs, I'll raise him t' be like me! (*He turns to leave them*) I'm goin' in an' dance!—sing an' celebrate! (*He walks to the porch—then turns with a great grin*) I don't calc'late it's left in him, but if he gits pesky, Abbie, ye jest sing out. I'll come a-runnin' an' by the Etarnal, I'll put him across my knee an' birch him! Ha-ha-ha! (*He goes into the house laughing. A moment later his loud "whoop" is heard*).

ABBIE. (*tenderly*) Eben. Air ye hurt? (*She tries to kiss him but he pushes her violently away and struggles to a sitting position*).

EBEN. (*gaspingly*) T'hell—with ye!

ABBIE. (*not believing her ears*) It's me, Eben—Abbie—don't ye know me?

EBEN. (*glowering at her with hatred*) Ay-eh—I know ye—now! (*He suddenly breaks down, sobbing weakly*).

ABBIE. (*fearfully*) Eben—what's happened t' ye—why did ye look at me 's if ye hated me?

EBEN. (*violently, between sobs and gasps*) I do hate ye! Ye're a whore—a damn trickin' whore!

ABBIE. (*shrinking back horrified*) Eben! Ye don't know what ye're sayin'!

EBEN. (*scrambling to his feet and following her—accusingly*) Ye're nothin' but a stinkin' passel o' lies! Ye've been lyin' t' me every word ye spoke, day an' night, since we fust—done it. Ye've kept sayin' ye loved me. . . .

ABBIE. (*frantically*) I do love ye! (*She takes his hand but he flings hers away*).

EBEN. (*unheeding*) Ye've made a fool o' me—a sick, dumb fool—a-purpose! Ye've been on'y playin' yer sneakin', stealin' game all along—gittin' me t' lie with ye so's ye'd hev a son he'd think was his'n, an' makin' him promise he'd give ye the farm and let me eat dust, if ye did git him a son! (*Staring at her with anguished, bewildered eyes*) They must be a devil livin' in ye! T'ain't human t' be as bad as that be!

ABBIE. (*stunned—dully*) He told yew . . . ?

EBEN. Hain't it true? It hain't no good in yew lyin'.

ABBIE. (*pleadingly*) Eben, listen—ye must listen—it was long ago —afore we done nothin'—yew was scornin' me—goin' t' see Min— when I was lovin' ye—an' I said it t' him t' git vengeance on ye!

EBEN. (*unheedingly. With tortured passion*) I wish ye was dead! I wish I was dead along with ye afore this come! (*Ragingly*) But I'll git my vengeance too! I'll pray Maw t' come back t' help me— t' put her cuss on yew an' him!

ABBIE. (*brokenly*) Don't ye, Eben! Don't ye! (*She throws herself on her knees before him, weeping*) I didn't mean t' do bad t'ye! Fergive me, won't ye?

EBEN. (*not seeming to hear her—fiercely*) I'll git squar' with the old skunk—an' yew! I'll tell him the truth 'bout the son he's so proud o'! Then I'll leave ye here t' pizen each other—with Maw comin' out o' her grave at nights—an' I'll go t' the gold fields o' Californi-a whar Sim an' Peter be!

ABBIE. (*terrified*) Ye won't—leave me? Ye can't!

EBEN. (*with fierce determination*) I'm a-goin', I tell ye! I'll git rich thar an' come back an' fight him fur the farm he stole—an' I'll kick ye both out in the road—t' beg an' sleep in the woods—an' yer son along with ye—t' starve an' die! (*He is hysterical at the end*).

ABBIE. (*with a shudder—humbly*) He's yewr son, too, Eben.

EBEN. (*torturedly*) I wish he never was born! I wish he'd die this minit! I wish I'd never sot eyes on him! It's him—yew havin' him— a-purpose t' steal—that's changed everythin'!

ABBIE. (*gently*) Did ye believe I loved ye—afore he come?

EBEN. Ay-eh—like a dumb ox!

ABBIE. An' ye don't believe no more?

EBEN. B'lieve a lyin' thief! Ha!

ABBIE. (*shudders—then humbly*) An' did ye r'ally love me afore?

EBEN. (*brokenly*) Ay-eh—an' ye was trickin' me!

ABBIE. An' ye don't love me now!

EBEN. (*violently*) I hate ye, I tell ye!

ABBIE. An' ye're truly goin' West—goin' t' leave me—all account o' him being born?

EBEN. I'm a-goin' in the mornin'—or may God strike me t' hell!

ABBIE. (*after a pause—with a dreadful cold intensity—slowly*) If that's what his comin's done t' me—killin' yewr love—takin' yew away—my on'y joy—the on'y joy I ever knowed—like heaven t' me— purtier'n heaven—then I hate him, too, even if I be his Maw!

EBEN. (*bitterly*) Lies! Ye love him! He'll steal the farm fur ye! (*Brokenly*) But t'ain't the farm so much—not no more—it's yew foolin' me—gittin' me t' love ye—lyin' yew loved me—jest t' git a son t' steal!

ABBIE. (*distractedly*) He won't steal! I'd kill him fust! I do love ye! I'll prove t' ye . . . !

EBEN. (*harshly*) T'ain't no use lyin' no more. I'm deaf t' ye! (*He turns away*) I hain't seein' ye agen. Good-by!

ABBIE. (*pale with anguish*) Hain't ye even goin' t' kiss me—not once—arter all we loved?

EBEN. (*in a hard voice*) I hain't wantin' t' kiss ye never agen! I'm wantin' t' forgit I ever sot eyes on ye!

ABBIE. Eben!—ye mustn't—wait a spell—I want t' tell ye. . . .

EBEN. I'm a-goin' in t' git drunk. I'm a-goin' t' dance.

ABBIE. (*clinging to his arm—with passionate earnestness*) If I could make it—'s if he'd never come up between us—if I could prove t' ye I wa'n't schemin' t' steal from ye—so's everythin' could be jest the same with us, lovin' each other jest the same, kissin' an' happy the same's we've been happy afore he come—if I could do it— ye'd love me agen, wouldn't ye? Ye'd kiss me agen? Ye wouldn't never leave me, would ye?

EBEN. (*moved*)I calc'late not. (*Then shaking her hand off his arm—with a bitter smile*) But ye hain't God, be ye?

ABBIE. (*exultantly*) Remember ye've promised! (*Then with strange intensity*) Mebbe I kin take back one thin' God does!

EBEN. (*peering at her*) Ye're gittin' cracked, hain't ye? (*Then going towards door*) I'm a-goin' t' dance.

ABBIE. (*calls after him intensely*) I'll prove t' ye! I'll prove I love ye better'n. . . . (*He goes in the door, not seeming to hear. She remains standing where she is, looking after him—then she finishes desperately*) Better'n everythin' else in the world!

SCENE THREE

Just before dawn in the morning—shows the kitchen and CABOT'S
bedroom. In the kitchen, by the light of a tallow candle on the table,
EBEN *is sitting, his chin propped on his hands, his drawn face blank
and expressionless. His carpetbag is on the floor beside him. In the
bedroom, dimly lighted by a small whale-oil lamp,* CABOT *lies asleep.*
ABBIE *is bending over the cradle, listening, her face full of terror yet
with an undercurrent of desperate triumph. Suddenly, she breaks down
and sobs, appears about to throw herself on her knees beside the
cradle; but the old man turns restlessly, groaning in his sleep, and
she controls herself, and, shrinking away from the cradle with a
gesture of horror, backs swiftly toward the door in rear and goes out.
A moment later she comes into the kitchen and, running to* EBEN,
*flings her arms about his neck and kisses him wildly. He hardens
himself, he remains unmoved and cold, he keeps his eyes straight
ahead.*

ABBIE. (*hysterically*) I done it, Eben! I told ye I'd do it! I've proved
I love ye—better'n everythin'—so's ye can't never doubt me no more!

EBEN. (*dully*) Whatever ye done, it hain't no good now.

ABBIE. (*wildly*) Don't say that! Kiss me, Eben, won't ye? I need
ye t' kiss me arter what I done! I need ye t' say ye love me!

EBEN. (*kisses her without emotion—dully*) That's fur good-by.
I'm a-goin' soon.

ABBIE. No! No! Ye won't go—not now!

EBEN. (*going on with his own thoughts*) I been a-thinkin'—an'
I hain't goin' t' tell Paw nothin'. I'll leave Maw t' take vengeance on
ye. If I told him, the old skunk'd jest be stinkin' mean enuf to take
it out on that baby. (*His voice showing emotion in spite of him*) An'
I don't want nothin' bad t' happen t' him. He hain't t' blame fur yew.
(*He adds with a certain queer pride*) An' he looks like me! An' by
God, he's mine! An' some day I'll be a-comin' back an' . . . !

ABBIE. (*too absorbed in her own thoughts to listen to him—pleadingly*) They's no cause fur ye t' go now—they's no sense—it's all the
same's it was—they's nothin' come b'tween us now—arter what I
done!

EBEN. (*something in her voice arouses him. He stares at her a
bit frightenedly*) Ye look mad, Abbie. What did ye do?

ABBIE. I—I killed him, Eben.

EBEN (*amazed*) Ye killed him?

ABBIE. (*dully*) Ay-eh.

EBEN. (*recovering from his astonishment—savagely*) An' serves
him right! But we got t' do somethin' quick t' make it look s'if the
old skunk'd killed himself when he was drunk. We kin prove by 'em
all how drunk he got.

ABBIE. (*wildly*) No! No! Not him! (*Laughing distractedly*) But that's what I ought t' done, hain't it? I oughter killed him instead! Why didn't ye tell me?

EBEN. (*appalled*) Instead? What d'ye mean?

ABBIE. Not him.

EBEN. (*his face grown ghastly*) Not—not that baby!

ABBIE. (*dully*) Ay-eh!

EBEN. (*falls to his knees as if he'd been struck—his voice trembling with horror*) Oh, God A'mighty! A'mighty God! Maw, whar was ye, why didn't ye stop her?

ABBIE. (*simply*) She went back t' her grave that night we fust done it, remember? I hain't felt her about since. (*A pause.* EBEN *hides his head in his hands, trembling all over as if he had the ague. She goes on dully*) I left the piller over his little face. Then he killed himself. He stopped breathin'. (*She begins to weep softly*).

EBEN. (*rage beginning to mingle with grief*) He looked like me. He was mine, damn ye!

ABBIE. (*slowly and brokenly*) I didn't want t' do it. I hated myself fur doin' it. I loved him. He was so purty—dead spit 'n' image o' yew. But I loved yew more—an' yew was goin' away—far off whar I'd never see ye agen, never kiss ye, never feel ye pressed agin me agen—an' ye said ye hated me fur havin' him—ye said ye hated him an' wished he was dead—ye said if it hadn't been fur him comin' it'd be the same's afore between us.

EBEN. (*unable to endure this, springs to his feet in a fury, threatening her, his twitching fingers seeming to reach out for her throat*) Ye lie! I never said—I never dreamed ye'd—I'd cut off my head afore I'd hurt his finger!

ABBIE. (*piteously, sinking on her knees*) Eben, don't ye look at me like that—hatin' me—not after what I done fur ye—fur us—so's we could be happy agen—

EBEN. (*furiously now*) Shut up, or I'll kill ye! I see yer game now—the same old sneakin' trick—ye're aimin' t' blame me fur the murder ye done!

ABBIE. (*moaning—putting her hands over her ears*) Don't ye, Eben! Don't ye! (*She grasps his legs*).

EBEN. (*his mood suddenly changing to horror, shrinks away from her*) Don't ye tech me! Ye're pizen! How could ye—t' murder a pore little critter—Ye must've swapped yer soul t' hell! (*Suddenly raging*) Ha! I kin see why ye done it! Not the lies ye jest told—but 'cause ye wanted t' steal agen—steal the last thin' ye'd left me—my part o' him—no, the hull o' him—ye saw he looked like me—ye knowed he was all mine—an' ye couldn't b'ar it—I know ye! Ye killed him fur bein' mine! (*All this has driven him almost insane. He makes a rush past her for the door—then turns—shaking both fists at her, violently*) But I'll take vengeance now! I'll git the Sheriff! I'll tell him everythin'!

Then I'll sing "I'm off to Californi-a!" an' go—gold—Golden Gate—
gold sun—fields o' gold in the West! (*This last he half shouts, half
croons incoherently, suddenly breaking off passionately*) I'm a-goin'
fur the Sheriff t' come an' git ye! I want ye tuk away, locked up from
me! I can't stand t' luk at ye! Murderer an' thief 'r not, ye still tempt
me! I'll give ye up t' the Sheriff! (*He turns and runs out, around the
corner of house, panting and sobbing, and breaks into a swerving
sprint down the road*).

    ABBIE. (*struggling to her feet, runs to the door, calling after him*)
I love ye, Eben! I love ye! (*She stops at the door weakly, swaying,
about to fall*) I don't care what ye do—if ye'll on'y love me agen—
(*She falls limply to the floor in a faint*).

SCENE FOUR

*About an hour later. Same as Scene Three. Shows the kitchen
and* CABOT's *bedroom. It is after dawn. The sky is brilliant with the
sunrise. In the kitchen,* ABBIE *sits at the table, her body limp and
exhausted, her head bowed down over her arms, her face hidden.
Upstairs,* CABOT *is still asleep but awakens with a start. He looks
toward the window and gives a snort of surprise and irritation—
throws back the covers and begins hurriedly pulling on his clothes.
Without looking behind him, he begins talking to* ABBIE *whom he
supposes beside him.*

    CABOT. Thunder 'n' lightin', Abbie! I hain't slept this late in fifty
year! Looks 's if the sun was full riz a'most. Must've been the dancin'
an' likker. Must be gittin' old. I hope Eben's t' wuk. Ye might've tuk
the trouble t' rouse me, Abbie. (*He turns—sees no one there—surprised*) Waal—whar air she? Gittin' vittles, I calc'late. (*He tiptoes to
the cradle and peers down—proudly*) Mornin', sonny. Purty's a picter!
Sleepin' sound. He don't beller all night like most o' 'em. (*He goes
quietly out the door in rear—a few moments later enters kitchen—
sees* ABBIE—*with satisfaction*) So thar ye be. Ye got any vittles cooked?
    ABBIE. (*without moving*) No.
    CABOT. (*coming to her, almost sympathetically*) Ye feelin' sick?
    ABBIE. No.
    CABOT. (*pats her on shoulder. She shudders*) Ye'd best lie down
a spell. (*Half jocularly*) Yer son'll be needin' ye soon. He'd ought t'
wake up with a gnashin' appetite, the sound way he's sleepin'.
    ABBIE. (*shudders—then in a dead voice*) He hain't never goin' t'
wake up.
    CABOT. (*jokingly*) Takes after me this mornin'. I hain't slept so
late in . . .
    ABBIE. He's dead.

CABOT. (*stares at her—bewilderedly*) What. . . .

ABBIE. I killed him.

CABOT. (*stepping back from her—aghast*) Air ye drunk—'r crazy—'r . . . !

ABBIE. (*suddenly lifts her head and turns on him—wildly*) I killed him, I tell ye! I smothered him. Go up an' see if ye don't b'lieve me! (CABOT *stares at her a second, then bolts out the rear door, can be heard bounding up the stairs, and rushes into the bedroom and over to the cradle.* ABBIE *has sunk back lifelessly into her former position.* CABOT *puts his hand down on the body in the crib. An expression of fear and horror comes over his face*).

CABOT. (*shrinking away—tremblingly*) God A'mighty! God A'mighty. (*He stumbles out the door—in a short while returns to the kitchen—comes to* ABBIE, *the stunned expression still on his face— hoarsely*) Why did ye do it? Why? (*As she doesn't answer, he grabs her violently by the shoulder and shakes her*) I ax ye why ye done it! Ye'd better tell me 'r . . . !

ABBIE. (*gives him a furious push which sends him staggering back and springs to her feet—with wild rage and hatred*) Don't ye dare tech me! What right hev ye t' question me 'bout him? He wa'n't yewr son! Think I'd have a son by yew? I'd die fust! I hate the sight o' ye an' allus did! It's yew I should've murdered, if I'd had good sense! I hate ye! I love Eben. I did from the fust. An' he was Eben's son—mine an' Eben's—not your'n!

CABOT. (*stands looking at her dazedly—a pause—finding words with an effort—dully*) That was it—what I felt—pokin' round the corners—while ye lied—holdin' yerself from me—sayin' ye'd a'ready conceived—(*He lapses into crushed silence—then with a strange emotion*) He's dead, sart'n. I felt his heart. Pore little critter! (*He blinks back one tear, wiping his sleeve across his nose*).

ABBIE. (*hysterically*) Don't ye! Don't ye! (*She sobs unrestrainedly*).

CABOT. (*with a concentrated effort that stiffens his body into a rigid line and hardens his face into a stony mask—through his teeth to himself*) I got t' be—like a stone—a rock o' jedgment! (*A pause. He gets complete control over himself—harshly*) If he was Eben's, I be glad he air gone! An' mebbe I suspicioned it all along. I felt they was somethin' onnateral—somewhars—the house got so lonesome—an' cold—drivin' me down t' the barn—t' the beasts o' the field. . . . Ay-eh. I must've suspicioned—somethin'. Ye didn't fool me— not altogether, leastways—I'm too old a bird—growin' ripe on the bough. . . . (*He becomes aware he is wandering, straightens again, looks at* ABBIE *with a cruel grin*) So ye'd like t' hev murdered me 'stead o' him, would ye? Waal, I'll live to a hundred! I'll live t' see ye hung! I'll deliver ye up t' the jedgment o' God an' the law! I'll git the Sheriff now. (*Starts for the door*).

ABBIE. (*dully*) Ye needn't. Eben's gone fur him.

CABOT. (*amazed*) Eben—gone fur the Sheriff?

ABBIE. Ay-eh.

CABOT. T' inform agen ye?

ABBIE. Ay-eh.

CABOT. (*considers this—a pause—then in a hard voice*) Waal, I'm thankful fur him savin' me the trouble. I'll git t' wuk. (*He goes to the door—then turns—in a voice of strange emotion*) He'd ought t' been my son, Abbie. Ye'd ought t' loved me. I'm a man. If ye'd loved me, I'd never told no Sheriff on ye no matter what ye did, if they was t' brile me alive!

ABBIE. (*defensively*) They's more to it nor yew know, makes him tell.

CABOT. (*dryly*) Fur yewr sake, I hope they be. (*He goes out—comes around to the gate—stares up at the sky. His control relaxes. For a moment he is old and weary. He murmurs despairingly*) God A'mighty, I be lonesomer'n ever! (*He hears running footsteps from the left, immediately is himself again.* EBEN *runs in, panting exhaustedly, wild-eyed and mad looking. He lurches through the gate.* CABOT *grabs him by the shoulder.* EBEN *stares at him dumbly*) Did ye tell the Sheriff?

EBEN. (*nodding stupidly*) Ay-eh.

CABOT. (*gives him a push away that sends him sprawling—laughing with withering contempt*) Good fur ye! A prime chip o' yer Maw ye be! (*He goes toward the barn, laughing harshly.* EBEN *scrambles to his feet. Suddenly* CABOT *turns—grimly threatening*) Git off this farm when the Sheriff takes her—or, by God, he'll have t' come back an' git me fur murder, too! (*He stalks off.* EBEN *does not appear to have heard him. He runs to the door and comes into the kitchen.* ABBIE *looks up with a cry of anguished joy.* EBEN *stumbles over and throws himself on his knees beside her—sobbing brokenly*).

EBEN. Fergive me!

ABBIE. (*happily*) Eben! (*She kisses him and pulls his head over against her breast*).

EBEN. I love ye! Fergive me!

ABBIE. (*ecstatically*) I'd fergive ye all the sins in hell fur sayin' that! (*She kisses his head, pressing it to her with a fierce passion of possession*).

EBEN. (*brokenly*) But I told the Sheriff. He's comin' fur ye!

ABBIE. I kin b'ar what happens t' me—now!

EBEN. I woke him up. I told him. He says, wait 'til I git dressed. I was waiting. I got to thinkin' o' yew. I got to thinkin' how I'd loved ye. It hurt like somethin' was bustin' in my chest an' head. I got t' cryin'. I knowed sudden I loved ye yet, an' allus would love ye!

ABBIE. (*caressing his hair—tenderly*) My boy, hain't ye?

EBEN. I begun t' run back. I cut across the fields an' through the woods. I thought ye might have time t' run away—with me—an' . . .

ABBIE. (*shaking her head*) I got t' take my punishment—t' pay fur my sin.

EBEN. Then I want t' share it with ye.

ABBIE. Ye didn't do nothin'.

EBEN. I put it in yer head. I wisht he was dead! I as much as urged ye t' do it!

ABBIE. No. It was me alone!

EBEN. I'm as guilty as yew be! He was the child o' our sin.

ABBIE. (*lifting her head as if defying God*) I don't repent that sin! I hain't askin' God t' fergive that!

EBEN. Nor me—but it led up t' the other—an' the murder ye did, ye did 'count o' me—an' it's my murder, too, I'll tell the Sheriff—an' if ye deny it, I'll say we planned it t'gether—an' they'll all b'lieve me, fur they suspicion everythin' we've done, an' it'll seem likely an' true to 'em. An' it is true—way down. I did help ye—somehow.

ABBIE. (*laying her head on his—sobbing*) No! I don't want yew t' suffer!

EBEN. I got t' pay fur my part o' the sin! An' I'd suffer wuss leavin' ye, goin' West, thinkin' o' ye day an' night, bein' out when yew was in—(*Lowering his voice*) 'r bein' alive when yew was dead. (*A pause*) I want t' share with ye, Abbie—prison 'r death 'r hell 'r anythin'! (*He looks into her eyes and forces a trembling smile*) If I'm sharin' with ye, I won't feel lonesome, leastways.

ABBIE. (*weakly*) Eben! I won't let ye! I can't let ye!

EBEN. (*kissing her—tenderly*) Ye can't he'p yerself. I got ye beat fur once!

ABBIE. (*forcing a smile—adoringly*) I hain't beat—s'long's I got ye!

EBEN. (*hears the sound of feet outside*) Ssshh! Listen! They've come t' take us!

ABBIE. No, it's him. Don't give him no chance to fight ye, Eben. Don't say nothin'—no matter what he says. An' I won't neither. (*It is* CABOT. *He comes up from the barn in a great state of excitement and strides into the house and then into the kitchen.* EBEN *is kneeling beside* ABBIE, *his arm around her, hers around him. They stare straight ahead*).

CABOT. (*stares at them, his face hard. A long pause—vindictively*) Ye make a slick pair o' murderin' turtle doves! Ye'd ought t' be both hung on the same limb an' left thar t' swing in the breeze an' rot—a warnin' t' old fools like me t' b'ar their lonesomeness alone—an' fur young fools like ye t' hobble their lust. (*A pause. The excitement returns to his face, his eyes snap, he looks a bit crazy*) I couldn't work today. I couldn't take no interest. T' hell with the farm! I'm leavin' it!

I've turned the cows an' other stock loose! I've druv 'em into the woods whar they kin be free! By freein' 'em, I'm freein' myself! I'm quittin' here today! I'll set fire t' house an' barn an' watch 'em burn, an' I'll leave yer Maw t' haunt the ashes, an' I'll will the fields back t' God, so that nothin' human kin never touch 'em! I'll be a-goin' to Californi-a —t' jine Simeon an' Peter—true sons o' mine if they be dumb fools— an' the Cabots'll find Solomon's Mines t'gether! (*He suddenly cuts a mad caper*) Whoop! What was the song they sung? "Oh, Californi-a! That's the land fur me." (*He sings this—then gets on his knees by the floor-board under which the money was hid*) An' I'll sail thar on one o' the finest clippers I kin find! I've got the money! Pity ye didn't know whar this was hidden so's ye could steal. . . . (*He has pulled up the board. He stares—feels—stares again. A pause of dead silence. He slowly turns, slumping into a sitting position on the floor, his eyes like those of a dead fish, his face the sickly green of an attack of nausea. He swallows painfully several times—forces a weak smile at last*) So—ye did steal it!

EBEN. (*emotionlessly*) I swapped it t' Sim an' Peter fur their share o' the farm—t' pay their passage t' Californi-a.

CABOT. (*with one sardonic*) Ha! (*He begins to recover. Gets slowly to his feet—strangely*) I calc'late God give it to 'em—not yew! God's hard, not easy! Mebbe they's easy gold in the West but it hain't God's gold. It hain't fur me. I kin hear His voice warnin' me agen t' be hard an' stay on my farm. I kin see his hand usin' Eben t' steal t' keep me from weakness. I kin feel I be in the palm o' His hand, His fingers guidin' me. (*A pause—then he mutters sadly*) It's a-goin' t' be lonesomer now than ever it was afore—an' I'm gittin' old, Lord—ripe on the bough. . . . (*Then stiffening*) Waal—what d'ye want? God's lonesome, hain't He? God's hard an' lonesome! (*A pause. The Sheriff with two men comes up the road from the left. They move cautiously to the door. The Sheriff knocks on it with the butt of his pistol*).

SHERIFF. Open in the name o' the Law! (*They start*).

CABOT. They've come fur ye. (*He goes to the rear door*) Come in, Jim! (*The three men enter.* CABOT *meets them in doorway*) Jest a minit, Jim. I got 'em safe here. (*The Sheriff nods. He and his companions remain in the doorway*).

EBEN. (*suddenly calls*) I lied this mornin', Jim. I helped her to do it. Ye kin take me, too.

ABBIE. (*brokenly*) No!

CABOT. Take 'em both. (*He comes forward—stares at* EBEN *with a trace of grudging admiration*) Purty good—fur yew! Waal, I got t' round up the stock. Good-by.

EBEN. Good-by.

ABBIE. Good-by. (*CABOT turns and strides past the men—comes out and around the corner of the house, his shoulders squared, his*

*face stony, and stalks grimly toward the barn. In the meantime the
Sheriff and men have come into the room).*

SHERIFF. (*embarrassedly*) Wall—we'd best start.

ABBIE. Wait. (*Turns to* EBEN) I love ye, Eben.

EBEN. I love ye, Abbie. (*They kiss. The three men grin and shuffle
embarrassedly.* EBEN *takes* ABBIE's *hand. They go out the door in rear,
the men following, and come from the house, walking hand in hand
to the gate.* EBEN *stops there and points to the sunrise sky*) Sun's
a-rizin'. Purty, hain't it?

ABBIE. Ay-eh. (*They both stand for a moment looking up raptly
in attitudes strangely aloof and devout).*

SHERIFF. (*looking around at the farm enviously—to his companion*) It's a jim-dandy farm, no denyin'. Wished I owned it!

CURTAIN

EARLIER
FICTION

Earlier Fiction (writers born before 1900)

How could fiction possibly have gone on after the example of Henry James, who, in those last three great novels of the first decade of the century—*The Ambassadors, The Wings of the Dove,* and *The Golden Bowl*—and in the splendid late stories like "The Beast in the Jungle," had shown how utterly dedicated to his art a writer of fiction could be? This body of work had brought him to a point of refinement in psychological realism and in the discrimination of values beyond which fiction could not go. There had been no such demonstration in American literature before, and it could hardly be matched again. Fiction would have to take a deep breath and start over. It did.

Even Edith Wharton, who had taken James as her master, apparently saw that necessity. The movement would be back to a harsher form of realism, to a realism more explicitly concerned than the later James's was with the class structure of society, with the pressures of that structure on the individual, and with the individual's struggle to find his place in it or to escape from it. There would be a turning away from James's emphasis on style as the great penetrating instrument of reality to a renewed emphasis on *things* for their own sake, to the details of physical reality, of social circumstance. In tone the writer could move away from James's Olympian and even rather glacial objectivity in a number of directions: into, for example, a sharper strain of satire than he was generally given to or into a looser strain of rapture than he cared to cultivate—in short, into something more subjective, invocative, "poetic."

The contrast with Jamesian subtleties presented by the novels of Theodore Dreiser is not only extreme, it is violent. And if other novelists could hardly carry fiction further in James's direction, similarly they could hardly go further in Dreiser's than he himself had taken it. His is exclusively the material world of American things, things so massively accumulated as to leave no room for spiritual nuances, but much for animal pain and some for sentiments. The things of this world themselves present extreme contrasts: horrid squalor and grinding poverty opposed to vulgar ostentation and gross luxury; but nowhere aristocratic refinements or considerations of taste. Dreiser's prose style is notoriously clumsy and inept, perhaps appropriate enough to the brutal world of his novels. That it serves their purpose is demonstrated by their undeniable power, these great weighty monoliths of impassive brooding.

Edith Wharton's best fiction is concerned with the top layer of old New York society, with its ethical and social rigidities, and at the same time, with its corruption by the "invaders," as she called them—the newly rich in all their aggressive pretentiousness. Between the two, fine spirits are forced to compromise, or they are destroyed. But the limitations of both classes enabled her to develop a resistant objectivity and a satiric talent that give her novels of manners a comic edge even when they end in individual disaster.

Learning from her, but broadening her satiric instrument in at least two ways—complete externalization of observed detail and linguistic mimicry—Sinclair Lewis moved into the middle classes, the world of small business and the professions in the Midwest. Again it is a world of total materialism, but now so benighted that it is also a world of buffoons. Buffoons, however, can be cruel as well as absurd, and again the finer spirits (and they are not so very "fine" as those in Edith Wharton) are forced into compromise or destruction by the relentless pressure of conventionality and philistinism.

Willa Cather's most memorable work moved the scene farther west than Lewis's and further back in time. With a power of observation at least equal to his, unlike him, she exercised a high degree of selection in detail. Never obscuring the harshness of the life she described, she yet managed to imbue it with a poetry of loneliness and yearning and, in her best moments, to invoke a strange sense of primeval continuity beneath the rough surfaces of things—the ancient, the perdurable, the cosmically ancestral—which gives her rude pastorals an expansive nobility.

It is some such sense of human ultimates that Sherwood Anderson, usually without success, sought to communicate. Stumbling into literature, fumbling his way through two novels, he then managed in the sketches that make up *Winesburg, Ohio,* and in a number of short stories, to bring his readers into a realm not, perhaps, of the mythic richness that he hoped for, but at least into one that gave them some hints of the experience of the dark underside of American life, where the inarticulate dreams of cosmic and simply human connection strive toward realization. If his later, longer fictions came no nearer to success in fulfilling this ambition, one must be all the more grateful for the shorter pieces that nearly did.

One gateway that he thought he saw into that richer, more poetic and fulfilling world than any that middle-class America was prepared to open was the life of black Americans. While Anderson's chief imaginative attempt to enter that life, his novel called *Dark Laughter,* can now be seen to be a lot of white folkloristic sentimentalization, it is interesting that Jean Toomer, who himself came much more directly out of that experience than Anderson, nevertheless now seems closer to Anderson than to any other fiction writer in white America. They share a mask of questioning naïveté as, in their plotless fictions, they present characters whose motives are

largely enigmatic; they share, too, in method, a drifting, unan-
chored impressionism that is more suggestive than definitive. In
both, but more particularly in Toomer, the effect is often a kind of
emotional strangling, as if the very materials of human experience
that they were trying to handle were impossibly intractable. If this
quality is stronger in Toomer than in Anderson, it may well be
because he was trying to push the language of fiction further. In
his long story, "Kabnis," the central character cries out that he
has "Been shapin words t fit m soul. . . . The form that burned int
my soul is some twisted awful thing that crept in from a dream, a
godam nightmare, an wont stay still unless I feed it. An it lives on
words. Not beautiful words. God Almighty no. Misshapen, split-gut,
tortured, twisted words."

One of Sherwood Anderson's characters might almost have made
that speech—but not quite. And the difference is what connects
Toomer with his own contemporaries, those writers who came up
in the 1920s and who were concerned above all with a new language for fiction, a language shaped to express most exactly the
particular kind of realism that each pursued—Hemingway, Dos
Passos, Faulkner.

F. Scott Fitzgerald, the first of that generation to break upon the scene,
did not feel that urgency for a new prose. Following Edith Wharton,
but cultivating a romantic, golden glow in his style rather than her
more steely glint, he too took as his favorite subject the lives of the
very rich. These were, of course, the rich of quite another generation, the postwar "beautiful and damned," and his account of their
lives made him not only the first chronicler of the "jazz age" but
also, in at least two of his books and in a number of stories, our
finest postwar novelist of manners.

Katherine Anne Porter, too, was content to refine traditional prose in
her own direction. When she was asked whether Walt Whitman or
Henry James had the greater relevance to current and future American writing, she chose James, ". . . holding as I do with the conscious,
disciplined artist." But while James no doubt represented a general
ideal for her, if her work is to be associated with any one earlier
novelist, it is probably Willa Cather, one of the few writers about
whom she has written critically and with great sympathy. Although
her stories are set in the present, she is, like Cather, profoundly
concerned with the past; and if the Porter past is more personal and
local, less historic and primitive, it nevertheless opens her best
stories to similar mythic reverberations and resonance. As in a
concerto, the past gives orchestral expansion to her solo account of
the present, and sometimes the very contrast that it offers is the
thematic core of the fiction.

When one designates the remaining three writers in this group as the great innovators in novelistic style and structure, one is not commenting on their achievement as such but on its special character. Hemingway was interested chiefly in a realism of the intensely personal and physical. The intensity is communicated mainly through the extraordinary concentration of his style. The other qualities, paradoxically enough, come from the very impersonality of the manner (at its best, Hemingway's style is at least the most apparently objective in our fiction) and its bareness, its stripped down spareness, the rigor with which he suppressed all but the most telling detail, all but the essential word.

Dos Passos, in his great trilogy, *U.S.A.*, was interested in a realism of social movement in an industrial culture, and to that end he developed not one but four styles, each appropriate to one of the four modes through which the narrative is presented. What they have in common is their swiftness—the flash, the speed, the cinematic mobility—the sometimes nearly mechanical click and purr, as if we were both listening to and watching the inner workings of an enormous, beautifully constructed, well-lubricated, and necessarily, completely impersonal dynamo.

Faulkner, finally, in the work for which he is most highly esteemed, is interested in a realism of history and tradition, or rather, of the individual psyche in its interchange and its attempt to maintain itself as its own history and tradition glide away into the dark labyrinth of an irrecoverable past. In his effort to explore the mazes of that past and of the psyche itself, Faulkner developed an expressive style of protracted sinuosities, curvings and turnings, twistings back and forth, involutions and exfoliations, that is as remarkable as it is often bewildering. Correspondingly, just as Hemingway developed his subject of mute and tough and lonely individual endurance; as Dos Passos developed his of capitalist clang and boom and crush, the individual lost in the grinding gears and the mass; so Faulkner worked out his endless myth of Yoknapatawpha County, the individual groping and searching in the bewildering caverns of his history and of his heart.

HENRY JAMES [JR.] (1843–1916)

By 1900 Henry James had already achieved more in quantity and distinction than is the lot of most fine novelists, but sixteen more years lay before him and, amazingly, his greatest work.

By 1900 he had published fourteen substantial novels including such great ones as The Portrait of a Lady (1881), The Princess Casamassima (1886), The Spoils of Poynton (1897), What Maisie Knew (1897), and The Awkward Age (1899); countless stories and novelettes including "Daisy Miller" (1878), "The Aspern Papers" (1888), "The Lesson of the Master" (1892), and "The Turn of the Screw" (1898), to name only a few of the most famous; many volumes of literary criticism, including the superb short book on Hawthorne (1879) which tells us as much about James in relation to America as it does about its nominal subject; and several books of plays and travel writings.

This body of work had established many facts about Henry James and his artistic concerns; we should remind ourselves of at least four of them. First, his faith in the literary art was absolute—unlike, for example, his contemporary and sometime friend, H. G. Wells—and he seemed to believe that its potentialities, if one worked with true dedication, were nearly limitless. Second, he took as his special province the most subtle inspection of psychological motivations and moral discriminations. Next, he presented his material over and over in modulations of his favorite theme, the "international" theme, in which, characteristically, "innocent" Americans confront the old European complexities of art, manners, and tradition. Finally, he dramatized that theme by presenting it through the observations of a single character or point of view, necessarily not omniscient but limited, and often the development of the observer himself is the essence of the story.

He liked to use the word pilgrim for his travelers, and he himself was a pilgrim from childhood on. Much of his education was accomplished through tutors in Europe. At the beginning of the Civil War he suffered some physical injury (an "obscure hurt," he called it) which kept him out of that conflict and probably decreed the rather passive role of spectator that he chose for himself and the inactive physical life (travel can be leisurely) that he was to lead. Interestingly, in 1862 he tried a year in the Harvard Law School, but he knew by then that his métier was to be letters, not law. He had, however, an early conviction that the American scene was not congenial to the growth of creative talent and that the materials it offered were thin and graceless. From the middle sixties on he lived chiefly in Europe, and after 1875 he lived there permanently. In *that year it was still possible, as James did, to meet such great writers as Flaubert and Turgenev in Paris; but after 1876 London became his home.*

In the first half of the nineties, James gave up fiction to write for the stage, but his talent was too subtle to accomplish truly theatrical effects, and his plays were not successful. At the opening performance of Guy Domville, *he was booed and hooted down, a traumatic experience. Yet the stage taught him a good deal about the method of the dramatized scene, and when he returned to fiction, his genius had been enriched.*

In the opening year of the new century he published one of his most baffling novels, The Sacred Fount, *in which the drama lies in the very myopia from which the narrative observer suffers as he theorizes about the relationships of the guests at an English weekend house party. This is a small work, in direct contrast to the immensity of the three great novels of the late years. Leon Edel, the American authority above all others on Henry James, describes them as follows:*

At the end, form and substance coalesced to give us the psychological drama of James's highest comedy, The Ambassadors, *the brooding tragedy of* The Wings of the Dove, *and what might be called James's supreme novel of manners,* The Golden Bowl.

During the same years he was writing his most accomplished long stories. Perhaps his best known is "The Beast in the Jungle," the story of a man who discovers at last the horror of possessing an empty self.

There were other works: travel books, more plays, two unfinished novels—The Ivory Tower (1917) and The Sense of the Past (1917)—*biography, criticism, three volumes of autobiography, and above all,* The American Scene (1907), *a brilliant account of James's extended visit to the United States when he returned to it at last in 1904.*

The outbreak of the war was a blow to James. He wrote in a desperate *"epistolary gasp": "To have to take it all for what the treacherous years were all the while really making for and meaning, is too tragic for any words." In a dramatic demonstration of allegiance to the Allied cause, he relinquished his American citizenship in 1915 and became a British subject. And in the next year he was dead.*

FURTHER READING

Leon Edel has published four volumes of his definitive biography, *Henry James: The Untried Years* (1953), *The Conquest of London*

(1962), *The Middle Years* (1962), *The Treacherous Years* (1969). Important early critical estimates are F. O. Matthiessen, *Henry James: The Major Phase* (1944); F. W. Dupee, *Henry James* (1951, revised 1966); and Quentin Anderson, *The American Henry James* (1957). More recent critical studies include, Richard Poirier, *The Comic Sense of Henry James* (1960); Dorothea Krook, *The Ordeal of Consciousness in Henry James* (1962); Laurence B. Holland, *The Expense of Vision: Essays on the Craft of Henry James* (1964); Robert Gale, *The Caught Image* (1964); Edward Stone, *The Battle and the Books: Some Aspects of Henry James* (1964); and Sallie Sears, *The Negative Imagination* (1968). S. Gorley Putt assembled *Henry James: A Reader's Guide* (1966). *Selected Letters of Henry James* was edited by Leon Edel in 1955.

The Beast in the Jungle (1903)

I

What determined the speech that startled him in the course of their encounter scarcely matters, being probably but some words spoken by himself quite without intention—spoken as they lingered and slowly moved together after their renewal of acquaintance. He had been conveyed by friends, an hour or two before, to the house at which she was staying; the party of visitors at the other house, of whom he was one, and thanks to whom it was his theory, as always, that he was lost in the crowd, had been invited over to luncheon. There had been after luncheon much dispersal, all in the interest of the original motive, a view of Weatherend itself and the fine things, intrinsic features, pictures, heirlooms, treasures of all the arts, that made the place almost famous; and the great rooms were so numerous that guests could wander at their will, hang back from the principal group, and, in cases where they took such matters with the last seriousness, give themselves up to mysterious appreciations and measurements. There were persons to be observed, singly or in couples, bending toward objects in out-of-the-way corners with their hands on their knees and their heads nodding quite as with the emphasis of an excited sense of smell. When they were two they either mingled their sounds of ecstasy or melted into silences of even deeper import, so that there were aspects of the occasion that gave it for Marcher much the air of the "look round," previous to a sale highly advertised, that excites or quenches, as may be, the dream of acquisition. The dream of acquisition at Weatherend would have had to be wild indeed, and John Marcher found himself, among such suggestions, disconcerted almost equally by the presence of those who knew too much and by that of those who knew nothing. The great rooms caused so much poetry and history to press upon him that he needed to wander apart to feel in a proper relation with them, though his doing so was not, as happened, like the gloating of some of his companions, to be compared to the movements of a dog sniffing a cupboard. It had an issue promptly enough in a direction that was not to have been calculated.

It led, in short, in the course of the October afternoon, to his closer meeting with May Bartram, whose face, a reminder, yet not quite a remembrance, as they sat, much separated, at a very long table, had begun merely by troubling him rather pleasantly. It affected him as the sequel of something of which he had lost the beginning. He knew it, and for the time quite welcomed it, as a continuation, but didn't know what it continued, which was an interest, or an amusement, the greater as he was also somehow aware—yet without a direct sign from her—that the young woman herself had not lost the thread. She had not lost it, but she wouldn't give it back to him, he saw, without some putting forth of his hand for it; and he not only saw that, but saw several things more, things odd enough in the light of the fact that at the moment some accident of grouping brought them face to face he was still merely fumbling with the idea that any contact between them in the past would have had no importance. If it had had no importance he scarcely knew why his actual impression of her should so seem to have so much; the answer to which, however, was that in such a life as they all appeared to be leading for the moment one could but take things as they came. He was satisfied, without in the least being able to say why, that this young lady might roughly have ranked in the house as a poor relation; satisfied also that she was not there on a brief visit, but was more or less a part of the establishment—almost a working, a remunerated part. Didn't she enjoy at periods a protection that she paid for by helping, among other services, to show the place and explain it, deal with the tiresome people, answer questions about the dates of the buildings, the styles of the furniture, the authorship of the pictures, the favourite haunts of the ghost? It wasn't that she looked as if you could have given her shillings—it was impossible to look less so. Yet when she finally drifted toward him, distinctly handsome, though ever so much older—older than when he had seen her before—it might have been as an effect of her guessing that he had, within the couple of hours, devoted more imagination to her than to all the others put together, and had thereby penetrated to a kind of truth that the others were too stupid for. She *was* there on harder terms than anyone; she was there as a consequence of things suffered, in one way and another, in the interval of years; and she remembered him very much as she was remembered—only a good deal better.

By the time they at last thus came to speech they were alone in one of the rooms—remarkable for a fine portrait over the chimney-place—out of which their friends had passed, and the charm of it was that even before they had spoken they had practically arranged with each other to stay behind for talk. The charm, happily, was in other things too; it was partly in there being scarce a spot at Weather-end without something to stay behind for. It was in the way the autumn day looked into the high windows as it waned; in the way the red light, breaking at the close from under a low, sombre sky, reached out in a long shaft and played over old wainscots, old tapestry, old gold, old colour. It was most of all perhaps in the way she came to him as if, since she had been turned on to deal with the simpler sort, he might, should he choose to keep the whole thing down, just take her mild attention for a part of her general business. As soon as he heard her voice, however, the gap was filled up and the missing link supplied; the slight irony he divined in her attitude lost its advantage. He almost jumped at it to get there before her. "I met you years and years ago in Rome. I remember all about it." She confessed to disappointment—she had been so sure he didn't; and to prove how well he did he began to pour forth the particular recollections that popped up as he called for them. Her face and her voice, all at his service now, worked the miracle—the impression operating like the torch of a lamplighter who touches into flame, one by one, a long row of gas jets. Marcher flattered himself that the illumination was brilliant, yet he was really still more pleased on her showing him, with amusement, that in his haste to make everything right he had got most things rather wrong. It hadn't been at Rome—it had been at Naples; and it hadn't been seven years before—it had been more nearly ten. She hadn't been either with her uncle and aunt, but with her mother and her brother; in addition to which it was not with the Pembles that *he* had been, but with the Boyers, coming down in their company from Rome—a point on which she insisted, a little to his confusion, and as to which she had her evidence in hand. The Boyers she had known, but she didn't know the Pembles, though she had heard of them, and it was the people he was with who had made them acquainted. The incident of the thunderstorm that had raged round them with such violence as to drive them for refuge into an excavation—this incident had not occurred at the Palace of the Cæsars, but at Pompeii, on an occasion when they had been present there at an important find.

He accepted her amendments, he enjoyed her corrections, though the moral of them was, she pointed out, that he *really* didn't remember the least thing about her; and he only felt it as a drawback that when all was made conformable to the truth there didn't appear much of anything left. They lingered together still, she neglecting her office—for from the moment he was so clever she had no proper right to him—and both neglecting the house, just waiting as to see if a memory or two more wouldn't again breathe upon them. It had not taken them many minutes, after all, to put down on the table, like the cards of a pack, those that constituted their respective hands; only what came out was that the pack was unfortunately not perfect— that the past, invoked, invited, encouraged, could give them, naturally, no more than it had. It had made them meet—her at twenty, him at twenty-five; but nothing was so strange, they seemed to say to each other, as that, while so occupied, it hadn't done a little more for them. They looked at each other as with the feeling of an occasion missed; the present one would have been so much better if the other, in the far distance, in the foreign land, hadn't been so stupidly meagre. There weren't, apparently, all counted, more than a dozen little old things that had succeeded in coming to pass between them; trivialities of youth, simplicities of freshness, stupidities of ignorance, small possible germs, but too deeply buried—too deeply (didn't it seem?) to sprout after so many years. Marcher said to himself that he ought to have rendered her some service—saved her from a cap- sized boat in the Bay, or at least recovered her dressing-bag, filched from her cab, in the streets of Naples, by a lazzarone with a stiletto. Or it would have been nice if he could have been taken with fever, alone, at his hotel, and she could have come to look after him, to write to his people, to drive him out in convalescence. *Then* they would be in possession of the something or other that their actual show seemed to lack. It yet somehow presented itself, this show, as too good to be spoiled; so that they were reduced for a few minutes more to wondering a little helplessly why—since they seemed to know a certain number of the same people—their reunion had been so long averted. They didn't use that name for it, but their delay from minute to minute to join the others was a kind of confession that they didn't quite want it to be a failure. Their attempted supposition of reasons for their not having met but showed how little they knew of each other. There came in fact a moment when Marcher felt a positive pang. It was vain to pretend she was an old friend, for all the com- munities were wanting, in spite of which it was as an old friend that he saw she would have suited him. He had new ones enough—was surrounded with them, for instance, at that hour at the other house; as a new one he probably wouldn't have so much as noticed her. He would have liked to invent something, get her to make-believe with him that some passage of a romantic or critical kind *had* originally occurred. He was really almost reaching out in imagination— as against time—for something that would do, and saying to himself that if it didn't come this new incident would simply and rather awkwardly close. They would separate, and now for no second or for no third chance. They would have tried and not succeeded. Then it was, just at the turn, as he afterwards made it out to himself, that, every- thing else failing, she herself decided to take up the case and, as it

were, save the situation. He felt as soon as she spoke that she had
been consciously keeping back what she said and hoping to get on
without it; a scruple in her that immensely touched him when, by the
end of three or four minutes more, he was able to measure it. What
she brought out, at any rate, quite cleared the air and supplied the
link—the link it was such a mystery he should frivolously have managed to lose.

"You know you told me something that I've never forgotten and
that again and again has made me think of you since; it was that
tremendously hot day when we went to Sorrento, across the bay, for
the breeze. What I allude to was what you said to me, on the way
back, as we sat, under the awning of the boat, enjoying the cool. Have
you forgotten?"

He had forgotten, and he was even more surprised than ashamed.
But the great thing was that he saw it was no vulgar reminder of any
"sweet" speech. The vanity of women had long memories, but she
was making no claim on him of a compliment or a mistake. With
another woman, a totally different one, he might have feared the recall
possibly even some imbecile "offer." So, in having to say that he had
indeed forgotten, he was conscious rather of a loss than of a gain;
he already saw an interest in the matter of her reference. "I try to
think—but I give it up. Yet I remember the Sorrento day."

"I'm not very sure you do," May Bartram after a moment said; "and
I'm not very sure I ought to want you to. It's dreadful to bring a person
back, at any time, to what he was ten years before. If you've lived
away from it," she smiled, "so much the better."

"Ah, if *you* haven't why should I?" he asked.

"Lived away, you mean, from what I myself was?"

"From what *I* was. I was of course an ass," Marcher went on;
"but I would rather know from you just the sort of ass I was than—
from the moment you have something in your mind—not know anything."

Still, however, she hesitated. "But if you've completely ceased to
be that sort——?"

"Why, I can then just so all the more bear to know. Besides, perhaps I haven't."

"Perhaps. Yet if you haven't," she added, "I should suppose you
would remember. Not indeed that *I* in the least connect with my
impression the invidious name you use. If I had only thought you
foolish," she explained, "the thing I speak of wouldn't so have remained
with me. It was about yourself." She waited, as if it might come to
him; but as, only meeting her eyes in wonder, he gave no sign, she
burnt her ships. "Has it ever happened?"

Then it was that, while he continued to stare, a light broke for
him and the blood slowly came to his face, which began to burn with
recognition. "Do you mean I told you——?" But he faltered, lest

what came to him shouldn't be right, lest he should only give himself
away.

"It was something about yourself that it was natural one shouldn't
forget—that is if one remembered you at all. That's why I ask you,"
she smiled, "if the thing you then spoke of has ever come to pass?"

Oh, then he saw, but he was lost in wonder and found himself
embarrassed. This, he also saw, made her sorry for him, as if her
allusion had been a mistake. It took him but a moment, however, to
feel that it had not been, much as it had been a surprise. After the
first little shock of it her knowledge on the contrary began, even if
rather strangely, to taste sweet to him. She was the only other person
in the world then who would have it, and she had had it all these
years, while the fact of his having so breathed his secret had unaccountably faded from him. No wonder they couldn't have met as if
nothing had happened. "I judge," he finally said, "that I know what
you mean. Only I had strangely enough lost the consciousness of having taken you so far into my confidence."

"Is it because you've taken so many others as well?"

"I've taken nobody. Not a creature since then."

"So that I'm the only person who knows?"

"The only person in the world."

"Well," she quickly replied, "I myself have never spoken. I've never,
never repeated of you what you told me." She looked at him so that
he perfectly believed her. Their eyes met over it in such a way that
he was without a doubt. "And I never will."

She spoke with an earnestness that, as if almost excessive, put him at
ease about her possible derision. Somehow the whole question was a
new luxury to him—that is, from the moment she was in possession.
If she didn't take the ironic view she clearly took the sympathetic, and
that was what he had had, in all the long time, from no one whom-
soever. What he felt was that he couldn't at present have begun to
tell her and yet could profit perhaps exquisitely by the accident of
having done so of old. "Please don't then. We're just right as it is."

"Oh, I am," she laughed, "if you are!" To which she added: "Then
you do still feel in the same way?"

It was impossible to him not to take to himself that she was really
interested, and it all kept coming as a sort of revelation. He had
thought of himself so long as abominably alone, and, lo, he wasn't
alone a bit. He hadn't been, it appeared, for an hour—since those
moments on the Sorrento boat. It was *she* who had been, he seemed
to see as he looked at her—she who had been made so by the graceless
fact of his lapse of fidelity. To tell her what he had told her—what
had it been but to ask something of her? something that she had given,
in her charity, without his having, by a remembrance, by a return
of the spirit, failing another encounter, so much as thanked her. What
he had asked of her had been simply at first not to laugh at him. She
had beautifully not done so for ten years, and she was not doing so

now. So he had endless gratitude to make up. Only for that he must see just how he had figured to her. "What, exactly, was the account I gave——?"

"Of the way you did feel? Well, it was very simple. You said you had from your earliest time, as the deepest thing within you, the sense of being kept for something rare and strange, possibly prodigious and terrible, that was sooner or later to happen to you, that you had in your bones the foreboding and the conviction of, and that would perhaps overwhelm you."

"Do you call that very simple?" John Marcher asked.

She thought a moment. "It was perhaps because I seemed, as you spoke, to understand it."

"You do understand it?" he eagerly asked.

Again she kept her kind eyes on him. "You still have the belief?"

"Oh!" he exclaimed helplessly. There was too much to say.

"Whatever it is to be," she clearly made out, "it hasn't yet come."

He shook his head in complete surrender now. "It hasn't yet come. Only, you know, it isn't anything I'm to *do*, to achieve in the world, to be distinguished or admired for. I'm not such as ass as *that*. It would be much better, no doubt, if I were."

"It's to be something you're merely to suffer?"

"Well, say to wait for—to have to meet, to face, to see suddenly break out in my life; possible destroying all further consciousness, possibly annihilating me; possibly, on the other hand, only altering everything, striking at the root of all my world and leaving me to the consequences, however they shape themselves."

She took this in, but the light in her eyes continued for him not to be that of mockery. "Isn't what you describe perhaps but the expectation—or, at any rate, the sense of danger, familiar to so many people—of falling in love?"

John Marcher thought. "Did you ask me that before?"

"No—I wasn't so free-and-easy then. But it's what strikes me now."

"Of course," he said after a moment, "it strikes you. Of course it strikes *me*. Of course what's in store for me may be no more than that. The only thing is," he went on, "that I think that if it had been that, I should by this time know."

"Do you mean because you've *been* in love?" And then as he but looked at her in silence: "You've been in love and it hasn't meant such a cataclysm, hasn't proved the great affair?"

"Here I am, you see. It hasn't been overwhelming."

"Then it hasn't been love," said May Bartram.

"Well, I at least thought it was. I took it for that—I've taken it till now. It was agreeable, it was delightful, it was miserable," he explained. "But it wasn't strange. It wasn't what *my* affair's to be."

"You want something all to yourself—something that nobody else knows or *has* known?"

"It isn't a question of what I 'want'—God knows I don't want

anything. It's only a question of the apprehension that haunts me—
that I live with day by day."

He said this so lucidly and consistently that, visibly, it further
imposed itself. If she had not been interested before she would have
been interested now. "Is it a sense of coming violence?"

Evidently now too, again, he liked to talk of it. "I don't think of it
as—when it does come—necessarily violent. I only think of it as
natural and as of course, above all, unmistakeable. I think of it simply
as *the* thing. *The* thing will of itself appear natural."

"Then how will it appear strange?"

Marcher bethought himself. "It won't—to *me*."

"To whom then?"

"Well," he replied, smiling at last, "say to you."

"Oh then, I'm to be present?"

"Why, you *are* present—since you know."

"I see." She turned it over. "But I mean at the catastrophe."

At this, for a minute, their lightness gave way to their gravity; it
was as if the long look they exchanged held them together. "It will only
depend on yourself—if you'll watch with me."

"Are you afraid?" she asked.

"Don't leave me *now*," he went on.

"Are you afraid?" she repeated.

"Do you think me simply out of my mind?" he pursued instead
of answering. "Do I merely strike you as a harmless lunatic?"

"No," said May Bartram. "I understand you. I believe you."

"You mean you feel how my obsession—poor old thing!—may
correspond to some possible reality?"

"To some possible reality."

"Then you *will* watch with me?"

She hesitated, then for the third time put her question. "Are you
afraid?"

"Did I tell you I was—at Naples?"

"No, you said nothing about it."

"Then I don't know. And I should *like* to know," said John Marcher.
"You'll tell me yourself whether you think so. If you'll watch with me
you'll see."

"Very good then." They had been moving by this time across the
room, and at the door, before passing out, they paused as if for the full
wind-up of their understanding. "I'll watch with you," said May
Bartram.

II

The fact that she "knew"—knew and yet neither chaffed him nor
betrayed him—had in a short time begun to constitute between them
a sensible bond, which became more marked when, within the year that

followed their afternoon at Weatherend, the opportunities for meeting
multiplied. The event that thus promoted these occasions was the
death of the ancient lady, her great-aunt, under whose wing, since
losing her mother, she had to such an extent found shelter, and who,
though but the widowed mother of the new successor to the property,
had succeeded—thanks to a high tone and a high temper—in not
forfeiting the supreme position at the great house. The deposition of
this personage arrived but with her death, which, followed by many
changes, made in particular a difference for the young woman in whom
Marcher's expert attention had recognised from the first a dependent
with a pride that might ache though it didn't bristle. Nothing for a
long time had made him easier than the thought that the aching must
have been much soothed by Miss Bartram's now finding herself able
to set up a small home in London. She had acquired property, to an
amount that made that luxury just possible, under her aunt's extremely
complicated will, and when the whole matter began to be straightened
out, which indeed took time, she let him know that the happy issue
was at last in view. He had seen her again before that day, both
because she had more than once accompanied the ancient lady to town
and because he had paid another visit to the friends who so conveniently made of Weatherend one of the charms of their own hospitality. These friends had taken him back there; he had achieved
there again with Miss Bartram some quiet detachment; and he had
in London succeeded in persuading her to more than one brief absence
from her aunt. They went together, on these latter occasions, to the
National Gallery and the South Kensington Museum, where, among
vivid reminders, they talked of Italy at large—not now attempting to
recover, as at first, the taste of their youth and their ignorance. That
recovery, the first day at Weatherend, had served its purpose well, had
given them quite enough; so that they were, to Marcher's sense, no
longer hovering about the head-waters of their stream, but had felt
their boat pushed sharply off and down the current.

They were literally afloat together; for our gentleman this was
marked, quite as marked as that the fortunate cause of it was just
the buried treasure of her knowledge. He had with his own hands dug
up this little hoard, brought to light—that is to within reach of the dim
day constituted by their discretions and privacies—the object of value
the hiding-place of which he had, after putting it into the ground himself, so strangely, so long forgotten. The exquisite luck of having again
just stumbled on the spot made him indifferent to any other question;
he would doubtless have devoted more time to the odd accident of his
lapse of memory if he had not been moved to devote so much to the
sweetness, the comfort, as he felt, for the future, that this accident
itself had helped to keep fresh. It had never entered into his plan that
anyone should "know," and mainly for the reason that it was not in him
to tell anyone. That would have been impossible, since nothing but

the amusement of a cold world would have waited on it. Since, however, a mysterious fate had opened his mouth in youth, in spite of him,
he would count that a compensation and profit by it to the utmost.
That the right person *should* know tempered the asperity of his secret
more even than his shyness had permitted him to imagine; and May
Bartram was clearly right, because—well, because there she was. Her
knowledge simply settled it; he would have been sure enough by this
time had she been wrong. There was that in his situation, no doubt,
that disposed him too much to see her as a mere confidant, taking all
her light for him from the fact—the fact only—of her interest in his
predicament, from her mercy, sympathy, seriousness, her consent not
to regard him as the funniest of the funny. Aware, in fine, that her
price for him was just in her giving him this constant sense of his being
admirably spared, he was careful to remember that she had, after all,
also a life of her own, with things that might happen to *her*, things
that in friendship one should likewise take account of. Something
fairly remarkable came to pass with him, for that matter, in this
connection—something represented by a certain passage of his consciousness, in the suddenest way, from one extreme to the other.

He had thought himself, so long as nobody knew, the most disinterested person in the world, carrying his concentrated burden, his
perpetual suspense, ever so quietly, holding his tongue about it, giving
others no glimpse of it nor of its effect upon his life, asking of them
no allowance and only making on his side all those that were asked.
He had disturbed nobody with the queerness of having to know a
haunted man, though he had had moments of rather special temptation
on hearing people say that they were "unsettled." If they were as
unsettled as he was—he who had never been settled for an hour in
his life—they would know what it meant. Yet it wasn't, all the same,
for him to make them, and he listened to them civilly enough. This
was why he had such good—though possibly such rather colourless—
manners; this was why, above all, he could regard himself, in a greedy
world, as decently—as, in fact, perhaps even a little sublimely—
unselfish. Our point is accordingly that he valued this character quite
sufficiently to measure his present danger of letting it lapse, against
which he promised himself to be much on his guard. He was quite
ready, none the less, to be selfish just a little, since, surely, no more
charming occasion for it had come to him. "Just a little," in a word,
was just as much as Miss Bartram, taking one day with another, would
let him. He never would be in the least coercive, and he would keep
well before him the lines on which consideration for her—the very
highest—ought to proceed. He would thoroughly establish the heads
under which her affairs, her requirements, her peculiarities—he went
so far as to give them the latitude of that name—would come into
their intercourse. All this naturally was a sign of how much he took
the intercourse itself for granted. There was nothing more to be done

about *that*. It simply existed; had sprung into being with her first
penetrating question to him in the autumn light there at Weatherend.
The real form it should have taken on the basis that stood out large
was the form of their marrying. But the devil in this was that the
very basis itself put marrying out of the question. His conviction, his
apprehension, his obsession, in short, was not a condition he could
invite a woman to share; and that consequence of it was precisely
what was the matter with him. Something or other lay in wait for
him, amid the twists and the turns of the months and the years, like
a crouching beast in the jungle. It signified little whether the crouching
beast were destined to slay him or to be slain. The definite point was
the inevitable spring of the creature; and the definite lesson from that
was that a man of feeling didn't cause himself to be accompanied by a
lady on a tiger-hunt. Such was the image under which he had ended
by figuring his life.

They had at first, none the less, in the scattered hours spent
together, made no allusion to that view of it; which was a sign he
was handsomely ready to give that he didn't expect, that he in fact
didn't care always to be talking about it. Such a feature in one's outlook
was really like a hump on one's back. The difference it made every
minute of the day existed quite independently of discussion. One discussed, of course, *like* a hunchback, for there was always, if nothing
else, the hunchback face. That remained, and she was watching him;
but people watched best, as a general thing, in silence, so that such
would be predominantly the manner of their vigil. Yet he didn't want,
at the same time, to be solemn; solemn was what he imagined he too
much tended to be with other people. The thing to be, with the one
person who knew, was easy and natural—to make the reference rather
than be seeming to avoid it, to avoid it rather than be seeming to make
it, and to keep it, in any case, familiar, facetious even, rather than
pedantic and portentous. Some such consideration as the latter was
doubtless in his mind, for instance, when he wrote pleasantly to Miss
Bartram that perhaps the great thing he had so long felt as in the
lap of the gods was no more than this circumstance, which touched
him so nearly, of her acquiring a house in London. It was the first
allusion they had yet again made, needing any other hitherto so little;
but when she replied, after having given him the news, that she was by
no means satisfied with such a trifle, as the climax to so special a
suspense, she almost set him wondering if she hadn't even a larger
conception of singularity for him than he had for himself. He was at
all events destined to become aware little by little, as time went by,
that she was all the while looking at his life, judging it, measuring it,
in the light of the thing she knew, which grew to be at last, with the
consecration of the years, never mentioned between them save as "the
real truth" about him. That had always been his own form of reference
to it, but she adopted the form so quietly that, looking back at the

end of a period, he knew there was no moment at which it was traceable that she had, as he might say, got inside his condition, or exchanged the attitude of beautifully indulging for that of still more beautifully believing him.

It was always open to him to accuse her of seeing him but as the most harmless of maniacs, and this, in the long run—since it covered so much ground—was his easiest description of their friendship. He had a screw loose for her, but she liked him in spite of it, and was practically, against the rest of the world, his kind, wise keeper, unremunerated, but fairly amused and, in the absence of other near ties, not disreputably occupied. The rest of the world of course thought him queer, but she, she only, knew how, and above all why, queer; which was precisely what enabled her to dispose the concealing veil in the right folds. She took his gaiety from him—since it had to pass with them for gaiety—as she took everything else; but she certainly so far justified by her unerring touch his finer sense of the degree to which he had ended by convincing her. *She* at least never spoke of the secret of his life except as "the real truth about you," and she had in fact a wonderful way of making it seem, as such, the secret of her own life too. That was in fine how he so constantly felt her as allowing for him; he couldn't on the whole call it anything else. He allowed for himself, but she, exactly, allowed still more; partly because, better placed for a sight of the matter, she traced his unhappy perversion through portions of its course into which he could scarce follow it. He knew how he felt, but, besides knowing that, she knew how he *looked* as well; he knew each of the things of importance he was insidiously kept from doing, but she could add up the amount they made, understand how much, with a lighter weight on his spirit, he might have done, and thereby establish how, clever as he was, he fell short. Above all she was in the secret of the difference between the forms he went through—those of his little office under Government, those of caring for his modest patrimony, for his library, for his garden in the country, for the people in London whose invitations he accepted and repaid— and the detachment that reigned beneath them and that made of all behaviour, all that could in the least be called behaviour, a long act of dissimulation. What it had come to was that he wore a mask painted with the social simper, out of the eyeholes of which there looked eyes of an expression not in the least matching the other features. This the stupid world, even after years, had never more than half discovered. It was only May Bartram who had, and she achieved, by an art indescribable, the feat of at once—or perhaps it was only alternately— meeting the eyes from in front and mingling her own vision, as from over his shoulder, with their peep through the apertures.

So, while they grew older together, she did watch with him, and so she let this association give shape and colour to her own existence.

Beneath *her* forms as well detachment had learned to sit, and behaviour had become for her, in the social sense, a false account of herself. There was but one account of her that would have been true all the while, and that she could give, directly, to nobody, least of all to John Marcher. Her whole attitude was a virtual statement, but the perception of that only seemed destined to take its place for him as one of the many things necessarily crowded out of his consciousness. If she had, moreover, like himself, to make sacrifices to their real truth, it was to be granted that her compensation might have affected her as more prompt and more natural. They had long periods, in this London time, during which, when they were together, a stranger might have listened to them without in the least pricking up his ears; on the other hand, the real truth was equally liable at any moment to rise to the surface, and the auditor would then have wondered indeed what they were talking about. They had from an early time made up their mind that society was, luckily, unintelligent, and the margin that this gave them had fairly become one of their commonplaces. Yet there were still moments when the situation turned almost fresh—usually under the effect of some expression drawn from herself. Her expressions doubtless repeated themselves, but her intervals were generous. "What saves us, you know, is that we answer so completely to so usual an appearance: that of the man and woman whose friendship has become such a daily habit, or almost, as to be at last indispensable." That, for instance, was a remark she had frequently enough had occasion to make, though she had given it at different times different developments. What we are especially concerned with is the turn it happened to take from her one afternoon when he had come to see her in honour of her birthday. This anniversary had fallen on a Sunday, at a season of thick fog and general outward gloom; but he had brought her his customary offering, having known her now long enough to have established a hundred little customs. It was one of his proofs to himself, the present he made her on her birthday, that he had not sunk into real selfishness. It was mostly nothing more than a small trinket, but it was always fine of its kind, and he was regularly careful to pay for it more than he thought he could afford. "Our habit saves you, at least, don't you see? because it makes you, after all, for the vulgar, indistinguishable from other men. What's the most inveterate mark of men in general? Why, the capacity to spend endless time with dull women— to spend it, I won't say without being bored, but without minding that they are, without being driven off at a tangent by it; which comes to the same thing. I'm your dull woman, a part of the daily bread for which you pray at church. That covers your tracks more than anything."

"And what covers yours?" asked Marcher, whom his dull woman could mostly to this extent amuse. "I see of course what you mean by your saving me, in one way and another, so far as other people are concerned—I've seen it all along. Only, what is it that saves *you?* I often think, you know, of that."

She looked as if she sometimes thought of that too, but in rather a different way. "Where other people, you mean, are concerned?"

"Well, you're really so in with me, you know—as a sort of result of my being so in with yourself. I mean of my having such an immense regard for you, being so tremendously grateful for all you've done for me. I sometimes ask myself if it's quite fair. Fair I mean to have so involved and—since one may say it—interested you. I almost feel as if you hadn't really had time to do anything else."

"Anything else but be interested?" she asked. "Ah, what else does one ever want to be? If I've been 'watching' with you, as we long ago agreed that I was to do, watching is always in itself an absorption."

"Oh, certainly," John Marcher said, "if you hadn't had your curiosity——! Only, doesn't it sometimes come to you, as time goes on, that your curiosity is not being particularly repaid?"

May Bartram had a pause. "Do you ask that, by any chance, because you feel at all that yours isn't? I mean because you have to wait so long."

Oh, he understood what she meant. "For the thing to happen that never does happen? For the beast to jump out? No, I'm just where I was about it. It isn't a matter as to which I can *choose*, I can decide for a change. It isn't one as to which there *can* be a change. It's in the lap of the gods. One's in the hands of one's law—there one is. As to the form the law will take, the way it will operate, that's its own affair."

"Yes," Miss Bartram replied; "of course one's fate is coming, of course it *has* come, in its own form and its own way, all the while. Only, you know, the form and the way in your case were to have been—well, something so exceptional and, as one may say, so particularly *your* own."

Something in this made him look at her with suspicion. "You say 'were to *have* been,' as if in your heart you had begun to doubt."

"Oh!" she vaguely protested.

"As if you believed," he went on, "that nothing will now take place."

She shook her head slowly, but rather inscrutably. "You're far from my thought."

He continued to look at her. "What then is the matter with you?"

"Well," she said after another wait, "the matter with me is simply that I'm more sure than ever my curiosity, as you call it, will be but too well repaid."

They were frankly grave now; he had got up from his seat, had turned once more about the little drawing-room to which, year after year, he brought his inevitable topic; in which he had, as he might have said, tasted their intimate community with every sauce, where every object was as familiar to him as the things of his own house and the very carpets were worn with his fitful walk very much as the desks in old counting-houses are worn by the elbows of generations of clerks. The generations of his nervous moods had been at work there, and the place was the written history of his whole middle life. Under the impression of what his friend has just said he knew himself, for some reason, more aware of these things, which made him, after a moment, stop again before her. "Is it, possibly, that you've grown afraid?"

"Afraid?" He thought, as she repeated the word, that his question had made her, a little, change colour; so that, lest he should have touched on a truth, he explained very kindly, "You remember that that was what you asked *me* long ago—that first day at Weatherend."

"Oh yes, and you told me you didn't know—that I was to see for myself. We've said little about it since, even in so long a time."

"Precisely," Marcher interposed—"quite as if it were too delicate a matter for us to make free with. Quite as if we might find, on pressure, that I *am* afraid. For then," he said, "we shouldn't, should we? quite know what to do."

She had for the time no answer to this question. "There have been days when I thought you were. Only, of course," she added, "there have been days when we have thought almost anything."

"Everything. Oh!" Marcher softly groaned as with a gasp, half spent, at the face, more uncovered just then than it had been for a long while, of the imagination always with them. It had always had its incalculable moments of glaring out, quite as with the very eyes of the very Beast, and, used as he was to them, they could still draw from him the tribute of a sigh that rose from the depths of his being. All that they had thought, first and last, rolled over him; the past seemed to have been reduced to mere barren speculation. This in fact was what the place had just struck him as so full of—the simplification of everything but the state of suspense. That remained only by seeming to hang in the void surrounding it. Even his original fear, if fear it had been, had lost itself in the desert. "I judge, however," he continued, "that you see I'm not afraid now."

"What I see is, as I make it out, that you've achieved something almost unprecedented in the way of getting used to danger. Living with it so long and so closely, you've lost your sense of it; you know it's there, but you're indifferent, and you cease even, as of old, to have to whistle in the dark. Considering what the danger is," May Bartram wound up, "I'm bound to say that I don't think your attitude could well be surpassed."

John Marcher faintly smiled. "It's heroic?"

"Certainly—call it that."

He considered. "I *am*, then, a man of courage?"

"That's what you were to show me."

He still, however, wondered. "But doesn't the man of courage know what he's afraid of—or *not* afraid of? I don't know *that,* you see. I don't focus it. I can't name it. I only know I'm exposed."

"Yes, but exposed—how shall I say?—so directly. So intimately. That's surely enough."

"Enough to make you feel, then—as what we may call the end of our watch—that I'm not afraid?"

"You're not afraid. But it isn't," she said, "the end of our watch. That is it isn't the end of yours. You've everything still to see."

"Then why haven't you?" he asked. He had had, all along, to-day, the sense of her keeping something back, and he still had it. As this was his first impression of that, it made a kind of date. The case was the more marked as she didn't at first answer; which in turn made him go on. "You know something I don't." Then his voice, for that of a man of courage, trembled a little. "You know what's to happen." Her silence, with the face she showed, was almost a confession—it made him sure. "You know, and you're afraid to tell me. It's so bad that you're afraid I'll find out."

All this might be true, for she did look as if, unexpectedly to her, he had crossed some mystic line that she had secretly drawn round her. Yet she might, after all, not have worried; and the real upshot was that he himself, at all events, needn't. "You'll never find out."

III

It was all to have made, none the less, as I have said, a date; as came out in the fact that again and again, even after long intervals, other things that passed between them wore, in relation to this hour, but the character of recalls and results. Its immediate effect had been indeed rather to lighten insistence—almost to provoke a reaction; as if their topic had dropped by its own weight and as if moreover, for that matter, Marcher had been visited by one of his occasional warnings against egotism. He had kept up, he felt, and very decently on the whole, his consciousness of the importance of not being selfish, and it was true that he had never sinned in that direction without promptly enough trying to press the scales the other way. He often repaired his fault, the season permitting, by inviting his friend to accompany him to the opera; and it not infrequently thus happened that, to show he didn't wish her to have but one sort of food for her mind, he was the cause of her appearing there with him a dozen nights in the month. It even happened that, seeing her home at such times, he occasionally went in with her to finish, as he called it, the evening, and, the better to make his point, sat down to the frugal but always careful little supper that awaited his pleasure. His point was made, he thought, by his not eternally insisting with her on himself; made for instance, at such hours, when it befell that, her piano at hand and each of them familiar with it, they went over passages of the opera together. It chanced to be on one of these occasions, however, that he reminded her of her not having answered a certain question he had put to her during the talk that had taken place between them on her last birthday. "What is it that saves *you?*"—saved her, he meant, from that appearance of variation from the usual human type. If he had practically escaped remark, as she pretended, by doing, in the most important particular, what most men do—find the answer to life in patching up an alliance of a sort with a woman no better than himself—how had she escaped it, and how could the alliance, such as it was, since they must suppose it had been more or less noticed, have failed to make her rather positively talked about?

"I never said," May Bartram replied, "that it hadn't made me talked about."

"Ah well then, you're not 'saved.'"

"It has not been a question for me. If you've had your woman, I've had," she said, "my man."

"And you mean that makes you all right?"

She hesitated. "I don't know why it shouldn't make me—humanly, which is what we're speaking of—as right as it makes you."

"I see," Marcher returned. "'Humanly,' no doubt, as showing that you're living for something. Not, that is, just for me and my secret."

May Bartram smiled. "I don't pretend it exactly shows that I'm not living for you. It's my intimacy with you that's in question."

He laughed as he saw what she meant. "Yes, but since, as you say, I'm only, so far as people make out, ordinary, you're—aren't you?—no more than ordinary either. You help me to pass for a man like another. So if I *am*, as I understand you, you're not compromised. Is that it?"

She had another hesitation, but she spoke clearly enough. "That's it. It's all that concerns me—to help you to pass for a man like another."

He was careful to acknowledge the remark handsomely. "How kind, how beautiful, you are to me! How shall I ever repay you?"

She had her last grave pause, as if there might be a choice of ways. But she chose. "By going on as you are."

It was into this going on as he was that they relapsed, and really for so long a time that the day inevitably came for a further sounding of their depths. It was as if these depths, constantly bridged over by a structure that was firm enough in spite of its lightness and of its occasional oscillation in the somewhat vertiginous air, invited on occasion, in the interest of their nerves, a dropping of the plummet and a measurement of the abyss. A difference had been made moreover, once for all, by the fact that she had, all the while, not appeared to feel the need of rebutting his charge of an idea within her that she didn't dare to express, uttered just before one of the fullest of their later discussions ended. It had come up for him then that she "knew" something and that what she knew was bad—too bad to tell him. When he had spoken of it as visibly so bad that she was afraid he might find it out, her reply had left the matter too equivocal to be let alone and yet, for Marcher's special sensibility, almost too formidable again to touch. He circled about it at a distance that alternately narrowed and widened and that yet was not much affected by the consciousness in him that there was nothing she could "know," after all, any better than he did. She had no source of knowledge that he hadn't equally—except of course that she might have finer nerves. That was what women had where they were interested; they made out things, where people were concerned, that the people often couldn't have made out for themselves. Their nerves, their sensibility, their imagination, were conductors and revealers, and the beauty of May Bartram was in particular that she had given herself so to his case. He felt in these days what, oddly enough, he had never felt before, the growth of a dread of losing her by some catastrophe—some catastrophe that yet wouldn't at all be *the* catastrophe: partly because she had, almost of a sudden, begun to strike him as useful to him as never yet, and partly by reason of an appearance of uncertainty in her health, coincident and equally new. It was characteristic of the inner detachment he had hitherto so successfully cultivated and to which our whole account of him is a reference, it was characteristic that his complications, such as they were, had never yet seemed so as at this crisis to thicken about him, even to the point of making him ask himself if he were, by any chance, of a truth, within sight or sound, within touch or reach, within the immediate jurisdiction of the thing that waited.

When the day came, as come it had to, that his friend confessed to him her fear of a deep disorder in her blood, he felt somehow the shadow of a change and the chill of a shock. He immediately began to imagine aggravations and disasters, and above all to think of her peril as the direct menace for himself of personal privation. This indeed gave him one of those partial recoveries of equanimity that were agreeable to him—it showed him that what was still first in his mind was the loss she herself might suffer. "What if she should have to die before knowing, before seeing——?" It would have been brutal, in the early stages of her trouble, to put that question to her; but it had immediately sounded for him to his own concern, and the possibility was what most made him sorry for her. If she did "know," moreover, in the sense of her having had some—what should he think?— mystical, irresistible light, this would make the matter not better, but worse, inasmuch as her original adoption of his own curiosity had quite become the basis of her life. She had been living to see what would *be* to be seen, and it would be cruel to her to have to give up before the accomplishment of the vision. These reflections, as I say, refreshed his generosity; yet, make them as he might, he saw himself, with the lapse of the period, more and more disconcerted. It lapsed for him with a strange, steady sweep, and the oddest oddity was that it gave him, independently of the threat of much inconvenience, almost the only positive surprise his career, if career it could be called, had yet offered him. She kept the house as she had never done; he had to go to her to see her—she could meet him nowhere now, though there was scarce a corner of their loved old London in which she had not in the past, at one time or another, done so; and he found her always seated by her fire in the deep, old-fashioned chair she was less and less able to leave. He had been struck one day, after an absence exceeding his usual measure, with her suddenly looking much older to him than he had ever thought of her being; then he recognized that the suddenness was all on his side—he had just been suddenly struck. She looked older because inevitably, after so many years, she *was* old, or almost; which was of course true in still greater measure of her companion. If she was old, or almost, John Marcher assuredly was, and yet it was her showing of the lesson, not his own, that brought the truth home to him. His surprises began here; when once they had begun they multiplied; they came rather with a rush: it was as if, in the oddest way in the world, they had all been kept back, sown in a thick cluster, for the late afternoon of life, the time at which, for people in general, the unexpected has died out.

One of them was that he should have caught himself—for he *had* so done—*really* wondering if the great accident would take form now as nothing more than his being condemned to see this charming woman, this admirable friend, pass away from him. He had never so unreservedly qualified her as while confronted in thought with such a possibility; in spite of which there was small doubt for him that as an answer to his long riddle the mere effacement of even so fine a feature of his situation would be an abject anticlimax. It would represent, as connected with his past attitude, a drop of dignity under the shadow of which his existence could only become the most grotesque of failures. He had been far from holding it a failure—long as he had waited for the appearance that was to make it a success. He had waited for a quite other thing, not for such a one as that. The breath of his good faith came short, however, as he recognized how long he had waited, or how long, at least, his companion had. That she, at all events, might be recorded as having waited in vain—this affected him sharply, and all the more because of his at first having done little more than amuse himself with the idea. It grew more grave as the gravity of her condition grew, and the state of mind it produced in him, which he ended by watching, himself, as if it had been some definite disfigurement of his outer person, may pass for another of his surprises. This conjoined itself still with another, the really stupefying consciousness of a question that he would have allowed to shape itself had he dared. What did everything mean—what, that is, did *she* mean, she and her vain waiting and her probable death and the soundless admonition of it all—unless that, at this time of day, it was simply, it was overwhelmingly too late? He had never, at any stage of his queer consciousness, admitted the whisper of such a correction; he had never, till within these last few months, been so false to his conviction as not to hold that what was to come to him had time, whether *he* struck himself as having it or not. That at last, at last, he certainly hadn't it, to speak of, or had it but in the scantiest measure— such, soon enough, as things went with him, became the inference with which his old obsession had to reckon: and this it was not helped to do by the more and more confirmed appearance that the great vagueness casting the long shadow in which he had lived had, to attest itself, almost no margin left. Since it was in Time that he was to have met his fate, so it was in Time that his fate was to have acted; and as he waked up to the sense of no longer being young, which was exactly the sense of being stale, just as that, in turn, was the sense of being weak, he waked up to another matter beside. It all hung together; they were subject, he and the great vagueness, to an equal and indivisible law. When the possibilities themselves had, accordingly, turned stale, when the secret of the gods had grown faint, had perhaps even quite evaporated, that, and that only, was failure. It wouldn't have been failure to be bankrupt, dishonoured, pilloried, hanged; it was failure not to be anything. And so, in the dark valley into which his path had taken its unlooked-for twist, he wondered not a little as he groped. He didn't care what awful crash might overtake him, with what ignominy or what monstrosity he might yet be associated— since he wasn't, after all, too utterly old to suffer—if it would only be decently proportionate to the posture he had kept, all his life, in the promised presence of it. He had but one desire left—that he shouldn't have been "sold."

IV

Then it was that one afternoon, while the spring of the year was young and new, she met, all in her own way, his frankest betrayal of these alarms. He had gone in late to see her, but evening had not settled, and she was presented to him in that long, fresh light of waning April days which affects us often with a sadness sharper than the greyest hours of autumn. The week had been warm, the spring was supposed to have begun early, and May Bartram sat, for the first time in the year, without a fire, a fact that, to Marcher's sense, gave the scene of which she formed part a smooth and ultimate look, an air of knowing, in its immaculate order and its cold, meaningless cheer, that it would never see a fire again. Her own aspect— he could scarce have said why—intensified this note. Almost as white as wax, with the marks and signs in her face as numerous and as fine as if they had been etched by a needle, with soft white draperies relieved by a faded green scarf, the delicate tone of which had been consecrated by the years, she was the picture of a serene, exquisite, but impenetrable sphinx, whose head, or indeed all whose person, might have been powdered with silver. She was a sphinx, yet with her white petals and green fronds she might have been a lily too—only an artificial lily, wonderfully imitated and constantly kept, without dust or stain, though not exempt from a slight droop and a complexity of faint creases, under some clear glass bell. The perfection of household care, of high polish and finish, always reigned in her rooms, but they especially looked to Marcher at present as if everything had been wound up, tucked in, put away, so that she might sit with folded hands and with nothing more to do. She was "out of it," to his vision; her work was over; she communicated with him as across some gulf, or from some island of rest that she had already reached, and it made him feel strangely abandoned. Was it—or, rather, wasn't it—that if for so long she had been watching with him the answer to their question had swum into her ken and taken on its name, so that her occupation was verily gone? He had as much as charged her with this in saying to her, many months before, that she even then knew something she was keeping from him. It was a point he had never since ventured to press, vaguely fearing, as he did, that it might become a difference, perhaps a disagreement, between them. He had in short, in this later time, turned nervous, which was what, in all the other years, he had never been; and the oddity was that his nervousness should have waited till he had begun to doubt, should have held off so long as he was sure. There was something, it seemed to him, that the wrong word would bring down on his head, something that would so at least put an end to his suspense. But he wanted not to speak the wrong word; that would make everything ugly. He wanted the knowledge he lacked to drop on him, if drop it could, by its own august weight. If she was to forsake him it was surely for her to take leave. This was why he didn't ask her again, directly, what she knew; but it was also why, approaching the matter from another side, he said to her in the course of his visit: "What do you regard as the very worst that, at this time of day, *can* happen to me?"

He had asked her that in the past often enough; they had, with the odd, irregular rhythm of their intensities and avoidances, exchanged ideas about it and then had seen the ideas washed away by cool intervals, washed like figures traced in sea-sand. It had ever been the mark of their talk that the oldest allusions in it required but a little dismissal and reaction to come out again, sounding for the hour as new. She could thus at present meet his inquiry quite freshly and patiently. "Oh yes, I've repeatedly thought, only it always seemed to me of old that I couldn't quite make up my mind. I thought of dreadful things, between which it was difficult to choose; and so must you have done."

"Rather! I feel now as if I had scarce done anything else. I appear to myself to have spent my life in thinking of nothing *but* dreadful things. A great many of them I've at different times named to you, but there were others I couldn't name."

"They were too, too dreadful?"

"Too, too dreadful—some of them."

She looked at him a minute, and there came to him as he met it an inconsequent sense that her eyes, when one got their full clearness, were still as beautiful as they had been in youth, only beautiful with a strange, cold light—a light that somehow was a part of the effect, if it wasn't rather a part of the cause, of the pale, hard sweetness of the season and the hour. "And yet," she said at last, "there are horrors we have mentioned."

It deepened the strangeness to see her, as such a figure in such a picture, talk of "horrors," but she was to do, in a few minutes, something stranger yet—though even of this he was to take the full measure but afterwards—and the note of it was already in the air. It was, for the matter of that, one of the signs that her eyes were having again such a high flicker of their prime. He had to admit, however, what she said. "Oh yes, there were times when we did go far." He caught himself in the act of speaking as if it all were over. Well, he wished it were; and the consummation depended, for him, clearly, more and more on his companion.

But she had now a soft smile. "Oh, far——!"

It was oddly ironic. "Do you mean you're prepared to go further?"

She was frail and ancient and charming as she continued to look at him, yet it was rather as if she had lost the thread. "Do you consider that we went so far?"

"Why, I thought it the point you were just making—that we *had* looked most things in the face."

"Including each other?" She still smiled. "But you're quite right. We've had together great imaginations, often great fears; but some of them have been unspoken."

"Then the worst—we haven't faced that. I *could* face it, I believe, if I knew what you think it. I feel," he explained, "as if I had lost my power to conceive such things." And he wondered if he looked as blank as he sounded. "It's spent."

"Then why do you assume," she asked, "that mine isn't?"

"Because you've given me signs to the contrary. It isn't a question for you of conceiving, imagining, comparing. It isn't a question now of choosing." At last he came out with it. You know something that I don't. You've shown me that before."

These last words affected her, he could see in a moment, remarkably, and she spoke with firmness. "I've shown you, my dear, nothing."

He shook his head. "You can't hide it."

"Oh, oh!" May Bartram murmured over what she couldn't hide. It was almost a smothered groan.

"You admitted it months ago, when I spoke of it to you as of something you were afraid I would find out. Your answer was that I couldn't, that I wouldn't, and I don't pretend I have. But you had something therefore in mind, and I see now that it must have been, that it still is, the possibility that, of all possibilities, has settled itself for you as the worst. This," he went on, "is why I appeal to you. I'm only afraid of ignorance now—I'm not afraid of knowledge." And then as for a while she said nothing: "What makes me sure is that I see in your face and feel here, in this air and amid these appearances, that you're out of it. You've done. You've had your experience. You leave me to my fate."

Well, she listened, motionless and white in her chair, as if she had in fact a decision to make, so that her whole manner was a virtual confession, though still with a small, fine, inner stiffness, an imperfect surrender. "It *would* be the worst," she finally let herself say. "I mean the thing that I've never said."

It hushed him a moment. "More monstrous than all the monstrosities we've named?"

"More monstrous. Isn't that what you sufficiently express," she asked, "in calling it the worst?"

Marcher thought. "Assuredly—if you mean, as I do, something that includes all the loss and all the shame that are thinkable."

"It would if it *should* happen," said May Bartram. "What we're speaking of, remember, is only my idea."

"It's your belief," Marcher returned. "That's enough for me. I feel your beliefs are right. Therefore if, having this one, you give me no more light on it, you abandon me."

"No, no!" she repeated. "I'm with you—don't you see?—still." And as if to make it more vivid to him she rose from her chair—a movement she seldom made in these days—and showed herself, all draped and all soft, in her fairness and slimness. "I haven't forsaken you."

It was really, in its effort against weakness, a generous assurance, and had the success of the impulse not, happily, been great, it would have touched him to pain more than to pleasure. But the cold charm in her eyes had spread, as she hovered before him, to all the rest of her person, so that it was, for the minute, almost like a recovery of youth. He couldn't pity her for that; he could only take her as she showed— as capable still of helping him. It was as if, at the same time, her light might at any instant go out; wherefore he must make the most of it. There passed before him with intensity the three or four things he wanted most to know; but the question that came of itself to his lips really covered the others. "Then tell me if I shall consciously suffer."

She promptly shook her head. "Never!"

It confirmed the authority he imputed to her, and it produced on him an extraordinary effect. "Well, what's better than that? Do you call that the worst?"

"You think nothing is better?" she asked.

She seemed to mean something so special that he again sharply wondered, though still with the dawn of a prospect of relief. "Why not, if one doesn't *know*?" After which, as their eyes, over his question, met in a silence, the dawn deepened and something to his purpose came, prodigiously, out of her very face. His own, as he took it in, suddenly flushed to the forehead, and he gasped with the force of a perception to which, on the instant, everything fitted. The sound of his gasp filled the air; then he became articulate. "I see—if I don't suffer!"

In her own look, however, was doubt. "You see what?"

"Why, what you mean—what you've always meant."

She again shook her head. "What I mean isn't what I've always meant. It's different."

"It's something new?"

She hesitated. "Something new. It's not what you think. I see what you think."

His divination drew breath then; only her correction might be wrong. "It isn't that I *am* a donkey?" he asked between faintness and grimness. "It isn't that it's all a mistake?"

"A mistake?" she pityingly echoed. *That* possibility, for her, he saw, would be monstrous; and if she guaranteed him the immunity from pain it would accordingly not be what she had in mind. "Oh, no," she declared; "it's nothing of that sort. You've been right."

Yet he couldn't help asking himself if she weren't, thus pressed, speaking but to save him. It seemed to him he should be most lost if his history should prove all a platitude. "Are you telling me the truth, so that I sha'n't have been a bigger idiot than I can bear to know? I *haven't* lived with a vain imagination, in the most besotted illusion? I haven't waited but to see the door shut in my face?"

She shook her head again. "However the case stands *that* isn't the truth. Whatever the reality, it *is* a reality. The door isn't shut. The door's open," said May Bartram.

"Then something's to come?"

She waited once again, always with her cold, sweet eyes on him. "It's never too late." She had, with her gliding step, diminished the distance between them, and she stood nearer to him, close to him, a minute, as if still full of the unspoken. Her movement might have been for some finer emphasis of what she was at once hesitating and deciding to say. He had been standing by the chimney-piece, fireless and sparely adorned, a small, perfect old French clock and two morsels of rosy Dresden constituting all its furniture; and her hand grasped the shelf while she kept him waiting, grasped it a little as for support and encouragement. She only kept him waiting, however; that is he only waited. It had become suddenly, from her movement and attitude, beautiful and vivid to him that she had something more to give him;

her wasted face delicately shone with it, and it glittered, almost as with the white lustre of silver, in her expression. She was right, incontestably, for what he saw in her face was the truth, and strangely, without consequence, while their talk of it as dreadful was still in the air, she appeared to present it as inordinately soft. This, prompting bewilderment, made him but gape the more gratefully for her revelation, so that they continued for some minutes silent, her face shining at him, her contact imponderably pressing, and his stare all kind, but all expectant. The end, none the less, was that what he had expected failed to sound. Something else took place instead, which seemed to consist at first in the mere closing of her eyes. She gave way at the same instant to a slow, fine shudder, and though he remained staring—though he stared, in fact, but the harder—she turned off and regained her chair. It was the end of what she had been intending, but it left him thinking only of that.

"Well, you don't say——?"

She had touched in her passage a bell near the chimney and had sunk back, strangely pale. "I'm afraid I'm too ill."

"Too ill to tell me?" It sprang up sharp to him, and almost to his lips, the fear that she would die without giving him light. He checked himself in time from so expressing his question, but she answered as if she had heard the words.

"Don't you know—now?"

" 'Now'——?" She had spoken as if something that had made a difference had come up within the moment. But her maid, quickly obedient to her bell, was already with them. "I know nothing." And he was afterwards to say to himself that he must have spoken with odious impatience, such an impatience as to show that, supremely disconcerted, he washed his hands of the whole question.

"Oh!" said May Bartram.

"Are you in pain?" he asked, as the woman went to her.

"No," said May Bartram.

Her maid, who had put an arm round her as if to take her to her room, fixed on him eyes that appealingly contradicted her; in spite of which, however, he showed once more his mystification. "What then has happened?"

She was once more, with her companion's help, on her feet, and, feeling withdrawal imposed on him, he had found, blankly, his hat and gloves and had reached the door. Yet he waited for her answer. "What *was* to," she said.

V

He came back the next day, but she was then unable to see him, and as it was literally the first time this had occurred in the long stretch of their acquaintance he turned away, defeated and sore, almost

angry—or feeling at least that such a break in their custom was really
the beginning of the end—and wandered alone with his thoughts,
especially with one of them that he was unable to keep down. She
was dying, and he would lose her; she was dying, and his life would
end. He stopped in the park, into which he had passed, and stared
before him at his recurrent doubt. Away from her the doubt pressed
again; in her presence he had believed her, but as he felt his forlorn-
ness he threw himself into the explanation that, nearest at hand,
had most of a miserable warmth for him and least of a cold torment.
She had deceived him to save him—to put him off with something
in which he should be able to rest. What could the thing that was to
happen to him be, after all, but just this thing that had begun to
happen? Her dying, her death, his consequent solitude—*that* was
what he had figured as the beast in the jungle, that was what had
been in the lap of the gods. He had had her word for it as he left her;
for what else, on earth, could she have meant? It wasn't a thing of
a monstrous order; not a fate rare and distinguished; not a stroke
of fortune that overwhelmed and immortalised; it had only the stamp
of the common doom. But poor Marcher, at this hour, judged the
common doom sufficient. It would serve his turn, and even as the
consummation of infiite waiting he would bend his pride to accept it.
He sat down on a bench in the twilight. He hadn't been a fool. Something had *been*, as she had said, to come. Before he rose indeed it had
quite struck him that the final fact really matched with the long
avenue through which he had had to reach it. As sharing his suspense,
and as giving herself all, giving her life, to bring it to an end, she
had come with him every step of the way. He had lived by her aid, and
to leave her behind would be cruelly, damnably to miss her. What
could be more overwhelming that that?

Well, he was to know within the week, for though she kept him a
while at bay, left him restless and wretched during a series of days
on each of which he asked about her only again to have to turn away,
she ended his trial by receiving him where she had always received
him. Yet she had been brought out at some hazard into the presence
of so many of the things that were, consciously, vainly, half their past,
and there was scant service left in the gentleness of her mere desire,
all too visible, to check his obsession and wind up his long trouble.
That was clearly what she wanted; the one thing more, for her own
peace, while she could still put out her hand. He was so affected by
her state that, once seated by her chair, he was moved to let everything go; it was she herself therefore who brought him back, took
up again, before she dismissed him, her last word of the other time.
She showed how she wished to leave their affair in order. "I'm not sure
you understood. You've nothing to wait for more. It *has* come."

Oh, how he looked at her! "Really?"

"Really."

"The thing that, as you said, *was* to?"

"The thing that we began in our youth to watch for."

Face to face with her once more he believed her; it was a claim to which he had so abjectly little to oppose. "You mean that it has come as a positive, definite occurrence, with a name and a date?"

"Positive. Definite. I don't know about the 'name,' but, oh, with a date!"

He found himself again too helplessly at sea. "But come in the night—come and passed me by?"

May Bartram had her strange, faint smile. "Oh no, it hasn't passed you by!"

"But if I haven't been aware of it, and it hasn't touched me——?"

"Ah, your not being aware of it," and she seemed to hesitate an instant to deal with this—"your not being aware of it is the strangeness *in* the strangeness. It's the wonder *of* the wonder." She spoke as with the softness almost of a sick child, yet now at last, at the end of all, with the perfect straightness of a sibyl. She visibly knew that she knew, and the effect on him was of something co-ordinate, in its high character, with the law that had ruled him. It was the true voice of the law; so on her lips would the law itself have sounded. "It *has* touched you," she went on. "It has done its office. It has made you all it's own."

"So utterly without my knowing it?"

"So utterly without your knowing it." His hand, as he leaned to her, was on the arm of her chair, and dimly smiling always now, she placed her own on it. "It's enough if *I* know it."

"Oh!" he confusedly sounded, as she herself of late so often had done.

"What I long ago said is true. You'll never know now, and I think you ought to be content. You've *had* it," said May Bartram.

"But had what?"

"Why, what was to have marked you out. The proof of your law. It has acted. I'm too glad," she then bravely added, "to have been able to see what it's *not*."

He continued to attach his eyes to her, and with the sense that it was all beyond him, and that *she* was too, he would still have sharply challenged her, had he not felt it an abuse of her weakness to do more than take devoutly what she gave him, take it as hushed as to a revelation. If he did speak, it was out of the foreknowledge of his loneliness to come. "If you're glad of what it's 'not,' it might then have been worse?"

She turned her eyes away, she looked straight before her with which, after a moment: "Well, you know our fears."

He wondered. "It's something then we never feared?"

On this, slowly, she turned to him. "Did we ever dream, with all our dreams, that we should sit and talk of it thus?"

He tried for a little to make out if they had; but it was as if their dreams, numberless enough, were in solution in some thick, cold mist, in which thought lost itself. "It might have been that we couldn't talk?"

"Well"—she did her best for him—"not from this side. This, you see," she said, "is the *other* side."

"I think," poor Marcher returned, "that all sides are the same to me." Then, however, as she softly shook her head in correction: "We mightn't, as it were, have got across——?"

"To where we are—no. We're *here*"—she made her weak emphasis.

"And much good does it do us!" was her friend's frank comment.

"It does us the good it can. It does us the good that *it* isn't here. It's past. It's behind," said May Bartram. "Before——" but her voice dropped.

He had got up, not to tire her, but it was hard to combat his yearning. She after all told him nothing but that his light had failed—which he knew well enough without her. "Before——?" he blankly echoed.

"Before, you see, it was always to *come*. That kept it present."

"Oh, I don't care what comes now! Besides," Marcher added, "it seems to me I liked it better present, as you say, than I can like it absent with *your* absence."

"Oh, mine!"—and her pale hands made light of it.

"With the absence of everything." He had a dreadful sense of standing there before her for—so far as anything but this proved, this bottomless drop was concerned—the last time of their life. It rested on him with a weight he felt he could scarce bear, and this weight it apparently was that still pressed out what remained in him of speakable protest. "I believe you; but I can't begin to pretend I understand. *Nothing*, for me, is past; nothing *will* pass until I pass myself, which I pray my stars may be as soon as possible. Say, however," he added, "that I've eaten my cake, as you contend, to the last crumb—how can the thing I've never felt at all be the thing I was marked out to feel?"

She met him, perhaps, less directly, but she met him unperturbed. "You take your 'feelings' for granted. You were to suffer your fate. That was not necessarily to know it."

"How in the world—when what is such knowledge but suffering?"

She looked up at him a while, in silence. "No—you don't understand."

"I suffer," said John Marcher.

"Don't, don't!"

"How can I help at least *that*?"

"*Don't!*" May Bartram repeated.

She spoke it in a tone so special, in spite of her weakness, that he stared an instant—stared as if some light, hitherto hidden, had shimmered across his vision. Darkness again closed over it, but the gleam had already become for him an idea. "Because I haven't the right——?"

"Don't *know*—when you needn't," she mercifully urged. "You needn't —for we shouldn't."

"Shouldn't?" If he could but know what she meant!

"No—it's too much."

"Too much?" he still asked—but with a mystification that was the next moment, of a sudden, to give way. Her words, if they meant something, affected him in this light—the light also of her wasted face—as meaning *all*, and the sense of what knowledge had been for herself came over him with a rush which broke through into a question. "Is it of that, then, you're dying?"

She but watched him, gravely at first, as if to see, with this, where he was, and she might have seen something, or feared something, that moved her sympathy. "I would live for you still—if I could." Her eyes closed for a little, as if, withdrawn into herself, she were, for a last time, trying. "But I can't!" she said as she raised them again to take leave of him.

She couldn't indeed, as but too promptly and sharply appeared, and he had no vision of her after this that was anything but darkness and doom. They had parted forever in that strange talk; access to her chamber of pain, rigidly guarded, was almost wholly forbidden him; he was feeling now moreover, in the face of doctors, nurses, the two or three relatives attracted doubtless by the presumption of what she had to "leave," how few were the rights, as they were called in such cases, that he had to put forward, and how odd it might even seem that their intimacy shouldn't have given him more of them. The stupidest fourth cousin had more, even though she had been nothing in such a person's life. She had been a feature of features in *his*, for what else was it to have been so indispensable? Strange beyond saying were the ways of existence, baffling for him the anomaly of his lack, as he felt it to be, of producible claim. A woman might have been, as it were, everything to him, and it might yet present him in no connection that anyone appeared obliged to recognise. If this was the case in these closing weeks it was the case more sharply on the occasion of the last offices rendered, in the great grey London cemetery, to what had been mortal, to what had been precious, in his friend. The concourse at her grave was not numerous, but he saw himself treated as scarce more nearly concerned with it than if there had been a thousand others. He was in short from this moment face to face with the fact that he was to profit extraordinarily little by the interest May Bartram had taken in him. He couldn't quite have said what he expected, but he had somehow not expected this approach to a double privation. Not only had her interest failed him, but he seemed to feel himself unattended—and for a reason he couldn't sound—by the distinction, the dignity, the propriety, if nothing else, of the man markedly bereaved. It was as if, in the view of society, he had not *been* markedly bereaved, as if there still failed some sign or proof of it, and as if, none the less, his character could never be affirmed, nor the deficiency ever made up. There were moments, as the weeks went by, when he would have liked, by some almost aggressive act, to take his stand on the intimacy of his loss, in order that it *might* be questioned and his retort, to the relief of his spirit, so recorded; but the moments of an irritation more helpless followed fast on these, the moments during which, turning things over with a good conscience but with a bare horizon, he found himself wondering if he oughtn't to have begun, so to speak, further back.

He found himself wondering indeed at many things, and this last speculation had others to keep it company. What could he have done, after all, in her lifetime, without giving them both, as it were, away? He couldn't have made it known she was watching him, for that would have published the superstition of the Beast. This was what closed his mouth now—now that the Jungle had been threshed to vacancy and that the Beast had stolen away. It sounded too foolish and too flat; the difference for him in this particular, the extinction in his life of the element of suspense, was such in fact as to surprise him. He could scarce have said what the effect resembled; the abrupt cessation, the positive prohibition, of music perhaps, more than anything else, in some place all adjusted and all accustomed to sonority and to attention. If he could at any rate have conceived lifting the veil from his image at some moment of the past (what had he done, after all, if not lift it to *her?*), so to do this to-day, to talk to people at large of the jungle cleared and confide to them that he now felt it as safe, would have been not only to see them listen as to a good-wife's tale, but really to hear himself tell one. What it presently came to in truth was that poor Marcher waded through his beaten grass, where no life stirred, where no breath sounded, where no evil eye seemed to gleam from a possible lair, very much as if vaguely looking for the Beast, and still more as if missing it. He walked about in an existence that had grown strangely more spacious, and, stopping fitfully in places where the undergrowth of life struck him as closer, asked himself yearningly, wondered secretly, and sorely, if it would have lurked here or there. It would have at all events *sprung;* what was at least complete was his belief in the truth itself of the assurance given him. The change from his old sense to his new was absolute and final: what was to happen *had* so absolutely and finally happened that he was as little able to know a fear for his future as to know a hope; so absent in short was any question of anything still to come. He was to live entirely with the other question, that of his unidentified past, that of his having to see his fortune impenetrably muffled and masked.

The torment of this vision became then his occupation; he couldn't perhaps have consented to live but for the possibility of guessing. She had told him, his friend, not to guess; she had forbidden him, so far as he might, to know, and she had even in a sort denied the power in him to learn: which were so many things, precisely, to deprive him of rest. It wasn't that he wanted, he argued for fairness, that anything that had happened to him should happen over again; it was only that he shouldn't as an anticlimax, have been taken sleeping so sound as not to be able to win back by an effort of thought the lost stuff of consciousness. He declared to himself at moments that he would either win it back or have done with consciousness for ever; he made this idea his one motive, in fine, made it so much his passion that none other, to compare with it, seemed ever to have touched him. The lost stuff of consciousness became thus for him as a strayed or stolen child to an unappeasable father; he hunted it up and down very much as if he were knocking at doors and inquiring of the police. This was the spirit in which, inevitably, he set himself to travel; he started on a journey that was to be as long as he could make it; it danced before him that, as the other side of the globe couldn't possibly have less to say to him, it might, by a possibility of suggestion, have more. Before he quitted London, however, he made a pilgrimage to May Bartram's grave, took his way to it through the endless avenues of the grim suburban necropolis, sought it out in the wilderness of tombs, and, though he had come but for the renewal of the act of farewell, found himself, when he had at last stood by it, beguiled into long intensities. He stood for an hour, powerless to turn away and yet powerless to penetrate the darkness of death; fixing with his eyes her inscribed name and date, beating his forehead against the fact of the secret they kept, drawing his breath, while he waited as if, in pity of him, some sense would rise from the stones. He kneeled on the stones, however, in vain; they kept what they concealed; and if the face of the tomb did become a face for him it was because her two names were like a pair of eyes that didn't know him. He gave them a last long look, but no palest light broke.

VI

He stayed away, after this, for a year; he visited the depths of Asia, spending himself on scenes of romantic interest, of superlative sanctity; but what was present to him everywhere was that for a man who had known what *he* had known the world was vulgar and vain. The state of mind in which he had lived for so many years shone out to him, in reflection, as a light that coloured and refined, a light beside which the glow of the East was garish, cheap and thin. The terrible truth was that he had lost—with everything else—a distinction as well; the things he saw couldn't help being common when he had become common to look at them. He was simply now one of them himself—he was in the dust, without a peg for the sense of difference; and there were hours when, before the temples of gods and the sepulchres of kings, his spirit turned, for nobleness of association, to the barely discriminated slab in the London suburb. That had become for him, and more intensely with time and distance, his one witness of a past glory. It was all that was left to him for proof or pride, yet the past glories of Pharaohs were nothing to him as he thought of it. Small wonder then that he came back to it on the morrow of his return. He was drawn there this time as irresistibly as the other, yet with a confidence, almost, that was doubtless the effect of the many months that had elapsed. He had lived, in spite of himself, into his change of feeling, and in wandering over the earth had wandered, as might be said, from the circumference to the centre of his desert. He had settled to his safety and accepted perforce his extinction; figuring to himself, with some colour, in the likeness of certain little old men he remembered to have seen, of whom, all meagre and wizened as they might look, it was related that they had in their time fought twenty duels or been loved by ten princesses. They indeed had been wondrous for others, while he was but wondrous for himself; which, however, was exactly the cause of his haste to renew the wonder by getting back, as he might put it, into his own presence. That had quickened his steps and checked his delay. If his visit was prompt it was because he had been separated so long from the part of himself that alone he now valued.

It is accordingly not false to say that he reached his goal with a certain elation and stood there again with a certain assurance. The creature beneath the sod *knew* of his rare experience, so that, strangely now, the place had lost for him its mere blankness of expression. It met him in mildness—not, as before, in mockery; it wore for him the air of conscious greeting that we find, after absence, in things that have closely belonged to us and which seem to confess of themselves to the connection. The plot of ground, the graven tablet, the tended flowers affected him so as belonging to him that he quite felt for the hour like a contended landlord reviewing a piece of property. Whatever had happened—well, had happened. He had not come back this time with the vanity of that question, his former worrying, "What, *what?*" now practically so spent. Yet he would, none the less, never again so cut himself off from the spot; he would come back to it every month, for if he did nothing else by its aid he at least held up his head. It thus grew for him, in the oddest way, a positive resource; he carried out his idea of periodical returns, which took their place at last among the most inveterate of his habits. What it all amounted to, oddly enough, was that, in his now so simplified world, this garden of death gave him the few square feet of earth on which he could still most live. It was as if, being nothing anywhere else for anyone, nothing even for himself, he were just everything here, and if not for a crowd of witnesses, or indeed for any witness but John Marcher, then by clear right of the register that he could scan like an open page. The open page was the tomb of his friend, and *there* were the facts of the past, there the truth of his life, there the backward reaches in which he could lose himself. He did this, from time to time, with such effect that he seemed to wander through the old years with his hand in the arm of a companion who was, in the most extraordinary manner, his other, his younger self; and to wander, which was more extraordinary yet, round and round a third presence—not wandering she, but stationary, still, whose eyes, turning with his revolution, never ceased to follow him, and whose seat was his point, so to speak, of orientation. Thus in short he settled to live—feeding only on the sense that he once *had* lived, and dependent on it not only for a support but for an identity.

It sufficed him, in its way, for months, and the year elapsed; it would doubtless even have carried him further but for an accident, superficially slight, which moved him, in a quite other direction, with a force beyond any of his impressions of Egypt or of India. It was a thing of the merest chance—the turn, as he afterwards felt, of a hair, though he was indeed to live to believe that if light hadn't come to him in this particular fashion it would still have come in another. He was to live to believe this, I say, though he was not to live, I may not less definitely mention, to do much else. We allow him at any rate the benefit of the conviction, struggling up for him at the end, that, whatever might have happened or not happened, he would have come round of himself to the light. The incident of an autumn day had put the match to the train laid from of old by his misery. With the light before him he knew that even of late his ache had only been smothered. It was strangely drugged, but it throbbed; at the touch it began to bleed. And the touch, in the event, was the face of a fellow-mortal. This face, one grey afternoon when the leaves were thick in the alleys, looked into Marcher's own, at the cemetery, with an expression like the cut of a blade. He felt it, that is, so deep down that he winced at the steady thrust. The person who so mutely assaulted him was a figure he had noticed, on reaching his own goal, absorbed by a grave a short distance away, a grave apparently fresh, so that the emotion of the visitor would probably match it for frankness. This fact alone forbade further attention, though during the time he stayed he remained vaguely conscious of his neighbour, a middle-aged man apparently, in mourning, whose bowed back, among the clustered monuments and mortuary yews, was constantly presented. Marcher's theory that these were elements in contact with which he himself revived, had suffered, on this occasion, it may be granted, a sensible though inscrutable check. The autumn day was dire for him as none had recently been, and he rested with a heaviness he had not yet known on the low stone table that bore May Bartram's name. He rested without power to move, as if some spring in him, some spell vouchsafed, had suddenly been broken forever. If he could have done that moment as he wanted he would simply have stretched himself on the slab that was ready to take him, treating it as a place prepared to receive his last sleep. What in all the wide world had he now to keep awake for? He stared before him with the question, and it was then that, as one of the cemetery walks passed near him, he caught the shock of the face.

His neighbour at the other grave had withdrawn, as he himself, with force in him to move, would have done by now, and was advancing along the path on his way to one of the gates. This brought him near, and his pace was slow, so that—and all the more as there was a kind of hunger in his look—the two men were for a minute directly confronted. Marcher felt him on the spot as one of the deeply stricken—a perception so sharp that nothing else in the picture lived for it, neither his dress, his age, nor his presumable character and class; nothing lived but the deep ravage of the features that he showed. He *showed* them—that was the point; he was moved, as he passed, by some impulse that was either a signal for sympathy or, more possibly, a challenge to another sorrow. He might already have been aware of our friend, might, at some previous hour, have noticed in him the smooth habit of the scene, with which the state of his own senses so scantly consorted, and might thereby have been stirred as by a kind of overt discord. What Marcher was at all events conscious of was, in the first place, that the image of scarred passion presented to him was conscious too—of something that profaned the air; and, in the second, that, roused, startled, shocked, he was yet the next moment looking after it, as it went, with envy. The most extraordinary thing that had happened to him—though he had given that name to other matters as well—took place, after his immediate vague stare, as a consequence of this impression. The stranger passed, but the raw glare of his grief remained, making our friend wonder in pity what wrong, what wound it expressed, what injury not to be healed. What had the man *had* to make him, by the loss of it, so bleed and yet live?

Something—and this reached him with a pang—that *he*, John Marcher, hadn't; the proof of which was precisely John Marcher's arid end. No passion had ever touched him, for this was what passion meant; he had survived and maundered and pined, but where had been *his* deep ravage? The extraordinary thing we speak of was the sudden rush of the result of this question. The sight that had just met his eyes named to him, as in letters of quick flame, something he had utterly, insanely missed, and what he had missed made these things a train of fire, made them mark themselves in an anguish of inward throbs. He had seen *outside* of his life, not learned it within, the way a woman was mourned when she had been loved for herself; such was the force of his conviction of the meaning of the stranger's face, which still flared for him like a smoky torch. It had not come to him, the knowledge, on the wings of experience; it had brushed him, jostled him, upset him, with the disrespect of chance, the insolence of an accident. Now that the illumination had begun, however, it blazed to the zenith, and what he presently stood there gazing at was the sounded void of his life. He gazed, he drew breath, in pain; he turned in his dismay, and, turning, he had before him in sharper incision than ever the open page of his story. The name on the table smote him as the passage of his neighbour had done, and what it said to him, full in the face, was that *she* was what he had missed. This was the awful thought, the answer to all the past, the vision at the dread clearness of which he turned as cold as the stone beneath him. Everything fell together, confessed, explained, overhelmed; leaving him

most of all stupefied at the blindness he had cherished. The fate he had
been marked for he had met with a vengeance—he had emptied the
cup to the lees; he had been the man of his time, *the* man, to whom
nothing on earth was to have happened. That was the rare stroke—that
was his visitation. So he saw it, as we say, in pale horror, while the pieces
fitted and fitted. So *she* had seen it, while he didn't, and so she served at
this hour to drive the truth home. It was the truth, vivid and monstrous,
that all the while he had waited the wait was itself his portion. This the
companion of his vigil had at a given moment perceived, and she had
then offered him the chance to baffle his doom. One's doom, however,
was never baffled, and on the day she had told him that his own had
come down she had seen him but stupidly stare at the escape she offered
him.

The escape would have been to love her; then, *then* he would have
lived. *She* had lived—who could say now with what passion?—since she
had loved him for himself; whereas he had never thought of her (ah,
how it hugely glared at him!) but in the chill of his egotism and the light
of her use. Her spoken words came back to him, and the chain stretched
and stretched. The beast had lurked indeed, and the beast, at its hour,
had sprung; it had sprung in that twilight of the cold April when, pale,
ill, wasted, but all beautiful, and perhaps even then recoverable, she had
risen from her chair to stand before him and let him imaginably guess.
It had sprung as he didn't guess; it had sprung as she hopelessly turned
from him, and the mark, by the time he left her, had fallen where it *was*
to fall. He had justified his fear and achieved his fate; he had failed,
with the last exactitude, of all he was to fail of; and a moan now rose to
his lips as he remembered she had prayed he mightn't know. This horror
of waking—*this* was knowledge, knowledge under the breath of which
the very tears in his eyes seemed to freeze. Through them, none the less,
he tried to fix it and hold it; he kept it there before him so that he might
feel the pain. That at least, belated and bitter, had something of the taste
of life. But the bitterness suddenly sickened him, and it was as if, horribly, he saw, in the truth, in the cruelty of his image, what had been appointed and done. He saw the Jungle of his life and saw the lurking
Beast; then, while he looked, perceived it, as by a stir of the air, rise,
huge and hideous, for the leap that was to settle him. His eyes darkened—it was close; and, instinctively turning, in his hallucination, to
avoid it, he flung himself, on his face, on the tomb.

THEODORE [HERMAN ALBERT] DREISER (1871–1945)

Dreiser was born in Terre Haute, Indiana, to a poor, fanatically religious, German immigrant father and a mother who could read but
could not write even her own name until this boy, at the age of
twelve, taught her. The father tried to bring up his many children
(there were finally ten living, five boys and five girls) in his own
prejudicial pieties, but without success. He soon discovered that
Theodore was a boy who yearned above all for success, luxury, and
"fast-living" society. The oldest son became a drunken tramp. Some
of the daughters, at least, lived scandalously loose lives. Emma,
like Sister Carrie, eloped with a married Chicago bartender who
rifled his employer's safe before they fled to New York. Theodore's
older brother, Paul, changed his name to Dresser and became a
Broadway dude and popular songwriter, the composer of "On the
Banks of the Wabash" (for which Theodore Dreiser is said to have
written the chorus) and many other such tunes.

Dreiser himself spent most of his youth in Warsaw, Indiana, where he
went to school. Through the generosity of a high school teacher he
had a year at Indiana University. He had already spent two years
in Chicago, and he returned there to work in a real estate office and
as a collector for a furniture company. For a time he worked on
newspapers, but in 1894 he went to New York to edit a music
magazine that also published cheap fiction, called Every Week. He
did not give up editorial work on popular magazines until 1911.

He had done some free-lance writing in the 1890s, but it was a fluke, a
friend's dare, that pushed him into beginning a novel that turned
out to be Sister Carrie. Through the efforts of Frank Norris, the
novelist, who was a reader for the Doubleday company, the novel
was accepted and published in 1900 but then immediately withdrawn when—the gossip has always had it—Mrs. Doubleday read
an advance copy. This novel about the rise of its mindless little
heroine from poverty to theatrical fame while her lover declines
into poverty, despair, and suicide may well be Dreiser's best. Certainly it established the method of enormously detailed realism, the
scene of sordid and gruelling circumstance, and the tone of melancholy, pity, and acceptance that was to make Dreiser the titan that
he is.

Big, slow-moving, given to rather foppish clothes once he could afford
them, Dreiser the man is not unlike his work, with its clumsy prose,
plodding structures, and jarring lapses in taste. These faults, and
others, were nearly always transcended by the works as wholes. The
very weight of his work crashed down the barriers of genteel critical preferences as well as those of censorship, with which two later

novels were also threatened. His example proved to be emancipatory for American fiction.

Jennie Gerhardt *(1911)*, *his second novel, is not unlike* Sister Carrie *in conception, but it is perhaps less impressive. Then he published the first two parts of his trilogy about Frank Cowperwood, the businessman who was determined to succeed lavishly, in* The Financier *(1912) and* The Titan *(1914); the final section,* The Stoic *(1947), was published many years later and fell off considerably. In 1915 came* The Genius, *the story of a presumably gifted but morally floundering painter. Ten years later came Dreiser's only other important novel,* An American Tragedy, *a slow, impressive account (based on a real murder case) of a poor ambitious boy's attempt to achieve status in an indifferent society.*

Dreiser wrote volumes more, most of which will be forgotten: local and foreign journalism, poetry, plays, many bad short stories, another novel or two, character sketches, "philosophy," autobiographies; it went on relentlessly. His life was not very interesting, perhaps chiefly because his mind was not. He was always an easy prey to oddball creeds. Toward the end of his life, for example, he was not only preaching Quakerism but also permitting himself to be used by the Communist Party and spouting a mindless Marxism.

Theodore Dreiser, from almost any point of view except one, was a great human muddle; the exception is that in a number of novels he was simply tremendous.

FURTHER READING

Critical biographies are Robert H. Elias, *Theodore Dreiser: Apostle of Nature* (1949); F. O. Matthiessen, *Theodore Dreiser* (1951); W. A. Swanberg, *Dreiser* (1965); and Marguerite Tjader, *Theodore Dreiser: A New Dimension* (1965). Robert H. Elias has also edited *Letters of Theodore Dreiser* (three volumes, 1959). More recent critical studies are Charles Shapiro, *Theodore Dreiser: Our Bitter Patriot* (1962); Philip L. Gerber, *Theodore Dreiser* (1964); and Ellen Moers, *Two Dreisers* (1969), devoted to the making of *Sister Carrie* and *An American Tragedy*.

FROM *Sister Carrie* (1900)

The Strike

There had been appearing in the papers about this time rumours and notices of an approaching strike on the trolley lines in Brooklyn. There was general dissatisfaction as to the hours of labour required and the wages paid. As usual—and for some inexplicable reason—the men chose the winter for the forcing of the hand of their employers and the settlement of their difficulties.

Hurstwood had been reading of this thing, and wondering concerning the huge tie-up which would follow. A day or two before this trouble with Carrie, it came. On a cold afternoon, when everything was grey and it threatened to snow, the papers announced that the men had been called out on all the lines.

Being so utterly idle, and his mind filled with the numerous predictions which had been made concerning the scarcity of labour this winter and the panicky state of the financial market, Hurstwood read this with interest. He noted the claims of the striking motormen and conductors, who said that they had been wont to receive two dollars a day in times past, but that for a year or more "trippers" had been introduced, which cut down their chance of livelihood one-half, and increased their hours of servitude from ten to twelve, and even fourteen. These "trippers" were men put on during the busy and *rush* hours, to take a car out for one trip. The compensation paid for such a trip was only twenty-five cents. When the rush or busy hours were over, they were laid off. Worst of all, no man might know when he was going to get a car. He must come to the barns in the morning and wait around in fair and foul weather until such time as he was needed. Two trips were an average reward for so much waiting—a little over three hours' work for fifty cents. The work of waiting was not counted.

The men complained that this system was extending, and that the time was not far off when but a few out of 7,000 employees would have regular two-dollar-a-day work at all. They demanded that the system be abolished, and that ten hours be considered a day's work, barring unavoidable delays, with $2.25 pay. They demanded immediate acceptance of these terms, which the various trolley companies refused.

Hurstwood at first sympathised with the demands of these men— indeed, it is a question whether he did not always sympathise with them to the end, belie him as his actions might. Reading nearly all the news, he was attracted first by the scare-heads with which the trouble was noted in the "World." He read it fully—the names of the seven companies involved, the number of men.

"They're foolish to strike in this sort of weather," he thought to himself. "Let 'em win if they can, though."

The next day there was even a larger notice of it. "Brooklynites Walk," said the "World." "Knights of Labour Tie up the Trolley Lines Across the Bridge." "About Seven Thousand Men Out."

Hurstwood read this, formulating to himself his own idea of what would be the outcome. He was a great believer in the strength of corporations.

"They can't win," he said, concerning the men. "They haven't any money. The police will protect the companies. They've got to. The public has to have its cars."

He didn't sympathise with the corporations, but strength was with them. So was property and public utility.

"Those fellows can't win," he thought.

Among other things, he noticed a circular issued by one of the companies, which read:

"Atlantic Avenue Railroad

"Special Notice

"The motormen and conductors and other employees of this company having abruptly left its service, an opportunity is now given to all loyal men who have struck against their will to be reinstated, providing they will make their applications by twelve o'clock noon on Wednesday, January 16th. Such men will be given employment (with guaranteed protection) in the order in which such applications are received, and runs and positions assigned them accordingly. Otherwise, they will be considered discharged, and every vacancy will be filled by a new man as soon as his services can be secured.

"(Signed)
"Benjamin Norton,
"President."

He also noted among the want ads, one which read:

"WANTED.—50 skilled motormen, accustomed to Westinghouse system, to run U. S. mail cars only, in the City of Brooklyn; protection guaranteed."

He noted particularly in each the "protection guaranteed." It signified to him the unassailable power of the companies.

"They've got the militia on their side," he thought. "There isn't anything those men can do."

While this was still in his mind, the incident with Oeslogge and Carrie occurred. There had been a good deal to irritate him, but this seemed much the worst. Never before had she accused him of stealing —or very near that. She doubted the naturalness of so large a bill. And he had worked so hard to make expenses seem light. He had been "doing" butcher and baker in order not to call on her. He had eaten very little—almost nothing.

"Damn it all!" he said. "I can get something. I'm not down yet."

He thought that he really must do something now. It was too cheap to sit around after such an insinuation as this. Why, after a little, he would be standing anything.

He got up and looked out the window into the chilly street. It came gradually into his mind, as he stood there, to go to Brooklyn.

"Why not?" his mind said. "Any one can get work over there. You'll get two a day."

"How about accidents?" said a voice. "You might get hurt."

"Oh, there won't be much of that," he answered. "They've called out the police. Any one who wants to run a car will be protected all right."

"You don't know how to run a car," rejoined the voice.

"I won't apply as a motorman," he answered. "I can ring up fares all right."

"They'll want motormen mostly."

"They'll take anybody; that I know."

For several hours he argued pro and con with this mental counsellor, feeling no need to act at once in a matter so sure of profit.

In the morning he put on his best clothes, which were poor enough, and began stirring about, putting some bread and meat into a page of a newspaper. Carrie watched him, interested in this new move.

"Where are you going?" she asked.

"Over to Brooklyn," he answered. Then, seeing her still inquisitive, he added: "I think I can get on over there."

"On the trolley lines?" said Carrie, astonished.

"Yes," he rejoined.

"Aren't you afraid?" she asked.

"What of?" he answered. "The police are protecting them."

"The paper said four men were hurt yesterday."

"Yes," he returned; "but you can't go by what the papers say. They'll run the cars all right."

He looked rather determined now, in a desolate sort of way, and Carrie felt sorry. Something of the old Hurstwood was here—the least shadow of what was once shrewd and pleasant strength. Outside, it was cloudy and blowing a few flakes of snow.

"What a day to go over there," thought Carrie.

Now he left before she did, which was a remarkable thing, and tramped eastward to Fourteenth Street and Sixth Avenue, where he took the car. He had read that scores of applicants were applying at the office of the Brooklyn City Railroad building and were being received. He made his way there by horse-car and ferry—a dark, silent man—to the offices in question. It was a long way, for no cars were running, and the day was cold; but he trudged along grimly. Once in Brooklyn, he could clearly see and feel that a strike was on. People showed it in their manner. Along the routes of certain tracks not a car was running. About certain corners and nearby saloons small groups of men were lounging. Several spring wagons passed him, equipped with plain wooden chairs, and labelled "Flatbush" or "Prospect Park.

Fare, Ten Cents." He noticed cold and even gloomy faces. Labour was having its little war.

When he came near the office in question, he saw a few men standing about, and some policemen. On the far corners were other men—whom he took to be strikers—watching. All the houses were small and wooden, the streets poorly paved. After New York, Brooklyn looked actually poor and hard-up.

He made his way into the heart of the small group, eyed by policemen and the men already there. One of the officers addressed him.

"What are you looking for?"

"I want to see if I can get a place."

"The offices are up those steps," said the bluecoat. His face was a very neutral thing to contemplate. In his heart of hearts, he sympathised with the strikers and hated this "scab." In his heart of hearts, also, he felt the dignity and use of the police force, which commanded order. Of its true social significance, he never once dreamed. His was not the mind for that. The two feelings blended in him—neutralised one another and him. He would have fought for this man as determinedly as for himself, and yet only so far as commanded. Strip him of his uniform, and he would have soon picked his side.

Hurstwood ascended a dusty flight of steps and entered a small, dust-coloured office, in which were a railing, a long desk, and several clerks.

"Well, sir?" said a middle-aged man, looking up at him from the long desk.

"Do you want to hire any men?" inquired Hurstwood.

"What are you—a motorman?"

"No; I'm not anything," said Hurstwood.

He was not at all abashed by his position. He knew these people needed men. If one didn't take him, another would. This man could take him or leave him, just as he chose.

"Well, we prefer experienced men, of course," said the man. He paused, while Hurstwood smiled indifferently. Then he added: "Still, I guess you can learn. What is your name?"

"Wheeler," said Hurstwood.

The man wrote an order on a small card. "Take that to our barns," he said, "and give it to the foreman. He'll show you what to do."

Hurstwood went down and out. He walked straight away in the direction indicated, while the policemen looked after.

"There's another wants to try it," said Officer Kiely to Officer Macey.

"I have my mind he'll get his fill," returned the latter, quietly.

They had been in strikes before.

The barn at which Hurstwood applied was exceedingly short-handed, and was being operated practically by three men as directors. There were a lot of green hands around—queer, hungry-looking men,

who looked as if want had driven them to desperate means. They tried
to be lively and willing, but there was an air of hang-dog diffidence
about the place.

Hurstwood went back through the barns and out into a large,
enclosed lot, where were a series of tracks and loops. A half-dozen cars
were there, manned by instructors, each with a pupil at the lever. More
pupils were waiting at one of the rear doors of the barn.

In silence Hurstwood viewed this scene, and waited. His companions took his eye for a while, though they did not interest him much
more than the cars. They were an uncomfortable-looking gang, however. One or two were very thin and lean. Several were quite stout.
Several others were rawboned and sallow, as if they had been beaten
upon by all sorts of rough weather.

"Did you see by the paper they are going to call out the militia?"
Hurstwood heard one of them remark.

"Oh, they'll do that," returned the other. "They always do."

"Think we're liable to have much trouble?" said another, whom
Hurstwood did not see.

"Not very."

"That Scotchman that went out on the last car," put in a voice,
"told me that they hit him in the ear with a cinder."

A small, nervous laugh accompanied this.

"One of those fellows on the Fifth Avenue line must have had a
hell of a time, according to the papers," drawled another. "They broke
his car windows and pulled him off into the street 'fore the police
could stop 'em."

"Yes; but there are more police around to-day," was added by another.

Hurstwood hearkened without much mental comment. These talkers
seemed scared to him. Their gabbling was feverish—things said to quiet
their own minds. He looked out into the yard and waited.

Two of the men got around quite near him, but behind his back.
They were rather social, and he listened to what they said.

"Are you a railroad man?" said one.

"Me? No. I've always worked in a paper factory."

"I had a job in Newark until last October," returned the other, with
reciprocal feeling.

There were some words which passed too low to hear. Then the
conversation became strong again.

"I don't blame these fellers for striking," said one "They've got the
right of it, all right, but I had to get something to do."

"Same here," said the other, "If I had any job in Newark I wouldn't
be over here takin' chances like these."

"It's hell these days, ain't it?" said the man. "A poor man ain't
nowhere. You could starve, by God, right in the streets, and there ain't
most no one would help you."

"Right you are," said the other. "The job I had I lost 'cause they shut down. They run all summer and lay up a big stock, and then shut down."

Hurstwood paid some little attention to this. Somehow, he felt a little superior to these two—a little better off. To him these were ignorant and commonplace, poor sheep in a driver's hand.

"Poor devils," he thought, speaking out of the thoughts and feelings of a bygone period of success.

"Next," said one of the instructors.

"You're next," said a neighbor, touching him.

He went out and climbed on the platform. The instructor took it for granted that no preliminaries were needed.

"You see this handle," he said, reaching up to an electric cut-off, which was fastened to the roof. "This throws the current off or on. If you want to reverse the car you turn it over here. If you want to send it forward, you put it over here. If you want to cut off the power, you keep it in the middle."

Hurstwood smiled at the simple information.

"Now, this handle here regulates your speed. To here," he said, pointing with his finger, "gives you about four miles an hour. This is eight. When it's full on, you make about fourteen miles an hour."

Hurstwood watched him calmly. He had seen motormen work before. He knew just about how they did it, and was sure he could do as well, with a very little practice.

The instructor explained a few more details, and then said:

"Now, we'll back her up."

Hurstwood stood placidly by, while the car rolled back into the yard.

"One thing you want to be careful about, and that is to start easy. Give one degree time to act before you start another. The one fault of most men is that they always want to throw her wide open. That's bad. It's dangerous, too. Wears out the motor. You don't want to do that."

"I see," said Hurstwood.

He waited and waited, while the man talked on.

"Now you take it," he said, finally.

The ex-manager laid hand to the lever and pushed it gently, as he thought. It worked much easier than he imagined, however, with the result that the car jerked quickly forward, throwing him back against the door. He straightened up sheepishly, while the instructor stopped the car with the brake.

"You want to be careful about that," was all he said.

Hurstwood found, however, that handling a brake and regulating speed were not so instantly mastered as he had imagined. Once or twice he would have ploughed through the rear fence if it had not been for the hand and word of his companion. The latter was rather patient with him, but he never smiled.

"You've got to get the knack of working both arms at once," he said. "It takes a little practice."

One o'clock came while he was still on the car practising, and he began to feel hungry. The day set in snowing, and he was cold. He grew weary of running to and fro on the short track.

They ran the car to the end and both got off. Hurstwood went into the barn and sought a car step, pulling out his paper-wrapped lunch from his pocket. There was no water and the bread was dry, but he enjoyed it. There was no ceremony about dining. He swallowed and looked about, contemplating the dull, homely labour of the thing. It was disagreeable—miserably disagreeable—in all its phases. Not because it was bitter, but because it was hard. It would be hard to any one, he thought.

After eating, he stood about as before, waiting until his turn came.

The intention was to give him an afternoon of practice, but the greater part of the time was spent in waiting about.

At last evening came, and with it hunger and a debate with himself as to how he should spend the night. It was half-past five. He must soon eat. If he tried to go home, it would take him two hours and a half of cold walking and riding. Besides, he had orders to report at seven the next morning, and going home would necessitate his rising at an unholy and disagreeable hour. He had only something like a dollar and fifteen cents of Carrie's money, with which he had intended to pay the two weeks' coal bill before the present idea struck him.

"They must have some place around here," he thought. "Where does that fellow from Newark stay?"

Finally he decided to ask. There was a young fellow standing near one of the doors in the cold, waiting a last turn. He was a mere boy in years—twenty-one about—but with a body lank and long, because of privation. A little good living would have made this youth plump and swaggering.

"How do they arrange this, if a man hasn't any money?" inquired Hurstwood, discreetly.

The fellow turned a keen, watchful face on the inquirer.

"You mean eat?" he replied.

"Yes, and sleep. I can't go back to New York tonight."

"The foreman 'll fix that if you ask him, I guess. He did me."

"That so?"

"Yes. I just told him I didn't have anything. Gee, I couldn't go home. I live way over in Hoboken."

Hurstwood only cleared his throat by way of acknowledgment.

"They've got a place upstairs here, I understand. I don't know what sort of a thing it is. Purty tough, I guess. He gave me a meal ticket this noon. I know that wasn't much."

Hurstwood smiled grimly, and the boy laughed.

"It ain't no fun, is it?" he inquired, wishing vainly for a cheery reply.

"Not much," answered Hurstwood.

"I'd tackle him now," volunteered the youth. "He may go 'way."

Hurstwood did so.

"Isn't there some place I can stay around here tonight?" he inquired. "If I have to go back to New York, I'm afraid I won't——"

"There're some cots upstairs," interrupted the man, "if you want one of them."

"That'll do," he assented.

He meant to ask for a meal ticket, but the seemingly proper moment never came, and he decided to pay himself that night.

"I'll ask him in the morning."

He ate in a cheap restaurant in the vicinity, and, being cold and lonely, went straight off to seek the loft in question. The company was not attempting to run cars after nightfall. It was so advised by the police.

The room seemed to have been a lounging place for night workers. There were some nine cots in the place, two or three wooden chairs, a soap box, and a small, round-bellied stove, in which a fire was blazing. Early as he was, another man was there before him. The latter was sitting beside the stove warming his hands.

Hurstwood approached and held out his own toward the fire. He was sick of the bareness and privation of all things connected with his venture, but was steeling himself to hold out. He fancied he could for a while.

"Cold, isn't it?" said the early guest.

"Rather."

A long silence.

"Not much of a place to sleep in, is it?" said the man.

"Better than nothing," replied Hurstwood.

Another silence.

"I believe I'll turn in," said the man.

Rising, he went to one of the cots and stretched himself, removing only his shoes, and pulling the one blanket and dirty old comforter over him in a sort of bundle. The sight disgusted Hurstwood, but he did not dwell on it, choosing to gaze into the stove and think of something else. Presently he decided to retire, and picked a cot, also removing his shoes.

While he was doing so, the youth who had advised him to come here entered, and, seeing Hurstwood, tried to be genial.

"Better'n nothin'," he observed, looking around.

Hurstwood did not take this to himself. He thought it to be an expression of individual satisfaction, and so did not answer. The youth imagined he was out of sorts, and set to whistling softly. Seeing another man asleep, he quit that and lapsed into silence.

Hurstwood made the best of a bad lot by keeping on his clothes and pushing away the dirty covering from his head, but at last he dozed in sheer weariness. The covering became more and more comfortable, its character was forgotten, and he pulled it about his neck and slept.

In the morning he was aroused out of a pleasant dream by several men stirring about in the cold, cheerless room. He had been back in Chicago in fancy, in his own comfortable home. Jessica had been arranging to go somewhere, and he had been talking with her about it. This was so clear in his mind, that he was startled now by the contrast of this room. He raised his head, and the cold, bitter reality jarred him into wakefulness.

"Guess I'd better get up," he said.

There was no water on this floor. He put on his shoes in the cold and stood up, shaking himself in his stiffness. His clothes felt disagreeable, his hair bad.

"Hell!" he muttered, as he put on his hat.

Downstairs things were stirring again.

He found a hydrant, with a trough which had once been used for horses, but there was no towel here, and his handkerchief was soiled from yesterday. He contented himself with wetting his eyes with the ice-cold water. Then he sought the foreman, who was already on the ground.

"Had your breakfast yet?" inquired that worthy.

"No," said Hurstwood.

"Better get it, then; your car won't be ready for a little while."

Hurstwood hesitated.

"Could you let me have a meal ticket?" he asked with an effort.

"Here you are," said the man, handing him one.

He breakfasted as poorly as the night before on some fried steak and bad coffee. Then he went back.

"Here," said the foreman, motioning him, when he came in. "You take this car out in a few minutes."

Hurstwood climbed up on the platform in the gloomy barn and waited for a signal. He was nervous, and yet the thing was a relief. Anything was better than the barn.

On this the fourth day of the strike, the situation had taken a turn for the worse. The strikers, following the counsel of their leaders and the newspapers, had struggled peaceably enough. There had been no great violence done. Cars had been stopped, it is true, and the men argued with. Some crews had been won over and led away, some windows broken, some jeering and yelling done; but in no more than five or six instances had men been seriously injured. These by crowds whose acts the leaders disclaimed.

Idleness, however, and the sight of the company, backed by the police, triumphing, angered the men. They saw that each day more cars were going on, each day more declarations were being made by the company officials that the effective opposition of the strikers was broken. This put desperate thoughts in the minds of the men. Peaceful methods meant, they saw, that the companies would soon run all their cars and those who had complained would be forgotten. There was nothing so helpful to the companies as peaceful methods.

All at once they blazed forth, and for a week there was storm and stress. Cars were assailed, men attacked, policemen struggled with, tracks torn up, and shots fired, until at last street fights and mob movements became frequent, and the city was invested with militia.

Hurstwood knew nothing of the change of temper.

"Run your car out." called the foreman, waving a vigorous hand at him. A green conductor jumped up behind and rang the bell twice as a signal to start. Hurstwood turned the lever and ran the car out through the door into the street in front of the barn. Here two brawny policemen got up beside him on the platform—one on either hand.

At the sound of a gong near the barn door, two bells were given by the conductor and Hurstwood opened his lever.

The two policemen looked about them calmly.

" 'Tis cold, all right, this morning," said the one on the left, who possessed a rich brogue.

"I had enough of it yesterday," said the other. "I wouldn't want a steady job of this."

"Nor I."

Neither paid the slightest attention to Hurstwood, who stood facing the cold wind, which was chilling him completely, and thinking of his orders.

"Keep a steady gait," the foreman had said. "Don't stop for any one who doesn't look like a real passenger. Whatever you do, don't stop for a crowd."

The two officers kept silent for a few moments.

"The last man must have gone through all right," said the officer on the left. "I don't see his car anywhere."

"Who's on there?" asked the second officer, referring, of course, to its complement of policemen.

"Schaeffer and Ryan."

There was another silence, in which the car ran smoothly along. There were not so many houses along this part of the way. Hurstwood did not see many people either. The situation was not wholly disagreeable to him. If he were not so cold, he thought he would do well enough.

He was brought out of this feeling by the sudden appearance of a curve ahead, which he had not expected. He shut off the current and did an energetic turn at the brake, but not in time to avoid an unnaturally quick turn. It shook him up and made him feel like making some apologetic remarks, but he refrained.

"You want to look out for them things," said the officer on the left, condescendingly.

"That's right," agreed Hurstwood, shamefacedly.

"There's lots of them on this line," said the officer on the right.

Around the corner a more populated way appeared. One or two pedestrians were in view ahead. A boy coming out of a gate with a tin milk bucket gave Hurstwood his first objectionable greeting.

"Scab!" he yelled. "Scab!"

Hurstwood heard it, but tried to make no comment, even to himself. He knew he would get that, and much more of the same sort, probably.

At a corner farther up a man stood by the track and signalled the car to stop.

"Never mind him," said one of the officers. "He's up to some game."

Hurstwood obeyed. At the corner he saw the wisdom of it. No sooner did the man perceive the intention to ignore him, than he shook his fist.

"Ah, you bloody coward!" he yelled.

Some half dozen men, standing on the corner, flung taunts and jeers after the speeding car.

Hurstwood winced the least bit. The real thing was slightly worse than the thoughts of it had been.

Now came in sight, three or four blocks farther on, a heap of something on the track.

"They've been at work, here, all right," said one of the policemen.

"We'll have an argument, maybe," said the other.

Hurstwood ran the car close and stopped. He had not done so wholly, however, before a crowd gathered about. It was composed of ex-motormen and conductors in part, with a sprinkling of friends and sympathisers.

"Come off the car, pardner," said one of the men in a voice meant to be conciliatory. "You don't want to take the bread out of another man's mouth, do you?"

Hurstwood held to his brake and lever, pale and very uncertain what to do.

"Stand back," yelled one of the officers, leaning over the platform railing. "Clear out of this, now. Give the man a chance to do his work."

"Listen, pardner," said the leader, ignoring the policeman and addressing Hurstwood. "We're all working men, like yourself. If you were a regular motorman, and had been treated as we've been, you wouldn't want any one to come in and take your place, would you? You wouldn't want any one to do you out of your chance to get your rights, would you?"

"Shut her off! shut her off!" urged the other of the policemen, roughly. "Get out of this, now," and he jumped the railing and landed before the crowd and began shoving. Instantly the other officer was down beside him.

"Stand back, now," they yelled. "Get out of this. What the hell do you mean? Out, now."

It was like a small swarm of bees.

"Don't shove me," said one of the strikers, determinedly. "I'm not doing anything."

"Get out of this!" cried the officer, swinging his club. "I'll give ye a bat on the sconce. Back, now."

"What the hell!" cried another of the strikers, pushing the other way, adding at the same time some lusty oaths.

Crack came an officer's club on his forehead. He blinked his eyes blindly a few times, wabbled on his legs, threw up his hands, and staggered back. In return, a swift fist landed on the officer's neck.

Infuriated by this, the latter plunged left and right, laying about madly with his club. He was ably assisted by his brother of the blue, who poured ponderous oaths upon the troubled waters. No severe damage was done, owing to the agility of the strikers in keeping out of reach. They stood about the sidewalk now and jeered.

"Where is the conductor?" yelled one of the officers, getting his eye on that individual, who had come nervously forward to stand by Hurstwood. The latter had stood gazing upon the scene with more astonishment than fear.

"Why don't you come down here and get these stones off the track?" inquired the officer. "What you standing there for? Do you want to stay here all day? Get down."

Hurstwood breathed heavily in excitement and jumped down with the nervous conductor as if he had been called.

"Hurry up, now," said the other policeman.

Cold as it was, these officers were hot and mad. Hurstwood worked with the conductor, lifting stone after stone and warming himself by the work.

"Ah, you scab, you!" yelled the crowd. "You coward! Steal a man's job, will you? Rob the poor, will you, you thief? We'll get you yet, now. Wait."

Not all of this was delivered by one man. It came from here and there, incorporated with much more of the same sort and curses.

"Work, you blackguards," yelled a voice. "Do the dirty work. You're the suckers that keep the poor people down!"

"May God starve ye yet," yelled an old Irish woman, who now threw open a nearby window and stuck out her head.

"Yes, and you," she added, catching the eye of one of the policemen. "You bloody, murtherin' thafe! Crack my son over the head, will you, you hardhearted, murtherin' divil? Ah, ye——"

But the officer turned a deaf ear.

"Go to the devil, you old hag," he half muttered as he stared round upon the scattered company.

Now the stones were off, and Hurstwood took his place again amid a continued chorus of epithets. Both officers got up beside him and the conductor rang the bell, when, bang! bang! through window and door came rocks and stones. One narrowly grazed Hurstwood's head. Another shattered the window behind.

"Throw open your lever," yelled one of the officers, grabbing at the handle himself.

Hurstwood complied and the car shot away, followed by a rattle of stones and a rain of curses.

"That — — — —— hit me in the neck," said one of the officers. "I gave him a good crack for it, though."

"I think I must have left spots on some of them," said the other.

"I know that big guy that called us a — — — ——," said the first. "I'll get him yet for that."

"I thought we were in for it sure, once there," said the second.

Hurstwood, warmed and excited, gazed steadily ahead. It was an astonishing experience for him. He had read of these things, but the reality seemed something altogether new. He was no coward in spirit. The fact that he had suffered this much now rather operated to arouse a stolid determination to stick it out. He did not recur in thought to New York or the flat. This one trip seemed a consuming thing.

They now ran into the business heart of Brooklyn uninterrupted. People gazed at the broken windows of the car and at Hurstwood in his plain clothes. Voices called "scab" now and then, as well as other epithets, but no crowd attacked the car. At the downtown end of the line, one of the officers went to call up his station and report the trouble.

"There's a gang out there," he said, "Trying for us yet. Better send some one over there and clean them out."

The car ran back more quietly—hooted, watched, flung at, but not attacked. Hurstwood breathed freely when he saw the barns.

"Well," he observed to himself, "I came out of that all right."

The car was turned in and he was allowed to loaf a while, but later he was again called. This time a new team of officers was aboard. Slightly more confident, he sped the car along the commonplace streets and felt somewhat less fearful. On one side, however, he suffered intensely. The day was raw, with a sprinkling of snow and a gusty wind, made all the more intolerable by the speed of the car. His clothing was not intended for this sort of work. He shivered, stamped his feet, and beat his arms as he had seen other motormen do in the past, but said nothing. The novelty and danger of the situation modified in a way his disgust and distress at being compelled to be here, but not enough to prevent him from feeling grim and sour. This was a dog's life, he thought. It was a tough thing to have to come to.

The one thought that strengthened him was the insult offered by Carrie. He was not down so low as to take all that, he thought. He could do something—this, even—for a while. It would get better. He would save a little.

A boy threw a clod of mud while he was thus reflecting and hit him upon the arm. It hurt sharply and angered him more than he had been any time since morning.

"The little cur!" he muttered.

"Hurt you?" asked one of the policemen.

"No," he answered.

At one of the corners, where the car slowed up because of a turn, an ex-motorman, standing on the sidewalk, called to him:

"Won't you come out, pardner, and be a man? Remember we're fighting for decent day's wages, that's all. We've got families to support." The man seemed most peaceably inclined.

Hurstwood pretended not to see him. He kept his eyes straight on before and opened the lever wide. The voice had something appealing in it.

All morning this went on and long into the afternoon. He made three such trips. The dinner he had was no stay for such work and the cold was telling on him. At each end of the line he stopped to thaw out, but he could have groaned at the anguish of it. One of the barnmen, out of pity, loaned him a heavy cap and a pair of sheepskin gloves, and for once he was extremely thankful.

On the second trip of the afternoon he ran into a crowd about half way along the line, that had blocked the car's progress with an old telegraph pole.

"Get that thing off the track," shouted the two policemen.

"Yah, yah, yah!" yelled the crowd. "Get it off yourself."

The two policemen got down and Hurstwood started to follow.

"You stay there," one called. "Some one will run away with your car."

Amid the babel of voices, Hurstwood heard one close beside him.

"Come down, pardner, and be a man. Don't fight the poor. Leave that to the corporations."

He saw the same fellow who had called to him from the corner. Now, as before, he pretended not to hear him.

"Come down," the man repeated gently. "You don't want to fight poor men. Don't fight at all." It was a most philosophic and jesuitical motorman.

A third policeman joined the other two from somewhere and some one ran to telephone for more officers. Hurstwood gazed about, determined but fearful.

A man grabbed him by the coat.

"Come off of that," he exclaimed, jerking at him and trying to pull him over the railing.

"Let go," said Hurstwood, savagely.

"I'll show you—you scab!" cried a young Irishman, jumping up on the car and aiming a blow at Hurstwood. The latter ducked and caught it on the shoulder instead of the jaw.

"Away from here," shouted an officer, hastening to the rescue, and adding, of course, the usual oaths.

Hurstwood recovered himself, pale and trembling. It was becoming serious with him now. People were looking up and jeering at him. One girl was making faces.

He began to waver in his resolution, when a patrol wagon rolled up and more officers dismounted. Now the track was quickly cleared and the release effected.

"Let her go now, quick," said the officer, and again he was off.

The end came with a real mob, which met the car on its return trip a mile or two from the barns. It was an exceedingly poor-looking neighbourhood. He wanted to run fast through it, but again the track was blocked. He saw men carrying something out to it when he was yet a half-dozen blocks away.

"There they are again!" exclaimed one policeman.

"I'll give them something this time," said the second officer, whose patience was becoming worn. Hurstwood suffered a qualm of body as the car rolled up. As before, the crowd began hooting, but now, rather than come near, they threw things. One or two windows were smashed and Hurstwood dodged a stone.

Both policeman ran out toward the crowd, but the latter replied by running toward the car. A woman—a mere girl in appearance—was among these, bearing a rough stick. She was exceedingly wrathful and struck at Hurstwood, who dodged. Thereupon, her companions, duly encouraged, jumped on the car and pulled Hurstwood over. He had hardly time to speak or shout before he fell.

"Let go of me," he said, falling on his side.

"Ah, you sucker," he heard some one say. Kicks and blows rained on him. He seemed to be suffocating. Then two men seemed to be dragging him off and he wrestled for freedom.

"Let up," said a voice, "you're all right. Stand up."

He was let loose and recovered himself. Now he recognised two officers. He felt as if he would faint from exhaustion. Something was wet on his chin. He put up his hand and felt, then looked. It was red.

"They cut me," he said, foolishly, fishing for his handkerchief.

"Now, now," said one of the officers. "It's only a scratch."

His senses became cleared now and he looked around. He was standing in a little store, where they left him for the moment. Outside, he could see, as he stood wiping his chin, the car and the excited crowd. A patrol wagon was there, and another.

He walked over and looked out. It was an ambulance, backing in.

He saw some energetic charging by the police and arrests being made.

"Come on, now, if you want to take your car," said an officer, opening the door and looking in.

He walked out, feeling rather uncertain of himself. He was very cold and frightened.

"Where's the conductor?" he asked.

"Oh, he's not here now," said the policeman.

Hurstwood went toward the car and stepped nervously on. As he did so there was a pistol shot. Something stung his shoulder.

"Who fired that?" he heard an officer exclaim. "By God! who did that?" Both left him, running toward a certain building. He paused a moment and then got down.

"George!" exclaimed Hurstwood, weakly, "this is too much for me."

He walked nervously to the corner and hurried down a side street.

"Whew!" he said, drawing in his breath.

A half block away, a small girl gazed at him.

"You'd better sneak," she called.

He walked homeward in a blinding snowstorm, reaching the ferry by dusk. The cabins were filled with comfortable souls, who studied him curiously. His head was still in such a whirl that he felt confused. All the wonder of the twinkling lights of the river in a white storm passed for nothing. He trudged doggedly on until he reached the flat. There he entered and found the room warm. Carrie was gone. A couple of evening papers were lying on the table where she left them. He lit the gas and sat down. Then he got up and stripped to examine his shoulder. It was a mere scratch. He washed his hands and face, still in a brown study, apparently, and combed his hair. Then he looked for something to eat, and finally, his hunger gone, sat down in his comfortable rocking-chair. It was a wonderful relief.

He put his hand to his chin, forgetting, for the moment, the papers.

"Well," he said, after a time, his nature recovering itself, "that's a pretty tough game over there."

Then he turned and saw the papers. With half a sigh he picked up the "World."

"Strike Spreading in Brooklyn," he read. "Rioting Breaks Out in all Parts of the City."

He adjusted his paper very comfortably and continued. It was the one thing he read with absorbing interest.

EDITH [NEWBOLD JONES] WHARTON (1862–1937)

When she was young, Edith Wharton's close associates called her "Pussy" Jones. This information breaks down a little the formidable facade presented by all her stately, posed photographs, such guarded information about her life as she permitted to be known, the sense one has of the impeccably cold establishment she maintained for so many years outside Paris, and the imposing surfaces of her own best work. And it is also pleasant knowledge!

She was born into the small, tight, upper level of New York society in 1862, a society whose complacency equaled its conventionality, one that respected education and European culture but by no means encouraged artists or even intellectuals within its own closed circle. That circle, soon enough, was to be punctured and broken down by the invasion of the post-Civil War nouveaux riches as the old austerity gave way to a new and gaudy ostentation. But Edith Jones was brought up strictly within the old limits.

At twenty-three she married Edward Robbins Wharton, an amiable Bostonian somewhat older than she; it was a marriage that offered her very little in personal fulfillment. She apparently suffered a nervous breakdown very early in her marriage, at about the same time that her husband developed some mental disease which led finally to insanity. (His family insisted that it was her obligation to attend to him, and it was only in 1910 that she was freed of that burden.) Annual visits to Europe and leisurely summers in Newport and later in Lenox, Massachusetts, no doubt offered something by way of amelioration, but not enough. She had tried to write since childhood (in Newport, at sixteen, she had privately published a little book called Verses), *a habit that her family had regarded as a whimsy that could be safely ignored. But now, perhaps under professional advice recommending it as therapy, she turned seriously to writing.*

Her first book was not fiction but, significantly, a collaborative effort on interior decoration published in 1897. Three books of short stories and a historical novel followed. Some of her early work is splendid, especially in its incisive thrusts at that New York society she knew so well, as in her remarkable story of 1904, "The Other Two," in which a third husband discovers that his wife expects him to make a place in their life for his predecessors. But it was not until 1905, with The House of Mirth, *that she emerged as a novelist of genuine distinction. All her best work is contained in the next fifteen years. Two more novels,* The Custom of the Country (1913) *and* The Age of Innocence (1920), *continue her exploration of New York society; the chief theme is usually the crushed aspirations of individuals by convention in a world of great wealth. The other fine achievements are set at the socially opposite pole, among the crude and bleak and hard-pressed, where the crushing power is poverty:* Ethan Frome (1911), The Bunner Sisters (1916), *and* Summer (1917).

In 1910 Mrs. Wharton had moved permanently to France, and the longer she stayed away from the United States, the less adequate her fictional account of it became. With a few exceptions (most notably, the four long stories that make up Old New York, 1924), *the work was inferior, some of it indistinguishable from run-of-the-mill women's magazine fiction. The vein of social satire grew coarser, and the old ethical austerity softened into tepid sentiment.*

*She bequeathed her private papers to Yale University. One can only
hope that when they can finally be opened, the lacunae in her biography, which may well go far in explaining both her growth into
distinction and her long artistic deterioration, will be filled.*

FURTHER READING

Biographical portraits are Percy Lubbock, *Portrait of Edith Wharton*
(1947), and Grace Kellogg, *The Two Lives of Edith Wharton:, The
Woman and Her Work* (1965). The major critical study is Blake
Nevius, *Edith Wharton: A Study of Her Fiction* (1953). Louis
Auchincloss's *Edith Wharton* (1961) is a brief survey of her work.
Irving Howe edited *Edith Wharton: A Collection of Critical Essays*
(1962).

The Other Two *(1904)*

I

Waythorn, on the drawing-room hearth, waited for his wife to come
down to dinner.

It was their first night under his own roof, and he was surprised
at his thrill of boyish agitation. He was not so old, to be sure—his
glass gave him little more than the five-and-thirty years to which his
wife confessed—but he had fancied himself already in the temperate
zone; yet here he was listening for her step with a tender sense of all
it symbolised, with some old trail of verse about the garlanded nuptial
door-posts floating through his enjoyment of the pleasant room and
the good dinner just beyond it.

They had been hastily recalled from their honeymoon by the illness
of Lily Haskett, the child of Mrs. Waythorn's first marriage. The little
girl, at Waythorn's desire, had been transferred to his house on the
day of her mother's wedding, and the doctor, on their arrival, broke
the news that she was ill with typhoid, but declared that all the symptoms were favourable. Lily could show twelve years of unblemished
health, and the case promised to be a light one. The nurse spoke as
reassuringly, and after a moment of alarm Mrs. Waythorn had adjusted herself to the situation. She was very fond of Lily—her affection for the child had perhaps been her decisive charm in Waythorn's eyes—but she had the perfectly balanced nerves which her
little girl had inherited, and no woman ever wasted less tissue in unpro-
ductive worry. Waythorn was therefore quite prepared to see her come
in presently, a little late because of a last look at Lily, but as serene
and well-appointed as if her good-night kiss had been laid on the

brow of health. Her composure was restful to him; it acted as ballast to his somewhat unstable sensibilities. As he pictured her bending over the child's bed he thought how soothing her presence must be in illness: her very step would prognosticate recovery.

His own life had been a gray one, from temperament rather than circumstance, and he had been drawn to her by the unperturbed gaiety which kept her fresh and elastic at an age when most women's activities are growing either slack or febrile. He knew what was said about her; for, popular as she was, there had always been a faint undercurrent of detraction. When she had appeared in New York, nine or ten years earlier, as the pretty Mrs. Haskett whom Gus Varick had unearthed somewhere—was it in Pittsburg or Utica?—society, while promptly accepting her, had reserved the right to cast a doubt on its own indiscrimination. Enquiry, however, established her undoubted connection with a socially reigning family, and explained her recent divorce as the natural result of a runaway match at seventeen; and as nothing was known of Mr. Haskett it was easy to believe the worst of him.

Alice Haskett's remarriage with Gus Varick was a passport to the set whose recognition she coveted, and for a few years the Varicks were the most popular couple in town. Unfortunately the alliance was brief and stormy, and this time the husband had his champions. Still, even Varick's stanchest supporters admitted that he was not meant for matrimony, and Mrs. Varick's grievances were of a nature to bear the inspection of the New York courts. A New York divorce is in itself a diploma of virtue, and in the semi-widowhood of this second separation Mrs. Varick took on an air of sanctity, and was allowed to confide her wrongs to some of the most scrupulous ears in town. But when it was known that she was to marry Waythorn there was a momentary reaction. Her best friends would have preferred to see her remain in the rôle of the injured wife, which was as becoming to her as crape to a rosy complexion. True, a decent time had elapsed, and it was not even suggested that Waythorn had supplanted his predecessor. People shook their heads over him, however, and one grudging friend, to whom he affirmed that he took the step with his eyes open, replied oracularly: "Yes—and with your ears shut."

Waythorn could afford to smile at these innuendoes. In the Wall Street phrase, he had "discounted" them. He knew that society has not yet adapted itself to the consequences of divorce, and that till the adaptation takes place every woman who uses the freedom the law accords her must be her own social justification. Waythorn had an amused confidence in his wife's ability to justify herself. His expectations were fulfilled, and before the wedding took place Alice Varick's group had rallied openly to her support. She took it all imperturbably: she had a way of surmounting obstacles without seeming to be aware of them, and Waythorn looked back with wonder at the trivialities over which he had worn his nerves thin. He had the sense of having found refuge in a richer, warmer nature than his own, and his satisfaction, at the moment, was humourously summed up in the thought that his wife, when she had done all she could for Lily, would not be ashamed to come down and enjoy a good dinner.

The anticipation of such enjoyment was not, however, the sentiment expressed by Mrs. Waythorn's charming face when she presently joined him. Though she had put on her most engaging teagown she had neglected to assume the smile that went with it, and Waythorn thought he had never seen her look so nearly worried.

"What is it?" he asked. "Is anything wrong with Lily?"

"No; I've just been in and she's still sleeping." Mrs. Waythorn hesitated. "But something tiresome has happened."

He had taken her two hands, and now perceived that he was crushing a paper between them.

"This letter?"

"Yes—Mr. Haskett has written—I mean his lawyer has written."

Waythorn felt himself flush uncomfortably. He dropped his wife's hands.

"What about?"

"About seeing Lily. You know the courts—"

"Yes, yes," he interrupted nervously.

Nothing was known about Haskett in New York. He was vaguely supposed to have remained in the outer darkness from which his wife had been rescued, and Waythorn was one of the few who were aware that he had given up his business in Utica and followed her to New York in order to be near his little girl. In the days of his wooing, Waythorn had often met Lily on the doorstep, rosy and smiling, on her way "to see papa."

"I am so sorry," Mrs. Waythorn murmured.

He roused himself. "What does he want?"

"He wants to see her. You know she goes to him once a week."

"Well—he doesn't expect her to go to him now, does he?"

"No—he has heard of her illness; but he expects to come here."

"*Here?*"

Mrs. Waythorn reddened under his gaze. They looked away from each other.

"I'm afraid he has the right . . . You'll see. . . ." She made a proffer of the letter.

Waythorn moved away with a gesture of refusal. He stood staring about the softly lighted room, which a moment before had seemed so full of bridal intimacy.

"I'm so sorry," she repeated. "If Lily could have been moved—"

"That's out of the question," he returned impatiently.

"I suppose so."

Her lip was beginning to tremble, and he felt himself a brute.

"He must come, of course," he said. "When is—his day?"

"I'm afraid—to-morrow."

"Very well. Send a note in the morning."

The butler entered to announce dinner.

Waythorn turned to his wife. "Come—you must be tired. It's beastly, but try to forget about it," he said, drawing her hand through his arm.

"You're so good, dear. I'll try," she whispered back.

Her face cleared at once, and as she looked at him across the flowers, between the rosy candle-shades, he saw her lips waver back into a smile.

"How pretty everything is!" she sighed luxuriously.

He turned to the butler. "The champagne at once, please. Mrs. Waythorn is tired."

In a moment or two their eyes met above the sparkling glasses. Her own were quite clear and untroubled: he saw that she had obeyed his injunction and forgotten.

II

Waythorn, the next morning, went down town earlier than usual. Haskett was not likely to come till the afternoon, but the instinct of flight drove him forth. He meant to stay away all day—he had thoughts of dining at his club. As his door closed behind him he reflected that before he opened it again it would have admitted another man who had as much right to enter it as himself, and the thought filled him with a physical repugnance.

He caught the "elevated" at the employés' hour, and found himself crushed between two layers of pendulous humanity. At Eighth Street the man facing him wriggled out, and another took his place. Waythorn glanced up and saw that it was Gus Varick. The men were so close together that it was impossible to ignore the smile of recognition on Varick's handsome overblown face. And after all—why not? They had always been on good terms, and Varick had been divorced before Waythorn's attentions to his wife began. The two exchanged a word on the perennial grievance of the congested trains, and when a seat at their side was miraculously left empty the instinct of self-preservation made Waythorn slip into it after Varick.

The latter drew the stout man's breath of relief. "Lord—I was beginning to feel like a pressed flower." He leaned back, looking unconcernedly at Waythorn. "Sorry to hear that Sellers is knocked out again."

"Sellers?" echoed Waythorn, starting at his partner's name.

Varick looked surprise. "You didn't know he was laid up with the gout?"

"No. I've been away—I only got back last night." Waythorn felt himself reddening in anticipation of the other's smile.

"Ah—yes; to be sure. And Sellers's attack came on two days ago. I'm afraid he's pretty bad. Very awkward for me, as it happens, because he was just putting through a rather important thing for me."

"Ah?" Waythorn wondered vaguely since when Varick had been dealing in "important things." Hitherto he had dabbled only in the shallow pools of speculation, with which Waythorn's office did not usually concern itself.

It occurred to him that Varick might be talking at random, to relieve the strain of their propinquity. That strain was becoming momentarily more apparent to Waythorn, and when, at Cortlandt Street, he caught sight of an acquaintance and had a sudden vision of the picture he and Varick must present to an initiated eye, he jumped up with a muttered excuse.

"I hope you'll find Sellers better," said Varick civilly, and he stammered back: "If I can be of any use to you—" and let the departing crowd sweep him to the platform.

At his office he heard that Sellers was in fact ill with the gout, and would probably not be able to leave the house for some weeks.

"I'm sorry it should have happened so, Mr. Waythorn," the senior clerk said with affable significance. "Mr. Sellers was very much upset at the idea of giving you such a lot of extra work just now."

"Oh, that's no matter," said Waythorn hastily. He secretly welcomed the pressure of additional business, and was glad to think that, when the day's work was over, he would have to call at his partner's on the way home.

He was late for luncheon, and turned in at the nearest restaurant instead of going to his club. The place was full, and the waiter hurried him to the back of the room to capture the only vacant table. In the cloud of cigar-smoke Waythorn did not at once distinguish his neighbours: but presently, looking about him, he saw Varick seated a few feet off. This time, luckily, they were too far apart for conversation, and Varick, who faced another way, had probably not even seen him; but there was an irony in their renewed nearness.

Varick was said to be fond of good living, and as Waythorn sat despatching his hurried luncheon he looked across half enviously at the other's leisurely regustation of his meal. When Waythorn first saw him he had been helping himself with critical deliberation to a bit of Camembert at the ideal point of liquefaction, and now, the cheese removed, he was just pouring his *café double* from its little two-storied earthen pot. He poured slowly, his ruddy profile bent above the task, and one beringed white hand steadying the lid of the coffee-pot; then he stretched his other hand to the decanter of cognac at his elbow, filled a liqueur-glass, took a tentative sip, and poured the brandy into his coffee-cup.

Waythorn watched him in a kind of fascination. What was he thinking of—only of the flavour of the coffee and the liqueur? Had the

morning's meeting left no more trace in his thoughts than on his face?
Had his wife so completely passed out of his life that even this odd
encounter with her present husband, within a week after her remarriage, was no more than an incident in his day? And as Waythorn
mused, another idea struck him: had Haskett ever met Varick as
Varick and he had just met? The recollection of Haskett perturbed him,
and he rose and left the restaurant, taking a circuitous way out to
escape the placid irony of Varick's nod.

It was after seven when Waythorn reached home. He thought the
footman who opened the door looked at him oddly.

"How is Miss Lily?" he asked in haste.

"Doing very well, sir. A gentleman—"

"Tell Barlow to put off dinner for half an hour," Waythorn cut him
off, hurrying upstairs."

He went straight to his room and dressed without seeing his wife.
When he reached the drawing-room she was there, fresh and radiant.
Lily's day had been good; the doctor was not coming back that evening.

At dinner Waythorn told her of Sellers's illness and of the resulting
complications. She listened sympathetically, adjuring him not to let
himself be over-worked, and asking vague feminine questions about
the routine of the office. Then she gave him the chronicle of Lily's day;
quoted the nurse and doctor, and told him who had called to inquire.
He had never seen her more serene and unruffled. It struck him, with
a curious pang, that she was very happy in being with him, so happy
that she found a childish pleasure in rehearsing the trival incidents of
her day.

After dinner they went to the library, and the servant put the coffee
and liqueurs on a low table before her and left the room. She looked
singularly soft and girlish in her rosy pale dress, against the dark
leather of one of his bachelor armchairs. A day earlier the contrast
would have charmed him.

He turned away now, choosing a cigar with affected deliberation.

"Did Haskett come?" he asked, with his back to her.

"Oh, yes—he came."

"You didn't see him, of course?"

She hesitated a moment. "I let the nurse see him."

That was all. There was nothing more to ask. He swung round
toward her, applying a match to his cigar. Well, the thing was over
for a week, at any rate. He would try not to think of it. She looked up
at him, a trifle rosier than usual, with a smile in her eyes.

"Ready for your coffee, dear?"

He leaned against the mantelpiece, watching her as she lifted the
coffee-pot. The lamplight struck a gleam from her bracelets and tipped
her soft hair with brightness. How light and slender she was, and
how each gesture flowed into the next! She seemed a creature all
compact of harmonies. As the thought of Haskett receded, Waythorn

felt himself yielding again to the joy of possessorship. They were his, those white hands with their flitting motions, his the light haze of hair, the lips and eyes. . . .

She set down the coffee-pot, and reaching for the decanter of cognac, measured off a liqueur-glass and poured it into his cup.

Waythorn uttered a sudden exclamation.

"What is the matter?" she said, startled.

"Nothing; only—I don't take cognac in my coffee."

"Oh, how stupid of me," she cried.

Their eyes met, and she blushed a sudden agonised red.

III

Ten days later, Mr. Sellers, still house-bound, asked Waythorn to call on his way down town.

The senior partner, with his swaddled foot propped up by the fire, greeted his associate with an air of embarrassment.

"I'm sorry, my dear fellow; I've got to ask you to do an awkward thing for me."

Waythorn waited, and the other went on, after a pause apparently given to the arrangement of his phrases: "The fact is, when I was knocked out I had just gone into a rather complicated piece of business for—Gus Varick."

"Well?" said Waythorn, with an attempt to put him at his ease.

"Well—it's this way: Varick came to me the day before my attack. He had evidently had an inside tip from somebody, and had made about a hundred thousand. He came to me for advice, and I suggested his going in with Vanderlyn."

"Oh, the deuce!" Waythorn exclaimed. He saw in a flash what had happened. The investment was an alluring one, but required negotiation. He listened quietly while Sellers put the case before him, and, the statement ended, he said: "You think I ought to see Varick?"

"I'm afraid I can't as yet. The doctor is obdurate. And this thing can't wait. I hate to ask you, but no one else in the office knows the ins and outs of it."

Waythorn stood silent. He did not care a farthing for the success of Varick's venture, but the honour of the office was to be considered, and he could hardly refuse to oblige his partner.

"Very well," he said, "I'll do it."

That afternoon, apprised by telephone, Varick called at the office. Waythorn, waiting in his private room, wondered what the others thought of it. The newspapers, at the time of Mrs. Waythorn's marriage, had acquainted their readers with every detail of her previous matrimonial ventures, and Waythorn could fancy the clerks smiling behind Varick's back as he was ushered in.

Varick bore himself admirably. He was easy without being undigni-

fied, and Waythorn was conscious of cutting a much less impressive
figure. Varick had no experience of business, and the talk prolonged
itself for nearly an hour while Waythorn set forth with scrupulous
precision the details of the proposed transaction.

"I'm awfully obliged to you," Varick said as he rose. "The fact is
I'm not used to having much money to look after, and I don't want to
make an ass of myself—" He smiled, and Waythorn could not help
noticing that there was something pleasant about his smile. "It feels
uncommonly queer to have enough cash to pay one's bills. I'd have sold
my soul for it a few years ago!"

Waythorn winced at the allusion. He had heard it rumoured that a
lack of funds had been one of the determining causes of the Varick
separation, but it did not occur to him that Varick's words were intentional. It seemed more likely that the desire to keep clear of embarrassing topics had fatally drawn him into one. Waythorn did not
wish to be outdone in civility.

"We'll do the best we can for you," he said. "I think this is a good
thing you're in."

"Oh, I'm sure it's immense. It's awfully good of you—" Varick
broke off, embarrassed. "I suppose the thing's settled now—but if—"

"If anything happens before Sellers is about, I'll see you again,"
said Waythorn quietly. He was glad, in the end, to appear the more
self-possessed of the two.

The course of Lily's illness ran smooth, and as the days passed
Waythorn grew used to the idea of Haskett's weekly visit. The first
time the day came round, he stayed out late, and questioned his wife
as to the visit on his return. She replied at once that Haskett had merely
seen the nurse downstairs, as the doctor did not wish any one in the
child's sick-room till after the crisis.

The following week Waythorn was again conscious of the recurrence of the day, but had forgotten it by the time he came home to
dinner. The crisis of the disease came a few days later, with a rapid
decline of fever, and the little girl was pronounced out of danger. In
the rejoicing which ensued the thought of Haskett passed out of
Waythorn's mind, and one afternoon, letting himself into the house
with a latch-key, he went straight to his library without noticing a
shabby hat and umbrella in the hall.

In the library he found a small effaced-looking man with a thinnish
gray beard sitting on the edge of a chair. The stranger might have been
a piano-tuner, or one of those mysteriously efficient persons who are
summoned in emergencies to adjust some detail of the domestic
machinery. He blinked at Waythorn through a pair of gold-rimmed
spectacles and said mildly: "Mr. Waythorn, I presume? I am Lily's
father."

Waythorn flushed. "Oh—" he stammered uncomfortably. He broke off, disliking to appear rude. Inwardly he was trying to adjust the actual Haskett to the image of him projected by his wife's reminiscences. Waythorn had been allowed to infer that Alice's first husband was a brute.

"I am sorry to intrude," said Haskett, with his over-the-counter politeness.

"Don't mention it," returned Waythorn, collecting himself. "I suppose the nurse has been told?"

"I presume so. I can wait," said Haskett. He had a resigned way of speaking, as though life had worn down his natural powers of resistance.

Waythorn stood on the threshold, nervously pulling off his gloves.

"I'm sorry you've been detained. I will send for the nurse," he said; and as he opened the door he added with an effort: "I'm glad we can give you a good report of Lily." He winced as the *we* slipped out, but Haskett seemed not to notice it.

"Thank you, Mr. Waythorn. It's been an anxious time for me."

"Ah, well, that's past. Soon she'll be able to go to you." Waythorn nodded and passed out.

In his own room he flung himself down with a groan. He hated the womanish sensibility which made him suffer so acutely from the grotesque chances of life. He had known when he married that his wife's former husbands were both living, and that amid the multiplied contacts of modern existence there were a thousand chances to one that he would run against one or the other, yet he found himself as much disturbed by his brief encounter with Haskett as though the law had not obligingly removed all difficulties in the way of their meeting.

Waythorn sprang up and began to pace the room nervously. He had not suffered half as much from his two meetings with Varick. It was Haskett's presence in his own house that made the situation so intolerable. He stood still, hearing steps in the passage.

"This way, please," he heard the nurse say. Haskett was being taken upstairs, then: not a corner of the house but was open to him. Waythorn dropped into another chair, staring vaguely ahead of him. On his dressing-table stood a photograph of Alice, taken when he had first known her. She was Alice Varick then—how fine and exquisite he had thought her! Those were Varick's pearls about her neck. At Waythorn's insistence they had been returned before her marriage. Had Haskett ever given her any trinkets—and what had become of them, Waythorn wondered? He realised suddenly that he knew very little of Haskett's past or present situation; but from the man's appearance and manner of speech he could reconstruct with curious precision the surroundings of Alice's first marriage. And it startled him to think that she had, in the background of her life, a phase of existence so different from anything with which he had connected her. Varick, whatever his faults, was a gentleman, in the conventional, traditional sense of the term: the sense which at that moment seemed, oddly enough, to have most meaning to Waythorn. He and Varick had the same social habits, spoke the same language, understood the same allusions. But this other man . . . it was grotesquely uppermost in Waythorn's mind that Haskett had worn a made up tie attached with an elastic. Why should that ridiculous detail symbolise the whole man? Waythorn was exasperated by his own paltriness, but the fact of the tie expanded, forced itself on him, became as it were the key to Alice's past. He could see her, as Mrs. Haskett, sitting in a "front parlour" furnished in plush, with a pianola, and a copy of "Ben Hur" on the centre-table. He could see her going to the theatre with Haskett—or perhaps even to a "Church Sociable"—she in a "picture hat" and Haskett in a black frock-coat, a little creased, with the made-up tie on an elastic. On the way home they would stop and look at the illuminated shop-windows, lingering over the photographs of New York actresses. On Sunday afternoons Haskett would take her for a walk, pushing Lily ahead of them in a white enamelled perambulator, and Waythorn had a vision of the people they would stop and talk to. He could fancy how pretty Alice must have looked, in a dress adroitly constructed from the hints of a New York fashion-paper, and how she must have looked down on the other women, chafing at her life, and secretly feeling that she belonged in a bigger place.

For the moment his foremost thought was one of wonder at the way in which she had shed the phase of existence which her marriage with Haskett implied. It was as if her whole aspect, every gesture, every inflection, every allusion, were a studied negation of that period of her life. If she had denied being married to Haskett she could hardly have stood more convicted of duplicity than in this obliteration of the self which had been his wife.

Waythorn started up, checking himself in the analysis of her motives. What right had he to create a fantastic effigy of her and then pass judgment on it? She had spoken vaguely of her first marriage as unhappy, had hinted, with becoming reticence, that Haskett had wrought havoc among her young illusions. . . . It was a pity for Waythorn's peace of mind that Haskett's very inoffensiveness shed a new light on the nature of those illusions. A man would rather think that his wife had been brutalised by her first husband than that the process has been reversed.

IV

"Mr. Waythorn, I don't like that French governess of Lily's."

Haskett, subdued and apologetic, stood before Waythorn in the library, revolving his shabby hat in his hand.

Waythorn, surprised in his armchair over the evening paper, stared back perplexedly at his visitor.

"You'll excuse my asking to see you," Haskett continued. "But this is my last visit, and I thought if I could have a word with you it would be a better way than writing to Mrs. Waythorn's lawyer."

Waythorn rose uneasily. He did not like the French governess either; but that was irrelevant.

"I am not so sure of that," he returned stiffly; "but since you wish it I will give your message to—my wife." He always hesitated over the possessive pronoun in addressing Haskett.

The latter sighed. "I don't know as that will help much. She didn't like it when I spoke to her"

Waythorn turned red. "When did you see her?" he asked.

"Not since the first day I came to see Lily—right after she was taken sick. I remarked to her then that I didn't like the governess."

Waythorn made no answer. He remembered distinctly that, after that first visit, he had asked his wife if she had seen Haskett. She had lied to him then, but she had respected his wishes since; and the incident cast a curious light on her character. He was sure she would not have seen Haskett that first day if she had divined that Waythorn would object, and the fact that she did not divine it was almost as disagreeable to the latter as the discovery that she had lied to him.

"I don't like the woman," Haskett was repeating with mild persistency. "She ain't straight, Mr. Waythorn—she'll teach the child to be underhand. I've noticed a change in Lily—she's too anxious to please—and she don't always tell the truth. She used to be the straightest child, Mr. Waythorn—" He broke off, his voice a little thick. "Not but what I want her to have a stylish education," he ended.

Waythorn was touched. "I'm sorry, Mr. Haskett; but frankly, I don't quite see what I can do."

Haskett hesitated. Then he laid his hat on the table, and advanced to the hearth-rug, on which Waythorn was standing. There was nothing aggressive in his manner, but he had the solemnity of a timid man resolved on a decisive measure.

"There's just one thing you can do, Mr. Waythorn," he said. "You can remind Mrs. Waythorn that, by the decree of the courts, I am entitled to have a voice in Lily's bringing up." He paused, and went on more deprecatingly: "I'm not the kind to talk about enforcing my rights, Mr. Waythorn. I don't know as I think a man is entitled to rights he hasn't known how to hold on to; but this business of the child is different. I've never let go there—and I never mean to."

The scene left Waythorn deeply shaken. Shame-facedly, in indirect ways, he had been finding out about Haskett; and all that he had learned was favourable. The little man, in order to be near his daughter, had sold out his share in a profitable business in Utica, and accepted a modest clerkship in a New York manufacturing house. He boarded in a shabby street and had few acquaintances. His passion for Lily filled his life. Waythorn felt that this exploration of Haskett was like groping about with a dark-lantern in his wife's past; but he saw now that there were recesses his lantern had not explored. He had never enquired into the exact circumstances of his wife's first matrimonial rupture. On the surface all had been fair. It was she who had obtained the divorce, and the court had given her the child. But Waythorn knew how many ambiguities such a verdict might cover. The mere fact that Haskett retained a right over his daughter implied an unsuspected compromise. Waythorn was an idealist. He always refused to recognise unpleasant contingencies till he found himself confronted with them, and then he saw them followed by a spectral train of consequences. His next days were thus haunted, and he determined to try to lay the ghosts by conjuring them up in his wife's presence.

When he repeated Haskett's request a flame of anger passed over her face; but she subdued it instantly and spoke with a slight quiver of outraged motherhood.

"It is very ungentlemanly of him," she said.

The word grated on Waythorn. "That is neither here nor there. It's a bare question of rights."

She murmured: "It's not as if he could ever be a help to Lily—"

Waythorn flushed. This was even less to his taste. "The question is," he repeated, "what authority has he over her?"

She looked downward, twisting herself a little in her seat. "I am willing to see him—I thought you objected," she faltered.

In a flash he understood that she knew the extent of Haskett's claims. Perhaps it was not the first time she had resisted them.

"My objecting has nothing to do with it," he said coldly; "if Haskett has a right to be consulted you must consult him."

She burst into tears, and he saw that she expected him to regard her as a victim.

Haskett did not abuse his rights. Waythorn had felt miserably sure that he would not. But the governess was dismissed and from time to time the little man demanded an interview with Alice. After the first outburst she accepted the situation with her usual adaptability. Haskett had once reminded Waythorn of the piano-tuner, and Mrs. Waythorn, after a month or two, appeared to class him with that domestic familiar. Waythorn could not but respect the father's tenacity. At first he had tried to cultivate the suspicion that Haskett might be "up to" something, that he had an object in securing a foothold in the house. But in his heart Waythorn was sure of Haskett's single-mindedness; he even guessed in the latter a mild contempt for such advantages as his relation with the Waythorns might offer. Haskett's sincerity of purpose made him invulnerable, and his succesor had to accept him as a lien on the property.

Mr. Sellers was sent to Europe to recover from his gout, and Varick's affairs hung on Waythorn's hands. The negotiations were prolonged and complicated; they necessitated frequent conferences between the two men, and the interests of the firm forbade Waythorn's suggesting that his client should transfer his business to another office.

Varick appeared well in the transaction. In moments of relaxation his coarse streak appeared, and Waythorn dreaded his geniality; but in the office he was concise and clear-headed, with a flattering deference to Waythorn's judgment. Their business relations being so affably established, it would have been absurd for the two men to ignore each other in society. The first time they met in a drawing-room, Varick took up their intercourse in the same easy key, and his hostess's grateful glance obliged Waythorn to respond to it. After that they ran across each other frequently, and one evening at a ball Waythorn, wandering through the remoter rooms, came upon Varick seated beside his wife. She coloured a little, and faltered in what she was saying; but Varick nodded to Waythorn without rising, and the latter strolled on.

In the carriage, on the way home, he broke out nervously: "I didn't know you spoke to Varick."

Her voice trembled a little. "It's the first time—he happened to be standing near me; I didn't know what to do. It's so awkward, meeting everywhere—and he said you had been very kind about some business."

"That's different," said Waythorn.

She paused a moment. "I'll do just as you wish," she returned pliantly. "I thought it would be less awkward to speak to him when we meet."

Her pliancy was beginning to sicken him. Had she really no will of her own—no theory about her relation to these men? She had accepted Haskett—did she mean to accept Varick? It was "less awkward," as she had said, and her instinct was to evade difficulties or to circumvent them. With sudden vividness Waythorn saw how the instinct had developed. She was "as easy as an old shoe"—a shoe that too many feet had worn. Her elasticity was the result of tension in too many different directions. Alice Haskett—Alice Varick—Alice Waythorn—she had been each in turn, and had left hanging to each name a little of her privacy, a little of her personality, a little of the inmost self where the unknown god abides.

"Yes—it's better to speak to Varick," said Waythorn wearily.

V

The winter wore on, and society took advantage of the Waythorns' acceptance of Varick. Harassed hostesses were grateful to them for bridging over a social difficulty, and Mrs. Waythorn was held up as a miracle of good taste. Some experimental spirits could not resist the diversion of throwing Varick and his former wife together, and there were those who thought he found a zest in the propinquity. But Mrs. Waythorn's conduct remained irreproachable. She neither avoided Varick nor sought him out. Even Waythorn could not but admit that she had discovered the solution of the newest social problem.

He had married her without giving much thought to that problem. He had fancied that a woman can shed her past like a man. But now he saw that Alice was bound to hers both by the circumstances which forced her into continued relation with it, and by the traces it had left on her nature. With grim irony Waythorn compared himself to a member of a syndicate. He held so many shares in his wife's personality and his predecessors were his partners in the business. If there had been any element of passion in the transaction he would have felt less deteriorated by it. The fact that Alice took her change of husbands like a change of weather reduced the situation to mediocrity. He could have forgiven her for blunders, for excesses; for resisting Haskett, for yielding to Varick; for anything but her acquiescence and her tact. She reminded him of a juggler tossing knives; but the knives were blunt and she knew they would never cut her.

And then, gradually, habit formed a protecting surface for his sensibilities. If he paid for each day's comfort with the small change of his illusions, he grew daily to value the comfort more and set less store upon the coin. He had drifted into a dulling propinquity with Haskett and Varick and he took refuge in the cheap revenge of satirising the situation. He even began to reckon up the advantages which accrued from it, to ask himself if it were not better to own a third of a wife who knew how to make a man happy than a whole one who had lacked opportunity to acquire the art. For it *was* an art, and made up, like all others, of concessions, eliminations and embellishments; of lights judiciously thrown and shadows skilfully softened. His wife knew exactly how to manage the lights, and he knew exactly to what training she owed her skill. He even tried to trace the source of his obligations, to discriminate between the influences which had combined to produce his domestic happiness: he perceived that Haskett's commonness had made Alice worship good breeding, while Varick's liberal construction of the marriage bond had taught her to value the conjugal virtues; so that he was directly indebted to his predecessors for the devotion which made his life easy if not inspiring.

From this phase he passed into that of complete acceptance. He ceased to satirise himself because time dulled the irony of the situation and the joke lost its humour with its sting. Even the sight of Haskett's hat on the hall table had ceased to touch the springs of epigram. The hat was often seen there now, for it had been decided that it was better for Lily's father to visit her than for the little girl to go to his boarding-house. Waythorn, having acquiesced in this arrangement, had been surprised to find how little difference it made. Haskett was never obtrusive, and the few visitors who met him on the stairs were unaware of his identity. Waythorn did not know how often he saw Alice, but with himself Haskett was seldom in contact.

One afternoon, however, he learned on entering that Lily's father was waiting to see him. In the library he found Haskett occupying a chair in his usual provisional way. Waythorn always felt grateful to him for not leaning back.

"I hope you'll excuse me, Mr. Waythorn," he said rising. "I wanted to see Mrs. Waythorn about Lily, and your man asked me to wait here till she came in."

"Of course," said Waythorn, remembering that a sudden leak had that morning given over the drawing-room to the plumbers.

He opened his cigar-case and held it out to his visitor, and Haskett's acceptance seemed to mark a fresh stage in their intercourse. The spring evening was chilly, and Waythorn invited his guest to draw up his chair to the fire. He meant to find an excuse to leave Haskett in a moment; but he was tired and cold, and after all the little man no longer jarred on him.

The two were enclosed in the intimacy of their blended cigar-smoke when the door opened and Varick walked into the room. Waythorn rose abruptly. It was the first time that Varick had come to the house, and the surprise of seeing him, combined with the singular inopportuneness of his arrival, gave a new edge to Waythorn's blunted sensibilities. He stared at his visitor without speaking.

Varick seemed too preoccupied to notice his host's embarrassment.

"My dear fellow," he exclaimed in his most expansive tone, "I must apologise for tumbling in on you in this way, but I was too late to catch you down town, and so I thought—"

He stopped short, catching sight of Haskett, and his sanguine colour deepened to a flush which spread vividly under his scant blond hair. But in a moment he recovered himself and nodded slightly. Haskett returned the bow in silence, and Waythorn was still groping for speech when the footman came in carrying a tea-table.

The intrusion offered a welcome vent to Waythorn's nerves. "What the deuce are you bringing this here for?" he said sharply.

"I beg your pardon, sir, but the plumbers are still in the drawing-room, and Mrs. Waythorn said she would have tea in the library." The footman's perfectly respectful tone implied a reflection on Waythorn's reasonableness.

"Oh, very well," said the latter resignedly, and the footman proceeded to open the folding tea-table and set out its complicated appointments. While this interminable process continued the three men stood motionless, watching it with a fascinated stare, till Waythorn, to break the silence, said to Varick: "Won't you have a cigar?"

He held out the case he had just tendered to Haskett, and Varick helped himself with a smile. Waythorn looked about for a match, and finding none, proffered a light from his own cigar. Haskett, in the background, held his ground mildly, examining his cigar-tip now and then, and stepping forward at the right moment to knock its ashes into the fire.

The footman at last withdrew, and Varick immediately began: "If I could just say half a word to you about this business—"

"Certainly," stammered Waythorn; "in the dining-room—"

But as he placed his hand on the door it opened from without, and his wife appeared on the threshold.

She came in fresh and smiling, in her street dress and hat, shedding a fragrance from the boa which she loosened in advancing.

"Shall we have tea in here, dear?" she began; and then she caught sight of Varick. Her smile deepened, veiling a slight tremor of surprise.

"Why, how do you do?" she said with a distinct note of pleasure.

As she shook hands with Varick she saw Haskett standing behind him. Her smile faded for a moment, but she recalled it quickly, with a scarcely perceptible side-glance at Waythorn.

"How do you do, Mr. Haskett?" she said, and shook hands with him a shade less cordially.

The three men stood awkwardly before her, till Varick, always the most self-possessed, dashed into an explanatory phrase.

"We—I had to see Waythorn a moment on business," he stammered, brick-red from chin to nape.

Haskett stepped forward with his air of mild obstinacy. "I am sorry to intrude; but you appointed five o'clock—" he directed his resigned glance to the timepiece on the mantel.

She swept aside their embarrassment with a charming gesture of hospitality.

"I'm so sorry—I'm always late; but the afternoon was so lovely." She stood drawing off her gloves, propitiatory and graceful, diffusing about her a sense of ease and familiarity in which the situation lost its grotesqueness. "But before talking business," she added brightly, "I'm sure every one wants a cup of tea."

She dropped into her low chair by the tea-table, and the two visitors, as if drawn by her smile, advanced to receive the cups she held out.

She glanced about for Waythorn, and he took the third cup with a laugh.

WILLA [SIBERT] CATHER (1873–1947)

For four generations her family had lived in Virginia, where she was born; but when she was eight years old, her parents moved to a ranch in Nebraska. This was still frontier country, largely populated (insofar as it was) by immigrants from more distant points—energetic, uncomplaining people whose stalwart efforts her writing was to memorialize much later.

The Cather household in Nebraska included both grandmothers—very literate women who provided her early education, not only in the English classics but in Latin and its literature. Virgil, in many ways, was to become her literary mentor in her best work. But while she studied him, she also enjoyed a much more rough-and-tumble pastoralism than his, a tomboy in the rude life of the Western prairies. When her family moved to the town of Red Cloud, she entered high school; after graduation, she worked her way through the University of Nebraska by newspaper jobs.

Her first book of short stories, The Troll Garden (1905), makes evident her passion for music: she wanted to live where concerts were accessible. She chose Pittsburgh, oddly enough, where she became dramatic critic for the Daily Leader. Her story, "Paul's Case," which was included in The Troll Garden, is about a Pittsburgh high school boy, a boy who believes that there must be some more meaningful life beyond the only one he knows; he tries to pursue it as best he can, in the only terms that he can imagine, and dies, one might say, because of the inadequacy of the vision that his life had made possible for him.

In this, as in some of her other early stories, Willa Cather seems quite primitive now, almost a female Dreiser in the rather clumsy, summarizing art, so flatly narrated, so little presented. One wonders what is still moving in such narratives and must conclude that it is our own continuing sense of that groping and inarticulate social history that we must still share, that terrifying American wish for some richer life than the one we know.

This view of the American experience did not satisfy Willa Cather for long, although she continued for a time the kind of professional experience that could have supported only such a bitter estimate. She tried teaching, and then, in New York, she worked on McClure's Magazine, the muckraking journal, until 1912. The success of her novel O Pioneers! (1913) freed her from these necessities, and living quietly in New York for many years, traveling some but never tempted to an expatriate experience, she wrote her books. A few were more honored than they should have been, but not many.

She is one of our few good writers who published almost no really bad novels. One of Ours (1922), which won the Pulitzer Prize, probably comes closest—an attempt to tell of the glories of being a soldier, an experience about which she naturally knew nothing. The Professor's House (1925), about academic life, is also quite unpersuasive. Some other work may seem to readers now as thin, willed rather than imagined, her very last novels included. But by turning away from the contemporary and metropolitan subject to her own Western past and a past before that—O Pioneers!, My Ántonia (1918), Death Comes for the Archbishop (1927), even Shadows on the Rock (1931)—she was able to explore a subject matter that was *congenial to her imagination without being abrasive to her sensibility. In these novels written in her clean, quite naked prose, she manages to strike some gong in the caverns of our consciousness.*

FURTHER READING

The fullest biography is a posthumous volume by E. K. Brown, completed by Leon Edel, *Willa Cather: A Critical Biography* (1953). See also Edith Lewis, *Willa Cather Living: A Personal Record* (1953), and Elizabeth Shepley Sargeant, *Willa Cather: A Memoir* (1953). Useful critical studies are David Daiches, *Willa Cather: A Critical Introduction* (1951), and John H. Randall, III, *The Landscape and the Looking Glass: Willa Cather's Search for Value* (1960). James Schroeter edited *Willa Cather and Her Critics* (1967).

Paul's Case (1905)

A Study in Temperament

It was Paul's afternoon to appear before the faculty of the Pittsburgh High School to account for his various misdemeanors. He had been suspended a week ago, and his father had called at the Principal's office and confessed his perplexity about his son. Paul entered the faculty room suave and smiling. His clothes were a trifle outgrown, and the tan velvet on the collar of his open overcoat was frayed and worn; but for all that there was something of the dandy about him, and he wore an opal pin in his neatly knotted black four-in-hand, and a red carnation in his buttonhole. This latter adornment the faculty somehow felt was not properly significant of the contrite spirit befitting a boy under the ban of suspension.

Paul was tall for his age and very thin, with high, cramped shoulders and a narrow chest. His eyes were remarkable for a certain hysterical brilliancy, and he continually used them in a conscious, theatrical sort of way, peculiarly offensive in a boy. The pupils were abnormally large, as though he were addicted to belladonna, but there was a glassy glitter about them which that drug does not produce.

When questioned by the Principal as to why he was there Paul stated, politely enough, that he wanted to come back to school. This was a lie, but Paul was quite accustomed to lying; found it, indeed, indispensable for overcoming friction. His teachers were asked to state their respective charges against him, which they did with such a rancor and aggrievedness as evinced that this was not a usual case. Disorder and impertinence were among the offenses named, yet each of his

instructors felt that it was scarcely possible to put into words the real
cause of the trouble, which lay in a sort of hysterically defiant manner
of the boy's; in the contempt which they all knew he felt for them, and
which he seemingly made not the least effort to conceal. Once, when
he had been making a synopsis of a paragraph at the blackboard,
his English teacher had stepped to his side and attempted to guide
his hand. Paul had started back with a shudder and thrust his hands
violently behind him. The astonished woman could scarcely have been
more hurt and embarrassed had he struck at her. The insult was so
involuntary and definitely personal as to be unforgettable. In one way
and another he had made all his teachers, men and women alike,
conscious of the same feeling of physical aversion. In one class he
habitually sat with his hand shading his eyes; in another he always
looked out of the window during the recitation; in another he made a
running commentary on the lecture, with humorous intention.

His teachers felt this afternoon that his whole attitude was symbolized by his shrug and his flippantly red carnation flower, and they fell
upon him without mercy, his English teacher leading the pack. He
stood through it smiling, his pale lips parted over his white teeth. (His
lips were continually twitching, and he had a habit of raising his eyebrows that was contemptuous and irritating to the last degree.) Older
boys than Paul had broken down and shed tears under that baptism of
fire, but his set smile did not once desert him, and his only sign of
discomfort was the nervous trembling of the fingers that toyed with
the buttons of his overcoat, and an occasional jerking of the other hand
that held his hat. Paul was always smiling, always glancing about him,
seeming to feel that people might be watching him and trying to detect
something. This conscious expression, since it was as far as possible
from boyish mirthfulness, was usually attributed to insolence or "smart-
ness."

As the inquisition proceeded one of his instructors repeated an
impertinent remark of the boy's, and the Principal asked him whether
he thought that a courteous speech to have made a woman. Paul
shrugged his shoulders slightly and his eyebrows twitched.

"I don't know," he replied. "I didn't mean to be polite or impolite,
either. I guess it's a sort of way I have of saying things regardless."

The Principal, who was a sympathetic man, asked him whether he
didn't think that a way it would be well to get rid of. Paul grinned and
said he guessed so. When he was told that he could go he bowed
gracefully and went out. His bow was but a repetition of the scandalous
red carnation.

His teachers were in despair, and his drawing master voiced the
feeling of them all when he declared there was something about the
boy which none of them understood. He added: "I don't really believe
that smile of his comes altogether from insolence; there's something
sort of haunted about it. The boy is not strong, for one thing. I happen

to know that he was born in Colorado, only a few months before his
mother died out there of a long illness. There is something wrong about
the fellow."

The drawing master had come to realize that, in looking at Paul,
one saw only his white teeth and the forced animation of his eyes. One
warm afternoon the boy had gone to sleep at his drawing board, and
his master had noted with amazement what a white, blue-veined face
it was; drawn and wrinkled like an old man's about the eyes, the lips
twitching even in his sleep, and stiff with a nervous tension that drew
them back from his teeth.

His teachers left the building dissatisfied and unhappy; humiliated
to have felt so vindictive toward a mere boy, to have uttered this feeling
in cutting terms, and to have set each other on, as it were, in the gruesome game of intemperate reproach. Some of them remembered having
seen a miserable street cat set at bay by a ring of tormentors.

As for Paul, he ran down the hill whistling the "Soldiers' Chorus"
from *Faust,* looking wildly behind him now and then to see whether
some of his teachers were not there to writhe under his lighthearted-
ness. As it was now late in the afternoon and Paul was on duty that
evening as usher at Carnegie Hall, he decided that he would not go
home to supper. When he reached the concert hall the doors were not
yet open and, as it was chilly outside, he decided to go up into the
picture gallery—always deserted at this hour—where there were some
of Raffelli's [1] gay studies of Paris streets and an airy blue Venetian
scene or two that always exhilarated him. He was delighted to find no
one in the gallery but the old guard, who sat in one corner, a newspaper on his knee, a black patch over one eye and the other closed.
Paul possessed himself of the place and walked confidently up and
down, whistling under his breath. After a while he sat down before a
blue Rico [2] and lost himself. When he bethought him to look at his
watch, it was after seven o'clock, and he rose with a start and ran
downstairs, making a face at Augustus,[3] peering out from the cast
room, and an evil gesture at the Venus de Milo as he passed her on the
stairway.

When Paul reached the ushers' dressing room half a dozen boys
were there already, and he began excitedly to tumble into his uniform.
It was one of the few that at all approached fitting, and Paul thought
it very becoming—though he knew that the tight, straight coat accentuated his narrow chest, about which he was exceedingly sensitive. He
was always considerably excited while he dressed, twanging all over
to the tuning of the strings and the preliminary flourishes of the horns

---

[1] Jean François Raffaelli (1850–1923), French painter and sculptor.

[2] Andrea Rico, twelfth-century Greek painter.

[3] The first Roman emperor (63 B.C.–A.D. 14), patron of arts.

in the music room; but tonight he seemed quite beside himself, and he teased and plagued the boys until, telling him that he was crazy, they put him down on the floor and sat on him.

Somewhat calmed by his suppression, Paul dashed out to the front of the house to seat the early comers. He was a model usher; gracious and smiling he ran up and down the aisles; nothing was too much trouble for him; he carried messages and brought programs as though it were his greatest pleasure in life, and all the people in his section thought him a charming boy, feeling that he remembered and admired them. As the house filled, he grew more and more vivacious and animated, and the color came to his cheeks and lips. It was very much as though this were a great reception and Paul were the host. Just as the musicians came out to take their places, his English teacher arrived with checks for the seats which a prominent manufacturer had taken for the season. She betrayed some embarrassment when she handed Paul the tickets, and a hauteur which subsequently made her feel very foolish. Paul was startled for a moment, and had the feeling of wanting to put her out; what business had she here among all these fine people and gay colors? He looked her over and decided that she was not appropriately dressed and must be a fool to sit downstairs in such togs. The tickets had probably been sent her out of kindness, he reflected as he put down a seat for her, and she had about as much right to sit there as he had.

When the symphony began Paul sank into one of the rear seats with a long sigh of relief, and lost himself as he had done before the Rico. It was not that symphonies, as such, meant anything in particular to Paul, but the first sigh of the instruments seemed to free some hilarious and potent spirit within him; something that struggled there like the genie in the bottle found by the Arab fisherman. He felt a sudden zest of life; the lights danced before his eyes and the concert hall blazed into unimaginable splendor. When the soprano soloist came on Paul forgot even the nastiness of his teacher's being there and gave himself up to the peculiar stimulus such personages always had for him. The soloist chanced to be a German woman, by no means in her first youth, and the mother of many children; but she wore an elaborate gown and a tiara, and above all she had that indefinable air of achievement, that world-shine upon her, which, in Paul's eyes, made her a veritable queen of Romance.

After a concert was over Paul was always irritable and wretched until he got to sleep, and tonight he was even more than usually restless. He had the feeling of not being able to let down, of its being impossible to give up this delicious excitement which was the only thing that could be called living at all. During the last number he withdrew and, after hastily changing his clothes in the dressing room, slipped out to the side door where the soprano's carriage stood. Here he began pacing rapidly up and down the walk, waiting to see her come out.

Over yonder, the Schenley, in its vacant stretch, loomed big and square through the fine rain, the windows of its twelve stories glowing like those of a lighted cardboard house under a Christmas tree. All the actors and singers of the better class stayed there when they were in the city, and a number of the big manufacturers of the place lived there in the winter. Paul had often hung about the hotel, watching the people go in and out, longing to enter and leave schoomasters and dull care behind him forever.

At last the singer came out, accompanied by the conductor, who helped her into her carriage and closed the door with a cordial *auf wiedersehen* which set Paul to wondering whether she were not an old sweetheart of his. Paul followed the carriage over to the hotel, walking so rapidly as not to be far from the entrance when the singer alighted, and disappeared behind the swinging glass doors that were opened by a Negro in a tall hat and a long coat. In the moment that the door was ajar it seemed to Paul that he, too, entered. He seemed to feel himself go after her up the steps, into the warm, lighted building, into an exotic, tropical world of shiny, glistening surfaces and basking ease. He reflected upon the mysterious dishes that were brought into the dining room, the green bottles in buckets of ice, as he had seen them in the supper party pictures of the *Sunday World* supplement. A quick gust of wind brought the rain down with sudden vehemence, and Paul was startled to find that he was still outside in the slush of the gravel driveway; that his boots were letting in the water and his scanty overcoat was clinging wet about him; that the lights in front of the concert hall were out and that the rain was driving in sheets between him and the orange glow of the windows above him. There it was, what he wanted—tangibly before him, like the fairy world of a Christmas pantomime—but mocking spirits stood guard at the doors, and, as the rain beat in his face, Paul wondered whether he were destined always to shiver in the black night outside, looking up at it.

He turned and walked reluctantly toward the car tracks. The end had to come sometime; his father in his night-clothes at the top of the stairs, explanations that did not explain, hastily improvised fictions that were forever tripping him up, his upstairs room and its horrible yellow wallpaper, the creaking bureau with the greasy plush collar-box, and over his painted wooden bed the pictures of George Washington and John Calvin, and the framed motto, "Feed my Lambs," which had been worked in red worsted by his mother.

Half an hour later Paul alighted from his car and went slowly down one of the side streets off the main thoroughfare. It was a highly respectable street, where all the houses were exactly alike, and where businessmen of moderate means begot and reared large families of children, all of whom went to Sabbath school and learned the shorter catechism, and were interested in arithmetic; all of whom were as exactly alike as their homes, and of a piece with the monotony in which they lived. Paul never went up Cordelia Street without a shudder of loathing. His home was next to the house of the Cumberland minister. He approached it tonight with the nerveless sense of defeat, the hopeless feeling of sinking back forever into ugliness and commonness that he had always had when he came home. The moment he turned into Cordelia Street he felt the waters close above his head. After each of these orgies of living he experienced all the physical depression which follows a debauch; the loathing of respectable beds, of common food, of a house penetrated by kitchen odors; a shuddering repulsion for the flavorless, colorless mass of everyday existence; a morbid desire for cool things and soft lights and fresh flowers.

The nearer he approached the house, the more absolutely unequal Paul felt to the sight of it all: his ugly sleeping chamber; the cold bathroom with the grimy zinc tub, the cracked mirror, the dripping spiggots; his father, at the top of the stairs, his hairy legs sticking out from his nightshirt, his feet thrust into carpet slippers. He was so much later than usual that there would certainly be inquiries and reproaches, Paul stopped short before the door. He felt that he could not be accosted by his father tonight; that he could not toss again on that miserable bed. He would not go in. He would tell his father that he had no carfare and it was raining so hard he had gone home with one of the boys and stayed all night.

Meanwhile, he was wet and cold. He went around to the back of the house and tried one of the basement windows, found it open, raised it cautiously, and scrambled down the cellar wall to the floor. There he stood, holding his breath, terrified by the noise he had made, but the floor above him was silent, and there was no creak on the stairs. He found a soapbox, and carried it over to the soft ring of light that streamed from the furnace door, and sat down. He was horribly afraid of rats, so he did not try to sleep, but sat looking distrustfully at the dark, still terrified lest he might have awakened his father. In such reactions, after one of the experiences which made days and nights out of the dreary blanks of the calendar, when his senses were deadened, Paul's head was always singularly clear. Suppose his father had heard him getting in at the window and had come down and shot him for a burglar? Then, again, suppose his father had come down, pistol in hand, and he had cried out in time to save himself, and his father had been horrified to think how nearly he had killed him? Then, again, suppose a day should come when his father would remember that night, and wish there had been no warning cry to stay his hand? With this last supposition Paul entertained himself until daybreak.

The following Sunday was fine; the sodden November chill was broken by the last flash of autumnal summer. In the morning Paul had to go to church and Sabbath school, as always. On seasonable Sunday afternoons the burghers of Cordelia Street always sat out on their front stoops and talked to their neighbors on the next stoop, or called to those across the street in neighborly fashion. The men usually sat on gay cushions placed upon the steps that led down to the sidewalk, while the women, in their Sunday "waists," sat in rockers on the cramped porches, pretending to be greatly at their ease. The children played in the streets; there were so many of them that the place resembled the recreation grounds of a kindergarten. The men on the steps—all in their shirt sleeves, their vests unbuttoned—sat with their legs well apart, their stomachs comfortably protruding, and talked of the prices of things, or told anecdotes of the sagacity of their various chiefs and overlords. They occasionally looked over the multitude of squabbling children, listened affectionately to their high pitched, nasal voices, smiling to see their own proclivities reproduced in their offspring, and interspersed their legends of the iron kings with remarks about their sons' progress at school, their grades in arithmetic, and the amounts they had saved in their toy banks.

On this last Sunday of November Paul sat all the afternoon on the lowest step of his stoop, staring into the street, while his sisters, in their rockers, were talking to the minister's daughters next door about how many shirtwaists they had made in the last week, and how many waffles someone had eaten at the last church supper. When the weather was warm, and his father was in a particularly jovial frame of mind, the girls made lemonade, which was always brought out in a red-glass pitcher, ornamented with forget-me-nots in blue enamel. This the girls thought very fine, and the neighbors always joked about the suspicious colour of the pitcher.

Today Paul's father sat on the top step, talking to a young man who shifted a restless baby from knee to knee. He happened to be the young man who was daily held up to Paul as a model, and after whom it was his father's dearest hope that he would pattern. This young man was of a ruddy complexion, with a compressed, red mouth, and faded, nearsighted eyes, over which he wore thick spectacles, with gold bows that curved about his ears. He was clerk to one of the magnates of a great steel corporation, and was looked upon in Cordelia Street as a young man with a future. There was a story that, some five years ago —he was now barely twenty-six—he had been a trifle dissipated, but in order to curb his appetites and save the loss of time and strength that a sowing of wild oats might have entailed, he had taken his chief's advice, oft reiterated to his employees, and at twenty-one had married the first woman whom he could persuade to share his fortunes. She happened to be an angular schoolmistress, much older than he, who also wore thick glasses, and who had now borne him four children, all nearsighted, like herself.

The young man was relating how his chief, now cruising in the Mediterranean, kept in touch with all the details of the business, arranging his office hours on his yacht just as though he were at home, and "knocking off work enough to keep two stenographers busy." His father told, in turn, the plan his corporation was considering, of putting in an electric railway plant at Cairo. Paul snapped his teeth; he had an awful apprehension that they might spoil it all before he got there. Yet he rather liked to hear these legends of the iron kings that were told and retold on Sundays and holidays; these stories of palaces in Venice, yachts on the Mediterranean, and high play at Monte Carlo appealed to his fancy, and he was interested in the triumphs of these cash boys who had become famous, though he had no mind for the cash-boy stage.

After supper was over and he had helped to dry the dishes, Paul nervously asked his father whether he could go to George's to get some help in his geometry, and still more nervously asked for carfare. This latter request he had to repeat, as his father, on principle, did not like to hear requests for money, whether much or little. He asked Paul whether he could not go to some boy who lived nearer, and told him that he ought not leave his schoolwork until Sunday; but he gave him the dime. He was not a poor man, but he had a worthy ambition to come up in the world. His only reason for allowing Paul to usher was that he thought a boy ought to be earning a little.

Paul bounded upstairs, scrubbed the greasy odor of the dishwater from his hands with the ill-smelling soap he hated, and then shook over his fingers a few drops of violet water from the bottle he kept hidden in his drawer. He left the house with his geometry conspicuously under his arm, and the moment he got out of Cordelia Street and boarded a downtown car, he shook off the lethargy of two deadening days and began to live again.

The leading juvenile of the permanent stock company which played at one of the downtown theaters was an acquaintance of Paul's, and the boy had been invited to drop in at the Sunday-night rehearsals whenever he could. For more than a year Paul had spent every available moment loitering about Charley Edwards's dressing room. He had won a place among Edwards's following not only because the young actor, who could not afford to employ a dresser, often found him useful, but because he recognized in Paul something akin to what churchmen term "vocation."

It was at the theater and at Carnegie Hall that Paul really lived; the rest was but a sleep and a forgetting. This was Paul's fairy tale, and it had for him all the allurement of a secret love. The moment he inhaled the gassy, painty, dusty odor behind the scenes, he breathed like a prisoner set free, and felt within him the possibility of doing or saying splendid, brilliant, poetic things. The moment the cracked orchestra beat out the overture from *Martha*, or jerked at the serenade from *Rigoletto,* all stupid and ugly things slid from him, and his senses were deliciously, yet delicately fired.

Perhaps it was because, in Paul's world, the natural nearly always wore the guise of ugliness, that a certain element of artificiality seemed to him necessary in beauty. Perhaps it was because his experience of life elsewhere was so full of Sabbath-school picnics, petty economies, wholesome advice as to how to succeed in life, and the inescapable odors of cooking, that he found this existence so alluring, these smartly clad men and women so attractive, that he was so moved by these starry apple orchards that bloomed perennially under the limelight.

It would be difficult to put it strongly enough how convincingly the stage entrance of that theater was for Paul the actual portal of Romance. Certainly none of the company ever suspected it, least of all Charley Edwards. It was very like the old stories that used to float about London of fabulously rich Jews, who had subterranean halls there, with palms, and fountains, and soft lamps and richly appareled women who never saw the disenchanting light of London day. So, in the midst of that smoke-palled city, enamored of figures and grimy toil, Paul had his secret temple, his wishing carpet, his bit of blue-and-white Mediterranean shore bathed in perpetual sunshine.

Several of Paul's teachers had a theory that his imagination had been perverted by garish fiction, but the truth was that he scarcely ever read at all. The books at home were not such as would either tempt or corrupt a youthful mind, and as for reading the novels that some of his friends urged upon him—well, he got what he wanted much more quickly from music; any sort of music, from an orchestra to a barrel organ. He needed only the spark, the indescribable thrill that made his imagination master of his senses, and he could make plots and pictures enough of his own. It was equally true that he was not stage-struck—not, at any rate, in the usual acceptation of that expression. He had no desire to become an actor, any more than he had to become a musician. He felt no necessity to do any of these things; what he wanted was to see, to be in the atmosphere, float on the wave of it, to be carried out, blue league after blue league, away from everything.

After a night behind the scenes Paul found the schoolroom more than ever repulsive; the bare floors and naked walls; the prosy men who never wore frock coats, or violets in their buttonholes; the women with their dull gowns, shrill voices, and pitiful seriousness about prepositions that govern the dative. He could not bear to have the other pupils think, for a moment, that he took these people seriously; he must convey to them that he considered it all trivial, and was there only by way of a jest, anyway. He had autographed pictures of all the members of the stock company which he showed his classmates, telling them the most incredible stories of his familiarity with these people, of his acquaintance with the soloists who came to Carnegie Hall, his suppers with them and the flowers he sent them. When these stories lost their effect, and his audience grew listless, he became desperate and would bid all the boys good-by, announcing that he was going to travel for a while; going to Naples, to Venice, to Egypt. Then, next Monday, he would slip back, conscious and nervously smiling; his sister was ill, and he should have to defer his voyage until spring.

Matters went steadily worse with Paul at school. In the itch to let his instructors know how heartily he despised them and their homilies, and how thoroughly he was appreciated elsewhere, he mentioned once or twice that he had no time to fool with theorems; adding—with a twitch of the eyebrows and a touch of that nervous bravado which so perplexed them—that he was helping the people down at the stock company; they were old friends of his.

The upshot of the matter was that the Principal went to Paul's father, and Paul was taken out of school and put to work. The manager at Carnegie Hall was told to get another usher in his stead; the door-keeper at the theater was warned not to admit him to the house; and Charley Edwards remorsefully promised the boy's father not to see him again.

The members of the stock company were vastly amused when some of Paul's stories reached them—especially the women. They were hard-working women, most of them supporting indigent husbands or brothers, and they laughed rather bitterly at having stirred the boy to such fervid and florid inventions. They agreed with the faculty and with his father that Paul's was a bad case.

The eastbound train was plowing through a January snowstorm; the dull dawn was beginning to show gray when the engine whistled a mile out of Newark. Paul started up from the seat where he had lain curled in uneasy slumber, rubbed the breath-misted window glass with his hand, and peered out. The snow was whirling in curling eddies above the white bottom lands, and the drifts lay already deep in the fields and along the fences, while here and there the long dead grass and dried weed stalks protruded black above it. Lights shone from the scattered houses, and a gang of laborers who stood beside the track waved their lanterns.

Paul had slept very little, and he felt grimy and uncomfortable. He had made the all-night journey in a day coach, partly because he was ashamed, dressed as he was, to go into a Pullman, and partly because he was afraid of being seen there by some Pittsburgh businessman, who might have noticed him in Denny & Carson's office. When the whistle awoke him, he clutched quickly at his breast pocket, glancing about him with an uncertain smile. But the little, clay-bespattered Italians were still sleeping, the slatternly women across the aisle were in open-

mouthed oblivion, and even the crumby, crying babies were for the
nonce stilled. Paul settled back to struggle with his impatience as best
he could.

When he arrived at the Jersey City station he hurried through his
breakfast, manifestly ill at ease and keeping a sharp eye about him.
After he reached the Twenty-third Street station, he consulted a cabman
and had himself driven to a men's furnishings establishment that was
just opening for the day. He spent upward of two hours there, buying
with endless reconsidering and great care. His new street suit he put on
in the fitting room; the frock coat and dress clothes he had bundled
into the cab with his linen. Then he drove to a hatter's and a shoe
house. His next errand was at Tiffany's, where he selected his silver
and a new scarf pin. He would not wait to have his silver marked, he
said. Lastly, he stopped at a trunk shop on Broadway and had his
purchases packed into various traveling bags.

It was a little after one o'clock when he drove up to the Waldorf,
and after settling with the cabman, went into the office. He registered
from Washington; said his mother and father had been abroad, and that
he had come down to await the arrival of their steamer. He told his
story plausibly and had no trouble, since he volunteered to pay for them
in advance, in engaging his rooms; a sleeping room, sitting room, and
bath.

Not once, but a hundred times, Paul had planned this entry into
New York. He had gone over every detail of it with Charley Edwards,
and in his scapbook at home there were pages of description about New
York hotels, cut from the Sunday papers. When he was shown to his
sitting room on the eighth floor he saw at a glance that everything was
as it should be; there was but one detail in his mental picture that the
place did, not realize, so he rang for the bellboy and sent him down for
flowers. He moved about nervously until the boy returned, putting away
his new linen and fingering it delightedly as he did so. When the flowers
came he put them hastily into water, and then tumbled into a hot bath.
Presently he came out of his white bathroom, resplendent in his new
silk underwear, and playing with the tassels of his red robe. The snow
was whirling so fiercely outside his windows that he could scarcely see
across the street, but within the air was deliciously soft and fragrant.
He put the violets and jonquils on the taboret beside the couch, and
threw himself down, with a long sigh, covering himself with a Roman
blanket. He was thoroughly tired; he had been in such haste, he had
stood up to such a strain, covered so much ground in the last twenty-
four hours, that he wanted to think how it had all come about. Lulled
by the sound of the wind, the warm air, and the cool fragrance of the
flowers, he sank into deep, drowsy retrospection.

It had been wonderfully simple; when they had shut him out of the
theater and concert hall, when they had taken away his bone, the whole
thing was virtually determined. The rest was a mere matter of oppor-

tunity. The only thing that at all surprised him was his own courage— for he realized well enough that he had always been tormented by fear, a sort of apprehensive dread that, of late years, as the meshes of the lies he had told closed about him, had been pulling the muscles of his body tighter and tighter. Until now he could not remember the time when he had not been dreading something. Even when he was a little boy it was always there—behind him, or before, or on either side. There had always been the shadowed corner, the dark place into which he dared not look, but from which something seemed always to be watching him—and Paul had done things that were not pretty to watch, he knew.

But now he had a curious sense of relief, as though he had at last thrown down the gauntlet to the thing in the corner.

Yet it was but a day since he had been sulking in the traces; but yesterday afternoon that he had been sent to the bank with Denny & Carson's deposit, as usual—but this time he was instructed to leave the book to be balanced. There was above two thousand dollars in checks, and nearly a thousand in the bank notes which he had taken from the book and quietly transferred to his pocket. At the bank he had made out a new deposit slip. His nerves had been steady enough to permit of his returning to the office, where he had finished his work and asked for a full day's holiday tomorrow, Saturday, giving a perfectly reasonable pretext. The bankbook, he knew, would not be returned before Monday or Tuesday, and his father would be out of town for the next week. From the time he slipped the bank notes into his pocket until he boarded the night train for New York, he had not known a moment's hesitation. It was not the first time Paul had steered through treacherous waters.

How astonishingly easy it had all been; here he was, the thing done; and this time there would be no awakening, no figure at the top of the stairs. He watched the snowflakes whirling by his window until he fell asleep.

When he awoke, it was three o'clock in the afternoon. He bounded up with a start; half of one of his precious days gone already! He spent more than an hour in dressing, watching every stage of his toilet carefully in the mirror. Everything was quite perfect; he was exactly the kind of boy he had always wanted to be.

When he went downstairs Paul took a carriage and drove up Fifth Avenue toward the Park. The snow had somewhat abated; carriages and tradesmen's wagons were hurrying soundlessly to and fro in the winter twilight; boys in woolen mufflers were shoveling off the doorsteps; the avenue stages made fine spots of color against the white street. Here and there on the corners were stands, with whole flower gardens blooming under glass cases, against the sides of which the snowflakes stuck and melted; violets, roses, carnations, lilies of the valley—somehow vastly more lovely and alluring that they blossomed thus unnaturally in the snow. The Park itself was a wonderful stage winter-piece.

When he returned, the pause of the twilight had ceased and the tune of the streets had changed. The snow was falling faster, lights streamed from the hotels that reared their dozen stories fearlessly up into the storm, defying the raging Atlantic winds. A long, black stream of carriages poured down the avenue, intersected here and there by other streams, tending horizontally. There were a score of cabs about the entrance of his hotel, and his driver had to wait. Boys in livery were running in and out of the awning stretched across the sidewalk, up and down the red velvet carpet laid from the door to the street. Above, about, within it all was the rumble and roar, the hurry and toss of thousands of human beings as hot for pleasure as himself, and on every side of him towered the glaring affirmation of the omnipotence of wealth.

The boy set his teeth and drew his shoulders together in a spasm of realization; the plot of all dramas, the text of all romances, the nerve-stuff of all sensations was whirling about him like the snowflakes. He burnt like a faggot in a tempest.

When Paul went down to dinner the music of the orchestra came floating up the elevator shaft to greet him. His head whirled as he stepped into the thronged corridor, and he sank back into one of the chairs against the wall to get his breath. The lights, the chatter, the perfumes, the bewildering medley of color—he had, for a moment, the feeling of not being able to stand it. But only for a moment; these were his own people, he told himself. He went slowly about the corridors, through the writing rooms, smoking rooms, reception rooms, as though he were exploring the chambers of an enchanted palace, built and peopled for him alone.

When he reached the dining room he sat down at a table near a window. The flowers, the white linen, the many-colored wineglasses, the gay toilettes of the women, the low popping of corks, the undulating repetitions of the *Blue Danube* from the orchestra, all flooded Paul's dream with bewildering radiance. When the roseate tinge of his champagne was added—that cold, precious, bubbling stuff that creamed and foamed in his glass—Paul wondered that there were honest men in the world at all. This was what all the world was fighting for, he reflected; this was what all the struggle was about. He doubted the reality of his past. Had he ever known a place called Cordelia Street, a place where fagged-looking businessmen got on the early car; mere rivets in a machine they seemed to Paul,—sickening men, with combings of children's hair always hanging to their coats, and the smell of cooking in their clothes. Cordelia Street—Ah, that belonged to another time and country; had he not always been thus, had he not sat here night after night, from as far back as he could remember, looking pensively over just such shimmering textures and slowly twirling the stem of a glass like this one between his thumb and middle finger? He rather thought he had.

He was not in the least abashed or lonely. He had no especial desire to meet or to know any of these people; all he demanded was the right to look on and conjecture, to watch the pageant. The mere stage properties were all he contended for. Nor was he lonely later in the evening, in his lodge at the Metropolitan. He was now entirely rid of his nervous misgivings, of his forced aggressiveness, of the imperative desire to show himself different from his surroundings. He felt now that his surroundings explained him. Nobody questioned the purple; he had only to wear it passively. He had only to glance down at his attire to reassure himself that here it would be impossible for anyone to humiliate him.

He found it hard to leave his beautiful sitting-room to go to bed that night, and sat long watching the raging storm from his turret window. When he went to sleep it was with the lights turned on in his bedroom; partly because of his old timidity, and partly so that, if he should wake in the night, there would be no wretched moment of doubt, no horrible suspicion of yellow wallpaper, or of Washington and Calvin above his bed.

Sunday morning the city was practically snowbound. Paul breakfasted late, and in the afternoon he fell in with a wild San Francisco boy, a freshman at Yale, who said he had run down for a "little flyer" over Sunday. The young man offered to show Paul the night side of the town, and the two boys went out together after dinner, not returning to the hotel until seven o'clock the next morning. They had started out in the confiding warmth of a champagne friendship, but their parting in the elevator was singularly cool. The freshman pulled himself together to make his train, and Paul went to bed. He awoke at two o'clock in the afternoon, very thirsty and dizzy, and rang for ice-water, coffee, and the Pittsburgh papers.

On the part of the hotel management, Paul excited no suspicion. There was this to be said for him, that he wore his spoils with dignity and in no way made himself conspicuous. Even under the glow of his wine he was never boisterous, though he found the stuff like a magician's wand for wonder-building. His chief greediness lay in his ears and eyes, and his excesses were not offensive ones. His dearest pleasures were the gray winter twilights in his sitting room; his quiet enjoyment of his flowers, his clothes, his wide divan, his cigarette, and his sense of power. He could not remember a time when he had felt so at peace with himself. The mere release from the necessity of petty lying, lying every day and every day, restored his self-respect. He had never lied for pleasure, even at school; but to be noticed and admired, to assert his difference from other Cordelia Street boys; and he felt a good deal more manly, more honest, even, now that he had no need for boastful pretensions, now that he could, as his actor friends used to say, "dress the part." It was characteristic that remorse did not occur to him. His golden days went by without a shadow, and he made each as perfect as he could.

On the eighth day after his arrival in New York he found the whole affair exploited in the Pittsburgh papers, exploited with a wealth of detail which indicated that local news of a sensational nature was at a low ebb. The firm of Denny & Carson announced that the boy's father had refunded the full amount of the theft and that they had no intention of prosecuting. The Cumberland minister had been interviewed, and expressed his hope of yet reclaiming the motherless lad, and his Sabbath-school teacher declared that she would spare no effort to that end. The rumor had reached Pittsburgh that the boy had been seen in a New York hotel, and his father had gone East to find him and bring him home.

Paul had just come in to dress for dinner; he sank into a chair, weak to the knees, and clasped his head in his hands. It was to be worse than jail, even; the tepid waters of Cordelia Street were to close over him finally and forever. The gray monotony stretched before him in hopeless unrelieved years; Sabbath school, Young People's Meeting, the yellow-papered room, the damp dishtowels; it all rushed back upon him with a sickening vividness. He had the old feeling that the orchestra had suddenly stopped; the sinking sensation that the play was over. The sweat broke out on his face, and he sprang to his feet, looked about him with his white, conscious smile, and winked at himself in the mirror. With something of the old childish belief in miracles with which he had so often gone to class, all his lessons unlearned, Paul dressed and dashed whistling down the corridor to the elevator.

He had no sooner entered the dining room and caught the measure of the music than his remembrance was lightened by his old elastic power of claiming the moment, mounting with it, and finding it all sufficient. The glare and glitter about him, the mere scenic accessories had again, and for the last time, their old potency. He would show himself that he was game, he would finish the thing splendidly. He doubted, more than ever, the existence of Cordelia Street, and for the first time he drank his wine recklessly. Was he not, after all, one of those fortunate beings born to the purple, was he not still himself and in his own place? He drummed a nervous accompaniment to the Pagliacci music and looked about him, telling himself over and over that it had paid.

He reflected drowsily, to the swell of the music and the chill sweetness of his wine, that he might have done it more wisely. He might have caught an outbound steamer and been well out of their clutches before now. But the other side of the world had seemed too far away and too uncertain then; he could not have waited for it; his need had been too sharp. If he had to choose over again, he would do the same thing tomorrow. He looked affectionately about the dining room, now gilded with a soft mist. Ah, it had paid indeed!

Paul was awakened next morning by a painful throbbing in his head and feet. He had thrown himself across the bed without undressing, and had slept with his shoes on. His limbs and hands were lead heavy, and his tongue and throat were parched and burnt. There came upon him one of those fateful attacks of clearheadedness that never occurred except when he was physically exhausted and his nerves hung loose. He lay still, closed his eyes, and let the tide of things wash over him.

His father was in New York; "stopping at some joint or other," he told himself. The memory of successive summers on the front stoop fell upon him like a weight of black water. He had not a hundred dollars left; and he knew now, more than ever, that money was everything, the wall that stood between all he loathed and all he wanted. The thing was winding itself up; he had thought of that on his first glorious day in New York, and had even provided a way to snap the thread. It lay on his dressing table now: he had got it out last night when he came blindly up from dinner, but the shiny metal hurt his eyes, and he disliked the looks of it.

He rose and moved about with a painful effort, succumbing now and again to attacks of nausea. It was the old depression exaggerated; all the world had become Cordelia Street. Yet somehow he was not afraid of anything, was absolutely calm; perhaps because he had looked into the dark corner at last and knew. It was bad enough, what he saw there, but somehow not so bad as his long fear of it had been. He saw everything clearly now. He had a feeling that he had made the best of it, that he had lived the sort of life he was meant to live, and for half an hour he sat staring at the revolver. But he told himself that was not the way, so he went downstairs and took a cab to the ferry.

When Paul arrived at Newark he got off the train and took another cab, directing the driver to follow the Pennsylvania tracks out of the town. The snow lay heavy on the roadways and had drifted deep in the open fields. Only here and there the dead grass or dried weed stalks projected, singularly black, above it. Once well into the country, Paul dismissed the carriage and walked, floundering along the tracks, his mind a medley of irrelevant things. He seemed to hold in his brain an actual picture of everything he had seen that morning. He remembered every feature of both his drivers, of the toothless old woman from whom he had bought the red flowers in his coat, the agent from whom he had got his ticket, and all of his fellow passengers on the ferry. His mind, unable to cope with vital matters near at hand, worked feverishly and deftly at sorting and grouping these images. They made for him a part of the ugliness of the world, of the ache in his head, and the bitter burning on his tongue. He stooped and put a handful of snow into his mouth as he walked, but that, too, seemed hot. When he reached a little hillside, where the tracks ran through a cut some twenty feet below him, he stopped and sat down.

The carnations in his coat were drooping with the cold, he noticed, their red glory all over. It occurred to him that all the flowers he had seen in the glass cases that first night must have gone the same way, long before this. It was only one splendid breath they had, in spite of their brave mockery at the winter outside the glass; and it was a losing

game in the end, it seemed, this revolt against the homilies by which
the world is run. Paul took one of the blossoms carefully from his coat
and scooped a little hole in the snow, where he covered it up. Then he
dozed a while, from his weak condition, seemingly insensible to the cold.

The sound of an approaching train awoke him, and he started to
his feet, remembering only his resolution, and afraid lest he should be
too late. He stood watching the approaching locomotive, his teeth
chattering, his lips drawn away from them in a frightened smile; once
or twice he glanced nervously sidewise, as though he were being
watched. When the right moment came, he jumped. As he fell, the folly
of his haste occurred to him with merciless clearness, the vastness of
what he had left undone. There flashed through his brain, clearer than
ever before, the blue of Adriatic water, the yellow of Algerian sands.

He felt something strike his chest, and that his body was being
thrown swiftly through the air, on and on, immeasurably far and fast,
while his limbs were gently relaxed. Then, because the picture-making
mechanism was crushed, the disturbing visions flashed into black, and
Paul dropped back into the immense design of things.

SHERWOOD ANDERSON (1876–1941)

*It seems now that he really wanted to be a myth rather than simply a
man; or perhaps he felt that if he was to be a man at all he had
first to create a myth of himself. At any rate, in book after book,
both autobiographical fiction and fictionalized autobiography, he
gave out the same legend: how, one day, unable any longer to put
up with his life as a businessman, he walked out of that life, out
of his marriage, his home, his constrictive office, his town, into the
freedom of a new life as artist. All nonsense; or to be less harsh, all
metaphor.*

*Born to a harried mother and a shiftless father in Camden, Ohio, he
spent his early years wandering from town to town, acquiring a
hit-and-miss education that ended after one year of high school at
fourteen, when his mother died (except, later, for one attempted
year at the Wittenberg Academy), living by odd jobs that finally
took him to Chicago and work in a cold-storage warehouse. From
that repellent employment he enlisted in the Army during the
Spanish-American War but saw no service; returned to Ohio to work
on a farm; returned to Chicago, where he drifted into advertising,
writing copy that glorified the "adventure" of business. He married,
then became the president of a mail-order firm in Cleveland, and
finally bought a paint company in Elyria, Ohio, an enterprising
family man determined to succeed and writing the ads for his
product called "Roof-Fix." In about 1910 he tried another kind of
writing, short fictional sketches, and by 1912 he had written drafts*

of two novels. An increasing conflict between his business efforts and his literary ambitions drove him to drink and to loose women and finally into a nervous breakdown. It was in that state of collapse that, on the great day of liberation, he presumably walked out of his office into the free creative life. Four days later he was found wandering around Cleveland—haggard, bewildered, suffering from aphasia. He was returned to Elyria, and in the next year he did indeed sell his business; but he went back to Chicago and back into advertising, and he stayed with that activity for the next ten years.

His brother, a painter, introduced him to some of the Chicago writers, and it was one of them, Floyd Dell, whose efforts found publishers for those first two novels, Windy McPherson's Son (1916) and Marching Men (1917). In the Chicago literary circle, he had met Margaret Anderson. He was at work on the pieces that would make up Winesburg, Ohio, to be published in 1919, and in the years immediately before, a number of the seperate sketches appeared in her magazine, The Little Review. The publication of this book about the frustrations of the bewildered grotesques who inhabit a decaying American village marked the height of his achievement, and he was still three years away from his liberation from business.

In 1920 he published his best novel, Poor White, and that, too, is an uneven performance. Chafing to leave his second wife, he began work on Many Marriages (1922), which is about a man who wants to escape the routine of business. Then he did leave her and presently married a third, and there was to be a fourth. In 1922 he began his wandering life. Except for a few remarkable stories of that decade, his work in fiction continued to decline. In spite of the popular success of Dark Laughter (1925), it is a foolish novel. He simply did not possess the kind of orderly imagination that could cope with the sustained demands of a long fictional form.

In the middle 1920s he moved to Marian, Virginia, where he bought and edited the two local newspapers, one Republican, the other Democratic. This is characteristic of Anderson's own permanently inconclusive state of mind. He was always asking questions, usually large woolly ones about the meaning of life, questions which he was quite incapable of answering. He had, to be sure, a central thesis, and a perfectly good one, that is, the sterilizing influence of a commercial industrial culture on the individual emotional life. His later work, half-fictionalized autobiographical reminiscences, continued to circle around this proposition. An enormous selection from his endless notebooks and other autobiographical reflections, the bulk of which will presumably remain in manuscript, was published in 1969 under the title Sherwood Anderson's Memoirs. Over and over it forces the suggestion upon us that his very resistance to brisk American efficiencies led him to adopt the role of a sleepwalker.

FURTHER READING

Sherwood Anderson's Memoirs (1969), edited by Ray Lewis White, and *Letters of Sherwood Anderson* (1953), edited by Howard Mumford Jones and Walter B. Rideout, are central sources for the study of Anderson's life. The chief critical studies are Irving Howe, *Sherwood Anderson* (1951); James E. Schevill, *Sherwood Anderson: His Life and Work* (1951); Brom Weber, *Sherwood Anderson* (1964); and Rex Burbank, *Sherwood Anderson* (1964). Ray Lewis White also edited *The Achievement of Sherwood Anderson: Essays in Criticism* (1966).

FROM **Winesburg, Ohio** *(1919)*

The Strength of God (Concerning the Reverend Curtis Hartman)

The Reverend Curtis Hartman was pastor of the Presbyterian Church of Winesburg, and had been in that position ten years. He was forty years old, and by his nature very silent and reticent. To preach, standing in the pulpit before the people, was always a hardship for him and from Wednesday morning until Saturday evening he thought of nothing but the two sermons that must be preached on Sunday. Early on Sunday morning he went into a little room called a study in the bell tower of the church and prayed. In his prayers there was one note that always predominated. "Give me strength and courage for Thy work, O Lord!" he pled, kneeling on the bare floor and bowing his head in the presence of the task that lay before him.

The Reverend Hartman was a tall man with a brown beard. His wife, a stout, nervous woman, was the daughter of a manufacturer of underwear at Cleveland, Ohio. The minister himself was rather a favorite in the town. The elders of the church liked him because he was quiet and unpretentious and Mrs. White, the banker's wife, thought him scholarly and refined.

The Presbyterian Church held itself somewhat aloof from the other churches of Winesburg. It was larger and more imposing and its minister was better paid. He even had a carriage of his own and on summer evenings sometimes drove about town with his wife. Through Main Street and up and down Buckeye Street he went, bowing gravely to the people, while his wife, afire with secret pride, looked at him out of the corners of her eyes and worried lest the horse become frightened and run away.

For a good many years after he came to Winesburg things went well with Curtis Hartman. He was not one to arouse keen enthusiasm among the worshippers in his church but on the other hand he made no enemies. In reality he was much in earnest and sometimes suffered prolonged periods of remorse because he could not go crying the word of God in the highways and byways of the town. He wondered if the flame of the spirit really burned in him and dreamed of a day when a strong sweet new current of power would come like a great wind into his voice and his soul and the people would tremble before the spirit of God made manifest in him. "I am a poor stick and that will never really happen to me," he mused dejectedly and then a patient smile lit up his features. "Oh well, I suppose I'm doing well enough," he added philosophically.

The room in the bell tower of the church, where on Sunday mornings the minister prayed for an increase in him of the power of God, had but one window. It was long and narrow and swung outward on a hinge like a door. On the window, made of little leaded panes, was a design showing the Christ laying his hand upon the head of a child. One Sunday morning in the summer as he sat by his desk in the room with a large Bible opened before him, and the sheets of his sermon scattered about, the minister was shocked to see, in the upper room of the house next door, a woman lying in her bed and smoking a cigarette while she read a book. Curtis Hartman went on tiptoe to the window and closed it softly. He was horror stricken at the thought of a woman smoking and trembled also to think that his eyes, just raised from the pages of the book of God, had looked upon the bare shoulders and white throat of a woman. With his brain in a whirl he went down into the pulpit and preached a long sermon without once thinking of his gestures or his voice. The sermon attracted unusual attention because of its power and clearness. "I wonder if she is listening, if my voice is carrying a message into her soul," he thought and began to hope that on future Sunday mornings he might be able to say words that would touch and awaken the woman apparently far gone in secret sin.

The house next door to the Presbyterian Church, through the windows of which the minister had seen the sight that had so upset him, was occupied by two women. Aunt Elizabeth Swift, a gray competent-looking widow with money in the Winesburg National Bank, lived there with her daughter Kate Swift, a school teacher. The school teacher was thirty years old and had a neat trim-looking figure. She had few friends and bore a reputation of having a sharp tongue. When he began to think about her, Curtis Hartman remembered that she had been to Europe and had lived for two years in New York City. "Perhaps after all her smoking means nothing," he thought. He began to remember that when he was a student in college and occasionally read novels, good, although somewhat worldly women, had smoked through the pages of a book that had once fallen into his hands. With a rush of new determination he worked on his sermons all through the week and forgot, in his zeal to reach the ears and the soul of this new listener, both his embarrassment in the pulpit and the necessity of prayer in the study on Sunday mornings.

Reverend Hartman's experience with women had been somewhat limited. He was the son of a wagon maker from Muncie, Indiana, and had worked his way through college. The daughter of the underwear manufacturer had boarded in a house where he lived during his school days and he had married her after a formal and prolonged courtship, carried on for the most part by the girl herself. On his marriage day the underwear manufacturer had given his daughter five thousand dollars and he promised to leave her at least twice that amount in his will. The minister had thought himself fortunate in marriage and had never permitted himself to think of other women. He did not want to think of other women. What he wanted was to do the work of God quietly and earnestly.

In the soul of the minister a struggle awoke. From wanting to reach the ears of Kate Swift, and through his sermons to delve into her soul, he began to want also to look again at the figure lying white and quiet in the bed. On a Sunday morning when he could not sleep because of his thoughts he arose and went to walk in the streets. When he had gone along Main Street almost to the old Richmond place he stopped and picking up a stone rushed off to the room in the bell tower. With the stone he broke out a corner of the window and then locked the door and sat down at the desk before the open Bible to wait. When the shade of the window to Kate Swift's room was raised he could see, through the hole, directly into her bed, but she was not there. She also had arisen and had gone for a walk and the hand that raised the shade was the hand of Aunt Elizabeth Swift.

The minister almost wept with joy at this deliverance from the carnal desire to "peep" and went back to his own house praising God. In an ill moment he forgot, however, to stop the hole in the window. The piece of glass broken out of the corner of the window just nipped off the bare heel of the boy standing motionless and looking with rapt eyes into the face of Christ.

Curtis Hartman forgot his sermon on that Sunday morning. He talked to his congregation and in his talk said that it was a mistake for people to think of their minister as a man set aside and intended by nature to lead a blameless life. "Out of my own experience I know that we, who are the ministers of God's word, are beset by the same temptations that assail you," he declared. "I have been tempted and have surrendered to temptation. It is only the hand of God, placed beneath my head, that has raised me up. As he has raised me so also will he raise you. Do not despair. In your hour of sin raise your eyes to the skies and you will be again and again saved."

Resolutely the minister put the thoughts of the woman in the bed out of his mind and began to be something like a lover in the presence of his wife. One evening when they drove out together he turned the horse out of Buckeye Street and in the darkness on Gospel Hill, above Waterworks Pond, put his arm about Sarah Hartman's waist. When he

had eaten breakfast in the morning and was ready to retire to his study
at the back of his house he went around the table and kissed his wife
on the cheek. When thoughts of Kate Swift came into his head, he
smiled and raised his eyes to the skies. "Intercede for me, Master," he
muttered, "keep me in the narrow path intent on Thy work."

And now began the real struggle in the soul of the brown-bearded
minister. By chance he discovered that Kate Swift was in the habit of
lying in her bed in the evenings and reading a book. A lamp stood on a
table by the side of the bed and the light streamed down upon her white
shoulders and bare throat. On the evening when he made the discovery
the minister sat at the desk in the study from nine until after eleven
and when her light was put out stumbled out of the church to spend
two more hours walking and praying in the streets. He did not want to
kiss the shoulders and the throat of Kate Swift and had not allowed his
mind to dwell on such thoughts. He did not know what he wanted. "I
am God's child and he must save me from myself," he cried, in the
darkness under the trees as he wandered in the streets. By a tree he
stood and looked at the sky that was covered with hurrying clouds. He
began to talk to God intimately and closely. "Please, Father, do not
forget me. Give me power to go tomorrow and repair the hole in the
window. Lift my eyes again to the skies. Stay with me, Thy servant, in
his hour of need."

Up and down through the silent streets walked the minister and
for days and weeks his soul was troubled. He could not understand the
temptation that had come to him nor could he fathom the reason for its
coming. In a way he began to blame God, saying to himself that he had
tried to keep his feet in the true path and had not run about seeking sin.
"Through my days as a young man and all through my life here I have
gone quietly about my work," he declared. "Why now should I be
tempted? What have I done that this burden should be laid on me?"

Three times during the early fall and winter of that year Curtis
Hartman crept out of his house to the room in the bell tower to sit in
the darkness looking at the figure of Kate Swift lying in her bed and
later went to walk and pray in the streets. He could not understand
himself. For weeks he would go along scarcely thinking of the school
teacher and telling himself that he had conquered the carnal desire to
look at her body. And then something would happen. As he sat in the
study of his own house, hard at work on a sermon, he would become
nervous and begin to walk up and down the room. "I will go out into
the streets," he told himself and even as he let himself in at the church
door he persistently denied to himself the cause of his being there. "I
will not repair the hole in the window and I will train myself to come
here at night and sit in the presence of this woman without raising my
eyes. I will not be defeated in this thing. The Lord has devised this
temptation as a test of my soul and I will grope my way out of darkness
into the light of righteousness."

One night in January when it was bitter cold and snow lay deep on the streets of Winesburg Curtis Hartman paid his last visit to the room in the bell tower of the church. It was past nine o'clock when he left his own house and he set out so hurriedy that he forgot to put on his over-shoes. In Main Street no one was abroad but Hop Higgins the night watchman and in the whole town no one was awake but the watchman and young George Willard, who sat in the office of the *Winesburg Eagle* trying to write a story. Along the street to the church went the minister, plowing through the drifts and thinking that this time he would utterly give way to sin. "I want to look at the woman and to think of kissing her shoulders and I am going to let myself think what I choose," he declared bitterly and tears came into his eyes. He began to think that he would get out of the ministry and try some other way of life. "I shall go to some city and get into business," he declared. "If my nature is such that I cannot resist sin, I shall give myself over to sin. At least I shall not be a hypocrite, preaching the word of God with my mind thinking of the shoulders and neck of a woman who does not belong to me."

It was cold in the room of the bell tower of the church on that January night and almost as soon as he came into the room Curtis Hartman knew that if he stayed he would be ill. His feet were wet from tramping in the snow and there was no fire. In the room in the house next door Kate Swift had not yet appeared. With grim determination the man sat down to wait. Sitting in the chair and gripping the edge of the desk on which lay the Bible he stared into the darkness thinking the blackest thoughts of his life. He thought of his wife and for the moment almost hated her. "She has always been ashamed of passion and has cheated me," he thought. "Man has a right to expect living passion and beauty in a woman. He has no right to forget that he is an animal and in me there is something that is Greek. I will throw off the woman of my bosom and seek other women. I will besiege this school teacher. I will fly in the face of all men and if I am a creature of carnal lusts I will live then for my lusts."

The distracted man trembled from head to foot, partly from cold, partly from the struggle in which he was engaged. Hours passed and a fever assailed his body. His throat began to hurt and his teeth chattered. His feet on the study floor felt like two cakes of ice. Still he would not give up. "I will see this woman and will think the thoughts I have never dared to think," he told himself, gripping the edge of the desk and waiting.

Curtis Hartman came near dying from the effects of that night of waiting in the church, and also he found in the thing that happened what he took to be the way of life for him. On other evenings when he had waited he had not been able to see, through the little hole in the glass, any part of the school teacher's room except that occupied by her bed. In the darkness he had waited until the woman suddenly appeared sitting in the bed in her white night-robe. When the light was turned

up she propped herself up among the pillows and read a book. Sometimes she smoked one of the cigarettes. Only her bare shoulders and
throat were visible.

On the January night, after he had come near dying with cold and
after his mind had two or three times actually slipped away into an odd
land of fantasy so that he had by an exercise of will power to force
himself back into consciousness, Kate Swift appeared. In the room next
door a lamp was lighted and the waiting man stared into an empty bed.
Then upon the bed before his eyes a naked woman threw herself. Lying
face downward she wept and beat with her fists upon the pillow. With a
final outburst of weeping she half arose, and in the presence of the man
who had waited to look and to think thoughts the woman of sin began
to pray. In the lamplight her figure, slim and strong, looked like the
figure of the boy in the presence of the Christ on the leaded window.

Curtis Hartman never remembered how he got out of the church.
With a cry he arose, dragging the heavy desk along the floor. The Bible
fell, making a great clatter in the silence. When the light in the house
next door went out he stumbled down the stairway and into the street.
Along the street he went and ran in at the door of the *Winesburg Eagle*.
To George Willard, who was tramping up and down in the office undergoing a struggle of his own, he began to talk half-incoherently. "The
ways of God are beyond human understanding," he cried, running in
quickly and closing the door. He began to advance upon the young man,
his eyes glowing and his voice ringing with fervor. "I have found the
light," he cried. "After ten years in this town, God has manifested himself to me in the body of a woman." His voice dropped and he began to
whisper. "I did not understand," he said. "What I took to be a trial of my
soul was only a preparation for a new and more beautiful fervor of the
spirit. God has appeared to me in the person of Kate Swift, the school
teacher, kneeling naked on a bed. Do you know Kate Swift? Although
she may not be aware of it, she is an instrument of God, bearing the
message of truth."

Reverend Curtis Hartman turned and ran out of the office. At the
door he stopped, and after looking up and down the deserted street,
turned again to George Willard. "I am delivered. Have no fear." He held
up a bleeding fist for the young man to see. "I smashed the glass of the
window," he cried. "Now it will have to be wholly replaced. The strength
of God was in me and I broke it with my fist."

The Teacher (Concerning Kate Swift)

Snow lay deep in the streets of Winesburg. It had begun to snow
about ten o'clock in the morning and a wind sprang up and blew the
snow in clouds along Main Street. The frozen mud roads that led into
town were fairly smooth and in places ice covered the mud. "There will
be good sleighing," said Will Henderson, standing by the bar in Ed

Griffith's saloon. Out of the saloon he went and met Sylvester West the druggist stumbling along in the kind of heavy overshoes called arctics. "Snow will bring the people into town on Saturday," said the druggist. The two men stopped and discussed their affairs. Will Henderson, who had on a light overcoat and no overshoes, kicked the heel of his left foot with the toe of the right. "Snow will be good for the wheat," observed the druggist sagely.

Young George Willard, who had nothing to do, was glad because he did not feel like working that day. The weekly paper had been printed and taken to the post office on Wednesday evening and the snow began to fall on Thursday. At eight o'clock, after the morning train had passed, he put a pair of skates in his pocket and went up to Waterworks Pond but did not go skating. Past the pond and along a path that followed Wine Creek he went until he came to a grove of beech trees. There he built a fire against the side of a log and sat down at the end of the log to think. When the snow began to fall and the wind to blow he hurried about getting fuel for the fire.

The young reporter was thinking of Kate Swift who had once been his school teacher. On the evening before he had gone to her house to get a book she wanted him to read and had been alone with her for an hour. For the fourth or fifth time the woman had talked to him with great earnestness and he could not make out what she meant by her talk. He began to believe she might be in love with him and the thought was both pleasing and annoying.

Up from the log he sprang and began to pile sticks on the fire. Looking about to be sure he was alone he talked aloud pretending he was in the presence of the woman. "Oh, you're just letting on, you know you are," he declared. "I am going to find out about you. You wait and see."

The young man got up and went back along the path toward town leaving the fire blazing in the wood. As he went through the streets the skates clanked in his pocket. In his own room in the New Willard House he built a fire in the stove and lay down on top of the bed. He began to have lustful thoughts and pulling down the shade of the window closed his eyes and turned his face to the wall. He took a pillow into his arms and embraced it thinking first of the school teacher, who by her words had stirred something within him and later of Helen White, the slim daughter of the town banker, with whom he had been for a long time half in love.

By nine o'clock of that evening snow lay deep in the streets and the weather had become bitter cold. It was difficult to walk about. The stores were dark and the people had crawled away to their houses. The evening train from Cleveland was very late but nobody was interested in its arrival. By ten o'clock all but four of the eighteen hundred citizens of the town were in bed.

Hop Higgins, the night watchman, was partially awake. He was lame and carried a heavy stick. On dark nights he carried a lantern. Between nine and ten o'clock he went his rounds. Up and down Main Street he stumbled through the drifts trying the doors of the stores. Then he went into alleyways and tried the back doors. Finding all tight he hurried around the corner to the New Willard House and beat on the door. Through the rest of the night he intended to stay by the stove. "You go to bed. I'll keep the stove going," he said to the boy who slept on a cot in the hotel office.

Hop Higgins sat down by the stove and took off his shoes. When the boy had gone to sleep he began to think of his own affairs. He intended to paint his house in the spring and sat by the stove calculating the cost of paint and labor. That led him into other calculations. The night watchman was sixty years old and wanted to retire. He had been a soldier in the Civil War and drew a small pension. He hoped to find some new method of making a living and aspired to become a professional breeder of ferrets. Already he had four of the strangely shaped savage little creatures, that are used by sportsmen in the pursuit of rabbits, in the cellar of his house. "Now I have one male and three females," he mused. "If I am lucky by spring I shall have twelve or fifteen. In another year I shall be able to begin advertising ferrets for sale in the sporting papers."

The night watchman settled into his chair and his mind became a blank. He did not sleep. By years of practice he had trained himself to sit for hours through the long nights neither asleep nor awake. In the morning he was almost as refreshed as though he had slept.

With Hop Higgins safely stowed away in the chair behind the stove only three people were awake in Winesburg. George Willard was in the office of the *Eagle* pretending to be at work on the writing of a story but in reality continuing the mood of the morning by the fire in the wood. In the bell tower of the Presbyterian Church the Reverend Curtis Hartman was sitting in the darkness preparing himself for a revelation from God, and Kate Swift, the school teacher, was leaving her house for a walk in the storm.

It was past ten o'clock when Kate Swift set out and the walk was unpremeditated. It was as though the man and the boy, by thinking of her, had driven her forth into the wintry streets. Aunt Elizabeth Swift had gone to the county seat concerning some business in connection with mortgages in which she had money invested and would not be back until the next day. By a huge stove, called a base burner, in the living room of the house sat the daughter reading a book. Suddenly she sprang to her feet and, snatching a cloak from a rack by the front door, ran out of the house.

At the age of thirty Kate Swift was not known in Winesburg as a pretty woman. Her complexion was not good and her face was covered with blotches that indicated ill health. Alone in the night in the winter streets she was lovely. Her back was straight, her shoulders square and her features were as the features of a tiny goddess on a pedestal in a garden in the dim light of a summer evening.

During the afternoon the school teacher had been to see Dr. Welling concerning her health. The doctor had scolded her and had declared she was in danger of losing her hearing. It was foolish for Kate Swift to be abroad in the storm, foolish and perhaps dangerous.

The woman in the streets did not remember the words of the doctor and would not have turned back had she remembered. She was very cold but after walking for five minutes no longer minded the cold. First she went to the end of her own street and then across a pair of hay scales set in the ground before a feed barn and into Trunion Pike. Along Trunion Pike she went to Ned Winter's barn and turning east followed a street of low frame houses that led over Gospel Hill and into Sucker Road that ran down a shallow valley past Ike Smead's chicken farm to Waterworks Pond. As she went along, the bold, excited mood that had driven her out of doors passed and then returned again.

There was something biting and forbidding in the character of Kate Swift. Everyone felt it. In the schoolroom she was silent, cold, and stern, and yet in an odd way very close to her pupils. Once in a long while something seemed to have come over her and she was happy. All of the children in the schoolroom felt the effect of her happiness. For a time they did not work but sat back in their chairs and looked at her.

With hands clasped behind her back the school teacher walked up and down in the schoolroom and talked very rapidly. It did not seem to matter what subject came into her mind. Once she talked to the children of Charles Lamb and made up strange intimate little stories concerning the life of the dead writer. The stories were told with the air of one who had lived in a house with Charles Lamb and knew all the secrets of his private life. The children were somewhat confused, thinking Charles Lamb must be someone who had once lived in Winesburg.

On another occasion the teacher talked to the children of Benvenuto Cellini. That time they laughed. What a bragging, blustering, brave, lovable fellow she made of the old artist! Concerning him also she invented anecdotes. There was one of a German music teacher who had a room above Cellini's lodgings in the city of Milan that made the boys guffaw. Sugar McNutts, a fat boy with red cheeks, laughed so hard that he became dizzy and fell off his seat and Kate Swift laughed with him. Then suddenly she became again cold and stern.

On the winter night when she walked through the deserted snow-covered streets, a crisis had come into the life of the school teacher. Although no one in Winesburg would have suspected it, her life had been very adventurous. It was still adventurous. Day by day as she worked in the schoolroom or walked in the streets, grief, hope, and desire fought within her. Behind a cold exterior the most extraordinary events transpired in her mind. The people of the town thought of her as a confirmed old maid and because she spoke sharply and went her own way thought her lacking in all the human feeling that did so much to make and mar their own lives. In reality she was the most eagerly passionate soul among them, and more than once, in the five years since she had come back from her travels to settle in Winesburg and become a school teacher, had been compelled to go out of the house and walk half through the night fighting out some battle raging within. Once on a night when it rained she had stayed out six hours and when she came home had a quarrel with Aunt Elizabeth Swift. "I am glad you're not a man," said the mother sharply. "More than once I've waited for your father to come home, not knowing what new mess he had got into. I've had my share of uncertainty and you cannot blame me if I do not want to see the worst side of him reproduced in you."

Kate Swift's mind was ablaze with thoughts of George Willard. In something he had written as a school boy she thought she had recognized the spark of genius and wanted to blow on the spark. One day in the summer she had gone to the *Eagle* office and finding the boy unoccupied had taken him out Main Street to the fair ground, where the two sat on a grassy bank and talked. The school teacher tried to bring home to the mind of the boy some conception of the difficulties he would have to face as a writer. "You will have to know life," she declared, and her voice trembled with earnestness. She took hold of George Willard's shoulders and turned him about so that she could look into his eyes. A passer-by might have thought them about to embrace. "If you are to become a writer you'll have to stop fooling with words," she explained. "It would be better to give up the notion of writing until you are better prepared. Now it's time to be living. I don't want to frighten you, but I would like to make you understand the import of what you think of attempting. You must not become a mere peddler of words. The thing to learn is to know what people are thinking about, not what they say."

On the evening before that stormy Thursday night, when the Reverend Curtis Hartman sat in the bell tower of the church waiting to look at her body, young Willard had gone to visit the teacher and to borrow a book. It was then the thing happened that confused and puzzled the boy. He had the book under his arm and was preparing to depart. Again Kate Swift talked with great earnestness. Night was coming on and the light in the room grew dim. As he turned to go she spoke his name softly and with an impulsive movement took hold of his hand. Because the reporter was rapidly becoming a man something of his man's appeal combined with the winsomeness of the boy, stirred the heart of the lonely woman. A passionate desire to have him understand the import of life, to learn to interpret it truly and honestly, swept over her. Leaning forward, her lips brushed his cheek. At the same moment he for the first time became aware of the marked beauty of her features. They were both embarrassed, and to relieve her feeling she became harsh and domineering. "What's the use? It will be ten years before you begin to understand what I mean when I talk to you," she cried passionately.

On the night of the storm and while the minister sat in the church waiting for her, Kate Swift went to the office of the *Winesburg Eagle,* intending to have another talk with the boy. After the long walk in the snow she was cold, lonely, and tired. As she came through Main Street she saw the light from the print shop window shining on the snow and on an impulse opened the door and went in. For an hour she sat by the stove in the office talking of life. She talked with passionate earnestness. The impulse that had driven her out into the snow poured itself out into talk. She became inspired as she sometimes did in the presence of the children in school. A great eagerness to open the door of life to the boy, who had been her pupil and whom she thought might possess a talent for the understanding of life, had possession of her. So strong was her passion that it became something physical. Again her hands took hold of his shoulders and she turned him about. In the dim light her eyes blazed. She arose and laughed, not sharply as was customary with her, but in a queer, hesitating way. "I must be going," she said. "In a moment, if I stay, I'll be wanting to kiss you."

In the newspaper office a confusion arose. Kate Swift turned and walked to the door. She was a teacher but she was also a woman. As she looked at George Willard the passionate desire to be loved by a man, that had a thousand times before swept like a storm over her body, took possession of her. In the lamplight George Willard looked no longer a boy, but a man ready to play the part of a man.

The school teacher let George Willard take her into his arms. In the warm little office the air became suddenly heavy and the strength went out of her body. Leaning against a low counter by the door she waited. When he came and put a hand on her shoulder she turned and let her body fall heavily against him. For George Willard the confusion was immediately increased. For a moment he held the body of the woman tightly against his body and then it stiffened. Two sharp little fists began to beat on his face. When the school teacher had run away and left him alone, he walked up and down in the office swearing furiously.

It was into this confusion that the Reverend Curtis Hartman protruded himself. When he came in George Willard thought the town had gone mad. Shaking a bleeding fist in the air, the minister proclaimed the woman George had only a moment before held in his arms an instrument of God bearing a message of truth.

George blew out the lamp by the window and locking the door of the print shop went home. Through the hotel office, past Hop Higgins lost in his dream of the raising of ferrets, he went and up into his own room. The fire in the stove had gone out and he undressed in the cold. When he got into bed the sheets were like blankets of dry snow.

George Willard rolled about in the bed on which he had lain in the afternoon hugging the pillow and thinking thoughts of Kate Swift. The words of the minister, who he thought had gone suddenly insane, rang in his ears. His eyes stared about the room. The resentment, natural to the baffled male, passed and he tried to understand what had happened. He could not make it out. Over and over he turned the matter in his mind. Hours passed and he began to think it must be time for another day to come. At four o'clock he pulled the covers up about his neck and tried to sleep. When he became drowsy and closed his eyes, he raised a hand and with it groped about in the darkness. "I have missed something. I have missed something Kate Swift was trying to tell me," he muttered sleepily. Then he slept and in all Winesburg he was the last soul on that winter night to go to sleep.

KATHERINE ANNE PORTER (1890–   )

Her ancestors had lived in the South for generations (Daniel Boone was one of them), but in her grandmother's lifetime they had moved from Kentucky to Louisiana to Texas. There, in the centrally situated town of Indian Creek, Katherine Anne Porter was born. The family was Roman Catholic, and her early education was in convent schools, apparently divided between Texas and Louisana. She is reticent about her background and negligent about dates, but in at least one account she speaks of being brought up among impressive collections of books and of her father's suggesting, when she was fourteen, that she read all of Voltaire's Dictionnaire philosophique *and that she did, over about five years' time; but she also says, in the same account, that "At sixteen I ran away from New Orleans and got married. And at twenty-one I bolted again, went to Chicago, got a newspaper job, and went into the movies." She had been sent to the movie set to do a story, got into the wrong line of people, and found herself an extra in a Francis X. Bushman film at $5 a day. When, after a week, she returned to the newspaper office, she was dismissed, and so she stayed with the film company until it moved to California. "That was 1914 and World War I had broken out, so in September I went home."*

Something of her early life can be inferred from her stories, where she presents herself in the character called Miranda; but those stories are, of course, imaginative reconstructions, not autobiographies. It is apparently a fact—as we read in "Pale Horse, Pale Rider"—that toward the end of the war she was in Denver, working again on a newspaper, when she contracted influenza, of which she nearly died. The experience cut her life in two: everything before it was "getting ready."

*Although she had been writing ever since childhood, she had published
nothing. Now and for a long time to come she supported herself in
any way she could—newspaper writing (which she deplored), editing, book reviewing, hack writing. In 1921 she was in Mexico,
teaching dancing in a girl's technical school. "I spent fifteen years
learning to trust myself," she has said. In 1922 she published her
first story, "Maria Concepçíon." Others followed rather quickly, and
her first collection,* Flowering Judas and Other Stories *(1930), was
published in a small limited edition (an expanded edition and a
regular printing appeared in 1934). In Mexico again, married to an
American government official, she won a Guggenheim award and
sailed for Europe in 1931. On her return she lived in Baton Rouge,
where her next husband was on the staff of* Southern Review, *in
which she published two of the three short novels that make up*
Pale Horse, Pale Rider *(1939). A third volume,* The Leaning Tower
and Other Stories, *appeared in 1944.*

*By then Miss Porter, single again, was living something of a hermit's
existence (when she was not, out of necessity, giving public lectures
or participating in writers' conferences) in rural New York and Connecticut. She had begun work on her only novel, based on recollections of her trip to Europe from Mexico in 1931, and she was to
work on it (publishing occasional parts) for twenty years, her later
residence having been Washington, D. C.* Ship of Fools *(1962) was
her first great commercial success, and it may well be this fact, in
part at least, that led some critics to pronounce it a falling off from
her generally high standard.*

*A few short stories, of which she is said to have a trunk full in manu-
script, have been published since then. For years she has been at
work on a book about Cotton Mather. Her book of essays,* The Days
Before *(1952), has been augmented by the publication of* Collected
Essays and Occasional Writings *(1970).*

*Even with these titles, her total production cannot be called extensive.
That it stands firmly with our best is certain, and it is almost certain
that no other American writer of fiction has maintained a level of
artistic achievement so consistently high.*

FURTHER READING

Brief studies include: Harry John Mooney, Jr., *The Fiction and Criti-
cism of Katherine Anne Porter* (1957, revised 1962); Ray B. West,
Jr., *Katherine Anne Porter* (1963); William L. Nance, *Katherine
Anne Porter and the Art of Rejection* (1964); and George Hendrick,
Katherine Anne Porter (1965). Lodwick Hartley and George Core
have edited *Katherine Anne Porter: A Critical Symposium* (1969).

The Downward Path to Wisdom (1944)

In the square bedroom with the big window Mama and Papa were lolling back on their pillows handing each other things from the wide black tray on the small table with crossed legs. They were smiling and they smiled even more when the little boy, with the feeling of sleep still in his skin and hair, came in and walked up to the bed. Leaning against it, his bare toes wriggling in the white fur rug, he went on eating peanuts which he took from his pajama pocket. He was four years old.

"Here's my baby," said Mama. "Lift him up, will you?"

He went limp as a rag for Papa to take him under the arms and swing him up over a broad, tough chest. He sank between his parents like a bear cub in a warm litter, and lay there comfortably. He took another peanut between his teeth, cracked the shell, picked out the nut whole and ate it.

"Running around without his slippers again," said Mama. "His feet are like icicles."

"He crunches like a horse," said Papa. "Eating peanuts before breakfast will ruin his stomach. Where did he get them?"

"You brought them yesterday," said Mama, with exact memory, "in a grisly little cellophane sack. I have asked you dozens of times not to bring him things to eat. Put him out, will you? He's spilling shells all over me."

Almost at once the little boy found himself on the floor again. He moved around to Mama's side of the bed and leaned confidingly near her and began another peanut. As he chewed he gazed solemnly in her eyes.

"Bright-looking specimen, isn't he?" asked Papa, stretching his long legs and reaching for his bathrobe. "I suppose you'll say it's my fault he's dumb as an ox."

"He's my little baby, my only baby," said Mama richly, hugging him, "and he's a dear lamb." His neck and shoulders were quite boneless in her firm embrace. He stopped chewing long enough to receive a kiss on his crumby chin. "He's sweet as clover," said Mama. The baby went on chewing.

"Look at him staring like an owl," said Papa.

Mama said, "He's an angel and I'll never get used to having him."

"We'd be better off if we never *had* had him," said Papa. He was walking about the room and his back was turned when he said that. There was silence for a moment. The little boy stopped eating, and stared deeply at his Mama. She was looking at the back of Papa's head, and her eyes were almost black. "You're going to say that just once too often," she told him in a low voice. "I hate you when you say that."

Papa said, "You spoil him to death. You never correct him for anything. And you don't take care of him. You let him run around eating peanuts before breakfast."

"You gave him the peanuts, remember that," said Mama. She sat up and hugged her only baby once more. He nuzzled softly in the pit of her arm. "Run along, my darling," she told him in her gentlest voice, smiling at him straight in the eyes. "Run along," she said, her arms falling away from him. "Get your breakfast."

The little boy had to pass his father on the way to the door. He shrank into himself when he saw the big hand raised above him. "Yes, get out of here and stay out," said Papa, giving him a little shove toward the door. It was not a hard shove, but it hurt the little boy. He slunk out, and trotted down the hall trying not to look back. He was afraid something was coming after him, he could not imagine what. Something hurt him all over, he did not know why.

He did not want his breakfast; he would not have it. He sat and stirred it round in the yellow bowl, letting it stream off the spoon and spill on the table, on his front, on the chair. He liked seeing it spill. It was hateful stuff, but it looked funny running in white rivulets down his pajamas.

"Now look what you're doing, dirty boy," said Marjory. "You dirty little old boy."

The little boy opened his mouth to speak for the first time. "You're dirty yourself," he told her.

"That's right," said Marjory, leaning over him and speaking so her voice would not carry. "That's right, just like your papa. Mean," she whispered, "mean."

The little boy took up his yellow bowl full of cream and oatmeal and sugar with both hands and brought it down with a crash on the table. It burst and some of the wreck lay in chunks and some of it ran all over everything. He felt better.

"You see?" said Marjory, dragging him out of the chair and scrubbing him with a napkin. She scrubbed him as roughly as she dared until he cried out. "That's just what I said. That's exactly it." Through his tears he saw her face terribly near, red and frowning under a stiff white band, looking like the face of somebody who came at night and stood over him and scolded him when he could not move or get away. "Just like your papa, *mean*."

The little boy went out into the garden and sat on a green bench dangling his legs. He was clean. His hair was wet and his blue woolly pull-over made his nose itch. His face felt stiff from the soap. He saw Marjory going past a window with the black tray. The curtains were still closed at the window he knew opened into Mama's room. Papa's room. Mommanpoppasroom, the word was pleasant, it made a mumbling snapping noise between his lips; it ran in his mind while his eyes wandered about looking for something to do, something to play with.

Mommanpoppas' voices kept attracting his attention. Mama was being cross with Papa again. He could tell by the sound. That was what Marjory always said when their voices rose and fell and shot up to a point and crashed and rolled like the two tomcats who fought at night. Papa was being cross, too, much crosser than Mama this time. He grew cold and disturbed and sat very still, wanting to go to the bathroom, but it was just next to Mommanpoppasroom; he didn't dare think of it. As the voices grew louder he could hardly hear them any more, he wanted so badly to go to the bathroom. The kitchen door opened suddenly and Marjory ran out, making the motion with her hand that meant he was to come to her. He didn't move. She came to him, her face still red and frowning, but she was not angry; she was scared just as he was. She said, "Come on, honey, we've got to go to your gran'ma's again." She took his hand and pulled him. "Come on quick, your gran'ma is waiting for you." He slid off the bench. His mother's voice rose in a terrible scream, screaming something he could not understand, but she was furious; he had seen her clenching her fists and stamping in one spot, screaming with her eyes shut; he knew how she looked. She was screaming in a tantrum, just as he remembered having heard himself. He stood still, doubled over, and all his body seemed to dissolve, sickly, from the pit of his stomach.

"Oh, my God," said Marjory. "Oh, my God. Now look at you. Oh, my God. I can't stop to clean you up."

He did not know how he got to his grandma's house, but he was there at last, wet and soiled, being handled with disgust in the big bathtub. His grandma was there in long black skirts saying, "Maybe he's sick; maybe we should send for the doctor."

"I don't think so, m'am," said Marjory. "He hasn't et anything; he's just scared."

The little boy couldn't raise his eyes, he was so heavy with shame. "Take this note to his mother," said Grandma.

She sat in a wide chair and ran her hands over his head, combing his hair with her fingers; she lifted his chin and kissed him. "Poor little fellow," she said. "Never you mind. You always have a good time at your grandma's, don't you? You're going to have a nice little visit, just like the last time."

The little boy leaned against the stiff, dry-smelling clothes and felt horribly grieved about something. He began to whimper and said, "I'm hungry. I want something to eat." This reminded him. He began to bellow at the top of his voice; he threw himself upon the carpet and rubbed his nose in a dusty woolly bouquet of roses. "I want my peanuts," he howled. "Somebody took my peanuts."

His grandma knelt beside him and gathered him up so tightly he could hardly move. She called in a calm voice above his howls to Old Janet in the doorway, "Bring me some bread and butter with strawberry jam."

"I want peanuts," yelled the little boy desperately.

"No, you don't, darling," said his grandma. "You don't want horrid old peanuts to make you sick. You're going to have some of grandma's nice fresh bread with good strawberries on it. That's what you're going to have." He sat afterward very quietly and ate and ate. His grandma sat near him and Old Janet stood by, near a tray with a loaf and a glass bowl of jam upon the table at the window. Outside there was a trellis with tube-shaped red flowers clinging all over it, and brown bees singing.

"I hardly know what to do," said Grandma, "it's very . . ."

"Yes, m'am," said Old Janet, "it certainly is . . ."

Grandma said, "I can't possibly see the end of it. It's a terrible . . ."

"It certainly is bad," said Old Janet, "all this upset all the time and him such a baby."

Their voices ran on soothingly. The little boy ate and forgot to listen. He did not know these women, except by name. He could not understand what they were talking about; their hands and their clothes and their voices were dry and far away; they examined him with crinkled eyes without any expression that he could see. He sat there waiting for whatever they would do next with him. He hoped they would let him go out and play in the yard. The room was full of flowers and dark red curtains and big soft chairs, and the windows were open, but it was still dark in there somehow; dark, and a place he did not know, or trust.

"Now drink your milk," said Old Janet, holding out a silver cup.

"I don't want any milk," he said, turning his head away.

"Very well, Janet, he doesn't have to drink it," said Grandma quickly. "Now run out in the garden and play, darling. Janet, get his hoop."

A big strange man came home in the evenings who treated the little boy very confusingly. "Say 'please,' and 'thank you,' young man," he would roar, terrifyingly, when he gave any smallest object to the little boy. "Well, fellow, are you ready for a fight?" he would say, again, doubling up huge, hairy fists and making passes at him. "Come on now, you must learn to box." After the first few times this was fun.

"Don't teach him to be rough," said Grandma. "Time enough for all that."

"Now, Mother, we don't want him to be a sissy," said the big man. "He's got to toughen up early. Come on now, fellow, put up your mitts." The little boy liked this new word for hands. He learned to throw himself upon the strange big man, whose name was Uncle David, and hit him on the chest as hard as he could; the big man would laugh and hit him back with his huge, loose fists. Sometimes, but not often, Uncle David came home in the middle of the day. The little boy missed him on the other days, and would hang on the gate looking down the street for him. One evening he brought a large square package under his arm.

"Come over here, fellow, and see what I've got," he said, pulling off quantities of green paper and string from the box which was full of flat, folded colors. He put something in the little boy's hand. It was limp and silky and bright green with a tube on the end. "Thank you," said the little boy nicely, but not knowing what to do with it.

"Balloons," said Uncle David in triumph. "Now just put your mouth here and blow hard." The little boy blew hard and the green thing began to grow round and thin and silvery.

"Good for your chest," said Uncle David. "Blow some more." The little boy went on blowing and the balloon swelled steadily.

"Stop," said Uncle David, "that's enough." He twisted the tube to keep the air in. "That's the way," he said. "Now I'll blow one, and you blow one, and let's see who can blow up a big balloon the fastest."

They blew and blew, especially Uncle David. He puffed and panted and blew with all his might, but the little boy won. His balloon was perfectly round before Uncle David could even get started. The little boy was so proud he began to dance and shout, "I beat, I beat," and blew in his balloon again. It burst in his face and frightened him so he felt sick. "Ha ha, ho ho ho," whooped Uncle David. "That's the boy. I bet I can't do that. Now let's see." He blew until the beautiful bubble grew and wavered and burst into thin air, and there was only a small colored rag in his hand. This was a fine game. They went on with it until Grandma came in and said, "Time for supper now. No, you can't blow baloons at the table. Tomorrow maybe." And it was all over.

The next day, instead of being given balloons, he was hustled out of bed early, bathed in warm soapy water and given a big breakfast of soft-boiled eggs with toast and jam and milk. His grandma came in to kiss him good morning. "And I hope you'll be a good boy and obey your teacher," she told him.

"What's teacher?" asked the little boy.

"Teacher is at school," said Grandma. "She'll tell you all sorts of things and you must do as she says."

Mama and Papa had talked a great deal about School, and how they must send him there. They had told him it was a fine place with all kinds of toys and other children to play with. He felt he knew about School. "I didn't know it was time, Grandma," he said. "Is it today?"

"It's this very minute," said Grandma. "I told you a week ago."

Old Janet came in with her bonnet on. It was a prickly looking bundle held with a black rubber band under her back hair. "Come on," she said. "This is my busy day." She wore a dead cat slung around her neck, its sharp ears bent over under her baggy chin.

The little boy was excited and wanted to run ahead. "Hold to my hand like I told you," said Old Janet. "Don't go running off like that and get yourself killed."

"I'm going to get killed, I'm going to get killed," sang the little boy, making a tune of his own.

"Don't say that, you give me the creeps," said Old Janet. "Hold to my hand now." She bent over and looked at him, not at his face but at something on his clothes. His eyes followed hers.

"I declare," said Old Janet, "I did forget. I was going to sew it up. I might have known. I *told* your grandma it would be that way from now on."

"What?" asked the little boy.

"Just look at yourself," said Old Janet crossly. He looked at himself.

There was a little end of him showing through the slit in his short blue flannel trousers. The trousers came halfway to his knees above, and his socks came halfway to his knees below, and all winter long his knees were cold. He remembered now how cold his knees were in cold weather. And how sometimes he would have to put the part of him that came through the slit back again, because he was cold there too. He saw at once what was wrong, and tried to arrange himself, but his mittens got in the way. Janet said, "Stop that, you bad boy," and with a firm thumb she set him in order, at the same time reaching under his belt to pull down and fold his knit undershirt over his front.

"There now," she said, "try not to disgrace yourself today." He felt guilty and red all over, because he had something that showed when he was dressed that was not supposed to show then. The different women who bathed him always wrapped him quickly in towels and hurried him into his clothes, because they saw something about him he could not see for himself. They hurried him so he never had a chance to see whatever it was they saw, and though he looked at himself when his clothes were off, he could not find out what was wrong with him. Outside, in his clothes, he knew he looked like everybody else, but inside his clothes there was something bad the matter with him. It worried him and confused him and he wondered about it. The only people who never seemed to notice there was something wrong with him were Momman-poppa. They never called him a bad boy, and all summer long they had taken all his clothes off and let him run in the sand beside a big ocean.

"Look at him, isn't he a love?" Mama would say and Papa would look, and say, "He's got a back like a prize fighter." Uncle David was a prize fighter when he doubled up his mitts and said, "Come on, fellow."

Old Janet held him firmly and took long steps under her big rustling skirts. He did not like Old Janet's smell. It made him a little quivery in the stomach; it was just like wet chicken feathers.

School was easy. Teacher was a square-shaped woman with square short hair and short skirts. She got in the way sometimes, but not often. The people around him were his size; he didn't have always to be stretching his neck up to faces bent over him, and he could sit on the chairs without having to climb. All the children had names, like Frances and Evelyn and Agatha and Edward and Martin, and his own name was Stephen. He was not Mama's "Baby," nor Papa's "Old Man"; he was not Uncle David's "Fellow," or Grandma's "Darling," or even Old Janet's "Bad Boy." He was Stephen. He was learning to read, and to sing a tune to some strange-looking letters or marks written in chalk on a blackboard. You talked one kind of lettering, and you sang another. All the children talked and sang in turn, and then all together. Stephen thought it a fine game. He felt awake and happy. They had soft clay and paper and wires and squares of colors in tin boxes to play with, colored blocks to build houses with. Afterward they all danced in a big ring, and then they danced in pairs, boys with girls. Stephen danced with Frances, and Frances kept saying, "Now you just follow me." She was a little taller than he was, and her hair stood up in short, shiny curls, the color of an ash tray on Papa's desk. She would say, "You can't dance." "I can dance too," said Stephen, jumping around holding her hands, "I can, too, dance." He was certain of it. "*You* can't dance," he told Frances, "you can't dance at all."

Then they had to change partners, and when they came round again, Frances said, "I don't *like* the way you dance." This was different. He felt uneasy about it. He didn't jump quite so high when the phonograph record started going dumdiddy dumdiddy again. "Go ahead, Stephen, you're doing fine," said Teacher, waving her hands together very fast. The dance ended, and they all played "relaxing" for five minutes. They relaxed by swinging their arms back and forth, then rolling their heads round and round. When Old Janet came for him he didn't want to go home. At lunch his grandma told him twice to keep his face out of his plate. "Is that what they teach you at school?" she asked. Uncle David was at home. "Here you are, fellow," he said and gave Stephen two balloons. "Thank you," said Stephen. He put the balloons in his pocket and forgot about them. "I told you that boy could learn something," said Uncle David to Grandma. "Hear him say 'thank you'?"

In the afternoon at school Teacher handed out big wads of clay and told the children to make something out of it. Anything they liked. Stephen decided to make a cat, like Mama's Meeow at home. He did not like Meeow, but he thought it would be easy to make a cat. He could not get the clay to work at all. It simply fell into one lump after another. So he stopped, wiped his hands on his pull-over, remembered his balloons and began blowing one.

"Look at Stephen's horse," said Frances. "Just look at it."

"It's not a horse, it's a cat," said Stephen. The other children gathered around. "It looks like a horse, a little," said Martin.

"It is a cat," said Stephen, stamping his foot, feeling his face turning hot. The other children all laughed and exclaimed over Stephen's cat that looked like a horse. Teacher came down among them. She sat usually at the top of the room before a big table covered with papers and playthings. She picked up Stephen's lump of clay and turned it round and examined it with her kind eyes. "Now, children," she said, "everybody has the right to make anything the way he pleases. If Stephen says this is a cat, it *is* a cat. Maybe you were thinking about a horse, Stephen?"

"It's a *cat*," said Stephen. He was aching all over. He knew then he should have said at first, "Yes, it's a horse." Then they would have let him alone. They would never have known he was trying to make a cat. "It's Meeow," he said in a trembling voice, "but I forgot how she looks."

His balloon was perfectly flat. He started blowing it up again, trying not to cry. Then it was time to go home, and Old Janet came looking for him. While Teacher was talking to other grown-up people who came to take other children home, Frances said, "Give me your balloon; I haven't got a balloon." Stephen handed it to her. He was happy to give it. He reached in his pocket and took out the other. Happily, he gave her that one too. Frances took it, then handed it back. "Now you blow up one and I'll blow up the other, and let's have a race," she said. When their balloons were only half filled Old Janet took Stephen by the arm and said, "Come on here, this is my busy day."

Frances ran after them, calling, "Stephen, you give me back my balloon," and snatched it away. Stephen did not know whether he was surprised to find himself going away with Frances' balloon, or whether he was surprised to see her snatching it as if it really belonged to her. He was badly mixed up in his mind, and Old Janet was hauling him along. One thing he knew, he liked Frances, he was going to see her again tomorrow, and he was going to bring her more balloons.

That evening Stephen boxed awhile with his uncle David, and Uncle David gave him a beautiful orange. "Eat that," he said, "it's good for your health."

"Uncle David, may I have some more balloons?" asked Stephen.

"Well, what do you say first?" asked Uncle David, reaching for the box on the top bookshelf.

"Please," said Stephen.

"That's the word," said Uncle David. He brought out two balloons, a red and a yellow one. Stephen noticed for the first time they had letters on them, very small letters that grew taller and wider as the balloon grew rounder. "Now that's all, fellow," said Uncle David. "Don't ask for any more because that's all." He put the box back on the bookshelf, but not before Stephen had seen that the box was almost full of balloons. He didn't say a word, but went on blowing, and Uncle David blew also. Stephen thought it was the nicest game he had ever known.

He had only one left, the next day, but he took it to school and gave it to Frances. "There are a lot," he said, feeling very proud and warm; "I'll bring you a lot of them."

Frances blew it up until it made a beautiful bubble, and said, "Look, I want to show you something." She took a sharp-pointed stick they used in working the clay; she poked the balloon, and it exploded. "Look at that," she said.

"That's nothing," said Stephen, "I'll bring you some more."

After school, before Uncle David came home, while Grandma was resting, when Old Janet had given him his milk and told him to run away and not bother her, Stephen dragged a chair to the bookshelf, stood upon it and reached into the box. He did not take three or four as he believed he intended; once his hands were upon them he seized what they could hold and jumped off the chair, hugging them to him. He stuffed them into his reefer pocket where they folded down and hardly made a lump.

He gave them all to Frances. There were so many, Frances gave most of them away to the other children. Stephen, flushed with his new joy, the lavish pleasure of giving presents, found almost at once still another happiness. Suddenly he was popular among the children; they invited him specially to join whatever games were up; they fell in at once with his own notions for play, and asked him what he would like to do next. They had festivals of blowing up the beautiful globes, fuller and rounder and thinner, changing as they went from deep color to lighter, paler tones, growing glassy thin, bubbly thin, then bursting with a thrilling loud noise like a toy pistol.

For the first time in his life Stephen had almost too much of something he wanted, and his head was so turned he forgot how this fullness came about, and no longer thought of it as a secret. The next day was Saturday, and Frances came to visit him with her nurse. The nurse and Old Janet sat in Old Janet's room drinking coffee and gossiping, and the children sat on the side porch blowing balloons. Stephen chose an apple-colored one and Frances a pale green one. Between them on the bench lay a tumbled heap of delights still to come.

"I once had a silver balloon," said Frances, "a beyootiful silver one, not round like these; it was a long one. But these are even nicer, I think," she added quickly, for she did want to be polite.

"When you get through with that one," said Stephen, gazing at her with the pure bliss of giving added to loving, "you can blow up a blue one and then a pink one and a yellow one and a purple one." He pushed the heap of limp objects toward her. Her clear-looking eyes, with fine little rays of brown in them like the spokes of a wheel, were full of approval for Stephen. "I wouldn't want to be greedy, though, and blow up all your balloons."

"There'll be plenty more left," said Stephen, and his heart rose under his thin ribs. He felt his ribs with his fingers and discovered with some surprise that they stopped somewhere in front, while Frances sat blowing balloons rather halfheartedly. The truth was, she was tired of balloons. After you blow six or seven your chest gets hollow and your lips feel puckery. She had been blowing balloons steadily for three days now. She had begun to hope they were giving out. "There's boxes and boxes more of them, Frances," said Stephen happily. "Millions more. I guess they'd last and last if we didn't blow too many every day."

Frances said somewhat timidly, "I tell you what. Let's rest awhile and fix some liquish water. Do you like liquish?"

"Yes, I do," said Stephen, "but I haven't got any."

"Couldn't we buy some?" asked Frances. "It's only a cent a stick, the nice rubbery, twisty kind. We can put it in a bottle with some water, and shake it and shake it, and it makes foam on top like soda pop and we can drink it. I'm kind of thirsty," she said in a small, weak voice. "Blowing balloons all the time makes you thirsty, I think."

Stephen, in silence, realized a dreadful truth and a numb feeling crept over him. He did not have a cent to buy licorice for Frances and she was tired of his balloons. This was the first real dismay of his whole life, and he aged at least a year in the next minute, huddled, with his deep, serious blue eyes focused down his nose in intense speculation. What could he do to please Frances that would not cost money? Only yesterday Uncle David had given him a nickel, and he had thrown it away on gumdrops. He regretted that nickel so bitterly his neck and forehead were damp. He was thirsty too.

"I tell you what," he said, brightening with a splendid idea, lamely trailing off on second thought, "I know something we can do, I'll—I . . ."

"I *am* thirsty," said Frances with gentle persistence. "I think I'm so thirsty maybe I'll have to go home." She did not leave the bench, though, but sat, turning her grieved mouth toward Stephen.

Stephen quivered with the terrors of the adventure before him, but he said boldly, "I'll make some lemonade. I'll get sugar and lemon and some ice and we'll have lemonade."

"Oh, I love lemonade," cried Frances. "I'd rather have lemonade than liquish."

"You stay right here," said Stephen, "and I'll get everything."

He ran around the house, and under Old Janet's window he heard the dry, chattering voices of the two old women whom he must outwit. He sneaked on tiptoe to the pantry, took a lemon lying there by itself, a handful of lump sugar and a china teapot, smooth, round, with flowers and leaves all over it. These he left on the kitchen table while he broke a piece of ice with a sharp metal pick he had been forbidden to touch. He put the ice in the pot, cut the lemon and squeezed it as well as he could—a lemon was tougher and more slippery than he had thought—and mixed sugar and water. He decided there was not enough sugar so he sneaked back and took another handful. He was back on the porch in an astonishingly short time, his face tight, his knees trembling, carrying iced lemonade to thirsty Frances with both his devoted hands.

A pace distant from her he stopped, literally stabbed through with a thought. Here he stood in broad daylight carrying a teapot with lemonade in it, and his grandma or Old Janet might walk through the door at any moment.

"Come on, Frances," he whispered loudly. "Let's go round to the back behind the rose bushes where it's shady." Frances leaped up and ran like a deer beside him, her face wise with knowledge of why they ran; Stephen ran stiffly, cherishing his teapot with clenched hands.

It was shady behind the rose bushes, and much safer. They sat side by side on the dampish ground, legs doubled under, drinking in turn from the slender spout. Stephen took his just share in large, cool, delicious swallows. When Frances drank she set her round pink mouth daintily to the spout and her throat beat steadily as a heart. Stephen was thinking he had really done something pretty nice for Frances. He did not know where his own happiness was; it was mixed with the sweet-sour taste in his mouth and a cool feeling in his bosom because Frances was there drinking his lemonade which he had got for her with great danger.

Frances said, "My, what big swallows you take," when his turn came next.

"No bigger than yours," he told her downrightly. "You take awfully big swallows."

"Well," said Frances, turning this criticism into an argument for her rightness about things, "that's the way to drink lemonade anyway." She peered into the teapot. There was quite a lot of lemonade left and she was beginning to feel she had enough. "Let's make up a game and see who can take the biggest swallows.'

This was such a wonderful notion they grew reckless, tipping the spout into their opened mouths above their heads until lemonade welled up and ran over their chins in rills down their fronts. When they tired of this there was still lemonade left in the pot. They played first at giving the rosebush a drink and ended by baptizing it. "Name father son holygoat," shouted Stephen, pouring. At this sound Old Janet's face appeared over the low hedge, with the tan, disgusted-looking face of Frances' nurse hanging over her shoulder.

"Well, just as I thought," said Old Janet. "Just as I expected." The bag under her chin waggled.

"We were thirsty," he said; "we were awfully thirsty." Frances said nothing, but she gazed steadily at the toes of her shoes.

"Give me that teapot," said Old Janet, taking it with a rude snatch. "Just because you're thirsty is no reason," said Old Janet. "You can ask for things. You don't have to steal."

"We didn't steal," cried Frances suddenly. "We didn't. We didn't!"

"That's enough from you, missy," said her nurse. "Come straight out of there. You have nothing to do with this."

"Oh, I don't know," said Old Janet with a hard stare at Frances' nurse. "*He* never did such a thing before, by himself."

"Come on," said the nurse to Frances, "this is no place for you." She held Frances by the wrist and started walking away so fast Frances had to run to keep up. "Nobody can call *us* thieves and get away with it."

"You don't have to steal, even if others do," said Old Janet to Stephen, in a high carrying voice. "If you so much as pick up a lemon in somebody else's house you're a little thief." She lowered her voice then and said, "Now I'm going to tell your grandma and you'll see what you get."

"He went in the icebox and left it open," Janet told Grandma, "and he got into the lump sugar and spilt it all over the floor. Lumps everywhere underfoot. He dribbled water all over the clean kitchen floor, and he baptized the rose bush, blaspheming. And he took your Spode teapot."

"I didn't either," said Stephen loudly, trying to free his hand from Old Janet's big hard fist.

"Don't tell fibs," said Old Janet; "that's the last straw."

"Oh, dear," said Grandma. "He's not a baby any more." She shut the book she was reading and pulled the wet front of his pullover toward her. "What's this sticky stuff on him?" she asked and straightened her glasses.

"Lemonade," said Old Janet. "He took the last lemon."

They were in the big dark room with the red curtains. Uncle David walked in from the room with the bookcases, holding a box in his up-lifted hand. "Look here," he said to Stephen. "What's become of all my balloons?"

Stephen knew well that Uncle David was not really asking a question.

Stephen, sitting on a footstool at his grandma's knee, felt sleepy. He leaned heavily and wished he could put his head on her lap, but he might go to sleep, and it would be wrong to go to sleep while Uncle David was still talking. Uncle David walked about the room with his hands in his pockets, talking to Grandma. Now and then he would walk over to a lamp and, leaning, peer into the top of the shade, winking in the light, as if he expected to find something there.

"It's simply in the blood, I told her," said Uncle David. "I told her she would simply have to come and get him, and keep him. She asked me if I meant to call him a thief and I said if she could think of a more exact word I'd be glad to hear it."

"You shouldn't have said that," commented Grandma calmly.

"Why not? She might as well know the facts. . . . I suppose he can't help it," said Uncle David, stopping now in front of Stephen and dropping his chin into his collar, "I shouldn't expect too much of him, but you can't begin too early—"

"The trouble is," said Grandma, and while she spoke she took Stephen by the chin and held it up so that he had to meet her eye; she talked steadily in a mournful tone, but Stephen could not understand. She ended, "It's not just about the balloons, of course."

"It *is* about the balloons," said Uncle David angrily, "because balloons now mean something worse later. But what can you expect? His father—well, it's in the blood. He—"

"That's your sister's husband you're talking about," said Grandma, "and there is no use making things worse. Besides, you don't really *know*."

"I *do* know," said Uncle David, And he talked again very fast, walking up and down. Stephen tried to understand, but the sounds were strange and floating just over his head. They were talking about his father, and they did not like him. Uncle David came over and stood above Stephen and Grandma. He hunched over them with a frowning face, a long, crooked shadow from him falling across them to the wall. To Stephen he looked like his father, and he shrank against his grandma's skirts.

"The question is, what to do with him now?" asked Uncle David. "If we keep him here, he'd just be a—I won't be bothered with him. Why can't they take care of their own child? That house is crazy. Too far gone already, I'm afraid. No training. No example."

"You're right, they must take him and keep him," said Grandma.

She ran her hands over Stephen's head; tenderly she pinched the nape of his neck between thumb and forefinger. "You're your Grandma's darling," she told him, "and you've had a nice long visit, and now you're going home. Mama is coming for you in a few minutes. Won't that be nice?"

"I want my mama," said Stephen, whimpering, for his grandma's face frightened him. There was something wrong with her smile.

Uncle David sat down. "Come over here, fellow," he said, wagging a forefinger at Stephen. Stephen went over slowly, and Uncle David drew him between his wide knees in their loose, rough clothes. "You ought to be ashamed of yourself," he said, "stealing Uncle David's balloons when he had already given you so many."

"It wasn't that," said Grandma quickly. "Don't say that. It will make an impression—"

"I hope it does," said Uncle David in a louder voice; "I hope he remembers it all his life. If he belonged to me I'd give him a good thrashing."

Stephen felt his mouth, his chin, his whole face jerking. He opened his mouth to take a breath, and tears and noise burst from him. "Stop that, fellow, stop that," said Uncle David, shaking him gently by the shoulders, but Stephen could not stop. He drew his breath again and it came back in a howl. Old Janet came to the door.

"Bring me some cold water," called Grandma. There was a flurry, a commotion, a breath of cool air from the hall, the door slammed, and Stephen heard his mother's voice. His howl died away, his breath sobbed and fluttered, he turned his dimmed eyes and saw her standing there. His heart turned over within him and he bleated like a lamb, "Maaaaama," running toward her. Uncle David stood back as Mama swooped in and fell on her knees beside Stephen. She gathered him to her and stood up with him in her arms.

"What are you doing to my baby?" she asked Uncle David in a thickened voice. "I should never have let him come here. I should have known better—"

"You always should know better," said Uncle David, "and you never do. And you never will. You haven't got it here," he told her, tapping his forehead.

"David," said Grandma, "that's your—"

"Yes, I know, she's my sister," said Uncle David. "I know it. But if she must run away and marry a—"

"Shut up," said Mama.

"And bring more like him into the world, let her keep them at home. I say let her keep—"

Mama set Stephen on the floor and, holding him by the hand, she said to Grandma all in a rush as if she were reading something, "Good-by, Mother. This is the last time, really the last. I can't bear it any longer. Say good-by to Stephen; you'll never see him again. You let this happen. It's your fault. You know David was a coward and a bully and a self-righteous little beast all his life and you never crossed him in anything. You let him bully me all my life and you let him slander my husband and call my baby a thief, and now this is the end. . . . He calls my baby a thief over a few horrible little balloons because he doesn't like my husband. . . ."

She was panting and staring about from one to the other. They were all standing. Now Grandma said, "Go home, daughter. Go away, David. I'm sick of your quarreling. I've never had a day's peace or comfort from either of you. I'm sick of you both. Now let me alone and stop this noise. Go away," said Grandma in a wavering voice. She took out her handkerchief and wiped first one eye and then the other and said, "All this hate, hate—what is it for? . . . So this is the way it turns out. Well, let me alone."

"You and your little advertising balloons," said Mama to Uncle David. "The big honest businessman advertises with balloons and if he loses one he'll be ruined. And your beastly little moral notions . . ."

Grandma went to the door to meet Old Janet, who handed her a glass of water. Grandma drank it all, standing there.

"Is your husband coming for you, or are you going home by yourself?" she asked Mama.

"I'm driving myself," said Mama in a far-away voice as if her mind had wandered. "You know he wouldn't set foot in this house."

"I should think not," said Uncle David.

"Come on, Stephen darling," said Mama. "It's far past his bedtime," she said, to no one in particular. "Imagine keeping a baby up to torture him about a few miserable little bits of colored rubber." She smiled at Uncle David with both rows of teeth as she passed him on the way to the door, keeping between him and Stephen. "Ah, where would we be without high moral standards," she said, and then to Grandma, "Good night, Mother," in quite her usual voice. "I'll see you in a day or so."

"Yes, indeed," said Grandma cheerfully, coming out into the hall with Stephen and Mama. "Let me hear from you. Ring me up tomorrow. I hope you'll be feeling better."

"I feel very well now," said Mama brightly, laughing. She bent down and kissed Stephen. "Sleepy, darling? Papa's waiting to see you. Don't go to sleep until you've kissed your papa good night."

Stephen woke with a sharp jerk. He raised his head and put out his chin a little. "I don't want to go home," he said; "I want to go to school. I don't want to see Papa, I don't like him."

Mama laid her palm over his mouth softly. "Darling, don't."

Uncle David put his head out with a kind of snort. "There you are," he said. "There you've got a statement from headquarters."

Mama opened the door and ran, almost carrying Stephen. She ran across the sidewalk, jerking open the car door and dragging Stephen in after her. She spun the car around and dashed forward so sharply Stephen was almost flung out of the seat. He sat braced then with all his might, hands digging into the cushions. The car speeded up and the trees and houses whizzed by all flattened out. Stephen began suddenly to sing to himself, a quiet, inside song so Mama would not hear. He sang his new secret; it was a comfortable, sleepy song: "I hate Papa, I hate Mama, I hate Grandma, I hate Uncle David, I hate Old Janet, I hate Marjory, I hate Papa, I hate Mama . . ."

His head bobbed, leaned, came to rest on Mama's knee, eyes closed. Mama drew him closer and slowed down, driving with one hand.

JEAN TOOMER (1894–1967)

Of all the writers of the so-called Harlem or Negro renaissance of the 1920s—a movement that included Claude McKay, Langston Hughes, Countee Cullen, Eric Walrond, Zora Neale Hurston, and others—the most exciting talent was that of Jean Toomer as it revealed itself in the single book, Cane *(1923). The excitment was not limited to young black writers, for whom it was a tremendous stimulus, but to many white writers, including Gorham Munson, Waldo Frank, Sherwood Anderson, Hart Crane, Eugene O'Neill.*

He was the grandson of P. B. S. Pinchbeck, who, in the period of the Reconstruction, with the support of the Negro vote, was elected lieutenant governor of Louisiana and, when the governor died, became acting governor. When his term was over, he moved to Washington, D.C., and it was there that Jean Toomer was born.

He was very light skinned, and in 1922 he said of himself:

I have lived equally amid the two race groups. Now white, now colored. From my own point of view I am naturally and inevitably an American. I have strived for a spiritual fusion analogous to the fact of racial intermingling. Without denying a single element in me, with no desire to subdue one to the other, I have sought to let them function as complements. I have tried to let them live in harmony. Within the last two or three years, however, my growing need for artistic expression has pulled me deeper and deeper into the Negro group. And as my powers of receptivity increased, I found myself loving it in a way that I could never love the other. It has stimulated and fertilized whatever creative talent I may contain within me.

He attended public schools in Washington, the University of Wisconsin (as a white man, one gathers) for a year, 1914 to 1915, then the City College of New York. He lived through the mental deterioration of his aged grandparent in Washington and, when he died, took his body back South. It was probably at this time that he taught school for four months in Sparta, Georgia, an experience that, quite obviously, lies behind "Kabnis," one of two expressionist plays that Toomer wrote in 1922, when he was again in New York. These plays found no producers, but "Kabnis," rewritten, is the final section of Cane. *His last piece of published fiction was the short novel, "York Beach," in* American Caravan *(1929).*

Cane *seemed then and remains now a very strange book, a mixture of*
fiction, poetry, and drama that moves from Georgia to Washington
and back to Georgia, and a mixture, too, of radical affirmation and
rage. Toomer continued his efforts for the stage in at least three
more experimental plays, all unproduced and unpublished: Balo
(1923), The Sacred Factory *(1927), and* The Gallonwergs *(1928).*

Cane *had made a splash, but it had not sold. The plays got nowhere.*
Friends wrote about him—Paul Rosenfeld in Men Seen *(1925) and*
Gorham Munson in Destinations *(1928)—and at the end of the*
decade the second and third volumes of American Caravan *pub-*
lished his work. But the experience had been discouraging on the
whole, and Toomer began to drift out of literature.

He was interested in the theories of Charles Gurdjieff about the possible
expansion of consciousness and the spiritual self through disci-
plined meditation, and he had spent much of the summer of 1926
at the Gurdjieff Institute at Fontainebleau. Then, in 1931, he set up
some similar establishment in a cottage outside the small town of
Portage, Wisconsin. In the following year he married one of the
participants, a promising young novelist who lived in the town,
Margery Latimer. They moved to Chicago, where she died in child-
birth in 1933.

He seems then to have drifted to New Mexico, where he lived for some
years and, then, remarried, to Bucks County, Pennsylvania, where
he became interested in the work of the Society of Friends, for
which he wrote an occasional paper.

Cane *was long since forgotten. Two years after his death it was repub-*
lished in a paperback series with the legend "A Perennial Classic."

FURTHER READING

For critical estimates see Alain Locke, editor, *Four Negro Poets* (1927);
Hugh M. Gloster, *Negro Voices in American Fiction* (1948); Robert
Bone, *The Negro Novel in America* (revised 1965); and Arna Bon-
temps, *Anger and Beyond: The Negro Writer in the United States*
(1966).

FROM **Cane** (1923)

Avey

For a long while she was nothing more to me than one of those
skirted beings whom boys at a certain age disdain to play with. Just how
I came to love her, timidly, and with secret blushes, I do not know.
But that I did was brought home to me one night, the first night that

Ned wore his long pants. Us fellers were seated on the curb before an
apartment house where she had gone in. The young trees had not
outgrown their boxes then. V Street was lined with them. When our
legs grew cramped and stiff from the cold of the stone, we'd stand
around a box and whittle it. I like to think now that there was a hidden
purpose in the way we hacked them with our knives. I like to feel that
something deep in me responded to the trees, the young trees that
whinnied like colts impatient to be let free. . . On the particular night
I have in mind, we were waiting for the top-floor light to go out. We
wanted to see Avey leave the flat. This night she stayed longer than
usual and gave us a chance to complete the plans of how we were
going to stone and beat that feller on the top floor out of town. Ned
especially had it in for him. He was about to throw a brick up at the
window when at last the room went dark. Some minutes passed. Then
Avey, as unconcerned as if she had been paying an old-maid aunt a
visit, came out. I don't remember what she had on, and all that sort of
thing. But I do know that I turned hot as bare pavements in the summertime at Ned's boast: "Hell, bet I could get her too if you little niggers
weren't always spying and crabbing everything." I didnt say a word to
him. It wasnt my way then. I just stood there like the others, and some-
think like a fuse burned up inside of me. She never noticed us, but
swung along lazy and easy as anything. We sauntered to the corner
and watched her till her door banged to. Ned repeated what he'd said.
I didn't seem to care. Sitting around old Mush-Head's bread box, the
discussions began. "Hang if I can see how she gets away with it," Doc
started. Ned knew, of course. There was nothing he didnt know when
it came to women. He dilated on the emotional needs of girls. Said they
werent much different from men in that respect. And concluded with
the solemn avowal: "It does em good." None of us liked Ned much. We
all talked dirt; but it was the way he said it. And then too, a couple of
the fellers had sisters and had caught Ned playing with them. But there
was no disputing the superiority of his smutty wisdom. Bubs Sanborn,
whose mother was friendly with Avey's, had overhead the old ladies
talking. "Avey's mother's ont her," he said. We thought that only
natural and began to guess at what would happen. Some one said she'd
marry that feller on the top floor. Ned called that a lie because Avey
was going to marry nobody but him. We had our doubts about that, but
we did agree that she'd soon leave school and marry some one. The
gang broke up, and I went home, picturing myself as married.

　　Nothing I did seemed able to change Avey's indifference to me. I
played basket-ball, and when I'd make a long clean shot she'd clap
with the others, louder than they, I thought. I'd meet her on the street,
and there'd be no difference in the way she said hello. She never took
the trouble to call me by my name. On the days for drill, I'd let my
voice down a tone and call for a complicated maneuver when I saw
her coming. She'd smile appreciation, but it was an impersonal smile,
never for me. It was on a summer excursion down to Riverview that

she first seemed to take me into account. The day had been spent riding merry-go-rounds, scenic-railways, and shoot-the-chutes. We had been in swimming and we had danced. I was a crack swimmer then. She didnt know how. I held her up and showed her how to kick her legs and draw her arms. Of course she didnt learn in one day, but she thanked me for bothering with her. I was also somewhat of a dancer. And I had already noticed that love can start on a dance floor. We danced. But though I held her tightly in my arms, she was way away. That college feller who lived on the top floor was somewhere making money for the next year. I imagined that she was thinking, wishing for him. Ned was along. He treated her until his money gave out. She went with another feller. Ned got sore. One by one the boys' money gave out. She left them. And they got sore. Every one of them but me got sore. This is the reason, I guess, why I had her to myself on the top deck of the *Jane Mosely* that night as we puffed up the Potomac, coming home. The moon was brilliant. The air was sweet like clover. And every now and then, a salt tang, a stale drift of sea-weed. It was not my mind's fault if it went romancing. I should have taken her in my arms the minute we were stowed in that old lifeboat. I dallied, dreaming. She took me in hers. And I could feel by the touch of it that it wasnt a man-to-woman love. It made me restless. I felt chagrined. I didnt know what it was, but I did know that I couldnt handle it. She ran her fingers through my hair and kissed my forehead. I itched to break through her tenderness to passion. I wanted her to take me in her arms as I knew she had that college feller. I wanted her to love me passionately as she did him. I gave her one burning kiss. Then she laid me in her lap as if I were a child. Helpless. I got sore when she started to hum a lullaby. She wouldnt let me go. I talked. I knew damned well that I could beat her at that. Her eyes were soft and misty, the curves of her lips were wistful, and her smile seemed indulgent of the irrelevance of my remarks. I gave up at last and let her love me, silently, in her own way. The moon was brilliant. The air was sweet like clover, and every now and then, a salt tang, a stale drift of sea-weed. . .

The next time I came close to her was the following summer at Harpers Ferry. We were sitting on a flat projecting rock they give the name of Lover's Leap. Some one is supposed to have jumped off it. The river is about six hundred feet beneath. A railroad track runs up the valley and curves out of sight where part of the mountain rock had to be blasted away to make room for it. The engines of this valley have a whistle, the echoes of which sound like iterated gasps and sobs. I always think of them as crude music from the soul of Avey. We sat there holding hands. Our palms were soft and warm against each other. Our fingers were not tight. She would not let them be. She would not let me twist them. I wanted to talk. To explain what I meant to her. Avey was as silent as those great trees whose tops we looked down upon. She has always been like that. At least, to me. I had the notion that if I really wanted to, I could do with her just what I pleased. Like one can strip a tree. I did kiss her. I even let my hands cup her breasts. When I was through, she'd seek my hand and hold it till my pulse cooled down. Evening after evening we sat there. I tried to get her to talk about that college feller. She never would. There was no set time to go home. None of my family had come down. And as for hers, she didnt give a hang about them. The general gossips could hardly say more than they had. The boarding-house porch was always deserted when we returned. No one saw us enter, so the time was set conveniently for scandal. This worried me a little, for I thought it might keep Avey from getting an appointment in the schools. She didnt care. She had finished normal school. They could give her a job if they wanted to. As time went on, her indifference to things began to pique me; I was ambitious. I left the Ferry earlier than she did. I was going off to college. The more I thought of it, the more I resented, yes, hell, thats what it was, her down-right laziness. Sloppy indolence. There was no excuse for a healthy girl taking life so easy. Hell! she was no better than a cow. I was certain that she was a cow when I felt an udder in a Wisconsin stock-judging class. Among those energetic Swedes, or whatever they are, I decided to forget her. For two years I thought I did. When I'd come home for the summer she'd be away. And before she returned, I'd be gone. We never wrote; she was too damned lazy for that. But what a bluff I put up about forgetting her. The girls up that way, at least the ones I knew, havent got the stuff: they dont know how to love. Giving themselves completely was tame beside just the holding of Avey's hand. One day I received a note from her. The writing, I decided, was slovenly. She wrote on a torn bit of note-book paper. The envelope had a faint perfume that I remembered. A single line told me she had lost her school and was going away. I comforted myself with the reflection that shame held no pain for one so indolent as she. Nevertheless, I left Wisconsin that year for good. Washington had seemingly forgotten her. I hunted Ned. Between curses, I caught his opinion of her. She was no better than a whore. I saw her mother on the street. The same old pinch-beck, jerky-gaited creature that I'd always known.

Perhaps five years passed. The business of hunting a job or something or other had bruised my vanity so that I could recognize it. I felt old. Avey and my real relation to her, I thought I came to know. I wanted to see her. I had been told that she was in New York. As I had no money, I hiked and bummed my way there. I got work in a ship-yard and walked the streets at night, hoping to meet her. Failing in this, I saved enough to pay my fare back home. One evening in early June, just at the time when dusk is most lovely on the eastern horizon, I saw Avey, idolent as ever, leaning on the arm of a man, strolling under the recently lit arc-lights of U Street. She had almost passed before she recognized me. She showed no surprise. The puff over her eyes had grown heavier. The eyes themselves were still sleepy-large, and beautiful. I had almost concluded—indifferent. "You look older," was what she said. I wanted to convince her that I was, so I asked her to walk with me. The man whom she was with, and whom she never took the trouble to introduce, at a nod from her, hailed a taxi, and drove away. That gave me a notion of what she had been used to. Her dress was of some fine, costly stuff. I suggested the park, and then added that the grass might stain her skirt. Let it get stained, she said, for where it came from there are others.

I have a spot in Soldier's Home to which I always go when I want the simple beauty of another's soul. Robins spring about the lawn all day. They leave their footprints in the grass. I imagine that the grass at night smells sweet and fresh because of them. The ground is high. Washington lies below. Its light spreads like a blush against the darkened sky. Against the soft dusk sky of Washington. And when the wind is from the South, soil of my homeland falls like a fertile shower upon the lean streets of the city. Upon my hill in Soldier's Home. I know the policeman who watches the place of nights. When I go there alone, I talk to him. I tell him I come there to find the truth that people bury in their hearts. I tell him that I do not come there with a girl to do the thing he's paid to watch out for. I look deep in his eyes when I say these things and he believes me. He comes over to see who it is on the grass. I say hello to him. He greets me in the same way and goes off searching for other black splotches upon the lawn. Avey and I went there. A band in one of the buildings a fair distance off was playing a march. I wished they would stop. Their playing was like a tin spoon in one's mouth. I wanted the Howard Glee Club to sing "Deep River," from the road. To sing "Deep River, Deep River," from the road. . . Other than the first comments, Avey had been silent. I started to hum a folk-tune. She slipped her hand in mine. Pillowed her head as best she could upon my arm. Kissed the hand that she was holding and listened, or so I thought, to what I had to say. I traced my development from the early days up to the present time, the phase in which I could understand her. I described her own nature and temperament. Told how they needed a larger life for their expression. How incapable Washington was of understanding that need. How it could not meet it. I pointed out that in lieu of proper channels, her emotions had overflowed into paths that dissipated them. I talked, beautifully I thought, about an art that would be born, an art that would open the way for women the likes of her. I asked her to hope, and build up an inner life against the coming of that day. I recited some of my own things to her. I sang, with a strange quiver in my voice, a promise-song. And then I began to wonder why her hand had not once returned a single pressure. My old-time feeling about her laziness came back. I spoke sharply. My policeman friend passed by. I said hello to him. As he went away, I began to visualize certain possibilities. An immediate and urgent passion swept over me. Then I looked at Avey. Her heavy eyes were closed. Her breathing was as faint and regular as a child's in slumber. My passion died. I was afraid to move lest I disturb her. Hours and hours, I guess it was, she lay there. My body grew numb. I shivered. I coughed. I wanted to get up and whittle at the boxes of young trees. I withdrew my hand. I raised her head to waken her. She did not stir. I got up and walked around. I found my policeman friend and talked to him. We both came up, and bent over her. He said it would be all right for her to stay there just so long as she got away before the workmen came at dawn. A blanket was borrowed from a neighbor house. I sat beside her through the night. I saw the dawn steal over Washington. The Capitol dome looked like a gray ghost ship drifting in from sea. Avey's face was pale, and her eyes were heavy. She did not have the gray crimson-splashed beauty of the dawn. I hated to wake her. Orphan-woman. . .

F[RANCIS] SCOTT [KEY] FITZGERALD (1896–1940)

Born in Minneapolis into an Irish family with some money but never quite enough (a situation to which F. Scott Fitzgerald later attribu-ted his "inferiority complex"), he was educated in private Catholic schools until he entered Princeton in 1913. He left without a degree to join the Army in 1917, but he had not got beyond training camps when the Armistice was declared. His army duties gave him enough leisure to attempt a novel, The Romantic Egotist, *which Scribner's declined in 1918.*

Out of the Army and in New York, Fitzgerald tried without success to find newspaper employment and then entered an advertising agency. He was determined to make enough money to marry Zelda Sayre, a Southern belle whom he had met in Montgomery, Alabama. Clearly, his work in advertising was not going to earn him that money. Having sold some fiction to Mencken's Smart Set, *he was encouraged to return to St. Paul to write. Scrapping much of* The Romantic Egotist *but retaining its possible parts, he finished a new novel,* This Side of Paradise, *which Scribner's at once accepted and published early in 1920. It was an immediate success: with it, the "jazz age" had been born, and Miss Sayre married him.*

There followed a decade of giddy dissipation and travel. The life of the Fitzgeralds was an imitation of his early art, and quite as gaudy. They had one child, Frances, nicknamed Scottie. Fitzgerald's success gave him immediate entree to high-paying commercial magazines like The Saturday Evening Post *and no less to more literary peri-odicals like* Scribner's Magazine. *He turned out story after story, some of them very fine, others hack work. The best were collected in two volumes,* Flappers and Philosophers (1920) *and* Tales of the Jazz Age (1922), *and he published a second novel with a sinister*

and prophetic title, The Beautiful and Damned *(1922). His play,*
The Vegetable *(1923), was a failure, and again he had to write
many stories to recoup his losses and pay his debts. Some of these
stories were collected in* All the Sad Young Men *(1926), and among
the very best is one called "Winter Dreams," a kind of miniature
Daisy Buchanan–Jay Gatsby situation set in St. Paul rather than
on Long Island. In the meantime he had published* The Great
Gatsby *(1925) itself, his first fine novel and without equal of its
kind in our fiction. "I want to write something* new," *Fitzgerald had
written his publisher, "something extraordinary and beautiful and
simple and intricately patterned." And he had.*

But then things began to fall to pieces. Living now chiefly in Paris and
on the Riviera, and living very high, Fitzgerald could not get on
with his next novel, in spite of a number of earnest if false starts.
In 1930 Zelda Fitzgerald suffered a mental collapse, and he brought
her to Baltimore for treatment in 1931. (It was in early 1932, in a
relatively lucid period, that she wrote her novel, Save Me the Waltz,
published that year and republished in 1967.) Reconceiving his novel
in terms of her collapse, Fitzgerald found himself finishing Tender
is the Night, when, after a second breakdown in 1932, she seemed
to have recovered. He was correcting the proofs of his novel in
1934 when she suffered her most severe breakdown. After that,
most of her life was in hospitals, and their life together was over.

Tender is the Night *does not have the perfect structure of* The Great
Gatsby, *but it is richer and more eloquent and perhaps an even
greater novelistic achievement. Its reception was cool: critics treated
it as a story about frivolous people written in a dark social time
that demanded more responsible efforts from writers. The stories
collected in* Taps at Reveille *(1935) were brushed off even more
coldly.*

And Fitzgerald, very poor now, and in debt, drifted to Hollywood,
where he spent most of the rest of his life, little regarded by the
powers there. He had the companionship of the columnist Sheilah
Graham, who loved him and helped him live a moderately stable
life, but it was a relatively joyless one, accounted for in his
confessional pieces published in Esquire under the title "The
Crack-up" and, with other pieces, in book form in 1945, collected
by his old college friend, Edmund Wilson. Wilson had also edited
the unfinished novel, The Last Tycoon (1941), on which Fitzgerald
was at work at the time of his death. Had he lived to finish it, it
might have been his best work, and certainly our best novel about
Hollywood.

He attempted suicide several times, but he died of a heart attack in
1940.

FURTHER READING

Two biographies are vital: Arthur Mizener, *The Far Side of Paradise* (1951, revised 1965), and Andrew Turnbull, *Scott Fitzgerald* (1962). See also, for important biographical information, Fitzgerald's *The Crack-up* (1945, edited by Edmund Wilson), Sheila Graham's *Beloved Infidel* (1958), and Nancy Milford's *Zelda* (1970). Andrew Turnbull edited *The Letters of F. Scott Fitzgerald* (1963) and *Letters to a Daughter* (1965). The chief critical studies are Kenneth Eble, *F. Scott Fitzgerald* (1963); James E. Miller, Jr., *F. Scott Fitzgerald: His Art and His Technique* (1964); Sergio Perosa, *The Art of F. Scott Fitzgerald* (1965); Henry Dan Piper, *F. Scott Fitzgerald: A Critical Portrait* (1965); Richard D. Lehan, *F. Scott Fitzgerald and the Craft of Fiction* (1966); Robert F. Sklar, *F. Scott Fitzgerald: The Last Laocoön* (1967); and Milton Hindus, *F. Scott Fitzgerald: An Introduction and Interpretation* (1968). Alfred Kazin edited *F. Scott Fitzgerald: The Man and His Work* (1951), the best volume of collected criticism on Fitzgerald.

Winter Dreams (1926)

Some of the caddies were poor as sin and lived in one-room houses with a neurasthenic cow in the front yard, but Dexter Green's father owned the second best grocery-store in Black Bear—the best one was "The Hub," patronized by the wealthy people from Sherry Island—and Dexter caddied only for pocket-money.

In the fall when the days became crisp and gray, and the long Minnesota winter shut down like the white lid of a box, Dexter's skis moved over the snow that hid the fairways of the golf course. At these times the country gave him a feeling of profound melancholy—it offended him that the links should lie in enforced fallowness, haunted by ragged sparrows for the long season. It was dreary, too, that on the tees where the gay colors fluttered in summer there were now only the desolate sand-boxes knee-deep in crusted ice. When he crossed the hills the wind blew cold as misery, and if the sun was out he tramped with his eyes squinted up against the hard dimensionless glare.

In April the winter ceased abruptly. The snow ran down into Black Bear Lake scarcely tarrying for the early golfers to brave the season with red and black balls. Without elation, without an interval of moist glory, the cold was gone.

Dexter knew that there was something dismal about this Northern spring, just as he knew there was something gorgeous about the fall. Fall made him clinch his hands and tremble and repeat idiotic sentences to himself, and make brisk abrupt gestures of command to imaginary audiences and armies. October filled him with hope which November raised to a sort of ecstatic triumph, and in this mood the fleeting brilliant impressions of the summer at Sherry Island were ready grist to his mill. He became a golf champion and defeated Mr. T. A. Hedrick in a marvellous match played a hundred times over the fairways of his imagination, a match each detail of which he changed about untiringly—sometimes he won with almost laughable ease, sometimes he came up magnificently from behind. Again, stepping from a Pierce-Arrow automobile, like Mr. Mortimer Jones, he strolled frigidly into the lounge of the Sherry Island Golf Club—or perhaps, surrounded by an admiring crowd, he gave an exhibition of fancy diving from the spring-board of the club raft. . . . Among those who watched him in open-mouthed wonder was Mr. Mortimer Jones.

And one day it came to pass that Mr. Jones—himself and not his ghost—came up to Dexter with tears in his eyes and said that Dexter was the — — best caddy in the club, and wouldn't he decide not to quit if Mr. Jones made it worth his while, because every other — — caddy in the club lost one ball a hole for him—regularly——

"No, sir," said Dexter decisively, "I don't want to caddy any more." Then, after a pause: "I'm too old."

"You're not more than fourteen. Why the devil did you decide just this morning that you wanted to quit? You promised that next week you'd go over to the state tournament with me."

"I decided I was too old."

Dexter handed in his "A Class" badge, collected what money was due him from the caddy master, and walked home to Black Bear Village.

"The best — — caddy I ever saw," shouted Mr. Mortimer Jones over a drink that afternoon. "Never lost a ball! Willing! Intelligent! Quiet! Honest! Grateful!"

The little girl who had done this was eleven—beautifully ugly as little girls are apt to be who are destined after a few years to be inexpressibly lovely and bring no end of misery to a great number of men. The spark, however, was perceptible. There was a general ungodliness in the way her lips twisted down at the corners when she smiled, and in the—Heaven help us!—in the almost passionate quality of her eyes. Vitality is born early in such women. It was utterly in evidence now, shining through her thin frame in a sort of glow.

She had come eagerly out on to the course at nine o'clock with a white linen nurse and five small new golf-clubs in a white canvas bag which the nurse was carrying. When Dexter first saw her she was standing by the caddy house, rather ill at ease and trying to conceal the fact by engaging her nurse in an obviously unnatural conversation graced by startling and irrelevant grimaces from herself.

"Well, it's certainly a nice day, Hilda," Dexter heard her say. She drew down the corners of her mouth, smiled, and glanced furtively around, her eyes in transit falling for an instant on Dexter.

Then to the nurse:

"Well, I guess there aren't very many people out here this morning, are there?"

The smile again—radiant, blatantly artificial—convincing.

"I don't know what we're supposed to do now," said the nurse, looking nowhere in particular.

"Oh, that's all right. I'll fix it up."

Dexter stood perfectly still, his mouth slightly ajar. He knew that if he moved forward a step his stare would be in her line of vision—if he moved backward he would lose his full view of her face. For a moment he had not realized how young she was. Now he remembered having seen her several times the year before—in bloomers.

Suddenly, involuntarily, he laughed, a short abrupt laugh—then startled by himself, he turned and began to walk quickly away.

"Boy!"

Dexter stopped.

"Boy——"

Beyond question he was addressed. Not only that, but he was treated to that absurd smile, that preposterous smile—the memory of which at least a dozen men were to carry into middle age.

"Boy, do you know where the golf teacher is?"

"He's giving a lesson."

"Well, do you know where the caddy-master is?"

"He isn't here yet this morning."

"Oh." For a moment this baffled her. She stood alternately on her right and left foot.

"We'd like to get a caddy," said the nurse. "Mrs. Mortimer Jones sent us out to play golf, and we don't know how without we get a caddy."

Here she was stopped by an ominous glance from Miss Jones, followed immediately by the smile.

"There aren't any caddies here except me," said Dexter to the nurse, "and I got to stay here in charge until the caddy-master gets here."

"Oh."

Miss Jones and her retinue now withdrew, and at a proper distance from Dexter became involved in a heated conversation, which was concluded by Miss Jones taking one of the clubs and hitting it on the ground with violence. For further emphasis she raised it again and was about to bring it down smartly upon the nurse's bosom, when the nurse seized the club and twisted it from her hands.

"You damn little mean old *thing!*" cried Miss Jones wildly.

Another argument ensued. Realizing that the elements of the comedy were implied in the scene, Dexter several times began to laugh, but each time restrained the laugh before it reached audibility. He could not resist the monstrous conviction that the little girl was justified in beating the nurse.

The situation was resolved by the fortuitous appearance of the caddy-master, who was appealed to immediately by the nurse.

"Miss Jones is to have a little caddy, and this one says he can't go."

"Mr. McKenna said I was to wait here till you came," said Dexter quickly.

"Well, he's here now." Miss Jones smiled cheerfully at the caddy-master. Then she dropped her bag and set off at a haughty mince toward the first tee.

"Well?" The caddy-master turned to Dexter. "What you standing there like a dummy for? Go pick up the young lady's clubs."

"I don't think I'll go out to-day," said Dexter.

"You don't——"

"I think I'll quit."

The enormity of his decision frightened him. He was a favorite caddy, and the thirty dollars a month he earned through the summer were not to be made elsewhere around the lake. But he had received a strong emotional shock, and his perturbation required a violent and immediate outlet.

It is not so simple as that, either. As so frequently would be the case in the future, Dexter was unconsciously dictated to by his winter dreams.

II

Now, of course, the quality and the seasonability of these winter dreams varied, but the stuff of them remained. They persuaded Dexter several years later to pass up a business course at the State university— his father, prospering now, would have paid his way—for the precarious advantage of attending an older and more famous university in the East, where he was bothered by his scanty funds. But do not get the impression, because his winter dreams happened to be concerned at first with musings on the rich, that there was anything merely snobbish in the boy. He wanted not association with glittering things and glittering people—he wanted the glittering things themselves. Often he reached out for the best without knowing why he wanted it—and sometimes he ran up against the mysterious denials and prohibitions in which life indulges. It is with one of those denials and not with his career as a whole that this story deals.

He made money. It was rather amazing. After college he went to the city from which Black Bear Lake draws its wealthy patrons. When he was only twenty-three and had been there not quite two years, there were already people who liked to say: "Now *there's* a boy——" All about him rich men's sons were peddling bonds precariously, or investing patrimonies precariously, or plodding through the two dozen volumes of the "George Washington Commercial Course," but Dexter borrowed a thousand dollars on his college degree and his confident mouth, and bought a partnership in a laundry.

It was a small laundry when he went into it, but Dexter made a specialty of learning how the English washed fine woolen golf-stockings without shrinking them, and within a year he was catering to the trade that wore knickerbockers. Men were insisting that their Shetland hose and sweaters go to his laundry, just as they had insisted on a caddy who could find golf-balls. A little later he was doing their wives' lingerie as well—and running five branches in different parts of the city. Before he was twenty-seven he owned the largest string of laundries in his section of the country. It was then that he sold out and went to New York. But the part of his story that concerns us goes back to the days when he was making his first big success.

When he was twenty-three Mr. Hart—one of the gray-haired men who like to say "Now there's a boy"—gave him a guest card to the Sherry Island Golf Club for a week-end. So he signed his name one day on the register, and that afternoon played golf in a foursome with Mr. Hart and Mr. Sandwood and Mr. T. A. Hedrick. He did not consider it necessary to remark that he had once carried Mr. Hart's bag over this same links, and that he knew every trap and gully with his eyes shut—but he found himself glancing at the four caddies who trailed them, trying to catch a gleam or gesture that would remind him of himself, that would lessen the gap which lay between his present and his past.

It was a curious day, slashed abruptly with fleeting, familiar impressions. One minute he had the sense of being a trespasser—in the next he was impressed by the tremendous superiority he felt toward Mr. T. A. Hedrick, who was a bore and not even a good golfer any more.

Then, because of a ball Mr. Hart lost near the fifteenth green, an enormous thing happened. While they were searching the stiff grasses of the rough there was a clear call of "Fore!" from behind a hill in their rear. And as they all turned abruptly from their search a bright new ball sliced abruptly over the hill and caught Mr. T. A. Hedrick in the abdomen.

"By Gad!" cried Mr. T. A. Hedrick, "they ought to put some of these crazy women off the course. It's getting to be outrageous."

A head and a voice came up together over the hill:

"Do you mind if we go through?"

"You hit me in the stomach!" declared Mr. Hedrick wildly.

"Did I?" The girl approached the group of men. "I'm sorry. I yelled 'Fore!'"

Her glance fell casually on each of the men—then scanned the fairway for her ball.

"Did I bounce into the rough?"

It was impossible to determine whether this question was ingenuous or malicious. In a moment, however, she left no doubt, for as her partner came up over the hill she called cheerfully:

"Here I am! I'd have gone on the green except that I hit something."

As she took her stance for a short mashie shot, Dexter looked at her closely. She wore a blue gingham dress, rimmed at throat and shoulders with a white edging that accentuated her tan. The quality of exaggeration, of thinness, which had made her passionate eyes and down-turning mouth absurd at eleven, was gone now. She was arrestingly beautiful. The color in her cheeks was centred like the color in a picture—it was not a "high" color, but a sort of fluctuating and feverish warmth, so shaded that it seemed at any moment it would recede and disappear. This color and the mobility of her mouth gave a continual impression of flux, of intense life, of passionate vitality—balanced only partially by the sad luxury of her eyes.

She swung her mashie impatiently and without interest, pitching the ball into a sand-pit on the other side of the green. With a quick, insincere smile and a careless "Thank you!" she went on after it.

"That Judy Jones!" remarked Mr. Hedrick on the next tee, as they waited—some moments—for her to play on ahead. "All she needs is to be turned up and spanked for six months and then to be married off to an old-fashioned cavalry captain."

"My God, she's good-looking!" said Mr. Sandwood, who was just over thirty.

"Good-looking!" cried Mr. Hedrick contemptuously, "she always looks as if she wanted to be kissed! Turning those big cow-eyes on every calf in town!"

It was doubtful if Mr. Hedrick intended a reference to the maternal instinct.

"She'd play pretty good golf if she'd try," said Mr. Sandwood.

"She has no form," said Mr. Hedrick solemnly.

"She has a nice figure," said Mr. Sandwood.

"Better thank the Lord she doesn't drive a swifter ball," said Mr. Hart, winking at Dexter.

Later in the afternoon the sun went down with a riotous swirl of gold and varying blues and scarlets, and left the dry, rustling night of Western summer. Dexter watched from the veranda of the Golf Club, watched the even overlap of the waters in the little wind, silver molasses under the harvest-moon. Then the moon held a finger to her lips and the lake became a clear pool, pale and quiet. Dexter put on his bathing-suit and swam out to the farthest raft, where he stretched dripping on the wet canvas of the springboard.

There was a fish jumping and a star shining and the lights around the lake were gleaming. Over on a dark peninsula a piano was playing the songs of last summer and of summers before that—songs from "Chin-Chin" and "The Count of Luxemburg" and "The Chocolate Soldier" [1]—and because the sound of a piano over a stretch of water had always seemed beautiful to Dexter he lay perfectly quiet and listened.

The tune the piano was playing at that moment had been gay and new five years before when Dexter was a sophomore at college. They had played it at a prom once when he could not afford the luxury of proms, and he had stood outside the gymnasium and listened. The

[1] Popular Broadway musical shows.

sound of the tune precipitated in him a sort of ecstasy and it was with that ecstasy he viewed what happened to him now. It was a mood of intense appreciation, a sense that, for once, he was magnificently attune to life and that everything about him was radiating a brightness and a glamour he might never know again.

A low, pale oblong detached itself suddenly from the darkness of the Island, spitting forth the reverberate sound of a racing motorboat. Two white streamers of cleft water rolled themselves out behind it and almost immediately the boat was beside him, drowning out the hot tinkle of the piano in the drone of its spray. Dexter raising himself on his arms was aware of a figure standing at the wheel, of two dark eyes regarding him over the lengthening space of water—then the boat had gone by and was sweeping in an immense and purposeless circle of spray round and round in the middle of the lake. With equal eccentricity one of the circles flattened out and headed back toward the raft.

"Who's that?" she called, shutting off her motor. She was so near now that Dexter could see her bathing-suit, which consisted apparently of pink rompers.

The nose of the boat bumped the raft, and as the latter tilted rakishly he was precipitated toward her. With different degrees of interest they recognized each other.

"Aren't you one of those men we played through this afternoon?" she demanded.

He was.

"Well, do you know how to drive a motor-boat? Because if you do I wish you'd drive this one so I can ride on the surf-board behind. My name is Judy Jones"—she favored him with an absurd smirk—rather, what tried to be a smirk, for, twist her mouth as she might, it was not grotesque, it was merely beautiful—"and I live in a house over there on the Island, and in that house there is a man waiting for me. When he drove up at the door I drove out of the dock because he says I'm his ideal."

There was a fish jumping and a star shining and the lights around the lake were gleaming. Dexter sat beside Judy Jones and she explained how her boat was driven. Then she was in the water, swimming to the floating surf-board with a sinuous crawl. Watching her was without effort to the eye, watching a branch waving or a sea-gull flying. Her arms, burned to butternut, moved sinuously among the dull platinum ripples, elbow appearing first, casting the forearm back with a cadence of falling water, then reaching out and down, stabbing a path ahead.

They moved out into the lake; turning, Dexter saw that she was kneeling on the low rear of the now uptilted surf-board.

"Go faster," she called, "fast as it'll go."

Obediently he jammed the lever forward and the white spray mounted at the bow. When he looked around again the girl was standing up on the rushing board, her arms spread wide, her eyes lifted toward the moon.

"It's awful cold," she shouted. "What's your name?"

He told her.

"Well, why don't you come to dinner to-morrow night?"

His heart turned over like the fly-wheel of the boat, and, for the second time, her casual whim gave a new direction to his life.

III

Next evening while he waited for her to come down-stairs, Dexter peopled the soft deep summer room and the sun-porch that opened from it with the men who had already loved Judy Jones. He knew the sort of men they were—the men who when he first went to college had entered from the great prep schools with graceful clothes and the deep tan of healthy summers. He had seen that, in one sense, he was better than these men. He was newer and stronger. Yet in acknowledging to himself that he wished his children to be like them he was admitting that he was but the rough, strong stuff from which they eternally sprang.

When the time had come for him to wear good clothes, he had known who were the best tailors in America, and the best tailors in America had made him the suit he wore this evening. He had acquired that particular reserve peculiar to his university, that set it off from other universities. He recognized the value to him of such a mannerism and he had adopted it; he knew that to be careless in dress and manner required more confidence than to be careful. But carelessness was for his children. His mother's name had been Krimslich. She was a Bohemian of the peasant class and she had talked broken English to the end of her days. Her son must keep to the set patterns.

At a little after seven Judy Jones came down-stairs. She wore a blue silk afternoon dress, and he was disappointed at first that she had not put on something more elaborate. This feeling was accentuated when, after a brief greeting, she went to the door of a butler's pantry and pushing it open called: "You can serve dinner, Martha." He had rather expected that a butler would announce dinner, that there would be a cocktail. Then he put these thoughts behind him as they sat down side by side on a lounge and looked at each other.

"Father and mother won't be here," she said thoughtfully.

He remembered the last time he had seen her father, and he was glad the parents were not to be here to-night—they might wonder who he was. He had been born in Keeble, a Minnesota village fifty miles farther north, and he always gave Keeble as his home instead of Black Bear Village. Country towns were well enough to come from if they weren't inconveniently in sight and used as footstools by fashionable lakes.

They talked of his university, which she had visited frequently during the past two years, and of the near-by city which supplied Sherry Island with its patrons, and whither Dexter would return next day to his prospering laundries.

During dinner she slipped into a moody depression which gave Dexter a feeling of uneasiness. Whatever petulance she uttered in her throaty voice worried him. Whatever she smiled at—at him, at a chicken liver, at nothing—it disturbed him that her smile could have no root in mirth, or even in amusement. When the scarlet corners of her lips curved down, it was less a smile than an invitation to a kiss.

Then, after dinner, she led him out on the dark sun-porch and deliberately changed the atmosphere.

"Do you mind if I weep a little?" she said.

"I'm afraid I'm boring you," he responded quickly.

"You're not. I like you. But I've just had a terrible afternoon. There was a man I cared about, and this afternoon he told me out of a clear sky that he was poor as a church-mouse. He'd never even hinted it before. Does this sound horribly mundane?"

"Perhaps he was afraid to tell you."

"Suppose he was," she answered. "He didn't start right. You see, if I'd thought of him as poor—well, I've been mad about loads of poor men, and fully intended to marry them all. But in this case, I hadn't thought of him that way, and my interest in him wasn't strong enough to survive the shock. As if a girl calmly informed her fiancé that she was a widow. He might not object to widows, but——

"Let's start right," she interrupted herself suddenly. "Who are you, anyhow?"

For a moment Dexter hesitated. Then:

"I'm nobody," he announced. "My career is largely a matter of futures."

"Are you poor?"

"No," he said frankly, "I'm probably making more money than any man my age in the Northwest. I know that's an obnoxious remark, but you advised me to start right."

There was a pause. Then she smiled and the corners of her mouth drooped and an almost imperceptible sway brought her closer to him, looking up into his eyes. A lump rose in Dexter's throat, and he waited breathless for the experiment, facing the unpredictable compound that would form mysteriously from the elements of their lips. Then he saw— she communicated her excitement to him, lavishly, deeply, with kisses that were not a promise but a fulfilment. They aroused in him not hunger demanding renewal but surfeit that would demand more surfeit . . . kisses that were like charity, creating want by holding back nothing at all.

It did not take him many hours to decide that he had wanted Judy Jones ever since he was a proud, desirous little boy.

IV

It began like that—and continued, with varying shades of intensity, on such a note right up to the dénouement. Dexter surrendered a part of himself to the most direct and unprincipled personality with which he had ever come in contact. Whatever Judy wanted, she went after with the full pressure of her charm. There was no divergence of method, no jockeying for position or premeditation of effects—there was a very little mental side to any of her affairs. She simply made men conscious to the highest degree of her physical loveliness. Dexter had no desire to change her. Her deficiencies were knit up with a passionate energy that transcended and justified them.

When, as Judy's head lay against his shoulder that first night, she whispered, "I don't know what's the matter with me. Last night I thought I was in love with a man and to-night I think I'm in love with you ——"—it seemed to him a beautiful and romantic thing to say. It was the exquisite excitability that for the moment he controlled and owned. But a week later he was compelled to view this same quality in a different light. She took him in her roadster to a picnic supper, and after supper she disappeared, likewise in her roadster, with another man. Dexter became enormously upset and was scarcely able to be decently civil to the other people present. When she assured him that she had not kissed the other man, he knew she was lying—yet he was glad that she had taken the trouble to lie to him.

He was, as he found before the summer ended, one of a varying dozen who circulated about her. Each of them had at one time been favored above all others—about half of them still basked in the solace of occasional sentimental revivals. Whenever one showed signs of dropping out through long neglect, she granted him a brief honeyed hour, which encouraged him to tag along for a year or so longer. Judy made these forays upon the helpless and defeated without malice, indeed half unconscious that there was anything mischievous in what she did.

When a new man came to town every one dropped out—dates were automatically cancelled.

The helpless part of trying to do anything about it was that she did it all herself. She was not a girl who could be "won" in the kinetic sense—she was proof against cleverness, she was proof against charm; if any of these assailed her too strongly she would immediately resolve the affair to a physical basis, and under the magic of her physical splendor the strong as well as the brilliant played her game and not their own. She was entertained only by the gratification of her desires and by the direct exercise of her own charm. Perhaps from so much youthful love, so many youthful lovers, she had come, in self-defense, to nourish herself wholly from within.

Succeeding Dexter's first exhilaration came restlessness and dissatisfaction. The helpless ecstasy of losing himself in her was opiate rather than tonic. It was fortunate for his work during the winter that those moments of ecstasy came infrequently. Early in their acquaintance it had seemed for a while that there was a deep and spontaneous mutual attraction—that first August, for example—three days of long evenings on her dusky veranda, of strange wan kisses through the late afternoon, in shadowy alcoves or behind the protecting trellises of the garden arbors, of mornings when she was fresh as a dream and almost shy at meeting him in the clarity of the rising day. There was all the ecstasy of an engagement about it, sharpened by his realization that there was no engagement. It was during those three days that, for the first time, he had asked her to marry him. She said "maybe some day," she said "kiss me," she said "I'd like to marry you," she said "I love you"—she said—nothing.

The three days were interrupted by the arrival of a New York man who visited at her house for half September. To Dexter's agony, rumor engaged them. The man was the son of the president of a great trust company. But at the end of a month it was reported that Judy was yawning. At a dance one night she sat all evening in a motor-boat with a local beau, while the New Yorker searched the club for her frantically. She told the local beau that she was bored with her visitor, and two days later he left. She was seen with him at the station, and it was reported that he looked very mournful indeed.

On this note the summer ended. Dexter was twenty-four, and he found himself increasingly in a position to do as he wished. He joined two clubs in the city and lived at one of them. Though he was by no means an integral part of the stag-lines at these clubs, he managed to be on hand at dances where Judy Jones was likely to appear. He could have gone out socially as much as he liked—he was an eligible young man, now, and popular with down-town fathers. His confessed devotion to Judy Jones had rather solidified his position. But he had no social aspirations and rather despised the dancing men who were always on tap for the Thursday or Saturday parties and who filled in at dinners with the younger married set. Already he was playing with the idea of going East to New York. He wanted to take Judy Jones with him. No disillusion as to the world in which she had grown up could cure his illusion as to her desirability.

Remember that—for only in the light of it can what he did for her be understood.

Eighteen months after he first met Judy Jones he became engaged to another girl. Her name was Irene Scheerer, and her father was one of the men who had always believed in Dexter. Irene was light-haired and sweet and honorable, and a little stout, and she had two suitors whom she pleasantly relinquished when Dexter formally asked her to marry him.

Summer, fall, winter, spring, another summer, another fall—so much he had given of his active life to the incorrigible lips of Judy Jones. She had treated him with interest, with encouragement, with malice, with indifference, with contempt. She had inflicted on him the innumerable little slights and indignities possible in such a case—as if in revenge for having ever cared for him at all. She had beckoned him and yawned at him and beckoned him again and he had responded often with bitterness and narrowed eyes. She had brought him ecstatic happiness and intolerable agony of spirit. She had caused him untold inconvenience and not a little trouble. She had insulted him, and she had ridden over him, and she had played his interest in her against his interest in his work—for fun. She had done everything to him except to criticise him—this she had not done—it seemed to him only because it might have sullied the utter indifference she manifested and sincerely felt toward him.

When autumn had come and gone again it occurred to him that he could not have Judy Jones. He had to beat this into his mind but he convinced himself at last. He lay awake at night for a while and argued it over. He told himself the trouble and the pain she had caused him, he enumerated her glaring deficiencies as a wife. Then he said to himself that he loved her, and after a while he fell asleep. For a week, lest he imagined her husky voice over the telephone or her eyes opposite him at lunch, he worked hard and late, and at night he went to his office and plotted out his years.

At the end of a week he went to a dance and cut in on her once. For almost the first time since they had met he did not ask her to sit out with him or tell her that she was lovely. It hurt him that she did not miss these things—that was all. He was not jealous when he saw that there was a new man to-night. He had been hardened against jealously long before.

He stayed late at the dance. He sat for an hour with Irene Scheerer and talked about books and about music. He knew very little about either. But he was beginning to be master of his own time now, and he had a rather priggish notion that he—the young and already fabulously successful Dexter Green—should know more about such things.

That was in October, when he was twenty-five. In January, Dexter and Irene became engaged. It was to be announced in June, and they were to be married three months later.

The Minnesota winter prolonged itself interminably, and it was almost May when the winds came soft and the snow ran down into Black Bear Lake at last. For the first time in over a year Dexter was enjoying a certain tranquillity of spirit. Judy Jones had been in Florida, and afterward in Hot Springs, and somewhere she had been engaged, and somewhere she had broken it off. At first, when Dexter had definitely given her up, it had made him sad that people still linked them together and asked for news of her, but when he began to be placed at dinner next to Irene Scheerer people didn't ask him about her any more—they told him about her. He ceased to be an authority on her.

May at last. Dexter walked the streets at night when the darkness was damp as rain, wondering that so soon, with so little done, so much of ectasy had gone from him. May one year back had been marked by Judy's poignant, unforgivable, yet forgiven turbulence—it had been one of those rare times when he fancied she had grown to care for him. That old penny's worth of happiness he had spent for this bushel of content. He knew that Irene would be no more than a curtain spread behind him, a hand moving among gleaming teacups, a voice calling to children . . . fire and loveliness were gone, the magic of nights and the wonder of the varying hours and seasons . . . slender lips, down-turning, dropping to his lips and bearing him up into a heaven of eyes. . . . The thing was deep in him. He was too strong and alive for it to die lightly.

In the middle of May when the weather balanced for a few days on the thin bridge that led to deep summer he turned in one night at Irene's house. Their engagement was to be announced in a week now— no one would be surprised at it. And to-night they would sit together on the lounge at the University Çlub and look on for an hour at the dancers. It gave him a sense of solidity to go with her—she was so sturdily popular, so intensely "great."

He mounted the steps of the brownstone house and stepped inside.

"Irene," he called.

Mrs. Scheerer came out of the living-room to meet him.

"Dexter," she said, "Irene's gone up-stairs with a splitting headache. She wanted to go with you but I made her go to bed."

"Nothing serious, I——"

"Oh, no. She's going to play golf with you in the morning. You can spare her for just one night, can't you, Dexter?"

Her smile was kind. She and Dexter liked each other. In the living-room he talked for a moment before he said good-night.

Returning to the University Club, where he had rooms, he stood in the doorway for a moment and watched the dancers. He leaned against the door-post, nodded at a man or two—yawned.

"Hello, darling."

The familiar voice at his elbow startled him. Judy Jones had left a man and crossed the room to him—Judy Jones, a slender enamelled doll in cloth of gold: gold in a band at her head, gold in two slipper points at her dress's hem. The fragile glow of her face seemed to blossom as she smiled at him. A breeze of warmth and light blew through the room. His hands in the pockets of his dinner-jacket tightened spasmodically. He was filled with a sudden excitement.

"When did you get back?" he asked casually.

"Come here and I'll tell you about it."

She turned and he followed her. She had been away—he could have wept at the wonder of her return. She had passed through enchanted streets, doing things that were like provocative music. All mysterious happenings, all fresh and quickening hopes, had gone away with her, come back with her now.

She turned in the doorway.

"Have you a car here? If you haven't, I have."

"I have a coupé."

In then, with a rustle of golden cloth. He slammed the door. Into so many cars she had stepped—like this—like that—her back against the leather, so—her elbow resting on the door—waiting. She would have been soiled long since had there been anything to soil her—except herself—but this was her own self outpouring.

With an effort he forced himself to start the car and back into the street. This was nothing, he must remember. She had done this before, and he had put her behind him, as he would have crossed a bad account from his books.

He drove slowly down-town and, affecting abstraction, traversed the deserted streets of the business section, peopled here and there where a movie was giving out its crowd or where consumptive or pugilistic youth lounged in front of pool halls. The clink of glasses and the slap of hands on the bars issued from saloons, cloisters of glazed glass and dirty yellow light.

She was watching him closely and the silence was embarrassing, yet in this crisis he could find no casual word with which to profane the hour. At a convenient turning he began to zigzag back toward the University Club.

"Have you missed me?" she asked suddenly.

"Everybody missed you."

He wondered if she knew of Irene Scheerer. She had been back only a day—her absence had been almost contemporaneous with his engagement.

"What a remark!" Judy laughed sadly—without sadness. She looked at him searchingly. He became absorbed in the dashboard.

"You're handsomer than you used to be," she said thoughtfully. "Dexter, you have the most rememberable eyes."

He could have laughed at this, but he did not laugh. It was the sort of thing that was said to sophomores. Yet it stabbed at him.

"I'm awfully tired of everything, darling." She called every one darling, endowing the endearment with careless, individual comraderie. "I wish you'd marry me."

The directness of this confused him. He should have told her now that he was going to marry another girl, but he could not tell her. He could as easily have sworn that he had never loved her.

"I think we'd get along," she continued, on the same note, "unless probably you've forgotten me and fallen in love with another girl."

Her confidence was obviously enormous. She had said, in effect, that she found such a thing impossible to believe, that if it were true he had merely committed a childish indiscretion—and probably to show off. She would forgive him, because it was not a matter of any moment but rather something to be brushed aside lightly.

"Of course you could never love anybody but me," she continued, "I like the way you love me. Oh, Dexter, have you forgotten last year?"

"No, I haven't forgotten."

"Neither have I!"

Was she sincerely moved—or was she carried along by the wave of her own acting?

"I wish we could be like that again," she said, and he forced himself to answer:

"I don't think we can."

"I suppose not. . . . I hear you're giving Irene Scheerer a violent rush."

There was not the faintest emphasis on the name, yet Dexter was suddenly ashamed.

"Oh, take me home," cried Judy suddenly; "I don't want to go back to that idiotic dance—with those children."

Then, as he turned up the street that led to the residence district, Judy began to cry quietly to herself. He had never seen her cry before.

The dark street lightened, the dwellings of the rich loomed up around them, he stopped his coupé in front of the great white bulk of the Mortimer Joneses' house, somnolent, gorgeous, drenched with the splendor of the damp moonlight. Its solidity startled him. The strong walls, the steel of the girders, the breadth and beam and pomp of it were there only to bring out the contrast with the young beauty beside him. It was sturdy to accentuate her slightness—as if to show what a breeze could be generated by a butterfly's wing.

He sat perfectly quiet, his nerves in wild clamor, afraid that if he moved he would find her irresistibly in his arms. Two tears had rolled down her wet face and trembled on her upper lip.

"I'm more beautiful than anybody else," she said brokenly, "why can't I be happy?" Her moist eyes tore at his stability—her mouth turned slowly downward with an exquisite sadness: "I'd like to marry you if you'll have me, Dexter. I suppose you think I'm not worth having, but I'll be so beautiful for you, Dexter."

A million phrases of anger, pride, passion, hatred, tenderness fought on his lips. Then a perfect wave of emotion washed over him, carrying off with it a sediment of wisdom, of convention, of doubt, of honor. This was his girl who was speaking, his own, his beautiful, his pride.

"Won't you come in?" He heard her draw in her breath sharply. Waiting.

"All right," his voice was trembling, "I'll come in."

V

It was strange that neither when it was over nor a long time afterward did he regret that night. Looking at it from the perspective of ten years, the fact that Judy's flare for him endured just one month seemed of little importance. Nor did it matter that by his yielding he subjected himself to a deeper agony in the end and gave serious hurt to Irene

Scheerer and to Irene's parents, who had befriended him. There was nothing sufficiently pictorial about Irene's grief to stamp itself on his mind.

Dexter was at bottom hard-minded. The attitude of the city on his action was of no importance to him, not because he was going to leave the city, but because any outside attitude on the situation seemed superficial. He was completely indifferent to popular opinion. Nor, when he had seen that it was no use, that he did not possess in himself the power to move fundamentally or to hold Judy Jones, did he bear any malice toward her. He loved her, and he would love her until the day he was too old for loving—but he could not have her. So he tasted the deep pain that is reserved only for the strong, just as he had tasted for a little while the deep happiness.

Even the ultimate falsity of the grounds upon which Judy terminated the engagement that she did not want to "take him away" from Irene—Judy who had wanted nothing else—did not revolt him. He was beyond any revulsion or any amusement.

He went East in February with the intention of selling out his laundries and settling in New York—but the war came to America in March and changed his plans. He returned to the West, handed over the management of the business to his partner, and went into the first officers' training-camp in late April. He was one of those young thousands who greeted the war with a certain amount of relief, welcoming the liberation from webs of tangled emotion.

VI

This story is not his biography, remember, although things creep into it which have nothing to do with those dreams he had when he was young. We are almost done with them and with him now. There is only one more incident to be related here, and it happens seven years farther on.

It took place in New York, where he had done well—so well that there were no barriers too high for him. He was thirty-two years old, and, except for one flying trip immediately after the war, he had not been West in seven years. A man named Devlin from Detroit came into his office to see him in a business way, and then and there this incident occurred, and closed out, so to speak, this particular side of his life.

"So you're from the Middle West," said the man Devlin with careless curiosity. "That's funny—I thought men like you were probably born and raised on Wall Street. You know—wife of one of my best friends in Detroit came from your city. I was an usher at the wedding."

Dexter waited with no apprehension of what was coming.

"Judy Simms," said Devlin with no particular interest; "Judy Jones she was once."

"Yes, I knew her." A dull impatience spread over him. He had heard, of course, that she was married—perhaps deliberately he had heard no more.

"Awfully nice girl," brooded Devlin meaninglessly, "I'm sort of sorry for her."

"Why?" Something in Dexter was alert, receptive, at once.

"Oh, Lud Simms has gone to pieces in a way. I don't mean he ill-uses her, but he drinks and runs around——"

"Doesn't she run around?"

"No. Stays at home with her kids."

"Oh."

"She's a little too old for him," said Devlin.

"Too old!" cried Dexter. "Why, man, she's only twenty-seven."

He was possessed with a wild notion of rushing out into the streets and taking a train to Detroit. He rose to his feet spasmodically.

"I guess you're busy," Devlin apologized quickly. "I didn't real-ize——"

"No, I'm not busy," said Dexter, steading his voice. "I'm not busy at all. Not busy at all. Did you say she was—twenty-seven? No, I said she was twenty-seven."

"Yes, you did," agreed Devlin dryly.

"Go on, then. Go on."

"What do you mean?"

"About Judy Jones."

Devlin looked at him helplessly.

"Well, that's—I told you all there is to it. He treats her like the devil. Oh, they're not going to get divorced or anything. When he's particularly outrageous she forgives him. In fact, I'm inclined to think she loves him. She was a pretty girl when she first came to Detroit."

A pretty girl! The phrase struck Dexter as ludicrous.

"Isn't she—a pretty girl, any more?"

"Oh, she's all right."

"Look here," said Dexter, sitting down suddenly. "I don't understand. You say she was a 'pretty girl' and now you say she's 'all right.' I don't understand what you mean—Judy Jones wasn't a pretty girl, at all. She was a great beauty. Why, I knew her, I knew her. She was——"

Devlin laughed pleasantly.

"I'm not trying to start a row," he said. "I think Judy's a nice girl and I like her. I can't understand how a man like Lud Simms could fall madly in love with her, but he did." Then he added: "Most of the women like her."

Dexter looked closely at Devlin, thinking wildly that there must be a reason for this, some insensitivity in the man or some private malice.

"Lots of women fade just like *that*," Devlin snapped his fingers. "You must have seen it happen. Perhaps I've forgotten how pretty she was at her wedding. I've seen her so much since then, you see. She has nice eyes."

A sort of dullness settled down upon Dexter. For the first time in his life he felt like getting very drunk. He knew that he was laughing loudly at something Devlin had said, but he did not know what it was or why it was funny. When, in a few minutes, Devlin went he lay down on his lounge and looked out the window at the New York sky-line into which the sun was sinking in dull lovely shades of pink and gold.

He had thought that having nothing else to lose he was invulnerable at last—but he knew that he had just lost something more, as surely as if he had married Judy Jones and seen her fade away before his eyes.

The dream was gone. Something had been taken from him. In a sort of panic he pushed the palms of his hands into his eyes and tried to bring up a picture of the waters lapping on Sherry Island and the moonlit veranda, and gingham on the golf links and the dry sun and the gold color of her neck's soft down. And her mouth damp to his kisses and her eyes plaintive with melancholy and her freshness like new fine linen in the morning. Why, these things were no longer in the world! They had existed and they existed no longer.

For the first time in years the tears were streaming down his face. But they were for himself now. He did not care about mouth and eyes and moving hands. He wanted to care, and he could not care. For he had gone away and he could never go back any more. The gates were closed, the sun was gone down, and there was no beauty but the gray beauty of steel that withstands all time. Even the grief he could have borne was left behind in the country of illusion, of youth, of the richness of life, where his winter dreams had flourished.

"Long ago," he said, "long ago, there was something in me, but now that thing is gone. Now that thing is gone, that thing is gone. I cannot cry. I cannot care. That thing will come back no more."

JOHN [RODERIGO] DOS PASSOS (1896–1970)

Dos Passos, born in Chicago, was the son of a Virginian mother and a Portugese immigrant who became a successful New York lawyer. He was educated at the Choate School and at Harvard. Upon his graduation in 1916, he went to Spain to study architecture, but when the war broke out, he joined the French ambulance service. Out of that experience came One Man's Initiation: 1917 (1920), *and he became a writer.*

His early efforts at verse and fiction, except for Three Soldiers (1921), *one of the first novels to "debunk" the war, are of no importance. But in his collective novel,* Manhattan Transfer (1925), *which takes a whole city as its subject, he arrived at the techniques for which he was to become famous.*

Some plays and the other novels that immediately followed reveal a growing social awareness and a nonpartisan but leftish point of view, which had been dramatized by his arrest in Boston during the Sacco-Vanzetti protests when he shared a cell with the Communist Michael Gold. His general position then is made clear in The 42nd Parallel *(1930).*

This is the first volume in the trilogy called U.S.A. *(1938)—the others are* 1919 *(1932) and* The Big Money *(1936)—Dos Passos's great achievement and probably the closest we have come, if only because of its scope, to that hypothetical monster, "the great American novel." It takes as its subject the entire social history of the United States in the twentieth century up to and into the Great Depression. Involving swarms of characters and constantly shifting scenes, it organizes this vast material through four quite distinct techniques: rapidly summarizing segmented narratives of typical characters from all social strata, their lives overlapping and running parallel; montagelike conglomerates of current events called "Newsreels"; impressionistic biographies of contemporary figures of historic importance; and the subjective, stream-of-consciousness, rather lyrical impressions of the narrator himself, called "The Camera Eye." Ultimately, in literary history, the whole may prove to be a grand* tour de force, *but it is hard to believe that, in its sweeping indictment of a deteriorating culture, it will ever lose its interest.*

In spite of certain early gestures, Dos Passos was never a political activist. For many years he lived a quiet life on Cape Cod, later on his father's old farm in Virginia. His books continued to appear steadily over the years, but he was never much in the public eye. The chief critical interest in his later life was his turn to the Right and his defense of that system of free enterprise that his best work deplored. This began to show itself in his next trilogy, called District of Columbia *(1951), in four following novels, in a number of biographical works about American heroes, and in his late expository work,* The Theme is Freedom *(1956),* Occasions and Protests *(1964), and above all,* Mr. Wilson's War *(1963), which studies the history of the United States from 1901 to 1921 from a point-of-view that reverses* U.S.A. *His very last volume, an autobiographical memoir called* The Best Times *(1966), is a soft look backward at his experiences in the first three decades of the century. He wrote well, in a casual way, of himself, and only a little acidly of his friendship with such people as Fitzgerald and Hemingway.*

FURTHER READING

Robert Gorham Davis has written an informative brief study in *John Dos Passos* (1962). The full-length treatment is John H. Wrenn, *John Dos Passos* (1962). See also Alfred Kazin, *On Native Grounds* (1942) for a useful chapter on Dos Passos.

Playboy (*1932*)

Jack Reed [1]
was the son of a United States Marshal, a prominent citizen of Portland Oregon.
He was a likely boy
so his folks sent him east to school
and to Harvard.

Harvard stood for the broad *a* and those contacts so useful in later life and good English prose . . . if the hedgehog cant be cultured at Harvard the hedgehog cant
at all and the Lowells only speak to the Cabots and the Cabots
and the Oxford Book of Verse.
Reed was a likely youngster, he wasnt a jew or a socialist and he didnt come from Roxbury [2]; he was husky greedy had appetite for everything; a man's got to like many things in his life.
Reed was a man; he liked men he liked women he liked eating and writing and foggy nights and drinking and foggy nights and swimming and football and rhymed verse and being cheerleader ivy orator making clubs (not the very best clubs, his blood didn't run thin enough for the very best clubs)
and Copey's [3] voice reading *The Man Who Would Be King*, the dying fall *Urnburial*,[4] good English prose the lamps coming on across the Yard, under the elms in the twilight
dim voices in lecturehalls,
the dying fall the elms the Discobolus [5] the bricks of the old buildings and the commemorative gates and the goodies and the deans and the instructors all crying in thin voices refrain,
refrain; the rusty machinery creaked, the deans quivered under their

---

[1] John [Silas] Reed (1887–1920), poet, reporter, foreign correspondent, adventurer.
[2] Boston suburb inhabited mainly by workers and their families.
[3] Charles Townsend Copeland (1860–1952), vastly popular Harvard professor of English for many years, famous for his public readings.
[4] Works by Rudyard Kipling and Sir Thomas Browne, favorites of Copeland.
[5] Well-known early-fifth-century-B.C. Greek statue of a discus thrower.

mortarboards, the cogs turned to Class Day, and Reed was out in the world:

Washington Square!
Conventional turns out to be a cussword;
Villon seeking a lodging for the night in the Italian tenements on Sullivan Street, Bleecker, Carmine; [6]
research proves R.L.S.[7] to have been a great cocksman,
and as for the Elizabethans

to hell with them.
Ship on a cattleboat and see the world have adventures you can tell funny stories about every evening; a man's got to love . . . the quickening pulse the feel that today in foggy evenings footsteps taxicabs women's eyes . . . many things in his life.
Europe with a dash of horseradish, gulp Paris like an oyster;
but there's more to it than the Oxford Book of English Verse. Linc Steffens [8] talked the cooperative commonwealth.

revolution in a voice as mellow as Copey's, Diogenes Steffens with Marx for a lantern going through the west looking for a good man, Socrates Steffens kept asking why not revolution?

Jack Reed wanted to live in a tub and write verses;
but he kept meeting bums workingmen husky guys he liked out of luck out of work why not revolution?
He couldnt keep his mind on his work with so many people out of luck;
in school hadnt he learned the Declaration of Independence by heart? Reed was a westerner and words meant what they said; when he said something standing with a classmate at the Harvard Club [9] bar, he meant what he said from the soles of his feet to the waves of his untidy hair (his blood didnt run thin enough for the Harvard Club and the Dutch Treat Club [10] and respectable New York freelance Bohemia).

Life, liberty, and the pursuit of happiness;
not much of that round the silkmills when
in 1913,

---

[6] Streets in Greenwich Village.

[7] Robert Louis Stevenson (1850–1894), another romantic adventurer.

[8] [Joseph] Lincoln Steffens (1866–1936), radical American journalist, father figure to younger radicals like Reed.

[9] At 27 West 44th Street, New York; its members are alumni of Harvard University.

[10] A New York men's club made up largely of commercially successful writers, artists, etc., for which Reed wrote *Everymagazine, an Immorality Play*, presented at its annual dinner at Delmonico's in 1912.

he went over to Paterson to write up the strike,[11] textile workers
parading beaten up by the cops, the strikers in jail; before he knew it
he was a striker parading beaten up by the cops in jail;

he wouldn't let the editor bail him out, he'd learn more with the
strikers in jail.

He learned enough to put on the pageant of the Paterson Strike in
Madison Square garden.

He learned the hope of a new society where nobody would be out of
luck,

why not revolution?

The Metropolitan Magazine sent him to Mexico
to write up Pancho Villa.

Pancho Villa taught him to write and the skeleton mountains and
the tall organ cactus and the armored trains and the bands playing in
little plazas full of dark girls in blue scarfs

and the bloody dust and the ping of rifleshots

in the enormous night of the desert, and the brown quietvoiced
peons dying starving killing for liberty

for land for water for schools.

Mexico taught him to write.

Reed was a westerner and words meant what they said.

The war was a blast that blew out all the Diogenes lanterns;
the good men began to gang up to call for machineguns. Jack Reed
was the last of the great race of warcorrespondents who ducked under
censorships and risked their skins for a story.

Jack Reed was the best American writer of his time, if anybody had
wanted to know about the war they could have read about it in the
articles he wrote

about the German front,[12]
the Serbian retreat,[13]
Saloniki; [14]
behind the lines in the tottering empire of the Czar,
dodging the secret police,
jail in Cholm.[15]

---

[11] The violent mill-workers' strike in Paterson, New Jersey, in 1913 drew many
other intellectuals and writers beside John Reed across the Hudson River in sympathy
with the workers. Reed's Madison Square Garden pageant in support of the strikers
involved the cooperation of many of them.

[12] Late in 1914 the German military allowed Reed to observe trench warfare behind
their lines.

[13] Under Austrian attack in 1914.

[14] Greek refugee center where Reed encountered seven carpenters, not tailors.

[15] Entering Russia illegally, Reed was held in his room in Cholm for two weeks.

The brasshats wouldnt let him go to France because they said one night in the German trenches kidding with the Boche guncrew he'd pulled the string on a Hun gun pointed at the heart of France . . . playboy stuff but after all what did it matter who fired the guns or which way they were pointed? Reed was with the boys who were being blown to hell,
    with the Germans the French the Russians the Bulgarians the seven little tailors in the Ghetto in Salonique,
      and in 1917
      he was with the soldiers and peasants
      in Petrograd in October:
      Smolny,
      Ten Days That Shook the Word; [16]

no more Villa picturesque Mexico, no more Harvard Club playboy stuff, plans for Greek theatres, rhyming verse, good stories of an oldtime warcorrespondent,
    this wasnt fun anymore
    this was grim.

    Delegate,
    back in the States indictments, the Masses [17] trial, the Wobbly trial,[18] Wilson [19] cramming the jails,
    forged passports, speeches, secret documents, riding the rods across the cordon sanitaire, hiding in the bunkers on steamboats;
    jail in Finland all his papers stolen,
    no more chance to write verses now, no more warm chats with every guy you met up with, the college boy with the nice smile talking himself out of trouble with the judge;
    at the Harvard Club they're all in the Intelligence Service making the world safe for the Morgan-Baker-Stillman combination of banks;
    that old tramp sipping his coffee out of a tomato-can's a spy of the General Staff.

    The world's no fun anymore,
    only machinegunfire and arson
    starvation lice bedbugs cholera typhus

[16] Reed's most important book, 1919, his account of the October Revolution based on his observations in and near Petrograd. Smolny Institute was the meeting place of the committee of the Petrograd Soviet.

[17] The editors of this radical periodical, including Reed, were arrested and tried for sedition in New York in 1918.

[18] Familiar term for a member of the Industrial Workers of the World, 101 of whom were tried for sedition in Chicago in 1918.

[19] [Thomas] Woodrow Wilson (1856–1924), twenty-eighth President of the United States (1913–1921).

no lint for bandages no chloroform or ether thousands dead of
gangrened wounds cordon sanitaire and everywhere spies.
The windows of Smolny glow whitehot like a bessemer,
no sleep in Smolny,
Smolny the giant rollingmill running twentyfour hours a day rolling
out men nations hopes millenniums impulses fears,
rawmaterial
for the foundations
of a new society.

A man has to do many things in his life.
Reed was a westerner words meant what they said.
He threw everything he had and himself into Smolny,
dictatorship of the proletariat;
U.S.S.R.
The first workers republic
was established and stands.
Reed wrote, undertook missions (there were spies everywhere),
worked till he dropped,
caught typhus and died in Moscow.

The Body of an American (1932)

Whereasthe Congressoftheunitedstates byaconcurrentresolutionadoptedon the-
4thdayofmarch lastauthorizedthe Secretaryofwar to cause to be brought to
theunitedstatesthe body of an Americanwhowasamemberoftheamericanexpedi-
tionaryforcesineurope   wholosthislifeduringtheworldwarandwhoseidentityhas-
notbeenestablished for burial inthememorialamphitheatreofthe nationalceme-
teryatarlingtonvirginia

In the tarpaper morgue at Chalons-sur-Marne in the reek of chloride
of lime and the dead, they picked out the pine box that held all that was
left of
enie menie minie moe plenty other pine boxes stacked up there
containing what they'd scraped up of Richard Roe
and other person or persons unknown. Only one can go. How did
they pick John Doe?
Make sure he aint a dinge, boys,
make sure he aint a guinea or a kike,
how can you tell a guy's a hundredpercent when all you've got's a
gunnysack full of bones, bronze buttons stamped with the screaming
eagle and a pair of roll puttees?
    . . . and the gagging chloride and the puky dirt-stench of the yearold
dead . . .

The day withal was too meaningful and tragic for applause. Silence, tears, songs and prayer, muffled drums and soft music were the instrumentalities today of national approbation.

John Doe was born (thudding din of blood in love into the shuddering soar of a man and a woman alone indeed together lurching into
and ninemonths sick drowse waking into scared agony and the pain and blood and mess of birth). John Doe was born
and raised in Brooklyn, in Memphis, near the lakefront in Cleveland, Ohio, in the stench of the stockyards in Chi, on Beacon Hill, in an old brick house in Alexandria Virginia, on Telegraph Hill, in a halftimbered Tudor cottage in Portland the city of roses,
in the Lying-In Hospital old Morgan endowed on Stuyvesant Square,
across the railroad tracks, out near the country club, in a shack cabin tenement apartmenthouse exclusive residential suburb;
scion of one of the best families in the social register, won first prize in the baby parade at Coronado Beach, was marbles champion of the Little Rock grammarschools, crack basketballplayer at the Booneville High, quarterback at the State Reformatory, having saved the sheriff's kid from drowning in the Little Missouri River was invited to Washington to be photographed shaking hands with the President on the White House steps;—

though this was a time of mourning, such an assemblage necessarily has about it a touch of color. In the boxes are seen the court uniforms of foreign diplomats, the gold braid of our own and foreign fleets and armies, the black of the conventional morning dress of American statesmen, the varicolored furs and outdoor wrapping garments of mothers and sisters come to mourn, the drab and blue of soldiers and sailors, the glitter of musical instruments and the white and black of a vested choir

—busboy harveststiff hogcaller boyscout champeen cornshucker of Western Kansas bellhop at the United States Hotel at Saratoga Springs office boy callboy fruiter telephone lineman longshoreman lumberjack plumber's helper,
worked for an exterminating company in Union City, filled pipes in an opium joint in Trenton, N. J.
Y.M.C.A. secretary, express agent, truckdriver, fordmechanic, sold books in Denver Colorado: Madam would you be willing to help a young man work his way through college?

President Harding, with a reverence seemingly more significant because of his high temporal station, concluded his speech:

We are met today to pay the impersonal tribute;
the name of him whose body lies before us took flight with his imperishable soul . . .
as a typical soldier of this representative democracy he fought and died believing in the indisputable justice of his country's cause . . .

by raising his right hand and asking the thousands within the sound of his
voice to join in the prayer:

Our Father which art in heaven hallowed be thy name . . .

Naked he went into the army;
they weighed you, measured you, looked for flat feet, squeezed your
penis to see if you had clap, looked up your anus to see if you had piles,
counted your teeth, made you cough, listened to your heart and lungs,
made you read the letters on the card, charted your urine and your
intelligence,
gave you a service record for a future (imperishable soul)
and an identification tag stamped with your serial number to hang
around your neck, issued O D regulation equipment, a condiment can
and a copy of the articles of war.
Atten'SHUN suck in your gut you c——r wipe that smile off your
face eyes right wattja tink dis is a choirch-social? For-war-D'ARCH.

John Doe
and Richard Roe and other person or persons unknown
drilled hiked, manual of arms, ate slum, learned to salute, to soldier,
to loaf in the latrines, forbidden to smoke on deck, overseas guard duty,
forty men and eight horses, shortarm inspection and the ping of shrap-
nel and the shrill bullets combing the air and the sorehead woodpeckers
the machineguns mud cooties gasmasks and the itch.
Say feller tell me how I can get back to my outfit.

John Doe had a head
for twentyodd years intensely the nerves of the eyes the ears the
palate the tongue the fingers the toes the armpits, the nerves warm-
feeling under the skin charged the coiled brain with hurt sweet warm
cold mine must dont sayings print headlines:
Thou shalt not the multiplication table long division, Now is the
time for all good men knocks but once at a young man's door, It's a great
life if Ish gebibbel, The first five years'll be the Safety First, Suppose a
hun tried to rape your my country right or wrong, Catch 'em young,
What he dont know wont treat 'em rough, Tell 'em nothin, He got what
was coming to him he got his, This is a white man's country, Kick the
bucket, Gone west, If you dont like it you can croaked him
Say buddy cant you tell me how I can get back to my outfit?

Cant help jumpin when them things go off, give me the trots them
things do. I lost my identification tag swimmin in the Marne, rough-
housin with a guy while we was waitin to be deloused, in bed with a
girl named Jeanne (Love moving picture wet French postcard dream
began with saltpeter in the coffee and ended at the propho [1] station);—

――――――――――
[1] Prophylactic.

Say soldier for chrissake cant you tell me how I can get back to my outfit?

John Doe's
heart pumped blood:
alive thudding silence of blood in your ears
down in the clearing in the Oregon [2] forest where the punkins were punkincolor pouring into the blood through the eyes and the fallcolored trees and the bronze hoopers were hopping through the dry grass, where tiny striped snails hung on the underside of the blades and the flies hummed, wasps droned, bumblebees buzzed, and the woods smelt of wine and mushrooms and apples, homey smell of fall pouring into the blood,
    and I dropped the tin hat and the sweaty pack and lay flat with the dogday sun licking my throat and adamsapple and the tight skin over the breastbone.

The shell had his number on it.

The blood ran into the ground.

The service record dropped out of the filing cabinet when the quartermaster sergeant got blotto that time they had to pack up and leave the billets in a hurry.
The identification tag was in the bottom of the Marne.

The blood ran into the ground, the brains oozed out of the cracked skull and were licked up by the trenchrats, the belly swelled and raised a generation of bluebottle flies,
    and the incorruptible skeleton,
    and the scraps of dried viscera and skin bundled in khaki

they took to Chalons-sur-Marne
and laid it out neat in a pine coffin
and took it home to God's Country on a battleship
and buried it in a sarcophagus in the Memorial Amphitheatre in the Arlington National Cemetery
and draped the Old Glory over it
and the bugler played taps
and Mr. Harding prayed to God and the diplomats and the generals and the admirals and the brasshats and the politicians and the handsomely dressed ladies out of the society column of the *Washington Post* stood up solemn
and thought how beautiful sad Old Glory God's Country it was to have the bugler play taps and the three volleys made their ears ring.

Where his chest ought to have been they pinned
    the Congressional Medal, the D.S.C., the Medaille Militaire, the

---

[2] His approximation of Argonne, scene of crucial battles.

Belgian Croix de Guerre, the Italian gold medal, the Vitutea Militara sent by Queen Marie of Rumania, the Czechoslovak war cross, the Virtuti Militari of the Poles, a wreath sent by Hamilton Fish, Jr.,[3] of New York, and a little wampum presented by a deputation of Arizona redskins in warpaint and feathers. All the Washingtonians brought flowers.

Woodrow Wilson brought a bouquet of poppies.

Vag (1936)[1]

The young man waits at the edge of the concrete, with one hand he grips a rubbed suitcase of phony leather, the other hand almost making a fist, thumb up

that moves in ever so slight an arc when a car slithers past, a truck roars clatters; the wind of cars passing ruffles his hair, slaps grit in his face.

Head swims, hunger has twisted the belly tight,

he has skinned a heel through the torn sock, feet ache in the broken shoes, under the threadbare suit carefully brushed off with the hand, the torn drawers have a crummy feel, the feel of having slept in your clothes; in the nostrils lingers the staleness of discouraged carcasses crowded into a transient camp, the carbolic stench of the jail, on the taut cheeks the shamed flush from the boring eyes of cops and deputies, railroadbulls (they eat three squares a day, they are buttoned into wellmade clothes, they have wives to sleep with, kids to play with after supper, they work for the big men who buy their way, they stick their chests out with the sureness of power behind their backs). Git the hell out, scram. Know what's good for you, you'll make yourself scarce. Gittin' tough, eh? Think you kin take it, eh?

The punch in the jaw, the slam on the head with the nightstick, the wrist grabbed and twisted behind the back, the big knee brought up sharp into the crotch,

the walk out of town with sore feet to stand and wait at the edge of the hissing speeding string of cars where the reek of ether and lead and gas melts into the silent grassy smell of the earth.

Eyes black with want seek out the eyes of the drivers, a hitch, a hundred miles down the road.

Overhead in the blue a plane drones. Eyes follow the silver Douglas that flashes once in the sun and bores its smooth way out of sight into the blue.

(The transcontinental passengers sit pretty, big men with bankaccounts, highlypaid jobs, who are saluted by doormen; telephonegirls

---

[3] (1849–1936); long a leader of the Republican Party in New York.

[1] Vagrant, in this instance a migrant hitch-hiker.

say goodmorning to them. Last night after a fine dinner, drinks with friends, they left Newark. Roar of climbing motors slanting up into the inky haze. Lights drop away. An hour staring along a silvery wing at a big lonesome moon hurrying west through curdling scum. Beacons flash in a line across Ohio.

At Cleveland the plane drops banking in a smooth spiral, the string of lights along the lake swings in a circle. Climbing roar of the motors again; slumped in the soft seat drowsing through the flat moonlight night.

Chi. A glimpse of the dipper. Another spiral swoop from cool into hot air thick with dust and the reek of burnt prairies.

Beyond the Mississippi dawn creeps up behind through the murk over the great plains. Puddles of mist go white in the Iowa hills, farms, fences, silos, steel glint from a river. The blinking eyes of the beacons reddening into day. Watercourses vein the eroded hills.

Omaha. Great cumulus clouds, from coppery churning to creamy to silvery white, trail brown skirts of rain over the hot plains. Red and yellow badlands, tiny horned shapes of cattle.

Cheyenne. The cool high air smells of sweetgrass.

The tightbaled clouds to westward burst and scatter in tatters over the strawcolored hills. Indigo mountains jut rimrock. The plane breasts a huge crumbling cloudbank and toboggans over bumpy air across green and crimson slopes into the sunny dazzle of Salt Lake.

The transcontinental passenger thinks contracts, profits, vacationtrips, mighty continent between Atlantic and Pacific, power, wires humming dollars, cities jammed, hills empty, the indiantrail leading into the wagonroad, the macadamed pike, the concrete skyway; trains, planes: history and billiondollar speedup,

and in the bumpy air over the desert ranges towards Las Vegas

sickens and vomits into the carton container the steak and mushrooms he ate in New York. No matter, silver in the pocket, greenbacks in the wallet, drafts, certified checks, plenty restaurants in L. A.)

The young man waits on the side of the road; the plane has gone; thumb moves in a small arc when a car tears hissing past. Eyes seek the driver's eyes. A hundred miles down the road. Head swims, belly tightens, wants crawl over his skin like ants:

went to school, books said opportunity, ads promised speed, own your home, shine bigger than your neighbor, the radiocrooner whispered girls, ghosts of platinum girls coaxed from the screen, millions in winnings were chalked up on the boards in the offices, paychecks were for hands willing to work, the cleared desk of an executive with three telephones on it;

waits with swimming head, needs knot the belly, idle hands numb, beside the speeding traffic.

A hundred miles down the road.

WILLIAM [HARRISON] FAULKNER (1897–1962)

His father's name was Murray C. Falkner; the u was mistakenly inserted by the printer who set the type for Faulkner's first book, some poems called The Marble Faun (1924), and he retained it. When the boy, one of four, was five years old, the family moved from New Albany, Mississippi, to nearby Oxford, seat of the state university, where the father first ran a livery stable and a hardware store and then became business manager of the university. Oxford is the Jefferson of Faulkner's many novels, insofar as Jefferson can be identified with any one place. In spite of occasional departures from Oxford, Faulkner himself must always be identified with that town, where he was to spend most of his life.

He was a poor student and dropped out of high school after two years. He worked in a bank for a time and read extensively on his own. He was very small, 5 feet 5 inches, and when he tried to enlist in the Army he was rejected on that account; but he was accepted by the British Royal Flying Corps in Canada, although he saw no active service. Returning to Oxford after the Armistice, he attended the University of Mississippi for a year and wrote a little for the student publication, dropped out to work in a bookstore in New York, returned to Oxford for a couple of years, doing odd jobs, and, at the expense of a willing friend, published his first book.

Starting out for Europe, he got no farther than New Orleans, where he wrote pieces for the Times-Picayune and the Double Dealer, completed his first novel, Soldiers' Pay, and came to know Sherwood Anderson through whose characteristic kindness that novel found a publisher in 1926. After a walking trip in Europe in 1925, he returned to Mississippi to write his second novel, Mosquitoes (1927), a satire on bohemian life in New Orleans, and returned to odd jobs and lounging around Oxford. Thus far he seemed to be a somewhat talented and quite unfocused young man.

In Sartoris (1929), a novel based on his own family history, he began to find his way; and in The Sound and the Fury (1929), based on his more immediate family (the Compsons), he established the fictional techniques by means of which he would explore those ancestral themes that were largely to concern him henceforth. As I Lay Dying (1930) developed the techniques and pushed the subject more deeply into the macabre. Sanctuary (1931), intended as a pot-boiler, heightened the emphasis on the violent and the deranged, and found him a wide audience. Hollywood invited him. He had it made, and henceforth, through many books and over thirty years, he wrote precisely as he pleased.

Light in August *(1932) brings everything together that had thus far appeared in more separate strands, and profoundly deepens it all; it may very well be Faulkner's best novel. But it is the next novel— omitting* Pylon *(1935), a lesser work—*Absalom, Absalom! *(1936), that really lays down the basis for the whole mythohistorical legend that Faulkner would continue to work out. It was for this novel that he drew his famous fold-out map with his legend spelled out in his neat printing:*

JEFFERSON,
Yoknapatawpha Co.,
MISSISSIPPI

Area, 2400 Sq. Mi.

Population, Whites, 6298
Negroes 9313

William Faulkner,
sole owner & proprietor

This legend itself must serve here to suggest the scope and the complexity, the dark anguish and the historic guilt, the corruption, the violence, and the occasional nobility with which Faulkner's novels and short stories had already been and would continue to be concerned in his tortured dramatization of the history of Yoknapatawpha County, Mississippi. He could handle these concerns, in his many novels and short stories, in moods ranging from the deeply tragic to the grotesquely comic, and sometimes, most effectively, in a mingling of the two. He could miscalculate seriously and fall into the merely melodramatic or the baldly allegorical. That he had no great critical powers is all too clear in his attempts to talk about his own work or to estimate the achievements of others. That he had no great discursive intellect is suggested by the empty rhetoric of his acceptance speech when he was awarded the Nobel Prize in Sweden in 1950. Sheer rhetoric, often enough, tended to substitute for insight and genuine feeling in some of even his best fiction.

Yet the fact remains that our literature has known no other such pyrotechnical display, and Southern literature none at once so demonic and profound. No one since Herman Melville, a hundred years before him, thrusts upon us with such immediacy the presence of human genius, perhaps untrammeled, often, with or without pity, trampling.

FURTHER READING

Joseph Blotner is preparing the authorized biography. Until it appears, the introductory chapter of Michael Millgate's *The Achievement of*

William Faulkner (1966) is a dependable source of information about Faulkner's life. Among the many critical studies, these are notable: Irving Howe, *William Faulkner: A Critical Study* (1952, revised 1962); Olga W. Vickery, *The Novels of William Faulkner: A Critical Interpretation* (1959, revised 1964); Hyatt H. Waggoner, *William Faulkner: From Jefferson to the World* (1959); Cleanth Brooks, *William Faulkner: The Yoknapatawpha Country* (1963); Lawrance Thompson, *William Faulkner: An Introduction and Interpretation* (1963); Warren Beck, *Man in Motion* (1963); and Michael Millgate, cited above. Frederick J. Hoffman and Olga W. Vickery have edited *William Faulkner: Three Decades of Criticism* (1960). The best Faulkner handbook is Robert W. Kirk and Marvin Klotz, *Faulkner's People: A Complete Guide and Index to Characters in the Fiction of William Faulkner* (1963).

The Old People (1942)

I

At first there was nothing. There was the faint, cold, steady rain, the gray and constant light of the late November dawn, with the voices of the hounds converging somewhere in it and toward them. Then Sam Fathers, standing just behind the boy as he had been standing when the boy shot his first running rabbit with his first gun and almost with the first load it ever carried, touched his shoulder and he began to shake, not with any cold. Then the buck was there. He did not come into sight; he was just there, looking not like a ghost but as if all of light were condensed in him and he were the source of it, not only moving in it but disseminating it, already running, seen first as you always see the deer, in that split second after he has already seen you, already slanting away in that first soaring bound, the antlers even in that dim light looking like a small rocking-chair balanced on his head.

"Now," Sam Fathers said, "shoot quick, and slow."

The boy did not remember that shot at all. He would live to be eighty, as his father and his father's twin brother and their father in his turn had lived to be, but he would never hear that shot nor remember even the shock of the gun-butt. He didn't even remember what he did with the gun afterward. He was running. Then he was standing over the buck where it lay on the wet earth still in the attitude of speed and not looking at all dead, standing over it shaking and jerking, with Sam Fathers beside him again, extending the knife. "Don't walk up to him in front," Sam said. "If he aint dead, he will cut you all to pieces with his feet. Walk up to him from behind and take him by the horn first, so you can hold his head down until you can jump away. Then slip your other hand down and hook your fingers in his nostrils."

The boy did that—drew the head back and the throat taut and drew Sam Fathers' knife across the throat and Sam stooped and dipped his hands in the hot smoking blood and wiped them back and forth across the boy's face. Then Sam's horn rang in the wet gray woods and again and again; there was a boiling wave of dogs about them, with Tennie's Jim and Boon Hogganbeck whipping them back after each had had a taste of the blood, then the men, the true hunters—Walter Ewell whose rifle never missed, and Major de Spain and old General Compson and the boy's cousin, McCaslin Edmonds, grandson of his father's sister, sixteen years his senior and, since both he and McCaslin were only children and the boy's father had been nearing seventy when he was born, more his brother than his cousin and more his father than either— sitting their horses and looking down at them: at the old man of seventy who had been a negro for two generations now but whose face and bearing were still those of the Chickasaw [1] chief who had been his father; and the white boy of twelve with the prints of the bloody hands on his face, who had nothing to do now but stand straight and not let the trembling show.

"Did he do all right, Sam?" his cousin McCaslin said.

"He done all right," Sam Fathers said.

They were the white boy, marked forever, and the old dark man sired on both sides by savage kings, who had marked him, whose bloody hands had merely formally consecrated him to that which, under the man's tutelage, he had already accepted, humbly and joyfully, with abnegation and with pride too; the hands, the touch, the first worthy blood which he had been found at last worthy to draw, joining him and the man forever, so that the man would continue to live past the boy's seventy years and then eighty years, long after the man himself had entered the earth as chiefs and kings entered it;—the child, not yet a man, whose grandfather had lived in the same country and in almost the same manner as the boy himself would grow up to live, leaving his descendants in the land in his turn as his grandfather had done, and the old man past seventy whose grandfathers had owned the land long before the white men ever saw it and who had vanished from it now with all their kind, what of blood they left behind them running now in another race and for a while even in bondage and now drawing toward the end of its alien and irrevocable course, barren, since Sam Fathers had no children.

His father was Ikkemotubbe himself, who had named himself Doom. Sam told the boy about that—how Ikkemotubbe, old Issetibbeha's sister's son, had run away to New Orleans in his youth and returned seven years later with a French companion calling himself the Chevalier Soeur-Blonde de Vitry, who must have been the Ikkemotubbe of his family too and who was already addressing Ikkemotubbe as *Du Homme;*

---

[1] A tribe of American Indians that originally settled in Mississippi and Alabama.

—returned, came home again, with his foreign Aramis and the quadroon slave woman who was to be Sam's mother, and a gold-laced hat and coat and a wicker wine-hamper containing a litter of month-old puppies and a gold snuff-box filled with a white powder resembling fine sugar. And how he was met at the River landing by three or four companions of his bachelor youth, and while the light of a smoking torch gleamed on the glittering braid of the hat and coat Doom squatted in the mud of the land and took one of the puppies from the hamper and put a pinch of the white powder on its tongue and the puppy died before the one who was holding it could cast it away. And how they returned to the Plantation where Issetibbeha, dead now, had been succeeded by his son, Doom's fat cousin Moketubbe, and the next day Moketubbe's eight-year-old son died suddenly and that afternoon, in the presence of Moketubbe and most of the others (the People, Sam Fathers called them) Doom produced another puppy from the wine-hamper and put a pinch of the white powder on its tongue and Moketubbe abdicated and Doom became in fact The Man which his French friend already called him. And how on the day after that, during the ceremony of accession, Doom pronounced a marriage between the pregnant quadroon and one of the slave men which he had just inherited (that was how Sam Fathers got his name, which in Chickasaw had been Had-Two-Fathers) and two years later sold the man and woman and the child who was his own son to his white neighbor, Carothers McCaslin.

That was seventy years ago. The Sam Fathers whom the boy knew was already sixty—a man not tall, squat rather, almost sedentary, flabby-looking though he actually was not, with hair like a horse's mane which even at seventy showed no trace of white and a face which showed no age until he smiled, whose only visible trace of negro blood was a slight dullness of the hair and the fingernails, and something else which you did notice about the eyes, which you noticed because it was not always there, only in repose and not always then—something not in their shape nor pigment but in their expression, and the boy's cousin McCaslin told him what that was: not the heritage of Ham,[2] not the mark of servitude but of bondage; the knowledge that for a while that part of his blood had been the blood of slaves. "Like an old lion or a bear in a cage." McCaslin said. "He was born in the cage and has been in it all his life; he knows nothing else. Then he smells something. It might be anything, any breeze blowing past anything and then into his nostrils. But there for a second was the hot sand or the cane-brake that he never even saw himself, might not even know if he did see it and probably does know he couldn't hold his own with it if he got back to it. But that's not what he smells then. It was the cage he smelled. He hadn't smelled the cage until that minute. Then the hot sand or the brake blew into his

---

[2] Ham is the second son of Noah (cf. Gen. 9:22ff.), who, for having seen his father naked, is cursed to be "a servant of servants."

nostrils and blew away, and all he could smell was the cage. That's what makes his eyes look like that."

"Then let him go!" the boy cried. "Let him go!"

His cousin laughed shortly. Then he stopped laughing, making the sound, that is. It had never been laughing. "His cage aint McCaslins," he said. "He was a wild man. When he was born, all his blood on both sides, except the little white part, knew things that had been tamed out of our blood so long ago that we have not only forgotten them, we have to live together in herds to protect ourselves from our own sources. He was the direct son not only of a warrior but of a chief. Then he grew up and began to learn things, and all of a sudden one day he found out that he had been betrayed, the blood of the warriors and chiefs had been betrayed. Not by his father," he added quickly. "He probably never held it against old Doom for selling him and his mother into slavery, because he probably believed the damage was already done before then and it was the same warriors' and chiefs' blood in him and Doom both that was betrayed through the black blood which his mother gave him. Not betrayed by the black blood and not wilfully betrayed by his mother, but betrayed by her all the same, who had bequeathed him not only the blood of slaves but even a little of the very blood which had enslaved it; himself his own battleground, the scene of his own vanquishment and the mausoleum of his defeat. His cage aint us," McCaslin said. "Did you ever know anybody yet, even your father and Uncle Buddy, that ever told him to do or not do anything that he ever paid any attention to?"

That was true. The boy first remembered him as sitting in the door of the plantation blacksmith-shop, where he sharpened plow-points and mended tools and even did rough carpenter-work when he was not in the woods. And sometimes, even when the woods had not drawn him, even with the shop cluttered with work which the farm waited on, Sam would sit there, doing nothing at all for half a day or a whole one, and no man, neither the boy's father and twin uncle in their day nor his cousin McCaslin after he became practical though not yet titular master, ever to say to him, "I want this finished by sundown," or "why wasn't this done yesterday?" And once each year, in the late fall, in November, the boy would watch the wagon, the hooped canvas top erected now, being loaded—the food, hams and sausage from the smokehouse, coffee and flour and molasses from the commissary, a whole beef killed just last night for the dogs until there would be meat in camp, the crate containing the dogs themselves, then the bedding, the guns, the horns and lanterns and axes, and his cousin McCaslin and Sam Fathers in their hunting clothes would mount to the seat and with Tennie's Jim sitting on the dog-crate they would drive away to Jefferson, to join Major de Spain and General Compson and Boon Hogganbeck and Walter Ewell and go on into the big bottom of the Tallahatchie where the deer and bear were, to be gone two weeks. But before the wagon was even loaded the boy would find that he could watch no longer. He would go away, running almost, to stand behind the corner where he could not see the wagon and nobody could see him, not crying, holding himself rigid except for the trembling, whispering to himself: "Soon now. Soon now. Just three more years" (or two more or one more) "and I will be ten. Then Cass said I can go."

White man's work, when Sam did work. Because he did nothing else: farmed no allotted acres of his own, as the other ex-slaves of old Carothers McCaslin did, performed no field-work for daily wages as the younger and newer negroes did—and the boy never knew just how that had been settled between Sam and old Carothers, or perhaps with old Carothers' twin sons after him. For, although Sam lived among the negroes, in a cabin among the other cabins in the quarters, and consorted with negroes (what of consorting with anyone Sam did after the boy got big enough to walk alone from the house to the blacksmith-shop and then to carry a gun) and dressed like them and talked like them and even went with them to the negro church now and then, he was still the son of that Chickasaw chief and the negroes knew it. And, it seemed to the boy, not only negroes. Boon Hogganbeck's grandmother had been a Chickasaw woman too, and although the blood had run white since and Boon was a white man, it was not chief's blood. To the boy at least, the difference was apparent immediately you saw Boon and Sam together, and even Boon seemed to know it was there—even Boon, to whom in his tradition it had never occurred that anyone might be better born than himself. A man might be smarter, he admitted that, or richer (luckier, he called it) but not better born. Boon was a mastiff, absolutely faithful, dividing his fidelity equally between Major de Spain and the boy's cousin McCaslin, absolutely dependent for his very bread and dividing that impartially too between Major de Spain and McCaslin, hardy, generous, courageous enough, a slave to all the appetites and almost unratiocinative. In the boy's eyes at least it was Sam Fathers, the negro, who bore himself not only toward his cousin McCaslin and Major de Spain but toward all white men, with gravity and dignity and without servility or recourse to that impenetrable wall of ready and easy mirth which negroes sustain between themselves and white men, bearing himself toward his cousin McCaslin not only as one man to another but as an older man to a younger.

He taught the boy the woods, to hunt, when to shoot and when not to shoot, when to kill and when not to kill, and better, what to do with it afterward. Then he would talk to the boy, the two of them sitting beneath the close fierce stars on a summer hilltop while they waited for the hounds to bring the fox back within hearing, or beside a fire in the November or December woods while the dogs worked out a coon's trail along the creek, or fireless in the pitch dark and heavy dew of April mornings while they squatted beneath a turkey-roost. The boy would never question him; Sam did not react to questions. The boy would just wait and then listen and Sam would begin, talking about the old days and the People whom he had not had time ever to know and so could not remember (he did not remember ever having seen his father's face), and in place of whom the other race into which his blood had run supplied him with no substitute.

And as he talked about those old times and those dead and vanished men of another race from either that the boy knew, gradually to the boy those old times would cease to be old times and would become a part of the boy's present, not only as if they had happened yesterday but as if they were still happening, the men who walked through them actually walking in breath and air and casting an actual shadow on the earth they had not quitted. And more: as if some of them had not happened yet but would occur tomorrow, until at last it would seem to the boy that he himself had not come into existence yet, that none of his race nor the other subject race which his people had brought with them into the land had come here yet; that although it had been his grandfather's and then his father's and uncle's and was now his cousin's and someday would be his own land which he and Sam hunted over, their hold upon it actually was as trivial and without reality as the now faded and archaic script in the chancery book in Jefferson which allocated it to them and that it was he, the boy, who was the guest here and Sam Father's voice the mouthpiece of the host.

Until three years ago there had been two of them, the other a full-blood Chickasaw, in a sense even more incredibly lost than Sam Fathers. He called himself Jobaker, as if it were one word. Nobody knew his history at all. He was a hermit, living in a foul little shack at the forks of the creek five miles from the plantation and about that far from any other habitation. He was a market hunter and fisherman and he consorted with nobody, black or white; no negro would even cross his path and no man dared approach his hut except Sam. And perhaps once a month the boy would find them in Sam's shop—two old men squatting on their heels on the dirt floor, talking in a mixture of negroid English and flat hill dialect and now and then a phrase of that old tongue which as time went on and the boy squatted there too listening, he began to learn. Then Jobaker died. That is, nobody had seen him in some time. Then one morning Sam was missing, nobody, not even the boy, knew when nor where, until that night when some negroes hunting in the creek bottom saw the sudden burst of flame and approached. It was Jobaker's hut, but before they got anywhere near it, someone shot at them from the shadows beyond it. It was Sam who fired, but nobody ever found Jobaker's grave.

The next morning, sitting at breakfast with his cousin, the boy saw Sam pass the dining-room window and he remembered then that never in his life before had he seen Sam nearer the house than the blacksmith-shop. He stopped eating even; he sat there and he and his cousin both heard the voices from beyond the pantry door, then the door opened and Sam entered, carrying his hat in his hand but without knocking as anyone else on the place except a house servant would have done, entered just far enough for the door to close behind him and stood looking at neither of them—the Indian face above the nigger clothes, looking at something over their heads or at something not even in the room.

"I want to go," he said. "I want to go to the Big Bottom to live."

"To live?" the boy's cousin said.

"At Major de Spain's and your camp, where you go to hunt," Sam said. "I could take care of it for you all while you aint there. I will build me a little house in the woods, if you rather I didn't stay in the big one."

"What about Isaac here?" his cousin said. "How will you get away from him? Are you going to take him with you?" But still Sam looked at neither of them, standing just inside the room with that face which showed nothing, which showed that he was an old man only when it smiled.

"I want to go," he said. "Let me go."

"Yes," the cousin said quietly. "Of course. I'll fix it with Major de Spain. You want to go soon?"

"I'm going now," Sam said. He went out. And that was all. The boy was nine then; it seemed perfectly natural that nobody, not even his cousin McCaslin, should argue with Sam. Also, since he was nine now, he could understand that Sam could leave him and their days and nights in the woods together without any wrench. He believed that he and Sam both knew that this was not only temporary but that the exigencies of his maturing, of that for which Sam had been training him all his life some day to dedicate himself, required it. They had settled that one night last summer while they listened to the hounds bringing a fox back up the creek valley; now the boy discerned in that very talk under the high, fierce August stars a presage, a warning, of this moment today. "I done taught you all there is of this settled country," Sam said. "You can hunt it good as I can now. You are ready for the Big Bottom now, for bear and deer. Hunter's meat," he said. "Next year you will be ten. You will write your age in two numbers and you will be ready to become a man. Your pa" (Sam always referred to the boy's cousin as his father, establishing even before the boy's orphanhood did that relation between them not of the ward to his guardian and kinsman and chief and head of his blood, but of the child to the man who sired his flesh and his thinking too) "promised you can go with us then." So the boy could understand Sam's going. But he couldn't understand why now, in March, six months before the moon for hunting.

"If Jobaker's dead like they say," he said, "and Sam hasn't got anybody but us at all kin to him, why does he want to go to the Big Bottom now, when it will be six months before we get there?"

"Maybe that's what he wants," McCaslin said. "Maybe he wants to get away from you a little while."

But that was all right. McCaslin and other grown people often said things like that and he paid no attention to them, just as he paid no attention to Sam saying he wanted to go to the Big Bottom to live. After all, he would have to live there for six months, because there would be no use in going at all if he was going to turn right around and come back. And, as Sam himself had told him, he already knew all about hunting in this settled country that Sam or anybody else could teach him. So it would be all right. Summer, then the bright days after the first frost, then the cold and himself on the wagon with McCaslin this time and the moment would come and he would draw the blood, the big blood which would make him a man, a hunter, and Sam would come back home with them and he too would have outgrown the child's pursuit of rabbits and 'possums. Then he too would make one before the winter fire, talking of the old hunts and the hunts to come as hunters talked.

So Sam departed. He owned so little that he could carry it. He walked. He would neither let McCaslin send him in the wagon, nor take a mule to ride. No one saw him go even. He was just gone one morning, the cabin whch had never had very much in it, vacant and empty, the shop in which there never had been very much done, standing idle. Then November came at last, and now the boy made one— himself and his cousin McCaslin and Tennie's Jim, and Major de Spain and General Compson and Walter Ewell and Boon and old Uncle Ash to do the cooking, waiting for them in Jefferson with the other wagon, and the surrey in which he and McCaslin and General Compson and Major de Spain would ride.

Sam was waiting at the camp to meet them. If he was glad to see them, he did not show it. And if, when they broke camp two weeks later to return home, he was sorry to see them go, he did not show that either. Because he did not come back with them. It was only the boy who returned, returning solitary and alone to the settled familiar land, to follow for eleven months the childish business of rabbits and such while he waited to go back, having brought with him, even from his brief first sojourn, an unforgettable sense of the big woods—not a quality dangerous or particularly inimical, but profound, sentient, gigantic and brooding, amid which he had been permitted to go to and fro at will, unscathed, why he knew not, but dwarfed and, until he had drawn honorably blood worthy of being drawn, alien.

Then November, and they would come back. Each morning Sam would take the boy out to the stand allotted him. It would be one of the poorer stands of course, since he was only ten and eleven and twelve and he had never even seen a deer running yet. But they would stand there, Sam a little behind him and without a gun himself, as he had been standing when the boy shot the running rabbit when he was eight years old. They would stand there in the November dawns, and after a while they would hear the dogs. Sometimes the chase would sweep up and past quite close, belling and invisible; once they heard the two heavy reports of Boon Hogganbeck's old gun with which he had never killed anything larger than a squirrel and that sitting, and twice they heard the flat unreverberant clap of Walter Ewell's rifle, following which you did not even wait to hear his horn.

"I'll never get a shot," the boy said. "I'll never kill one."

"Yes you will," Sam said. "You wait. You'll be a hunter. You'll be a man."

But Sam wouldn't come out. They would leave him there. He would come as far as the road where the surrey waited, to take the riding horses back, and that was all. The men would ride the horses and Uncle Ash and Tennie's Jim and the boy would follow in the wagon with Sam, with the camp equipment and the trophies, the meat, the heads, the antlers, the good ones, the wagon winding on among the tremendous gums and cypresses and oaks where no axe save that of the hunter had ever sounded, between the impenetrable walls of cane and brier—the two changing yet constant walls just beyond which the wilderness whose mark he had brought away forever on his spirit even from that first two weeks seemed to lean, stooping a little, watching them and listening, not quite inimical because they were too small, even those such as Walter and Major de Spain and old General Compson who had killed many deer and bear, their sojourn too brief and too harmless to excite to that, but just brooding, secret, tremendous, almost inattentive.

Then they would emerge, they would be out of it, the line as sharp as the demarcation of a doored wall. Suddenly skeleton cotton- and corn-fields would flow away on either hand, gaunt and motionless beneath the gray rain; there would be a house, barns, fences, where the hand of man had clawed for an instant, holding, the wall of the wilderness behind them now, tremendous and still and seemingly impenetrable in the gray and fading light, the very tiny orifice through which they had emerged apparently swallowed up. The surrey would be waiting, his cousin McCaslin and Major de Spain and General Compson and Walter and Boon dismounted beside it. Then Sam would get down from the wagon and mount one of the horses and, with the others on a rope behind him, he would turn back. The boy would watch him for a while against that tall and secret wall, growing smaller and smaller against it, never looking back. Then he would enter it, returning to what the boy believed, and thought that his cousin McCaslin believed, was his loneliness and solitude.

II

So the instant came. He pulled trigger and Sam Fathers marked his face with the hot blood which he had spilled and he ceased to be a child and became a hunter and a man. It was the last day. They broke camp that afternoon and went out, his cousin and Major de Spain and

General Compson and Boon on the horses. Walter Ewell and the negroes in the wagon with him and Sam and his hide and antlers. There could have been (and were) other trophies in the wagon. But for him they did not exist, just as for all practical purposes he and Sam Fathers were still alone together as they had been that morning. The wagon wound and jolted between the slow and shifting yet constant walls from beyond and above which the wilderness watched them pass, less than inimical now and never to be inimical again since the buck still and forever leaped, the shaking gun-barrels coming constantly and forever steady at last, crashing, and still out of his instant of immortality the buck sprang, forever immortal;—the wagon jolting and bouncing on, the moment of the buck, the shot, Sam Fathers and himself and the blood with which Sam had marked him forever one with the wilderness which had accepted him since Sam said that he had done all right, when suddenly Sam reined back and stopped the wagon and they all heard the unmistakable and unforgettable sound of a deer breaking cover.

Then Boon shouted from beyond the bend of the trail and while they sat motionless in the halted wagon, Walter and the boy already reaching for their guns, Boon came galloping back, flogging his mule with his hat, his face wild and amazed as he shouted down at them. Then the other riders came around the bend, also spurring.

"Get the dogs!" Boon cried. "Get the dogs! If he had a nub on his head, he had fourteen points! Laying right there by the road in that pawpaw thicket! If I'd a knowed he was there, I could have cut his throat with my pocket knife!"

"Maybe that's why he run," Walter said. "He saw you never had your gun." He was already out of the wagon with his rifle. Then the boy was out too with his gun, and the other riders came up and Boon got off his mule somehow and was scrabbling and clawing among the duffel in the wagon, still shouting, "Get the dogs! Get the dogs!" And it seemed to the boy too that it would take them forever to decide what to do—the old men in whom the blood ran cold and slow, in whom during the intervening years between them and himself the blood had become a different and colder substance from that which ran in him and even in Boon and Walter.

"What about it, Sam?" Major de Spain said. "Could the dogs bring him back?"

"We wont need the dogs," Sam said. "If he dont hear the dogs behind him, he will circle back in here about sundown to bed."

"All right," Major de Spain said. "You boys take the horses. We'll go on out to the road in the wagon and wait there." He and General Compson and McCaslin got into the wagon and Boon and Walter and Sam and the boy mounted the horses and turned back and out of the trail. Sam led them for an hour through the gray and unmarked afternoon whose light was little different from what it had been at dawn and which would become darkness without any graduation between. Then Sam stopped them.

"This is far enough," he said. "He'll be coming upwind, and he dont want to smell the mules." They tied the mounts in a thicket. Sam led them on foot now, unpathed through the markless afternoon, the boy pressing close behind him, the two others, or so it seemed to the boy, on his heels. But they were not. Twice Sam turned his head slightly and spoke back to him across his shoulder, still walking: "You got time. We'll get there fore he does."

So he tried to go slower. He tried deliberately to decelerate the dizzy rushing of time in which the buck which he had not even seen was moving, which it seemed to him must be carrying the buck farther and farther and more and more irretrievably away from them even though there were no dogs behind him now to make him run, even though, according to Sam, he must have completed his circle now and was heading back toward them. They went on; it could have been another hour or twice that or less than half, the boy could not have said. Then they were on a ridge. He had never been in here before and he could not see that it was a ridge. He just knew that the earth had risen slightly because the underbrush had thinned a little, the ground sloping invisibly away toward a dense wall of cane. Sam stopped. "This is it," he said. He spoke to Walter and Boon: "Follow this ridge and you will come to two crossings. You will see the tracks. If he crosses, it will be at one of these three."

Walter looked about for a moment. "I know it," he said. "I've even seen your deer. I was in here last Monday. He aint nothing but a yearling."

"A yearling?" Boon said. He was panting from the walking. His face still looked a little wild. "If the one I saw was any yearling, I'm still in kindergarden."

"Then I must have seen a rabbit," Walter said. "I always heard you quit school altogether two years before the first grade."

Boon glared at Walter. "If you dont want to shoot him, get out of the way," he said. "Set down somewhere. By God, I—"

"Aint nobody going to shoot him standing here," Sam said quietly.

"Sam's right," Walter said. He moved, slanting the worn, silver-colored barrel of his rifle downward to walk with it again. "A little more moving and a little more quiet too. Five miles is still Hogganbeck range, even if he wasn't downwind." They went on. The boy could still hear Boon talking, though presently that ceased too. Then once more he and Sam stood motionless together against a tremendous pin oak in a little thicket, and again there was nothing. There was only the soaring and sombre solitude in the dim light, there was the thin murmur of the faint cold rain which had not ceased all day. Then, as if it had waited for them to find their positions and become still, the wilderness breathed again. It seemed to lean inward above them, above himself and Sam and Walter and Boon in their separate lurking-places, tremendous, attentive, impartial and omniscient, the buck moving in it somewhere, not running yet since he had not been pursued, not frightened yet and never fearsome but just alert also as they were alert, perhaps already circling back, perhaps quite near, perhaps conscious also of the eye of the ancient immortal Umpire. Because he was just twelve then, and that morning something had happened to him: in less than a second he had ceased forever to be the child he was yesterday. Or perhaps that made no difference, perhaps even a city-bred man, let alone a child, could not have understood it; perhaps only a country-bred one could comprehend loving the life he spills. He began to shake again.

"I'm glad it's started now," he whispered. He did not move to speak; only his lips shaped the expiring words: "Then it will be gone when I raise the gun—"

Nor did Sam. "Hush," he said.

"Is he that near?" the boy whispered. "Do you think—"

"Hush," Sam said. So he hushed. But he could not stop the shaking. He did not try, because he knew it would go away when he needed the steadiness—had not Sam Fathers already consecrated and absolved him from weakness and regret too?—not from love and pity for all which lived and ran and then ceased to live in a second in the very midst of splendor and speed, but from weakness and regret. So they stood motionless, breathing deep and quiet and steady. If there had been any sun, it would be near to setting now; there was a condensing, a densifying, of what he had thought was the gray and unchanging light until he realised suddenly that it was his own breathing, his heart, his blood—something, all things, and that Sam Fathers had marked him indeed, not as a mere hunter, but with something Sam had had in his turn of his vanished and forgotten people. He stopped breathing then; there was only his heart, his blood, and in the following silence the wilderness ceased to breathe also, leaning, stooping overhead with its breath held, tremendous and impartial and waiting. Then the shaking stopped too, as he had known it would, and he drew back the two heavy hammers of the gun.

Then it had passed. It was over. The solitude did not breathe again yet; it had merely stopped watching him and was looking somewhere else, even turning its back on him, looking on away up the ridge at another point, and the boy knew as well as if he had seen him that the buck had come to the edge of the cane and had either seen or scented them and faded back into it. But the solitude did not breathe again. It should have suspired again then but it did not. It was still facing, watching, what it had been watching and it was not here, not where he and Sam stood; rigid, not breathing himself, he thought, cried *No! No!*, knowing already that it was too late, thinking with the old despair of two and three years ago: *I'll never get a shot.* Then he heard it—the flat single clap of Walter Ewell's rifle which never missed. Then the mellow sound of the horn came down the ridge and something went out of him and he knew then he had never expected to get the shot at all.

"I reckon that's it," he said. "Walter got him." He had raised the gun slightly without knowing it. He lowered it again and had lowered one of the hammers and was already moving out of the thicket when Sam spoke.

"Wait."

"Wait?" the boy cried. And he would remember that—how he turned upon Sam in the truculence of a boy's grief over the missed opportunity, the missed luck. "What for? Dont you hear that horn?"

And he would remember how Sam was standing. Sam had not moved. He was not tall, squat rather and broad, and the boy had been growing fast for the past year or so and there was not much difference between them in height, yet Sam was looking over the boy's head and up the ridge toward the sound of the horn and the boy knew that Sam did not even see him; that Sam knew he was still there beside him but he did not see the boy. Then the boy saw the buck. It was coming down the ridge, as if it were walking out of the very sound of the horn which related its death. It was not running, it was walking, tremendous, unhurried, slanting and tilting its head to pass the antlers through the undergrowth, and the boy standing with Sam beside him now instead of behind him as Sam always stood, and the gun still partly aimed and one of the hammers still cocked.

Then it saw them. And still it did not begin to run. It just stopped for an instant, taller than any man, looking at them; then its muscles suppled, gathered. It did not even alter its course, not fleeing, not even running, just moving with that winged and effortless ease with which deer move, passing within twenty feet of them, its head high and the eye not proud and not haughty but just full and wild and unafraid, and Sam standing beside the boy now, his right arm raised at full length, palm-outward, speaking in that tongue which the boy had learned from listening to him and Jobaker in the blacksmith-shop, while up the ridge Walter Ewell's horn was still blowing them in to a dead buck.

"Oleh, Chief," Sam said. "Grandfather."

When they reached Walter, he was standing with his back toward them, quite still, bemused almost, looking down at his feet. He didn't look up at all.

"Come here Sam," he said quietly. When they reached him he still did not look up, standing above a little spike buck which had still been a fawn last spring. "He was so little I pretty near let him go," Walter said. "But just look at the track he was making. It's pretty near big as a cow's. If there were any more tracks here besides the ones he is laying in, I would swear there was another buck here that I never even saw."

III

It was dark when they reached the road where the surrey waited. It was turning cold, the rain had stopped, and the sky was beginning to blow clear. His cousin and Major de Spain and General Compson had a fire going. "Did you get him?" Major de Spain said.

"Got a good-sized swamp-rabbit with spike horns," Walter said. He slid the little buck down from his mule. The boy's cousin McCaslin looked at it.

"Nobody saw the big one?" he said.

"I dont even believe Boon saw it," Walter said. "He probably jumped somebody's straw cow in that thicket." Boon started cursing, swearing at Walter and at Sam for not getting the dogs in the first place and at the buck and all.

"Never mind," Major de Spain said. "He'll be here for us next fall. Let's get started home."

It was after midnight when they let Walter out at his gate two miles from Jefferson and later still when they took General Compson to his house and then returned to Major de Spain's, where he and McCaslin would spend the rest of the night, since it was still seventeen miles home. It was cold, the sky was clear now; there would be a heavy frost by sunup and the ground was already frozen beneath the horses' feet and the wheels and beneath their own feet as they crossed Major de Spain's yard and entered the house, the warm dark house, feeling their way up the dark stairs until Major de Spain found a candle and lit it, and into the strange room and the big deep bed, the still cold sheets until they began to warm to their bodies and at last the shaking stopped and suddenly he was telling McCaslin about it while McCaslin listened, quietly until he had finished. "You dont believe it," the boy said. "I know you dont—"

"Why not?" McCaslin said. "Think of all that has happened here, on this earth. All the blood hot and strong for living, pleasuring, that has soaked back into it. For grieving and suffering too, of course, but still getting something out of it for all that, getting a lot out of it, because after all you dont have to continue to bear what you believe is suffering; you can always choose to stop that, put an end to that. And even suffering and grieving is better than nothing; there is only one thing worse than not being alive, and that's shame. But you cant be alive forever, and you always wear out life long before you have exhausted the possibilities of living. And all that must be somewhere; all that could not have been invented and created just to be thrown away. And the earth is shallow; there is not a great deal of it before you come to the rock. And the earth dont want to just keep things, hoard then; it wants to use them again. Look at the seed, the acorns, at what happens even to carrion when you try to bury it: it refuses too, seethes and struggles too until it reaches light and air again, hunting the sun still. And they—" the boy saw his hand in silhouette for a moment against the

window beyond which, accustomed to the darkness now, he could see
sky where the scoured and icy stars glittered "—they dont want it, need
it. Besides, what would it want, itself, knocking around out there, when
it never had enough time about the earth as it was, when there is plenty
of room about the earth, plenty of places still unchanged from what they
were when the blood used and pleasured in them while it was still
blood?"

"But we want them," the boy said. "We want them too. There is
plenty of room for us and them too."

"That's right," McCaslin said. "Suppose they dont have substance,
cant cast a shadow—"

"But I saw it!" the boy cried. "I saw him!"

"Steady," McCaslin said. For an instant his hand touched the boy's
flank beneath the covers. "Steady. I know you did. So did I. Sam took
me in there once after I killed my first deer."

ERNEST [MILLER] HEMINGWAY (1899–1961)

*Hemingway's early life was divided between the settled routines of
upper-middle-class Oak Park, Illinois, where he was born, and the
more rugged activities of the northern Michigan woods, where he
spent his summers. The Oak Park life was dominated by his aggressive, "artistic" mother, about whom, in his later life, he was
very abusive; the summers were dominated by his physician father,
a sportsman who is said to have given the boy a fishing rod when
he was two and a gun when he was ten. It was from the summer
life and the relationship with his father that most of his early
fiction came. His mother's influence was to show itself in more
negative ways—in the many portraits of "bitches" that he was to
draw, domineering women intent on destroying their men, or,
inversely, in the "ideal" female who appears and reappears as his
heroine, the beautiful creature happily submissive to the masculine
will.*

*When he was fifteen he ran away from Oak Park, but he returned
to finish high school in 1917 and, with that, his formal education.
He had written a good deal for high school publications, much in
imitation of certain newspaper columnists, and his first employment was as a reporter on the Kansas City* Star. *He left this job
to become an honorary lieutenant in the Red Cross ambulance
corps serving on the Italian front, but in three months he was
wounded, hospitalized in Milan for three more months, and returned home. He never recovered from the shock of his wound,
which became a central symbol in his fiction until the end of his
life. Although it is not even mentioned (nor the war either, for that*

matter), no story shows its effect on the "Hemingway hero" more precisely than "Big Two-hearted River." Hemingway also became, whether or not as some by-product of his war experience, the most famous accident-prone man in literary history.

In 1920 *he went to Canada to work on the Toronto* Star Weekly, *and then to Chicago to an advertising firm. In his spare time he tried to write poems and stories and was encouraged by Sherwood Anderson, whose own stories had their influence on him. With the promise of employment as roving correspondent abroad for the Toronto* Star, *he married in 1921 and left for Paris. Very soon he met Gertrude Stein and Ezra Pound, two people who had no high regard for one another but both of whom were to supplement the influence of Anderson in shaping Hemingway's early style. His European newspaper experience, meantime, was playing its part too, both in expanding the store of his subject matter and in the development of that early, spare, and understated prose.*

The ten years that followed saw the flowering of his remarkable talent and the publication of his best books: Three Stories and Ten Poems *(1923)—the poems are nothing, the stories are everything; more stories in* In Our Time *(1924); the two novels,* The Sun Also Rises *(1926) and* A Farewell to Arms *(1929); more stories in* Men without Women *(1927) and* Winner Take Nothing *(1933).*

This body of fiction is extraordinary in that it altered the sensibility and the experience of an entire reading generation. In the work of the nearly thirty years that followed, he rose sporadically to the great achievements of his triumphant decade—in a few stories, in occasional scenes in For Whom the Bell Tolls *(1940)—but more and more he yielded to self-imitation and self-indulgence. The public exploitation of his favorite activities—bullfighting, big-game hunting, deep-sea fishing—had always been discomfiting, but at last it became simply tiresome. He brutally destroyed devoted friendships, marriages (he had four), bit by bit himself, and it was as if his general destructiveness could not exclude his own genius.*

In the late 1930s it seemed as though his deep involvement in the Spanish Civil War might save him by pushing him out and beyond his increasingly bellicose (and confining) self. But the literary work that resulted—the big novel, The Fifth Column *(his only play), and a half dozen stories (in 1969 the play was republished together with four of the stories, not previously collected)—did not accomplish that aesthetic therapy through politics.*

Nor did all the moving about across Europe and Africa, to China, to Key West, to Cuba, to Wyoming, and finally to a ranch near Ketchum, Idaho. Nor did all the public and critical acclaim, all the

*honors, including what he called "that Swedish thing"—the Nobel
award in 1954.*

*The deterioration of his personality into the blustering, boastful, vain,
and often petty figure that became so familiar through the wide publicity his very flamboyance commanded may well be the con-
comitant of the deterioration of his art. And yet, remembering his
greatest works, even some of those very short stories of the 1920s,
one grieved for his end when, following the example of his father
thirty-three years before, he shot off most of his head. Posthumous
publications are* A Movable Feast *(1964), a fictionalized memoir of
his Paris years, and* Islands in the Stream *(1970), an unfinished
novel of the Cuba period. He was not responsible for the publication
of these works, and we should not blame him for this indiscretion.*

FURTHER READING

The major biographical study is Carlos Baker, *Ernest Hemingway:
A Life Story* (1969). Lillian Ross, *Portrait of Hemingway* (1962),
Leicester Hemingway *My Brother Ernest Hemingway* (1962),
Morley Callaghan, *That Summer in Paris* (1963), and Marcelline
Hemingway Sanford, *At the Hemingways* (1962), are also important
sources of the facts of Hemingway's life. Carlos Baker published
the first comprehensive critical survey in *Hemingway: The Writer
as Artist* (1952, revised 1963). Philip Young wrote a more suggestive critique, *Ernest Hemingway* (1952, revised 1966). Charles A.
Fenton's *The Apprenticeship of Ernest Hemingway* (1954) treats
the early years. Three valuable short surveys of Hemingway's writing
are Sheridan Baker, *Ernest Hemingway: An Introduction and
Interpretation* (1967); Leo Gurko, *Ernest Hemingway and the Pursuit of Heroism* (1968); and Richard B. Hovey, *Hemingway: The
Inward Terrain* (1968).

Big Two-hearted River *(1925)*

The train went on up the track out of sight, around one of the hills
of burnt timber. Nick sat down on the bundle of canvas and bedding
the baggage man had pitched out of the door of the baggage car. There
was no town, nothing but the rails and the burned-over country. The
thirteen saloons that had lined the one street of Seney had not left a
trace. The foundations of the Mansion House hotel stuck up above the
ground. The stone was chipped and split by the fire. It was all that was
left of the town of Seney. Even the surface had been burned off the
ground.

Nick looked at the burned-over stretch of hillside, where he had
expected to find the scattered houses of the town and then walked down
the railroad track to the bridge over the river. The river was there. It

swirled against the log spiles of the bridge. Nick looked down into the clear, brown water, colored from the pebbly bottom, and watched the trout keeping themselves steady in the current with wavering fins. As he watched them they changed their positions by quick angles, only to hold steady in the fast water again. Nick watched them a long time.

He watched them holding themselves with their noses into the current, many trout in deep, fast moving water, slightly distorted as he watched far down through the glassy convex surface of the pool, its surface pushing and swelling smooth against the resistance of the log-driven piles of the bridge. At the bottom of the pool were the big trout. Nick did not see them at first. Then he saw them at the bottom of the pool, big trout looking to hold themselves on the gravel bottom in a varying mist of gravel and sand, raised in spurts by the current.

Nick looked down into the pool from the bridge. It was a hot day. A kingfisher flew up the stream. It was a long time since Nick had looked into a stream and seen trout. They were very satisfactory. As the shadow of the kingfisher moved up the stream, a big trout shot upstream in a long angle, only his shadow marking the angle, then lost his shadow as he came through the surface of the water, caught the sun, and then, as he went back into the stream under the surface, his shadow seemed to float down the stream with the current, unresisting, to his post under the bridge where he tightened facing up into the current.

Nick's heart tightened as the trout moved. He felt all the old feeling.

He turned and looked down the stream. It stretched away, pebbly-bottomed with shallows and big boulders and a deep pool as it curved away around the foot of a bluff.

Nick walked back up the ties to where his pack lay in the cinders beside the railway track. He was happy. He adjusted the pack harness around the bundle, pulling straps tight, slung the pack on his back, got his arms through the shoulder straps and took some of the pull off his shoulders by leaning his forehead against the wide band of the tump-line. Still, it was too heavy. It was much too heavy. He had his leather rod-case in his hand and leaning forward to keep the weight of the pack high on his shoulders he walked along the road that paralleled the railway track, leaving the burned town behind in the heat, and then turned off around a hill with a high, fire-scarred hill on either side onto a road that went back into the country. He walked along the road feeling the ache from the pull of the heavy pack. The road climbed steadily. It was hard work walking up-hill. His muscles ached and the day was hot, but Nick felt happy. He felt he had left everything behind, the need for thinking, the need to write, other needs. It was all back of him.

From the time he had gotten down off the train and the baggage man had thrown his pack out of the open car door things had been different. Seney was burned, the country was burned over and changed, but it did not matter. It could not all be burned. He knew that. He hiked along the road, sweating in the sun, climbing to cross the range of hills that separated the railway from the pine plains.

The road ran on, dipping occasionally, but always climbing. Nick went on up. Finally the road after going parallel to the burnt hillside reached the top. Nick leaned back against a stump and slipped out of the pack harness. Ahead of him, as far as he could see, was the pine plain. The burned country stopped off at the left with the range of hills. On ahead islands of dark pine trees rose out of the plain. Far off to the left was the line of the river. Nick followed it with his eye and caught glints of the water in the sun.

There was nothing but the pine plain ahead of him, until the far blue hills that marked the Lake Superior height of land. He could hardly see them, faint and far away in the heat-light over the plain. If he looked too steadily they were gone. But if he only half-looked they were there, the far-off hills of the height of land.

Nick sat down against the charred stump and smoked a cigarette. His pack balanced on the top of the stump, harness holding ready, a hollow molded in it from his back. Nick sat smoking, looking out over the country. He did not need to get his map out. He knew where he was from the position of the river.

As he smoked, his legs stretched out in front of him, he noticed a grasshopper walk along the ground and up onto his woolen sock. The grasshopper was black. As he had walked along the road, climbing, he had started many grasshoppers from the dust. They were all black. They were not the big grasshoppers with yellow and black or red and black wings whirring out from their black wing sheathing as they fly up. These were just ordinary hoppers, but all a sooty black in color. Nick had wondered about them as he walked, without really thinking about them. Now, as he watched the black hopper that was nibbling at the wool of his sock with its fourway lip, he realized that they had all turned black from living in the burned-over land. He realized that the fire must have come the year before, but the grasshoppers were all black now. He wondered how long they would stay that way.

Carefully he reached his hand down and took hold of the hopper by the wings. He turned him up, all his legs walking in the air, and looked at his jointed belly. Yes, it was black too, iridescent where the back and head were dusty.

"Go on, hopper," Nick said, speaking out loud for the first time. "Fly away somewhere."

He tossed the grasshopper up into the air and watched him sail away to a charcoal stump across the road.

Nick stood up. He leaned his back against the weight of his pack where it rested upright on the stump and got his arms through the shoulder straps. He stood with the pack on his back on the brow of the hill looking out across the country, toward the distant river and then struck down the hillside away from the road. Underfoot the ground was good walking. Two hundred yards down the hillside the fire line stopped. Then it was sweet fern, growing ankle high, to walk through, and clumps of jack pines; a long undulating country with frequent rises and descents, sandy underfoot and the country alive again.

Nick kept his direction by the sun. He knew where he wanted to strike the river and he kept on through the pine plain, mounting small rises to see other rises ahead of him and sometimes from the top of a rise a great solid island of pines off to his right or his left. He broke off some sprigs of the heathery sweet fern, and put them under his pack straps. The chafing crushed it and he smelled it as he walked.

He was tired and very hot, walking across the uneven, shadeless pine plain. At any time he knew he could strike the river by turning off to his left. It could not be more than a mile away. But he kept on toward the north to hit the river as far upstream as he could go in one day's walking.

For some time as he walked Nick had been in sight of one of the big islands of pine standing out above the rolling high ground he was crossing. He dipped down and then as he came slowly up to the crest of the bridge he turned and made toward the pine trees.

There was no underbrush in the island of pine trees. The trunks of the trees went straight up or slanted toward each other. The trunks were straight and brown without branches. The branches were high above. Some interlocked to make a solid shadow on the brown forest floor. Around the grove of trees was a bare space. It was brown and soft underfoot as Nick walked on it. This was the over-lapping of the pine needle floor, extending out beyond the width of the high branches. The trees had grown tall and the branches moved high, leaving in the sun this bare space they had once covered with shadow. Sharp at the edge of this extension of the forest floor commenced the sweet fern.

Nick slipped off his pack and lay down in the shade. He lay on his back and looked up into the pine trees. His neck and back and the small of his back rested as he stretched. The earth felt good against his back. He looked up at the sky, through the branches, and then shut his eyes. He opened them and looked up again. There was a wind high up in the branches. He shut his eyes again and went to sleep.

Nick woke stiff and cramped. The sun was nearly down. His pack was heavy and the straps painful as he lifted it on. He leaned over with the pack on and picked up the leather rod-case and started out from the pine trees across the sweet fern swale, toward the river. He knew it could not be more than a mile.

He came down a hillside covered with stumps into a meadow. At the edge of the meadow flowed the river. Nick was glad to get to the river. He walked upstream through the meadow. His trousers were soaked with the dew as he walked. After the hot day, the dew had come quickly and heavily. The river made no sound. It was too fast and smooth. At the edge of the meadow, before he mounted to a piece of high ground to make camp, Nick looked down the river at the trout rising. They were rising to insects come from the swamp on the other side of the stream when the sun went down. The trout jumped out of water to take them. While Nick walked through the little stretch of meadow alongside the stream, trout had jumped high out of water. Now as he looked down the river, the insects must be settling on the surface, for the trout were feeding steadily all down the stream. As far down the long stretch as he could see, the trout were rising, making circles all down the surface of the water, as though it were starting to rain.

The ground rose, wooded and sandy, to overlook the meadow, the stretch of river and the swamp. Nick dropped his pack and rod-case and looked for a level piece of ground. He was very hungry and he wanted to make his camp before he cooked. Between two jack pines, the ground was quite level. He took the ax out of the pack and chopped out two projecting roots. That leveled a piece of ground large enough to sleep on. He smoothed out the sandy soil with his hand and pulled all the sweet fern bushes by their roots. His hands smelled good from the sweet fern. He smoothed the uprooted earth. He did not want anything making lumps under the blankets. When he had the ground smooth, he spread his three blankets. One he folded double, next to the ground. The other two he spread on top.

With the ax he slit off a bright slab of pine from one of the stumps and split it into pegs for the tent. He wanted them long and solid to hold in the ground. With the tent unpacked and spread on the ground, the pack, leaning against a jackpine, looked much smaller. Nick tied the rope that served the tent for a ridge-pole to the trunk of one of the pine trees and pulled the tent up off the ground with the other end of the rope and tied it to the other pine. The tent hung on the rope like a canvas blanket on a clothesline. Nick poked a pole he had cut up under the back peak of the canvas and then made it a tent by pegging out the sides. He pegged the sides out taut and drove the pegs deep, hitting them down into the ground with the flat of the ax until the rope loops were buried and the canvas was drum tight.

Across the open mouth of the tent Nick fixed cheesecloth to keep out mosquitoes. He crawled inside under the mosquito bar with various things from the pack to put at the head of the bed under the slant of the canvas. Inside the tent the light came through the brown canvas. It smelled pleasantly of canvas. Already there was something mysterious and homelike. Nick was happy as he crawled inside the tent. He had not been unhappy all day. This was different though. Now things were done. There had been this to do. Now it was done. It had been a hard trip. He was very tired. That was done. He had made his camp. He was settled. Nothing could touch him. It was a good place to camp. He was there, in the good place. He was in his home where he had made it. Now he was hungry.

He came out, crawling under the cheesecloth. It was quite dark outside. It was lighter in the tent.

Nick went over to the pack and found, with his fingers, a long nail in a paper sack of nails, in the bottom of the pack. He drove it into the pine tree, holding it close and hitting it gently with the flat of the ax. He hung the pack up on the nail. All his supplies were in the pack. They were off the ground and sheltered now.

Nick was hungry. He did not believe he had ever been hungrier. He opened and emptied a can of pork and beans and a can of spaghetti into the frying pan.

"I've got a right to eat this kind of stuff, if I'm willing to carry it," Nick said. His voice sounded strange in the darkening woods. He did not speak again.

He started a fire with some chunks of pine he got with the ax from a stump. Over the fire he stuck a wire grill, pushing the four legs down into the ground with his boot. Nick put the frying pan on the grill over the flames. He was hungrier. The beans and spaghetti warmed. Nick stirred them and mixed them together. They began to bubble, making little bubbles that rose with difficulty to the surface. There was a good smell. Nick got out a bottle of tomato catchup and cut four slices of bread. The little bubbles were coming faster now. Nick sat down beside the fire and lifted the frying pan off. He poured about half the contents out into the tin plate. It spread slowly on the plate. Nick knew it was too hot. He poured on some tomato catchup. He knew the beans and spaghetti were still too hot. He looked at the fire, then at the tent, he was not going to spoil it all by burning his tongue. For years he had never enjoyed fried bananas because he had never been able to wait for them to cool. His tongue was very sensitive. He was very hungry. Across the river in the swamp, in the almost dark, he saw a mist rising. He looked at the tent once more. All right. He took a full spoonful from the plate.

"Chrise," Nick said, "Geezus Chrise," he said happily.

He ate the whole plateful before he remembered the bread. Nick finished the second plateful with the bread, mopping the plate shiny. He had not eaten since a cup of coffee and a ham sandwich in the station restaurant at St. Ignace. It had been a very fine experience. He had been that hungry before, but had not been able to satisfy it. He could have made camp hours before if he had wanted to. There were plenty of good places to camp on the river. But this was good.

Nick tucked two big chips of pine under the grill. The fire flared up. He had forgotten to get water for the coffee. Out of the pack he got a folding canvas bucket and walked down the hill, across the edge of the meadow, to the stream. The other bank was in the white mist. The grass was wet and cold as he knelt on the bank and dipped the canvas bucket into the stream. It bellied and pulled hard in the current. The water was ice cold. Nick rinsed the bucket and carried it full up to the camp. Up away from the stream it was not so cold.

Nick drove another big nail and hung up the bucket full of water. He dipped the coffee pot half full, put some more chips under the grill onto the fire and put the pot on. He could not remember which way he made coffee. He could remember an argument about it with Hopkins, but not which side he had taken. He decided to bring it to a boil. He remembered now that was Hopkins's way. He had once argued about everything with Hopkins. While he waited for the coffee to boil, he opened a small can of apricots. He liked to open cans. He emptied the can of apricots out into a tin cup. While he watched the coffee on the fire, he drank the juice syrup of the apricots, carefully at first to keep from spilling, then meditatively, sucking the apricots down. They were better than fresh apricots.

The coffee boiled as he watched. The lid came up and coffee and grounds ran down the side of the pot. Nick took it off the grill. It was a triumph for Hopkins. He put sugar in the empty apricot cup and poured some of the coffee out to cool. It was too hot to pour and he used his hat to hold the handle of the coffee pot. He would not let it steep in the pot at all. Not the first cup. It should be straight Hopkins all the way. Hop deserved that. He was a very serious coffee drinker. He was the most serious man Nick had ever known. Not heavy, serious. That was a long time ago. Hopkins spoke without moving his lips. He had played polo. He made millions of dollars in Texas. He had borrowed carfare to go to Chicago, when the wire came that his first big well had come in. He could have wired for money. That would have been too slow. They called Hop's girl the Blonde Venus. Hop did not mind because she was not his real girl. Hopkins said very confidently that none of them would make fun of his real girl. He was right. Hopkins went away when the telegram came. That was on the Black River. It took eight days for the telegram to reach him. Hopkins gave away his .22 caliber Colt automatic pistol to Nick. He gave his camera to Bill. It was to remember him always by. They were all going fishing again next summer. The Hop Head was rich. He would get a yacht and they would all cruise along the north shore of Lake Superior. He was excited but serious. They said good-bye and all felt bad. It broke up the trip. They never saw Hopkins again. That was a long time ago on the Black River.

Nick drank the coffee, the coffee according to Hopkins. The coffee was bitter. Nick laughed. It made a good ending to the story. His mind was starting to work. He knew he could choke it because he was tired enough. He spilled the coffee out of the pot and shook the grounds loose into the fire. He lit a cigarette and went inside the tent. He took off his shoes and trousers, sitting on the blankets, rolled the shoes up inside the trousers for a pillow and got in between the blankets.

Out through the front of the tent he watched the glow of the fire, when the night wind blew on it. It was a quiet night. The swamp was perfectly quiet. Nick stretched under the blanket comfortably. A mosquito hummed close to his ear. Nick sat up and lit a match. The mosquito was on the canvas, over his head. Nick moved the match quickly up to it. The mosquito made a satisfactory hiss in the flame. The match went out. Nick lay down again under the blanket. He turned on his side and shut his eyes. He was sleepy. He felt sleep coming. He curled up under the blanket and went to sleep.

In the morning the sun was up and the tent was starting to get hot. Nick crawled out under the mosquito netting stretched across the mouth of the tent, to look at the morning. The grass was wet on his hands as he came out. He held his trousers and his shoes in his hands. The sun was just up over the hill. There was the meadow, the river and the swamp. There were birch trees in the green of the swamp on the other side of the river.

The river was clear and smoothly fast in the early morning. Down about two hundred yards were three logs all the way across the stream. They made the water smooth and deep above them. As Nick watched, a mink crossed the river on the logs and went into the swamp. Nick was excited. He was excited by the early morning and the river. He was really too hurried to eat breakfast, but he knew he must. He built a little fire and put on the coffee pot.

While the water was heating in the pot he took an empty bottle and went down over the edge of the high ground to the meadow. The meadow was wet with dew and Nick wanted to catch grasshoppers for bait before the sun dried the grass. He found plenty of good grass-hoppers. They were at the base of the grass stems. Sometimes they clung to a grass stem. They were cold and wet with the dew, and could not jump until the sun warmed them. Nick picked them up, taking only the medium-sized brown ones, and put them into the bottle. He turned over a log and just under the shelter of the edge were several hundred hoppers. It was a grasshopper lodging house. Nick put about fifty of the medium browns into the bottle. While he was picking up the hoppers the others warmed in the sun and commenced to hop away. They flew when they hopped. At first they made one flight and stayed stiff when they landed, as though they were dead.

Nick knew that by the time he was through with breakfast they would be as lively as ever. Without dew in the grass it would take him all day to catch a bottle full of good grasshoppers and he would have to crush many of them, slamming at them with his hat. He washed his hands at the stream. He was excited to be near it. Then he walked up to the tent. The hoppers were already jumping stiffly in the grass. In the bottle, warmed by the sun, they were jumping in a mass. Nick put in a pine stick as a cork. It plugged the mouth of the bottle enough, so the hoppers could not get out and left plenty of air passage.

He had rolled the log back and knew he could get grasshoppers there every morning.

Nick laid the bottle full of jumping grasshoppers against a pine trunk. Rapidly he mixed some buckwheat flour with water and stirred it smooth, one cup of flour, one cup of water. He put a handful of coffee in the pot and dipped a lump of grease out of a can and slid it sputter-

ing across the hot skillet. On the smoking skillet he poured smoothly
the buckwheat batter. It spread like lava, the grease spitting sharply.
Around the edges the buckwheat cake began to firm, then brown, then
crisp. The surface was bubbling slowly to porousness. Nick pushed
under the browned under surface with a fresh pine chip. He shook the
skillet sideways and the cake was loose on the surface. I won't try and
flop it, he thought. He slid the chip of clean wood all the way under the
cake, and flopped it over onto its face. It sputtered in the pan.

When it was cooked Nick regreased the skillet. He used all the
batter. It made another big flapjack and one smaller one.

Nick ate a big flapjack and a smaller one, covered with apple butter.
He put apple butter on the third cake, folded it over twice, wrapped it in
oiled paper and put it in his shirt pocket. He put the apple butter jar
back in the pack and cut bread for two sandwiches.

In the pack he found a big onion. He sliced it in two and peeled the
silky outer skin. Then he cut one half into slices and made onion sandwiches. He wrapped them in oiled paper and buttoned them in the other
pocket of his khaki shirt. He turned the skillet upside down on the grill,
drank the coffee, sweetened and yellow brown with the condensed milk
in it, and tidied up the camp. It was a good camp.

Nick took his fly rod out of the leather rod-case, jointed it, and
shoved the rod-case back into the tent. He put on the reel and threaded
the line through the guides. He had to hold it from hand to hand, as
he threaded it, or it would slip back through its own weight. It was a
heavy, double tapered fly line. Nick had paid eight dollars for it a long
time ago. It was made heavy to lift back in the air and come forward
flat and heavy and straight to make it possible to cast a fly which has no
weight. Nick opened the aluminum leader box. The leaders were coiled
between the damp flannel pads. Nick had wet the pads at the water
cooler on the train up to St. Ignace. In the damp pads the gut leaders
had softened and Nick unrolled one and tied it by a loop at the end to
the heavy fly line. He fastened a hook on the end of the leader. It was
a small hook; very thin and springy.

Nick took it from his hook book, sitting with the rod across his lap.
He tested the knot and the spring of the rod by pulling the line taut. It
was a good feeling. He was careful not to let the hook bite into his
finger.

He started down to the stream, holding his rod, the bottle of grasshoppers hung from his neck by a thong tied in half hitches around the
neck of the bottle. His landing net hung by a hook from his belt. Over
his shoulder was a long flour sack tied at each corner into an ear. The
cord went over his shoulder. The sack flapped against his legs.

Nick felt awkward and professionally happy with all his equipment
hanging from him. The grasshopper bottle swung against his chest. In
his shirt the breast pockets bulged against him with the lunch and his
fly book.

He stepped into the stream. It was a shock. His trousers clung tight to his legs. His shoes felt the gravel. The water was a rising cold shock.

Rushing, the current sucked against his legs. Where he stepped in, the water was over his knees. He waded with the current. The gravel slid under his shoes. He looked down at the swirl of water below each leg and tipped up the bottle to get a grasshopper.

The first grasshopper gave a jump in the neck of the bottle and went out into the water. He was sucked under in the whirl by Nick's right leg and came to the surface a little way down stream. He floated rapidly, kicking. In a quick circle, breaking the smooth surface of the water, he disappeared. A trout had taken him.

Another hopper poked his face out of the bottle. His antennæ wavered. He was getting his front legs out of the bottle to jump. Nick took him by the head and held him while he threaded the slim hook under his chin, down through his thorax and into the last segments of his abdomen. The grasshopper took hold of the hook with his front feet, spitting tobacco juice on it. Nick dropped him into the water.

Holding the rod in his right hand he let out line against the pull of the grasshopper in the current. He stripped off line from the reel with his left hand and let it run free. He could see the hopper in the little waves of the current. It went out of sight.

There was a tug on the line. Nick pulled against the taut line. It was his first strike. Holding the now living rod across the current, he brought in the line with his left hand. The rod bent in jerks, the trout pumping against the current. Nick knew it was a small one. He lifted the rod straight up in the air. It bowed with the pull.

He saw the trout in the water jerking with his head and body against the shifting tangent of the line in the stream.

Nick took the line in his left hand and pulled the trout, thumping tiredly against the current, to the surface. His back was mottled the clear, water-over-gravel color, his side flashing in the sun. The rod under his right arm, Nick stooped, dipping his right hand into the current. He held the trout, never still, with his moist right hand, while he unhooked the barb from his mouth, then dropped him back into the stream.

He hung unsteadily in the current, then settled to the bottom beside a stone. Nick reached down his hand to touch him, his arm to the elbow under water. The trout was steady in the moving stream, resting on the gravel, beside a stone. As Nick's fingers touched him, touched his smooth, cool, underwater feeling he was gone, gone in a shadow across the bottom of the stream.

He's all right, Nick thought. He was only tired.

He had wet his hand before he touched the trout, so he would not disturb the delicate mucus that covered him. If a trout was touched with a dry hand, a white fungus attacked the unprotected spot. Years before when he had fished crowded streams, with fly fishermen ahead of him and behind him, Nick had again and again come on dead trout, furry with white fungus, drifted against a rock, or floating belly up in some pool. Nick did not like to fish with other men on the river. Unless they were of your party, they spoiled it.

He wallowed down the stream, above his knees in the current, through the fifty yards of shallow water above the pile of logs that crossed the stream. He did not rebait his hook and held it in his hand as he waded. He was certain he could catch small trout in the shallows, but he did not want them. There would be no big trout in the shallows this time of day.

Now the water deepened up his thighs sharply and coldly. Ahead was the smooth dammed-back flood of water above the logs. The water was smooth and dark; on the left the lower edge of the meadow; on the right the swamp.

Nick leaned back against the current and took a hopper from the bottle. He threaded the hopper on the hook and spat on him for good luck. Then he pulled several yards of line from the reel and tossed the hopper out ahead onto the fast, dark water. It floated down towards the logs, then the weight of the line pulled the bait under the surface. Nick held the rod in his right hand, letting the line run out through his fingers.

There was a long tug. Nick struck and the rod came alive and dangerous, bent double, the line tightening, coming out of water, tightening, all in a heavy, dangerous, steady pull. Nick felt the moment when the leader would break if the strain increased and let the line go.

The reel ratcheted into a mechanical shriek as the line went out in a rush. Too fast. Nick could not check it, the line rushing out, the reel note rising as the line ran out.

With the core of the reel showing, his heart feeling stopped with the excitement, leaning back against the current that mounted icily his thighs, Nick thumbed the reel hard with his left hand. It was awkward getting his thumb inside the fly reel frame.

As he put on pressure the line tightened into sudden hardness and beyond the logs a huge trout went high out of water. As he jumped, Nick lowered the tip of the rod. But he felt, as he dropped the tip to ease the strain, the moment when the strain was too great; the hardness too tight. Of course, the leader had broken. There was no mistaking the feeling when all spring left the line and it became dry and hard. Then it went slack.

His mouth dry, his heart down, Nick reeled in. He had never seen so big a trout. There was a heaviness, a power not to be held, and then the bulk of him, as he jumped. He looked as broad as a salmon.

Nick's hand was shaky. He reeled in slowly. The thrill had been too much. He felt, vaguely, a little sick, as though it would be better to sit down.

The leader had broken where the hook was tied to it. Nick took it in his hand. He thought of the trout somewhere on the bottom, holding himself steady over the gravel, far down below the light, under the logs, with the hook in his jaw. Nick knew the trout's teeth would cut through the snell of the hook. The hook would imbed itself in his jaw. He'd bet the trout was angry. Anything that size would be angry. That was a trout. He had been solidly hooked. Solid as a rock. He felt like a rock, too, before he started off. By God, he was a big one. By God, he was the biggest one I ever heard of.

Nick climbed out onto the meadow and stood, water running down his trousers and out of his shoes, his shoes squelchy. He went over and sat on the logs. He did not want to rush his sensations any.

He wriggled his toes in the water, in his shoes, and got out a cigarette from his breast pocket. He lit it and tossed the match into the fast water below the logs. A tiny trout rose at the match, as it swung around in the fast current. Nick laughed. He would finish the cigarette.

He sat on the logs, smoking, drying in the sun, the sun warm on his back, the river shallow ahead entering the woods, curving into the woods, shallows, light glittering, big water-smooth rocks, cedars along the bank and white birches, the logs warm in the sun, smooth to sit on, without bark, gray to the touch; slowly the feeling of disappointment left him. It went away slowly, the feeling of disappointment that came sharply after the thrill that made his shoulders ache. It was all right now. His rod lying out on the logs, Nick tied a new hook on the leader, pulling the gut tight until it crimped into itself in a hard knot.

He baited up, then picked up the rod and walked to the far end of the logs to get into the water, where it was not too deep. Under and beyond the logs was a deep pool. Nick walked around the shallow shelf near the swamp shore until he came out on the shallow bed of the stream.

On the left, where the meadow ended and the woods began, a great elm tree was uprooted. Gone over in a storm, it lay back into the woods, its roots clotted with dirt, grass growing in them, rising a solid bank beside the stream. The river cut to the edge of the uprooted tree. From where Nick stood he could see deep channels, like ruts, cut in the shallow bed of the stream by the flow of the current. Pebbly where he stood and pebbly and full of boulders beyond; where it curved near the tree roots, the bed of the stream was marly and between the ruts of deep water green weed fronds swung in the current.

Nick swung the rod back over his shoulder and forward, and the line, curving forward, laid the grasshopper down on one of the deep channels in the weeds. A trout struck and Nick hooked him.

Holding the rod far out toward the uprooted tree and sloshing backward in the current, Nick worked the trout, plunging, the rod bending alive, out of the danger of the weeds into the open river. Holding the rod, pumping alive against the current, Nick brought the trout in. He rushed, but always came, the spring of the rod yielding to the rushes, sometimes jerking under water, but always bringing him in. Nick eased downstream with the rushes. The rod above his head he led the trout over the net, then lifted.

The trout hung heavy in the net, mottled trout back and silver sides in the meshes. Nick unhooked him; heavy sides, good to hold, big under-shot jaw, and slipped him, heaving and big sliding, into the long sack that hung from his shoulders in the water.

Nick spread the mouth of the sack against the current and it filled, heavy with water. He held it up, the bottom in the stream, and the water poured out through the sides. Inside at the bottom was the big trout, alive in the water.

Nick moved downstream. The sack out ahead of him sunk heavy in the water, pulling from his shoulders.

It was getting hot, the sun hot on the back of his neck.

Nick had one good trout. He did not care about getting many trout. Now the stream was shallow and wide. There were trees along both banks. The trees of the left bank made short shadows on the current in the forenoon sun. Nick knew there were trout in each shadow. In the afternoon, after the sun had crossed toward the hills, the trout would be in the cool shadows on the other side of the stream.

The very biggest ones would lie up close to the bank. You could always pick them up there on the Black. When the sun was down they all moved out into the current. Just when the sun made the water blind-ing in the glare before it went down, you were liable to strike a big trout anywhere in the current. It was almost impossible to fish then, the surface of the water was blinding as a mirror in the sun. Of course, you could fish upstream, but in a stream like the Black, or this, you had to wallow against the current and in a deep place, the water piled up on you. It was no fun to fish upstream with this much current.

Nick moved along through the shallow stretch watching the banks for deep holes. A beech tree grew close beside the river, so that the branches hung down into the water. The stream went back in under the leaves. There were always trout in a place like that.

Nick did not care about fishing that hole. He was sure he would get hooked in the branches.

It looked deep though. He dropped the grasshopper so the current took it under water, back in under the overhanging branch. The line pulled hard and Nick struck. The trout threshed heavily, half out of water in the leaves and branches. The line was caught. Nick pulled hard and the trout was off. He reeled in and holding the hook in his hand, walked down the stream.

Ahead, close to the left bank, was a big log. Nick saw it was hollow; pointing up river the current entered it smoothly, only a little ripple spread each side of the log. The water was deepening. The top of the hollow log was gray and dry. It was partly in the shadow.

Nick took the cork out of the grasshopper bottle and a hopper clung to it. He picked him off, hooked him and tossed him out. He held the rod far out so that the hopper on the water moved into the current flowing into the hollow log. Nick lowered the rod and the hopper floated in. There was a heavy strike. Nick swung the rod against the pull. It felt as though he were hooked into the log itself, except for the live feeling.

He tried to force the fish out into the current. It came, heavily.

The line went slack and Nick thought the trout was gone. Then he saw him, very near, in the current, shaking his head, trying to get the hook out. His mouth was clamped shut. He was fighting the hook in the clear flowing current.

Looping in the line with his left hand, Nick swung the rod to make the line taut and tried to lead the trout toward the net, but he was gone, out of sight, the line pumping. Nick fought him against the current, letting him thump in the water against the spring of the rod. He shifted the rod to his left hand, worked the trout upstream, holding his weight, fighting on the rod, and then let him down into the net. He lifted him clear of the water, a heavy half circle in the net, the net dripping, unhooked him and slid him into the sack.

He spread the mouth of the sack and looked down in at the two big trout alive in the water.

Through the deepening water, Nick waded over to the hollow log. He took the sack off, over his head, the trout flopping as it came out of water, and hung it so the trout were deep in the water. Then he pulled himself up on the log and sat, the water from his trousers and boots running down into the stream. He laid his rod down, moved along to the shady end of the log and took the sandwiches out of his pocket. He dipped the sandwiches in the cold water. The current carried away the crumbs. He ate the sandwiches and dipped his hat full of water to drink, the water running out through his hat just ahead of his drinking.

It was cool in the shade, sitting on the log. He took a cigarette out and struck a match to light it. The match sunk into the gray wood, making a tiny furrow. Nick leaned over the side of the log, found a hard place and lit the match. He sat smoking and watching the river.

Ahead the river narrowed and went into a swamp. The river became smooth and deep and the swamp looked solid with cedar trees, their trunks close together, their branches solid. It would not be possible to walk through a swamp like that. The branches grew so low. You would have to keep almost level with the ground to move at all. You could not crash through the branches. That must be why the animals that lived in swamps were built the way they were, Nick thought.

He wished he had brought something to read. He felt like reading. He did not feel like going on into the swamp. He looked down the river. A big cedar slanted all the way across the stream. Beyond that the river went into the swamp.

Nick did not want to go in there now. He felt a reaction against deep wading with the water deepening up under his armpits, to hook big trout in places impossible to land them. In the swamp the banks were bare, the big cedars came together overhead, the sun did not come through, except in patches; in the fast deep water, in the half light, the fishing would be tragic. In the swamp fishing was a tragic adventure. Nick did not want it. He did not want to go down the stream any further today.

He took out his knife, opened it and stuck it in the log. Then he pulled up the sack, reached into it and brought out one of the trout. Holding him near the tail, hard to hold, alive, in his hand, he whacked him against the log. The trout quivered, rigid. Nick laid him on the log in the shade and broke the neck of the other fish the same way. He laid them side by side on the log. They were fine trout.

Nick cleaned them, slitting them from the vent to the tip of the jaw. All the insides and the gills and tongue came out in one piece. They were both males; long gray-white strips of milt, smooth and clean. All the insides clean and compact, coming out all together. Nick tossed the offal ashore for the minks to find.

He washed the trout in the stream. When he held them back up in the water they looked like live fish. Their color was not gone yet. He washed his hands and dried them on the log. Then he laid the trout on the sack spread out on the log, rolled them up in it, tied the bundle and put it in the landing net. His knife was still standing, blade stuck in the log. He cleaned it on the wood and put it in his pocket.

Nick stood up on the log, holding his rod, the landing net hanging heavy, then stepped into the water and splashed ashore. He climbed the bank and cut up into the woods, toward the high ground. He was going back to camp. He looked back. The river just showed through the trees. There were plenty of days coming when he could fish the swamp.

CRITICS OF THE CULTURE: BETWEEN WARS

H[ENRY] L[OUIS] MENCKEN (1880–1956)

H. L. Mencken was the noisiest of the iconoclasts, the "bad boys" of the 1920s, a fact which makes his generally quiet personal life the more surprising. Born in Baltimore, he lived almost his entire life in the same house there, although his work was for many years centered in New York. From 1899 to 1941 he was regularly employed in one capacity or another by two Baltimore newspapers, first the Morning Herald, then the Evening Sun. With George Jean Nathan, he edited Smart Set in New York from 1914 to 1923, and from 1924 to 1933, The American Mercury. In its pages he achieved his great influence with the young and constantly outraged the sedate.

His attack was always on what he called "Puritanism," by which he meant any restrictive force that attempted to impose itself on any show of individualism. His raucous denunciations of all conformity, of all bigotry, of commercial culture in general, of middle-class stupidities and plutocratic power, of censorship, of literary and academic timidity—of everything, in short, that was constrictive in American life—are best shown in the six volumes of his Prejudices, essays collected between 1919 and 1927, of which "The National Letters" (1920) is as good an example as any.

He was neither a political nor an economic radical, a fact not very closely observed until after 1929, when his basic, indeed fanatical, conservatism became more and more clear, especially in his unremitting attacks on the policies of Franklin D. Roosevelt and the New Deal.

He published many books, the most scholarly and enduring of which is probably The American Language (1919), with its several revisions and the supplementary volumes of 1945 and 1948. Among his most engaging works are a series of autobiographical memoirs, Happy Days (1940), Newspaper Days, 1899–1906 (1941), and Heathen Days (1943).

His most notable service to literature probably lay in his encouragement and defense of dissident novelists such as Theodore Dreiser, Sinclair Lewis, and Sherwood Anderson, and in his unremitting war on literary censorship.

Long a bachelor, he was married for the five happy years between 1930 and 1935, when his wife died. In 1948 he was stricken by a cerebral thrombosis which ended his literary life, and eight years later he died in his sleep of a coronary occlusion.

FURTHER READING

The most recent biography is Carl Bode's Mencken (1969), but these older volumes are still not supplanted: Walter Lippman, H. L.

Mencken (1926); Edgar Kemler, *The Irreverent Mr. Mencken* (1950); and William Manchester, *Disturber of the Peace* (1951). Sara Mayfield's *The Constant Circle* (1968) is limited to reminiscence of Mencken and his friends. Guy J. Forgue has selected and annotated *Letters of H. L. Mencken* (1961). Philip Wagner's *H. L. Mencken* (1966) is a useful introductory pamphlet. More specialized studies are M. K. Singleton, *H. L. Mencken and The American Mercury* (1962), and William H. Nolte, *H. L. Mencken, Literary Critic* (1966).

The National Letters *(1920)*

It is convenient to begin, like the gentlemen of God, with a glance at a text or two. The first, a short one, is from Ralph Waldo Emerson's celebrated oration, "The American Scholar," delivered before the Phi Beta Kappa Society at Cambridge on August 31st, 1837. Emerson was then thirty-four years old and almost unknown in his own country, though he had already published "Nature" and established his first contacts with Landor and Carlyle. But "The American Scholar" brought him into instant notice at home, partly as man of letters but more importantly as seer and prophet, and the fame thus founded has endured without much diminution, at all events in New England, to this day. Oliver Wendell Holmes, giving words to what was undoubtedly the common feeling, hailed the address as the intellectual declaration of independence of the American people, and that judgment, amiably passed on by three generations of pedagogues, still survives in the literature books. I quote from the first paragraph:

Our day of dependence, our long apprenticeship to the learning of other lands, draws to a close. . . . Events, actions arise, that must be sung, that will sing themselves. Who can doubt that poetry will revive and lead in a new age, as the star in the constellation Harp, which now flames in our zenith, astronomers announce, shall one day be the pole-star for a thousand years?

This, as I say, was in 1837. Thirty-three years later, in 1870, Walt Whitman echoed the prophecy in his even more famous "Democratic Vistas." What he saw in his vision and put into his gnarled and gasping prose was

a class of native authors, literatuses, far different, far higher in grade, than any yet known, sacerdotal, modern, fit to cope with our occasions, lands, permeating the whole mass of American morality, taste, belief, breathing into it a new breath of life, giving it decision, affecting politics far more than the popular superficial suffrage, with results inside and underneath the elections of Presidents or Congress—radiating, begetting appropriate teachers, schools, manners, and, as its grandest result, accomplishing, (what neither the schools nor the churches and their clergy have hitherto accomplished, and without which this nation will no more stand, permanently, soundly, than a house will stand without a substratum,) a religious and moral character beneath the political and productive and intellectual bases of the States.

The promulgation and belief in such a class or order—a new and greater literatus order—its possibility, (nay, certainty,) underlies these entire speculations. . . . Above all previous lands, a great original literature is sure to become the justification and reliance, (in some respects the sole reliance,) of American democracy.

Thus Whitman in 1870, the time of the first draft of "Democratic Vistas." He was of the same mind, and said so, in 1888, four years before his death. I could bring up texts of like tenor in great number, from the years before 1837, from those after 1888, and from every decade between. The dream of Emerson, though the eloquence of its statement was new and arresting, embodied no novel projection of the fancy; it merely gave a sonorous *Waldhorn* [1] tone to what had been dreamed and said before. You will find almost the same high hope, the same exuberant confidence in the essays of the elder Channing [2] and in the "Lectures on American Literature" of Samuel Lorenzo Knapp,[3] L.L.D., the first native critic of beautiful letters—the primordial tadpole of all our later Mores, Brownells, Phelpses, Mabies, Brander Matthewses [4] and other such grave and glittering fish. Knapp believed, like Whitman long after him, that the sheer physical grandeur of the New World would inflame a race of bards to unprecedented utterance. "What are the Tibers and Scamanders," he demanded, "measured by the Missouri and the Amazon? Or what the loveliness of Illysus or Avon by the Connecticut or the Potomack? Whenever a nation wills it, prodigies are born." That is to say, prodigies literary and ineffable as well as purely material— prodigies aimed, in his own words, at "the olympick crown" as well as at mere railroads, ships, wheatfields, droves of hogs, factories and money. Nor were Channing and Knapp the first of the haruspices. Noah Webster, the lexicographer, who "taught millions to spell but not one to

---

[1] A French horn; bugle.

[2] William Ellery Channing (1780–1842), Congregational pastor and essayist, author of *Remarks on American Literature* (1830). In the catalog beginning with Channing, Mencken is attacking the high priests of that officialdom in American letters in the nineteenth and early-twentieth centuries that George Santayana dubbed "the genteel tradition" in a famous essay with that term in its title.

[3] (1783–1838), popular but unreliable Massachusetts essayist, author of *Lectures on American Literature* (1829).

[4] Paul Elmer More (1864–1937), critic prominent in the New Humanist school; William Crary Brownell (1851–1928), critic; William Lyon Phelps (1865–1943) ["Billy"], popular Yale professor long associated with the New Humanism; Hamilton Wright Mabie (1845–1916), editor and critic; James Brander Matthews (1852– 1929), critic and Columbia professor of drama.

sin," had seen the early starlight of the same Golden Age so early as 1789, as the curious will find by examining his "Dissertations on the English Language," a work fallen long since into undeserved oblivion. Nor was Whitman, taking sober second thought exactly a century later, the last of them. Out of many brethren of our own day, extravagantly articulate in print and among the chautauquas, I choose one—not because his hope is of purest water, but precisely because, like Emerson, he dilutes it with various discreet whereases. He is Van Wyck Brooks,[5] a young man far more intelligent, penetrating and hospitable to fact than any of the reigning professors—a critic who is sharply differentiated from them, indeed, by the simple circumstance that he has information and sense. Yet this extraordinary Mr. Brooks, in his "Letters and Leadership," published in 1918, rewrites "The American Scholar" in terms borrowed almost bodily from "Democratic Vistas"—that is to say, he prophesies with Emerson and exults with Whitman. First there is the Emersonian doctrine of the soaring individual made articulate by freedom and realizing "the responsibility that lies upon us, each in the measure of his own gift." And then there is Whitman's vision of a self-interpretative democracy, forced into high literary adventures by Joseph Conrad's "obscure inner necessity," and so achieving a "new synthesis adaptable to the unique conditions of our life." And finally there is the specific prediction, the grandiose, Adam Forepaugh [6] mirage: "We shall become a luminous people, dwelling in the light and sharing our light. . . ."

As I say, the roll of such soothsayers might be almost endlessly lengthened. There is, in truth, scarcely a formal discourse upon the national letters (forgetting, perhaps, Barrett Wendell's sour threnody upon the New England *Aufklärung* [7]) that is without some touch of this previsional exultation, this confident hymning of glories to come, this fine assurance that American literature, in some future always ready to dawn, will burst into so grand a flowering that history will cherish its loveliest blooms even above such salient American gifts to culture as the moving-picture, the phonograph, the New Thought and the bichloride tablet. If there was ever a dissenter from the national optimism, in this as in other departments, it was surely Edgar Allan Poe—without question the bravest and most original, if perhaps also the least orderly and judicious, of all the critics that we have produced. And yet even Poe, despite his general habit of disgust and dismay, caught a flash or two of that engaging picture—even Poe, for an instant, in 1846, thought that he saw the beginnings of a solid and autonomous native literature, its roots deep in the soil of the republic—as you will discover by turning

[5] See pages 51 to 64.
[6] (1831–1890), American circus proprietor.
[7] "Enlightenment."

to his forgotten essay on J. G. C. Brainard,[8] a thrice-forgotten doggereleer of Jackson's time. Poe, of course, was too cautious to let his imagination proceed to details; one feels that a certain doubt, a saving peradventure or two, played about the unaccustomed vision as he beheld it. But, nevertheless, he unquestionably beheld it. . . .

Now for the answering fact. How has the issue replied to these visionaries? It has replied in a way that is manifestly to the discomfiture of Emerson as a prophet, to the dismay of Poe as a pessimist disarmed by transient optimism, and to the utter collapse of Whitman. We have, as everyone knows, produced no such "new and greater literatus order" as that announced by old Walt. We have given a gaping world no books that "radiate," and surely none intelligibly comparable to stars and constellations. We have achieved no prodigies of the first class, and very few of the second class, and not many of the third and fourth classes. Our literature, despite several false starts that promised much, is chiefly remarkable, now as always, for its respectable mediocrity. Its typical great man, in our own time, has been Howells, as its typical great man a generation ago was Lowell, and two generations ago, Irving. Viewed largely, its salient character appears as a sort of timorous flaccidity, an amiable hollowness. In bulk it grows more and more formidable, in ease and decorum it makes undoubted progress, and on the side of mere technic, of the bald capacity to write, it shows an ever-widening competence. But when one proceeds from such agencies and externals to the intrinsic substance, to the creative passion within, that substance quickly reveals itself as thin and watery, and that passion fades to something almost puerile. In all that mass of suave and often highly diverting writing there is no visible movement toward a distinguished and singular excellence, a signal national quality, a ripe and stimulating flavor, or, indeed, toward any other describable goal. What one sees is simply a general irresolution, a pervasive superficiality. There is no sober grappling with fundamentals, but only a shy sporting on the surface; there is not even any serious approach, such as Whitman dreamed of, to the special experiences and emergencies of the American people. When one turns to any other national literature—to Russian literature, say, or French, or German or Scandinavian—one is conscious immediately of a definite attitude toward the primary mysteries of existence, the unsolved and ever-fascinating problems at the bottom of human life, and of a definite preoccupation with some of them, and a definite way of translating their challenge into drama. These attitudes and preoccupations raise a literature above mere poetizing and tale-telling; they give it dignity and importance; above all, they give it national character. But it is

[8] John Gardiner Calkins Brainard (1796–1828), pious and sentimental American poet and romancer.

precisely here that the literature of America, and especially the later literature, is most colorless and inconsequential. As if paralyzed by the national fear of ideas, the democratic distrust of whatever strikes beneath the prevailing platitudes, it evades all resolute and honest dealing with what, after all, must be every healthy literature's elementary materials. One is conscious of no brave and noble earnestness in it, of no generalized passion for intellectual and spiritual adventure, of no organized determination to think things out. What is there is a highly self-conscious and insipid correctness, a bloodless respectability, a submergence of matter in manner—in brief, what is there is the feeble, uninspiring quality of German painting and English music.

It was so in the great days and it is so today. There has always been hope and there has always been failure. Even the most optimistic prophets of future glories have been united, at all times, in their discontent with the here and now. "The mind of this country," said Emerson, speaking of what was currently visible in 1837, "is taught to aim at low objects. . . . There is no work for any but the decorous and the complaisant. . . . Books are written . . . by men of talent . . . who start wrong, who set out from accepted dogmas, not from their own sight of principles." And then, turning to the way out: "The office of the scholar (*i.e.*, of Whitman's 'literatus') is to cheer, to raise and to guide men by showing them *facts amid appearances*." Whitman himself, a full generation later, found that office still unfilled. "Our fundamental want to-day in the United States," he said, "with closest, amplest reference to present conditions, and to the future, is of a class, and the clear idea of a class, of native authors, literatuses, far different, far higher in grade, than any yet known"—and so on, as I have already quoted him. And finally, to make an end of the prophets, there is Brooks, with nine-tenths of his book given over, not to his prophecy—it is crowded, indeed, into the last few pages—but to a somewhat heavy mourning over the actual scene before him. On the side of letters, the aesthetic side, the side of ideas, we present to the world at large, he says, "the spectacle of a vast, undifferentiated herd of good-humored animals"—Knights of Pythias, Presbyterians, standard model Ph.D.'s, readers of the *Saturday Evening Post*, admirers of Richard Harding Davis and O. Henry, devotees of Hamilton Wright Mabie's "white list" of books, members of the Y.M.C.A. or the Drama League, weepers at chautauquas, wearers of badges, 100 per cent patriots, children of God. Poe I pass over; I shall turn to him again later on. Nor shall I repeat the parrotings of Emerson and Whitman in the jeremiads of their innumerable heirs and assigns. What they all establish is what is already obvious: that American thinking, when it concerns itself with beautiful letters as when it concerns itself with religious dogma or political theory, is extraordinarily timid and superficial—that it evades the genuinely serious problems of life and art as if they were stringently taboo—that the outward virtues it undoubtedly shows are always the virtues, not of profundity, not of courage, not of originality, but merely those of an emasculated and often very trashy dilettantism.

The current scene is surely depressing enough. What one observes is a literature in three layers, and each inordinately doughy and uninspiring—each almost without flavor or savor. It is hard to say, with much critical plausibility, which layer deserves to be called the upper, but for decorum's sake the choice may be fixed upon that which meets with the approval of the reigning Lessings.[9] This is the layer of the novels of the late Howells, Judge Grant, Alice Brown and the rest of the dwindling survivors of New England *Kultur,* of the brittle, academic poetry of Woodberry and the elder Johnson, of the tea-party essays of Crothers, Miss Repplier and company, and of the solemn, highly judicial, coroner's inquest criticism of More, Brownell, Babbitt and their imitators.[10] Here we have manner, undoubtedly. The thing is correctly done; it is never crude or gross; there is in it a faint perfume of college-town society. But when this highly refined and attenuated manner is allowed for, what remains is next to nothing. One never remembers a character in the novels of these aloof and de-Americanized Americans; one never encounters an idea in their essays; one never carries away a line out of their poetry. It is literature as an academic exercise for talented grammarians, almost as a genteel recreation for ladies and gentlemen of fashion—the exact equivalent, in the field of letters, of eighteenth-century painting and German *Augenmusik.*[11]

What ails it, intrinsically, is a dearth of intellectual audacity and of aesthetic passion. Running through it, and characterizing the work of almost every man and woman producing it, there is an unescapable suggestion of the old Puritan suspicion of the fine arts as such—of the doctrine that they offer fit asylum for good citizens only when some ulterior and superior purpose is carried into them. This purpose, naturally enough, most commonly shows a moral tinge. The aim of poetry, it appears, is to fill the mind with lofty thoughts—not to give it joy, but to give it a grand and somewhat gaudy sense of virtue. The essay is a weapon against the degenerate tendencies of the age. The novel,

---

[9] Gotthold Ephraim Lessing (1729–1781), influential German critic, the title of whose essay on aesthetics, *Laokoön* (1766), suggested that of Irving Babbitt's *The New Laokoön* (1910).

[10] The names cataloged in this sentence, some mentioned earlier, are Mencken's representation of the "genteel tradition": William Dean Howells (1837–1920), Robert Grant (1852–1940), Alice Brown (1857–1948), George Edward Woodberry (1855–1930), Robert Underwood Johnson (1853–1937), Samuel McChord Crothers (1857–1927), Agnes Repplier (1858–1950), Irving Babbitt (1865–1933).

[11] Strictly speaking, an Italian attempt, especially in the writing of madrigals, to represent musical motifs graphically in the notation.

properly conceived, is a means of uplifting the spirit; its aim is to inspire, not merely to satisfy the low curiosity of man in man. The Puritan, of course, is not entirely devoid of aesthetic feeling. He has a taste for good form; he responds to style; he is even capable of something approaching a purely aesthetic emotion. But he fears this aesthetic emotion as an insinuating distraction from his chief business in life: the sober consideration of the all-important problem of conduct. Art is a temptation, a seduction, a Lorelei, and the Good Man may safely have traffic with it only when it is broken to moral uses—in other words, when its innocence is pumped out of it, and it is purged of gusto. It is precisely this gusto that one misses in all the work of the New England school, and in all the work of the formal schools that derive from it. One observes in such a fellow as Dr. Henry Van Dyke [12] an excellent specimen of the whole clan. He is, in his way, a genuine artist. He has a hand for pretty verses. He wields a facile rhetoric. He shows, in indiscreet moments, a touch of imagination. But all the while he remains a sound Presbyterian, with one eye on the devil. He is a Presbyterian first and an artist second, which is just as comfortable as trying to be a Presbyterian first and a chorus girl second. To such a man it must inevitably appear that a Molière, a Wagner, a Goethe or a Shakespeare was more than a little bawdy.

The criticism that supports this decaying caste of literary Brahmins is grounded almost entirely upon ethical criteria. You will spend a long while going through the works of such typical professors as More, Phelps, Boynton, Burton, Perry, Brownell and Babbitt before ever you encounter a purely aesthetic judgment upon an aesthetic question. It is almost as if a man estimating daffodils should do it in terms of artichokes. Phelps' whole body of "we church-goers" criticism—the most catholic and tolerant, it may be said in passing, that the faculty can show—consists chiefly of a plea for correctness, and particularly for moral correctness; he never gets very far from "the axiom of the moral law." Brownell argues eloquently for standards that would bind an imaginative author as tightly as a Sunday-school superintendent is bound by the Ten Commandments and the Mann Act. Sherman tries to save Shakespeare for the right-thinking by proving that he was an Iowa Methodist—a member of his local Chamber of Commerce, a contemner of Reds, an advocate of democracy and the League of Nations, a patriotic dollar-a-year-man during the Armada scare. Elmer More devotes himself, year in and year out, to denouncing the Romantic movement, *i.e.*, the effort to emancipate the artist from formulae and categories, and so make him free to dance with arms and legs. And Babbitt, to make an end, gives over his days and his nights to deploring Rousseau's anarchistic abrogation of "the veto power" over the imagination, leading to such

---

[12] (1852–1933), Presbyterian minister, professor at Princeton, popular critic; see especially Sinclair Lewis's "The American Fear of Literature," page 647.

"wrongness" in both art and life that it threatens "to wreck civilization."
In brief, the alarms of schoolmasters. Not many of them deal specifically
with the literature that is in being. It is too near to be quite nice. To
More or Babbitt only death can atone for the primary offense of the
artist. But what they preach nevertheless has its echoes contemporane-
ously, and those echoes, in the main, are woefully falsetto. I often
wonder what sort of picture of These States is conjured up by foreigners
who read, say, Crothers, Van Dyke, Babbitt, the later Winston
Churchill,[13] and the old maids of the Freudian suppression school. How
can such a foreigner, moving in those damp, asthmatic mists, imagine
such phenomena as Roosevelt, Billy Sunday, Bryan, the Becker case, the
I.W.W., Newport, Palm Beach, the University of Chicago, Chicago
itself—the whole, gross, glittering, excessively dynamic, infinitely grotesque, incredibly stupendous drama of American life?

As I have said, it is not often that the *ordentlichen Professoren*[14]
deign to notice contemporary writers, even of their own austere kidney.
In all the Shelburne Essays[15] there is none on Howells, or on Churchill,
or on Mrs. Wharton; More seems to think of American literature as
expiring with Longfellow and Donald G. Mitchell.[16] He has himself
hinted that in the department of criticism of criticism there enters into
the matter something beyond mere aloof ignorance. "I soon learned (as
editor of the pre-Bolshevik *Nation*)," he says, "that it was virtually
impossible to get fair consideration for a book written by a scholar not
connected with a university from a reviewer so connected." This class-
consciousness, however, should not apply to artists, who are admittedly
inferior to professors, and it surely does not show itself in such men as
Phelps and Spingarn,[17] who seem to be very eager to prove that they are
not professorial. Yet Phelps, in the course of a long work on the novel,
pointedly omits all mention of such men as Dreiser, and Spingarn, as
the aforesaid Brooks has said, "appears to be less inclined even than the
critics with whom he is theoretically at war to play an active, public part
in the secular conflict of darkness and light." When one comes to the
Privat-Dozenten[18] there is less remoteness, but what takes the place of
it is almost as saddening. To Sherman and Percy Boynton the one aim

---

[13] American novelist (1871–1947), not the famous prime minister.

[14] A tenured professor.

[15] A series of volumes containing literary essays (1904–1935) by Paul Elmer More.

[16] Donald Grant Mitchell (1822–1908), once a popular, but always minor, American
prose writer.

[17] Joel Elias Spingarn (1875–1939), professor of comparative literature in Columbia University and involved in the New Humanism controversy.

[18] Literally, unsalaried lecturers in German universities. Mencken seems to be using
the term to denigrate the two American professors he then names—Stuart Pratt
Sherman (1881–1926), at Illinois, and Percy Holmes Boynton (1875–1946), at
Chicago.

of criticism seems to be the enforcement of correctness—in Emerson's phrase, the upholding of "some great decorum, some fetish of a government, some ephemeral trade, or war, or man"—*e.g.*, Puritanism, democracy, monogamy, the League of Nations, the Wilsonian piffle. Even among the critics who escape the worst of this schoolmastering frenzy there is some touch of the heavy "culture" of the provincial school-ma'm. For example, consider Clayton Hamilton, M.A., vice-president of the National Institute of Arts and Letters. Here are the tests he proposes for dramatic critics, *i.e.*, for gentlemen chiefly employed in reviewing such characteristic American compositions as the Ziegfeld Follies, "Up in Mabel's Room," "Ben-Hur" and "The Witching Hour":

1   Have you ever stood bareheaded in the nave of Amiens?
2   Have you ever climbed to the Acropolis by moonlight?
3   Have you ever walked with whispers into the hushed presence of the Frari Madonna of Bellini?[19]

What could more brilliantly evoke an image of the eternal Miss Birch, blue veil flying and Baedeker in hand, plodding along faithfully through the interminable corridors and catacombs of the Louvre, the while bands are playing across the river, and young bucks in three-gallon hats are sparking the gals, and the Jews and harlots uphold the traditions of French *hig leef* [20] at Longchamps, and American deacons are frisked and debauched up on martyrs' hill? [21] The banality of it is really too exquisite to be borne; the lack of humor is almost that of a Fifth Avenue divine. One seldom finds in the pronunciamentoes of these dogged professors, indeed, any trace of either Attic or Gallic salt. When they essay to be jocose, the result is usually simply an elephantine whimsicality, by the chautauqua out of the *Atlantic Monthly.* Their satire is mere ill-nature. One finds it difficult to believe that they have ever read Lewes, or Hazlitt, or, above all, Saintsbury. I often wonder, in fact, how Saintsbury would fare, an unknown man, at the hands of, say, Brownell or More. What of his iconoclastic gayety, his boyish weakness for tweaking noses and pulling whiskers, his obscene delight in slang? . . .

So far, the disease. As to the cause, I have delivered a few hints. I now describe it particularly. It is, in brief, a defect in the general culture of the country—one reflected, not only in the national literature, but also in the national political theory, the national attitude toward religion and morals, the national habit in all departments of thinking. It is the lack of civilized aristocracy, secure in its position, animated by an intelligent curiosity, skeptical of all facile generalizations, superior to the

---

[19] Giovanni Bellini (1430?–1516). The painting is in the church of Santa Maria dei Frari, Venice.
[20] "High life"?
[21] Montmartre, a northern district of Paris, former artists' quarter.

sentimentality of the mob, and delighting in the battle of ideas for its own sake.

The word I use, despite the qualifying adjective, has got itself meanings, of course, that I by no means intend to convey. Any mention of an aristocracy, to a public fed upon democratic fustian, is bound to bring up images of stockbrokers' wives lolling obscenely in opera boxes, or of haughty Englishmen slaughtering whole generations of grouse in an inordinate and incomprehensible manner, or of Junkers with tight waists elbowing American schoolmarms off the sidewalks of German beer towns, or of perfumed Italians coming over to work their abominable magic upon the daughters of breakfast-food and bathtub kings. Part of this misconception, I suppose, has its roots in the gaudy imbecilities of the yellow press, but there is also a part that belongs to the general American tradition, along with the oppression of minorities and the belief in political panaceas. Its depth and extent are constantly revealed by the naïve assumption that the so-called fashionable folk of the large cities—chiefly wealthy industrials in the interior-decorator and country-club stage of culture—constitute an aristocracy, and by the scarcely less remarkable assumption that the peerage of England is identical with the gentry—that is, that such men as Lord Northcliffe, Lord Iveagh and even Lord Reading are English gentlemen, and of the ancient line of the Percys.[22]

Here, as always, the worshiper is the father of the gods, and no less when they are evil than when they are benign. The inferior man must find himself superiors, that he may marvel at his political equality with them, and in the absence of recognizable superiors *de facto* he creates superiors *de jure*. [23] The sublime principle of one man, one vote must be translated into terms of dollars, diamonds, fashionable intelligence; the equality of all men before the law must have clear and dramatic proofs. Sometimes, perhaps, the thing goes further and is more subtle. The inferior man needs an aristocracy to demonstrate not only his mere equality, but also his actual superiority. The society columns in the newspapers may have some such origin: they may visualize once more the accomplished journalist's understanding of the mob mind that he plays upon so skillfully, as upon some immense and cacophonous organ, always going *fortissimo*. What the inferior man and his wife see in the sinister revels of those amazing first families, I suspect, is often a massive witness to their own higher rectitude—to their relative innocence of cigarette-smoking, poodle-coddling, child-farming and the more abstruse branches of adultery—in brief, to their firmer grasp upon the immutable axioms of Christian virtue, the one sound boast of the nether nine-tenths of humanity in every land under the cross.

[22] These men were knighted in recent times for commercial achievements and are being contrasted with the knights of old, notably, perhaps, Sir Henry Percy (1364–1403), called Hotspur in Shakespeare's *Henry IV*.

[23] The actually existing, as opposed to the legally decreed.

But this bugaboo aristocracy, as I hint, is actually bogus, and the evidence of its bogusness lies in the fact that it is insecure. One gets into it only onerously, but out of it very easily. Entrance is effected by dint of a long and bitter struggle, and the chief incidents of that struggle are almost intolerable humiliations. The aspirant must school and steel himself to sniffs and sneers; he must see the door slammed upon him a hundred times before ever it is thrown open to him. To get in at all he must show a talent for abasement—and abasement makes him timorous. Worse, that timorousness is not cured when he succeeds at last. On the contrary, it is made even more tremulous, for what he faces within the gates is a scheme of things made up almost wholly of harsh and often unintelligible taboos, and the penalty for violating even the least of them is swift and disastrous. He must exhibit exactly the right social habits, appetites and prejudices, public and private. He must harbor exactly the right political enthusiasms and indignations. He must have a hearty taste for exactly the right sports. His attitude toward the fine arts must be properly tolerant and yet not a shade too eager. He must read and like exactly the right books, pamphlets and public journals. He must put up at the right hotels when he travels. His wife must patronize the right milliners. He himself must stick to the right haberdashery. He must live in the right neighborhood. He must even embrace the right doctrines of religion. It would ruin him, for all opera box and society column purposes, to set up a plea for justice to the Bolsheviki, or even for ordinary decency. It would ruin him equally to wear celluloid collars, or to move to Union Hill, N.J., or to serve ham and cabbage at his table. And it would ruin him, too, to drink coffee from his saucer, or to marry a chambermaid with a gold tooth, or to join the Seventh Day Adventists. Within the boundaries of his curious order he is worse fettered than a monk in a cell. Its obscure conception of propriety, its nebulous notion that this or that is honorable, hampers him in every direction, and very narrowly. What he resigns when he enters, even when he makes his first deprecating knock at the door, is every right to attack the ideas that happen to prevail within. Such as they are, he must accept them without question. And as they shift and change in response to great instinctive movements (or perhaps, now and then, to the punished but not to be forgotten revolts of extraordinary rebels) he must shift and change with them, silently and quickly. To hang back, to challenge and dispute, to preach reforms and revolutions—these are crimes against the brummagem Holy Ghost of the order.

Obviously, that order cannot constitute a genuine aristocracy, in any rational sense. A genuine aristocracy is grounded upon very much different principles. Its first and most salient character is its interior security, and the chief visible evidence of that security is the freedom that goes with it—not only freedom in act, the divine right of the aristocrat to do what he jolly well pleases, so long as he does not violate the primary guarantees and obligations of his class, but also and more importantly freedom in thought, the liberty to try and err, the right to be his own man. It is the instinct of a true aristocracy, not to punish eccentricity by expulsion, but to throw a mantle of protection about it—to safeguard it from the suspicions and resentments of the lower orders. Those lower orders are inert, timid, inhospitable to ideas, hostile to changes, faithful to a few maudlin superstitions. All progress goes on on the higher levels. It is there that salient personalities, made secure by artificial immunities, may oscillate most widely from the normal track. It is within that entrenched fold, out of reach of the immemorial certainties of the mob, that extraordinary men of the lower orders may find their city of refuge, and breathe a clear air. This, indeed, is at once the hall-mark and the justification of an aristocracy—that it is beyond responsibility to the general masses of men, and hence superior to both their degraded longings and their no less degraded aversions. It is nothing if it is not autonomous, curious, venturesome, courageous, and everything if it is. It is the custodian of the qualities that make for change and experiment; it is the class that organizes danger to the service of the race; it pays for its high prerogatives by standing in the forefront of the fray.

No such aristocracy, it must be plain, is now on view in the United States. The makings of one were visible in the Virginia of the later eighteenth century, but with Jefferson and Washington the promise died. In New England, it seems to me, there was never any aristocracy, either in being or in nascency: there was only a theocracy that degenerated very quickly into a plutocracy on the one hand and a caste of sterile *Gelehrten*[24] on the other—the passion for God splitting into a lust for dollars and a weakness for mere words. Despite the common notion to the contrary—a notion generated by confusing literacy with intelligence —New England has never shown the slightest sign of a genuine enthusiasm for ideas. It began its history as a slaughter-house of ideas, and it is to-day not easily distinguishable from a cold-storage plant. Its celebrated adventures in mysticism, once apparently so bold and significant, are now seen to have been little more than an elaborate hocus-pocus— respectable Unitarians shocking the peasantry and scaring the horned cattle in the fields by masquerading in the robes of Rosicrucians. The ideas that it embraced in those austere and far-off days were stale, and when it had finished with them they were dead: to-day one hears of Jakob Böhme almost as rarely as one hears of Allen G. Thurman.[25] So in politics. Its glory is Abolition—an English invention, long under the interdict of the native plutocracy. Since the Civil War its six states have produced fewer political ideas, as political ideas run in the Republic, than any average county in Kansas or Nebraska. Appomattox seemed to

---

[24] "Scholars."

[25] Allen Granbery Thurman (1813–1895), forgotten Ohio politician repeatedly defeated in presidential primaries and in 1888 as the nominee for Vice President with Grover Cleveland.

be a victory for New England idealism. It was actually a victory for the New England plutocracy, and that plutocracy has dominated thought above the Housatonic ever since. The sect of professional idealists has so far dwindled that it has ceased to be of any importance, even as an opposition. When the plutocracy is challenged now, it is challenged by the proletariat.

Well, what is on view in New England is on view in all other parts of the nation, sometimes with ameliorations, but usually with the colors merely exaggerated. What one beholds, sweeping the eye over the land, is a culture that, like the national literature, is in three layers—the plutocracy on top, a vast mass of undifferentiated human blanks at the bottom, and a forlorn *intelligentsia* gasping out a precarious life between. I need not set out at any length, I hope, the intellectual deficiencies of the plutocracy—its utter failure to show anything even remotely resembling the makings of an aristocracy. It is badly educated, it is stupid, it is full of low-caste superstitions and indignations, it is without decent traditions or informing vision; above all, it is extraordinarily lacking in the most elemental independence and courage. Out of this class comes the grotesque fashionable society of our big towns, already described. Imagine a horde of peasants incredibly enriched and with almost infinite power thrust into their hands, and you will have a fair picture of its habitual state of mind. It shows all the stigmata of inferiority—moral certainty, cruelty, suspicion of ideas, fear. Never did it function more revealingly than in the late *pogrom* against the so-called Reds,[26] *i.e.*, against humorless idealists who, like Andrew Jackson, took the platitudes of democracy quite seriously. The machinery brought to bear upon these feeble and scattered fanatics would have almost sufficed to repel an invasion by the united powers of Europe. They were hunted out of their sweat-shops and coffee-houses as if they were so many Carranzas or Ludendorffs,[27] dragged to jail to the tooting of horns, arraigned before quaking judges on unintelligible charges, condemned to deportation without the slightest chance to defend themselves, torn from their dependent families, herded into prison-ships, and then finally dumped in a snow waste, to be rescued and fed by the Bolsheviki. And what was the theory at the bottom of all these astounding proceedings? So far as it can be reduced to comprehensible terms it was much less a theory than a fear—a shivering, idiotic, discreditable fear of a mere banshee—an overpowering, paralyzing dread that some extra-eloquent Red, permitted to emit his balderdash unwhipped, might eventually con-

[26] Radicals; "the late *pogrom*" refers to the hysterical arrests and trials of discontented workers and intellectuals at the end of World War I; see Dos Passos' "Playboy," pages 555 to 559.

[27] Venustiano Carranza (1859–1920), Mexican reformist politician; Erich Ludendorff (1865–1937), German general prominent in Hitler's Munich "beer-hall *putsch*," 1923.

vert a couple of courageous men, and that the courageous men, filled with indignation against the plutocracy, might take to the highroad, burn down a nail-factory or two, and slit the throat of some virtuous profiteer. In order to lay this fear, in order to ease the jangled nerves of the American successors to the Hapsburgs and Hohenzollerns, all the constitutional guarantees of the citizen were suspended, the statute-books were burdened with laws that surpass anything heard of in the Austria of Maria Theresa, the country was handed over to a frenzied mob of detectives, informers and *agents provocateurs*—and the Reds departed laughing loudly, and were hailed by the Bolsheviki as innocents escaped from an asylum for the criminally insane.

Obviously, it is out of reason to look for any hospitality to ideas in a class so extravagantly fearful of even the most palpably absurd of them. Its philosophy is firmly grounded upon the thesis that the existing order must stand forever free from attack, and not only from attack, but also from mere academic criticism, and its ethics are as firmly grounded upon the thesis that every attempt at any such criticism is a proof of moral turpitude. Within its own ranks, protected by what may be re-garded as the privilege of the order, there is nothing to take the place of this criticism. A few feeble platitudes by Andrew Carnegie and a book of moderate merit by John D. Rockefeller's press-agent constitute almost the whole of the interior literature of ideas. In other countries the plu-tocracy has often produced men of reflective and analytical habit, eager to rationalize its instincts and to bring it into some sort of relationship to the main streams of human thought. The case of David Ricardo [28] at once comes to mind. There have been many others: John Bright, Richard Cobden, George Grote, and, in our own time, Walther von Rathenau.[29] But in the United States no such phenomenon has been visible. There was a day, not long ago, when certain young men of wealth gave signs of an unaccustomed interest in ideas on the political side, but the most they managed to achieve was a banal sort of Social-ism, and even this was abandoned in sudden terror when the war came, and Socialism fell under suspicion of being genuinely international—in brief, of being honest under the skin. Nor has the plutocracy of the country ever fostered an inquiring spirit among its intellectual valets and footmen, which is to say, among the gentlemen who compose headlines and leading articles for its newspapers. What chiefly distinguishes the daily press of the United States from the press of all other countries pre-tending to culture is not its lack of truthfulness or even its lack of dignity and honor, for these deficiencies are common to the newspapers everywhere, but its incurable fear of ideas, its constant effort to evade

[28] (1772–1823), British economist.
[29] Bright (1811–1889), English champion of laissez faire; Cobden (1804–1865), political coworker of Bright's; Grote (1794–1871), English historian of ancient Greece; Rathenau (1867–1922), German industrialist and statesman.

the discussion of fundamentals by translating all issues into a few elemental fears, its incessant reduction of all reflection to mere emotion. It is, in the true sense, never well-informed. It is seldom intelligent, save in the arts of the mob-master. It is never courageously honest. Held harshly to a rigid correctness of opinion by the plutocracy that controls it with less and less attempt at disguise, and menaced on all sides by censorships that it dare not flout, it sinks rapidly into formalism and feebleness. Its yellow section is perhaps its most respectable section for there the only vestige of the old free journalist survives. In the more conservative papers one finds only a timid and petulant animosity to all questioning of the existing order, however urbane and sincere—a pervasive and ill-concealed dread that the mob now heated up against the orthodox hobgoblins may suddenly begin to unearth hobgoblins of its own, and so run amok. For it is upon the emotions of the mob, of course, that the whole comedy is played. Theoretically the mob is the repository of all political wisdom and virtue; actually it is the ultimate source of all political power. Even the plutocracy cannot make war upon it openly, or forget the least of its weaknesses. The business of keeping it in order must be done discreetly, warily, with delicate technique. In the main that business consists of keeping alive its deep-seated fears—of strange faces, of unfamiliar ideas, of unhackneyed gestures, of untested liberties and responsibilities. The one permanent emotion of the inferior man, as of all the simpler mammals, is fear—fear of the unknown, the complex, the inexplicable. What he wants beyond everything else is safety. His instincts incline him toward a society so organized that it will protect him at all hazards, and not only against perils to his hide but also against assaults upon his mind—against the need to grapple with unaccustomed problems, to weigh ideas, to think things out for himself, to scrutinize the platitudes upon which his everyday thinking is based. Content under kaiserism so long as it functions efficiently, he turns, when kaiserism falls, to some other and perhaps worse form of paternalism, bringing to its benign tyranny only the docile tribute of his pathetic allegiance. In America it is the newspaper that is his boss. From it he gets support for his elemental illusions. In it he sees a visible embodiment of his own wisdom and consequence. Out of it he draws fuel for his simple moral passion, his congenital suspicion of heresy, his dread of the unknown. And behind the newspaper stands the plutocracy, ignorant, unimaginative and timorous.

Thus at the top and at the bottom. Obviously, there is no aristocracy here. One finds only one of the necessary elements, and that only in the plutocracy, to wit, a truculent egoism. But where is intelligence? Where are ease and surety of manner? Where are enterprise and curiosity? Where, above all, is courage, and in particular, moral courage—the capacity for independent thinking, for difficult problems, for what Nietzsche called the joys of the labyrinth? As well look for these things in a society of half-wits. Democracy, obliterating the old aristocracy, has left only a vacuum in its place; in a century and a half it has failed either to lift up the mob to intellectual autonomy and dignity or to purge the plutocracy of its inherent stupidity and swinishness. It is precisely here, the first and favorite scene of the Great Experiment, that the culture of the individual has been reduced to the most rigid and absurd regimentation. It is precisely here, of all civilized countries, that eccentricity in demeanor and opinion has come to bear the heaviest penalties. The whole drift of our law is toward the absolute prohibition of all ideas that diverge in the slightest from the accepted platitudes, and behind that drift of law there is a far more potent force of growing custom, and under that custom there is a national philosophy which erects conformity into the noblest of virtues and the free functioning of personality into a capital crime against society.

MALCOLM COWLEY (1898–   )

The classic account of American literary life in the 1920s, especially in its expatriate phases, is Malcolm Cowley's Exile's Return: A Narrative of Ideas *(1934; revised, with important additions about Pound, Fitzgerald, Crane, and others, in 1954).*

He was born in Belsano, Pennsylvania, and educated at Pittsburgh until his enrollment in Harvard College in 1915. His education there was interrupted several times, first when he went to France with the American Ambulance Service in 1917, and then in 1918 when he left again for an officers' training school and his first marriage. After a total of three years, he completed his college work at the end of the fall term in 1919–1920.

In the early 1920s, an American Field Service Fellowship gave him several years in France, where he helped edit a number of expatriate little magazines. In New York, again, he worked for periodicals and did free-lance book reviewing and translations from the French. His book of autobiographical poems, Blue Juniata *(1929), appeared just before he became literary editor of* New Republic *(1930–1940), following Edmund Wilson.* A Dry Season *(1942), further poems, contains interesting reflections on the "lost generation." Since 1948 he has been literary adviser and editor at the Viking Press, commuting once or twice a week from his remodeled barn in Sherman, Connecticut, where he has lived for many years now with his second wife.*

His The Literary Situation *(1954) is an instructive study in the sociology of contemporary American writing. Over the years, Cowley has edited some very useful books, notably* After the Genteel Tradition:

American Writers since 1910 *(1937); important texts of Hawthorne, Whitman, Hemingway, Fitzgerald, and Faulkner; and the first volume of* Paris Review *interviews called* Writers at Work *(1959). One of his most fascinating works is* The Faulkner-Cowley File: Letters and Memories, 1944–1962 *(1966).*

When he was seventy, he published Blue Juniata: Collected Poems *(1968), a reissue of his first volume with seventeen poems from his second volume and nineteen later poems. He has arranged them not in the usual chronology according to publication, but rather according to their relation to his life at a given time, making a poetic "autobiography" that is both charming and instructive. His most recent publication is* A Many-Windowed House *(1970), selected essays on American writers.*

FURTHER READING

For a critical essay on Cowley's work see John W. Aldridge, *In Search of Heresy: American Literature in the Age of Conformity* (1956).

FROM *Exile's Return: A Narrative of Ideas* (1934)

The French Line Pier, 1921

... there was one idea that was held in common by the older and the younger inhabitants of the Village—the idea of salvation by exile. "They do things better in Europe: let's go there." This was not only the undertone of discussions at Luke O'Connor's saloon; it was also the recurrent melody of an ambitious work, a real symposium, which was then being prepared for the printer.

Civilization in the United States [1] was written by thirty intellectuals, of whom only a few, say ten at the most, had been living in the Village. There were no Communists or even right-wing Socialists among the thirty. "Desirous of avoiding merely irrelevant criticism," said Harold Stearns [2] in his Preface, "we provided that all contributors to the volume must be American citizens. For the same reason, we likewise provided that in the list there should be no professional propagandists ... no martyrs, and no one who was merely disgruntled." All Village cranks were strictly excluded. But Harold Stearns, the editor, lived in a remodeled house at 31 Jones Street. The editorial meetings were conducted in his basement while often a Village party squeaked and thundered on the floor above. And the book that resulted from the labors of these

[1] *Civilization in the United States: An Inquiry by Thirty Americans* (1922).
[2] (1891–1943), writer, editor, critic.

thirty intellectuals embodied what might be called the more sober side of Village opinion.

Rereading it today, one is chiefly impressed by the limited vision of these men who were trying to survey and evaluate the whole of American civilization. They knew nothing about vast sections of the country, particularly the South and the Southwest. They knew little about the life of the upper classes and nothing (except statistically) about the life of the industrial proletariat. They were city men: if any one of the thirty had been familiar with farming, he would have prevented the glaring pommicultural error made by Lewis Mumford on the second page of the book. They were ridiculously ignorant of the younger generation. The civilization which they really surveyed was the civilization shared in by people over thirty, with incomes between $2,000 and $20,000, living in cities north of the Ohio and east of the Rockies.

As a matter of fact, their book was more modest than its pretentious title. They were not trying to present or solve the problem of American civilization as a whole. They were trying to answer one question that touched them more closely: why was there, in America, no satisfying career open to talent? Every year hundreds, thousands, of gifted young men and women were graduated from our colleges; they entered life as these thirty intellectuals had entered it; they brought with them a rich endowment, but they accomplished little. Why did all this promise result in so few notable careers?

It was Van Wyck Brooks, in his essay on "The Literary Life," who stated this problem most eloquently and with the deepest conviction:

What immediately strikes one as one surveys the history of our literature during the last half century, is the singular impotence of its creative spirit. . . . One can count on one's two hands the American writers who are able to carry on the development and unfolding of their individualities, year in, year out, as every competent man of affairs carries on his business. What fate overtakes the rest? Shall I begin to run over some of those names, familiar to us all, names that have signified so much promise and are lost in what Gautier calls "the limbo where moan (in the company of babes) stillborn vocations, abortive attempts, larvae of ideas that have won neither wings nor shapes"? Shall I mention the writers—but they are countless!—who have lapsed into silence, or have involved themselves in barren eccentricities, or have been turned into machines? The poets who, at the very outset of their careers, find themselves extinguished like so many candles? The novelists who have been unable to grow up, and remain withered boys of seventeen? The critics who find themselves overtaken in mid-career by a hardening of the spiritual arteries? . . . Weeds and wild flowers! Weeds without beauty or fragrance, and wild flowers that cannot survive the heat of the day.

Nowhere else is the problem stated with such deep feeling. But the other contributors are conscious of it: each in his own field they make the same report. "Journalism in America is no longer a profession through which a man can win to a place of real dignity among his neighbors." As for politics, the average congressman "is incompetent and imbecile, and not only incompetent and imbecile, but also incurably dishonest. . . . It is almost impossible to imagine a man of genuine self-respect and dignity offering himself as a candidate for the lower house." In music, art, medicine, scholarship, advertising, the theatre, everywhere the story is the same: there is no scope for individualism; ignorance, unculture or, at the best, mediocrity has triumphed; the doors are closed to talent. And what is the explanation?

Here again the thirty intellectuals have the same story to tell. "In view both of the fact that every contributor has full liberty of opinion and that the personalities and points of view finding expression in these essays are all highly individualistic, the underlying unity which binds the volume together is really surprising." The individualistic army has its own uniform. There were three or four who didn't wear it—thus, Conrad Aiken's essay on American Poetry is an appraisal, not an indictment, and has about it an air of final justice; Leo Wolman [3] writing on Labor and George Soule [4] on Radicalism are objective and critical, and analyze the weaknesses of these movements with an eye to the possibility of correcting them in the future. But most of the contributors may be treated conjointly and anonymously. One after another they come forward to tell us that American civilization itself is responsible for the tragedy of American talent.

Life in this country is joyless and colorless, universally standardized, tawdry, uncreative, given over to the worship of wealth and machinery. "The highest achievements of our material civilization . . . count as so many symbols of its spiritual failure." It is possible that this failure can be explained by a fundamental sexual inadequacy. The wife of the American business man "finds him so sexually inapt that she refuses to bear him children and so driveling in every way except as a money-getter that she compels him to expend his energies solely in that direction while she leads a discontented, sterile, stunted life." She seeks compensation by making herself the empress of culture. "Hardly any intelligent foreigner has failed to observe and comment upon the extraordinary feminization of American social life, and oftenest he has coupled this observation with a few biting remarks concerning the intellectual anemia or torpor that seems to accompany it."—"In almost every branch of American life there is a sharp dichotomy between preaching and practice . . . the moral code resolves itself into the one cardinal heresy of being found out."—"The most moving and pathetic fact in the social life of America today is emotional and esthetic starvation." And what is the remedy?

On this topic the chorus, so united in attack, becomes weak and dis-

[3] (1890–1966), economist, author, professor.
[4] (1887–   ), economist, one-time editor of *New Republic*.

cordant. Since the thirty contributors are city men, and for the most part New Yorkers, they feel that some good might be done by increasing the influence of the city at the expense of the small town, of the metropolis at the expense of the provinces. Since they are intellectuals and extremely class-conscious, they feel that the various professions should organize to better their own position and support intellectual standards. Being critics they assume that criticism will help "in making a real civilization possible . . . a field cannot be ploughed until it has first been cleared of rocks." They have a vague belief in aristocracy and in the possibility of producing real aristocrats through education. Beyond this point, their remedies differ. Van Wyck Brooks gives a moral lecture to writers, adjuring them to be creative. H. L. Mencken believes that our political life might be made over merely by abolishing the residential qualification for elective offices. Harold Stearns is inclined to cynicism: "One shudders slightly," he says, "and turns to the impeccable style, the slightly tired and sensuous irony of Anatole France for relief." On the whole, they question the efficacy of their own prescriptions. "One can feel the whole industrial and economic system as so maladjusted to the primary and simple needs of men and women"—that we ought to change the system? No, these are sensible men, not propagandists, and they see no possibility of changing the system. Instead they bring forth a milder remedy—"that the futility of a rationalistic attack on these infantilisms of compensation becomes obvious. There must be an entirely new deal of the cards in one sense; we must change our hearts." But is this remedy really simpler? Is a change in heart any easier to accomplish than a change in the system?

The intellectuals had explored many paths; they had found no way of escape; one after another they had opened doors that led only into the cupboards and linen closets of the mind. "What should a young man do?" asked Harold Stearns in an article written for the *Freeman*.[5] This time his answer was simple and uncompromising. A young man had no future in this country of hypocrisy and repression. He should take ship for Europe, where people know how to live.

Early in July, 1921, just after finishing his Preface and delivering the completed manuscript to the publisher, Mr. Stearns left this country, perhaps forever. His was no ordinary departure: he was Alexander marching into Persia and Byron shaking the dust of England from his feet. Reporters came to the gangplank to jot down his last words. Everywhere young men were preparing to follow his example. Among the contributors to *Civilization in the United States*, not many could go: most of them were moderately successful men who had achieved security without achieving freedom. But the younger and richer intellectuals went streaming up the longest gangplank in the world; they were preparing a great migration eastward into new prairies of the mind. "I'm going to Paris,"

[5] Weekly periodical of political and aesthetic criticism (1920–1924, 1930–1931).

they said at first, and then, "I'm going to the South of France. . . . I'm sailing Wednesday—next month—as soon as I can scrape together money enough for a ticket. Goodbye, so long," they said, "I'll meet you in Europe, I'll drink your health in good red Burgundy, I'll kiss all the girls for you. I'm sick of this country. I'm going abroad to write one good novel."

And we ourselves, the newcomers to the Village, were leaving it if we could. The long process of deracination had reached its climax. School and college had uprooted us in spirit; the War had physically uprooted us, carried us into strange countries and left us finally in the metropolis of the uprooted. Now even New York seemed too American, too close to home. On its river side, Greenwich Village is bounded by the French Line pier.

Hardly anybody came to the ship to say goodbye. All our friends had sailed already, except a few wistful people who promised to follow in a few months. The Village was almost deserted, except for the pounding feet of the young men from Davenport and Pocatello who came to make a name for themselves and live in glamor—who came because there was nowhere else to go.

Form and Matter

Early on a hot August morning in 1921, I started to write an essay on "This Youngest Generation." Six weeks had passed since leaving New York: it was still too early to be affected by a new intellectual climate. But the essay expressed clearly enough the ideas which the exiles of that year had packed in their baggage and carried duty-free across the Atlantic.

"As an organized body of opinion," I said, "the youngest generation in American letters does not exist. There is no group, but there are individuals. There is no solidarity, but there are prevailing habits of thought. Certain characteristics held in common unify the work of the youngest writers, the generation that has just turned twenty."

Most of these traits, I found, were negative. "One can safely assert that these new writers are not gathered in a solid phalanx behind H. L. Mencken to assault our American puritanism. Certainly they are not puritans themselves, but they are willing to leave the battle to their elder cousins and occupy themselves elsewhere. In the same way the controversy about Queen Victoria does not excite them. She died when they were still in bloomers, and the majority of the Browning Clubs died with her. Time has allowed enough perspective for them to praise Tennyson a little and Browning a great deal."

I am setting all this down as I wrote it that morning under the grape arbor, when everything was simpler and it was possible to annihilate in a phrase the life work of an internationally famous man of letters, without fear of being in turn annihilated. "It follows as a corollary," I said, "that they have little sympathy with the belated revolt of the Georgians. Little with the huge, uninspired documents of the Georgian novelists, as informative and formless as a cookbook. Little with the divine journalism of Mr. Wells. None with the *fausse-naïveté* of Georgian poets. It does not follow that they dislike the 'movements' popular among Georgians on both sides the water, and yet one meets few that are either feminist, Freudian or Communist.

"Let us picture the American writer at the age of twenty-five." In reality I was just about to celebrate my twenty-third birthday, and was in no way precocious. "He has already adopted," I said, "the enthusiams of the generation that preceded him, and has abandoned them one by one—at least they no longer exist in his mind as enthusiams. He cannot be described as Wildian, Wellsian, Shavian, Georgian or Menckenian, as esthetic, ecstatic or naturalistic. The great literary controversies of the last generation he has solved by the simplest of all logical processes: he ignores them. Thus, he is neither puritan nor anti-puritan, romantic nor realistic. He has a great many literary prejudices and could easily write little essays beginning with 'I hate people who . . . ' or smart poems whose refrain is 'I am tired of . . . ' Unfortunately, he equally hates and is tired of this form of literary inanity. He has no movement of his own to support and he has no audience. . . . It is the picture of a very negative young man; but it is only one side of the picture."

I began to sketch in some positive traits. "The writers of this newest generation show more respect, if not reverence, for the work of the past. Before the War the belief was rapidly gaining ground that literature and the drama began together on that night when Nora first slammed the door of the doll's house. To be a rebel from convention, one had only to say that one liked Shakespeare better than Ibsen or Shaw. . . . The youngest writers not only prefer to read Shakespeare: they may even prefer Jonson, Webster and Marlowe, Racine and Molière. They are more interested in Swift and Defoe than in Samuel Butler. Their enthusiam for the New Russians is temperate, even lukewarm. In other words, the past that they respect ended about forty years ago—not long after Nora slammed the door.

"If strange modern gods must be imported and worshiped, they are more likely to be French than Slavic, Scandinavian or English. In this respect, however, the youngest writers are developing the tendency of their elders rather than revolting from it. The last half-century of American literature might be diagramed as a progression away from London. This new interest in French prose and poetry almost completes the progression, for no city is intellectually so far from London as is Paris.

'They read Flaubert. They read Remy de Gourmont. These writers usually serve as their introduction to modern French literature; these are the two fixed points from which their reading diverges. Gourmont's *Book of Masks* may set them to following French poetry from Baudelaire and Laforgue down through the most recent and most involved Parisian schools. Or they may read the New Catholics, beginning with Huysmans. . . . Certainly the French influence is acting on us today; there remains to be seen just what effect it will bring forth."

It was very still under the arbor; flies were buzzing outside among the late Glory of Dijon roses; New York was centuries away. I tried to remember Manhattan conversations and translate them into terms of prophecy. "One of these effects," I said, "is almost sure to be a new interest in form. Flaubert and Gourmont spent too much time thinking of the balance and movement of their work for this subject to be neglected by their pupils. Already the tendency is manifesting itself strongly among the younger writers: they seem to have little desire to record inchoate episodes out of their own lives. I have heard one of them speak learnedly of line and mass, of planes, circles and tangents. Without going to the geometrical extremes of Kenneth Burke, one can forecast safely that our younger literature will be at least as well composed as a good landscape; it may even attain to the logical organization of music.

"Another characteristic of the younger writers is their desire for simplification; this also is partly a result of the French influence. 'What is needed of art,' said T. S. Eliot in the *Dial*, 'is a simplification of current life into something rich and strange.' One hears the same idea expressed elsewhere; it is coupled usually with a desire for greater abstractness.

"Form, simplification, strangeness, respect for literature as an art with traditions, abstractness . . . these are the catchwords repeated most often among the younger writers. They represent ideas that have characterized French literature hitherto, rather than English or American. They are the nearest approach to articulate doctrine of a generation without a school and without a manifesto."

There was more of the essay, but this was the heart of it. Rereading it now, after thirteen years, I am struck by two questions, both of which concern a larger question absent from our calculations: I mean the position of the artist in society. Why did our theories, slogans and catchwords all center about the unfruitful distinction between form and matter? Why did we abandon them, not without a struggle, but swiftly none the less, in the course of a few months?

The questions are not impossible to answer. . . . I have said that ours was a humble generation, but the truth is that all writers are ambitious: if they were really humble they would choose a craft that involved less risk of failure and milder penalties for the crime of being average. All writers thirst to excel. In many, even the greatest, this passion takes a vulgar form: they want to get rich quick, be invited to meet the Duchess —thus, Voltaire was a war profiteer; Shakespeare disgracefully wangled himself a coat of arms. But always, mingled with cheaper ambitions, is the desire to exert an influence on the world outside, to alter the course of history. And always, when this path seems definitely closed, ambition turns elsewhere, eating its way like a torrent into other channels—till it finally bursts forth, if not in life, why then, in the imagination. "Art for art's sake," "pure art," "form triumphant over matter"—all these slogans bear some relation to an old process of thought. "Matter" is equivalent to the outside world in which the writer is powerless; but in his rich interior world he can satisfy his ambition by subjugating "matter," by making it the slave of "form," of himself.

The writers of our generation were humble in the sense that they did not hope to alter the course of events or even to build themselves an honored place in society. Their class, the urban middle class, was lacking in political power; it was indeed so empty of political ideas as not to realize that such power was being exercised by others. Society was either regarded as a sort of self-operating, self-repairing, self-perpetuating machine, or else it was not regarded. Perhaps in their apprentice years, during Mr. Wilson's crusade[6] or the Russian revolution, the younger writers had the brief vision of a world adventurously controlled by men, guided by men in conflict, but the vision died. Once more society became an engine whose course they could not direct, whether to glory or destruction—nor did they much care, since the splendors and defeats of history were equally the material for art, the stone for the chisel. And, though their lives might be dingy and cluttered, they had one privilege: to write a poem in which all was but order and beauty, a poem rising like a clean tower above the tin cans and broken dishes of their days. In the world of "form," their failures, our failures, would be avenged.

This, I think, was the emotional attitude lying behind the ideas I was trying to express that morning in the grape arbor at Dijon, while flies buzzed among the August roses. The arbor itself, and the garden with its graveled walks, its fruit trees geometrically trained against the north wall, were triumphs of art over nature, were matter subjugated to form. Indeed, to young writers like ourselves, a long sojourn in France was almost a pilgrimage to Holy Land.

France was the birthplace of our creed. It was in France that poets had labored for days over a single stanza, while bailiffs hammered at the door; in France that novelists like Gourmont had lived as anchorites, while imagining seductions more golden and mistresses more harmoniously yielding than life could ever reproduce; in France that Flaubert had described "the quaint mania of passing one's life wearing oneself out over words," and had transformed this mania into a religion. Everything admirable in literature began in France, was developed in France; and though we knew that the great French writers quarreled among themselves, Parnassians giving way to Decadents, who gave way to Symbolists, who in turn were giving way to the new school, whatever it was, that would soon reign in Paris—though none achieved perfection, we were eager to admire them all. And this, precisely, was the privilege we should not be granted.

In the year 1921, Flaubert had ceased to be admired by the younger writers and Gourmont was almost despised. The religion of art is an un-

---

6 President Wilson's effort to gain support for his hope that the United States would enter the League of Nations.

stable religion which yearly makes over its calendar of saints. Changes come rapidly, convolutions are piled on convolutions; schools, leaders, manifestoes, follow and cancel each other—and into this mad steeplechase we arrived with our innocent belief that Flaubert was great and that form ought to be cultivated at the expense of matter. In a few months we were exposed to the feverish intellectual development of half a century.

This suggests, I think, the answer to my second question, why we abandoned our theories after so brief a struggle. As school superseded school, the religion of art had extended its domain. Esthetic standards of judgment, after being applied to works of art, had been applied to the careers of their authors and finally to the world at large. Cities, nations, were admired for the qualities that were then being accepted as making books admirable—for being picturesque, surprising, dramatic, swift, exuberant, vigorous, "original." What nation more than America possessed these qualities? It happened that the American writers who admired French literature were confronted by young French writers who admired American civilization. "Gourmont," we said, "is a great stylist."—"Nonsense, my dear friend. New York has houses of fifty-six stories."

It was a contest of politeness, an Alphonse-Gaston [7] argument in which, at the end, we were glad to yield. America was after all our country, and we were beginning to feel a little homesick for it. But our friends in New York were unaware of the change.

LEWIS MUMFORD (1895–   )

Mumford was born on Long Island and attended various colleges and universities in New York City. He has always been interested in the culture of cities and, beyond that, in the potentialities of human culture generally as the expression of the physical environment that human beings do and can create for themselves. An early book, Sticks and Stones *(1924), was an interpretation of American life and thought in terms of its architecture. The next,* The Golden Day *(1926), was an interpretation of the same material in terms of American literature, especially in its great mid-nineteenth-century flowering, but this in turn in relation to its colonial precedents, its contemporary pioneer efforts, its postfrontier effects; the final chapter, "Envoi," is an appeal for that "full human existence," that "full culture" of which, in 1926, American life still seemed capable.*

Many Americans stopped thinking in such terms after about 1930, still many more after 1945; Mumford never has. Through all his

[7] Inefficient, overly polite characters in a comic strip of the 1900s drawn by F. Opper.

years of service with a variety of civic, academic, professional, national, and international institutes, groups, and commissions; through all his many published volumes—his major work is probably his "Renewal of Life" series, consisting of Technics and Civilization *(1934),* The Culture of Cities *(1938),* The Condition of Man *(1944), and* The Conduct of Life *(1951)—he has made the same plea for an intelligent utilization of our resources, natural no less than technological, on behalf of a* human *culture.*

In 1965, in the speech he delivered as retiring president of the National Academy of Arts and Letters, he caused a furor when he denounced, on the grounds of simple human decency, our involvement in Vietnam; today, not even the people whom he then most outraged would disagree with him. More recently, when a number of prominent persons were asked to comment on the significance of our adventure on the moon, a younger, presumably "with-it" person like Paul Goodman could say,

It's good to "waste" money on such a moral and esthetic venture. These are our cathedrals. I don't think it is fair to say they are our circuses, for that is not the tone.

Among these men Lewis Mumford, alone, had the courage to be forthright. He began by saying:

The most conspicuous scientific and technical achievements of our age— nuclear bombs, rockets, computers—are all direct products of war, and are still being promoted, under the guise of "Research and Development," for military and political ends that would shrivel under rational examination and candid moral appraisal. The moon-landing program is no exception: it is a symbolic act of war, and the slogan the astronauts will carry, proclaiming that it is for the benefit of mankind, is on the same level as the Air Force's monstrous hypocrisy—"Our Profession is Peace."

And he concluded:

Only a return to full waking consciousness, with an overwhelming transfer of interest from our dehumanized technology to the human person, will suffice to bring our moonstruck nation back to earth. Meanwhile, thanks to the very triumphs of technology, the human race hovers on the edge of catastrophe.

Lewis Mumford is a great literal humanist, perhaps one of the few surviving. But can he still confidently cry, as he did at the end of The Golden Day in 1926, "Allons! the road is before us!"?

FURTHER READING

See Thomas Reed West, *Flesh of Steel: Literature and the Machine in American Culture* (1967), and *The Van Wyck Brooks-Lewis*

Mumford Letters: The Record of a Literary Friendship, 1921–1963 (1970), edited by Robert E. Spiller.

FROM **The Golden Day** *(1926)*

Envoi

Entering our own day, one finds the relations of culture and experience a little difficult to trace out. With the forces that have come over from the past, it is fairly easy to reckon: but how these are being modified or supplanted by new efforts of experience and new stores of culture one cannot with any assurance tell. Is Robert Frost the evening star of New England, or the first streak of a new dawn? Will the Dewey [1] who is struggling to step outside his old preoccupations influence the coming generation, or will the more passive and utilitarian thinker continue to dominate? Will our daily activities center more completely in metropolises, for which the rest of the country serves merely as raw material, or will the politics and economics which produce this state give place to programs of regional development? What is the meaning of Lindsay and Sandburg and Mrs. Mary Austin? [2] What is the promise of regional universities like Nebraska and North Carolina and New Mexico? May we look forward to a steady process of re-settlement; or will the habits of nomadry, expansion, and standardization prevail?

The notion that the forces that are now dominant will inevitably continue and grow stronger will not stand a close examination. Those who take refuge in this comfortable view are merely accepting facts as hopes when they think this would be desirable, or hopes as facts, when they profess that it is unavoidable. The effort of an age may not lead to its prolongation: it may serve to sharpen its antithesis and prepare the way for its own demise. So the stiffening of the old Renaissance motifs in the Eighteenth Century did not lead to their persistence: they formed the thorny nest in which Romanticism was hatched. It was in the decade of Watt's steam engine that Percy's *Reliques* [3] were published; it was in the decade of the steamboat that Scott published his Waverley novels. Romanticism, for all its superficialities, gave men the liberty to breathe again; out of the clever imitations of Chatterton grew Wordsworth, and out of the meretricious Gothic of Walpole, Hugo and Viollet-le-Duc took possession anew of Notre Dame. I do not say that the Romantic poets changed the course of industrialism; but they altered the mood in which industrialism was received and quickened the recognition of its poten-

[1] John Dewey (1859–1952), philosopher and educator.
[2] (1868–1934), novelist of the Far West.
[3] Thomas Percy (1729–1811), *Reliques of Ancient English Poetry* (1765).

tialities for evil, which a blind and complacent utilitarianism might have ignored for generations.

We have seen American culture as formed largely by two events: the breakdown of the medieval synthesis, in the centuries that preceded America's settlement and by the transferal to the new soil of an abstract and fragmentary culture, given definitive form by the Protestants of the Sixteenth Century, by the philosophers and scientists of the Seventeenth, and by the political thinkers of the Eighteenth Century. Faced with the experience of the American wilderness, we sought, in the capacity of pioneers, to find a new basis for culture in the primitive ways of forest and field, in the occupations of hunter, woodman, miner and pastoral nomad: but these occupations, practiced by people who were as much influenced by the idola of utilitarianism as by the deeper effort of the Romantic Movement, did not lead towards a durable culture: the pioneer environment became favorable to an even bleaker preoccupation with the abstractions of matter, money, and political rights. In this situation, the notion of a complete society, carrying on a complete and symmetrical life, tended to disappear from the minds of every one except the disciples of Fourier; with the result that business, technology, and science not merely occupied their legitimate place but took to themselves all that had hitherto belonged to art, religion, and poetry. Positive knowledge and practical action, which are indispensable elements in every culture, became the only living sources of our own; and as the Nineteenth Century wore on, we moved within an ever narrower circle of experience, living mean and illiberal lives.

The moving out of Europe was not merely due to the lure of free land and a multitude of succulent foods: it pointed to cultural vacancy. For three centuries the best minds in Europe had either been trying to get nourishment from the leftovers of classic culture or the Middle Ages, or they had been trying to reach some older source of experience, in order to supplement their bare spiritual fare. Science built up a new conception of the universe, and it endowed its disciples with the power to understand—and frequently to control—external events; but it achieved these results by treating men's central interests and desires as negligible, ignoring the fact that science itself was but a mode of man's activity as a living creature, and that its effort to cancel out the human element was only a very ingenious human expedient. In America, it was easy for an Emerson or a Whitman to see the importance of welding together the interests which science represented, and those which, through the accidents of its historic development, science denied. Turning from a limited European past to a wider heritage, guiding themselves by all the reports of their own day, these poets continued the old voyages of exploration on the plane of the mind, and, seeking passage to India, found themselves coasting along strange shores. None of the fine minds of the Golden Day [4] was afraid to welcome the new forces that were at large in the

---

[4] The period from 1830 to 1860.

world. Need I recall that Whitman wrote an apostrophe to the locomotive, that Emerson said a steamship sailing promptly between America and Europe might be as beautiful as a star, and that Thoreau, who loved to hear the wind in the pine needles, listened with equal pleasure to the music of the telegraph wires?

That practical instrumentalities were to be worshiped, never occurred to these writers; but that they added a new and significant element to our culture, which the poet was ready to absorb and include in his report upon the universe, was profoundly true. It is this awareness of new sources of experience that distinguishes the American writers of the Golden Day from their contemporaries in Europe. That the past was merely provisional, and that the future might be formed afresh were two patent generalizations which they drew directly from their environment. These perceptions called, of course, for great works of the imagination; for in proportion as intelligence was dealing more effectually with the instrumentalities of life, it became more necessary for the imagination to project more complete and satisfying ends. The attempt to pre-figure in the imagination a culture which should grow out of and refine the experiences the transplanted European encountered on the new soil, mingling the social heritage of the past with the experience of the present, was the great activity of the Golden Day: the essays of Emerson, the poems of Whitman, the solitary musings of Melville all clustered around this central need. None of these men was caught by the dominant abstractions: each saw life whole, and sought a whole life.

We cannot return to the America of the Golden Day, nor keep it fixed in the postures it once naturally assumed; and we should be far from the spirit of Emerson or Whitman if we attempted to do this. But the principal writers of that time are essential links between our own lives and that earlier, that basic, America. In their work, we can see in pristine state the essential characteristics that still lie under the surface: and from their example, we can more readily find our own foundations, and make our own particular point of departure. In their imaginations, a new world began to form out of the distracting chaos: wealth was in its place, and science was in its place, and the deeper life of man began again to emerge, no longer stunted or frustrated by the instrumentalities it had conceived and set to work. For us who share their vision, a revival of the moribund, or a relapse into the pragmatic acquiescence is equally impossible; and we begin again to dream Thoreau's dream—of what it means to live a whole human life.

A complete culture leads to the nurture of the good life; it permits the fullest use, or sublimation, of man's natural functions and activities. Confronted by the raw materials of existence, a culture works them over into new patterns, in which the woof of reality is crossed by the warp of desire. Love is the type of desire in all its modes; and in the recent emergence of a handful of artists who by the force of their inner life have seen the inessential and makeshift character of a large part of the daily routine, there is perhaps the prophecy of a new stream of tendency in American life.

Henry Adams, in his *Education*, observed that the American artist, in distinction to all the great writers of classic times, seemed scarcely conscious of the power of sex: he was aware of neither a Virgin nor a Venus. In the works of Sherwood Anderson, Edna Millay, Eugene O'Neill, and Waldo Frank this aversion has disappeared: human passion comes back to the scene with almost volcanic exuberance, drawing all the habits and conventionalties and prudences in its wake. It is through brooding over their sexual experience that Mr. Anderson's characters begin to perceive the weaknesses, the limitations, the sordidness of the life about them: they awaken with the eagerness of a new adolescence to discover, like the father in *Many Marriages*, that what seemed to them "real life," the externalisms, the business arrangements, the neat routine of office and factory, was in fact an unrelated figment, something which drew upon a boyish self that made sandpiles, whittled sticks, or played soldier and wanted to be captain. Whereas the deep and disruptive force that rouses them, and makes beauty credible and desire realizable, is not, as the Gradgrinds [5] would have it, a dream at all, but the prelude to every enduring reality.

Desire is real! Sherwood Anderson's people come to this, as to a final revelation. But if sexual desire, why not every human desire? In full lust of life man is not merely a poor creature, wryly adjusting himself to external circumstances: he is also a creator, an artist, making circumstances conform to the aims and necessities he himself freely imposes. "Sooner murder an infant in its cradle," wrote William Blake, "than nurse unacted desires", [6] and in the deep sense of Blake's application, this covers every aspect of life, since a failure of desire, imagination, and vision tends to spread over into every activity. Practical intelligence and a prudent adjustment to externalities are useful only in a secondary position: they are but props to straighten the plant when it begins to grow: at the bottom of it all must be a soil and a seed, an inner burgeoning, an eagerness of life. Art in its many forms is a union of imaginative desire, desire sublimated and socialized, with actuality: without this union, desires become idiotic, and actualities perhaps even a little more so. It is not that our instrumental activities are mean: far from it: but that life is mean when it is entirely absorbed in instrumental activities. Beneath the organized vivacity of our American communities, who is not aware of a blankness, a sterility, a boredom, a despair? Their activity, their very lust, is the galvanic response to an external stimulus, given by an organism that is dead.

The power to escape from this sinister world can come only by the double process of encountering more complete modes of life, and of re-

[5] Thomas Gradgrind, leading character in Dickens' *Hard Times* (1854).

[6] "Proverbs of Hell," from *The Marriage of Heaven and Hell* (1793).

formulating a more vital tissue of ideas and symbols to supplant those which have led us into the stereotyped interests and actions which we endeavor in vain to identify with a full human existence. We must rectify the abstract framework of ideas which we have used, in lieu of a full culture these last few centuries. In part, we shall achieve this by a criticism of the past, which will bring into the foreground those things that have been left out of the current scheme of life and thought. Mr. A. N. Whitehead's *Science and the Modern World* [1925], and Mr. Victor Branford's *Science and Sanctity* [1923] are landmarks towards this new exploration; for they both suggest the groundwork of a philosophy which shall be oriented as completely towards Life as the dominant thought since Descartes has been directed towards the Machine. To take advantage of our experience and our social heritage and to help in creating this new idolum is not the smallest adventure our generation may know. It is more imaginative than the dreams of the transcendentalist, more practical than the work of the pragmatists, more drastic than the criticisms of the old social revolutionists, and more deeply cultural than all our early attempts to possess the simulacra of culture. It is nothing less than the effort to conceive a new world.

Allons! the road is before us!

[HARRY] SINCLAIR LEWIS (1885–1951)

Sinclair Lewis was born in Sauk Centre, Minnesota, a raw little town less than thirty years old then, the town that he was to make famous as the Gopher Prairie of his first very successful novel, Main Street *(1920). Physically, the young Lewis was as unattractive, as uncouth and awkward, as the village in which he grew up, but he was early resentful of the kind of restrictions that it wanted to impose upon any independence of spirit. When he was seventeen, his father, a country physician whose forebears had lived near New Haven, Connecticut, sent him to the Oberlin Academy for six months to prepare for his entrance into Yale College.*

At Yale he was an unhappy social pariah, but even as a freshman he wrote assiduously, both verse and prose, and was soon publishing in the undergraduate literary periodicals. He was so unhappy at Yale that in the beginning of his senior year he left it abruptly to become a janitor in Upton Sinclair's experiment in communal living, Helican Hall, at Englewood on the Palisades, where he lasted for a month. Then followed months of near starvation in New York, when he tried to live by writing, before he decided to return to Yale, from which he was graduated in 1908.

For *several years he traveled all over the United States, trying to be a
newspaperman, trying to be a writer, collecting a whole file of plots
for stories and novels (some of which he sold to Jack London while
he lived in Carmel), now and then selling a poor piece of fiction of
his own to one obscure periodical or another. From 1910 until
1915 he worked in publishing houses and on various periodicals.
In one summer he wrote, on commission, a book for boys called
Hike and the Aeroplane (1912), published under the pseudonym
of Tom Graham; but all the time he was working on his first novel,
Our Mr. Wrenn (1914), a competent imitation of H. G. Wells,
adapted to American circumstances. It combined rather arch satire
with a broad optimism, had a fairly good critical press, and won
him his first wife, the latter an accomplishment that he was presently to regret.*

Four *novels of no great distinction and a series of stories sold to commercial magazines made the Lewises independent of other employment. Then in 1920 came the first extraordinary success and, two
years later, with Babbitt, the second and even greater. These novels
set the Lewis pattern: satire of American provincialism and materialism that seemed positively acerbic at the time, flat characters,
loosely episodic structures, a basis of nearly systematic research
into the given subject, and an amazing gift for catching the current
speech patterns of the middle class in the Middle West. The decade
of the 1920s saw three further highly successful novels: Arrowsmith
(1925), Elmer Gantry (1927), and Dodsworth (1929). This achievement was climaxed in 1930 when Sinclair Lewis became the first
American to win the Nobel Prize in literature—to the horror of
most Americans.*

"The American Fear of Literature," *delivered in 1930, was a quite
belated attack on the academicism and gentility of American literature, forces no longer of any consequence at all, as Lewis's own
ten years of phenomenal success more than demonstrated. The very
writers whom Lewis named as brushed aside in the United States—
Dreiser, Cather, Anderson, O'Neill, Mencken, Sinclair, Hemingway—were, of course, the writers who for some years had been the
most favorably received by any audience of critical consequence.
The decade of the 1920s, now over, had freed American literature
once and for all from that timidity and chauvinism that Lewis
attacked. Yet perhaps a spokesman was required to announce to
the world that such a development had indeed taken place: "The
American Fear of Literature" really said that American literature
had for some time been without fear.*

He *was now widely traveled, divorced, remarried to an internationally
known journalist, Dorothy Thompson; and although he was to pub-*

lish ten more novels and much else, from a literary point of view he was finished. His marriage to Dorothy Thompson soon collapsed, and he was a poor father to his two sons. In novel after novel, attempting always to deal with a topic of immediate interest, he came to seem more and more repetitious, self-parodying, and old-fashioned, even though most of these novels were great commercial successes. History was moving, but Sinclair Lewis was not.

In the end he was a miserably lonely, sometimes clowning, but generally ill-tempered old man, still believing as he always had that something better must be ahead. For years liquor had been his curse, but behind the liquor was, of course, his tormented, divided self. One of his problems was that he could never confront and thereby objectify his own anxieties, and shunning the subjective, he fell deeper and deeper into the sentimental. Yet there are other realities than those that pertain to the subjective life, and even now no one can dismiss him as unimportant. He managed, in fact, a great thing, whether he knew it or not: he was the first of our novelists to make literally millions of commonplace Americans aware of the terrors of the commonplace. Not, of course, that the lesson did much good.

FURTHER READING

The comprehensive biography is Mark Schorer, *Sinclair Lewis: An American Life* (1961). Vincent Sheean, in *Dorothy and Red* (1963), and Grace Hegger Lewis, in *With Love from Gracie; Sinclair Lewis: 1912–1925* (1955), also provide details about the writer's life. Harrison Smith has edited *From Main Street to Stockholm: Letters of Sinclair Lewis, 1919–1930* (1952). For critical estimates see Sheldon Norman Grebstein, *Sinclair Lewis* (1962); D. J. Dooley, *The Art of Sinclair Lewis* (1967); and Mark Schorer, *Sinclair Lewis: A Collection of Critical Essays* (1962).

The American Fear of Literature *(1930)*

Members of the Swedish Academy; Ladies and Gentlemen:

Were I to express my feeling of honor and pleasure in having been awarded the Nobel Prize in Literature, I should be fulsome and perhaps tedious, and I present my gratitude with a plain "Thank you."

I wish, in this address, to consider certain trends, certain dangers, and certain high and exciting promises in present-day American literature. To discuss this with complete and unguarded frankness—and I should not insult you by being otherwise than completely honest, how-ever indiscreet—it will be necessary for me to be a little impolite regard-ing certain institutions and persons of my own greatly beloved land.

But I beg of you to believe that I am in no case gratifying a grudge. Fortune has dealt with me rather too well. I have known little struggle, not much poverty, many generosities. Now and then I have, for my books or myself, been somewhat warmly denounced—there was one good pas-tor in California who upon reading my *Elmer Gantry* desired to lead a mob and lynch me, while another holy man in the State of Maine won-dered if there was no respectable and righteous way of putting me in jail. And, much harder to endure than any raging condemnation, a cer-tain number of old acquaintances among journalists, what in the gallop-ing American slang we call the "I Knew Him When Club," have scribbled that since they know me personally, therefore I must be a rather low sort of fellow and certainly no writer. But if I have now and then received such cheering brickbats, still I, who have heaved a good many bricks my-self, would be fatuous not to expect a fair number in return.

No, I have for myself no conceivable complaint to make, and yet for American literature in general, and its standing in a country where in-dustrialism and finance and science flourish and the only arts that are vital and respected are architecture and the film, I have a considerable complaint.

I can illustrate by an incident which chances to concern the Swedish Academy and myself and which happened a few days ago, just before I took ship at New York for Sweden. There is in America a learned and most amiable old gentleman who has been a pastor, a university profes-sor, and a diplomat. He is a member of the American Academy of Arts and Letters [1] and no few universities have honored him with degrees. As a writer he is chiefly known for his pleasant little essays on the joy of fishing. I do not suppose that professional fishermen, whose lives depend on the run of cod or herring, find it altogether an amusing occupation, but from these essays I learned, as a boy, that there is something very important and spiritual about catching fish, if you have no need of doing so.

This scholar [2] stated, and publicly, that in awarding the Nobel Prize to a person who has scoffed at American institutions as much as I have, the Nobel Committee and the Swedish Academy had insulted America. I don't know whether, as an ex-diplomat, he intends to have an inter-national incident made of it, and perhaps demand of the American Gov-

---

[1] Founded in 1904, an honorary circle of fifty members within the National Institute of Arts and Letters, to the membership of which Sinclair Lewis had declined an invitation in 1922. Sometime after the Nobel award, he became an enthusiastic member of the Academy.

[2] Henry Van Dyke (1852–1933), Presbyterian minister, Princeton professor, polite and popular essayist.

ernment that they land Marines in Stockholm to protect American literary rights, but I hope not.

I should have supposed that to a man so learned as to have been made a Doctor of Divinity, a Doctor of Letters, and I do not know how many other imposing magnificences, the matter would have seemed different; I should have supposed that he would have reasoned, "Although personally I dislike this man's books, nevertheless the Swedish Academy has in choosing him honored America by assuming that the Americans are no longer a puerile backwoods clan, so inferior that they are afraid of criticism, but instead a nation come of age and able to consider calmly and maturely any dissection of their land, however scoffing."

I should even have supposed that so international a scholar would have believed that Scandinavia, accustomed to the works of Strindberg, Ibsen, and Pontoppidan, would not have been peculiarly shocked by a writer whose most anarchistic assertion has been that America, with all her wealth and power, has not yet produced a civilization good enough to satisfy the deepest wants of human creatures.

I believe that Strindberg rarely sang the "Star-Spangled Banner" or addressed Rotary Clubs, yet Sweden seems to have survived him.

I have at such length discussed this criticism of the learned fisherman not because it has any conceivable importance in itself, but because it does illustrate the fact that in America most of us—not readers alone but even writers—are still afraid of any literature which is not a glorification of everything American, a glorification of our faults as well as our virtues. To be not only a best-seller in America but to be really beloved, a novelist must assert that all American men are tall, handsome, rich, honest, and powerful at golf; that all country towns are filled with neighbors who do nothing from day to day save go about being kind to one another; that although American girls may be wild, they change always into perfect wives and mothers; and that, geographically, America is composed solely of New York, which is inhabited entirely by millionaires; of the West, which keeps unchanged all the boisterous heroism of 1870; and of the South, where every one lives on a plantation perpetually glossy with moonlight and scented with magnolias.

It is not today vastly more true than it was twenty years ago that such novelists of ours as you have read in Sweden, novelists like Dreiser and Willa Cather, are authentically popular and influential in America. As it was revealed by the venerable fishing Academician whom I have quoted, we still most revere the writers for the popular magazines who in a hearty and edifying chorus chant that the America of a hundred and twenty million population is still as simple, as pastoral, as it was when it had but forty million; that in an industrial plant with ten thousand employees, the relationship between the worker and the manager is still as neighborly and uncomplex as in a factory of 1840, with five employees; that the relationships between father and son, between husband and wife, are precisely the same in an apartment in a thirty-story palace today, with three motor cars awaiting the family below and five books on the library shelves and a divorce imminent in the family next week, as were those relationships in a rose-veiled five-room cottage in 1880; that, in fine, America has gone through the revolutionary change from rustic colony to world-empire without having in the least altered the bucolic and Puritanic simplicity of Uncle Sam.

I am, actually, extremely grateful to the fishing Academician for having somewhat condemned me. For since he is a leading member of the American Academy of Arts and Letters, he has released me, has given me the right to speak as frankly of that Academy as he has spoken of me. And in any honest study of American intellectualism today, that curious institution must be considered.

Before I consider the Academy, however, let me sketch a fantasy which has pleased me the last few days in the unavoidable idleness of a rough trip on the Atlantic. I am sure that you know, by now, that the award to me of the Nobel Prize has by no means been altogether popular in America. Doubtless the experience is not new to you. I fancy that when you gave the award even to Thomas Mann, whose *Zauberberg* [3] seems to me to contain the whole of intellectual Europe, even when you gave it to Kipling, whose social significance is so profound that it has been rather authoritatively said that he created the British Empire, even when you gave it to Bernard Shaw, there were countrymen of those authors who complained because you did not choose another.

And I imagined what would have been said had you chosen some American other than myself. Suppose you had taken Theodore Dreiser.

Now to me, as to many other American writers, Dreiser more than any other man, marching alone, usually unappreciated, often hated, has cleared the trail from Victorian and Howellsian [4] timidity and gentility in American fiction to honesty and boldness and passion of life. Without his pioneering, I doubt if any of us could, unless we liked to be sent to jail, seek to express life and beauty and terror.

My great colleague Sherwood Anderson has proclaimed this leadership of Dreiser. I am delighted to join him. Dreiser's great first novel, *Sister Carrie*, which he dared to publish thirty long years ago and which I read twenty-five years ago, came to housebound and airless America like a great free Western wind, and to our stuffy domesticity gave us the first fresh air since Mark Twain and Whitman.

Yet had you given the Prize to Mr. Dreiser, you would have heard groans from America; you would have heard that his style—I am not exactly sure what this mystic quality "style" may be, but I find the word so often in the writings of minor critics that I suppose it must exist—you would have heard that his style is cumbersome, that his choice of words is insensitive, that his books are interminable. And certainly respectable

[3] *The Magic Mountain* (1924).

[4] Adjectival form derived from the name William Dean Howells (1837–1920), American novelist and editor.

scholars would complain that in Mr. Dreiser's world, men and women are often sinful and tragic and despairing, instead of being forever sunny and full of song and virtue, as befits authentic Americans.

And had you chosen Mr. Eugene O'Neill, who has done nothing much in American drama save to transform it utterly, in ten or twelve years, from a false world of neat and competent trickery to a world of splendor and fear and greatness, you would have been reminded that he has done something far worse than scoffing—he has seen life as not to be neatly arranged in the study of a scholar but as a terrifying, magnificent and often quite terrible thing akin to the tornado, the earthquake, the devastating fire.

And had you given Mr. James Branch Cabell the Prize, you would have been told that he is too fantastically malicious. So would you have been told that Miss Willa Cather, for all the homely virtue of her novels concerning the peasants of Nebraska, has in her novel, *The Lost Lady* [1923], been so untrue to America's patent and perpetual and possibly tedious virtuousness as to picture an abandoned woman who remains, nevertheless, uncannily charming even to the virtuous, in a story without any moral; that Mr. Henry Mencken is the worst of all scoffers; that Mr. Sherwood Anderson viciously errs in considering sex as important a force in life as fishing; that Mr. Upton Sinclair, being a Socialist, sins against the perfectness of American capitalistic mass-production; that Mr. Joseph Hergesheimer is un-American in regarding graciousness of manner and beauty of surface as of some importance in the endurance of daily life; and that Mr. Ernest Hemingway is not only too young but, far worse, uses language which should be unknown to gentlemen; that he acknowledges drunkenness as one of man's eternal ways to happiness, and asserts that a soldier may find love more significant that the hearty slaughter of men in battle.

Yes, they are wicked, these colleagues of mine; you would have done almost as evilly to have chosen them as to have chosen me; and as a chauvinistic American—only, mind you, as an American of 1930 and not of 1880—I rejoice that they are my countrymen and countrywomen, and that I may speak of them with pride even in the Europe of Thomas Mann, H. G. Wells, Galsworthy, Knut Hamsun, Arnold Bennett, Feuchtwanger, Selma Lagerlöf, Sigrid Undset, Werner von Heidenstam, D'Annuzio, Romain Rolland.

It is my fate in this paper to swing constantly from optimism to pessimism and back, but so is it the fate of any one who writes or speaks of anything in America—the most contradictory, the most depressing, the most stirring, of any land in the world today.

Thus, having with no muted pride called the roll of what seem to me to be great men and women in American literary life today, and having indeed omitted a dozen other names of which I should like to boast were there time. I must turn again and assert that in our contemporary American Literature, indeed in all American arts save architecture and the film, we—yes, we who have such pregnant and vigorous standards in commerce and science—have no standards, no healing communication, no heroes to be followed nor villains to be condemned, no certain ways to be pursued and no dangerous paths to be avoided.

The American novelist or poet or dramatist or sculptor or painter must work alone, in confusion, unassisted save by his own integrity.

That, of course, has always been the lot of the artist. The vagabond and criminal François Villon had certainly no smug and comfortable refuge in which elegant ladies would hold his hand and comfort his starveling soul and more starved body. He, veritably a great man, destined to outlive in history all the dukes and puissant cardinals whose robes he was esteemed unworthy to touch, had for his lot the gutter and the hardened crust.

Such poverty is not for the artist in America. They pay us, indeed, only too well; that writer is a failure who cannot have his butler and motor and his villa at Palm Beach, where he is permitted to mingle almost in equality with the barons of banking. But he is oppressed ever by something worse than poverty—by the feeling that what he creates does not matter, that he is expected by his readers to be only a decorator or a clown, or that he is good-naturedly accepted as a scoffer whose bark probably is worse than his bite and who probably is a good fellow at heart, who in any case certainly does not count in a land that produces eighty-story buildings, motors by the million, and wheat by the billions of bushels. And he has no institution, no group, to which he can turn for inspiration, whose criticism he can accept and whose praise will be precious to him.

What institutions have we?

The American Academy of Arts and Letters does contain along with several excellent painters and architects and statesmen, such a really distinguished university-president as Nicholas Murray Butler, so admirable and courageous a scholar as Wilbur Cross, and several first-rate writers: the poets Edwin Arlington Robinson and Robert Frost, the free-minded publicist James Truslow Adams, and the novelists Edith Wharton, Hamlin Garland, Owen Wister, Brand Whitlock and Booth Tarkington.

But it does not include Theodore Dreiser, Henry Mencken, our most vivid critic, George Jean Nathan who, though still young, is certainly the dean of our dramatic critics, Eugene O'Neill, incomparably our best dramatist, the really original and vital poets, Edna St. Vincent Millay and Carl Sandburg, Robinson Jeffers and Vachel Lindsay and Edgar Lee Masters, whose *Spoon River Anthology* [1915] was so utterly different from any other poetry ever published, so fresh, so authoritative, so free from any gropings and timidities that it came like a revelation, and created a new school of native American poetry. It does not include the novelists and short-story writers, Willa Cather, Joseph Hergesheimer, Sherwood Anderson, Ring Lardner, Ernest Hemingway, Louis Bromfield, Wilbur Daniel Steele, Fannie Hurst, Mary Austin, James Branch Cabell, Edna Ferber, nor Upton Sinclair, of whom you must say, whether you admire or detest his aggressive Socialism, that he is internationally better known than any other American artist whosoever, be he novelist, poet, painter, sculptor, musician, architect.

I should not expect any Academy to be so fortunate as to contain all these writers, but one which fails to contain any of them, which thus cuts itself off from so much of what is living and vigorous and original in American letters, can have no relationship whatever to our life and aspirations. It does not represent literary America of today—it represents only Henry Wadsworth Longfellow.

It might be answered that, after all, the Academy is limited to fifty members; that, naturally, it cannot include every one of merit. But the fact is that while most of our few giants are excluded, the Academy does have room to include three extraordinarily bad poets, two very melodramatic and insignificant playwrights, two gentlemen who are known only because they are university presidents, a man who was thirty years ago known as a rather clever humorous draughtsman, and several gentlemen of whom—I sadly confess my ignorance—I have never heard.

Let me again emphasize the fact—for it is a fact—that I am not attacking the American Academy. It is a hospitable and generous and decidedly dignified institution. And it is not altogether the Academy's fault that it does not contain many of the men who have significance in our letters. Sometimes it is the fault of those writers themselves. I cannot imagine that grizzly bear Theodore Dreiser being comfortable at the serenely Athenian dinners of the Academy, and were they to invite Mencken, he would infuriate them with his boisterous jeering. No, I am not attacking—I am reluctantly considering the Academy because it is so perfect an example of the divorce in America of intellectual life from all authentic standards of importance and reality.

Our universities and colleges, or gymnasia, most of them, exhibit the same unfortunate divorce. I can think of four of them, Rollins College in Flordia, Middlebury College in Vermont, the University of Michigan, and the University of Chicago—which has had on its roll so excellent a novelist as Robert Herrick, so courageous a critic as Robert Morss Lovett—which have shown an authentic interest in contemporary creative literature. Four of them. But universities and colleges and musical emporiums and schools for the teaching of theology and plumbing and sign-painting are as thick in America as the motor traffic. Whenever you see a public building with Gothic fenestration on a sturdy backing of Indiana concrete, you may be certain that it is another university, with anywhere from two hundred to twenty thousand students equally ardent about avoiding the disadvantage of becoming learned and about gaining the social prestige contained in the possession of a B.A. degree.

Oh, socially our universities are close to the mass of our citizens, and so are they in the matter of athletes. A great college football game is passionately witnessed by eighty thousand people, who have paid five dollars apiece and motored anywhere from ten to a thousand miles for the ecstasy of watching twenty-two men chase one another up and down a curiously marked field. During the football season, a capable player ranks very nearly with our greatest and most admired heroes—even with Henry Ford, President Hoover, and Colonel Lindbergh.

And in one branch of learning, the sciences, the lords of business who rule us are willing to do homage to the devotees of learning. However bleakly one of our trader aristocrats may frown upon poetry or the visions of a painter, he is graciously pleased to endure a Millikan,[5] a Michelson,[6] a Banting,[7] a Theobald Smith.[8]

But the paradox is that in the arts our universities are as cloistered, as far from reality and living creation, as socially and athletically and scientifically they are close to us. To a true-blue professor of literature in an American university, literature is not something that a plain human being, living today, painfully sits down to produce. No; it is something dead; it is something magically produced by superhuman beings who must, if they are to be regarded as artists at all, have died at least one hundred years before the diabolical invention of the typewriter. To any authentic don, there is something slightly repulsive in the thought that literature could be created by any ordinary human being, still to be seen walking the streets, wearing quite commonplace trousers and coat and looking not so unlike a chauffeur or a farmer. Our American professors like their literature clear and cold and pure and very dead.

I do not suppose that American universities are alone in this. I am aware that to the dons of Oxford and Cambridge, it would seem rather indecent to suggest that Wells and Bennett and Galsworthy and George Moore may, while they commit the impropriety of continuing to live, be compared to any one so beautifully and safely dead as Samuel Johnson. I suppose that in the universities of Sweden and France and Germany there exist plenty of professors who prefer dissection to understanding. But in the new and vital and experimental land of America, one would expect the teachers of literature to be less monastic, more human, than in the traditional shadows of old Europe.

They are not.

There has recently appeared in America, out of the universities, an astonishing circus called "the New Humanism." [9] Now of course "humanism" means so many things that it means nothing. It may infer anything from a belief that Greek and Latin are more inspiring than the dialect of contemporary peasants to a belief that any living peasant is more interesting than a dead Greek. But it is a delicate bit of justice that this nebulous word should have been chosen to label this nebulous cult.

Insofar as I have been able to comprehend them—for naturally in a world so exciting and promising at this today, a life brilliant with Zeppe-

---

[5] Robert Andrews Millikan (1868–1955), physicist.
[6] Albert Abraham Michelson (1852–1931), physicist.
[7] Sir Frederick Grant Banting (1891–1941), Canadian physicist.
[8] (1859–1934), American pathologist.
[9] A conservative aesthetic creed dominated by Professor Irving Babbitt of Harvard.

lins and Chinese revolutions and the Bolshevik industrialization of farming and ships and the Grand Canyon and young children and terrifying
hunger and the lonely quest of scientists after God, no creative writer
would have time to follow all the chilly enthusiams of the New Humanists—this newest of sects reasserts the dualism of man's nature. It would
confine literature to the fight between man's soul and God, or man's soul
and evil.

But, curiously, neither God nor the devil may wear modern dress, but
must retain Grecian vestments. Oedipus is a tragic figure for the New
Humanists; man, trying to maintain himself as the image of God under
the menace of dynamos, in a world of high-pressure salesmanship, is not.
And the poor comfort which they offer is that the object of life is to
develop self-discipline—whether or not one ever accomplishes anything
with this self-discipline. So this whole movement results in the not particularly novel doctrine that both art and life must be resigned and negative. It is a doctrine of the blackest reaction introduced into a stirringly
revolutionary world.

Strangely enough, this doctrine of death, this escape from the complexities and danger of living into the secure blankness of the monastery,
has become widely popular among professors in a land where one would
have expected only boldness and intellectual adventure, and it has more
that ever shut creative writers off from any benign influence which
might conceivably have come from the universities.

But it has always been so. America has never had a Brandes, a
Taine, a Goethe, a Croce.

With a wealth of creative talent in America, our criticism has most
of it been a chill and insignificant activity pursued by jealous spinsters,
ex-baseball-reporters, and acid professors. Our Erasmuses have been village schoolmistresses. How should there be any standards when there
has been no one capable of setting them up?

The great Cambridge-Concord circle of the middle of the Nineteenth
Century—Emerson, Longfellow, Lowell, Holmes, the Alcotts—were sentimental reflections of Europe, and they left no school, no influence.
Whitman and Thoreau and Poe and, in some degree, Hawthorne, were
outcasts, men alone and despised, berated by the New Humanists of
their generation. It was with the emergence of William Dean Howells
that we first began to have something like a standard, and a very bad
standard it was.

Mr. Howells was one of the gentlest, sweetest, and most honest of
men, but he had the code of a pious old maid whose greatest delight was
to have tea at the vicarage. He abhorred not only profanity and obscenity
but all of what H. G. Wells has called "the jolly coarseness of life." In
his fantastic vision of life, which he innocently conceived to be realistic,
farmers and seamen and factory-hands might exist, but the farmer must
never be covered with muck, the seaman must never roll out bawdy
chanteys, the factory-hand must be thankful to his good employer, and

all of them must long for the opportunity to visit Florence and smile gently at the quaintness of the beggars.

So strongly did Howells feel this genteel, this New Humanistic philosophy that he was able vastly to influence his contemporaries, down even to 1914 and the turmoil of the Great War.

He was actually able to tame Mark Twain, perhaps the greatest of our writers, and to put that fiery old savage into an intellectual frock coat and top hat. His influence is not altogether gone today. He is still worshipped by Hamlin Garland, an author who should in every way have been greater than Howells but who under Howells' influence was changed from a harsh and magnificent realist into a genial and insignificant lecturer. Mr. Garland is, so far as we have one, the dean of American letters today, and as our dean, he is alarmed by all of the younger writers who are so lacking in taste as to suggest that men and women do not always love in accordance with the prayer-book, and that common people sometimes use language which would be inappropriate at a women's literary club on Main Street. Yet this same Hamlin Garland, as a young man, before he had gone to Boston and become cultured and Howellized, wrote two most valiant and revelatory works of realism, *Main-Travelled Roads* [1891] and *Rose of Dutcher's Cooly* [1895].

I read them as a boy in a prairie village in Minnesota—just such an environment as was described in Mr. Garland's tales. They were vastly exciting to me. I had realized in reading Balzac and Dickens that it was possible to describe French and English common people as one actually saw them. But it had never occurred to me that one might without indecency write of the people of Sauk Centre, Minnesota, as one felt about them. Our fictional tradition, you see, was that all of us in Midwestern villages were altogether noble and happy; that not one of us would exchange the neighborly bliss of living on Main Street for the heathen gaudiness of New York or Paris or Stockholm. But in Mr. Garland's *Main-Travelled Roads* I discovered that there was one man who believed that Midwestern peasants were sometimes bewildered and hungry and vile— and heroic. And, given this vision, I was released; I could write of life as living life.

I am afraid that Mr. Garland would not be pleased but acutely annoyed to know that he made it possible for me to write of America as I see it, and not as Mr. William Dean Howells so sunnily saw it. And it is his tragedy, it is a completely revelatory American tragedy, that in our land of freedom, men like Garland, who first blast the roads to freedom, become themselves the most bound.

But, all this time, while men like Howells were so effusively seeking to guide America into becoming a pale edition of an English cathedral town, there were surly and authentic fellows—Whitman and Melville, then Dreiser and James Huneker and Mencken—who insisted that our land had something more than tea-table gentility.

And so, without standards, we have survived. And for the strong young men, it has perhaps been well that we should have no standards. For, after seeming to be pessimistic about my own and much beloved land, I want to close this dirge with a very lively sound of optimism.

I have, for the future of American literature, every hope and every eager belief. We are coming out, I believe, of the stuffiness of safe, sane, and incredibly dull provincialism. There are young Americans today who are doing such passionate and authentic work that it makes me sick to see that I am a little too old to be one of them.

There is Ernest Hemingway, a bitter youth, educated by the most intense experience, disciplined by his own high standards, an authentic artist whose home is in the whole of life; there is Thomas Wolfe, a child of, I believe, thirty or younger, whose one and only novel, *Look Homeward, Angel* [1929] is worthy to be compared with the best in our literary production, a Gargantuan creature with great gusto of life; there is Thornton Wilder, who in an age of realism dreams the old and lovely dreams of the eternal romantics; there is John Dos Passos, with his hatred of the safe and sane standards of Babbitt and his splendor of revolution; there is Stephen Benét who, to American drabness, has restored the epic poem with his glorious memory of old John Brown; there are Michael Gold, who reveals the new frontier of the Jewish East Side, and William Faulkner, who has freed the South from hoop-skirts; and there are a dozen other young poets and fictioneers, most of them living now in Paris, most of them a little insane in the tradition of James Joyce, who, however insane they may be, have refused to be genteel and traditional and dull.

I salute them, with a joy in being not yet too far removed from their determination to give to the America that has mountains and endless prairies, enormous cities and lost farm cabins, billions of money and tons of faith, to an America that is as strange as Russia and as complex as China, a literature worthy of her vastness.

MICHAEL GOLD [IRVING GRANICH] (1896–1967)

For many years Mike Gold, as he was familiarly known, was the most famous Communist in America, with the possible exception of Earl Browder, who for just as many years (it now seems) was—while the Party was legal—its persistent candidate for the Presidency of the United States.

Gold was the son of impoverished Rumanian immigrants, a boy born and brought up on New York's East Side, who went to work at the age of thirteen. In the middle of the second decade of the century he became a Socialist and worked for the New York Call, *a Socialist daily paper; but after the Russian Revolution he joined the Communist Party and for the rest of his writing life wrote for Communist journals. He was on the staff of* The Masses *and* The Liberator, *and in 1933 he was one of the founders of* The New Masses, *with which he was associated until it expired in 1948. During the same years he was a constant contributor to* The Daily Worker.

He published a number of books but only one novel, Jews without Money *(1930), a work based on his own past and for some years regarded, by Marxist sympathizers, as the model of the "proletarian" novel.*

For most people who remember him, he was the aggressive editorialist of The New Masses *in the years when quite a few non-Communists were reading, with close attention, that journal of opinion.*

FURTHER READING

For critical estimates, see Walter Rideout, *The Radical Novel in the United States, 1900–1954* (1956), and David Madden, editor, *Proletarian Writers of the Thirties* (1968), and for the whole movement of which Gold was a part, Daniel Aaron, *Writers on The Left* (1961).

Wilder: Prophet of the Genteel Christ *(1927)*

The Cabala, by Thornton Wilder. New York: Albert and Charles Boni. $2.50.
The Bridge of San Luis Rey, by Thornton Wilder. New York: Albert and Charles Boni. $2.50.
The Woman of Andros, by Thornton Wilder. New York: Albert and Charles Boni. $2.50.
The Angel That Troubled the Waters, by Thornton Wilder. New York: Coward-McCann. $2.50.

"Here's a group of people losing sleep over a host of notions that the rest of the world has outgrown several centuries ago: one duchess's right to enter a door before another; the word order in a dogma of the Church; the divine right of Kings, especially of Bourbons."

In these words Thorton Wilder describes the people in his first book, "The Cabala." They are some eccentric old aristocrats in Rome, seen through the eyes of a typical American art "pansy" who is there as a student.

Marcantonio is the sixteen-year-old son of one of the group; he is burned out with sex and idleness, and sexualizes with his sister, and then commits suicide. Another character is a beautiful, mad Princess, who hates her dull Italian husband, falls in love with many Nordics and is regularly rejected by them. Others are a moldy old aristocrat woman who "believes," and a moldly old Cardinal who doesn't, and some other fine worm-eaten authentic speciments of the rare old Italian antique.

Wilder views these people with tender irony. He makes no claim as to their usefulness to the world that feeds them; yet he hints that their palace mustiness is a most important fact in the world of today. He writes with a brooding seriousness of them as if all the gods were watching their little lavender tragedies. The style is a diluted Henry James.

Wilder's second novel was "The Bridge of San Luis Rey." This famous and vastly popular yarn made a bold leap backward in time. Mr. Wilder, by then, had evidently completed his appraisal of our own age. The scene is laid in Lima, Peru; the time is Friday noon, July 20, 1714. In this volume Wilder perfected the style which is now probably permanent with him; the diluted and veritable Anatole France.

Among the characters of San Luis Rey are: (1) A sweet old duchess who loves her grown daughter to madness, but is not loved in return; (2) A beautiful unfortunate genius of an actress who after much sexualizing turns nun; (3) Her tutor, a jolly old rogue, but a true worshipper of literature; (4) Two strange brothers who love each other with a passion and delicacy that again brings the homosexual bouquet into a Wilder book, and a few other minor sufferers.

Some of the characters in this novel die in the fall of a Bridge. Our author points out the spiritual lessons imbedded in this Accident; viz: that God is Love.

The third novel is the recent "The Woman of Andros." This marks a still further masterly retreat into time and space. The scene is one of the lesser Greek islands, the hour somewhere in B. C.

The fable: a group of young Greeks spend their evenings in alternate sexual bouts and lofty Attic conversations with the last of the Aspasias. One young man falls in love with her sister, who is "pure." His father objects. Fortunately, the Aspasia dies. The father relents. But then the sister dies, too. Wistful futility and sweet soft sadness of Life. Hints of the coming of Christ: "and in the East the stars shone tranquilly down upon the land that was soon to be called Holy and that even then was preparing its precious burden." (Palestine.)

Then Mr. Wilder has published some pretty, tinkling, little three-minute playlets. These are on the most erudite and esoteric themes one could ever imagine; all about Angels, and Mozart, and King Louis, and Fairies, and a Girl of the Renaissance, and a whimsical old Actress (1780) and her old Lover; Childe Harold to the Dark Tower Came [1];

---

[1] *Childe Roland to the Dark Tower Came*, title of a play in *The Angel That Troubled the Waters* (1928). Gold, perhaps deliberately, confused this title, taken from an old Scottish ballad and a poem by Robert Browning (1855), with Lord Byron's title, *Childe Harold's Pilgrimage* (1809–1818).

Prosperina [*sic*] and the Devil[2]; The Flight into Egypt[3]; a Venetian Prince
and a Mermaid; Shelley, Judgment Day, Centaurs, God, The Woman in
the Chlamys, Christ; Brigomeide [4], Leviathan, Isben; every waxwork in
Wells's *Outline*,[5] in fact, except Buffalo Bill.

And this, to date, is the garden cultivated by Mr. Thornton Wilder.
It is a museum, it is not a world. In the devitalized air move the wan
ghosts he has called up, each in "romantic" costume. It is an historic
junkshop over which our author presides.

Here one will not find the heroic archæology of a Walter Scott or
Eugene Sue. Those men had social passions, and used the past as a
weapon to affect the present and future. Scott was the poet of feudalism.
The past was a glorious myth he created to influence the bourgeois anti-
feudal present. Eugene Sue was the poet of the proletariat. On every
page of history he traced the bitter, neglected facts of the working-class
martyrdom. He wove these into an epic melodrama to strengthen the
heart and hand of the revolutionary workers, to inspire them with a
proud consciousness of their historic mission.

That is how the past should be used; as a rich manure, as a spring-
board, as a battle cry, as a deepening, clarifying and sublimation of the
struggles in the too-immediate present. But Mr. Wilder is the poet of the
genteel bourgeoisie. They fear any such disturbing lessons out of the
past. Their goal is comfort and status quo. Hence, the vapidity of these
little readings in history.

Mr. Wilder, in a foreword to his book of little plays tells himself and
us the object of his esthetic striving.

"I hope," he says, "through many mistakes, to discover that spirit that
is not unequal to the elevation of the great religious themes, yet which
does not fall into a repellant didacticism. Didacticism is an attempt at
the coercion of another's free mind, even though one knows that in these
matters beyond logic, beauty is the only persuasion. Here the schoolmaster enters again. He sees all that is fairest in the Christian tradition
made repugnant to the new generations by reason of the diction in
which it is expressed. . . . So that the revival of religion is almost a matter of rhetoric. The work is difficult, perhaps impossible (perhaps all religions die out with the exhaustion of the language), but it at least reminds us that Our Lord asked us in His work to be not only gentle as
doves, but as wise as serpents."

Mr. Wilder wishes to restore he says, through Beauty and Rhetoric,
the Spirit of Religion in American Literature. One can respect any writer
in America who sets himself a goal higher than the usual racketeering.
But what is this religious spirit Mr. Wilder aims to restore? Is it the
crude self-torture of the Holy Rollers, or the brimstone howls and fears

---

2 Title of another play in this volume.

3 A third play in the same volume.

4 Brigomeide is a mermaid in *Leviathan*, another play in the group.

5 H. G. Wells, *The Outline of History* (1920).

of the Baptists, or even the mad, titanic sincerities and delusions of a Tolstoy or Dostoievsky?

No, it is that newly fashionable literary religion that centers around Jesus Christ, the First British Gentleman. It is a pastel, pastiche, dilettante religion, without the true neurotic blood and fire, a daydream of homosexual figures in graceful gowns moving archaically among the lilies. It is Anglo-Catholicism, that last refuge of the American literary snob.

This genteel spirit of the new parlor-Christianity pervades every phrase of Mr. Wilder's rhetoric. What gentle theatrical sighs! what lovely, well composed deaths and martyrdoms! what languishings and flutterings of God's sinning doves! what little jewels of Sunday-school wisdom, distributed modestly here and there through the softly flowing narrative like delicate pearls, diamonds and rubies on the costume of a meek, wronged Princess gracefully drowning herself for love (if my image is clear).

Wilder has concocted a synthesis of all the chambermaid literature, Sunday-school tracts and boulevard piety there ever were. He has added a dash of the prep-school teacher's erudition, then embalmed all this in the speciously glamorous style of the late Anatole France. He talks much of art, of himself as Artist, of style. He is a very conscious craftsman. But his is the most irritating and pretentious style pattern I have read in years. It has the slick, smug finality of the lesser Latins; that shallow clarity and tight little good taste that remind one of nothing so much as the conversation and practice of a veteran cocotte.

Mr. Wilder strains to be spiritual; but who could reveal any real agonies and exaltations of spirit in this neat, tailormade rhetoric? It is a great lie. It is Death. Its serenity is that of the corpse. Prick it, and it will bleed violet ink and *apéritif*. It is false to the great stormy music of Anglo-Saxon speech. Shakespeare is crude and disorderly beside Mr. Wilder. Neither Milton, Fielding, Burns, Blake, Byron, Chaucer nor Hardy could ever receive a passing mark in Mr. Wilder's classroom of style.

And this is the style with which to express America? Is this the speech of a pioneer continent? Will this discreet French drawing-room hold all the blood, horror and hope of the world's new empire? Is this the language of the intoxicated Emerson? Or the clean, rugged Thoreau, or vast Whitman? Where are the modern streets of New York, Chicago and New Orleans in these little novels? Where are the cotton mills, and the murder of Ella May [6] and her songs? Where are the child slaves of the beet fields? Where are the stockbroker suicides, the labor racketeers

---

[6] Ella May Wiggins, a widow with five children who had written songs for the Gastonia, North Carolina, strikers in the textile industry, 1929; killed by a shot from an armed mob attempting to prevent a union meeting. Her death provided a rallying cry for the Communist Party.

or passion and death of the coal miners? Where are Babbitt,[7] Jimmy
Higgins [8] and Anita Loos's Blonde [9]? Is Mr. Wilder a Swede or a Greek,
or is he an American? No stranger would know from these books he has
written.

But is it right to demand this "nativism" of him? Yes, for Mr. Wilder
has offered himself as a spiritual teacher; therefore one may say: Father,
what are your lessons? How will your teaching help the "spirit" trapped
in American capitalism? But Wilder takes refuge in the rootless cosmo-
politanism which marks every *emigré* trying to flee the problems of his
community. Internationalism is a totally different spirit. It begins at
home. Mr. Wilder speaks much of the "human heart" and its eternal
problems. It is with these, he would have us believe, that he concerns
himself; and they are the same in any time and geography, he says. Another banal evasion. For the human heart, as he probes it in Greece,
Peru, Italy and other remote places, is only the "heart" of a small futile
group with whom few Americans have the faintest kinship.

For to repeat, Mr. Wilder remains the poet of a small sophisticated
class that has recently arisen in America—our genteel bourgeoisie. His
style is their style; it is the new fashion. Their women have taken to
wearing his Greek chlamys and faintly indulge themselves in his smart
Victorian pieties. Their men are at ease in his Paris and Rome.

America won the War. The world's wealth flowed into it like a red
Mississippi. The newest and greatest of all leisure classes was created.
Luxury-hotels, golf, old furniture and *Vanity Fair* [10] sophistication were
some of their expressions.

Thorstein Veblen foretold all this in 1899, in an epoch-making book
that every American critic ought to study like a Bible. In *The Theory of
the Leisure Class* he painted the hopeless course of most American
culture for the next three decades. The grim, ironic prophet has been
justified. Thornton Wilder is the perfect flower of the new prosperity. He
has all the virtues Veblen said this leisure class would demand; the air
of good breeding, the decorum, priestliness, glossy high finish as against
intrinsic qualities, conspicuous inutility, caste feeling, love of the archaic, etc. . . .

All this is needed to help the parvenu class forget its lowly origins in
American industrialism. It yields them a short cut to the aristocratic
emotions. It disguises the barbaric sources of their income, the billions
wrung from American workers and foreign peasants and coolies. It lets
them feel spiritually worthy of that income.

Babbitt made them ashamed of being crude American climbers. Mr.
Wilder, "gentle as the dove and wise as the serpent," is a more construc-

---

[7] Sinclair Lewis's title character (1922).

[8] Upton Sinclair's title character, *Jimmie Higgins* (1919).

[9] *Gentlemen Prefer Blondes* (1925).

[10] Monthly review of American manners (1808–1936); merged with *Vogue*.

tive teacher. Taking them patiently by the hand, he leads them into castles, palaces and far-off Greek islands, where they may study the human heart when it is nourished by blue blood. This Emily Post of culture will never reproach them; or remind them of Pittsburgh or the breadlines. He is always in perfect taste; he is the personal friend of Gene Tunney.

"For there is a land of the living and a land of the dead and the bridge is love, the only survival, the only meaning." And nobody works in a Ford plant, and nobody starves looking for work, and there is nothing but Love in God's ancient Peru, Italy, Greece, if not in God's capitalist America 1930!

Let Mr. Wilder write a book about modern America. We predict it will reveal all his fundamental silliness and superficiality, now hidden under a Greek chlamys.

GRANVILLE HICKS (1901–   )

After his graduation from Harvard College in 1923, Granville Hicks, whose family had a New England Puritan background, spent two years in theological study directed at the ministry, and although he gave up that intention, his first teaching at Smith College was in Biblical literature. He went on to Rensselaer Polytechnic Institute as professor of English in 1929. He became interested in Marxism and joined the Communist Party, and when The New Masses *was founded in 1934, he became its literary editor. In the meantime he had published* The Great Tradition *(1933), one of our first sustained efforts in so-called "Marxist" criticism. He was dismissed from Rensselaer for his political affiliations in 1935. He again became a figure of controversy when he was appointed Counsellor in American Civilization at Harvard in 1938–1939. With the Soviet-German pact in 1939, he left both* The New Masses *and the Party. In the meantime he had published a collaborative biography,* John Reed *(1936); the* Letters of Lincoln Steffens *(1938) with his widow, Ella Winters; and* I Like America *(1938), an autobiographical defense of his Communist allegiance. This was followed by* Figures of Transition *(1939), a Marxist interpretation of British literature at the end of the nineteenth century and his last work written from that point of view. "The Natural History of an Intellectual" in* Small Town *(1946) and* Where We Came Out *(1954) look back on that whole troubled time in American political history.*

Granville Hicks has published three novels and an autobiography called Part of the Truth *(1965), and he continues very actively on the literary scene as critic and editor. He is a regular if long distance contributor to* The Saturday Review; *for years he has lived quietly on a farm in Grafton, New York.*

FURTHER READING

See Daniel Aaron, *Writers on The Left* (1961).

Call for an American Writers' Congress *(1935)*

The New Masses [1] welcomes the call for an American Writers' Congress sponsored by those writers whose names appear below. It fully endorses the purposes as set forth in the call. This Congress, we believe, can effectively counteract the new wave of race-hatred, the organized anti-Communist campaign, and the growth of Fascism, all of which can only be understood as part of the Administration's war program. Unlike the Anti-War Congress in Chicago,[2] and the National Congress for Unemployment Insurance just concluded in Washington,[3] the American Writers' Congress will not be a delegated body. Each writer will represent his own personal allegiance. With hundreds of writers attending from all sections, however, and united in a basic program, the Congress will be the voice of many thousands of intellectuals, and middle class people allied with the working class. In the coming weeks, *The New Masses* will publish from time to time articles by well known writers, outlining the basic discussions to be proposed at the Congress. Of those invited to sign the call a few—whose support of its program is unquestioned— were at too great a distance to be heard from in time for this publication.— *The Editors.*

The capitalist system crumbles so rapidly before our eyes that, whereas ten years ago scarely more than a handful of writers were sufficiently far-sighted and courageous to take a stand for proletarian revolution, today hundreds of poets, novelists, dramatists, critics, short story writers and journalists recognize the necessity of personally helping to accelerate the destruction of capitalism and the establishment of a workers' government.

We are faced by two kinds of problems. First, the problems of effective political action. The dangers of war and fascism are everywhere ap-

[1] (1926–1948), weekly journal of social criticism and aesthetics, affiliated with the Communist Party.

[2] August, 1932. As an aftermath of World War I, revulsion against war and fervent isolationism were widespread throughout the United States. Radicals and many other thoughtful men feared that, according to the Marxian prediction of the later phase of capitalism, the United States would embark on a policy of militarism, war, and dictatorship. Communists feared an attack on Russia by the capitalist countries; fascism was in full control in Italy and in the next year Hitler's National Socialist party would take over Germany.

[3] January, 1935. Later that year, President Roosevelt and the Congress would adopt the Social Security Act.

parent; we all can see the steady march of the nations towards war and
the transformation of sporadic violence into organized fascist terror.

The question is: how can we function most successfully against
these twin menaces?

In the second place, there are the problems peculiar to us as writers,
the problems of presenting in our work the fresh understanding of the
American scene that has come from our enrollment in the revolutionary
cause. A new Renaissance is upon the world; for each writer there is
the opportunity to proclaim both the new way of life and the revolutionary way to attain it. Indeed, in the historical perspective, it will be
seen that only these two things matter. The revolutionary spirit is penetrating the ranks of the creative writers.

Many revolutionary writers live virtually in isolation, lacking opportunities to discuss vital problems with their fellows. Others are so absorbed in the revolutionary cause that they have few opportunities for
thorough examination and analysis. Never have the writers of the nation
come together for fundamental discussion.

We propose, therefore, that a Congress of American revolutionary
writers be held in New York City on May 1, 1935; that to this Congress
shall be invited all writers who have achieved some standing in their
respective fields; who have clearly indicated their sympathy to the revolutionary cause; who do not need to be convinced of the decay of capitalism, of the inevitability of revolution. Subsequently, we will seek to
influence and win to our side those writers not yet so convinced.

This Congress will be devoted to exposition of all phases of a writer's
participation in the struggle against war, the preservation of civil liberties, and the destruction of facist tendencies everywhere. It will develop
the possibilities for wider distribution of revolutionary books and the
improvement of the revolutionary press, as well as the relations between
revolutionary writers and bourgeois publishers and editors. It will provide technical discussion of the literary applications of Marxist philosophy and of the relations between critic and creator. It will solidify our
ranks.

We believe such a Congress should create the League of American
Writers, affiliated with the International Union of Revolutionary
Writers.[4] In European countries, the I.U.R.W. is in the vanguard of liter-
ature and political action. In France, for example, led by such men as
Henri Barbusse, Romain Rolland, Andre Malraux, Andre Gide and Louis
Aragon, it has been in the forefront of the magnificent fight of the united
militant working class against Fascism.

The program for the League of American Writers would be evolved
at the Congress, basing itself on the following: fight against imperialist
war and fascism; defend the Soviet Union against capitalist aggression;
for the development and strengthening of the revolutionary labor move-

---

[4] An organization of the twenties and thirties with an international membership
but directed from Moscow.

ment; against white chauvinism (against all forms of Negro discrimination or persecution) and against the persecution of minority groups and of the foreign-born; solidarity with colonial people in their struggles for freedom; against the influence of bourgeois ideas in American liberalism; against the imprisonment of revolutionary writers and artists, as well as other class-war prisoners throughout the world.

By its very nature our organization would not occupy the time and energy of its members in administrative tasks; instead, it will reveal, through collective discussion, the most effective ways in which writers, *as writers*, can function in the rapidly developing crisis.

The undersigned are among those who have thus far signed the call to the Congress.[5]

Nelson Algren	Herbert Kline
Arnold B. Armstrong	Joshua Kunitz
Nathan Asch	John Howard Lawson
Maxwell Bodenheim	Tillie Lerner
Thomas Boyd	Meridel Le Sueur
Earl Browder	Melvin Levy
Bob Brown	Louis Lozowick
Fielding Burke	Grace Lumpkin
Kenneth Burke	Edward Newhouse
Erskine Caldwell	Joseph North
Alan Calmer	Moissaye Olgin
Robert Cantwell	Samuel Ornitz
Lester Cohen	Myra Page
Jack Conroy	Paul Peters
Malcolm Cowley	Allan Porter
Edward Dahlberg	Harold Preece
Theodore Dreiser	William Rollins
Guy Endore	Paul Romaine
James T. Farrell	Isidor Schneider
Ben Field	Edwin Seaver
Waldo Frank	Claire Sifton
Joseph Freeman	Paul Sifton
Michael Gold	George Sklar
Eugene Gordon	John L. Spivak
Horace Gregory	Lincoln Steffens
Henry Hart	Philip Stevenson
Clarence Hathaway	Bernhard J. Stern
Josephine Herbst	Genevieve Taggard
Granville Hicks	Alexander Trachtenberg
Langston Hughes	Nathanael West
Orrick Johns	Ella Winter
Arthur Kallet	Richard Wright

[5] This group of writers, many of them distinguished, many of them not, was made up of Communists, "fellow travellers," and a few left-leaning liberals.

JAMES AGEE (1909–1955)

Born and brought up in Tennessee, Agee was enrolled in the Exeter
Academy and in 1932 was graduated from Harvard College, where
he had edited The Advocate. Two years later he won the Yale
Younger Poets competition, and Permit Me Voyage (1934) was published in that series. In the same year he went to work for Fortune
magazine, which presently assigned him to a story on Southern
sharecroppers. He spent most of the summer of 1936 living with a
sharecropper family in Alabama, and Fortune did not find the
literary result appropriate to its pages. Written in passionate bitterness and accompanied by the superb photographs of Walker Evans,
Agee published his Let Us Now Praise Famous Men (1941) after
leaving Fortune.

In 1939 he went to Time magazine, for which he wrote film criticism,
and in 1943 he became the film reviewer for The Nation. His superior work in this area is collected in Agee on Film (1958). He resigned from The Nation in 1948 to write independently, and much
of his later work was in television and for Hollywood, where among
other scripts he wrote The African Queen. Agee on Film: II (1960)
contains five of his film scripts including two based on stories by
Stephen Crane.

A beautiful novelette, The Morning Watch (1951), tells of a day in the
life of a Tennessee boy and leads to his masterpiece in fiction, A
Death in the Family (1957), another reminiscent story, this one
about the death of a father in Tennessee and as moving as Agee's
own premature death in 1955.

It remains to be seen whether or not the publication of his Collected
Poems (1969) will bring out and extend his essentially underground reputation.

FURTHER READING

Biographical data are available in Letters of James Agee to Father
Flye (1962). Good critical estimates are Peter H. Olin, Agee (1966),
and Kenneth Seib, James Agee: Promise and Fulfillment (1968).

FROM *Let Us Now Praise Famous Men* (*1941*)

Emma

   Just a half-inch beyond the surface of this wall I face is another
surface, one of the four walls which square and collaborate against the
air another room, and there lie sleeping, on two iron beds and on pallets
on the floor, a man and his wife and her sister, and four children, a girl,
and three harmed boys. Their lamp is out, their light is done this long
while, and not in a long while has any one of them made a sound. Not
even straining, can I hear their breathing: rather, I have a not quite
sensuous knowledge of a sort of suspiration, less breathing than that in-
discernible drawing-in of heaven by which plants live, and thus I know
they rest and the profundity of their tiredness, as if I were in each one
of these seven bodies whose sleeping I can almost touch through this
wall, and which in the darkness I so clearly see, with the whole touch
and weight of my body: George's red body, already a little squat with the
burden of thirty years, knotted like oakwood, in its clean white cotton
summer union suit that it sleeps in; and his wife's beside him, Annie
Mae's, slender, and sharpened through with bone, that ten years past
must have had such beauty, and now is veined at the breast, and the skin
of the breast translucent, delicately shriveled, and blue, and she and her
sister Emma are in plain cotton shifts; and the body of Emma, her sister,
strong, thick and wide, tall, the breasts set wide and high, shallow and
round, not yet those of a full woman, the legs long thick and strong;
and Louise's green lovely body, the dim breasts faintly blown between
wide shoulders, the thighs long, clean and light in their line from hip to
knee, the head back steep and silent to the floor, the chin highest, and
the white shift up to her divided thighs; and the tough little body of
Junior, hardskinned and gritty, the feet crusted with sores; and the
milky and strengthless littler body of Burt whose veins are so bright in
his temples; and the shriveled and hopeless, most pitiful body of
Squinchy, which will not grow:
   But it is not only their bodies but their postures that I know, and
their weight on the bed or on the floor, so that I lie down inside each one
as if exhausted in a bed, and I become not my own shape and weight
and self, but that of each of them, the whole of it, sunken in sleep like
stones; so that I know almost the dreams they will not remember, and the
soul and body of each of these seven, and of all of them together in this
room in sleep, as if they were music I were hearing, each voice in relation to all the others, and all audible, singly, and as one organism, and
a music that cannot be communicated: and thus they lie in this silence,
and rest.

   Burt half-woke, whimpering before he was awake, an inarticulated
soprano speaking through not quite weeping in complaint to his mother

as before a sure jury of some fright of dream: the bed creaked and I heard her bare feet slow, the shuffling soles, and her voice, not whispering but stifled and gentle, Go to sleep now, git awn back to sleep, they aint nothin agoin to pester ye, git awn back to sleep, in that cadence of strength and sheltering comfort which anneals all fence of language and surpasses music; and George's grouched, sleepy voice, and hers to him, no words audible; and the shuffling; and a twisting in beds, and grumbling of weak springs; and the whimpering sinking, and expired; and the sound of breathing, strong, not sleeping, now, slowed, shifted across into sleep, now, steadier; and now, long, long, drawn off as lightest lithest edge of bow, thinner, thinner, a thread, a filament; nothing: and once more that silence wherein more deep than starlight this home is foundered.

I am fond of Emma, and very sorry for her, and I shall probably never see her again after a few hours from now. I want to tell you what I can about her.

She is a big girl, almost as big as her sister is wiry, though she is not at all fat: her build is rather that of a young queen of a child's magic story who throughout has been coarsened by peasant and earth living and work, and that of her eyes and her demeanor, too, kind, not fully formed, resolute, bewildered, and sad. Her soft abundant slightly curling brown hair is cut in a square bob which on her large fine head is particularly childish, and indeed Emma is rather a big child, sexual beyond propriety to its years, than a young woman; and this can be seen in a kind of dimness of definition in her features, her skin, and the shape of her body, which will be lost in a few more years. She wears a ten cent store necklace and a sunday cotton print dress because she is visiting, and is from town, but she took off her slippers as soon as she came, and worked with Annie Mae. According to her father she is the spitn image of her mother when her mother was young; Annie Mae favors her father and his people, who were all small and lightly built.

Emma is very fond of her father and very sorry for him, as her sister is, and neither of them can stand his second wife. I have an idea that his marrying her had a lot to do with Emma's own marriage, which her father so strongly advised her against. He married the second time when Emma was thirteen, and for a long while they lived almost insanely, as I will tell you of later, far back in a swamp: and when Emma was sixteen she married a man her father's age, a carpenter in Cherokee City. She has been married to him two years; they have no children. Emma loves good times, and towns, and people her own age, and he is jealous and mean to her and suspicious of her. He has given her no pretty dresses nor the money to buy cloth to make them. Every minute he is in the house he keeps his eye right on her as if she was up to something, and when he goes out, which is as seldom as he can, he locks her in: so that twice already she has left him and come home to stay, and then after a

while he has come down begging, and crying, and swearing he'll treat
her good, and give her anything she asks for, and that he'll take to drink
or kill himself if she leaves him, and she has gone back: for it isn't any
fun at home, hating that woman the way she does, and she can't have
fun with anyone else because she is married and nobody will have fun
with her that way: and now (and I think it may be not only through the
depression but through staying in the house because of jealousy and
through fear of living in a town with her, and so near a home she can
return to), her husband can no longer get a living in Cherokee City; he
has heard of a farm on a plantation over in the red hills in Mississippi
and has already gone, and taken it, and he has sent word to Emma that
she is to come in a truck in which a man he knows, who has business to
drive out that way, is moving their furniture; and this truck is leaving
tomorrow. She doesn't want to go at all, and during the past two days
she has been withdrawing into rooms with her sister and crying a good
deal, almost tearlessly and almost without voice, as if she knew no more
how to cry than how to take care for her life; and Annie Mae is strong
against her going, all that distance, to a man who leaves her behind and
then just sends for her, saying, Come on along, now; and George too is
as committal over it as he feels will appear any right or business of his
to be, he a man, and married, to the wife of another man, who is no kin
to him, but only the sister of his wife, and to whom he is himself uncon-
cealably attracted: but she is going all the same, without at all understanding why. Annie Mae is sure she won't stay out there long, not all
alone in the country away from her kinfolks with that man; that is what
she keeps saying, to Emma, and to George, and even to me; but actually
she is surer than not that she may never see her young sister again, and
she grieves for her, and for the loss of her to her own loneliness, for she
loves her, both for herself and her dependence and for that softness of
youth which already is drawn so deep into the trap, and in which Annie
Mae can perceive herself as she was ten years past; and she gives no appearance of noticing the clumsy and shamefaced would-be-subtle demeanors of flirtation which George is stupid enough to believe she does
not understand for what they are: for George would only be shocked
should she give him open permission, and Emma could not be too well
trusted either. So this sad comedy has been going on without comment
from anyone, which will come to nothing: and another sort has been
going on with us, of a kind fully as helpless. Each of us is attractive to
Emma, both in sexual immediacy and as symbols or embodiments of a
life she wants and knows she will never have; and each of us is fond of
her, and attracted toward her. We are not only strangers to her, but we
are strange, unexplainable, beyond what I can begin yet fully to realize.
We have acted toward her with the greatest possible care and shyness
and quiet, yet we have been open or 'clear' as well, so that she knows we
understand her and like her and care for her almost intimately. She is
puzzled by this and yet not at all troubled, but excited; but there is

nothing to do about it on either side. There is tenderness and sweetness and mutual pleasure in such a 'flirtation' which one would not for the world restrain or cancel, yet there is also an essential cruelty, about which nothing can be done, and strong possibility of cruelty through mis-understanding, and inhibition, and impossibility, which can be re-strained, and which one would rather die than cause any of: but it is a cruel and ridiculous and restricted situation, and everyone to some ex-tent realizes it. Everyone realizes it, I think, to such a degree even as this: supposing even that nothing can be helped about the marriage, sup-posing she is going away and on with it, which she shouldn't, then if only Emma could spend her last few days alive having a gigantic good time in bed, with George, a kind of man she is best used to, and with Walker and with me, whom she is curious about and attracted to, and who are at the same moment tangible and friendly and not at all to be feared, and on the other hand have for her the mystery or glamour almost of mythological creatures. This has a good many times in the past couple of days come very clearly through between all of us except the children, and without fear, in sudden and subtle but unmistakable expressions of the eyes, or ways of smiling: yet not one of us would be capable of trust-ing ourselves to it unless beyond any doubt each knew all the others to be thus capable: and even then how crazily the conditioned and inferior parts of each of our beings would rush in, and take revenge. But this is just a minute specialization of a general brutal pity: almost any person, no matter how damaged and poisoned and blinded, is infinitely more capable of intelligence and of joy than he can let himself be or than he usually knows; and even if he had no reason to fear his own poisons, he has those that are in others to fear, to assume and take care for, if he would not hurt both himself and that other person and the pure act itself beyond cure.

But here I am going to shift ahead of where I am writing, to a thing which is to happen, or which happened, the next morning (you mustn't be puzzled by this, I'm writing in a continuum), and say what came of it.

The next morning was full of the disorganized, half listless, yet very busy motions of ordinary life broken by an event: Emma's going away. I was going to take her and Annie Mae to her brother Gallatin's house near Cookstown, where she was to meet the man with his truck, and I was waiting around on the front porch in the cool-hot increasing morning sunlight, working out my notes, while the morning housework was done up in special speed. (George was gone an hour or more ago, immediately after the breakfast they had all sat through, not talking much. There had been a sort of lingering in eating and in silences, and a little when the food was done, broken by talk to keep the silences from becoming too frightening; I had let the breakfast start late by telling him I would take him in the car; then abruptly he got up saying, 'Well, Jimmy, if you —' Whether he would kiss Emma goodbye, as a sort of relative, was on everybody's mind. He came clumsily near it: she half got from her chair, and their bodies were suddenly and sharply drawn toward each other a few inches: but he was much too shy, and did not even touch her with the hand he reached out to shake hers. Annie Mae drawled, smiling, What's wrong with ye George; she ain't agoin' to bite ye; and everyone laughed, and Emma stood up and they embraced, laughing, and he kissed her on her suddenly turned cheek, a little the way a father and an adolescent son kiss, and told her goodbye and wished her good luck, and I took him to work in the car, and came back. And now here I was, as I have said, on the porch.) Here I was on the porch, diddling around in a notebook and hearing the sounds of work and the changing patterns of voices inside, and the unaccustomed noise of shoeleather on the floor, because someone was dressed up for travel; and a hen thudded among dried watermelon seeds on the oak floor, looking, as they usually do, like a nearsighted professor; and down hill beyond the open field a little wind laid itself in a wall against the glistening leaves of the high forest and lay through with a long sweet granular noise of rustling water; and the hen dropped from the ledge of the porch to the turded dirt with a sodden bounce, and an involuntary cluck as her heaviness hit the ground on her sprung legs; and the long lithe little wind released the trees and was gone on, wandering the fringed earth in its affairs like a saturday schoolchild in the sun, and the leaves hung troubling in the aftermath; and I heard footsteps in the hall and Emma appeared, all dressed to go, looking somehow as if she had come to report a decision that had been made in a conference, for which I, without knowing it, seemed to have been waiting. She spoke in that same way, too, not wasting any roundabout time or waiting for an appropriate rhythm, yet not in haste, looking me steadily and sweetly in the eyes, and said, I want you and Mr. Walker to know how much we all like you, because you make us feel easy with you; we don't have to act any different from what it comes natural to act, and we don't have to worry what you're thinking about us, it's just like you was our own people and had always lived here with us, you all are so kind, and nice, and quiet, and easygoing, and we wisht you wasn't never going to go away but stay on here with us, and I just want to tell you how much we all keer about you; Annie Mae says the same, and you please tell Mr. Walker, too, if I don't see him afore I go. (I knew she could never say it over again, and I swore I certainly would tell him.)

What's the use trying to say what I felt. It took her a long time to say what she wanted so much to say, and it was hard for her, but there she stood looking straight into my eyes, and I straight into hers, longer than you'd think it would be possible to stand it. I would have done anything in the world for her (that is always characteristic, I guess, of the seizure of the strongest love you can feel: pity, and the wish to die for a person, because there isn't anything you can do for them that is at all measurable to your love), and all I could do, the very most, for this girl who was so soon going on out of my existence into so hopeless a one of hers, the very most I could do was not to show all I cared for her and for what she was saying, and not to even try to do, or to indicate the good I wished I might do her and was so utterly helpless to do. I had such tenderness and such gratitude toward her that while she spoke I very strongly, as something steadier than an 'impulse,' wanted in answer to take her large body in my arms and smooth the damp hair back from her forehead and to kiss and comfort and shelter her like a child, and I can swear that I now as then almost believe that in that moment she would have so well understood this, and so purely and quietly met it, that now as then I only wish to God I had done it; but instead the most I did was to stand facing her, and to keep looking into her eyes (doing her the honor at least of knowing that she did not want relief from this), and, managing to keep the tears from running down my face, to smile to her and say that there was nothing in my whole life that I had cared so much to be told, and had been so grateful for (and I believe this is so); and that I wanted her to know how much I like them, too, and her herself, and that I certainly felt that they were my own people, and wanted them to be, more than any other kind of people in the world, and that if they felt that of me, and that I belonged with them, and we all felt right and easy with each other and fond of each other, then there wasn't anything in the world I could be happier over, or be more glad to know (and this is so, too); and that I knew I could say all of the same of Walker (and this, too, I know I was true in saying). I had stood up, almost without realizing I was doing it, the moment she appeared and began to speak, as though facing some formal, or royal, or ritual action, and we stayed thus standing, not leaning against or touching anything, about three feet apart, facing each other. I went on to say that whatever might happen to her or that she might do in all her life I wished her the best luck anyone could think of, and not ever to forget it, that nobody has a right to be unhappy, or to live in a way that makes them unhappy, for the sake of being afraid, or what people will think of them, or for the sake of anyone else, if there is any way they can possibly do better, that won't hurt other people too much. She slowly and lightly blushed while I spoke and her eyes became damp and bright, and said that she sure did wish me the same. Then we had nothing to say, unless we should invent something, and nothing to do, and quite suddenly and at the same instant we smiled, and she said well, she reckoned she'd better git on in and help Annie Mae, and I nodded, and she went, and a half-hour later I was driving her, and Annie Mae, and her father, and Louise, and Junior, and Burt, and the baby, to her brother's house near Cooks-town. The children were silent and intent with the excitement of riding in the car, stacked on top of each other around their mother on the back seat and looking out of the windows like dogs, except Louise, whose terrible gray eyes met mine whenever I glanced for them in the car mirror. Emma rode between me and her father, her round sleeveless arms cramped a little in front of her. My own sleeves were rolled high, so that in the crowding our flesh touched. Each of us at the first few of these contacts drew quietly away, then later she relaxed her arms, and her body and thighs as well, and so did I, and for perhaps fifteen minutes we lay quietly and closely side to side, and intimately communicated also in our thoughts. Our bodies were very hot, and the car was packed with hot and sweating bodies, and with a fine salt and rank odor like that of crushed grass: and thus in a short while, though I knew speed was not in the mood of anyone and was going as slowly as I felt I could with propriety, we covered the short seven mileage of clay, then slag, to Cookstown, and slowed through the town (eyes, eyes on us, of men, from beneath hatbrims), and down the meandering now sandy road to where her brother lived. I had seen him once before, a man in his thirties with a bitter, intelligent, skull-formed face; and his sour wife, and their gold skinned children: and now here also was another man, forty or so, leathery-strong, blackshaven, black-hatted, booted, his thin mouth tightened round a stalk of grass showing gold stained teeth, his cold, mean eyes a nearly white blue; and he was sardonically waiting, and his truck, loaded with chairs and bed-iron, stood in the sun where the treeshade had slid beyond it. He was studying Emma coldly and almost without furtiveness, and she was avoiding his eyes. It was impossible to go quite immediately. We all sat around a short while and had lemonade from a pressed-glass pitcher, from which he had already taken at least two propitiatory glasses. It had been made in some hope of helping the leave-taking pass off as a sort of party, from two lemons and spring water, without ice, and it was tepid, heavily sweetened (as if to compensate the lack of lemons), and scarcely tart; there was half a glass for each of us, out of five tumblers, and we all gave most of it to the children. The children of the two families stayed very quiet, shy of each other; the others, save the black-hatted man, tried to talk, without managing much; they tried especially hard when Emma got up, as suddenly as if she had to vomit, and went into the next room and shut the door, and Annie Mae followed her. Gallatin said it was mighty hard on a girl so young as that leaving her kinfolks so far behind. The man in the hat twisted his mouth on the grass and, without opening his teeth, said Yeah-ah, as if he had his own opinions about that. We were trying not to try to hear the voices in the next room, and that same helpless, frozen, creaky weeping I had heard before; and after a little it quieted; and after a little more they came out, Emma flourily powdered straight to the eyes, and the eyes as if she had cried sand instead of tears; and the man said—it was the first kind gesture I had seen in him and one of the few I suspect in his life, and I am sure it was kind by no intention of his: 'Well, we can't hang around here all day. Reckon you'd better come on along, if you're coming.'

With that, Emma and her father kiss, shyly and awkwardly, children doing it before parents; so do she and her brother; she and Annie Mae embrace; she and I shake hands and say goodbye: all this in the sort of broken speed in which a family takes leave beside the black wall of a steaming train when the last crates have been loaded and it seems certain that at any instant the windows, and the leaned unpitying faces, will begin to slide past on iron. Emma's paper suitcase is lifted into the truck beside the bedsprings which will sustain the years on years of her cold, hopeless nights; she is helped in upon the hard seat beside the driver above the hot and floorless engine, her slippered feet propped askew at the ledges of that pit into the road; the engine snaps and coughs and catches and levels on a hot white moistureless and thin metal roar, and with a dreadful rending noise that brings up the mild heads of cattle a quarter of a mile away the truck rips itself loose from the flesh of the planed dirt of the yard and wrings into the road and chucks ahead, we waving, she waving, the black hat straight ahead, she turned away, not bearing it, our hands drooped, and we stand disconsolate and emptied in the sun; and all through these coming many hours while we slow move within the anchored rondures of our living, the hot, screaming, rattling, twenty-mile-an-hour traveling elongates steadily crawling, a lost, earnest, and frowning ant, westward on red roads and on white in the febrile sun above no support, suspended, sustained from falling by force alone of its outward growth, like that long and lithe incongruous slender runner a vine spends swiftly out on the vast blank wall of the earth, like snake's head and slim stream feeling its way, to fix, and anchor, so far, so wide of the strong and stationed stalk: and that is Emma.

But as yet this has not happened, and now she sleeps, here in this next room, among six others dear in their lives to me, and if I were but to section and lift away a part of this so thin shell and protection of wall, there they would be as in a surgery, or a medical drawing, the brain beneath the lifted, so light helmet of the skull, the deep-chambered, powerful and so vulnerable, so delicately ruined, emboweled, most vital organs behind the placid lovedelighting skin; and a few hours past, they were going to bed, and not long before, they were eating supper, and because of their sadness, and because of the excitement of her being here, supper had in its speaking and its whole manner a tone out of the ordinary, a quality of an occasion, almost of a party, almost of gaiety, with a pale chocolate pudding, made out of cocoa and starch, for dessert, and a sort of made-conversation and joking half forced by fear of sadness, and half genuinely stimulated by her presence and by a shyness and liking for us; and in the middle of the table stood the flower of the lighted lamp, more kind, more friendly in the still not departed withering daylight and more lovely, than may be set in words beneath its fact: and when the supper was finished, it disintegrated without suture or transition into work, sleep, rest: Annie Mae, Emma, Louise, the three women, rising to the work they had scarcely ceased during the meal (for they had served us, eating between times), clearing, scraping, crumbing the damp oilcloth with damp cloth in the light, dishwashing, meanwhile talking (Louise not talking, listening to them, the older women, absorbing, absorbing deeply, grain by grain, ton by ton, that which she shall not escape): the women lifting themselves from their chairs into this work; the children meanwhile sinking and laid out five fathom five mile deep along the exhausted floor: and we, following manners, transferred with George, a few feet beyond the kitchen door, in the open porch hall, leaned back in chairs against the wall, or leaned between our knees and our planted feet, he, with his work shoes off, his feet taking, thirstily drinking like the sunken heads of horses at the trough, the cool and beauty quiet of the grained and gritted boards of the floor; and he talking a little, but too tired for talk, and rolling a damp cigarette and smoking its short sweetness through to the scorching of the stony thumb, with a child's body lifted sleeping between his knees:

and when the women are through, they may or may not come out too, with their dresses wet in front with the dishwashing and their hard hands softened and seamed as if withered with water, and sit a little while with the man or the men: and if they do, it is not for long, for everyone is much too tired, and has been awake and at work since daylight whitened a little behind the trees on the hill, and it is now very close to dark, with daylight scarcely more than a sort of tincture on the air, and this diminishing, and the loudening frogs, and the locusts, the crickets, and the birds of night, tentative, tuning, in that great realm of hazy and drowned dew, who shall so royally embroider the giant night's fragrant cloud of earthshade: and so, too, the talking is sporadic, and sinks into long unembarrassed silences; the sentences, the comments, the monosyllables, drawn up from deepest within them without thought and with faint creaking of weight as if they were wells, and spilled out in a cool flat drawl, and quietly answered; and a silence; and again, some words: and it is not really talking, or meaning, but another and profounder kind of communication, a rhythm to be completed by answer and made whole by silence, a lyric song, as horses who nudge one another in pasture, or like drowsy birds who are heavying a dark branch with their tiredness before sleep: and it is their leisure after work; but it does not last; and in fifteen minutes, or a half-hour at most, it is done, and they draw themselves into motion for bed:

one by one, in a granite-enameled, still new basin which is for that single purpose, they wash their feet in cold water—for this is a very cleanly and decent family—and begin to move into the bedroom: first the children, then the women, last George: the pallets are laid; the lamp is in the bedroom; George sits in the porch dark, smoking another cigarette. Junior, morose and whimpering and half blind with sleep, undresses himself, sliding the straps from his shoulders and the overalls from his nakedness and sinking in his shirt asleep already, along the thin cotton pallet. Burt scarely half awakens as his sister strips him, a child of dough, and is laid like a corpse beside his cruel brother. Squinchy is drugged beyond doomcrack: his heavy tow head falls back across her bent arm loose as that of a dead bird, the mouth wide open, the eyelids oily gleaming, as his mother slips from his dwarf body the hip length, one-button dress; and the women, their plain shifts lifted from the closet nails, undress themselves, turned part away from each other, and careful not to look: the mother, whose body already at twenty-seven is so wrung and drained and old, a scrawny, infinitely tired, delicate animal, the poor emblems of delight no longer practicable to any but most weary and grunting use: her big young sister, childless still, and dim, soft as a bloomed moon, and still in health, who emanates some disordering or witless violation: and the still inviolate, lyric body of a child, very much of the earth, yet drawn into that short and seraphic phase of what seems unearthliness which it will so soon lose: each aware of herself and of the others, and each hiding what shames or grieves her: and the two elder talking (and the child, the photographic plate, receiving: These are women, I am a woman, I am not a child any more, I am undressing with women, and this is how women are, and how they talk), talking ahead, the two women, in flat, secure, drawled, reedy voices, neither shy nor deliberately communicative, but utterly communicative, the talk loosening out of them serenely and quietly steady and in no restraint of uncertainty of one another like the alternate and plaited music of two slow-dribbling taps; and they are in bed and George throws his cigarette, hurdling its spark into the night yard, and comes in, and they turn their faces away while he undresses; and he takes the clean thin union suit from its nail by the scrolled iron head of the bed; and he slides between the coarse sheets and lets down his weight; and for a little while more, because they are stimulated, they keep talking, while the children sleep, and while Louise lies looking and listening, with the light still on, and there is almost volubility in the talk, and almost gaiety again, and inaudible joking, and little runs of laughter like startled sparrows; and gradually this becomes more quiet, and there is a silence full of muted thought; and George, says; Well; and fluffs out the lamp, and its light from the cracks in my wall, and there is silence; and George speaks, low, and is answered by both women; and a silence; and Emma murmurs something; and after a few seconds Annie Mae murmurs a reply; and there is a silence, and a slow and constrained twisting on springs and extension of a body, and silence; and a long silence in the darkness of the peopled room that is chambered in the darkness of the continent before the unwatching stars; and Louise says, Good night Immer, and Emma says, Good night Louise; and Louise says, Good night mamma; and Annie Mae says, Good night Louise; and Louise says, Good night daddy; and George says, Good night Louise; good night George; night, Immer; night, Annie Mae; night, George; night, Immer; night, Annie Mae; night, Louise; night; good night, good night:

LATER POETRY

Later Poetry (poets born after 1900)

In an interview with the *New York Times* on the occasion of his eightieth birthday in the summer of 1969, Conrad Aiken took a very dim view of American writing since the Second World War. "I think we're going through a very depressing decline in taste, which is on all levels everywhere," he was quoted as "ruefully" saying. "I don't think there is any first-rate fiction, and I mean to include everybody in that—Nabokov, Bellow and so on." Poets came off no better. Wallace Stevens, Aiken said, was our last great poet; since Stevens, American poetry "has come to a temporary pause." The achievement of Robert Lowell, for example, "is greatly overestimated." As for Allen Ginsberg, "I don't care for him at all. It's a howl and that's all you can say."

These may be the cranky views of a disappointed man whose great gifts have never been properly recognized and who now confronts his end; but coming from Conrad Aiken, they cannot be so easily dismissed. For who indeed is to say with any certainty what is even the relative value of this abundant writing in which we are now immersed—relative, that is, not only to what had gone before but also, or only, to what is immediate? Of the poets represented in the following selections, most responsible judges would argue that, beyond Lowell himself, at least six are of enduring interest: Warren, Roethke, Schwartz, Shapiro, Jarrell, Berryman. For each of the remaining fourteen, many readers might well wish to substitute some other poet and could plausibly defend the substitution. But an editor of immediately contemporary work wishes, within the limitations of the available space, not only to represent insofar as possible the full variety of the contemporary effort, but also, finally and necessarily, to fall back on his own judgment and taste.

Taking a very different view from Aiken's toward American writing since the Second World War, Stephen Spender announced at a British "Festival of Literature" in October 1967, that "The centre of poetic activity in the English language has shifted from London to New York and San Francisco, just as that of painting has shifted from Paris to New York." English poetry was now the provincial poetry, and it stood in relation to America as Ireland had to England at the end of the last century. "... there will be no swing of the pendulum back in our direction." And Spender suggested that if the young English poet does not choose to become an American poet (following the example of W. H. Auden, one supposes him to mean) but yet wishes to break out of his provinciality, "... he must relate his English situation very carefully to four things: the American outpouring of confessional poetry written in cities; a Dostoevskian passion for crime and salvation; academies of learning immensely subsidized in a country where universities come more and more to resemble city-states; With-Itness where there is a violence really to be With."

One might consider the third point first: Of the fifteen poets in our earlier group, only two, Ransom and Tate, held regular academic appointments. Of the twenty-one poets in this later group, only five have not had or do not have such appointments, and even most of these five are familiar campus figures. Does this shift suggest a change in poets and necessarily in the poetry they produce? Or a change in the academy, which employs and "protects" them? The remaining three items in Spender's catalog hardly suggest that poets have put on a new academic discretion and conventionality, but rather that, the university now having become so large, it has also become sufficiently flexible to easily assimilate poetic talent without, on its part, restraining even the most extreme eccentricity. Whether the atmosphere of academic life—however that may have altered in recent years—is good for poetry remains as one of the questions that literary history must ultimately answer. But the evidence of even so limited a selection as we have here demonstrates that freedom of expression, at least, has not been curbed, but encouraged.

As a matter of fact, none of these later poets, even the older ones like Eberhart, Warren, Kunitz, and Roethke, are as academic as Eliot or Pound, Stevens, Marianne Moore, or Tate—which is to say, in the first place, that their poetry does not exploit their learning. It is to say, in the second place, that they are not "system builders": they have no interest in constructing frameworks of mythological or historical, intellectual or dogmatic or aesthetic reference, and when they are allusive, they are unsystematically so, simply meeting the demands of a given moment in a given poem. And then, in the third place, they are much more direct: they do not, generally, speak through masks, *personae*, to use Pound's term, giving to their utterance a dramatized objectification, but speak immediately for themselves, in their own voices, without that earlier kind of technical guile. And finally, in many of these poets, at least, we can see a resurgence of romantic ardor, a reassertion of faith in the spontaneity of the creative act, even of that old-fashioned concept of inspiration, which, while it presumably shuns merely studied effects, does not dispel craft.

This change in poetry came about without any revolutionary bravura, without the fanfare of manifestoes and ultimatums that had characterized the earlier period, without public disavowals, renunciations and denunciations, splendid statements of new allegiances. It was a quiet shift of emphasis only, and in fact the first ten years after the end of the war were generally quiet years in American poetry. "These are the tranquillized Fifties," wrote Robert Lowell, "and I am forty." Then, in the middle fifties, a sudden current of change did make itself felt. In 1956 Robert Lowell published his prose reminiscence, "91 Revere Street," which was a prelude to the poems that were to follow, the autobiographical, so-called "confessional" poems of *Life Studies*. Now he abandoned his earlier intense, rhetorically packed forms for open forms, and he wrote with apparently perfect candor about his most intimate personal experiences in poems at once gentle and shocking, deeply sad and grotesque. At about the same time John Berryman began to publish his "dream songs," poems that showed a no less surprising shift in a poet who had already firmly established himself by a quite different manner. If these later poems are hardly less personal that those of Lowell, the change is to a form of statement more enigmatic, dark, jagged, irreverent, hallucinatory. At the same time, a whole new generation of poets began to publish—a generation represented here by six or eight of the best—each in his way pursuing the new revelatory personalization. The change in the mid-fifties was probably most strikingly announced by the anarchistic "beat" group, who provide, perhaps, only the extreme and disheveled example of a general aim. Theirs has become a kind of "street poetry," and it is not surprising that they, among others, point to Whitman as their precursor and, more recently, to William Carlos Williams.

It can now be seen that this recent activity in poetry is an intensification of the qualities, ennumerated above, that carried these poets, even when they had assimilated the lessons of Eliot, in a direction away from him. And it is in this recent activity that Spender's 1967 characterization becomes almost universally applicable. Allowing for exceptions, one can yet say that this is generally a city poetry, thick with all the experienced contingency and multiplicity of the immediate present ("With-Itness"), violent in action as in feeling, deeply personal, abrasive, anguished, crying for release, sometimes heart-breaking in its often baffled rage and even in its often baffling obscurity. It is, after all, 1970, and how far we have moved, in poetry no less than in history, from Eliot's gentle "now, under conditions / That seem unpropitious"!

RICHARD EBERHART (1904–   )

*Eberhart has said that the protracted and painful death of his mother,
when he was eighteen, probably made him a poet; the major theme
of his early poetry no doubt is the shocking discovery of death. The
shock of that early poetry itself lies in a kind of Blakean break from
Innocence into Experience, Experience being, as it was for Blake,
one's first full awareness of death, Dylan Thomas's knowledge that
"After the first death [birth] there is no other."*

*Some such awareness has haunted Eberhart through all his poetry,
giving it, at its best, glimpses of that "otherness" that exists in and
beyond the life of natural things. When his poems communicate
those glimpses, he writes with great simplicity and immediacy.
Sometimes, however, he labors with abstractions and with astonishingly awkward verbalisms, almost as if he were beating his way
through impossible thickets or up rocky, pathless mountain sides
to reach the open, imaginative clearing where the profoundest experiences can be contemplated, once passed through.*

*He was brought up in Minnesota but was graduated from Dartmouth,
then he was awarded several degrees at Cambridge University,
where his real education in poetry took place. He tutored the son of
a Siamese king, taught for several years at St. Mark's School, went
into the Navy (and wrote some of our best war poems), and after
working for a while in his father's business, became a professor of
English and poet in residence at Dartmouth College.*

His first seven volumes of poems were reduced to Selected Poems
(1951) and then, after two more volumes, expanded in Collected
Poems 1930–1960 *(1960). Since then, he has published* The Quarry:
New Poems *(1964) and* Shifts of Being *(1967). The problem still
seems to be the same, to get out of all the second-growth, rocky,
bookish terrain to the high, clear place where, when he ach·eves it,
he lets us share what he names as his meaning, "The light beyond
compare . . ."*

Inescapable brotherhood of the living,
Our mystery of time, the only hopeful light.

FURTHER READING

Ralph J. Mills, Jr., *Richard Eberhart* (1966), is the first comprehensive
survey of the poet's work. *The Achievement of Richard Eberhart*
(1968), by Bernard F. Engel, is a selection of his poems with a
critical introduction. Joel E. Roache's *Richard Eberhart: The Progress
of an American Poet* (1970) is the most recent critical study.

FROM **Reading the Spirit** *(1936)*

The Groundhog

In June, amid the golden fields,
I saw a groundhog lying dead.
Dead lay he; my senses shook,
And mind outshot our naked frailty.
There lowly in the vigorous summer
His form began its senseless change,
And made my senses waver dim
Seeing nature ferocious in him.
Inspecting close his maggots' might
And seething cauldron of his being,   10
Half with loathing, half with a strange love,
I poked him with an angry stick.
The fever arose, became a flame
And Vigour circumscribed the skies,
Immense energy in the sun,
And through my frame a sunless trembling.
My stick had done nor good nor harm.
Then stood I silent in the day
Watching the object, as before;
And kept my reverence for knowledge   20
Trying for control, to be still,
To quell the passion of the blood;
Until I had bent down on my knees
Praying for joy in the sight of decay.
And so I left; and I returned
In Autumn strict of eye, to see
The sap gone out of the groundhog,
But the bony sodden hulk remained.
But the year had lost its meaning,
And in intellectual chains   30
I lost both love and loathing,
Mured up in the wall of wisdom.
Another summer took the fields again
Massive and burning, full of life,
But when I chanced upon the spot
There was only a little hair left,
And bones bleaching in the sunlight
Beautiful as architecture;
I watched them like a geometer,
And cut a walking stick from a birch.   40
It has been three years, now.
There is no sign of the groundhog.

I stood there in the whirling summer,
My hand capped a withered heart,
And thought of China and of Greece,
Of Alexander in his tent;
Of Montaigne in his tower,
Of Saint Theresa in her wild lament.

In a Hard Intellectual Light

In a hard intellectual light
I will kill all delight,
And I will build a citadel
Too beautiful to tell

O too austere to tell
And far too beautiful to see,
Whose evident distance
I will call the best of me.

And this light of intellect
Will shine on all my desires,   10
It will my flesh protect
And flare my bold constant fires,

For the hard intellectual light
Will lay the flesh with nails.
And it will keep the world bright
And closed the body's soft jails.

And from this fair edifice
I shall see, as my eyes blaze,
The moral grandeur of man
Animating all his days.   20

And peace will marry purpose,
And purity married to grace
Will make the human absolute
As sweet as the human face.

Until my hard vision blears,
And Poverty and Death return
In organ music like the years,
Making the spirit leap, and burn

For the hard intellectual light
That kills all delight   30
And brings the solemn, inward pain
Of truth into the heart again.

ROBERT PENN WARREN (1905–   )

He was born in Todd County, Kentucky, the scene of his first novel, Night Rider (1939). At Vanderbilt University he intended to study the sciences, but his excellent English teachers, Donald Davidson and John Crowe Ransom, turned him to the study of literature. Like his friend Allen Tate, he was an undergraduate member of the Fugitive group, and his first poems were published in that periodical. After his graduation in 1925 and further studies in various universities, he was at Oxford as a Rhodes Scholar, and there he wrote his contribution to I'll Take My Stand—his defense of segregation. At Oxford, too, he "stumbled on" the writing of fiction when he wrote "Prime Leaf," a long story that finally developed into Night Rider.

Ten years before, he had published his first book, a biography of John Brown, and three years before, Thirty-six Poems. Since 1934 he had been teaching at Louisiana State University, and there in association with Cleanth Brooks, he helped found Southern Review. With Brooks, too, he collaborated on Understanding Poetry (1938) and Understanding Fiction (1943), two textbooks that had an inestimable influence on the teaching of college English in the United States.

In 1942 he went to the University of Minnesota, and in 1950 to Yale. In the meantime and after, he produced a series of long and powerful and richly tapestried novels, the best of which is All the King's Men (1946), a complex account of provincial political tyranny that has no equal in American fiction in the treatment of that subject.

He published eight novels between 1939 and 1964, and shorter fiction as well. During those years he was also publishing poetry, critical essays, a play, and occasional polemical prose. His books of poems, after the first, are Eleven Poems on the Same Theme (1942); Selected Poems, 1923–1943 (1944); Brother to Dragons: A Tale in Verse and Voices (1953); Promises: Poems, 1954–1956 (1957); You, Emperors, and Others: Poems, 1957–1960 (1960); Selected Poems New and Old: 1923–1966 (1966); Incarnations: Poems, 1966–1968 (1968); and Audubon: A Vision (1969).

His poetry, beginning in a knotty metaphysical vein presented in tightly wrought structures, has become increasingly more casual, colloquial, lyrical, sensuous, and finally, personal to the point of idiosyncracy. Where now, one wonders, are his old "classical" English teachers? They are present still, conceivably, in Warren's continued but much intensified theme of man's sense of guilt in his collaboration with history.

Warren's short critical studies were published as Selected Essays (1958). His more generally discursive prose works are Segregation: The

Inner Conflict of the South (1956), *in which his youthful views are much altered;* The Legacy of the Civil War (1961); *and* Who Speaks for the Negro? (1965), *one of the most eloquent works in the contemporary literature of civil rights.*

FURTHER READING

The first full-length critique of Warren's work is Leonard Casper, *Robert Penn Warren: The Dark and Bloody Ground* (1960). More recent studies are Charles H. Bohner, *Robert Penn Warren* (1964), and Victor H. Strandberg, *A Colder Fire: The Poetry of Robert Penn Warren* (1965). Paul West's *Robert Penn Warren* (1964) is a brief general introduction. John Lewis Longley edited *Robert Penn Warren: A Collection of Critical Essays* (1965). See also John M. Bradbury, *The Fugitives: A Critical Account* (1958), and Louise Cowan, *The Fugitive Group: A Literary History* (1959).

FROM *Eleven Poems on the Same Theme* (1942)

Original Sin: A Short Story

Nodding, its great head rattling like a gourd,
And locks like seaweed strung on the stinking stone,
The nightmare stumbles past, and you have heard
It fumble your door before it whimpers and is gone:
It acts like the old hound that used to snuffle your door and moan.

You thought you had lost it when you left Omaha,
For it seemed connected then with your grandpa, who
Had a wen on his forehead and sat on the veranda
To finger the precious protuberance, as was his habit to do,
Which glinted in sun like rough garnet or the rich old brain bulging
    through.   10

But you met it in Harvard Yard as the historic steeple
Was confirming the midnight with its hideous racket,
And you wondered how it had come, for it stood so imbecile,
With empty hands, humble, and surely nothing in pocket:
Riding the rods, perhaps—or Grandpa's will paid the ticket.

You were almost kindly then, in your first homesickness,
As it tortured its stiff face to speak, but scarely mewed.
Since then you have outlived all your homesickness,
But have met it in many another distempered latitude:
Oh, nothing is lost, ever lost! at last you understood.   20

It never came in the quantum glare of sun
To shame you before your friends, and had nothing to do
With your public experience or private reformation:
But it thought no bed too narrow—it stood with lips askew
And shook its great head sadly like the abstract Jew.

Never met you in the lyric arsenical meadows
When children call and your heart goes stone in the bosom—
At the orchard anguish never, nor ovoid horror,
Which is furred like a peach or avid like the delicious plum.
It takes no part in your classic prudence or fondled axiom.   30

Not there when you exclaimed: "Hope is betrayed by
Disastrous glory of sea-capes, sun-torment of whitecaps
—There must be a new innocence for us to be stayed by."
But there it stood, after all the timetables, all the maps,
In the crepuscular clutter of *always, always,* or *perhaps.*

You have moved often and rarely left an address,
And hear of the deaths of friends with a sly pleasure,
A sense of cleansing and hope which blooms from distress;
But it has not died, it comes, its hand childish, unsure,
Clutching the bribe of chocolate or a toy you used to treasure.   40

It tries the lock. You hear, but simply drowse:
There is nothing remarkable in that sound at the door.
Later you may hear it wander the dark house
Like a mother who rises at night to seek a childhood picture;
Or it goes to the backyard and stands like an old horse cold in the
    pasture.

Bearded Oaks

The oaks, how subtle and marine,
Bearded, and all the layered light
Above them swims; and thus the scene,
Recessed, awaits the positive night.

So, waiting, we in the grass now lie
Beneath the languorous tread of light:
The grasses, kelp-like, satisfy
The nameless motions of the air.

Upon the floor of light, and time,
Unmurmuring, of polyp made,   10
We rest; we are, as light withdraws,
Twin atolls on a shelf of shade.

Ages to our construction went,
Dim architecture, hour by hour:
And violence, forgot now, lent
The present stillness all its power.

The storm of noon above us rolled,
Of light the fury, furious gold,
The long drag troubling us, the depth:
Dark is unrocking, unrippling, still.   20

Passion and slaughter, ruth, decay
Descend, minutely whispering down,
Silted down swaying steams, to lay
Foundation for our voicelessness.

All our debate is voiceless here,
As all our rage, the rage of stone;
If hope is hopeless, then fearless is fear,
And history is thus undone.

Our feet once wrought the hollow street
With echo when the lamps were dead   30
At windows, once our headlight glare
Disturbed the doe that, leaping fled.

I do not love you less that now
The caged heart makes iron stroke,
Or less that all that light once gave
The graduate dark should now revoke.

We live in time so little time
And we learn all so painfully,
That we may spare this hour's term
To practice for eternity.   40

STANLEY [JASSPON] KUNITZ (1905–   )

Does Kunitz's poem "Father and Son" take on additional meaning or weight if one happens to know that his father committed suicide just before this boy was born? One doubts it. The situation is evident in the poem itself. But beyond that, all our fathers die in the swamps of our wishes, even as we implore them for guidance; and their ghosts, which persist, cannot help us anymore than their living selves, suicidal or murdered or merely dead, which are all the same condition in the end. And in the end, every father probably must turn to his son "the white ignorant hollow of his face."

It is difficult to respond to any poem of Stanley Kunitz's without such
   a personal (and probably disgraceful) response as that. Kunitz is an
   extremely intellectual (metaphysical is the more favored word) poet
   who forces us out of mere intellectuality into the most private
   recesses of our inner lives, which, without poetry, we tend to
   forget.

He himself said, "A poet cannot concern himself with being fair to the
   reader. All poems contain a degree of mystery, as poetry is a discovery of one's hidden self. . . . Poetry is not concerned with communication; it has roots in magic, incantation, and spell-casting."
   All very true, but he, of course, does communicate through those
   very means, and to our profoundest understanding.

Brought up by a mother left with the problems of a bankrupt business,
   Stanley Kunitz managed his public school education in Worcester,
   Massachusetts, and with scholarship assistance, he took an A.B.
   (1926, summa cum laude) and an M.A. at Harvard. For a time he
   was a Sunday feature writer on the Worcester Telegraph, during
   which he wrote a novel that he "heroically destroyed."

In 1927 he became an editor with the H. W. Wilson Company, for
   whom he wrote a book of biographies entitled Living Authors under
   the pseudonymn of "Dilly Tante." Then, with Howard Haycraft, he
   brought out a series of very useful biographical reference works
   on literary figures, present and past, British and American, from
   which he modestly excluded himself. He resigned in 1943, when he
   was called to the Army, for which, as a staff sergeant, he edited a
   news magazine for service men called Ten Minute Break.

Out of the Army, he held teaching assignments at Bennington,
   Potsdam (N.Y.) State Teachers College (where he directed the Summer Workshop in Creative Arts from 1949 to 1953), and the New
   School for Social Research. He has been a visitor on many faculties
   and, since 1963, a lecturer at Columbia.

He has published three volumes of poems—Intellectual Things (1930),
   Passport to the War (1944), and Selected Poems (1958), which won
   the Pulitzer Prize. Ever since winning a Harvard undergraduate
   prize for poetry, he has been the recipient of honors and awards. He
   was among the first group, for example, to receive Ford Foundation
   support in the creative arts (1959). But, honors apart, his fine and
   piercing work has not had the recognition that it merits.

FURTHER READING

For critical estimates see Poets in Progress (1962), edited by Edward
   Hungerford, and Ralph J. Mills, Jr., Contemporary American Poetry
   (1965).

FROM *Passport to the War* *(1944)*

Father and Son

Now in the suburbs and the falling light
I followed him, and now down sandy road
Whiter than bone-dust, through the sweet
Curdle of fields, where the plums
Dropped with their load of ripeness, one by one.
Mile after mile I followed, with skimming feet,
After the secret master of my blood,
Him, steeped in the odor of ponds, whose indomitable love
Kept me in chains. Strode years; stretched into bird:
Raced through the sleeping country where I was young,   10
The silence unrolling before me as I came,
The night nailed like an orange to my brow.

How should I tell him my fable and the fears,
How bridge the chasm in a casual tone,
Saying, "The house, the stucco one you built,
We lost. Sister married and went from home,
And nothing comes back, it's strange, from where she goes.
I lived on a hill that had too many rooms:
Light we could make, but not enough of warmth,
And when the light failed, I climbed under the hill.   20
The papers are delivered every day;
I am alone and never shed a tear."

At the water's edge, where the smothering ferns lifted
Their arms, "Father!" I cried, "Return! You know
The way. I'll wipe the mudstains from your clothes;
No trace, I promise, will remain. Instruct
Your son, whirling between two wars,
In the Gemara of your gentleness,
For I would be a child to those who mourn
And brother to the foundlings of the field   30
And friend of innocence and all bright eyes.
O teach me how to work and keep me kind."
Among the turtles and the lilies he turned to me
The white ignorant hollow of his face.

The Daughters of the Horseleech

The daughters of the horseleech crying "Give! Give!"[1]
Implore the young men for the blood of martyrs.
How shall we keep the old senator alive
Unless we satisfy his thirst for cultures?

Entreat the rat, the weasel, and the fox
To forage for a toothless master;
Have mercy, boys, on the monkey in his box;
Dear. Judas goat, lead out the sheep to slaughter,

For if the warlock with the gilded claws
Withers away, and of his bones are waters,   10
Who will transmute our foreheads into brass
And who will keep his five charming daughters?

THEODORE ROETHKE (1908–1963)

*Physically, Roethke was a great lumbering bear of a man, and it was a
charming and moving experience to hear this unlikely creature recite
his fleeting, notional Blakean poems—some of them about bears—
for children, whom he loved (perhaps because, like Blake, he had
none). I Am! Says the Lamb (1961) is a collection of some of these
verses. But Roethke was also very agile, swift, and quick in his
reflexes. He was a great tennis player, and that points to the quality
of his serious poetry which, as James Dickey has said, reveals "his
beautifully personal sense of form."*

*He was born in Saginaw, Michigan, and he grew up in and around
the greenhouses which were the center of the large floral establishment owned by his family and operated by his father and his uncle.
He was graduated from the University of Michigan and after a brief
period at Harvard held teaching appointments at Lafayette, Pennsylvania State, and Bennington. At the time of his death, he was
professor of English and poet in residence at the University of
Washington in Seattle. He was recognized from the outset as a poet
of consequence (W. H. Auden, for example, praised his earliest
work), and the many prizes and honors and awards that he won
were climaxed by the Pulitzer Prize in 1954. His untimely death cut
off a poetic career that was still in the process of growth, of deepening perceptions into himself and his experience, of an expanding
sense of the possibilities of language.*

[1] Proverbs, 30:15.

His first book, Open House *(1941), contained short, intense lyrics that suggest the influence of W. B. Yeats, but they also mark the qualities that he was to cultivate as particularly his own, notably his openness to experience ("My heart keeps open house / My doors are widely swung") and his imaginative identification with natural things—stones, weeds, flowers. But it was his second volume,* The Lost Son *(1948), in biographical poems that present the experiences of the growing boy in the atmosphere and imagery of greenhouses, that he begins his exploration of his favorite theme, the cycle of birth, growth, decay, and death. In later works—*Praise to the End! *(1951) and* The Waking *(1953) and* Words for the Wind *(1958)— he expands his forms in a new kind of meditativeness and extends his subject matter in the celebration of the spirit in bodily love.*

The Far Field (1964) was the volume at which he was at work when he died. This discovery of the self in the rhythms of nature, of spirituality in physicality, a nearly mystical awareness of wholeness of being within the entirety of things—all this he expressed with an increasing sharpness of detail that in itself seemed to give rise to an often heard ecstatic cry. Even as a strain of melancholy (and premonitions of his own death) deepened, the strain of joy in being swelled.

His selected prose, On the Poet and His Craft *(1965), is a valuable supplement to his* Collected Poems *(1966).*

FURTHER READING

The only biography is Allan Seager, *The Glass House: The Life of Theodore Roethke* (1968); but see also *Selected Letters, 1908–1963* (1968), edited by Ralph J. Mills, Jr. The major critical study is Karl Malkoff, *Theodore Roethke: An Introduction to the Poetry* (1966). Nine briefer critiques have been collected by Arnold Stein in *Theodore Roethke: Essays on the Poetry* (1965). *The Achievement of Theodore Roethke* (1966) is a comprehensive selection of his poetry with an introduction by William J. Martz. Ralph J. Mills, Jr., published a useful brief survey of the poet's work, *Theodore Roethke* (1963).

FROM *The Lost Son and Other Poems* *(1948)*

Frau Bauman, Frau Schmidt, and Frau Schwartze

Gone the three ancient ladies
Who creaked on the greenhouse ladders,
Reaching up white strings
To wind, to wind
The sweet-pea tendrils, the smilax,
Nasturtiums, the climbing
Roses, to straighten
Carnations, red
Chrysanthemums; the stiff
Stems, jointed like corn,   10
They tied and tucked,—
These nurses of nobody else.
Quicker than birds, they dipped
Up and sifted the dirt;
They sprinkled and shook;
They stood astride pipes,
Their skirts billowing out wide into tents,
Their hands twinkling with wet;
Like witches they flew along rows
Keeping creation at ease;   20
With a tendril for needle
They sewed up the air with a stem;
They teased out the seed that the cold kept asleep,—
All the coils, loops, and whorls.
They trellised the sun; they plotted for more than themselves.

I remember how they picked me up, a spindly kid,
Pinching and poking my thin ribs
Till I lay in their laps, laughing,
Weak as a whiffet;
Now, when I'm alone and cold in my bed,   30
They still hover over me,
These ancient leathery crones,
With their bandannas stiffened with sweat,
And their thorn-bitten wrists,
And their snuff-laden breath blowing lightly over me in my first sleep.

Dolor

I have known the inexorable sadness of pencils,
Neat in their boxes, dolor of pad and paper-weight,
All the misery of manilla folders and mucilage,
Desolation in immaculate public places,
Lonely reception room, lavatory, switchboard,
The unalterable pathos of basin and pitcher,
Ritual of multigraph, paper-clip, comma,
Endless duplication of lives and objects.
And I have seen dust from the walls of institutions,
Finer than flour, alive, more dangerous than silica,   10
Sift, almost invisible, through long afternoons of tedium,
Dropping a fine film on nails and delicate eyebrows,
Glazing the pale hair, the duplicate gray standard faces.

FROM **Words for the Wind** (1958)

I Knew a Woman

I knew a woman, lovely in her bones,
When small birds sighed, she would sigh back at them;
Ah, when she moved, she moved more ways than one:
The shapes a bright container can contain!
Of her choice virtues only gods should speak,
Or English poets who grew up on Greek
(I'd have them sing in chorus, cheek to cheek).

How well her wishes went! She stroked my chin,
She taught me Turn, and Counter-turn, and Stand;
She taught me Touch, that undulant white skin;   10
I nibbled meekly from her proffered hand;
She was the sickle; I, poor I, the rake,
Coming behind her for her pretty sake
(But what prodigious mowing we did make).

Love likes a gander, and adores a goose;
Her full lips pursed, the errant note to seize;
She played it quick, she played it light and loose;
My eyes, they dazzled at her flowing knees;
Her several parts could keep a pure repose,
Or one hip quiver with a mobile nose   20
(She moved in circles, and those circles moved).

Let seed be grass, and grass turn into hay:
I'm martyr to a motion not my own;
What's freedom for? To know eternity.
I swear she cast a shadow white as stone.
But who would count eternity in days?
These old bones live to learn her wanton ways:
(I measure time by how a body sways).

ELIZABETH BISHOP (1911–   )

*Elizabeth Bishop is the supreme living poet of what one can only call
the matter of fact—and by that one means to suggest something
about both her subjects and her special style. She never raises her
voice, she never beats her breast, she never importunes us, she
never bangs down a resounding conclusion, or, really, any conclusion at all. She drifts into her poems on a quiet observation that is
probably, for all her quietness, in fact astonishing:*

Think of the storm roaming the sky uneasily
like a dog looking for a place to sleep in,
listen to it growling; . . .

*Then, as if from a considerable distance, she lets us observe the
progress of the storm (lets us? Makes us know a storm, as we never
have, but out of it), and ends with a man sleeping in a boat, a man
who had hardly "been disturbed." And she has drifted out of the
poem, but we are still in it, rounding it out from the echoes she has
left in our heads.*

*She is the calm observer of fact, of landscape and seascape, of terrain,
of creatures; of things simply themselves, not symbols; but in the
very clarity of their actuality, mysterious and extraordinary. There is
something of Marianne Moore here, but without the exoticism;
something of Stevens, without the luxury. Her very plainness is her
wonder.*

*Miss Bishop was born in Worcester, Massachusetts, and was graduated
from Vassar College in 1934. For two years she traveled all over
Europe, and then for four years she lived in Key West and, after
that, in Mexico and Nova Scotia. Her first book,* North and South
*(1946), was completed on a Houghton Mifflin Fellowship, and she
has had many awards since then. In 1949–1950 she was Consultant
in Poetry at the Library of Congress. In 1951 she moved to South
America where she lived for some years in a mountain town near
Rio de Janeiro; with the editors of* Life *magazine, she has written a*

prose work called Brazil *(1962). Her second book of verse,* Poems:
North and South—A Cold Spring *(1955), consisted of thirty poems
from her first book and nineteen new ones, and it won the Pulitzer
Prize. This was followed with a volume appropriately entitled* Questions of Travel *(1965), and that by* The Ballad of the Burglar of
Babylon *(1968). She has published occasional short stories, and we
now have her* Complete Poems *(1969).*

FURTHER READING

For a critical estimate see Anne Stevenson, *Elizabeth Bishop* (1966),
and Ralph J. Mills, Jr., *Contemporary American Poetry* (1965).

FROM *Poems: North and South—*
A Cold Spring (1955)

Little Exercise

Think of the storm roaming the sky uneasily
like a dog looking for a place to sleep in,
listen to it growling.

Think how they must look now, the mangrove keys
lying out there unresponsive to the lightning
in dark, coarse-fibred families,

where occasionally a heron may undo his head,
shake up his feathers, make an uncertain comment
when the surrounding water shines.

Think of the boulevard and the little palm trees   10
all stuck in rows, suddenly revealed
as fistfuls of limp fish-skeletons.

It is raining there. The boulevard
and its broken sidewalks with weeds in every crack,
are relieved to be wet, the sea to be freshened.

Now the storm goes away again in a series
of small, badly lit battle-scenes,
each in "Another part of the field."

Think of someone sleeping in the bottom of a row-boat
tied to a mangrove root or the pile of a bridge;   20
think of him as uninjured, barely disturbed.

FROM *Questions of Travel* (1965)

Sunday, 4 a.m.

An endless and flooded
dreamland, lying low,
cross-and wheel-studded
like a tick-tack-toe.

At the right, ancillary,
"Mary"'s close and blue.
Which Mary? Aunt Mary?
Tall Mary Stearns I knew?

The old kitchen knife box,
full of rusty nails,   10
is at the left. A high *vox*
humana somewhere wails:

The gray horse needs shoeing!
It's always the same!
What are you doing,
there, beyond the frame?

If you're the donor,
you might do that much!
Turn on the light. Turn over.
On the bed a smutch—   20

black-and-gold gesso
on the altered cloth.
The cat jumps to the window;
in his mouth's a moth.

Dream dream confronting,
now the cupboard's bare.
The cat's gone a-hunting.
The brook feels for the stair.

The world seldom changes,
but the wet foot dangles   30
until a bird arranges
two notes at right angles.

JOSEPHINE MILES (1911–   )

Josephine Miles was born in Chicago, but she was brought to California as a young child and, except for very occasional travel, has spent her entire life there. She was an undergraduate at the University of California at Los Angeles and then did graduate work at Berkeley, where she took her Ph.D. in 1938, became a member of the department of English, and has been one of its most distinguished teachers ever since. As the only woman holding a tenure appointment in a group of about forty-five men, despite physical handicaps that condemn most people to helpless invalidism, she is known as the teacher who has the widest and deepest acquaintance in the department among both graduate and undergraduate students. Her office is always thronged with students, and they flow in and out of her little house in streams for informal conversations about poetry and ideas. She corresponds with an astonishing number of former students, some of whom have not been on campus for years. Within her department, she gives particular attention to the course in freshman composition and is a constant source of ideas for the vitalization of this pedagogical area that can so readily lapse into the dull, the mechanical, the plodding.

Through her many critical and scholarly works, climaxed by Eras and Modes in English Poetry *(1957), she is widely known as a student of poetics and stylistics. Through her poems, beginning with* Lines at Intersection *(1957) and proceeding through three more volumes to* Poems: 1930–1960 *(1960)—this latter followed by* Kinds of Affection *(1967) and a number of pamphlets of verses coming out of the immediate civic and social problems of the sixties—she has established herself as a poet who always speaks in what is distinctively her own tone and manner. She cannot be mistaken for any other poet.*

Most of her poems are very short, wasting no words, spelling out no directional comments on themselves. They are shrewd and, as has been said, "narrow-eyed" in their observations, quick, penetrating, and odd. They deliberately choose the small over the large and expansive, which is not at all to say that they are not ample in their wisdom. They are like intense gnomic statements chiseled on stones, and if they sometimes puzzle, they continue to reverberate like ancient sayings.

FROM **Poems on Several Occasions** *(1941)*

**Purchase of a Blue, Green, or
Orange Ode**

Jake's store past Pindaric mountain
Over the wash is the only place in a day's ride
To get odes at except close to Mesa City side.

He has one glass a dusty one there
Full of blue green and orange odes sticky but o k,
And many come by on that account that way.

Scramble down off the hot flats, swallow a lot of universal wind,
Hear that lone freight pushing around sandy acre,
And they need for the slow swipes one green jawbreaker.

A slug of sweet, a globe of a barber's pole,   10
A suck of a human victory out of a crowd,
Sugared, colored, out of a jar, an ode.

FROM **Poems: 1930—1960** *(1960)*

The Savages

As we rowed from our ships and set foot on the shore
In the still coves,
We met our images.

Our brazen images emerged from the mirrors of the wood
Like yelling shadows,
So we searched our souls,

And in that hell and pit of everyman
Placed the location of their ruddy shapes.
We must be cruel to ourselves.

Then through the underbrush we cut our hopes   10
Forest after forest to within
The inner hush where Mississippi flows

And were in ambush at the very source,
Scalped to the cortex. Yet bought them off.
It was an act of love to seek their salvation.

President Jackson asked,
What good man would prefer a forested country ranged with savages

To our extensive republic studded with cities
With all the improvements art can devise or industry execute? [1]

Pastor Smiley [2] inquired,   20
What good man would allow his sins or his neighbors'
To put on human dress and run in the wilds
To leap out on innocent occasions?

Miss Benedict proposed,
The partial era of enlightenment in which we live
Bring Dionysus to the mesa and the cottonwood grove,
And floats Apollo to the barrows of the civic group
To ratify entreaties and to harp on hope. [3]

Professor Roy Harvey Pearce [4] quoted,
These savages are outlandish Tartars and Cain's children,   30
Though someone reported once, "They do not withhold assent
From the truth set forth in a credible manner."
Is it possible?

Henry David Thoreau,
The most popular highbrow overseas reading-material
For our armed forces, because while they work and wait
They see before them in the green shade
His ruddy image, said, as his last word when he died, *Indians*. [5]

Reading today this manual of wisdom,
In the still coves   40
We meet our images

And, in ambush at the very source,
Would buy them off. It is an act of love
To seek their salvation.

One party to the purchase
Receipts the purchase price and hands us back
His token of negotiation which redeems:

We cannibals must help these Christians. [6]

[1] From his Second Annual Message, December 6, 1830; in Roy Harvey Pearce, *The Savages of America* (1953), 2, 1, note 4.

[2] The poet's invention.

[3] Ruth Benedict, *Patterns of Culture* (1934), 4.

[4] Scholar-teacher (1919–   ). *Savages*, 10, 4; the poet has rearranged the original and substituted Cain for Noah. The following quotation is from *Annual Letter of the English Province of the Society of Jesus* (1639), *Savages*, 1, 3, note 29.

[5] *Savages*, 5, 2, note 32.

[6] Queequeg in Melville's *Moby Dick* (1851), end of chapter 13; *Savages*, 7, note 5.

DELMORE SCHWARTZ (1913–1966)

Of all these poets, Delmore Schwartz was the "golden boy." He began publishing his poetry when he was hardly twenty. When Jay Laughlin founded his avant-garde press, New Directions, *in 1936, Delmore Schwartz was among his earliest discoveries and appeared in the first annual,* New Directions in Prose and Poetry *(1937). Later he was to publish an essay on T. S. Eliot as "culture hero," but he himself was a culture hero to liberal intellectuals and other poets in those early years. And he had some strong sense of his special being, of his uniqueness, of his identity ("Delmore! What a pretty name, Mrs. Goldmark—" one of the characters in his play,* Shenandoah *[1941], observes)—and this without any arrogance, simply as fact. But he also labored under some sense of special doom. He brings to mind the young Rimbaud, whose* A Season in Hell *Schwartz translated (1939). He was tortured by a feeling of betrayal. (He is said to have remarked to a friend, in self-defense, "Even paranoids have real enemies.") His torment grew to a cruel disease. Drinking did not help. Nervous collapses hacked into his work. His academic career ended. Marriages were wrecked. Old friendships were destroyed when those who held him dearest tried to help him. One felt a wild despair when in 1966 the newspapers announced that a body found dead of a heart attack in the hallway of a sordid Broadway hotel had been identified as his.*

*He was born into a Brooklyn Jewish family that figures in much of his writing—*Shenandoah: A Verse Play; Genesis: Book One *(1943); and in many of the short stories of* The World Is a Wedding *(1948). He was educated at Columbia, the University of Wisconsin, New York University, and Harvard, where his interest was in philosophy, as it always would be. He had the power of dramatizing ideas in poetry as few have had, and his first book of poems,* In Dreams Begin Responsibilities *(1938), seemed to open a career that would be more than brilliant, that would be splendid and profound and triumphant. He became an editor for* Partisan Review *in its liveliest years. He published many critical essays (which should be collected) in* Partisan, Kenyon, Southern Review—*essays still marked by their fresh independence and easy, ranging qualities. Finally, he brought together the volume called* Selected Poems: Summer Knowledge *(1959), which contains many new poems (including the lovely echoing "Gold Morning, Sweet Prince") and many revisions of earlier poems.*

The life and the work took on the quality of legend, which lingers: in 1968, John Berryman dedicated his volume, His Toy, His Dream, His Rest, *to "the sacred memory of Delmore Schwartz."*

FROM **In Dreams Begin Responsibilities** (1938)

In the Naked Bed, in Plato's Cave

In the naked bed, in Plato's cave,[1]
Reflected headlights slowly slid the wall,
Carpenters hammered under the shaded window,
Wind troubled the window curtains all night long,
A fleet of trucks strained uphill, grinding,
Their freights covered, as usual.
The ceiling lightened again, the slanting diagram
Slid slowly forth.
                         Hearing the milkman's chop,
His striving up the stair, the bottle's chink,   10
I rose from bed, lit a cigarette,
And walked to the window. The stony street
Displayed the stillness in which buildings stand,
The street-lamp's vigil and the horse's patience.
The winter sky's pure capital
Turned me back to bed with exhausted eyes.

Strangeness grew in the motionless air. The loose
Film grayed. Shaking wagons, hooves' waterfalls,
Sounded far off, increasing, louder and nearer.
A car coughed, starting. Morning, softly   20
Melting the air, lifted the half-covered chair
From underseas, kindled the looking-glass,
Distinguished the dresser and the white wall.
The bird called tentatively, whistled, called,
Bubbled and whistled, so! Perplexed, still wet
With sleep, affectionate, hungry and cold. So, so,
O son of man, the ignorant night, the travail
Of early morning, the mystery of beginning
Again and again,
                         while History is unforgiven.   30

[1] *The Republic*, beginning of book 7.

FROM **Summer Knowledge** (1959)

Gold Morning, Sweet Prince [1]

What the sad and passionate gay player of Avon [2] avowed
With vivid exactness, eloquent variety is, as immense
As the sea is. The sea which neither the humble nor the proud
Can dam, control or master. No matter what our sense
Of existence, or whence we come or where we hope and seek
He knew us all before we were, he knew the strong, the weak,
The silly, the reticent, the pious, the powerful, the experience
Of fortune, sudden fame, extremes reversed, inevitable loss
Whether on land or sea. He knew mortality's immortality
And essential uncertainty, as he knew the land and sea.   10

He knew the reality of nobility.
He saw the cowering, towering power of treachery.
He hated the flakes and butterflies of lechery.
And he believed, at times, in truth, hope, loyalty and charity.

See: he saw what was and what is and what has yet to come to be: [3]
A gentle monarch murdered in helpless sleep.[4]
A girl by Regent Hypocrisy seduced.[5]
A child by Archduke Ambition stabbed and killed.[6]
A loving loyal wife by a husband loyal and brave,
Falsely suspected, by a handkerchief accused,[7]   20
Stabbed by his love, his innocence, his trust
In the glib cleverness of a self-hating knave.[8]

Look: Ophelia lolls and babbles in the river named Forever,[9]
Never Never Never Never Never.[10]
Cordelia is out of breath [11] *and Lear*
Has learned at last that flattery is clever

[1] Cf. Horatio's farewell in *Hamlet*, 5, 2.

[2] Shakespeare himself.

[3] A general recognition of the amplitude of Shakespeare's vision, the line seems to echo *Macbeth* particularly.

[4] Duncan in *Macbeth*, or Hamlet's father.

[5] The attempted seduction of Isabella by the Lord Deputy Angelo in *Measure for Measure*?

[6] The murder of Macduff's son in *Macbeth*, 4, 3; or of the young princes in *Richard III*, 4, 3?

[7] Desdemona's murder by Othello.

[8] Iago in *Othello*.

[9] Ophelia's suicide by drowning in *Hamlet*.

[10] *King Lear*, 5, 3.

[11] Cordelia's death by hanging at the end of *King Lear*.

That words are free, sentiments inexpensive, vows
And declarations worthless and priceless: at last he knows
How true love is sometimes speechless, always sincere.
He knows—and knows too late—that love was very near and dear.　　　**30**

Are all hearts and all girls always betrayed?
Is love never beyond lust, disgust, and distrust?
See: it is clear: Duncan is in his grave,
While Desdemona weeps beneath the willow tree,
Having been granted little time to weep, pray or rave:
Is this the truth, the truth which is one, eternal, and whole?
Surely the noble, the innocent, the gifted and the brave
Sometimes—surely, at times—prevail. Yet if one living soul
Is caught by cruelty and killed by trust
Whence is our consolation above or before the grave?　　　**40**

Ripeness is all: [12] *the rest is silence.* [13] Love
Is all; we are such stuff as love has made us [14]
And our little life, green, ripe, or rotten, is what it is
Because of love accepted, rejected, refused and jilted, faded, raided,
　　neglected or betrayed.
Some are defeated, some are mistreated, some are fulfilled, some come to
　　flower and succeed
In knowing the patience of energy from the dark root to the rounding
　　fruit.
And if this were not true, if love were not kind and cruel,
Generous and unjust, heartless and irresistible, painful to the savant and
　　gentle to the fool,
Fecund and various, wasteful and precarious, lavish, savage, greedy and
　　tender, begetting the lion and the lamb
The peacock, the spaniel, the tiger, the lizard, the chicken hawk and the
　　dove,　　　**50**
All would be nothing much, all would be trivial, nothing would be
　　enough, love would not be love.
For, as there is no game and no victory when no one loses
So there is no choice but the choice of love, unless one chooses
Never to love, seeking immunity, discovering nothingness.

This is the only sanctuary, this is the one asylum unless
We hide in a dark ark, and deny, refuse to believe in hope's conscious-
　　ness,
Deny hope's reality, until hope descends, in the unknown, hidden and
　　ultimate love,

[12] *King Lear,* 5, 2; Edgar's speech to his father, Gloucester, at end of the scene.
[13] *Hamlet,* 5, 2; Hamlet's last words.
[14] Cf. *The Tempest,* 4, 1, Prospero's speech to Ferdinand and Miranda, "We are
such stuff /As dreams are made on," etc.

Crying forever with all the others who are damned and hopeless that *love
is not love*.[15]

Gold morning, sweet prince, black night has always descended and has
    always ended,
Gold morning, prince of Avon, sovereign and king   60
Of reality, hope, and speech, may all the angels sing
With all the sweetness and all the truth with which you sang of anything
    and everything.

KARL [JAY] SHAPIRO (1913–   )

*Karl Shapiro was born and brought up in Baltimore, where he attended
public schools from which he went on to the University of Virginia.
There he was more interested in writing poetry than in hard studying, and he left to work and study on his own. He wrote a good deal,
including long poems and verse plays, and destroyed nearly everything; but in 1935 he published, at his own expense, a small volume
called* Poems. *In 1937 scholarship assistance enabled him to enroll
at the Johns Hopkins for two years. Again he withdrew, this time
to become a salaried library student in the Pratt Library, Baltimore,
but he had not finished a year there when he was drafted into the
Army (March, 1941), was shipped into the Pacific theater, and did
not return to the United States until 1945.*

*In the meantime, however, he established a considerable reputation as
a poet, with a devoted fiancée (later his wife) acting as editor and
agent at home. In 1941 New Directions published a group of his
poems in* Five Young American Poets. Person, Place and Thing
*(1942) was praised by people like Allen Tate, who said that not since
the advent of Eliot had poetry seen "that final honesty which is rare,
unpleasant, and indispensable in a poet of our time." This work,
like the poems that followed in* V-Letter and Other Poems *(1944),
while written in conventional forms (he even wrote an occasional
sonnet), had something of Eliot's irony and weariness. A change
was evident in his blank-verse* Essay on Rime *(1945), which attacked
the "confusions" of contemporary poetry "in Prosody, in Language,
and in Belief," and while it was praised by many, it infuriated most
poets.*

*From this point on there was a turning away from what Shapiro re-
garded as fashionable attitudes and fashionable models to, finally, a
reassertion of the importance of Whitman, a free prosody, and a
large cosmic view of things. The new work in* Poems, 1940–1953,

---

[15] Shakespeare's sonnet 116, "Let me not to the marriage of true minds," line 2.

(1953); Poems of a Jew (1958); The Bourgeois Poet *(1964), which consists of prose poems;* Selected Poems *(1968); and* White-haired Lover *(1968) all carry on this later antimodernist view and more informal practice.*

After a year as Consultant in Poetry to the Library of Congress (1947), Shapiro taught for a time at the Johns Hopkins, then went to Chicago to edit Poetry *and teach at Loyola (1950 to 1956), and then to the University of Nebraska, where he edited* Prairie Schooner. *In recent years he has been on the faculty of the University of California at Davis.*

His polemical prose, contained in Beyond Criticism *(1953) and* In Defense of Ignorance *(1960), carries on what can only be called his "anti-intellectual" position.*

FURTHER READING

For a critical opinion of Shapiro's work, see Stephen Stepanchev, *American Poetry Since 1945* (1965), and Hyatt H. Waggoner, *American Poets from the Puritans to the Present* (1968).

FROM **Poems of a Jew** *(1958)*

University

To hurt the Negro and avoid the Jew
Is the curriculum. In mid-September
The entering boys, identified by hats,
Wander in a maze of mannered brick
    Where boxwood and magnolia brood
    And columns with imperious stance
    Like rows of ante-bellum girls
        Eye them, outlanders.

In whited cells, on lawns equipped for peace,
Under the arch, and lofty banister,   10
Equals shake hands, unequals blankly pass;
The exemplary weather whispers, "Quiet, quiet"
    And visitors on tiptoe leave
    For the raw North, the unfinished West,
    As the young, detecting an advantage,
        Practice a face.

Where, on their separate hill, the colleges,
Like manor houses of an older law,

Gaze down embankments on a land in fee,
The Deans, dry spinsters over family plate,   *20*
    Ring out the English name like coin,
    Humor the snob and lure the lout.
    Within the precincts of this world
        Poise is a club.

But on the neighboring range, misty and high,
The past is absolute: some luckless race
Dull with inbreeding and conformity
Wears out its heart, and comes barefoot and bad
    For charity or jail. The scholar
    Sanctions their obsolete disease;   *30*
    The gentleman revolts with shame
        At his ancestor.

And the true nobleman, once a democrat,
Sleeps on his private mountain. He was one
Whose thought was shapely and whose dream was broad;
This school he held his art and epitaph.
    But now it takes from him his name,
    Falls open like a dishonest look,
    And shows us, rotted and endowed,
        Its senile pleasure.   *40*

Lord, I Have Seen Too Much

Lord, I have seen too much for one who sat
In quiet at his window's luminous eye
And puzzled over house and street and sky,
Safe only in the narrowest habitat;
Who studied peace as if the world were flat,
The edge of nature linear and dry,
But faltered at each brilliant entity
Drawn like a prize from some magician's hat.

Too suddenly this lightning is disclosed:
Lord, in a day the vacuum of Hell,   *10*
The mouth of blood, the ocean's ragged jaw,
More than embittered Adam ever saw
When driven from Eden to the East to dwell,
The lust of godhead hideously exposed!

RANDALL JARRELL (1914–1965)

Although Randall Jarrell even in his lifetime was recognized as one of the most remarkable poets of the Second World War and the two decades that followed, he was remarkable beyond that in sheer versatility. He published some of our best and most caustic essays, both literary and general, in Poetry and the Age *(1953),* A Sad Heart at the Supermarket *(1962), and* A Third Book of Criticism *(1969). He made translations of Rilke and Chekhov and Goethe, most of them not yet published but promised. He wrote three pleasing books for children and, more notably, one of the most readable, witty, and corrosive novels of this century in* Pictures from an Institution *(1954), a satirical novel about faculty life in a progressive college for women.*

Such versatility seems to be characteristic of men who, even if they were not born in Tennessee as Jarrell was, were students at Vanderbilt University, from which he was graduated in 1935. Certainly he lived up to the example of men like Ransom, Tate, and Warren. Like them, too, he taught in various colleges and universities— Kenyon, Texas, Sarah Lawrence, North Carolina.

In the year that he published Blood for a Stranger *(1942), he enlisted in the Army Air Corps, and his military service, which did not end until the end of the war, had everything to do with the character of his next two books,* Little Friend, Little Friend *(1945) and* Losses *(1948). About his war poems, including the famous "Death of the Ball Turret Gunner," some readers have complained that Jarrell did not write about the suffering of individual men in wartime but about generalized man. That, of course, was his whole point—war does not recognize the individual.*

Of his poems, Wilfred Owen, coming out of an earlier war, could write, "The poetry is in the pity." Alas, no more! we are in the space age, far beyond pity. One more book, The Seven-League Crutches *(1951), preceded Jarrell's Selected Poems (1955), which made quite clear his central question—and in his poems it is a question, only by our collaboration is it a denunciation: How can the human being survive inside a machine? His language was always unvarnished and direct; he wrote, as Karl Shapiro said, in "Plain American, which dogs and cats can read."*

There were two further volumes before the publication of The Complete Poems *(1969), which appeared several years after his accidental death in a dark night on a country road.*

FURTHER READING

Randall Jarrell, 1914–1965 (1967) is a commorative volume of reminiscences by friends and fellow poets, edited by Robert Lowell, Peter Taylor, and Robert Penn Warren. See also *Poets in Progress* (1962), edited by Edward Hungerford.

FROM **Little Friend, Little Friend** *(1945)*

The Death of the Ball Turret Gunner

From my mother's sleep I fell into the State,
And I hunched in its belly till my wet fur froze.
Six miles from earth, loosed from its dream of life,
I woke to black flak and the nightmare fighters.
When I died they washed me out of the turret with a hose.

FROM **The Seven-League Crutches** *(1951)*

The Orient Express

One looks from the train
Almost as one looked as a child. In the sunlight
What I see still seems to me plain,
I am safe; but at evening
As the lands darken, a questioning
Precariousness comes over everything.

Once after a day of rain
I lay longing to be cold; and after a while
I was cold again, and hunched shivering
Under the quilt's many colors, gray   10
With the dull ending of the winter day.
Outside me there were a few shapes
Of chairs and tables, things from a primer;
Outside the window
There were the chairs and tables of the world. . . .
I saw that the world
That had seemed to me the plain

Gray mask of all that was strange
Behind it—of all that *was*—was all.

But it is beyond belief.   20
One thinks, "Behind everything
An unforced joy, an unwilling
Sadness (a willing sadness, a forced joy)
Moves changelessly"; one looks from the train
And there is something, the same thing
Behind everything: all these little villages,
A passing woman, a field of grain,
The man who says good-bye to his wife—
A path through a wood full of lives, and the train
Passing, after all unchangeable   30
And not now ever to stop, like a heart—

It is like any other work of art.
It is and never can be changed.
Behind everything there is always
The unknown unwanted life.

JOHN BERRYMAN (1914–   )

Berryman's one hundred and fifty-third Dream Song begins:

I'm cross with god who has wrecked this generation.
First he seized Ted, then Richard, Randall and now Delmore.
In between he gorged on Sylvia Plath.
That was a first rate haul. He left alive
fools I could number like a kitchen knife
but Lowell he did not touch.

> *Nor Berryman himself; except with some madness as well as out-
> rage. His poems have always been characterized by their nervous
> intensity, but this has now reached such a high degree that it
> threatens to explode into the inarticulate.*

Born in McAlester, Oklahoma, he took degrees from Columbia and
  Cambridge and returned to the United States to teach, first at
  Wayne, then at Harvard and Princeton, and since 1955, at the
  University of Minnesota. By then he had published widely: "Twenty
  Poems" in the New Directions Five Young American Poets (1940);
  Poems (1942); The Dispossessed (1948); and a biography of Stephen
  Crane (1950). Then came the long poem that established his repu-
  tation, Homage to Mistress Bradstreet (1956). "He bided his time

and made the poem of his generation," said his fellow poet, Robert Fitzgerald, and Edmund Wilson pronounced it the most distinguished American long poem since The Waste Land.

Some of his more recent work is included in Berryman's Sonnets *(1967), a sequence of 115 Petrarchan sonnets about an illicit summer love affair, and* Short Poems *(1967), new work together with some previously published. But the later work that has aroused the most interest is the* Dream Songs, *which he began in 1955, published in part in* 77 Dream Songs *(1964), more amply in* His Toy, His Dream, His Rest: 308 Dream Songs *(1968), and, presumably in their totality, in* The Dream Songs *(1969).*

The idiom of these poems is as surprising as it is new. The technique seems to have developed out of Mistress Bradstreet, *in which the two poets' voices alternate in a kind of dialog and often seem to merge, as if, in the suggestion of M. L. Rosenthal, they are the voices of a divided self. In* The Dream Songs, *all the multiple voices of a much divided self speak (and mock and grieve and cajole and jeer and sing). But the major voice is that of the persona, Henry Pussy-Cat, not the whole poet perhaps but a large part of him, as the obvious autobiographical elements demonstrate, particularly the elegies for all the "dear men," those dead poets who were Berryman's friends and mentors. The influences that speak in this long poem, consisting of 385 short ones (usually eighteen lines each) are, among others, Hopkins, Pound, and Williams. Certainly it suggests both the* Cantos *and* Paterson *in that it has no definable structural limits; it could continue forever. What it is about is hard to say (the life of memory, perhaps), unless one wishes to say that it is about a poet writing a poem that is the poem one is reading.*

Berryman's most recent volume, a long poem called Love and Fame *(1970), is a kind of biographia literaria in difficult and fascinating verse.*

FURTHER READING

Carol Holmes Johnson treats the body of Berryman's work in *Reason's Double Agents* (1966).

FROM **77 Dream Songs** (1964)

There sat down, once, a thing on Henry's heart

29

There sat down, once, a thing on Henry's [1] heart
só heavy, if he had a hundred years
& more, & weeping, sleepless, in all them time
Henry could not make good.
Starts again always in Henry's ears
the little cough somewhere, and odour, a chime.

And there is another thing he has in mind
like a grave Sienese face a thousand years
would fail to blur the still profiled reproach of. Ghastly,
with open eyes, he attends, blind.   10
All the bells say: too late. This is not for tears;
thinking.

But never did Henry, as he thought he did,
end anyone and hacks her body up
and hide the pieces, where they may be found.
He knows: he went over everyone, & nobody's missing.
Often he reckons, in the dawn, them up.
Nobody is ever missing.

[1] The poet has said: "The poem then [meaning the entire sequence from which this and the following selection are taken] ... is essentially about an imaginary character (not the poet, not me) named Henry, a white American in early middle age sometimes in blackface, who has suffered an irreversible loss and talks about himself sometimes in the first person, sometimes in the third, sometimes even in the second; he has a friend, never named, who addresses him as Mr Bones and variants thereof." The reference is to a minstrel show, a form of theatrical entertainment popular in the late nineteenth and early twentieth centuries in the United States.

He lay in the middle of
the world, and twitcht

53
He lay in the middle of the world, and twitcht.
More Sparine [1] for Pelides,
human (half) & down here as he is,
with probably insulting mail to open
and certainly unworthy words to hear
and his unforgivable memory.

—I seldom *go* to *films*. They are too exciting,
said the Honourable Possum.[2]
—It takes me so long to read the 'paper,
said to me one day a novelist hot as a firecracker,   10
because I have to identify myself with everyone in it,
including the corpses, pal.'

Kierkegaard wanted a society, to refuse to read 'papers,
and that was not, friends, his worst idea.
Tiny Hardy, toward the end, refused to say *anything*,
a programme adopted early on by long Housman,
and Gottfried Benn [3]
said:—We are using our own skins for wallpaper and we cannot win.

ROBERT [TRAILL SPENCE] LOWELL [JR.] (1917–   )

*Lowell's distinguished family background is apparently at once his
burden and a large source of his strength, as it is of his subject
matter. Born in Boston, he was sent to the St. Mark's School, where
Richard Eberhart was then teaching. He disliked Harvard and what
seemed to him the stuffy pedantry of its literature professors, and
after a summer with the Allen Tates in Tennessee, he soon transferred to Kenyon College, where in John Crowe Ransom and Randall
Jarrell he found sympathetic mentors for his early poetry, which
was highly compressed, opaque, intense, intricately symbolic. Just
before his graduation in 1940, he married the novelist Jean Stafford
and was converted to Roman Catholicism.*

*Living in New York during the Second World War, he was refused the
status of conscientious objector and was sent to jail. After his re-*

---

[1] Pharmaceutical trademark for promazine, a tranquilizer.
[2] T. S. Eliot?
[3] (1886–1956), German physician, critic, and expressionistic poet.

lease, he and his wife moved to Damariscotta Mills, Maine, and he published his first volume of poems, Land of Unlikeness (1944), rebellious poems that saw war as the great sign of the world's corruption and sought for peace in his new faith. Many of these poems, together with many new ones, appeared in his second volume, Lord Weary's Castle (1946), which won him the Pulitzer Prize at twenty-nine. He led a tortured inner life and neither honors nor his marriage nor his religion could calm it; in 1948 he renounced both of the latter.

Remarried in the next year to the writer Elizabeth Hardwick, he tried teaching here and there, but most of the next three years he spent abroad and published a third volume, The Mills of the Kavanaughs (1951). After the death of his mother in 1954, the Lowells moved to Boston in the hope of recapturing his roots.

And indeed an extraordinary development did take place. The Lowells had their first child Harriet, and they lived a pleasant social life, seeing many poets, and for five years Lowell taught at Boston University. But the great thing was that he wrote his prose autobiography, "91 Revere Street," and, contemplating his own heritage and his own immediate chaotic psychological situation within the larger chaos of the world, he wrote his first astonishing "autobiographical" poems. The old, tight, choked forms would no longer do. Speaking of much contemporary poetry, he said that in its devotion to craft and skill, "...the writing seems divorced from culture somehow...this Alexandrian poetry is very brilliant," but "I thought it was getting increasingly stifling." And turning then to himself: "I couldn't get my experience into tight metrical forms...the meter plastered difficulties and mannerisms on what I was trying to say...."

In the looser lines and more open forms that have characterized his later poems, he finds that he must work just as hard, but he hopes that—even when he alters autobiographical fact—his readers feel they are "getting the real Robert Lowell."

The publication of Life Studies (1959), which appeared at about the time that the Lowells moved back to New York, was the turning point in our later poetry. It contained, beside many new poems and the prose memoir, a number of translations, or "imitations." Of these he has now done many including those in the volumes called Imitations (1961) and The Voyage & Other Versions of Poems by Baudelaire. For the Union Dead (1964) extended and deepened his own liberation. He has published three verse dramas on American themes in The Old Glory (1965); Prometheus Bound (1969), an adaptation of Aeschylus with powerful contemporary overtones; and a translation of Racine's Phaedra (1967). His own poems keep coming: Near the Ocean (1967) and Notebook: 1967–1968 (1969), revised and expanded in 1970. Deeply concerned with the problems of our diseased

*times, his always generous mind presents his own racked experience
as a troubled, troubling reflection of them. His reputation now and
the amplitude of his production suggest that it is time for his first
volume of collected poems.*

FURTHER READING

The major study is Hugh B. Staples, *Robert Lowell: The First Twenty
Years* (1962). See also two books by Jerome Mazzaro: *The Achievement of Robert Lowell, 1939–1959* (1960), and *The Poetic Themes
of Robert Lowell* (1965); Ralph J. Mills, Jr., *Contemporary American Poetry* (1965); and M. L. Rosenthal, *The New Poets* (1967).
Thomas Parkinson edited *Robert Lowell: A Collection of Critical
Essays* (1968).

FROM **Life Studies** *(1959)*

Grandparents

They're altogether otherworldly now,
those adults champing for their ritual Friday spin
to pharmacist and five-and-ten in Brockton.
Back in my throw-away and shaggy span
of adolescence, Grandpa still waves his stick
like a policeman;
Grandmother, like a Mohammedan, still wears her thick
lavender mourning and touring veil;
the Pierce Arrow clears its throat in a horse-stall.
Then the dry road dust rises to whiten   10
the fatigued elm leaves—
the nineteenth century, tired of children, is gone.
They're all gone into a world of light; the farm's my own.

The farm's my own!
Back there alone,
I keep indoors, and spoil another season.
I hear the rattley little country gramophone
racking its five foot horn:
"O Summer Time!"
Even at noon here the formidable   20
Ancien Régime still keeps nature at a distance. Five
green shaded light bulbs spider the billiards-table;
no field is greener than its cloth,
where Grandpa, dipping sugar for us both,
once spilled his demitasse.
His favorite ball, the number three,
still hides the coffee stain.

Never again
to walk there, chalk our cues,
insist on shooting for us both.   *30*
Grandpa! Have me, hold me, cherish me!
Tears smut my fingers. There
half my life-lease later,
I hold an *Illustrated London News*—;
disloyal still,
I doodle handlebar
mustaches on the last Russian Czar.

FROM **For the Union Dead** *(1964)*

For the Union Dead

"Relinquunt Omnia Servare Rem Publicam." [1]

The old South Boston Aquarium stands
in a Sahara of snow now. Its broken windows are boarded.
The bronze weathervane cod has lost half its scales.
The airy tanks are dry.

Once my nose crawled like a snail on the glass;
my hand tingled
to burst the bubbles
drifting from the noses of the cowed, compliant fish.

My hand draws back. I often sigh still
for the dark downward and vegetating kingdom   *10*
of the fish and reptile. One morning last March,
I pressed against the new barbed and galvanized

fence on the Boston Common. Behind their cage,
yellow dinosaur steamshovels were grunting
as they cropped up tons of mush and grass
to gouge their underworld garage.

Parking spaces luxuriate like civic
sandpiles in the heart of Boston.
A girdle of orange, Puritan-pumpkin colored girders
braces the tingling Statehouse,   *20*

---

[1] "They gave up everything to save the republic." The inscription on the frieze that
the poem describes is nearly identical yet significantly different: "Omnia relinquit"
("He gives up everything"), etc.

shaking over the excavations, as it faces Colonel Shaw [2]
and his bell-cheeked Negro infantry
on St. Gaudens' [3] shaking Civil War relief,
propped by a plank splint against the garage's earthquake.

Two months after marching through Boston,
half the regiment was dead;
at the dedication,
William James [4] could almost hear the bronze Negroes breathe.

Their monument sticks like a fishbone
in the city's throat.   30
Its Colonel is as lean
as a compass-needle.

He has an angry wrenlike vigilance,
a greyhound's gentle tautness;
he seems to wince at pleasure,
and suffocate for privacy.

He is out of bounds now. He rejoices in man's lovely,
peculiar power to choose life and die—
when he leads his black soldiers to death,
he cannot bend his back.   40

On a thousand small town New England greens,
the old white churches hold their air
of sparse, sincere rebellion; frayed flags
quilt the graveyards of the Grand Army of the Republic.

The stone statues of the abstract Union Soldier
grow slimmer and younger each year—
wasp-waisted, they doze over muskets
and muse through their sideburns . . .

Shaw's father wanted no monument
except the ditch,   50
where his son's body was thrown
and lost with his "niggers."

The ditch is nearer.
There are no statues for the last war here;
on Boylston Street, a commercial photograph
shows Hiroshima boiling

[2] Robert Gould Shaw (1837–1863), colonel of first Negro regiment in the Civil War.
[3] Augustus Saint-Gaudens (1848–1907), foremost sculptor in nineteenth-century America.
[4] Who delivered the dedicatory address at the unveiling of the Shaw monument.

over a Mosler Safe, the "Rock of Ages"
that survived the blast. Space is nearer.
When I crouch to my television set,
the drained faces of Negro school-children rise like balloons.   60

Colonel Shaw
is riding on his bubble,
he waits
for the blessed break.

The Aquarium is gone. Everywhere,
giant finned cars nose forward like fish;
a savage servility
slides by on grease.

GWENDOLYN BROOKS (1917–   )

*The fourth poem in Gwendolyn Brooks's sonnet sequence called "The
  Children of the Poor," from* Annie Allen *(1949), ends as follows:*

Win war. Rise bloody, maybe not too late
For having first to civilize a space
Wherein to play your violin with grace.

> *This injunction, coming from her, is so eloquent and said with such
> simple finality that one is almost tempted to let it stand as the full
> comment on her work.*

*Her mother went from Chicago to Topeka, Kansas, for her birth and
  then returned at once to her home in Chicago; there, in a music-
  loving family, Gwendolyn Brooks grew up and has lived ever since.
  She finished Englewood High School in 1934 and entered Wilson
  Junior College. She began to submit poems to the* Chicago Defender,
  *a Negro newspaper, when she was seventeen, and about seventy-five
  of these were published in a column called "Lights and Shadows."
  She finished college at nineteen, worked as a typist and on a newspaper, married in 1934, had two children, and, for a number of
  years between their births (they are about a decade apart), she
  attended writing classes at the South Side Community Art Center,
  where, she has said, she learned about modern poetry.*

*Her poems show no particular traces of such study: their style has a
  clarity and purity that is entirely her own. She was twenty-eight
  years old when she published her first volume,* A Street in Bronzeville
  (1945). Her next, Annie Allen, *won not only a major prize from*
  Poetry *magazine, but also the Pulitzer Prize in 1950. Only five women
  had preceded her in that award, and no black poet had ever won it.
  Her single novel,* Maud Martha *(1953), is an impressionistic account
  of a black girl's growing up in Chicago. In 1956 she published a book*

for children, Bronzeville Boys and Girls. *Since then she has published three more volumes of poems,* The Bean Eaters *(1960),* Selected Poems *(1963), and* In the Mecca *(1968). She has frequently read her poetry in public appearances including one at the Library of Congress. Her writing classes in a number of Illinois colleges have been attended by devoted students, and in 1967 she began full-time faculty duties at Chicago Teachers College North.*

She writes with calmed simplicity (one is aware of the experienced suffering and turmoil under the poised surface), with a delicate sadness; she has suggested to young writers and literary aspirants, with quiet magnanimity, that they "live richly with eyes open, and heart, too."

FURTHER READING

To Gwen with Love (1970) is an anthology dedicated to Miss Brooks by fifty contributing black writers.

FROM **The Bean Eaters** (1960)

The Ballad of Rudolph Reed

Rudolph Reed was oaken.
His wife was oaken too.
And his two good girls and his good little man
Oakened as they grew.

"I am not hungry for berries.
I am not hungry for bread.
But hungry hungry for a house
Where at night a man in bed

"May never hear the plaster
Stir as if in pain.   10
May never hear the roaches
Falling like fat rain.

"Where never wife and children need
Go blinking through the gloom.
Where every room of many rooms
Will be full of room.

"Oh my home may have its east or west
Or north or south behind it.
All I know is I shall know it,
And fight for it when I find it."   20

It was in a street of bitter white
That he made his application.
For Rudolph Reed was oakener
Than others in the nation.

The agent's steep and steady stare
Corroded to a grin.
Why, you black old, tough old hell of a man,
Move your family in!

Nary a grin grinned Rudolph Reed,
Nary a curse cursed he,   30
But moved in his House. With his dark little wife,
And his dark little children three.

A neighbor would *look,* with a yawning eye
That squeezed into a slit.
But the Rudolph Reeds and the children three
Were too joyous to notice it.

For were they not firm in a home of their own
With windows everywhere
And a beautiful banistered stair
And a front yard for flowers and a back yard for grass?   40

The first night, a rock, big as two fists.
The second, a rock big as three.
But nary a curse cursed Rudolph Reed.
(Though oaken as man could be.)

The third night, a silvery ring of glass.
Patience ached to endure.
But he looked, and lo! small Mabel's blood
Was staining her gaze so pure.

Then up did rise our Rudolph Reed
And pressed the hand of his wife,   50
And went to the door with a thirty-four
And a beastly butcher knife.

He ran like a mad thing into the night.
And the words in his mouth were stinking.
By the time he had hurt his first white man
He was no longer thinking.

By the time he had hurt his fourth white man
Rudolph Reed was dead.
His neighbors gathered and kicked his corpse.
"Nigger—" his neighbors said.   60

Small Mabel whimpered all night long,
For calling herself the cause.
Her oak-eyed mother did no thing
But change the bloody gauze.

RICHARD WILBUR (1921–   )

Richard Wilbur first came to public attention as a poet of consequence
toward the end of the Second World War, and his first book of
poems, The Beautiful Changes (1947), was warmly received as the
work of a fine new poet. This friendly view continued through the
next few books—Ceremony (1950), A Bestiary (1955), Things of
This World (1956), and Poems (1957), which won the Pulitzer Prize.

At about that point the critical view of him seemed to change. Until
then everyone had approved of him. His work was delicate, skillful,
sensuous, mystical, musical, speculative, beautifully controlled,
above all, charming. And all these qualities represented virtues. But
then a chill set in, and while critics did not find him less charming,
charming itself had become a belittling word. No one abused him;
he was only damned with such praise as "elegant," "cerebral," "well-
controlled." And as the late fifties roared into the "with-it" sixties,
one detected some patronizing tone in the critical air, as though he
were that merely "charming" verse maker, poor Richard Wilbur.

From the point of view of our disheveled times, we can see that
everything was against him. He was the son of cultivated people (his
father was a painter), was brought up in pleasant pastoral circumstances in New Jersey, went to Amherst, did army service in the
European theater during the Second World War, entered the Harvard graduate school and had three years with the Society of Fellows
there, married and had three children and lived in Concord (a
suburb!), won prizes including the Prix de Rome Fellowship to the
American Academy, was courted by a dozen universities and finally
settled on Wesleyan at Middletown, Connecticut, in 1955. And all
the while he wrote that pleasant poetry, most of it for The New
Yorker. How straight can one be?

He was not only over thirty, he was forty when he published Advice to
a Prophet (1961). He translated Molière's Misanthrope (1955) and
Tartuffe (1963). He wrote the lyrics for Lillian Hellman's libretto
for an opera based on Candide (1957). He minded his own business
and continued to write poems, the most recent collected in Walking
to Sleep: New Poems and Translations (1969).

His poems continue to be "controlled" in form (can there be a real poem, in any final sense, that is not controlled?), and his feeling for language continues to be "elegant" (why else would we want to have poets bothering us?). These are not limitations on the imagination, nor are clarity, lucidity, irony that is humane, intelligence. Wilbur's poems have not only always urged us, but more than that they have enabled us to rejoice in "the things of this world." That is all that one can ask of the world itself, and almost everything that one can ask of its poets.

FURTHER READING

Donald L. Hill's *Richard Wilbur* (1967) is the first full-length study of the poet's work. See also *Poets in Progress* (1962), edited by Edward Hungerford, and *Contemporary American Poetry* (1965), a collection of essays by Ralph J. Mills, Jr.

FROM **Things of This World** (1956)

Love Calls Us to the Things of This World

The eyes open to a cry of pulleys,
And spirited from sleep, the astounded soul
Hangs for a moment bodiless and simple
As false dawn.
           Outside the open window
The morning air is all awash with angels.

Some are in bed-sheets, some are in blouses,
Some are in smocks: but truly there they are.
Now they are rising together in calm swells
Of halcyon feeling, filling whatever they wear   *10*
With the deep joy of their impersonal breathing;

Now they are flying in place, conveying
The terrible speed of their omnipresence, moving
And staying like white water; and now of a sudden
They swoon down into so rapt a quiet
That nobody seems to be there.
             The soul shrinks

From all that it is about to remember,
From the punctual rape of every blessed day,
And cries,   *20*

"Oh, let there be nothing on earth but laundry,
Nothing but rosy hands in the rising steam
And clear dances done in the sight of heaven."

Yet, as the sun acknowledges
With a warm look the world's hunks and colors,
The soul descends once more in bitter love
To accept the waking body, saying now
In a changed voice as the man yawns and rises,

"Bring them down from their ruddy gallows,
Let there be clean linen for the backs of thieves;   *30*
Let lovers go fresh and sweet to be undone,
And the heaviest nuns walk in a pure floating
Of dark habits,
                    keeping their difficult balance."

FROM *Advice to a Prophet and Other Poems* (1961)

Shame

It is a cramped little state with no foreign policy,
Save to be thought inoffensive. The grammar of the language
Has never been fathomed, owing to the national habit
Of allowing each sentence to trail off in confusion.
Those who have visited Scusi,[1] the capital city,
Report that the railway-route from Schuldig [2] passes
Through country best described as unrelieved.
Sheep are the national product. The faint inscription
Over the city gates may perhaps be rendered,
"I'm afraid you won't find much of interest here."   *10*
Census-reports which give the population
As zero are, of course, not to be trusted,
Save as reflecting the natives' flustered insistence
That they do not count, as well as their modest horror
Of letting one's sex be known in so many words.
The uniform grey of the nondescript buildings, the absence
Of churches or comfort-stations, have given observers
An odd impression of ostentatious meanness,
And it must be said of the citizens (muttering by
In their ratty sheepskins, shying at cracks in the sidewalk)   *20*
That they lack the peace of mind of the truly humble.

[1] "Exuse me!" ("My fault!")
[2] "My guilt!"

The tenor of life is careful, even in the stiff
Unsmiling carelessness of the border-guards
And *douaniers*,[3] who admit, whenever they can,
Not merely the usual carloads of deodorant
But gypsies, g-strings, hasheesh, and contraband pigments.
Their complete negligence is reserved, however,
For the hoped-for invasion, at which time the happy people
(Sniggering, ruddily naked, and shamelessly drunk)
Will stun the foe by their overwhelming submission,   30
Corrupt the generals, infiltrate the staff,
Usurp the throne, proclaim themselves to be sun-gods,
And bring about the collapse of the whole empire.

JAMES DICKEY (1923–   )

*James Dickey was born in Atlanta, Georgia, and went to public schools
   there. In high school, he was an athlete given to "wild motorcycle
   riding" (the motorcycle appears frequently in his poems) and the
   guitar ("years of guitar playing" contribute, he believes, to his special
   rhythm). For a time he attended Clemson Agricultural College in
   South Carolina but left to serve in the Air Force in the Second World
   War (and later in the Korean war) and was decorated with the Air
   medal. He enrolled in Vanderbilt University and took two degrees
   there; he was married in his junior year (the Dickeys have two sons)
   at about the time that he seriously began to write poetry. For six
   years he worked in an advertising agency, and he also taught at Rice
   Institute and the University of Florida. He was publishing widely,
   and his books began to appear:* Into the Stone *(1960),* Drowning with
   Others *(1962),* Helmets *(1964). He was poet in residence at Reed
   College in 1963–1964, at San Fernando (California) Valley State
   College in 1964–1965, and at the University of Wisconsin in 1966.
   For two years he was Consultant in Poetry to the Library of Congress. He had been winning prizes and fellowships since 1958, and
   when* Buckdancer's Choice *(1965) appeared, no one was surprised
   that it won the National Book Award. From his previously published
   volumes he selected those poems he wished to retain, added twenty-
   four new ones ("growing encounters"), and published* Poems: 1957–
   1967 *(1967). One volume has followed,* The Eye-Beaters, Blood,
   Victory, Madness, Buckhead and Mercy *(1970).*

His two volumes of criticism, The Suspect in Poetry *(1964) and* Babel
   to Byzantium: Poets & Poetry Now *(1968), reveal a strong critic
   with wide tastes and a consuming love of the art of poetry. His
   astonishing novel,* Deliverance *(1970), enjoyed a popular as well as*

---

[3] "Customs officers."

a critical success. Self-Interviews (1970) *is a series of tape-recorded informal conversations on a wide range of literary subjects.*

He has characterized his themes as follows:

...the continuity of the human family, the necessity of both caused and causeless joy, and the permanent interest of what the painter John Marin called "the big basic forms"—rivers, mountains, woods, clouds, oceans, and the creatures that live naturally among them. The forfeited animal grace of human beings, occasionally redeemed by athletes, interests me also, and the hunter's sense of understanding with the hunted animal.

More generally, he has said that "All poetry, I suspect, is nothing more or less than an attempt to discover or invent conditions under which one can live with oneself."

For a long time his favorite line was anapaestic, with a "strong carrying rhythm." More recently he has cultivated the "split line," in which spaces between groups of words take the place of punctuation. He works for an "optimum 'presentational immediacy.'" He likes to base his poems on a narrative situation that moves through a short period of time and in which there is no clear distinction between what is objectively happening and what is happening in the mind of the narrator or character. His poems are poems of process, of a compulsive action driving through a thick welter of physicality. Often they are incantatory in effect, and no other poet writes with such unremitting energy, such prosodic urgency.

FURTHER READING

For studies of Dickey's work, see Paul Carroll, *The Poem in Its Skin* (1968), and Richard Howard, *Alone with America* (1969).

FROM **Buckdancer's Choice** (1965)

The War Wound

It wounded well—one time and
A half: once with instant blood and again
Reinfecting blackly, years later. Now all
    Is calm at the heel of my hand

    Where I grabbed, in a bellied-
in airplane, and caught the dark glass
Offered once in a lifetime by
    The brittle tachometer.

Moons by the thousands
Have risen in all that time; I hold   10
The healed half-moon of that night.
        I tell it to shine as still

    As it can in the temperate flesh
That never since has balled into a fist,
To hover on nylon guitar strings
        Like the folk-moon itself;

    I tell it to burn like a poison
When my two children threaten themselves,
Wall-walking, or off the deep end
        Of a county swimming pool,   20

And with, thousands of moons
Coming over me year after year,
I lie with it well under cover,
        The war of the millions,

    Through glass ground under
Heel twenty-one years ago
Concentrating its light on my hand,
        Small, but with world-fury.

Dust

Lying at home
Anywhere   it can change not only the color
But the shape of the finger that runs along it   leaving a trail
That disappears from the earth; nothing can follow
Where that hand has walked and withdrawn.
And I have lain in bed at home and watched

Through a haze
Of afternoon liquor   the sun come down through it
Dropping off from the window sill from which the dust has risen
With no voice   the voices of children   to spin   10
In a stunned silence   the individual motes
All with a shape apiece   wool fragments

Small segments
Of rope tricks   spirochetes boring into the very
Body of light   and if you move your hand through their air
They dip   weave   then assume in the altered brightness
The places they have had, and all
Their wandering. Wherever it is,

It rises;
The place stands up and whirls   as in valleys   20
Of Arizona   where the world-armies of dust gather in sleeping
Hordes. I have seen them walking
Nearly out of the world   on a crazed foot
Spinning the ground beneath them

Into chaos.
These are dust-devils, and in that sunny room
With the shape of their motes unmassed   not given a desert
I have closed my eyes and changed them into forms
Of fire   the dying's vision
Of incandescent worms: 30

For moment
After moment have lain as though whirling
Toward myself from the grains of the earth   in a cone
Of sunlight   massing my forces
To live in time   drawn into a shape
Of dust   and in that place

A woman
Came from my spinning side. There we lay
And stared at the ceiling of our house   at the extra motes
That danced about the raising of our hands   40
Unable to get in—
to a human form at this time

But ready
For children we might raise and call our own,
Teach to sing   to sweep the sills   to lift their hands
And make the dust dance in the air
Like bodies: ready:
Ready, always, for the next.

W[ILLIAM] D[e WITT] SNODGRASS (1926–   )

*W. D. Snodgrass was born in Wilkinsburg, Pennsylvania, and enrolled
at Geneva College in that state for one year before serving in the
Navy for two. In 1946 he returned to Geneva for another year and
then transferred to the State University of Iowa, where he took three
degrees and where Robert Lowell was one of his teachers. He had
been married and divorced, and in 1954, the year after he left Iowa,
he was remarried. He taught for two years at Cornell and for one
at the University of Rochester, and in the year 1958–1959 he was*

unable "to find either a publisher or a job." In 1959, however, he was appointed to the faculty of Wayne State University, and Alfred A. Knopf, Inc., published his first volume, Heart's Needle, which promptly won the Pulitzer Prize.

Snodgrass, like Lowell, writes "confessional" poetry, and because Lowell was his teacher for a time, critics have tended to assume that he was also his model; but Lowell himself says that, if anything, it was the other way round. "He did these things before I did, though he's younger than I am. . . . He may have influenced me. . . ." The confession, in Snodgrass, usually has to do with some opposition, confrontation, or division. It can be as simple as in "The Operation," where the "I," the poet's self, is a different entity from the body, under sedation, and where, in the final lines, the world of offices, headlights, and traffic is really there outside, but also reflected in the brandy bowl on the window sill, "the crystal world . . . inverted, slow and gay." In "The Campus on the Hill" the poet's house is on an opposite hill, and he, as a teacher, wonders how he can communicate his knowledge of the dire state of the world to his childlike, self-immured students who do not want to hear of it, as time, in the last line, has literally run out.

These are modest, quiet poems and successful. But sometimes, in his more ambitious efforts, Snodgrass is less so; his personal experience is not always adequate as a reflector of universal chaos, or he cannot make it so. Yet he has developed a special technique toward this end, an antiphonal play of voices against one another in, as he believes, a sonatalike fashion. Thus the title poem of his next volume, After Experience (1968), alternates lines from a passage in Spinoza with the tough voice of a naval instructor telling his men how to kill in single, hand-to-hand combat. And another poem, "A Visitation," is a dialog between the ghost of Adolf Eichmann and the poet-soldier, who, finally, recognizing his own aggressions, takes on Eichmann's guilt.

Besides his original poems, Snodgrass has published translations from the German, including (with Lore Segal) the Gallows Songs (1959) of Christian Morgenstern.

His less solemn verse has a wry humor that was illustrated in his biographical entry in the anthology, A Controversy of Poets (1965), where he says that he was "Deeply influenced by the Texas poet S. S. Gardons." He has published a number of poems under that name, which is of course his own, spelled almost backwards.

FURTHER READING

For studies of Snodgrass's work, see Paul Carroll, The Poem in Its Skin (1968), and Richard Howard, Alone with America (1969).

FROM **Heart's Needle** (1957)

The Operation

From stainless steel basins of water
They brought warm cloths and they washed me,
From spun aluminum bowls, cold Zephiran sponges, fuming;
Gripped in the dead yellow glove, a bright straight razor
Inched on my stomach, down my groin,
Paring the brown hair off. They left me
White as a child, not frightened. I was not
Ashamed. They clothed me, then,
In the thin, loose, light, white garments,
The delicate sandals of poor Pierrot,   10
A schoolgirl first offering her sacrament.

I was drifting, inexorably, on toward sleep.
In skullcaps, masked, in blue-green gowns, attendants
Towed my cart, afloat in its white cloths,
The body with its tributary poisons borne
Down corridors of the diseased, thronging:
The scrofulous faces, contagious grim boys,
The huddled families, weeping, a staring woman
Arched to her gnarled stick,—a child was somewhere
Screaming, screaming—then, blind silence, the elevator rising   20
To the arena, humming, vast with lights; blank hero,
Shackled and spellbound, to enact my deed.

Into flowers, into women, I have awakened.
Too weak to think of strength, I have thought all day,
Or dozed among standing friends. I lie in night, now,
A small mound under linen like the drifted snow.
Only by nurses visited, in radiance, saying, Rest.
Opposite, ranked office windows glare; headlamps, below,
Trace out our highways; their cargoes under dark tarpaulins,
Trucks climb, thundering, and sirens may   30
Wail for the fugitive. It is very still. In my brandy bowl
Of sweet peas at the window, the crystal world
Is inverted, slow and gay.

The Campus on the Hill

Up the reputable walks of old established trees
They stalk, children of the *nouveaux riches;* chimes
Of the tall Clock Tower drench their heads in blessing:
"I don't wanna play at your house;
I don't like you any more."
My house stands opposite, on the other hill,
Among meadows, with the orchard fences down and falling;
Deer come almost to the door.
You cannot see it, even in this clearest morning.
White birds hang in the air between   10
Over the garbage landfill and those homes thereto adjacent,
Hovering slowly, turning, settling down
Like the flakes sifting imperceptibly onto the little town
In a waterball of glass.
And yet, this morning, beyond this quiet scene,
The floating birds, the backyards of the poor,
Beyond the shopping plaza, the dead canal, the hillside lying tilted in
    the air,
Tomorrow has broken out today:
Riot in Algeria, in Cyprus, in Alabama;
Aged in wrong, the empires are declining,   20
And China gathers, soundlessly, like evidence.
What shall I say to the young on such a morning?—
Mind is the one salvation?—also grammar?—
No; my little ones lean not toward revolt. They
Are the Whites, the vaguely furiously driven, who resist
Their souls with such passivity
As would make Quakers swear. All day, dear Lord, all day
They wear their godhead lightly.
They look out from their hill and say,
To themselves, "We have nowhere to go but down;   30
The great destination is to stay."
Surely the nations will be reasonable;
They look at the world—don't they?—the world's way?
The clock just now has nothing more to say.

ROBERT [WHITE] CREELEY (1926–   )

Nearly the whole substance of Robert Creeley's many small and fugitive books and pamphlets are available in three volumes: For Love: Poems, 1950–1960 *(1962),* Words *(1967), and* Pieces *(1969). Further poems, "early and uncollected," are now available in* The Charm *(1970), and his "notes and essays" in* A Quick Graph *(1970).*

He was born in Arlington, Massachusetts, next to Cambridge, and in 1943 he went to Harvard, but the war took him away almost at once with the American Field Service in Burma and India. He returned to Harvard, but only briefly. After wide travels he went to Black Mountain College in North Carolina and took his B.A. in 1954. There he worked with Charles Olson, helping him edit The Black Mountain Review, *and was influenced—formed, really—by his theory of "projectivist verse." The theory accounts not only for Creeley's ideas about the proper form and content of poetry, but also for the typography of his poems, their brevity and the short lines. Olson said that ". . . the line comes (I swear it) from the breath, from the breathing of the man who writes, at that moment that he writes," and Creeley put the notion into a poem: "the lines / talking, taking, always the beat from / the breath." Later he took an M.A. at the University of New Mexico, and for a time he was a lecturer there in the department of English, but in 1963 he went to New York State University at Buffalo and is now a professor of English there, a colleague of Leslie Fiedler and John Barth, among others. Creeley has written prose as well as verse, notably a novel called* The Island *(1963).*

His poems are countless, infinitely minute islands, tiny fragments of experience, each a moment chopped off, suspended, incomplete, caught just before it becomes something else. This is a poetry of discontinuities, a poetry of what someone has called "presentative simultaneity." It wishes to dispense with memory, with connection, with recurrence, almost with what is conventionally thought of as subject matter.

Creeley has a poem called "Joy," which speaks for all this. It goes as follows:

I could look at
an empty hole for hours
thinking it will
get something in it,

will collect
things. There is
an infinite emptiness
placed there.

FURTHER READING
See Richard Howard, *Alone with America* (1969).

FROM *For Love: Poems, 1950—1960* *(1962)*

The Rain

All night the sound had
come back again,
and again falls
this quiet, persistent rain.

What am I to myself
that must be remembered,
insisted upon
so often? Is it

that never the ease,
even the hardness,   *10*
of rain falling
will have for me

something other than this,
something not so insistent—
am I to be locked in this
final uneasiness.

Love, if you love me,
lie next to me.
Be for me, like rain,
the getting out   *20*

of the tiredness, the fatuousness, the semi-
lust of intentional indifference.
Be wet
with a decent happiness.

Jack's Blues

I'm going to roll up
a monkey and smoke it, put
an elephant in the pot. I'm going out
and never come back.

What's better than that.
Lying on your back, flat
on your back with your
eyes to the view.

Oh the view is blue, I saw that
too, yesterday and you,   10
red eyes and blue,
funked.

I'm going to roll up
a rug and smoke it, put
the car in the garage and I'm
gone, like a sad old candle.

FROM **Words** *(1967)*

For No Clear Reason

I dreamt last night
the fright was over, that
the dust came, and then water,
and women and men, together
again, and all was quiet
in the dim moon's light.

A paean of such patience—
laughing, laughing at me,
and the days extend over
the earth's great cover,   10
grass, trees, and flower-
ing season, for no clear reason.

DAVID WAGONER (1926–   )

One would like to think that anyone who can conceive of and write such a happily attractive novel as The Escape Artist *(1965), a story about a boy who in spite of all obstacles, even the most unexpected, always comes out on top, is also writing an allegory of his own imaginative (and personal) life. That may very well be what David Wagoner was in fact doing in that novel, although perhaps without that intention, given his modesty.*

He was born in Ohio, took his bachelor's degree at Pennsylvania State University and a master's at Indiana, where his thesis was a sheaf of poems. Then he taught at De Pauw and Pennsylvania State before going on to the University of Washington in Seattle, where he has been since 1954. In various interstices in his academic life he worked as a railroad section hand, a park policeman, a restaurant grillman; he has worked on newspapers, acted in summer theaters, hovered about at writers' conferences, studied stage problems (on a Ford Foundation grant), and wrote a play, Everyman for Himself, *lectured and read his poems widely and often, edited periodicals, accepted prizes. Since 1961 he has been the editor of* Poetry Northwest.

As a writer, he has balanced almost every volume of poetry with a novel, and out of each novel came better poetry. First came his poems in Dry Sun, Dry Wind *(1953), very gifted, perhaps a little constricted; then two novels,* The Man in the Middle *(1954) and* Money Money Money *(1955), the title of the latter taken from a poem by Theodore Roethke, Wagoner's colleague and friend; the next poems,* A Place to Stand *(1958), opening up in both form and view; almost simultaneously, another novel,* Rock *(1958); more poems in* The Nesting Ground *(1963), jousting happily with ultimate (and tragic) questions with a novelist's ease;* The Escape Artist, *that enchanting novel that has been called a "romance," in Hawthorne's sense of the word; more poems in* Staying Alive *(1966), with its extraordinary title piece, the brilliant, bemused, low-pitched handbook of directions for the survival of Being, all in the imagery of the wilderness; then two more novels,* Baby, Come on Inside *(1968) and* Where Is My Wandering Boy Tonight? *(1970), comic outrages and both in counterpoint, one before and one after, to* New and Selected Poems *(1969), which includes a number of quite stunning, large and free hymns, invocations, no less, to human life, its dangers, its desperate beauty; it carries a dedication to the poet's wife that must be one of the most gracious dedications in all literature: " . . . with love, new and unselected." This is important to what one wishes to say about Wagoner finally.*

Every now and then in the history of literature—but not very often—a writer (usually a poet) appears who, in the very development of his work (and behind it, of course, that of his person), gives us what is in its totality a work of art, by which one means a composed progress into amplitude, into triumph, so that one begins to hear the piercing sound of bugles, to see banners flying on ramparts. It is difficult to describe something so exhilarating, and nothing that has been said here demonstrates it. But David Wagoner's career is one of those, and some day—if we stay alive—history will know it. As of now he does not seem to have an entry in Who's Who.

FURTHER READING

A study of Wagoner's work appears in Richard Howard, *Alone with America* (1969).

FROM *New and Selected Poems* (1969)

Staying Alive

Staying alive in the woods is a matter of calming down
At first and deciding whether to wait for rescue,
Trusting to others,
Or simply to start walking and walking in one direction
Till you come out—or something happens to stop you.
By far the safer choice
Is to settle down where you are, and try to make a living
Off the land, camping near water, away from shadows.
Eat no white berries;
Spit out all bitterness. Shooting at anything   10
Means hiking further and further every day
To hunt survivors;
It may be best to learn what you have to learn without a gun,
Not killing but watching birds and animals go
In and out of shelter
At will. Following their example, build for a whole season:
Facing across the wind in your lean-to,
You may feel wilder,
But nothing, not even you, will have to stay in hiding.
If you have no matches, a stick and a fire-bow   20
Will keep you warmer,
Or the crystal of your watch, filled with water, held up to the sun
Will do the same, in time. In case of snow,
Drifting toward winter,
Don't try to stay awake through the night, afraid of freezing—
The bottom of your mind knows all about zero;
It will turn you over
And shake you till you waken. If you have trouble sleeping
Even in the best of weather, jumping to follow
With eyes strained to their corners   30
The unidentifiable noises of the night and feeling
Bears and packs of wolves nuzzling your elbow,
Remember the trappers
Who treated them indifferently and were left alone.
If you hurt yourself, no one will comfort you
Or take your temperature,
So stumbling, wading, and climbing are as dangerous as flying.
But if you decide, at last, you must break through
In spite of all danger,
Think of yourself by time and not by distance, counting   40
Wherever you're going by how long it takes you;
No other measure

Will bring you safe to nightfall. Follow no streams: they run
Under the ground or fall into wilder country.
Remember the stars
And moss when your mind runs into circles. If it should rain,
Or the fog should roll the horizon in around you,
Hold still for hours
Or days, if you must, or weeks, for seeing is believing
In the wilderness. And if you find a pathway,   50
Wheel rut, or fence wire,
Retrace it left or right—someone knew where he was going
Once upon a time, and you can follow
Hopefully, somewhere,
Just in case. There may even come, on some uncanny evening
A time when you're warm and dry, well fed, not thirsty,
Uninjured, without fear,
When nothing, either good or bad, is happening.
This is called staying alive. It's temporary.
What occurs after   60
Is doubtful. You must always be ready for something to come bursting
Through the far edge of a clearing, running toward you,
Grinning from ear to ear
And hoarse with welcome. Or something crossing and hovering
Overhead, as light as air, like a break in the sky,
Wondering what you are.
Here you are face to face with the problem of recognition.
Having no time to make smoke, too much to say,
You should have a mirror
With a tiny hole in the back for better aiming, for reflecting   70
Whatever disaster you can think of, to show
The way you suffer
These body signals have universal meaning: If you are lying
Flat on your back with arms outstretched behind you,
You say you require
Emergency treatment; If you are standing erect and holding
Arms horizontal, you mean you are not ready;
If you hold them over
Your head, you want to be picked up. Three of anything
Is a sign of distress. Afterward, if you see   80
No ropes, no ladders,
No maps or messages falling, no searchlights or trails blazing,
Then chances are, you should be prepared to burrow
Deep for a deep winter.

JAMES MERRILL (1926–   )

James Merrill's problem as a poet was to make himself less poetical.

He was born in New York City and into great wealth—the son of Charles Edward Merrill, the financier and founder of the international brokerage firm that prominently bears his name. Much of his work draws directly on that lavish background, in physical detail, in domestic situation, in emotional reproach, perhaps malaise.

He was educated at the Lawrenceville School and at Amherst, from which, after a year's interruption for army service, he was graduated in 1947. He has traveled widely and ceaselessly, a central fact in his development as a poet, and he now alternates his place of residence between Stonington, Connecticut, and Athens.

His earliest work, a collection of verse and short stories called Jim's Book, *was privately printed when he was sixteen years old, and he was only twenty-five when his earliest commercially published volume appeared,* First Poems *(1951). These are in large part the poems of an obvious prodigy who is also an exquisite. They are precious, lapidary, lacquered, obsessed with decor, and largely static. They are presented in glittering, involuted sentences that are like the coils of a brilliant but motionless reptile. They evoke an operatic setting that is studded with cold marble statuary out of the museums of mythology. But here and there a wind blows, a different voice speaks, something moves—as in this subtly conversational blank verse:*

> Love merely as the best
> There is, and one would make the best of that
> By saying how it grows and in what climates,
> By trying to tell the crystals from the branch,
> Stretching that wand then toward the sparkling wave.
> To say at the end, however we find it, good,
> Bad, or indifferent, it helps us, and the air
> Is sweetest there. The air is very sweet.

Merrill's problem was to free consistently that second voice without choking off what was original and valid, or truly personal, in the first, only sloughing off the acquired and affected accents of a second language.

A privately printed book of ten dramatic monologs of sorts, or at any rate spoken narratives, called Short Stories *(1954), went far in that direction, and the disciplines of prose in his full-length play,* The Immortal Husband *(1956), and in a novel,* The Seraglio *(1957), carried him further. The next poetry,* The Country of a Thousand Years of Peace *(1959), showed that the transformation had been accomplished. The poems are no longer decorative objects; now the poet can use them as occasions for self-confrontation. This move-*

ment continues in Water Street *(1962), largely taking off from his
own, not his family's domestic world. A second novel, daring and
experimental,* The (Diblos) Notebook *(1965), again serves the poet
well, or so it would appear from the confident maturity of the poems
in the most recent volumes,* Nights and Days *(1966) and* The Fire
Screen *(1969), many of which are steep descents into the self. He
has learned to trust himself, both in his dreams and his waking,
nights and days, and that trust is our pleasure.*

FURTHER READING

See Richard Howard, *Alone with America* (1969).

FROM *The Country of a Thousand Years
of Peace and Other Poems* (1959)

*The Country of a Thousand
Years of Peace*

to Hans Lodeizen (1924–1950)[1]

Here they all come to die,
Fluent therein as in a fourth tongue.
But for a young man not yet of their race
It was a madness you should lie

Blind in one eye, and fed
By the blood of a scrubbed face;
It was a madness to look down
On the toy city where

The glittering neutrality
Of clock and chocolate and lake and cloud   *10*
Made every morning somewhat
Less than you could bear;

And makes me cry aloud
At the old masters of disease
Who dangling high above you on a hair
The sword that, never falling, kills

Would coax you still back from that starry land
Under the world, which no one sees
Without a death, its finish and sharp weight
Flashing in his own hand.   *20*

[1] Dutch poet.

FROM **Nights and Days** *(1966)*

The Mad Scene

Again last night I dreamed the dream called Laundry.
In it, the sheets and towels of a life we were going to share,
The milk-stiff bibs, the shroud, each rag to be ever
Trampled or soiled, bled on or groped for blindly,
Came swooming out of an enormous willow hamper
Onto moon-marbly boards. We had just met. I watched
From outer darkness. I had dressed myself in clothes
Of a new fiber that never stains or wrinkles, never
Wears thin. The opera house sparkled with tiers
And tiers of eyes, like mine enlarged by belladonna,   10
Trained inward. There I saw the cloud-clot, gust by gust,
Form, and the lightning bite, and the roan mane unloosen.
Fingers were running in panic over the flute's nine gates.
Why did I flinch? I loved you. And in the downpour laughed
To have us wrung white, gnarled together, one
Topmost mordent of wisteria,
As the lean tree burst into grief.

ALLEN GINSBERG (1926–   )

The term beat *(together with its derivative,* beatnik) *implies a number of meanings: exhaustion in the competitive scramble; beaten* up,
impossibly abused by society; beaten out *of it, drop-out; beatitude, a
new serenity. Of the poets of the "beat generation," only Allen Ginsberg seems to retain any influence fifteen years after that "movement" made itself felt; but it is hard to know whether that influence
comes from his work, which in its published form is hardly extensive, or from his public role as the bearded* guru *speaking for protest
and freedom and flower power by way of Zen Buddhism, the prophet
of pot and homosexual love and "holy ecstasy," the performer in
coffee houses, museums, and colleges who sometimes decides that
his audience can best be edified by his taking off his clothes.*

*Allen Ginsberg was born in Newark, New Jersey, and the almost un-
believable circumstances of his early life are detailed in the "Narrative" section of his best poem, an elegy for his mother, "Kaddish
for Naomi Ginsberg 1894–1956," the title work of* Kaddish *and*
Other Poems, 1958–1960 *(1961). His father was a school teacher
and a conventional poet, the author of volumes called* The Attic of
the Past *(1920),* The Everlasting Minute *(1937), and* Morning in
Spring: and Other Poems *(1970), and (from Ginsberg's own account),*

a defeated man; his mother, a woman with radical political convictions, was, over a long period, insane, and died in madness.

Allen Ginsberg attended Columbia College, and before he left it in 1948 he had many adventures and misadventures there and had worked at many odd jobs—floor washer, diswasher, spot welder, night porter, etc; and after leaving it, he was book reviewer for Newsweek *and a market research consultant in both New York City and San Francisco. It was in San Francisco that he made his great splash with the publication of* Howl and Other Poems *(1955), the work that announced his allegiance to the William Blake of the long prophetic poems, to Christopher Smart in his street prayers, to Walt Whitman, to Ezra Pound of the later Cantos, and to William Carlos Williams.*

The publicity attendant on the publication of Howl *and the public role that Ginsberg subsequently assumed led to his poetry readings all over the world, to the translation of his work into any number of languages, to his acting in a half dozen underground films beginning with* Pull My Daisy *(1961), to his wide popularity among dissident students, and to a number of stately awards and honors from the "establishment" he scorned.*

Would Howl *have caused even a ripple on the literary stream if the San Francisco police had not been so silly as to try to suppress it? Who is to say? As it was, it unquestionably crashed like a tidal wave over the neatly restricted beaches of poetic subject matter and language, and, to mix the watery metaphor, opened the floodgates. It also made room for the publication of Ginsberg's own not very interesting earlier poems in* Empty Mirror *(1961) and* Reality Sandwiches *(1963). It also thrust him into his evangelical role, which becomes increasingly insistent in the later books,* T.V. Baby Poems *and* Planet News, 1961–1967 *(1968). His evangelism obscures his most interesting talent, the ability to pinpoint in exact and sourly comic detail the scrofulous filth of American life. The "holy" generalizations and adjurations one can do without.*

Still, it is pleasant to know that he is setting the songs of William Blake to music, and that in his role of blithe saintliness he is indifferent to all material concerns. In the spring of 1969, when the National Institute of Arts and Letters gave him one of its awards, he was observed stuffing its $5000 check into the embroidered tote bag that hangs from his shoulder as if it were a piece of used Kleenex.

FURTHER READING

The first full-length study is Jane Kramer's *Allen Ginsberg in America* (1969). See also Richard Howard, *Alone with America* (1969).

FROM *Howl and Other Poems* (1956)

Howl

for Carl Solomon [1]

I

I saw the best minds of my generation destroyed by madness, starving
　　hysterical naked,
dragging themselves through the negro streets at dawn looking for an
　　angry fix,
angelheaded hipsters burning for the ancient heavenly connection to the
　　starry dynamo in the machinery of night,
who poverty and tatters and hollow-eyed and high sat up smoking in the
　　supernatural darkness of cold-water flats floating across the tops of
　　cities contemplating jazz,
who bared their brains to Heaven under the El and saw Mohammedan
　　angels staggering on tenement roofs illuminated,
who passed through universities with radiant cool eyes hallucinating
　　Arkansas and Blake-light tragedy among the scholars of war,
who were expelled from the academies for crazy & publishing obscene
　　odes on the windows of the skull,
who cowered in unshaven rooms in underwear, burning their money in
　　wastebaskets and listening to the Terror through the wall,
who got busted in their pubic beards returning through Laredo with a
　　belt of marijuana for New York,
who ate fire in paint hotels or drank turpentine in Paradise Alley,[2] death,
　　or purgatoried their torsos night after night   10
with dreams, with drugs, with waking nightmares, alcohol and cock
　　and endless balls,
incomparable blind streets of shuddering cloud and lightning in the
　　mind leaping toward poles of Canada & Paterson, illuminating all
　　the motionless world of Time between,
Peyote solidities of halls, backyard green tree cemetery dawns, wine
　　drunkenness over the rooftops, storefront boroughs of teahead joy-
　　ride neon blinking traffic light, sun and moon and tree vibrations in
　　the roaring winter dusks of Brooklyn, ashcan rantings and kind king
　　light of mind,
who chained themselves to subways for the endless ride from Battery to

---

[1] (1931–　　　), author of *Mishaps, Perhaps* (1966), edited by Mary Beach, and of
More Mishaps (1968); the former contains poems and autobiographical fragments
including a letter to Governor Rockefeller from Pilgrim State Hospital.

[2] In the 1950s, a slum courtyard in lower East Side Manhattan, setting of Jack
Kerouac's *The Subterraneans* (1958). Most of Ginsberg's personal allusions in this
poem are made clear in his *Paris Review* interview, reprinted in *Writers at Work:
Third Series* (1968), edited by Alfred Kazin.

holy Bronx on benzedrine until the noise of wheels and children
brought them down shuddering mouth-wracked and battered bleak
of brain all drained of brilliance in the drear light of Zoo,[3]
who sank all night in submarine light of Bickford's [4] floated out and sat
through the stale beer afternoon in desolate Fugazzi's,[5] listening to
crack of doom on the hydrogen jukebox,
who talked continuously seventy hours from park to pad to bar to
Bellevue [6] to museum to the Brooklyn Bridge,
a lost battalion of platonic conversationalists jumping down the stoops
off fire escapes off windowsills off Empire State [7] out of the moon,
yacketayakking screaming vomiting whispering facts and memories and
anecdotes and eyeball kicks and shocks of hospitals and jails and
wars,
whole intellects disgorged in total recall for seven days and nights with
brilliant eyes, meat for the Synagogue cast on the pavement,
who vanished into nowhere Zen New Jersey leaving a trail of ambiguous
picture postcards of Atlantic City Hall,
suffering Eastern sweats and Tangerian bone-grindings and migraines
of China under junk-withdrawal in Newark's bleak furnished room,
who wandered around and around at midnight in the railroad yard wondering where to go, and went, leaving no broken hearts,
who lit cigarettes in boxcars boxcars boxcars racketing through snow
toward lonesome farms in grandfather night,
who studied Plotinus Poe St. John of the Cross telepathy and bop kaballa
because the cosmos instinctively vibrated at their feet in Kansas,
who loned it through the streets of Idaho seeking visionary indian angels
who were visionary indian angels,
who thought they were only mad when Baltimore gleamed in supernatural ecstasy,
who jumped in limousines with the Chinaman of Oklahoma on the
impulse of winter midnight streetlight smalltown rain,
who lounged hungry and lonesome through Houston seeking jazz or
sex or soup, and followed the brilliant Spaniard to converse about
America and Eternity, a hopeless task, and so took ship to Africa,
who disappeared into the volcanoes of Mexico leaving behind nothing but

20

---

[3] The Bronx Zoo.

[4] Cafeteria chain.

[5] Bar on lower Sixth Avenue, New York, near Greenwich Village, where many
"early martyrs" [author's phrase] sat waiting for connections in the late 1940s and
early 1950s.

[6] New York City hospital, best known as the central Manhattan receiving station
for the mentally deranged.

[7] Manhattan skyscraper, the official nickname of New York State.

the shadow of dungarees and the lava and ash of poetry scattered in
 fireplace Chicago,
who reappeared on the West Coast investigating the F.B.I. in beards
 and shorts with big pacifist eyes sexy in their dark skin passing out
 incomprehensible leaflets,   30
who burned cigarette holes in their arms protesting the narcotic tobacco
 haze of Capitalism,
who distributed Supercommunist pamphlets in Union Square [8] weeping
 and undressing while the sirens of Los Alamos wailed them down,
 and wailed down Wall,[9] and the Staten Island ferry also wailed,
who broke down crying in white gymnasiums naked and trembling before the machinery of other skeletons,
who bit detectives in the neck and shrieked with delight in policecars for
 committing no crime but their own wild cooking pederasty and intoxication,
who howled on their knees in the subway and were dragged off the roof
 waving genitals and manuscripts,
who let themselves be fucked in the ass by saintly motorcyclists, and
 screamed with joy,
who blew and were blown by those human seraphim, the sailors, caresses
 of Atlantic and Carribbean love,
who balled in the morning in the evenings in rosegardens and the grass
 of public parks and cemeteries scattering their semen freely to
 whomever come who may,
who hiccupped endlessly trying to giggle but wound up with a sob behind a partition in a Turkish Bath when the blonde & naked angel
 came to pierce them with a sword,
who lost their loveboys to the three old shrews of fate the one eyed shrew
 of the heterosexual dollar the one eyed shrew that winks out of the
 womb and the one eyed shrew that does nothing but sit on her ass
 and snip the intellectual golden threads of the craftsman's loom,   40
who copulated ecstatic and insatiate with a bottle of beer a sweetheart
 a package of cigarettes a candle and fell off the bed, and continued
 along the floor and down the hall and ended fainting on the wall
 with a vision of ultimate cunt and come eluding the last gyzym [10] of
 consciousness,
who sweetened the snatches of a million girls trembling in the sunset,
 and were red eyed in the morning but prepared to sweeten the

---

[8] Celebrated radical and workingmen's meeting place in New York City (14th
Street and 4th Avenue); like Hyde Park Corner, London, the traditional place for
soapbox rhetoric.
[9] Wall Street in lower Manhattan; wailing wall.
[10] Variant spelling of slang word for seminal matter.

snatch of the sunrise, flashing buttocks under barns and naked in
the lake.

who went out whoring through Colorado in myriad stolen night-cars,
N.C., secret hero of these poems,[11] cocksman and Adonis of Denver
—joy to the memory of his innumerable lays of girls in empty lots &
diner backyards, moviehouses' rickety rows, on mountaintops in
caves or with gaunt waitresses in familiar roadside lonely petticoat
upliftings & especially secret gas-station solipisims of johns, &
hometown alleys too,

who faded out in vast sordid movies, were shifted in dreams, woke on
a sudden Manhattan, and picked themselves up out of basements
hungover with heartless Tokay and horrors of Third Avenue iron
dreams & stumbled to unemployment offices.

who walked all night with their shoes full of blood on the snowbank
docks waiting for a door in the East River to open to a room full of
steamheat and opium,

who created great suicidal dramas on the apartment cliff-banks of the
Hudson under the wartime blue floodlight of the moon & their heads
shall be crowned with laurel in oblivion,

who ate the lamb stew of the imagination or digested the crab at the
muddy bottom of the rivers of Bowery,

who wept at the romance of the streets with their pushcarts full of
onions and bad music,

who sat in boxes breathing in the darkness under the bridge, and rose up
to build harpsichords in their lofts,

who coughed on the sixth floor of Harlem crowned with flame under the
tubercular sky surrounded by orange crates of theology,   50

who scribbled all night rocking and rolling over lofty incantations which
in the yellow morning were stanzas of gibberish,

who cooked rotten animals lung heart feet tail borsht & tortillas dreaming of the pure vegetable kingdom,

who plunged themselves under meat trucks looking for an egg,

who threw their watches off the roof to cast their ballot for Eternity outside of Time, & alarm clocks fell on their heads every day for the
next decade,

who cut their wrists three times successively unsuccessfully, gave up and
were forced to open antique stores where they thought they were
growing old and cried,

who were burned alive in their innocent flannel suits on Madison Avenue
amid blasts of leaden verse & the tanked-up clatter of the iron regi-
ments of fashion & the nitroglycerine shrieks of the fairies of advertising & the mustard gas of sinister intelligent editors, or were run
down by the drunken taxicabs of Absolute Reality,

[11] Neal Cassady.

who jumped off the Brooklyn Bridge this actually happened and walked
away unknown and forgotten into the ghostly daze of Chinatown
soup alleyways & firetrucks, not even one free beer,
who sang out of their windows in despair, fell out of the subway window,
jumped in the filthy Passaic, leaped on negroes, cried all over the
street, danced on broken wineglasses barefoot smashed phonograph
records of nostalgic European 1930's German jazz finished the whiskey and threw up groaning into the bloody toilet, moans in their ears
and the blast of colossal steamwhistles,
who barreled down the highways of the past journeying to each other's
hotrod-Golgotha jail-solitude watch or Birmingham jazz incarnation,
who drove crosscountry seventytwo hours to find out if I had a vision or
you had a vision or he had a vision to find out Eternity,   60
who journeyed to Denver, who died in Denver, who came back to Denver
& waited in vain, who watched over Denver & brooded & loned in
Denver and finally went away to find out the Time, & now Denver
is lonesome for her heroes,
who fell on their knees in hopeless cathedrals praying for each other's
salvation and light and breasts, until the soul illuminated its hair for
a second,
who crashed through their minds in jail waiting for impossible criminals
with golden heads and the charm of reality in their hearts who sang
sweet blues to Alcatraz,
who retired to Mexico to cultivate a habit, or Rocky Mount [12] to tender
Buddha or Tangiers to boys or Southern Pacific [13] to the black locomotive or Harvard to Narcissus to Woodlawn [14] to the daisychain or
grave,
who demanded sanity trials accusing the radio of hypnotism & were left
with their insanity & their hands & a hung jury,
who threw potato salad at CCNY [15] lecturers on Dadaism and subsequently presented themselves on the granite steps of the mad-
house with shaven heads and harlequin speech of suicide, demanding instantaneous lobotomy,
and who were given instead the concrete void of insulin metrasol electricity hydrotherapy psychotherapy occupational therapy pingpong
& amnesia,
who in humorless protest overturned only one symbolic pingpong table,
resting briefly in catatonia,

---

[12] Town in North Carolina where Jack Kerouac lived at the time of the composition of this poem.
[13] California railroad on which Neal Cassady worked at the time of the composition
of this poem.
[14] A cemetery in the Bronx; Edgar Allan Poe lived nearby.
[15] City College, New York.

returning years later truly bald except for a wig of blood, and tears and
fingers, to the visible madman doom of the wards of the madtowns
of the East,

Pilgrim State's [16] Rockland's [17] and Greystone's [18] foetid halls, bickering
with the echoes of the soul, rocking and rolling in the midnight soli-
tude-bench dolmen-realms of love, dream of life a nightmare, bodies
turned to stone as heavy as the moon,   70

with mother finally ******, and the last fantastic book flung out of the
tenement window, and the last door closed at 4 AM and the last telephone slammed at the wall in reply and the last furnished room
emptied down to the last piece of mental furniture, a yellow paper
rose twisted on a wire hanger in the closet, and even that imaginary,
nothing but a hopeful little bit of hallucination—

ah, Carl, while you are not safe I am not safe, and now you're really in
the total animal soup of time—

and who therefore ran through the icy streets obsessed with a sudden
flash of the alchemy of the use of the ellipse the catalog the meter &
the vibrating plane,

who dreamt and made incarnate gaps in Time & Space through images
juxtaposed, and trapped the archangel of the soul between 2 visual
images and joined the elemental verbs and set the noun and dash of
consciousness together jumping with sensation of Pater Omnipotens Aeterna Deus [19]

to recreate the syntax and measure of poor human prose and stand before you speechless and intelligent and shaking with shame, rejected
yet confessing out the soul to conform to the rhythm of thought
in his naked and endless head,

the madman bum and angel beat in Time, unknown, yet putting down
here what might be left to say in time come after death,

and rose reincarnate in the ghostly clothes of jazz in the goldhorn shadow of the band and blew the suffering of America's naked mind for
love into an eli eli lamma lamma sabacthani [20] saxophone cry that
shivered the cities down to the last radio

with the absolute heart of the poem of life butchered out of their own
bodies good to eat a thousand years.

[16] Psychiatric hospital in West Brentwood, New York.

[17] Psychiatric hospital in Orangeburg, New York.

[18] Psychiatric hospital near Morristown, New Jersey.

[19] All-powerful Father, Eternal God. Quoted from Paul Cézanne's letter to Émile
Bernard (April 15, 1904), first published in Bernard's *Souvenirs sur Paul Cézanne*
(1912), a famous statement of Cézanne's concept of perspective in painting and
meant by Ginsberg to suggest art's saving function as eternal human communication.

[20] "Lord, Lord, why hast thou forsaken me?" Christ's words on the Cross.

II

What sphinx of cement and aluminum bashed open their skulls and ate up their brains and imagination?

Moloch! Solitude! Filth! Ugliness! Ashcans and unobtainable dollars! Children screaming under the stairways! Boys sobbing in armies! Old men weeping in the parks!　　80

Moloch! Moloch! Nightmare of Moloch! Moloch the loveless! Mental Moloch! Moloch the heavy judger of men!

Moloch the incomprehensible prison! Moloch the crossbone soulless jailhouse and Congress of sorrows! Moloch whose buildings are judgement! Moloch the vast stone of war! Moloch the stunned governments!

Moloch whose mind is pure machinery! Moloch whose blood is running money! Moloch whose fingers are ten armies! Moloch whose breast is a cannibal dynamo! Moloch whose ear is a smoking tomb!

Moloch whose eyes are a thousand blind windows! Moloch whose skyscrapers stand in the long streets like endless Jehovahs! Moloch whose factories dream and croak in the fog! Moloch whose smokestacks and antennae crown the cities!

Moloch whose love is endless oil and stone! Moloch whose soul is electricity and banks! Moloch whose poverty is the specter of genius! Moloch whose fate is a cloud of sexless hydrogen! Moloch whose name is the Mind!

Moloch in whom I sit lonely! Moloch in whom I dream Angels! Crazy in Moloch! Cocksucker in Moloch! Lacklove and manless in Moloch!

Moloch who entered my soul early! Moloch in whom I am a consciousness without a body! Moloch who frightened me out of my natural ecstasy! Moloch whom I abandon! Wake up in Moloch! Light streaming out of the sky!

Moloch! Moloch! Robot apartments! invisible suburbs! skeleton treasuries! blind capitals! demonic industries! spectral nations! invincible madhouses! granite cocks! monstrous bombs!

They broke their backs lifting Moloch to Heaven! Pavements, trees, radios, tons! lifting the city to Heaven which exists and is everywhere about us!　　90

Visions! omens! hallucinations! miracles! ecstasies! gone down the American river!

Dreams! adorations! illuminations! religions! the whole boatload of sensitive bullshit!

Breakthroughs! over the river! flips and crucifixions! gone down the flood! Highs! Epiphanies! Despairs! Ten years' animal screams and suicides! Minds! New loves! Mad generation! down on the rocks of Time

Real holy laughter in the river! They saw it all! the wild eyes! the holy yells! They bade farewell! They jumped off the roof! to solitude! waving! carrying flowers! Down to the river! into the street!

III

Carl Solomon! I'm with you in Rockland
    where you're madder than I am
I'm with you in Rockland
    where you must feel very strange
I'm with you in Rockland
    where you imitate the shade of my mother   100
I'm with you in Rockland
    where you've murdered your twelve secretaries
I'm with you in Rockland
    where you laugh at this invisible humor
I'm with you in Rockland
    where we are great writers on the same dreadful typewriter
I'm with you in Rockland
    where your condition has become serious and is reported on the radio
I'm with you in Rockland
    where the faculties of the skull no longer admit the worms of the
    senses   110
I'm with you in Rockland
    where you drink the tea of the breasts of the spinsters of Utica
I'm with you in Rockland
    where you pun on the bodies of your nurses the harpies of the Bronx
I'm with you in Rockland
    where you scream in a straightjacket that you're losing the game of
    the actual pingpong of the abyss
I'm with you in Rockland
    where you bang on the catatonic piano the soul is innocent and im-
    mortal it should never die ungodly in an armed madhouse
I'm with you in Rockland
    where fifty more shocks will never return your soul to its body again
    from its pilgrimage to a cross in the void   120
I'm with you in Rockland
    where you accuse your doctors of insanity and plot the Hebrew
    socialist revolution against the fascist national Golgotha
I'm with you in Rockland
    where you will split the heavens of Long Island and resurrect your
    living human Jesus from the superhuman tomb
I'm with you in Rockland
    where there are twentyfive-thousand mad comrades all together sing-
    ing the final stanzas of the Internationale
I'm with you in Rockland
    where we hug and kiss the United States under our bedsheets the
    United States that coughs all night and won't let us sleep
I'm with you in Rockland
    where we wake up electrified out of the coma by our own souls' air-
    planes roaring over the roof they've come to drop angelic bombs the

hospital illuminates itself imaginary walls collapse O skinny legions
  run outside O starry-spangled shock of mercy the eternal war is here
  O victory forget your underwear we're free   130
I'm with you in Rockland
  in my dreams you walk dripping from a sea-journey on the highway
  across America in tears to the door of my cottage in the Western
  night
San Francisco 1955-56

FOOTNOTE TO HOWL

Holy! Holy! Holy! Holy! Holy! Holy! Holy! Holy! Holy! Holy! Holy! Holy!
  Holy! Holy! Holy!
The world is holy! The soul is holy! The skin is holy! The nose is holy!
  The tongue and cock and hand and asshole holy!
Everything is holy! everybody's holy! everywhere is holy! everyday is in
  eternity! Everyman's an angel!
The bum's as holy as the seraphim! the madman is holy as you my soul
  are holy!
The typewriter is holy the poem is holy the voice is holy the hearers are
  holy the ecstasy is holy!
Holy Peter holy Allen holy Solomon holy Lucien holy Kerouac holy
  Huncke holy Burroughs holy Cassady [21] holy the unknown buggered
  and suffering beggars holy the hideous human angels!
Holy my mother in the insane asylum! Holy the cocks of the grand-
  fathers of Kansas!
Holy the groaning saxophone! Holy the bop apocalypse! Holy the jazz-
  bands marijuana hipsters peace & peyote pipes & drums!   140
Holy the solitudes of skyscraper and pavements! Holy the cafeterias
  filled with the millions! Holy the mysterious rivers of tears under the
  streets!
Holy the lone juggernaut! Holy the vast lamb of the middleclass! Holy
  the crazy shepherds of rebellion! Who digs Los Angeles IS Los
  Angeles!
Holy New York Holy San Francisco Holy Peoria & Seattle Holy Paris
  Holy Tangiers Holy Moscow Holy Istanbul!
Holy time in eternity holy eternity in time holy the clocks in space holy
  the fourth dimension holy the fifth International holy the Angel in
  Moloch!

[21] Peter Orlovsky (1933–   ), poet; Ginsberg himself; the subject of the dedication; "Lucien" (1925–   ) prefers to remain anonymous; Herbert E. Huncke
(1922–   ), writer; William S. Burroughs (1914–   ), novelist; Neal Cassady
(1926–1968), prototype of Moriarity in Kerouac's *On the Road* (1957) and, ten
years later, driver of Ken Kesey's "cosmos-patterned Merry Pranksters psychedelic
bus throughout the nation" [author's explanation].

Holy the sea holy the desert holy the railroad holy the locomotive holy
   the visions holy the hallucinations holy the miracles, holy the eyeball
   holy the abyss!
Holy forgiveness! mercy! charity! faith! Holy! Ours! bodies! suffering!
   magnanimity!
Holy the supernatural extra brilliant intelligent kindness of the soul!

ANNE [HARVEY] SEXTON (1928–   )

*Anne Sexton was brought up in Wellesley, Massachusetts, attended
local schools, and enrolled in Garland Junior College (1947–1948).
The daugther of a salesman, at twenty she married a salesman,
became a fashion model in Boston (1950–1951), and had two
daughters. With the birth of her second child, she suffered a mental
breakdown. She attempted suicide twice and was in and out of
mental hospitals. Her mother-in-law took one daughter until she was
past four. Her parents died within three months of one another in
1959.*

In an interview published in Hudson Review *(Winter 1965–1966) she
said that "The Double Image" in her first book,* To Bedlam and Part
Way Back *(1960), gives the truth of these years with some distortion of literal fact. Her life before her breakdown is implied in her
return to life,*

back into my own
seven rooms, visited the swan boats,
the market, answered the phone,
served cocktails as a wife
should, made love among my petticoats

and August tan.

*But she was back knowing what she was, a poet. Erik H. Erikson has
described what apparently happened to her: drastic, dramatic re-
orderings of the personality in religious trance, ecstasies, madness,
before a creative or historic personality comes into being. "It was a
kind of rebirth," Anne Sexton said.*

*Her education was her breakdown; the sanatariums and the analysts
were her alma mater, the nourishing mother through whom she
became able to cope with her rejecting mother and with her own
rejecting motherhood. These presented her with her themes—the
mother-child relation, death (with the awareness of one who had
tried to try it), madness.*

*From 1961 to 1963 she attended the Radcliffe Institute for Independent
Study, with Robert Lowell as her teacher; but she has said that if*

any poet influenced her, it was W. D. Snodgrass in Heart's Needle.
*When her friends told her that her poems were too impossibly per-
sonal, his poems gave her courage to go on with them. And also to
go over to her mother-in-law's house and bring her daughter home.*

All My Pretty Ones *(1962), with its title taken from the scene in*
Macbeth *where Macduff learns of the death of his children and his
wife, continues in the confessional vein. The title poem is about
the death of her parents. An inner epigraph from Kafka ("A book
should serve as an axe for the frozen sea within us") suggests the
literal aim of the book: to make her shock treatments shock her
reader into awareness too.*

*The later volumes tend to present her material in retrospect, and they
gain by that distancing. "Flee on Your Donkey" is an example, and
the poem called "Self in 1958" bears the dates "June 1958–June
1965." These poems appear in* Live or Die *(1966), which won the
Pulitzer Prize. In* Love Poems *(1969) there is a further distancing
through a greater involvement in the outside world than was characteristic of the early poems: "December 12th" presents an "I" who
is working in a state school for the retarded; there is love, to be
sure, but there are also the draft and the burning of draft cards,
the war and marches for peace. Her play,* Mercy Street, *opened the
1969 autumn season of the off-Broadway theater, American Place.*

FURTHER READING

For critical studies see Ralph J. Mills, Jr., *Contemporary American
Poetry* (1965); M. L. Rosenthal, *The New Poets* (1967); and
Richard Howard, *Alone with America* (1969).

FROM *All My Pretty Ones* (1962)

The Starry Night

That does not keep me from having a terrible need of—shall I say the word—
religion. Then I go out at night to paint the stars.

> Vincent Van Gogh in a letter to his brother [1]

The town does not exist
except where one black-haired tree slips
up like a drowned woman into the hot sky.

---

[1] *Letters*, no. 543, September, 1888, from Arles.

The town is silent. The night boils with eleven stars.
Oh starry starry night! This is how
I want to die.

It moves. They are all alive.
Even the moon bulges in its orange irons
to push children, like a god, from its eye.
The old unseen serpent swallows up the stars.   *10*
Oh starry starry night! This is how
I want to die:

into that rushing beast of the night,
sucked up by that great dragon, to split
from my life with no flag,
no belly,
no cry.

FROM **Live or Die** *(1966)*

Flee on Your Donkey

Ma Faim, Anne, Anne, Fuis sur ton âne. . . .—Rimbaud.[1]

Because there was no other place
to flee to,
I came back to the scene of the disordered senses,
came back last night at midnight,
arriving in the thick June night
without luggage or defenses,
giving up my car keys and my cash,
keeping only a pack of Salem cigarettes
the way a child holds on to a toy.
I signed myself in where a stranger   *10*
puts the inked-in X's—
for this is a mental hospital,
not a child's game.

Today an interne knocks my knees,
testing for reflexes.
Once I would have winked and begged for dope.
Today I am terribly patient.

[1] "My hunger, Anne, Anne, flee on your donkey . . ." from a poem entitled "*Fêtes de la Faim*" in *Poesies complètes* (1895).

Today crows play blackjack
on the stethoscope.

Everyone has left me   20
except my muse,
that good nurse.
She stays in my hand,
a mild white mouse.

The curtains, lazy and delicate,
billow and flutter and drop
like the Victorian skirts
of my two maiden aunts
who kept an antique shop.

Hornets have been sent.   30
They cluster like floral arrangements on the screen.
Hornets, dragging their thin stingers,
hover outside, all knowing,
hissing: *the hornet knows.*
I heard it as a child
but what was it that he meant?
The hornet knows!
What happened to Jack and Doc and Reggy? [2]
Who remembers what lurks in the heart of man? [3]
What did the Green Hornet mean, *he knows?*   40
Or have I got it wrong?
Is it the Shadow who had seen
me from my bedside radio?

Now it's *Dinn, Dinn, Dinn!* [4]
while the ladies in the next room argue
and pick their teeth.
Upstairs a girl curls like a snail;
in another room someone tries to eat a shoe;
meanwhile an adolescent pads up and down
the hall in his white tennis socks.   50
A new doctor makes rounds
advertising tranquilizers, insulin, or shock
to the uninitiated.

Six years of such small preoccupations!
Six years of shuttling in and out of this place!

[2] Characters in "The Green Hornet," radio serial of the 1940s, and a comic book.
[3] "Who knows what lurks in the hearts of men? The Shadow knows." Opening of
the 1940s radio serial, "The Shadow."
[4] From "*Fêtes de la Faim.*"

Oh, my hunger! My hunger!
I could have gone around the world twice
or had new children—all boys.
It was a long trip with little days in it
and no new places.   60

In here,
it's the same old crowd,
the same ruined scene.
The alcoholic arrives with his golf clubs.
The suicide arrives with extra pills sewn
into the lining of her dress.
The permanent guests have done nothing new.
Their faces are still small
like babies with jaundice.

Meanwhile,   70
they carried out my mother
wrapped like somebody's doll, in sheets,
bandaged her jaw and stuffed up her holes.
My father, too. He went out on the rotten blood
he used up on other women in the Middle West.
He went out, a cured old alcoholic
on crooked feet and useless hands.
He went out calling for his father
who died all by himself long ago—
that fat banker who got locked up,   80
his genes suspended like dollars,
wrapped up in his secret,
tied up securely in a straitjacket.

But you, my doctor, my enthusiast,
were better than Christ;
you promised me another world
to tell me who
I was.

I spent most of my time,
a stranger,   90
damned and in trance—that little hut,
that naked blue-veined place,
my eyes shut on the confusing office,
eyes circling into my childhood,
eyes newly cut.
Years of hints
strung out—a serialized case history—
thirty-three years of the same dull incest
that sustained us both.

You, my bachelor analyst,   *100*
who sat on Marborough Street,
sharing your office with your mother
and giving up cigarettes each New Year,
were the new God,
the manager of the Gideon Bible.

I was your third-grader
with a blue star on my forehead.
In trance I could be any age,
voice, gesture—all turned backward
like a drugstore clock.   *110*
Awake, I memorized dreams.
Dreams came into the ring
like third-string fighters,
each one a bad bet
who might win
because there was no other.

I stared at them,
concentrating on the abyss
the way one looks down into a rock quarry,
uncountable miles down,   *120*
my hands swinging down like hooks
to pull dreams up out of their cage.
Oh, my hunger! My hunger!

Once,
outside your office,
I collapsed in the old-fashioned swoon
between the illegally parked cars.
I threw myself down,
pretending dead for eight hours.
I thought I had died   *130*
into a snowstorm.
Above my head
chains crackled along like teeth
digging their way through the snowy street.
I lay there
like an overcoat
that someone had thrown away.
You carried me back in,
awkwardly, tenderly,
with the help of the red-haired secretary   *140*
who was built like a lifeguard.
My shoes,
I remember,

were lost in the snowbank
as if I planned never to walk again.

That was the winter
that my mother died,
half mad on morphine,
blown up, at last,
like a pregnant pig.   *150*
I was her dreamy evil eye.
In fact,
I carried a knife in my pocketbook—
my husband's good L. L. Bean [5] hunting knife.
I wasn't sure if I should slash a tire
or scrape the guts out of some dream.

You taught me
to believe in dreams;
thus I was the dredger.
I held them like an old woman with arthritic fingers,   *160*
carefully straining the water out—
sweet, dark playthings,
and above all mysterious
until they grew mournful and weak.
Oh, my hunger! My hunger!
I was the one
who opened the warm eyelid
like a surgeon
and brought forth young girls
to grunt like fish.   *170*
I told you,
I said—
but I was lying—
that the knife was for my mother . . .
and then I delivered her.

The curtains flutter out
and slump against the bars.
They are my two thin ladies
named Blanche and Rose.

The grounds outside   *180*
are pruned like an estate at Newport.
Far off, in the field,
something yellow grows.

Was it last month or last year
that the ambulance ran like a hearse

[5] Maine retail and mail order house that specializes in woodsmen's equipment.

with its siren blowing on suicide—
Dinn, dinn, dinn!—
a noon whistle that kept insisting on life
all the way through the traffic lights?

I have come back   *190*
but disorder is not what it was.
I have lost the trick of it!
The innocence of it!
That fellow-patient in his stovepipe hat,
with his fiery joke, his manic smile—
even he seems blurred, small and pale.
I have come back,
recommitted,
fastened to the wall like a bathroom plunger,
held like a prisoner   *200*
who was so poor
he fell in love with jail.

I stand at this old window
complaining of the soup,
examining the grounds,
allowing myself the wasted life.
Soon I will raise my face for a white flag,
and, when God enters the fort,
I won't spit or gag on his finger.
I will eat it like a white flower.   *210*
Is this the old trick, the wasting away,
the skull that waits for its dose
of electric power?

This is madness
but a kind of hunger.
What good are my questions
in this hierarchy of death
where the earth and the stones go
Dinn! Dinn! Dinn!
It is hardly a feast.   *220*
It is my stomach that makes me suffer.[6]

Turn, my hungers!
For once make a deliberate decision.
There are brains that rot here
like black bananas.
Hearts have grown as flat as dinner plates.
Anne, Anne,
flee on your donkey,

[6] From "*Fêtes de la Faim.*"

flee this sad hotel,
ride out on some hairy beast,   230
gallop backward pressing
your buttocks to his withers,
sit to his clumsy gait somehow.
Ride out
any old way you please!
In this place everyone talks to his own mouth.
That's what it means to be crazy.
Those I loved best died of it—
the fool's disease.

SYLVIA PLATH (1932–1963)

*Sylvia Plath was born in Boston; both her parents were teachers and
both were of German origin. Her mother was Austrian. Her father
was born in East Prussia, became a professor of entomology at
Boston University, and is described in her poems as a Nazi with "a
love of the rack and the screw." The child Sylvia adored him, and at
three, to please him, she had learned the Latin names of hundreds
of insects. He died when she was ten, a traumatic betrayal, she
thought, and the event apparently caused her first nervous crisis and
beyond that, thrust her into her compulsion to be supreme. At eight
and a half she had published her first poem in a Boston newspaper,
and now writing became an obsession. She wrote plays, poems,
stories, and some of them presently of sufficiently professional
quality to appear in magazines like* Seventeen *and* Mademoiselle.

*She won a scholarship to Smith College where she was a compulsive
learner and had a straight-A record, graduating* summa cum laude.
One summer a "scholarship" from Mademoiselle *gave her an unhappy month in New York (the background of her single novel,* The
Bell Jar, *1963), and when she came home she crept under the front
porch and swallowed fifty sleeping pills. She was found three days
later, barely alive. "They had to call and call / And pick the worms
off me like sticky pearls." After a time in a mental hospital, she then
returned to Smith.*

*In 1955, on a Fulbright scholarship she went to Newnham College,
Cambridge, and in England met the young poet, Ted Hughes, whom
she married in 1956. They came to the United States, and she taught
for a year at Smith, but in 1959 they returned to England for good.*

*In 1960 her first child, a girl, was born, and she published her first
volume,* The Colossus. *These are distinguished poems, brilliant in
their imagery and the felt pulse of life, but perhaps a little rhetorical,*

too, as though she had not yet got down to the bedrock of her subject, which was her own intense suffering and her identification of
it with the agonized, anonymous suffering of the world—Dachau,
Hiroshima, the terrible technological extinctions.

In the fall of 1962, just after the birth of a son, her marriage broke up.
Living alone with her children, after an orderly housewife's day, she
threw herself into a frenzy of composition at night, and now came
the extraordinary poems like "Daddy" and "Lady Lazarus." Of the
first, she said:

The poem is spoken by a girl with an Electra complex. Her father died while
she thought he was God. Her case is complicated by the fact that her father
was also a Nazi and her mother very possibly part Jewish. In the daughter
the two strains marry and paralyze each other—she has to act out the awful
little allegory before she is free of it.

In the second poem she thinks of the first two crises in her life and
predicts the third. On February 11, 1963, she put her head in the
oven with the gas jets wide open and died.

Her second book of poems, Ariel, containing many of those late excrutiating confrontations with the self, was published two years
later. Her Uncollected Poems (1965) have been published in London,
but as of the present writing this publication has not been announced
in the United States. She liked to draw, and the cover of the English
volume reproduces her sketch of Wuthering Heights.

FURTHER READING

An invaluable introduction to the poet and her work is a symposium
edited by Charles Newman, The Art of Sylvia Plath (1969). See
also Richard Howard, Alone with America (1969).

FROM **Ariel** (1965)

Lady Lazarus

I have done it again.
One year in every ten
I manage it——

A sort of walking miracle, my skin
Bright as a Nazi lampshade,
My right foot

A paperweight,
My face a featureless, fine
Jew linen.

Peel off the napkin   *10*
O my enemy.
Do I terrify?——

The nose, the eye pits, the full set of teeth?
The sour breath
Will vanish in a day.

Soon, soon the flesh
The grave cave ate will be
At home on me

And I a smiling woman.
I am only thirty.   *20*
And like the cat I have nine times to die.

This is Number Three.
What a trash
To annihilate each decade.

What a million filaments.
The peanut-crunching crowd
Shoves in to see

Them unwrap me hand and foot——
The big strip tease.
Gentlemen, ladies   *30*

These are my hands
My knees.
I may be skin and bone,

Nevertheless, I am the same, identical woman.
The first time it happened I was ten.
It was an accident.

The second time I meant
To last it out and not come back at all.
I rocked shut

As a seashell.   *40*
They had to call and call
And pick the worms off me like sticky pearls.

Dying
Is an art, like everything else.
I do it exceptionally well.

I do it so it feels like hell.
I do it so it feels real.
I guess you could say I've a call.

It's easy enough to do it in a cell.
It's easy enough to do it and stay put.   50
It's the theatrical

Comeback in broad day
To the same place, the same face, the same brute
Amused shout:

'A miracle!'
That knocks me out.
There is a charge

For the eyeing of my scars, there is a charge
For the hearing of my heart— —
It really goes.   60

And there is a charge, a very large charge
For a word or a touch
Or a bit of blood

Or a piece of my hair or my clothes.
So, so, Herr Doktor.
So, Herr Enemy.

I am your opus,
I am your valuable,
The pure gold baby

That melts to a shriek.   70
I turn and burn.
Do not think I underestimate your great concern.

Ash, ash—
You poke and stir.
Flesh, bone, there is nothing there— —

A cake of soap,
A wedding ring,
A gold filling.

Herr God, Herr Lucifer
Beware   80
Beware.

Out of the ash
I rise with my red hair
And I eat men like air.

Daddy

You do not do, you do not do
Any more, black shoe
In which I have lived like a foot
For thirty years, poor and white,
Barely daring to breathe or Achoo.

Daddy, I have had to kill you.
You died before I had time——
Marble-heavy, a bag full of God,
Ghastly statue with one grey toe
Big as a Frisco seal   *10*

And a head in the freakish Atlantic
Where it pours bean green over blue
In the waters off beautiful Nauset.
I used to pray to recover you.
Ache, du.

In the German tongue, in the Polish town
Scraped flat by the roller
Of wars, wars, wars.
But the name of the town is common.
My Polack friend   *20*

Says there are a dozen or two.
So I never could tell where you
Put your foot, your root,
I never could talk to you.
The tongue stuck in my jaw.

It stuck in a barb wire snare.
Ich, ich, ich, ich,
I could hardly speak.
I thought every German was you.
And the language obscene   *30*

An engine, an engine
Chuffing me off like a Jew.
A Jew to Dachau, Auschwitz, Belsen.
I began to talk like a Jew.
I think I may well be a Jew.

The snows of the Tyrol, the clear beer of Vienna
Are not very pure or true.
With my gypsy ancestress and my weird luck
And my Taroc ¹ pack and my Taroc pack
I may be a bit of a Jew.   *40*

¹ Variant spelling of Tarot.

I have always been scared of *you,*
With your Luftwaffe, your gobbledygoo.
And your neat moustache
And your Aryan eye, bright blue.
Panzer-man, panzer-man, O You——

Not God but a swastika
So black no sky could squeak through.
Every woman adores a Fascist,
The boot in the face, the brute
Brute heart of a brute like you.   50

You stand at the blackboard, daddy,
In the picture I have of you,
A cleft in your chin instead of your foot
But no less a devil for that, no not
Any less the black man who

Bit my pretty red heart in two.
I was ten when they buried you.
At twenty I tried to die
And get back, back, back to you.
I thought even the bones would do.   60

But they pulled me out of the sack,
And they stuck me together with glue.
And then I knew what to do.
I made a model of you,
A man in black with a Meinkampf look

And a love of the rack and the screw.
And I said I do, I do.
So daddy, I'm finally through.
The black telephone's off at the root,
The voices just can't worm through.   70

If I've killed one man, I've killed two——
The vampire who said he was you
And drank my blood for a year,
Seven years, if you want to know.
Daddy, you can lie back now.

There's a stake in your fat black heart
And the villagers never liked you.
They are dancing and stamping on you.
They always *knew* it was you.
Daddy, daddy, you bastard, I'm through.   80

LATER DRAMA

Later Drama

Since the end of the Second World War, the American theater (again, most of Broadway's marketable staples to the contrary) has been in a state of dizzying ferment. The innovations of the "little theater" movement of the 1910s and 1920s had been absorbed by the commercial theater long before the war, and that movement found its successor and continuation in the off-Broadway theaters of the fifties and in the off-off-Broadway theaters of the sixties, in newly developing repertory companies and experimental performing groups in many cities throughout the United States, and in the laboratory studios of university theaters. Again, any new development that attracted interest in these theaters was quickly absorbed by the commercial theater, and often, but not necessarily, vulgarized. Often enough the vulgarization was accomplished in the place of origin, but again, not necessarily.

Many things happened. In the first place, these smaller theaters introduced American audiences (and actors and playwrights) to new European styles and particularly to the theater of the absurd as exemplified in such plays as those of Beckett, Ionesco, and Genêt. These models in themselves encouraged a new drama of psychological crisis and introspection, but the very physical circumstances of these noncommercial theaters—relatively limited seating capacity, small performing space—in themselves almost necessitated a narrowing in the scope of subject matter, from the large social preoccupations often involving a generous *dramatis personae* in considerable theatrical movement, to the tighter, close-up presentation of the psychological situation of a few characters, often in quite static physical circumstances. The smaller size of these theaters also encouraged a new intimacy between the actors and their audience, until, finally, in what is called the "environment" theater, the audience is encouraged to join the action, often absurdly. The breakdown of that invisible fourth wall between actors and audience that the traditional proscenium arch had decreed was made possible by the development of the concept of theater in the round, or three-quarters round, or half round. When a conventional stage was still employed, the sets could still be highly unconventional—the old physical realism of furniture and painted flats being merely suggested, or sometimes not there at all. In many instances this simplification in production put a new emphasis on the language of drama; in many others, because of the new intimacy, it put the emphasis on the physical presence and the personality of the actors, a less happy development. Acting styles, in either case, and under the influence of certain new modish schools such as the Actors Studio, changed considerably. And then again the new influence of television plays, with their loose scenic structure and their tight scenic presentation, necessarily focusing on only a few characters in cramped quarters, contributed to the change in the nature of plays themselves. In reaction to that development, the most recent turn, the "democratized" theater of the "environment," has violently burst out of those bounds and turned the performing area into an arena for masses of bodies participating in sometimes orgiastic sports that can even spill out into the streets and the police station. In these curious excesses, language has ceased to be of any importance, and whatever it is that we are concerned with here (and whatever the merits may be), these are no longer a matter of literature.

To turn back from such spectacles as *Hair* and *Futz* to the plays of Thornton Wilder is like coming into a gracious shelter from a violent storm. Yet surely Wilder is a major link, unhappy as this thought might make him, between the experimental theater of Eugene O'Neill and the current extremities. Like O'Neill, Wilder began his theatrical career with experiments in very short plays (some of them not plays at all, or at least not intended to be staged), then produced his full-length *Our Town*, with its very simple story and multiple new devices of presentation, and brought things to a climax in *The Skin of Our Teeth*, written just before we entered the war and produced during it. The wartime context signifies, because this is a fable about the survival of the human race in spite of all the stupidity, folly, wickedness, and disaster that beset it. In its disregard for the conventions of time and space, in its employment of mythical and fabulous expansions, in its high-spirited disrespect for stage "decorum," especially its amusing (because relevant) device of audience participation, it was a high-water mark in American theatrical experiment. To this assertion one must quickly add another: taking the entire history of mankind as its subject, it was the last truly *ample* experiment that our theater has known.

Turning to Edward Albee's first play, *The Zoo Story*, presented at the Provincetown Playhouse in Greenwich Village eighteen years later, one sees all the difference in striking contrast. This play about the absurdity of existence involves only two characters, an "outsider" and a conformist. The first spends most of his time pacing up and down, the second, sitting on a park bench. The action is minimal but what there is is violent. The language—tense, idiomatic, elliptical—is nearly everything, and Albee's gift for dialog when he is willing to exercise it (as recently, he has not been) is remarkable. His theme is the reverse of Wilder's: man's compulsive self-destructiveness.

Between Wilder and Albee many new dramatists came into prominence, and of these at least two in a few of their plays may prove to have some enduring interest: Tennessee Williams and Arthur Miller. The two are quite different: Williams writes darkly and evocatively of the perverse and tortured homeless psyche; Miller writes lucidly and explicitly of the bewildered and defeated familial and social being. They share one quality: each imitates himself, so that the later work of both is not only exasperating but unfortunately stale, and it now seems very doubtful that either will ever again rise to the theatrical eloquence of his first success.

Some mention, even in a very compressed comment, must be made of the formidable presence of T. S. Eliot. For years he was concerned with bringing the poetic drama back to the living stage, believing as he did, and as W. B. Yeats had before him and many a younger dramatist has since, that the realistic play was a dead end. His greatest success was his earliest full-length attempt, *Murder in the Cathedral*. Ironically, that play was in itself a dead end; written, as it was, not to be performed in a theater (although that has been done many times to great effect), but in the charter house of the cathedral whose history it celebrates, it was a unique effort that can lead nowhere beyond itself. After that, in four more plays, Eliot tried to locate his double theme of secularity and redemption in modern settings, but using, almost to the end, classic Greek models to give both skeletal structure and reverberation to his plots. Attempting to adjust his exalted subject, the salvation of the Christian soul, to modern circumstances was not a simple task, and as one play followed another, while it seemed easier and easier for the characters to get a mundane drink, the realistic setting became more and more important and the poetic speech became more and more like prose. Yet there was always a portentous quality about these plays that annoyed some people, a kind of cold arrogance even as they made their plea for Christian humility, a certain pretentiousness—or so, at any rate, one contemporary of Eliot's, William Carlos Williams, felt. He wrote in exasperation to a friend, saying that he was writing a poetic drama, and he gave his friend a little sample of the dialog from this hypothetical work:

Christ: In my house there are many mansions.
Eliot: I'll take the corner room on the second floor overlooking the lawns and the river. And who is this rabble that follows you about?
Christ: Oh, some of the men I've met in my travels.
Eliot: Well, if I am to follow you I'd like to know something more of your sleeping arrangements.
Christ: Yes sir.

Except for the plays of Eliot, religious aspiration has had no important part in the American theatrical effort. Most recently, the issues that have animated it have been very mundane indeed and immediately contemporary, most notably, the Vietnam war and the situation of black people in a repressive white society. On this last issue, the most vigorous spokesman is LeRoi Jones.

To further the cause of Black Power, he was instrumental in organizing the revolutionary Black Arts Repertory Theatre in Harlem and, more recently, the Spirit House Movers and Players in Newark, New Jersey. His more personal contribution to this cause has been in a series of relatively short plays, all off-Broadway productions, of which *Dutchman* is perhaps the most effective. He is an enraged man, and rage is the first quality of these explosive works. They are deadly serious in a double sense: LeRoi Jones is not being metaphorical when he says that white blood must flow in the gutters. In their violence of feeling as of action, his plays stand at the opposite extreme from the orgiastic capers of the "flower people," whirling about to hard-rock music, intent only on sensation, mind expansion, and what they call love. LeRoi Jones's may or may not be a revolutionary theater; it is unquestionably a theater of hate, and hate unleashed, rampant, perhaps justified by the history of these times.

THORNTON [NIVEN] WILDER (1897–   )

Thornton Wilder, a quiet and urbane man, has twice been the center of noisy controversies from both of which he held himself coolly aloof. The first was Michael Gold's attack in the New Republic *in 1930, a "Marxist" denunciation of Wilder's aesthetic remoteness from the affairs of real life. Gold charged that his work created "a museum, not a world."* [1] *The second was in 1942, when the authors of* A Skeleton Key to Finnegans Wake *accused him of having plagiarized from Joyce's last book in* The Skin of Our Teeth. *While Wilder has always been interested in Joyce and while Joyce's book may well have given him certain suggestions for his play, the charge of plagiarism was absurd and irresponsible. Wilder emerged from both controversies unruffled and unharmed.*

He was born in Madison, Wisconsin, the son of the editor of one of the two local newspapers, and it must have been a considerably literary household, since not only Wilder himself, but both his brother and sister also became writers. When Wilder was nine, the family moved to China, where the father was American Consul-General at Hong Kong and Shanghai. The boy went to school there for a time but continued his education at Ojai, California, and Berkeley, Oberlin, and finally Yale (A.B., 1920). During the next two years he studied at the American Academy in Rome, where he began work on his first novel, The Cabala *(1926), an ironic treatment of decadent Italian aristocrats. He had appeared in print before: in 1919–1920,* The Yale Literary Magazine *had published his first work, a play called* The Trumpet Shall Sound, *which was produced by the American Laboratory Theatre in 1925.*

He continued to write and publish short, experimental plays, but his major effort first went into fiction. The Bridge of San Luis Rey *(1927), his great success, and* The Woman of Andros *(1930) were both set in past times.* Heaven's My Destination *(1935) presented an abrupt reversal, a satirical account of an American salesman that abandoned the elegant and rhythmical prose of the earlier novels for a skillful plunge into the vernacular.* Our Town *(1938), that nostalgic recreation of the daily routines of life in a small New England town, as simple and quiet as a poem by Robert Frost, while effectively experimental, also involved a reversal, now from the poetic and intellectual aspirations of the earlier shorter plays.*

For some years he had taught at the Lawrenceville School and, from 1930 to 1936, at the University of Chicago. He left teaching to set up residence outside New Haven and to travel. While he was to publish two more novels, The Ides of March *(1948), about the life*

[1] See pages 881–886.

of Julius Caesar, and The Eighth Day *(1967), an American chronicle, the theater held him:* The Merchant of Yonkers *(1938) became* The Matchmaker *(1954) and, in other hands, finally,* Hello, Dolly! *(1963). The great triumph came, of course, in* The Skin of Our Teeth, *a kind of climax and a kind of final curtain to thirty years of American stage history.*

FURTHER READING

The pioneering work is Rex Burbank's *Thornton Wilder* (1961), followed by Malcolm Goldstein's *The Art of Thornton Wilder* (1965). A limited but important critical study is Donald Haberman, *The Plays of Thornton Wilder* (1967). Bernard Grebanier published a brief pamphlet, *Thornton Wilder* (1964). Three German studies of the author are Helmut Papajewski, *Thornton Wilder* (1961); Hermann Stresau, *Thornton Wilder* (1963); and Heinz Beckmann, *Thornton Wilder* (1966).

The Skin of Our Teeth (1942)

CHARACTERS (IN ORDER OF THEIR APPEARANCE)

Announcer	*Miss E. Muse*
Sabina	*Miss T. Muse*
Mr. Fitzpatrick	*Miss M. Muse*
Mrs. Antrobus	*Two Ushers*
Dinosaur	*Two Drum Majorettes*
Mammoth	*Fortune Teller*
Telegraph Boy	*Two Chair-pushers*
Gladys	*Six Conveeners*
Henry	*Broadcast Official*
Mr. Antrobus	*Defeated Candidate*
Doctor	*Mr. Tremayne*
Professor	*Hester*
Judge	*Ivy*
Homer	*Fred Bailey*

Act I   Home, Excelsior, New Jersey

Act II   Atlantic City Boardwalk

Act III   Home, Excelsior, New Jersey

ACT I

A projection screen in the middle of the curtain. The first lantern slide: the name of the theatre, and the words: NEWS EVENTS OF THE WORLD. An ANNOUNCER'S *voice is heard.*

ANNOUNCER. The management takes pleasure in bringing to you— The News Events of the World:

Slide of the sun appearing above the horizon.

Freeport, Long Island:
The sun rose this morning at 6:32 a.m. This gratifying event was first reported by Mrs. Dorothy Stetson of Freeport, Long Island, who promptly telephoned the Mayor.

The Society for Affirming the End of the World at once went into a special session and postponed the arrival of that event for TWENTY-FOUR HOURS.

All honor to Mrs. Stetson for her public spirit.

New York City:

Slide of the front doors of the theatre in which this play is playing; three cleaning WOMEN *with mops and pails.*

The X Theatre. During the daily cleaning of this theatre a number of lost objects were collected as usual by Mesdames Simpson, Pateslewski, and Moriarty.

Among these objects found today was a wedding ring, inscribed: To Eva from Adam. Genesis II:18.

The ring will be restored to the owner or owners, if their credentials are satisfactory.

Tippehatchee, Vermont:

Slide representing a glacier.

The unprecedented cold weather of this summer has produced a condition that has not yet been satisfactorily explained. There is a report that a wall of ice is moving southward across these counties. The disruption of communications by the cold wave now crossing the country has rendered exact information difficult, but little credence is given to the rumor that the ice had pushed the Cathedral of Montreal as far as St. Albans, Vermont.

For further information see your daily papers.

Excelsior, New Jersey:

Slide of a modest suburban home.

The home of Mr. George Antrobus, the inventor of the wheel. The discovery of the wheel, following so closely on the discovery of the lever, has centered the attention of the country on Mr. Antrobus of this attractive suburban residence district. This is his home, a commodious seven-room house, conveniently situated near a public school, a Methodist church, and a firehouse; it is right handy to an A and P.

Slide of MR. ANTROBUS *on his front steps, smiling and lifting his straw hat. He holds a wheel.*

Mr. Antrobus, himself. He comes of very old stock and has made his way up from next to nothing.

It is reported that he was once a gardener, but left that situation under circumstances that have been variously reported.

Mr. Antrobus is a veteran of foreign wars, and bears a number of scars, front and back.

Slide of MRS. ANTROBUS, *holding some roses.*

This is Mrs. Antrobus, the charming and gracious president of the Excelsior Mothers' Club.

Mrs. Antrobus is an excellent needlewoman; it is she who invented the apron on which so many interesting changes have been rung since.

Slide of the FAMILY *and* SABINA.

Here we see the Antrobuses with their two children, Henry and Gladys, and friend. The friend in the rear, is Lily Sabina, the maid.

I know we all want to congratulate this typical American family on its enterprise. We all wish Mr. Antrobus a successful future. Now the management takes you to the interior of this home for a brief visit.

Curtain rises. Living room of a commuter's home. SABINA—*straw-blonde, over-rouged—is standing by the window back center, a feather duster under her elbow.*

SABINA. Oh, oh, oh! Six o'clock and the master not home yet.

Pray God nothing serious has happened to him crossing the Hudson River. If anything happened to him, we would certainly be inconsolable and have to move into a less desirable residence district.

The fact is I don't know what'll become of us. Here it is the middle of August and the coldest day of the year. It's simply freezing; the dogs are sticking to the sidewalks; can anybody explain that? No.

But I'm not surprised. The whole world's at sixes and sevens, and why the house hasn't fallen down about our ears long ago is a miracle to me.

A fragment of the right wall leans precariously over the stage. SABINA *looks at it nervously and it slowly rights itself.*

Every night this same anxiety as to whether the master will get home safely: whether he'll bring home anything to eat. In the midst of life we are in the midst of death, a truer word was never said.

The fragment of scenery flies up into the lofts. SABINA *is struck dumb with surprise, shrugs her shoulders and starts dusting* MR. ANTROBUS' *chair, including the under side.*

Of course, Mr. Antrobus is a very fine man, an excellent husband and father, a pillar of the church, and has all the best interests of the community at heart. Of course, every muscle goes tight every time he passes a policeman; but what I think is that there are certain charges that ought not to be made, and I think I may add, ought not to be allowed to be made; we're all human; who isn't? [*She dusts* MRS. ANTROBUS' *rocking chair.*] Mrs. Antrobus is as fine a woman as you could hope to see. She lives only for her children; and if it would be any benefit to her children she'd see the rest of us stretched out dead at her feet without turning a hair,—that's the truth. If you want to know anything more about Mrs. Antrobus, just go and look at a tigress, and look hard.

As to the children—

Well, Henry Antrobus is a real, clean-cut American boy. He'll graduate from High School one of these days, if they make the alphabet any easier.—Henry, when he has a stone in his hand, has a perfect aim; he can hit anything from a bird to an older brother—Oh! I didn't mean to say that!—but it certainly was an unfortunate accident, and it was very hard getting the police out of the house.

Mr. and Mrs. Antrobus' daughter is named Gladys. She'll make some good man a good wife some day, if he'll just come down off the movie screen and ask her.

So here we are!

We've managed to survive for some time now, catch as catch can, the fat and the lean, and if the dinosaurs don't trample us to death, and if the grasshoppers don't eat up our garden, we'll all live to see better days, knock on wood.

Each new child that's born to the Antrobuses seems to them to be sufficient reason for the whole universe's being set in motion; and each new child that dies seems to them to have been spared a whole world of sorrow, and what the end of it will be is still very much an open question.

We've rattled along, hot and cold, for some time now—[*A portion of the wall above the door, right, flies up into the air and disappears.*]—and my advice to you is not to inquire into why or whither, but just enjoy your ice cream while it's on your plate,—that's my philosophy.

Don't forget that a few years ago we came through the depression by the skin of our teeth! One more tight squeeze like that and where will we be? [*This is a cue line.* SABINA *looks angrily at the kitchen door and repeats:*] ... we came through the depression by the skin of our teeth; one more tight squeeze like that and where will we be? [*Flustered, she looks through the opening in the right wall; then goes to the window and reopens the Act.*] Oh, oh, oh! Six o'clock and the master not home yet. Pray God nothing has happened to him crossing the Hudson. Here it is the middle of August and the coldest day of the year. It's simply freezing; the dogs are sticking. One more tight squeeze like that and where will we be?

VOICE. [*Off stage.*] Make up something! Invent something!

SABINA. Well ... uh ... this certainly is a fine American home ... and—uh ... everybody's very happy ... and—uh ... [*Suddenly flings pretense to the winds and coming downstage says with indignation:*] I can't invent any words for this play, and I'm glad I can't. I hate this play and every word in it.

As for me, I don't understand a single word of it, anyway,—all about the troubles the human race has gone through, there's a subject for you.

Besides the author hasn't made up his silly mind as to whether we're all living back in caves or in New Jersey today, and that's the way it is all the way through.

Oh—why can't we have plays like we used to have—*Peg o' My Heart,* and *Smilin' Thru,* and *The Bat,* good entertainment with a message you can take home with you?

I took this hateful job because I had to. For two years I've sat up in my room living on a sandwich and a cup of tea a day, waiting for better times in the theatre. And look at me now: I—I who've played *Rain* and the *Barretts of Wimpole Street* and *First Lady*—God in Heaven!

MR. FITZPATRICK. [*The* STAGE MANAGER *puts his head out from the hole in the scenery.*] Miss Somerset!! Miss Somerset!

SABINA. Oh! Anyway!—nothing matters! It'll all be the same in a hundred years. [*Loudly.*] We came through the depression by the skin of our teeth,—that's true!—one more tight squeeze like that and where will we be?

Enter MRS. ANTROBUS, *a mother.*

MRS. ANTROBUS. Sabina, you've let the fire go out.

SABINA. [*In a lather.*] One-thing-and-another; don't-know-whether-my-wits-are-upside-or-down; might-as-well-be-dead-as-alive-in-a-house-all-sixes-and-sevens. ...

MRS. ANTROBUS. You've let the fire go out. Here it is the coldest day of the year right in the middle of August, and you've let the fire go out.

SABINA. Mrs. Antrobus, I'd like to give my two weeks' notice, Mrs. Antrobus. A girl like I can get a situation in a home where they're rich enough to have a fire in every room, Mrs. Antrobus, and a girl don't have to carry the responsibility of the whole house on her two shoulders. And a home without children, Mrs. Antrobus, because children are a thing only a parent can stand, and a truer word was never said; and a home, Mrs. Antrobus, where the master of the house don't pinch decent, self-respecting girls when he meets them in a dark corridor. I mention no names and make no charges. So you have my notice, Mrs. Antrobus. I hope that's perfectly clear.

MRS. ANTROBUS. You've let the fire go out!—Have you milked the mammoth?

SABINA. I don't understand a word of this play.—Yes, I've milked the mammoth.

MRS. ANTROBUS. Until Mr. Antrobus comes home we have no food and we have no fire. You'd better go over to the neighbors and borrow some fire.

SABINA. Mrs. Antrobus! I can't! I'd die on the way, you know I would. It's worse than January. The dogs are sticking to the sidewalks. I'd die.

MRS. ANTROBUS. Very well, I'll go.

SABINA. [*Even more distraught, coming forward and sinking on her knees.*] You'd never come back alive; we'd all perish; if you weren't here, we'd just perish. How do we know Mr. Antrobus'll be back? We don't know. If you go out, I'll just kill myself.

MRS. ANTROBUS. Get up, Sabina.

SABINA. Every night it's the same thing. Will he come back safe, or won't he? Will we starve to death, or freeze to death, or boil to death or will we be killed by burglars? I don't know why we go on living. I don't know why we go on living at all. It's easier being dead.

She flings her arms on the table and buries her head in them. In each of the succeeding speeches she flings her head up—and sometimes her hands— then quickly buries her head again.

MRS. ANTROBUS. The same thing! Always throwing up the sponge, Sabina. Always announcing your own death. But give you a new hat— or a plate of ice cream—or a ticket to the movies, and you want to live forever.

SABINA. You don't care whether we live or die; all you care about is those children. If it would be any benefit to them you'd be glad to see us all stretched out dead.

MRS. ANTROBUS. Well, maybe I would.

SABINA. And what do they care about? Themselves—that's all they care about. [*Shrilly.*] They make fun of you behind your back. Don't tell me: they're ashamed of you. Half the time, they pretend they're someone else's children. Little thanks you get from them.

MRS. ANTROBUS. I'm not asking for any thanks.

SABINA. And Mr. Antrobus—you don't understand *him*. All that work he does—trying to discover the alphabet and the multiplication table. Whenever he tries to learn anything you fight against it.

MRS. ANTROBUS. Oh, Sabina, I know you.

When Mr. Antrobus raped you home from your Sabine hills, he did it to insult me.

He did it for your pretty face, and to insult me.

You were the new wife, weren't you?

For a year or two you lay on your bed all day and polished the nails on your hands and feet:

You made puff-balls of the combings of your hair and you blew them up to the ceiling.

And I washed your underclothes and I made you chicken broths.

I bore children and between my very groans I stirred the cream that you'd put on your face.

But I knew you wouldn't last.

You didn't last.

SABINA. But it was I who encouraged Mr. Antrobus to make the alphabet. I'm sorry to say it, Mrs. Antrobus, but you're not a beautiful woman, and you can never know what a man could do if he tried. It's girls like I who inspire the multiplication table.

I'm sorry to say it, but you're not a beautiful woman, Mrs. Antrobus, and that's the God's truth.

MRS. ANTROBUS. And you didn't last—you sank to the kitchen. And what do you do there? *You let the fire go out!*

No wonder to you it seems easier being dead.

Reading and writing and counting on your fingers is all very well in their way,—but I keep the home going.

MRS. ANTROBUS.—There's that dinosaur on the front lawn again.— Shoo! Go away. Go away.

The baby DINOSAUR *puts his head in the window.*

DINOSAUR. It's cold.

MRS. ANTROBUS. You go around to the back of the house where you belong.

DINOSAUR. It's cold.

The DINOSAUR *disappears.* MRS. ANTROBUS *goes calmly out.*

SABINA *slowly raises her head and speaks to the audience. The central portion of the center wall rises, pauses, and disappears into the loft.*

SABINA. Now that you audience are listening to this, too, I understand it a little better.

I wish eleven o'clock were here; I don't want to be dragged through this whole play again.

The TELEGRAPH BOY *is seen entering along the back wall of the stage from the right. She catches sight of him and calls:*

Mrs. Antrobus! Mrs. Antrobus! Help! There's a strange man coming to the house. He's coming up the walk, help!

Enter MRS. ANTROBUS *in alarm, but efficient.*

MRS. ANTROBUS. Help me quick! [*They barricade the door by piling the furniture against it.*] Who is it? What do you want?

TELEGRAPH BOY. A telegram for Mrs. Antrobus from Mr. Antrobus in the city.

SABINA. Are you sure, are you sure? Maybe it's just a trap!

MRS. ANTROBUS. I know his voice, Sabina. We can open the door.

Enter the TELEGRAPH BOY, *12 years old, in uniform. The* DINOSAUR *and* MAMMOTH *slip by him into the room and settle down front right.*

I'm sorry we kept you waiting. We have to be careful, you know. [*To the* ANIMALS.] Hm! . . . Will you be quiet? [*They nod.*] Have you had your supper? [*They nod.*] Are you *ready* to come in? [*They nod.*]

Young man, have you any fire with you? Then light the grate, will you? [*He nods, produces something like a briquet; and kneels by the imagined fireplace, footlights center. Pause.*] What are people saying about this cold weather? [*He makes a doubtful shrug with his shoulders.*] Sabina, take this stick and go and light the stove.

SABINA. Like I told you, Mrs. Antrobus; two weeks. That's the law. I hope that's perfectly clear. [*Exit.*]

MRS. ANTROBUS. What about this cold weather?

TELEGRAPH BOY. [*Lowered eyes.*] Of course, I don't know anything . . . but they say there's a wall of ice moving down from the North, that's what they say. We can't get Boston by telegraph, and they're burning pianos in Hartford.

. . . It moves everything in front of it, churches and post offices and city halls.

I live in Brooklyn myself.

MRS. ANTROBUS. What are people doing about it?

TELEGRAPH BOY. Well . . . uh . . . Talking, mostly.

Or just what you'd do a day in February.

There are some that are trying to go South and the roads are crowded; but you can't take old people and children very far in a cold like this.

MRS. ANTROBUS.—What's this telegram you have for me?

TELEGRAPH BOY. [*Fingertips to his forehead.*] If you wait just a minute; I've got to remember it.

The ANIMALS *have left their corner and are nosing him. Presently they take places on either side of him, leaning against his hips, like heraldic beasts.*

This telegram was flashed from Murray Hill to University Heights! And then by puffs of smoke from University Heights to Staten Island.

And then by lantern from Staten Island to Plainfield, New Jersey. What hath God wrought! [*He clears his throat.*] "To Mrs. Antrobus, Excelsior, New Jersey: My dear wife, will be an hour late. Busy day at the office. Don't worry the children about the cold just keep them warm burn everything except Shakespeare." [*Pause.*]

MRS. ANTROBUS. Men!—He knows I'd burn ten Shakespeares to prevent a child of mine from having one cold in the head. What does it say next?

Enter SABINA.

TELEGRAPH BOY. "Have made great discoveries today have separated em from en."

SABINA. I know what that is, that's the alphabet, yes it is. Mr. Antrobus is just the cleverest man. Why, when the alphabet's finished, we'll be able to tell the future and everything.

TELEGRAPH BOY. Then listen to this: "Ten tens make a hundred semi-colon consequences far-reaching." [*Watches for effect.*]

MRS. ANTROBUS. The earth's turning to ice, and all he can do is to make up new numbers.

TELEGRAPH BOY. Well, Mrs. Antrobus, like the head man at our office said: a few more discoveries like that and we'll be worth freezing.

MRS. ANTROBUS. What does he say next?

TELEGRAPH BOY. I . . . I can't do this last part very well. [*He clears his throat and sings.*] "Happy w'dding ann'vers'ry to you, Happy ann'vers'ry to you—"

The ANIMALS *begin to howl soulfully;* SABINA *screams with pleasure.*

MRS. ANTROBUS. Dolly! Frederick! Be quiet.

TELEGRAPH BOY. [*Above the din.*] "Happy w'dding ann'vers'ry, dear Eva; happy w'dding ann'vers'ry to you."

MRS. ANTROBUS. Is that in the telegram? Are they singing telegrams now? [*He nods.*] The earth's getting so silly no wonder the sun turns cold.

SABINA. Mrs. Antrobus, I want to take back the notice I gave you. Mrs. Antrobus, I don't want to leave a house that gets such interesting telegrams and I'm sorry for anything I said. I really am.

MRS. ANTROBUS. Young man, I'd like to give you something for all this trouble; Mr. Anthrobus isn't home yet and I have no money and no food in the house—

TELEGRAPH BOY. Mrs. Antrobus . . . I don't like to . . . appear to . . . ask for anything, but . . .

MRS. ANTROBUS. What is it you'd like?

TELEGRAPH BOY. Do you happen to have an old needle you could spare? My wife just sits home all day thinking about needles.

SABINA. [*Shrilly.*] We only got two in the house, Mrs. Antrobus, you know we only got two in the house.

MRS. ANTROBUS. [*After a look at* SABINA *taking a needle from her collar.*] Why yes, I can spare this.

TELEGRAPH BOY. [*Lowered eyes.*] Thank you, Mrs. Antrobus. Mrs. Antrobus, can I ask you something else? I have two sons of my own; if the cold gets worse, what should I do?

SABINA. I think we'll all perish, that's what I think. Cold like this in August is just the end of the whole world. [*Silence.*]

MRS. ANTROBUS. I don't know. After all, what does one do about anything? Just keep as warm as you can. And don't let your wife and children see that you're worried.

TELEGRAPH BOY. Yes. . . . Thank you, Mrs. Antrobus. Well, I'd better be going.—Oh, I forgot! There's one more sentence in the telegram. "Three cheers have invented the wheel."

MRS. ANTROBUS. A wheel? What's a wheel?

TELEGRAPH BOY. I don't know. That's what it said. The sign for it is like this. Well, goodbye.

The WOMEN *see him to the door, with goodbyes and injunctions to keep warm.*

SABINA. [*Apron to her eyes, wailing.*] Mrs. Antrobus, it looks to me like all the nice men in the world are already married; I don't know why that is. [*Exit.*]

MRS. ANTROBUS. [*Thoughtful; to the* ANIMALS.] Do you ever remember hearing tell of any cold like this in August? [*The* ANIMALS *shake their heads.*] From your grandmothers or anyone? [*They shake their heads.*] Have you any suggestions? [*They shake their heads. She pulls her shawl around, goes to the front door and opening it an inch calls:*]

HENRY. GLADYS. CHILDREN. Come right in and get warm. No, no, when mama says a thing she means it.

Henry! HENRY. Put down that stone. You know what happened last time. [*Shriek.*] HENRY! Put down that stone!

Gladys! Put down your dress!! Try and be a lady.

The CHILDREN *bound in and dash to the fire. They take off their winter things and leave them in heaps on the floor.*

GLADYS. Mama, I'm hungry. Mama, why is it so cold?

HENRY. [At the same time.] Mama, why doesn't it snow? Mama, when's supper ready? Maybe, it'll snow and we can make snowballs.

GLADYS. Mama, it's so cold that in one more minute I just couldn't of stood it.

MRS. ANTROBUS. Settle down, both of you, I want to talk to you.

She draws up a hassock and sits front center over the orchestra pit before the imaginary fire. The CHILDREN *stretch out on the floor, leaning against her lap. Tableau by Raphael. The* ANIMALS *edge up and complete the triangle.*

It's just a cold spell of some kind. Now listen to what I'm saying: When your father comes home I want you to be extra quiet. He's had a hard day at the office and I don't know but what he may have one of his moods.

I just got a telegram from him very happy and excited, and you

know what that means. Your father's temper's uneven; I guess you know
that. [*Shriek.*]

Henry! Henry!

Why—why can't you remember to keep your hair down over your
forehead? You must keep that scar covered up. Don't you know that
when your father sees it he loses all control over himself? He goes crazy.
He wants to die.

*After a moment's despair she collects herself decisively, wets the hem of her
apron in her mouth and starts polishing his forehead vigorously.*

Lift your head up. Stop squirming. Blessed me, sometimes I think
that it's going away—and then there it is: just as red as ever.

HENRY. Mama, today at school two teachers forgot and called me by
my old name. They forgot, Mama. You'd better write another letter to
the principal, so that he'll tell them I've changed my name. Right out in
class they called me: Cain.

MRS. ANTROBUS. [*Putting her hand on his mouth, too late; hoarsely.*]
Don't say it. [*Polishing feverishly.*] If you're good they'll forget it. Henry,
you didn't hit anyone . . . today, did you?

HENRY. Oh . . . no-o-o!

MRS. ANTROBUS. [*Still working, not looking at Gladys.*] And, Gladys,
I want you to be especially nice to your father tonight. You know what
he calls you when you're good—his little angel, his little star. Keep your
dress down like a little lady. And keep your voice nice and low. Gladys
Antrobus!! What's that red stuff you have on your face? [*Slaps her.*]
You're a filthy detestable child! [*Rises in real, though temporary, repudiation and despair.*]

Get away from me, both of you! I wish I'd never seen sight or sound
of you. Let the cold come! I can't stand it. I don't want to go on. [*She
walks away.*]

GLADYS. [*Weeping.*] All the girls at school do, Mama.

MRS. ANTROBUS. [*Shrieking.*] I'm through with you, that's all!—
Sabina! Sabina!—Don't you know your father'd go crazy if he saw that
paint on your face? Don't you know your father thinks you're perfect?
Don't you know he couldn't live if he didn't think you were perfect?—
Sabina!

Enter SABINA.

SABINA. Yes, Mrs. Antrobus!

MRS. ANTROBUS. Take this girl out into the kitchen and wash her
face with the scrubbing brush.

MR. ANTROBUS. [*Outside, roaring.*] "I've been working on the railroad, all the livelong day . . . etc."

The ANIMALS *start running around in circles, bellowing.* SABINA *rushes to the
window.*

MRS. ANTROBUS. Sabina, what's that noise outside?

SABINA. Oh, it's a drunken tramp. It's a giant, Mrs. Antrobus. We'll all be killed in our beds, I know it!

MRS. ANTROBUS. Help me quick. Quick. Everybody.

Again they stack all the furniture against the door. MR. ANTROBUS *pounds and bellows.*

Who is it? What do you want?—Sabina, have you any boiling water ready?—Who is it?

MR. ANTROBUS. Broken-down camel of a pig's snout, open this door.

MRS. ANTROBUS. God be praised! It's your father.—Just a minute, George!—Sabina, clear the door, quick. Gladys, come here while I clean your nasty face!

MR. ANTROBUS. She-bitch of a goat's gizzard, I'll break every bone in your body. Let me in or I'll tear the whole house down.

MRS. ANTROBUS. Just a minute, George, something's the matter with the lock.

MR. ANTROBUS. Open the door or I'll tear your livers out. I'll smash your brains on the ceiling, and Devil take the hindmost.

MRS. ANTROBUS. Now, you can open the door, Sabina. I'm ready.

The door is flung open. Silence. MR. ANTROBUS—*face of a Keystone Comedy Cop—stands there in fur cap and blanket. His arms are full of parcels, including a large stone wheel with a center in it. One hand carries a railroad man's lantern. Suddenly he bursts into joyous roar.*

MR. ANTROBUS. Well, how's the whole crooked family?

Relief. Laughter. Tears. Jumping up and down. ANIMALS *cavorting.* ANTROBUS *throws the parcels on the ground. Hurls his cap and blanket after them. Heroic embraces. Melee of* HUMANS *and* ANIMALS, SABINA *included.*

I'll be scalded and tarred if a man can't get a little welcome when he comes home. Well, Maggie, you old gunny-sack, how's the broken down old weather hen?—Sabina, old fishbait, old skunkpot.—And the children,—how've the little smellers been?

GLADYS. Papa, Papa, Papa, Papa, Papa.

MR. ANTROBUS. How've they been, Maggie?

MRS. ANTROBUS. Well, I must say, they've been as good as gold. I haven't had to raise my voice once. I don't know what's the matter with them.

ANTROBUS. [*Kneeling before* GLADYS.] Papa's little weasel, eh?—Sabina, there's some food for you.—Papa's little gopher?

GLADYS. [*Her arm around his neck.*] Papa, you're always teasing me.

ANTROBUS. And Henry? Nothing rash today, I hope. Nothing rash?

HENRY. No, Papa.

ANTROBUS. [*Roaring.*] Well that's good, that's good—I'll bet Sabina let the fire go out.

SABINA. Mr. Antrobus, I've given my notice. I'm leaving two weeks from today. I'm sorry, but I'm leaving.

ANTROBUS. [*Roar.*] Well, if you leave now you'll freeze to death, so go and cook the dinner.

SABINA. Two weeks, that's the law. [*Exit.*]

ANTROBUS. Did you get my telegram?

MRS. ANTROBUS. Yes.—What's a wheel?

He indicates the wheel with a glance. HENRY *is rolling it around the floor. Rapid, hoarse interchange:* MRS. ANTROBUS: *What does this cold weather mean? It's below freezing.* ANTROBUS: *Not before the children!* MRS. ANTROBUS: *Shouldn't we do something about it?—start off, move?* ANTROBUS: *Not before the children!!! He gives* HENRY *a sharp slap.*

HENRY. Papa, you hit me!

ANTROBUS. Well, remember it. That's to make you remember today. Today. The day the alphabet's finished; and the day that we *saw* the hundred—the hundred, the hundred, the hundred, the hundred, the hundred—there's no end to 'em.

I've had a day at the office!

Take a look at that wheel, Maggie—when I've got that to rights: you'll see a sight.

There's a reward there for all the walking you've done.

MRS. ANTROBUS. How do you mean?

ANTROBUS. [*On the hassock looking into the fire; with awe.*] Maggie, we've reached the top of the wave. There's not much more to be done. We're there!

MRS. ANTROBUS. [*Cutting across his mood sharply.*] And the ice?

ANTROBUS. The ice!

HENRY. [*Playing with the wheel.*] Papa, you could put a chair on this.

ANTROBUS. [*Broodingly.*] Ye-e-s, any booby can fool with it now,—but I thought of it first.

MRS. ANTROBUS. Children, go out in the kitchen. I want to talk to your father alone. [*The* CHILDREN *go out.*]

ANTROBUS *has moved to his chair up left. He takes the goldfish bowl on his lap; pulls the canary cage down to the level of his face. Both the* ANIMALS *put their paws up on the arm of his chair.* MRS. ANTROBUS *faces him across the room, like a judge.*

MRS. ANTROBUS. Well?

ANTROBUS. [*Shortly.*] It's cold.—How things been, eh? Keck, keck, keck.—And you, Millicent?

MRS. ANTROBUS. I know it's cold.

ANTROBUS. [*To the canary.*] No spilling of sunflower seed, eh? No singing after lights-out, y'know what I mean?

MRS. ANTROBUS. You can try and prevent us freezing to death, can't you? You can do something? We can start moving. Or we can go on the animals' backs?

ANTROBUS. The best thing about animals is that they don't talk much.

MAMMOTH. It's cold.

ANTROBUS. Eh, eh, eh! Watch that!—

By midnight we'd turn to ice. The roads are full of people now who can scarcely lift a foot from the ground. The grass out in front is like iron,—which reminds me, I have another needle for you.—The people up north—where are they?

Frozen . . . crushed. . . .

MRS. ANTROBUS. Is that what's going to happen to us?—Will you answer me?

ANTROBUS. I don't know. I don't know anything. Some say that the ice is going slower. Some say that it's stopped. The sun's growing cold. What can I do about that? Nothing we can do but burn everything in the house, and the fenceposts and the barn. Keep the fire going. When we have no more fire, we die.

MRS. ANTROBUS. Well, why didn't you say so in the first place?

MRS. ANTROBUS *is about to march off when she catches sight of two* REFUGEES, *men, who have appeared against the back wall of the theatre and who are soon joined by others.*

REFUGEES. Mr. Antrobus! Mr. Antrobus! Mr. An-nn-tro-bus!

MRS. ANTROBUS. Who's that? Who's that calling you?

ANTROBUS. [*Clearing his throat guiltily.*] Mm—let me see.

Two REFUGEES *come up to the window.*

REFUGEE. Could we warm our hands for a moment, Mr. Antrobus. It's very cold, Mr. Antrobus.

ANOTHER REFUGEE. Mr. Antrobus, I wonder if you had a piece of bread or something that you could spare.

Silence. They wait humbly. MRS. ANTROBUS *stands rooted to the spot. Suddenly a knock at the door, then another hand knocking in short rapid blows.*

MRS. ANTROBUS. Who are these people? Why, they're all over the front yard. What have they come *here* for?

Enter SABINA.

SABINA. Mrs. Antrobus! There are some tramps knocking at the back door.

MRS. ANTROBUS. George, tell these people to go away. Tell them to move right along. I'll go and send them away from the back door. Sabina, come with me. [*She goes out energetically.*]

ANTROBUS. Sabina! Stay here! I have something to say to you. [*He goes to the door and opens it a crack and talks through it.*]

Ladies and gentlemen! I'll have to ask you to wait a few minutes longer. It'll be all right . . . while you're waiting you might each one pull up a stake of the fence. We'll need them all for the fireplace. There'll be coffee and sandwiches in a moment.

SABINA *looks out door over his shoulder and suddenly extends her arm pointing, with a scream.*

SABINA. Mr. Antrobus, what's that??—that big white thing? Mr. Antrobus, it's ICE. It's ICE!!

ANTROBUS. Sabina, I want you to go in the kitchen and make a lot of coffee. Make a whole pail full.

SABINA. Pail full!!

ANTROBUS. [*With gesture.*] And sandwiches . . . piles of them . . . like this.

SABINA. Mr. An . . . !! [*Suddenly she drops the play, and says in her own person as* MISS SOMERSET, *with surprise.*] Oh, I see what this part of the play means now! This means refugees. [*She starts to cross to the proscenium.*] Oh, I don't like it. I don't like it. [*She leans against the proscenium and bursts into tears.*]

ANTROBUS. Miss Somerset!

Voice of the STAGE MANAGER.

Miss Somerset!

SABINA. [*Energetically, to the audience.*] Ladies and gentlemen! Don't take this play serious. The world's not coming to an end. You know it's not. People exaggerate! Most people really have enough to eat and a roof over their heads. Nobody actually starves—you can always eat grass or something. That ice-business—why, it was a long, long time ago. Besides they were only savages. Savages don't love their families—not like we do.

ANTROBUS *and* STAGE MANAGER. Miss Somerset!!

There is renewed knocking at the door.

SABINA. All right. I'll say the lines, but I won't think about the play.

Enter MRS. ANTROBUS.

SABINA. [*Parting thrust at the audience.*] And I advise *you* not to think about the play, either. [*Exit* SABINA.]

MRS. ANTROBUS. George, these tramps say that you asked them to come to the house. What does this mean?

Knocking at the door.

ANTROBUS. Just . . . uh. . . . There are a few friends, Maggie, I met on the road. Real nice, real useful people. . . .

MRS. ANTROBUS. [*Back to the door.*] Now, don't you ask them in! George Antrobus, not another soul comes in here over my dead body.

ANTROBUS. Maggie, there's a doctor there. Never hurts to have a good doctor in the house. We've lost a peck of children, one way and another. You can never tell when a child's throat will be stopped up. What you and I have seen—! ! ! [*He puts his fingers on his throat, and imitates diphtheria.*]

MRS. ANTROBUS. Well, just one person then, the Doctor. The others can go right along the road.

ANTROBUS. Maggie, there's an old man, particular friend of mine—

MRS. ANTROBUS. I won't listen to you—

ANTROBUS. It was he that really started off the A.B.C.'s.

MRS. ANTROBUS. I don't care if he perishes. We can do without reading or writing. We can't do without food.

ANTROBUS. Then let the ice come!! Drink your coffee!! I don't want any coffee if I can't drink it with some good people.

MRS. ANTROBUS. Stop shouting. Who else is there trying to push us off the cliff?

ANTROBUS. Well, there's the man . . . who makes all the laws. Judge Moses!

MRS. ANTROBUS. Judges can't help us now.

ANTROBUS. And if the ice melts? . . . and if we pull through? Have you and I been able to bring up Henry? What have we done?

MRS. ANTROBUS. Who are those old women?

ANTROBUS. [*Coughs.*] Up in town there are nine sisters. There are three or four of them here. They're sort of music teachers . . . and one of them recites and one of them—

MRS. ANTROBUS. That's the end. A singing troupe! Well, take your choice, live or die. Starve your own children before your face.

ANTROBUS. [*Gently.*] These people don't take much. They're used to starving.

They'll sleep on the floor.

Besides, Maggie, listen: no, listen:

Who've we got in the house, but Sabina? Sabina's always afraid the worst will happen. Whose spirits can she keep up? Maggie, these people never give up. They think they'll live and work forever.

MRS. ANTROBUS. [*Walks slowly to the middle of the room.*] All right, let them in. Let them in. You're master here. [*Softly.*]—But these animals must go. Enough's enough. They'll soon be big enough to push the walls down, anyway. Take them away.

ANTROBUS. [*Sadly.*] All right. The dinosaur and mammoth—! Come on, baby, come on Frederick. Come for a walk. That's a good little fellow.

DINOSAUR. It's cold.

ANTROBUS. Yes, nice cold fresh air. Bracing.

He holds the door open and the ANIMALS *go out. He beckons to his friends. The* REFUGEES *are typical elderly out-of-works from the streets of New York today.* JUDGE MOSES *wears a skull cap.* HOMER *is a blind beggar with a guitar. The seedy crowd shuffles in and waits humbly and expectantly.* ANTROBUS *introduces them to his wife who bows to each with a stately bend of her head.*

Make yourself at home, Maggie, this the doctor ... m ... Coffee'll be here in a minute. ... Professor, this is my wife. ... And: ... Judge ... Maggie, you know the Judge. [*An old blind man with a guitar.*] Maggie, you know ... you know Homer?—Come right in, Judge.—Miss Muse—are some of your sisters here? Come right in. ... Miss E. Muse; Miss T. Muse, Miss M. Muse.

MRS. ANTROBUS. Pleased to meet you.

Just ... make yourself comfortable. Supper'll be ready in a minute. [*She goes out, abruptly.*]

ANTROBUS. Make yourself at home, friends. I'll be right back. [*He goes out.*]

The REFUGEES *stare about them in awe. Presently several voices start whispering "Homer! Homer!" All take it up.* HOMER *strikes a chord or two on his guitar, then starts to speak:*

HOMER. Μῆνιν ἄειδε, θεὰ, Πηληϊάδεω Ἀχιλῆος, οὐλομένην, ἣ μυρί' Ἀχαιοῖς ἄλγε' ἔθηκεν, πολλὰς δ' ἰφθίμους ψυχὰς—[1]

HOMER'S *face shows he is lost in thought and memory and the words die away on his lips. The* REFUGEES *likewise nod in dreamy recollection. Soon the whisper "Moses, Moses!" goes around. An aged Jew parts his beard and recites dramatically:*

MOSES. בְּרֵאשִׁית בָּרָא אֱלֹהִים אֵת הַשָּׁמַיִם וְאֵת הָאָרֶץ: וְהָאָרֶץ הָיְתָה תֹהוּ

וָבֹהוּ וְחֹשֶׁךְ עַל־פְּנֵי תְהוֹם וְרוּחַ אֱלֹהִים מְרַחֶפֶת עַל־פְּנֵי הַמָּיִם:[2]

The same dying away of the words take place, and on the part of the REFUGEES *the same retreat into recollection. Some of them murmur, "Yes, yes."*

The mood is broken by the abrupt entrance of MR. *and* MRS. ANTROBUS

---

[1] Opening lines of Homer's *Iliad:* "The wrath of Achilles is my theme, that fatal wrath, which, in fulfillment of the will of Zeus, brought the Achaeans so much suffering and many brave souls...."

[2] The opening lines of Genesis: "In the beginning God created the heavens and the earth. And the earth was waste and void; and darkness was on the face of the deep...."

and SABINA *bearing platters of sandwiches and a pail of coffee.* SABINA *stops and stares at the guests.*

MR. ANTROBUS. Sabina, pass the sandwiches.

SABINA. I thought I was working in a respectable house that had respectable guests. I'm giving my notice, Mr. Antrobus: two weeks, that's the law.

MR. ANTROBUS. Sabina! Pass the sandwiches.

SABINA. Two weeks, that's the law.

MR. ANTROBUS. There's the law. That's Moses.

SABINA. [*Stares.*] The Ten Commandments—FAUGH!!—(*To Audience*) That's the worst line I've ever had to say on any stage.

ANTROBUS. I think the best thing to do is just not to stand on ceremony, but pass the sandwiches around from left to right.—Judge, help yourself to one of these.

MRS. ANTROBUS. The roads are crowded, I hear?

THE GUESTS. [*All talking at once.*] Oh, ma'am, you can't imagine. . . . You can hardly put one foot before you . . . people are trampling one another. [*Sudden silence.*]

MRS. ANTROBUS. Well, you know what I think it is,—I think it's sunspots!

THE GUESTS. [*Discreet hubbub.*] Oh, you're right, Mrs. Antrobus . . . that's what it is. . . . That's what I was saying the other day. [*Sudden silence.*]

ANTROBUS. Well, I don't believe the whole world's going to turn to ice. [*All eyes are fixed on him, waiting:*] I can't believe it. Judge! Have we worked for nothing? Professor! Have we just failed in the whole thing?

MRS. ANTROBUS. It is certainly very strange—well fortunately on both sides of the family we come of very hearty stock.—Doctor, I want you to meet my children. They're eating their supper now. And of course I want them to meet you.

MISS M. MUSE. How many children have you, Mrs. Antrobus?

MRS. ANTROBUS. I have two,—a boy and a girl.

THE JUDGE. [MOSES, *softly.*] I understood you had two sons, Mrs. Antrobus.

MRS. ANTROBUS *in blind suffering; she walks toward the footlights.*

MRS. ANTROBUS. [*In a low voice.*] Abel, Abel, my son, my son, Abel, my son, Abel, Abel, my son.

The REFUGEES *move with few steps toward her as though in comfort murmuring words in Greek, Hebrew, German, et cetera.*

*A piercing shriek from the kitchen,—*SABINA'S *voice. All heads turn.*

ANTROBUS. What's that?

SABINA *enters, bursting with indignation, pulling on her gloves.*

SABINA. Mr. Antrobus—that son of yours, that boy Henry Antrobus —I don't stay in this house another moment!—He's not fit to live among respectable folks and that's a fact.

MRS. ANTROBUS. Don't say another word, Sabina. I'll be right back. [*Without waiting for an answer she goes past her into the kitchen.*]

SABINA. Mr. Antrobus, Henry has thrown a stone again and if he hasn't killed the boy that lives next door, I'm very much mistaken. He finished his supper and went out to play; and I heard such a fight; and then I saw it. I saw it with my own eyes. And it looked to me like stark murder.

MRS. ANTROBUS *appears at the kitchen door, shielding* HENRY *who follows her. When she steps aside, we see on* HENRY'S *forehead a large ochre and scarlet scar in the shape of a C.* MR. ANTROBUS *starts toward him. A pause.* HENRY *is heard saying under his breath:*

HENRY. He was going to take the wheel away from me. He started to throw a stone at me first.

MRS. ANTROBUS. George, it was just a boyish impulse. Remember how young he is. [*Louder, in an urgent wail.*] George, he's only four thousand years old.

SABINA. And everything was going along so nicely!

Silence. ANTROBUS *goes back to the fireplace.*

ANTROBUS. Put out the fire! Put out all the fires. [*Violently.*] No wonder the sun grows cold. [*He starts stamping on the fireplace.*]

MRS. ANTROBUS. Doctor! Judge! Help me!—George, have you lost your mind?

ANTROBUS. There is no mind. We'll not try to live. [*To the guests.*] Give it up. Give up trying.

MRS. ANTROBUS *seizes him.*

SABINA. Mr. Antrobus! I'm downright ashamed of you.

MRS. ANTROBUS. George, have some more coffee.—Gladys! Where's Gladys gone?

GLADYS *steps in, frightened.*

GLADYS. Here I am, mama.

MRS. ANTROBUS. Go upstairs and bring your father's slippers. How could you forget a thing like that, when you know how tired he is?

ANTROBUS *sits in his chair. He covers his face with his hands.* MRS. ANTROBUS *turns to the* REFUGEES:

Can't some of you sing? It's your business in life to sing, isn't it? Sabina!

Several of the women clear their throats tentatively, and with frightened faces gather around HOMER'S *guitar. He establishes a few chords. Almost inaudibly they start singing, led by* SABINA: *"Jingle Bells."* MRS. ANTROBUS *continues to* ANTROBUS *in a low voice, while taking off his shoes:*

George, remember all the other times. When the volcanoes came right up in the front yard.

And the time the grasshoppers ate every single leaf and blade of grass, and all the grain and spinach you'd grown with your own hands. And the summer there were earthquakes every night.

ANTROBUS. Henry! Henry! [*Puts his hand on his forehead.*] Myself. All of us, we're covered with blood.

MRS. ANTROBUS. Then remember all the times you were pleased with him and when you were proud of yourself.—Henry! Henry! Come here and recite to your father the multiplication table that you do so nicely.

HENRY *kneels on one knee beside his father and starts whispering the multiplication table.*

HENRY. [*Finally.*] Two times six is twelve; three times six is eighteen—I don't think I know the sixes.

Enter GLADYS *with the slippers.* MRS. ANTROBUS *makes stern gestures to her: Go in there and do your best. The* GUESTS *are now singing "Tenting Tonight."*

GLADYS. [*Putting slippers on his feet.*] Papa . . . papa . . . I was very good in school today. Miss Conover said right out in class that if all the girls had as good manners as Gladys Antrobus, that the world would be a very different place to live in.

MRS. ANTROBUS. You recited a piece at assembly, didn't you? Recite it to your father.

GLADYS. Papa, do you want to hear what I recited in class? [*Fierce directorial glance from her mother.*] "THE STAR" by Henry Wadsworth LONGFELLOW.

MRS. ANTROBUS. Wait!!! The fire's going out. There isn't enough wood! Henry, go upstairs and bring down the chairs and start breaking up the beds.

Exit HENRY. *The singers return to "Jingle Bells," still very softly.*

GLADYS. Look, Papa, here's my report card. Lookit. Conduct A! Look, Papa, Papa, do you want to hear the Star, by Henry Wadsworth Longfellow? Papa, you're not mad at me, are you?—I know it'll get warmer. Soon it'll be just like spring, and we can go to a picnic at the Hibernian Picnic Grounds like you always like to do, don't you remember? Papa, just look at me once.

Enter HENRY *with some chairs.*

ANTROBUS. You recited in assembly, did you? [*She nods eagerly.*] You didn't forget it?

GLADYS. No!!! I was perfect.

Pause. Then ANTROBUS *rises, goes to the front door and opens it. The* REFUGEES *draw back timidly; the song stops; he peers out of the door, then closes it.*

ANTROBUS. [*With decision, suddenly.*] Build up the fire. It's cold. Build up the fire. We'll do what we can. Sabina, get some more wood. Come around the fire, everybody. At least the young ones may pull through. Henry, have you eaten something?

HENRY. Yes, papa.

ANTROBUS. Gladys, have you had some supper?

GLADYS. I ate in the kitchen, papa.

ANTROBUS. If you do come through this—what'll you be able to do? What do you know? Henry, did you take a good look at that wheel?

HENRY. Yes, papa.

ANTROBUS. [*Sitting down in his chair.*] Six times two are—

HENRY.—twelve; six times three are eighteen; six times four are— Papa, it's hot and cold. It makes my head all funny. It makes me sleepy.

ANTROBUS. [*Gives him a cuff.*] Wake up. I don't care if your head is sleepy. Six times four are twenty-four. Six times five are—

HENRY. Thirty. Papa!

ANTROBUS. Maggie, put something into Gladys head on the chance she can use it.

MRS. ANTROBUS. What do you mean, George?

ANTROBUS. Six times six are thirty-six. Teach her the beginning of the Bible.

GLADYS. But, Mama, it's so cold and close.

HENRY *has all but drowsed off. His father slaps him sharply and the lesson goes on.*

MRS. ANTROBUS. "In the beginning God created the heavens and the earth; and the earth was waste and void; and the darkness was upon the face of the deep—"

The singing starts up again louder. SABINA *has returned with wood.*

SABINA. [*After placing wood on the fireplace comes down to the footlights and addresses the audience:*] Will you please start handing up your chairs? We'll need everything for this fire. Save the human race.— Ushers, will you pass the chairs up here? Thank you.

HENRY. Six times nine are fifty-four; six times ten are sixty.

In the back of the auditorium the sound of chairs being ripped up can be heard. USHERS *rush down the aisles with chairs and hand them over.*

GLADYS. "And God called the light Day and the darkness he called Night."

SABINA. Pass up your chairs, everybody. Save the human race.

CURTAIN

ACT II

*Toward the end of the intermission, though with the houselights
still up, lantern slide projections begin to appear on the curtain. Timetables for trains leaving Pennsylvania Station for Atlantic City. Advertisements of Atlantic City hotels, drugstores, churches, rug merchants;
fortune tellers; Bingo parlors.*

When the house-lights go down, the voice of an ANNOUNCER *is
heard.*

ANNOUNCER. The Management now brings you the News Events of
the World. Atlantic City, New Jersey:

*Projection of a chrome postcard of the waterfront, trimmed in mica with the
legend: FUN AT THE BEACH.*

This great convention city is playing host this week to the anniversary
convocation of that great fraternal order,—the Ancient and Honorable
Order of Mammals, Subdivision Humans. This great fraternal, militant
and burial society is celebrating on the Boardwalk, ladies and gentlemen, its six hundred thousandth Annual Convention.

It has just elected its president for the ensuing term,—

Projection of MR. *and* MRS. ANTROBUS *posed as they will be shown a few
moments later.*

Mr. George Antrobus of Excelsior, New Jersey. We show you President
Antrobus and his gracious and charming wife, every inch a mammal.
Mr. Antrobus has had a long and chequered career. Credit has been paid
to him for many useful enterprises including the introduction of the
lever, of the wheel and the brewing of beer. Credit has been also extended to President Antrobus's gracious and charming wife for many
practical suggestions, including the hem, the gore, and the gusset; and
the novelty of the year,—frying in oil. Before we show you Mr. Antrobus
accepting the nomination, we have an important announcement to
make. As many of you know, this great celebration of the Order of the
Mammals has received delegations from the other rival Orders,—or
shall we say: esteemed concurrent Orders: the WINGS, the FINS, the
SHELLS, and so on. These Orders are holding their conventions also,
in various parts of the world, and have sent representatives to our own,
two of a kind.

Later in the day we will show you President Antrobus broadcasting
his words of greeting and congratulation to the collected assemblies of
the whole natural world.

Ladies and Gentlemen! We give you President Antrobus!

The screen becomes a Transparency. MR. ANTROBUS *stands beside a pedestal;*
MRS. ANTROBUS *is seated wearing a corsage of orchids.* ANTROBUS *wears an
untidy Prince Albert; spats; from a red rosette in his buttonhole hangs a fine*

long purple ribbon of honor. He wears a gay lodge hat,—something between a fez and a legionnaire's cap.

ANTROBUS. Fellow-mammals, fellow-vertebrates, fellow-humans, I thank you. Little did my dear parents think,—when they told me to stand on my own two feet,—that I'd arrive at this place.

My friends, we have come a long way.

During this week of happy celebration it is perhaps not fitting that we dwell on some of the difficult times we have been through. The dinosaur is extinct—[*Applause.*]—the ice has retreated; and the common cold is being pursued by every means within our power.

MRS. ANTROBUS *sneezes, laughs prettily, murmurs: "I beg your pardon."*

In our memorial service yesterday we did honor to all our friends and relatives who are no longer with us, by reason of cold, earthquakes, plagues and . . . and . . . [*Coughs.*] differences of opinion.

As our Bishop so ably said . . . uh . . . so ably said. . . .

MRS. ANTROBUS. [*Closed lips.*] Gone, but not forgotten.

ANTROBUS. 'They are gone, but not forgotten.'

I think I can say, I think I can prophecy with complete . . . .uh . . . with complete. . . .

MRS. ANTROBUS. Confidence.

ANTROBUS. Thank you, my dear,—With complete lack of confidence, that a new day of security is about to dawn.

The watchword of the closing year was: Work. I give you the watchword for the future: Enjoy Yourselves.

MRS. ANTROBUS. George, sit down!

ANTROBUS. Before I close, however, I wish to answer one of those unjust and malicious accusations that were brought against me during this last electoral campaign.

Ladies and gentlemen, the charge was made that at various points in my career I leaned toward joining some of the rival orders,—that's a lie.

As I told reporters of the *Atlantic City Herald*, I do not deny that a few months before my birth I hesitated between . . . uh . . . between pinfeathers and gill-breathing,—and so did many of us here,—but for the last million years I have been viviparous, hairy and diaphragmatic.

Applause. Cries of 'Good old Antrobus,' 'The Prince chap!' 'Georgie,' etc.

ANNOUNCER. Thank you. Thank you very much, Mr. Antrobus.

Now I know that our visitors will wish to hear a word from that gracious and charming mammal, Mrs. Antrobus, wife and mother,— Mrs. Antrobus!

MRS. ANTROBUS *rises, lays her program on her chair, bows and says:*

MRS. ANTROBUS. Dear friends, I don't really think I should say anything. After all, it was my husband who was elected and not I.

Perhaps, as president of the Women's Auxiliary Bed and Board Society,—I had some notes here, oh, yes, here they are:—I should give a short report from some of our committees that have been meeting in this beautiful city.

Perhaps it may interest you to know that it has at last been decided that the tomato is edible. Can you all here me? The tomato *is* edible.

A delegate from across the sea reports that the thread woven by the silkworm gives a cloth . . . I have a sample of it here . . . can you see it? smooth, elastic. I should say that it's rather attractive,—though personally I prefer less shiny surfaces. Should the windows of a sleeping apartment be open or shut? I know all mothers will follow our debates on this matter with close interest. I am sorry to say that the most expert authorities have not yet decided. It does seem to me that the night air would be bound to be unhealthy for our children, but there are many distinguished authorities on both sides. Well, I could go on talking forever,—as Shakespeare says: a woman's work is seldom done; but I think I'd better join my husband in saying thank you, and sit down.

Thank you. [*She sits down.*]

ANNOUNCER. Oh, Mrs. Antrobus!

MRS. ANTROBUS. Yes?

ANNOUNCER. We understand that you are about to celebrate a wedding anniversary. I know our listeners would like to extend their felicitations and hear a few words from you on that subject.

MRS. ANTROBUS. I have been asked by this kind gentleman . . . yes, my friends, this Spring Mr. Antrobus and I will be celebrating our five thousandth wedding anniversary.

I don't know if I speak for my husband, but I can say that, as for me, I regret every moment of it. [*Laughter of confusion.*]

I beg your pardon. What I *mean* to say is that I do not regret one moment of it. I hope none of you catch my cold. We have two children. we've always had two children, though it hasn't always been the same two. But as I say, we have two fine children, and we're very grateful for that. Yes, Mr. Antrobus and I have been married five thousand years. Each wedding anniversary reminds me of the times when there were no weddings. We had to crusade for marriage. Perhaps there are some women within the sound of my voice who remember that crusade and those struggles; we fought for it, didn't we? We chained ourselves to lampposts and we made disturbances in the Senate,—anyway, at last we women got the ring.

A few men helped us, but I must say that most men blocked our way at every step: they said we were unfeminine.

I only bring up these unpleasant memories, because I see some signs of backsliding from that great victory.

Oh, my fellow mammals, keep hold of that.

My husband says that the watchword for the year is Enjoy Yourselves. I think that's very open to misunderstanding. My watchword for the year is: Save the Family. It's held together for over five thousand years: Save it! Thank you.

ANNOUNCER. Thank you, Mrs. Antrobus.

The transparency disappears.

We had hoped to show you the Beauty Contest that took place here today.

President Antrobus, an experienced judge of pretty girls, gave the title of Miss Atlantic City 1942, to Miss Lily-Sabina Fairweather, charming hostess of our Boardwalk Bingo Parlor.

Unfortunately, however, our time is up, and I must take you to some views of the Convention City and conveeners,—enjoying themselves.

A burst of music; the curtain rises.

The Boardwalk. The audience is sitting in the ocean. A handrail of scarlet cord stretches across the front of the stage. A ramp—also with scarlet hand rail—descends to the right corner of the orchestra pit where a great scarlet beach umbrella or a cabana stands. Front and right stage left are benches facing the sea; attached to each bench is a street-lamp.

The only scenery is two cardboard cut-outs six feet high, representing shops at the back of the stage. Reading front left to right they are: SALT WATER TAFFY: FORTUNE TELLER; then the blank space; BINGO PARLOR; TURKISH BATH. They have practical doors, that of the Fortune Teller's being hung with bright gypsy curtains.

By the left proscenium and rising from the orchestra pit is the weather signal; it is like the mast of a ship with cross bars. From time to time black discs are hung on it to indicate the storm and hurricane warnings. Three roller chairs, pushed by melancholy NEGROES file by empty. Throughout the act they traverse the stage in both directions.

From time to time, CONVEENERS, dressed like MR. ANTROBUS, cross the stage. Some walk sedately by; others engage in inane horseplay. The old gypsy FORTUNE TELLER is seated at the door of her shop, smoking a corncob pipe.

From the Bingo Parlor comes the voice of the CALLER.

BINGO CALLER. A-Nine; A-Nine. C-Twenty-six; C-Twenty-six. A-Four; A-Four. B-Twelve.

CHORUS. [*Back-stage.*] Bingo!!!

The front of the Bingo Parlor shudders, rises a few feet in the air and returns to the ground trembling.

FORTUNE TELLER. [*Mechanically, to the unconscious back of a passerby, pointing with her pipe.*] Bright's disease! Your partner's deceiving you in that Kansas City deal. You'll have six grandchildren. Avoid high places. [*She rises and shouts after another:*] Cirrhosis of the liver!

SABINA *appears at the door of the Bingo Parlor. She hugs about her a blue raincoat that almost conceals her red bathing suit. She tries to catch the* FORTUNE TELLER'S *attention.*

SABINA. Ssssst! Esmeralda! Ssssst!

FORTUNE TELLER. Keck!

SABINA. Has President Antrobus come along yet?

FORTUNE TELLER. No, no, no. Get back there. Hide yourself.

SABINA. I'm afraid I'll miss him. Oh, Esmeralda, if I fail in this, I'll die; I know I'll die. President Antrobus!!! And I'll be his wife! If it's the last thing I'll do, I'll be Mrs. George Antrobus.—Esmeralda, tell me my future.

FORTUNE TELLER. Keck!

SABINA. All right, I'll tell *you* my future. [*Laughing dreamily and tracing it out with one finger on the palm of her hand.*] I've won the Beauty Contest in Atlantic City,—well, I'll win the Beauty Contest of the whole world. I'll take President Antrobus away from that wife of his. Then I'll take every man away from his wife. I'll turn the whole earth upside down.

FORTUNE TELLER. Keck!

SABINA. When all those husbands just think about me they'll get dizzy. They'll faint in the streets. They'll have to lean against lamp-posts.—Esmeralda, who was Helen of Troy?

FORTUNE TELLER. [*Furiously.*] Shut your foolish mouth. When Mr. Antrobus comes along you can see what you can do. Until then,—go away.

SABINA *laughs. As she returns to the door of her Bingo Parlor a group of* CONVEENERS *rush over and smother her with attentions: "Oh, Miss Lily, you know me. You've known me for years."*

SABINA. Go away, boys, go away. I'm after bigger fry than you are.— Why, Mr. Simpson!! How *dare* you!! I expect that even you nobodies must have girls to amuse you; but where you find them and what you do with them, is of absolutely no interest to me.

Exit. The CONVEENERS *squeal with pleasure and stumble in after her.*

The FORTUNE TELLER *rises, puts her pipe down on the stool, unfurls her voluminous skirts, gives a sharp wrench to her bodice and strolls towards the audience, swinging her hips like a young woman.*

FORTUNE TELLER. I tell the future. Keck. Nothing easier. Everybody's future is in their face. Nothing easier.

But who can tell your past,—eh? Nobody!

Your youth,—where did it go? It slipped away while you weren't looking. While you were asleep. While you were drunk? Puh! You're like our friends, Mr. and Mrs. Antrobus; you lie awake nights trying to know your past. What did it mean? What was it trying to say to you?

Think! Think! Split your heads. I can't tell the past and neither can you. If anybody tries to tell you the past, take my word for it, they're charlatans! Charlatans! But I can tell the future. [*She suddenly barks at a passing chair-pusher.*] Apoplexy! [*She returns to the audience.*] Nobody listens.—Keck! I see a face among you now—I won't embarrass him by pointing him out, but, listen, it may be you: Next year the watchsprings inside you will crumple up. Death by regret,—Type Y. It's in the corners of your mouth. You'll decide that you should have lived for pleasure, but that you missed it. Death by regret,—Type Y. . . . Avoid mirrors. You'll try to be angry,—but no!—no anger. [*Far forward, confidentially.*] And now what's the immediate future of our friends, the Antrobuses? Oh, you've seen it as well as I have, keck,—that dizziness of the head; that Great Man dizziness? The inventor of beer and gunpowder. The sudden fits of temper and then the long stretches of inertia? "I'm a sultan; let my slave-girls fan me?"

You know as well as I what's coming. Rain. Rain. Rain in floods. The deluge. But first you'll see shameful things—shameful things. Some of you will be saying: "Let him drown. He's not worth saving. Give the whole thing up." I can see it in your faces. But you're wrong. Keep your doubts and despairs to yourselves.

Again there'll be the narrow escape. The survival of a handful. From destruction,—total destruction. [*She points sweeping with her hand to the stage.*] Even of the animals, a few will be saved: two of a kind, male and female, two of a kind.

The heads of CONVEENERS *appear about the stage and in the orchestra pit, jeering at her.*

CONVEENERS. Charlatan! Madam Kill-joy! Mrs. Jeremiah! Charlatan!

FORTUNE TELLER. And you! Mark my words before it's too late. Where'll *you* be?

CONVEENERS. The croaking raven. Old dust and ashes. Rags, bottles, sacks.

FORTUNE TELLER. Yes, stick out your tongues. You can't stick your tongues out far enough to lick the death-sweat from your foreheads. It's too late to work now—bail out the flood with your soup spoons. You've had your chance and you've lost.

CONVEENERS. Enjoy yourselves!!!

They disappear. The FORTUNE TELLER *looks off left and puts her finger on her lip.*

FORTUNE TELLER. They're coming—the Antrobuses. Keck. Your hope. Your despair. Your selves.

Enter from the left, MR. *and* MRS. ANTROBUS *and* GLADYS.

MRS. ANTROBUS. Gladys Antrobus, stick your stummick in.

GLADYS. But it's easier this way.

MRS. ANTROBUS. Well, it's too bad the new president has such a clumsy daughter, that's all I can say. Try and be a lady.

FORTUNE TELLER. Aijah! That's been said a hundred billion times.

MRS. ANTROBUS. Goodness! Where's Henry? He was here just a minute ago. Henry!

Sudden violent stir. A roller-chair appears from the left. About it are dancing in great excitement HENRY *and a* NEGRO CHAIR-PUSHER.

HENRY. [*Slingshot in hand.*] I'll put your eye out. I'll make you yell, like you never yelled before.

NEGRO. [*At the same time.*] Now, I warns you. I warns you. If you make me mad, you'll get hurt.

ANTROBUS. Henry! What is this? Put down that slingshot.

MRS. ANTROBUS. [*At the same time.*] Henry! HENRY! Behave yourself.

FORTUNE TELLER. That's right, young man. There are too many people in the world as it is. Everybody's in the way, except one's self.

HENRY. All I wanted to do was—have some fun.

NEGRO. Nobody can't touch my chair, nobody, without I allow 'em to. You get clean away from me and you get away fast. [*He pushes his chair off, muttering.*]

ANTROBUS. What were you doing, Henry?

HENRY. Everybody's always getting mad. Everybody's always trying to push you around. I'll make him sorry for this; I'll make him sorry.

ANTROBUS. Give me that slingshot.

HENRY. I won't. I'm sorry I came to this place. I wish I weren't here. I wish I weren't anywhere.

MRS. ANTROBUS. Now, Henry, don't get so excited about nothing. I declare I don't know what we're going to do with you. Put your slingshot in your pocket, and don't try to take hold of things that don't belong to you.

ANTROBUS. After this you can stay home. I wash my hands of you.

MRS. ANTROBUS. Come now, let's forget all about it. Everybody take a good breath of that sea air and calm down.

A passing CONVEENER *bows to* ANTROBUS *who nods to him.*

Who was that you spoke to, George?

ANTROBUS. Nobody, Maggie. Just the candidate who ran against me in the election.

MRS. ANTROBUS. The man who ran against you in the election!! [*She turns and waves her umbrella after the disappearing* CONVEENER.] My husband didn't speak to you and he never will speak to you.

ANTROBUS. Now, Maggie.

MRS. ANTROBUS. After those lies you told about him in your speeches! Lies, that's what they were.

GLADYS AND HENRY. Mama, everybody's looking at you. Everybody's laughing at you.

MRS. ANTROBUS. If you must know, my husband's a SAINT, a downright SAINT, and you're not fit to speak to him on the street.

ANTROBUS. Now, Maggie, now, Maggie, that's enough of that.

MRS. ANTROBUS. George Antrobus, you're a perfect worm. If you won't stand up for yourself, I will.

GLADYS. Mama, you just act awful in public.

MRS. ANTROBUS. [*Laughing.*] Well, I must say I enjoyed it. I feel better. Wish his wife had been there to hear it. Children, what do you want to do?

GLADYS. Papa, can we ride in one of those chairs? Mama, I want to ride in one of those chairs.

MRS. ANTROBUS. No, sir. If you're tired you just sit where you are. We have no money to spend on foolishness.

ANTROBUS. I guess we have money enough for a thing like that. It's one of the things you do at Atlantic City.

MRS. ANTROBUS. Oh, we have? I tell you it's a miracle my children have shoes to stand up in. I didn't think I'd ever live to see them pushed around in chairs.

ANTROBUS. We're on a vacation, aren't we? We have a right to some treats, I guess. Maggie, some day you're going to drive me crazy.

MRS. ANTROBUS. All right, go. I'll just sit here and laugh at you. And you can give me my dollar right in my hand. Mark my words, a rainy day is coming. There's a rainy day ahead of us. I feel it in my bones. Go on, throw your money around. I can starve. I've starved before. I know how.

A CONVEENER *puts his head through Turkish Bath window, and says with raised eyebrows:*

CONVEENER. Hello, George. How are ya? I see where you brought the WHOLE family along.

MRS. ANTROBUS. And what do you mean by that?

CONVEENER *withdraws head and closes window.*

ANTROBUS. Maggie, I tell you there's a limit to what I can stand. God's Heaven, haven't I worked *enough*? Don't I get *any* vacation? Can't I even give my children so much as a ride in a roller-chair?

MRS. ANTROBUS. [*Putting out her hand for raindrops.*] Anyway, it's going to rain very soon and you have your broadcast to make.

ANTROBUS. Now, Maggie, I warn you. A man can stand a family only just so long. I'm warning you.

Enter SABINA *from the Bingo-Parlor. She wears a flounced red silk bathing suit, 1905. Red stockings, shoes, parasol. She bows demurely to* ANTROBUS *and starts down the ramp.* ANTROBUS *and the* CHILDREN *stare at her.* ANTROBUS *bows gallantly.*

MRS. ANTROBUS. Why, George Antrobus, how can you say such a thing! You have the best family in the world.

ANTROBUS. Good morning, Miss Fairweather.

SABINA *finally disappears behind the beach umbrella or in a cabana in the orchestra pit.*

MRS. ANTROBUS. Who on earth was that you spoke to, George?

ANTROBUS. [*Complacent; mock-modest.*] Hm ... m ... just a ... solambaka keray.

MRS. ANTROBUS. What? I can't understand you.

GLADYS. Mama, wasn't she beautiful?

HENRY. Papa, introduce her to me.

MRS. ANTROBUS. Children, will you be quiet while I ask your father a simple question?—Who did you say it was, George?

ANTROBUS. Why-uh ... a friend of mine. Very nice refined girl.

MRS. ANTROBUS. I'm waiting.

ANTROBUS. Maggie, that's the girl I gave the prize to in the beauty contest,—that's Miss Atlantic City 1942.

MRS. ANTROBUS. Hm! She looked like Sabina to me.

HENRY. [*At the railing.*] Mama, the life-guard knows her, too. Mama, he knows her well.

ANTROBUS. Henry, come here.—She's a very nice girl in every way and the sole support of her aged mother.

MRS. ANTROBUS. So was Sabina, so was Sabina; and it took a wall of ice to open your eyes about Sabina.—Henry, come over and sit down on this bench.

ANTROBUS. She's a very different matter from Sabina. Miss Fairweather is a college graduate, Phi Beta Kappa.

MRS. ANTROBUS. Henry, you sit here by mama. Gladys—

ANTROBUS. [*Sitting.*] Reduced circumstances have required her taking a position as hostess in a Bingo Parlor; but there isn't a girl with higher principles in the country.

MRS. ANTROBUS. Well, let's not talk about it.—Henry, I haven't seen a whale yet.

ANTROBUS. She speaks seven languages and has more culture in her little finger than you've acquired in a lifetime.

MRS. ANTROBUS. [*Assumed amiability.*] All right, all right, George. I'm glad to know there are such superior girls in the Bingo Parlors.— Henry, what's that? [*Pointing at the storm signal, which has one black disk.*]

HENRY. What is it, Papa?

ANTROBUS. What? Oh, that's the storm signal. One of those black disks means bad weather; two means storm; three means hurricane; and four means the end of the world. [*As they watch it a second black disk rolls into place.*]

MRS. ANTROBUS. Goodness! I'm going this very minute to buy you all some raincoats.

GLADYS. [*Putting her cheek against her father's shoulder.*] Mama, don't go yet. I like sitting this way. And the ocean coming in and coming in. Papa, don't you like it?

MRS. ANTROBUS. Well, there's only one thing I lack to make me a perfectly happy woman: I'd like to see a whale.

HENRY. Mama, we saw two. Right out there. They're delegates to the convention. I'll find you one.

GLADYS. Papa, ask me something. Ask me a question.

ANTROBUS. Well . . . how big's the ocean?

GLADYS. Papa, you're teasing me. It's—three-hundred and sixty million square-miles—and—it—covers—three-fourths—of—the—earth's—surface —and —its —deepest-place —is —five —and —a —half —miles—deep — and — its — average — depth — is — twelve-thousand — feet. No, Papa, ask me something hard, real hard.

MRS. ANTROBUS. [*Rising.*] Now I'm going off to buy those raincoats. I think that bad weather's going to get worse and worse. I hope it doesn't come before your broadcast. I should think we have about an hour or so.

HENRY. I hope it comes and zzzzzz everything before it. I hope it—

MRS. ANTROBUS. Henry!—George, I think . . . maybe, it's one of those storms that are just as bad on land as on sea. When you're just as safe and safer in a good stout boat.

HENRY. There's a boat out at the end of the pier.

MRS. ANTROBUS. Well, keep your eye on it. George, you shut your eyes and get a good rest before the broadcast.

ANTROBUS. Thundering Judas, do I have to be told when to open and shut my eyes? Go and buy your raincoats.

MRS. ANTROBUS. Now, children, you have ten minutes to walk around. Ten minutes. And, Henry: control yourself. Gladys, stick by your brother and don't get lost. [*They run off.*]

MRS. ANTROBUS. Will you be all right, George?

CONVEENERS *suddenly stick their heads out of the Bingo Parlor and Salt Water Taffy store, and voices rise from the orchestra pit.*

CONVEENER. George. Geo-r-r-rge! George! Leave the old hen-coop at home, George. Do-mes-ticated Georgie!

MRS. ANTROBUS. [*Shaking her umbrella.*] Low common oafs! That's what they are. Guess a man has a right to bring his wife to a convention, if he wants to. [*She starts off.*] What's the matter with a family, I'd like to know. What else have they got to offer?

Exit. ANTROBUS *has closed his eyes. The* FORTUNE TELLER *comes out of her shop and goes over to the left proscenium. She leans against it watching* SABINA *quizzically.*

FORTUNE TELLER. Heh! Here she comes!

SABINA. [*Loud whisper.*] What's he doing?

FORTUNE TELLER. Oh, he's ready for you. Bite your lips, dear, take a long breath and come on up.

SABINA. I'm nervous. My whole future depends on this. I'm nervous.

FORTUNE TELLER. Don't be a fool. What more could you want? He's forty-five. His head's a little dizzy. He's just been elected president. He's never known any other woman than his wife. Whenever he looks at her he realizes that she knows every foolish thing he's ever done.

SABINA. [*Still whispering.*] I don't know why it is, but every time I start one of these I'm nervous.

The FORTUNE TELLER *stands in the center of the stage watching the following:*

FORTUNE TELLER. You make me tired.

SABINA. First tell me my fortune.

The FORTUNE TELLER *laughs drily and makes the gesture of brushing away a nonsensical question.* SABINA *coughs and says:*

Oh, Mr. Antrobus,—dare I speak to you for a moment?

ANTROBUS. What?—Oh, certainly, certainly, Miss Fairweather.

SABINA. Mr. Antrobus . . . I've been so unhappy. I've wanted . . . I've wanted to make sure that you don't think that I'm the kind of girl who goes out for beauty contests.

FORTUNE TELLER. That's the way!

ANTROBUS. Oh, I understand, I understand perfectly.

FORTUNE TELLER. Give it a little more. Lean on it.

SABINA. I knew you would. My mother said to me this morning: Lily, she said, that fine Mr. Antrobus gave you the prize because he saw at once that you weren't the kind of girl who'd go in for a thing like that. But, honestly, Mr. Antrobus, in this world, honestly, a good girl doesn't know where to turn.

FORTUNE TELLER. Now you've gone too far.

ANTROBUS. My dear Miss Fairweather!

SABINA. You wouldn't know how hard it is. With that lovely wife and daughter you have. Oh, I think Mrs. Antrobus is the finest woman I ever saw. I wish I were like her.

ANTROBUS. There, there. There's . . . uh . . . room for all kinds of people in the world, Miss Fairweather.

SABINA. How wonderful of you to say that. How generous!—Mr. Antrobus, have you a moment free? . . . I'm afraid I may be a little conspicuous here ... could you come down, for just a moment, to my beach cabana ... ?

ANTROBUS. Why-uh ... yes, certainly ... for a moment ... just for a moment.

SABINA. There's a deck chair there. Because: you know you *do* look tired. Just this morning my mother said to me: Lily, she said, I hope Mr. Antrobus is getting a good rest. His fine strong face has deep lines in it. Now isn't it true, Mr. Antrobus: you work too hard?

FORTUNE TELLER. Bingo! [*She goes into her shop.*]

SABINA. Now you will just stretch out. No, I shan't say a word, not a word. I shall just sit there,—privileged. That's what I am.

ANTROBUS. [*Taking her hand.*] Miss Fairweather ... you'll ... spoil me.

SABINA. Just a moment. I have something I wish to say to the audience.—Ladies and gentlemen. I'm not going to play this particular scene tonight. It's just a short scene and we're going to skip it. But I'll tell you what takes place and then we can continue the play from there on. Now in this scene—

ANTROBUS. [*Between his teeth.*] But, Miss Somerset!

SABINA. I'm sorry. I'm sorry. But I have to skip it. In this scene, I talk to Mr. Antrobus, and at the end of it he decides to leave his wife, get a divorce at Reno and marry me. That's all.

ANTROBUS. Fitz!—Fitz!

SABINA. So that now I've told you we can jump to the end of it,— where you say:

Enter in fury MR. FITZPATRICK, *the stage manager.*

MR. FITZPATRICK. Miss Somerset, we insist on your playing this scene.

SABINA. I'm sorry, Mr. Fitzpatrick, but I can't and I won't. I've told the audience all they need to know and now we can go on.

Other ACTORS *begin to appear on the stage, listening.*

MR. FITZPATRICK. And *why* can't you play it?

SABINA. Because there are some lines in that scene that would hurt some people's feelings and I don't think the theatre is a place where people's feelings ought to be hurt.

MR. FITZPATRICK. Miss Somerset, you can pack up your things and go home. I shall call the understudy and I shall report you to Equity.

SABINA. I sent the understudy up to the corner for a cup of coffee and if Equity tries to penalize me I'll drag the case right up to the Supreme Court. Now listen, everybody, there's no need to get excited.

MR. FITZPATRICK *and* ANTROBUS. Why can't you play it ... what's the matter with the scene?

SABINA. Well, if you must know, I have a personal guest in the audience tonight. Her life hasn't been exactly a happy one. I wouldn't have

my friend hear some of these lines for the whole world. I don't suppose
it occurred to the author that some other women might have gone
through the experience of losing their husbands like this. Wild horses
wouldn't drag from me the details of my friend's life, but ... well,
they'd been married twenty years, and before he got rich, why, she'd
done the washing and everything.

MR. FITZPATRICK. Miss Somerset, your friend will forgive you. We
must play this scene.

SABINA. Nothing, nothing will make me say some of those lines ...
about "a man outgrows a wife every seven years" and ... and that one
about "the Mohammedans being the only people who looked the subject
square in the face." Nothing.

MR. FITZPATRICK. Miss Somerset! Go to your dressing room. I'll *read*
your lines.

SABINA. Now everybody's nerves are on edge.

MR. ANTROBUS. Skip the scene.

MR. FITZPATRICK *and the other* ACTORS *go off.*

SABINA. Thank you. I knew you'd understand. We'll do just what I
said. So Mr. Antrobus is going to divorce his wife and marry me. Mr.
Antrobus, you say: "It won't be easy to lay all this before my wife."

The ACTORS *withdraw.* ANTROBUS *walks about, his hand to his forehead
muttering:*

ANTROBUS. Wait a minute. I can't get back into it as easily as all
that. "My wife is a very obstinate woman." Hm ... then you say ... hm
... Miss Fairweather, I mean Lily, it won't be easy to lay all this before
my wife. It'll hurt her feelings a little.

SABINA. Listen, George: *other* people haven't got feelings. Not in the
same way that we have,—we who are presidents like you and prize-
winners like me. Listen, other people haven't got feelings; they just
imagine they have. Within two weeks they go back to playing bridge and
going to the movies.

Listen, dear: everybody in the world except a few people like you
and me are just people of straw. Most people have no insides at all. Now
that you're president you'll see that. Listen, darling, there's a kind of
secret society at the top of the world,—like you and me,—that know
this. The world was made for us. What's life anyway? Except for two
things, pleasure and power, what is life? Boredom! Foolishness. You
know it is. Except for those two things, life's nau-se-at-ing. So,—come
here! [*She moves close. They kiss.*] So.

Now when your wife comes, it's really very simple; just tell her.

ANTROBUS. Lily, Lily: you're a wonderful woman.

SABINA. Of course I am.

*They enter the cabana and it hides them from view. Distant roll of thunder.
A third black disk appears on the weather signal. Distant thunder is heard.*

MRS. ANTROBUS *appears carrying parcels. She looks about, seats herself on the bench left, and fans herself with her handkerchief. Enter* GLADYS *right, followed by two* CONVEENERS. *She is wearing red stockings.*

MRS. ANTROBUS. Gladys!

GLADYS. Mama, here I am.

MRS. ANTROBUS. Gladys Antrobus!!! Where did you get those dreadful things?

GLADYS. Wha-a-t? Papa liked the color.

MRS. ANTROBUS. You go back to the hotel this minute!

GLADYS. I won't. I won't. Papa liked the color.

MRS. ANTROBUS. All right. All right. You stay here. I've a good mind to let your father see you that way. You stay right here.

GLADYS. I . . . I don't want to stay if . . . if you don't think he'd like it.

MRS. ANTROBUS. Oh . . . It's all one to me. I don't care what happens. I don't care if the biggest storm in the whole world comes. Let it come. [*She folds her hands.*] Where's your brother?

GLADYS. [*In a small voice.*] He'll be here.

MRS. ANTROBUS. Will he? Well, let him get into trouble. I don't care. I don't know where your father is, I'm sure. [*Laughter from the cabana.*]

GLADYS. [*Leaning over the rail.*] I think he's . . . Mama, he's talking to the lady in the red dress.

MRS. ANTROBUS. Is that so? [*Pause.*] We'll wait till he's through. Sit down here beside me and stop fidgeting . . . what are you crying about? [*Distant thunder. She covers* GLADYS's *stockings with a raincoat.*]

GLADYS. You don't like my stockings.

Two CONVEENERS *rush in with a microphone on a standard and various paraphernalia. The* FORTUNE TELLER *appears at the door of her shop. Other characters gradually gather.*

BROADCAST OFFICIAL. Mrs. Antrobus! Thank God we've found you at last. Where's Mr. Antrobus? We've been hunting everywhere for him. It's about time for the broadcast to the conventions of the world.

MRS. ANTROBUS. [*Calm.*] I expect he'll be here in a minute.

BROADCAST OFFICIAL. Mrs. Antrobus, if he doesn't show up in time, I hope you will consent to broadcast in his place. It's the most important broadcast of the year.

SABINA *enters from cabana followed by* ANTROBUS.

MRS. ANTROBUS. No, I shan't. I haven't one single thing to say.

BROADCAST OFFICIAL. Then won't you help us find him, Mrs. Antrobus? A storm's coming up. A hurricane. A deluge!

SECOND CONVEENER. [*Who has sighted* ANTROBUS *over the rail.*] Joe! Joe! Here he is.

BROADCAST OFFICIAL. In the name of God, Mr. Antrobus, you're on the air in five minutes. Will you kindly please come and test the instrument? That's all we ask. If you just please begin the alphabet slowly.

ANTROBUS, *with set face, comes ponderously up the ramp. He stops at the point where his waist is level with the stage and speaks authoritatively to the* OFFICIALS.

ANTROBUS. I'll be ready when the time comes. Until then, move away. Go away. I have something I wish to say to my wife.

BROADCASTING OFFICIAL. [*Whimpering.*] Mr. Antrobus! This is the most important broadcast of the year.

The OFFICIALS *withdraw to the edge of the stage.* SABINA *glides up the ramp behind* ANTROBUS.

SABINA. [*Whispering.*] Don't let her argue. Remember arguments have nothing to do with it.

ANTROBUS. Maggie, I'm moving out of the hotel. In fact, I'm moving out of everything. For good. I'm going to marry Miss Fairweather. I shall provide generously for you and the children. In a few years you'll be able to see that it's all for the best. That's all I have to say.

BROADCAST OFFICIAL. Mr. Antrobus! I hope you'll be ready. This is the most important broadcast of the year.

GLADYS. What did Papa say, Mama? I didn't hear what papa said.

BINGO ANNOUNCER. A—nine; A—nine. D—forty-two; D—forty-two. C—thirty; C—thirty. B—seventeen; B-seventeen. C—forty; C—forty.

CHORUS. Bingo!!

BROADCAST OFFICIAL. Mr. Antrobus. All we want to do is test your voice with the alphabet.

ANTROBUS. Go away. Clear out.

MRS. ANTROBUS. [*Composedly with lowered eyes.*] George, I can't talk to you until you wipe those silly red marks off your face.

ANTROBUS. I think there's nothing to talk about. I've said what I have to say.

SABINA. Splendid!!

ANTROBUS. You're a fine woman, Maggie, but . . . but a man has his own life to lead in the world.

MRS. ANTROBUS. Well, after living with you for five thousand years I guess I have a right to a word or two, haven't I?

ANTROBUS. [*To* SABINA.] What can I answer to that?

SABINA. Tell her that conversation would only hurt her feelings. It's-kinder-in-the-long-run-to-do-it-short-and-quick.

ANTROBUS. I want to spare your feelings in every way I can, Maggie.

BROADCAST OFFICIAL. Mr. Antrobus, the hurricane signal's gone up. We could begin right now.

MRS. ANTROBUS. [*Calmly, almost dreamily.*] I didn't marry you because you were perfect. I didn't even marry you because I loved you. I married you because you gave me a promise. [*She takes off her ring and looks at it.*] That promise made up for your faults. And the promise I gave you made up for mine. Two imperfect people got married and it was the promise that made the marriage.

ANTROBUS. Maggie, . . . I was only nineteen.

MRS. ANTROBUS. [*She puts her ring back on her finger.*] And when our children were growing up, it wasn't a house that protected them; and it wasn't our love, that protected them—it was that promise.

And when that promise is broken—this can happen! [*With a sweep of the hand she removes the raincoat from* GLADYS' *stockings.*]

ANTROBUS. [*Stretches out his arm, apoplectic.*] Gladys!! Have you gone crazy? Has everyone gone crazy? [*Turning on* SABINA.] You did this. You gave them to her.

SABINA. I never said a word to her.

ANTROBUS. [*To* GLADYS.] You go back to the hotel and take those horrible things off.

GLADYS. [*Pert.*] Before I go, I've got something to tell you,—it's about Henry.

MRS. ANTROBUS. [*Claps her hands peremptorily.*] Stop your noise,— I'm taking her back to the hotel, George. Before I go I have a letter. . . . I have a message to throw into the ocean. [*Fumbling in her handbag.*] Where is the plagued thing? Here it is. [*She flings something—invisible to us—far over the heads of the audience to the back of the auditorium.*] It's a bottle. And in the bottle's a letter. And in the letter is written all the things that a woman knows.

It's never been told to any man and it's never been told to any woman, and if it finds its destination, a new time will come. We're not what books and plays say we are. We're not what advertisements say we are. We're not in the movies and we're not on the radio.

We're not what you're all told and what you think we are: We're ourselves. And if any man can find one of us he'll learn why the whole universe was set in motion. And if any man harm any one of us, his soul—the only soul he's got—had better be at the bottom of that ocean,—and that's the only way to put it. Gladys, come here. We're going back to the hotel. [*She drags* GLADYS *firmly off by the hand, but* GLADYS *breaks away and comes down to speak to her father.*]

SABINA. Such goings-on. Don't give it a minute's thought.

GLADYS. Anyway, I think you ought to know that Henry hit a man with a stone. He hit one of those colored men that push the chairs and the man's very sick. Henry ran away and hid and some policemen are looking for him very hard. And I don't care a bit if you don't want to have anything to do with mama and me, because I'll never like you again and I hope nobody ever likes you again,—so there! [*She runs off.* ANTROBUS *starts after her.*]

ANTROBUS. I . . . I have to go and see what I can do about this.

SABINA. You stay right here. Don't you go now while you're excited. Gracious sakes, all these things will be forgotten in a hundred years. Come, now, you're on the air. Just say anything.—it doesn't matter what. Just a lot of birds and fishes and things.

BROADCAST OFFICIAL. Thank you, Miss Fairweather. Thank you very much. Ready, Mr. Antrobus.

ANTROBUS. [*Touching the microphone.*] What is it, what is it? Who am I talking to?

BROADCAST OFFICIAL. Why, Mr. Antrobus! To our order and to all the other orders.

ANTROBUS. [*Raising his head.*] What are all those birds doing?

BROADCAST OFFICIAL. Those are just a few of the birds. Those are the delegates to our convention,—two of a kind.

ANTROBUS. [*Pointing into the audience.*] Look at the water. Look at them all. Those fishes jumping. The children should see this!—There's Maggie's whales!! Here are your whales, Maggie!!

BROADCAST OFFICIAL. I hope you're ready, Mr. Antrobus.

ANTROBUS. And look on the beach! You didn't tell me these would be here!

SABINA. Yes, George. Those are the animals.

BROADCAST OFFICIAL. [*Busy with the apparatus.*] Yes, Mr. Antrobus, those are the vertebrates. We hope the lion will have a word to say when you're through. Step right up, Mr. Antrobus, we're ready. We'll just have time before the storm. [*Pause. In a hoarse whisper:*] They're wait-ing.

It has grown dark. Soon after he speaks a high whistling noise begins. Strange veering lights start whirling about the stage. The other characters disappear from the stage.

ANTROBUS. Friends. Cousins. Four score and ten billion years ago our forefather brought forth upon this planet the spark of life,—

He is drowned out by thunder. When the thunder stops the FORTUNE TELLER *is seen standing beside him.*

FORTUNE TELLER. Antrobus, there's not a minute to be lost. Don't you see the four disks on the weather signal? Take your family into that boat at the end of the pier.

ANTROBUS. My family? I have no family. Maggie! Maggie! They won't come.

FORTUNE TELLER. They'll come.—Antrobus! Take these animals into that boat with you. All of them,—two of each kind.

SABINA. George, what's the matter with you? This is just a storm like any other storm.

ANTROBUS. Maggie!

SABINA. Stay with me, we'll go . . . [*Losing conviction.*] This is just another thunderstorm,—isn't it? Isn't it?

ANTROBUS. Maggie!!!

MRS. ANTROBUS *appears beside him with* GLADYS.

MRS. ANTROBUS. [*Matter-of-fact.*] Here I am and here's Gladys.

ANTROBUS. Where've you been? Where have you been? Quick, we're going into that boat out there.

MRS. ANTROBUS. I know we are. But I haven't found Henry. [*She wanders off into the darkness calling "Henry!"*]

SABINA. [*Low urgent babbling, only occasionally raising her voice.*] I don't believe it. I don't believe it's anything at all. I've seen hundreds of storms like this.

FORTUNE TELLER. There's no time to lose. Go. Push the animals along before you. Start a new world. Begin again.

SABINA. Esmeralda! George! Tell me,—is it really serious?

ANTROBUS. [*Suddenly very busy.*] Elephants first. Gently, gently.— Look where you're going.

GLADYS. [*Leaning over the ramp and striking an animal on the back.*] Stop it or you'll be left behind!

ANTROBUS. Is the Kangaroo there? *There* you are! Take those turtles in your pouch, will you? [*To some other animals, pointing to his shoulder.*] Here! You jump up here. You'll be trampled on.

GLADYS. [*To her father, pointing below.*] Papa, look,—the snakes!

MRS. ANTROBUS. I can't find Henry. Hen-ry!

ANTROBUS. Go along. Go along. Climb on their backs.—Wolves! Jackals,—whatever you are,—tend to your own business!

GLADYS. [*Pointing, tenderly.*] Papa,—look.

SABINA. Mr. Antrobus—take me with you. Don't leave me here. I'll work. I'll help. I'll do anything.

THREE CONVEENERS *cross the stage, marching with a banner.*

CONVEENERS. George! What are you scared of?—George! Fellas, it looks like rain.—"Maggie, where's my umbrella?"—George, setting up for Barnum and Bailey.

ANTROBUS. [*Again catching his wife's hand.*] Come on now, Maggie, —the pier's going to break any minute.

MRS. ANTROBUS. I'm not going a step without Henry. Henry!

GLADYS. [*On the ramp.*] Mama! Papa! Hurry. The pier's cracking, Mama. It's going to break.

MRS. ANTROBUS. Henry! Cain! CAIN!

HENRY *dashes into the stage and joins his mother.*

HENRY. Here I am, Mama.

MRS. ANTROBUS. Thank God!—now come quick.

HENRY. I didn't think you wanted me.

MRS. ANTROBUS. Quick! [*She pushes him down before her into the aisle.*]

SABINA. [*All the* ANTROBUSES *are now in the theatre aisle.* SABINA *stands at the top of the ramp.*] Mrs. Antrobus, take me. Don't you remember me? I'll work. I'll help. Don't leave me here!

MRS. ANTROBUS. [*Impatiently, but as though it were of no importance.*] Yes, yes. There's a lot of work to be done. Only hurry.

FORTUNE TELLER. [*Now dominating the stage. To* SABINA *with a grim smile.*] Yes, go—back to the kitchen with you.

SABINA. [*Half-down the ramp. To* FORTUNE TELLER.] I don't know why my life's always being interrupted—just when everything's going fine!! [*She dashes up the aisle.*]

Now the CONVEENERS *emerge doing a serpentine dance on the stage. They jeer at the* FORTUNE TELLER.

CONVEENERS. Get a canoe—there's not a minute to be lost! Tell me my future, Mrs. Croaker.

FORTUNE TELLER. Paddle in the water, boys—enjoy yourselves.

VOICE from the BINGO PARLOR. A-nine; A-nine. C-twenty-four. C-twenty-four.

CONVEENERS. Rags, bottles, and sacks.

FORTUNE TELLER. Go back and climb on your roofs. Put rags in the cracks under your doors.—Nothing will keep out the flood! You've had your chance. You've had your day. You've failed. You've lost.

VOICE from the BINGO PARLOR. B-fifteen. B-fifteen.

FORTUNE TELLER. [*Shading her eyes and looking out to sea.*] They're safe. George Antrobus! Think it over! A new world to make.—think it over!

CURTAIN

ACT III

Just before the curtain rises, two sounds are heard from the stage: a cracked bugle call.

The curtain rises on almost total darkness. Almost all the flats composing the walls of MR. ANTROBUS's *house, as of Act I, are up, but they lean helter-skelter against one another, leaving irregular gaps. Among the flats missing are two in the back wall, leaving the frames of the window and door crazily out of line. Off stage, back right, some red Roman fire is burning. The bugle call is repeated. Enter* SABINA *through the tilted door. She is dressed as a Napoleonic camp follower, "la fille du regiment," in begrimed reds and blues.*

SABINA. Mrs. Antrobus! Gladys! Where are you?

The war's over. The war's over. You can come out. The peace treaty's been signed.

Where are they?—Hmpf! Are they dead, too? Mrs. Annnntrobus!

Glaaaadus! Mr. Antrobus'll be here this afternoon. I just saw him down-town. Huuuuurry and put things in order. He says that now that the war's over we'll all have to settle down and be perfect.

Enter MR. FITZPATRICK, *the stage manager, followed by the whole company, who stand waiting at the edges of the stage.* MR. FITZPATRICK *tries to interrupt* SABINA.

    MR. FITZPATRICK. Miss Somerset, we have to stop a moment.
    SABINA. They may be hiding out in the back—
    MR. FITZPATRICK. Miss Somerset! We have to stop a moment.
    SABINA. What's the matter?
    MR. FITZPATRICK. There's an explanation we have to make to the audience.—Lights, please. [*To the actor who plays* MR. ANTROBUS.] Will you explain the matter to the audience?

The lights go up. We now see that a balcony or elevated runway has been erected at the back of the stage, back of the wall of the Antrobus house. From its extreme right and left ends ladder-like steps descend to the floor of the stage.

    ANTROBUS. Ladies and gentlemen, an unfortunate accident has taken place back stage. Perhaps I should say *another* unfortunate accident.
    SABINA. I'm sorry. I'm sorry.
    ANTROBUS. The management feels, in fact, we all feel that you are due an apology. And now we have to ask your indulgence for the most serious mishap of all. Seven of our actors have . . . have been taken ill. Apparently, it was something they ate. I'm not exactly clear what hap-pened. [*All the* ACTORS *start to talk at once.* ANTROBUS *raises his hand.*] Now, now—not all at once. Fitz, do you know what it was?
    MR. FITZPATRICK. Why, it's perfectly clear. These seven actors had dinner together, and they ate something that disagreed with them.
    SABINA. Disagreed with them!!! They have ptomaine poisoning. They're in Bellevue Hospital this very minute in agony. They're having their stomachs pumped out this very minute, in perfect agony.
    ANTROBUS. Fortunately, we've just heard they'll all recover.
    SABINA. It'll be a miracle if they do, a downright miracle. It was the lemon meringue pie.
    ACTORS. It was the fish . . . it was the canned tomatoes . . . it was the fish.
    SABINA. It was the lemon meringue pie. I saw it with my own eyes; it had blue mould all over the bottom of it.
    ANTROBUS. Whatever it was, they're in no condition to take part in this performance. Naturally, we haven't enough understudies to fill all those roles; but we do have a number of splendid volunteers who have kindly consented to help us out. These friends have watched our re-hearsals, and they assure me that they know the lines and the business

very well. Let me introduce them to you—my dresser, Mr. Tremayne,—himself a distinguished Shakespearean actor for many years; our wardrobe mistress, Hester; Miss Somerset's maid, Ivy; and Fred Bailey, captain of the ushers in this theatre.

These persons bow modestly. IVY *and* HESTER *are colored girls.*

Now this scene takes place near the end of the act. And I'm sorry to say we'll need a short rehearsal, just a short run-through. And as some of it takes place in the auditorium, we'll have to keep the curtain up. Those of you who wish can go out in the lobby and smoke some more. The rest of you can listen to us, or . . . or just talk quietly among yourselves, as you choose. Thank you. Now will you take it over Mr. Fitzpatrick?

MR. FITZPATRICK. Thank you.—Now for those of you who are listening perhaps I should explain that at the end of this act, the men have come back from the War and the family's settled down in the house. And the author wants to show the hours of the night passing by over their heads, and the planets crossing the sky . . . uh . . . over their heads. And he says—this is hard to explain—that each of the hours of the night is a philosopher, or a great thinker. Eleven o'clock, for instance, is Aristotle. And nine o'clock is Spinoza. Like that. I don't suppose it means anything. It's just a kind of poetic effect.

SABINA. Not mean anything! Why, it certainly does. Twelve o'clock goes by saying those wonderful things. I think it means that when people are asleep they have all those lovely thoughts, much better than when they're awake.

IVY. Excuse me, I think it means,—excuse me, Mr. Fitzpatrick—

SABINA. What were you going to say, Ivy?

IVY. Mr. Fitzpatrick, you let my father come to a rehearsal; and my father's a Baptist minister, and he said that the author meant that—just like the hours and stars go by over our heads at night, in the same way the ideas and thoughts of the great men are in the air around us all the time and they're working on us, even when we don't know it.

MR. FITZPATRICK. Well, well, maybe that's it. Thank you, Ivy. Anyway,—the hours of the night are philosophers. My friends, are you ready? Ivy, can you be eleven o'clock? "This good estate of the mind possessing its object in energy we call divine." Aristotle.[3]

IVY. Yes, sir. I know that and I know twelve o'clock and I know nine o'clock.

MR. FITZPATRICK. Twelve o'clock? Mr. Tremayne, the Bible.

TREMAYNE. Yes.

MR. FITZPATRICK. Ten o'clock? Hester,—Plato? [*She nods eagerly.*] Nine o'clock, Spinoza,—Fred?

[3] *Metaphysics,* 7, 7.

BAILEY. Yes, *sir*.

FRED BAILEY *picks up a great gilded cardboard numeral IX and starts up the steps to the platform.* MR. FITZPATRICK *strikes his forehead.*

MR. FITZPATRICK. The planets!! We forgot all about the planets.
SABINA. O my God! The planets! Are they sick too?

ACTORS *nod.*

MR. FITZPATRICK. Ladies and gentlemen, the planets are singers. Of course, we can't replace them, so you'll have to imagine them singing in this scene. Saturn sings from the orchestra pit down here. The Moon is way up there. And Mars with a red lantern in his hand, stands in the aisle over there—Tz-tz-tz. It's too bad; it all makes a very fine effect. However! Ready—nine o'clock: Spinoza.
BAILEY. [*Walking slowly across the balcony, left to right.*] "After experience had taught me that the common occurrences of daily life are vain and futile—"
FITZPATRICK. Louder, Fred. "And I saw that all the objects of my desire and fear—"
BAILEY. "And I saw that all the objects of my desire and fear were in themselves nothing good nor bad save insofar as the mind was affected by them—"[4]
FITZPATRICK. Do you know the rest? All right. Ten o'clock. Hester. Plato.
HESTER. "Then tell me, O Critias, how will a man choose the ruler that shall rule over him? Will he not—"[5]
FITZPATRICK. Thank you. Skip to the end, Hester.
HESTER. "... can be multiplied a thousand fold in its effects among the citizens."
FITZPATRICK. Thank you.—Aristotle, Ivy?
IVY. "This good estate of the mind possessing its object in energy we call divine. This we mortals have occasionally and it is this energy which is pleasantest and best. But God has it always. It is wonderful in us; but in Him how much more wonderful."[6]
FITZPATRICK. Midnight. Midnight, Mr. Tremayne. That's right,— you've done it before.—All right, everybody. You know what you have to do.—Lower the curtain. House lights up. Act Three of THE SKIN OF OUR TEETH. [*As the curtain descends he is heard saying:*] You volunteers, just wear what you have on. Don't try to put on the costumes today.

---

[4] Spinoza, opening of the *Treatise on the Correction of the Understanding* (1677).
[5] Although Critias is present or takes part in five of the Platonic *Dialogues*, this question seems never to have been addressed to him. Plato brings up the general question in several places; see, for example, *The Republic*, 7.
[6] *Metaphysics*, 12, 7.

*House lights go down. The Act begins again. The Bugle call. Curtain rises.
Enter* SABINA.

SABINA. Mrs. Antrobus! Gladys! Where are you?
The war's over.—You've heard all this—[*She gabbles the main
points.*]
Where—are—they? Are—they—dead, too, et cetera.
I—just—saw—Mr.—Antrobus—down town, et cetera. [*Slowing up:*]
He says that now that the war's over we'll all have to settle down
and be perfect. They may be hiding out in the back somewhere. Mrs.
An-tro-bus.

She wanders off. It has grown lighter.
A trapdoor is cautiously raised and MRS. ANTROBUS *emerges waist-high
and listens. She is disheveled and worn; she wears a tattered dress and a
shawl half covers her head. She talks down through the trapdoor.*

MRS. ANTROBUS. It's getting light. There's still something burning
over there—Newark, or Jersey City. What? Yes, I could swear I heard
someone moving about up here. But I can't see anybody. I say: I can't
see anybody.

She starts to move about the stage. GLADYS' *head appears at the trapdoor. She
is holding a* BABY.

GLADYS. Oh, Mama. Be careful.
MRS. ANTROBUS. Now, Gladys, you stay out of sight.
GLADYS. Well, let me stay here just a minute. I want the baby to get
some of this fresh air.
MRS. ANTROBUS. All right, but keep your eyes open. I'll see what I
can find. I'll have a good hot plate of soup for you before you can say
Jack Robinson. Gladys Antrobus! Do you know what I think I see?
There's old Mr. Hawkins sweeping the sidewalk in front of his A. and P.
store. Sweeping it with a broom. Why, he must have gone crazy, like the
others! I see some other people moving about, too.
GLADYS. Mama, come back, come back.

MRS. ANTROBUS *returns to the trapdoor and listens.*

MRS. ANTROBUS. Gladys, there's something in the air. Everybody's
movement's sort of different. I see some women walking right out in the
middle of the street.
SABINA'S VOICE. Mrs. An-tro-bus!
MRS. ANTROBUS AND GLADYS. What's that?!!
SABINA'S VOICE. Glaaaadys! Mrs. An-tro-bus!

Enter SABINA.

MRS. ANTROBUS. Gladys, that's Sabina's voice as sure as I live.—
Sabina! Sabina!—Are you *alive?!!*

SABINA. Of course, I'm alive. How've you girls been?—*Don't* try and kiss me. I never want to kiss another human being as long as I live. Sh-sh, there's nothing to get emotional about. Pull yourself together, the war's over. Take a deep breath,—the war's over.

MRS. ANTROBUS. The war's over!! I don't believe you. I don't believe you. I can't believe you.

GLADYS. Mama!

SABINA. Who's that?

MRS. ANTROBUS. That's Gladys and her baby. I don't believe you. Gladys, Sabina says the war's over. Oh, Sabina.

SABINA. [*Leaning over the* BABY.] Goodness! Are there any babies left in the world! Can it *see*? And can it cry and everything?

GLADYS. Yes, he can. He notices everything very well.

SABINA. Where on earth did you get it? Oh, I won't ask.—Lord, I've lived all these seven years around camp and I've forgotten how to behave.—Now we've got to think about the men coming home.—Mrs. Antrobus, go and wash your face, I'm ashamed of you. Put your best clothes on. Mr. Antrobus'll be here this afternoon. I just saw him downtown.

MRS. ANTROBUS AND GLADYS. He's alive!! He'll be here!! Sabina, you're not joking?

MRS. ANTROBUS. And Henry?

SABINA. [*Dryly.*] Yes, Henry's alive, too, that's what they say. Now don't stop to talk. Get yourselves fixed up. Gladys, you look terrible. Have you any decent clothes? [SABINA *has pushed them toward the trapdoor.*]

MRS. ANTROBUS. [*Half down.*] Yes, I've something to wear just for this very day. But, Sabina,—who won the war?

SABINA. Don't stop now,—just wash your face. [*A whistle sounds in the distance.*] Oh, my God, what's that silly little noise?

MRS. ANTROBUS. Why, it sounds like . . . it sounds like what used to be the noon whistle at the shoe-polish factory. [*Exit.*]

SABINA. That's what it is. Seems to me like peacetime's coming along pretty fast—shoe polish!

GLADYS. [*Half down.*] Sabina, how soon after peacetime begins does the milkman start coming to the door?

SABINA. As soon as he catches a cow. Give him time to catch a cow, dear. [*Exit* GLADYS. SABINA *walks about a moment, thinking.*] Shoe polish! My, I'd forgotten what peacetime was like. [*She shakes her head, then sits down by the trapdoor and starts talking down the hole.*] Mrs. Antrobus, guess what I saw Mr. Antrobus doing this morning at dawn. He was tacking up a piece of paper on the door of the Town Hall. You'll die when you hear: it was a recipe for grass soup, for a grass soup that doesn't give you the diarrhea. Mr. Antrobus is still thinking up new things.—He told me to give you his love. He's got all sorts of ideas for peacetime, he says. No more laziness and idiocy, he says. And oh, yes! Where are his books? What? Well, pass them up. The first thing he wants to see are his books. He says if you've burnt those books, or if the rats have eaten them, he says it isn't worthwhile starting over again. Everybody's going to be beautiful, he says, and diligent, and very intelligent.

A hand reaches up with two volumes.

What language is that? Pu-u-gh,—mold! And he's got such plans for you, Mrs. Antrobus. You're going to study history and algebra—and so are Gladys and I—and philosophy. You should hear him talk: [*Taking two more volumes.*] Well, these are in English, anyway.—To hear him talk, seems like he expects you to be a combination, Mrs. Antrobus, of a saint and a college professor, and a dancehall hostess, if you know what I mean. [*Two more volumes.*] Ugh. German! [*She is lying on the floor; one elbow bent, her cheek on her hand, meditatively.*] Yes, peace will be here before we know it. In a week or two we'll be asking the Perkinses in for a quiet evening of bridge. We'll turn on the radio and hear how to be big successes with a new toothpaste. We'll trot down to the movies and see how girls with wax faces live—all *that* will begin again. Oh, Mrs. Antrobus, God forgive me but I enjoyed the war. Everybody's at their best in wartime. I'm sorry it's over. And, oh, I forgot! Mr. Antrobus sent you another message—can you hear me?—

Enter HENRY, *blackened and sullen. He is wearing torn overalls, but has one gaudy admiral's epaulette hanging by a thread from his right shoulder, and there are vestiges of gold and scarlet braid running down his left trouser leg. He stands listening.*

Listen! Henry's never to put foot in this house again, he says. He'll kill Henry on sight, if he sees him.

You don't know about Henry??? Well, where have you been? What? Well, Henry rose right to the top. Top of *what?* Listen, I'm telling you. Henry rose from corporal to captain, to major, to general.—I don't know how to say it, but the enemy is *Henry;* Henry *is* the enemy. Everybody knows that.

HENRY. He'll kill me, will he?

SABINA. Who are *you?* I'm not afraid of you. The war's over.

HENRY. I'll kill him so fast. I've spent seven years trying to find him; the others I killed were just substitutes.

SABINA. Goodness! It's Henry!—[*He makes an angry gesture.*] Oh, I'm not afraid of you. The war's over, Henry Antrobus, and you're not any more important than any other unemployed. You go away and hide yourself, until we calm your father down.

HENRY. The first thing to do is to burn up those old books; it's the ideas he gets out of those old books that . . . that makes the whole world so you can't live in it. [*He reels forward and starts kicking the books about, but suddenly falls down in a sitting position.*]

SABINA. You leave those books alone!! Mr. Antrobus is looking forward to them a-special.—Gracious sakes, Henry, you're so tired you can't stand up. Your mother and sister'll be here in a minute and we'll think what to do about you.

HENRY. What did they ever care about me?

SABINA. There's that old whine again. All you people think you're not loved enough, nobody loves you. Well, you start being lovable and we'll love you.

HENRY. [*Outraged.*] I don't want anybody to love me.

SABINA. Then stop talking about it all the time.

HENRY. I never talk about it. The last thing I want is anybody to pay any attention to me.

SABINA. I can hear it behind every word you say.

HENRY. I want everybody to hate me.

SABINA. Yes, you've decided that's second best, but it's still the same thing.—Mrs. Antrobus! Henry's here. He's so tired he can't stand up.

MRS. ANTROBUS *and* GLADYS, *with her* BABY, *emerge. They are dressed as in Act I.* MRS. ANTROBUS *carries some objects in her apron, and* GLADYS *has a blanket over her shoulder.*

MRS. ANTROBUS AND GLADYS. Henry! Henry! Henry!

HENRY. [*Glaring at them.*] Have you anything to eat?

MRS. ANTROBUS. Yes, I have, Henry. I've been saving it for this very day,—two good baked potatoes. No! Henry! one of them's for your father. Henry!! Give me that other potato back this minute.

SABINA *sidles up behind him and snatches the other potato away.*

SABINA. He's so dog-tired he doesn't know what he's doing.

MRS. ANTROBUS. Now you just rest there, Henry, until I can get your room ready. Eat that potato good and slow, so you can get all the nourishment out of it.

HENRY. You all might as well know right now that I haven't come back here to live.

MRS. ANTROBUS. Sh. ... I'll put this coat over you. Your room's hardly damaged at all. Your football trophies are a little tarnished, but Sabina and I will polish them up tomorrow.

HENRY. Did you hear me? I don't live here. I don't belong to anybody.

MRS. ANTROBUS. Why, how can you say a thing like that! You certainly do belong right here. Where else would you want to go? Your forehead's feverish, Henry, seems to me. You'd better give me that gun, Henry. You won't need that any more.

GLADYS. [*Whispering.*] Look, he's fallen asleep already, with his potato half-chewed.

SABINA. Puh! The terror of the world.

MRS. ANTROBUS. Sabina, you mind your own business, and start putting the room to rights.

HENRY *has turned his face to the back of the sofa,* MRS. ANTROBUS *gingerly puts the revolver in her apron pocket, then helps* SABINA. SABINA *has found a rope hanging from the ceiling. Grunting, she hangs all her weight on it, and as she pulls the walls begin to move into their right places.* MRS. ANTROBUS *brings the overturned tables, chairs and hassock into the positions of Act I.*

SABINA. That's all we do—always beginning again! Over and over again. Always beginning again. [*She pulls on the rope and a part of the wall moves into place. She stops. Meditatively:*] How do we know that it'll be any better than before? Why do we go on pretending? Some day the whole earth's going to have to turn cold anyway, and until that time all these other things'll be happening again: it will be more wars and more walls of ice and floods and earthquakes.

MRS. ANTROBUS. Sabina!! Stop arguing and go on with your work.

SABINA. All right. I'll go on just out of habit, but I won't believe in it.

MRS. ANTROBUS. [*Aroused.*] Now, Sabina. I've let you talk long enough. I don't want to hear any more of it. Do I have to explain to you what everybody knows,—everybody who keeps a home going? Do I have to say to you what nobody should ever *have* to say, because they can read it in each other's eyes?

Now listen to me: [MRS. ANTROBUS *takes hold of the rope.*] I could live for seventy years in a cellar and make soup out of grass and bark, without ever doubting that this world has a work to do and will do it.

Do you hear me?

SABINA. [*Frightened.*] Yes, Mrs. Antrobus.

MRS. ANTROBUS. Sabina, do you see this house,—216 Cedar Street,—do you see it?

SABINA. Yes, Mrs. Antrobus.

MRS. ANTROBUS. Well, just to have known this house is to have seen the idea of what we can do someday if we keep our wits about us. Too many people have suffered and died for my children for us to start reneging now. So we'll start putting this house to rights. Now Sabina, go and see what you can do in the kitchen.

SABINA. Kitchen! Why is it that however far I go away, I always find myself back in the kitchen? [*Exit.*]

MRS. ANTROBUS. [*Still thinking over her last speech, relaxes and says with a reminiscent smile:*] Goodness, gracious, wouldn't you know that my father was a parson? It was just like I heard his own voice speaking and he's been dead five thousand years. There! I've gone and almost waked Henry up.

HENRY. [*Talking in his sleep, indistinctly.*] Fellows . . . what have they done for us? . . . Blocked our way at every step. Kept everything in their own hands, And you've stood it. When are you going to wake up?

MRS. ANTROBUS. Sh, Henry. Go to sleep. Go to sleep. Go to sleep.— Well, that looks better. Now let's go and help Sabina.

GLADYS. Mama, I'm going out into the backyard and hold the baby right up in the air. And show him that we don't have to be afraid any more. [*Exit* GLADYS *to the kitchen.*]

MRS. ANTROBUS *glances at* HENRY, *exits into kitchen.* HENRY *thrashes about in his sleep. Enter* ANTROBUS, *his arms full of bundles, chewing the end of a carrot. He has a slight limp. Over the suit of Act I he is wearing an overcoat too long for him, its skirts trailing on the ground. He lets his bundles fall and stands looking about. Presently his attention is fixed on* HENRY, *whose words grow clearer.*

HENRY. All right! What have you got to lose? What have they done for us? That's right—nothing. Tear everything down. I don't care what you smash. We'll begin again and we'll show 'em.

ANTROBUS *takes out his revolver and holds it pointing downwards. With his back towards the audience he moves toward the footlights.*

HENRY'S *voice grows louder and he wakes with a start. They stare at one another. Then* HENRY *sits up quickly. Throughout the following scene* HENRY *is played, not as a misunderstood or misguided young man, but as a representation of strong unreconciled evil.*

All right! Do something. [*Pause.*] Don't think I'm afraid of you, either. All right, do what you were going to do. Do it. [*Furiously.*] Shoot me, I tell you. You don't have to think I'm any relation of yours. I haven't got any father or any mother, or brothers or sisters. And I don't want any. And what's more I haven't got anybody over me; and I never will have. I'm alone, and that's all I want to be: alone. So you can shoot me.

ANTROBUS. You're the last person I wanted to see. The sight of you dries up all my plans and hopes. I wish I were back at war still, because it's easier to fight you than to live with you. War's a pleasure—do you hear me?—War's a pleasure compared to what faces us now: trying to build up a peacetime with you in the middle of it. [ANTROBUS *walks up to the window.*]

HENRY. I'm not going to be a part of any peacetime of yours. I'm going a long way from here and make my own world that's fit for a man to live in. Where a man can be free, and have a chance, and do what he wants to do in his way.

ANTROBUS. [*His attention arrested; thoughtfully. He throws the gun out of the window and turns with hope.*] . . . Henry, let's try again.

HENRY. Try what? Living *here?*—Speaking polite downtown to all the old men like you? Standing like a sheep at the street corner until the red light turns to green? Being a good boy and a good sheep, like all the stinking ideas you get out of your books? Oh, no, I'll make a world, and I'll show you.

ANTROBUS. [*Hard.*] How can you make a world for people to live in, unless you've first put order in yourself? Mark my words: I shall continue fighting you until my last breath as long as you mix up your idea of liberty with your idea of hogging everything for yourself. I shall have no pity on you. I shall pursue you to the far corners of the earth. You and I want the same thing; but until you think of it as something that everyone has a right to, you are my deadly enemy and I will destroy you.—I hear your mother's voice in the kitchen. Have you seen her?

HENRY. I have no mother. Get it into your head. I don't belong here. I have nothing to do here. I have no home.

ANTROBUS. Then why did you come here? With the whole world to choose from, why did you come to this one place: 216 Cedar Street, Excelsior, New Jersey. . . . Well?

HENRY. What if I did? What if I wanted to look at it once more, to see if—

ANTROBUS. Oh, you're related, all right—When your mother comes in you must behave yourself. Do you hear me?

HENRY. [*Wildly.*] What is this?—*must behave* yourself. Don't you say *must* to me.

ANTROBUS. Quiet! [*Enter* MRS. ANTROBUS *and* SABINA.]

HENRY. Nobody can say *must* to me. All my life everybody's been crossing me,—everybody, everything, all of you. I'm going to be free, even if I have to kill half the world for it. Right now, too. Let me get my hands on his throat. I'll show him.

He advances toward ANTROBUS. *Suddenly,* SABINA *jumps between them and calls out in her own person:*

SABINA. Stop! Stop! Don't play this scene. You know what happened last night. Stop the play. [*The men fall back, panting.* HENRY *covers his face with his hands.*] Last night you almost strangled him. You became a regular savage. Stop it!

HENRY. It's true. I'm sorry. I don't know what comes over me. I have nothing against him personally. I respect him very much . . . I . . . I admire him. But something comes over me. It's like I become fifteen years old again. I . . . I . . . listen: my own father used to whip me and lock me up every Saturday night. I never had enough to eat. He never let me have enough money to buy decent clothes. I was ashamed to go downtown. I never could go to the dances. My father and my uncle put rules in the way of everything I wanted to do. They tried to prevent my living at all.—I'm sorry. I'm sorry.

MRS. ANTROBUS. [*Quickly.*] No, go on. Finish what you were saying. Say it all.

HENRY. In this scene it's as though I were back in High School again. It's like I had some big emptiness inside me,—the emptiness of being hated and blocked at every turn. And the emptiness fills up with the one thought that you have to strike and fight and kill. Listen, it's as though you have to kill somebody else so as not to end up killing yourself.

SABINA. That's not true. I knew your father and your uncle and your mother. You imagined all that. Why, they did everything they could for you. How can you say things like that? They didn't lock you up.

HENRY. They did. They did. They wished I hadn't been born.

SABINA. That's not true.

ANTROBUS. [*In his own person, with self-condemnation, but cold and proud.*] Wait a minute. I have something to say, too. It's not wholly his fault that he wants to strangle me in this scene. It's my fault, too. He wouldn't feel that way unless there were something in me that reminded him of all that. He talks about an emptiness. Well, there's an emptiness in me, too. Yes,—work, work, work,—that's all I do. I've ceased to *live*. No wonder he feels that anger coming over him.

MRS. ANTROBUS. There! At least you've said it.

SABINA. We're all just as wicked as we can be, and that's the God's truth.

MRS. ANTROBUS. [*Nods a moment, then comes forward; quietly:*] Come. Come and put your head under some cold water.

SABINA. [*In a whisper.*] I'll go with him. I've known him a long while. You have to go on with the play. Come with me.

HENRY *starts out with* SABINA, *but turns at the exit and says to* ANTROBUS.

HENRY. Thanks. Thanks for what you said. I'll be all right tomorrow. I won't lose control in that place. I promise. [*Exeunt* HENRY *and* SABINA.]

ANTROBUS *starts toward the front door, fastens it.* MRS. ANTROBUS *goes up stage and places the chair close to table.*

MRS. ANTROBUS. George, do I see you limping?

ANTROBUS. Yes, a little. My old wound from the other war started smarting again. I can manage.

MRS. ANTROBUS. [*Looking out of the window.*] Some lights are coming on,—the first in seven years. People are walking up and down looking at them. Over in Hawkins' open lot they've built a bonfire to celebrate the peace. They're dancing around it like scarecrows.

ANTROBUS. A bonfire! As though they hadn't seen enough things burning.—Maggie,—the dog died?

MRS. ANTROBUS. Oh, yes. Long ago. There are no dogs left in Excelsior.—You're back again! All these years. I gave up counting on letters. The few that arrived were anywhere from six months to a year late.

ANTROBUS. Yes, the ocean's full of letters, along with the other things.

MRS. ANTROBUS. George, sit down, you're tired.

ANTROBUS. No, you sit down. I'm tired but I'm restless. [*Suddenly, as she comes forward:*] Maggie! I've lost it. I've lost it.

MRS. ANTROBUS. What, George? What have you lost?

ANTROBUS. The most important thing of all: The desire to begin again to start building.

MRS. ANTROBUS. [*Sitting in the chair right of the table.*] Well, it will come back.

ANTROBUS. [*At the window.*] I've lost it. This minute I feel like all those people dancing around the bonfire—just relief. Just the desire to settle down; to slip into the old grooves and keep the neighbors from walking over my lawn.—Hm. But during the war,—in the middle of all that blood and dirt and hot and cold—every day and night. I'd have moments, Maggie, when I *saw* the things that we could do when it was over. When you're at war you think about a better life; when you're at peace you think about a more comfortable one. I've lost it. I feel sick and tired.

MRS. ANTROBUS. Listen! The baby's crying.

I hear Gladys talking. Probably she's quieting Henry again. George, while Gladys and I were living here—like moles, like rats, and when we were at our wits' end to save the baby's life—the only thought we clung to was that you were going to bring something good out of this suffering. In the night, in the dark, we'd whisper about it, starving and sick.—Oh, George, you'll have to get it back again. Think! What else kept us alive all these years? Even now, it's not comfort we want. We can suffer whatever's necessary; only give us back that promise.

Enter SABINA *with a lighted lamp. She is dressed as in Act I.*

SABINA. Mrs. Antrobus . . .

MRS. ANTROBUS. Yes, Sabina?

SABINA. Will you need me?

MRS. ANTROBUS. No, Sabina, you can go to bed.

SABINA. Mrs. Antrobus, if it's all right with you, I'd like to go to the bonfire and celebrate seeing the war's over. And, Mrs. Antrobus, they've opened the Gem Movie Theatre and they're giving away a hand-painted soup tureen to every lady, and I thought one of us ought to go.

ANTROBUS. Well, Sabina, I haven't any money. I haven't seen any money for quite a while.

SABINA. Oh, you don't need money. They're taking anything you can give them. And I have some . . . some . . . Mrs. Antrobus, promise you won't tell anyone. It's a little against the law. But I'll give you some, too.

ANTROBUS. What is it?

SABINA. I'll give you some, too. Yesterday I picked up a lot of . . . of beef-cubes!

MRS. ANTROBUS *turns and says calmly:*

MRS. ANTROBUS. But, Sabina, you know you ought to give that in to the Center downtown. They know who needs them most.

SABINA. [*Outburst.*] Mrs. Antrobus, I didn't make this war. I didn't ask for it. And, in my opinion, after anybody's gone through what we've gone through, they have a right to grab what they can find. You're a very nice man, Mr. Antrobus, but you'd have got on better in the world if you'd realized that dog-eat-dog was the rule in the beginning and always will be. And most of all now. [*In tears.*] Oh, the world's an awful place, and you know it is. I used to think something could be done about it; but I know better now. I hate it. I hate it. [*She comes forward slowly and brings six cubes from the bag.*] All right. All right. You can have them.

ANTROBUS. Thank you, Sabina.

SABINA. Can I have . . . can I have one to go to the movies? [ANTRO-BUS *in silence gives her one.*] Thank you.

ANTROBUS. Good night, Sabina.

SABINA. Mr. Antrobus, don't mind what I say. I'm just an ordinary girl, you know what I mean, I'm just an ordinary girl. But you're a bright man, you're a very bright man, and of course you invented the alphabet and the wheel, and, my God, a lot of things . . . and if you've got any other plans, my God, don't let me upset them. Only every now and then I've got to go to the movies. I mean my nerves can't stand it. But if you have any ideas about improving the crazy old world, I'm really with you. I really am. Because it's . . . it's . . . Good night.

She goes out. ANTROBUS *starts laughing softly with exhilaration.*

ANTROBUS. Now I remember what three things always went together when I was able to see things most clearly: three things. Three things: [*He points to where* SABINA *has gone out.*] The voice of the people in their confusion and their need. And the thought of you and the children and this house . . . And . . . Maggie! I didn't dare ask you: my books! They haven't been lost, have they?

MRS. ANTROBUS. No. There are some of them right here. Kind of tattered.

ANTROBUS. Yes.—Remember, Maggie, we almost lost them once before? And when we finally did collect a few torn copies out of old cellars they ran in everyone's head like a fever. They as good as rebuilt the world. [*Pauses, book in hand, and looks up.*] Oh, I've never forgotten for long at a time that living is struggle. I know that every good and excellent thing in the world stands moment by moment on the razor-edge of danger and must be fought for—whether it's a field, or a home, or a country. All I ask is the chance to build new worlds and God has always given us that. And has given us [*Opening the book.*] voices to guide us; and the memory of our mistakes to warn us. Maggie, you and I will remember in peacetime all the resolves that were so clear to us in the days of war. We've come a long ways. We've learned. We're learning. And the steps of our journey are marked for us here. [*He stands by the table turning the leaves of a book.*] Sometimes out there in the war,—standing all night on a hill—I'd try and remember some of the words in these books. Parts of them and phrases would come back to me. And after a while I used to give names to the hours of the night. [*He sits, hunting for a passage in the book.*] Nine o'clock I used to call Spinoza. Where is it: "After experience had taught me—"

The back wall has disappeared, revealing the platform. FRED BAILEY *carrying his numeral has started from left to right.* MRS. ANTROBUS *sits by the table sewing.*

BAILEY. "After experience had taught me that the common occurrences of daily life are vain and futile; and I saw that all the objects of my desire and fear were in themselves nothing good nor bad save insofar as the mind was affected by them; I at length determined to search out whether there was something truly good and communicable to man." [7]

Almost without break HESTER, *carrying a large Roman numeral ten, starts crossing the platform.* GLADYS *appears at the kitchen door and moves towards her mother's chair.*

HESTER. "Then tell me, O Critias, how will a man choose the ruler that shall rule over him? Will he not choose a man who has first established order in himself, knowing that any decision that has its spring from anger or pride or vanity can be multiplied a thousand fold in its effects upon the citizens?" [8]

HESTER *disappears and* IVY, *as eleven o'clock starts speaking.*

IVY. "This good estate of the mind possessing its object in energy we call divine. This we mortals have occasionally and it is this energy which is pleasantest and best. But God has it always. It is wonderful in us; but in Him how much more wonderful." [9]

As MR. TREMAYNE *starts to speak,* HENRY *appears at the edge of the scene, brooding and unreconciled, but present.*

TREMAYNE. "In the beginning, God created the Heavens and the earth; And the Earth was waste and void; And the darkness was upon the face of the deep. And the Lord said let there be light and there was light." [10]

Sudden black-out and silence, except for the last strokes of the midnight bell. Then just as suddenly the lights go up, and SABINA *is standing at the window, as at the opening of the play.*

SABINA. Oh, oh, oh. Six o'clock and the master not home yet. Pray God nothing serious has happened to him crossing the Hudson River.

[7] Opening of *The Treatise on the Correction of the Understanding.*

[8] See page 820, note 5.

[9] Continuation of the quotation from *Metaphysics*, 12, 7; see page 820.

[10] Partial quotation from the opening lines of *Genesis.*

But I wouldn't be surprised. The whole world's at sixes and sevens, and why the house hasn't fallen down about our ears long ago is a miracle to me. [*She comes down to the footlights.*]

This is where you came in. We have to go on for ages and ages yet. You go home.

The end of this play isn't written yet.

Mr. and Mrs. Antrobus! Their heads are full of plans and they're as confident as the first day they began,—and they told me to tell you: good night.

EDWARD [FRANKLIN] ALBEE (1928–   )

Abandoned as an infant and adopted by wealthy theatrical people who could give him luxury but apparently little else, Albee's childhood and youth were troubled and his expensive schooling disastrous. He broke with his parents at twenty and for nearly a decade led a precarious existence in Greenwich Village and environs. The Zoo Story, he has said, was his birthday present to himself at thirty.

The play found no American producer until the Provincetown Players presented it as part of a double bill with Beckett's Krapp's Last Tape (1960). The play brought him a good deal of attention and introduced the endless debate on how Albee's "absurd" is different from the European "Absurd."

A number of short plays followed: The Death of Bessie Smith (1960),* The Sandbox (1960), Fam and Yam (1960), The American Dream (1960). In some of these plays, Mommy and Daddy play their perhaps expectedly vicious roles. In Who's Afraid of Virginia Woolf (1962), Mommy and Daddy—or Martha and George—have no child at all, but they have a secret fictional child between them, which they destroy at the end of the play.

Such mysteries keep even attempts at art interesting when they might otherwise be only exasperating. And exasperating many people have found most of Albee's later plays to be—exasperating because they try so hard to be interesting by being enigmatic, as if the playwright were saying, "My secrets are my secrets and I won't tell you"—that sort of thing. He showed, in his early plays, a wonderful feeling for the interchange of speech, and that was the drama; but recently, toying with what has always been his central theme, the slippery difference between illusion and reality, he has become more inter-

---

* Dates given for Albee's plays are those of the first American performance.

ested in the elaboration of elusive thematic structures than in the basic fact of dramatic interchange.

That Tiny Alice (1964), for example, is telling us something about illusion and reality, about shadow and substance, is obvious enough; but what? It is an elaborate puzzle or a series of mirrored reflections that extend into infinity. If well acted, it can, through Albee's sheer power of theatricality, compel one's attention during the span of the performance, but once the performance is over, it is all too likely to seem to have been only a dark exercise in the arbitrary and the willful. Does it become impressive, or even clear, if we acknowledge that somewhere there is some kind of enormous (or tiny) allegory, but we still are unable to define it? Is the exercise itself conceivably too tiny, too constricted?

A Delicate Balance *(1966) cannot be written off as tiresome. One repeats: Albee has a superb theatrical sense, and with any group of competent actors, he holds his audience like a ringmaster, but it is not an interesting reading experience, as* The Zoo Story *and many of the plays through* Virginia Woolf *are.*

*His adaptations of the work of other people—*Malcolm *(1966),* Everything in the Garden *(1967)—seem to be kindnesses to friends and perhaps misguided. And his most recent original plays,* Box *and* Quotations from Chairman Mao Tse-Tung *(1968), suggest that even mystery, at last, can become dull.*

FURTHER READING

The first full-length study is Gilbert Debusscher, *Edward Albee: Tradition and Renewal* (translated from the French by Ann D. Williams, 1968). See also Gerald Weales, *American Drama Since World War II* (1962), and Nelvin Vos, *Eugene Ionesco and Edward Albee: A Critical Essay* (1968). Ruby Cohn's pamphlet, *Edward Albee* (1969), is instructive.

The Zoo Story *(1960)*
A Play in One Scene

For William Flanagan [1]

THE PLAYERS:

Peter: A man in his early forties, neither fat nor gaunt, neither handsome nor homely. He wears tweeds, smokes a pipe, carries horn-rimmed glasses. Although he is moving into middle age, his dress and his manner would suggest a man younger.

Jerry: A man in his late thirties, not poorly dressed, but carelessly. What was once a trim and lightly muscled body has begun to go to fat; and while he is no longer handsome, it is evident that he once was. His fall from physical grace should not suggest debauchery; he has, to come closest to it, a great weariness.

The Scene: It is Central Park; a Sunday afternoon in summer; the present. There are two park benches, one toward either side of the stage; they both face the audience. Behind them: foliage, trees, sky. At the beginning, Peter is seated on one of the benches.

Stage Directions: As the curtain rises, PETER *is seated on the bench stage-right. He is reading a book. He stops reading, cleans his glasses, goes back to reading.* JERRY *enters.*

JERRY. I've been to the zoo. (PETER *doesn't notice*) I said, I've been to the zoo. MISTER, I'VE BEEN TO THE ZOO!
PETER. Hm? . . . What? . . . I'm sorry, were you talking to me?
JERRY. I went to the zoo, and then I walked until I came here. Have I been walking north?
PETER. (*Puzzled*) North? Why . . . I . . . I think so. Let me see.
JERRY. (*Pointing past the audience*) Is that Fifth Avenue?
PETER. Why yes; yes, it is.
JERRY. And what is that cross street there; that one, to the right?
PETER. That? Oh, that's Seventy-fourth Street.
JERRY. And the zoo is around Sixty-fifth Street; so, I've been walking north.

[1] (1923–1969), composer and friend of the dramatist for some of whose plays he wrote incidental music; the dramatist wrote the libretto for Flanagan's opera, *Bartleby* (1961).

PETER. (*Anxious to get back to his reading*) Yes; it would seem so.

JERRY. Good old north.

PETER. (*Lightly, by reflex*) Ha, ha.

JERRY. (*After a slight pause*) But not due north.

PETER. I . . . well, no, not due north; but, we . . . call it north. It's northerly.

JERRY. (*Watches as* PETER, *anxious to dismiss him, prepares his pipe*) Well, boy; *you're* not going to get lung cancer, are you?

PETER. (*Looks up, a little annoyed, then smiles*) No, sir. Not from this.

JERRY. No, sir. What you'll probably get is cancer of the mouth, and then you'll have to wear one of those things Freud wore after they took one whole side of his jaw away. What do they call those things?

PETER. (*Uncomfortable*) A prosthesis?

JERRY. The very thing! A prosthesis. You're an educated man, aren't you? Are you a doctor?

PETER. Oh, no; no. I read about it somewhere; *Time* magazine, I think. (*He turns to his book*)

JERRY. Well, *Time* magazine isn't for blockheads.

PETER. No, I suppose not.

JERRY. (*After a pause*) Boy, I'm glad that's Fifth Avenue there.

PETER. (*Vaguely*) Yes.

JERRY. I don't like the west side of the park much.

PETER. Oh? (*Then, slightly wary, but interested*) Why?

JERRY. (*Offhand*) I don't know.

PETER. Oh. (*He returns to his book*)

JERRY. (*He stands for a few seconds, looking at* PETER, *who finally looks up again, puzzled*) Do you mind if we talk?

PETER. (*Obviously minding*) Why . . . no, no.

JERRY. Yes you do; you do.

PETER. (*Puts his book down, his pipe out and away, smiling*) No, really; I don't mind.

JERRY. Yes you do.

PETER. (*Finally decided*) No; I don't mind at all, really.

JERRY. It's . . . it's a nice day.

PETER. (*Stares unnecessarily at the sky*) Yes. Yes, it is; lovely.

JERRY. I've been to the zoo.

PETER. Yes, I think you said so . . . didn't you?

JERRY. You'll read about it in the papers tomorrow, if you don't see it on your TV tonight. You have TV, haven't you?

PETER. Why yes, we have two; one for the children.

JERRY. You're married!

PETER. (*With pleased emphasis*) Why, certainly.

JERRY. It isn't a law, for God's sake.

PETER. No . . . no, of course not.

JERRY. And you have a wife.

PETER. *(Bewildered by the seeming lack of communication)* Yes!

JERRY. And you have children.

PETER. Yes; two.

JERRY. Boys?

PETER. No, girls . . . both girls.

JERRY. But you wanted boys.

PETER. Well . . . naturally, every man wants a son, but . . .

JERRY. *(Lightly mocking)* But that's the way the cookie crumbles?

PETER. *(Annoyed)* I wasn't going to say that.

JERRY. And you're not going to have any more kids, are you?

PETER. *(A bit distantly)* No. No more. *(Then back, and irksome)* Why did you say that? How would you know about that?

JERRY. The way you cross your legs, perhaps; something in the voice. Or maybe I'm just guessing. Is it your wife?

PETER. *(Furious)* That's none of your business! *(A silence)* Do you understand? *(JERRY nods. PETER is quiet now)* Well, you're right. We'll have no more children.

JERRY. *(Softly)* That *is* the way the cookie crumbles.

PETER. *(Forgiving)* Yes . . . I guess so.

JERRY. Well, now; what else?

PETER. What were you saying about the zoo . . . that I'd read about it, or see . . . ?

JERRY. I'll tell you about it, soon. Do you mind if I ask you questions?

PETER. Oh, not really.

JERRY. I'll tell you why I do it; I don't talk to many people—except to say like: give me a beer, or where's the john, or what time does the feature go on, or keep your hands to yourself, buddy. You know—things like that.

PETER. I must say I don't . . .

JERRY. But every once in a while I like to talk to somebody, really *talk;* like to get to know somebody, know all about him.

PETER. *(Lightly laughing, still a little uncomfortable)* And am I the guinea pig for today?

JERRY. On a sun-drenched Sunday afternoon like this? Who better than a nice married man with two daughters and . . . uh . . . a dog? *(PETER shakes his head)* No? Two dogs. *(PETER shakes his head again)* Hm. No dogs? *(PETER shakes his head, sadly)* Oh, that's a shame. But you look like an animal man. CATS? *(PETER nods his head, ruefully)* Cats! But, that can't be your idea. No, sir. Your wife and daughters? *(PETER nods his head)* Is there anything else I should know?

PETER. *(He has to clear his throat)* There are . . . there are two parakeets. One . . . uh . . . one for each of my daughters.

JERRY. Birds.

PETER. My daughters keep them in a cage in their bedroom.

JERRY. Do they carry disease? The birds.

PETER. I don't believe so.

JERRY. That's too bad. If they did you could set them loose in the house and the cats could eat them and die, maybe. (PETER *looks blank for a moment, then laughs*) And what else? What do you do to support your enormous household?

PETER. I . . . uh . . . I have an executive position with a . . . a small publishing house. We . . . uh . . . we publish textbooks.

JERRY. That sounds nice; very nice. What do you make?

PETER. (*Still cheerful*) Now look here!

JERRY. Oh, come on.

PETER. Well, I make around eighteen thousand a year, but I don't carry more than forty dollars at any one time . . . in case you're a . . . a holdup man . . . ha, ha, ha.

JERRY. (*Ignoring the above*) Where do you live? (PETER *is reluctant*) Oh, look; I'm not going to rob you, and I'm not going to kidnap your parakeets, your cats, or your daughters.

PETER. (*Too loud*) I live between Lexington and Third Avenue, on Seventy-fourth Street.

JERRY. That wasn't so hard, was it?

PETER. I didn't mean to seem . . . ah . . . it's that you don't really carry on a conversation; you just ask questions. And I'm . . . I'm normally . . . uh . . . reticent. Why do you just stand there?

JERRY. I'll start walking around in a little while, and eventually I'll sit down. (*Recalling*) Wait until you see the expression on his face.

PETER. What? Whose face? Look here; is this something about the zoo?

JERRY. (*Distantly*) The what?

PETER. The zoo; the zoo. Something about the zoo.

JERRY. The zoo?

PETER. You've mentioned it several times.

JERRY. (*Still distant, but returning abruptly*) The zoo? Oh, yes; the zoo. I was there before I came here. I told you that. Say, what's the dividing line between upper-middle-middle-class and lower-upper-middle-class?

PETER. My dear fellow, I . . .

JERRY. Don't my dear fellow me.

PETER. (*Unhappily*) Was I patronizing? I believe I was; I'm sorry. But, you see, your question about the classes bewildered me.

JERRY. And when you're bewildered you become patronizing?

PETER. I . . . I don't express myself too well, sometimes. (*He attempts a joke on himself*) I'm in publishing, not writing.

JERRY. (*Amused, but not at the humor*) So be it. The truth *is:* I was being patronizing.

PETER. Oh, now; you needn't say that.

(It is at this point that Jerry may begin to move about the stage with slowly increasing determination and authority, but pacing himself, so that the long speech about the dog comes at the high point of the arc)

JERRY. All right. Who are your favorite writers? Baudelaire and J. P. Marquand?

PETER. *(Wary)* Well, I like a great many writers; I have a considerable . . . catholicity of taste, if I may say so. Those two men are fine, each in his way. *(Warming up)* Baudelaire, of course . . . uh . . . is by far the finer of the two, but Marquand has a place . . . in our . . . uh . . . national . . .

JERRY. Skip it.

PETER. I . . . sorry.

JERRY. Do you know what I did before I went to the zoo today? I walked all the way up Fifth Avenue from Washington Square; all the way.

PETER. Oh; you live in the Village! *(This seems to enlighten PETER)*

JERRY. No, I don't. I took the subway down to the Village so I could walk all the way up Fifth Avenue to the zoo. It's one of those things a person has to do; sometimes a person has to go a very long distance out of his way to come back a short distance correctly.

PETER. *(Almost pouting)* Oh, I thought you lived in the Village.

JERRY. What were you trying to do? Make sense out of things? Bring order? The old pigeonhole bit? Well, that's easy; I'll tell you. I live in a four-story brownstone roominghouse on the upper West Side between Columbus Avenue and Central Park West. I live on the top floor; rear; west. It's a laughably small room, and one of my walls is made of beaverboard; this beaverboard separates my room from another laughably small room, so I assume that the two rooms were once one room, a small room, but not necessarily laughable. The room beyond my beaverboard wall is occupied by a colored queen who always keeps his door open; well, not always but *always* when he's plucking his eyebrows, which he does with Buddhist concentration. This colored queen has rotten teeth, which is rare, and he has a Japanese kimono, which is also pretty rare; and he wears this kimono to and from the john in the hall, which is pretty frequent. I mean, he goes to the john a lot. He never bothers me, and he never brings anyone up to his room. All he does is pluck his eyebrows, wear his kimono and go to the john. Now, the two front rooms on my floor are a little larger, I guess; but they're pretty small, too. There's a Puerto Rican family in one of them, a husband, a wife, and some kids; I don't know how many. These people entertain a lot. And in the other front room, there's somebody living there, but I don't know who it is. I've never seen who it is. Never. Never ever.

PETER. *(Embarrassed)* Why . . . why do you live there?

JERRY. *(From a distance again)* I don't know.

PETER. It doesn't sound like a very nice place . . . where you live.

JERRY. Well, no; it isn't an apartment in the East Seventies. But, then again, I don't have one wife, two daughters, two cats and two parakeets. What I do have, I have toilet articles, a few clothes, a hot plate that I'm not supposed to have, a can opener, one that works with a key, you know; a knife, two forks, and two spoons, one small, one large; three plates, a cup, a saucer, a drinking glass, two picture frames, both empty, eight or nine books, a pack of pornographic playing cards, regular deck, and old Western Union typewriter that prints nothing but capital letters, and a small strongbox without a lock which has in it . . . what? Rocks! Some rocks . . . sea-rounded rocks I picked up on the beach when I was a kid. Under which . . . weighed down . . . are some letters . . . please letters . . . please why don't you do this, and please when will you do that letters. And when letters, too. When will you write? When will you come? When? These letters are from more recent years.

PETER. *(Stares glumly at his shoes, then)* About those two empty picture frames . . .?

JERRY. I don't see why they need any explanation at all. Isn't it clear? I don't have pictures of anyone to put in them.

PETER. Your parents . . . perhaps . . . a girl friend . . .

JERRY. You're a very sweet man, and you're possessed of a truly enviable innocence. But good old Mom and good old Pop are dead . . . you know? . . . I'm broken up about it, too . . . I mean really. BUT. That particular vaudeville act is playing the cloud circuit now, so I don't see how I can look at them, all neat and framed. Besides, or, rather, to be pointed about it, good old Mom walked out on good old Pop when I was ten and a half years old; she embarked on an adulterous turn of our southern states . . . a journey of a year's duration . . . and her most constant companion . . . among others, among many others . . . was a Mr. Barleycorn. At least, that's what good old Pop told me after he went down . . . came back . . . brought her body north. We'd received the news between Christmas and New Year's, you see, that good old Mom had parted with the ghost in some dump in Alabama. And, without the ghost . . . she was less welcome. I mean, what was she? A stiff . . . a northern stiff. At any rate, good old Pop celebrated the New Year for an even two weeks and then slapped into the front of a somewhat moving city omnibus, which sort of cleaned things out family-wise. Well no; then there was Mom's sister, who was given neither to sin nor the consolations of the bottle. I moved in on her, and my memory of her is slight excepting I remember still that she did all things dourly: sleeping, eating, working, praying. She dropped dead on the stairs to her apartment, my apartment then, too, on the afternoon of my high school graduation. A terribly middle-European joke, if you ask me.

PETER. Oh, my; oh, my.

JERRY. Oh, your what? But that was a long time ago, and I have no feeling about any of it that I care to admit to myself. Perhaps you can see, though, why good old Mom and good old Pop are frameless. What's your name? Your first name?

PETER. I'm Peter.

JERRY. I'd forgotten to ask you. I'm Jerry.

PETER. *(With a slight, nervous laugh)* Hello, Jerry.

JERRY. *(Nods his hello)* And let's see now; what's the point of having a girl's picture, especially in two frames? I have two picture frames, you remember. I never see the pretty little ladies more than once, and most of them wouldn't be caught in the same room with a camera. It's odd, and I wonder if it's sad.

PETER. The girls?

JERRY. No. I wonder if it's sad that I never see the little ladies more than once. I've never been able to have sex with, or, how is it put? . . . make love to anybody more than once. Once; that's it. . . . Oh, wait; for a week and a half, when I was fifteen . . . and I hang my head in shame that puberty was late . . . I was a h-o-m-o-s-e-x-u-a-l. I mean, I was queer . . . *(Very fast)* . . . queer, queer, queer . . . with bells ringing, banners snapping in the wind. And for those eleven days, I met at least twice a day with the park superintendent's son . . . a Greek boy, whose birthday was the same as mine, except he was a year older. I think I was very much in love . . . maybe just with sex. But that was the jazz of a very special hotel, wasn't it? And now; oh, do I love the little ladies; really, I love them. For about an hour.

PETER. Well, it seems perfectly simple to me. . . .

JERRY. *(Angry)* Look! Are you going to tell me to get married and have parakeets?

PETER. *(Angry himself)* Forget the parakeets! And stay single if you want to. It's no business of mine. I didn't start this conversation in the . . .

JERRY. All right, all right. I'm sorry. All right? You're not angry?

PETER. *(Laughing)* No, I'm not angry.

JERRY. *(Relieved)* Good. *(Now back to his previous tone)* Interesting that you asked me about the picture frames. I would have thought that you would have asked me about the pornographic playing cards.

PETER. *(With a knowing smile)* Oh, I've seen those cards.

JERRY. That's not the point. *(Laughs)* I suppose when you were a kid you and your pals passed them around, or you had a pack of your own.

PETER. Well, I guess a lot of us did.

JERRY. And you threw them away just before you got married.

PETER. Oh, now; look here. I didn't *need* anything like that when I got older.

JERRY. No?

PETER. *(Embarrassed)* I'd rather not talk about these things.

JERRY. So? Don't. Besides, I wasn't trying to plumb your postadolescent sexual life and hard times; what I wanted to get at is the value difference between pornographic playing cards when you're a kid, and pornographic playing cards when you're older. It's that when you're a kid you use the cards as a substitute for a real experience, and when you're older you use real experience as a substitute for the fantasy. But I imagine you'd rather hear about what happened at the zoo.

PETER. *(Enthusiastic)* Oh, yes; the zoo. *(Then, awkward)* That is . . . if you. . . .

JERRY. Let me tell you about why I went . . . well, let me tell you some things. I've told you about the fourth floor of the roominghouse where I live. I think the rooms are better as you go down, floor by floor. I guess they are; I don't know. I don't know any of the people on the third and second floors. Oh, wait! I do know that there's a lady living on the third floor, in the front. I know because she cries all the time. Whenever I go out or come back in, whenever I pass her door, I always hear her crying, muffled, but . . . very determined. Very determined indeed. But the one I'm getting to, and all about the dog, is the landlady. I don't like to use words that are too harsh in describing people. I don't like to. But the landlady is a fat, ugly, mean, stupid, unwashed, misanthropic, cheap, drunken bag of garbage. And you may have noticed that I very seldom use profanity, so I can't describe her as well as I might.

PETER. You describe her . . . vividly.

JERRY. Well, thanks. Anyway, she has a dog, and I will tell you about the dog, and she and her dog are the gatekeepers of my dwelling. The woman is bad enough; she leans around in the entrance hall, spying to see that I don't bring in things or people, and when she's had her mid-afternoon pint of lemon-flavored gin she always stops me in the hall, and grabs ahold of my coat or my arm, and she presses her disgusting body up against me to keep me in a corner so she can talk to me. The smell of her body and her breath . . . you can't imagine it . . . and some-where, somewhere in the back of that pea-sized brain of hers, an organ developed just enough to let her eat, drink, and emit, she has some foul parody of sexual desire. And I, Peter, I am the object of her sweaty lust.

PETER. That's disgusting. That's . . . horrible.

JERRY. But I have found a way to keep her off. When she talks to me, when she presses herself to my body and mumbles about her room and how I should come there, I merely say: but, Love; wasn't yesterday enough for you, and the day before? Then she puzzles, she makes slits of her tiny eyes, she sways a little, and then, Peter . . . and it is at this moment that I think I might be doing some good in that tormented house . . . a simple-minded smile begins to form on her unthinkable face, and she giggles and groans as she thinks about yesterday and the day before; as she believes and relives what never happened. Then, she motions to that black monster of a dog she has, and she goes back to her room. And I am safe until our next meeting.

PETER. It's so . . . unthinkable. I find it hard to believe that people such as that really *are*.

JERRY. *(Lightly mocking)* It's for reading about, isn't it?

PETER. *(Seriously)* Yes.

JERRY. And fact is better left to fiction. You're right, Peter. Well, what I have been meaning to tell you about is the dog; I shall, now.

PETER. *(Nervously)* Oh, yes; the dog.

JERRY. Don't go. You're not thinking of going, are you?

PETER. Well . . . no, I don't think so.

JERRY. *(As if to a child)* Because after I tell you about the dog, do you know what then? Then . . . then I'll tell you about what happened at the zoo.

PETER. *(Laughing faintly)* You're . . . you're full of stories, aren't you?

JERRY. You don't *have* to listen. Nobody is holding you here; remember that. Keep that in your mind.

PETER. *(Irritably)* I know that.

JERRY. You do? Good.

(The following long speech, it seems to me, should be done with a great deal of action, to achieve a hypnotic effect on Peter, and on the audience, too. Some specific actions have been suggested, but the director and the actor playing Jerry might best work it out for themselves)

ALL RIGHT. *(As if reading from a huge billboard)* THE STORY OF JERRY AND THE DOG! *(Natural again)* What I am going to tell you has something to do with how sometimes it's necessary to go a long distance out of the way in order to come back a short distance correctly; or, maybe I only think that it has something to do with that. But, it's why I went to the zoo today, and why I walked north . . . northerly, rather . . . until I came here. All right. The dog, I think I told you, is a black monster of a beast: an oversized head, tiny, tiny ears, and eyes . . . bloodshot, infected, maybe; and a body you can see the ribs through the skin. The dog is black, all black; all black except for the bloodshot eyes, and . . . yes . . . and an open sore on its . . . *right* forepaw; that is red, too. And, oh yes; the poor monster, and I do believe it's an old dog . . . it's certainly a misused one . . . almost always has an erection . . . of sorts. That's red, too. And . . . what else? . . . oh, yes; there's a gray-yellow-white color, too, when he bares his fangs. Like this: Grrrrrrr! Which is what he did when he saw me for the first time . . . the day I moved in. I worried about that animal the very first minute I met him. Now, animals don't take to me like Saint Francis had birds hanging off him all the time. What I mean is: animals are indifferent to me . . . like people *(He smiles slightly)* . . . most of the time. But this dog wasn't indifferent. From the very beginning he'd snarl and then go for me, to get one of my legs. Not like he was rabid, you know; he was sort of a stumbly dog, but he wasn't half-assed, either. It was a good, stumbly run; but I always got away. He got a piece of my trouser leg, look, you can see right here, where it's mended; he got that the second day I lived there; but, I kicked free and got upstairs fast, so that was that. *(Puzzles)* I still don't know to this day

how the other roomers manage it, but you know what I *think:* I think
it had to do only with me. Cozy. So. Anyway, this went on for over a
week, whenever I came in; but never when I went out. That's funny. Or,
it *was* funny. I could pack up and live in the street for all the dog cared.
Well, I thought about it up in my room one day, one of the times after
I'd bolted upstairs, and I made up my mind. I decided: First, I'll kill the
dog with kindness, and if that doesn't work . . . I'll just kill him. (PETER
winces) Don't react, Peter: just listen. So, the next day I went out and
bought a bag of hamburgers, medium rare, no catsup, no onion; and on
the way home I threw away all the rolls and kept just the meat.

(Action for the following, perhaps)

When I got back to the roominghouse the dog was waiting for me. I half
opened the door that led into the entrance hall, and there he was; waiting for me. It figured. I went in, very cautiously, and I had the hamburgers, you remember; I opened the bag, and I set the meat down about
twelve feet from where the dog was snarling at me. Like so! He snarled;
stopped snarling; sniffed; moved slowly; then faster; then faster toward
the meat. Well, when he got to it he stopped, and he looked at me. I
smiled; but tentatively, you understand. He turned his face back to the
hamburgers, smelled, sniffed some more, and then . . . RRRAAAA-
GGGGGHHHH, like that . . . he tore into them. It was as if he had never
eaten anything in his life before, except like garbage. Which might very
well have been the truth. I don't think the landlady ever eats anything
but garbage. But. He ate all the hamburgers, almost all at once, making
sounds in his throat like a woman. *Then,* when he'd finished the meat,
the hamburger, and tried to eat the paper, too, he sat down and smiled.
I think he smiled; I know cats do. It was a very gratifying few moments.
Then, BAM, he snarled and made for me again. He didn't get me this
time, either. So, I got upstairs, and I lay down on my bed and started to
think about the dog again. To be truthful, I was offended, and I was
damn mad, too. It was six perfectly good hamburgers with not enough
pork in them to make it disgusting. I was offended. But, after a while, I
decided to try it for a few more days. If you think about it, this dog had
what amounted to an antipathy toward me; really. And, I wondered if
I mightn't overcome this antipathy. So, I tried it for five more days, but
it was always the same: snarl, sniff; move; faster; stare; gobble; RAA-
GGGHHH; smile; snarl; BAM. Well, now; by this time Columbus Avenue
was strewn with hamburger rolls and I was less offended than disgusted.
So, I decided to kill the dog.

(PETER raises a hand in protest)

Oh, don't be so alarmed, Peter; I didn't succeed. The day I tried to kill
the dog I bought only one hamburger and what I thought was a murderous portion of rat poison. When I bought the hamburger I asked the
man not to bother with the roll, all I wanted was the meat. I expected

some reaction from him, like: we don't sell no hamburgers without rolls; or, wha' d'ya wanna do, eat it out'a ya han's? But no; he smiled benignly,- wrapped up the hamburger in waxed paper, and said: A bite for ya pussy-cat? I wanted to say: No, not really; it's part of a plan to poison a dog I know. But, you can't say "a dog I know" without sounding funny; so I said, a little too loud, I'm afraid, and too formally: YES, A BITE FOR MY PUSSY-CAT. People looked up. It always happens when I try to simplify things, people look up. But that's neither hither nor thither. So. On my way back to the roominghouse, I kneaded the hamburger and the rat poison together between my hands, at that point feeling as much sadness as disgust. I opened the door to the entrance hall, and there the monster was, waiting to take the offering and then jump me. Poor bastard; he never learned that the moment he took to smile before he went for me gave me time enough to get out of range. BUT, there he was; malevolence with an erection, waiting. I put the poison patty down, moved toward the stairs and watched. The poor animal gobbled the food down as usual, smiled, which made me almost sick, and then, BAM. But, I sprinted up the stairs, as usual, and the dog didn't get me, as usual. AND IT CAME TO PASS THAT THE BEAST WAS DEATHLY ILL. I knew this because he no longer attended me, and because the landlady sobered up. She stopped me in the hall the same evening of the attempted murder and confided the information that God had struck her puppy-dog a surely fatal blow. She had forgotten her bewildered lust, and her eyes were wide open for the first time. They looked like the dog's eyes. She sniveled and implored me to pray for the animal. I wanted to say to her: Madam, I have myself to pray for, the colored queen, the Puerto Rican family, the person in the front room whom I've never seen, the woman who cries deliberately behind her closed door, and the rest of the people in all roominghouses, everywhere; besides, Madam, I don't understand how to pray. But . . . to simplify things . . . I told her I would pray. She looked up. She said that I was a liar, and that I probably wanted the dog to die. I told her, and there was so much truth here, that I didn't want the dog to die. I didn't and not just because I'd poisoned him. I'm afraid that I must tell you I wanted the dog to live so that I could see what our new relationship might come to.

(PETER *indicates his increasing displeasure and slowly growing antagonism*)

Please understand, Peter; that sort of thing is important. You must be-lieve me; it *is* important. We have to know the effect of our actions. (*Another deep sigh*) Well, anyway; the dog recovered. I have no idea why, unless he was a descendant of the puppy that guarded the gates of hell or some such resort. I'm not up on my mythology. (*He pronounces the word myth-o-*logy) Are you?

(PETER *sets to thinking, but* JERRY *goes on*)

At any rate, and you've missed the eight-thousand-dollar question, Peter;

at any rate, the dog recovered his health and the landlady recovered her thirst, in no way altered by the bow-wow's deliverance. When I came home from a movie that was playing on Forty-second Street, a movie I'd seen, or one that was very much like one or several I'd seen, after the landlady told me puppykins was better, I was so hoping for the dog to be waiting for me. I was . . . well, how would you put it . . . enticed? . . . fascinated? . . . no, I don't think so . . . heart-shatteringly anxious, that's it; I was heart-shatteringly anxious to confront my friend again.

(PETER *reacts scoffingly*)

Yes, Peter; friend. That's the only word for it. I was heart-shatteringly et cetera to confront my doggy friend again. I came in the door and advanced, unafraid, to the center of the entrance hall. The beast was there . . . looking at me. And, you know, he looked better for his scrape with the nevermind. I stopped; I looked at him; he looked at me. I think . . . I think we stayed a long time that way . . . still, stone-statue . . . just looking at one another. I looked more into his face than he looked into mine. I mean, I can concentrate longer at looking into a dog's face than a dog can concentrate at looking into mine, or into anybody else's face, for that matter. But during that twenty seconds or two hours that we looked into each other's face, we made contact. Now, here is what I had wanted to happen: I loved the dog now, and I wanted him to love me. I had tried to love, and I had tried to kill, and both had been unsuccessful by themselves. I hoped . . . and I don't really know why I expected the dog to understand anything, much less my motivations . . . I hoped that the dog would understand.

(PETER *seems to be hypnotized*)

It's just . . . it's just that . . . (JERRY *is abnormally tense, now*) . . . it's just that if you can't deal with people, you have to make a start somewhere. WITH ANIMALS! (*Much faster now, and like a conspirator*) Don't you see? A person has to have some way of dealing with SOMETHING. If not with people . . . if not with people . . . SOMETHING. With a bed, with a cockroach, with a mirror . . . no, that's too hard, that's one of the last steps. With a cockroach, with a . . . with a . . . with a carpet, a roll of toilet paper . . . no, not that, either . . . that's a mirror, too; always check bleeding. You see how hard it is to find things? With a street corner, and too many lights, all colors reflecting on the oily-wet streets . . . with a wisp of smoke, a wisp . . . of smoke . . . with . . . with pornographic playing cards, with a strongbox . . . WITHOUT A LOCK . . . with love, with vomiting, with crying, with fury because the pretty little ladies aren't pretty little ladies, with making money with your body which is an act of love and I could prove it, with howling because you're alive; with God. How about that? WITH GOD WHO IS A COLORED QUEEN WHO WEARS A KIMONO AND PLUCKS HIS EYEBROWS, WHO IS A WOMAN WHO CRIES WITH DETERMINATION BEHIND

HER CLOSED DOOR ... with God who, I'm told, turned his back on the whole thing some time ago ... with ... some day, with people. (JERRY *sighs the next word heavily*) People. With an idea; a concept. And where better, where ever better in this humiliating excuse for a jail, where better to communicate one single, simple-minded idea than in an entrance hall? Where? It would be A START! Where better to make a beginning ... to understand and just possibly be understood ... a beginning of an understanding, than with ...

(*Here* JERRY *seems to fall into almost grotesque fatigue*)

... than with A DOG. Just that; a dog.

(*Here there is a silence that might be prolonged for a moment or so; then* JERRY *wearily finishes his story*)

A dog. It seemed like a perfectly sensible idea. Man is a dog's best friend, remember. So: the dog and I looked at each other. I longer than the dog. And what I saw then has been the same ever since. Whenever the dog and I see each other we both stop where we are. We regard each other with a mixture of sadness and suspicion, and then we feign indifference. We walk past each other safely; we have an understanding. It's very sad, but you'll have to admit that it is an understanding. We had made many attempts at contact, and we had failed. The dog has returned to garbage, and I to solitary but free passage. I have not returned. I mean to say. I have *gained* solitary free passage, if that much further loss can be said to be gain. I have learned that neither kindness nor cruelty by themselves, independent of each other, creates any effect beyond themselves; and I have learned that the two combined, together, at the same time, are the teaching emotion. And what is gained is loss. And what has been the result: the dog and I have attained a compromise; more of a bargain, really. We neither love nor hurt because we do not try to reach each other. And, *was* trying to feed the dog an act of love? And, perhaps, was the dog's attempt to bite me *not* an act of love? If we can so misunderstand, well then, why have we invented the word love in the first place?

(*There is silence.* JERRY *moves to* PETER'S *bench and sits down beside him. This is the first time* JERRY *has sat down during the play*)

The Story of Jerry and the Dog: the end.

(PETER *is silent*)

Well, Peter? (JERRY *is suddenly cheerful*) Well, Peter? Do you think I could sell that story to the *Reader's Digest* and make a couple of hundred bucks for *The Most Unforgettable Character I've Ever Met*? Huh?

(JERRY *is animated, but* PETER *is disturbed*)

Oh, come on now, Peter; tell me what you think.

PETER. *(Numb)* I . . . I don't understand what . . . I don't think I . . . *(Now, almost tearfully)* Why did you tell me all of this?

JERRY. Why not?

PETER. I DON'T UNDERSTAND!

JERRY. *(Furious, but whispering)* That's a lie.

PETER. No. No, it's not.

JERRY. *(Quietly)* I tried to explain it to you as I went along. I went slowly; it all has to do with . . .

PETER. I DON'T WANT TO HEAR ANY MORE. I don't understand you, or your landlady, or her dog. . . .

JERRY. *Her* dog! I thought it was my . . . No. No, you're right. It *is* her dog. *(Looks at* PETER *intently, shaking his head)* I don't know what I was thinking about; of course you don't understand. *(In a monotone, wearily)* I don't live in your block; I'm not married to two parakeets, or whatever your setup is. I am a *permanent transient,* and my home is the sickening roominghouses on the West Side of New York City, which is the greatest city in the world. Amen.

PETER. I'm . . . I'm sorry; I didn't mean to . . .

JERRY. Forget it. I suppose you don't quite know what to make of me, eh?

PETER. *(A joke)* We get all kinds in publishing. *(Chuckles)*

JERRY. You're a funny man. *(He forces a laugh)* You know that? You're a very . . . a richly comic person.

PETER. *(Modestly, but amused)* Oh, now, not really. *(Still chuckling)*

JERRY. Peter, do I annoy you, or confuse you?

PETER. *(Lightly)* Well, I must confess that this wasn't the kind of afternoon I'd anticipated.

JERRY. You mean, I'm not the gentleman you were expecting.

PETER. I wasn't expecting anybody.

JERRY. No, I don't imagine you were. But I'm here, and I'm not leaving.

PETER. *(Consulting his watch)* Well, you may not be, but I must be getting home soon.

JERRY. Oh, come on; stay a while longer.

PETER. I really should get home; you see . . .

JERRY. *(Tickles* PETER'S *ribs with his fingers)* Oh, come on.

PETER. *(He is very ticklish; as* JERRY *continues to tickle him his voice becomes falsetto)* No, I . . . OHHHHH! Don't do that. Stop, Stop. Ohhh, no, no.

JERRY. Oh, come on.

PETER. *(As* JERRY *tickles)* Oh, hee, hee, hee. I must go. I . . . hee, hee, hee. After all, stop, stop, hee, hee, hee, after all, the parakeets will be getting dinner ready soon. Hee, hee. And the cats are setting the table. Stop, stop, and, and . . . *(PETER is beside himself now)* . . . and we're having . . . hee, hee . . . uh . . . ho, ho, ho.

(JERRY *stops tickling* PETER, *but the combination of the tickling and his own mad whimsy has* PETER *laughing almost hysterically. As his laughter continues, then subsides,* JERRY *watches him, with a curious fixed smile*)

JERRY. Peter?

PETER. Oh, ha, ha, ha, ha, ha. What? What?

JERRY. Listen, now.

PETER. Oh, ho, ho. What . . . what is it, Jerry? Oh, my.

JERRY. (*Mysteriously*) Peter, do you want to know what happened at the zoo?

PETER. Ah, ha, ha. The what? Oh, yes; the zoo. Oh, ho, ho. Well, I had my own zoo there for a moment with . . . hee, hee, the parakeets getting dinner ready, and the . . . ha, ha, whatever it was, the . . .

JERRY. (*Calmly*) Yes, that was very funny, Peter. I wouldn't have expected it. But do you want to hear about what happened at the zoo, or not?

PETER. Yes. Yes, by all means; tell me what happened at the zoo. Oh, my. I don't know what happened to me.

JERRY. Now I'll let you in on what happened at the zoo; but first, I should tell you why I went to the zoo. I went to the zoo to find out more about the way people exist with animals, and the way animals exist with each other, and with people too. It probably wasn't a fair test, what with everyone separated by bars from everyone else, the animals for the most part from each other, and always the people from the animals. But, if it's a zoo, that's the way it is. (*He pokes* PETER *on the arm*) Move over.

PETER (*Friendly*) I'm sorry, haven't you enough room? (*He shifts a little*)

JERRY. (*Smiling slightly*) Well, all the animals are there, and all the people are there, and it's Sunday and all the children are there. (*He pokes* PETER *again*) Move over.

PETER. (*Patiently, still friendly*) All right.

(*He moves some more, and* JERRY *has all the room he might need*)

JERRY. And it's a hot day, so all the stench is there, too, and all the balloon sellers, and all the ice cream sellers, and all the seals are barking, and all the birds are screaming. (*Pokes* PETER *harder*) Move over!

PETER. (*Beginning to be annoyed*) Look here, you have more than enough room! (*But he moves more, and is now fairly cramped at one end of the bench*)

JERRY. And I am there, and it's feeding time at the lions' house, and the lion keeper comes into the lion cage, one of the lion cages, to feed one of the lions. (*Punches* PETER *on the arm, hard*) MOVE OVER!

PETER. (*Very annoyed*) I can't move over any more, and stop hitting me. What's the matter with you?

JERRY. Do you want to hear the story? (*Punches* PETER'S *arm again*)

PETER. (*Flabbergasted*) I'm not so sure! I certainly don't want to be punched in the arm.

JERRY. (*Punches* PETER's *arm again*) Like that?

PETER. Stop it! What's the matter with you?

JERRY. I'm crazy, you bastard.

PETER. That isn't funny.

JERRY. Listen to me, Peter. I want this bench. You go sit on the bench over there, and if you're good I'll tell you the rest of the story.

PETER. (*Flustered*) But . . . whatever for? What *is* the matter with you? Besides, I see no reason why I should give up this bench. I sit on this bench almost every Sunday afternoon, in good weather. It's secluded here; there's never anyone sitting here, so I have it all to myself.

JERRY. (*Softly*) Get off this bench, Peter; I want it.

PETER. (*Almost whining*) No.

JERRY. I said I want this bench, and I'm going to have it. Now get over there.

PETER. People can't have everything they want. You should know that; it's a rule; people can have some of the things they want, but they can't have everything.

JERRY. (*Laughs*) Imbecile! You're slow-witted!

PETER. Stop that!

JERRY. You're a vegetable! Go lie down on the ground.

PETER. (*Intense*) Now *you* listen to me. I've put up with you all afternoon.

JERRY. Not really.

PETER. LONG ENOUGH. I've put up with you long enough. I've listened to you because you seemed . . . well, because I thought you wanted to talk to somebody.

JERRY. You put things well; economically, and, yet . . . oh, what is the word I want to put justice to your . . . JESUS, you make me sick . . . get off here and give me my bench.

PETER. MY BENCH!

JERRY. (*Pushes* PETER *almost, but not quite, off the bench*) Get out of my sight.

PETER. (*Regaining his position*) God da . . . mn you. That's enough! I've had enough of you. I will not give up this bench; you can't have it, and that's that. Now, go away.

(JERRY *snorts but does not move*)

Go away, I said.

(JERRY *does not move*)

Get away from here. If you don't move on . . . you're a bum . . . that's what you are . . . If you don't move on, I'll get a policeman here and make you go.

(JERRY *laughs, stays*)

I warn you, I'll call a policeman.

JERRY. (*Softly*) You won't find a policeman around here; they're all over on the west side of the park chasing fairies down from trees or out of the bushes. That's all they do. That's their function. So scream your head off; it won't do you any good.

PETER. POLICE! I warn you, I'll have you arrested. POLICE! (*Pause*) I said POLICE! (*Pause*) I feel ridiculous.

JERRY. You look ridiculous: a grown man screaming for the police on a bright Sunday afternoon in the park with nobody harming you. If a policeman *did* fill his quota and come sludging over this way he'd probably take you in as a nut.

PETER. (*With disgust and impotence*) Great God, I just came here to read, and now you want me to give up the bench. You're mad.

JERRY. Hey, I got news for you, as they say. I'm on your precious bench, and you're never going to have it for yourself again.

PETER. (*Furious*) Look, you; get off my bench. I don't care if it makes any sense or not. I want this bench to myself; I want you OFF IT!

JERRY. (*Mocking*) Aw . . . look who's mad.

PETER. GET OUT!

JERRY. No.

PETER. I WARN YOU!

JERRY. Do you know how ridiculous you look *now*?

PETER. (*His fury and self-consciousness have possessed him*) It doesn't matter. (*He is almost crying*) GET AWAY FROM MY BENCH!

JERRY. Why? You have everything in the world you want; you've told me about your home, and your family, and *your own* little zoo. You have everything, and now you want this bench. Are these the things men fight for? Tell me, Peter, is this bench, this iron and this wood, is this your honor? Is this the thing in the world you'd fight for? Can you think of anything more absurd?

PETER. Absurd? Look, I'm not going to talk to you about honor, or even try to explain it to you. Besides, it isn't a question of honor; but even if it were, you wouldn't understand.

JERRY. (*Contemptuously*) You don't even know what you're saying, do you? This is probably the first time in your life you've had anything more trying to face than changing your cats' toilet box. Stupid! Don't you have any idea, not even the slightest, what other people *need*?

PETER. Oh, boy, listen to you; well, you don't need this bench. That's for sure.

JERRY. Yes; yes, I do.

PETER. (*Quivering*) I've come here for years; I have hours of great pleasure, great satisfaction, right here. And that's important to a man. I'm a responsible person, and I'm a GROWNUP. This is my bench, and you have no right to take it away from me.

JERRY. Fight for it, then. Defend yourself; defend your bench.

PETER. You've *pushed* me to it. Get up and fight.

JERRY. Like a man?

PETER. (*Still angry*) Yes, like a man, if you insist on mocking me even further.

JERRY. I'll have to give you credit for one thing: you *are* a vegetable, and a slightly nearsighted one, I think . . .

PETER. THAT'S ENOUGH. . . .

JERRY. . . . but, you know, as they say on TV all the time—you know—and I mean this, Peter, you have a certain dignity; it surprises me. . . .

PETER. STOP!

JERRY. (*Rises lazily*) Very well, Peter, we'll battle for the bench, but we're not evenly matched.

(*He takes out and clicks open an ugly looking knife*)

PETER. (*Suddenly awakening to the reality of the situation*) You *are* mad! You're stark raving mad! YOU'RE GOING TO KILL ME!

(*But before* PETER *has time to think what to do,* JERRY *tosses the knife at* PETER's *feet*)

JERRY. There you go. Pick it up. You have the knife and we'll be more evenly matched.

PETER. (*Horrified*) No!

JERRY.

(*Rushes over to* PETER, *grabs him by the collar;* PETER *rises; their faces almost touch*)

Now you pick up that knife and you fight with me. You fight for your self-respect; you fight for that goddamned bench.

PETER. (*Struggling*) No! Let . . . let go of me! He . . . Help!

JERRY. (*Slaps* PETER *on each "fight"*) You fight, you miserable bastard; fight for that bench; fight for your parakeets; fight for your cats, fight for your two daughters; fight for your wife; fight for your manhood, you pathetic little vegetable. (*Spits in* PETER's *face*) You couldn't even get your wife with a male child.

PETER. (*Breaks away, enraged*) It's a matter of genetics, not manhood, you . . . you monster.

(*He darts down, picks up the knife and backs off a little; he is breathing heavily*)

I'll give you one last chance; get out of here and leave me alone!

(*He holds the knife with a firm arm, but far in front of him, not to attack, but to defend*)

JERRY. (*Sighs heavily*) So be it!

(*With a rush he charges* PETER *and impales himself on the knife. Tableau: For just a moment, complete silence,* JERRY *impaled on the knife at the end of* PETER's *still firm arm. Then* PETER *screams, pulls away, leaving the knife in* JERRY. JERRY *is motionless, on point. Then he, too, screams, and it must be the sound of an infuriated and fatally wounded animal. With the knife in him, he stumbles back to the bench that* PETER *had vacated. He crumbles there, sitting, facing* PETER, *his eyes wide in agony, his mouth open)*

PETER. (*Whispering*) Oh my God, oh my God, oh my God. . . . (*He repeats these words many times, very rapidly*)

JERRY.

(JERRY *is dying; but now his expression seems to change. His features relax, and while his voice varies, sometimes wrenched with pain, for the most part he seems removed from his dying. He smiles*)

Thank you, Peter. I mean that, now; thank you very much.

(PETER'S *mouth drops open. He cannot move; he is transfixed*)

Oh, Peter, I was so afraid I'd drive you away. (*He laughs as best he can*) You don't know how afraid I was you'd go away and leave me. And now I'll tell you what happened at the zoo. I think . . . I think this is what happened at the zoo . . . I think. I think that while I was at the zoo I decided that I would walk north . . . northerly, rather . . . until I found you . . . or somebody . . . and I decided that I would talk to you . . . I would tell you things . . . and things that I would tell you would . . . Well, here we are. You see? Here we *are.* But . . . I don't know . . . could I have planned all this? No . . . no, I couldn't have. But I think I did. And now I've told you what you wanted to know, haven't I? And now you know all about what happened at the zoo. And now you know what you'll see in your TV, and the face I told you about . . . you remember . . . the face I told you about . . . my face, the face you see right now. Peter . . . Peter? . . . Peter . . . thank you. I came unto you (*He laughs, so faintly*) and you have comforted me. Dear Peter.

PETER. (*Almost fainting*) Oh my God!

JERRY. You'd better go now. Somebody might come by, and you don't want to be here when anyone comes.

PETER. (*Does not move, but begins to weep*) Oh my God, oh my God.

JERRY. (*Most faintly, now; he is very near death*) You won't be coming back here any more, Peter; you've been dispossessed. You've lost your bench, but you've defended your honor. And Peter, I'll tell you something now; you're not really a vegetable; it's all right, you're an animal. You're an animal, too. But you're better hurry now, Peter. Hurry, you'd better go . . . see?

(JERRY *takes a handkerchief and with great effort and pain wipes the knife handle clean of fingerprints*)

Hurry away, Peter.

(PETER *begins to stagger away*)

Wait . . . wait, Peter. Take your book . . . book. Right here . . . beside
me . . . on your bench . . . my bench, rather. Come . . . take your book.

(PETER *starts for the book, but retreats*)

Hurry . . . Peter.

(PETER *rushes to the bench, grabs the book, retreats*)

Very good, Peter . . . very good. Now . . . hurry away.

(PETER *hesitates for a moment, then flees, stage left*)

Hurry away. . . . (*His eyes are closed now*) Hurry away, your parakeets
are making the dinner . . . the cats . . . are setting the table . . .
    PETER. (*Off stage*) (*A pitiful howl*) OH MY GOD!
    JERRY.

(*His eyes still closed, he shakes his head and speaks; a combination of scornful mimicry and supplication*)

Oh . . . my . . . God.

(*He is dead*)

CURTAIN

LEROI JONES (1934–   )

*LeRoi Jones's mother was a social worker and his father was a postal
supervisor in Newark, New Jersey, where he was born and brought
up. In the seventh grade at the Central Avenue School he improvised
a comic strip called "The Crime Wave," and for the Barringer High
School magazine he produced short works of science fiction. He
attended Rutgers University for a year but found the atmosphere
uncongenial and left it for Howard University in Washington D.C.,
where he was an English major. In 1954 he began two years of
service with the Strategic Air Command, stationed in Puerto Rico.
He returned to New York to study at Columbia and the New School
for Social Research. He married a white woman, had two children,
and was later divorced in order to marry a black woman as his
increasingly militant ethnic allegiance defined itself. He now calls
himself Imamu Amiri Baraka.*

*He taught poetry writing at the New School in the late 1950s, and,
later, lectured on theater arts at Columbia. In 1961 he published his
first book of poems,* Preface to a Twenty Volume Suicide Note, *and
in 1964, his second,* The Dead Lecturer. *At just this point his first
plays began to find off-Broadway productions.*

It is said that he considers himself primarily a poet. His own utterances on the subject of poetry, fifty years after Carl Sandburg, are not very reassuring:

Accentual verse, the regular metric of rumbling iambics, is dry as slivers of sand. Nothing happens in that frame anymore. We can get nothing from England. And the diluted formalism of the academy (the formal culture of the U.S.) is anaemic & fraught with incompetence & unreality.

Fraught?

Jones's poems, in fact, are old-fashioned Village chants on current topics. His plays are his forte. They are short, staccato, abusive, highly theatrical, and without literary echoes, his own. Dutchman, The Slave, The Toilet—all of the middle sixties—and perhaps one or two of the later ones, especially Slave Ship, are, as of now, his best work. His energetic involvement in and leadership of a number of theatrical enterprises for black people on behalf of their art as integral to their revolutionary cause and needs will, one hopes, stimulate his own contribution to the stage. His short plays lead his admirers to hope for some longer plays.

He published an apparently autobiographical novel called The System of Dante's Hell *(1965), a book of militant social essays called* Home *(1966), some short fiction collected in* Tales *(1967), more verse in* Black Magic *(1969), and two instructive books on music,* Blues People: Negro Music in White America *(1963) and* Black Music *(1967).*

FURTHER READING

Jones's place in the American theater is described in Loften Mitchell, *Black Drama* (1967); C. W. E. Bigsby, *Confrontation and Commitment* (1967); Doris E. Abramson, *Negro Playwrights in the American Theatre, 1925–1959* (1969); and especially Gerald Weales, *The Jumping-off Place: American Drama in the 1960's* (1969).

Dutchman (1964)

CHARACTERS

Clay, twenty-year-old Negro
Lula, thirty-year-old white woman
Riders of Coach, white and black
Young Negro
Conductor

In the flying underbelly of the city. Steaming hot, and summer on top, outside. Underground. The subway heaped in modern myth.

Opening scene is a man sitting in a subway seat, holding a magazine but looking vacantly just above its wilting pages. Occasionally he looks blankly toward the window on his right. Dim lights and darkness whistling by against the glass. (Or paste the lights, as admitted props, right on the subway windows. Have them move, even dim and flicker. But give the sense of speed. Also stations, whether the train is stopped or the glitter and activity of these stations merely flashes by the windows.)

The man is sitting alone. That is, only his seat is visible, though the rest of the car is outfitted as a complete subway car. But only his seat is shown. There might be, for a time, as the play begins, a loud scream of the actual train. And it can recur throughout the play, or continue on a lower key once the dialogue starts.

The train slows after a time, pulling to a brief stop at one of the stations. The man looks idly up, until he sees a woman's face staring at him through the window; when it realizes that the man has noticed the face, it begins very premeditatedly to smile. The man smiles too, for a moment, without a trace of self-consciousness. Almost an instinctive though undesirable response. Then a kind of awkwardness or embarrassment sets in, and the man makes to look away, is further embarrassed, so he brings back his eyes to where the face was, but by now the train is moving again, and the face would seem to be left behind by the way the man turns his head to look back through the other windows at the slowly fading platform. He smiles then; more comfortably confident, hoping perhaps that his memory of this brief encounter will be pleasant. And then he is idle again.

SCENE I

Train roars. Light flash outside the windows.
LULA enters from the rear of the car in bright, skimpy summer

clothes and sandals. She carries a net bag full of paper books, fruit, and other anonymous articles. She is wearing sunglasses, which she pushes up on her forehead from time to time. LULA *is a tall, slender, beautiful woman with long red hair hanging straight down her back, wearing only loud lipstick in somebody's good taste. She is eating an apple, very daintily. Coming down the car toward* CLAY.

She stops beside CLAY's *seat and hangs languidly from the scrap, still managing to eat the apple. It is apparent that she is going to sit in the seat next to* CLAY, *and that she is only waiting for him to notice her before she sits.*

CLAY *sits as before, looking just beyond his magazine, now and again pulling the magazine slowly back and forth in front of his face in a hopeless effort to fan himself. Then he sees the woman hanging there beside him and he looks up into her face, smiling quizzically.*

LULA. Hello.

CLAY. Uh, hi're you?

LULA. I'm going to sit down. . . . O.K.?

CLAY. Sure.

LULA. [*Swings down onto the seat, pushing her legs straight out as if she is very weary*] Oooof! Too much weight.

CLAY. Ha, doesn't look like much to me. [*Leaning back against the window, a little surprised and maybe stiff*]

LULA. It's so anyway. [*And she moves her toes in the sandals, then pulls her right leg up on the left knee, better to inspect the bottoms of the sandals and the back of her heel. She appears for a second not to notice that* CLAY *is sitting next to her or that she has spoken to him just a second before.* CLAY *looks at the magazine, then out the black window. As he does this, she turns very quickly toward him*] Weren't you staring at me through the window?

CLAY. [*Wheeling around and very much stiffened*] What?

LULA. Weren't you staring at me through the window? At the last stop?

CLAY. Staring at you? What do you mean?

LULA. Don't you know what staring means?

CLAY. I saw you through the window . . . if that's what it means. I don't know if I was staring. Seems to me you were staring through the window at me.

LULA. I was. But only after I'd turned around and saw you staring through that window down in the vicinity of my ass and legs.

CLAY. Really?

LULA. Really. I guess you were just taking those idle potshots. Nothing else to do. Run your mind over people's flesh.

CLAY. Oh boy. Wow, now I admit I was looking in your direction. But the rest of that weight is yours.

LULA. I suppose.

CLAY. Staring through train windows is weird business. Much weirder than staring very sedately at abstract asses.

LULA. That's why I came looking through the window . . . so you'd have more than that to go on. I even smiled at you.

CLAY. That's right.

LULA. I even got into this train, going some other way than mine. Walked down the aisle . . . searching you out.

CLAY. Really? That's pretty funny.

LULA. That's pretty funny. . . . God, you're dull.

CLAY. Well, I'm sorry, lady, but I really wasn't prepared for party talk.

LULA. No, you're not. What are you prepared for? [*Wrapping the apple core in a Kleenex and dropping it on the floor*]

CLAY. [*Takes her conversation as pure sex talk. He turns to confront her squarely with this idea*] I'm prepared for anything. How about you?

LULA. [*Laughing loudly and cutting it off abruptly*] What do you think you're doing?

CLAY. What?

LULA. You think I want to pick you up, get you to take me somewhere and screw me, huh?

CLAY. Is that the way I look?

LULA. You look like you been trying to grow a beard. That's exactly what you look like. You look like you live in New Jersey with your parents and are trying to grow a beard. That's what. You look like you've been reading Chinese poetry and drinking lukewarm sugarless tea. [*Laughs, uncrossing and recrossing her legs*] You look like death eating a soda cracker.

CLAY. [*Cocking his head from one side to the other, embarrassed and trying to make some comeback, but also intrigued by what the woman is saying . . . even the sharp city coarseness of her voice, which is still a kind of gentle sidewalk throb*] Really? I look like all that?

LULA. Not all of it. [*She feints a seriousness to cover an actual somber tone*] I lie a lot. [*Smiling*] It helps me to control the world.

CLAY. [*Relieved and laughing louder than the humor*] Yeah, I bet.

LULA. But it's true, most of it, right? Jersey? Your bumpy neck?

CLAY. How'd you know all that? Huh? Really, I mean about Jersey . . . and even the beard. I met you before? You know Warren Enright?

LULA. You tried to make it with your sister when you were ten. [CLAY *leans back hard against the back of the seat, his eyes opening now, still trying to look amused*] But I succeeded a few weeks ago. [*She starts to laugh again*]

CLAY. What're you talking about? Warren tell you that? You're a friend of Georgia's?

LULA. I told you I lie. I don't know your sister. I don't know Warren Enright.

CLAY. You mean you're just picking these things out of the air?

LULA. Is Warren Enright a tall skinny black black boy with a phony English accent?

CLAY. I figured you knew him.

LULA. But I don't. I just figured you would know somebody like that. [*Laughs*]

CLAY. Yeah, yeah.

LULA. You're probably on your way to his house now.

CLAY. That's right.

LULA. [*Putting her hand on Clay's closest knee, drawing it from the knee up to the thigh's hinge, then removing it, watching his face very closely, and continuing to laugh, perhaps more gently than before*] Dull, dull, dull. I bet you think I'm exciting.

CLAY. You're O.K.

LULA. Am I exciting you now?

CLAY. Right. That's not what's supposed to happen?

LULA. How do I know? [*She returns her hand, without moving it, then takes it away and plunges it in her bag to draw out an apple*] You want this?

CLAY. Sure.

LULA. [*She gets one out of the bag for herself*] Eating apples together is always the first step. Or walking up uninhabited Seventh Avenue in the twenties on weekends. [*Bites and giggles, glancing at Clay and speaking in loose singsong*] Can get you involved . . . boy! Get us involved. Um-huh. [*Mock seriousness*] Would you like to get involved with me, Mister Man?

CLAY. [*Trying to be as flippant as Lula, whacking happily at the apple*] Sure. Why not? A beautiful woman like you. Huh, I'd be a fool not too.

LULA. And I bet you're sure you know what you're talking about. [*Taking him a little roughly by the wrist, so he cannot eat the apple, then shaking the wrist*] I bet you're sure of almost everything anybody ever asked you about . . . right? [*Shakes his wrist harder*] Right?

CLAY. Yeah, right. . . . Wow, you're pretty strong, you know? Whatta you, a lady wrestler or something?

LULA. What's wrong with lady wrestlers? And don't answer because you never knew any. Huh. [*Cynically*] That's for sure. They don't have any lady wrestlers in that part of Jersey. That's for sure.

CLAY. Hey, you still haven't told me how you know so much about me.

LULA. I told you I didn't know anything about *you* . . . you're a well-known type.

CLAY. Really?

LULA. Or at least I know the type very well. And your skinny English friend too.

CLAY. Anonymously?

LULA. [*Settles back in seat, single-mindedly finishing her apple and humming snatches of rhythm and blues song*] What?

CLAY. Without knowing us specifically?

LULA. Oh boy. [*Looking quickly at Clay*] What a face. You know, you could be a handsome man.

CLAY. I can't argue with you.

LULA. [*Vague, off-center response*] What?

CLAY. [*Raising his voice, thinking the train noise has drowned part of his sentence*] I can't argue with you.

LULA. My hair is turning gray. A gray hair for each year and type I've come through.

CLAY. Why do you want to sound so old?

LULA. But it's always gentle when it starts. [*Attention drifting*] Hugged against tenements, day or night.

CLAY. What?

LULA. [*Refocusing*] Hey, why don't you take me to that party you're going to?

CLAY. You must be a friend of Warren's to know about the party.

LULA. Wouldn't you like to take me to the party? [*Imitates clinging vine*] Oh, come on, ask me to your party.

CLAY. Of course I'll ask you to come with me to the party. And I'll bet you're a friend of Warren's.

LULA. Why not be a friend of Warren's? Why not? [*Taking his arm*] Have you asked me yet?

CLAY. How can I ask you when I don't know your name?

LULA. Are you talking to my name?

CLAY. What is it, a secret?

LULA. I'm Lena the Hyena.

CLAY. The famous woman poet?

LULA. Poetess! The same!

CLAY. Well, you know so much about me . . . what's my name?

LULA. Morris the Hyena.

CLAY. The famous woman poet?

LULA. The same. [*Laughing and going into her bag*] You want another apple?

CLAY. Can't make it, lady. I only have to keep one doctor away a day.

LULA. I bet your name is . . . something like . . . uh, Gerald or Walter. Huh?

CLAY. God, no.

LULA. Lloyd, Norman? One of those hopeless colored names creeping out of New Jersey. Leonard? Gag. . . .

CLAY. Like Warren?

LULA. Definitely. Just exactly like Warren. Or Everett.

CLAY. Gag. . . .

LULA. Well, for sure, it's not Willie.

CLAY. It's Clay.

LULA. Clay? Really? Clay what?

CLAY. Take your pick. Jackson, Johnson, or Williams.

LULA. Oh, really? Good for you. But it's got to be Williams. You're too pretentious to be a Jackson or Johnson.

CLAY. Thass right.

LULA. But Clay's O.K.

CLAY. So's Lena.

LULA. It's Lula.

CLAY. Oh?

LULA. Lula the Hyena.

CLAY. Very good.

LULA. [*Starts laughing again*] Now you say to me, "Lula, Lula, why don't you go to this party with me tonight?" It's your turn, and let those be your lines.

CLAY. Lula, why don't you go to this party with me tonight, Huh?

LULA. Say my name twice before you ask, and no huh's

CLAY. Lula, Lula, why don't you go to this party with me tonight?

LULA. I'd like to go, Clay, but how can you ask me to go when you barely know me?

CLAY. That is strange, isn't it?

LULA. What kind of reaction is that? You're supposed to say, "Aw, come on, we'll get to know each other better at the party."

CLAY. That's pretty corny.

LULA. What are you into anyway? [*Looking at him half sullenly but still amused*] What thing are you playing at, Mister? Mister Clay Williams? [*Grabs his thigh, up near the crotch*] What are *you* thinking about?

CLAY. Watch it now, you're gonna excite me for real.

LULA. [*Taking her hand away and throwing her apple core through the window*] I bet. [*She slumps in the seat and is heavily silent*]

CLAY. I thought you knew everything about me? What happened? [LULA *looks at him, then looks slowly away, then over where the other aisle would be. Noise of the train. She reaches in her bag and pulls out one of the paper books. She puts it on her leg and thumbs the pages listlessly.* CLAY *cocks his head to see the title of the book. Noise of the train.* LULA *flips pages and her eyes drift. Both remain silent*] Are you going to the party with me, Lula?

LULA. [*Bored and not even looking*] I don't even know you.

CLAY. You said you know my type.

LULA. [*Strangely irritated*] Don't get smart with me, Buster. I know you like the palm of my hand.

CLAY. The one you eat the apples with?

LULA. Yeh. And the one I open doors late Saturday evening with. That's my door. Up at the top of the stairs. Five flights. Above a lot of Italians and lying Americans. And scrape carrots with. Also . . . [*Looks *at him*] the same hand I unbutton my dress with, or let my skirt fall down. Same hand. Lover.

CLAY. Are you angry about anything? Did I say something wrong?

LULA. Everything you say is wrong. [*Mock smile*] That's what makes you so attractive. Ha. In that funnybook jacket with all the buttons. [*More animate, taking hold of his jacket*] What've you got that jacket and tie on in all this heat for? And why're you wearing a jacket and tie like that? Did your people ever burn witches or start revolutions over the price of tea? Boy, those narrow-shoulder clothes come from a tradition you ought to feel oppressed by. A three-button suit. What right do you have to be wearing a three-button suit and striped tie? Your grandfather was a slave, he didn't go to Harvard.

CLAY. My grandfather was a night watchman.

LULA. And you went to a colored college where everybody thought they were Averell Harriman.[1]

CLAY. All except me.

LULA. And who did you think you were? Who do you think you are now?

CLAY. [*Laughs as if to make light of the whole trend of the conversation*] Well, in college I thought I was Baudelaire. But I've slowed down since.

LULA. I bet you never once thought you were a black nigger. [*Mock serious, then she howls with laughter.* CLAY *is stunned but after initial reaction, he quickly tries to appreciate the humor.* LULA *almost shrieks*] A black Baudelaire.

CLAY. That's right.

LULA. Boy, are you corny. I take back what I said before. Everything you say is not wrong. It's perfect. You should be on television.

CLAY. You act like you're on television already.

LULA. That's because I'm an actress.

CLAY. I thought so.

LULA. Well, you're wrong. I'm no actress. I told you I always lie. I'm nothing, honey, and don't you ever forget it. [*Lighter*] Although my mother was a Communist. The only person of my family ever to amount to anything.

CLAY. My mother was a Republican.

LULA. And your father voted for the man rather than the party.

CLAY. Right!

LULA. Yea for him. Yea, yea for him.

CLAY. Yea!

LULA. And yea for America where he is free to vote for the mediocrity of his choice! Yea!

CLAY. Yea!

LULA. And yea for both your parents who even though they differ

---

[1] W. Averell Harriman (1891–   ), liberal U.S. government official and diplomat.

about so crucial a matter as the body politic still forged a union of love and sacrifice that was destined to flower at the birth of the noble Clay . . . what's your middle name?

CLAY. Clay.

LULA. A union of love and sacrifice that was destined to flower at the birth of the noble Clay Clay Williams. Yea! And most of all yea yea for you, Clay Clay. The Black Baudelaire! Yes! [*And with knifelike cynicism*] My Christ. My Christ.

CLAY. Thank you, ma'am.

LULA. May the people accept you as a ghost of the future. And love you, that you might not kill them when you can.

CLAY. What?

LULA. You're a murderer, Clay, and you know it. [*Her voice darkening with significance*] You know goddamn well what I mean.

CLAY. I do?

LULA. So we'll pretend the air is light and full of perfume.

CLAY. [*Sniffing at her blouse*] It is.

LULA. And we'll pretend the people cannot see you. That is, the citizens. And that you are free of your own history. And I am free of my history. We'll pretend that we are both anonymous beauties smashing along through the city's entrails. [*She yells as loud as she can*] GROOVE!

                                                                BLACK

SCENE II

Scene is the same as before, though now there are other seats visible in the car. And throughout the scene other people get on the subway. There are maybe one or two seated in the car as the scene opens, though neither CLAY *nor* LULA *notices them.* CLAY'S *tie is open.* LULA *is hugging his arm.*

CLAY. The party!

LULA. I know it'll be something good. You can come in with me, looking casual and significant. I'll be strange, haughty, and silent, and walk with long slow strides.

CLAY. Right.

LULA. When you get drunk, pat me once, very lovingly on the flanks, and I'll look at you cryptically, licking my lips.

CLAY. It sounds like something we can do.

LULA. You'll go around talking to young men about your mind, and to old men about your plans. If you meet a very close friend who is also with someone like me, we can stand together, sipping our drinks and exchanging codes of lust. The atmosphere will be slithering in love and half-love and very open moral decision.

CLAY. Great. Great.

LULA. And everyone will pretend they don't know your name, and then ... [*She pauses heavily*] later, when they have to, they'll claim a friendship that denies your sterling character.

CLAY. [*Kissing her neck and fingers*] And then what?

LULA. Then? Well, then we'll go down the street, late night, eating apples and winding very deliberately toward my house.

CLAY. Deliberately?

LULA. I mean, we'll look in all the shopwindows, and make fun of the queers. Maybe we'll meet a Jewish Buddhist and flatten his conceits over some very pretentious coffee.

CLAY. In honor of whose God?

LULA. Mine.

CLAY. Who is ... ?

LULA. Me ... and you?

CLAY. A corporate Godhead.

LULA. Exactly. Exactly. [*Notices one of the other people entering*]

CLAY. Go on with the chronicle. Then what happens to us?

LULA. [*A mild depression, but she still makes her description triumphant and increasingly direct*] To my house, of course.

CLAY. Of course.

LULA. And up the narrow steps of the tenement.

CLAY. You live in a tenement?

LULA. Wouldn't live anywhere else. Reminds me specifically of my novel form of insanity.

CLAY. Up the tenement stairs.

LULA. And with my apple-eating hand I push open the door and lead you, my tender big-eyed prey, into my ... God, what can I call it ... into my hovel.

CLAY. Then what happens?

LULA. After the dancing and games, after the long drinks and long walks, the real fun begins.

CLAY. Ah, the real fun. [*Embarrassed, in spite of himself*] Which is ... ?

LULA. [*Laughs at him*] Real fun in the dark house. Hah! Real fun in the dark house, high up above the street and the ignorant cowboys. I lead you in, holding your wet hand gently in my hand ...

CLAY. Which is not wet?

LULA. Which is dry as ashes.

CLAY. And cold?

LULA. Don't think you'll get out of your responsibility that way. It's not cold at all. You Fascist! Into my dark living room. Where we'll sit and talk endlessly, endlessly.

CLAY. About what?

LULA. About what? About your manhood, what do you think? What do you think we've been talking about all this time?

CLAY. Well, I didn't know it was that. That's for sure.

Every other thing in the world but that. [*Notices another person entering, looks quickly, almost involuntarily up and down the car, seeing the other people in the car*] Hey, I didn't even notice when those people got on.

LULA. Yeah, I know.

CLAY. Man, this subway is slow.

LULA. Yeah, I know.

CLAY. Well, go on. We were talking about my manhood.

LULA. We still are. All the time.

CLAY. We were in your living room.

LULA. My dark living room. Talking endlessly.

CLAY. About my manhood.

LULA. I'll make you a map of it. Just as soon as we get to my house.

CLAY. Well, that's great.

LULA. One of the things we do while we talk. And screw.

CLAY. [*Trying to make his smile broader and less shaky*] We finally got there.

LULA. And you'll call my rooms black as a grave. You'll say, "This place is like Juliet's tomb."

CLAY. [*Laughs*] I might.

LULA. I know. You've probably said it before.

CLAY. And is that all? The whole grand tour?

LULA. Not all. You'll say to me very close to my face, many, many times, you'll say, even whisper, that you love me.

CLAY. Maybe I will.

LULA. And you'll be lying.

CLAY. I wouldn't lie about something like that.

LULA. Hah. It's the only thing you will lie about. Especially if you think it'll keep me alive.

CLAY. Keep you alive? I don't understand.

LULA. [*Bursting out laughing, but too shrilly*] Don't understand? Well, don't look at me. It's the path I take, that's all. Where both feet take me when I set them down. One in front of the other.

CLAY. Morbid. Morbid. You sure you're not an actress? All that self-aggrandizement.

LULA. Well, I told you I wasn't an actress . . . but I also told you I lie all the time. Draw your own conclusions.

CLAY. Morbid. Morbid. You sure you're not an actress? All scribed? There's no more?

LULA. I've told you all I know. Or almost all.

CLAY. There's no funny parts?

LULA. I thought it was all funny.

CLAY. But you mean peculiar, not ha-ha.

LULA. You don't know what I mean.

CLAY. Well, tell me the almost part then. You said almost all. What else? I want the whole story.

LULA. [*Searching aimlessly through her bag. She begins to talk breathlessly, with a light and silly tone*] All stories are whole stories. All of 'em. Our whole story ... nothing but change. How could things go on like that forever? Huh? [*Slaps him on the shoulder, begins finding things in her bag, taking them out and throwing them over her shoulder into the aisle*] Except I do go on as I do. Apples and long walks with deathless intelligent lovers. But you mix it up. Look out the window, all the time. Turning pages. Change change change. Till, shit, I don't know you. Wouldn't, for that matter. You're too serious. I bet you're even too serious to be psychoanalyzed. Like all those Jewish poets from Yonkers, who leave their mothers looking for other mothers, or others' mothers, on whose baggy tits they lay their fumbling heads. Their poems are always funny, and all about sex.

CLAY. They sound great. Like movies.

LULA. But you change. [*Blankly*] And things work on you till you hate them. [*More people come into the train. They come closer to the couple, some of them not sitting, but swinging drearily on the straps, staring at the two with uncertain interest*]

CLAY. Wow. All these people, so suddenly. They must all come from the same place.

LULA. Right. That they do.

CLAY. Oh? You know about them too?

LULA. Oh yeah. About them more than I know about you. Do they frighten you?

CLAY. Frighten me? Why should they frighten me?

LULA. 'Cause you're an escaped nigger.

CLAY. Yeah?

LULA. 'Cause you crawled through the wire and made tracks to my side.

CLAY. Wire?

LULA. Don't they have wire around plantations?

CLAY. You must be Jewish. All you can think about is wire. Plantations didn't have any wire. Plantations were big open whitewashed places like heaven, and everybody on 'em was grooved to be there. Just strummin' and hummin' all day.

LULA. Yes, yes.

CLAY. And that's how the blues was born.

LULA. Yes, yes. And that's how the blues was born. [*Begins to make up a song that becomes quickly hysterical. As she sings she rises from her seat, still throwing things out of her bag into the aisle, beginning a rhythmical shudder and twistlike wiggle, which she continues up and down the aisle, bumping into many of the standing people and tripping over the feet of those sitting. Each time she runs into a person she lets out a very vicious piece of profanity, wiggling and stepping all the time*] And that's how the blues was born. Yes. Yes. Son of a bitch, get out of the way. Yes. Quack. Yes. Yes. And that's how the blues was born. Ten little niggers sitting on a limb, but none of them ever looked like him. [*Points to* CLAY, *returns toward the seat, with her hands extended for him to rise and dance with her*] And that's how blues was born. Yes. Come on, Clay. Let's do the nasty. Rub bellies. Rub bellies.

CLAY. [*Waves his hands to refuse. He is embarrassed, but determined to get a kick out of the proceedings*] Hey, what was in those apples? Mirror, mirror on the wall, who's the fairest one of all? Snow White, baby, and don't you forget it.

LULA. [*Grabbing for his hands, which he draws away*] Come on, Clay. Let's rub bellies on the train. The nasty. The nasty. Do the gritty grind, like your ol' rag-head mammy. Grind till you lose your mind. Shake it, shake it, shake it, shake it! OOOOweeee! Come on, Clay. Let's do the choo-choo train shuffle, the navel scratcher.

CLAY. Hey, you coming on like the lady who smoked up her grass skirt.

LULA. [*Becoming annoyed that he will not dance, and becoming more animated as if to embarrass him still further*] Come on, Clay . . . let's do the thing. Uhh! Uhh! Clay! Clay! You middle-class black bastard. Forget your social-working mother for a few seconds and let's knock stomachs. Clay, you liver-lipped white man. You would-be Christian. You ain't no nigger, you're just a dirty white man. Get up, Clay. Dance with me, Clay.

CLAY. Lula! Sit down, now. Be cool.

LULA. [*Mocking him, in wild dance*] Be cool. Be cool. That's all you know . . . shaking that wildroot cream-oil on your knotty head, jackets buttoning up to your chin, so full of white man's words. Christ. God. Get up and scream at these people. Like scream meaningless shit in these hopeless faces. [*She screams at people in train, still dancing*] Red trains cough Jewish underwear for keeps! Expanding smells of silence. Gravy snot whistling like sea birds. Clay. Clay, you got to break out. Don't sit there dying the way they want you to die. Get up.

CLAY. Oh, sit the fuck down. [*He moves to restrain her*] Sit down, goddamn it.

LULA. [*Twisting out of his reach*] Screw yourself, Uncle Tom. Thomas Woolly-head. [*Begins to dance a kind of jig, mocking Clay with loud forced humor*] There is Uncle Tom . . . I mean, Uncle Thomas Woolly-Head. With old white matted mane. He hobbles on his wooden cane. Old Tom. Old Tom. Let the white man hump his ol' mama, and he jes' shuffle off in the woods and hide his gentle gray head. Ol' Thomas Woolly-Head. [*Some of the other riders are laughing now. A drunk gets up and joins* LULA *in her dance, singing, as best he can, her "song."* CLAY *gets up out of his seat and visibly scans the faces of the other riders*]

CLAY. Lula! Lula! [*She is dancing and turning, still shouting as loud as she can. The drunk too is shouting, and waving his hands wildly*] Lula . . . you dumb bitch. Why don't you stop it? [*He rushes half stumbling from his seat, and grabs one of her flailing arms*]

LULA. Let me go! You black son of a bitch. [*She struggles against him*] Let me go! Help! [CLAY *is dragging her towards her seat, and the drunk seeks to interfere. He grabs* CLAY *around the shoulders and begins wrestling with him.* CLAY *clubs the drunk to the floor without releasing* LULA, *who is still screaming.* CLAY *finally gets her to the seat and throws her into it*]

CLAY. Now you shut the hell up. [*Grabbing her shoulders*] Just shut up. You don't know what you're talking about. You don't know anything. So just keep your stupid mouth closed.

LULA. You're afraid of white people. And your father was. Uncle Tom Big Lip!

CLAY. [*Slaps her as hard as he can, across the mouth.* LULA's *head bangs against the back of the seat. When she raises it again,* CLAY *slaps her again*] Now shut up and let me talk. [*He turns toward the other riders, some of whom are sitting on the edge of their seats. The drunk is on one knee, rubbing his head, and singing softly the same song. He shuts up too when he sees* CLAY *watching him. The others go back to newspapers or stare out the windows*] Shit, you don't have any sense, Lula, nor feelings either. I could murder you now. Such a tiny ugly throat. I could squeeze it flat, and watch you turn blue, on a humble. For dull kicks. And all these weak-faced ofays squatting around here, staring over their papers at me. Murder them too. Even if they expected it. That man there . . . [*Points to well-dressed man*] I could rip that *Times* right out of his hand, as skinny and middle-classed as I am, I could rip that paper out of his hand and just as easily rip out his throat. It takes no great effort. For what? To kill you soft idiots? You don't understand anything but luxury.

LULA. You fool!

CLAY. [*Pushing her against the seat*] I'm not telling you again, Tallulah Bankhead! Luxury. In your face and your fingers. You telling me what I ought to do. [*Sudden scream frightening the whole coach*] Well, don't! Don't you tell me anything! If I'm a middle-class fake white man . . . let me be. And let me be in the way I want. [*Through his teeth*] I'll rip your lousy breasts off! Let me be who I feel like being. Uncle Tom. Thomas. Whoever. It's none of your business. You don't know anything except what's there for you to see. An act. Lies. Device. Not the pure heart, the pumping black heart. You don't ever know that. And I sit here, in this buttoned-up suit, to keep myself from cutting all your throats. I mean wantonly. You great liberated whore! You fuck some black man, and right away you're an expert on black people. What a lotta shit that is. The only thing you know is that you come if he bangs you hard enough. And that's all. The belly rub? You wanted to do the belly rub? Shit, you don't even know how. You don't know how. That ol'dipty-dip shit you do, rolling your ass like an elephant. That's not my kind of belly rub. Belly rub is not Queens. Belly rub is dark places, with big hats and overcoats held up with one arm. Belly rub hates you. Old bald-headed four-eyed ofays popping their fingers . . . and don't know yet what they're doing. They say, "I love Bessie Smith." [2] And don't even understand that Bessie Smith is saying, "Kiss my ass, kiss my black unruly ass." Before love, suffering, desire, anything you can explain, she's saying, and very plainly, "Kiss my black ass." And if you don't know that, it's you that's doing the kissing.

Charlie Parker? Charlie Parker. [3] All the hip white boys scream for Bird. And Bird saying, "Up your ass, feeble-minded ofay! Up your ass." And they sit there talking about the tortured genius of Charlie Parker. Bird would've played not a note of music if he just walked up to East Sixty-seventh Street and killed the first ten white people he saw. Not a note! And I'm the great would-be poet. Yes. That's right! Poet. Some kind of bastard literature . . . all it needs is a simple knife thrust. Just let me bleed you, you loud whore, and one poem vanished. A whole people of neurotics, struggling to keep from being sane. And the only thing that would cure the neurosis would be your murder. Simple as that. I mean if I murdered you, then other white people would begin to understand me. You understand? No. I guess not. If Bessie Smith had killed some white people she wouldn't have needed that music. She could have talked very straight and plain about the world. No metaphors. No grunts. No wiggles in the dark of her soul. Just straight two and two are four. Money. Power. Luxury. Like that. All of them. Crazy niggers turning their backs on sanity. When all it needs is that simple act. Murder. Just murder! Would make us all sane. [*Suddenly weary*] Ahhh. Shit. But who needs it? I'd rather be a fool. Insane. Safe with my words, and no deaths, and clean, hard thoughts, urging me to new conquests. My people's madness. Hah! That's a laugh. My people. They don't need me to claim them. They got legs and arms of their own. Personal insanities. Mirrors. They don't need all those words. They don't need any defense. But listen, though, one more thing. And you tell this to your father, who's probably the kind of man who needs to know at once. So he can plan ahead. Tell him not to preach so much rationalism and cold logic to these niggers. Let them alone. Let them sing curses at you in code and see your filth as simple lack of style. Don't make the mistake, through some irresponsible surge of Christian charity, of talking too much about the advantages of Western rationalism, or the great intellectual legacy of the white man, or maybe they'll begin to listen. And then, maybe one day, you'll find they actually do understand exactly what you are talking about, all these fantasy people. All these blues people. And on that day, as sure as shit, when you really believe you can "accept" them into your fold, as half-white trusties late of the subject peoples. With no more blues, except the very old ones, and not a watermelon in sight, the great missionary heart will have triumphed, and all of those ex-coons will be stand-up Western men, with eyes for clean hard useful lives, sober, pious

---

[2] (1896?–1937), perhaps the greatest of all blues singers.
[3] Charlie ["Bird"] Parker (1920–1955), great jazz saxophonist.

and sane, and they'll murder you. They'll murder you, and have very rational explanations. Very much like your own. They'll cut your throats, and drag you out to the edge of your cities so the flesh can fall away from your bones, in sanitary isolation.

LULA. [*Her voice takes on a different, more businesslike quality*] I've heard enough.

CLAY. [*Reaching for his books*] I bet you have. I guess I better collect my stuff and get off this train. Looks like we won't be acting out that little pageant you outlined before.

LULA. No. We won't. You're right about that, at least. [*She turns to look quickly around the rest of the car*] All right! [*The others respond*]

CLAY. [*Bending across the girl to retrieve his belongings*] Sorry, baby, I don't think we could make it. [*As he is bending over her, the girl brings up a small knife and plunges it into* CLAY's *chest. Twice. He slumps across her knees, his mouth working stupidly*]

LULA. Sorry is right. [*Turning to the others in the car who have already gotten up from their seats*] Sorry is the rightest thing you've said. Get this man off me! Hurry, now! [*The others come and drag* CLAY's *body down the aisle*] Open the door and throw his body out. [*They throw him off*] And all of you get off at the next stop.

[LULA *busies herself straightening her things. Getting everything in order. She takes out a notebook and makes a quick scribbling note. Drops it in her bag. The train apparently stops and all the others get off, leaving her alone in the coach.*

Very soon a young Negro of about twenty comes into the coach, with a couple of books under his arm. He sits a few seats in back of LULA. *When he is seated she turns and gives him a long slow look. He looks up from his book and drops the book on his lap. Then an old Negro conductor comes into the car, doing a sort of restrained soft shoe, and half mumbling the words of some song. He looks at the young man, briefly, with a quick greeting*]

CONDUCTOR. Hey, brother!
YOUNG MAN. Hey.

[*The conductor continues down the aisle with his little dance and the mumbled song.* LULA *turns to stare at him and follows his movements down the aisle. The conductor tips his hat when he reaches her seat, and continues out the car*]

CURTAIN

LATER FICTION

Later Fiction (writers born after 1900)

In the "tranquilized Fifties," the Eisenhower years, *Life* magazine felt
it incumbent upon itself to comment editorially upon the state of
American fiction. Taking off from a remark made by a then commercially successful novelist named Sloan Wilson ("These are, we
forget, pretty good times. Yet too many novelists are writing as if
we were back in the Depression years"), the *Life* editorialists pon-
tificated as follows:

Ours is the most powerful nation in the world. It has had a decade of unparalleled prosperity. It has gone further than any other society in the history of
man toward creating a truly classless society. Yet it is still producing a
literature which sounds sometimes as if it were written by an unemployed
homosexual living in a packing box shanty on the city dump while awaiting
admission to the county poorhouse.

Now, of course, eighty years after Howells so mildly suggested that the
"more smiling aspects" of life were "more American" than some of
the grimmer aspects that attracted the early realists, one can only
be repelled by those easily militant clichés—*most powerful nation
in the world, unparalleled prosperity, a truly classless society, unemployed homosexual*—and all that other chauvinistic lingo that composed the *Life* article.

Now, of course, we have the dubious benefit of the hindsight conferred
upon us by the bitter history of those fifteen years that have since
elapsed, and we can only ask questions: A nation so powerful that it
cannot extricate itself from a wretched war with one of the smallest
and most backward nations in the world? A nation so prosperous
that a grotesque and widespread poverty is one of its major problems? A society so truly classless that we are engaged in the most
violent racial antagonisms in history? A society that, passing
through a revolution in sexual mores, has pushed emancipation
into anarchy? A nation in which city life has become almost unendurable, natural resources and beauties continue to be plundered,
and assassinations are nearly a commonplace?

Yet one hardly needed the experience of all this recent anguish to
recognize the absurdity of the *Life* article at the time of its publication. That studied composition appeared in the magazine on September 12, 1955. What it was asking for was a body of fiction that
affirmed the splendors of life here, splendors such as those that *Life*
and other publicists regularly presented to the world as their "image"
of the United States. Any serious writer happening upon the *Life*

articles naturally turned away and vomited, or more probably, puked—and in that mood continued his pursuit of a more forthright vocabulary and a more honest vision than any that can interest our commercial purveyors of opinion.

The article appeared a quarter of a century after the publication of Thomas Wolfe's first book, *Look Homeward, Angel*. That was in October, 1929, the month in which the stock-market collapse ushered us into the years of the Great Depression. Wolfe was probably the last of our novelists who dedicated his work to a search for meaning in American life, who tried to make a kind of poetry out of its very enormity and sweep and power, but who ended as he began with a lamentation for the loneliness and the isolation of the searching individual. The writers who followed him in the Depression could hardly afford to interest themselves in his kind of poetry. Like Richard Wright, their concern was the sheer problem of survival in a brutally hostile world.

For most of the 1930s, with its widespread economic distress and unrest, a downright naturalism underscored by an angry mood of protest such as Wright's seemed the nearly inevitable technique for fiction, but very soon it began to seem inadequate to the materials of fiction, as these themselves began to shift. Eudora Welty, for example, has always been concerned with what is natural (including prominently the eccentricities of human nature), but behind the curtain of nature as she and most of her characters perceive it, there has from the beginning been an element of mystery and magic that only a language beyond that of naturalism could suggest. A similar quality and adjustment in language is to be observed in the stories of Carson McCullers and Flannery O'Connor; in the first, the quality that lurks behind things is chiefly the inevitable sadness that in fact informs them, and in the second, behind the gray and drab human scene that preoccupies her, a sacramental quality that can, like revelation, burst drastically upon the individual.

With these writers, the direction is toward poetry and the landscape of myth. Another direction is toward fantasy and fable. Thus, John Cheever, long the witty chronicler of suburbia, abruptly writes an astonishing story in which his hero, in one afternoon, swims through country house pools into his wasted future. In his novel, *Invisible Man*, Ralph Ellison did something of the same sort on a grand scale: we begin in the horrid everyday world that naturalism can spell out for us, but then presently we are in the baffling horrors of a Kafka world in which the opposition is undefined, as the identity itself struggles to survive against encompassing odds that it is unable to see, in large part because it is not seen. But the identity persists, and finally there is a great statement in this amazing novel that can stand as the epigraph for most of our later fiction: "I condemn and affirm, say no and say yes, say yes and say no."

The speech is not without its ambiguity, but we can be certain of one thing—that the nameless hero of this novel is not saying yes to such absurdities as the editors of *Life*, a few years later, asked American novelists to say yes to. He is saying yes to the creative force of life itself and to everything that would encourage the discovery and the survival of his own identity in it; and no to everything that would circumscribe it, limit it, deny it, and finally, destroy it.

"I condemn and affirm, say no and say yes, say yes and say no." This marvelous utterance suggests a third way in which the later fiction moves—into the comic. For only the comic can be so blithe—after so much suffering. This, at any rate, seems to epitomize the imaginative motives behind the work of Bernard Malamud and Saul Bellow (the latter beginning with *The Adventures of Augie March*, his third novel). With Malamud and the mature Bellow we do move into the comic, with heroes who themselves are often comic figures (clowns), making an exhilarating assertion of the freedom of their existence in the face of a constant experience that would put chains around it. This is comedy in an ultimate sense: the human spirit can at last, in spite of all the travail and through all the guilt and suffering, be free. Happy ending. The individual, without either joining it or leaving it, can "tell off" the world, not to mention the United States of America, which is only a rather small part of it.

Most of our later fiction that is worth our time is written in this mood, and the work of writers like John Barth and Donald Barthelme pursues not only the comic vein of Malamud and Bellow, but makes it wild by joining it with those other nonnaturalistic tendencies toward poetry and myth, fantasy and fable. Barthelme's "Report" is a very funny (very tragic) account of the dehumanization of modern life, whereas fiction has always depended on accounting for the human. John Barth's "Lost in the Funhouse," even while telling about the not yet experienced experience of being lost in the maze of distorting mirrors which is the world we live in (because we are there all the time), derides in the very telling the form of fiction in which he is telling it. The forms of fiction, as we have known them, are probably no longer adequate to the experience that fiction must attempt to deal with if it is to survive at all.

This is the implication behind a discussion on "The Future of Fiction" (a subject tirelessly debated for the past fifty years) that took place in New York in March of 1969. On this occasion, a brilliant new fiction writer, William Gass, who is also a professor of philosophy, asserted that the future of American fiction is bright, and for the very reason that it is becoming more and more free of its traditional preoccupations. Fiction, he argued, no longer fills the function of entertainment that it once did, because that function has been taken over by other forms of communication—the films, television, light shows, who knows?—and so can forego its old concern with plot, suspense, character engagement and conflict, physical setting. It is no longer obliged to deal with the problems of the self in its social involvements because that is now the business of sociologists (Lionel Trilling some years ago suggested that David Riesman's kind of sociology had taken over the functions of the novel). And fiction, said William Gass, need no longer be very concerned with the problems of the human heart because that has become the province of psychoanalysis. Having rid itself of all these traditional concerns, he argued, the novel is now free to develop in a wholly new way, into a fiction of "concepts."[1] He was not very clear about what he meant by "concepts," but perhaps this is the sort of fiction that we are now reading by writers like Barth and Barthelme and many others. Yet one wonders: can the heart really be successfully removed from the concerns of fiction? We might remind ourselves that until now, at least, people who have heart transplants die rather quickly; the body rejects the transplant as alien.

Who knows what the body of fiction will do? All that we can be certain of is that it is not going to take its directions from the public oracles of respectability, tired convention, class allegiance. That kind of direction from the higher echelons of established authority it will certainly reject: in *order* to survive, or to evolve into something different.

---

[1] William H. Gass, in his book of essays, *Fiction and the Figures of Life* (1970), has more to say about a "fiction of concepts," but perhaps these essays still require a philosopher's intuitions.

THOMAS [CLAYTON] WOLFE (1900–1938)

Thomas Wolfe was a big man with big appetites, appetites not only for enormous amounts of food but for enormous amounts of experience, or at least, for experience that presented itself as enormous. He could never get enough of it, because nothing was ever as big as he wanted it to be. He died, one might say, swallowing air.

He was born and brought up in Asheville, North Carolina, and his first novel, Look Homeward, Angel (1929), all its rapturous and elegiac apostrophes and interruptions notwithstanding, gives us a better account of his early life, the character of his Gothic parents, the weird and bloody family web, his education, and his unending adolescence, than any objective biography possibly could.

He left Asheville for Chapel Hill and was graduated from the University of North Carolina in 1920; then he went to Harvard to study play-writing for two years. After another two years in Europe, he taught English at New York University for six years. After Look Homeward, Angel finally found a publisher (twelve houses declined it before Scribner's took it), he devoted himself entirely to writing and to trying to appease his hunger for some kind of cosmic satisfaction that he was never to find.

His other novels are extended accounts of that same fascinating but finally nebulous effort. Only one more, Of Time and the River (1935), appeared in his lifetime. But he wrote prodigiously, and out of his enormous collection of manuscripts and notebooks, literally trunks of writing, his editor (and his devoted editors from the beginning had to do much of the selecting, reducing, cutting, arranging of his masses of material in order to make possible books) produced two more, The Web and the Rock (1939) and You Can't Go Home Again (1940).

These are extraordinary books. They will always be, at the least, literary curiosities. In fiction there has never been such a protracted demonstration of frank self-involvement. Trying to see these novels as an entirety, one has to imagine some huge mythical spider endlessly spinning vast webs out of itself, webs spanning continents, unlimited mazes of tortured autobiography, brutally repetitious, not really very interesting, and yet somehow never to be dismissed as boring. He wanted something bigger in human relations, in nationality, in nature than he could ever find. Still a young man, he died of a cerebral infection.

In the blasting course of all that rhetoric and wild and often dogged lyricism to which he gave himself, he wrote a restrained and instruc-

tive account of the history of his first book, The Story of a Novel *(1936). He also published a volume of short stories,* From Death to Morning *(1935), and perhaps his best work is in these more limited forms, where, quite simply, he was forced to fence in his hungry striding, loping, ranging. Obviously he was a man of great gifts. One of them, and not the least, was in his ear—the capacity to record the accents of the human voice. His story, "Only the Dead Know Brooklyn," is a fair example of that pervasive quality. And yet, beyond the brilliantly reported talk in this story, which is its essence, there is the echoing, unasked question of the narrator, Thomas Wolfe, brooding on the vast mystery of things, even of the shabby streets of a drab city, never really to be known by anyone.*

Born in the opening year of the new century, Thomas Wolfe was also, somehow, in his aspiring hungers, the last man of the old America. No one after him expected to find so much, or even very much.

FURTHER READING

Two biographies give a full account of Wolfe's life and times: Elizabeth Nowell, *Thomas Wolfe: A Biography* (1960), and Andrew Turnbull, *Thomas Wolfe* (1968). For more specialized reminiscence see Mabel Wheaton and Legette Blythe, *Thomas Wolfe and His Family* (1961), and Robert Raynolds, *Thomas Wolfe: Memoir of a Friendship* (1965). Elizabeth Nowell edited *The Letters of Thomas Wolfe* (1956). A briefer volume is *The Correspondence of Thomas Wolfe and Homer Andrew Watts* (1954), edited by Oscar Cargill and Thomas Clark Pollock. The most recent is *The Letters of Thomas Wolfe to His Mother* (1968), edited by C. Hugh Holman and Sue F. Ross.

Brief critical surveys are C. Hugh Holman, *Thomas Wolfe* (1960), and Bruce R. McElderry, Jr., *Thomas Wolfe* (1964). The first extended critical study was Herbert J. Muller's *Thomas Wolfe* (1947), and it was followed by Louis D. Rubin, Jr., *Thomas Wolfe: The Weather of His Youth* (1955); Floyd C. Watkins, *Thomas Wolfe's Characters: Portraits from Life* (1957); and Richard S. Kennedy, *The Window of Memory: The Literary Career of Thomas Wolfe* (1962). Three collections of essays offer a wide choice of critiques: *The Enigma of Thomas Wolfe* (1953), edited by Richard Walser; *The World of Thomas Wolfe* (1962), edited by C. Hugh Holman; and *Thomas Wolfe: Three Decades of Criticism* (1968), edited by Leslie Field.

Only the Dead Know Brooklyn (1935)

Dere's no guy livin' dat knows Brooklyn t'roo an' t'roo, because it'd take a guy a lifetime just to find his way aroun' duh f—— town.

So like I say, I'm waitin' for my train t' come when I sees dis big guy standin' deh—dis is duh foist I eveh see of him. Well, he's lookin' wild, y'know, an' I can see dat he's had plenty, but still he's holdin' it; he talks good an' is walkin' straight enough. So den, dis big guy steps up to a little guy dat's standin' deh, an' says, "How d'yuh get t' Eighteent' Avenoo an' Sixty-sevent' Street?" he says.

"Jesus! Yuh got me, chief," duh little guy says to him. "I ain't been heah long myself. Where is duh place?" he says. "Out in duh Flatbush section somewhere?"

"Nah," duh big guy says. "It's out in Bensonhoist. But I was neveh deh befoeh. How d'yuh get deh?"

"Jesus," duh little guy says, scratchin' his head, y'know—yuh could see duh little guy didn't know his way about—"yuh got me, chief. I neveh hoid of it. Do any of youse guys know where it is?" he says to me.

"Sure," I says. "It's out in Bensonhoist. Yuh take duh Fourt' Avenoo express, get off at Fifty-nint' Street, change to a Sea Beach local deh, get off at Eighteent' Avenoo an' Sixty-toid, an' den walk down foeh blocks. Dat's all yuh got to do," I says.

"G'wan!" some wise guy dat I neveh seen befoeh pipes up. "Whatcha talkin' about?" he says—oh, he was wise, y'know. "Duh guy is crazy! I tell you what yuh do," he says to duh big guy. "Yuh change to duh West End line at Toity-sixt'," he tells him. "Get off at Noo Utrecht an' Sixteent' Avenoo," he says. "Walk two blocks oveh, foeh blocks up," he says, "an' you'll be right deh." Oh, a *wise* guy, y'know.

"Oh, yeah?" I says. "Who told *you* so much?" He got me sore because he was so wise about it. "How long you been livin' heah?" I says.

"All my life," he says. "I was bawn in Williamsboig," he says. "An' I can tell you t'ings about dis town you neveh hoid of," he says.

"Yeah?" I says.

"Yeah," he says.

"Well, den, you can tell me t'ings about dis town dat nobody else has eveh hoid of, either. Maybe you make it all up yoehself at night," I says, "befoeh you go to sleep—like cuttin' out papeh dolls, or somp'n."

"Oh, yeah?" he says. "You're pretty wise, ain't yuh?"

"Oh, I don't know," I says. "Duh boids ain't usin' my head for Lincoln's statue yet," I says. "But I'm wise enough to know a phony when I see one."

"Yeah?" he says. "A wise guy, huh? Well, you're so wise dat some one's goin' t'bust yuh one right on duh snoot some day," he says. "Dat's how wise *you* are."

Well, my train was comin', or I'da smacked him den and dere, but when I seen duh train was comin', all I said was, All right, mugg! I'm sorry I can't stay to take keh of you, but I'll be seein' yuh sometime, I hope, out in duh cemetery." So den I says to duh big guy, who'd been standin' deh all duh time, "You come wit me," I says. So when we gets onto duh train I says to him, "Where yuh goin' out in Bensonhoist?" I says. "What numbeh are yuh lookin' for?" I says. *You* know—I t'ought if he told me duh address I might be able to help him out.

"Oh," he says, "I'm not lookin' for no one. I don't know no one out deh."

"Then whatcha goin' out deh for?" I says.

"Oh," duh guy says, "I'm just goin' out to see duh place," he says. "I like duh sound of duh name—Bensonhoist, y'know—so I t'ought I'd go out an' have a look at it."

"Whatcha tryin' t'hand me?" I says. "Whatcha tryin' t'do—kid me?" *You* know, I t'ought duh guy was bein' wise wit me.

"No," he says, "I'm tellin' you duh troot. I like to go out an' take a look at places wit nice names like dat. I like to go out an' look at all kinds of places," he says.

"How'd yuh know deh was such a place," I says, "if yuh neveh been deh befoeh?"

"Oh," he says, "I got a map."

"A *map*?" I says.

"Sure," he says, "I got a map dat tells me about all dese places. I take it wit me every time I come out heah," he says.

And Jesus! Wit dat, he pulls it out of his pocket, an' so help me, but he's *got* it—he's tellin' duh troot—a big map of duh whole f—— place with all duh different pahts mahked out. You know—Canarsie an' East Noo Yawk an' Flatbush, Bensonhoist, Sout' Brooklyn, duh Heights, Bay Ridge, Greenpernt—duh whole goddam layout, he's got it right deh on duh map.

"You been to any of dose places?" I says.

"Sure," he says, "I been to most of 'em. I was down in Red Hook just last night," he says.

"Jesus! Red Hook!" I says. "Whatcha do down deh?"

"Oh," he says, "nuttin' much. I just walked aroun'. I went into a coupla places an' had a drink," he says, "but most of the time I just walked aroun'."

"Just walked aroun'?" I says.

"Sure," he says, "just lookin' at t'ings, y'know."

"Where'd yuh go?" I asts him.

"Oh," he says, "I don't know duh name of duh place, but I could find it on my map," he says. "One time I was walkin' across some big fields where deh ain't no houses," he says, "but I could see ships oveh deh all lighted up. Dey was loadin'. So I walks across duh fields," he says, "to where duh ships are."

"Sure," I says, "I know where you was. You was down to duh Erie Basin."

"Yeah," he says, "I guess dat was it. Dey had some of dose big elevators an' cranes an' dey was loadin' ships, an' I could see some ships in drydock all lighted up, so I walks across duh fields to where dey are," he says.

"Den what did yuh do?" I says.

"Oh," he says, "nuttin' much. I came on back across duh fields after a while an' went into a coupla places an' had a drink."

"Didn't nuttin' happen while yuh was in dere?" I says.

"No," he says. "Nuttin' much. A coupla guys was drunk in one of duh places an' started a fight, but dey bounced 'em out," he says, "an' den one of duh guys stahted to come back again, but duh bartender gets his baseball bat out from under duh counteh, so duh guy goes on."

"Jesus!" I said. "Red Hook!"

"Sure," he says. "Dat's where it was, all right."

"Well, you keep outa deh," I says. "You stay away from deh."

"Why?" he says. "What's wrong wit it?"

"Oh," I says, "it's a good place to stay away from, dat's all. It's a good place to keep out of."

"Why?" he says. "Why is it?"

Jesus! Whatcha gonna do wit a guy as dumb as dat? I saw it wasn't no use to try to tell him nuttin', he wouldn't know what I was talkin' about, so I just says to him, "Oh, nuttin'. Yuh might get lost down deh, dat's all."

"Lost?" he says. "No, I wouldn't get lost. I got a map," he says.

A map! Red Hook! Jesus!

So den duh guy begins to ast me all kinds of nutty questions: how big was Brooklyn an' could I find my way aroun' in it, an' how long would it take a guy to know duh place.

"Listen!" I says. "You get dat idea outa yoeh head right now," I says. "You ain't neveh gonna get to know Brooklyn," I says. "Not in a hundred yeahs. I been livin' heah all my life," I says, "an' I don't even know all deh is to know about it, so how do you expect to know duh town," I says, "when you don't even live heah?"

"Yes," he says, "but I got a map to help me find my way about."

"Map or no map," I says, "yuh ain't gonna get to know Brooklyn wit no map," I says.

"Can you swim?" he says, just like dat. Jesus! By dat time, y'know, I begun to see dat duh guy was some kind of nut. He'd had plenty to drink, of course, but he had dat crazy look in his eye I didn't like. "Can you swim?" he says.

"Sure," I says. "Can't you?"

"No," he says. "Not more'n a stroke or two. I neveh loined good."

"Well, it's easy," I says. "All yuh need is a little confidence. Duh way I loined, me older bruddeh pitched me off duh dock one day when I was eight yeahs old, cloes an' all. 'You'll swim,' he says. 'You'll swim all right—or drown.' An', believe me, I *swam!* When yuh know yuh got to, you'll do it. Duh only t'ing yuh need is confidence. An' once you've loined," I says, "you've got nuttin' else to worry about. You'll neveh forget it. It's somp'n dat stays wit yuh as long as yuh live."

"Can yuh swim good?" he says.

"Like a fish," I tells him. "I'm a regulah fish in duh wateh," I says. "I loined to swim right off duh docks wit all duh oddeh kids," I says.

"What would you do if yuh saw a man drownin'?" duh guy says.

"Do? Why, I'd jump in an' pull him out," I says. "Dat's what I'd do."

"Did yuh eveh see a man drown?" he says.

"Sure," I says. "I see two guys—bot' times at Coney Island. Dey got out too far, an' neider one could swim. Dey drowned befoeh any one could get to 'em."

"What becomes of people after dey've drowned out heah?" he says.

"Drowned out where?" I says.

"Out heah in Brooklyn."

"I don't know whatcha mean," I says. "Neveh hoid of no one drownin' heah in Brooklyn, unless you mean a swimmin' pool. Yuh can't drown in Brooklyn," I says. "Yuh gotta drown somewhere else—in duh ocean, where dere's wateh."

"Drownin'," duh guy says, lookin' at his map. "Drownin'." Jesus! I could see by den he was some kind of nut, he had dat crazy expression in his eyes when he looked at you, an' I didn't know what he might do. So we was comin' to a station, an' it wasn't my stop, but I got off anyway, an' waited for duh next train.

"Well, so long, chief," I says. "Take it easy, now."

"Drownin'," duh guy says, lookin' at his map. "Drownin'."

Jesus! I've t'ought about dat guy a t'ousand times since den an' wondered what eveh happened to 'm goin' out to look at Bensonhoist because he liked duh name! Walkin' aroun' t'roo Red Hook by himself at night an' lookin' at his map! How many people did I see get drowned out heah in Brooklyn! How long would it take a guy wit a good map to know all deh was to know about Brooklyn!

Jesus! What a nut *he* was! I wondeh what eveh happened to 'im, anyway! I wondeh if some one knocked him on duh head, or if he's still wanderin' aroun' in duh subway in duh middle of duh night wit his little map! Duh poor guy! Say, I've got to laugh, at dat, when I t'ink about him! Maybe he's found out by now dat he'll neveh live long enough to know duh whole of Brooklyn. It'd take a guy a lifetime to know Brooklyn t'roo an' t'roo. An' even den, yuh wouldn't know it all.

RICHARD WRIGHT (1908–1960)

When Richard Wright was five years old, his father, a sharecropper and mill worker living in a plantation shack outside Natchez, Mississippi, abandoned his wife and two young sons to a life of poverty, hunger, and violence. His mother, who did her best to hold the family together through domestic labor, became partially paralyzed, and by the time the boy was ten she was totally paralyzed. For a time he was put in an orphanage and then shunted about from one relative to another, ending up in Jackson, Mississippi, with an aunt who was a devout Seventh Day Adventist. The life of fanatical piety and denial so repelled the adolescent boy that he relinquished all religious ideas and at fifteen fled to Memphis, where he lived by any odd jobs he could find. His schooling, needless to say, had been less than random, but now, through the discovery of H. L. Mencken, he was swept into an intellectual and literary fervor.

In 1927 he arrived in Chicago, lived again by odd jobs, and, in the Depression, went on relief. In 1934 he joined the Communist Party and began to write for various Marxist publications, and in 1935 he found a place in the Federal Writers' Project. Two years later, in New York, he wrote the WPA Guide to Harlem, and in 1938 he won a $500 Story magazine prize for the best piece of fiction from a Writers' Project author—the novelette, "Uncle Tom's Children," which became the title story in his volume of four long stories published later that year. On a Guggenheim Fellowship, living in Brooklyn, in eight months he wrote his first novel, Native Son (1940).

This brutally violent story of a young black man in Chicago whose frustrated circumstances force him into murder and his own death was Wright's economic emancipation. Unrelievedly naturalistic in method, it yet forcefully explored the black man's psychology of alienation, and it established Wright as a major writer and a hero to his people. A successful play from the novel followed and finally a film, in which Wright himself played the central role.

He wrote the text for a photographic history, 12 Million Black Voices (1941), broke with the Communist Party in 1944 (that experience is the substance of his contribution to the book of essays called The God That Failed, 1950), and published an autobiographical account of his first seventeen years in Black Boy (1945), perhaps his best book. A man now held in international esteem, he was invited by the French government to visit France in 1946, and from 1947 until his death, he lived in Paris and a Normandy village. His best work was behind him.

Honored by French intellectuals and writers, a friend, for example, of Jean-Paul Sartre, he tried in his following novels—The Outsider

(1953), Savage Holiday (1954), and The Long Dream (1958)—*to
extend his social alienation into the cosmic alienation of existential-
ism. He became interested in the collapse of imperialist power in
Asia and Africa and journeyed to both continents, as well as to
Spain; a book came from each journey:* Black Power (1954), The
Color Curtain (1956), *and* Pagan Spain (1957). White Man, Listen!
(1957) *summarizes his experience of colonial revolution.*

He died of a heart attack at fifty-two. An early and unimportant novel,
Lawd Today (1963), *and a book of stories,* Eight Men (1961), *did not
embellish his fame, but the publication in 1969 of uniform editions
of his four major works memorialized it.*

*It was not only his impressive writing that made of him a heroic figure
on whom younger black writers could fix their faith; it was his
whole extraordinary, self-willed development from abandoned Mississippi waif to international intellectual. Perhaps we have no more
dramatic instance than this of truth—of truth telling, in this case—
setting a man free.*

FURTHER READING

Constance Webb has written the first biography, *Richard Wright* (1968),
and Thomas Knipp edited *Richard Wright: Letters to Joe C. Brown*
(1968). Recent critical studies are Dan McCall, *The Example of
Richard Wright* (1969), and Edward Margolies, *The Art of Richard
Wright* (1969). See also Richard Crossman, editor, *The God That
Failed* (1949).

Big Boy Leaves Home (1938)

*Is it true what they say about Dixie?
Does the sun really shine all the time?
Do sweet magnolias blossom at everybody's door?
Do folks keep eating 'possum, till they can't eat no more?
Is it true what they say about Swanee?
Is a dream by that stream so sublime?
Do they laugh, do they love, like they say in ev'ry song? . . .
If it's true, that's where I belong.*

Popular Song

I

Yo mama don wear no drawers . . .
Clearly, the voice rose out of the woods, and died away. Like an echo

another voice caught it up:
Ah seena when she pulled em off . . .
Another, shrill, cracking, adolescent:
N she washed 'em in alcohol . . .
Then a quartet of voices, blending in harmony, floated high above
the tree tops:
N she hung 'em out in the hall . . .
Laughing easily, four black boys came out of the woods into cleared
pasture. They walked lollingly in bare feet, beating tangled vines and
bushes with long sticks.
"Ah wished Ah knowed some mo lines t tha song."
"Me too."
"Yeah, when yuh gits t where she hangs em out in the hall yuh has t
stop."
"Shucks, what goes wid *hall?*"
"*Call.*"
"*Fall.*"
"*Wall.*"
"*Quall.*"
They threw themselves on the grass, laughing.
"Big Boy?"
"Huh?"
"Yuh know one thing?"
"Whut?"
"Yuh sho is crazy!"
"Crazy?"
"Yeah, yuh crazys a bed-bug!"
"Crazy bout whut?"
"Man, whoever hearda *quall?*"
"Yuh said yuh wanted something t go wid *hall,* didnt yuh?"
"Yeah, but whuts a *quall?*"
"Nigger, a *qualls* a *quall.*"
They laughed easily, catching and pulling long green blades of grass
with their toes.
"Waal, ef a *qualls* a *quall,* whut IS a *quall?*"
"Oh, Ah know."
"Whut?"
"Tha ol song goes something like this:

Yo mama don wear no drawers,
Ah seena when she pulled em off,
N she washed em in alcohol,
N she hung em out in the hall,
N then she put em back on her QUALL!"

They laughed again. Their shoulders went flat to the earth, their
knees propped up, and their faces square to the sun.

"Big Boy, yuhs CRAZY!"
"Don ax me nothin else."
"Nigger, yuhs CRAZY!"
They fell silent, smiling, drooping the lids of their eyes softly against the sunlight.
"Man, don the groun feel warm?"
"Jus lika bed."
"Jeeesus, Ah could stay here ferever."
"Me too."
"Ah kin feel tha ol sun goin all thu me."
"Feels like mah bones is warm."
In the distance a train whistled mournfully.
"There goes number fo!"
"Hittin on all six!"
"Highballin it down the line!"
"Boun fer up Noth, Lawd, boun fer up Noth!"
They began to chant, pounding bare heels in the grass.

Dis train boun fo Glory
Dis train, Oh Hallelujah
Dis train boun fo Glory
Dis train, Oh Hallelujah
Dis train boun fo Glory
Ef yuh ride no need fer fret er worry
Dis train, Oh Hallelujah
Dis train . . .

Dis train don carry no gambler
Dis train, Oh Hallelujah
Dis train don carry no gambler
Dis train, Oh Hallelujah
Dis train don carry no gambler
No fo day creeper er midnight rambler
Dis train, Oh Hallelujah
Dis train . . .

When the song ended they burst out laughing, thinking of a train bound for Glory.
"Gee, thas a good ol song!"
"Huuuuummmmmmmmmman . . ."
"Whut?"
"Geeee whiiiiiiz . . ."
"Whut?"
"Somebody don let win! Das whut!"
Buck, Bobo and Lester jumped up. Big Boy stayed on the ground, feigning sleep.

"Jeeesus, tha sho stinks!"

"Big Boy!"

Big Boy feigned to snore.

"Big Boy!"

Big Boy stirred as though in sleep.

"Big Boy!"

"Hunh?"

"Yuh rotten inside!"

"Rotten?"

"Lawd, cant yuh smell it?"

"Smell whut?"

"Nigger, yuh mus gotta bad col!"

"Smell whut?"

"NIGGER, YUH BROKE WIN!"

Big Boy laughed and fell back on the grass, closing his eyes.

"The hen whut cackles is the hen whut laid the egg."

"We ain no hens."

"Yuh cackled, didnt yuh?"

The three moved off with noses turned up.

"C mon!"

"Where yuh-all goin?"

"T the creek fer a swim."

"Yeah, les swim."

"Naw buddy naw!" said Big Boy, slapping the air with a scornful
palm.

"Aw, c mon! Don be a heel!"

"N git *lynched?* Hell naw!"

"He ain gonna see us."

"How yuh know?"

"Cause he ain."

"Yuh-all go on. Ahma stay right here," said Big Boy.

"Hell, let im stay! C mon, les go," said Buck.

The three walked off, swishing at grass and bushes with sticks. Big
Boy looked lazily at their backs.

"Hey!"

Walking on, they glanced over their shoulders.

"Hey, niggers!"

"C mon!"

Big Boy grunted, picked up his stick, pulled to his feet, and stumbled
off.

"Wait!"

"C mon!"

He ran, caught up with them, leaped upon their backs, bearing them
to the ground.

"Quit, Big Boy!"

"Gawddam, nigger!"

"Git t hell offa me!"

Big Boy sprawled in the grass beside them, laughing and pounding his heels in the ground.

"Nigger, whut yuh think we is, hosses?"

"How come yuh awways hoppin on us?"

"Lissen, wes gonna double-team on yuh one of these days n beat yo ol ass good."

Big Boy smiled.

"Sho nough?"

"Yeah, don yuh like it?"

"We gonna beat yuh sos yuh cant walk!"

"N dare yuh t do nothin erbout it!"

Big Boy bared his teeth.

"C mon! Try it now!"

The three circled around him.

"Say, Buck, yuh grab his feets!"

"N yuh git his head, Lester!"

"N Bobo, yuh git berhin n grab his arms!"

Keeping more than arm's length, they circled round and round Big Boy.

"C mon!" said Big Boy, feinting at one and then the other.

Round and round they circled, but could not seem to get any closer. Big Boy stopped and braced his hands on his hips.

"Is all three of yuh-all scareda me?"

"Les git im some other time," said Bobo, grinning.

"Yeah, we kin ketch yuh when yuh ain thinkin," said Lester.

"We kin trick yuh," said Buck.

They laughed and walked together.

Big Boy belched.

"Ahm hongry," he said.

"Me too."

"Ah wished Ah hada big hot pota belly-busters!"

"Cooked wid some good ol salty ribs . . ."

"N some good ol egg cornbread . . ."

"N some buttermilk . . ."

"N some hot peach cobbler swimmin in juice . . ."

"Nigger, hush!"

They began to chant, emphasizing the rhythm by cutting at grass with sticks.

Bye n bye
Ah wanna piece of pie
Pies too sweet
Ah wanna piece of meat
Meats too red

Ah wanna piece of bread
Breads too brown
Ah wanna go t town
Towns too far
Ah wanna ketch a car
Cars too fas
Ah fall n break mah ass
Ahll understan it better bye n bye . . .

They climbed over a barbed-wire fence and entered a stretch of thick woods. Big Boy was whistling softly, his eyes half-closed.

"LES GIT IM!"

Buck, Lester, and Bobo whirled, grabbed Big Boy about the neck, arms, and legs, bearing him to the ground. He grunted and kicked wildly as he went back into weeds.

"Hol im tight!"

"Git his arms! Git his arms!"

"Set on his legs so he cant kick!"

Big Boy puffed heavily, trying to get loose.

"WE GOT YUH NOW, GAWDDAMMIT, WE GOT YUH NOW!"

"Thas a Gawddam lie!" said Big Boy. He kicked, twisted, and clutched for a hold on one and then the other.

"Say, yuh-all hep me hol his arms!" said Bobo.

"Aw, we got this bastard now!" said Lester.

"Thas a Gawddam lie!" said Big Boy again.

"Say, yuh-all hep me hol his arms!" called Bobo.

Big Boy managed to encircle the neck of Bobo with his left arm. He tightened his elbow scissors-like and hissed through his teeth:

"Yuh got me, ain yuh?"

"Hol im"

"Les beat this bastard's ass!"

"Say, hep me hol his *arms!* Hes got aholda mah *neck!*" cried Bobo.

Big Boy squeezed Bobo's neck and twisted his head to the ground.

"Yuh got me, ain yuh?"

"Quit, Big Boy, yuh chokin me; yuh hurtin mah neck!" cried Bobo.

"Turn me loose!" said Big Boy.

"Ah ain got yuh! Its the others whut got yuh!" pleaded Bobo.

"Tell them others t git t hell offa me or Ahma break yo neck," said Big Boy.

"Ssssay, yyyuh-all gggit ooooffa Bbig Boy. Hhhes got me," gurgled Bobo.

"Cant yuh hol im?"

"Nnaw, hhes ggot mmah nneck . . ."

Big Boy squeezed tighter.

"N Ahma break it too less yuh tell em t git t hell offa me!"

"Ttturn mmmeee lllloose," panted Bobo, tears gushing.

"Cant yuh hol im, Bobo?" asked Buck.

"Nnaw, yuh-all tturn im lloose; hhhes got mah nnneck . . ."

"Grab his neck, Bobo . . ."

"Ah cant; yugurgur . . ."

To save Bobo, Lester and Buck got up and ran to a safe distance. Big Boy released Bobo, who staggered to his feet, slobbering and trying to stretch a crick out of his neck.

"Shucks, nigger, yuh almos broke mah neck," whimpered Bobo.

"Ahm gonna break yo ass nex time," said Big Boy.

"Ef Bobo coulda hel yuh we woulda had yuh," yelled Lester.

"Ah waznt gonna let im do that," said Big Boy.

They walked together again, swishing sticks.

"Yuh see," began Big Boy, "when a ganga guys jump on yuh, all yuh gotta do is just put the heat on one of them n make im tell the others t let up, see?"

"Gee, thas a good idee!"

"Yeah, thas a good idee!"

"But yuh almos broke mah neck, man," said Bobo.

"Ahma smart nigger," said Big Boy, thrusting out his chest.

II

They came to the swimming hole.

"Ah ain goin in," said Bobo.

"Done got scared?" asked Big Boy.

"Naw, Ah ain scared . . ."

"How come yuh ain goin in?"

"Yuh know ol man Harvey don erllow no niggers t swim in this hole."

"N jus las year he took a shot at Bob fer swimmin in here," said Lester.

"Shucks, ol man Harvey ain studyin bout us niggers," said Big Boy.

"Hes at home thinkin about his jelly-roll," said Buck.

They laughed.

"Buck, yo mins lowern a snakes belly," said Lester.

"Ol man Harveys too doggone ol t think erbout jelly-roll," said Big Boy.

"Hes dried up: all the saps done lef im," said Bobo.

"C mon, les go!" said Big Boy.

Bobo pointed.

"See tha sign over yonder?"

"Yeah."

"Whut it say?"

"NO TRESPASSIN," read Lester.

"Know whut tha mean?"

"Mean ain no dogs n niggers erllowed," said Buck.

"Waal, wes here now," said Big Boy. "Ef he ketched us even like this thered be trouble, so we just as waal go on in . . ."

"Ahm wid the nex one!"

"Ahl go ef anybody else goes!"

Big Boy looked carefully in all directions. Seeing nobody, he began jerking off his overalls.

"LAS ONE INS A OL DEAD DOG!"

"THAS YO MA!"

"THAS YO PA!"

"THAS BOTH YO MA N YO PA!"

They jerked off their clothes and threw them in a pile under a tree. Thirty seconds later they stood, black and naked, on the edge of the hole under a sloping embankment. Gingerly Big Boy touched the water with his foot.

"Man, this waters col," he said.

"Ahm gonna put mah cloes back on," said Bobo, withdrawing his foot.

Big Boy grabbed him about the waist.

"Like hell yuh is!"

"Git outta the way, nigger!" Bobo yelled.

"Throw im in!" said Lester.

"Duck im!"

Bobo crouched, spread his legs, and braced himself against Big Boy's body. Locked in each other's arms, they tussled on the edge of the hole, neither able to throw the other.

"C mon, les me n yuh push em in."

Laughing, Lester and Buck gave the two locked bodies a running push. Big Boy and Bobo splashed, sending up silver spray in the sunlight. When Big Boy's head came up he yelled:

"Yuh bastard!"

"That wuz yo ma yuh pushed!" said Bobo, shaking his head to clear the water from his eyes.

They did a surface dive, came up and struck out across the creek. The muddy water foamed. They swam back, waded into shallow water, breathing heavily and blinking eyes.

"C mon in!"

"Man, the waters fine!"

Lester and Buck hesitated.

"Les wet em," Big Boy whispered to Bobo.

Before Lester and Buck could back away, they were dripping wet from handsful of scooped water.

"Hey, quit!"

"Gawddam, nigger! Tha waters col!"

"C mon in!" called Big Boy.

"We jus as waal go on in now," said Buck.

"Look n see ef anybodys comin."

Kneeling, they squinted among the trees.

"Ain nobody."

"C mon, les go."

They waded in slowly, pausing each few steps to catch their breath. A desperate water battle began. Closing eyes and backing away, they shunted water into one another's faces with the flat palms of hands.

"Hey, cut it out!"

"Yeah, Ahm bout drownin!"

They came together in water up to their navels, blowing and blinking. Big Boy ducked, upsetting Bobo.

"Look out, nigger!"

"Don holler so loud!"

"Yeah, they kin hear yo ol big mouth a mile erway."

"This waters too col fer me."

"Thas cause it rained yistiddy."

They swam across and back again.

"Ah wish we hada bigger place t swim in."

"The white folks got plenty swimmin pools n we ain got none."

"Ah useta swim in the ol Missippi when we lived in Vicksburg."

Big Boy put his head under the water and blew his breath. A sound came like that of a hippopotamus.

"C mon, les be hippos."

Each went to a corner of the creek and put his mouth just below the surface and blew like a hippopotamus. Tiring, they came and sat under the embankment.

"Look like Ah gotta chill."

"Me too."

"Les stay here n dry off."

"Jeeesus, Ahm col!"

They kept still in the sun, suppressing shivers. After some of the water had dried off their bodies they began to talk through clattering teeth.

"Whut would yuh do ef ol man Harveyd come erlong right now?"

"Run like hell"

"Man, Ahd run so fas hed thinka black streaka lightnin shot pass im."

"But spose he hada gun?"

"Aw, nigger, shut up!"

They were silent. They ran their hands over wet, trembling legs, brushing water away. Then their eyes watched the sun sparkling on the restless creek.

Far away a train whistled.

"There goes number seven!"

"Headin fer up Noth!"

"Blazin it down the line!"

"Lawd, Ahm goin Noth some day."

"Me too, man."

"They say colored folks up Noth is got ekual rights."

They grew pensive. A black winged butterfly hovered at the water's edge. A bee droned. From somewhere came the sweet scent of honeysuckles. Dimly they could hear sparrows twittering in the woods. They rolled from side to side, letting sunshine dry their skins and warm their blood. They plucked blades of grass and chewed them.

"Oh!"

They looked up, their lips parting.

"Oh!"

A white woman, poised on the edge of the opposite embankment, stood directly in front of them, her hat in her hand and her hair lit by the sun.

"Its a woman!" whispered Big Boy in an underbreath. "A *white* woman!"

They stared, their hands instinctively covering their groins. Then they scrambled to their feet. The white woman backed slowly out of sight. They stood for a moment, looking at one another.

"Les git outta here!" Big Boy whispered.

"Wait till she goes erway."

"Les run, theyll ketch us here naked like this!"

"Mabbe theres a man wid her."

"C mon, les git our cloes," said Big Boy.

They waited a moment longer, listening.

"Whut t hell! Ahma git mah cloes," said Big Boy.

Grabbing at short tufts of grass, he climbed the embankment.

"Don run out there now!"

"C mon back, fool!"

Bobo hesitated. He looked at Big Boy, and then at Buck and Lester.

"Ahm goin wid Big Boy n git mah cloes," he said.

"Don run out there naked like tha, fool!" said Buck. "Yuh don know whos out there!"

Big Boy was climbing over the edge of the embankment.

"C mon," he whispered.

Bobo climbed after. Twenty-five feet away the woman stood. She had one hand over her mouth. Hanging by fingers, Buck and Lester peeped over the edge.

"C mon back; that womans scared," said Lester.

Big Boy stopped, puzzled. He looked at the woman. He looked at the bundle of clothes. Then he looked at Buck and Lester.

"C mon, les git our cloes!"

He made a step.

"Jim!" the woman screamed.

Big Boy stopped and looked around. His hands hung loosely at his sides. The woman, her eyes wide, her hand over her mouth, backed away to the tree where their clothes lay in a heap.

"Big Boy, come back n wait till shes gone!"

Bobo ran to Big Boy's side.

"Les go home! Theyll ketch us here," he urged.

Big Boy's throat felt tight.

"Lady, we wanna git our cloes," he said.

Buck and Lester climbed the embankment and stood indecisively. Big Boy ran toward the tree.

"Jim!" the woman screamed. "Jim! Jim!"

Black and naked, Big Boy stopped three feet from her.

"We wanna git our cloes," he said again, his words coming mechanically.

He made a motion.

"You go away! You go away! I tell you, you go away!"

Big Boy stopped again, afraid. Bobo ran and snatched the clothes. Buck and Lester tried to grab theirs out of his hands.

"You go away! You go away! You go away!" the woman screamed.

"Les go!" said Bobo, running toward the woods.

CRACK!

Lester grunted, stiffened, and pitched forward. His forehead struck a toe of the woman's shoes.

Bobo stopped, clutching the clothes. Buck whirled. Big Boy stared at Lester, his lips moving.

"Hes gotta gun; hes gotta gun!" yelled Buck, running wildly.

CRACK!

Buck stopped at the edge of the embankment, his head jerked backward, his body arched stiffly to one side; he toppled headlong, sending up a shower of bright spray to the sunlight. The creek bubbled.

Big Boy and Bobo backed away, their eyes fastened fearfully on a white man who was running toward them. He had a rifle and wore an army officer's uniform. He ran to the woman's side and grabbed her hand.

"You hurt, Bertha, you hurt?"

She stared at him and did not answer.

The man turned quickly. His face was red. He raised the rifle and pointed it at Bobo. Bobo ran back, holding the clothes in front of his chest.

"Don shoot me, Mistah, don shoot me . . ."

Big Boy lunged for the rifle, grabbing the barrel.

"You black sonofabitch!"

Big Boy clung desperately.

"Let go, you black bastard!"

The barrel pointed skyward.

CRACK!

The white man, taller and heavier, flung Big Boy to the ground. Bobo dropped the clothes, ran up, and jumped onto the white man's back.

"You black sonsofbitches!"

The white man released the rifle, jerked Bobo to the ground, and began to batter the naked boy with his fists. Then Big Boy swung, striking the man in the mouth with the barrel. His teeth caved in, and he fell, dazed. Bobo was on his feet.

"C mon, Big Boy, les go!"

Breathing hard, the white man got up and faced Big Boy. His lips were trembling, his neck and chin wet with blood. He spoke quietly.

"Give me that gun, boy!"

Big Boy leveled the rifle and backed away.

The white man advanced.

"Boy, I say give me that gun!"

Bobo had the clothes in his arms.

"Run, Big Boy, run!"

The man came at Big Boy.

"Ahll kill yuh; Ahll kill yuh!" said Big Boy.

His fingers fumbled for the trigger.

The man stopped, blinked, spat blood. His eyes were bewildered. His face whitened. Suddenly, he lunged for the rifle, his hands outstretched.

CRACK!

He fell forward on his face.

"Jim!"

Big Boy and Bobo turned in surprise to look at the woman.

"Jim!" she screamed again, and fell weakly at the foot of the tree.

Big Boy dropped the rifle, his eyes wide. He looked around. Bobo was crying and clutching the clothes.

"Big Boy, Big Boy . . ."

Big Boy looked at the rifle, started to pick it up, but didn't. He seemed at a loss. He looked at Lester, then at the white man; his eyes followed a thin stream of blood that seeped to the ground.

"Yuh don killed im," mumbled Bobo.

"Les go home!"

Naked, they turned and ran toward the woods. When they reached the barbed-wire fence they stopped.

"Les git our cloes on," said Big Boy.

They slipped quickly into overalls. Bobo held Lester's and Buck's clothes.

"Whut we gonna do wid these?"

Big Boy stared. His hands twitched.

"Leave em."

They climbed the fence and ran through the woods. Vines and leaves switched their faces. Once Bobo tripped and fell.

"C mon!" said Big Boy.

Bobo started crying, blood streaming from his scratches.

"Ahm scared!"

"C mon! Don cry! We wanna git home fo they ketches us!"

"Ahm scared!" said Bobo again, his eyes full of tears.

Big Boy grabbed his hand and dragged him along.

"C mon!"

III

They stopped when they got to the end of the woods. They could see the open road leading home, home to ma and pa. But they hung back, afraid. The thick shadows cast from the trees were friendly and sheltering. But the wide glare of sun stretching out over the fields was pitiless. They crouched behind an old log.

"We gotta git home," said Big Boy.

"Theys gonna lynch us," said Bobo, half questioningly.

Big Boy did not answer.

"Theys gonna lynch us," said Bobo again.

Big Boy shuddered.

"Hush!" he said. He did not want to think of it. He could not think of it; there was but one thought, and he clung to that one blindly. He had to get home, home to ma and pa.

Their heads jerked up. Their ears had caught the rhythmic jingle of a wagon. They fell to the ground and clung flat to the side of a log. Over the crest of the hill came the top of a hat. A white face. Then shoulders in a blue shirt. A wagon drawn by two horses pulled into full view.

Big Boy and Bobo held their breath, waiting. Their eyes followed the wagon till it was lost in dust around a bend of the road.

"We gotta git home," said Big Boy.

"Ahm scared," said Bobo.

"C mon! Les keep t the fields."

They ran till they came to the cornfields. Then they went slower, for last year's corn stubbles bruised their feet.

They came in sight of a brickyard.

"Wait a minute," gasped Big Boy.

They stopped.

"Ahm goin on t mah home n yuh better go on t yos."

Bobo's eyes grew round.

"Ahm scared!"

"Yuh better go on!"

"Lemme go wid yuh; theyll ketch me . . ."

"Ef yuh kin git home mabbe yo folks kin hep yuh t git erway."

Big Boy started off. Bobo grabbed him.

"Lemme go wid yuh!"

Big Boy shook free.

"Ef yuh stay here theys gonna lynch yuh!" he yelled, running.

After he had gone about twenty-five yards he turned and looked; Bobo was flying through the woods like the wind.

Big Boy slowed when he came to the railroad. He wondered if he ought to go through the streets or down the track. He decided on the tracks. He could dodge a train better than a mob.

He trotted along the ties, looking ahead and back. His cheek itched, and he felt it. His hand came away smeared with blood. He wiped it nervously on his overalls.

When he came to his back fence he heaved himself over. He landed among a flock of startled chickens. A bantam rooster tried to spur him. He slipped and fell in front of the kitchen steps, grunting heavily. The ground was slick with greasy dishwater.

Panting, he stumbled through the doorway.

"Lawd, Big Boy, whuts wrong wid yuh?"

His mother stood gaping in the middle of the floor. Big Boy flopped wordlessly onto a stool, almost toppling over. Pots simmered on the stove. The kitchen smelled of food cooking.

"Whuts the matter, Big Boy?"

Mutely, he looked at her. Then he burst into tears. She came and felt the scratches on his face.

"Whut happened t yuh, Big Boy? Somebody been botherin yuh?"

"They after me, Ma! They after me . . ."

"Who!"

"Ah . . . Ah . . . We . . ."

"Big Boy, whuts wrong wid yuh?"

"He killed Lester n Buck," he muttered simply.

"Killed!"

"Yessum."

"Lester n Buck!"

"Yessum, Ma!"

"How killed?"

"He shot em, Ma!"

"Lawd Gawd in Heaven, have mercy on us all! This is mo trouble, mo trouble," she moaned, wringing her hands.

"N Ah killed im, Ma . . ."

She stared, trying to understand.

"Whut happened, Big Boy?"

"We tried t git our cloes from the tree . . ."

"Whut tree?"

"We wuz swimmin, Ma. N the white woman . . ."

"*White* woman? . . ."

"Yessum. She wuz at the swimmin hole . . ."

"Lawd have mercy! Ah knowed yuh boys wuz gonna keep on till yuh got into somethin like this!"

She ran into the hall.

"Lucy!"

"Mam?"

"C mere!"

"Mam?"

"C mere, Ah say!"

"Wutcha wan, Ma? Ahm sewin."

"Chile, will yuh c mere like Ah ast yuh?"

Lucy came to the door holding an unfinished apron in her hands. When she saw Big Boy's face she looked wildly at her mother.

"Whuts the matter?"

"Wheres Pa?"

"Hes out front, Ah reckon."

"Git im, quick!"

"Whuts the matter, Ma?"

"Go git yo Pa, Ah say!"

Lucy ran out. The mother sank into a chair, holding a dish rag. Suddenly, she sat up.

"Big Boy, Ah thought yuh wuz at school?"

Big Boy looked at the floor.

"How come yuh didnt go t school?"

"We went t the woods."

She sighed.

"Ah done done all Ah kin fer yuh, Big Boy. Only Gawd kin hep yuh now."

"Ma, don let em git me; don let em git me . . ."

His father came into the doorway. He stared at Big Boy, then at his wife.

"Whuts Big Boy inter now?" he asked sternly.

"Saul, Big Boys done gone n got inter trouble wid the white folks."

The old man's mouth dropped, and he looked from one to the other.

"Saul, we gotta git im erway from here."

"Open yo mouth n talk! Whut yuh been doin?" The old man gripped Big Boy's shoulders and peered at the scratches on his face.

"Me n Lester n Buck n Bobo wuz out on ol man Harveys place swimmin . . ."

"Saul, its a *white* woman!"

Big Boy winced. The old man compressed his lips and stared at his wife. Lucy gaped at her brother as though she had never seen him before.

"Whut happened? Cant yuh-all talk?" the old man thundered with a certain helplessness in his voice.

"We wuz swimmin," Big Boy began, "n then a white woman comes up t the hole. We got up right erway t git our cloes sos we could git erway, n she started screamin. Our cloes wuz right by the tree where she wuz standin, n when we started t git em she jus screamed. We tol her we wanted our cloes . . . Yuh see, Pa, she wuz standin right *by* our cloes; n when we went t git em she jus screamed . . . Bobo got the cloes, n then he shot Lester . . ."

"*Who* shot Lester?"

"The white man."

"Whut white man?"

"Ah dunno, Pa. He wuz a soljer, n he had a rifle."

"A soljer?"

"Yessuh."

"A *soljer?*"

"Yessuh, Pa. A soljer."

The old man frowned.

"N then whut yuh-all do?"

"Waal, Buck said, 'He's gotta gun!' N we started runnin. N then he shot Buck, n he fell in the swimmin hole. We didnt see im no mo . . . He wuz close on us then. He looked at the white woman n then he started t shoot Bobo. Ah grabbed the gun, n we started fightin. Bobo jumped on his back. He started beatin Bobo. Then Ah hit im wid the gun. The he started at me n Ah shot im. Then we run . . ."

"Who seen?"

"Nobody."

"Wheres Bobo?"

"He went home."

"Anybody run after yuh-all?"

"Nawsuh."

"Yuh see anybody?"

"Nawsuh. Nobody but a white man. But he didnt see us."

"How long fo yuh-all lef the swimmin hole?"

"Little while ergo."

The old man nervously brushed his hand across his eyes and walked to the door. His lips moved, but no words came.

"Saul, whut we gonna do?"

"Lucy," began the old man, "go t Brother Sanders n tell im Ah said c mere; n go t Brother Jenkins n tell im Ah said c mere; n go t Elder Peters n tell im Ah said c mere. N don say nothin t nobody but whut Ah tol yuh. N when yuh git thu come straight back. Now go!"

Lucy dropped her apron across the back of a chair and ran down the steps. The mother bent over, crying and praying. The old man walked slowly over to Big Boy.

"Big Boy?"

Big Boy swallowed.

"Ahm talkin t yuh!"

"Yessuh."

"How come yuh didnt go t school this mawnin?"

"We went t the woods."

"Didnt yo ma send yuh t school?"

"Yessuh."

"How come yuh didnt go?"

"We went t the woods."

"Don yuh know thas wrong?"

"Yessuh."

"How come yuh go?"

Big Boy looked at his fingers, knotted them, and squirmed in his seat.

"AHM TALKIN T YUH!"

His wife straightened up and said reprovingly:

"Saul!"

The old man desisted, yanking nervously at the shoulder straps of his overalls.

"How long wuz the woman there?"

"Not long."

"Wuz she young?"

"Yessuh. Lika gal."

"Did yuh-all say anythin t her?"

"Nawsuh. We jus said we wanted our cloes."

"N whut she say?"

"Nothin, Pa. She jus backed erway t the tree n screamed."

The old man stared, his lips trying to form a question.

"Big Boy, did yuh-all bother her?"

"Nawsuh, Pa. We didnt *touch* her."

"How long fo the white man come up?"

"Right erway."

"Whut he say?"

"Nothin. He jus cussed us."

Abruptly the old man left the kitchen.

"Ma, cant Ah go fo they ketches me?"

"Sauls doin whut he kin."

"Ma, Ma, Ah don wan em t ketch me . . ."

"Sauls doin whut he kin. Nobody but the good Lawd kin hep us now."

The old man came back with a shotgun and leaned it in a corner. Fascinatedly, Big Boy looked at it.

There was a knock at the front door.

"Liza, see whos there."

She went. They were silent, listening. They could hear her talking.

"Whos there?"

"Me."

"Who?"

"Me, Brother Sanders."

"C mon in. Sauls waitin fer yuh."

Sanders paused in the doorway, smiling.

"Yuh sent fer me, Brother Morrison?"

"Brother Sanders, wes in deep trouble here."

Sanders came all the way into the kitchen.

"Yeah?"

"Big Boy done gone n killed a white man."

Sanders stopped short, then came forward, his face thrust out, his mouth open. His lips moved several times before he could speak.

"A *white* man?"

"They gonna kill me; they gonna kill me!" Big Boy cried, running to the old man.

"Saul, cant we git im erway somewhere?"

"Here now, take it easy; take it easy," said Sanders, holding Big Boy's wrists.

"They gonna kill me; they gonna lynch me!"

Big Boy slipped to the floor. They lifted him to a stool. His mother held him closely, pressing his head to her bosom.

"Whut we gonna do?" asked Sanders.

"Ah done sent fer Brother Jenkins n Elder Peters."

Sanders leaned his shoulders against the wall. Then, as the full meaning of it all came to him, he exclaimed:

"Theys gonna git a mob! ...." His voice broke off and his eyes fell on the shotgun.

Feet came pounding on the steps. They turned toward the door. Lucy ran in crying. Jenkins followed. The old man met him in the middle of the room, taking his hand.

"Wes in bad trouble here, Brother Jenkins. Big Boy's done gone n killed a white man. Yuh-alls gotta hep me ..."

Jenkins looked hard at Big Boy.

"Elder Peters says hes comin," said Lucy.

"When all this happen?" asked Jenkins.

"Near bout a hour ergo, now," said the old man.

"Whut we gonna do?" asked Jenkins.

"Ah wanna wait till Elder Peters come," said the old man helplessly.

"But we gotta work fas ef we gonna do anythin," said Sanders. "Well git in trouble jus standin here like this."

Big Boy pulled away from his mother.

"Pa, lemme go now! Lemme go now!"

"Be still, Big Boy!"

"Where kin yuh go?"

"Ah could ketch a freight!"

"Thas *sho* death!" said Jenkins. "Theyll be watchin em all!"

"Kin yuh-all hep me wid some money?" the old man asked.

They shook their heads.

"Saul, whut kin we do? Big Boy cant stay here."

There was another knock at the door.

The old man backed stealthily to the shotgun.

"Lucy go!"

Lucy looked at him, hesitating.

"Ah better go," said Jenkins.

It was Elder Peters. He came in hurriedly.

"Good evenin, everybody!"

"How yuh, Elder?"

"Good evenin."

"How yuh today?"

Peters looked around the crowded kitchen.

"Whuts the matter?"

"Elder, wes in deep trouble," began the old man. "Big Boy n some mo boys . . ."

". . . Lester n Buck n Bobo . . ."

". . . wuz over on ol man Harveys place swimmin . . ."

"N he don like us niggers *none*," said Peters emphatically. He widened his legs and put his thumbs in the armholes of his vest.

". . . n some white woman . . ."

"Yeah?" said Peters, coming closer.

". . . comes erlong n the boys tries t git their cloes where they done lef em under a tree. Waal, she started screamin n all, see? Reckon she thought the boys wuz after her. Then a white man in a soljers suit shoots two of em . . ."

". . . Lester n Buck . . ."

"Huummm," said Peters. "Tha wuz ol man Harveys son."

"Harveys son?"

"Yuh mean the one tha wuz in the Army?"

"Yuh mean Jim?"

"Yeh," said Peters. "The papers said he wuz here for a vacation from his regiment. N tha woman the boys saw wuz jus erbout his wife . . ."

They stared at Peters. Now that they knew what white person had been killed, their fears became definite.

"N whut else happened?"

"Big Boy shot the man . . ."

"Harveys *son*?"

"He had t, Elder. He wuz gonna shoot im ef he didnt . . ."

"Lawd!" said Peters. He looked around and put his hat back on.

"How long ergo wuz this?"

"Mighty near an hour, now, Ah reckon."

"Do the white folks know yit?"

"Don know, Elder."

"Yuh-all better git this boy outta here right now," said Peters. "Cause ef yuh don theres gonna be a lynchin . . ."

"Where kin Ah go, Elder?" Big Boy ran up to him.

They crowded around Peters. He stood with his legs wide apart, looking up at the ceiling.

"Mabbe we kin hide im in the church till he kin git erway," said Jenkins.

Peters' lips flexed.

"Naw, Brother, thall never do! Theyll git im there sho. N anyhow, ef they ketch im there itll ruin us all. We gotta git the boy outta town . . ."

Sanders went up to the old man.

"Lissen," he said in a whisper. "Mah son, Will, the one whut drives for the Magnolia Express Company, is taking a truck o goods t Chicawgo in the mawnin. If we kin hide Big Boy somewhere till then, we kin put put im on the truck . . ."

"Pa, please, lemme go wid Will when he goes in the mawnin," Big Boy begged.

The old man stared at Sanders.

"Yuh reckon thas safe?"

"Its the only thing yuh *kin* do," said Peters.

"But where we gonna hide im till then?"

"Whut time yo boy leavin out in the mawnin?"

"At six."

They were quiet, thinking. The water kettle on the stove sang.

"Pa, Ah knows where Will passes erlong wid the truck out on Bullards Road. Ah kin hide in one of them ol kilns . . ."

"Where?"

"In one of them kilns we built . . ."

"But theyll git yuh there," wailed the mother.

"But there ain no place else fer im t go."

"Theres some holes big ernough fer me t git in n stay till Will comes erlong," said Big Boy. "Please, Pa, lemme go fo they ketches me . . ."

"Let im go!"

"Please, Pa . . ."

The old man breathed heavily.

"Lucy, git his things!"

"Saul, theyll git im out there!" wailed the mother, grabbing Big Boy.

Peters pulled her way.

"Sister Morrison, ef yuh don let im go n git erway from here hes gonna be caught shos theres a Gawd in Heaven!"

Lucy came running with Big Boy's shoes and pulled them on his feet. The old man thrust a battered hat on his head. The mother went to the stove and dumped the skillet of corn pone into her apron. She wrapped it, and unbuttoning Big Boy's overalls, pushed it into his bosom.

"Heres somethin fer yuh t eat; n pray, Big Boy, cause thas all anybody kin do now . . ."

Big Boy pulled to the door, his mother clinging to him.

"Let im go, Sister Morrison!"

"Run fas, Big Boy!"

Big Boy raced across the yard, scattering the chickens. He paused at the fence and hollered back:

"Tell Bobo where Ahm hidin n tell im t c mon!"

IV

He made for the railroad, running straight toward the sunset. He held his left hand tightly over his heart, holding the hot pone of corn bread there. At times he stumbled over the ties, for his shoes were tight and hurt his feet. His throat burned from thirst; he had had no water since noon.

He veered off the track and trotted over the crest of a hill, following Bullard's Road. His feet slipped and slid in the dust. He kept his eyes straight ahead, fearing every clump of shrubbery, every tree. He wished it were night. If he could only get to the kilns without meeting anyone. Suddenly a thought came to him like a blow. He recalled hearing the old folks tell tales of blood-hounds, and fear made him run slower. None of them had thought of that. Spose blood-houns wuz put on his trail? Lawd! Spose a whole pack of em, foamin n howlin, tore im t pieces? He went limp and his feet dragged. Yeah, thas whut they wuz gonna send after im, blood-houns! N then thered be no way fer im to dodge! Why hadnt Pa let im take tha shotgun? He stopped. He oughta go back n git tha shotgun. And then when the mob came he would take some with him.

In the distance he heard the approach of a train. It jarred him back to a sharp sense of danger. He ran again, his big shoes sopping up and down in the dust. He was tired and his lungs were bursting from running. He wet his lips, wanting water. As he turned from the road across a plowed field he heard the train roaring at his heels. He ran faster, gripped in terror.

He was nearly there now. He could see the black clay on the sloping hillside. Once inside a kiln he would be safe. For a little while, at least. He thought of the shotgun again. If he only had something! Someone to talk to ... Thas right! Bobo! Bobod be wid im. Hed almost fergot Bobo. Bobod bringa gun; he knowed he would. N tergether they could kill the whole mob. Then in the mawning theyd git inter Will's truck n go far erway, t Chicawgo ...

He slowed to a walk, looking back and ahead. A light wind skipped over the grass. A beetle lit on his cheek and he brushed it off. Behind the dark pines hung a red sun. Two bats flapped against that sun. He shivered, for he was growing cold; the sweat on his body was drying.

He stopped at the foot of the hill, trying to choose between two patches of black kilns high above him. He went to the left, for there lay the ones he, Bobo, Lester, and Buck had dug only last week. He looked around again; the landscape was bare. He climbed the embankment and stood before a row of black pits sinking four and five feet deep into the earth. He went to the largest and peered in. He stiffened when his ears caught the sound of a whir. He ran back a few steps and poised on his toes. Six foot of snake slid out of the pit and went into coil. Big Boy looked around wildly for a stick. He ran down the slope, peering into the grass. He stumbled over a tree limb. He picked it up and tested it by striking it against the ground.

Warily, he crept back up the slope, his stick poised. When about seven feet from the snake he stopped and waved the stick. The coil grew tighter, the whir sounded louder, and a flat head reared to strike. He went to the right, and the flat head followed him, the blue-black tongue darting forth; he went to the left, and the flat head followed him there too.

He stopped, teeth clenched. He had to kill this snake. Jus had t kill im! This wuz the safest pit on the hillside. He waved the stick again, looking at the snake before, thinking of a mob behind. The flat head reared higher. With stick over shoulder, he jumped in, swinging. The stick sang through the air, catching the snake on the side of the head, sweeping him out of coil. There was a brown writhing mass. Then Big Boy was upon him, pounding blows home, one on top of the other. He fought viciously, his eyes red, his teeth bared in a snarl. He beat till the snake lay still; then he stomped it with his heel, grinding its head into the dirt.

He stopped, limp, wet. The corners of his lips were white with spittle. He spat and shuddered.

Cautiously, he went to the hole and peered. He longed for a match. He imagined whole nests of them in there waiting. He put the stick into the hole and waved it around. Stooping, he peered again. It mus be awright. He looked over the hillside, his eyes coming back to the dead snake. Then he got to his knees and backed slowly into the hole.

When inside he felt there must be snakes all about him, ready to strike. It seemed he could see and feel them there, waiting tensely in coil. In the dark he imagined long white fangs ready to sink into his neck, his side, his legs. He wanted to come out, but kept still. Shucks, he told himself, ef there wuz any snakes in here they sho woulda done bit me by now. Some of his fear left, and he relaxed.

With elbows on ground and chin on palms, he settled. The clay was cold to his knees and thighs, but his bosom was kept warm by the hot pone of corn bread. His thirst returned and he longed for a drink. He was hungry, too. But he did not want to eat the corn pone. Naw, not now. Mabbe after erwhile, after Bobo came. Then theyd both eat the corn pone.

The view from his hole was fringed by the long tufts of grass. He could see all the way to Bullard's Road, and even beyond. The wind was blowing, and in the east the first touch of dusk was rising. Every now and then a bird floated past, a spot of wheeling black printed against the sky. Big Boy sighed, shifted his weight, and chewed at a blade of grass. A wasp droned. He heard number nine, far away and mournful.

The train made him remember how they had dug these kilns on

long hot summer days, how they had made boilers out of big tin cans, filled them with water, fixed stoppers for steam, cemented them in holes with wet clay, and built fires under them. He recalled how they had danced and yelled when a stopper blew out of a boiler, letting out a big spout of steam and a shrill whistle. There were times when they had the whole hillside blazing and smoking. Yeah, yuh see, Big Boy wuz Casey Jones n wuz speedin it down the gleamin rails of the Southern Pacific. Bobo had number two on the Santa Fe. Buck wuz on the Illinoy Central. Lester the Nickel Plate. Lawd, how they shelved the wood in! The boiling water would almost jar the cans loose from the clay. More and more pine-knots and dry leaves would be piled under the cans. Flames would grow so tall they would have to shield their eyes. Sweat would pour off their faces. Then, suddenly, a peg would shoot high into the air, and

Pssseeeezzzzzzzzzzzzzzzzzzzzzz . . .

Big Boy sighed and stretched out his arm, quenching the flames and scattering the smoke. Why didnt Bobo c mon? He looked over the fields; there was nothing but dying sunlight. His mind drifted back to the kilns. He remembered the day when Buck, jealous of his winning, had tried to smash his kiln. Yeah, that ol sonofabitch! Naw, Lawd! He didnt go t say tha! Whut wuz he thinkin erbout? Cussin the dead! Yeah, po ol Buck wuz dead now. N Lester too. Yeah, it wuz awright fer Buck t smash his kiln. Sho. N he wished he hadnt socked ol Buck so hard tha day. He wuz sorry fer Buck now. N he sho wished he hadnt cussed po ol Bucks ma, neither. Tha wuz sinful! Mabbe Gawd would git im fer tha? But he didnt go t do it! Po Buck! Po Lester! Hed never treat anybody like tha ergin, never . . .

Dusk was slowly deepening. Somewhere, he could not tell exactly where, a cricket took up a fitful song. The air was growing soft and heavy. He looked over the fields, longing for Bobo . . .

He shifted his body to ease the cold damp of the ground, and thought back over the day. Yeah, hed been dam right erbout not wantin t go swimmin. N ef hed followed his right min hed neverve gone n got inter all this trouble. At first hed said naw. But shucks, somehow hed just went on wid the res. Yeah, he shoulda went on t school tha mawnin, like Ma told im t do. But, hell, who wouldnt git tireda school? T hell wid school! Tha wuz the big trouble, awways drivin a guy t school. He wouldnt be in all this trouble now ef it wuznt for that Gawddam school! Impatiently, he took the grass out of his mouth and threw it away, demolishing the little red school house . . .

Yeah, ef they had all kept still n quiet when that ol white woman showed-up, mabbe shedve went on off. But yuh never kin tell erbout these white folks. Mabbe she wouldntve went. Mabbe that white man woulda killed all of em! All *fo* of em! Yeah, yuh never kin tell erbout white folks. Then, ergin, mabbe tha white woman woulda went on off n laffed. Yeah, mabbe tha white man woulda said: *Yuh nigger bastards*

git t hell outta here! Yuh know Gawddam well yuh don berlong here!
N then they woulda grabbed their cloes n run like all hell . . . He blinked
the white man away. Where wuz Bobo? Why didnt he hurry up n
c mon?

He jerked another blade and chewed. Yeah, ef pa had only let im
have tha shotgun? He could stan off a whole mob wid a shotgun. He
looked at the ground as he turned a shotgun over in his hands. Then
he leveled it at an advancing white man. *Boooom!* The man curled up.
Another came. He reloaded quickly, and let him have what the other
had got. He too curled up. Then another came. He got the same medicine. Then the whole mob swirled around him, and he blazed away,
getting as many as he could. They closed in; but, by Gawd, he had done
his part, hadnt he? N the newspapersd say: NIGGER KILLS DOZEN
OF MOB BEFO LYNCHED! Er mabbe theyd say: TRAPPED NIGGER
SLAYS TWENTY BEFO KILLED! He smiled a little. Tha wouldnt be
so bad, would it? Blinking the newspaper away, he looked over the
fields. Where wuz Bobo? Why didnt he hurry up n c mon?

He shifted, trying to get a crick out of his legs. Shucks, he wuz
gittin tireda this. N it wuz almos dark now. Yeah, there wuz a little
bittie star way over yonder in the eas. Mabbe that white man wuznt
dead? Mabbe they wuznt even lookin for im? Mabbe he could go back
home now? Naw, better wait erwhile. Thad be bes. But, Lawd, ef he
only had some water! He could hardly swallow, his throat was so dry.
Gawddam them white folks! Thas all they wuz good fer, t run a nigger
down lika rabbit! Yeah, they git yuh in a corner n then they let yuh
have it. A thousan of em! He shivered, for the cold of the clay was
chilling his bones. Lawd, spose they foun im here in this hole? N wid
nobody t hep im? . . . But ain no use in thinkin erbout tha; wait till
trouble come fo yuh start fightin it. But ef tha mob came one by one
hed wipe em all out. Clean up the whole bunch. He caught one by the
neck and choked him long and hard, choked him till his tongue and
eyes popped out. Then he jumped upon his chest and stomped him like
he had stomped that snake. When he had finished with one, another
came. He choked him too. Choked till he sank slowly to the ground,
gasping . . .

"Hoalo!"

Big Boy snatched his fingers from the white man's neck and looked
over the fields. He saw nobody. Had someone spied him? He was sure
that somebody had hollered. His heart pounded. But, shucks, nobody
couldnt see im here in this hole . . . But mabbe theyd seen im when he
wuz comin n had laid low n wuz now closin in on im! Praps they wuz
signalin fer the others? Yeah, they wuz creepin up on im! Mabbe he
oughta git up n run . . . Oh! Mabbe tha wuz Bobo! Yeah, Bobo! He
oughta clim out n see ef Bobo wuz lookin fer im . . . He stiffened.

"Hoalo!"

"Hoalo!"

"Wheres yuh?"

"Over here on Bullards Road!"

"C mon over!"

"Awright!"

He heard footsteps. Then voices came again, low and far away this time.

"Seen anybody?"

"Naw. Yuh?"

"Naw."

"Yuh reckon they got erway?"

"Ah dunno. Its hard t tell."

"Gawddam them sonofabitchin niggers!"

"We oughta kill ever black bastard in this country!"

"Waal, Jim got two of em, anyhow."

"But Bertha said there wuz *fo!*"

"Where in hell they hidin?"

"She said one of em wuz named Big Boy, or somethin like tha."

"We went t his shack lookin fer im."

"Yeah?"

"But we didnt fin im."

"These niggers stick tergether; they don never tell on each other."

"We looked all thu the shack n couldnt fin hide ner hair of im. Then we drove the ol woman n man out n set the shack on fire . . ."

"Jeesus! Ah wished Ah coulda been there!"

"Yuh shoulda heard the ol nigger woman howl . . ."

"Hoalo!"

"C mon over!"

Big Boy eased to the edge and peeped. He saw a white man with a gun slung over his shoulder running down the slope. Wuz they gonna search the hill? Lawd, there wuz no way fer im t git erway now; he wuz caught! He shoulda knowed theyd git im here. N he didnt hava thing, notta thing t fight wid. Yeah, soon as the blood-houns came theyd fin im. Lawd, have mercy! Theyd lynch im right here on the hill . . . Theyd git im n tie im t a stake n burn im erlive! Lawd! Nobody but the good Lawd could hep im now, nobody . . .

He heard more feet running. He nestled deeper. His chest ached. Nobody but the good Lawd could hep now. They wuz crowdin all round im n when they hada big crowd theyd close in on im. Then itd be over . . . The good Lawd would have t hep im, cause nobody could hep im now, nobody . . .

And then he went numb when he remembered Bobo. Spose Bobod come now? Hed be caught sho! Both of em would be caught! They'd make Bobo tell where he wuz! Bobo oughta not try to come now. Somebody oughta tell im . . . But there wuz nobody; there wuz no way . . .

He eased slowly back to the opening. There was a large group of men. More were coming. Many had guns. Some had coils of rope slung over shoulders.

"Ah tell yuh they still here, somewhere . . ."

"But we looked all over!"

"What t hell! Wouldnt do t let em git erway!"

"Naw. Ef they git erway notta woman in this town would be safe."

"Say, whuts tha yuh got?"

"Er pillar."

"Fer whut?"

"Feathers, fool!"

"Chris! Thisll be hot ef we kin ketch them niggers!"

"Ol Anderson said he wuz gonna bringa barrela tar!"

"Ah got some gasoline in mah car ef yuh need it."

Big Boy had no feelings now. He was waiting. He did not wonder if they were coming after him. He just waited. He did not wonder about Bobo. He rested his cheek against the cold clay, waiting.

A dog barked. He stiffened. It barked again. He balled himself into a knot at the bottom of the hole, waiting. Then he heard the patter of dog feet.

"Look!"

"Whuts he got?"

"Its a snake!"

"Yeah, the dogs foun a snake!"

"Gee, its a big one!"

"Shucks, Ah wish he could fin one of them sonofabitchin niggers!"

The voices sank to low murmurs. Then he heard number twelve, its bell tolling and whistle crying as it slid along the rails. He flattened himself against the clay. Someone was singing:

"We'll hang ever nigger t a sour apple tree . . ."

When the song ended there was hard laughter. From the other side of the hill he heard the dog barking furiously. He listened. There was more than one dog now. There were many and they were barking their throats out.

"Hush, Ah hear them dogs!"

"When theys barkin like tha theys foun somethin!"

"Here they come over the hill!"

"WE GOT IM! WE GOT IM!"

There came a roar. Tha mus be Bobo; tha mus be Bobo . . . In spite of his fear, Big Boy looked. The road, and half of the hillside across the road, were covered with men. A few were at the top of the hill, stenciled against the sky. He could see dark forms moving up the slopes. They were, yelling.

"By Gawd, we got im!"

"C mon!"

"Where is he?"

"Theyre bringin im over the hill!"

"Ah got a rope fer im!"

"Say, somebody go n git the others!"

"Where is he? Cant we see im, Mister?"

"They say Berthas comin, too."

"Jack! Jack! Don leave me! Ah wanna see im!"

"Theyre bringin im over the hill, sweetheart!"

"AH WANNA BE THE FIRS T PUT A ROPE ON THA BLACK BASTARDS NECK!"

"Les start the fire!"

"Heat the tar!"

"Ah got some chains t chain im."

"Bring im over this way!"

"Chris, Ah wished Ah hada drink . . ."

Big Boy saw men moving over the hill. Among them was a long dark spot. Tha mus be Bobo; tha mus be Bobo theys carryin . . . They'll git im here. He oughta git up n run. He clamped his teeth and ran his hand across his forehead, bringing it away wet. He tried to swallow, but could not; his throat was dry.

They had started the song again:

"We'll hang ever nigger t a sour apple tree . . ."

There were women singing now. Their voices made the song round and full. Song waves rolled over the top of pine trees. The sky sagged low, heavy with clouds. Wind was rising. Sometimes cricket cries cut surprisingly across the mob song. A dog had gone to the utmost top of the hill. At each lull of the song his howl floated full into the night.

Big Boy shrank when he saw the first tall flame light the hillside. Would they see im here? Then he remembered you could not see into the dark if you were standing in the light. As flames leaped higher he saw two men rolling a barrel up the slope.

"Say, gimme a han here, will yuh?"

"Awright, heave!"

"C mon! Straight up! Git t the other end!"

"Ah got the feathers here in this pillar!"

"BRING SOME MO WOOD!"

Big Boy could see the barrel surrounded by flames. The mob fell back, forming a dark circle. Theyd fin im here! He had a wild impulse to climb out and fly across the hills. But his legs would not move. He stared hard, trying to find Bobo. His eyes played over a long dark spot near the fire. Fanned by wind, flames leaped higher. He jumped. That dark spot had moved. Lawd, thas Bobo; thas Bobo . . .

He smelt the scent of tar, faint at first, then stronger. The wind brought it full into his face, then blew it away. His eyes burned and he rubbed them with his knuckles. He sneezed.

"LES GIT SOURVINEERS!"

He saw the mob close in around the fire. Their faces were hard and sharp in the light of the flames. More men and women were coming over the hill. The long dark spot was smudged out.

"Everybody git back!"

"Look! Hes gotta finger!"

"C MON! GIT THE GALS BACK FROM THE FIRE!"

"Hes got one of his ears, see?"

"Whuts the matter!"

"A woman fell out! Fainted, Ah reckon . . ."

The stench of tar permeated the hillside. The sky was black and the wind was blowing hard.

"HURRY UP N BURN THE NIGGER FO IT RAINS!"

Big Boy saw the mob fall back, leaving a small knot of men about the fire. Then, for the first time, he had a full glimpse of Bobo. A black body flashed in the light. Bobo was struggling, twisting; they were binding his arms and legs. . .

When he saw them tilt the barrel he stiffened. A scream quivered. He knew the tar was on Bobo. The mob fell back. He saw a tar-drenched body glistening and turning.

"THE BASTARDS GOT IT!"

There was a sudden quiet. Then he shrank violently as the wind carried, like a flurry of snow, a widening spiral of white feathers into the night. The flames leaped tall as the trees. The scream came again. Big Boy trembled and looked. The mob was running down the slopes, leaving the fire clear. Then he saw a writhing white mass cradled in yellow flame, and heard screams, one on top of the other, each shriller and shorter than the last. The mob was quiet now, standing still, looking up the slopes at the writhing white mass gradually growing black, growing black in a cradle of yellow flame.

"PO ON MO GAS!"

"Gimme a lif, will yuh!"

Two men were struggling, carrying between them a heavy can. They set it down, tilted it, leaving it so that the gas would trickle down to the hollowed earth around the fire.

Big Boy slid back into the hole, his face buried in clay. He had no feelings now, no fears. He was numb, empty, as though all blood had been drawn from him. Then his muscles flexed taut when he heard a faint patter. A tiny stream of cold water seeped to his knees, making him push back to a drier spot. He looked up; rain was beating in the grass.

"Its rainin!"

"C mon, les git t town!"

". . . don worry, when the fire git thu wid im hell be gone . . ."

"Wait, Charles! Don leave me; its slippery here . . ."

"Ahll take some of yuh ladies back in mah car . . ."

Big Boy heard the dogs barking again, this time closer. Running feet pounded past. Cold water chilled his ankles. He could hear raindrops steadily hissing.

Now a dog was barking at the mouth of the hole, barking furiously, sensing a presence there. He balled himself into a knot and clung to the bottom, his knees and shins buried in water. The bark came louder. He heard paws scraping and felt the hot scent of dog breath on his face. Green eyes glowed and drew nearer as the barking, muffled by the closeness of the hole, beat upon his eardrums. Backing till his shoulders pressed against the clay, he held his breath. He pushed out his hands, his fingers stiff. The dog yawped louder, advancing, his bark rising sharp and thin. Big Boy rose to his knees, his hands before him. Then he flattened out still more against the bottom, breathing lungsful of hot dog scent, breathing it slowly, hard, but evenly. The dog came closer, bringing hotter dog scent. Big Boy could go back no more. His knees were slipping and slopping in the water. He braced himself, ready. Then, he never exactly knew how—he never knew whether he had lunged or the dog had lunged—they were together, rolling in the water. The green eyes were beneath him, between his legs. Dognails bit into his arms. His knees slipped backward and he landed full on the dog; the dog's breath left in a heavy gasp. Instinctively, he fumbled for the throat as he felt the dog twisting between his knees. The dog snarled, long and low, as though gathering strength. Big Boy's hands traveled swiftly over the dog's back, groping for the throat. He felt dognails again and saw green eyes, but his fingers had found the throat. He choked, feeling his fingers sink; he choked, throwing back his head and stiffening his arms. He felt the dog's body heave, felt dognails digging into his loins. With strength flowing from fear, he closed his fingers, pushing his full weight on the dog's throat. The dog heaved again, and lay still . . . Big Boy heard the sound of his own breathing filling the hole, and heard shouts and footsteps above him going past.

For a long, long time he held the dog, held it long after the last footstep had died out, long after the rain had stopped.

V

Morning found him still on his knees in a puddle of rainwater, staring at the stiff body of a dog. As the air brightened he came to himself slowly. He held still for a long time, as though waking from a dream, as though trying to remember.

The chug of a truck came over the hill. He tried to crawl to the opening. His knees were stiff and a thousand needle-like pains shot from the bottom of his feet to the calves of his legs. Giddiness made his eyes blur. He pulled up and looked. Through brackish light he saw Will's truck standing some twenty-five yards away, the engine running. Will stood on the running board, looking over the slopes of the hill.

Big Boy scuffled out, falling weakly in the wet grass. He tried to call to Will, but his dry throat would make no sound. He tried again.

"Will!"

Will heard, answering:

"Big Boy, c mon!"

He tried to run, and fell. Will came, meeting him in the tall grass.

"C mon," Will said, catching his arm.

They struggled to the truck.

"Hurry up!" said Will, pushing him onto the runningboard.

Will pushed back a square trapdoor which swung above the back of the driver's seat. Big Boy pulled through, landing with a thud on the bottom. On hands and knees he looked around in the semi-darkness.

"Wheres Bobo?"

Big Boy stared.

"Wheres Bobo?"

"They got im."

"When?"

"Las night."

"The mob?"

Big Boy pointed in the direction of a charred sapling on the slope of the opposite hill. Will looked. The trapdoor fell. The engine purred, the gears whined, and the truck lurched forward over the muddy road, sending Big Boy on his side.

For a while he lay as he had fallen, on his side, too weak to move. As he felt the truck swing around a curve he straightened up and rested his back against a stack of wooden boxes. Slowly, he began to make out objects in the darkness. Through two long cracks fell thin blades of daylight. The floor was of smooth steel, and cold to his thighs. Splinters and bits of sawdust danced with the rumble of the truck. Each time they swung around a curve he was pulled over the floor; he grabbed at corners of boxes to steady himself. Once he heard the crow of a rooster. It made him think of home, of ma and pa. He thought he remembered hearing somewhere that the house had burned, but could not remember where . . . It all seemed unreal now.

He was tired. He dozed, swaying with the lurch. Then he jumped awake. The truck was running smoothly, on gravel. Far away he heard two short blasts from the Buckeye Lumber Mill. Unconsciously, the thought sang through his mind: Its six erclock . . .

The trapdoor swung in. Will spoke through a corner of his mouth.

"How yuh comin?"

"Awright."

"How they git Bobo?"

"He wuz comin over the hill."

"What they do?"

"They burnt im . . . Will, Ah wan some water; mah throats like fire . . ."

"Well git some when we pass a fillin station."

Big Boy leaned back and dozed. He jerked awake when the truck stopped. He heard Will git out. He wanted to peep through the trapdoor, but was afraid. For a moment, the wild fear he had known in the hole came back. Spose theyd search n fin im? He quieted when he heard Will's footstep on the runningboard. The trapdoor pushed in. Will's hat came through dripping.

"Take it quick!"

Big Boy grabbed, spilling water into his face. The truck lurched. He drank. Hard cold lumps of brick rolled into his hot stomach. A dull pain made him bend over. His intestines seemed to be drawing into a tight knot. After a bit it eased, and he sat up, breathing softly.

The truck swerved. He blinked his eyes. The blades of daylight had turned brightly golden. The sun had risen.

The truck sped over the asphalt miles, sped northward, jolting him, shaking out of his bosom the crumbs of corn bread, making them dance with the splinters and sawdust in the golden blades of sunshine.

He turned on his side and slept.

EUDORA WELTY (1909–   )

The publishing career of Eudora Welty began in 1936 with the appearance of one of her most remarkable stories—"Death of a Travelling Salesman"—in a rather obscure little magazine called Manuscript. *Anyone fortunate enough to have come upon this drama of a nearly dreamlike lapse into death, with its orchestral overtones of pathos and loss, isolation and pain, pity and terror, would have known that he had had a fresh experience of life, an experience different from any that he had had before in literature; in short, he would have known that he had just read an original writer.*

The story was prophetic in the sense that Eudora Welty's best writing proved to be in the shorter forms of fiction. These began to appear at once in a number of distinguished periodicals, particularly Southern Review, *and they attracted highly discriminating readers who spoke for her—Ford Madox Ford, Robert Penn Warren, and Katherine Anne Porter, among others. But the publication of volumes of short stories by writers who have not published successful novels has never been easy in the United States, and it was five years before Eudora Welty's first collection appeared,* A Curtain of Green *(1941), with an introduction by Miss Porter. This was followed by three more collections:* The Wide Net *(1943),* The Golden Apples *(1949), and* The Bride of the Innisfallen *(1955). Her scene generally has remained the same—that perhaps narrow, but humanly complex, South that she knows best. But with each successive volume, the thematic reverberations grew deeper and thrust themselves out farther. There is, indeed, a kind of echoing limitlessness to her stories for all their precise particularity in the detail of place and manners.*

She has published four novels, each quite different from the others: The
Robber Bridegroom *(1942), half fantasy and fairy tale, half prose
ballad;* Delta Wedding *(1946), a realistic account of modern plantation life;* The Ponder Heart *(1954), a warm and hilarious comedy
dramatized from the point of view of a woman who cannot stop
talking; and* Losing Battles *(1969), a grave and funny family chronicle in which no one, very nearly, can stop talking. Her inventiveness
is inexhaustible.*

*She has written some of the most suggestive essays we have on the
problems that a writer of fiction daily confronts. These are not,
unfortunately, readily available; delivered as talks at Smith College
in a year when she was in residence there as visiting writer, they
appeared separately in periodicals and were published as a group by
Smith College,* Three Papers on Fiction *(1962).*

*Eudora Welty has lived almost all her life in the place where she was
born, Jackson, Mississippi. After spending two years at the Mississippi State College for Women, she went North and took her A.B.
at the University of Wisconsin (1929). A year in the Columbia
University School of Advertising persuaded her that advertising was
not her* métier, *but she now knew what was, and in 1932 she settled
down in Jackson to pursue it. She soon had a whole world at her
door.*

FURTHER READING

The fullest study to date is *A Season of Dreams: The Fiction of Eudora
Welty* (1965) by Alfred Appel, Jr., but it does not supplant Ruth M.
Vande Kieft's *Eudora Welty* (1962). J. A. Bryant, Jr., *Eudora Welty*
(1968) is a useful introductory pamphlet.

Livvie *(1943)*

Solomon carried Livvie twenty-one miles away from her home when
he married her. He carried her away up on the Old Natchez Trace into
the deep country to live in his house. She was sixteen—an only girl,
then. Once people said he thought nobody would ever come along there.
He told her himself that it had been a long time, and a day she did not
know about, since that road was a traveled road with *people* coming and
going. He was good to her, but he kept her in the house. She had not
thought that she could not get back. Where she came from, people said
an old man did not want anybody in the world to ever find his wife, for
fear they would steal her back from him. Solomon asked her before he
took her, "Would she be happy?"—very dignified, for he was a colored

man that owned his land and had it written down in the courthouse; and she said, "Yes, sir," since he was an old man and she was young and just listened and answered. He asked her, if she was choosing winter, would she pine for spring, and she said, "No indeed." Whatever she said, always, was because he was an old man . . . while nine years went by. All the time, he got old, and he got so old he gave out. At last he slept the whole day in bed, and she was young still.

It was a nice house, inside and outside both. In the first place, it had three rooms. The front room was papered in holly paper, with green palmettos from the swamp spaced at careful intervals over the walls. There was fresh newspaper cut with fancy borders on the mantel-shelf, on which were propped photographs of old or very young men printed in faint yellow—Solomon's people. Solomon had a houseful of furniture. There was a double settee, a tall scrolled rocker and an organ in the front room, all around a three-legged table with a pink marble top, on which was set a lamp with three gold feet, besides a jelly glass with pretty hen feathers in it. Behind the front room, the other room had the bright iron bed with the polished knobs, like a throne, in which Solomon slept all day. There were snow-white curtains of wiry lace at the window, and a lace bed-spread belonged on the bed. But what old Solomon slept so sound under was a big feather-stitched piece-quilt in the pattern "Trip Around the World," which had twenty-one different colors, four hundred and forty pieces, and a thousand yards of thread, and that was what Solomon's mother made in her life and old age. There was a table holding the Bible, and a trunk with a key. On the wall were two calendars, and a diploma from somewhere in Solomon's family, and under that Livvie's one possession was nailed, a picture of the little white baby of the family she worked for, back in Natchez before she was married. Going through that room and on to the kitchen, there was a big wood stove and a big round table always with a wet top and with the knives and forks in one jelly glass and the spoons in another, and a cut-glass vinegar bottle between, and going out from those, many shallow dishes of pickled peaches, fig preserves, watermelon pickles and blackberry jam always sitting there. The churn sat in the sun, the doors of the safe were always both shut, and there were four baited mouse-traps in the kitchen, one in every corner.

The outside of Solomon's house looked nice. It was not painted, but across the porch was an even balance. On each side there was one easy chair with high springs, looking out, and a fern basket hanging over it from the ceiling, and a dishpan of zinnia seedlings growing at its foot on the floor. By the door was a plow-wheel, just a pretty iron circle, nailed up on one wall and a square mirror on the other, a turquoise-blue comb stuck up in the frame, with the wash stand beneath it. On the door was a wooden knob with a pearl in the end, and Solomon's black hat hung on that, if he was in the house.

Out front was a clean dirt yard with every vestige of grass patiently

uprooted and the ground scarred in deep whorls from the strike of
Livvie's broom. Rose bushes with tiny blood-red roses blooming every
month grew in threes on either side of the steps. On one side was a
peach tree, on the other a pomegranate. Then coming around up the
path from the deep cut of the Natchez Trace below was a line of bare
crape-myrtle trees with every branch of them ending in a colored bottle,
green or blue. There was no word that fell from Solomon's lips to say
what they were for, but Livvie knew that there could be a spell put in
trees, and she was familiar from the time she was born with the way
bottle trees kept evil spirits from coming into the house—by luring
them inside the colored bottles, where they cannot get out again.
Solomon had made the bottle trees with his own hands over the nine
years, in labor amounting to about a tree a year, and without a sign
that he had any uneasiness in his heart, for he took as much pride in
his precautions against spirits coming in the house as he took in the
house, and sometimes in the sun the bottle trees looked prettier than
the house did.

It was a nice house. It was in a place where the days would go by and
surprise anyone that they were over. The lamplight and the firelight would shine out the door after dark, over the still and breathing
country, lighting the roses and the bottle trees, and all was quiet there.

But there was nobody, nobody at all, not even a white person. And
if there had been anybody, Solomon would not have let Livvie look at
them, just as he would not let her look at a field hand, or a field hand
look at her. There was no house near, except for the cabins of the tenants that were forbidden to her, and there was no house as far as she
had been, stealing away down the still, deep Trace. She felt as if she
waded a river when she went, for the dead leaves on the ground reached
as high as her knees, and when she was all scratched and bleeding she
said it was not like a road that went anywhere. One day, climbing up
the high bank, she had found a graveyard without a church, with
ribbon-grass growing about the foot of an angel (she had climbed up
because she thought she saw angel wings), and in the sun, trees shining like burning flames through the great caterpillar nets which enclosed them. Scarey thistles stood looking like the prophets in the Bible
in Solomon's house. Indian paint brushes grew over her head, and the
mourning dove made the only sound in the world. Oh for a stirring of
the leaves, and a breaking of the nets! But not by a ghost, prayed Livvie,
jumping down the bank. After Solomon took to his bed, she never went
out, except one more time.

Livvie knew she made a nice girl to wait on anybody. She fixed
things to eat on a tray like a surprise. She could keep from singing when
she ironed, and to sit by a bed and fan away the flies, she could be so
still she could not hear herself breathe. She could clean up the house
and never drop a thing, and wash the dishes without a sound, and she
would step outside to churn, for churning sounded too sad to her, like

sobbing, and if it made her home-sick and not Solomon, she did not think of that.

But Solomon scarcely opened his eyes to see her, and scarcely tasted his food. He was not sick or paralyzed or in any pain that he mentioned, but he was surely wearing out in the body, and no matter what nice hot thing Livvie would bring him to taste, he would only look at it now, as if he were past seeing how he could add anything more to himself. Before she could beg him, he would go fast asleep. She could not surprise him any more, if he would not taste, and she was afraid that he was never in the world going to taste another thing she brought him—and so how could he last?

But one morning it was breakfast time and she cooked his eggs and grits, carried them in on a tray, and called his name. He was sound asleep. He lay in a dignified way with his watch beside him, on his back in the middle of the bed. One hand drew the quilt up high, though it was the first day of spring. Through the white lace curtains a little puffy wind was blowing as if it came from round cheeks. All night the frogs had sung out in the swamp, like a commotion in the room, and he had not stirred, though she lay wide awake and saying "Shh, frogs!" for fear he would mind them.

He looked as if he would like to sleep a little longer, and so she put back the tray and waited a little. When she tiptoed and stayed so quiet, she surrounded herself wih a little reverie, and sometimes it seemed to her when she was so stealthy that the quiet she kept was for a sleeping baby, and that she had a baby and was its mother. When she stood at Solomon's bed and looked down at him, she would be thinking. "He sleeps so well," and she would hate to wake him up. And in some other way, too, she was afraid to wake him up because even in his sleep he seemed to be such a strict man.

Of course, nailed to the wall over the bed—only she would forget who it was—there was a picture of him when he was young. Then he had a fan of hair over his forehead like a king's crown. Now his hair lay down on his head, the spring had gone out of it. Solomon had a lightish face, with eyebrows scattered but rugged, the way privet grows, strong eyes, with second sight, a strict mouth, and a little gold smile. This was the way he looked in his clothes, but in bed in the daytime he looked like a different and smaller man, even when he was wide awake, and holding the Bible. He looked like somebody kin to himself. And then sometimes when he lay in sleep and she stood fanning the flies away, and the light came in, his face was like new; so smooth and clear that it was like a glass of jelly held to the window, and she could almost look through his forehead and see what he thought.

She fanned him and at length he opened his eyes and spoke her name, but he would not taste the nice eggs she had kept warm under a pan.

Back in the kitchen she ate heartily, his breakfast and hers, and looked out the open door at what went on. The whole day, and the whole night before, she had felt the stir of spring close to her. It was as present in the house as a young man would be. The moon was in the last quarter and outside they were turning the sod and planting peas and beans. Up and down the red fields, over which smoke from the brush-burning hung showing like a little skirt of sky, a white horse and a white mule pulled the plow. At intervals hoarse shouts came through the air and roused her as if she dozed neglectfully in the shade, and they were telling her, "Jump up!" She could see how over each ribbon of field were moving men and girls, on foot and mounted on mules, with hats set on their heads and bright with tall hoes and forks as if they carried streamers on them and were going to some place on a journey—and how as if at a signal now and then they would all start at once shouting, hollering, cajoling, calling and answering back, running, being leaped on and breaking away, flinging to earth with a shout and lying motionless in the trance of twelve o'clock. The old women came out of the cabins and brought them the food they had ready for them, and then all worked together, spread evenly out. The little children came too, like a bouncing stream overflowing the fields, and set upon the men, the women, the dogs, the rushing birds, and the wave-like rows of earth, their little voices almost too high to be heard. In the middle distance like some white and gold towers were the haystacks, with black cows coming around to eat their edges. High above everything, the wheel of fields, house, and cabins, and the deep road surrounding like a moat to keep them in, was the turning sky, blue with long, far-flung white mare's-tail clouds, serene and still as high flames. And sound asleep while all this went around him that was his, Solomon was like a little still spot in the middle.

Even in the house the earth was sweet to breathe. Solomon had never let Livvie go any farther than the chicken house and the well. But what if she would walk now into the heart of the fields and take a hoe and work until she fell stretched out and drenched with her efforts, like other girls, and laid her cheek against the laid-open earth, and shamed the old man with her humbleness and delight? To shame him! A cruel wish would come in uninvited and so fast while she looked out the back door. She washed the dishes and scrubbed the table. She could hear the cries of the little lambs. Her mother, that she had not seen since her wedding day, had said one time, "I rather a man be anything, than a woman be mean."

So all morning she kept tasting the chicken broth on the stove, and when it was right she poured off a nice cup-ful. She carried it in to Solomon, and there he lay having a dream. Now what did he dream about? For she saw him sigh gently as if not to disturb some whole thing he held round in his mind, like a fresh egg. So even an old man dreamed about something pretty. Did he dream of her, while his eyes were shut and sunken, and his small hand with the wedding ring curled close in sleep around the quilt? He might be dreaming of what time it was, for even through his sleep he kept track of it like a clock, and knew how much of it went by, and waked up knowing where the hands were even before he consulted the silver watch that he never let go. He would sleep with the watch in his palm, and even holding it to his cheek like a child that loves a plaything. Or he might dream of journeys and travels on a steamboat to Natchez. Yet she thought he dreamed of her; but even while she scrutinized him, the rods of the foot of the bed seemed to rise up like a rail fence between them, and she could see that people never could be sure of anything as long as one of them was asleep and the other awake. To look at him dreaming of her when he might be going to die frightened her a little, as if he might carry her with him that way, and she wanted to run out of the room. She took hold of the bed and held on, and Solomon opened his eyes and called her name, but he did not want anything. He would not taste the good broth.

Just a little after that, as she was taking up the ashes in the front room for the last time in the year, she heard a sound. It was somebody coming. She pulled the curtains together and looked through the slit.

Coming up the path under the bottle trees was a white lady. At first she looked young, but then she looked old. Marvelous to see, a little car stood steaming like a kettle out in the field-track—it had come without a road.

Livvie stood listening to the long, repeated knockings at the door, and after a while she opened it just a little. The lady came in through the crack, though she was more than middle-sized and wore a big hat.

My name is Miss Baby Marie, she said.

Livvie gazed respectfully at the lady and at the little suitcase she was holding close to her by the handle until the proper moment. The lady's eyes were running over the room, from palmetto to palmetto, but she was saying, "I live at home . . . out from Natchez . . . and get out and show these pretty cosmetic things to the white people and the colored people both . . . all around . . . years and years. . . . Both shades of powder and rouge. . . . It's the kind of work a girl can do and not go clear 'way from home . . ." And the harder she looked, the more she talked. Suddenly she turned up her nose and said, "It is not Christian or sanitary to put feathers in a vase," and then she took a gold key out of the front of her dress and began unlocking the locks on her suitcase. Her face drew the light, the way it was covered with intense white and red, with a little patty-cake of white between the wrinkles by her upper lip. Little red tassels of hair bobbed under the rusty wires of her picture-hat, as with an air of triumph and secrecy she now drew open her little suitcase and brought out bottle after bottle and jar after jar, which she put down on the table, the mantel-piece, the settee, and the organ.

"Did you ever see so many cosmetics in your life?" cried Miss Baby Marie.

"No'm," Livvie tried to say, but the cat had her tongue.

"Have you ever applied cosmetics?" asked Miss Baby Marie next.

"No'm," Livvie tried to say.

"Then look! she said, and pulling out the last thing of all, "Try this!" she said. And in her hand was unclenched a golden lipstick which popped open like magic. A fragrance came out of it like incense, and Livvie cried out suddenly, "Chinaberry flowers!"

Her hand took the lipstick, and in an instant she was carried away in the air through the spring, and looking down with a half-drowsy smile from a purple cloud she saw from above a chinaberry tree, dark and smooth and neatly leaved, neat as a guinea hen in the dooryard, and there was her home that she had left. On one side of the tree was her mama holding up her heavy apron, and she could see it was loaded with ripe figs, and on the other side was her papa holding a fish-pole over the pond, and she could see it transparently, the little clear fishes swimming up to the brim.

"Oh, no, not chinaberry flowers—secret ingredients," said Miss Baby Marie. "My cosmetics have secret ingredients—not chinaberry flowers."

"It's purple," Livvie breathed, and Miss Baby Marie said, "Use it freely. Rub it on."

Livvie tiptoed out to the wash stand on the front porch and before the mirror put the paint on her mouth. In the wavery surface her face danced before her like a flame. Miss Baby Marie followed her out, took a look at what she had done, and said, "That's it."

Livvie tried to say "Thank you" without moving her parted lips where the paint lay so new.

By now Miss Baby Marie stood behind Livvie and looked in the mirror over her shoulder, twisting up the tassles of her hair. "The lipstick I can let you have for only two dollars," she said, close to her neck.

"Lady, but I don't have no money, never did have," said Livvie.

"Oh, but you don't pay the first time. I make another trip, that's the way I do. I come back again—later."

"Oh," said Livvie, pretending she understood everything so as to please the lady.

"But if you don't take it now, this may be the last time I'll call at your house," said Miss Baby Marie sharply. "It's far away from any-where. I'll tell you that. You don't live close to anywhere."

"Yes'm. My husband, he keep the *money*," said Livvie, trembling. "He is strict as he can be. He don't know *you* walk in here—Miss Baby Marie!"

"Where is he?"

"Right now, he in yonder sound asleep, an old man. I wouldn't ever ask him for anything."

Miss Baby Marie took back the lipstick and packed it up. She gathered up the jars for both black and white and got them all inside the suitcase, with the same little fuss of triumph with which she had brought them out. She started away.

"Goodbye," she said, making herself look grand from the back, but at the last minute she turned around in the door. Her old hat wobbled as she whispered, "Let me see your husband."

Livvie obediently went on tiptoe and opened the door to the other room. Miss Baby Marie came behind her and rose on her tiptoes and looked in.

"My, what a little tiny old, old man!" she whispered, clasping her hands and shaking her head over them. "What a beautiful quilt! What a tiny old, old man!"

"He can sleep like that all day," whispered Livvie proudly.

They looked at him awhile so fast asleep, and then all at once they looked at each other. Somehow that was as if they had a secret, for he had never stirred. Livvie then politely, but all at once closed the door.

"Well! I'd certainly like to leave you with a lipstick!" said Miss Baby Marie vivaciously. She smiled in the door.

"Lady, but I told you I don't have no money, and never did have."

"And never will?" In the air and all around, like a bright halo around the white lady's nodding head, it was a true spring day.

"Would you take eggs, lady?" asked Livvie softly.

"No, I have plenty of eggs—plenty," said Miss Baby Marie.

"I still don't have no money," said Livvie, and Miss Baby Marie took her suitcase and went on somewhere else.

Livvie stood watching her go, and all the time she felt her heart beating in her left side. She touched the place with her hand. It seemed as if her heart beat and her whole face flamed from the pulsing color of her lips. She went to sit by Solomon and when he opened his eyes he could not see a change in her. "He's fixin' to die," she said inside. That was the secret. That was when she went out of the house for a little breath of air.

She went down the path and down the Natchez Trace a way, and she did not know how far she had gone, but it was not far, when she saw a sight. It was a man, looking like a vision—she standing on one side of the Old Natchez Trace and he standing on the other.

As soon as this man caught sight of her, he began to look himself over. Starting at the bottom with his pointed shoes, he began to look up, lifting his peg-top pants the higher to see fully his bright socks. His coat long and wide and leaf-green he opened like doors to see his high-up tawny pants and his pants he smoothed downward from the points of his collar, and he wore a luminous baby-pink satin shirt. At the end, he reached gently above his wide platter-shaped round hat, the color of a plum, and one finger touched at the feather, emerald green, blowing in the spring winds.

No matter how she looked, she could never look so fine as he did, and she was not sorry for that, she was pleased.

He took three jumps, one down and two up, and was by her side.

"My name is Cash," he said.

He had a guinea pig in his pocket. They began to walk along. She stared on and on at him, as if he were doing some daring spectacular thing, instead of just walking beside her. It was not simply the city way he was dressed that made her look at him and see hope in its insolence looking back. It was not only the way he moved along kicking the flowers as if he could break through everything in the way and destroy anything in the world, that made her eyes grow bright. It might be, if he had not appeared the way he did appear that day she would never have looked so closely at him, but the time people come makes a difference.

They walked through the still leaves of the Natchez Trace, the light and the shade falling through trees about them, the white irises shining like candles on the banks and the new ferns shining like green stars up in the oak branches. They came out at Solomon's house, bottle trees and all. Livvie stopped and hung her head.

Cash began whistling a little tune. She did not know what it was, but she had heard it before from a distance, and she had a revelation. Cash was a field hand. He was a transformed field hand. Cash belonged to Solomon. But he had stepped out of his overalls into this. There in front of Solomon's house he laughed. He had a round head, a round face, all of him was young, and he flung his head up, rolled it against the mare's-tail sky in his round hat, and he could laugh just to see Solomon's house sitting there. Livvie looked at it, and there was Solomon's black hat hanging on the peg on the front door, the blackest thing in the world.

"I been to Natchez," Cash said, wagging his head around against the sky. "I taken a trip, I ready for Easter!"

How was it possible to look so fine before the harvest? Cash must have stolen the money, stolen it from Solomon. He stood in the path and lifted his spread hand high and brought it down again and again in his laughter. He kicked up his heels, A little chill went through her. It was as if Cash was bringing that strong hand down to beat a drum or to rain blows upon a man, such an abandon and menace were in his laugh. Frowning, she went closer to him and his swinging arm drew her in at once and the fright was crushed from her body, as a little match-flame might be smothered out by what it lighted. She gathered the folds of his coat behind him and fastened her red lips to his mouth, and she was dazzled by herself then, the way he had been dazzled at himself to begin with.

In that instant she felt something that could not be told—that Solomon's death was at hand, that he was the same to her as if he were dead now. She cried out, and uttering little cries turned and ran for the house.

At once Cash was coming, following after, he was running behind her. He came close, and halfway up the path he laughed and passed her. He even picked up a stone and sailed it into the bottle trees. She put her hands over her head, and sounds clattered through the bottle trees like cries of outrage. Cash stamped and plunged zigzag up the front steps and in at the door.

When she got there, he had stuck his hands in his pockets and was turning slowly about in the front room. The little guinea pig peeped out. Around Cash, the pinned-up palmettoes looked as if a lazy green monkey had walked up and down and around the walls leaving green prints of his hands and feet.

She got through the room and his hands were still in his pockets, and she fell upon the closed door to the other room and pushed it open. She ran to Solomon's bed calling "Solomon! Solomon!" The little shape of the old man never moved at all, wrapped under the quilt as if it were winter still.

"Solomon!" She pulled the quilt away, but there was another one under that, and she fell on her knees beside him. He made no sound except a sigh, and then she could hear in the silence the light springy steps of Cash walking and walking in the front room, and the ticking of Solomon's silver watch, which came from the bed. Old Solomon was far away in his sleep, his face looked small, relentless, and devout, as if he were walking somewhere where she could imagine the snow falling.

Then there was a noise like a hoof pawing the floor, and the door gave a creak, and Cash appeared beside her. When she looked up, Cash's face was so black it was bright, and so bright and bare of pity that it looked sweet to her. She stood up and held her head. Cash was so powerful that his presence gave her strength even when she did not need any.

Under their eyes Solomon slept. People's faces tell of things and places not known to the one who looks at them while they sleep, and while Solomon slept under the eyes of Livvie and Cash his face told them like a mythical story that all his life he had built, little scrap by scrap, respect. A beetle could not have been more laborious or more ingenious in the task of its destiny. When Solomon was young, as he was in his picture overhead, it was the infinite thing with him, and he could see no end to the respect he would contrive and keep in a house. He had built a lonely house, the way he would make a cage, but it grew to be the same with him as a great monumental pyramid and sometimes in his absorption of getting it erected he was like the builder-slaves of Egypt who forgot or never knew the origin and the using of the thing to which they gave all the strength of their bodies and used up all their days. Livvie and Cash could see that as a man might rest from a life-labor he lay in his bed, and they could hear how, wrapped in his quilt, he sighed to himself comfortably in sleep, while in his dreams he might have been an ant, a beetle, a bird, an Egyptian, assembling and carrying on his back and building with his hands, or he might have been an old man of India or a swaddled baby, about to smile and brush all away.

Then without warning old Solomon's eyes flew wide open under the hedge-like brows. He was wide awake.

And instantly Cash raised his quick arm. A radiant sweat stood on his temples. But he did not bring his arm down—it stayed in the air, as if something might have taken hold.

It was not Livvie—she did not move. As if something said "Wait," she stood waiting. Even while her eyes burned under motionless lids, her lips parted in a stiff grimace, and her arms stiff at her sides she stood above the prone old man and the panting young one, erect and apart.

Movement when it came came in Solomon's face. It was an old and strict face, a frail face, but behind it, like a covered light, came an animation that could play hide and seek, that would dart and escape, had always escaped. The mystery flickered in him, and invited from his eyes. It was that very mystery that Cash with his quick arm would have to strike, and that Livvie could not weep for. But Cash only stood holding his arm in the air, when the gentlest flick of his great strength, almost a puff of his breath, would have been enough, if he had known how to give it, to send the old man over the obstruction that kept him away from death.

If it could not be that the tiny illumination in the fragile and ancient face caused a crisis, a mystery in the room that would not permit a blow to fall, at least it was certain that Cash, throbbing in his Easter clothes, felt a pang of shame that the vigor of a man would come to such an end that he could not be struck without warning. He took down his hand and stepped back behind Livvie, like a round-eyed schoolboy on whose unsuspecting head the dunce cap has been set.

"Young ones can't wait," said Solomon.

Livvie shuddered violently, and then in a gush of tears she stooped for a glass of water and handed it to him, but he did not see her.

"So here come the young man Livvie wait for. Was no prevention. No prevention. Now I lay eyes on young man and it come to be somebody I know all the time, and been knowing since he were born in a cotton patch, and watched grow up year to year, Cash McCord, growed to size, growed up to come in my house in the end—ragged and barefoot."

Solomon gave a cough of distaste. Then he shut his eyes vigorously, and his lips began to move like a chanter's.

"When Livvie married, her husband were already somebody. He had paid great cost for his land. He spread sycamore leaves over the ground from wagon to door, day he brought her home, so her foot would not have to touch ground. He carried her through his door. Then he growed old and could not lift her, and she were still young."

Livvie's sobs followed his words like a soft melody repeating each thing as he stated it. His lips moved for a little without sound, or she cried too fervently, and unheard he might have been telling his whole life, and then he said, "God forgive Solomon for sins great and small. God forgive Solomon for carrying away too young girl for wife and keeping her away from her people and from all the young people would clamor for her back."

Then he lifted up his right hand toward Livvie where she stood by the bed and offered her his silver watch. He dangled it before her eyes, and she hushed crying; her tears stopped. For a moment the watch could be heard ticking as it always did, precisely in his proud hand. She lifted it away. Then he took hold of the quilt; then he was dead.

Livvie left Solomon dead and went out of the room. Stealthily, nearly without noise, Cash went beside her. He was like a shadow, but his shiny shoes moved over the floor in spangles, and the green downy feather shone like a light in his hat. As they reached the front room, he seized her deftly as a long black cat and dragged her hanging by the waist round and round him, while he turned in a circle, his face bent down to hers. The first moment, she kept one arm and its hand stiff and still, the one that held Solomon's watch. Then the fingers softly let go, all of her was limp, and the watch fell somewhere on the floor. It ticked away in the still room, and all at once there began outside the full song of a bird.

They moved around and around the room and into the brightness of the open door, then he stopped and shook her once. She rested in silence in his trembling arms, unprotesting as a bird on a nest. Outside the redbirds were flying and criss-crossing, the sun was in all the bottles on the prisoned trees, and the young peach was shining in the middle of them with the bursting light of spring.

JOHN CHEEVER (1912–   )

John Cheever was born in Quincy, Massachusetts, to parents whom, according to his later remarks, he respected and liked—a refreshing novelty. But when he was sent to the Thayer Academy at nearby South Braintree, he found himself in an educational atmosphere that he could neither respect nor like, and in his junior year he was expelled for what one might call academic lassitude. He recorded his experience in a series of sketches under the general title, "Expelled," which was published in New Republic *in October, 1930. He may have thought that he had not learned much at Thayer, but how amazingly well he could already write!*

Once started, he published stories regularly—more in New Republic, *but some also in* Colliers, The Yale Review, Story, The Atlantic Monthly, *and then, finally, a long series over the years chiefly in* The New Yorker. *Most of these stories have been collected in five volumes.*

The first, The Way Some People Live *(1943), was published during his four-year hitch with the Army. The second,* The Enormous Radio and Other Stories *(1953), was published while he was working for the Columbia Broadcasting System (he wrote the script for "Life with Father," among others). There followed* The Housebreaker of Shady Hill and Other Stories *(1958);* Some People, Places and Things That Will Not Appear in My Next Novel *(1961); and* The Brigadier and the Golf Widow *(1964). The settings of most of these stories are New York City and, more frequently, New York suburbs; but in the last two volumes, the settings have been much extended, including a group set in Italy. The characters are almost always drawn from the same upper-middle-class world of people who are professional, knowledgeable, and bewildered.*

He has published three novels: The Wapshot Chronicle *(1957) and* The Wapshot Scandal *(1964)—the episodic, witty, sad, and rather gamey story of the Wapshot men in the old Massachusetts inland port of Saint Botolphs—and, most recently,* Bullet Park *(1969), set in suburbia again, a mordant dramatization of life among the Wasps.*

He himself now lives in Ossining, New York, and he says that he enjoys living in and writing about suburbia. Certainly he is one of its supreme historians. "The Swimmer," in the view of many, is its great epitaph.

FURTHER READING

For critical estimates see Ihab Hassan, Radical Innocence: Studies in the Contemporary American Novel *(1961), and John W. Aldridge,* Time to Murder and Create: The Contemporary Novel in Crisis *(1966).*

The Swimmer *(1964)*

It was one of those midsummer Sundays when everyone sits around saying, "I *drank* too much last night." You might have heard it whispered by the parishioners leaving church, heard it from the lips of the priest himself, struggling with his cassock in the *vestiarium,* heard it on the golf links and the tennis courts, heard it in the wildlife preserve, where the leader of the Audubon group was suffering from a terrible hangover.

"I *drank* too much," said Donald Westerhazy, at the edge of the Westerhazy's pool.

"We all *drank* too much," said Lucinda Merrill.

"It must have been the wine," said Helen Westerhazy. "I *drank* too much of that claret."

The pool, fed by an artesian well with a high iron content, was a pale shade of green. It was a fine day. In the west there was a massive stand of cumulus clouds, so like a city seen from a distance—from the bow of an approaching ship—that it might have had a name. Lisbon. Hackensack. The sun was hot. Neddy Merrill sat by the green water, one hand in it, one around a glass of gin. He was a slender man—he seemed to have the special slenderness of youth—and while he was far from young, he had slid down his banister that morning and given the bronze backside of Aphrodite on the hall table a smack, as he jogged toward the smell of coffee in his dining room. He might have been compared to a summer's day, particularly the last hours of one, and while he lacked a tennis racket or a sail bag, the impression was definitely one of youth, sport, and clement weather. He had been swimming, and now he was breathing deeply, stertorously, as if he could gulp into his lungs the components of that moment, the heat of the sun, the intenseness of his pleasure. It all seemed to flow into his chest. His own house stood in Bullet Park, eight miles to the south, where his four beautiful daughters would have had their lunch and might be playing tennis. Then it occurred to him that, by taking a dog-leg to the southwest, he could reach his home by water.

His life was not confining, and the delight he took in this thought could not be explained by its suggestion of escape. In his mind he saw, with a cartographer's eye, a string of swimming pools, a quasi-subterranean stream that curved across the county. He had made a discovery, a contribution to modern geography; he would name the stream Lucinda, after his wife. He was not a practical joker, nor was he a fool, but he was determinedly original, and had a vague and modest idea of himself as a legendary figure. The day was beautiful, and it seemed to him that a long swim might enlarge and celebrate its beauty.

He took off a sweater that was hung over his shoulders and dove in. He had a simple contempt for men who did not hurl themselves into pools. He swam a choppy crawl, breathing either with every other stroke or every fourth stroke, and counting somewhere well in the back of his mind the one-two one-two of a flutter kick. It was not a serviceable stroke for long distances, but the domestication of swimming had saddled the sport with some customs, and in his part of the world a crawl was customary. Being embraced and sustained by the light-green water seemed not as much a pleasure as the resumption of a natural condition, and he would have liked to swim without trunks, but this was not possible, considering his project. He hoisted himself up on the far curb—he never used the ladder—and started across the lawn. When Lucinda asked where he was going, he said he was going to swim home.

The only maps and charts he had to go by were remembered or imaginary, but these were clear enough. First there were the Grahams', the Hammers', the Lears', the Howlands', and the Crosscups'. He would cross Ditmar Street to the Bunkers' and come, after a short portage, to the Levys', the Welchers', and the public pool in Lancaster. Then there were the Hallorans', the Sachs', the Biswangers', the Shirley Abbot's, the Gilmartins', and the Clydes'. The day was lovely, and that he lived in a world so generously supplied with water seemed like a clemency, a beneficence. His heart was high, and he ran across the grass. Making his way home by an uncommon route gave him the feeling that he was a pilgrim, an explorer, a man with a destiny, and he knew that he would find friends all along the way; friends would line the banks of the Lucinda River.

He went through a hedge that separated the Westerhazy's land from the Grahams', walked under some flowering apple trees, passed the shed that housed their pump and filter, and came out at the Grahams' pool. "Why, Neddy," Mrs. Graham said, "what a marvellous surprise. I've been trying to get you on the phone all morning. Here, let me get you a drink." He saw then, like any explorer, that the hospitable customs and traditions of the natives would have to be handled with diplomacy if he was ever going to reach his destination. He did not want to mystify or seem rude to the Grahams, nor did he have time to linger there. He swam the length of their pool and joined them in the sun. A few minutes later, two carloads of friends arrived from Connecticut. During the uproarious reunions he was able to slip away. He went down by the front of the Grahams' house, stepped over a thorny hedge, and crossed a vacant lot to the Hammers'. Mrs. Hammer, looking up from her roses, saw him swim by, although she wasn't quite sure who it was. The Lears heard him splashing past the open windows of their living room. The Howlands and the Crosscups were away. After leaving the Crosscups', he crossed Ditmar Street and started for the Bunkers', where he could hear, even at that distance, the noise of a party.

The water refracted the sound of voices and laughter and seemed to suspend it in midair. The Bunkers' pool was on a rise, and he climbed some stairs to a terrace where twenty-five or thirty men and women were drinking. The only person in the water was Rusty Towers, who floated there on a rubber raft. Oh, how bonny and lush were the banks of the Lucinda River! Prosperous men and women gathered by the sapphire-colored waters while caterer's men in white coats passed them cold gin. Overhead, a red de Havilland trainer was circling around and around and around in the sky, with something like the glee of a child in a swing. Ned felt a passing affection for the scene, a tenderness for the gathering, as if it was something he might touch. In the distance he heard thunder.

As soon as Enid Bunker saw him, she began to scream, "Oh, look who's here! What a marvellous surprise! When Lucinda said that you couldn't come, I thought I'd *die*. . . ." She made her way to him through the crowd, and when they had finished kissing, she led him to the bar, a progress that was slowed by the fact that he stopped to kiss eight or ten other women and shake the hands of as many men. A smiling bartender

he had seen at a hundred parties gave him a gin-and-tonic, and Ned
stood by the bar for a moment, anxious not to get stuck in any conversation that would delay his voyage. When he seemed about to be surrounded, he dove in and swam close to the side, to avoid colliding with
Rusty's raft. He climbed out at the far end of the pool, bypassed the
Tomlinsons with a broad smile, and jogged up the garden path. The
gravel cut his feet, but this was the only unpleasantness.

The party was confined to the pool, and as he went toward the
house he heard the brilliant, watery sound of voices fade, heard the
noise of a radio from the Bunkers' kitchen, where someone was listening to a ball game. Sunday afternoon. He made his way through the
parked cars and down the grassy border of their driveway to Alewives'
Lane. He did not want to be seen on the road in his bathing trunks, but
there was no traffic, and he made the short distance to the Levys' driveway, marked with a "Private Property" sign and a green tube for the
Times. All the doors and windows of the big house were open, but there
were no signs of life, not even a barking dog. He went around the side of
the house to the pool and saw that the Levys had only recently left. Glasses
and bottles and dishes of nuts were on a table at the deep end, where
there was a bathhouse or gazebo, hung with Japanese lanterns. After
swimming the pool, he got himself a glass and poured a drink. It was
his fourth or fifth drink, and he had swum nearly half the length of the
Lucinda River. He felt tired, clean, and pleased at that moment to be
alone, pleased with everything.

It would storm. The stand of cumulus cloud—that city—had risen
and darkened, and while he sat there, he heard thunder. The de Havi-
land trainer was still circling overhead, and it seemed to Ned that he
could almost hear the pilot laugh with pleasure in the afternoon; but
when there was another peal of thunder, he took off for home. A train
whistle blew, and he wondered what time it had gotten to be. Four?
Five? He thought of the station where, at that hour, a waiter, his tuxedo
concealed by a raincoat, a dwarf with some flowers wrapped in newspaper, and a woman who had been crying would be waiting for the
local. It was suddenly growing dark—it was that moment when the pin-
headed birds seem to organize their song into some acute and knowledgeable recognition of the storms' approach. From the crown of an oak
at his back, there was a fine noise of rushing water, as if a spigot there
had been turned on. Then the noise of fountains came from the crowns
of all the tall trees. Why did he love storms? What was the meaning of
his excitement when the front door sprang open and the rain wind fled
rudely up the stairs? Why had the simple task of shutting the windows
of an old house seemed fitting and urgent? Why did the first watery
notes of a storm wind have for him the unmistakable sound of good
news, cheer, glad tidings? There was an explosion, a smell of cordite,
and rain lashed the Japanese lanterns that Mrs. Levy had bought in
Kyoto the year before last, or was it the year before that?

He stayed in the Levys' gazebo until the storm had passed. The rain had cooled the air and he shivered. The force of the wind had stripped a maple of its red and yellow leaves and scattered them over the grass and the water. Since it was midsummer, the tree must be blighted, and yet he felt a sadness at this sign of autumn. He braced his shoulders, emptied his glass, and started for the Welchers' pool. This meant crossing the Pasterns' riding ring, and he was surprised to find it overgrown with grass and all the jumps dismantled. Had the Pasterns sold their horses or gone away for the summer and put them out to board? He seemed to remember having heard something about the Pasterns and their horses, but the memory was unclear. On he went, barefoot, through the wet grass to the Welchers', where he found that their pool was dry.

This breach in his chain of water disappointed him absurdly, and he felt like an explorer who is seeking a torrential headwater and finds a dead stream. He was disappointed and mystified. It was common enough to go away for the summer, but people never drained their pools. The Welchers' had definitely gone away. The pool furniture was folded, stacked, and covered with a tarpaulin. The bathhouse was locked. All the windows of the house were shut, and when he went around to the driveway in front, he saw a "For Sale" sign nailed to a tree. When had he last heard from the Welchers—when, that is, had he and Lucinda last regretted an invitation to dine with them? It seemed only a week or so ago. Was his memory failing, or had he so disciplined it in the repression of unpleasant facts that he had damaged his sense of the truth? In the distance he heard the sound of a tennis game. This cheered him, cleared away all his apprehensions, and let him regard the overcast sky and the cold air with indifference. This was the day that Neddy Merrill swam across the county. That was the day! He started off then for his most difficult portage.

Had you gone for a Sunday-afternoon ride that day, you might have seen him, close to naked, standing on the shoulder of Route 424, waiting for a chance to cross. You might have wondered if he was the victim of foul play, or had his car broken down, or was he merely a fool? Standing barefoot in the deposits of the highway—beer cans, rags, and blowout patches—exposed to all kinds of ridicule, he seemed pitiful. He had known when he started that this was a part of his journey—it had been on his imaginary maps—but, confronted with the lines of traffic worming through the summery light, he found himself unprepared. He was laughed at, jeered at, a beer can was thrown at him, and he had no dignity or humor to bring to the situation. He could have gone back, back to the Westerhazy's, where Lucinda would still be sitting in the sun. He had signed nothing, vowed nothing, pledged nothing—not even to himself. Why, believing as he did that all human obduracy was susceptible to common sense, was he unable to turn back?

Why was he determined to complete his journey, even if it meant putting his life in danger? At what point had this prank, this joke, this piece of horseplay become serious? He could not go back, he could not even recall with any clearness the green water at the Westerhazys', the sense of inhaling the day's components, the friendly and relaxed voices saying that they had *drunk* too much. In the space of an hour, more or less, he had covered a distance that made his return impossible.

An old man, tooling down the highway at fifteen miles an hour, let him get to the middle of the road, where there was a grass divider. Here he was exposed to the ridicule of the northbound traffic, but after ten or fifteen minutes he was able to cross. From here he had only a short walk to the Recreation Center at the edge of the village of Lancaster, where there were some handball courts and a public pool.

The effect of water on voices, the illusion of brilliance and suspense, was the same here as it had been at the Bunkers', but the sounds here were louder, harsher, and more shrill, and as soon as he entered the crowded enclosure he was confronted with regimentation. "ALL SWIMMERS MUST TAKE A SHOWER BEFORE USING THE POOL. ALL SWIMMERS MUST USE THE FOOT-BATH. ALL SWIMMERS MUST WEAR THEIR IDENTIFICATION DISCS." He took a shower, washed his feet in a cloudy and bitter solution, and made his way to the edge of the water. It stank of chlorine and looked to him like a sink. A pair of lifeguards in a pair of towers blew police whistles at what seemed to be regular intervals, and abused the swimmers through a public-address system. Neddy remembered the sapphire water at the Bunkers' with longing, and thought that he might contaminate himself—damage his own prosperousness and charm—by swimming in this murk, but he reminded himself that he was an explorer, a pilgrim, and that this was merely a stagnant bend in the Lucinda River. He dove, scowling with distaste, into the chlorine, and had to swim with his head above water to avoid collisions, but even so he was bumped into, splashed, and jostled. When he got to the shallow end, both lifeguards were shouting at him: "Hey, you, you without the identification disc, get outa the water!" He did. They had no way of pursuing him, and he went through the reek of sun-tan oil and chlorine, out through the hurricane fence and past the handball courts. Crossing the road, he entered the wooded part of the Halloran estate. The woods were not cleared, and the footing was treacherous and difficult, until he reached the lawn and the clipped beech hedge that encircled the pool.

The Hallorans were friends, an elderly couple of enormous wealth who seemed to bask in the suspicion that they might be Communists. They were zealous reformers, but they were not Communists, and yet when they were accused, as they sometimes were, of subversion, it seemed to gratify and excite them. Their beech hedge was yellow, and he guessed it was suffering from a blight, like the Levys' maple. He called "Hullo, hullo," to warn the Hallorans of his approach. The Hallorans, for reasons that had never been explained to him, did not wear bathing suits. No explanations were in order, really. Their nakedness was a detail in their uncompromising zeal for reform, and he stepped politely out of his trunks before he went through the opening in the hedge.

Mrs. Halloran, a stout woman with white hair and a serene face, was reading the *Times*. Mr. Halloran was taking beech leaves out of the water with a scoop. They seemed neither surprised nor displeased to see him. Their pool was perhaps the oldest in the neighborhood, a fieldstone rectangle fed by a brook. It had no filter or pump, and its waters were the opaque gold of the stream.

"I'm swimming across the county," Ned said.

"Why, I didn't know one could!" exclaimed Mrs. Halloran.

"Well, I've made it from the Westerhazys'," Ned said. "That must be about four miles."

He left his trunks at the deep end, walked to the shallow end, and swam back. As he was pulling himself out of the water, he heard Mrs. Halloran say, "We've been *terribly* sorry to hear about all your misfortunes, Neddy."

"My misfortunes?" Ned asked. "I don't know what you mean."

"Why, we heard that you'd sold the house, and that your poor children . . ."

"I don't recall having sold the house," Ned said, "and the girls are at home."

"Yes," Mrs. Halloran sighed. "Yes . . ."

Her voice filled the air with an unseasonable melancholy, and Ned said briskly, "Thank you for the swim."

"Well, have a nice trip," said Mrs. Halloran.

Beyond the hedge, he pulled on his trunks and fastened them. They were loose, and he wondered if during the space of an afternoon he could have lost some weight. He was cold, and he was tired, and the naked Hallorans and their dark water had depressed him. The swim was too much for his strength, but how could he have guessed this, sliding down the banister that morning and sitting in the Westerhazys' sun? His arms were lame. His legs felt rubbery and ached at the joints. The worst of it was the cold in his bones, and the feeling that he might never be warm again. Leaves were falling around him and he smelled woodsmoke on the wind. Who would be burning wood in the fireplace at this time of year?

He needed a drink. Whiskey would warm him, pick him up, carry him through the last of his journey, refresh his feeling that it was original and valorous to swim across the county. Channel swimmers took brandy. He needed a stimulant. He crossed the lawn in front of the Hallorans' house and went down a little path to where they had built a house for their only daughter, Helen, and her husband, Eric Sachs. The Sachs' pool was small, and he found Helen and her husband there.

"Oh, *Neddy!*" Helen said. "Did you lunch at Mother's?"

"Not *really*," Ned said. "I *did* stop to see your parents." This seemed to be explanation enough. "I'm terribly sorry to break in on you like this, but I've taken a chill, and I wonder if you'd give me a drink."

"Why, I'd *love* to," Helen said, "but there hasn't been anything in this house to drink since Eric's operation. That was three years ago."

Was he losing his memory, had his gift for concealing painful facts let him forget that he had sold his house, that his children were in trouble, and that his friend had been ill? Ned's eyes slipped from Eric's face to his abdomen, where he saw three pale, sutured scars, two of them at least a foot long. Gone was his navel, and what, Neddy thought, would the roving hand, bed-checking one's gifts at 3 A.M., make of a belly with no navel, no link to birth, this breach in the succession?

"I'm sure you can get a drink at the Biswangers'," Helen said. "They're having an enormous do. You can hear it from here. Listen!"

She raised her head, and from across the road, the lawns, the gardens, the woods, the fields he heard again the brilliant noise of voices over water. "Well, I'll get wet," he said, still feeling that he had no freedom of choice about his means of travel. He dove into the Sachs' cold water, and, gasping, close to drowning, made his way from one end of the pool to the other. " Lucinda and I want *terribly* to see you," he said over his shoulder, his face set toward the Biswangers'. "We're sorry it's been so long, and we'll call you *very* soon."

He crossed some fields to the Biswangers' and the sounds of revelry there. They would be honored to give him a drink, they would be happy to give him a drink, they would, in fact, be lucky to give him a drink. The Biswangers invited him and Lucinda for dinner four times a year, six weeks in advance. They were always rebuffed, and yet they continued to send out their invitations, unwilling to comprehend the rigid and undemocratic realities of their society. They were the sort of people who discussed the price of things at cocktails, exchanged market tips during dinner, and after dinner told dirty stories to mixed company. They did not belong to Neddy's set—they were not even on Lucinda's Christmas-card list. He went toward their pool with feelings of indifference, charity, and some unease, since it seemed to be getting dark and these were the longest days of the year. The party when he joined it was noisy and large. Grace Biswanger was the kind of hostess who asked the ophthalmologist, the veterinarian, the real-estate dealer, and the dentist. No one was swimming, and the twilight, reflected on the water of the pool, had a wintery gleam. There was a bar, and he started for it. When Grace Biswanger saw him, she came toward him, not affectionately, as he had every right to expect, but bellicosely.

"Why, this party has everything," she said loudly, "including a gate-crasher."

She could not deal him a social blow—there was no question about this—and he did not flinch. "As a gate-crasher," he asked politely, "do I rate a drink?"

"Suit yourself," she said.

She turned her back on him and joined some guests, and he went to the bar and ordered a whiskey. The bartender served him, but rudely. His was a world in which the caterer's men kept the social score, and to be rebuffed by a part-time barkeep meant that he had suffered some loss of social esteem. Or perhaps the man was new and uninformed. Then at his back he heard Grace say, "They went broke overnight—nothing but income—and he showed up drunk one Sunday and asked us to loan him five thousand dollars. . . ." She was always talking about money. It was worse than eating your peas off a knife. He dove into the pool, swam its length, and went away.

The next pool on his list, the last but two, belonged to his old mistress, Shirley Abbott. If he had suffered any injuries at the Biswangers', they would be cured here. Love—sexual roughhouse, in fact—was the supreme elixir, the painkiller, the brightly colored pill that would put the spring back into his step, the joy of life in his heart. They had had an affair last week, last month, last year. He couldn't remember. It was he who had broken it off, his was the upper hand, and as he stepped through the gate of the wall that surrounded her pool it seemed to be his pool, since the lover, particularly the illicit lover, enjoys the possessions of his mistress with an authority unknown to holy matrimony. She was there, her hair the color of brass, but her figure, at the edge of the lighted, cerulean water, excited in him no profound memories. It had been, he thought, a lighthearted affair, although she wept when he broke it off. She seemed confused to see him. If she was still wounded, would she, God forbid, weep again?

"What do you want?" she asked.

"I'm swimming across the county."

"Good Christ. Will you ever grow up?"

"What's the matter?"

"If you've come here for money," she said, "I won't give you another cent."

"You could give me a drink."

"I could, but I won't. I'm not alone."

"Well, I'm on my way."

He dove in and swam the pool, but when he tried to haul himself up onto the curb, he found that the strength in his arms and his shoulders had gone, and he paddled to the ladder and climbed out. Looking over his shoulder, he saw, in the lighted bathhouse, a young man. Going out onto the dark lawn, he smelled chrysanthemums or marigolds—some stubborn autumnal fragrance on the night air, strong as gas. Looking overhead, he saw that the stars had come out, but why should he seem to see Andromeda, Cepheus, and Cassiopeia? What had become of the constellations of midsummer? He began to cry.

It was probably the first time in his adult life that he had ever cried—certainly the first time in his life that he had ever felt so miserable, cold, tired, and bewildered. He could not understand the rudeness of the caterer's barkeep, or the rudeness of a mistress who had once come to him on her knees and showered his trousers with tears. He had swum too long, he had been immersed too long, and his nose and his throat were sore from the water. What he needed then was a drink, some company, and some clean dry clothes, and while he could have cut directly across the road to his home, he went on, instead, to the Gilmartins' pool. Here, for the first time in his life, he did not dive but went down the steps into the icy water and swam a hobbled sidestroke that he might have learned as a child. He staggered with fatigue on his way to the Clydes', and paddled the length of their pool, stopping again and again, with his hand on the curb, to rest. He climbed up the ladder and wondered if he had the strength to get home. He had done what he wanted—he had swum the county—but he was so stupefied with exhaustion that his triumph seemed vague. Stooped, holding onto the gateposts for support, he turned up the driveway of his own house.

The place was dark. Had Lucinda stayed at the Westerhazys' for supper? Had the girls joined her there, or gone someplace else? Hadn't they agreed, as they usually did on Sunday, to regret all their invitations and stay at home?

He tried the garage doors, to see what cars were in, but the doors were locked and rust came off the handles. Going toward the house, he saw that the force of the thunderstorm had knocked one of the rain gutters loose. It hung down over the front door like an umbrella rib, but it could be fixed in the morning. The house was locked, and he thought that the stupid cook or the stupid maid must have locked the place up, until he remembered that it had been some time since they had employed a maid or a cook. He shouted, pounded on the door, tried to force it with his shoulder, and then, looking in at the windows, saw that the place was empty.

RALPH [WALDO] *ELLISON* (1914–   )

*Ralph Ellison was born in Oklahoma City, Oklahoma, and while he
   suffered from the limitations and the indignities that we have
   always imposed upon people of his race, he did not suffer them with
   that excess that has characterized the youth of many other black
   writers, and he could later write, "I felt no innate sense of inferiority
   which would keep me from getting those things I desired out of life."
   He attended segregated schools, but many of his teachers were good,
   and he could cultivate not only his interest in jazz music through the*

community but also his deep interest in classical music through programs offered at school. He also read omnivorously, as his father had before him.

He *attended Tuskegee Institute from 1933 to 1936 with the hope of becoming a composer of symphonies. He went to New York where he met Richard Wright, who was about to publish "Uncle Tom's Children," and through Wright he wrote and published his first review and his first story and became interested in radical politics. Much of his work in the late thirties and early forties appeared in* The New Masses, *although he was never a Communist, and indeed, after about 1943 he ceased to have any very active interest in politics of any kind. But his stories, as they continued to appear, were consistently concerned with the problem of racial identity and of the imperative necessity that the white man recognize it in its full complexity. These stories, up and through "King of the Bingo Game" (1941), have not been collected; they should be, and on their own account, not only because in their underlying concerns and in their developing techniques, their excursions into the fantastic, the macabre, the absurd, they prefigure that major work,* Invisible Man *(1953), to which Ellison was now to dedicate himself.*

Later *he published a book of essays,* Shadow and Act *(1964), and in one of these, "Hidden Name and Complex Fate," he tells how, as a small boy, he was bewildered and plagued by his name, Ralph Waldo Ellison. Who was Ralph Waldo Emerson? He denied the middle name until he learned who Emerson was and what Emerson believed in.*

Ironically *enough, in* Invisible Man, *the white philanthropist urges the young black narrator to read Emerson, assuring him that "Self-reliance is a most worthy virtue." The young man does, and, in the course of his following appalling experiences, satirizes the actualities of that American virtue. And yet, at the end of the novel, as he is about to emerge from underground, he himself vows to "affirm the principle on which the country was built and not the men, or at least not the men who did the violence." At the end of his essay Ellison himself writes, ". . . remember that I did not destroy that troublesome middle name of mine, I only suppressed it."*

It *is probably a strain of Emersonian optimism, surviving and tempered by a full imaginative experience of the most debasing horrors, that marks Ellison off from other black writers. Like the hero of "Out of the Hospital and Under the Bar"—a long section of* Invisible Man *that did not finally fit there and was eliminated—his people must be freed from the monolithic machine of a repressive white culture and from a moral and psychological underground life, into their full humanity in all its individual differences; and—more than that— they can be.*

FURTHER READING

Although Ellison has published only one novel, he has received considerable critical attention. See Robert Bone, *The Negro Novel in America* (1958); Joseph J. Waldmeir, editor, *Recent American Fiction: Some Critical Views* (1960); Ihab Hassan, *Radical Innocence: Studies in the Contemporary American Novel* (1961); Marcus Klein, *After Alienation* (1964); Jonathan Baumbach, *The Landscape of Nightmare* (1965); and Seymour L. Gross and John Edward Hardy, editors, *Images of the Negro in American Literature* (1966).

Author's Note

The following narrative formed a part of the original version of a novel called *Invisible Man*, and it marked an attempt to get the hero of that memoir out of the hospital into the world of Harlem. It was Mary's world, the world of the urbanized (or partially urbanized), Negro folk, and I found it quite pleasurable to discover, during those expansive days of composition before the necessities of publication became a reality, that it was Mary, a woman of the folk, who helped release the hero from the machine. I was quite sorry that considerations of space made it necessary that I reconceive the development.

I am pleased for Mary's sake to see this version in print. She deserved more space in the novel and would, I think, have made it a better book. . . .

Reading it now, almost ten years after it was put aside, I have the feeling that it stands on its own if only as one of those pieces of writing which consists mainly of one damned thing after another sheerly happening. If I am right, then it is still in tune with our times and an amusing *riff* on the old theme of "Ain't Life the Damndest?"—with the added advantage that it's happening to the hero (who is something of a liar, if you ask me) and not the reader.

For those who would care to fit it back into *Invisible Man* let them start at the point where the explosion occurs in the paint factory, substitute the following happenings, and leave them once the hero is living in Mary's home.

For those who desire more than the sheer narrative ride, who hunger and thirst for "meaning," let them imagine what this country would be without its Marys. Let them imagine, indeed, what the American Negro would be without the Marys of our ever-expanding Harlems. Better still, since fiction is always a collaboration between writer and reader, let them take this proffered middle, this *agon*, this passion, and supply their own beginning, and if an ending, a moral, or a perception is needed, let them supply their own. For me, of course, the narrative *is* the meaning.

Out of the Hospital
and Under the Bar *(1961)*

When I awakened she stood looking down. Her newly straightened hair gleamed glossily in the intense light, her blue uniform freshly ironed and stiffly starched. Seeing me awake she shook her head and grinned. I tensed, expecting a trick. But not this time. Instead, she tried seriously to communicate with me. Her mood was solemn, and I was almost sure that I understood some of her shouted questions. But just as I had been unable to put my own ideas into words, now I could not put the movements of her lips into definite patterns. Who was she anyway? Why this feeling that I had known her for a long time? Whatever it was she was saying seemed very serious and it included both of us. I watched her, puzzled. Her question was escaping me. She threw up her hands, "Shucks!" she said.

"Shucks!" She froze, her eyes looking into the case, studying something I could not see. What's happening? Was this another trick? She was as still as a mountain. Will she spit upon the lid again? I thought with disgust. My mind overflowed with fore-bodings of danger. My mouth grew dry. Yet above me she stood as still as before—until, drawn by some almost imperceptible movement of her hands, I saw the whorls of her fingertips pressing worn and fish-belly white now from her blood-draining pressure upon the lids, her worn fingers arching back to palms I could not see.

She drummed upon the glass making a series of light padding sounds, her eyes lost in abstraction. It stopped abruptly, her fingers darting out of my range of vision, disappearing completely. I could not see them about her face, which still leaned over my case; nor below, where through the glass side, I saw her harsh blue uniform. They had to be somewhere along the chromium upper edge of the case where the lid joined the side. Then with a start, I saw them darting along the side of the case. A grating sound began. What on earth! Was she insane? She was twisting the bolts! Visions of calamity flashed through my head. I was in a panic. Suddenly I no longer wanted to be freed. What if she was opening the case too soon? Before my treatment was complete? Suppose she turned the wrong bolts and set the machinery in motion? A strange animal sound filled the case. I tugged at the arm straps, both afraid and furious, seeing her calm and controlled above me as though freeing people from intricate machines was a usual thing. "Stop it! Stop it!" I thought, tugging vainly at the straps. For though I wanted release, I was frightened lest it should come through this ignorant, unscientific old woman. Where was the doctor? Why didn't somebody come? The grating of bolts continued. She frowned, saying "Shhhh, shhhh!" and the animal sounds ceased. Straightening, she looked in with deep conspiratorial expression as she spread her arms along the edge of the lid and lifted. "No," I thought, pressing against the bottom of the case, "oh no!"

I held my breath waiting for the flash of short-circuited wires, the blasting shock into oblivion, waiting an eternity, it seemed, but nothing happened. The lid failed to budge. Not even a charge of static flashed over me.

"Shucks!" her lips made.

I shut my eyes as she set herself, lifting. There came a small quick sound, then a click. I looked up. A wave of nausea struck me. There, beneath the lid and inches above my head protruded her work-swollen fingers. I felt an irrational desire to retch as I watched them strain with the heavy lid. My eyes were drawn to their scarred, leather-brown texture, the smooth polish of the knuckles. Suddenly I saw them straighten and work in the air, like the legs of an obscene insect rolled upon its back. The finger-tips turned alternately white and pink as she tried to bring back circulation. I was seized by a savage impulse to bite them. But my head could not raise that far. A new sound arose! I had started to moan, when before my eyes the lid now raised a few inches, brought a rush of ether-laden air, and my stomach heaved. The air set off a thermostatic device inside the machine which, as I saw the lid come trembling down, clicked off. A mixture of relief and despair flooded over me as I saw an expression of pain grip her features. Sweat popped upon her forehead, her fingers were caught beneath the lid. Her face glowed up with pain. The rasping of tense breathing came to me. I saw her face set in determined lines as, with the heavy lid still knifing into her fingers, she studied the side of the case. Abruptly I saw her jaws snap shut, the muscles of her throat, roping out as she lifted, the lid rising a tortuous fraction and halting in precarious balance as she sent her right hand sliding swiftly along the edge of the case, giving a sudden twist. I saw a shiny bolt flip between the side of the case and the lid, landing with a faint click. Amazed, I saw her pull her fingers free, then turn quickly to the other end of the case. Another bolt fell into place, and I saw her step back, holding her fingers and breathing heavily. The strange outside air rushed upon me, making me suddenly light-headed. A turmoil of emotions filled me.

"How's that?" she said, peering in through the crack. "I knowed I could get that doggone thing open if I tried. How you feeling?"

I stared dumbly into her bright eyes.

Well you could be sociable," she said. "How come you don't say nothing? Is you all right?"

I looked into her face, feeling things begin to rush inside of me. A single drop of blood showed on a fingertip that rested upon the edge of the case. "Like dark red wine," I though light-headedly, her voice was strangely familiar. Who was she? A lost relative, a member of my forgotten family come to the North leaving no forwarding address? An aunt whom I didn't know? Hell no, she's crazy, I thought, realizing what she had done. She *must* be crazy. Why doesn't someone come? But for the slight sighing moan of the machine, it was quiet. Time itself seemed to move to the dragging moans of the mechanism, punctuated by her rasping breath. Far back within me, crouching on the bottom of the case, I waited for an explosion, feeling that an outrageous crime had been committed—for which I would be sacrificed. A furious resentment grew within me.

"Say, son!" she said. "Is you a dummy or something? You look intelligent, so how come you don't say something? Why these white folks got you in this iron straight-jacket?"

A ringing set up in my ears.

Her eyes swept the machine and as she soothed her mashed fingers she snickered, "You must be awful strong for them to have to put you under all this pile of junk. *Awful* strong. Who they think you is, Jack the Bear or John Henry [1] or somebody like that? . . . Say something, fool!"

Something seemed to give way. "You, you, you! . . ." I shouted angrily, a vile name fighting for expression, and stopped short, surprised. I still had a voice! I could talk! My eyes filled with uncontrollable tears. My anger faded. I looked at her and she seemed to understand.

"Well, at least you can talk," she said. "How you feel?"

"Fine," I whispered hoarsely, "I feel fine."

"What's supposed to be wrong with you?"

"I don't remember, but I'm all right now."

"What you mean you don't remember? You in there, ain't you? Now when *I* was in the hospital I had a tumor. They damn near took out all my works—all but the important ones, that is," she added coyly. "So don't come telling me you don't remember."

"But, I don't," I said. "I've forgotten nearly everything!"

"You *what?*"

"That's right, my memory's gone. I've lost it."

"Shucks, boy, I ain't one of them doctors. You don't have to tell me that stuff. How long you been from down home?"

"I don't remember," I said, "but I don't think it's been long."

She grinned through the crack knowingly. "You must have left in a hurry. Yeah, a heap leaves in a hurry, you know. But you ain't fooling me. I heard them nurses talking 'bout you. They say they even got one of the psychiatristses and a socialist or sociologist or something looking at you all the time."

"A psychiatrist!"

"Sho. I was in here cleaning one day when they come in and I liked to laughed myself sick seeing them write you all them questions when a fool could see you couldn't answer through all that glass anyway. And I says to myself, that there is the gamest young scamp I most ever seen, laying up there making a fool outa them doctors. He ain't no more sick than I am!"

---

[1] Folklore strongmen of work-camp gangs in the nineteenth century.

I tried to piece it together. "How long have I been here?" I asked.

"Eight or nine days—say, don't you want something to eat?"

"Eat?"

"Yeah," she said, straightening and looking around. "They don't never feed nobody enough in this place."

Then stooping to the crack again she said, "I be back in a minute. You don't have to worry 'bout the nurse, she won't be looking in here for a while, cause she's off with her intern boy friend. Be right back."

She moved away. I heard a door open and close. So old friendly face was a psychiatrist. Perhaps I *was* crazy, crazy in my private room. All by myself. "Food." My stomach growled. Breathing the outside air seemed to have given me a sharp appetite. This old Mary, she'd probably get me confined to this machine for months and months—and get herself fired. Who was she and why had she bothered?

"Here," she said, her bright eyes peeping through the cracked lid. "All I could find was some kind of canned meat, but it's got some good ole pork in it and that's what a down-home boy like you needs."

Saliva welled from the wall of my mouth as I saw the trimmed sandwich bread appear near the crack. "Here," she said. Then we both realized that I could not reach it.

"You'd think it was enough for them to have you in that thing," she scolded, "but here they have to tie your hands as well. Let's see . . ." she said, trying to reach beneath the lid to release my arm. The space was too narrow.

She shook her head. "Guess I'll have to feed you myself," she said. "Open your mouth."

"What?"

"I say open your mouth . . . Lord, here I is feeding another baby. A big ole rusty baby!"

I saw her break off a piece of the sandwich and push her fingers beneath the lid. I didn't like the idea.

"Aw here, boy!" she snapped, tossing the bit of sandwich. For a moment it balanced beneath my nose—long enough for me to catch its odor and snap it up viciously. It was delicious; strange and yet familiar in my mouth. So delicious that I swallowed my anger with the bread and waited eagerly for the next morsel. She sat beside me, looking through with a pleased expression—as though actually feeding a baby.

I could taste the sweet starch of the bread ball and the meat spreading beneath the motion of my teeth. As soon as I swallowed she dropped in another.

"Just look at him eat," she said. "I bet ain't nothing wrong with you a few square meals won't cure. And maybe you a little lonesome too. That's it, you need some company. But I bet you that's all."

I continued to chew, thinking, "No, it isn't all." I wasn't lonesome for people, because I didn't remember anyone. If anything, I was lonesome for my lost name—whatever it was. Suppose it's Cootie Brown! I Thought, or "Dobby Hicks" or "Mr. I. P. Freely"?

"Son, you was fooling about forgetting your name, warn't you?" she said as though reading my mind.

"No, I've really forgotten it."

"Well, what you going to do when they send you to the other hospital?"

"*Other* hospital?"

"Sho. They suppose to transfer you. I heard them saying something about it the other day."

Looking into her eyes shining through the cracked lid I felt myself slipping into a bottomless hole. I was sure that I was not asleep, yet it was as though I dreamed.

"They intends to watch you a while," she was saying. "They wants to study your case."

"I've got to get out of here," I said. "I've got to get out right away."

"Boy, you can't go nowhere," she said, her voice rising. "You too weak."

"I'm not weak," I said.

"Sho, you weak. You ain't had no exercise."

"I'm not weak," I insisted. "It's just that my hands are strapped."

She looked at me. "That's right."

"Sure, that's why I seem to be weak. If my hands were freed, I'd show you."

She hesitated. "You don't have to worry right away," she said. "They ain't going to transfer you until sometime next week."

"Are you sure?"

"That's right."

"I've got to get out of here," I said.

"Son, you sho you ain't in some kind of trouble?"

"Trouble?"

"You can tell me," she said, her voice kindly.

"I think so," I said, "I must be. But I can't remember what I did."

"Shucks, there you go lying to me agin!"

"But you're wrong. I'm telling the truth."

She shook her head in silent disbelief.

"Look," I said, "these people might kill me. Nobody knows me. They can do anything they want with me and no one would say a word."

I began to cough, my throat was dry. It became violent.

"Wait, I'll get you some water," she said. "I be back in a second."

I had to get away, how would I do it? If only she'd release my hands! Perhaps then I could think much better. I had to leave, for I feared that now that I was becoming adjusted to this machine, they planned to place me in one that was smaller—more severe. I'd probably be killed next time. If only she'd release my arms, I thought as she appeared with a glass of water.

"Here." She pushed the glass toward the crack and discovering that it was too narrow I had an idea.

"How you get your water?" she asked.

"Through a tube they stick through the lid," I said.

"I don't see no tube. . . . Wonder where they keep it."

"I don't know," I said, pretending to go into a fit of coughing. She looked around hastily, then attempted to push the glass of water into the case. I continued coughing.

"I'll have to open this thing wider," she said fretfully, leaving to get rid of the glass and returning to lift upon the lid. It didn't budge. I coughed more violently, gasping for breath. She lifted again.

"Hurry please," I gasped between coughs. But it was too heavy. After a moment she stopped, breathing tiredly, looking into my distorted face. I had actually started myself to coughing now. For a minute it got completely out of hand, sending great gusts of saliva spraying against the glass.

"Loosen my arm," I managed to gasp, "I'll help you lift it . . ."

Without a word she began to squeeze her arm into the case. "Where is the strap?"

"Here, under the sheet," I sputtered.

"There here's the tightest place I ever tried to get into," she said. Now I could see her forearm groping down the inside of the case. Then her fingers touched my shoulder.

"That's it!" I shouted eagerly.

"I know it," she said between grunts. "You suppose to be coughing, ain't you?"

And I was taken with such an urgent desire to laugh that in suppressing it, I began coughing again.

"All right, all right, I'll have you loose in a second. I thought you was trying to jive old Mary."

"NO, no," I gasped, feeling her loosening the strap that bound my left arm. Suddenly I heard the sound of metal striking against glass.

"There it is," she said, standing up.

Still coughing, I tried to lift my arm. Swift arrow flights of needling pain shot from my wrist to my shoulder, as when a newly mended limb is first removed from its cast. I stopped for a moment.

"Here," she said, "let's get you some water in there before you start coughing again."

"My arm feels strange," I said.

"Sho, it feels strange. You ain't been using it."

I flexed my fingers, clinched them, tried again, vainly. A great sense of impotence took me. I couldn't lift my arm. I looked at it lying beside me, feeling a profound emptiness. It was as though the bone had been removed and my arm become a flabby grey mass of atrophying flesh. I moved my fingers, watching them respond sluggishly. A feeling of a complete drainage and shame grew within me.

"Come on, son," she said, waiting with her hands upon the lid, prepared to lift it further. I wanted to turn my face away.

"What's the matter?"

"I can't," I said.

"You cain't what?"

"I can't raise my arm."

"You just ain't trying. Stop being such a sissy and come on."

"I've tried. It's too weak to raise."

"You'd better hurry," she said with impatience. "I ain't got much more time before the nurse comes back."

"Something's happened to it," I said, gritting my teeth and straining. "Look, I'm really trying."

I began to sweat from the effort, the muscles of my shoulder ached, but the arm lay rubbery at my side.

She shook her head. "I ain't *never* seen no man in the shape you in. . . . Why don't you tell me what you done for them to put you in this thing, so I can help you?"

"But I don't know," I said.

Without a word she reached for one of the bolts that propped the lid. "I got to go," she said, "I cain't help nobody who don't trust me. . . ."

"Wait," I said, filling with a dread of being left alone with the knowledge of my weakness.

"I got no time," she said coldly.

"Please, I'll tell you what I did," I begged, sparring desperately.

"I ain't interested no more," she said, tugging at the bolt.

"Please."

"Naw! You been lying to me all the time."

"I'm sorry," I said, "I was afraid."

"Tell that lie to the white folks; they the ones what wants to believe it. . . . You young Negroes is pass being afraid. . . ."

"But I *was* afraid."

"I got to go," she said, attacking the last bolt. "You young'ns ain't never scaird o'nothing."

"Stay just a minute," I pleaded. "I had to do it. . . ."

"You had to do what? . . . Naw, don't bother me, boy, I told you I got to go. Tell me next time."

"But I had to get him . . ."

"I got to go . . . Get who?" she asked, her eyes narrowing.

"The man."

"What man?"

"He was white . . ."

"A white man, boy?"

"Yes," I said, desperately talking at random. "He had a loaf of bread . . ."

"Some bread, yeah? . . ."

"And he had a bottle . . ."

"Uh huh, and what else he have?" she said shrewdly.

"He had something that looked like a microscope," I said, remembering the instruments pointed at me by the physicians.

"Yes . . . and just as I was going past an alley he tried to stop me . . ."

"Good God! What you do then?"

"Well, he said something that I couldn't understand and then he started after me . . ."

"No he didn't!"

"Yes, he did," I said, watching her closely. "He came after me with the microscope as though he meant to hit me with it . . ."

"He did? And then what happen?"

"Well, when I saw him coming toward me I got scared and hollered, 'Don't come any closer. Don't come any closer—' "

"And the fool kept coming?"

"That's right. . . ."

"And what you do then?"

"I saw a bottle on the ground and stooped and picked it up . . ."

"An' what he do then? He keep on coming?"

"No," I said, suddenly gripped by a feeling that I was relating an actual happening, something that had occurred sometime, somewhere, in my past. "He didn't keep coming, he stopped in his tracks and looked up and down the street. I was in the dark and I could see the freckles on the side of his face that was in the light. And he said, 'Look at me, black boy, what kind of man am I?' "

"What kinda man he was?" she said, frowning.

"Yes. And I . . ."

"And what you tell him?"

"I said, 'You're a white man, sir,' and his eyes got bright and he started laughing and said, 'That's right, but what *other* kind of man am I?'

"I didn't know. So I had to tell him I didn't know. And that made him angry.

"He said, 'Don't play dumb, boy. You nigger boys always try to play dumb!'

" 'But I'm telling the truth, sir,' I said. And he said, 'All right, all right, so I'm a white man, and what are you?' "

"And what you say then, boy?" she asked.

"I said, 'I'm colored, sir,' but it seemed to make him very angry. . . . His face changed while I was looking at it fast."

"Yeah, he wanted you to call yourself a nigger. How he look, how he look, son?"

"I couldn't see all of it because he was in the shadow of the street light . . . standing in a kind of half light. . . . But his face got tight and started to quiver like he had a tic."

"Go on, boy," she said.

"Well, he became very angry and said, 'That's right, you're a black, stinking, low-down nigger bastard that's probably got the syph and I'm white and you're supposed to do whatever I say, understand . . . ?' "

"And what'd you say?"

"Nothing . . ."

"You ought to have hit the old thing with that bottle. . . . These white folks . . . It oughta been me!"

"I was thinking about trying to run past him, when all at once he jammed his hand in his pocket and brought out a big roll of bills. He said, 'Now, nigger, I want you to stand still while I put this twenty-dollar bill in your pocket.' And I looked at him, and saw that the side of his mouth was twitching and his voice was shaky. I had never heard a man's voice sound like that . . ."

"What happen, boy?"

"He said, 'See, this is a real twenty-dollar bill. You can have it,' and I said, 'No, thank you, sir, I'm on my way to work.' He looked at me and said softly, 'Please don't be like that, boy.' 'I'm sorry, sir,' I said, 'but I've got to be going . . .'"

She looked dubious, her head to one side. "Boy, you ain't lying to me, is you?" she asked.

"I'm not lying. He said, 'Nigger, do you want to get in trouble?'

"I said, 'No, sir, I always try to keep out of trouble.'

" 'You're not keeping out of trouble now,' he said, 'real trouble. I don't believe I ever saw a nigger boy get himself in trouble as fast as you are with me.'

" 'No, sir, I don't want to get into trouble with anybody, sir.'

" 'Well, if you don't come on and take the money—'

" 'No, sir, I'm afraid.'

" 'What are you afraid of?'

" 'I don't know—I think it's because I didn't do anything to earn it, sir.'

" 'You will, you will,' he said, looking at me and starting to laugh again. 'You don't have to worry about that. That's my worry. Nigger,' he said in a hard voice, 'I'm asking you again, what kinda man am I?'

" 'You're a white man, sir,' I said.

" 'Is that all you can say?'

" 'Yes, sir.'

"He seemed to think about it a moment. 'Well, didn't your mammy teach you better than to disobey a white man?'

" 'Yes, sir, she taught me.'

" 'And don't you know I can have you taken care of? . . .'"

"Good God, boy, what'd you do then?" she interrupted.

"I look at him and thought about fighting him. I thought about trying to run past him, too. He was only a small, slender man, nice-looking in the face that had been beaten up a lot. I said, 'Yes, sir, but I haven't done anything . . .'

"He said, 'You don't *have* to do anything, you know that.'

" 'Yes, sir, I know it.'

" 'All I have to do is step into the diner up there on the corner and speak to the truck drivers, and what'd you do? I wouldn't want to have to do that,' he said.

"I was very worried, so I asked him: 'Please, can't you wait until Saturday, sir. I'll have plenty of time on Saturday, and I always come right past here . . .'

" 'Oh, no,' he said. 'You won't pull that one on me. I know that one. Once before one of you tried to do that. Some of you nigger boys try to be smart. I'm on to you. Now why don't you stop arguing and take the money? I bet you never had a twenty-dollar bill in your whole life, did you?'

" 'No, sir.'

" 'Well, you're going to have this one. Hold still,' he said and started towards me . . .''

"He still have that what-you-ma-call-it in his hand?"

"The microscope? Yes . . ."

"And what you do?"

"That's when I did it."

"Did what, boy?"

"I didn't know what else to do. He kept coming up on me and I tried to tell him not to do it, but he kept on coming and I decided to run past him, and he said, 'You want to be smart? You can have this microscope, too. I won't be needing it any more.' And by then he had rolled the money into a little wad like a spit-ball, rolling it slowly between his fingers. He said, 'It won't take but a minute,' and then he reached out and touched me and I swung the bottle at him and ran. . . .''

"You hit him, boy?"

"I think so. . . .''

"You kill him? You think you killed him?" she asked excitedly.

"I ran, I've been running ever since."

"You run a long ways, didn't you, son?"

"Yes," I said.

"And hopped them freight trains and everything."

"I don't want to talk about it," I said. "I've got to get out of here. Can't you see why I have to get out?"

"Yeah," she said, looking at me with dead seriousness. "I see it now. You probably killed him, or hurt him bad, and they looking for you. . . . I tell you what, it's too late to do anything right now 'cause it's time for me to go and that nurse'll be coming in here. . . ."

"You can't help me?"

"Yeah, but not tonight. You stay here like nothing happen until I get back tomorrow and I'll help you git outa here."

"But they might transfer me," I protested.

"No they won't. They don't aim to do that till next week. You just have to be patient awhile. Besides, you oughta told me the truth when I first ask you."

And before I could protest further she proceeded to lower the lid and bolt it, and I felt a profound loneliness take hold of me. When she was done, she stood above me looking in. Suddenly she gestured frantically toward the case. With despair I discovered that she had forgotten to cover my naked arm, lying impotent and partly exposed beside me. Above me she made frantic signs, but my muscles couldn't respond. She gestured furiously—only to stop off, listening, and leave hurriedly, her face full of dismay. I seemed to boil inside. I would be discovered. She had rushed away as though someone was coming. I looked at my arm, trying with all my will to make it respond. It was as though it betrayed me of a separate will. I had thought all that need be done to free myself was to have my arms released, but now I was as far from freedom as before, perhaps farther. A sharp, helpless anger formed within me as I struggled, squirming like a pinioned worm, seeing the sheet dank, clinging, as though plastered to me. Soon I was bathed in sweat. If only I could turn on my side! . . . or my stomach! Why hadn't old Mary been a nurse, a technician, a doctor? Or a lawyer with a writ of *habeas corpus*? Then instead of getting me into a worse predicament than before she might have given me some real assistance. I froze.

Under the strain my ears had grown extremely sensitive, for when she entered the room I heard her through the walls of the soundproof case. It's all over, I thought, it's all over now. She loomed, framed in empty space, above my head, holding a bottle of rubbing alcohol. She looked strange, her face highly flushed, as though delicately bruised or stung by peach fuzz, her lipstick badly blurred. I stared. She seemed to look straight at me, but not to see me. She's daydreaming. I thought with a sense of wonder. She seemed lost in some delicious dream. I waited to see her plummet the instant she saw the obscene nakedness of my arm. I steeled myself, waiting for the cry of alarm, already hearing the excited arrival of the technicians and physicians. But she hardly noticed me! I watched her make inscriptions upon my chart as though in a delightful fog. Was she baiting me, trying to give me a false sense of security before sounding the alarm? Maybe she's afraid and plans to call the others when she's safely out of the room. . . . If only the case were open, I thought, I could plead with her or frighten her with threats. Finishing with the charts now she raised her hand lovingly to the light and, with her fingers curved delicately, gazed with admiration upon the flashing of a fiery stone. It was amazing. She seemed to fall into a trance, smiling dreamily into the flashing fire as upon some bright inward happening; then closing her eyes, she turned her head languidly from side to side— a movement of sweet swooning surrender; like a spellbound dancer, or a child dizzy with turning, she took a swirling step toward the case, gliding as in a dream waltz, her mouth upturned invitingly, to receive an invisible kiss. What on earth? I thought. She was transformed! Before my eyes she had become the heroine of a thousand colorful picture ads, motion picture reels. I could not believe I saw the same plain face. It was lovely, and absurd; the loveliness peeping out of the absurdity, and she seemingly aware of it, carried away with the image of herself reflected in the flashing jewel. For a moment she was still, her flushed face smiling as though listening to an inner voice, then as though dancing a pantomine of tenderness and delicacy, she caressingly adjusted the pressure control of the machine and left wide-eyed without detecting that anything about me was changed.

I fought against the descending pressures filled with a feeling that I had seen something forbidden, something which would get me destroyed even though I didn't understand its meaning. I would have to get free of the machine before the doctors discovered that I had seen. . . .

Suddenly I was clearly awake, as though plunged into an icy pool. Two physicians stood above me, one with a microscope-like instrument focusing its twin eyes with a deadly stare into the case. I stole a look at my exposed arm and watched: My body ached with rigidity. But strangely they seemed unaware of it. They concentrated upon the instrument (one focusing, the other making notes) and I waited for it to tell them what their eyes ignored. But still, with the lenses directed full upon me from a point less than four feet away, nothing happened. I became uneasy. Why didn't they say something? Didn't they see that my arm was free? Yet they made no move. I waited, filled with a sense of angry indignation. They were deliberately ignoring me! Deliberately filling me with suspense. Secretly they were laughing at me! These peckerwoods! My anger grew. I had succeeded in partly freeing myself, something I was sure they were against, and now they ignored me. It was insulting! I felt myself filling with silent rage as I realized that I really was no freer than before—simply because *they* refused to acknowledge my freedom. Yes, and if they should consider me free, if they had only the faintest hallucination of it, then even though I remained in the case with only one arm unstrapped, I would indeed be free. It was crystal clear. These bastards! They had me locked in their eyes like a tadpole in a jug. Looking at the sparkling lenses, the polished cylinders, the smooth forehead topped by blond hair, the calm cheeks . . . I became so angry that I experienced the strange sensation of clenching my fist. There it was, a knuckled ball beside me. I looked up hastily expecting them to look alarmed. Instead they merely became a bit more active with their instruments. Nobody bothered to notice the bare arm, the clenched fist. Defeated, I closed my eyes, trying to shut them out.

My thoughts turned to old Mary. Where had she gone? I grew resentful that by meddling, she had partly freed me and rendered me more insecure. And yet, for all my resentment, I wished for her. I imagined her returning subtly transformed into a young pink nurse; one trained in the intricacies of the machine; but who yet, for some nameless reason, was interested in helping me escape. Yes, she'd come and open the case, bearing with her a clean light smell that was neither the odor of ether nor disinfectant. And I would be set completely free and my impotent arms and legs would be strong and well and I would take her away with me—where, I didn't know. What was the weather outside? I wondered. Was it fall or winter, or some unnamed season in between winter and spring? Oh, well it wouldn't happen like that. Not if they had noticed my arm, without giving a sign. Old Mary wouldn't return in *any* form. Perhaps she was already fired never to return again. It was up to me, I had to get free of the case and find my way to the street. But what if the rest of my body was as naked as my arm. Even that wouldn't stop me, I'd walk into the street naked. I'd find clothes somewhere out there. . . .

But how would I walk? If my legs were as weak as my arm I'd fall on my face. Still I'd have to risk it. Then once again I heard the tinkling of keys and looked up to see old Mary. I was so relieved to see her that tears formed in my eyes. This time she wasted no time trying to communicate through the glass, but unbolted the case and started lifting the lid. And in the excitement I forgot my impotent arm and discovered myself helping her from the inside.

"You laying in there gitting strong," she said. "Last time I was here you couldn't do nothing but eat." She winked.

"You were gone a long time."

"You think I wasn't coming back?"

"I was worried."

"I had to send home to get something for you. It took longer than I thought."

"What did you send for?"

"Just a little something to give you some strength."

"Something for me to *take*?"

"Sho, just a little home remedy, something I got from my mama."

Was she kidding again? "You have a mother?" I said.

"Sure, haven't you? Everybody got a mother."

"Of course, but I thought . . ."

"I know, you think I'm too old to have a mama still living. But I have. The Lawd willing, Mama's gonna be 104 years old on her next birthday. And her hearing's good and she don't need no glasses *and* her teeth's better'n mine."

"She must be a remarkable woman."

"Us think she is," she said. "She's a smart woman too. Useta sing alto, grow the best crops in the county, and right now she knows more about roots and herbs and midwifery and things than anybody you ever seen. Here," she said, "take this and swaller it."

I saw her removing something from her apron pocket. "That's what I sent to Mama to get. It'll make you strong. Go on, eat it."

I stared at the substance. It was green, like balled grape leaves that had dried without fading. . . .

"Go on, boy."

I looked at it. I wanted both to reject and accept it. I was fascinated.

Around the outer leaf the ribs spread tree-shaped, with the root and uppermost branches beginning inside the ball and ending there. . . . *"What's the matter, boy, you scared?"* I distrusted it, yet I had to draw strength from some source. . . . Fearfully, I put it into my mouth and bit it in half, swallowing part and holding the rest between my teeth.

"You swaller it?"

I bowed my head.

"How's it?" she said.

"All right." As dry as it seemed, it went down smoothly, a bittersweet taste that suddenly seemed to set my throat aflame.

"Ah," I began. "Aaaaah!"

"Hush, boy! Keep your mouth shut!"

I wanted to vomit, but already it was burning my stomach.

"You're trying to kill me. . . ."

"Kill you? Fool, that's going to make you strong. . . ."

". . . Get the nurse. . . ."

". . . Sho, if you want to stay in that junk pile. . . ."

"Then give me some water. . . ."

"No water. You be all right in a minute. Don't you know ain't no medicine any good unless it's hard to take? You ought to know that. . . ."

I writhed. Drops of scalding sweat seemed to pop out over my scalp, my eyes went out of focus, distorting her image, my skin flamed. I thought I was going to die.

"That's some good stuff," she said. "You'll be all right now. That stuff'll make a baby strong. Now less see, you better stay at my house. The address ——. You remember it, you hear me. But first we gotta get you out."

"What was that stuff?" I said.

"Never mind. You don't have to worry, we been knowing about it a long time. Least Mama is, and her mama's mama knowed about it. . . ."

"But what is it?"

"Look, boy, ain't no use in your asking me, 'cause I done tole you all I'm going to. It's in you now, so let's think about getting you out of there."

"O.K. I think I can help you with the lid."

"Sho, but the problem is to get you out of the building, and I can't go along with you. That you got to do by yourself. Maybe we better wait till next week. . . ."

"No, I've got to go *tonight!*"

"But liable to get caught. . . ."

"I don't care, I'll have to take the chance."

"Huh, looks like the herb is working. You sho you want to try? All right, all I can do is help you open the lid and then you have ta go for yourself. You might make it, but I don't know. Lucky this here's the third floor." Suddenly I saw her turn. "Oh my Lord, they calling me. . . ."

"Mary, the lid!" I called as started for the door.

"I be right back," she hissed, her hand on the knob.

"Then turn off the lights!"

As she opened the door I saw her hand dart at the wall and the room went black, " Mary!" The voice was cut off by the shutting door. She was gone and I was aware of my pounding heart.

It had to be now, alone. I raised my head to the cracked lid, listening. Silence. My eyes pressed against a total blackness, without form. An absolute, ether-drenched blackness that poured into my lungs as my mind cursed the voice that had called old Mary away. I would have to do it alone. Go out there alone. But first I had to get from the inside. I rested, my hands exploring the inside of the case.

Beneath the sheet swathing my body I found the electrodes strapped over my navel and my spine. I tugged at the first, hearing a motor click sinisterly in the bowels of the case and, snatching my hands away, it stopped. I would leave it until later. The straps that bound my legs were easy—smooth leather linked with a simple metal buckle. But there were still the two binding my ankles, too far to reach until the lid was further raised. Resting, I planned my next move. I would escape now, before old Mary changed her mind, or became afraid and turned me in. It had to be now. Beyond the door lay a hall, the first problem was to get there. After that I wouldn't think. With my back pressing the bottom I moved my palms upward against the glass and pushed. The smooth hardness of the lid slanted steeply to my right. I pushed upward, my soft muscles seeming to stiffen and burn inwardly as my arms extended and slid toward the outer edge like an impersonal tool. The lid rose slightly. Now, now! With a burst of energy I strained upward, raising it. My hands grew hot with friction, rubbing against the glass. It was stubborn. My arms ached. My ears rang. A wave of nausea boiled up within me, bringing a green bittersweet taste; the rest of the old woman's medicine had dissolved beneath my tongue. I swallowed it down, tasting fire. It seemed to act directly upon my muscles, giving me new strength. I felt the heavy lid swinging like a stone now, smoothly silent in the benevolent blackness. And all the time I was listening, praying a crazy prayer: "Lord, give me the strength of Jack-the-Bear," grunting and straining against the lid.

Jack the rabbit
Jack the Bear,
Lift it, lift it,
Just a hair . . .

Make poetry of it, sing it—no, they might hear. Sing a song in silence. Sing a song of silence in a strange land. Jack it up, bear it in the dark. It's heavy as the world. With my arms straight above me now, numbing aches lost in the metal and glass, and the glass and metal inseparable from the blackness, I listened for footsteps beyond the door, expecting the intrusion of the hated light, the swish of a starched uniform, then pushed again. Suddenly there was a click. I felt the slanting plane become perpendicular, the weight left my hands. The lid had clicked back upon its hinges. Hesitantly I sat up, feeling the sheet drop from my back into the case. My body was wet. The ringing in my ears increased swiftly in volume, then faded. There was a silence punctuated by my breathing. For an instant it seemed I had struggled through a dream. I needed to see, if only there were some kind of *black* light present. . . . My body shuddered, then tensed with a swift insistent urge. Rising to my knees I braced myself against the side of the case, feeling the nodes come with me and becoming aware of the danger of electrocution at the instant. I could hear the dull splattering below, seeing it arching downward with a faintly phosphorescent glowing. I held on. At last it ended. I was disgusted, yet amused; for I would have to step in it on my way out. It's your River Jordan, you have to cross over it, I thought. Still kneeling I went after the node, again hearing the machinery click on and whirr. I'd have to hurry before they noticed the fluctuation of the current and came to make an inspection. Releasing it, I searched into the case. The rest of the cord was folded neatly beneath the sheet. I tugged it violently, hearing the machinery whirr up. Enraged, I dropped it cursing, then stopped, petrified by a sudden loud sound outside the door. I seemed to wait a hundred years, the cord tight around my hand. The knob clicked, then silence. Have they come in? But they couldn't, there was no flash of light. But what if the hall lights had been killed? I leaned against the case listening, the tension tearing at my nerves. Something heavy struck again.

"All right," I whispered in a rage. "Why don't you do something? Come and get me! Say something!"

Silence.

"Let's not play games—come on and get me. I'm sick and tired of lying at the bottom of this piece of nickle-plated junk, I'm climbing out! . . ."

I listened, seeming to hear my own voice echoing around the walls.

"Listen, I've learned to control it. Hear that sound? I started it with my finger. Now get away from that door so I can get through. . . ."

Silence.

"Get away from that door," I said, giving voice to something I had felt for a long time. "Do I have to make you a speech? All right, Lincoln freed the slaves and I'm getting out! Say amen! You didn't cure me, you took my energy. That's it, you probably have a hospital full of us, using our energy to run your stupid machinery! What do you care about my name? How'd you get us in here, anyway? With a cold pork chop and a loaf of bread? With a black snake whip, with handcuffs and a log chain? You see, I'm leaving, I'm remembering. Lincoln freed the slaves, I remember that. He freed the field niggers, and the house niggers and the stud niggers; the red niggers and the white niggers, and the yellow niggers and the blue niggers—and I'm freeing me. . . . I'm climbing out. . . ."

Suddenly I seemed to plunge into space, then thudded against the damp floor; and still falling inside of me, falling through a blacker darkness than that in which I sprawled, striking out wildly with my fists ex-

pecting them to reach out and grab me. But no hand fell. I lay still.
Were they teasing me? I swept my arm in a circle, through emptiness.
I crawled a step. Still empty. I whipped the slack cord about in the dark,
hearing a dry smacking sound. Had they left in the swift interval of my
fall? Had I been unconscious? "No," I said aloud, listening and trying to
calm myself, "there was no one; you imagined it all." And lucky too, for
I must have sounded insane even though it was a relief to get it out. I
crawled again, then something was holding me back. Turning, my hand
struck the cord, making it twang like a bass viol. I gave it a sharp tug,
and again, this time hearing the creak of rolling wheels, the machine!
This wouldn't do.

I tried to stand, feeling the blood rushing dizzily from my head. What
had she given me? A strange sensation, to stand; blackness seemed to
swirl about me like ink awhirl in a bowl. Now I found the belt that held
the nodes in place. It seemed endless, part of my flesh. I snatched the
front cord until my hand ached. If only I knew where it entered the
machine, I thought, going back. Forcing my thumbs beneath the elastic
web of the belt, I tried to slip it down around my hips and it was as
though I tried to peel off my flesh. Suddenly in a flash of out-of-focus
memory I remembered standing with a string leading from one of my
teeth to a doorknob. I headed for the door, pulling the machine behind
me. Slow going, as against the steady pressure of a current. Suddenly
a flash of red fire filled my head, and I struck out, feeling a pain in my
hand. It was the wall. Reaching the wall, I shuffled sideways, an inch at
a time, until my hands found a break in the surface, then down the cool
panel to the knob, egg-smooth and silent as I turned it cautiously. With
my ear against the door, it seemed as though the surface had come alive
with the roar of invisible tides; the muffled and rhythmical thunder of
remote machinery. Voices, other sounds, washed underneath, creating
a near sub-aural harmony. But still no footsteps. Hurriedly I wrapped the
length of the rear cord around the knob, tightening it, then I was turning
and falling face forward, stiff as a man of stone, feeling the darkness
plunging above me as though falling from a great height. Then jerking
taut for a moment I slanted at a dangerous angle, then something
snapped loudly and I lay upon the labyrinthine pattern of the floor, drawing upon my nerve to touch the node. It had snapped completely. The
belt had given way! I was free of both. Only fine cat whiskers of wire
brushed beneath my finger. Crawling excitedly back to the door I pulled
myself erect and listened. There was a furor in the depths of the building, like the country choir which I had known somewhere rendering
Handel's *Messiah*:

Hallelujah—Boom!   Hallelujah—Bong!
Hallelujah—Crash!
He's risen—Smash!

And suddenly I was certain someone was coming! So I would stand
behind the door and slip out unseen. Let them come now and I'm free,

I thought, just open the door. . . . A sound arose outside the door, moved on. My heart beat madly. I stood hating the men who had shanghaied me into the machine. Waiting. It became quiet now! Cautiously I turned the knob. A flash of light struck my eyes and I stood blinded and exposed, feeling the air upon my naked body. Then I could see the long, white, disinfected corridor, brightly lighted and empty. Far ahead it turned off. Back of me was a similar emptiness. I started to move and blacked out. But now I found myself crawling down the corridor, trying to rise, stumbling, crawling again, moving past several doors before getting a grip on myself and trying to stand. Pressing against the smooth surface of the wall, I pushed erect and proceeded, holding on to the wall, lurching fearfully to the turn in the corridor which lay ahead.

Reaching the turn I looked back. The cord lay curled upon the labyrinthine pattern of the floor, like a trampled snake. But already I was trying to remember old Mary's address and falling to my knees to better control my legs. Rounding the curve I came to an operating table, its rubber-tired wheels turned inward toward the wall. The corridor was quiet, empty. Gripping a table leg I raised myself, seeing the outline of a form, covered with white. Who sleeps with his head beneath the sheet? As of their own volition, my hands reached out, seizing one white enameled leg. Then the other, as though remembering the principle of some forgotten stroller or kiddie-car. Trying to pull myself upright, I felt the table begin to move—in a circle! I held on trying to guide it away from the wall, my knees knocking against the floor as I tried to stand; trying to guide it back in the other direction as it circled back towards the room from which I'd escaped. But each attempt to stand sent it ahead, wobbling crazily back down the corridor. Stop, you bastard. . . . Why . . . why doesn't he protest? I wonder with swift dread. . . . Stop! Stop! I whisper fiercely, addressing it. And as though in answer the table rolled to a stop. Disarranging the sheet as I pulled upright, I looked into a face, a youth's face. The cheeks were drawn, the eyes closed as though in sleep. I wanted to run but the face held me, as though by some hypnotic spell cast by the eyes beneath the puckered lids. I couldn't move. My eyes refused to look away. I could not turn—until back down the corridor I could hear the sliding of metal gates: an elevator. Holding to the table I opened the door to my old room, and started the table into the darkness, half-stumbling. I felt my foot press upon the discarded cord and it clinging to me for a step and dropping off. The table rolled forward and stopped. I tugged at it desperately, feeling it give suddenly and shoot me backwards. Hard metal pressed into my back: the machine. It was like a dream. I started back toward the door, still holding on to the table, but laughing softly—a muted hysteria that stopped suddenly as my hand found the door; then I was holding my breath, half-expecting, half-hoping, to hear him breathing behind me. All was silence, suspense, vacuum and blackness. "Why'd you let them kill you?" I whispered crazily. Perhaps he had been confined to a machine just as I.

Too bad, and I'd better get out of here before they put me back beneath the lid. . . . I started back to the door on wobbly legs, remembering the table. It would be useful. I was swinging it around, broadside to the case, hearing the clink of metal against metal as I pressed it close. But the case was too high, and there was only one thing to do. Nausea washed over me as my hands came in contact with cool flesh. For a moment I started to turn away, then one hand finding the neck and the other slipping beneath the curve spine, I pushed it gently, feeling it come up as though weightless rolling toward the case. If only I could see! I pushed again. Something plunked lightly against the bottom of the case; and with a heave I sent it over the side into the machine. "Get in there, you bastard!" I whispered with sudden anger. "I should shut the lid on you. . . ." How easy it would be now if he had been dressed. I could walk forth into the street fully clothed. Starting away, something stopped the table. My hands groped about. It was a leg, caught in the sheet. Lifting it clear I pushed the table out into the corridor. Looking back, as I shut the door I saw it dangling as though broken in the flash of light.

The corridor was empty, quiet. Where had they gone? Who had it been? Were there machines behind all the doors? With each step my legs seemed to grow stronger. I passed the spot where I found the table, holding it firmly now, careful not to bump the walls. My eyes swept the ceiling, the shut doors. Were they watching from some hidden peepsight in the ceiling? Testing me like a rat in a maze? Let them! I'd show them how intelligent a rat could be. . . . Why didn't I meet someone? Around the curve now, the corridor swept ahead, bringing a wave of indistinct sound. I picked up speed, almost running. Nameless voices from the past seemed to whisper warnings. A new alertness grew. My throat burned with outrage. Tense sensations crackled the length of my spine, in my crouch. Then I saw the elevator shaft and stopped. Was it exit or trap? There was no time to decide. Already it groaned with movement. I swung around, hesitating. Where could I hide? The well-lighted corridors stretched away for thirty feet in three directions, then curved—too far to race before being seen. Back of me, a wall set with a small high window. And now the shaft filled with light and the car was stopping. And as the gate swung open I swung the table around and ran it close. Almost upsetting a small blonde, who carried a covered tray, who, imaculate in her uniform, gave a startled "Oh, my God!"

"Between you and me, it's hot as hell back there," I said, noticing the gleaming breast-pin, the glint of pearly teeth.

"Oh . . . oh yes," she said. "Yes, yes . . ."

"And it's even hotter downstairs," I said, shoving the table inside.

She stood petrified and I pushed her gently as I closed the door. "Better watch your tray," I said. . . . Then I was dropping beneath her, hearing the shrill stab of her scream. The car dropped past lighted floors on which, through the glass door, I could see uniformed men and women caught grotesquely in mid-gesture, the precise contortions of the modern dance. All the floors were occupied. My one chance was to make for the basement, the one place that I was sure the car would stop. I shoved the handle toward the extreme position marked "B," feeling the nerves twitch in my legs as I dropped, seeming to hear the little nurse's scream falling featherlike upon me. The car landed with a thud, throwing me to my knees and bouncing as though preparing to spring above. Yanking the control I felt it settle and I broke from the car.

I faced two gloomy corridors, hesitating an instant, then ran for the dimmest, the left, plunging through an atmosphere heavy with medicine, machinery, food, seeing the passage narrowing but afraid to retreat. Then I ran smack against the cart. My hands shooting out landed upon heated metal, jostling the cart and releasing a cloud of steam, as I tried to see the man behind its wavering strands.

"Hy, man," he said. "Look like you're in a hurry." Then the steam was thinning and I could see his white suit in the dim light.

"I didn't see you . . ." I said.

"You were in a hurry. Even so, you think you'll ever get rich?"

"Rich . . . ?" I said through the veil of steam as my mind weighed his question formally, without curiosity. . . . "In here?"

"Sure—step around there, daddy, so I can get past you. . . . Sometimes I think a dope fiend dreamed up this here basement. It's crowded as a barrel of snakes. I say, you think you'll be in the money?"

"Not soon. . . ."

"Shucks, man, you can't tell," he said, beginning to move. "You might dream you up a good one. . . ."

"Dream? It's a nightmare," I said, my voice growing loud, angry as his broad back bent over the handles and he started to push away. "A nightmare," I repeated, my voice rising.

"Shucks, man," he said laughing over his shoulder. "You dream you up a right good nightmare, you liable to break the bank. . . ."

I watched him go still laughing. What if he sounds the alarm? I backed several steps, then turned and ran, his laughter behind me. Voices arose around a passage to the right. Ahead there was light, a dim bulb by which I could see a door marked "Engine Room." I ran for it, thinking, "There will be men, lights. Kill the lights, your only chance is in darkness. . . ."

It opened easily. A wave of bright heat and vibration struck my body. It was a huge room. My teeth chattered as to my right I saw a large man reading at a table, his head down, unaware. I stood paralyzed with alertness, my back arched with tension, my eyes sweeping past three huge engines to the far blank wall set with a small door far to the rear, and seeing on the left stretching behind him a series of furnaces and back around, looking for the switch panel, thinking, "It's got to be here, it's got to . . ." and seeing him look up, his calm freezing into rigid surprise as I yelled desperately, "Where's the switch?" His mouth moved silently, his eyes widening. . . .

"The switch, hurry!" I called.

"Switch?" his mouth said through the machine noise. Then his arm raised, pointing, extending; my eyes following. And there it was attached to pipes cemented into the floor. I ran over, watching him start amazed, beginning to stand, seeing the question looming in his eyes as I gained the bakelite panel and yanked for the largest switch, hearing him yell, "Hey," his voice shrill, disjointed and dreamlike as I saw the room still bright despite the switch in my hand, and now seeing his astonishment changing to indignation as I broke another switch and another, sending blue sparks flying and still the light; and reaching now for a brace of smaller switches and seeing him start forward, as now, at last, one part of the room and then the other fell black. For an instant I was still. His voice was growing more distinct, in the swiftly dying roar of the room, drawing closer, seeming to advance out of the slowing hum of the dynamos. Gaging my direction by the intensity of the heat upon my body, I ran to my right, remembering the small door far across the room, running past the furnaces, veering away from the heat and feeling the shock as he ran against me. Going down then, hearing him yelling, and me crawling and getting to my feet and leaping back as he scrambled on the floor. Upright now, I danced my indecision, pivoting this way and that, then remembering and bearing again for the floor. "Hey, hey!" his voice came, and I seemed to race on a treadmill until a crack of intense red light leaped suddenly through to the back of my skull. I had hit the wall, grabbing my head and rolling, feeling my shoulder strike cool metal and beating upon it frantically with my fists. It was the door. I pushed it, grabbing the handle, shaking it, hearing a popping sound. The man yelled again. Then came a crash. I looked back, seeing space flash out of the blackness as the far door burst open. Several men loomed in the rectangle of light, poised like dancers at the climax of a powerful leap. . . . "He's back there!" a voice cried and they shot into the darkness. I lunged. The metal scraped against my shoulder like a rasp, as at my back the huge loping rhythm of an engine whirled into motion beneath the sound of men's yells and rapid footfalls. Again I lunged, this time it gave, opening outwardly, a seldom used door. I squeezed my body through and plunged into another blackness. It was swiftly cold, dank. I shot along on a level, the floor bouncing roughly against my feet, feeling as though falling endlessly into a black shaft through which damp currents sped upward against me. But no shaft at all, I saw now in a dim filtering of sourceless light, but a storage celler of indeterminate size. And behind me they had found the door.

"This way," someone yelled, then in a sudden whirlpool of flickering light I could see a narrow passage winding through a jumble of packing cases. Behind me, moving down an incline I could see a group of wavering flashlights; then the men above them, their faces skull-like in the shadows shooting from below. I backed a step and stumbled, hearing a large object crash to the floor. Something looked out of the darkness

ahead. For a second beams of light boiled around me, then I tripped
and went to my knees, thinking, they have me, they have me! But still
I crawled, scrambling, feeling rough wood tearing at my sides and hearing the men come close as I stopped, still, listening. They breathed heavily, whispered, stepping softly. Even with their lights they moved slower
than I. But hardly had they passed when they returned. More cautiously
now, the flashlights crawling over packing cases ... watching their
white-clad legs and thinking, "All right now, it's time you stopped this
dreaming. ..."

"I tell you he kept going," someone said.

"Then where'd he go?"

"How do I know? He certainly didn't walk through us and go back
into the engine room. ..."

"Come on, let's see how far we can go up this way." They moved off.
Then, "Shhhh, listen!" I heard, my heart in my mouth now, as somewhere close by a furious struggle began. It went in a circle, a desperate
lunging scramble that banged here and there against something for a
second, then trailed drily off building in my mind a series of bright
sounds scratching rapidly upon the wall of darkness.

"There he goes!"

"Get him this time, understand? We've got to get him!"

I heard them go. "It was a rat," I thought. "They're chasing a rat!
Or maybe only a mouse." Perhaps the rat went in the true direction of
escape. ... I got up. I'd have to take the other direction, the rat and I
were caught in different mazes. I'd have to find my own way out. The
men were still going away from me. If only the rat keeps running,
doesn't double back on his trail!

"I hear him up there," a voice called as I moved out into the passageway, thinking, "Sure, up there, maybe two miles. Get after him—"

At first the ether fumes seemed part of the underground air, then
the light focused into my eyes, blinding me.

"All right, boy, I've got you cornered. Don't move!"

I crouched, muscles aching with tension, whispering, "No, no ... !"

"Oh, but yes," the voice said, the light wavering in my eyes as he
moved forward, a step at a time. "Oh, yes."

I lowered my head seeing some sort of garment stretched between
his hands and I thought, "It's—! He's got a strait-jacket!"

"You might as well come quietly," he said, his nervous laugh hollow
in the low cellar. "Here, put this on, you're ill. You'll catch pneumonia
in this dampness. ..."

"No, no," I repeated, recording the nuances of his voice as though
hearing it played on a sluggish phonograph and feeling my fear flowing
to contempt, thinking, "He's unsure. Unsure ... !"

"It's for your own good, you'll be released when its time. ... You're
still ill, very ill, you know. ..."

I saw him still shuffling forward. "You're ill," he repeated.

"Maybe you're the one . . ." I whispered, stalling for time.

He stopped shuffling.

"Ha! Ha! See, you have a sense of humor. You boys always show a sense of humor when you're improving. A few weeks more . . . and you'll . . . be . . . released—"

I could see the gleam of his white buttons now and suddenly I feinted to rush past him, seeing the flashlight beam streak to the ceiling, revealing his white-swathed body crouching before me, his irises dilated like a cat's.

"Don't try that, boy. I can play rough. Why not be a good patient? In time you'll be properly released. . . ."

"Come and get me," I whispered. "I'm already released."

"Oh, I'm going to get you, boy," he said, the cautious ease coming back into his voice. "But why not come peacefully? Why have a setback?"

"Sure," I whispered, "only come on. . . ."

"Here, let me put this around you. . . ."

"What?"

"A robe, you'll be more comfortable. . . ."

"Will it fit? I'm fastidious about my clothes. . . ."

"Oh, it'll fit perfectly . . . my, but you're a character, ha! ha! . . . It'll fit, all right, it's endlessly adjustable. Here, let me show you." Again he inched forward.

"Toss it," I said.

"Sure, sure," he said. "Sure . . ."

I saw his head come forward, the light flashing downward, causing his eyes to gleam for an instant as he lunged toward me—then the shock. I grabbed, feeling the rough canvas brush my arm and him grappling for me, his grip like steel. Slipping off, I jabbed, my fist going deep. He grunted and I hammered him, feeling him burst away, grunting, his head dropping down, and I was already running furiously. But in the same spot, my high-driving knees drumming fiercely against him, making a sound like a boy dragging a stick along a picket fence. He was down, the flash rolling crazily upon the floor, throwing a hot, bright light against a wall as I shot out of the corner and was past, hearing him begin to yell.

It was tortuous going. I felt my way swiftly. I found the upturned case and felt along in the direction from which the men had returned. He yelled, his words growing more articulate all the time. I moved, afraid to run because of the unseen objects, yet moving as fast as possible. Far behind and to my right I could hear the men following the rat. "Keep on, boys," I thought. "You'll flush him soon." I went around something cold and smooth beneath the dust, following its long smooth lines until it curved away, then touching here and there the rough surface of a wall. "This way, this way!" he yelled behind me. Suddenly I was amused, remembering how my fist had sunk in. And I was conscious of

being somehow different. It was not only that I had forgotten my name,
or that I had been processed in the machine, or even that I had taken
Mary's medicine—but something internal. My thoughts seemed to be the
thoughts of another. Impressions flashed through my mind, too fleeting
and secretly meaningful to have been my own—whoever I was. And yet
somehow they were. It was as though I had become capable of new
powers of understanding. Perhaps I was insane. But it wasn't so
simple. . . .

His voice was stronger now. And far behind a door slammed and I
ran again. Ahead it was brightening. A new light grew to my left and
I entered a larger room, a kind of storage section, filled with old medical
cabinets, stools, bathtubs—all dappled with spots of light filtering down
from what looked like a sidewalk studded with thick glass discs. I could
feel the damp descend. A cobweb clung to my face. I brushed it away,
moving, listening. . . . The sound arose far ahead, a roar, like a roll on an
out-of-tune tympany, approached me, setting up a shrill vibration within
the dark, beneath which I heard the sound of footsteps and plunged
wildly to my left. I felt myself going over, landing against something that
creaked and groaned, filling my nose and mouth with dust. Rooting,
scrambling, listening, I found myself in a kneeling position on what
seemed to be an ancient leather couch. I gripped it, strangling a sneeze
and hearing it going over me, passing me, rumbling above the passage
like thunder echoing in high clouds.

"We lost him again," a voice said. "There's just too much down here
that we don't know about. . . ."

They were close by, but I couldn't see them! I pressed against the
dried leather feeling cornered, helpless.

"But I tell you he's up here somewhere. I had him cornered, he didn't
come past you so he has to be up here. . . ."

"It's a matter for the police," another voice said.

"But, Doctor . . ."

"Why would he think of coming down *here*?"

"Probably some buried memory guided him. Perhaps this storage
basement corresponds to the structure of his mind. . . ."

"He's down here, that's certain, and I think it's our job and not that
of the police to find him. . . ."

"That fellow must be crazy," an indignant voice said. "Came in stark
naked and started pulling switches!"

"Let's search over this way, then if we don't find him we'll get the
police down here with tear gas and floodlights. . . . Talking about a nigger in a wood pile! Whew!"

"Tear gas will flush him! . . . Say . . ."

"What is it—?"

"That door there!"

Shoes scraped upon the concrete floor, turning. "Where?"

"Over there. Maybe he went in there. . . ."

"For Christ's sake—can't you see that it's just leaning there, that it
isn't hung?"

"Sure, it's leaning against the wall."

"Can't you see it?"

"I do now. Let's go."

They left, their voices receding, seeming to move before them with
the lights.

What should I do? They'd return soon with the police and tear gas.
Standing, I could see the dappling lights continuing for about twenty feet
to my right, then fading off. I was in a tight place and now in attempting
to turn between the couch and something, the floor had tilted. I stumbled, falling against the door, feeling it swing inward, almost throwing
me into space. It was not dismantled at all, only deceptively hung. Fascinated, I pushed it gently, hearing the men again, but this time they
seemed on the other side of some sort of partition, drawing closer. The
door sighed. I looked into sheer blackness. A narrow rectangle of blackness set into the dark grey of the basement. Where did it lead? To escape or danger, to dismemberment, insanity or death? It was not a finished doorway, my hands told me, but a kind of improvisation, crude,
like a tunnel in a mine, something cut in haste, used furtively and left
unexpectedly. . . .

I seemed to feel the light before I saw it stabbing, slanting at the
ceiling above me. And for an instant I felt an impulse to walk out into
its circular beam with my hands above my head, but the machine loomed
in my mind and I stepped into the blackness and pulled the door softly
closed. Silence. The passage moved straight ahead, then rose abruptly.
Moving with outstretched arms I felt my fingers flickering the narrow
sides, touching marks left in the sheer earth, wooden post, and then another. Suddenly something rolled beneath my foot and I lurched forward,
hearing the clatter of glass. I felt about, finding bottles, bundles of paper.
I kneeled, listening for sound behind me, then pulling up I limped cautiously ahead. It became warm. An image of three huge ovens built
themselves up in my mind. Somewhere back there in the past I had been
inside a bakery, had seen the hot loaves lined in heated tins, and rows of
gingerbread-boys cooling brown upon the well-scrubbed boards. . . . Had
I been running even then?

At first it sounded like an engine pounding, then the rasping insinua-
tions of trumpets and saxophones cut through and I realized that it was
music. I stood still, breathing in the fumes of stale alcohol. Was the
sound coming from straight ahead or from above? I moved forward—
until my toes were striking against a wall that seemed to move away.
I drew back. The air had suddenly changed, the sound booming out. I
swung my foot, encountering void. It was another basement! Another
damn basement! And the music came from above. The beery air grew
stronger. Cautiously, I moved forward again. Behind there would be
tear gas, ahead at least there was music. . . . What had I blundered into?

Why should it be connected with the hospital? Was it a bar, a restaurant, some kind of clubroom located in another wing of the building? I hesitated, for minutes it seemed, wishing they'd come and end my indecision. For a moment the music stopped, then boomed out again. I moved, keeping close to the wall. The smell of beer became heavy, I had come to a row of barrels. I could feel their squat shapes following one after another as I felt my way. "I'm under a bar," I thought. That's the jukebox playing. Who would believe that, underneath, the hospital was connected with a bar? There was relief in the idea and I stopped moving and tried to figure my next move. If it was a bar then I could wait until closing time and then go up after they had left and escape—I was tired now. Perhaps Mary's medicine was wearing off. What on earth was the bitter stuff anyway? I had to wait, to sit down, but the floor was covered with sharp pieces of coal. I moved a step, coming upon a wooden structure, a series of rails, a fence, and stopped lest I upset something and give myself away. . . . I leaned against a post, my body seeming still to move. Overhead the jukebox boomed again, a familiar number. A blues. Where had I heard it, what did it mean? Some muted instrument sounded all the world like a muffled voice. Or was it a voice that sounded like a muted horn? What was the voice in the jukebox saying? Another instrument, like a bear growling, took up the refrain. It sounds like Jack-the-Bear, I thought for no reason at all. . . . If only I dare lie down and rest. . . . How long, baby, tell me how long? . . . When would they close up above? What if they were open twenty-four hours? Never closed? The mere idea of time repulsed me. I tried to think of other things. I dozed. . . .

At first I thought it was the jukebox. I was sitting on the floor beside a coal bin blinking my eyes in disbelief, a man stood atop the stairs.

"What the hell!" he yelled. "Hey you! Hey you!"

My vision sharpened. He held a crate of bottles against his white apron, a fat brown man whose large head caught the light upon its baldness. I rolled over and crawled behind the partition and dived behind into the coal bin, lumps of pea coal cutting sharply into my unprotected knees. Now behind me a new voice, "He's over yonder!"

"Where? Just you show me where!"

"He was standing right back yonder!"

"Yonder *where*?"

"Behind them boards!"

"And naked?"

"As ever he come into this world."

"You sure he wasn't painted green, ain't you?"

"Hell, Pritchett, don't be trying to make no fool out of me. I know what I saw."

"You saw him all right, but he ain't there. It was your whiskey that showed him to you."

"So I guess I'm lying?"

"Naw, you ain't lying, you drunk. How the hell's anybody going to get down here behind the bar and past me?"

"I don't know, Pritchett, but I damn sho saw a man down here. I damn sho did! . . . Hey, mister," he called out plaintively. "Mister, if you down there, please will you come out or we'll have to call the cops and the boss don't want no cops fooling round down there. . . ."

"Oh shut up, man, and let's get back to work. . . ."

"You see there, mister, if you don't come up I'll never hear the end of it," the first voice said. "They'll swear I'm drunk and dock me a day's pay. . . ."

I held my breath, amazed at the sincerity in the voice. For a moment it was silent. Then: "You hear me, man?"

I wanted to laugh.

"You speak to him, Pritchett."

"I tell you, man, you drunk. Sloppy drunk!"

"Go on, Pritchett, I swear he's down there."

"Hell! All right. . . . Hey you, down there, if you *is* down there, if you don't come the hell on outa there, we'll know you trying to steal something and we have ta be hard on you," he called, sounding as though he had become convinced, as though by addressing me I *had* to exist. And again I felt an impulse to surrender, fighting it down. I had gone too far to give up now.

"See there," I heard. "Ain't a damn soul down there."

"He's down there all right." the voice said. "He just don't want to do the right thing. I ought to go down there with a baseball bat—he's trying to mess up a whole day's pay for me! Go get the pistol."

Pistol? I burrowed further into the pile of coal, moving slowly lest it slide, or smother me. Behind me they argued heatedly as I worked my way. The coal had spilled into the shape of a pyramid several feet high and I bored between the pile and the wall . . . hearing them coming across the floor.

"Well, you ain't supposed to drink on the job."

"You just come on, you'll see."

I saw them now, two men peering over the partition near where I had dozed off, looking over into the coal toward where I lay afraid to breathe.

"Now where's he?" one of them said.

"He must be here somewhere. He gotta be, 'cause I seen him."

"All right, you find him. He didn't come up by me, so he's got to still be down here."

They moved slowly now, focusing the feeble rays of a flashlight into the darkness.

"Maybe he's got a gun. . . ."

"Gun?"

"Yeah. Let's get out of here."

"Hell, he didn't have nothing. His hands was empty."

"You cain't tell."

"But he's naked. . . ."

"Maybe he's got a knife. . . ."

They moved away. What if they discovered the passage to the hospital? I heard them breathing tensely now, coming toward me from the other side of the coal bin. Pressing closely to the wall, I froze, hearing someone yell, "There he is!"

"Where?"

"Back over there."

"You mean that noise?"

"Yeah, it was him."

"Hell, man, I knowed you was drunk. That was somebody walking across that manhole in the sidewalk. You git drunk just one more time on this job and it'll be the last."

A trickle of coal slid over me, sounding like a crash.

"Hey, Roscoe!" a voice called from the stairs. "What's going on down there?"

"Nothing, we're coming right up."

"Nothing, and the house full of customers?"

"Okey, it was just a big rat."

"A rat?"

"That's right."

"Hell, they're *our* rats ain't they? Leave 'em alone and get the hell on up here, will you?"

"Come on, before that bastard gets mad. We don't get paid for chasing nobody out of the basement anyway."

I watch them wobble in arm-swinging haste back to the stairs, the first shaking his head in puzzlement. Going up, their distorted shadows flowed swiftly against a circular banquet table top and disappeared. The lights snapped off, the jukebox muffled down. What now? I tried to stand, reaching out for support and feeling my hand contact a piece of metal. It was set in the wall, I reached upwarding finding three more at regular intervals. And before my mind could build the image of a ladder, I was climbing, peering upward. Just as a scraping sound began, then the dull clang of metal and something showering into my face, eyes. I ducked, thinking, "It's the sidewalk," as by some chain reaction the sound of barking came from the stairs. Looking past the vague pyramid of coal I saw several men with flashlights coming down. At first I thought they were from the hospital, then I heard, "I bet twenty to one he'll kill any rat living in three seconds by the clock!"

"Let's find him first."

"Put up your money!"

The dog barked tentatively, searching, sniffing, whining; its nails scratching crisply across the floor. Quietly, I climbed another rung, feeling the bars cold against my body.

"Where I live they got rats that don't give a damn about *no* cats, and only but a few great big dogs! Weigh fifteen, twenty pounds, man."

"Get him, Little Brother! Sick him, boy!"

The dog barked. I climbed, expecting any moment to hear him scramble into the bin. I was above the pale now, and reaching upward I felt a circular, steel-ringed hole, and above that the dome of a manhole cover that showered down another tuft of dirt. Suddenly the dog grew hysterical.

"He's smelled the rat," a voice yelled.

"Where'd he go?"

"Over there in the coal."

"He better leave that rat get out of that corner!"

"He's over there in the bin!"

"He'll cut a dog's throat in a corner, man!"

I could feel the fury of the dog's malicious bark as they urged him on. I climbed until the steel ring stopped me and clung with my back pressed against the curved mouth of the hole, my knees drawn up to my chin like a boy rolling down a hill in an auto tire.

"Hey, why's he barking up that ladder?"

"He's after the rat!"

"Shine some light up there."

"What the hell! Hey, give me the light, somebody! You see what I see?"

"Sasay—it's a man's leg!"

I went weak inside, hearing, "Bring the other light!"

"Good God!"

"Somebody done stuffed a dead body down that hole!"

I clung like a treed coon, hearing them climbing over the partition, scattering the coal.

"That's all I need to lose my license, to have a dead man found in my basement!"

"I *bet* it's that labor leader."

There was nothing to do but break out and face whatever dangers lay above the surface. Holding with one hand I pushed firmly against the cover, feeling a heavy weight upon my shoulders. Dry dirt showered down. "There's been no rain," I thought distantly. "Outside it's dry. . . ." Then my knee slipped from the ring. For a second it was quiet. Then: "Hey! He moved! That ain't no dead man, that guy's alive!"

"I didn't see anything. . . ."

"Maybe something jarred the walk. . . ."

"Hell no, he *moved!*"

"I tole you, Pritchett! I know damn well I seen somebody down here!"

"Hey!"

I could cling no longer. I felt myself slipping and kicked out, getting one foot on the top ring, then the other, crouching like a monkey on a limb, and pushing upward with one arm. The cover gave, settled back. Something struck the wall beneath me.

"Come down from there, you bastard!"

"Watch him, he might have a gun!"

A blow struck my foot. "Come down!"

I pushed, feeling a hand close around my ankle, pulling down. I kicked, stubbing my toe against something hard, feeling the hand go away.

"Get him!"

"I'm getting the cops!"

"No cops! Hell, no! You want to put me out of business?"

"Watch out the way, you all, I'll get this sonofabitch!"

I looked down. A man's face, half-illuminated from below, started steadily upward. If only I had on shoes, I thought. I could see his eyes. My lips puckered but when I tried to spit my mouth was dry.

"You better watch him, now, Talmadge!"

I pushed again, thrusting my head into the steel cover, muck and all.

"All right now, buddy," the man said, gripping my ankle. Holding on with my hands, I gave him my heel swiftly, three times, feeling his grip tighten. Steadying myself, I measured the next kick, hearing him slip away, yelling, "Get the club from behind the bar," as now, crouching on the topmost rung, I pushed upward from the hips. The weight pressing into my skull, neck, shoulders, then a rush of outside air. For a second the cap tittered upon my head, making a wavering crack through which I could see the glint of street lights. Then it clanged to the side and I pushed it away and seemed to shoot through the hole, moving so furiously that I stumbled and sprawled on the walk, my head striking the pavement, dazing me. Then from above there came a sound like thunder and a woman yelled, "Lord, God, what in the world is this!"

I rolled, looking into the faces of two women dressed in white.

"Police! A naked man, a naked . . . !" the woman screamed. "Police!"

"Oh no! No!" called a woman who crouched against a building front. "Not *naked!* Is he, Sis Spencer? Let's us be sure 'fore we call the cops. Wait'll I change my glasses."

"As ever he was born in the world! Police! Out here on the street like that. . . ."

I got to my knees, breathing hard. I saw a bar with the neon signs in the window behind me. Below the walk men called me names. Then it thundered again and I stood up, feeling the first drops of rain.

"Lawd, God, have mercy, Jesus!" the woman moaned, leaving the building and taking the other's arm. "Come on, Sis Spencer! Come on away from that sinful man!"

"Call the police," I called to them. "They're murdering a man in the basement."

There was a movement at my feet. A hand showed on the ring of the hole and I bent and pushed the manhole cover into place, hearing a curse and a second tremendous clash of thunder. Seeing the women dash scurrying down the street, I ran in the opposite direction, entering a side street of old brownstones. The rain poured. Keeping to the dark side of the street and searching in vain for an alley and remembering that none existed. What sort of people would build a city without alleys? Where did the honey-dipper carts travel? But this was Harlem, I remembered, and I must make my way to old Mary's house.

Rounding the corner in the huge drops of rain, I saw the men looming ahead. They turned and stared.

"Hey, Jack!" one of them called to the others who stood in a doorway passing a bottle between them. "Dig this here game stud!"

I turned and started across the street but a line of cars drove me back. They staggered after me catching my arm before I could cross, bringing the sickening odor of cheap sweet wine. I was surrounded. They stared in drunken amusement.

"Now here's a stud that's naked as a jaybird."

"He had to leave in a hurry, maybe."

"Look, fellows," I said, "he's after me. Let me go."

"Who's this that's after you, old man?"

"Yeah, daddy-o, who's this that's making you cut out? Her Husband?"

"Yeah, that's right—"

"Well, no better for you," one of them said. "I'm a husband myself."

"Looks like he had hold to you already, Jack. Your leg is bleeding."

I looked, realizing that I had scratched myself emerging from the manhole.

"I got away," I said, "but if he catches me he's liable to kill me!"

"Yeah, but if the cops see you running round like that, they liable to put you under the jail."

"Aw, let the man go."

Another came up and tried to pry his fingers from my arm. "Let him alone."

"Hell, Bridgewater, I'm fixing to help the man."

"Well help him then, and let him go. I once had to grab me a armful of window myself."

"Sure, Bridgewater, who hasn't?" Then to me he said, "Come on upstairs with us, daddy-o, I'll see if I got something you can wear."

I looked at him, then at the others; they were all about my own age, slightly high from the wine and amused at what they thought had been my adventure.

"Okey!" I said and followed them up the steps. We climbed three flights of narrow stairs that reeked with urine, stale cabbage. Then kidding loudly, they steered me down a hall so narrow that it was impossible to walk two abreast until we came to a door, which Bridgewater opened and we pushed inside.

A single dim bulb burned in the ceiling. It was a small room, painted a milky blue gloss. I saw a bed, two old upholstered chairs, a dresser and a beautifully made radio-phonograph.

"Sit down, Tyrone," the owner said, addressing me. "You must be tired!"

"Tyrone? That man's name ain't no Tyrone. How come you call him Tyrone?" one of them asked, laughing.

"Hell, 'cause he's a lover, that's why."

Then turning to me he grinned. "Don't pay me no mind, ole man. I'm just kidding. You want a drink?"

"No thanks."

"You got some gage? Bridgewater, give the man some gage."

"You know I don't fool with that stuff," Bridgewater said, producing a bottle and several glasses from a cabinet. He gravely poured a round of drinks. "Here you go, lover, drink this while I find you a pair of pants and a shirt. They won't be no hell, but good enough for you to get home in."

"That'll be good enough," I said. I drank it down.

'Here's one to hold it down," he said refilling the glass before I could refuse. "You all better drink up too," he said. " 'Cause my gal's due here pretty soon and I don't want her to have to look at all you half-high squares eyeballing her and all that mess."

Soon he quit rummaging in a closet and produced a brown and blue-sleeved sweater and a pair of grey slacks.

"Slip these on, man," he said.

He showed me into a small bedroom where I pulled into the slacks and sweater. The shoes were tight. When I entered the room two girls had come who looked me over as they drank. I took Bridgewater's address, promising to return his clothes, and left.

Outside the rain had begun to pour. I headed for old Mary's.

I hobbled along, keeping to side streets as much as possible, entering the avenues only when necessary and taking only a block at a time, then cutting back into a side street. The side streets were free of policemen and I saw only two on the avenues, each standing whitefaced and grim in a doorway, avoiding the rain.

I had reached the forking of three streets and started across when the man bumped against me.

"Pardon me," the voice said.

"Sure," I said, stepping into the street over the water streaming and gurgling in the gutter, only a passing stream of trucks keeping me from bolting.

"This is a dangerous crossing," the man said, his voice crotchety yet gentle.

"Thanks," I mumbled, disguising my voice. The lights were red, I had forgotten about such things. Cars shot past, their tires singing on the road. I silently repeated old Mary's address. If I were lucky, I'd soon be there.

"Would you give me a hand, please?" the old man said.

I turned, seeing him for the first time: An old man standing stiffly erect with his head held back at an angle, holding a gleaming white cane, and beneath his broad-brimmed hat, eyes, focused not at me, but out past the falling rain to some point of infinity above the gleaming street and the cars. "He's blind," I thought with relief. "He can't see me."

"All right," I said, reluctant to bother with him even for the short time it would take to cross the street. For not only was there the possibility that I was being searched for at that very moment, but the need to know something definite about myself now filled me with frantic urgency. Indeed, only the presence of a couple that had come up waiting for the lights to change kept me from insulting the old man and going off in another direction. I had to get to old Mary's. Already I had stopped thinking about the old man and taking his arm automatically without waiting for the lights to change, started across.

"How light he is," flashed through my mind as I guided him along. "It's like floating a body buoyed up by water. . . ."

I failed to see the car. It seemed to roll out of nowhere, it's brakes screeching as I snatched the old man aside, causing him to stumble on the wet asphalt as the car careened around us and ahead, with the driver's curses bursting upon my ears like acid through the rain. He breathed tensely beside me as I looked up and down the street. A car approached, passed, its horn blowing. Taking his arm, I started off, my nerves screaming with tension. I was furious, both with the driver and myself. It was as though I had deliberately tried to guide this stranger, whom I'd barely seen, into the path of a car.

"Are you all right?" the couple called behind us.

"Yes, everything's all right," the old man called, his head cocked to the side. Then to me, "That was pretty close. I felt the air from his wings as he passed. . . ."

"I'd like to take a shot at him," I said impulsively, "but it was really my fault."

"It's all right," he said.

"I was in too much of a hurry to get to an appointment. I'm sorry."

"Don't worry about it, they almost hit me at least once a day." Our feet made soft steady splashings through the swift water. Cars threw spray that slapped from fenders and humming tires.

"It's like a second flood," he said. "Such rain should purify the world."

We had reached the other side now and I slowed so that he could step upon the curb. What was he jabbering about?

"Well, here you are," I said.

"Thank you, I hope I didn't make you late."

"No, no," I said, suddenly irritated again. "I was in too much of a hurry. . . ." I started away.

"Well, a young fellow has to keep moving. . . ."

I spun in my tracks, as though I had been hit with a club, grasping his arms, there in the middle of the walk, staring into his face as his words beat in my head like the rain.

"Say it again!" I shouted.

"What?" he said. "Whaat?"

"Say it!"

"But what?"

"Goddamit, repeat it! Say the word!"

"Say what, young man?" his voice came patiently.

I cursed him seeing his sightless eyes full upon me, his expression puzzled like one struck suddenly deaf. I shook furiously. "Repeat it!"

"But I don't know—"

"Say what you said about keeping moving!" I managed.

"I don't . . . Oh yes, I said, 'I guess they keep a young fellow like you moving. . . .' "

I searched his face as his words spattered through my mind, seeing the rain dripping and lacing from his hat brim onto my arm. Why was his face so familiar? I mumbled his words like some magic formula, the key word of which I had forgotten. . . .

"Is there something wrong?" he asked.

"No . . ." I said, bewildered. "I guess not. I misunderstood you."

I stared into his eyes, smelling the aura of a strong old pipe about him as he stood quietly in my grasp.

"I don't know," I repeated. "You sound like someone I know."

"Oh, like whom?"

"I can't remember," I said, continuing to stare and hold him.

"Where is your home?" he asked. "Down South?"

"Yes, but I can't remember where. Do you believe me?"

"Yes, I do," he said quietly. "Such things happen—but you'll be late, won't you, son?"

"Late? Late for what?"

"Your appointment. What is it, a party? You've been drinking sweet wine."

Suddenly I laughed; so he was a blind detective. "No, it's not that kind of an appointment. But I'd better be getting there."

And though suddenly atremble with agitation I mumbled an apology and released his arms. He didn't seem at all alarmed by my strange behavior.

"Good night," he said softly, tapping the sidewalk three times with his cane, then after a few cautious steps, moved smoothly away through the rain. I watched him going with a sense of turmoil. There was the weight of a name on my tongue, but I couldn't pronounce it. Watching him I tried vainly to shake the feeling away. The rain was driving now. I was in an awful state, knowing that I should be on my way, yet riveted to the spot. I wiped rain streaming from my face, listening to the tapping cane. Was I going crazy? I repeated the words. Was it his face or his voice that caused this feeling? Or was it both his face *and* his words? Suddenly his face glowed luminously before my eyes as though projected against the falling rain, and it was as though my whole life depended upon my seeing his face once more.

I whirled, to run after him. It was dark. A wide, empty street of apartment buildings on my right and on the left a broad concrete playground fenced with heavy wire. Except for a woman entering one of the dark buildings, the street was empty. My eyes swept along the bleak stoops of the buildings. Where had he gone? Had I dreamed him, had I bumped my head too hard when emerging from the manhole? But that was impossible, I could still feel the lightness of him in my hands, smell the strong tobacco. Slowing to a walk I could now hear the faint tapping of the cane once more and plunged forward. If only I hadn't been so annoyed with him for having interrupted me I would have seen him back there at the crossing. . . .

"Hey, you. Blind man! Hey! You, Mr. ——" I called and stopped dead in my tracks. I had called him by a name—my grandfather's name! I looked about me, seized with a guilty uneasiness. Where had he gone? I listened, expecting a laugh or a curse. Gone. There was no sound except the racing rain. I ran again, moving painfully in my borrowed shoes, a movement part hobble, part limp, part skip and part crawl; until forced to stop of tiredness. It was a long block and I had not come to its end, but no sign of him. I was sure now that the face in which his sightless eyes were set was a face that haunted my dream. Although more patient and refined, it was the face of my grandfather.

Stopping, I found myself leaning against a stoop guarded by two weather-beaten stone lions when I seemed to hear the taps again. But oddly, this time from above a window in an upper apartment, a hollow sound in the night. Up there, several stories above, I watched a man's extended arm knocking his pipe against the sill, the ash glowing up, then dying in the rain. Then as I heard him clear his throat and start lowering the window, someone began a poorly executed flourish upon a tinny trumpet. Cursing, I plunged ahead. He must have gone into one of the buildings, I thought. He couldn't have been grandfather. Forget about him, he's been dead and you saw him die. There's too much to be done now for you to go chasing off after a ghost. . . . But still I strained my eyes and ears for a glimpse or sound of him. The street was empty, not even a car.

Turning, I started back, searching the dark for a sign. Across the street beneath the floodlighted playground the grey ground glistened with rain and there inexplicably played one small boy who alone in the great grey square bounced a ball and sang, oblivious to the rain or hour, his voice so small and distant.

For a moment I watched him in bewilderment, then retraced my steps. Where were his parents? I was tired and hungry, too much had burst upon me at once. That which should have been the past had become mixed with the present again, clashing with it, and memory beat upon me like the rain. And though I tried not to think about it, it all came back: the illness in the street, the letters to the trustees; my room at the Young Men's House (retreat), my interrupted career at the college, Bledsoe—everything. How long had it been? I had to get to my room immediately. No, I must have time to think about it. I resolved there and then that every move I made must be weighed carefully before I put it into action. I could take no chances. They might have policemen and attendants stationed at the Men's House to return me to the hospital. How long had it been since I was carried away in the ambulance? Perhaps the best course was to find old Mary's and hide there until I could fill in the blank part of my experience. I would get there as swiftly as possible.

BERNARD MALAMUD (1914–   )

Bernard Malamud writes like no one else. He is, to borrow one of his own titles, a natural, an original. He is as much his own writer as, shall we say, Chagall is his own painter. And there is, in fact, a closer imaginative affinity between these two men than there is between Malamud and those other Jewish writers, his contemporaries, with whom popular criticism tends to associate him—writers like Mailer, Bellow, Roth, and so on. The fractural nature of experience, the incongruities, the flights and the fantasies, the mythical overtones, the birds and beasts and flowers hovering on the edge of the mind, the sense of eruption and of renovation, the anxious but accepted suffering, the pervasive pathos and comedy, but over both of those, the joy—does any of this suggest the kind of imaginative character one is trying to indicate if not define?

He was born in Brooklyn, the son of immigrant Russian parents. He was graduated from the City College of New York after working at a variety of jobs, and he supported himself by teaching night classes while he did graduate study at Columbia. It was while he taught English at Oregon State University (1949 to 1961) that his first stories began to appear with refreshing regularity, and then his first four books.

The earliest of these was The Natural (1952), a comic treatment of the American hero, a baseball player, seen in terms of the great heroes of myth and legend and romance, all growing out of a simple newspaper report that Malamud had read about a player who was offered a bribe and accepted. Another novel followed: The Assistant (1957). More realistic in treatment, it is the story of a young Italian drifter who works in a poor Jewish grocery store; but the grocery is more than a store, it is also a purgatory in which suffering literally turns the hero into a Jew and morally into a human being.

In the next year came the first volume of stories, The Magic Barrel (1958), which contains some of Malamud's best stories including the title work, which many of his critics believe to be the best. The third

novel, A New Life *(1961), as its title suggests, again has to do with
the moral renovation of a man's life; its setting is something like that
Oregon college that Malamud left in the year of its publication.*

Since then he has published more stories in Idiot's First *(1963) and*
Pictures of Fidelman *(1969) and a novel,* The Fixer *(1966), quite
different from anything that came before or followed, a dark story of
unjust suffering set in Tsarist Russia that shows a little cipher of a
man becoming, through a steadfast assertion of his own courageous
humanity, a hero so big that he may move into mythology, the far
reaches of humanistic aspiration.*

*For all the comedy, the clownishness, the color, the poverty and the
pain in Malamud's fiction, it is probably its assertion of the dignity
and moral order that the suffering human individual can attain that
is basic.*

FURTHER READING

The first full-length study is Sidney Richman, *Bernard Malamud*
(1967). Glenn Meeter has written a brief study, *Bernard Malamud
and Philip Roth: A Critical Essay* (1968). See also Ihab Hassan,
Radical Innocence: Studies in the Contemporary American Novel
(1961), and Philip Rahv's introduction to *A Malamud Reader*
(1967).

Still Life *(1963)*

Months after vainly seeking a studio on the vie Margutta, del
Babuino, della Croce,[1] and elsewhere in that neighborhood, Arthur
Fidelman settled for part of a crowded, windowy, attic-like atelier on
a cobblestone street in the Trastevere,[2] strung high with sheets and
underwear. He had, a week before, in "personal notices" in the American
language newspaper in Rome, read: "Studio to share, cheap, many
advantages, etc., A Oliovino," and after much serious anguish (the curt
advertisement having recalled dreams he had dreamed were dead),
many indecisions, enunciations and renunciations, Fidelman had, one
very cold late-December morning, hurried to the address given, a worn
four-story building with a yellowish façade stained brown along the
edges. On the top floor, in a thickly cluttered artist's studio smelling
aromatically of turpentine and oil paints, the inspiring sight of an easel
lit in unwavering light from the three large windows setting the former

[1] Streets in Rome peopled by chic artists.
[2] A section of Rome immediately across the Tiber.

art student on fire once more to paint, he had dealt not with a pittore,[3] as expected, but with a pittrice,[4] Annamaria Aliovino.

The pittrice, a thin, almost gaunt, high-voiced, restless type, with short black uncombed hair, violet mouth, distracted eyes and tense neck, a woman with narrow buttocks and piercing breasts, was in her way attractive if not in truth beautiful. She had on a thick black woolen sweater, eroded black velveteen culottes, black socks, and leather sandals spotted with drops of paint. Fidelman and she eyed each other stealthily and he realized at once she was, as a woman, indifferent to him or his type, who or which made no difference. But after ten minutes, despite the turmoil she exuded even as she dispassionately answered his hesitant questions, the art student, ever a sucker for strange beauty and all sorts of experiences, felt himself involved with and falling for her. Not my deep dish, he warned himself, aware of all the dangers to him and his renewed desire to create art; yet he was already half in love with her. It can't be, he thought in desperation; but it could. It had happened to him before. In her presence he tightly shut both eyes and wholeheartedly wished against what might be. Really he trembled, and though he labored to extricate his fate from hers, he was already a plucked bird, greased, and ready for frying. Fidelman protested within—cried out severely against the weak self, called himself ferocious names but could do not much, a victim of his familiar response, a too passionate fondness for strangers. So Annamaria, who had advertised a twenty thousand lire monthly rental, in the end doubled the sum, and Fidelman paid through both nostrils, cash for first and last months (should he attempt to fly by night) plus a deposit of ten thousand for possible damages. An hour later he moved in with his imitation leather suitcase. This happened in the dead of winter. Below the cold sunlit windows stood two frozen umbrella pines and beyond, in the near distance, sparkled the icy Tiber.

The studio was well heated, Annamaria had insisted, but the cold leaked in through the wide windows. It was more a blast; the art student shivered but was kept warm by his hidden love for the pittrice. It took him most of a day to clear himself a space to work, about a third of the studio was as much as he could manage. He stacked her canvases five deep against her portion of the walls, curious to examine them but Annamaria watched his every move (he noticed several self-portraits) although she was at the same time painting a monumental natura morta of a loaf of bread with two garlic bulbs ("Pane ed Aglii").[5] He moved stacks of *Oggi*,[6] piles of postcards and yellowed letters, and a bundle of calendars going back to many years ago; also a Perugina candy box

---

[3] "Painter."

[4] "Female painter."

[5] "Bread and Garlic."

[6] *"Today"*; a popular picture magazine.

full of broken pieces of Etruscan pottery, one of small sea shells, and a third of medallions of various saints and of the Virgin, which she warned him to handle with care. He had uncovered a sagging cot by a dripping stone sink in his corner of the studio and there he slept. She furnished an old chafing dish and a broken table, and he bought a few household things he needed. Annamaria rented the art student an easel for a thousand lire a month. Her quarters were private, a room at the other end of the studio whose door she kept locked, handing him the key when he had to use the toilet. The wall was thin and the instrument noisy. He could hear the whistle and rush of her water, and though he tried to be quiet, because of the plumbing the bowl was always brimful and the pour of his stream embarrassed him. At night, if there was need, although he was tempted to use the sink, he fished out the yellowed, sedimented pot under his bed; once or twice, as he was using it in the thick of night, he had the impression she was awake and listening.

They painted in their overcoats, Annamaria wearing a black babushka, Fidelman a green wool hat pulled down over his frozen ears. She kept a pan of hot coals at her feet and every so often lifted a sandaled foot to toast it. The marble floor of the studio was sheer thick ice; Fidelman wore two pairs of tennis socks his sister Bessie had recently sent him from the States. Annamaria, a leftie, painted with a smeared leather glove on her hand, and theoretically his easel had been arranged so that he couldn't see what she was doing but he often sneaked looks at her work. The pittrice, to his surprise, painted with flicks of her fingers and wrists, peering at her performance with almost shut eyes. He noticed she alternated still lifes with huge lyric abstractions—massive whorls of red and gold exploding in all directions, these built on, entwined with, and ultimately concealing a small black religious cross, her first two brush strokes on every abstract canvass. Once when Fidelman gathered the nerve to ask her why the cross, she answered it was the symbol that gave the painting its meaning.

He was eager to know more but she was impatient. "Eh," she shrugged, "who can explain art."

Though her response to his various attempts to become better acquainted were as a rule curt, and her voluntary attention to him, shorter still—she was able, apparently, to pretend he wasn't there—Fidelman's feeling for Annamaria grew, and he was as unhappy in love as he had ever been.

But he was patient, a persistent virtue, served her often in various capacities, for instance carrying down four flights of stairs her two bags of garbage shortly after supper—the portinaia was crippled and the portiere never around—sweeping the studio clean each morning, even running to retrieve a brush or paint tube when she happened to drop one—offering any service any time, you name it. She accepted these small favors without giving them notice.

One morning after reading a many-paged letter she had just got in the mail, Annamaria was sad, sullen, unable to work; she paced around restlessly, it troubled him. But after feverishly painting a widening purple spiral that continued off the canvas, she regained a measure of repose. This heightened her beauty, lent it somehow a youthful quality it didn't ordinarily have—he guessed her to be no older than twenty-seven or -eight; so Fidelman, inspired by the change in her, hoping it might foretoken better luck for him, approached Annamaria, removed his hat and suggested since she went out infrequently why not lunch for a change at the trattoria at the corner, Guido's, where workmen assembled and the veal and white wine were delicious? She, to his surprise, after darting an uneasy glance out of the window at the tops of the motionless umbrella pines, abruptly assented. They ate well and conversed like human beings, although she mostly limited herself to answering his modest questions. She informed Fidelman she had come from Naples to Rome two years ago, although it seemed much longer, and he told her he was from the United States. Being so physically close to her, able to inhale the odor of her body—like salted flowers—and intimately eating together, excited Fidelman, and he sat very still, not to rock the boat and spill a drop of what was so precious to him. Anna-maria ate hungrily, her eyes usually lowered. Once she looked at him with a shade of a smile and he felt beatitude; the art student contemplated many such meals though he could ill afford them, every cent he spent, saved and sent by Bessie.

After zuppa inglese and a peeled apple she patted her lips with a napkin, and still in good humor, suggested they take the bus to the Piazza del Popolo and visit some painter friends of hers.

"I'll introduce you to Alberto Moravia."

"With pleasure," Fidelman said, bowing.

But when they stepped into the street and were walking to the bus stop near the river a cold wind blew up and Annamaria turned pale.

"Something wrong?" Fidelman inquired.

"The East Wind," she answered testily.

"What wind?"

"The Evil Eye," she said with irritation. "Malocchio."

He had heard something of the sort. They returned quickly to the studio, their heads lowered against the noisy wind, the pittrice from time to time furtively crossing herself. A black-habited old nun passed them at the trattoria corner, from whom Annamaria turned in torment, muttering, "Jettatura! Porca miseria!"[7] When they were upstairs in the studio she insisted Fidelman touch his testicles three times to undo or dispel who knows what witchcraft, and he modestly obliged. Her request had inflamed him although he cautioned himself to remember it was in purpose and essence, theological.

Later she received a visitor, a man who came to see her on Monday

---

[7] Italian expletives, approximating our "Get lost, you muthah. . . ."

and Friday afternoons after his work in a government bureau. Her visitors, always men, whispered with her a minute, then left restlessly; most of them, excepting also Giancarlo Balducci, a crosseyed illustrator—Fidelman never saw again. But the one who came oftenest stayed longest, a solemn gray-haired gent. Augusto Ottogalli, with watery blue eyes and missing side teeth, old enough to be her father for sure. He wore a slanted black fedora, and a shabby gray overcoat too large for him, greeted Fidelman vacantly and made him inordinately jealous. When Augusto arrived in the afternoon the pittrice usually dropped anything she was doing and they retired to her room, at once locked and bolted. The art student wandered alone in the studio for dreadful hours. When Augusto ultimately emerged, looking disheveled, and if successful, defeated, Fidelman turned his back on him and the old man hastily let himself out of the door. After his visits, and only his, Annamaria did not appear in the studio for the rest of the day. Once when Fidelman knocked on her door to invite her out to supper, she told him to use the pot because she had a headache and was sound asleep. On another occasion when Augusto was locked long in her room with her, after a tormenting two hours Fidelman tip-toed over and put his jealous ear to the door. All he could hear was the buzz and sigh of their whispering. Peeking through the keyhole he saw them both in their overcoats, sitting on her bed. Augusto tightly clasping her hands, whispering passionately, his nose empurpled with emotion, Annamaria's white face averted. When the art student checked an hour afterward, they were still at it, the old man imploring, the pittrice weeping. The next time, Augusto came with a priest, a portly, heavy-breathing man with a doubtful face. But as soon as they appeared in the studio Annamaria, enraged to fury, despite the impassioned entreatments of Augusto, began to throw at them anything of hers or Fidelman's she could lay hands on.

"Bloodsuckers!" she shouted, "scorpions! parasites!" until they had hastily retreated. Yet when Augusto, worn and harried, returned alone, without complaint she retired to her room with him.

2

Fidelman's work, despite the effort and despair he gave it, was going poorly. Every time he looked at unpainted canvas he saw harlequins, whores, tragic kings, fragmented musicians, the sick and the dread. Still, tradition was tradition and what if he should want to make more? Since he had always loved art history he considered embarking on a "Mother and Child," but was afraid her image would come out too much Bessie—after all, fifteen years between them. Or maybe a moving "Pietà," the dead son's body held like a broken wave in mama's frail arms? A curse on art history—he fought the fully prefigured picture though some of his former best paintings had jumped in every detail to the mind. Yet if so, where's true engagement? Sometimes I'd like to forget every picture I've seen, Fidelman thought. Almost in panic he sketched in charcoal a coat-tailed "Figure of a Jew Fleeing" and quickly hid it away. After that, ideas, prefigured or not, were scarce. "Astonish me," he muttered to himself, wondering whether to return to surrealism. He also considered a series of "Relations to Place and Space," constructions in squares and circles, the pleasures of tri-dimensional geometry of linear abstraction, only he had little heart for it. The furthest abstraction, Fidelman thought, is the blank canvas. A moment later he asked himself, if painting shows who you are, why should not painting?

After the incident with the priest Annamaria was despondent for a week, stayed in her room sometimes bitterly crying, Fidelman often standing helplessly by her door. However this was a prelude to a burst of creativity by the pittrice. Works by the dozens leaped from her brush and stylus. She continued her lyric abstractions based on the theme of a hidden cross and spent hours with a long black candle, burning holes in heavy white paper ("Buchi Spontanei").[8] Having mixed coffee grounds, sparkling bits of crushed mirror and ground-up sea shells, she blew the dust on mucilaged paper ("Velo nella Nebbia").[9] She composed collages of rags and toilet tissue. After a dozen linear studies ("Linee Discendenti"),[10] she experimented with gold leaf sprayed with umber, the whole while wet combed in long undulations with a fine comb. She framed this in a black frame and hung it on end like a diamond ("Luce di Candela").[11] Annamaria worked intently, her brow furrowed, violet mouth tightly pursed, eyes lit, nostrils palpitating in creative excitement. And when she had temporarily run out of new ideas she did a mythological bull in red clay ("La Donna Toro"),[12] afterwards returning to nature morte [13] with bunches of bananas; then self-portraits.

The pittrice occasionally took time out to see what Fidelman was up to, although not much, and then editing his efforts. She changed lines and altered figures, or swabbed paint over whole compositions that didn't appeal to her. There was not much that did, but Fidelman was grateful for any attention she gave his work, and even kept at it to incite her criticism. He could feel his heart beat in his teeth whenever she stood close to him modifying his work, he deeply breathing her intimate smell of sweating flowers. She used perfume only when Augusto came and it disappointed Fidelman that the old man should evoke the use of bottled fragrance; yet he was cheered that her

[8] "Spontaneous Holes."
[9] "Veil in the Fog."
[10] "Descending Lines."
[11] "Candlelight."
[12] "The Lady Bull
[13] "Still life."

natural odor which he, so to say, got for free, was so much more exciting than the stuff she doused herself with for her decrepit Romeo. He
had noticed she had a bit of soft belly but he loved the pliant roundness
and often daydreamed of it. Thinking it might please her, for he pleased
her rarely (he reveried how it would be once she understood the true
depth of his love for her), the art student experimented with some of
the things Annamaria had done—the spontaneous holes, for instance,
several studies of "Lines Ascending," and two lyrical abstract expressionistic pieces based on, interwoven with, and ultimately concealing a
Star of David, although for these attempts he soon discovered he had
earned, instead of her good will, an increased measure of scorn.

However, Annamaria continued to eat lunch with him at Guido's,
and more often than not, supper, although she said practically nothing
during meals and afterwards let her eye roam over the faces of the men
at the other tables. But there were times after they had eaten when she
would agree to go for a short walk with Fidelman, if there was no serious wind; and once in a while they entered a movie in the Trastevere,
for she hated to cross any of the bridges of the Tiber, and then only in
a bus, sitting stiffly, staring ahead. As they were once riding, Fidelman
seized the opportunity to hold her tense fist in his, but as soon as they
were across the river she tore it out of his grasp. He was by now giving
her presents—tubes of paints, the best brushes, a few yards of Belgian
linen, which she accepted without comment; she also borrowed small
sums from him, nothing startling—a hundred lire today, five hundred
tomorrow. And she announced one morning that he would thereafter,
since he used so much of both, have to pay additional for water and
electricity—he already paid extra for the heatless heat. Fidelman,
though continually worried about money, assented. He would have given
his last lira to lie on her soft belly, but she offered niente, not so much
as a caress; until one day, he was permitted to look on as she sketched
herself nude in his presence. Since it was bitter cold the pittrice did
this in two stages. First she removed her sweater and brassiere, and
viewing herself in a long, faded mirror, quickly sketched the upper half
of her body before it turned blue. He was dizzily enamored of her form
and flesh. Hastily fastening the brassiere and pulling on her sweater,
Annamaria stepped out of her sandals and peeled off her culottes,
and white panties torn at the crotch, then drew the rest of herself down
to her toes. The art student begged permission to sketch along with her
but the pittrice denied it, so he had, as best one can, to commit to
memory her lovely treasures—the hard, piercing breasts, narrow shapely
buttocks, vine-hidden labia, the font and sweet beginning of time. After
she had drawn herself and dressed, and when Augusto appeared and
they had retired behind her bolted door. Fidelman sat motionless on his
high stool before the glittering blue-skied windows, slowly turning to
ice to faint strains of Bach.

3

The art student increased his services to Annamaria, her increase was scorn, or so it seemed. This severely bruised his spirit. What have I done to deserve such treatment? That I pay my plenty of rent on time? That I buy her all sorts of presents, not to mention two full meals a day? That I live in flaming hot and freezing cold? That I passionately adore each sweet-and-sour bit of her? He figured it bored her to see so much of him. For a week Fidelman disappeared during the day, sat in cold libraries or stood around in frosty museums. He tried painting after midnight and into the early morning hours but the pittrice found out and unscrewed the bulbs before she went to bed. "Don't waste my electricity, this isn't America." He screwed in a dim blue bulb and worked silently from one a.m. to five. At dawn he discovered he had painted a blue picture. Fidelman wandered in the streets of the city. At night he slept in the studio and could hear her sleeping in her room. She slept restlessly, dreamed badly, and often moaned. He dreamed he had three eyes.

For two weeks he spoke to no one but a dumpy four-and-a-half foot female on the third floor, and to her usually to say no. Fidelman, having often heard the music of Bach drifting up from below, had tried to picture the lady piano player, imagining a quiet blonde with a slender body, a woman of grace and beauty. It had turned out to be Clelia Montemaggio, a middle-aged old maid music teacher, who sat at an old upright piano, her apartment door open to let out the cooking smells, particularly fried fish on Friday. Once when coming up from bringing down the garbage, Fidelman had paused to listen to part of a partita at her door and she had lassoed him in for an espresso and pastry. He ate and listened to Bach, her plump bottom moving spryly on the bench as she played not badly. "Lo spirito," she called to him raptly over her shoulder, "l'architettura!" [14] Fidelman nodded. Thereafter whenever she spied him in the hall she attempted to entice him with cream-filled pastries and J.S.B., whom she played apparently exclusively.

"Come een," she called in English, "I weel play for you. We weel talk. There is no use for too much solitude." But the art student, burdened by his, spurned hers.

Unable to work, he wandered in the streets in a desolate mood, his spirit dusty in a city of fountains and leaky water taps. Water, water everywhere, spouting, flowing, dripping, whispering secrets, love love love, but not for him. If Rome's so sexy, where's mine? Fidelman's Romeless Rome. It belonged least to those who yearned most for it. With slow steps he climbed the Pincio,[15] if possible to raise his spirits gazing down at the rooftops of the city, spires, cupolas, towers, monuments, compounded history and past time. It was in sight, possessible,

14 "The spirit . . . the structure!"
15 Hill in Rome.

all but its elusive spirit; after so long he was still straniero. He was then struck by a thought: if you could paint this sight, give it its quality in yours, the spirit belonged to you. History become esthetic! Fidelman's scalp thickened. A wild rush of things he might paint swept sweetly through him: saints in good and bad health, whole or maimed, in gold and red; nude gray rabbis at Auschwitz, black or white Negroes—what not when *any* color dripped from your brush? And if these, so also ANNAMARIA ES PULCHRA.[16] He all but cheered. What more intimate possession of a woman! He would paint her, whether she permitted or not, posed or not—she was his to paint, he could with eyes shut. Maybe something will come after all of my love for her. His spirits elevated, Fidelman ran most of the way home.

It took him eight days, a labor of love. He tried her as nude and although able to imagine every inch of her, could not commit it to canvas. Then he suffered until it occurred to him to paint her as "Virgin with Child." The idea astonished and elated him. Fidelman went ferverishly to work and caught an immediate likeness in paint. Annamaria, saintly beautiful, held in her arms the infant resembling his little nephew Georgie. The pittrice, aware, of course, of his continuous activity, cast curious glances his way, but Fidelman, painting in the corner by the stone sink, kept the easel turned away from her. She pretended unconcern. Done for the day he covered the painting and carefully guarded it. The art student was painting Annamaria in a passion of tenderness for the infant at her breast, her face responsive to its innocence. When, on the ninth day, in trepidation Fidelman revealed his work, the pittrice's eyes clouded and her underlip curled. He was about to grab the canvas and smash it up all over the place when her expression fell apart. The art student postponed all movement but visible trembling. She seemed at first appalled, a darkness descended on her, she was undone. She wailed wordlessly, then sobbed, "You have seen my soul." They embraced tempestuously, her breasts stabbing him, Annamaria bawling on his shoulder. Fidelman kissed her wet face and salted lips, she murmuring as he fooled with the hook of her brassiere under her sweater, "Aspetta, aspetta, caro, Augusto viene."[17] He was mad with expectation and suspense.

Augusto, who usually arrived punctually at four, did not appear that Friday afternoon. Uneasy as the hour approached, Annamaria seemed relieved as the streets grew dark. She had worked badly after viewing Fidelman's painting, sighed frequently, gazed at him with sweet-sad smiles. At six she gave in to his urging and they retired to her room, his unframed "Virgin with Child" already hanging above her bed, replacing a gaunt self-portrait. He was curiously disappointed in the picture—surfacy thin—and made a mental note to borrow it back in the

16 "ANNAMARIA IS BEAUTIFUL."
17 "Wait, wait, dear, Augusto is coming."

morning to work on it more. But the conception, at least, deserved the reward. Annamaria cooked supper. She cut his meat for him and fed him forkfuls. She peeled Fidelman's orange and stirred sugar in his coffee. Afterwards, at his nod, she locked and bolted the studio and bedroom doors and they undressed and slipped under her blankets. How good to be for a change on this side of the locked door, Fidelman thought, relaxing marvelously. Annamaria, however, seemed tensely alert to the noises of the old building, including a parrot screeching, some shouting kids running up the stairs, a soprano singing "Ritorna, vincitor!"[18] But she calmed down and then hotly embraced Fidelman. In the middle of a passionate kiss the doorbell rang.

Annamaria stiffened in his arms. "Diavolo! Augusto!"

"He'll go away," Fidelman advised. "Both doors locked."

But she was at once out of bed, drawing on her culottes. "Get dressed," she said.

He hopped up and hastily got into his pants.

Annamaria unlocked and unbolted the inner door and then the outer one. It was the postman waiting to collect ten lire for an overweight letter from Naples.

After she had read the long letter and wiped away a tear they undressed and got back into bed.

"Who is he to you?" Fidelman asked.

"Who?"

"Augusto."

"An old friend. Like a father. We went through much together."

"Were you lovers?"

"Look, if you want me, take me. If you want to ask questions, go back to school."

He determined to mind his business.

"Warm me," she said, "I'm freezing."

Fidelman stroked her slowly. After ten minutes she said, " 'Gioco di mano, gioco di villano.'[19] Use your imagination."

He used his imagination and she responded with excitement. "Dolce tesoro,"[20] she whispered, flicking the tip of her tongue into his ear, then with little bites biting his ear lobe.

The door bell rang loudly.

"For Christ's sake, don't answer," Fidelman groaned. He tried to hold her down but she was already up, hunting her robe.

"Put on your pants," she hissed.

He had thoughts of waiting for her in bed but it ended with his dressing fully. She sent him to the door. It was the crippled portinaia, the art student having neglected to take down the garbage.

[18] "Come back, conqueror!" an aria from Verdi's *Aïda*.
[19] "Play of the hand, impolite play."
[20] "Sweet treasure."

Annamaria furiously got the two bags and handed them to her.

In bed she was so cold her teeth chattered.

Tense with desire Fidelman warmed her.

"Angelo mio," she murmured. "Amore, possess me."

He was about to when she rose in a hurry. "The cursed door again!" Fidelman gnashed his teeth. "I heard nothing."

In her torn yellow silk robe she hurried to the front door, opened and shut it, quickly locked and bolted it, did the same in her room and slid into bed.

"You were right, it was nobody."

She embraced him, her hairy armpits perfumed. He responded with postponed passion.

"Enough of antipasto," Annamaria said. She reached for his member.

Overwrought, Fidelman though fighting himself not to, spent himself in her hand. Although he mightily willed resurrection, his wilted flower bit the dust.

She furiously shoved him out of bed, into the studio, flinging his clothes after him.

"Pig, beast, onanist!"

4

At least she lets me love her. Daily Fidelman shopped, cooked, and cleaned for her. Every morning he took her shopping sack off the hook, went to the street market and returned with the bag stuffed full of greens, pasta, eggs, meat, cheese, wine, bread. Annamaria insisted on three hearty meals a day although she had once told him she no longer enjoyed eating. Twice he had seen her throw up her supper. What she enjoyed he didn't know except it wasn't Fidelman. After he had served her at her table he was allowed to eat alone in the studio. At two every afternoon she took her siesta, and though it was forbidden to make noise, he was allowed to wash the dishes, dust and clean her room, swab the toilet bowl. She called, Fatso, and in he trotted to get her anything she had run out of—drawing pencils, sanitary belt, safety pins. After she waked from her nap, rain or shine, snow or hail, he was now compelled to leave the studio so she could work in peace and quiet. He wandered, in the tramontana,[21] from one cold two-bit movie to another. At seven he was back to prepare her supper, and twice a week Augusto's, who sported a new black hat and spiffy overcoat, and pitied the art student with both wet blue eyes but wouldn't look at him. After supper, another load of dishes, the garbage downstairs, and when Fidelman returned, with or without Augusto Annamaria was already closeted behind her bolted door. He checked through the keyhole on Mondays

21 "North wind."

and Fridays but she and the old gent were always fully clothed. Fidel-man had more than once complained to her that his punishment ex-ceeded his crime, but the pittrice said he was a type she would never have any use for. In fact he did not exist for her. Not existing how could he paint, although he told himself he must? He couldn't. He aim-lessly froze wherever he went, a mean cold that seared his lungs, although under his overcoat he wore a new thick sweater Bessie had knitted for him, and two woolen scarves around his neck. Since the night Annamaria had kicked him out of bed he had not been warm; yet he often dreamed of ultimate victory. Once when he was on his lonely way out of the house—a night she was giving a party for some painter friends, Fidelman, a drooping butt in the corner of his mouth, carrying the garbage bags, met Clelia Montemaggio coming up the stairs.

"You look like a frozen board," she said. "Come in and enjoy the warmth and a little Bach."

Unable to unfreeze enough to say no, he continued down with the garbage.

"Every man gets the woman he deserves," she called after him.

"Who got," Fidelman muttered. "Who gets."

He considered jumping into the Tiber but it was full of ice that winter.

One night at the end of February, Annamaria, to Fidelman's aston-ishment—it deeply affected him—said he might go with her to a party at Giancarlo Balducci's studio on the Via dell'Oca; she needed somebody to accompany her in the bus across the bridge and Augusto was flat on his back with the Asian flu. The party was lively—painters, sculptors, some writers, two diplomats, a prince and a visiting Hindu sociologist, their ladies and three hotsy-totsy, scantily dressed, unattached girls. One of them, a shapely beauty with orange hair, bright eyes, and warm ways became interested in Fidelman, except that he was dazed by Anna-maria, seeing her in a dress for the first time, a ravishing, rich, ruby-colored affair. The crosseyed host had provided simply a huge cut-glass bowl of spiced mulled wine, and the guests dipped ceramic glasses into it, and guzzled away. Everyone but the art student seemed to be enjoy-ing· himself. One or two of the men disappeared into other rooms with female friends or acquaintances and Annamaria, in a gay mood, did a fast shimmy to rhythmic handclapping. She was drinking steadily and when she wanted her glass filled, politely called him "Arturo." He began to have mild thoughts of possibly possessing her.

The party bloomed, at least forty, and turned wildish. Practical jokes were played. Fidelman realized his left shoe had been smeared with mustard. Balducci's black cat mewed at a fat lady's behind, a slice of sausage pinned to her dress. Before midnight there were two fist fights, Fidelman enjoying both but not getting involved, though once he was socked on the neck by a sculptor who had aimed at a painter.

The girl with the orange hair, still interested in the art student, invited him to join her in Balducci's bedroom, but he continued to be devoted to Annamaria, his eyes tied to her every move. He was jealous of the illustrator, who whenever near her, nipped her bottom.

One of the sculptors, Orazio Pinello, a slender man with a darkish face, heavy black brows, and bleached blond hair, approached Fidelman. "Haven't we met before, caro?"

"Maybe," the art student said, perspiring lightly. "I'm Arthur Fidelman, an American painter."

"You don't say? Action painter?"

"Always active."

"I refer of course to Abstract Expressionism."

"Of course. Well, sort of. On and off."

"Haven't I seen some of your work around? Galleria Schneider? Some symmetric, hard-edge, biomorphic forms? Not bad as I remember."

Fidelman thanked him, in full blush.

"Who are you here with?" Orazio Pinello asked.

"Annamaria Oliovino."

"Her?" said the sculptor. "But she's a fake."

"Is she?" Fidelman said with a sigh.

"Have you looked at her work?"

"With one eye. Her art is bad but I find her irresistable."

"Peccato." [22] The sculptor shrugged and drifted away.

A minute later there was another fist fight, during which the bright-eyed orange head conked Fidelman with a Chinese vase. He went out cold and when he came to, Annamaria and Balducci were undressing him in the illustrator's bedroom. Fidelman experienced an almost overwhelming pleasure, then Balducci explained that the art student had been chosen to pose in the nude for drawings both he and the pittrice would do of him. He explained there had been a discussion as to which of them did male nudes best and they had decided to settle it in a short contest. Two easels had been wheeled to the center of the studio; a half hour was allotted to the contestants, and the guests would judge who had done the better job. Though he at first objected because it was a cold night, Fidelman nevertheless felt warmish from wine so he agreed to pose; besides he was proud of his muscles and maybe if she sketched him nude it might arouse her interest for a tussle later. And if he wasn't painting he was at least being painted.

So the pittrice and Giancarlo Balducci, in paint-smeared smocks, worked for thirty minutes by the clock, the whole party silently looking on, with the exception of the orange-haired tart, who sat in the corner eating a prosciutto sandwich. Annamaria, her brow furrowed, lips pursed, drew intensely with crayon; Balducci worked calmly in colored chalk. The guests were absorbed, although after ten minutes the Hindu

---

22 "Too bad."

went home. A journalist locked himself in the painter's bedroom with orange head and would not admit his wife who pounded on the door. Fidelman, standing barefoot on a bathmat, was eager to see what Annamaria was accomplishing but had to be patient. When the half hour was up he was permitted to look. Balducci had drawn a flock of green and black abstract testiculate circles, Fidelman shuddered. But Annamaria's drawing was representational, not Fidelman although of course inspired by him: A gigantic funereal phallus that resembled a broken-backed snake. The blond sculptor inspected it with half-closed eyes, then yawned and left. By now the party was over, the guests departed, lights out except for a few dripping white candles. Balducci was collecting his ceramic glasses and emptying ash trays, and Annamaria had thrown up. The art student afterwards heard her begging the illustrator to sleep with her but Balducci complained of fatigue.

"I will if he won't," Fidelman offered.

Annamaria, enraged, spat on her picture of his unhappy phallus.

"Don't dare come near me," she cried. "Malocchio! Jettatura!" [23]

5

The next morning he awoke sneezing, a nasty cold. How can I go on? Annamaria, showing no signs of pity or remorse, continued shrilly to berate him. "You've brought me nothing but bad luck since you came here. I'm letting you stay because you pay well but I warn you to keep out of my sight."

"But how—" he asked hoarsely.

"That doesn't concern me."

"—how will I paint?"

"Who cares? Paint at night."

"Without light—"

"Paint in the dark. I'll buy you a can of black paint."

"How can you be so cruel to a man who loves—"

"I'll scream," she said.

He left in anguish. Later while she was at her siesta he came back, got some of things and tried to paint in the hall. No dice. Fidelman wandered in the rain. He sat for hours on the Spanish Steps. Then he returned to the house and went slowly up the stairs. The door was locked. "Annamaria," he hoarsely called. Nobody answered. In the street he stood at the river wall, watching the dome of St. Peter's in the distance. Maybe a potion, Fidelman thought, or an amulet? He doubted either would work. How do you go about hanging yourself? In the late afternoon he went back to the house—would say he was sick, needed rest, possibly a doctor. He felt feverish. She could hardly refuse.

But she did, although explaining she felt bad herself. He held onto

[23] "Evil eye! Scram!"

the bannister as he went down the stairs. Clelia Montemaggio's door was open. Fidelman paused, then continued down but she had seen him. "Come een, come een."

He went reluctantly in. She fed him camomile tea and panettone. He ate in a wolfish hurry as she seated herself at the piano.

"No Bach, please, my head aches from various troubles."

"Where's your dignity?" she asked.

"Try Chopin, that's lighter."

"Respect yourself, please."

Fidelman removed his hat as she began to play a Bach prelude, her bottom rhythmic on the bench. Though his cold oppressed him and he could hardly breathe, tonight the spirit, the architecture, moved him. He felt his face to see if he were crying but only his nose was wet. On the top of the piano Clelia had placed a bowl of white carnations in full bloom. Each white petal seemed a white flower. If I could paint those gorgeous flowers, Fidelman thought. If I could paint something. By Jesus, if I could paint myself, that'd show them! Astonished by the thought he ran out of the house.

The art student hastened to a costume shop and settled on a cassock and fuzzy black soupbowl biretta, envisaging another Rembrandt: "Portrait of the Artist as Priest." He hurried with his bulky package back to the house. Annamaria was handing the garbage to the portinaia as Fidelman thrust his way into the studio. He quickly changed into the priest's vestments. The pittrice came in wildly to tell him where he got off, but when she saw Fidelman already painting himself as priest, with a moan she rushed into her room. He worked with smoking intensity and in no time created an amazing likeness. Annamaria, after stealthily re-entering the studio, with heaving bosom and agitated eyes closely followed his progress. At last, with a cry she threw herself at his feet.

"Forgive me, Father, for I have sinned—"

Dripping brush in hand, he stared down at her. "Please, I—"

"Oh, Father, if you knew how I have sinned. I've been a whore—"

After a moment's thought, Fidelman said, "If so, I absolve you."

"Not without penance. First listen to the rest. I've had no luck with men. They're all bastards. Or else I jinx them. If you want the truth I am an Evil Eye myself. Anybody who loves me is cursed."

He listened, fascinated.

"Augusto is really my uncle. After many others he became my lover. At least he's gentle. My father found out and swore he'd kill us both. When I got pregnant I was scared to death. A sin can go too far. Augusto told me to have the baby and leave it at an orphanage, but the night it was born I was confused and threw it into the Tiber. I was afraid it was an idiot."

She was sobbing. He drew back.

"Wait," she wept. "The next time in bed Augusto was impotent. Since then he's been imploring me to confess so he can get back his powers. But everytime I step into the confessional my tongue turns to bone. The priest can't tear a word out of me. That's how it's been all my life, don't ask my why because I don't know."

She grabbed his knees, "Help me, Father, for Christ's sake."

Fidelman, after a short tormented time, said in a quavering voice, "I forgive you, my child."

"The penance," she wailed, "first the penance."

After reflecting, he replied, "say one hundred times each, Our Father and Hail Mary."

"More," Annamaria wept. "More, more. Much more."

Gripping his knees so hard they shook she burrowed her head into his black-buttoned lap. He felt the surprised beginnings of an erection.

"In that case," Fidelman said, shuddering a little, "better undress."

"Only," Annamaria said, "if you keep your vestments on."

"Not the cassock, too clumsy."

"At least the biretta."

He agreed to that.

Annamaria undressed in a swoop. Her body was extraordinarily lovely, the flesh glowing. In her bed they tightly embraced. She clasped his buttocks, he cupped hers. Pumping slowly he nailed her to her cross.

SAUL BELLOW (1915–   )

Bellow's story, "Looking for Mr. Green," is the attempt of a quite anonymous character, the narrator, to locate another character who refuses to answer to his name. This story can stand as emblematic of Bellow's central fictional concern: what is identity, and, more than that, can one possibly bear to know?

His stories, long and short, have a curious similarity in the way that they end, hanging in the air. Dangling Man (1944), his first novel, could give a perfectly appropriate title to every book that has followed. His characters always seem to be spending their energies in trying to escape the nets that would keep them from being what they are, and then in hovering over the unknown declivities in which they might find out and which they themselves have been struggling toward but into which they are finally unwilling to plunge.

It is difficult to know whether Saul Bellow, with all his great gift of narrative style (ranging from the most colloquial and relaxed to the most literary and "ordered," mixing these styles when he wishes and always handling both, and all the variations between, exactly as he wants them), is dramatizing a psychological crisis of our time, a continuing psychological problem of his own, or an identification of one of these with the other.

He has given lectures on and written essays about the situation of the writer today, including himself. These do not throw much light on the question one asks. Nor does his biography as it is publicly available.

He was born in Quebec of Russian immigrant parents but brought up in Chicago, where he attended the university for a time and then was graduated from Northwestern (1937). He taught at Chicago and then Minnesota, traveled, won awards, lectured in many places, and finally settled into membership of the Committee on Social Thought at the University of Chicago, which he still inhabits.

His novels are an admirable attempt to imagine a hero who, coping with, confronting, finally demanding to meet his own experience, hopes at the end to meet himself, and in the course of this "heroic" effort, Bellow of course takes us through the basic problems of his and our time. In the course of it, too, he attempts many literary strategies in all of which he is expert, from the simply and completely persuasive realistic to the outer frontiers of fantasy where a wholly different kind of persuasiveness pertains, one in which he is equally expert. The novels, after the first, are The Victim *(1947),* The Adventures of Augie March *(1953),* Henderson the Rain King *(1959), and* Herzog *(1964). The books of shorter fiction are* Seize the Day *(1956) and* Mosby's Memoirs and Other Stories *(1968). There is also a play,* The Last Analysis *(1964). His most recent publication is a novel,* Mr. Sammler's Planet *(1969). The disturbing account of a wise old man trying to maintain himself in an increasingly irrational world.*

His writing asks the biggest and, probably, in the end, the only relevant question. Perhaps it is too much to expect that he should answer it. In reading Bellow, no matter how far he may go beyond what we know are the limits of his biography, one still feels that one is always tracking him through his problem. Perhaps, because it is the major problem for all of us, we can continue to follow his tracks and hope to find the answer that he apparently continues to expect.

FURTHER READING

Three introductory surveys are Tony Tanner, *Saul Bellow* (1965); Earl Rovit, *Saul Bellow* (1967); and Robert Detweiler, *Saul Bellow: A Critical Essay* (1967). Recent full-length studies are Keith Michael Opdahl, *The Novels of Saul Bellow: An Introduction* (1967); Pierre Dommergues, *Saul Bellow* (1967); John Jacob Clayton, *Saul Bellow: In Defense of Man* (1968); and Irving Malin, *Saul Bellow's Fiction* (1969). Malin has also edited a collection of twelve essays, *Saul Bellow and the Critics* (1967).

Looking for Mr. Green (1968)

Whatsoever thy hand findeth to do, do it with thy might.[1] . . .

Hard work? No, it wasn't really so hard. He wasn't used to walking and stair-climbing, but the physical difficulty of his new job was not what George Grebe felt most. He was delivering relief checks in the Negro district, and although he was a native Chicagoan this was not a part of the city he knew much about—it needed a depression to introduce him to it. No, it wasn't literally hard work, not as reckoned in foot-pounds, but yet he was beginning to feel the strain of it, to grow aware of its peculiar difficulty. He could find the streets and numbers, but the clients were not where they were supposed to be, and he felt like a hunter inexperienced in the camouflage of his game. It was an unfavorable day, too—fall, and cold, dark weather, windy. But, anyway, instead of shells in his deep trenchcoat pocket he had the cardboard of checks, punctured for the spindles of the file, the holes reminding him of the holes in player-piano paper. And he didn't look much like a hunter, either; his was a city figure entirely, belted up in this Irish conspirator's coat. He was slender without being tall, stiff in the back, his legs looking shabby in a pair of old tweed pants gone through and fringy at the cuffs. With this stiffness, he kept his head forward, so that his face was red from the sharpness of the weather; and it was an indoors sort of face with gray eyes that persisted in some kind of thought and yet seemed to avoid definiteness of conclusion. He wore sideburns that surprised you somewhat by the tough curl of the blond hair and the effect of assertion in their length. He was not so mild as he looked, nor so youthful; and nevertheless there was no effort on his part to seem what he was not. He was an educated man; he was a bachelor; he was in some ways simple; without lushing, he liked a drink; his luck had not been good. Nothing was deliberately hidden.

He felt that his luck was better than usual today. When he had reported for work that morning he had expected to be shut up in the relief office at a clerk's job, for he had been hired downtown as a clerk, and he was glad to have, instead, the freedom of the streets and welcomed, at least at first, the vigor of the cold and even the blowing of the hard wind. But on the other hand he was not getting on with the distribution of the checks. It was true that it was a city job; nobody expected you to push too hard at a city job. His supervisor, that young Mr. Raynor, had practically told him that. Still, he wanted to do well at it. For one thing, when he knew how quickly he could deliver a batch of checks, he would know also how much time he could expect to clip for himself. And then, too, the clients would be waiting for their money. That was not the most important consideration, though it certainly mattered to him. No, but he wanted to do well, simply for doing-well's

[1] Ecclesiastes, 10:10.

sake, to acquit himself decently of a job because he so rarely had a job to do that required just this sort of energy. Of this peculiar energy he now had a superabundance; once it had started to flow, it flowed all too heavily. And, for the time being anyway, he was balked. He could not find Mr. Green.

So he stood in his big-skirted trenchcoat with a large envelope in his hand and papers showing from his pocket, wondering why people should be so hard to locate who were too feeble or sick to come to the station to collect their own checks. But Raynor had told him that tracking them down was not easy at first and had offered him some advice on how to proceed. "If you can see the postman, he's your first man to ask, and your best bet. If you can't connect with him, try the stores and tradespeople around. Then the janitor and the neighbors. But you'll find the closer you come to your man the less people will tell you. They don't want to tell you anything."

"Because I'm a stranger."

"Because you're white. We ought to have a Negro doing this, but we don't at the moment, and of course you've got to eat, too, and this is public employment. Jobs have to be made. Oh, that holds for me too. Mind you, I'm not letting myself out. I've got three years of seniority on you, that's all. And a law degree. Otherwise, you might be back of the desk and I might be going out into the field this cold day. The same dough pays us both and for the same, exact, identical reason. What's my law degree got to do with it? But you have to pass out these checks, Mr. Grebe, and it'll help if you're stubborn, so I hope you are."

"Yes, I'm fairly stubborn."

Raynor sketched hard with an eraser in the old dirt of his desk, left-handed, and said, "Sure, what else can you answer to such a question. Anyhow, the trouble you're going to have is that they don't like to give information about anybody. They think you're a plain-clothes dick or an installment collector, or summons-server or something like that. Till you've been seen around the neighborhood for a few months and people know you're only from the relief."

It was dark, ground-freezing, pre-Thanksgiving weather; the wind played hob with the smoke, rushing it down, and Grebe missed his gloves, which he had left in Raynor's office. And no one would admit knowing Green. It was past three o'clock and the postman had made his last delivery. The nearest grocer, himself a Negro, had never heard the name Tulliver Green, or said he hadn't. Grebe was inclined to think that it was true, that he had in the end convinced the man that he wanted only to deliver a check. But he wasn't sure. He needed experience in interpreting looks and signs and, even more, the will not to be put off or denied and even the force to bully if need be. If the grocer did know, he had got rid of him easily. But since most of his trade was with re-liefers, why should he prevent the delivery of a check? Maybe Green, or Mrs. Green, if there was a Mrs. Green, patronized another grocer.

And was there a Mrs. Green? It was one of Grebe's great handicaps that he hadn't looked at any of the case records. Raynor should have let him read files for a few hours. But he apparently saw no need for that, probably considering the job unimportant. Why prepare systematically to deliver a few checks?

But now it was time to look for the janitor. Grebe took in the building in the wind and gloom of the late November day—trampled, frost-hardened lots on one side; on the other, an automobile junk yard and then the infinite work of Elevated frames, weak-looking, gaping with rubbish fires; two sets of leaning brick porches three stories high and a flight of cement stairs to the cellar. Descending, he entered the underground passage, where he tried the doors until one opened and he found himself in the furnace room. There someone rose toward him and approached, scraping on the coal grit and bending under the canvas-jacketed pipes.

"Are you the janitor?"

"What do you want?"

"I'm looking for a man who's supposed to be living here. Green."

"What Green?"

"Oh, you maybe have more than one Green?" said Grebe with new, pleasant hope. "This is Tulliver Green."

"I don't think I c'n help you, mister. I don't know any."

"A crippled man."

The janitor stood bent before him. Could it be that he was crippled? Oh, God! what if he was. Grebe's gray eyes sought with excited difficulty to see. But no, he was only very short and stooped. A head awakened from meditation, a strong-haired beard, low, wide shoulders. A staleness of sweat and coal rose from his black shirt and the burlap sack he wore as an apron.

"Crippled how?"

Grebe thought and then answered with the light voice of unmixed candor, "I don't know. I've never seen him." This was damaging, but his only other choice was to make a lying guess, and he was not up to it. "I'm delivering checks for the relief to shut-in cases. If he weren't crippled he'd come to collect himself. That's why I said crippled. Bed-ridden, chairridden—is there anybody like that?"

This sort of frankness was one of Grebe's oldest talents, going back to childhood. But it gained him nothing here.

"No suh. I've got four buildin's same as this that I take care of. I don' know all the tenants, leave alone the tenants' tenants. The rooms turn over so fast, people movin' in and out every day. I can't tell you."

"Then where should I ask?"

The janitor opened his grimy lips but Grebe did not hear him in the piping of the valves and the consuming pull of air to flame in the body of the furnace. He knew, however, what he had said.

"Well, all the same, thanks. Sorry I bothered you. I'll prowl around upstairs again and see if I can turn up someone who knows him."

Once more in the cold air and early darkness he made the short circle from the cellarway to the entrance crowded between the brick-work pillars and began to climb to the third floor. Pieces of plaster ground under his feet; strips of brass tape from which the carpeting had been torn away marked old boundaries at the sides. In the passage, the cold reached him worse than in the street; it touched him to the bone. The hall toilets ran like springs. He thought grimly as he heard the wind burning around the building with a sound like that of the furnace, that this was a great piece of constructed shelter. Then he struck a match in the gloom and searched for names and numbers among the writings and scribbles on the walls. He saw WHOODY-DOODY GO TO JESUS, and zigzags, caricatures, sexual scrawls, and curses. So the sealed rooms of pyramids were also decorated, and the caves of human dawn.

The information on his card was, TULLIVER GREEN—APT 3D. There were no names, however, and no numbers. His shoulders drawn up, tears of cold in his eyes, breathing vapor, he went the length of the corridor and told himself that if he had been lucky enough to have the temperament for it he would bang on one of the doors and bawl out "Tulliver Green!" until he got results. But it wasn't in him to make an uproar and he continued to burn matches, passing the light over the walls. At the rear, in a corner off the hall, he discovered a door he had not seen before and he thought it best to investigate. It sounded empty when he knocked, but a young Negress answered, hardly more than a girl. She opened only a bit, to guard the warmth of the room.

"Yes suh?"

"I'm from the district relief station on Prairie Avenue. I'm looking for a man named Tulliver Green to give him his check. Do you know him?"

No, she didn't; but he thought she had not understood anything of what he had said. She had a dream-bound, dream-blind face, very soft and black, shut off. She wore a man's jacket and pulled the ends together at her throat. Her hair was parted in three directions, at the sides and transversely, standing up at the front in a dull puff.

"Is there somebody around here who might know?"

"I jus' taken this room las' week."

He observed that she shivered, but even her shiver was somnam-bulistic and there was no sharp consciousness of cold in the big smooth eyes of her handsome face.

"All right, miss, thank you. Thanks," he said, and went to try an-other place.

Here he was admitted. He was grateful, for the room was warm. It was full of people, and they were silent as he entered—ten people, or a dozen, perhaps more, sitting on benches like a parliament. There was no light, properly speaking, but a tempered darkness that the window gave, and everyone seemed to him enormous, the men padded out in heavy work clothes and winter coats, and the women huge, too, in their sweaters, hats, and old furs. And, besides, bed and bedding, a black cooking range, a piano piled towering to the ceiling with papers, a dining-room table of the old style of prosperous Chicago. Among these people Grebe, with his cold-heightened fresh color and his smaller stature, entered like a schoolboy. Even though he was met with smiles and good will, he knew, before a single word was spoken, that all the currents ran against him and that he would make no headway. Nevertheless he began. "Does anybody here know how I can deliver a check to Mr. Tulliver Green?"

"Green?" It was the man that had let him in who answered. He was in short sleeves, in a checkered shirt, and had a queer, high head, profusely overgrown and long as a shako; the veins entered it strongly from his forehead. "I never heard mention of him. Is this where he live?"

"This is the address they gave me at the station. He's a sick man, and he'll need his check. Can't anybody tell me where to find him?"

He stood his ground and waited for a reply, his crimson wool scarf wound about his neck and drooping outside his trenchcoat, pockets weighted with the block of checks and official forms. They must have realized that he was not a college boy employed afternoons by a bill collector, trying foxily to pass for a relief clerk, recognized that he was an older man who knew himself what need was, who had had more than an average seasoning in hardship. It was evident enough if you looked at the marks under his eyes and at the sides of his mouth.

"Anybody know this sick man?"

"No suh." On all sides he saw heads shaken and smiles of denial. No one knew. And maybe it was true, he considered, standing silent in the earthen, musky human gloom of the place as the rumble continued. But he could never really be sure.

"What's the matter with this man?" said shako-head.

"I've never seen him. All I can tell you is that he can't come in person for his money. It's my first day in this district."

"Maybe they given you the wrong number?"

"I don't believe so. But where else can I ask about him?" He felt that his persistence amused them deeply, and in a way he shared their amusement that he should stand up so tenaciously to them. Though smaller, though slight, he was his own man, he retracted nothing about himself, and he looked back at them, gray-eyed, with amusement and also with a sort of courage. On the bench some man spoke in his throat, the words impossible to catch, and a woman answered with a wild, shrieking laugh, which was quickly cut off.

"Well, so nobody will tell me?"

"Ain't nobody who knows."

"At least, if he lives here, he pays rent to someone. Who manages the building?"

"Greatham Company. That's on Thirty-ninth Street."

Grebe wrote it in his pad. But, in the street again, a sheet of wind-driven paper clinging to his leg while he deliberated what direction to take next, it seemed a feeble lead to follow. Probably this Green didn't rent a flat, but a room. Sometimes there were as many as twenty people living in an apartment; the real-estate agent would know only the lessee. And not even the agent could tell you who the renters were. In some places the beds were even used in shifts, watchmen or jitney drivers or short-order cooks in night joints turning out after a day's sleep and sur-rendering their beds to a sister, a nephew, or perhaps a stranger, just off the bus. There were large numbers of newcomers in this terrific, blight-bitten portion of the city between Cottage Grove and Ashland, wandering from house to house and room to room. When you saw them, how could you know them? They didn't carry bundles on their backs or look picturesque. You only saw a man, a Negro, walking in the street or riding in the car, like everyone else, with his thumb closed on a trans-fer. And therefore how were you supposed to tell? Grebe thought the Greatham agent would only laugh at his question.

But how much it would have simplified the job to be able to say that Green was old, or blind, or consumptive. An hour in the files, taking a few notes, and he needn't have been at such a disadvantage. When Raynor gave him the block of checks he had asked, "How much should I know about these people?" Then Raynor had looked as though he were preparing to accuse him of trying to make the job more important than it was. He smiled, because by then they were on fine terms, but never-theless he had been getting ready to say something like that when the confusion began in the station over Staika and her children.

Grebe had waited a long time for this job. It came to him through the pull of an old schoolmate in the Corporation Counsel's office, never a close friend, but suddenly sympathetic and interested—pleased to show, moreover, how well he had done, how strongly he was coming on even in these miserable times. Well, he was coming through strongly, along with the Democratic administration itself. Grebe had gone to see him in City Hall, and they had had a counter lunch or beers at least once a month for a year, and finally it had been possible to swing the job. He didn't mind being assigned the lowest clerical grade, nor even being a messenger, though Raynor thought he did.

This Raynor was an original sort of guy and Grebe had taken to him immediately. As was proper on the first day, Grebe had come early, but he waited long, for Raynor was late. At last he darted into his cubicle of an office as though he had just jumped from one of those hurtling huge red Indiana Avenue cars. His thin, rough face was wind-stung and he was grinning and saying something breathlessly to him-self. In his hat, a small fedora and his coat, the velvet collar a neat fit about his neck, and his silk muffler that set off the nervous twist of his chin, he swayed and turned himself in his swivel chair, feet leaving the ground; so that he pranced a little as he sat. Meanwhile he took Grebe's measure out of his eyes, eyes of an unusual vertical length and slightly sardonic. So the two men sat for a while, saying nothing, while the supervisor raised his hat from his miscombed hair and put it in his lap. His cold-darkened hands were not clean. A steel beam passed through the little makeshift room, from which machine belts once had hung. The building was an old factory.

"I'm younger than you; I hope you won't find it hard taking orders from me," said Raynor. "But I don't make them up, either. You're how old, about?"

"Thirty-five."

"And you thought you'd be inside doing paper-work. But it so happens I have to send you out."

"I don't mind."

"And it's mostly a Negro load we have in this district."

"So I thought it would be."

"Fine. You'll get along. *C'est un bon boulot.*[2] Do you know French?"

"Some."

"I thought you'd be a university man."

"Have you been in France?" said Grebe.

"No, that's the French of the Berlitz School. I've been at it for more than a year, just as I'm sure people have been, all over the world, office boys in China and braves in Tanganyika. In fact, I damn well know it. Such is the attractive power of civilization. It's overrated, but what do you want? *Que voulez vous?*[3] I get *Le Rire*[4] and all the spicy papers, just like in Tanganyika. It must be mystifying, out there. But my reason is that I'm aiming at the diplomatic service. I have a cousin who's a courier, and the way he describes it is awfully attractive. He rides in the *wagon-lits* and reads books. While we—What did you do before?"

"I sold."

"Where?"

"Canned meat at Stop and Shop. In the basement."

"And before that?"

"Window shades, at Goldblatt's."

"Steady work?"

"No, Thursdays and Saturdays. I also sold shoes."

"You've been a shoe-dog, too. Well. And prior to that? Here it is in your folder." He opened the record. "St. Olaf's College, instructor in classical languages. Fellow, University of Chicago, 1926–27. I've had Latin, too. Let's trade quotations—'*Dum spiro spero.*' "

[2] "You're a good worker."
[3] "What do you want?"
[4] French satrical periodical.

" '*Da dextram misero.*' "
" '*Alea jacta est.*' "
" '*Excelsior.*' " [5]

Raynor shouted with laughter, and other workers came to look at him over the partition. Grebe also laughed, feeling pleased and easy. The luxury of fun on a nervous morning.

When they were done and no one was watching or listening, Raynor said rather seriously, "What made you study Latin in the first place. Was it for the priesthood?"

"No."

"Just for the hell of it? For the culture? Oh, the things people think they can pull!" He made his cry hilarious and tragic. "I ran my pants off so I could study for the bar, and I've passed the bar, so I get twelve dollars a week more than you as a bonus for having seen life straight and whole. I'll tell you, as a man of culture, that even though nothing looks to be real, and everything stands for something else, and that thing for another thing, and that thing for a still further one—there ain't any comparison between twenty-five and thirty-seven dollars a week, regardless of the last reality. Don't you think that was clear to your Greeks? They were a thoughtful people, but they didn't part with their slaves."

This was a great deal more than Grebe had looked for in his first interview with his supervisor. He was too shy to show all the astonishment he felt. He laughed a little, aroused, and brushed at the sunbeam that covered his head with its dust. "Do you think my mistake was so terrible?"

"Damn right it was terrible, and you know it now that you've had the whip of hard times laid on your back. You should have been preparing yourself for trouble. Your people must have been well off to send you to the university. Stop me, if I'm stepping on your toes. Did your mother pamper you? Did your father give in to you? Were you brought up tenderly, with permission to go out and find out what were the last things that everything else stands for while everybody else labored in the fallen world of appearances?"

"Well, no, it wasn't exactly like that." Grebe smiled. *The fallen world of appearances!* no less. But now it was his turn to deliver a surprise. "We weren't rich. My father was the last genuine English butler in Chicago—"

"Are you kidding?"

"Why should I be?"

"In a livery?"

"In livery. Up on the Gold Coast."

[5] " 'As long as I breathe, I hope.' "
" 'Give the right hand to the wretched.' "
" 'The die is cast.' "
" 'Onward and upward.' "

"And he wanted you to be educated like a gentleman?"

"He did not. He sent me to the Armour Institute to study chemical engineering. But when he died I changed schools."

He stopped himself, and considered how quickly Raynor had reached him. In no time he had your valise on the table and all your stuff unpacked. And afterward, in the streets, he was still reviewing how far he might have gone, and how much he might have been led to tell if they had not been interrupted by Mrs. Staika's great noise.

But just then a young woman, one of Raynor's workers, ran into the cubicle exclaiming, "Haven't you heard all the fuss?"

"We haven't heard anything."

"It's Staika, giving out with all her might. The reporters are coming. She said she phoned the papers, and you know she did."

"But what is she up to?" said Raynor.

"She brought her wash and she's ironing it here, with our current, because the relief won't pay her electric bill. She has her ironing board set up by the admitting desk, and her kids are with her, all six. They never are in school more than once a week. She's always dragging them around with her because of her reputation."

"I don't want to miss any of this," said Raynor, jumping up. Grebe, as he followed with the secretary, said, "Who is this Staika?"

"They call her the 'Blood Mother of Federal Street.' She's a professional donor at the hospitals. I think they pay ten dollars a pint. Of course it's no joke, but she makes a very big thing out of it and she and the kids are in the papers all the time."

A small crowd, staff and clients divided by a plywood barrier, stood in the narrow space of the entrance, and Staika was shouting in a gruff, mannish voice, plunging the iron on the board and slamming it on the metal rest.

"My father and mother came in a steerage, and I was born in our own house, Robey by Huron. I'm no dirty immigrant. I'm a US citizen. My husband is a gassed veteran from France with lungs weaker'n paper, that hardly can he go to the toilet by himself. These six children of mine, I have to buy the shoes for their feet with my own blood. Even a lousy little white communion necktie, that's a couple of drops of blood; a little piece of mosquito veil for my Vadja so she won't be ashamed in church for the other girls, they take my blood for it by Goldblatt. That's how I keep goin'. A fine thing if I had to depend on the relief. And there's plenty of people on the rolls—fakes! There's nothin' *they* can't get, that can go and wrap bacon at Swift and Armour any time. They're lookin' for them by the Yards. They never have to be out of work. Only they rather lay in their lousy beds and eat the public's money." She was not afraid, in a predominantly Negro station, to shout this way about Negroes.

Grebe and Raynor worked themselves forward to get a closer view of the woman. She was flaming with anger and with pleasure at herself,

broad and huge, a golden-headed woman who wore a cotton cap laced
with pink ribbon. She was barelegged and had on black gym-shoes, her
hoover apron was open and her great breasts, not much restrained by
a man's undershirt, hampered her arms as she worked at the kid's dress
on the ironing board. And the children, silent and white, with a kind of
locked obstinacy, in sheepskins and lumberjackets, stood behind her.
She had captured the station, and the pleasure this gave her was enormous. Yet her grievances were true grievances. She was telling the
truth. But she behaved like a liar. The look of her small eyes was hidden, and while she raged she also seemed to be spinning and planning.

"They send me out college case-workers in silk pants to talk me out
of what I got comin'. Are they better'n me? Who told them? Fire them.
Let 'em go and get married, and then you won't have to cut electric from
people's budget."

The chief supervisor, Mr. Ewing, couldn't silence her and he stood
with folded arms at the head of his staff, bald, bald-headed, saying to
his subordinates like the ex-school principal he was, "Pretty soon she'll
be tired and go."

"No she won't," said Raynor to Grebe. "She'll get what she wants.
She knows more about the relief even than Ewing. She's been on the
rolls for years, and she always gets what she wants because she puts
on a noisy show. Ewing knows it. He'll give in soon. He's only saving
face. If he gets bad publicity, the Commissioner'll have him on the
carpet, downtown. She's got him submerged; she'll submerge everybody
in time, and that includes nations and governments."

Grebe replied with his characteristic smile, disagreeing completely.
Who would take Staika's orders, and what changes could her yelling
ever bring about?

No, what Grebe saw in her, the power that made people listen, was
that her cry expressed the war of flesh and blood, perhaps turned a little
crazy and certainly intensely ugly, on this place and this condition. And
at first, when he went out, the spirit of Staika somehow presided over
the whole district for him, and it took color from her; he saw her color,
in the spotty curb-fires, and the fires under the El, the straight alley of
flamey gloom. Later, too, when he went into a tavern for a shot of rye,
the sweat of beer, association with West Side Polish streets, made him
think of her again.

He wiped the corners of his mouth with his muffler, his handkerchief being inconvenient to reach for, and went out again to get on with
the delivery of his checks. The air bit cold and hard and a few flakes
of snow formed near him. A train struck by and left a quiver in the
frames and a bristling icy hiss over the rails.

Crossing the street, he descended a flight of board steps into a basement grocery, setting off a little bell. It was a dark, long store and it
caught you with its stinks of smoked meat, soap, dried peaches, and
fish. There was a fire wrinkling and flapping in the little stove, and the

proprietor was waiting, an Italian with a long, hollow face and stubborn bristles. He kept his hands warm under his apron.

No, he didn't know Green. You knew people, but not names. The same man might not have the same name twice. The police didn't know, either, and mostly didn't care. When somebody was shot or knifed they took the body away and didn't look for the murderer. In the first place, nobody would tell them anything. So they made up a name for the coroner and called it quits. And in the second place, they didn't give a goddam anyhow. But they couldn't get to the bottom of a thing even if they wanted to. Nobody would get to know even a tenth of what went on among these people. They stabbed and stole, they did every crime and abomination you ever heard of, men and men, women and women, parents and children, worse than the animals. They carried on their own way, and the horrors passed off like a smoke. There was never anything like it in the history of the whole world.

It was a long speech, deepening with every word in its fantasy and passion and becoming increasingly senseless and terrible: a swarm amassed by suggestion and invention, a huge, hugging, despairing knot, a human wheel of heads, legs, bellies, arms, rolling through his shop.

Grebe felt that he must interrupt him. He said sharply, "What are you talking about! All I asked was whether you knew this man."

"That isn't even the half of it. I been here six years. You probably don't want to believe this. But suppose it's true?"

"All the same," said Grebe, "there must be a way to find a person."

The Italian's close-spaced eyes had been queerly concentrated, as were his muscles, while he leaned across the counter trying to convince Grebe. Now he gave up the effort and sat down on his stool. "Oh—I suppose. Once in a while. But I been telling you, even the cops don't get anywhere."

"They're always after somebody. It's not the same thing."

"Well, keep trying if you want. I can't help you."

But he didn't keep trying. He had no more time to spend on Green. He slipped Green's check to the back of the block. The next name on the list was FIELD, WINSTON.

He found the back-yard bungalow without the least trouble; it shared a lot with another house, a few feet of yard between. Grebe knew these two-shack arrangements. They had been built in vast numbers in the days before the swamps were filled and the streets raised, and they were all the same—a boardwalk along the fence, well under street level, three or four ball-headed posts for clotheslines, greening wood, dead shingles, and a long, long flight of stairs to the rear door.

A twelve-year-old boy let him into the kitchen, and there the old man was, sitting by the table in a wheel chair.

"Oh, it's d' government man," he said to the boy when Grebe drew out his checks. "Go bring me my box of papers." He cleared a space on the table.

"Oh, you don't have to go to all that trouble," said Grebe. But Field laid out his papers: Social Security card, relief certification, letters from the state hospital in Manteno, and a naval discharge dated San Diego, 1920.

"That's plenty," Grebe said. "Just sign."

"You got to know who I am," the old man said, "You're from the government. It's not your check, it's a government check and you got no business to hand it over till everything is proved."

He loved the ceremony of it, and Grebe made no more objections. Field emptied his box and finished out the circle of cards and letters.

"There's everything I done and been. Just the death certificate and they can close book on me." He said this with a certain happy pride and magnificence. Still he did not sign; he merely held the little pen upright on the golden-green corduroy of his thigh. Grebe did not hurry him. He felt the old man's hunger for conversation.

"I got to get better coal," he said. "I send my little gran'son to the yard with my order and they fill his wagon with screening. The stove ain't made for it. It fall through the grate. The order says Franklin County egg-size coal."

"I'll report it and see what can be done."

"Nothing can be done, I expect. You know and I know. There ain't no little ways to make things better, and the only big thing is money. That's the only sunbeams, money. Nothing is black where it shines, and the only place you see black is where it ain't shining. What we colored have to have is our own rich. There ain't no other way."

Grebe sat, his reddened forehead bridged levelly by his close-cut hair and his cheeks lowered in the wings of his collar—the caked fire shone hard within the isinglass and iron frames but the room was not comfortable—sat and listened while the old man unfolded his scheme. This was to create one Negro millionaire a month by subscription. One clever, good-hearted young fellow elected every month would sign a contract to use the money to start a business employing Negroes. This would be advertised by chain letters and word of mouth, and every Negro wage-earner would contribute a dollar a month. Within five years there would be sixty millionaires.

"That'll fetch respect," he said with a throat-stopped sound that came out like a foreign syllable. "You got to take and organize all the money that gets thrown away on the policy wheel and horse race. As long as they can take it away from you, they got no respect for you. Money, that's d' sun of human kind!" Field was a Negro of mixed blood, perhaps Cherokee, or Natchez; his skin was reddish. And he sounded, speaking about a golden sun in this dark room, and looked, shaggy and slab-headed, with the mingled blood of his face and broad lips, the little pen still upright in his hand, like one of the underground kings of mythology, old judge Minos himself.

And now he accepted the check and signed. Not to soil the slip, he held it down with his knuckles. The table budged and creaked, the center of the gloomy, heathen midden of the kitchen covered with bread, meat, and cans, and the scramble of papers.

"Don't you think my scheme'd work?"

"It's worth thinking about. Something ought to be done, I agree."

"It'll work if people will do it. That's all. That's the only thing, any time. When they understand it in the same way, all of them."

"That's true," said Grebe, rising. His glance met the old man's.

"I know you got to go," he said. "Well, God bless you, boy, you ain't been sly with me, I can tell it in a minute."

He went back through the buried yard. Someone nursed a candle in a shed, where a man unloaded kindling wood from a sprawl-wheeled baby buggy and two voices carried on a high conversation. As he came up the sheltered passage he heard the hard boost of the wind in the branches and against the house fronts, and then, reaching the sidewalk, he saw the needle-eye red of cable towers in the open icy height hundreds of feet above the river and the factories—those keen points. From here, his view was unobstructed all the way to the South Branch and its timber banks, and the cranes beside the water. Rebuilt after the Great Fire, this part of the city was, not fifty years later, in ruins again, factories boarded up, buildings deserted or fallen, gaps of prairie between. But it wasn't desolation that this made you feel, but rather a faltering of organization that set free a huge energy, an escaped, unattached, unregulated power from the giant raw place. Not only must people feel it but, it seemed to Grebe, they were compelled to match it. In their very bodies. He no less than others, he realized. Say that his parents had been servants in their time, whereas he was not supposed to be one. He thought that they had never done any service like this, which no one visible asked for, and probably flesh and blood could not even perform. Nor could anyone show why it should be performed; or see where the performance would lead. That did not mean that he wanted to be released from it, he realized with a grimly pensive face. On the contrary. He had something to do. To be compelled to feel this energy and yet have no task to do—that was horrible; that was suffering; he knew what that was. It was now quitting time. Six o'clock. He could go home if he liked, to his room, that is, to wash in hot water, to pour a drink, lie down on his quilt, read the paper, eat some liver paste on crackers before going out to dinner. But to think of this actually made him feel a little sick, as though he had swallowed hard air. He had six checks left, and he was determined to deliver at least one of these: Mr. Green's check.

So he started again. He had four or five dark blocks to go, past open lots, condemned houses, old foundations, closed schools, black churches, mounds, and he reflected that there must be many people alive who had once seen the neighborhood rebuilt and new. Now there was a second layer of ruins; centuries of history accomplished through human massing. Numbers had given the place forced growth; enormous numbers had also broken it down. Objects once so new, so concrete that it could never have occurred to anyone they stood for other things, had crumbled. Therefore, reflected Grebe, the secret of them was out. It was that they stood for themselves by agreement, and were natural and not unnatural by agreement, and when the things themselves collapsed the agreement became visible. What was it, otherwise, that kept cities from looking peculiar? Rome, that was almost permanent, did not give rise to thoughts like these. And was it abidingly real? But in Chicago, where the cycles were so fast and the familiar died out, and again rose changed, and died again in thirty years, you saw the common agreement or covenant, and you were forced to think about appearances and realities. (He remembered Raynor and he smiled. Raynor was a clever boy.) Once you had grasped this, a great many things became intelligible. For instance, why Mr. Field should conceive such a scheme. Of course, if people were to agree to create a millionaire, a real millionaire would come into existence. And if you wanted to know how Mr. Field was inspired to think of this, why, he had within sight of his kitchen window the chart, the very bones of a successful scheme—the El with its blue and green confetti of signals. People consented to pay dimes and ride the crash-box cars, and so it was a success. Yet how absurd it looked; how little reality there was to start with. And yet Yerkes, the great financier who built it, had known that he could get people to agree to do it. Viewed as itself, what a scheme of a scheme it seemed, how close to an appearance. Then why wonder at Mr. Field's idea? He had grasped a principle. And then Grebe remembered, too, that Mr. Yerkes had established the Yerkes Observatory and endowed it with millions. Now how did the notion come to him in his New York museum of a palace or his Aegean-bound yacht to give money to astronomers? Was he awed perhaps by the success of his bizarre enterprise and therefore ready to spend money to find out where in the universe being and seeming were identical? Yes, he wanted to know what abides; and whether flesh is Bible-grass; and he offered money to be burned in the fire of suns. Okay, then, Grebe thought further, these things exist because people consent to exist with them—we have got so far—and also there is a reality which doesn't depend on consent but within which consent is a game. But what about need, the need that keeps so many vast thousands in position? You tell me that, you *private* little gentleman and *decent* soul—he used these words against himself scornfully. Why is the consent given to misery? And why so painfully ugly? Because there *is something* that is dismal and permanently ugly? Here he sighed and gave it up, and thought it was enough for the present moment that he had a real check in his pocket for a Mr. Green who must be real beyond question. If only his neighbors didn't think they had to conceal him.

This time he stopped at the second floor. He struck a match and found a door. Presently a man answered his knock and Grebe had the

check ready and showed it even before he began. "Does Tulliver Green
live here? I'm from the relief."

The man narrowed the opening and spoke to someone at his back.
"Does he live here?"

"Uh-uh. No."

"Or anywhere in this building? He's a sick man and he can't come
for his dough." He exhibited the check in the light, which was smoky—
the air smelled of charred lard—and the man held off the brim of his
cap to study it.

"Uh-uh. Never seen the name."

"There's nobody around here that uses crutches?"

He seemed to think, but it was Grebe's impression that he was
simply waiting for a decent interval to pass.

"No, suh. Nobody I ever see."

"I've been looking for this man all afternoon," Grebe spoke out with
sudden force, "and I'm going to have to carry this check back to the
station. It seems strange not to be able to find a person to *give* him something when you're looking for him for a good reason. I suppose if I had
bad news for him I'd find him quick enough."

There was a responsive motion in the other man's face. "That's
right, I reckon."

"It almost doesn't do any good to have a name if you can't be found
by it. It doesn't stand for anything. He might as well not have any,"
he went on, smiling. It was as much of a concession as he could make to
his desire to laugh.

"Well, now, there's a little old knot-back man I see once in a while.
He might be the one you lookin' for. Downstairs."

"Where? Right side or left? Which door?"

"I don't know which. Thin face little knot-back with a stick."

But no one answered at any of the doors on the first floor. He went
to the end of the corridor, searching by matchlight, and found only a
stairless exit to the yard, a drop of about six feet. But there was a
bungalow near the alley, an old house like Mr. Field's. To jump was
unsafe. He ran from the front door, through the underground passage
and into the yard. The place was occupied. There was a light through
the curtains, upstairs. The name on the ticket under the broken, scoop-
shaped mailbox was Green! He exultantly rang the bell and pressed
against the locked door. Then the lock clicked faintly and a long staircase opened before him. Someone was slowly coming down—a woman.
He had the impression in the weak light that she was shaping her hair
as she came, making herself presentable, for he saw her arms raised.
But it was for support that they were raised; she was feeling her way
downward, down the walls, stumbling. Next he wondered about the
pressure of her feet on the treads; she did not seem to be wearing shoes.
And it was a freezing stairway. His ring had got her out of bed, perhaps,
and she had forgotten to put them on. And then he saw that she was
not only shoeless but naked; she was entirely naked, climbing down

while she talked to herself, a heavy woman, naked and drunk. She blundered into him. The contact of her breasts, though they touched only his coat, made him go back against the door with a blind shock. See what he had tracked down, in his hunting game!

The woman was saying to herself, furious with insult, "So I cain't ——k, huh? I'll show that son-of-a-bitch kin I, cain't I."

What should he do now? Grebe asked himself. Why, he should go. He should turn away and go. He couldn't talk to this woman. He couldn't keep her standing naked in the cold. But when he tried he found himself unable to turn away.

He said, "Is this where Mr. Green lives?"

But she was still talking to herself and did not hear him.

"Is this Mr. Green's house?"

At last she turned her furious drunken glance on him. "What do you want?"

Again her eyes wandered from him; there was a dot of blood in their enraged brilliance. He wondered why she didn't feel the cold.

"I'm from the relief."

"Awright, what?"

"I've got a check for Tulliver Green."

This time she heard him and put out her hand.

"No, no, for *Mr.* Green. He's got to sign," he said. How was he going to get Green's signature tonight!

"I'll take it. He cain't."

He desperately shook his head, thinking of Mr. Field's precautions about identification. "I can't let you have it. It's for him. Are you Mrs. Green?"

"Maybe I is, and maybe I ain't. Who want to know?"

"Is he upstairs?"

"Awright. Take it up yourself, you goddam fool."

Sure, he was a goddamned fool. Of course he could not go up because Green would probably be drunk and naked, too. And perhaps he would appear on the landing soon. He looked eagerly upward. Under the light was a high narrow brown wall. Empty! It remained empty!

"Hell with you, then!" he heard her cry. To deliver a check for coal and clothes, he was keeping her in the cold. She did not feel it, but his face was burning with frost and self-ridicule. He backed away from her.

"I'll come tomorrow, tell him."

"Ah, hell with you. Don' never come. What you doin' here in the nighttime? Don' come back." She yelled so that he saw the breadth of her tongue. She stood astride in the long cold box of the hall and held on to the banister and the wall. The bungalow itself was shaped something like a box, a clumsy, high box pointing into the freezing air with its sharp, wintry lights.

"If you are Mrs. Green, I'll give you the check," he said, changing his mind.

"Give here, then." She took it, took the pen offered with it in her left hand, and tried to sign the receipt on the wall. He looked around, almost as though to see whether his madness was being observed, and came near believing that someone was standing on a mountain of used tires in the auto-junking shop next door.

"But are you Mrs. Green?" he now thought to ask. But she was already climbing the stairs with the check, and it was too late, if he had made an error, if he was now in trouble, to undo the thing. But he wasn't going to worry about it. Though she might not be Mrs. Green, he was convinced that Mr. Green was upstairs. Whoever she was, the woman stood for Green, whom he was not to see this time. Well, you silly bastard, he said to himself, so you think you found him. So what? Maybe you really did find him—what of it? But it was important that there was a real Mr. Green whom they could not keep him from reaching because he seemed to come as an emissary from hostile appearances. And though the self-ridicule was slow to diminish, and his face still blazed with it, he had, nevertheless, a feeling of elation, too. "For after all," he said, "he *could* be found!"

CARSON [SMITH] McCULLERS (1917–1967)

It would be a challenge to write a detailed biography of Carson McCullers, who always made such a point of obscuring her own history in evasion, inaccuracy, irrelevance, invention, and fantasy. Presumably one can be fairly certain that she was born in Columbus, Georgia, and that in 1937 she married a man named Reeves McCullers, who died in 1953. It is certain that in her later years she lived in her own house at Nyack, New York, that for a long time she suffered heroically from an intolerable disease, and that she died too early.

We can also be certain of the dates of her remarkable books: The Heart Is a Lonely Hunter *(1940);* Reflections in a Golden Eye *(1941);* The Member of the Wedding *(1946);* The Ballad of the Sad Café *(1951);* The Square Root of Wonderful *(1958), a play;* The Ballad of the Sad Café: The Novels and Stories of Carson McCullers *(1959), a collection that for the first time presented her short stories in book form; and* Clock without Hands *(1961), her last novel.*

She always had one theme ("spiritual isolation," she called it) which necessarily provided the pivotal dilemma of her plots. For that dilemma, her plots suggested one answer, love, which usually, in the world as she saw it, could not work any wonders of solution.

Her two fine novels, the first, The Heart Is a Lonely Hunter, *and the third,* The Member of the Wedding, *and that weird and moving novella,* The Ballad of the Sad Café, *are her most commanding presentations of her theme and demonstrations of the usual human inadequacy to her answer. Of her short stories, "A Tree. A Rock. A Cloud," is the best example of both the theme and the dilemma. Before sunrise a young boy and an old man have an encounter in a shabby all-night hamburger joint. The old man lectures the boy on the "science" of love, and the boy has no idea what he is talking about. They move off, each into his own separateness. The very periods in her title suggest the character of the human situation as she saw it.*

Her theme in itself was not remarkable, but she had an unusual depth of feeling about it that animated in unforgettable ways certain characters (Frankie Addams of The Member of the Wedding *above all*), put heart-breaking speeches into their casual mouths, and created works of art. One can quote Mick Kelly, the young heroine of The Heart Is a Lonely Hunter, *as, talking to herself, she fades out of that scene: "It was some good."*

The Mortgaged Heart, *Carson McCuller's previously uncollected writings, edited by her sister, Margarita Smith, has been announced for 1971.*

FURTHER READING

Oliver Evans, *The Ballad of Carson McCullers: A Biography* (1966), first appeared under the title *Carson McCullers: Her Life and Work.* Briefer estimates are Irving Malin, *New American Gothic* (1962); Harry T. Moore, editor, *Contemporary American Novelists* (1964); Louise Y. Gossett, *Violence in Recent Southern Fiction* (1965); Louis Auchincloss, *Pioneers and Caretakers: A Study of Nine American Women Novelists* (1965); Frederick J. Hoffman, *The Art of Southern Fiction* (1967); and Mark Schorer, *The World We Imagine* (1968).

A Tree. A Rock. A Cloud (1959)

It was raining that morning, and still very dark. When the boy reached the streetcar café he had almost finished his route and he went in for a cup of coffee. The place was an all-night café owned by a bitter and stingy man called Leo. After the raw, empty street the café seemed friendly and bright: along the counter there were a couple of soldiers, three spinners from the cotton mill, and in a corner a man who sat hunched over with his nose and half his face down in a beer mug. The boy wore a helmet such as aviators wear. When he went into the café he unbuckled the chin strap and raised the right flap up over his pink little ear; often as he drank his coffee someone would speak to him in a friendly way. But this morning Leo did not look into his face and none

of the men were talking. He paid and was leaving the café when a voice
called out to him:

'Son! Hey Son!'

He turned back and the man in the corner was crooking his finger
and nodding to him. He had brought his face out of the beer mug and
he seemed suddenly very happy. The man was long and pale, with a
big nose and faded orange hair.

'Hey Son!'

The boy went toward him. He was an undersized boy of about
twelve, with one shoulder drawn higher than the other because of the
weight of the paper sack. His face was shallow, freckled, and his eyes
were round child eyes.

'Yeah Mister?'

The man laid one hand on the paper boy's shoulders, then grasped
the boy's chin and turned his face slowly from one side to the other.
The boy shrank back uneasily.

'Say! What's the big idea?'

The boy's voice was shrill; inside the café it was suddenly very quiet.

The man said slowly: 'I love you.'

All along the counter the men laughed. The boy, who had scowled
and sidled away, did not know what to do. He looked over the counter
at Leo, and Leo watched him with a weary, brittle jeer. The boy tried to
laugh also. But the man was serious and sad.

'I did not mean to tease you, Son,' he said. 'Sit down and have a
beer with me. There is something I have to explain.'

Cautiously, out of the corner of his eye, the paper boy questioned
the men along the counter to see what he should do. But they had gone
back to their beer or their breakfast and did not notice him. Leo put a
cup of coffee on the counter and a little jug of cream.

'He is a minor,' Leo said.

The paper boy slid himself up onto the stool. His ear beneath the
upturned flap of the helmet was very small and red. The man was
nodding at him soberly. 'It is important,' he said. Then he reached in
his hip pocket and brought out something which he held up in the palm
of his hand for the boy to see.

'Look very carefully,' he said.

The boy stared, but there was nothing to look at very carefully.
The man held in his big, grimy palm a photograph. It was the face of
a woman, but blurred, so that only the hat and the dress she was wearing stood out clearly.

'See?' the man asked.

The boy nodded and the man placed another picture in his palm.
The woman was standing on a beach in a bathing suit. The suit made
her stomach very big, and that was the main thing you noticed.

'Got a good look?' He leaned over closer and finally asked: 'You ever
seen her before?'

The boy sat motionless, staring slantwise at the man. 'Not so I know of.'

'Very well.' The man blew on the photographs and put them back into his pocket. 'That was my wife.'

'Dead?' the boy asked.

Slowly the man shook his head. He pursed his lips as though about to whistle and answered in a long-drawn way: 'Nuuu—' he said. 'I will explain.'

The beer on the counter before the man was in a large brown mug. He did not pick it up to drink. Instead he bent down and, putting his face over the rim, he rested there for a moment. Then with both hands he tilted the mug and sipped.

'Some night you'll go to sleep with your big nose in a mug and drown,' said Leo. 'Prominent transient drowns in beer. That would be a cute death.'

The paper boy tried to signal to Leo. While the man was not looking he screwed up his face and worked his mouth to question soundlessly: 'Drunk?' But Leo only raised his eyebrows and turned away to put some pink strips of bacon on the grill. The man pushed the mug away from him, straightened himself, and folded his loose crooked hands on the counter. His face was sad as he looked at the paper boy. He did not blink, but from time to time the lids closed down with delicate gravity over his pale green eyes. It was nearing dawn and the boy shifted the weight of the paper sack.

'I am talking about love,' the man said. 'With me it is a science.'

The boy half slid down from the stool. But the man raised his forefinger, and there was something about him that held the boy and would not let him go away.

'Twelve years ago I married the woman in the photograph. She was my wife for one year, nine months, three days, and two nights. I loved her. Yes . . .' He tightened his blurred, rambling voice and said again: 'I loved her. I thought also that she loved me. I was a railroad engineer. She had all home comforts and luxuries. It never crept into my brain that she was not satisfied. But do you know what happened?'

'Mgneeow!' said Leo.

The man did not take his eyes from the boy's face. 'She left me. I came in one night and the house was empty and she was gone. She left me.'

'With a fellow?' the boy asked.

Gently the man placed his palm down on the counter. 'Why naturally, Son. A woman does not run off like that alone.'

The café was quiet, the soft rain black and endless in the street outside. Leo pressed down the frying bacon with the prongs of his long fork. 'So you have been chasing the floozie for eleven years. You frazzled old rascal!'

For the first time the man glanced at Leo. 'Please don't be vulgar.

Besides, I was not speaking to you.' He turned back to the boy and said in a trusting and secretive undertone: 'Let's not pay any attention to him. O.K.?'

The paper boy nodded doubtfully.

'It was like this,' the man continued. 'I am a person who feels many things. All my life one thing after another has impressed me. Moonlight. The leg of a pretty girl. One thing after another. But the point is that when I had enjoyed anything there was a peculiar sensation as though it was laying around loose in me. Nothing seemed to finish itself up or fit in with the other things. Women? I had my portion of them. The same. Afterwards laying around loose in me. I was a man who had never loved.'

Very slowly he closed his eyelids, and the gesture was like a curtain drawn at the end of a scene in a play. When he spoke again his voice was excited and the words came fast—the lobes of his large, loose ears seemed to tremble.

'Then I met this woman. I was fifty-one years old and she always said she was thirty. I met her at a filling station and we were married within three days. And do you know what it was like? I just can't tell you. All I had ever felt was gathered together around this woman. Nothing lay around loose in me any more but was finished up by her.'

The man stopped suddenly and stroked his long nose. His voice sank down to a steady and reproachful undertone: 'I'm not explaining this right. What happened was this. There were these beautiful feelings and loose little pleasures inside me. And this woman was something like an assembly line for my soul. I run these little pieces of myself through her and I come out complete. Now do you follow me?'

'What was her name?' the boy asked.

'Oh,' he said. 'I called her Dodo. But that is immaterial.'

'Did you try to make her come back?'

The man did not seem to hear. 'Under the circumstances you can imagine how I felt when she left me.'

Leo took the bacon from the grill and folded two strips of it between a bun. He had a gray face, with slitted eyes, and a pinched nose saddled by faint blue shadows. One of the mill workers signaled for more coffee and Leo poured it. He did not give refills on coffee free. The spinner ate breakfast there every morning, but the better Leo knew his customers the stingier he treated them. He nibbled his own bun as though he grudged it to himself.

'And you never got hold of her again?'

The boy did not know what to think of the man, and his child's face was uncertain with mingled curiosity and doubt. He was new on the paper route; it was still strange to him to be out in the town in the black, queer early morning.

'Yes,' the man said. 'I took a number of steps to get her back. I went

around trying to locate her. I went to Tulsa where she had folks. And
to Mobile. I went to every town she had ever mentioned to me, and I
hunted down every man she had formerly been connected with. Tulsa,
Atlanta, Chicago, Cheehaw, Memphis. . . . For the better part of two
years I chased around the country trying to lay hold of her.'

'But the pair of them had vanished from the face of the earth!' said
Leo.

'Don't listen to him,' the man said confidentially. 'And also just forget those two years. They are not important. What matters is that
around the third year a curious thing begun to happen to me.'

'What?' the boy asked.

The man leaned down and tilted his mug to take a sip of beer. But
as he hovered over the mug his nostrils fluttered slightly; he sniffed the
staleness of the beer and did not drink. 'Love is a curious thing to begin
with. At first I thought only of getting her back. It was a kind of mania.
But then as time went on I tried to remember her. But do you know what
happened?'

'No,' the boy said.

'When I laid myself down on a bed and tried to think about her my
mind became a blank. I couldn't see her. I would take out her pictures
and look. No good. Nothing doing. A blank. Can you imagine it?'

'Say Mac!' Leo called down the counter. 'Can you imagine this
bozo's mind a blank!'

Slowly, as though fanning away flies, the man waved his hand. His
green eyes were concentrated and fixed on the shallow little face of the
paper boy.

'But a sudden piece of glass on a sidewalk. Or a nickel tune in a
music box. A shadow on a wall at night. And I would remember. It
might happen in a street and I would cry or bang my head against a
lamppost. You follow me?'

'A piece of glass . . .' the boy said.

'Anything. I would walk around and I had no power of how and
when to remember her. You think you can put up a kind of shield. But
remembering don't come to a man face forward—it corners around
sideways. I was at the mercy of everything I saw and heard. Suddenly
instead of me combing the countryside to find her she begun to chase
me around in my very soul. *She* chasing *me*, mind you! And in my soul.'

The boy asked finally: 'What part of the country were you in then?'

'Ooh,' the man groaned. 'I was a sick mortal. It was like smallpox.
I confess, Son, that I boozed. I fornicated. I committed any sin that sud-
denly appealed to me. I am loath to confess it but I will do so. When
I recall that period it is all curdled in my mind, it was so terrible.'

The man leaned his head down and tapped his forehead on the
counter. For a few seconds he stayed bowed over in this position, the
back of his stringy neck covered with orange furze, his hands with their

long warped fingers held palm to palm in an attitude of prayer. Then the man straightened himself; he was smiling and suddenly his face was bright and tremulous and old.

'It was in the fifth year that it happened,' he said. 'And with it I started my science.'

Leo's mouth jerked with a pale, quick grin. 'Well none of we boys are getting any younger,' he said. Then with sudden anger he balled up a dishcloth he was holding and threw it down hard on the floor. 'You draggle-tailed old Romeo!'

'What happened?' the boy asked.

The old man's voice was high and clear: 'Peace,' he answered.

'Huh?'

'It is hard to explain scientifically, Son,' he said. 'I guess the logical explanation is that she and I had fleed around from each other for so long that finally we just got tangled up together and lay down and quit. Peace. A queer and beautiful blankness. It was spring in Portland and the rain came every afternoon. All evening I just stayed there on my bed in the dark. And that is how the science come to me.'

The windows in the streetcar were pale blue with light. The two soldiers paid for their beers and opened the door—one of the soldiers combed his hair and wiped off his muddy puttees before they went outside. The three mill workers bent silently over their breakfasts. Leo's clock was ticking on the wall.

'It is this. And listen carefully. I meditated on love and reasoned it out. I realized what is wrong with us. Men fall in love for the first time. And what do they fall in love with?'

The boy's soft mouth was partly open and he did not answer.

'A woman,' the old man said. 'Without science, with nothing to go by, they undertake the most dangerous and sacred experience in God's earth. They fall in love with a woman. Is that correct, Son?'

'Yeah,' the boy said faintly.

'They start at the wrong end of love. They begin at the climax. Can you wonder it is so miserable? Do you know how men should love?'

The old man reached over and grasped the boy by the collar of his leather jacket. He gave him a gentle little shake and his green eyes gazed down unblinking and grave.

'Son, do you know how love should be begun?'

The boy sat small and listening and still. Slowly he shook his head. The old man leaned closer and whispered:

'A tree. A rock. A cloud.'

It was still raining outside in the street: a mild, gray, endless rain. The mill whistle blew for the six o'clock shift and the three spinners paid and went away. There was no one in the café but Leo, the old man, and the little paper boy.

'The weather was like this in Portland,' he said. 'At the time my science was begun. I meditated and I started very cautious. I would

pick up something from the street and take it home with me. I bought
a goldfish and I concentrated on the goldfish and I loved it. I graduated
from one thing to another. Day by day I was getting this technique. On
the road from Portland to San Diego——'

'Aw shut up!' screamed Leo suddenly. 'Shut up! Shut up!'

The old man still held the collar of the boy's jacket; he was trembling and his face was earnest and bright and wild. 'For six years now
I have gone around by myself and built up my science. And now I am
a master. Son. I can love anything. No longer do I have to think about
it even. I see a street full of people and a beautiful light comes in me.
I watch a bird in the sky. Or I meet a traveler on the road. Everything,
Son. And anybody. All stranger and all loved! Do you realize what a
science like mine can mean?'

The boy held himself stiffly, his hands curled tight around the
counter edge. Finally he asked: 'Did you ever really find that lady?'

'What? What say, Son?'

'I mean,' the boy asked timidly. 'Have you fallen in love with a
woman again?'

The old man loosened his grasp on the boy's collar. He turned away
and for the first time his green eyes had a vague and scattered look. He
lifted the mug from the counter, drank down the yellow beer. His head
was shaking slowly from side to side. Then finally he answered: 'No,
Son. You see that is the last step in my science. I go cautious. And I
am not quite ready yet.'

'Well!' said Leo. 'Well well well!'

The old man stood in the open doorway. 'Remember,' he said.
Framed there in the gray damp light of the early morning he looked
shrunken and seedy and frail. But his smile was bright. 'Remember I
love you,' he said with a last nod. And the door closed quietly behind
him.

The boy did not speak for a long time. He pulled down the bangs
on his forehead and slid his grimy little forefinger around the rim of his
empty cup. Then without looking at Leo he finally asked:

'Was he drunk?'

'No,' said Leo shortly.

The boy raised his clear voice higher. 'Then was he a dope fiend?'

'No.'

The boy looked up at Leo, and his flat little face was desperate, his
voice urgent and shrill. 'Was he crazy? Do you think he was a lunatic?'
The paper boy's voice dropped suddenly with doubt. 'Leo? Or not?'

But Leo would not answer him. Leo had run a night café for fourteen years, and he held himself to be a critic of craziness. There were
the town characters and also the transients who roamed in from the
night. He knew the manias of all of them. But he did not want to satisfy
the questions of the waiting child. He tightened his pale face and was
silent.

So the boy pulled down the right flap of his helmet and as he turned to leave he made the only comment that seemed safe to him, the only remark that could not be laughed down and despised:

'He sure has done a lot of traveling.'

[MARY] FLANNERY O'CONNOR (1925–1964)

Hers was a short, unbearable, and, it would seem, happy life. Fortunately, from the point of view of her own suffering—and, more than that, but no doubt also out of it—of her art, she was a staunch Roman Catholic in a part of the world largely inhabited by Baptists and Methodists.

She was born in Savannah, Georgia, where she attended parochial schools, but when she was thirteen years old it was discovered that her father was suffering from an incurable disease called disseminated lupus, in which the body forms antibodies to its own tissues. They moved to her mother's family house in Milledgeville, and there in the year before she finished the local high school, her father died.

In Milledgeville she attended and was graduated from the Georgia Woman's College. A recommendation from one of her English teachers (and samples of her own work) won her a scholarship to the Writers' Workshop at the State University of Iowa, where she spent several years, took a degree, and published her first story. At the Yaddo colony and later in New York she worked on her first novel, Wise Blood *(1952), parts of which she published in a number of magazines in 1948 and 1949. In 1950 she became very ill and it was soon discovered that she had inherited her father's disease. With her mother, she moved to a dairy farm outside Milledgeville. Her illness was arrested through new drugs, but by 1955 she had to use crutches to get about, and in less than ten years, after other physical problems, the lupus became active. Knowing that she must die very soon, she continued her writing—her best writing—until she did.*

In her lifetime, she published two short novels, Wise Blood *and* The Violent Bear It Away *(1960), and one book of short stories,* A Good Man Is Hard to Find *(1955). The stories that she was working on at the time of her death were published as* Everything That Rises Must Converge *(1965). Later, her friends Sally and Robert Fitzgerald selected and edited a collection of her occasional prose—essays, lectures, and various notes—under the title* Mystery and Manners *(1969). Robert Fitzgerald wrote the introduction to her posthumous collection of stories, and anyone who wants to know what she was*

*really like and what her bold, often grotesque, understated fiction is
all about, must read his essay.*

*Here it should only be said that the religious faith that no doubt sus-
tained her in her life is never apparent in the forefront of her
fiction; but it profoundly illuminated the astonishing muscular
imagination that made that fiction possible.*

FURTHER READING

Carter W. Martin's *The True Country: Themes in the Fiction of Flannery O'Connor* (1969) is the major critical study. Stanley Edgar
Hyman, *Flannery O'Connor* (1966), and Robert Drake, *Flannery
O'Connor, A Critical Essay*, are brief introductions. Melvin J. Friedman and Lewis A. Lawson collected ten essays on the author's work
in *The Added Dimension: The Art and Mind of Flannery O'Connor*
(1966). The most recent study is Josephine Hendin's *The World of
Flannery O'Connor* (1970).

Everything That Rises
Must Converge *(1965)*

Her doctor had told Julian's mother that she must lose twenty
pounds on account of her blood pressure, so on Wednesday nights Julian
had to take her downtown on the bus for a reducing class at the Y.
The reducing class was designed for working girls over fifty, who
weighed from 165 to 200 pounds. His mother was one of the slimmer
ones, but she said ladies did not tell their age or weight. She would not
ride the buses by herself at night since they had been integrated, and
because the reducing class was one of her few pleasures, necessary for
her health, and *free*, she said Julian could at least put himself out to
take her, considering all she did for him. Julian did not like to consider
all she did for him, but every Wednesday night he braced himself and
took her.

She was almost ready to go, standing before the hall mirror, putting
on her hat, while he, his hands behind him, appeared pinned to the
door frame, waiting like Saint Sebastian for the arrows to begin piercing
him. The hat was new and had cost her seven dollars and a half. She
kept saying, "Maybe I shouldn't have paid that for it. No, I shouldn't
have. I'll take it off and return it tomorrow. I shouldn't have bought it."

Julian raised his eyes to heaven. "Yes, you should have bought it,"
he said. "Put it on and let's go." It was a hideous hat. A purple velvet
flap came down on one side of it and stood up on the other; the rest of
it was green and looked like a cushion with the stuffing out. He decided

it was less comical than jaunty and pathetic. Everything that gave her pleasure was small and depressed him.

She lifted the hat one more time and set it down slowly on top of her head. Two wings of gray hair protruded on either side of her florid face, but her eyes, sky-blue, were as innocent and untouched by experience as they must have been when she was ten. Were it not that she was a widow who had struggled fiercely to feed and clothe and put him through school and who was supporting him still, "until he got on his feet," she might have been a little girl that he had to take to town.

"It's all right, it's all right," he said. "Let's go." He opened the door himself and started down the walk to get her going. The sky was a dying violet and the houses stood out darkly against it, bulbous liver-colored monstrosities of a uniform ugliness though no two were alike. Since this had been a fashionable neighborhood forty years ago, his mother persisted in thinking they did well to have an apartment in it. Each house had a narrow collar of dirt around it in which sat, usually, a grubby child. Julian walked with his hands in his pockets, his head down and thrust forward and his eyes glazed with the determination to make himself completely numb during the time he would be sacrificed to her pleasure.

The door closed and he turned to find the dumpy figure, surmounted by the atrocious hat, coming toward him. "Well," she said, "you only live once and paying a little more for it, I at least won't meet myself coming and going."

"Some day I'll start making money," Julian said gloomily—he knew he never would—"and you can have one of those jokes whenever you take the fit." But first they would move. He visualized a place where the nearest neighbors would be three miles away on either side.

"I think you're doing fine," she said, drawing on her gloves. "You've only been out of school a year. Rome wasn't built in a day."

She was one of the few members of the Y reducing class who arrived in hat and gloves and who had a son who had been to college. "It takes time," she said, "and the world is in such a mess. This hat looked better on me than any of the others, though when she brought it out I said, 'Take that thing back. I wouldn't have it on my head,' and she said, 'Now wait till you see it on,' and when she put it on me, I said, 'We-ull,' and she said, 'If you ask me, that hat does something for you and you do something for the hat, and besides,' she said, 'with that hat, you won't meet yourself coming and going.'"

Julian thought he could have stood his lot better if she had been selfish, if she had been an old hag who drank and screamed at him. He walked along, saturated in depression, as if in the midst of his martyrdom he had lost his faith. Catching sight of his long, hopeless, irritated face, she stopped suddenly with a grief-stricken look, and pulled back on his arm. "Wait on me," she said. "I'm going back to the house and take this thing off and tomorrow I'm going to return it. I was out of my head. I can pay the gas bill with that seven-fifty."

He caught her arm in a vicious grip. "You are not going to take it back," he said. "I like it."

"Well," she said, "I don't think I ought . . ."

"Shut up and enjoy it," he muttered, more depressed than ever.

"With the world in the mess it's in," she said, "it's a wonder we can enjoy anything. I tell you, the bottom rail is on the top."

Julian sighed.

"Of course," she said, "if you know who you are, you can go anywhere." She said this every time he took her to the reducing class. "Most of them in it are not our kind of people," she said, "but I can be gracious to anybody. I know who I am."

"They don't give a damn for your graciousness," Julian said savagely. "Knowing who you are is good for one generation only. You haven't the foggiest idea where you stand now or who you are."

She stopped and allowed her eyes to flash at him. "I most certainly do know who I am," she said, "and if you don't know who you are, I'm ashamed of you."

"Oh hell," Julian said.

"Your great-grandfather was a former governor of this state," she said. "Your grandfather was a prosperous landowner. Your grandmother was a Godhigh."

"Will you look around you," he said tensely, "and see where you are now?" and he swept his arm jerkily out to indicate the neighborhood, which the growing darkness at least made less dingy.

"You remain what you are," she said. "Your great-grandfather had a plantation and two hundred slaves."

"There are no more slaves," he said irritably.

"They were better off when they were," she said. He groaned to see that she was off on that topic. She rolled onto it every few days like a train on an open track. He knew every stop, every junction, every swamp along the way, and knew the exact point at which her conclusion would roll majestically into the station: "It's ridiculous. It's simply not realistic. They should rise, yes, but on their own side of the fence."

"Let's skip it," Julian said.

"The ones I feel sorry for," she said, "are the ones that are half white. They're tragic."

"Will you skip it?"

"Suppose we were half white. We would certainly have mixed feelings."

"I have mixed feelings now," he groaned.

"Well let's talk about something pleasant," she said. "I remember going to Grandpa's when I was a little girl. Then the house had double stairways that went up to what was really the second floor—all the cooking was done on the first. I used to like to stay down in the kitchen on account of the way the walls smelled. I would sit with my nose pressed against the plaster and take deep breaths. Actually the place belonged to the Godhighs but your grandfather Chestny paid the mortgage and saved it for them. They were in reduced circumstances," she said, "but reduced or not, they never forgot who they were."

"Doubtless that decayed mansion reminded them," Julian muttered. He never spoke of it without contempt or thought of it without longing. He had seen it once when he was a child before it had been sold. The double stairways had rotted and been torn down. Negroes were living in it. But it remained in his mind as his mother had known it. It appeared in his dreams regularly. He would stand on the wide porch, listening to the rustle of oak leaves, then wander through the high-ceilinged hall into the parlor that opened onto it and gaze at the worn rugs and faded draperies. It occurred to him that it was he, not she, who could have appreciated it. He preferred its threadbare elegance to anything he could name and it was because of it that all the neighborhoods they had lived in had been a torment to him—whereas she had hardly known the difference. She called her insensitivity "being adjustable."

"And I remember the old darky who was my nurse, Caroline. There was no better person in the world. I've always had a great respect for my colored friends," she said. "I'd do anything in the world for them and they'd . . ."

"Will you for God's sake get off that subject?" Julian said. When he got on a bus by himself, he made it a point to sit down beside a Negro, in reparation as it were for his mother's sins.

"You're mighty touchy tonight," she said. "Do you feel all right?"

"Yes I feel all right," he said. "Now lay off."

She pursed her lips. "Well, you certainly are in a vile humor," she observed. "I just won't speak to you at all."

They had reached the bus stop. There was no bus in sight and Julian, his hands still jammed in his pockets and his head thrust forward, scowled down the empty street. The frustration of having to wait on the bus as well as ride on it began to creep up his neck like a hot hand. The presence of his mother was borne in upon him as she gave a pained sigh. He looked at her bleakly. She was holding herself very erect under the preposterous hat, wearing it like a banner of her imaginary dignity. There was in him an evil urge to break her spirit. He suddenly unloosened his tie and pulled it off and put it in his pocket.

She stiffened. "Why must you look like *that* when you take me to town?" she said. "Why must you deliberately embarrass me?"

"If you'll never learn where you are," he said, "you can at least learn where I am."

"You look like a—thug," she said.

"Then I must be one," he murmured.

"I'll just go home," she said. "I will not bother you. If you can't do a little thing like that for me . . ."

Rolling his eyes upward, he put his tie back on. "Restored to my class," he muttered. He thrust his face toward her and hissed, "True culture is in the mind, the *mind*," he said, and tapped his head, "the mind."

"It's in the heart," she said, "and in how you do things and how you do things is because of who you *are*."

"Nobody in the damn bus cares who you are."

"I care who I am," she said icily.

The lighted bus appeared on top of the next hill and as it approached, they moved out into the street to meet it. He put his hand under her elbow and hoisted her up on the creaking step. She entered with a little smile, as if she were going into a drawing room where everyone had been waiting for her. While he put in the tokens, she sat down on one of the broad front seats for three which faced the aisle. A thin woman with protruding teeth and long yellow hair was sitting on the end of it. His mother moved up beside her and left room for Julian beside herself. He sat down and looked at the floor across the aisle where a pair of thin feet in red and white canvas sandals were planted.

His mother immediately began a general conversation meant to attract anyone who felt like talking. "Can it get any hotter?" she said and removed from her purse a folding fan, black with a Japanese scene on it, which she began to flutter before her.

"I reckon it might could," the woman with the protruding teeth said, "but I know for a fact my apartment couldn't get no hotter."

"It must get the afternoon sun," his mother said. She sat forward and looked up and down the bus. It was half filled. Everybody was white. "I see we have the bus to ourselves," she said. Julian cringed.

"For a change," said the woman across the aisle, the owner of the red and white canvas sandals. "I come on one the other day and they were thick as fleas—up front and all through."

"The world is in a mess everywhere," his mother said. "I don't know how we've let it get in this fix."

"What gets my goat is all those boys from good families stealing automobile tires," the woman with the protruding teeth said. "I told my boy, I said you may not be rich but you been raised right and if I ever catch you in any such mess, they can send you on to the reformatory. Be exactly where you belong."

"Training tells," his mother said. "Is your boy in high school?"

"Ninth grade," the woman said.

"My son just finished college last year. He wants to write but he's selling typewriters until he gets started," his mother said.

The woman leaned forward and peered at Julian. He threw her such a malevolent look that she subsided against the seat. On the floor across the aisle there was an abandoned newspaper. He got up and got it and opened it out in front of him. His mother discreetly continued the conversation in a lower tone but the woman across the aisle said in a loud voice, "Well that's nice. Selling typewriters is close to writing. He can go right from one to the other."

"I tell him," his mother said, "that Rome wasn't built in a day."

Behind the newspaper Julian was withdrawing into the inner compartment of his mind where he spent most of his time. This was a kind of mental bubble in which he established himself when he could not bear to be a part of what was going on around him. From it he could see out and judge but in it he was safe from any kind of penetration from without. It was the only place where he felt free of the general idiocy of his fellows. His mother had never entered it but from it he could see her with absolute clarity.

The old lady was clever enough and he thought that if she had started from any of the right premises, more might have been expected of her. She lived according to the laws of her own fantasy world, outside of which he had never seen her set foot. The law of it was to sacrifice herself for him after she had first created the necessity to do so by making a mess of things. If he had permitted her sacrifices, it was only because her lack of foresight had made them necessary. All of her life had been a struggle to act like a Chestny without the Chestny goods, and to give him everything she thought a Chestny ought to have; but since, said she, it was fun to struggle, why complain? And when you had won, as she had won, what fun to look back on the hard times! He could not forgive her that she had enjoyed the struggle and that she thought *she* had won.

What she meant when she said she had won was that she had brought him up successfully and had sent him to college and that he had turned out so well—good looking (her teeth had gone unfilled so that his could be straightened), intelligent (he realized he was too intelligent to be a success), and with a future ahead of him (there was of course no future ahead of him). She excused his gloominess on the grounds that he was still growing up and his radical ideas on his lack of practical experience. She said he didn't yet know a thing about "life," that he hadn't even entered the real world—when already he was as disenchanted with it as a man of fifty.

The further irony of all this was that in spite of her, he had turned out so well. In spite of going to only a third-rate college, he had, on his own initiative, come out with a first-rate education; in spite of growing up dominated by a small mind, he had ended up with a large one; in spite of all her foolish views, he was free of prejudice and unafraid to face facts. Most miraculous of all, instead of being blinded by love for her as she was for him, he had cut himself emotionally free of her and could see her with complete objectivity. He was not dominated by his mother.

The bus stopped with a sudden jerk and shook him from his meditation. A woman from the back lurched forward with little steps and barely escaped falling in his newspaper as she righted herself. She got off and a large Negro got on. Julian kept his paper lowered to watch. It gave him a certain satisfaction to see injustice in daily operation. It confirmed his view that with a few exceptions there was no one worth knowing within a radius of three hundred miles. The Negro was well dressed and carried a briefcase. He looked around and then sat down on the other end of the seat where the woman with the red and white canvas sandals was sitting. He immediately unfolded a newspaper and obscured himself behind it. Julian's mother's elbow at once prodded insistently into his ribs. "Now you see why I won't ride on these buses by myself," she whispered.

The woman with the red and white canvas sandals had risen at the same time the Negro sat down and had gone further back in the bus and taken the seat of the woman who had got off. His mother leaned forward and cast her an approving look.

Julian rose, crossed the aisle, and sat down in the place of the woman with the canvas sandals. From this position, he looked serenely across at his mother. Her face had turned an angry red. He stared at her, making his eyes the eyes of a stranger. He felt his tension suddenly lift as if he had openly declared war on her.

He would have liked to get in conversation with the Negro and to talk with him about art or politics or any subject that would be above the comprehension of those around them, but the man remained entrenched behind his paper. He was either ignoring the change of seating or had never noticed it. There was no way for Julian to convey his sympathy.

His mother kept her eyes fixed reproachfully on his face. The woman with the protruding teeth was looking at him avidly as if he were a type of monster new to her.

"Do you have a light?" he asked the Negro.

Without looking away from his paper, the man reached in his pocket and handed him a packet of matches.

"Thanks," Julian said. For a moment he held the matches foolishly. A NO SMOKING sign looked down upon him from over the door. This alone would not have deterred him; he had no cigarettes. He had quit smoking some months before because he could not afford it. "Sorry," he muttered and handed back the matches. The Negro lowered the paper and gave him an annoyed look. He took the matches and raised the paper again.

His mother continued to gaze at him but she did not take advantage of his momentary discomfort. Her eyes retained their battered look. Her face seemed to be unnaturally red, as if her blood pressure had risen. Julian allowed no glimmer of sympathy to show on his face. Having got the advantage, he wanted desperately to keep it and carry it through. He would have liked to teach her a lesson that would last her a while, but there seemed no way to continue the point. The Negro refused to come out from behind his paper.

Julian folded his arms and looked stolidly before him, facing her but as if he did not see her, as if he had ceased to recognize her existence.

He visualized a scene in which, the bus having reached their stop, he would remain in his seat and when she said, "Aren't you going to get off?" he would look at her as at a stranger who had rashly addressed him. The corner they got off on was usually deserted, but it was well lighted and it would not hurt her to walk by herself the four blocks to the Y. He decided to wait until the time came and then decide whether or not he would let her get off by herself. He would have to be at the Y at ten to bring her back, but he could leave her wondering if he was going to show up. There was no reason for her to think she could always depend on him.

He retired again into the high-ceilinged room sparsely settled with large pieces of antique furniture. His soul expanded momentarily but then he became aware of his mother across from him and the vision shriveled. He studied her coldly. Her feet in little pumps dangled like a child's and did not quite reach the floor. She was training on him an exaggerated look of reproach. He felt completely detached from her. At that moment he could with pleasure have slapped her as he would have slapped a particularly obnoxious child in his charge.

He began to imagine various unlikely ways by which he could teach her a lesson. He might make friends with some distinguished Negro professor or lawyer and bring him home to spend the evening. He would be entirely justified but her blood pressure would rise to 300. He could not push her to the extent of making her have a stroke, and moreover, he had never been successful at making any Negro friends. He had tried to strike up an acquaintance on the bus with some of the better types, with ones that looked like professors or ministers or lawyers. One morning he had sat down next to a distinguished-looking dark brown man who had answered his questions with a sonorous solemnity but who had turned out to be an undertaker. Another day he had sat down beside a cigar-smoking Negro with a diamond ring on his finger, but after a few stilted pleasantries, the Negro had rung the buzzer and risen, slipping two lottery tickets into Julian's hand as he climbed over him to leave.

He imagined his mother lying desperately ill and his being able to secure only a Negro doctor for her. He toyed with that idea for a few minutes and then dropped it for a momentary vision of himself participating as a sympathizer in a sit-in demonstration. This was possible but he did not linger with it. Instead, he approached the ultimate horror. He brought home a beautiful suspiciously Negroid woman. Prepare yourself, he said. There is nothing you can do about it. This is the woman I've chosen. She's intelligent, dignified, even good, and she's suffered and she hasn't thought it *fun*. Now persecute us, go ahead and persecute us. Drive her out of here, but remember, you're driving me too. His eyes were narrowed and through the indignation he had generated, he saw his mother across the aisle, purple-faced, shrunken to the dwarf-like proportions of her moral nature, sitting like a mummy beneath the ridiculous banner of her hat.

He was tilted out of his fantasy again as the bus stopped. The door opened with a sucking hiss and out of the dark a large, gaily dressed, sullen-looking colored woman got on with a little boy. The child, who might have been four, had on a short plaid suit and a Tyrolean hat with a blue feather in it. Julian hoped that he would sit down beside him and that the woman would push in beside his mother. He could think of no better arrangement.

As she waited for her tokens, the woman was surveying the seating possibilities—he hoped with the idea of sitting where she was least wanted. There was something familiar-looking about her but Julian could not place what it was. She was a giant of a woman. Her face was set not only to meet opposition but to seek it out. The downward tilt of her large lower lip was like a warning sign: DON'T TAMPER WITH ME. Her bulging figure was encased in a green crepe dress and her feet overflowed in red shoes. She had on a hideous hat. A purple velvet flap came down on one side of it and stood up on the other; the rest of it was green and looked like a cushion with the stuffing out. She carried a mammoth red pocketbook that bulged throughout as if it were stuffed with rocks.

To Julian's disappointment, the little boy climbed up on the empty seat beside his mother. His mother lumped all children, black and white, into the common category, "cute," and she thought little Negroes were on the whole cuter than little white children. She smiled at the little boy as he climbed on the seat.

Meanwhile the woman was bearing down upon the empty seat beside Julian. To his annoyance, she squeezed herself into it. He saw his mother's face change as the woman settled herself next to him and he realized with satisfaction that this was more objectionable to her than it was to him. Her face seemed almost gray and there was a look of dull recognition in her eyes, as if suddenly she had sickened at some awful confrontation. Julian saw that it was because she and the woman had, in a sense, swapped sons. Though his mother would not realize the symbolic significance of this, she would feel it. His amusement showed plainly on his face.

The woman next to him muttered something unintelligible to herself. He was conscious of a kind of bristling next to him, a muted growling like that of an angry cat. He could not see anything but the red pocketbook upright on the bulging green thighs. He visualized the woman as she had stood waiting for her tokens—the ponderous figure, rising from the red shoes upward over the solid hips, the mammoth bosom, the haughty face, to the green and purple hat.

His eyes widened.

The vision of the two hats, identical, broke upon him with the radiance of a brilliant sunrise. His face was suddenly lit with joy. He could not believe that Fate had thrust upon his mother such a lesson. He gave a loud chuckle so that she would look at him and see that he saw. She turned her eyes on him slowly. The blue in them seemed to have turned a bruised purple. For a moment he had an uncomfortable sense of her innocence, but it lasted only a second before principle rescued him. Justice entitled him to laugh. His grin hardened until it said to her as plainly as if he were saying aloud: Your punishment exactly fits your pettiness. This should teach you a permanent lesson.

Her eyes shifted to the woman. She seemed unable to bear looking at him and to find the woman preferable. He became conscious again of the bristling presence at his side. The woman was rumbling like a volcano about to become active. His mother's mouth began to twitch slightly at one corner. With a sinking heart, he saw incipient signs of recovery on her face and realized that this was going to strike her suddenly as funny and was going to be no lesson at all. She kept her eyes on the woman and an amused smile came over her face as if the woman were a monkey that had stolen her hat. The little Negro was looking up at her with large fascinated eyes. He had been trying to attract her attention for some time.

"Carver!" the woman said suddenly. "Come heah!"

When he saw that the spotlight was on him at last Carver drew his feet and turned himself toward Julian's mother and giggled.

"Carver!" the woman said. "You heah me? Come heah!"

Carver slid down from the seat but remained squatting with his back against the base of it, his head turned slyly around toward Julian's mother, who was smiling at him. The woman reached a hand across the aisle and snatched him to her. He righted himself and hung backwards on her knees, grinning at Julian's mother. "Isn't he cute?" Julian's mother said to the woman with the protruding teeth.

"I reckon he is," the woman said without conviction.

The Negress yanked him upright but he eased out of her grip and shot across the aisle and scrambled giggling wildly, onto the seat beside his love.

"I think he likes me," Julian's mother said, and smiled at the woman. It was the smile she used when she was being particularly gracious to an inferior. Julian saw everything lost. The lesson had rolled off her like rain on a roof.

The woman stood up and yanked the little boy off the seat as if she were snatching him from contagion. Julian could feel the rage in her at having no weapon like his mother's smile. She gave the child a sharp slap across his leg. He howled once and then thrust his head into her stomach and kicked his feet against her shins. "Be-have," she said vehemently.

The bus stopped and the Negro who had been reading the newspaper got off. The woman moved over and set the little boy down with a thump between herself and Julian. She held him firmly by the knee. In a moment he put his hands in front of his face and peeped at Julian's mother through his fingers.

"I see yoooooooo!" she said and put her hand in front of her face and peeped at him.

The woman slapped his hand down. "Quit yo' foolishness," she said, "before I knock the living Jesus out of you!"

Julian was thankful that the next stop was theirs. He reached up and pulled the cord. The woman reached up and pulled it at the same time. Oh my God, he thought. He had the terrible intuition that when they got off the bus together, his mother would open her purse and give the little boy a nickel. The gesture would be as natural to her as breathing. The bus stopped and the woman got up and lunged to the front, dragging the child, who wished to stay on, after her. Julian and his mother got up and followed. As they neared the door, Julian tried to relieve her of her pocketbook.

"No," she murmured, "I want to give the little boy a nickel."

"No!" Julian hissed. "No!"

She smiled down at the child and opened her bag. The bus door opened and the woman picked him up by the arm and descended with him, hanging at her hip. Once in the street she set him down and shook him.

Julian's mother had to close her purse while she got down the bus step but as soon as her feet were on the ground, she opened it again and began to rummage inside. "I can't find but a penny," she whispered, "but it looks like a new one."

"Don't do it!" Julian said fiercely between his teeth. There was a streetlight on the corner and she hurried to get under it so that she could better see into her pocketbook. The woman was heading off rapidly down the street with the child still hanging backward on her hand.

"Oh little boy!" Julian's mother called and took a few quick steps and caught up with them just beyond the lamp-post. "Here's a bright new penny for you," and she held out the coin, which shone bronze in the dim light.

The huge woman turned and for a moment stood, her shoulders lifted and her face frozen with frustrated rage, and stared at Julian's mother. Then all at once she seemed to explode like a piece of machinery that had been given one ounce of pressure too much. Julian saw the black fist swing out with the red pocketbook. He shut his eyes and cringed as he heard the woman shout, "He don't take nobody's pennies!" When he opened his eyes, the woman was disappearing down the street with the little boy staring wide-eyed over her shoulder. Julian's mother was sitting on the sidewalk.

"I told you not to do that," Julian said angrily. "I told you not to do that!"

He stood over her for a minute, gritting his teeth. Her legs were stretched out in front of her and her hat was on her lap. He squatted down and looked her in the face. It was totally expressionless. "You got exactly what you deserved," he said. "Now get up."

He picked up her pocketbook and put what had fallen out back in it. He picked the hat up off her lap. The penny caught his eye on the sidewalk and he picked that up and let it drop before her eyes into the purse. Then he stood up and leaned over and held his hands out to pull her up. She remained immobile. He sighed. Rising above them on either side were black apartment buildings, marked with irregular rectangles of light. At the end of the block a man came out of a door and walked off in the opposite direction. "All right," he said, "suppose somebody happens by and wants to know why you're sitting on the sidewalk?"

She took the hand and, breathing hard, pulled heavily up on it and then stood for a moment, swaying slightly as if the spots of light in the darkness were circling around her. Her eyes, shadowed and confused, finally settled on his face. He did not try to conceal his irritation. "I hope this teaches you a lesson," he said. She leaned forward and her eyes raked his face. She seemed trying to determine his identity. Then, as if she found nothing familiar about him, she started off with a headlong movement in the wrong direction.

"Aren't you going on to the Y?" he asked.

"Home," she muttered.

"Well, are we walking?"

For answer she kept going. Julian followed along, his hands behind him. He saw no reason to let the lesson she had had go without backing it up with an explanation of its meaning. She might as well be made to understand what had happened to her. "Don't think that was just an uppity Negro woman," he said. "That was the whole colored race which will no longer take your condescending pennies. That was your black double. She can wear the same hat as you, and to be sure," he added gratuitously (because he thought it was funny), "it looked better on her than it did on you. What all this means," he said, "is that the old world is gone. The old manners are obsolete and your graciousness is not worth a damn." He thought bitterly of the house that had been lost for him. "You aren't who you think you are," he said.

She continued to plow ahead, paying no attention to him. Her hair had come undone on one side. She dropped her pocketbook and took no notice. He stooped and picked it up and handed it to her but she did not take it.

"You needn't act as if the world had come to an end," he said, "because it hasn't. From now on you've got to live in a new world and face a few realities for a change. Buck up," he said, "it won't kill you."

She was breathing fast.

"Let's wait on the bus," he said.

"Home," she said thickly.

"I hate to see you behave like this," he said. "Just like a child. I should be able to expect more of you." He decided to stop where he was and make her stop and wait for a bus. "I'm not going any farther," he said, stopping. "We're going on the bus."

She continued to go on as if she had not heard him. He took a few steps and caught her arm and stopped her. He looked into her face and caught his breath. He was looking into a face he had never seen before. "Tell Grandpa to come get me," she said.

He stared, stricken.

"Tell Caroline to come get me," she said.

Stunned, he let her go and she lurched forward again, walking as if one leg were shorter than the other. A tide of darkness seemed to be sweeping her from him. "Mother!" he cried. "Darling, sweetheart, wait!" Crumpling, she fell to the pavement. He dashed forward and fell at her side, crying, "Mamma, Mamma!" He turned her over. Her face was fiercely distorted. One eye, large and staring, moved slightly to the left as if it had become unmoored. The other remained fixed on him, raked his face again, found nothing and closed.

"Wait here, wait here!" he cried and jumped up and began to run for help toward a cluster of lights he saw in the distance ahead of him. "Help, help!" he shouted, but his voice was thin, scarcely a thread of sound. The lights drifted farther away the faster he ran and his feet moved numbly as if they carried him nowhere. The tide of darkness seemed to sweep him back to her, postponing from moment to moment his entry into the world of guilt and sorrow.

JOHN [SIMMONS] BARTH (1930–)

John Barth looks like a rather solemn and conventional young man; he has published five outrageously unconventional books.

The conventional externals are these: he was born in Cambridge, Maryland; he took his B.A. at the Johns Hopkins University in 1951 and his M.A. in 1952; before taking either degree he was married; he is now the father of three children; for three years he taught English at Pennsylvania State University, and since 1965 he has been a professor of English at the State University of New York, Buffalo. These externals tell us almost nothing.

When he was twenty-six years old, he published his first novel, The Floating Opera *(1956), the story of a man's life as he recalls it on the day that he contemplates his suicide. His next novel,* The End of the Road *(1958), parodying the conventional love triangle of popular fiction, reduces human relations to the absurd. His next, the novel that made his reputation as an innovator with a considerable debt to Rabelais,* The Sot-Weed Factor *(1960)—another parody, now of eighteenth-century fiction like* Tom Jones, *with a plot at least as elaborately complicated and finally as tidy—is the ostensible life of Ebenezer Cook, the author of an early-eighteenth-century satirical poem called "The Sot-Weed Factor," about whose personal life nothing at all is known; Barth brilliantly improvised a life for him. In 1966 he published the work that many of his admirers regard as his most important,* Giles Goat-Boy, or, The Revised New Syllabus. *While he was at work on this book, he was asked what it was about, and he replied: "It's a longish story about a young man who is raised as a goat, later learns he's human and commits himself to the heroic project of discovering the secret of things." John Barth's comments on his own work do not illuminate it much more than do the bare facts of his biography.*

His most recent book, Lost in the Funhouse *(1968), bears the subtitle "Fiction for Print, Tape, Live Voice." It is a single work, meant to be designed like a funhouse, a structure that the reader enters blithely enough, only to be fooled, bewildered, booby-trapped, talked to by the voices of unseen recordings, shouted at, tossed about until he staggers out, severely shaken but conceivably wiser—at least about funhouses. The title piece cannot communicate the effect of the whole, but it successfully suggests it.*

The author comments:

These are "experimental" pieces and the word "experimental" is a pejorative term now. We tend to think of experiment as being cold exercises in technique. My feeling about technique in art is that it has about the same value as technique in love-making. That is to say, heartfelt ineptitude has its appeal and so does heartless skill; but what you want is passionate virtuosity.

FURTHER READING

For a good introduction to Barth's world, see Robert Scholes, *The Fabulators* (1967).

Lost in the Funhouse (1968)

For whom is the funhouse fun? Perhaps for lovers. For Ambrose it is *a place of fear and confusion.* He has come to the seashore with his family for the holiday, *the occasion of their visit is Independence Day, the most important secular holiday of the United States of America.* A single straight underline is the manuscript mark for italic type, *which in turn* is the printed equivalent to oral emphasis of words and phrases as well as the customary type for titles of complete works, not to mention. Italics are also employed, in fiction stories especially, for "outside," intrusive, or artificial voices, such as radio announcements, the texts of telegrams and newspaper articles, et cetera. They should be used *sparingly*. If passages originally in roman type are italicized by someone repeating them, it's customary to acknowledge the fact. *Italics mine.*

Ambrose was "at that awkward age." His voice came out high-pitched as a child's if he let himself get carried away; to be on the safe side, therefore, he moved and spoke with *deliberate calm* and *adult gravity.* Talking soberly of unimportant or irrelevant matters and listening consciously to the sound of your own voice are useful habits for maintaining control in this difficult interval. *En route* to Ocean City he sat in the back seat of the family car with his brother Peter, age fifteen, and Magda G——, age fourteen, a pretty girl an exquisite young lady, who lived not far from them on B—— Street in the town of D——, Maryland. Initials, blanks, or both were often substituted for proper names in nineteenth-century fiction to enhance the illusion of reality. It is as if the author felt it necessary to delete the names for reasons of tact or legal liability. Interestingly, as with other aspects of realism, it is an *illusion* that is being enhanced, by purely artificial means. Is it likely, does it violate the principle of verisimilitude, that a thirteen-year-old boy could make such a sophisticated observation? A girl of fourteen is *the psychological coeval* of a boy of fifteen or sixteen; a thirteen-year-old boy, therefore, even one precocious in some other respects, might be three years *her emotional junior.*

Thrice a year—on Memorial, Independence, and Labor Days—the family visits Ocean City for the afternoon and evening. When Ambrose and Peter's father was their age, the excursion was made by train, as mentioned in the novel *The 42nd Parallel* by John Dos Passos. Many families from the same neighborhood used to travel together, with dependent relatives and often with Negro servants; schoolfuls of children swarmed through the railway cars; everyone shared everyone else's Maryland fried chicken, Virginia ham, deviled eggs, potato salad, beaten biscuits, iced tea. Nowadays (that is, in 19—, the year of our story) the journey is made by automobile—more comfortably and quickly though without the extra fun though without the *camaraderie* of a general excursion. It's all part of the deterioration of American life, their father declares; Uncle Karl supposes that when the boys take *their* families to Ocean City for the holidays they'll fly in Autogiros. Their mother, sitting in the middle of the front seat like Magda in the second, only with her arms on the seat-back behind the men's shoulders, wouldn't want the good old days back again, the steaming trains and stuffy long dresses; on the other hand she can do without Autogiros, too, if she has to become a grandmother to fly in them.

Description of physical appearance and mannerisms is one of several standard methods of characterization used by writers of fiction. It is also important to "keep the senses operating"; when a detail from one of the five senses, say visual, is "crossed" with a detail from another, say auditory, the reader's imagination is oriented to the scene, perhaps unconsciously. This procedure may be compared to the way surveyors and navigators determine their positions by two or more compass bearings, a process known as triangulation. The brown hair on Ambrose's mother's forearms gleamed in the sun like. Though right-handed, she took her left arm from the seat-back to press the dashboard cigar lighter for Uncle Karl. When the glass bead in its handle glowed red, the lighter was ready for use. The smell of Uncle Karl's cigar smoke reminded one of. The fragrance of the ocean came strong to the picnic ground where they always stopped for lunch, two miles inland from Ocean City. Having to pause for a full hour almost within sound of the breakers was difficult for Peter and Ambrose when they were younger; even at their present age it was not easy to keep their anticipation, *stimulated by the briny spume,* from turning into short temper. The Irish author James Joyce, in his unusual novel entitled *Ulysses,* now available in this country, uses the adjectives *snot-green* and *scrotum-tightening* to describe the sea. Visual, auditory, tactile, olfactory, gustatory. Peter and Ambrose's father, while steering their black 1936 LaSalle sedan with one hand, could with the other remove the first cigarette from a white pack of Lucky Strikes and, more remarkably, light it with a match forefingered from its book and thumbed against the flint paper without being detached. The matchbook cover merely advertised U. S. War Bonds and Stamps. A fine metaphor, simile, or other figure of speech, in addition to its obvious "first-order" relevance to the thing it describes, will be seen upon reflection to have a second order of significance: it may be drawn from the *milieu* of the action, for example, or be particularly appropriate to the sensibility of the narrator, even hinting to the reader things of which the narrator is unaware; or it may cast further and subtler lights upon the thing it describes, sometimes ironically qualifying the more evident sense of the comparison.

To say that Ambrose's and Peter's mother was *pretty* is to accomplish nothing; the reader may acknowledge the proposition, but his imagination is not engaged. Besides, Magda was also pretty, yet in an altogether different way. Although she lived on B—— Street she had very good manners and did better than average in school. Her figure was very well developed for her age. Her right hand lay casually on the plush upholstery of the seat, very near Ambrose's left leg, on which his own hand rested. The space between their legs, between her right and his left leg, was out of the line of sight of anyone sitting on the other side of Magda, as well as anyone glancing into the rear-view mirror. Uncle Karl's face resembled Peter's—rather, vice versa. Both had dark hair and eyes, short husky statures, deep voices. Magda's left hand was probably in a similar position on her left side. The boy's father is difficult to describe; no particular feature of his appearance or manner stood out. He wore glasses and was principal of a T—— County grade school. Uncle Karl was a masonry contractor.

Although Peter must have known as well as Ambrose that the latter, because of his position in the car, would be the first to see the electrical towers of the power plant at V——, the halfway point of their trip, he leaned forward and slightly toward the center of the car and pretended to be looking for them through the flat pinewoods and tuckahoe creeks along the highway. For as long as the boys could remember, "looking for the Towers" had been a feature of the first half of their excursions to Ocean City, "looking for the standpipe" of the second. Though the game was childish, their mother preserved the tradition of rewarding the first to see the Towers with a candy-bar or piece of fruit. She insisted now that Magda play the game; the prize, she said, was "something hard to get nowadays." Ambrose decided not to join in; he sat far back in his seat. Magda, like Peter, leaned forward. Two sets of straps were discernible through the shoulders of her sun dress; the inside right one, a brassiere-strap, was fastened or shortened with a small safety pin. The right armpit of her dress, presumably the left as well, was damp with perspiration. The simple strategy for being first to espy the Towers, which Ambrose had understood by the age of four, was to sit on the right-hand side of the car. Whoever sat there, however, had also to put up with the worst of the sun, and so Ambrose, without mentioning the matter, chose sometimes the one and sometimes the other. Not impossibly Peter had never caught on to the trick, or thought that his brother hadn't simply because Ambrose on occasion preferred shade to a Baby Ruth or tangerine.

The shade-sun situation didn't apply to the front seat, owing to the windshield; if anything the driver got more sun, since the person on the passenger side not only was shaded below by the door and dashboard but might swing down his sunvisor all the way too.

"Is that them?" Magda asked. Ambrose's mother teased the boys for letting Magda win, insinuating that "somebody [had] a girlfriend." Peter and Ambrose's father reached a long thin arm across their mother to butt his cigarette in the dashboard ashtray, under the lighter. The prize this time for seeing the Towers first was a banana. Their mother bestowed it after chiding their father for wasting a half-smoked cigarette when everything was so scarce. Magda, to take the prize, moved her hand from so near Ambrose's that he could have touched it as though accidentally. She offered to share the prize, things like that were so hard to find; but everyone insisted it was hers alone. Ambrose's mother sang an iambic trimeter couplet from a popular song, femininely rhymed:

"What's good is in the Army;
What's left will never harm me."

Uncle Karl tapped his cigar ash out the ventilator window; some particles were sucked by the slipstream back into the car through the rear window on the passenger side. Magda demonstrated her ability to hold a banana in one hand and peel it with her teeth. She still sat forward; Ambrose pushed his glasses back onto the bridge of his nose with his left hand, which he then negligently let fall to the seat cushion immediately behind her. He even permitted the single hair, gold, on the second joint of his thumb to brush the fabric of her skirt. Should she have sat back at that instant, his hand would have been caught under her.

Plush upholstery prickles uncomfortably through gabardine slacks in the July sun. The function of the *beginning* of a story is to introduce the principal characters, establish their initial relationships, set the scene for the main action, expose the background of the situation if necessary, plant motifs and foreshadowings where appropriate, and initiate the first complication or whatever of the "rising action." Actually, if one imagines a story called "The Funhouse," or "Lost in the Funhouse," the details of the drive to Ocean City don't seem especially relevant. The *beginning* should recount the events between Ambrose's first sight of the funhouse early in the afternoon and his entering it with Magda and Peter in the evening. The *middle* would narrate all relevant events from the time he goes in to the time he loses his way; middles have the double and contradictory function of delaying the climax while at the same time preparing the reader for it and fetching him to it. Then the *ending* would tell what Ambrose does while he's lost, how he finally finds his way out, and what everybody makes of the experience. So far there's been no real dialogue, very little sensory detail, and nothing in the way of a *theme*. And a long time has gone by already without anything happening; it makes a person wonder. We haven't even reached Ocean City yet: we will never get out of the funhouse.

The more closely an author identifies with the narrator, literally or metaphorically, the less advisable it is, as a rule, to use the first-person narrative viewpoint. Once three years previously the young people *afore-mentioned* played Niggers and Masters in the backyard; when it was Ambrose's turn to be Master and theirs to be Niggers Peter had to go serve his evening papers; Ambrose was afraid to punish Magda alone, but she led him to the whitewashed Torture Chamber between the woodshed and the privy in the Slaves Quarters; there she knelt sweating among bamboo rakes and dusty Mason jars, pleadingly embraced his knees, and while bees droned in the lattice as if on an ordinary summer afternoon, purchased clemency at a surprising price set by herself. Doubtless she remembered nothing of this event; Ambrose on the other hand seemed unable to forget the least detail of his life. He even recalled how, standing beside himself with awed impersonality in the reeky heat, he'd stared the while at an empty cigar box in which Uncle Karl kept stone-cutting chisels: beneath the words *El Producto*, a laureled, loose-toga'd lady regarded the sea from a marble bench; beside her, forgotten or not yet turned to, was a five-stringed lyre. Her shin reposed on the back of her right hand; her left depended negligently from the bench-arm. The lower half of scene and lady was peeled away; the words EX-AMINED BY —— were inked there into the wood. Nowadays cigar boxes are made of pasteboard. Ambrose wondered what Magda would have done, Ambrose wondered what Magda would do when she sat back on his hand as he resolved she should. Be angry. Make a teasing joke of it. Give no sign at all. For a long time she leaned forward, playing cow-poker with Peter against Uncle Karl and Mother and watching for the first sign of Ocean City. At nearly the same instant, picnic ground and Ocean City standpipe hove into view; an Amoco filling station on their side of the road cost Mother and Uncle Karl fifty cows and the game; Magda bounced back, clapping her right hand on Mother's right arm; Ambrose moved clear "in the nick of time."

At this rate our hero, at this rate our protagonist will remain in the funhouse forever. Narrative ordinarily consists of alternating dramatization and summarization. One sympton of nervous tension, paradoxically, is repeated and violent yawning; neither Peter nor Magda nor Uncle Karl nor Mother reacted in this manner. Although they were no longer small children, Peter and Ambrose were each given a dollar to spend on board-walk amusements in addition to what money of their own they'd brought along. Magda too, though she protested she had ample spending money. The boys' mother made a little scene out of distributing the bills; she pretended that her sons and Magda were small children and cautioned them not to spend the sum too quickly or in one place. Magda promised with a merry laugh and, having both hands free, took the bill with her left. Peter laughed also and pledged in a falsetto to be a good boy. His imitation of a child was not clever. The boys' father was tall and thin, balding, fair-complexioned. Assertions of that sort are not effective; the reader may acknowledge the proposition, but. We should be much farther along than we are; something has gone wrong; not much of this preliminary rambling seems relevant. Yet everyone begins in the same place; how is it that most go along without difficulty but a few lose their way?

"Stay out from under the boardwalk," Uncle Karl growled from the side of his mouth. The boys' mother pushed his shoulder *in mock annoyance.* They were all standing before Fat May the Laughing Lady who advertised the funhouse. Larger than life, Fat May mechanically shook, rocked on her heels, slapped her thighs while recorded laughter—uproarious, female—came amplified from a hidden loudspeaker. It chuckled, wheezed, wept; tried in vain to catch its breath; tittered, groaned, exploded raucous and anew. You couldn't hear it without laughing yourself, no matter how you felt. Father came back from talking to a Coast-Guardsman on duty and reported that the surf was spoiled with crude oil from tankers recently torpedoed offshore. Lumps of it, difficult to remove, made tarry tidelines on the beach and stuck on swimmers. Many bathed in the surf nevertheless and came out speckled; others paid to use a municipal pool and only sunbathed on the beach. We would do the latter. We would do the latter. We would do the latter.

Under the boardwalk, matchbook covers, grainy other things. What is the story's theme? Ambrose is ill. He perspires in the dark passages; candied apples-on-a-stick, delicious-looking, disappointing to eat. Funhouses need men's and ladies' room at intervals. Others perhaps have also vomited in corners and corridors; may even have had bowel movements liable to be stepped in in the dark. The word *fuck* suggests suction and/or and/or flatulence. Mother and Father; grandmothers and grandfathers on both sides; great-grandmothers and great-grandfathers on four sides, et cetera. Count a generation as thirty years: in approximately the year when Lord Baltimore was granted charter to the province of Maryland by Charles I, five hundred twelve women—English, Welsh, Bavarian, Swiss—of every class and character, received into themselves the penises the intromittent organs of five hundred twelve men, ditto, in every circumstance and posture, to conceive the five hundred twelve ancestors of the two hundred fifty-six ancestors of the et cetera et cetera et cetera et cetera et cetera et cetera et cetera et cetera of the author, of the narrator, of this story, *Lost in the Funhouse*. In alleyways, ditches, canopy beds, pinewoods, bridal suites, ship's cabins, coach-and-fours, coaches-and-four, sultry toolsheds; on the cold sand under boardwalks, littered with *El Producto* cigar butts, treasured with Lucky Strike cigarette stubs, Coca-Cola caps, gritty turds, cardboard lollipop sticks, matchbook covers warning that A Slip of the Lip Can Sink a Ship. The shluppish whisper, continuous as seawash round the globe, tidelike falls and rises with the circuit of dawn and dusk.

Magda's teeth. She *was* left-handed. Perspiration. They've gone all the way, through, Magda and Peter, they've been waiting for hours with Mother and Uncle Karl while Father searches for his lost son; they draw french-fried potatoes from a paper cup and shake their heads. They've named the children they'll one day have and bring to Ocean City on holidays. Can spermatozoa properly be thought of as male animalcules when there are no female spermatozoa? They grope through hot, dark windings, past Love's Tunnel's fearsome obstacles. Some perhaps lose their way.

Peter suggested then and there that they do the funhouse; he had been through it before, so had Magda, Ambrose hadn't and suggested, his voice cracking on account of Fat May's laughter, that they swim first. All were chuckling, couldn't help it; Ambrose's father, Ambrose's and Peter's father came up grinning like a lunatic with two boxes of syrup-coated popcorn, one for Mother, one for Magda; the men were to help themselves. Ambrose walked on Magda's right; being by nature left-handed, she carried the box in her left hand. Up front the situation was reversed.

"What are you limping for?" Magda inquired of Ambrose. He supposed in a husky tone that his foot had gone to sleep in the car. Her teeth flashed. "Pins and needles?" It was the honeysuckle on the lattice of the former privy that drew the bees. Imagine being stung there. How long is this going to take?

The adults decided to forgo the pool; but Uncle Karl insisted they change into swimsuits and do the beach. "He wants to watch the pretty girls," Peter teased, and ducked behind Magda from Uncle Karl's pretended wrath. "You've got all the pretty girls you need right here," Magda declared, and Mother said: "Now that's the gospel truth." Magda scolded Peter, who reached over her shoulder to sneak some popcorn. "Your brother and father aren't getting any." Uncle Karl wondered if they were going to have fireworks that night, what with the shortages. It wasn't the shortages, Mr. M—— replied; Ocean City had fireworks from prewar. But it was too risky on account of the enemy submarines, some people thought.

"Don't seem like Fourth of July without fireworks," said Uncle Karl. *The inverted tag in dialogue writing is still considered permissible with proper names or epithets, but sounds old-fashioned with personal pronouns.* "We'll have 'em again soon enough," predicted the boys' father. Their mother declared she could do without fireworks: they reminded her too much of the real thing. Their father said all the more reason to shoot off a few now and again. Uncle Karl asked *rhetorically* who needed reminding, just look at people's hair and skin.

"The oil, yes," said Mrs. M——.

Ambrose had a pain in his stomach and so didn't swim but enjoyed watching the others. He and his father burned red easily. Magda's figure was exceedingly well developed for her age. She too declined to swim, and got mad, and became angry when Peter attempted to drag her into the pool. She always swam, he insisted; what did she mean not swim? Why did a person come to Ocean City?

"Maybe I want to lay here with Ambrose," Magda teased.

Nobody likes a pedant.

"Aha," said Mother. Peter grabbed Magda by one ankle and ordered Ambrose to grab the other. She squealed and rolled over on the beach blanket. Ambrose pretended to help hold her back. Her tan was darker that even Mother's and Peter's. "Help out, Uncle Karl!" Peter cried. Uncle Karl went to seize the other ankle. Inside the top of her swimsuit, however, you could see the line where the sunburn ended and, when she hunched her shoulders and squealed again, one nipple's auburn edge. Mother made them behave themselves. "*You* should certainly know," she said to Uncle Karl. *Archly.* "That when a lady says she doesn't feel like swimming, a gentleman doesn't ask questions." Uncle Karl said excuse *him;* Mother winked at Magda; Ambrose blushed; stupid Peter kept saying "Phooey on *feel like!*" and tugging at Magda's ankle; then even he got the point, and cannonballed with a holler into the pool.

"I swear," Magda said, in mock *in feigned* exasperation.

The diving would make a suitable literary symbol. To go off the high board you had to wait in a line along the poolside and up the ladder. Fellows tickled girls and goosed one another and shouted to the ones at the top to hurry up, or razzed them for bellyfloppers. Once on the springboard some took a great while posing or clowning or deciding on a dive or getting up their nerve; others ran right off. Especially among the younger fellows the idea was to strike the funniest pose or do the craziest stunt as you fell, a thing that got harder to do as you kept on and kept on. But whether you hollered *Geronimo!* or *Sieg heil!*, held your nose or "rode a bicycle," pretended to be shot or did a perfect jacknife or changed your mind halfway down and ended up with nothing, it was over in two seconds, after all that wait. Spring, pose, splash. Spring, neat-o, splash. Spring, aw fooey, splash.

The grown-ups had gone on; Ambrose wanted to converse with Magda; she was remarkably well developed for her age; it was said that that came from rubbing with a turkish towel, and there were other theories. Ambrose could think of nothing to say except how good a diver Peter was, who was showing off for her benefit. You could pretty well tell by looking at their bathing suits and arm muscles how far along the different fellows were. Ambrose was glad he hadn't gone in swimming, the cold water shrank you up so. Magda pretended to be uninterested in the diving; she probably weighed as much as he did. If you knew your way around in the funhouse like your own bedroom, you could wait until a girl came along and then slip away without ever getting caught, even if her boyfriend was right with her. She'd think *he* did it! It would be better to be the boyfriend, and act outraged, and tear the funhouse apart.

Not act; *be.*

"He's a master diver," Ambrose said. In feigned admiration. "You really have to slave away at it to get that good." What would it matter anyhow if he asked her right out whether she remembered, even teased her with it as Peter would have?

There's no point in going farther; this isn't getting anybody anywhere; they haven't even come to the funhouse yet. Ambrose is off the track, in some new or old part of the place that's not supposed to be used; he strayed into it by some one-in-a-million chance, like the time the roller-coaster car left the tracks in the nineteen-teens against all the laws of physics and sailed over the boardwalk in the dark. And they can't locate him because they don't know where to look. Even the designer and operator have forgotten this other part, that winds around on itself like a whelk shell. That winds around the right part like the snakes on Mercury's caduceus. Some people, perhaps, don't "hit their stride" until their twenties, when the growing-up business is over and women appreciate other things besides wisecracks and teasing and strutting. Peter didn't have one-tenth the imagination *he* had, not one-tenth. Peter did this naming-their-children thing as a joke, making up names like Aloysius and Murgatroyd, but Ambrose knew *exactly* how it would feel to be married and have children of your own, and be a loving husband and father, and go comfortably to work in the mornings and to bed with your wife at night, and wake up with her there. With a breeze coming through the sash and birds and mockingbirds singing in the Chinese-cigar trees. His eyes watered, there aren't enough ways to say that. He would be quite famous in his line of work. Whether Magda was his wife or not, one evening when he was wise-lined and gray at the temples he'd smile gravely, at a fashionable dinner party, and remind her of his youthful passion. The time they went with his family to Ocean City; the *erotic fantasies* he used to have about her. How long ago it seemed, and childish! Yet tender, too, *n'est-ce pas?* Would she have imagined that the world-famous whatever remembered how many strings were on the lyre on the bench beside the girl on the label of the cigar box he'd stared at in the toolshed at age ten while she, age eleven. Even then he had felt *wise beyond his years;* he'd stroked her hair and said in his deepest voice and correctest English, as to a dear child: "I shall never forget this moment."

But though he had breathed heavily, groaned as if ecstatic, what he'd really felt throughout was an odd detachment, as though someone else were Master. Strive as he might to be transported, he heard his mind take notes upon the scene: *This is what they call* passion. *I am experiencing it.* Many of the digger machines were out of order in the penny arcades and could not be repaired or replaced for the duration. Moreover the prizes, made now in USA, were less interesting than formerly, pasteboard items for the most part, and some of the machines wouldn't work on white pennies. The gypsy fortune-teller machine might have provided a foreshadowing of the climax of this story if Ambrose had operated it. It was even dilapidateder than most: the silver coating was worn off the brown metal handles, the glass windows around the dummy were cracked and taped, her kerchiefs and silks long-faded. If a man lived by himself, he could take a department-store mannequin with flexible joints and modify her in certain ways. *However:* by the time he was that old he'd have a real woman. There was a machine that stamped your name around a white-metal coin with a star in the middle: A——. His son would be the second, and when the lad reached thirteen or so he would put a strong arm around his shoulder and tell him calmly: "It is perfectly normal. We have all been through it. It will not last forever." Nobody knew how to be what they were right. He'd smoke a pipe, teach his son how to fish and softcrab, assure him he needn't worry about himself. Magda would certainly give, Magda would certainly yield a great deal of milk, although guilty of occasional solecisms. It don't taste so bad. Suppose the lights came on now!

The day wore on. You think you're yourself, but there are other persons in you. Ambrose gets hard when Ambrose doesn't want to, *and obversely.* Ambrose watches them disagree; Ambrose watches him watch. In the funhouse mirror-room you can't see yourself go on forever, because no matter how you stand, your head gets in the way. Even if you had a glass periscope, the image of your eye would cover up the thing you really wanted to see. The police will come; there'll be a story in the papers. That must be where it happened. Unless he can find a surprise exit, an unofficial backdoor or escape hatch opening on an alley, say, and

then stroll up to the family in front of the funhouse and ask where ever-
body's been; *he's* been out of the place for ages. That's just where it happened, in that last lighted room: Peter and Magda found the right exit;
he found one that you weren't supposed to find and strayed off into the
works somewhere. In a perfect funhouse you'd be able to go only one
way, like the divers off the highboard; getting lost would be impossible;
the doors and halls would work like minnow traps or the valves in veins.

On account of German U-boats, Ocean City was "browned out":
streetlights were shaded on the seaward side; shop-windows and boardwalk amusement places were kept dim, not to silhouette tankers and
Liberty-ships for torpedoing. In a short story about Ocean City, Maryland, during World War II, the author could make use of the image of
sailors on leave in the penny arcades and shooting galleries, sighting
through the crosshairs of toy machine guns at swastika'd subs, while out
in the black Atlantic a U-boat skipper squints through his periscope at
real ships outlined by the glow of penny arcades. After dinner the family
strolled back to the amusement end of the boardwalk. The boys' father
had burnt red as always and was masked with Noxzema, a minstrel in
reverse. The grownups stood at the end of the boardwalk where the Hurricane of '33 had cut an inlet from the ocean to Assawoman Bay.

"Pronounced with a long *o*," Uncle Karl reminded Magda with a
wink. His shirt sleeves were rolled up; Mother punched his brown biceps
with the arrowed heart on it and said his mind was naughty. Fat May's
laugh came suddenly from the funhouse, as if she'd just got the joke;
the family laughed too at the coincidence. Ambrose went under the
boardwalk to search for out-of-town matchbook covers with the aid of
his pocket flashlight; he looked out from the edge of the North American
continent and wondered how far their laughter carried over the water.
Spies in rubber rafts; survivors in lifeboats. If the joke had been beyond
his understanding, he could have said: *"The laughter was over his head."*
And let the reader see the serious wordplay on second reading.

He turned the flashlight on and then off at once even before the
woman whooped. He sprang away, heart athud, dropping the light. What
had the man grunted? Perspiration drenched and chilled him by the
time he scrambled up to the family. "See anything?" his father asked.
His voice wouldn't come; he shrugged and violently brushed sand from
his pants legs.

"Let's ride the old flying horses!" Magda cried. I'll never be an
author. It's been forever already, everybody's gone home, Ocean City's
deserted, the ghost-crabs are tickling across the beach and down the
littered cold streets. And the empty halls of clabboard hotels and abandoned funhouses. A tidal wave; an enemy air raid; a monster-crab swelling like an island from the sea. *The inhabitants fled in terror.* Magda
clung to his trouser leg; he alone knew the maze's secret. "He gave his
life that we might live," said Uncle Karl with a scowl of pain, as he. The
fellow's hands had been tattooed; the woman's legs, the woman's fat white

legs had. *An astonishing coincidence.* He yearned to tell Peter. He wanted to throw up for excitement. They hadn't even chased him. He wished he were dead.

One possible ending would be to have Ambrose come across another lost person in the dark. They'd match their wits together against the funhouse, struggle like Ulysses past obstacle after obstacle, help and encourage each other. Or a girl. By the time they found the exit they'd be closest friends, sweethearts if it were a girl; they'd know each other's inmost souls, be bound together *by the cement of shared adventure;* then they'd emerge into the light and it would turn out that his friend was a Negro. A blind girl. President Roosevelt's son. Ambrose's former archenemy.

Shortly after the mirror room he'd groped along a musty corridor, his heart already misgiving him at the absence of phosphorescent arrows and other signs. He'd found a crack of light—not a door, it turned out, but a seam between the plyboard wall panels—and squinting up to it, espied a small old man, *in appearance not unlike* the photographs at home of Ambrose's late grandfather, nodding upon a stool beneath a bare, speckled bulb. A crude panel of toggle- and knife-switches hung beside the open fuse box near his head; elsewhere in the little room were wooden levers and ropes belayed to boat cleats. At the time, Ambrose wasn't lost enough to rap or call; later he couldn't find that crack. Now it seemed to him that he'd possibly dozed off for a few minutes somewhere along the way; certainly he was exhausted from the afternoon's sunshine and the evening's problems; he couldn't be sure he hadn't dreamed part or all of the sight. Had an old black wall fan droned like bees and shimmied two flypaper streamers? Had the funhouse operator—gentle, somewhat said and tired-appearing, in expression not unlike the photographs at home of Ambrose's late Uncle Konrad—murmured in his sleep? Is there really such a person as Ambrose, or is he a figment of the author's imagination? Was it Assawoman Bay or Sinepuxent? Are there other errors of fact in this fiction? Was there another sound besides the little slap slap of thigh on ham, like water sucking at the chine-boards of a skiff?

When you're lost, the smartest thing to do is stay put till you're found, hollering if necessary. But to holler guarantees humiliation as well as rescue; keeping silent permits some saving of face—you can act surprised at the fuss when your rescuers find you and swear you weren't lost, if they do. What's more you might find your own way yet, *however belatedly.*

"Don't tell me your foot's still asleep!" Magda exclaimed as the three young people walked from the inlet to the area set aside for ferris wheels, carrousels, and other carnival rides, they having decided in favor of the vast and ancient merry-go-round instead of the funhouse. What a sentence, everything was wrong from the outset. People don't know what to make of him, he doesn't know what to make of himself, he's only thirteen, *athletically and socially inept,* not astonishingly bright, but there are antennae; he has . . . some sort of receivers in his head; things speak to him, he understands more than he should, the world winks at him through its objects, grabs grinning at his coat. Everybody else is in on some secret he doesn't know; they've forgotten to tell him. Through simple *procrastination* his mother put off his baptism until this year. Everyone else had it done as a baby; he'd assumed the same of himself, as had his mother, so she claimed, until it was time for him to join Grace Methodist-Protestant and the oversight came out. He was mortified, but pitched sleepless through his private catechizing, intimidated by the ancient mysteries, a thirteen year old would never say that, resolved to experience conversion like St. Augustine. When the water touched his brow and Adam's sin left him, he contrived by a strain like defecation to bring tears into his eyes—but felt nothing. There was some simple, radical difference about him; he hoped it was genius, feared it was madness, devoted himself to amiability and inconspicuousness. Alone on the seawall near his house he was seized by the terrifying transports he'd thought to find in toolshed, in Communion-cup. The grass was alive! The town, the river, himself, were not imaginary; time roared in his ears like wind; the world was *going on!* This part ought to be dramatized. The Irish author James Joyce once wrote. Ambrose M—— is going to scream.

There is no *texture of rendered sensory detail,* for one thing. The faded distorting mirrors beside Fat May; the impossibility of choosing a mount when one had but a single ride on the great carrousel; the *vertigo attendant on his recognition* that Ocean City was worn out, the place of fathers and grandfathers, straw-boatered men and parasoled ladies survived by their amusements. Money spent, the three paused at Peter's insistence beside Fat May to watch the girls get their skirts blown up. The object was to tease Magda, who said: "I swear, Peter M——, you've got a one-track mind! Amby and me aren't *interested* in such things." In the tumbling-barrel, too, just inside the Devil's-mouth entrance to the funhouse, the girls were upended and their boyfriends and others could see up their dresses if they cared to. Which was the whole point, Ambrose realized. Of the entire funhouse! If you looked around, you noticed that almost all the people on the boardwalk were paired off into couples except the small children; in a way, that was the whole point of Ocean City! If you had X-ray eyes and could see everything going on at that instant under the boardwalk and in all the hotel rooms and cars and alleyways, you'd realize that all that normally *showed,* like restaurants and dance halls and clothing and test-your-strength machines, was merely preparation and intermission. Fat May screamed.

Because he watched the goings-on from the corner of his eye, it was Ambrose who spied the half-dollar on the boardwalk near the tumbling-barrel. Losers weepers. The first time he'd heard some people moving through a corridor not far away, just after he'd lost sight of the crack of

light, he'd decided not to call to them, for fear they'd guess he was scared
and poke fun; it sounded like roughnecks; he'd hoped they'd come by
and he could follow in the dark without their knowing. Another time
he'd heard just one person, unless he imagined it, bumping along as if
on the other side of the plywood; perhaps Peter coming back for him, or
Father, or Magda lost too. Or the owner and operator of the funhouse.
He'd called out once, as though merrily: "Anybody know where the heck
we are?" But the query was too stiff, his voice cracked, when the sounds
stopped he was terrified: maybe it was a queer who waited for fellows to
get lost, or a longhaired filthy monster that lived in some cranny of the
funhouse. He stood rigid for hours it seemed like, scarely respiring. His
future was shockingly clear, in outline. He tried holding his breath to the
point of unconsciousness. There ought to be a button you could push to
end your life absolutely without pain; disappear in a flick, like turning
out a light. He would push it instantly! He despised Uncle Karl. But he
despised his father too, for not being what he was supposed to be. Perhaps his father hated *his* father, and so on, and his son would hate him,
and so on. Instantly!

Naturally he didn't have nerve enough to ask Magda to go through
the funhouse with him. With incredible nerve and to everyone's surprise
he invited Magda, quietly and politely, to go through the funhouse with
him. "I warn you, I've never been through it before," he added, *laughing
easily;* "but I reckon we can manage somehow. The important thing to
remember, after all, is that it's meant to be a *fun*house; that is, a place
of amusement. If people really got lost or injured or too badly frightened
in it, the owner'd go out of business. There'd even be lawsuits. No character in a work of fiction can make a speech this long without interruption or acknowledgment from the other characters."

Mother teased Uncle Karl: "Three's a crowd, I always heard." But
actually Ambrose was relieved that Peter now had a quarter too. Nothing
was what it looked like. Every instant, under the surface of the Atlantic
Ocean, millions of living animals devoured one another. Pilots were falling in flames over Europe; women were being forcibly raped in the South
Pacific. His father should have taken him aside and said: "There is a
simple secret to getting through the funhouse, as simple as being first to
see the Towers. Here it is. Peter does not know it; neither does your
Uncle Karl. You and I are different. Not surprisingly, you've often
wished you weren't Don't think I haven't noticed how unhappy your
childhood has been! But you'll understand, when I tell you, why it had
to be kept secret until now. And you won't regret not being like your
brother and your uncle. *On the contrary!*" If you knew all the stories behind all the people on the boardwalk, you'd see that *nothing* was what it
looked like. Husbands and wives often hated each other; parents didn't
necessarily love their children; et cetera. A child took things for granted
because he had nothing to compare his life to and everybody acted as if
things were as they should be. Therefore each saw himself as the hero

of the story, when the truth might turn out to be that he's the villain, or the coward. And there wasn't one thing you could do about it!

Hunchbacks, fat ladies, fools—that no one chose what he was was unbearable. In the movies he'd meet a beautiful young girl in the funhouse; they'd have hairs-breadth escapes from real dangers; he'd do and say the right things; she also; in the end they'd be lovers; their dialogue lines would match up; he'd be perfectly at ease; she'd not only like him well enough, she'd think he was *marvelous;* she'd lie awake thinking about *him,* instead of vice versa—the way *his* face looked in different lights and how he stood and exactly what he'd said—and yet that would be only one small episode in his wonderful life, among many many others. Not a *turning point* at all. What had happened in the toolshed was nothing. He hated, he loathed his parents! One reason for not writing a lost-in-the-funhouse story is that either everybody's felt what Ambrose feels, in which case it goes without saying, or else no normal person feels such things, in which case Ambrose is a freak. "Is anything more tiresome, in fiction, than the problems of sensitive adolescents?" And it's all too long and rambling, as if the author. For all a person knows the first time through, the end could be just around any corner; perhaps, *not impossibly* it's been within reach any number of times. On the other hand he may be scarely past the start, with everything yet to get through, an intolerable idea.

Fill in: His father's raised eyebrows when he announced his decision to do the funhouse with Magda. Ambrose understands now, but didn't then, that his father was wondering whether he knew what the funhouse was *for*—especially since he didn't object, as he should have, when Peter decided to come along too. The ticket-woman, witchlike, mortifying him when inadvertently he gave her his name-coin instead of the half-dollar, then unkindly calling Magda's attention to the birthmark on his temple: "Watch out for him, girlie, he's a marked man!" She wasn't even cruel, he understood, only vulgar and insensitive. Somewhere in the world there was a young woman with such splendid understanding that she'd see him entire, like a poem or story, and find his words so valuable after all that when he confessed his apprehensions she would explain why they were in fact the very things that made him precious to her . . . and to Western Civilization! There was no such girl, the simple truth being. Violent yawns as they approached the mouth. Whispered advice from an old-timer on a bench near the barrel: "Go crabwise and ye'll get an eyeful without upsetting!" Composure vanished at the first pitch: Peter hollered joyously, Magda tumbled, shrieked, clutched her skirt; Ambrose scrambled crabwise, tight-lipped with terror, was soon out, watched his dropped name-coin slide among the couples. Shame-faced he saw that to get through expeditiously was not the point; Peter feigned assistance in order to trip Magda up, shouted "I see Christmas!" when her legs went flying. The old man, his latest betrayer, cacked approval. A dim hall then of black-thread cobwebs and recorded gibber: he took Magda's elbow to steady her against revolving discs set in the slanted floor to throw your feet out from under, and explained to her in a calm, deep voice his theory that each phase of the funhouse was triggered either automatically, by a series of photoelectric devices, or else manually by operators stationed at peepholes. But he lost his voice thrice as the discs unbalanced him; Magda was anyhow squealing; but at one point she clutched him about the waist to keep from falling, and her right cheek pressed for a moment against his belt-buckle. Heroically he drew her up, it was his chance to clutch her close as if for support and say: "I love you." He even put an arm lightly about the small of her back before a sailor-and-girl pitched into them from behind, sorely treading his left big toe and knocking Magda asprawl with them. The sailor's girl was a string-haired hussy with a loud laugh and light blue drawers; Ambrose realized that he wouldn't have said "I love you" anyhow, and was smitten with self-contempt. How much better it would be to be that common sailor! A wiry little Seaman 3rd, the fellow squeezed a girl to each side and stumbled hilarious into the mirror room, closer to Magda in thirty seconds than Ambrose had got in thirteen years. She giggled at something the fellow said to Peter; she drew her hair from her eyes with a movement so womanly it struck Ambrose's heart; Peter's smacking her backside then seemed particularly coarse. But Magda made a pleased indignant face and cried, "All right for *you*, mister!" and pursued Peter into the maze without a backward glance. The sailor followed after, leisurely, drawing his girl against his hip; Ambrose understood not only that they were all so relieved to be rid of his burdensome company that they didn't even notice his absence, but that he himself shared their relief. Stepping from the treacherous passage at last into the mirror-maze, he saw once again, more clearly than ever, how readily he deceived himself into supposing he was a person. He even foresaw, wincing at his dreadful self-knowledge, that he would repeat the deception, at ever-rarer intervals, all his wretched life, so fearful were the alternatives. Fame, madness, suicide; perhaps all three. It's not believable that so young a boy could articulate that reflection, and in fiction the merely true must always yield to the plausible. Moreover, the symbolism is in places heavy-footed. Yet Ambrose M—— understood, as few adults do, that the famous loneliness of the great was no popular myth but a general truth—furthermore, that it was as much cause as effect.

All the preceding except the last few sentences is exposition that should've been done earlier or interspersed with the present action instead of lumped together. No reader would put up with so much with such *prolixity*. It's interesting that Ambrose's father, though presumably an intelligent man (as indicated by his role as grade-school principal), neither encouraged nor discouraged his sons at all in any way—as if he either didn't care about them or cared all right but didn't know how to act. If this fact should contribute to one of them's becoming a celebrated but wretchedly unhappy scientist, was it a good thing or not? He too might someday face the question; it would be useful to know whether it had tortured his father for years, for example, or never once crossed his mind.

In the maze two important things happened. First, our hero found a name-coin someone else had lost or discarded: *AMBROSE,* suggestive of the famous lightship and of his late grandfather's favorite dessert, which his mother used to prepare on special occasions out of coconut, oranges, grapes, and what else. Second, as he wondered at the endless replication of his image in the mirrors, second, as he *lost himself in the reflection* that the necessity for an observer makes perfect observation impossible, better make him eighteen at least, yet that would render other things unlikely, he heard Peter and Magda chuckling somewhere together in the maze. "Here!" "No, here!" they shouted to each other; Peter said, "Where's Amby?" Magda murmured. "Amb?" Peter called. In a pleased, friendly voice. He didn't reply. The truth was, his brother was a *happy-go-lucky youngster* who'd've been better off with a regular brother of his own, but who seldom complained of his lot and was generally cordial. Ambrose's throat ached; there aren't enough different ways to say that. He stood quietly while the two young people giggled and thumped through the glittering maze, hurrah'd their discovery of its exit, cried out in joyful alarm at what next beset them. Then he set his mouth and followed after, as he supposed, took a wrong turn, strayed into the pass *wherein he lingers yet.*

The action of conventional dramatic narrative may be represented by a diagram called Freitag's Triangle:

$$\underset{\displaystyle A\diagup\;\diagdown C}{B}$$

or more accurately by a variant of that diagram:

$$\underset{\displaystyle A\!-\!\!\!-\!\!\!-\overset{B}{\diagup}\;\diagdown D}{C}$$

in which *AB* represents the exposition, *B* the introduction of conflict, *BC* the "rising action," complication, or development of the conflict, *C* the climax, or turn of the action, *CD* the dénouement, or resolution of the conflict. While there is no reason to regard this pattern as an absolute necessity, like many other conventions it became conventional because great numbers of people over many years learned by trial and error that it was effective; one ought not to forsake it, therefore, unless one wishes to forsake as well the effect of drama or has clear cause to feel that deliberate violation of the "normal" pattern can better can better effect that effect. This can't go on much longer; it can go on forever. He died telling stories to himself in the dark; years later, when that vast unsuspected area of the funhouse came to light, the first expedition found his skeleton in one of its labyrinthine corridors and mistook it for part of the entertainment. He died of starvation telling himself stories in the dark; but unbeknownst unbeknownst to him, an assistant operator of the funhouse, happening to overhear him, crouched just behind the plyboard partition and wrote down his every word. The operator's daughter, an exquisite young woman with a figure unusually well developed for her age, crouched just behind the partition and transcribed his every word. Though she had never laid eyes on him, she recognized that here was one of Western Culture's truly great imaginations, the eloquence of whose suffering would be an inspiration to unnumbered. And her heart was torn between her love for the misfortunate young man (yes, she loved him, though she had never laid though she knew him only—but how well!—through his words, and the deep, calm voice in which he spoke them) between her love et cetera and her womanly intuition that only in suffering and isolation could he give voice et cetera. Lone dark dying. Quietly she kissed the rough plyboard, and a tear fell upon the page. Where she had written in shorthand *Where she had written in shorthand* Where she had written in shorthand *Where she* et cetera. A long time ago we should have passed the apex of Freitag's Triangle and made brief work of the *dénouement;* the plot doesn't rise by meaningful steps but winds upon itself, digresses, retreats, hesitates, sighs, collapses, expires. The climax of the story must be its protagonist's discovery of a way to get through the funhouse. But he has found none, may have ceased to search.

What relevance does the war have to the story? Should there be fireworks outside or not?

Ambrose wandered, languished, dozed. Now and then he fell into his habit of rehearsing to himself the unadventurous story of his life, narrated from the third-person point of view, from his earliest memory parenthesis of maple leaves stirring in the summer breath of tidewater Maryland end of parenthesis to the present moment. Its principal events, on this telling, would appear to have been *A, B, C,* and *D.*

He imagined himself years hence, successful, married, at ease in the world, the trials of his adolescence far behind him. He has come to the seashore with his family for the holiday: how Ocean City has changed! But at one seldom at one ill-frequented end of the boardwalk a few derelict amusements survive from times gone by: the great carrousel from the turn of the century, with its monstrous griffins and mechanical concert band; the roller coaster rumored since 1916 to have been condemned; the mechanical shooting gallery in which only the image of our enemies changed. His own son laughs with Fat May and wants to know what a funhouse is; Ambrose hugs the sturdy lad close and smiles around his pipestem at his wife.

The family's going home. Mother sits between Father and Uncle Karl, who teases him good-naturedly who chuckles over the fact that the comrade with whom he'd fought his way shoulder to shoulder through the funhouse had turned out to be a blind Negro girl—to their mutual discomfort, as they'd opened their souls. But such are the walls of custom, which even. Whose arm is where? How must it feel. He dreams of a funhouse vaster by far than any yet constructed; but by then they may be out of fashion, like steamboats and excursion trains. Already quaint and seedy: the draperied ladies on the frieze of the carrousel are his father's father's mooncheeked dreams; if he thinks of it more he will vomit his apple-on-a-stick.

He wonders: will he become a regular person? Something has gone wrong; his vaccination didn't take; at the Boy-Scout initiation campfire he only pretended to be deeply moved, as he pretends to this hour that it is not so bad after all in the funhouse, and that he has a little limp. How long will it last? He envisions a truly astonishing funhouse, incredibly complex yet utterly controlled from a great central switchboard like the console of a pipe organ. Nobody had enough imagination. He could design such a place himself, wiring and all, and he's only thirteen years old. He would be its operator: panel lights would show what was up in every cranny of its cunning of its multifarious vastness; a switch-flick would ease this fellow's way, complicate that's, to balance things out; if anyone seemed lost or frightened, all the operator had to do was.

He wishes he had never entered the funhouse. But he has. Then he wishes he were dead. But he's not. Therefore he will construct funhouses for others and be their secret operator—though he would rather be among the lovers for whom funhouses are designed.

DONALD BARTHELME (1933–   )

Donald Barthelme must surely be the least talkative man ever to have come out of the garrulous state of Texas. It is impossible to discover any but the baldest facts of his life. To be sure, he was not born in Texas but in Philadelphia, and perhaps some strain of Main Line reticence has adhered even though he was brought up in Houston. The son of an architect, he served in the Army in Korea and Japan, and he has worked on a newspaper, on a magazine, and as a museum director. He has red hair and a short beard and lives with his third wife and small daughter in New York City. That is about all one knows, except that in the early sixties his surprising stories began to appear in well-known periodicals, chiefly The New Yorker, *and they have continued to appear with quiet persistence.*

His stories have been collected in three volumes, Come Back, Dr. Caligari *(1964),* Unspeakable Practices, Unnatural Acts *(1968), and* City Life *(1970). He has also published a short fantastic novel,* Snow White *(1967).*

Donald Barthelme's stories are, on the whole, as short as they are
  enigmatic, but there must be some great compression of content
  within that brevity, because the best of these stories, after one has
  finished, continue to resound. They are still there, knocking at the
  back door of one's mind, after one has closed that door on them.

The clue to his special effects is not hard to name: it is that he tells of
  the most grotesque, illogical, inane, discontinuous, and parodic
  events in an utterly matter-of-fact voice, which by its very pitch is
  assuring us that this grotesquerie, illogic, and disorientation is in-
  deed the condition of the world. And these stories, funny as they
  often are in their macabre inventiveness, do indeed tell us a good
  deal about that condition, and above all about the struggle to be
  human in a society that seems intent only on depersonalization.

"Report," for example, satirizes that whole cold and appalling lingo with
  which technocracy has replaced language, that fuzzy gibberish of
  what is called the military-industrial complex. And the conclusion
  is clearly that those very persons who mastermind wars are finally
  in themselves the merest robots—cogs in their own machine.

FURTHER READING

See William H. Gass, "The Leading Edge of the Trash Phenomenon" in
Fiction and the Figures of Life (1970).

Report (1969)

Our group is against the war. But the war goes on. I was sent to
Cleveland to talk to the engineers. The engineers were meeting in Cleveland. I was supposed to persuade them not to do what they are going to
do. I took United's 4:45 from LaGuardia arriving in Cleveland at 6:13.
Cleveland is dark blue at that hour. I went directly to the motel, where
the engineers were meeting. Hundreds of engineers attended the Cleveland meeting. I noticed many fractures among the engineers, bandages,
traction. I noticed what appeared to be fracture of the carpal scaphoid in
six examples. I noticed numerous fractures of the humeral shaft, of the
os calcis, of the pelvic girdle. I noticed a high incidence of clay-shovel-
ler's fracture. I could not account for these fractures. The engineers were
making calculations, taking measurements, sketching on the blackboard, drinking beer, throwing bread, buttonholing employers, hurling
glasses into the fireplace. They were friendly.

They were friendly. They were full of love and information. The
chief engineer wore shades. Patella in Monk's traction, clamshell fracture by the look of it. He was standing in a slum of beer bottles and

microphone cable. "Have some of this chicken à la Isambard Kingdom Brunel the Great Ingineer," he said. "And declare who you are and what we can do for you. What is your line, distinguished guest?"

"Software," I said. "In every sense. I am here representing a small group of interested parties. We are interested in your thing, which seems to be functioning. In the midst of so much dysfunction, function is interesting. Other people's things don't seem to be working. The State Department's thing doesn't seem to be working. The U.N.'s thing doesn't seem to be working. The democratic left's thing doesn't seem to be working. Buddha's thing—"

"Ask us anything about our thing, which seems to be working," the chief engineer said. "We will open our hearts and heads to you, Software Man, because we want to be understood and loved by the great lay public, and have our marvels appreciated by that public, for which we daily unsung produce tons of new marvels each more life-enhancing than the last. Ask us anything. Do you want to know about evaporated thin-film metallurgy? Monolithic and hybrid integrated-circuit processes? The algebra of inequalities? Optimization theory? Complex high-speed microminiature closed and open loop systems? Fixed variable mathematical cost searches? Epitaxial deposition of semi-conductor materials? Gross interfaced space gropes? We also have specialists in the cuckooflower, the doctorfish, and the dumdum bullet as these relate to aspects of today's expanding technology, and they do in the damnedest ways."

I spoke to him then about the war. I said the same things people always say when they speak against the war. I said that the war was wrong. I said that large countries should not burn down small countries. I said that the government had made a series of errors. I said that these errors once small and forgivable were now immense and unforgivable. I said that the government was attempting to conceal its original errors under layers of new errors. I said that the government was sick with error, giddy with it. I said that ten thousand of our soldiers had already been killed in pursuit of the government's errors. I said that tens of thousands of the enemy's soldiers and civilians had been killed because of various errors, ours and theirs. I said that we are responsible for errors made in our name. I said that the government should not be allowed to make additional errors.

"Yes, yes," the chief engineer said, "there is doubtless much truth in what you say, but we can't possibly *lose* the war, can we? And stopping is losing, isn't it? The war regarded as a process, stopping regarded as an abort? We don't know *how* to lose a war. That skill is not among our skills. Our array smashes their array, that is what we know. That is the process. That is what is.

"But let's not have any more of this dispiriting downbeat counterproductive talk. I have a few new marvels here I'd like to discuss with you just briefly. A few new marvels that are just about ready to be gaped at by the admiring layman. Consider for instance the area of realtime online computer-controlled wish evaporation. Wish evaporation is going to be crucial in meeting the rising expectations of the world's peoples, which are as you know rising entirely too fast."

I noticed then distributed about the room a great many transverse fractures of the ulna. "The development of the pseudo-ruminant stomach for underdeveloped peoples," he went on, "is one of our interesting things you should be interested in. With the pseudo-ruminant stomach they can chew cuds, that is to say, eat grass. Blue is the most popular color worldwide and for that reason we are working with certain strains of your native Kentucky *Poa pratensis,* or bluegrass, as the staple input for the p/r stomach cycle, which would also give a shot in the arm to our balance-of-payments thing don't you know. . . ." I noticed about me then a great number of metatarsal fractures in banjo splints. "The kangaroo initiative . . . eight hundred thousand harvested last year . . . highest percentage of edible protein of any herbivore yet studied . . ."

"Have new kangaroos been planted?"

The engineer looked at me.

"I intuit your hatred and jealousy of our thing," he said. "The ineffectual always hate our thing and speak of it as anti-human, which is not at all a meaningful way to speak of our thing. Nothing mechanical is alien to me," he said (amber spots making bursts of light in his shades), "because I am human, in a sense, and if I think it up, then 'it' is human too, whatever 'it' may be. Let me tell you, Software Man, we have been damned forbearing in the matter of this little war you declare yourself to be interested in. Function is the cry, and our thing is functioning like crazy. There are things we could do that we have not done. Steps we could take that we have not taken. These steps are, regarded in a certain light, the light of our enlightened self-interest, quite justifiable steps. We could, of course, get irritated. We could, of course, *lose patience.*

"We could, of course, release thousands upon thousands of self-powered crawling-along-the-ground lengths of titanium wire eighteen inches long with a diameter of .0005 centimetres (that is to say, invisible) which, scenting an enemy, climb up his trouser leg and wrap themselves around his neck. We have developed those. They are within our capabilities. We could, of course, release in the arena of the upper air our new improved pufferfish toxin which precipitates an identity crisis. No special technical problems there. That is almost laughably easy. We could, of course, place up to two million maggots in their rice within twenty-four hours. The maggots are ready, massed in secret staging areas in Alabama. We have hypodermic darts capable of piebalding the enemy's pigmentation. We have rots, blights, and rusts capable of attacking his alphabet. Those are dandies. We have a hut-shrinking chemical which penetrates the fibres of the bamboo, causing it, the hut, to strangle its occupants. This operates only after 10 P.M., when people are sleeping. Their mathematics are at the mercy of a suppurating surd we have invented. We have a family of fishes trained to attack their fishes. We have the deadly testicle-destroying telegram. The cable companies are coöperating. We have a green substance that, well, I'd rather not talk about. We have a secret word that, if pronounced, produces multiple fractures in all living things in an area the size of four football fields."

"That's why—"

"Yes. Some damned fool couldn't keep his mouth shut. The point is that the whole structure of enemy life is within our power to *rend, vitiate, devour,* and *crush.* But that's not the interesting thing."

"You recount these possibilities with uncommon relish."

"Yes I realize that there is too much relish here. But *you* must realize that these capabilities represent in and of themselves highly technical and complex and interesting problems and hurdles on which our boys have expended many thousands of hours of hard work and brilliance. And that the effects are often grossly exaggerated by irresponsible victims. And that the whole thing represents a fantastic series of triumphs for the multi-disciplined problem-solving team concept."

"I appreciate that."

"We *could* unleash all this technology at once. You can imagine what would happen then. But that's not the interesting thing."

"What is the interesting thing?"

"The interesting thing is that we have a *moral sense.* It is on punched cards, perhaps the most advanced and sensitive moral sense the world has ever known."

"Because it is on punched cards?"

"It considers all considerations in endless and subtle detail," he said. "It even quibbles. With this great new moral tool, how can we go wrong? I confidently predict that, although we *could* employ all this splendid new weaponry I've been telling you about, *we're not going to do it.*"

"We're not going to do it?"

I took United's 5:44 from Cleveland arriving at Newark at 7:19. New Jersey is bright pink at that hour. Living things move about the surface of New Jersey at that hour molesting each other only in traditional ways. I made my report to the group. I stressed the friendliness of the engineers. I said, It's all right. I said, We have a moral sense. I said, *We're not going to do it.* They didn't believe me.

CRITICS
OF THE
CULTURE:
AFTER A WAR

JAMES BALDWIN (1924–   )

*From the point of view of sheer literary power and virtuosity, James
Baldwin is probably the most gifted black writer now at work in the
United States. He has written a good deal of fiction long and short,
a number of plays, and many essays including some of the most
brilliantly polemical in this century. Beyond this variety, he commands a powerful and pervasive style, a style that ranges from the
subtle, the sinuous, the gently lyrical, to the bold, the denunciatory,
the outraged. When he loses his grip, the range of this style can tip
at one end into the sentimental, at the other into the rhetorically
bombastic.*

*He was the oldest of nine children of a Harlem store-front church
preacher, and he was brought up in rigid pieties and a revivalist
atmosphere. At the age of fourteen he himself became a boy
preacher, and he has acknowledged that the hymn-singing, gospel-
shouting, Biblical-chanting atmosphere with which he was first
familiar profoundly colored his prose when he began to write it.
Nevertheless, at seventeen, when he was graduated from high
school, he decided that this religion was not for him, and he abandoned it together with his family.*

*For a few years he lived as best he could, but in 1945, through the
efforts of Richard Wright (an early inspiration to him although
he later deplored some of the qualities of Wright's fiction), he won
his first literary fellowship on the basis of an early draft of what
would be his first novel. He decided, however, that living in the
midst of racial tensions in the United States would inhibit his development as a writer, and he went to France to live as an expatriate in
Paris for some years. There he finished his novel,* Go Tell It on the
Mountain *(1953), the story of the individuals who comprise a
Harlem congregation, told in one day, the fourteenth birthday of
the autobiographical hero. He returned to the United States in
1958.*

The novels that followed were Giovanni's Room *(1956), about white
people in Paris and a hetero-homo–sexual conflict;* Another Country
*(1962), largely concerned with the violent complexities of sexual
relations between the races; and* Tell Me How Long the Train's
Been Gone *(1968). His short stories, showing the whole range of his
fictional moods, have been collected in* Going to Meet the Man
(1965). His two plays are called Blues for Mister Charlie *(1964) and*
The Amen Corner *(1968).*

*It is now conventional to say that his best prose is in his essays, and
there is no doubt that these have commanded the widest attention.
They are gathered in* Notes of a Native Son *(1955);* Nobody Knows

My Name *(1961); and* The Fire Next Time *(1963), two "letters" (the term does not in the least describe their tone), hortatory and accusatory, uttered in a voice near to breaking with the pure weight and passion of its moral urgency.*

FURTHER READING

The first book on Baldwin's work is Fern Marja Eckman, *The Furious Passage of James Baldwin* (1966). See also Norman Podhoretz, *Doings and Undoings: The Fifties and After in American Writing* (1964); Marcus Klein, *After Alienation* (1964); Seymour L. Gross and John Edward Hardy, editors, *Images of the Negro in American Literature* (1966); and Howard M. Harper, Jr., *Desperate Faith* (1967).

Notes of a Native Son *(1955)*

On the 29th of July, in 1943, my father died. On the same day, a few hours later, his last child was born. Over a month before this, while all our energies were concentrated in waiting for these events, there had been, in Detroit, one of the bloodiest race riots of the century. A few hours after my father's funeral, while he lay in state in the undertaker's chapel, a race riot broke out in Harlem. On the morning of the 3rd of August, we drove my father to the graveyard through a wilderness of smashed plate glass.

The day of my father's funeral had also been my nineteenth birthday. As we drove him to the graveyard, the spoils of injustice, anarchy, discontent, and hatred were all around us. It seemed to me that God himself had devised, to mark my father's end, the most sustained and brutally dissonant of codas. And it seemed to me, too, that the violence which rose all about us as my father left the world had been devised as a corrective for the pride of his eldest son. I had declined to believe in that apocalypse which had been central to my father's vision; very well, life seemed to be saying, here is something that will certainly pass for an apocalypse until the real thing comes along. I had inclined to be contemptuous of my father for the conditions of his life, for the conditions of our lives. When his life had ended I began to wonder about that life and also, in a new way, to be apprehensive about my own.

I had not known my father very well. We had got on badly, partly because we shared, in our different fashions, the vice of stubborn pride. When he was dead I realized that I had hardly ever spoken to him. When he had been dead a long time I began to wish I had. It seems to be typical of life in America, where opportunities, real and fancied, are thicker than anywhere else on the globe, that the second generation has no time to talk to the first. No one, including my father, seems to have known exactly how old he was, but his mother had been born during slavery. He was of the first generation of free men. He, along with thousands of other Negroes, came North after 1919 and I was part of that generation which had never seen the landscape of what Negroes sometimes call the Old Country.

He had been born in New Orleans and had been a quite young man there during the time that Louis Armstrong, a boy, was running errands for the dives and honky-tonks of what was always presented to me as one of the most wicked of cities—to this day, whenever I think of New Orleans, I also helplessly think of Sodom and Gomorrah. My father never mentioned Louis Armstrong, except to forbid us to play his records; but there was a picture of him on our wall for a long time. One of my father's strong-willed female relatives had placed it there and forbade my father to take it down. He never did, but he eventually maneuvered her out of the house and when, some years later, she was in trouble and near death, he refused to do anything to help her.

He was, I think, very handsome. I gather this from photographs and from my own memories of him, dressed in his Sunday best and on his way to preach a sermon somewhere, when I was little. Handsome, proud, and ingrown, "like a toe-nail," somebody said. But he looked to me, as I grew older, like pictures I had seen of African tribal chieftains: he really should have been naked, with war-paint on and barbaric mementos, standing among spears. He could be chilling in the pulpit and indescribably cruel in his personal life and he was certainly the most bitter man I have ever met; yet it must be said that there was something else in him, buried in him, which lent him his tremendous power and, even, a rather crushing charm. It had something to do with his blackness, I think— he was very black—with his blackness and his beauty, and with the fact that he knew that he was black but did not know that he was beautiful. He claimed to be proud of his blackness but it had also been the cause of much humiliation and it had fixed bleak boundaries to his life. He was not a young man when we were growing up and he had already suffered many kinds of ruin; in his outrageously demanding and protective way he loved his children, who were black like him and menaced, like him; and all these things sometimes showed in his face when he tried, never to my knowledge with any success, to establish contact with any of us. When he took one of his children on his knee to play, the child always became fretful and began to cry; when he tried to help one of us with our homework the absolutely unabating tension which emanated from him caused our minds and our tongues to become paralyzed, so that he, scarcely knowing why, flew into a rage and the child, not knowing why, was punished. If it ever entered his head to bring a surprise home for his children, it was, almost unfailingly, the wrong surprise and even the big watermelons he often brought home on his back in the summertime led to the most appalling scenes. I do not remember, in all those years, that one of his children was ever glad to see him come home. From what I was able to gather of his early life, it seemed that this inability to establish contact with other people had always marked him and had been one of the things which had driven him out of New Orleans. There was something in him, therefore, groping and tentative, which was never expressed and which was buried with him. One saw it most clearly when he was facing new people and hoping to impress them. But he never did, not for long. We went from church to smaller and more improbable church, he found himself in less and less demand as a minister, and by the time he died none of his friends had come to see him for a long time. He had lived and died in an intolerable bitterness of spirit and it frightened me, as we drove him to the graveyard through those unquiet, ruined streets, to see how powerful and overflowing this bitterness could be and to realize that this bitterness now was mine.

When he died I had been away from home for a little over a year. In that year I had had time to become aware of the meaning of all my father's bitter warnings, had discovered the secret of his proudly pursed lips and rigid carriage: I had discovered the weight of white people in the world. I saw that this had been for my ancestors and now would be for me an awful thing to live with and that the bitterness which had helped to kill my father could also kill me.

He had been ill a long time—in the mind, as we now realized, reliving instances of his fantastic intransigence in the new light of his affliction and endeavoring to feel a sorrow for him which never, quite, came true. We had not known that he was being eaten up by paranoia, and the discovery that his cruelty, to our bodies and our minds, had been one of the symptoms of his illness was not, then, enough to enable us to forgive him. The younger children felt, quite simply, relief that he would not be coming home anymore. My mother's observation that it was he, after all, who had kept them alive all these years meant nothing because the problems of keeping children alive are not real for children. The older children felt, with my father gone, that they could invite their friends to the house without fear that their friends would be insulted or, as had sometimes happened with me, being told that their friends were in league with the devil and intended to rob our family of everything we owned. (I didn't fail to wonder, and it made me hate him, what on earth we owned that anybody else would want.)

His illness was beyond all hope of healing before anyone realized that he was ill. He had always been so strange and had lived, like a prophet, in such unimaginably close communion with the Lord that his long silences which were punctuated by moans and hallelujahs and snatches of old songs while he sat at the living-room window never seemed odd to us. It was not until he refused to eat because, he said, his family was trying to poison him that my mother was forced to accept as a fact what had, until then, been only an unwilling suspicion. When he was committed, it was discovered that he had tuberculosis and, as it turned out, the disease of his mind allowed the disease of his body to destroy him. For the doctors could not force him to eat, either, and, though he was fed intravenously, it was clear from the beginning that there was no hope for him.

In my mind's eye I could see him, sitting at the window, locked up in his terrors; hating and fearing every living soul including his children who had betrayed him, too, by reaching towards the world which had despised him. There were nine of us. I began to wonder what it could have felt like for such a man to have had nine children whom he could barely feed. He used to make little jokes about our poverty, which never, of course, seemed very funny to us; they could not have seemed very funny to him, either, or else our all too feeble response to them would never have caused such rages. He spent great energy and achieved, to our chagrin, no small amount of success in keeping us away from the people who surrounded us, people who had all-night rent parties to which we listened when we should have been sleeping, people who cursed and drank and flashed razor blades on Lenox Avenue. He could not understand why, if they had so much energy to spare, they could not use it to make their lives better. He treated almost everybody on our block with a most uncharitable asperity and neither they, nor, of course, their children were slow to reciprocate.

The only white people who came to our house were welfare workers and bill collectors. It was almost always my mother who dealt with them, for my father's temper, which was at the mercy of his pride, was never to be trusted. It was clear that he felt their very presence in his home to be a violation: this was conveyed by his carriage, almost ludicrously stiff, and by his voice, harsh and vindictively polite. When I was around nine or ten I wrote a play which was directed by a young, white schoolteacher, a woman, who then took an interest in me, and gave me books to read and, in order to corroborate my theatrical bent, decided to take me to see what she somewhat tactlessly referred to as "real" plays. Theater-going was forbidden in our house, but, with the really cruel intuitiveness of a child, I suspected that the color of this woman's skin would carry the day for me. When, at school, she suggested taking me to the theater, I did not, as I might have done if she had been a Negro, find a way of discouraging her, but agreed that she should pick me up at my house one evening. I then, very cleverly, left all the rest to my mother, who suggested to my father, as I knew she would, that it would not be very nice to let such a kind woman make the trip for nothing. Also, since it was a schoolteacher, I imagine that my mother countered the idea of sin with the idea of "education," which word, even with my father, carried a kind of bitter weight.

Before the teacher came my father took me aside to ask *why* she was coming, what *interest* she could possibly have in our house, in a boy like me. I said I didn't know but I, too, suggested that it had something to do with education. And I understood that my father was waiting for me to say something—I didn't quite know what; perhaps that I wanted his protection against this teacher and her "education." I said none of these things and the teacher came and we went out. It was clear, during the brief interview in our living room, that my father was agreeing very much against his will and that he would have refused permission if he had dared. The fact that he did not dare caused me to despise him: I had no way of knowing that he was facing in that living room a wholly unprecedented and frightening situation.

Later, when my father had been laid off from his job, this woman became very important to us. She was really a very sweet and generous woman and went to a great deal of trouble to be of help to us, particularly during one awful winter. My mother called her by the highest name she knew: she said she was a "christian." My father could scarcely disagree but during the four or five years of our relatively close association he never trusted her and was always trying to surprise in her open, Midwestern face the genuine, cunningly hidden, and hideous motivation. In later years, particularly when it began to be clear that this "education" of mine was going to lead me to perdition, he became more explicit and warned me that my white friends in high school were not really my friends and that I would see, when I was older, how white people would do anything to keep a Negro down. Some of them could be nice, he admitted, but none of them were to be trusted and most of them were not even nice. The best thing was to have as little to do with them as possible. I did not feel this way and I was certain, in my innocence, that I never would.

But the year which preceded my father's death had made a great change in my life. I had been living in New Jersey, working in defense plants, working and living among southerners, white and black. I knew about the south, of course, and about how southerners treated Negroes and how they expected them to behave, but it had never entered my mind that anyone would look at me and expect *me* to behave that way. I learned in New Jersey that to be a Negro meant, precisely, that one was never looked at but was simply at the mercy of the reflexes the color of one's skin caused in other people. I acted in New Jersey as I had always acted, that is as though I thought a great deal of myself—I had to *act* that way—with results that were, simply, unbelievable. I had scarcely arrived before I had earned the enmity, which was extraordinarily ingenious, of all my superiors and nearly all my co-workers. In the beginning, to make matters worse, I simply did not know what was happening. I did not know what I had done, and I shortly began to wonder what *anyone* could possibly do, to bring about such unanimous, active, and unbearably vocal hostility. I knew about jim-crow but I had never experienced it. I went to the same self-service restaurant three times and stood with all the Princeton boys before the counter, waiting for a hamburger and coffee; it was always an extraordinarily long time before anything was set before me; but it was not until the fourth visit that I learned that, in fact, nothing had ever been set before me: I had simply picked something up. Negroes were not served there, I was told, and they had been waiting for me to realize that I was always the only Negro present. Once I was told this, I determined to go there all the time. But now they were ready for me and, though some dreadful scenes were subsequently enacted in that restaurant, I never ate there again.

It was the same story all over New Jersey, in bars, bowling alleys, diners, places to live. I was always being forced to leave, silently, or with mutual imprecations. I very shortly became notorious and children giggled behind me when I passed and their elders whispered or shouted— they really believed that I was mad. And it did begin to work on my mind, of course; I began to be afraid to go anywhere and to compensate for this I went places to which I really should not have gone and where, God knows, I had no desire to be. My reputation in town naturally enhanced my reputation at work and my working day became one long series of acrobatics designed to keep me out of trouble. I cannot say that these acrobatics succeeded. It began to seem that the machinery of the organization I worked for was turning over, day and night, with but one aim: to eject me. I was fired once, and contrived, with the aid of a friend from New York, to get back on the payroll; was fired again, and bounced back again. It took a while to fire me for the third time, but the third time took. There were no loopholes anywhere. There was not even any way of getting back inside the gates.

That year in New Jersey lives in my mind as though it were the year during which, having an unsuspected predilection for it, I first contracted some dread, chronic disease, the unfailing symptom of which is a kind of blind fever, a pounding in the skull and fire in the bowels. Once this disease is contracted, one can never be really carefree again, for the fever, without an instant's warning, can recur at any moment. It can wreck more important things than race relations. There is not a Negro alive who does not have this rage in his blood—one has the choice, merely, of living with it consciously or surrendering to it. As for me, this fever has recurred in me, and does, and will until the day I die.

My last night in New Jersey, a white friend from New York took me to the nearest big town, Trenton, to go to the movies and have a few drinks. As it turned out, he also saved me from, at the very least, a violent whipping. Almost every detail of that night stands out very clearly in my memory. I even remember the name of the movie we saw because its title impressed me as being so patly ironical. It was a movie about the German occupation of France, starring Maureen O'Hara and Charles Laughton and called *This Land Is Mine*. I remember the name of the diner we walked into when the movie ended: it was the "American Diner." When we walked in the counterman asked what we wanted and I remember answering with the casual sharpness which had become my habit: "We want a hamburger and a cup of coffee, what do you think we want?" I do not know why, after a year of such rebuffs, I so completely failed to anticipate his answer, which was, of course, "We don't serve Negroes here." This reply failed to discompose me, at least for the moment. I made some sardonic comment about the name of the diner and we walked out into the streets.

This was the time of what was called the "brown-out," when the lights in all American cities were very dim. When we re-entered the streets something happened to me which had the force of an optical illusion, or a nightmare. The streets were very crowded and I was facing north. People were moving in every direction but it seemed to me, in that instant, that all of the people I could see, and many more than that, were moving toward me, against me, and that everyone was white. I remember how their faces gleamed. And I felt, like a physical sensation, a *click* at the nape of my neck as though some interior string connecting my head to my body had been cut. I began to walk. I heard my friend call after me, but I ignored him. Heaven only knows what was going on in his mind, but he had the good sense not to touch me—I don't know what would have happened if he had—and to keep me in sight. I don't know what was going on in my mind, either; I certainly had no conscious plan. I wanted to do something to crush these white faces, which were crushing me. I walked for perhaps a block or two until I came to an enormous, glittering, and fashionable restaurant in which I knew not even the intercession of the Virgin would cause me to be served. I pushed through the doors and took the first vacant seat I saw, at a table for two, and waited.

I do not know how long I waited and I rather wonder, until today, what I could possibly have looked like. Whatever I looked like, I frightened the waitress who shortly appeared, and the moment she appeared all of my fury flowed towards her. I hated her for her white face, and for her great, astounded, frightened eyes. I felt that if she found a black man so frightening I would make her fright worth-while.

She did not ask me what I wanted, but repeated, as though she had learned it somewhere, "We don't serve Negroes here." She did not say it with the blunt, derisive hostility to which I had grown so accustomed, but, rather, with a note of apology in her voice, and fear. This made me colder and more murderous than ever. I felt I had to do something with my hands. I wanted her to come close enough for me to get her neck between my hands.

So I pretended not to have understood her, hoping to draw her closer. And she did step a very short step closer, with her pencil poised incongruously over her pad, and repeated the formula: ". . . don't serve Negroes here."

Somehow, with the repetition of that phrase, which was already ringing in my head like a thousand bells of a nightmare, I realized that she would never come any closer and that I would have to strike from a distance. There was nothing on the table but an ordinary water-mug half

full of water, and I picked this up and hurled it with all my strength at
her. She ducked and it missed her and shattered against the mirror behind the bar. And, with that sound, my frozen blood abruptly thawed, I
returned from wherever I had been, I *saw*, for the first time the restaurant, the people with their mouths open, already, as it seemed to me,
rising as one man, and I realized what I had done, and where I was, and
I was frightened. I rose and began running for the door. A round, pot-
bellied man grabbed me by the nape of the neck just as I reached the
doors and began to beat me about the face. I kicked him and got loose
and ran into the streets. My friend whispered, *"Run!"* and I ran.

My friend stayed outside the restaurant long enough to misdirect
my pursuers and the police, who arrived, he told me, at once. I do not
know what I said to him when he came to my room that night. I could
not have said much. I felt, in the oddest, most awful way, that I had
somehow betrayed him. I lived it over and over and over again, the way
one relives an automobile accident after it has happened and one finds
oneself alone and safe. I could not get over two facts, both equally difficult for the imagination to grasp, and one was that I could have been
murdered. But the other was that I had been ready to commit murder.
I saw nothing very clearly but I did see this: that my life, my *real* life,
was in danger, and not from anything other people might do but from
the hatred I carried in my own heart.

II

I had returned home around the second week in June—in great
haste because it seemed that my father's death and my mother's confinement were both but a matter of hours. In the case of my mother, it soon
became clear that she had simply made a miscalculation. This had always been her tendency and I don't believe that a single one of us arrived in the world, or has since arrived anywhere else, on time. But none
of us dawdled so intolerably about the business of being born as did my
baby sister. We sometimes amused ourselves, during those endless, stifling weeks, by picturing the baby sitting within in the safe, warm dark,
bitterly regretting the necessity of becoming a part of our chaos and
stubbornly putting it off as long as possible. I understood her perfectly
and congratulated her on showing such good sense so soon. Death, however, sat as purposefully at my father's bedside as life stirred within my
mother's womb and it was harder to understand why he so lingered in
that long shadow. It seemed that he had bent, and for a long time, too,
all of his energies towards dying. Now death was ready for him but my
father held back.

All of Harlem, indeed, seemed to be infected by waiting. I had never
before known it to be so violently still. Racial tensions throughout this
country were exacerbated during the early years of the war, partly because the labor market brought together hundreds of thousands of ill-

prepared people and partly because Negro soldiers, regardless of where they were born, received their military training in the south. What happened in defense plants and army camps had repercussions, naturally, in every Negro ghetto. The situation in Harlem had grown bad enough for clergymen, policemen, educators, politicians, and social workers to assert in one breath that there was no "crime wave" and to offer, in the very next breath, suggestions as to how to combat it. These suggestions always seemed to involve playgrounds, despite the fact that racial skirmishes were occurring in the playgrounds, too. Playground or not, crime wave or not, the Harlem police force had been augmented in March, and the unrest grew—perhaps, in fact, partly as a result of the ghetto's instinctive hatred of policemen. Perhaps the most revealing news item, out of the steady parade of reports of muggings, stabbings, shootings, assaults, gang wars, and accusations of police brutality, is the item concerning six Negro girls who set upon a white girl in the subway because, as they all too accurately put it, she was stepping on their toes. Indeed she was, all over the nation.

I had never before been so aware of policemen, on foot, on horseback, on corners, everywhere, always two by two. Nor had I ever been so aware of small knots of people. They were on stoops and on corners and in doorways, and what was striking about them, I think, was that they did not seem to be talking. Never, when I passed these groups, did the usual sound of a curse or a laugh ring out and neither did there seem to be any hum of gossip. There was certainly, on the other hand, occurring between them communication extraordinarily intense. Another thing that was striking was the unexpected diversity of the people who made up these groups. Usually, for example, one would see a group of sharpies standing on the street corner, jiving the passing chicks; or a group of older men, usually, for some reason, in the vicinity of a barber shop, discussing baseball scores, or the numbers, or making rather chilling observations about women they had known. Women, in a general way, tended to be seen less often together—unless they were church women, or very young girls, or prostitutes met together for an unprofessional instant. But that summer I saw the strangest combinations: large, respectable, churchly matrons standing on the stoops or the corners with their hair tied up, together with a girl in sleazy satin whose face bore the marks of gin and the razor, or heavy-set, abrupt, no-nonsense older men, in company with the most disreputable and fanatical "race" men, or these same "race" men with the sharpies, or these sharpies with the churchly women. Seventh Day Adventists and Methodists and Spiritualists seemed to be hobnobbing with Holyrollers and they were all, alike, entangled with the most flagrant disbelievers; something heavy in their stance seemed to indicate that they had all, incredibly, seen a common vision, and on each face there seemed to be the same strange, bitter shadow.

The churchly women and the matter-of-fact, no-nonsense men had children in the Army. The sleazy girls they talked to had lovers there, the sharpies and the "race" men had friends and brothers there. It would have demanded an unquestioning patriotism, happily as uncommon in this country as it is undesirable, for these people not to have been disturbed by the bitter letters they received, by the newspaper stories they read, not to have been enraged by the posters, then to be found all over New York, which described the Japanese as "yellow-bellied Japs." It was only the "race" men, to be sure, who spoke ceaselessly of being revenged —how this vengeance was to be exacted was not clear—for the indignities and dangers suffered by Negro boys in uniform; but everybody felt a directionless, hopeless bitterness, as well as that panic which can scarcely be suppressed when one knows that a human being one loves is beyond one's reach, and in danger. This helplessness and this gnawing uneasiness does something, at length, to even the toughest mind. Perhaps the best way to sum all this up is to say that the people I knew felt, mainly, a peculiar kind of relief when they knew that their boys were being shipped out of the south, to do battle overseas. It was, perhaps, like feeling that the most dangerous part of a dangerous journey had been passed and that now, even if death should come, it would come with honor and without the complicity of their countrymen. Such a death would be, in short, a fact with which one could hope to live.

It was on the 28th of July, which I believe was a Wednesday, that I visited my father for the first time during his illness and for the last time in his life. The moment I saw him I knew why I had put off this visit so long. I had told my mother that I did not want to see him because I hated him. But this was not true. It was only that I *had* hated him and I wanted to hold on to this hatred. I did not want to look on him as a ruin: it was not a ruin I had hated. I imagine that one of the reasons people cling to their hates so stubbornly is because they sense, once hate is gone, that they will be forced to deal with pain.

We traveled out to him, his older sister and myself, to what seemed to be the very end of a very Long Island. It was hot and dusty and we wrangled, my aunt and I, all the way out, over the fact that I had recently begun to smoke and, as she said, to give myself airs. But I knew that she wrangled with me because she could not bear to face the fact of her brother's dying. Neither could I endure the reality of her despair, her unstated bafflement as to what had happened to her brother's life, and her own. So we wrangled and I smoked and from time to time she fell into a heavy reverie. Covertly, I watched her face, which was the face of an old woman; it had fallen in, the eyes were sunken and lightless; soon she would be dying, too.

In my childhood—it had not been so long ago—I had thought her beautiful. She had been quick-witted and quick-moving and very generous with all the children and each of her visits had been an event. At one time one of my brothers and myself had thought of running away to live with her. Now she could no longer produce out of her handbag some unexpected and yet familiar delight. She made me feel pity and revulsion and fear. It was awful to realize that she no longer caused me to feel affection. The closer we came to the hospital the more querulous she became and at the same time, naturally, grew more dependent on me. Between pity and guilt and fear I began to feel that there was another me trapped in my skull like a jack-in-the-box who might escape my control at any moment and fill the air with screaming.

She began to cry the moment we entered the room and she saw him lying there, all shriveled and still, like a little black monkey. The great, gleaming apparatus which fed him and would have compelled him to be still even if he had been able to move brought to mind, not beneficence, but torture; the tubes entering his arm made me think of pictures I had seen when a child, of Gulliver, tied down by the pygmies on that island. My aunt wept and wept, there was a whistling sound in my father's throat; nothing was said; he could not speak. I wanted to take his hand, to say something. But I do not know what I could have said, even if he could have heard me. He was not really in that room with us, he had at last really embarked on his journey; and though my aunt told me that he said he was going to meet Jesus, I did not hear anything except that whistling in his throat. The doctor came back and we left, into that unbearable train again, and home. In the morning came the telegram saying that he was dead. Then the house was suddenly full of relatives, friends, hysteria, and confusion and I quickly left my mother and the children to the care of those impressive women, who, in Negro communities at least, automatically appear at times of bereavement armed with lotions, proverbs, and patience, and an ability to cook. I went downtown. By the time I returned, later the same day, my mother had been carried to the hospital and the baby had been born.

III

For my father's funeral I had nothing black to wear and this posed a nagging problem all day long. It was one of those problems, simple, or impossible of solution, to which the mind insanely clings in order to avoid the mind's real trouble. I spent most of that day at the downtown apartment of a girl I knew, celebrating my birthday with whiskey and wondering what to wear that night. When planning a birthday celebration one naturally does not expect that it will be up against competition from a funeral and this girl had anticipated taking me out that night, for a big dinner and a night club afterwards. Sometime during the course of that long day we decided that we would go out anyway, when my father's funeral service was over. I imagine I decided it, since, as the funeral hour approached, it became clearer and clearer to me that I would not know what to do with myself when it was over. The girl, stifling her very lively concern as to the possible effects of the whiskey on one of my father's chief mourners, concentrated on being conciliatory and practically helpful. She found a black shirt for me somewhere and ironed it and, dressed in the darkest pants and jacket I owned, and slightly drunk, I made my way to my father's funeral.

The chapel was full, but not packed, and very quiet. There were, mainly, my father's relatives, and his children, and here and there I saw faces I had not seen since childhood, the faces of my father's one-time friends. They were very dark and solemn now, seeming somehow to suggest that they had known all along that something like this would happen. Chief among the mourners was my aunt, who had quarreled with my father all his life; by which I do not mean to suggest that her mourning was insincere or that she had not loved him. I suppose that she was one of the few people in the world who had, and their incessant quarreling proved precisely the strength of the tie that bound them. The only other person in the world, as far as I knew, whose relationship to my father rivaled my aunt's in depth was my mother, who was not there.

It seemed to me, of course, that it was a very long funeral. But it was, if anything, a rather shorter funeral than most, nor since there were no overwhelming, uncontrollable expressions of grief, could it be called—if I dare to use the word—successful. The minister who preached my father's funeral sermon was one of the few my father had still been seeing as he neared his end. He presented to us in his sermon a man whom none of us had ever seen—a man thoughtful, patient, and forbearing, a Christian inspiration to all who knew him, and a model for his children. And no doubt the children, in their disturbed and guilty state, were almost ready to believe this; he had been remote enough to be anything and, anyway, the shock of the incontrovertible, that it was really our father lying up there in that casket, prepared the mind for anything. His sister moaned and this grief-stricken moaning was taken as corroboration. The other faces held a dark, non-committal thoughtfulness. This was not the man they had known, but they had scarcely expected to be confronted with *him;* this was, in a sense deeper than questions of fact, the man they had not known, and the man they had not known may have been the real one. The real man, whoever he had been, had suffered and now he was dead: this was all that was sure and all that mattered now. Every man in the chapel hoped that when his hour came he, too, would be eulogized, which is to say forgiven, and that all of his lapses, greeds, errors, and strayings from the truth would be invested with coherence and looked upon with charity. This was perhaps the last thing human beings could give each other and it was what they demanded, after all, of the Lord. Only the Lord saw the midnight tears, only He was present when one of His children, moaning and wringing hands, paced up and down the room. When one slapped one's child in anger the recoil in the heart reverberated through heaven and became part of the pain of the universe. And when the children were hungry and

sullen and distrustful and one watched them, daily, growing wilder, and
further away, and running headlong into danger, it was the Lord who
knew what the charged heart endured as the strap was laid to the backside; the Lord alone who knew what one *would* have said if one had had,
like the Lord, the gift of the living word. It was the Lord who knew of
the impossibility every parent in that room faced: how to prepare the
child for the day when the child would be despised and how to *create*
in the child—by what means?—a stronger antidote to this poison than
one had found for oneself. The avenues, side streets, bars, billiard halls,
hospitals, police stations, and even the playgrounds of Harlem—not to
mention the houses of correction, the jails, and the morgue—testified
to the potency of the poison while remaining silent as to the efficacy of
whatever antidote, irresistibly raising the question of whether or not
such an antidote existed; raising, which was worse, the question of
whether or not an antidote was desirable; perhaps poison should be
fought with poison. With these several schisms in the mind and with
more terrors in the heart than could be named, it was better not to judge
the man who had gone down under an impossible burden. It was better
to remember: *Thou knowest this man's fall; but thou knowest not his
wrassling.*

     While the preacher talked and I watched the children—years of
changing their diapers, scrubbing them, slapping them, taking them to
school, and scolding them had had the perhaps inevitable result of
making me love them, though I am not sure I knew this then—my mind
was busily breaking out with a rash of disconnected impressions.
Snatches of popular songs, indecent jokes, bits of books I had read,
movie sequences, faces, voices, political issues—I thought I was going
mad; all these impressions suspended, as it were, in the solution of the
faint nausea produced in me by the heat and liquor. For a moment I
had the impression that my alcoholic breath, inefficiently disguised with
chewing gum, filled the entire chapel. Then someone began singing one
of my father's favorite songs and, abruptly, I was with him, sitting on
his knee, in the hot, enormous, crowded church which was the first
church we attended. It was the Abyssinia Baptist Church on 138th
Street. We had not gone there long. With this image, a host of others
came. I had forgotten, in the rage of my growing up, how proud my
father had been of me when I was little. Apparently, I had had a voice
and my father had liked to show me off before the members of the
church. I had forgotten what he had looked like when he was pleased
but now I remembered that he had always been grinning with pleasure
when my solos ended. I even remembered certain expressions on his
face when he teased my mother—had he loved her? I would never
know. And when had it all begun to change? For now it seemed that he
had not always been cruel. I remembered being taken for a haircut and
scraping my knee on the footrest of the barber's chair and I remembered
my father's face as he soothed my crying and applied the stinging iodine.

Then I remembered our fights, fights which had been of the worst possible kind because my technique had been silence.

I remembered the one time in all our life together when we had really spoken to each other.

It was on a Sunday and it must have been shortly before I left home. We were walking, just the two of us, in our usual silence, to or from church. I was in high school and had been doing a lot of writing and I was, at about this time, the editor of the high school magazine. But I had also been a Young Minister and had been preaching from the pulpit. Lately, I had been taking fewer engagements and preached as rarely as possible. It was said in the church, quite truthfully, that I was "cooling off."

My father asked me abruptly, "You'd rather write than preach, wouldn't you?"

I was astonished at his question—because it was a real question. I answered, "Yes."

That was all we said. It was awful to remember that that was all we had *ever* said.

The casket now was opened and the mourners were being led up the aisle to look for the last time on the deceased. The assumption was that the family was too overcome with grief to be allowed to make this journey alone and I watched while my aunt was led to the casket and, muffled in black, and shaking, led back to her seat. I disapproved of forcing the children to look on their dead father, considering that the shock of his death, or, more truthfully, the shock of death as a reality, was already a little more than a child could bear, but my judgment in this matter had been overruled and there they were, bewildered and frightened and very small, being led, one by one, to the casket. But there is also something very gallant about children at such moments. It has something to do with their silence and gravity and with the fact that one cannot help them. Their legs, somehow, seem *exposed* so that it is at once incredible and terribly clear that their legs are all they have to hold them up.

I had not wanted to go to the casket myself and I certainly had not wished to be led there, but there was no way of avoiding either of these forms. One of the deacons led me up and I looked on my father's face. I cannot say that it looked like him at all. His blackness had been equivocated by powder and there was no suggestion in that casket of what his power had or could have been. He was simply an old man dead, and it was hard to believe that he had ever given anyone either joy or pain. Yet, his life filled that room. Further up the avenue his wife was holding his newborn child. Life and death so close together, and love and hatred, and right and wrong, said something to me which I did not want to hear concerning man, concerning the life of man.

After the funeral, while I was downtown desperately celebrating my birthday, a Negro soldier, in the lobby of the Hotel Braddock, got into a fight with a white policeman over a Negro girl. Negro girls, white police-men, in or out of uniform, and Negro males—in or out of uniform—were part of the furniture of the lobby of the Hotel Braddock and this was certainly not the first time such an incident had occurred. It was destined, however, to receive an unprecedented publicity, for the fight between the policeman and the soldier ended with the shooting of the soldier. Rumor, flowing immediately to the streets outside, stated that the soldier had been shot in the back, an instantaneous and revealing invention, and that the soldier had died protecting a Negro woman. The facts were somewhat different—for example, the soldier had not been shot in the back, and was not dead, and the girl seems to have been as dubious a symbol of womanhood as her white counterpart in Georgia usually is, but no one was interested in the facts. They preferred the invention because this invention expressed and corroborated their hates and fears so perfectly. It is just as well to remember that people are always doing this. Perhaps many of those legends, including Christianity, to which the world clings began their conquest of the world with just some such concerted surrender to distortion. The effect, in Harlem, of this particular legend was like the effect of a lit match in a tin of gasoline. The mob gathered before the doors of the Hotel Braddock simply began to swell and to spread in every direction, and Harlem exploded.

The mob did not cross the ghetto lines. It would have been easy, for example, to have gone over Morningside Park on the west side or to have crossed the Grand Central railroad tracks at 125th Street on the east side, to wreak havoc in white neighborhoods. The mob seems to have been mainly interested in something more potent and real than the white face, that is, in white power, and the principal damage done during the riot of the summer of 1943 was to white business establishments in Harlem. It might have been a far bloodier story, of course, if, at the hour the riot began, these establishments had still been open. From the Hotel Braddock the mob fanned out, east and west along 125th Street, and for the entire length of Lenox, Seventh, and Eighth avenues. Along each of these avenues, and along each major side street—116th, 125th, 135th, and so on—bars, stores, pawnships, restaurants, even little luncheonettes had been smashed open and entered and looted—looted, it might be added, with more haste than efficiency. The shelves really looked as though a bomb had struck them. Cans of beans and soup and dog food, along with toilet paper, corn flakes, sardines, and milk tumbled every which way, and abandoned cash registers and cases of beer leaned crazily out of the splintered windows and were strewn along the avenues. Sheets, blankets, and clothing of every description formed a kind of path, as though people had dropped them while running. I truly had not realized that Harlem *had* so many stores until I saw them all smashed open; the first time the word *wealth* ever entered my mind in relation to Harlem was when I saw it scattered in the streets. But one's first, incongruous impression of plenty was countered immediately by an impression of waste. None of this was doing anybody any good. It would have been better to have left the plate glass as it had been and the goods lying in the stores.

It would have been better, but it would also have been intolerable, for Harlem had needed something to smash. To smash something is the ghetto's chronic need. Most of the time it is the members of the ghetto who smash each other, and themselves. But as long as the ghetto walls are standing there will always come a moment when these outlets do not work. That summer, for example, it was not enough to get into a fight on Lenox Avenue, or curse out one's cronies in the barber shops. If ever, indeed, the violence which fills Harlem's churches, pool halls, and bars erupts outward in a more direct fashion, Harlem and its citizens are likely to vanish in an apocalyptic flood. That this is not likely to happen is due to a great many reasons, most hidden and powerful among them the Negro's real relation to the white American. This relation prohibits, simply, anything as uncomplicated and satisfactory as pure hatred. In order really to hate white people, one has to blot so much out of the mind—and the heart—that this hatred itself becomes an exhausting and self-destructive pose. But this does not mean, on the other hand, that love comes easily: the white world is too powerful, too complacent, too ready with gratuitous humiliation, and, above all, too ignorant and too innocent for that. One is absolutely forced to make perpetual qualifications and one's own reactions are always canceling each other out. It is this, really, which has driven so many people mad, both white and black. One is always in the position of having to decide between amputation and gangrene. Amputation is swift but time may prove that the amputation was not necessary—or one may delay the amputation too long. Gangrene is slow, but it is impossible to be sure that one is reading one's symptoms right. The idea of going through life as a cripple is more than one can bear, and equally unbearable is the risk of swelling up slowly, in agony, with poison. And the trouble, finally, is that the risks are real even if the choices do not exist.

"But as for me and my house," my father had said, "we will serve the Lord." I wondered, as we drove him to his resting place, what this line had meant for him. I had heard him preach it many times. I had preached it once myself, proudly giving it an interpretation different from my father's. Now the whole thing came back to me, as though my father and I were on our way to Sunday school and I were memorizing the golden text: *And if it seem evil unto you to serve the Lord, choose you this day whom you will serve; whether the gods which your fathers served that were on the other side of the flood, or the gods of the Amorites, in whose land ye dwell: but as for me and my house, we will serve the Lord.*[1] I suspected in these familiar lines a meaning which had never been there for me before. All of my father's texts and songs, which

[1] *Joshua,* 24:15.

I had decided were meaningless, were arranged before me at his death like empty bottles, waiting to hold the meaning which life would give them for me. This was his legacy: nothing is ever escaped. That bleakly memorable morning I hated the unbelievable streets and the Negroes and whites who had, equally, made them that way. But I knew that it was folly, as my father would have said, this bitterness was folly. It was necessary to hold on to the things that mattered. The dead man mattered, the new life mattered; blackness and whiteness did not matter; to believe that they did was to acquiesce in one's own destruction. Hatred, which could destroy so much, never failed to destroy the man who hated and this was an immutable law.

It began to seem that one would have to hold in the mind forever two ideas which seemed to be in opposition. The first idea was acceptance, the acceptance, totally without rancor, of life as it is, and men as they are: in the light of this idea, it goes without saying that injustice is a commonplace. But this did not mean that one could be complacent, for the second idea was of equal power: that one must never, in one's own life, accept these injustices as commonplace but must fight them with all one's strength. This fight begins, however, in the heart and it now had been laid to my charge to keep my own heart free of hatred and despair. This intimation made my heart heavy and, now that my father was irrecoverable, I wished that he had been beside me so that I could have searched his face for the answers which only the future would give me now.

NORMAN MAILER (1923–   )

A line in one of Mildred Bailey's old songs goes, "You may have been a bring-down but you never were a bore," and perhaps it suits Mailer. Anyone who has been so persistently flamboyant must surely at some point have been tiresome, but the curious fact is that he has not been. Often funny, when he probably did not mean to be, he was never tiresome. But in the course of his career, he has certainly repeatedly let us down.

He was born in Long Branch, New Jersey, but when he was still very young his family moved to Brooklyn, and there he was brought up. When, as a sophomore at Harvard, he won Story magazine's college contest, he knew that he was going to be a writer. And, with many ups and downs, he has never ceased to be, or even paused.

His most famous novel is still his first, The Naked and the Dead (1948), and none of those that have followed, for all their striving toward new and sometimes extraordinary forms, has won the general acclaim received by that novel of the Second World War in the

Pacific. *The others are* Barbary Shore *(1951),* The Deer Park *(1955),* An American Dream *(1965), and* Why Are We in Vietnam? *(1967).*

But in the 1950s Mailer began to publish widely as an essayist and (highly) informal cultural historian—pieces like "The White Negro" —and tried to develop his special stance of involved observer on the social and political scene, a self-appointed master of the Now. Advertisements for Myself *(1959) was not only a collection of such pieces as he had written up to then, but also (including as it did much of his then uncollected short fiction and large samples of his longer work and many of his poems as well—here is where he risks becoming tiresome) an anthological outline of his own development. Then followed, in the same mood,* The Presidential Papers *(1963) and* Cannibals and Christians *(1966).*

Then History itself reached down and touched his by now furrowed brow; "Norman, be mine," it murmured. This was history in the form of a peace march on Washington in 1967 and of the major political conventions in 1968. Two quite extraordinary works of reporting resulted: The Armies of the Night: History as a Novel, the Novel as History *(1968) and* Miami and the Siege of Chicago: An Informal History of the Republican and Democratic Conventions of 1968 *(1968).*

He was always at his best as a reporter. The readable parts of The Naked and the Dead *now are the objective reports, not the psychological investigations. But even then he had a psychological need of his own to be inside the action. In* Armies of the Night *he found the form he needed. To write another such book, he will need the blessing of History again, but he can almost depend on it, in these times. Perhaps the series on the American foray into space that he has begun for* Life *magazine will have this blessing; the title of the announced book is* Of a Fire on the Moon *(1970).*

FURTHER READING

A brief pamphlet surveying Mailer's career is Richard J. Foster, *Norman Mailer* (1968). Earlier critical estimates include Ihab Hassan, *Radical Innocence: Studies in the Contemporary American Novel* (1961); Norman Podhoretz, *Doings and Undoings: The Fifties and After in American Writing* (1964); John W. Aldridge, *Time to Murder and Create: The Contemporary Novel in Crisis* (1966); and Ronald Berman, *America in the Sixties: An Intellectual History* (1968).

The White Negro

Superficial Reflections on the Hipster (1957)

Our search for the rebels of the generation led us to the hipster. The hipster is an *enfant terrible* turned inside out. In character with his time, he is trying to get back at the conformists by lying low . . . You can't interview a hipster because his main goal is to keep out of a society which, he thinks, is trying to make everyone over in its own image. He takes marijuana because it supplies him with experiences that can't be shared with "squares." He may affect a broad-brimmed hat or a zoot suit, but usually he prefers to skulk unmarked. The hipster may be a jazz musician; he is rarely an artist, almost never a writer. He may earn his living as a petty criminal, a hobo, a carnival roustabout or a free-lance moving man in Greenwich Village, but some hipsters have found a safe refuge in the upper income brackets as television comics or movie actors. (The late James Dean,[1] for one, was a hipster hero.) . . . It is tempting to describe the hipster in psychiatric terms as infantile, but the style of his infantilism is a sign of the times. He does not try to enforce his will on others, Napoleon-fashion, but contents himself with a magical omnipotence never disproved because never tested. . . . As the only extreme nonconformist of his generation, he exercises a powerful if underground appeal for conformists, through newspaper accounts of his delinquencies, his structureless jazz, and his emotive grunt words.

—"Born 1930: The Unlost Generation"
by Caroline Bird
Harper's Bazaar, Feb. 1957

Probably, we will never be able to determine the psychic havoc of the concentration camps and the atom bomb upon the unconscious mind of almost everyone alive in these years. For the first time in civilized history, perhaps for the first time in all of history, we have been forced to live with the suppressed knowledge that the smallest facets of our personality or the most minor projection of our ideas, or indeed the absence of ideas and the absence of personality could mean equally well that we might still be doomed to die as a cipher in some vast statistical operation in which our teeth would be counted, and our hair would be saved, but our death itself would be unknown, unhonored, and unremarked, a death which could not follow with dignity as a possible consequence to serious actions we had chosen, but rather a death by *deus ex machina* in a gas chamber or a radioactive city; and so if in the midst of civilization—that civilization founded upon the Faustian urge to dominate nature by mastering time, mastering the links of social cause and effect—in the middle of an economic civilization founded upon the confidence that time could indeed be subjected to our will, our psyche was subjected itself to the intolerable anxiety that death being causeless, life

---

[1] (1931–1955), film star who was killed in a motor accident.

was causeless as well, and time deprived of cause and effect had come to a stop.

The Second World War presented a mirror to the human condition which blinded anyone who looked into it. For if tens of millions were killed in concentration camps out of the inexorable agonies and contractions of super-states founded upon the always insoluble contradictions of injustice, one was then obliged also to see that no matter how crippled and perverted an image of man was the society he had created, it was nonetheless his creation, his collective creation (at least his collective creation from the past) and if society was so murderous, then who could ignore the most hideous of questions about his own nature?

Worse. One could hardly maintain the courage to be individual, to speak with one's own voice, for the years in which one could complacently accept oneself as part of an elite by being a radical were forever gone. A man knew that when he dissented, he gave a note upon his life which could be called in any year of overt crisis. No wonder then that these have been the years of conformity and depression. A stench of fear has come out of every pore of American life, and we suffer from a collective failure of nerve. The only courage, with rare exceptions, that we have been witness to, has been the isolated courage of isolated people.

2

It is on this bleak scene that a phenomenon has appeared: the American existentialist—the hipster, the man who knows that if our collective condition is to live with instant death by atomic war, relatively quick death by the State as *l'univers concentrationnaire,*[2] or with a slow death by conformity with every creative and rebellious instinct stifled (at what damage to the mind and the heart and the liver and the nerves no research foundation for cancer will discovery in a hurry), if the fate of twentieth-century man is to live with death from adolescence to premature senescence, why then the only life-giving answer is to accept the terms of death, to live with death as immediate danger, to divorce oneself from society, to exist without roots, to set out on that uncharted journey into the rebellious imperatives of the self. In short, whether the life is criminal or not, the decision is to encourage the psychopath in oneself, to explore that domain of experience where security is boredom and therefore sickness, and one exists in the present, in that enormous present which is without past or future, memory or planned intention, the life where a man must go until he is beat, where he must gamble with his energies through all those small or large crises of courage and unforeseen situations which beset his day, where he must be with it or doomed not to swing. The unstated essence of Hip, its psychopathic brilliance, quivers with the knowledge that new kinds of victories increase one's power for new kinds of perception; and defeats, the wrong kind of

2 "Universe as concentration camp."

defeats, attack the body and imprison one's energy until one is jailed in the prison air of other people's habits, other people's defeats, boredom, quiet desperation, and muted icy self-destroying rage. One is Hip or one is Square (the alternative which each new generation coming into American life is beginning to feel), one is a rebel or one conforms, one is a frontiersman in the Wild West of American night life, or else a Square cell, trapped in the totalitarian tissues of American society, doomed willy-nilly to conform if one is to succeed.

A totalitarian society makes enormous demands on the courage of men, and a partially totalitarian society makes even greater demands, for the general anxiety is greater. Indeed if one is to be a man, almost any kind of unconventional action often takes disproportionate courage. So it is no accident that the source of Hip is the Negro for he has been living on the margin between totalitarianism and democracy for two centuries. But the presence of Hip as a working philosophy in the sub-worlds of American life is probably due to jazz, and its knifelike entrance into culture, its subtle but so penetrating influence on an avant-garde generation—that postwar generation of adventurers who (some consciously, some by osmosis) had absorbed the lessons of disillusionment and disgust of the twenties, the depression, and the war. Sharing a collective disbelief in the words of men who had too much money and controlled too many things, they knew almost as powerful a disbelief in the socially monolithic ideas of the single mate, the solid family and the respectable love life. If the intellectual antecedents of this generation can be traced to such separate influences as D. H. Lawrence, Henry Miller, and Wilhelm Reich, the viable philosophy of Hemingway fit most of their facts: in a bad world, as he was to say over and over again (while taking time out from his parvenu snobbery and dedicated gourmandize), in a bad world there is no love nor mercy nor charity nor justice unless a man can keep his courage, and this indeed fitted some of the facts. What fitted the need of the adventurer even more precisely was Hemingway's categorical imperative that what made him feel good became therefore The Good.

So no wonder that in certain cities of America, in New York of course, and New Orleans, in Chicago and San Francisco and Los Angeles, in such American cities as Paris and Mexico, D.F., this particular part of a generation was attracted to what the Negro had to offer. In such places as Greenwich Village, a ménage-à-trois [3] was completed—the bohemian and the juvenile delinquent came face-to-face with the Negro, and the hipster was a fact in American life. If marijuana was the wedding ring, the child was the language of Hip for its argot gave expression to abstract states of feeling which all could share, at least all who were Hip. And in this wedding of the white and the black it was the Negro who brought the cultural dowry. Any Negro who wishes to live must live with danger from his first day, and no experience can ever be

[3] Domestic establishment for three.

casual to him, no Negro can saunter down a street with any real certainty that violence will not visit him on his walk. The cameos of security
for the average white: mother and the home, job and the family, are not
even a mockery to millions of Negroes; they are impossible. The Negro
has the simplest of alternatives: live a life of constant humility or ever-
threatening danger. In such a pass where paranoia is as vital to survival
as blood, the Negro had stayed alive and begun to grow by following the
need of his body where he could. Knowing in the cells of his existence
that life was war, nothing but war, the Negro (all exceptions admitted)
could rarely afford the sophisticated inhibitions of civilization, and so
he kept for his survival the art of the primitive, he lived in the enormous
present, he subsisted for his Saturday night kicks, relinquishing the
pleasures of the mind for the more obligatory pleasures of the body, and
in his music he gave voice to the character and quality of his existence,
to his rage and the infinite variations of joy, lust, languor, growl, cramp,
pinch, scream and despair of his orgasm. For jazz is orgasm, it is the
music of orgasm, good orgasm and bad, and so it spoke across a nation,
it had the communication of art even where it was watered, perverted,
corrupted, and almost killed, it spoke in no matter what laundered popular way of instantaneous existential states to which some whites could
respond, it was indeed a communication by art because it said, "I feel
this, and now you do too."

So there was a new breed of adventurers, urban adventurers who
drifted out at night looking for action with a black man's code to fit their
facts. The hipster had absorbed the existentialist synapses of the Negro,
and for practical purposes could be considered a white Negro.

To be an existentialist, one must be able to feel oneself—one must
know one's desires, one's rages, one's anguish, one must be aware of the
character of one's frustration and know what would satisfy it. The over-
civilized man can be an existentialist only if it is chic, and deserts it
quickly for the next chic. To be a real existentialist (Sartre admittedly
to the contrary) one must be religious, one must have one's sense of
the "purpose"—whatever the purpose may be—but a life which is directed by one's faith in the necessity of action is a life committed to the
notion that the substratum of existence is the search, the end meaningful
but mysterious; it is impossible to live such a life unless one's emotions
provide their profound conviction. Only the French, alienated beyond
alienation from their unconscious could welcome an existential philosophy without ever feeling it at all; indeed only a Frenchman by declaring
that the unconscious did not exist could then proceed to explore the delicate involutions of consciousness, the microscopically sensuous and all
but ineffable *firissons* [1] of mental becoming, in order finally to create the
theology of atheism and so submit that in a world of absurdities the
existential absurdity is most coherent.

In the dialogue between the atheist and the mystic, the atheist is

---

[1] "Thrills."

on the side of life, rational life, undialectical life—since he conceives of death as emptiness, he can, no matter how weary or despairing, wish for nothing but more life; his pride is that he does not transpose his weakness and spiritual fatigue into a romantic longing for death, for such appreciation of death is then all too capable of being elaborated by his imagination into a universe of meaningful structure and moral orchestration.

Yet this masculine argument can mean very little for the mystic. The mystic can accept the atheist's description of his weakness, he can agree that his mysticism was a response to despair. And yet . . . . and yet his argument is that he, the mystic, is the one finally who has chosen to live with death, and so death is his experience and not the atheist's, and the atheist by eschewing the limitless dimensions of profound despair has rendered himself incapable to judge the experience. The real argument which the mystic must always advance is the very intensity of his private vision—his argument depends from the vision precisely because what was felt in the vision is so extraordinary that no rational argument, no hypotheses of "oceanic feelings" and certainly no skeptical reductions can explain away what has become for him the reality more real than the reality of closely reasoned logic. His inner experience of the possibilities within death is his logic. So, too, for the existentialist. And the psychopath. And the saint and the bullfighter and the lover. The common denominator for all of them is their burning consciousness of the present, exactly that incandescent consciousness which the possibilities within death has opened for them. There is a depth of desperation to the condition which enables one to remain in life only by engaging death, but the reward is their knowledge that what is happening at each instant of the electric present is good or bad for them, good or bad for their cause, their love, their action, their need.

It is this knowledge which provides the curious community of feeling in the world of the hipster, a muted cool religious revival to be sure, but the element which is exciting, disturbing, nightmarish perhaps, is that incompatibles have come to bed, the inner life and the violent life, the orgy and the dream of love, the desire to murder and the desire to create, a dialectical conception of existence with a lust for power, a dark, romantic, and yet undeniably dynamic view of existence for it sees every man and woman as moving individually through each moment of life forward into growth or backward into death.

3

It may be fruitful to consider the hipster a philosophical psychopath, a man interested not only in the dangerous imperatives of his psychopathy but in codifying, at least for himself, the suppositions on which his inner universe is constructed. By this premise the hipster is a psychopath, and yet not a psychopath but the negation of the psychopath, for he possesses the narcissistic detachment of the philosopher, that absorption in the recessive nuances of one's own motive which is so alien to the unreasoning drive of the psychopath. In this country where new millions of psychopaths are developed each year, stamped with the mint of our contradictory popular culture (where sex is sin and yet sex is paradise), it is as if there has been room already for the development of the antithetical psychopath who extrapolates from his own condition, from the inner certainty that his rebellion is just, a radical vision of the universe which thus separates him from the general ignorance, reactionary prejudice, and self-doubt of the more conventional psychopath. Having converted his unconscious experience into much conscious knowledge, the hipster has shifted the focus of his desire from immediate gratification toward that wider passion for future power which is the mark of civilized man. Yet with an irreducible difference. For Hip is the sophistication of the wise primitive in a giant jungle, and so its appeal is still beyond the civilized man. If there are ten million Americans who are more or less psychopathic (and the figure is most modest), there are probably not more than one hundred thousand men and women who consciously see themselves as hipsters, but their importance is that they are an elite with the potential ruthlessness of an elite, and a language most adolescents can understand instinctively, for the hipster's intense view of existence matches their experience and their desire to rebel.

Before one can say more about the hipster, there is obviously much to be said about the psychic state of the psychopath—or, clinically, the psychopathic personality. Now, for reasons which may be more curious than the similarity of the words, even many people with a psychoanalytical orientation often confuse the psychopath with the psychotic. Yet the terms are polar. The psychotic is legally insane, the psychopath is not; the psychotic is almost always incapable of discharging in physical acts the rage of his frustration, while the psychopath at his extreme is virtually as incapable of restraining his violence. The psychotic lives in so misty a world that what is happening at each moment of his life is not very real to him whereas the psychopath seldom knows any reality greater than the face, the voice, the being of the particular people among whom he may find himself at any moment. Sheldon and Eleanor Glueck [5] describe him as follows:

The psychopath . . . can be distinguished from the person sliding into or clambering out of a "true psychotic" state by the long tough persistence of his anti-social attitude and behaviour and the absence of hallucinations, delusions, manic flight of ideas, confusion, disorientation, and other dramatic signs of psychosis.

The late Robert Lindner,[6] one of the few experts on the subject, in

---

[5] (1896–   ) and (1898–   ), criminologists. The quotation is from their introduction to the Lindner book next cited.

[6] (1914–1956), American psychoanalyst whose book was published in 1944.

his book *Rebel Without a Cause—The Hypnoanalysis of a Criminal Psychopath* presented part of his definition in this way:

... the psychopath is a rebel without a cause, an agitator without a slogan, a revolutionary without a program: in other words, his rebelliousness is aimed to achieve goals satisfactory to himself alone; he is incapable of exertions for the sake of others. All his efforts, hidden under no matter what disguise, represent investments designed to satisfy his immediate wishes and desires.... The psychopath, like the child, cannot delay the pleasures of gratification; and this trait is one of his underlying, universal characteristics. He cannot wait upon erotic gratification which convention demands should be preceded by the chase before the kill: he must rape. He cannot wait upon the development of prestige in society; his egoistic ambitions lead him to leap into headlines by daring performances. Like a red thread the predominance of this mechanism for immediate satisfaction runs through the history of every psychopath. It explains not only his behaviour but also the violent nature of his acts.

Yet even Lindner who was the most imaginative and most sympathetic of the psychoanalysts who have studied the psychopathic personality was not ready to project himself into the essential sympathy—which is that the psychopath may indeed be the perverted and dangerous front-runner of a new kind of personality which could become the central expression of human nature before the twentieth century is over. For the psychopath is better adapted to dominate those mutually contradictory inhibitions upon violence and love which civilization has exacted of us, and if it be remembered that not every psychopath is an extreme case, and that the condition of psychopathy is present in a host of people including many politicians, professional soldiers, newspaper columnists, entertainers, artists, jazz musicians, call-girls, promiscuous homosexuals and half the executives of Hollywood, television, and advertising, it can be seen that there are aspects of psychopathy which already exert considerable cultural influence.

What characterizes almost every psychopath and part-psychopath is that they are trying to create a new nervous system for themselves. Generally we are obliged to act with a nervous system which has been formed from infancy, and which carries in the style of its circuits the very contradictions of our parents and our early milieu. Therefore, we are obliged, most of us, to meet the tempo of the present and the future with reflexes and rhythms which come from the past. It is not only the "dead weight of the institutions of the past" but indeed the inefficient and often antiquated nervous circuits of the past which strangle our potentiality for responding to new possibilities which might be exciting for our individual growth.

Through most of modern history, "sublimation" was possible: at the expense of expressing only a small portion of oneself, that small portion could be expressed intensely. But sublimation depends on a reasonable tempo to history. If the collective life of a generation has moved too quickly, the "past" by which particular men and women of that generation may function is not, let us say, thirty years old, but relatively a hundred or two hundred years old. And so the nervous system is overstressed beyond the possibility of such compromises as sublimation especially since the stable middle-class values so prerequisite to sublimation have been virtually destroyed in our time, at least as nourishing values free of confusion or doubt. In such a crisis of accelerated historical tempo and deteriorated values, neurosis tends to be replaced by psychopathy, and the success of psychoanalysis (which even ten years ago gave promise of becoming a direct major force) diminishes because of its inbuilt and characteristic incapacity to handle patients more complex, more experienced, or more adventurous than the analyst himself. In practice, psychoanalysis has by now become all too often no more than a psychic blood-letting. The patient is not so much changed as aged, and the infantile fantasies which he is encouraged to express are condemned to exhaust themselves against the analyst's nonresponsive reactions. The result for all too many patients is a diminution, a "tranquilizing" of their most interesting qualities and vices. The patient is indeed not so much altered as worn out— less bad, less good, less bright, less willful, less destructive, less creative. He is thus able to conform to that contradictory and unbearable society which first created his neurosis. He can conform to what he loathes because he no longer has the passion to feel loathing so intensely.

The psychopath is notoriously difficult to analyze because the fundamental decision of his nature is to try to live the infantile fantasy, and in this decision (given the dreary alternative of psychoanalysis) there may be a certain instinctive wisdom. For there is a dialectic to changing one's nature, the dialectic which underlies all psychoanalytic method: it is the knowledge that if one is to change one's habits, one must go back to the source of their creation, and so the psychopath exploring backward along the road of the homosexual, the orgiast, the drug-addict, the rapist, the robber and the murderer seeks to find those violent parallels to the violent and often hopeless contradictions he knew as an infant and as a child. For if he has the courage to meet the parallel situation at the moment when he is ready, then he has a chance to act as he has never acted before, and in satisfying the frustration—if he can succeed —he may then pass by symbolic substitute through the locks of incest. In thus giving expression to the buried infant in himself, he can lessen the tension of those infantile desires and so free himself to remake a bit of his nervous system. Like the neurotic he is looking for the opportunity to grow up a second time, but the psychopath knows instinctively that to express a forbidden impulse actively is far more beneficial to him than merely to confess the desire in the safety of a doctor's room. The psychopath is inordinately ambitious, too ambitious ever to trade his warped brilliant conception of his possible victories in life for the grim if peaceful attrition of the analyst's couch. So his associational journey into the past is lived out in the theatre of the present, and he exists for those charged situations where his senses are so alive that he can be aware actively (as the analysand is aware passively) of what his habits are, and how he can change them. The strength of the psychopath is that he knows (where most of us can only guess) what is good for him and what is bad for him at exactly those instants when an old crippling habit has become so attacked by experience that the potentiality exists to change it, to replace a negative and empty fear with an outward action, even if—and here I obey the logic of the extreme psychopath—even if the fear is of himself, and the action is to murder. The psychopath murders—if he has the courage—out of the necessity to purge his violence, for if he cannot empty his hatred then he cannot love, his being is frozen with implacable self-hatred for his cowardice. (It can of course be suggested that it takes little courage for two strong eighteen-year-old hoodlums, let us say, to beat in the brains of a candy-store keeper, and indeed the act—even by the logic of the psychopath—is not likely to prove very therapeutic, for the victim is not an immediate equal. Still, courage of a sort is necessary, for one murders not only a weak fifty-year-old man but an institution as well, one violates private property, one enters into a new relation with the police and introduces a dangerous element into one's life. The hoodlum is therefore daring the unknown, and so no matter how brutal the act, it is not altogether cowardly.)

At bottom, the drama of the psychopath is that he seeks love. Not love as the search for a mate, but love as the search for an orgasm more apocalyptic than the one which preceded it. Orgasm is his therapy—he knows at the seed of his being that good-orgasm opens his possibilities and bad orgasm imprisons him. But in this search, the psychopath becomes an embodiment of the extreme contradictions of the society which formed his character, and the apocalyptic orgasm often remains as remote as the Holy Grail, for there are clusters and nests and ambushes of violence in his own necessities and in the imperatives and retaliations of the men and women among whom he lives his life, so that even as he drains his hatred in one act or another, so the conditions of his life create it anew in him until the drama of his movements bears a sardonic resemblance to the frog who climbed a few feet in the well only to drop back again.

Yet there is this to be said for the search after the good orgasm: when one lives in a civilized world, and still can enjoy none of the cultural nectar of such a world because the paradoxes on which civilization is built demand that there remain a cultureless and alienated bottom of exploitable human material, then the logic of becoming a sexual outlaw (if one's psychological roots are bedded in the bottom) is that one has at least a running competitive chance to be physically healthy so long as one stays alive. It is therefore no accident that psychopathy is most prevalent with the Negro. Hated from outside and therefore hating himself, the Negro was forced into the position of exploring all those moral wildernesses of civilized life which the Square automatically condemns as delinquent or evil or immature or morbid or self-destructive or corrupt. (Actually the terms have equal weight. Depending on the telescope of the cultural clique from which the Square surveys the universe, "evil" or "immature" are equally strong terms of condemnation.) But the Negro, not being privileged to gratify his self-esteem with the heady satisfactions of categorical condemnation, chose to move instead in that other direction where all situations are equally valid, and in the worst of perversion, promiscuity, pimpery, drug addiction, rape, razor-slash, bottle-break, what-have-you, the Negro discovered and elaborated a morality of the bottom, an ethical differentiation between the good and the bad in every human activity from the go-getter pimp (as opposed to the lazy one) to the relatively dependable pusher or prostitute. Add to this, the cunning of their language, the abstract ambiguous alternatives in which from the danger of their oppression they learned to speak ("Well, now, man, like I'm looking for a cat to turn me on . . ."), add even more the profound sensitivity of the Negro jazzman who was the cultural mentor of a people, and it is not too difficult to believe that the language of Hip which evolved was an artful language, tested and shaped by an intense experience and therefore different in kind from white slang, as different as the special obscenity of the soldier, which in its emphasis upon "ass" as the soul and "shit" as circumstance, was able to express the existential states of the enlisted man. What makes Hip a special language is that it cannot really be taught—if one shares none of the experiences of elation and exhaustion which it is equipped to describe, then it seems merely arch or vulgar or irritating. It is a pictorial language, but pictorial like non-objective art, imbued with the dialectic of small but intense change, a language for the microcosm, in this case, man, for it takes the immediate experiences of any passing man and magnifies the dynamic of his movements, not specifically but abstractly so that he is seen more as a vector in a network of forces than as a static character in a crystallized field. (Which latter is the practical view of the snob.) For example, there is real difficulty in trying to find a Hip substitute for "stubborn." The best possibility I can come up with is: "That cat will never come off his groove, dad." But groove implies movement, narrow movement but motion nonetheless. There is really no way to describe someone who does not move at all. Even a creep does move—if at a pace exasperatingly more slow than the pace of the cool cats.

4

Like children, hipsters are fighting for the sweet, and their language is a set of subtle indications of their success or failure in the competition for pleasure. Unstated but obvious is the social sense that there is not nearly enough sweet for everyone. And so the sweet goes only to the victor, the best, the most, the man who knows the most about how to find his energy and how not to lose it. The emphasis is on energy because the psychopath and the hipster are nothing without it since they do not have the protection of a position or a class to rely on when they have overextended themselves. So the language of Hip is a language of energy, how it is found, how it is lost.

But let us see. I have jotted down perhaps a dozen words, the Hip perhaps most in use and most likely to last with the minimum of variation. The words are man, go, put down, make, beat, cool, swing, with it, crazy, dig, flip, creep, hip, square. They serve a variety of purposes and the nuance of the voice uses the nuance of the situation to convey the subtle contextual difference. If the hipster moves through his life on a constant search with glimpses of Mecca in many a turn of his experience (Mecca being the apocalyptic orgasm) and if everyone in the civilized world is at least in some small degree a sexual cripple, the hipster lives with the knowledge of how he is sexually crippled and where he is sexually alive, and the faces of experience which life presents to him each day are engaged, dismissed or avoided as his need directs and his life-manship makes possible. For life is a contest between people in which the victor generally recuperates quickly and the loser takes long to mend, a perpetual competition of colliding explorers in which one must grow or else pay more for remaining the same (pay in sickness, or depression, or anguish for the lost opportunity), but pay or grow.

Therefore one finds words like go, and make it, and with it, and swing: "Go" with its sense that after hours or days or months or years of monotony, boredom, and depression one has finally had one's chance, one has amassed enough energy to meet an exciting opportunity with all one's present talents for the flip (up or down) and so one is ready to go, ready to gamble. Movement is always to be preferred to inaction. In motion a man has a chance, his body is warm, his instincts are quick, and when the crisis comes, whether of love or violence, he can make it, he can win, he can release a little more energy for himself since he hates himself a little less, he can make a little better nervous system, make it a little more possible to go again, to go faster next time and so make more and thus find more people with whom he can swing. For to swing is to communicate, is to convey the rhythms of one's own being to a lover, a friend, or an audience, and—equally necessary—be able to feel the rhythms of their response. To swing with the rhythms of another is to enrich oneself—the conception of the learning process as dug by Hip is that one cannot really learn until one contains within oneself the implicit rhythm of the subject or the person. As an example, I remember once hearing a Negro friend have an intellectual discussion at a party for half an hour with a white girl who was a few years out of college. The Negro literally could not read or write, but he had an extraordinary ear and a fine sense of mimicry. So as the girl spoke, he would detect the particular formal uncertainties in her argument, and in a pleasant (if slightly Southern) English accent, he would respond to one or another facet of her doubts. When she would finish what she felt was a particularly well-articulated idea, he would smile privately and say, "Other-direction . . . do you really believe in that?"

"Well . . . No," the girl would stammer, "now that you get down to it, there is something disgusting about it to me," and she would be off again for five more minutes.

Of course the Negro was not learning anything about the merits and demerits of the argument, but he was learning a great deal about a type of girl he had never met before, and that was what he wanted. Being unable to read or write, he could hardly be interested in ideas nearly as much as in lifemanship, and so he eschewed any attempt to obey the precision or lack of precision in the girl's language, and instead sensed her character (and the values of her social type) by swinging with the nuances of her voice.

So to swing is to be able to learn, and by learning take a step toward making it, toward creating. What is to be created is not nearly so important as the hipster's belief that when he really makes it, he will be able to turn his hand to anything, even to self-discipline. What he must do before that is find his courage at the moment of violence, or equally make it in the act of love, find a little more between his woman and himself, or indeed between his mate and himself (since many hipsters are bisexual), but paramount, imperative, is the necessity to make it because in making it, one is making the new habit, unearthing the new talent which the old frustration denied.

Whereas if you goof (the ugliest word in Hip), if you lapse back into being a frightened stupid child, or if you flip, if you lose your control, reveal the buried weaker more feminine part of your nature, then it is more difficult to swing the next time, your ear is less alive, your bad and energy-wasting habits are further confirmed, you are farther away from being with it. But to be with it is to have grace, is to be closer to the secrets of that inner unconscious life which will nourish you if you can hear it, for you are then nearer to that God which every hipster believes is located in the senses of his body, that trapped, mutilated and nonetheless megalomaniacal God who is It, who is energy, life, sex, force, the Yoga's *prana*, the Reichian's orgone, Lawrence's "blood," Hemingway's "good," the Shavian life-force; "It"; God; not the God of the churches but the unachievable whisper of mystery within the sex, the paradise of limitless energy and perception just beyond the next wave of the next orgasm.

To which a cool cat might reply, "Crazy, man!"

Because, after all, what I have offered above is an hypothesis, no more, and there is not the hipster alive who is not absorbed in his own tumultuous hypotheses. Mine is interesting, mine is way out (on the avenue of the mystery along the road to "It") but still I am just one cat in a world of cool cats, and everything interesting is crazy, or at least so the Squares who do not know how to swing would say.

(And yet crazy is also the self-protective irony of the hipster. Living with questions and not with answers, he is so different in his isolation and in the far reach of his imagination from almost everyone with whom he deals in the outer world of the Square, and meets generally so much enmity, competition, and hatred in the world of Hip, that his isolation is always in danger of turning upon itself, and leaving him indeed just that, crazy.)

If, however, you agree with my hypothesis, if you as a cat are way out too, and we are in the same groove (the universe now being glimpsed as a series of ever-extending radii from the center), why then you say simply, "I dig," because neither knowledge nor imagination comes easily, it is buried in the pain of one's forgotten experience, and so one must work to find it, one must occasionally exhaust oneself by digging into the self in order to perceive the outside. And indeed it is essential to dig the most, for if you do not dig you lose your superiority over the Square, and so you are less likely to be cool (to be in control of a situation because you have swung where the Square has not, or because you have allowed to come to consciousness a pain, a guilt, a shame or a desire which the other has not had the courage to face). To be cool is to be equipped, and if you are equipped it is more difficult for the next cat who comes along to put you down. And of course one can hardly afford to be put down too often, or one is beat, one has lost one's confidence, one has lost one's will, one is impotent in the world of action and so closer to the demeaning flip of becoming a queer, or indeed closer to dying, and therefore it is even more difficult to recover enough energy to try to make it again, because once a cat is beat he has nothing to give, and no one is interested any longer in making it with him. This is the terror of the hipster—to be beat—because once the sweet of sex has deserted him, he still cannot give up the search. It is not granted to the hipster to grow old gracefully—he has been captured too early by the oldest dream of power, the gold fountain of Ponce de León, the fountain of youth where the gold is in the orgasm.

To be beat is therefore a flip, it is a situation beyond one's experience, impossible to anticipate—which indeed in the circular vocabulary of Hip is still another meaning for flip, but then I have given just a few of the connotations of these words. Like most primitive vocabularies each word is a prime symbol and serves a dozen or a hundred functions of communication in the instinctive dialectic through which the hipster perceives his experience, that dialectic of the instantaneous differentials of existence in which one is forever moving forward into more or retreating into less.

5

It is impossible to conceive a new philosophy until one creates a new language, but a new popular language (while it must implicitly contain a new philosophy) does not necessarily present its philosophy overtly. It can be asked then what really is unique in the life-view of Hip which raises its argot above the passing verbal whimsies of the bohemian or the lumpenproletariat.[7]

The answer would be in the psychopathic element of Hip which has almost no interest in viewing human nature, or better, in judging human nature, from a set of standards conceived a priori to the experience, standards inherited from the past. Since Hip sees every answer as posing immediately a new alternative, a new question, its emphasis is on complexity rather than simplicity (such complexity that its language without the illumination of the voice and the articulation of the face and body remains hopelessly incommunicative). Given its emphasis on complexity, Hip abdicates from any conventional moral responsibility because it would argue that the result of our actions are unforeseeable, and so we cannot know if we do good or bad, we cannot even know (in the Joycean sense of the good and the bad) whether we have given energy to another, and indeed if we could, there would still be no idea of what ultimately the other would do with it.

Therefore, men are not seen as good or bad (that they are good-and-bad is taken for granted) but rather each man is glimpsed as a collection of possibilities, some more possible than others (the view of character implicit in Hip) and some humans are considered more capable than others of reaching more possibilities within themselves in less time, provided, and this is the dynamic, provided the particular character can swing at the right time. And here arises the sense of context which differentiates Hip from a Square view of character. Hip sees the context as generally dominating the man, dominating him because his character is less significant than the context in which he must function. Since it is arbitrarily five times more demanding of one's energy to accomplish even an inconsequential action in an unfavorable context than a favorable one, man is then not only his character but his context, since the success or failure of an action in a given context reacts upon the character and therefore affects what the character will be in the next context. What dominates both character and context is the energy available at the moment of intense context.

Character being thus seen as perpetually ambivalent and dynamic enters then into an absolute relativity where there are no truths other than the isolated truths of what each observer feels at each instant of his existence. To take a perhaps unjustified metaphysical extrapolation, it

[7] Rabble; nonrevolutionary workers (literally, "ragged").

is as if the universe which has usually existed conceptually as a Fact (even if the Fact were Berkeley's [8] God) but a Fact which it was the aim of all science and philosophy to reveal, becomes instead a changing reality whose laws are remade at each instant by everything living, but most particularly man, man raised to a neo-medieval summit where the truth is not what one has felt yesterday or what one expects to feel tomorrow but rather truth is no more nor less than what one feels at each instant in the perpetual climax of the present.

What is consequent therefore is the divorce of man from his values, the liberation of the self from the Super-Ego of society. The only Hip morality (but of course it is an ever-present morality) is to do what one feels whenever and wherever it is possible, and—this is how the war of the Hip and the Square begins—to be engaged in one primal battle: to open the limits of the possible for oneself, for oneself alone, because that is one's need. Yet in widening the arena of the possible, one widens it reciprocally for others as well, so that the nihilistic fulfillment of each man's desire contains its antithesis of human co-operation.

If the ethic reduces to Know Thyself and Be Thyself, what makes it radically different from Socratic moderation with its stern conservative respect for the experience of the past is that the Hip ethic is immoderation, childlike in its adoration of the present (and indeed to respect the past means that one must also respect such ugly consequences of the past as the collective murders of the State). It is this adoration of the present which contains the affirmation of Hip, because its ultimate logic surpasses even the unforgettable solution of the Marquis de Sade to sex, private property, and the family, that all men and women have absolute but temporary rights over the bodies of all other men and women—the nihilism of Hip proposes as its final tendency that every social restraint and category be removed, and the affirmation implicit in the proposal is that man would then prove to be more creative than murderous and so would not destroy himself. Which is exactly what separates Hip from the authoritarian philosophies which now appeal to the conservative and liberal temper—what haunts the middle of the twentieth century is that faith in man has been lost, and the appeal of authority has been that it would restrain us from ourselves. Hip, which would return us to ourselves, at no matter what price in individual violence, is the affirmation of the barbarian, for it requires a primitive passion about human nature to believe that individual acts of violence are always to be preferred to the collective violence of the State; it takes literal faith in the creative possibilities of the human being to envisage acs of violence as the catharsis which prepares growth.

Whether the hipster's desire for absolute sexual freedom contains any genuinely radical conception of a different world is of course another matter, and it is possible, since the hipster lives with his hatred,

[8] George Berkeley (1685–1753), philosophical idealist.

that many of them are the material for an elite of storm troopers ready to follow the first truly magnetic leader whose view of mass murder is phrased in a language which reaches their emotions. But given the desperation of his condition as a psychic outlaw, the hipster is equally a candidate for the most reactionary and most radical of movements, and so it is just as possible that many hipsters will come—if the crisis deepens—to a radical comprehension of the horror of society, for even as the radical has had his incommunicable dissent confirmed in his experience by precisely the frustration, the denied opportunities, and the bitter years which his ideas have cost him, so the sexual adventurer deflected from his goal by the implacable animosity of a society constructed to deny the sexual radical as well, may yet come to an equally bitter comprehension of the slow relentless inhumanity of the conservative power which controls him from without and from within. And in being so controlled, denied, and starved into the attrition of conformity, indeed the hipster may come to see that his condition is no more than an exaggeration of the human condition, and if he would be free, then everyone must be free. Yes, this is possible too, for the heart of Hip is its emphasis upon courage at the moment of crisis, and it is pleasant to think that courage contains within itself (as the explanation of its existence) some glimpse of the necessity of life to become more than it has been.

It is obviously not very possible to speculate with sharp focus on the future of the hipster. Certain possibilities must be evident, however, and the most central is that the organic growth of Hip depends on whether the Negro emerges as a dominating force in American life. Since the Negro knows more about the ugliness and danger of life than the white, it is probable that if the Negro can win his equality, he will possess a potential superiority, a superiority so feared that the fear itself has become the underground drama of domestic politics. Like all conservative political fear it is the fear of unforeseeable consequences, for the Negro's equality would tear a profound shift into the psychology, the sexuality, and the moral imagination of every white alive.

With this possible emergence of the Negro, Hip may erupt as a psychically armed rebellion whose sexual impetus may rebound against the antisexual foundation of every organized power in America, and bring into the air such animosities, antipathies, and new conflicts of interest that the mean empty hypocrisies of mass conformity will no longer work. A time of violence, new hysteria, confusion and rebellion will then be likely to replace the time of conformity. At that time, if the liberal should prove realistic in his belief that there is peaceful room for every tendency in American life, then Hip would end by being absorbed as a colorful figure in the tapestry. But if this is not the reality, and the economic, the social, the psychological, and finally the moral crises accompanying the rise of the Negro should prove insupportable, then a time is coming when every political guidepost will be gone, and millions

of liberals will be faced with political dilemmas they have so far succeeded in evading, and with a view of human nature they do not wish to
accept. To take the desegregation of the schools in the South as an example, it is quite likely that the reactionary sees the reality more closely
than the liberal when he argues that the deeper issue is not desegregation but miscegenation. (As a radical I am of course facing in the opposite direction from the White Citizen's Councils—obviously I believe
it is the absolute human right of the Negro to mate with the white, and
matings there will undoubtedly be, for there will be Negro high school
boys brave enough to chance their lives.) But for the average liberal
whose mind has been dulled by the committee-ish cant of the professional liberal, miscegenation is not an issue because he has been told
that the Negro does not desire it. So, when it comes, miscegenation will
be a terror, comparable perhaps to the derangement of the American
Communists when the icons to Stalin came tumbling down. The average
American Communist held to the myth of Stalin for reasons which had
little to do with the political evidence and everything to do with their
psychic necessities. In this sense it is equally a psychic necessity for the
liberal to believe that the Negro and even the reactionary Southern
white are eventually and fundamentally people like himself, capable of
becoming good liberals too if only they can be reached by good liberal
reason. What the liberal cannot bear to admit is the hatred beneath the
skin of a society so unjust that the amount of collective violence buried
in the people is perhaps incapable of being contained, and therefore if
one wants a better world one does well to hold one's breath, for a worse
world is bound to come first, and the dilemma may well be this: given
such hatred, it must either vent itself nihilistically or become turned
into the cold murderous liquidations of the totalitarian state.

6

No matter what its horrors the twentieth century is a vastly exciting
century for its tendency is to reduce all of life to its ultimate alternatives.
One can well wonder if the last war of them all will be between the
blacks and the whites, or between the women and the men, or between
the beautiful and ugly, the pillagers and managers, or the rebels and
the regulators. Which of course is carrying speculation beyond the point
where speculation is still serious, and yet despair at the monotony and
bleakness of the future have become so engrained in the radical temper
that the radical is in danger of abdicating from all imagination. What
a man feels is the impulse for his creative effort, and if an alien but
nonetheless passionate instinct about the meaning of life has come so
unexpectedly from a virtually illiterate people, come out of the most intense conditions of exploitation, cruelty, violence, frustration, and lust,
and yet has succeeded as an instinct in keeping this tortured people alive,
then it is perhaps possible that the Negro holds more of the tail of the

expanding elephant of truth than the radical, and if this is so, the radical humanist could do worse than to brood upon the phenomenon. For if a revolutionary time should come again, there would be a crucial difference if someone had already delineated a neo-Marxian calculus aimed at comprehending every circuit and process of society from ukase to kiss as the communications of human energy—a calculus capable of translating the economic relations of man into his psychological relations and then back again, his productive relations thereby embracing his sexual relations as well, until the crises of capitalism in the twentieth century would yet be understood as the unconscious adaptations of a society to solve its economic imbalance at the expense of a new mass psychological imbalance. It is almost beyond the imagination to conceive of a work in which the drama of human energy is engaged, and a theory of its social currents and dissipations, its imprisonments, expressions, and tragic wastes are fitted into some gigantic synthesis of human action where the body of Marxist thought, and particulary the epic grandeur of *Das Kapital* (that first of the major *psychologies* to approach the mystery of social cruelty so simply and practically as to say that we are a collective body of humans whose life-energy is wasted, displaced, and procedurally stolen as it passes from one of us to another)—where particularly the epic grandeur of *Das Kapital* would find its place in an even more God-like view of human justice and injustice, in some more excrutiating vision of those intimate and institutional processes which lead to our creations and disasters, our growth, our attrition, and our rebellion.

[LEROY] *ELDRIDGE CLEAVER* [JR.] (1935–   )

Eldridge Cleaver, the son of a piano player, was born in Wabaseka, Arkansas, but when his father became a Pullman car waiter, the family moved to Los Angeles, where his parents soon separated. When he was a student in junior high school he was arrested for bicycle theft and sent to the Fred C. Nelles School for Boys. There he learned about hustling pot, and it was on that charge that he was arrested again (he was now in high school and on the football team) and, in 1953, sentenced to the Preston School of Industry and later to Soledad. There he read widely and developed a theory that justified the rape of white women as "an insurrectionary act." Released again, he put his unhappy theory into practice, was arrested, and sentenced to from two to fourteen years in Folsom Prison for assault with intent to kill.

In prison he recognized his folly and began to write "to save myself." He was a follower of Malcolm X, but with his assassination broke with the Black Muslims. In the meantime, he was corresponding

*with civil rights lawyers, first Charles R. Garry and then Beverly
Alexrod, and they interested Edward Keating, one of the founders
of* Ramparts, *in his writing. When Cleaver was paroled in November,
1966, he had already written most of the pieces that were to make
up his book,* Soul on Ice *(1968).*

*That book was published in February, and in the same month
Cleaver began his association with the Black Panthers, under the
leadership of Huey P. Newton. At the end of that year he married
Kathleen Neal. The object of constant police harrassment, he was
arrested again on the charge of violating his parole and was confined to Vacaville for two months, before Charles Garry succeeded in
obtaining his release on a writ of habeas corpus. Ultimately, that
ruling was reversed.*

*In the meantime, as Minister of Information for the Black Panthers,
Cleaver was instrumental in founding the California Peace and
Freedom Party and became its Presidential candidate in the summer
of 1968. But with the reversal of the ruling that had freed him from
Vacaville, he was ordered to give himself up to the police to finish
out his long sentence at Folsom. He was determined not to go back
to prison, convinced that it would mean the end of his life, and on
the day before he was to surrender, he disappeared.*

*Objective observers who have interviewed him are convinced that only
the force of circumstances impelled him into his life of political
activism and that under other circumstances he would have dedicated himself to what he truly wanted, the life of a writer.* Soul on
Ice *is unquestionably the most important book to have come out of
our late years of racial violence. His recently published* Post-Prison
Writings and Speeches *(1969), eloquent in their fury as many of
them are, do not make up for the potential writing that we have
lost.*

FROM **Soul on Ice** *(1968)*[1]

In the autobiographical notes of *Notes of a Native Son,*[2] Baldwin is
frank to confess that, in growing into his version of manhood in Harlem,
he discovered that, since his African heritage had been wiped out and
was not accessible to him, he would appropriate the white man's heritage
and make it his own. This terrible reality, central to the psychic stance

[1] This book is dedicated to the author's attorney, Beverly Axelrad, and contains
moving letters written to her from prison.
[2] See page 1276.

of all American Negroes, revealed to Baldwin that he hated and feared white people. Then he says: "This did not mean that I loved black people; on the contrary, I despised them, possibly because they failed to produce Rembrandt." The psychic distance between love and hate could be the mechanical difference between a smile and a sneer, or it could be the journey of a nervous impulse from the depths of one's brain to the tip of one's toe. But this impulse in its path through North American nerves may, if it is honest, find the passage disputed: may find the leap from the fiber of hate to that of love too taxing on its meager store of energy—and so the long trip back may never be completed, may end in a reconnaissance, a compromise, and then a lie.

Self-hatred takes many forms; sometimes it can be detected by no one, not by the keenest observer, not by the self-hater himself, not by his most intimate friends. Ethnic self-hate is even more difficult to detect. But in American Negroes, this ethnic self-hatred often takes the bizarre form of a racial death-wish, with many and elusive manifestations. Ironically, it provides much of the impetus behind the motivations of integration. And the attempt to suppress or deny such drives in one's psyche leads many American Negroes to become ostentatious separationists, Black Muslims,[3] and back-to-Africa advocates. It is no wonder that Elijah Muhammad[4] could conceive of the process of controlling evolution whereby the white race was brought into being. According to Elijah, about 6300 years ago all the people of the earth were Original Blacks. Secluded on the island of Patmos, a mad black scientist by the name of Yacub set up the machinery for grafting whites out of blacks through the operation of a birth-control system. The population on this island of Patmos was 59,999 and whenever a couple on this island wanted to get married they were only allowed to do so if there was a difference in their color, so that by mating black with those in the population of a brownish color and brown with brown—but never black with black—all traces of the black were eventually eliminated; the process was repeated until all the brown was eliminated, leaving only men of the red race; the red was bleached out, leaving only yellow; then the yellow was bleached out, and only white was left. Thus Yacub, who was long since dead, because this whole process took hundreds of years, had finally succeeded in creating the white devil with the blue eyes of death.

This myth of the creation of the white race, called "Yacub's History," is an inversion of the racial death-wish of American Negroes. Yacub's plan is still being followed by many Negroes today. Quite simply, many Negroes believe, as the principle of assimilation into white America implies, that the race problem in America cannot be settled until all traces of the black race are eliminated. Toward this end, many Negroes loathe

---

[3] A religious organization which stresses the superiority of the black race and urges its separation from the white.

[4] (1897–   ), founder of the Black Muslims.

the very idea of two very dark Negroes mating. The children, they say, will come out ugly. What they mean is that the children are sure to be black, and this is not desirable. From the widespread use of cosmetics to bleach the black out of one's skin and other concoctions to take Africa out of one's hair, to the extreme, resorted to by more Negroes than one might wish to believe, of undergoing nose-thinning and lip-clipping operations, the racial death-wish of American Negroes—Yacub's goal—takes its terrible toll. What has been happening for the past four hundred years is that the white man, through his access to black women, has been pumping his blood and genes into the blacks, has been diluting the blood and genes of the blacks—i.e., has been fulfilling Yacub's plan and accelerating the Negroes' racial death-wish.

The case of James Baldwin aside for a moment, it seems that many Negro homosexuals, acquiescing in this racial death-wish, are outraged and frustrated because in their sickness they are unable to have a baby by a white man. The cross they have to bear is that, already bending over and touching their toes for the white man, the fruit of their miscegenation is not the little half-white offspring of their dreams but an increase in the unwinding of their nerves—though they redouble their efforts and intake of the white man's sperm.

In this land of dichotomies and disunited opposites, those truly concerned with the resurrection of black Americans have had eternally to deal with black intellectuals who have become their own opposites, taking on all of the behavior patterns of their enemy, vices and virtues, in an effort to aspire to alien standards in all respects. The gulf between an audacious, bootlicking Uncle Tom and an intellectual buckdancer is filled only with sophistication and style. On second thought, Uncle Tom comes off much cleaner here because usually he is just trying to survive, choosing to pretend to be something other than his true self in order to please the white man and thus receive favors. Whereas the intellectual sycophant does not pretend to be other than he actually is, but hates what he is and seeks to redefine himself in the image of his white idols. He becomes a white man in a black body. A self-willed, automated slave, he becomes the white man's most valuable tool in oppressing other blacks.

The black homosexual, when his twist has a racial nexus, is an extreme embodiment of this contradiction. The white man has deprived him of his masculinity, castrated him in the center of his burning skull, and when he submits to this change and takes the white man for his lover as well as Big Daddy, he focuses on "whiteness" all the love in his pent up soul and turns the razor edge of hatred against "blackness"—upon himself, what he is, and all those who look like him, remind him of himself. He may even hate the darkness of night.

The racial death-wish is manifested as the driving force in James Baldwin. His hatred for blacks, even as he pleads what he conceives as their cause, makes him the apotheosis of the dilemma in the ethos of the black bourgeoisie who have completely rejected their African heritage, consider the loss irrevocable, and refuse to look again in that direction. This is the root of Baldwin's violent repudiation of Mailer's *The White Negro*.[5]

To understand what is at stake here, and to understand it in terms of the life of this nation, is to know the central fact that the relationship between black and white in America is a power equation, a power struggle, and that this power struggle is not only manifested in the aggregate (civil rights, black nationalism, etc.) but also in the interpersonal relationships, actions, and reactions between blacks and whites where taken into account. When those "two lean cats," Baldwin and Mailer, met in a French living room, it was precisely this power equation that was at work.

It is fascinating to read (in *Nobody Knows My Name*)[6] in what terms this power equation was manifested in Baldwin's immediate reaction to that meeting: "And here we were, suddenly, circling around each other. We liked each other at once, but each was frightened that the other would pull rank. He could have pulled rank on me because he was more famous and *had more money* and also *because he was white;* but I could have pulled rank on him precisely because I was black and knew more about that periphery he so helplessly maligns in *The White Negro* than he could ever hope to know." [Italics added.]

Pulling rank, it would seem, is a very dangerous business, especially when the troops have mutinied and the basis of one's authority, or rank, is devoid of that interdictive power and has become suspect. One would think that for Baldwin, of all people, these hues of black and white were no longer armed with the power to intimidate—and if one thought this, one would be exceedingly wrong: for behind the structure of the thought of Baldwin's quoted above, there lurks the imp of Baldwin's unwinding, of his tension between love and hate—love of the white and hate of the black. And when we dig into this tension we will find that when those "two lean cats" crossed tracks in that French living room, one was a Pussy Cat, the other a Tiger. Baldwin's purr was transmitted magnificently in *The Fire Next Time*.[7] But his work is the fruit of a tree with a poison root. Such succulent fruit, such a painful tree, what a malignant root!

It is ironic, but fascinating for what it reveals about the ferment in the North American soul in our time, that Norman Mailer, the white boy, and James Baldwin, the black boy, encountered each other in the eye of a social storm, traveling in opposite directions; the white boy, with knowledge of white Negroes, was traveling toward a confrontation with

[5] See page 1294.
[6] See page 1275.
[7] See page 1276.

the black, with Africa; while the black boy, with a white mind, was on his way to Europe. Baldwin's nose, like the North-seeking needle on a compass, is forever pointed toward his adopted fatherland, Europe, his by intellectual osmosis and in Africa's stead. What he says of Aimé Césaire [8] one of the greatest black writers of the twentieth century, and intending it as an ironic rebuke, that "he had penetrated into the heart of the great wilderness which was Europe and stolen the sacred fire . . . which . . . was . . . the assurance of his power," seems only too clearly to speak more about Peter than it does about Paul. What Baldwin seems to forget is that Césaire explains that fire, whether sacred or profane, burns. In Baldwin's case, though the fire could not burn the black off his face, it certainly did burn it out of his heart.

I am not interested in denying anything to Baldwin. I, like the entire nation, owe a great debt to him. But throughout the range of his work, from *Go Tell It on the Mountain*, through *Notes of a Native Son*, *Nobody Knows My Name*, *Another Country*, to *The Fire Next Time*,[9] all of which I treasure, there is a decisive quirk in Baldwin's vision which corresponds to his relationship to black people and to masculinity. It was this same quirk, in my opinion, that compelled Baldwin to slander Rufus Scott in *Another Country*, venerate André Gide, repudiate *The White Negro*, and drive the blade of Brutus into the corpse of Richard Wright.[10] As Baldwin has said in *Nobody Knows My Name*, "I think that I know something about the American masculinity which most men of my generation do not know because they have not been menaced by it in the way I have been." O.K., Sugar, but isn't it true that Rufus Scott, the weak, craven-hearted ghost of *Another Country*, bears the same relation to Bigger Thomas of *Native Son*, the black rebel of the ghetto and a man, as you yourself bore to the fallen gaint, Richard Wright, a rebel and a man?

GEORGE WALD (1906–   )

Dr. George Wald is not a literary man by profession or even avocation. He is a distinguished professor of biology at Harvard who has received many honors, among them the Nobel Prize for physiology and medicine (1967) for his achievements in the biochemistry of vision. When the New York Times, *commenting on this award, said that he had "gone far to explain the miracle of vision," its editorialists could hardly have known how many thousands, hundreds of thousands, of people would presently come to think of*

---

[8] (1913–   ), influential French-Martinique politician.
[9] See page 1276.
[10] See page 1103.

George Wald as an expert on perception, on vision, on seeing *in a sense much larger than the precise one for which he had been so justly honored. The daily concerns of life for some men have an astonishing way of turning into powerful metaphors.*

George Wald was born in New York City and took his academic degrees at New York University and Columbia (many honorary degrees followed in due course) and began teaching at Harvard in 1934. Over the years, before the Nobel award, honors fell upon him. They did not seem to touch him, nor did that great one. He pursued his research and he devoted himself to his teaching. He made his rather special subject matter intensely interesting to many of his Radcliffe and Harvard students, but he was not in himself an intense man or much of a public man. He had published his "introductory laboratory manual" called Twenty-six Afternoons of Biology *(1962), and he had, of course, delivered his internationally reported Nobel address, "The Molecular Basis of Visual Excitation" (1968). In our recent bitter years he occasionally took a public position—in 1967, for example, he appeared before the Cambridge City Council to support a petition that a referendum about the war in Vietnam be allowed to be placed on the city's ballot. Generally, however, he was not identified with "causes."*

Nevertheless, he was asked to attend a conference of students and teachers at the Massachusetts Institute of Technology on March 4, 1969, where the general subject to be discussed throughout the day was the responsibility of scientists in a dubious wartime situation. When he arrived, the talk sessions had been going on for some time, they had become increasingly dull, people were becoming noisy, shuffling about, and beginning to drift out of the auditorium after they had endured a long harangue from a California congressman. Then Professor Wald stood up and started talking in what is his characteristic way—voice soft and precise in its enunciation, head thrown back a bit, eyes half closed, no notes. He began: "All of you know that in the last couple of years there has been student unrest breaking at times into violence in many parts of the world. . . ."

At once there was a hush. People who had started to leave came back. People standing sat down. Silence, except for the single uninsistent voice, continuing for twenty dramatic minutes.

Even a person who had spent some years studying William Blake may have felt that for the first time he really knew what Blake meant when he said, "The eye sees more than the heart knows."

A Generation in Search of a Future (1969)

All of you know that in the last couple of years there has been student unrest breaking at times into violence in many parts of the world: in England, Germany, Italy, Spain, Mexico and needless to say, in many parts of this country. There has been a great deal of discussion as to what it all means. Perfectly clearly it means something different in Mexico from what it does in France, and something different in France from what it does in Tokyo, and something different in Tokyo from what it does in this country. Yet unless we are to assume that students have gone crazy all over the world, or that they have just decided that it's the thing to do, there must be some common meaning.

I don't need to go so far afield to look for that meaning. I am a teacher, and at Harvard, I have a class of about 350 students—men and women—most of them freshmen and sophomores. Over these past few years I have felt increasingly that something is terribly wrong—and this year ever so much more than last. Something has gone sour, in teaching and in learning. It's almost as though there were a widespread feeling that education has become irrelevant.

A lecture is much more of a dialogue than many of you probably appreciate. As you lecture, you keep watching the faces; and information keeps coming back to you all the time. I began to feel, particularly this year, that I was missing much of what was coming back. I tried asking the students, but they didn't or couldn't help me very much.

But I think I know what's the matter, even a little better than they do. I think that this whole generation of students is beset with a profound uneasiness. I don't think that they have yet quite defined its source. I think I understand the reasons for their uneasiness even better than they do. What is more, I share their uneasiness.

What's bothering those students? Some of them tell you it's the Vietnam War. I think the Vietnam War is the most shameful episode in the whole of American history. The concept of War Crimes is an American invention. We've committed many War Crimes in Vietnam; but I'll tell you something interesting about that. We were committing War Crimes in World War II, even before Nuremberg trials [1] were held and the principle of war crimes started. The saturation bombing of German cities was a War Crime. Dropping atom bombs on Hiroshima and Nagasaki was a War Crime. If we had lost the war, some of our leaders might have had to answer for those actions.

I've gone through all of that history lately, and I find that there's a gimmick in it. It isn't written out, but I think we established it by precedent. That gimmick is that if one can allege that one is repelling or retaliating for an aggression—after that everything goes. And you see

---

[1] (1945–1946), first international trial for war crimes, when Britain, the United States, and the U.S.S.R. tried National Socialist leaders.

we are living in a world in which all wars are wars of defense. All War Departments are now Defense Departments. This is all part of the double talk of our time. The aggressor is always on the other side. And I suppose this is why our ex-Secretary of State, Dean Rusk [2]—a man in whom repetition takes the place of reason, and stubbornness takes the place of character—went to such pains to insist, as he still insists, that in Vietnam we are repelling an aggression. And if that's what we are doing—so runs the doctrine—anything goes. If the concept of war crimes is ever to mean anything, they will have to be defined as categories of acts, regardless of alleged provocation. But that isn't so now.

I think we've lost that war, as a lot of other people think, too. The Vietnamese have a secret weapon. It's their willingness to die, beyond our willingness to kill. In effect they've been saying, you can kill us, but you'll have to kill a lot of us, you may have to kill all of us. And thank heavens, we are not yet ready to do that.

Yet we have come a long way—far enough to sicken many Americans, far enough even to sicken our fighting men. Far enough so that our national symbols have gone sour. How many of you can sing about "the rockets' red glare, bombs bursting in air" without thinking, those are *our* bombs and *our* rockets bursting over South Vietnamese villages? When those words were written, we were a people struggling for freedom against oppression. Now we are supporting real or thinly disguised military dictatorships all over the world, helping them to control and repress peoples struggling for their freedom.

But that Vietnam War, shameful and terrible as it is, seems to me only an immediate incident in a much larger and more stubborn situation.

Part of my trouble with students is that almost all the students I teach were born since World War II. Just after World War II, a series of new and abnormal procedures came into American life. We regarded them at the time as temporary aberrations. We thought we would get back to normal American life some day. But those procedures have stayed with us now for more than 20 years, and those students of mine have never known anything else. They think those things are normal. They think we've always had a Pentagon, that we have always had a big army, and that we always had a draft. But those are all new things in American life; and I think that they are incompatible with what America meant before.

How many of you realize that just before World War II the entire American army including the Air Force numbered 139,000 men? Then World War II started, but we weren't yet in it; and seeing that there was great trouble in the world, we doubled this army to 268,000 men. Then in World War II it got to be 8 million. And then World War II

---

[2] (1909–   ), ex-professor, appointed Secretary of State (1961–1968) by President Kennedy.

came to an end, and we prepared to go back to a peacetime army somewhat as the American army had always been before. And indeed in 1950 —you think about 1950, our international commitments, the Cold War, the Truman Doctrine, and all the rest of it—in 1950 we got down to 600,000 men.

Now we have 3.5 million men under arms: about 600,000 in Vietnam, about 300,000 more in "support areas" elsewhere in the Pacific, about 250,000 in Germany. And there are a lot at home. Some months ago we were told that 300,000 National Guardsmen and 200,000 reservists—so half a million men—had been specially trained for riot duty in the cities.

I say the Vietnam War is just an immediate incident, because so long as we keep that big an army, it will always find things to do. If the Vietnam War stopped tomorrow, with that big a military establishment, the chances are that we would be in another such adventure abroad or at home before you knew it.

As for the draft: Don't reform the draft—get rid of it.

A peacetime draft is the most un-American thing I know. All the time I was growing up I was told about oppressive Central European countries and Russia, where young men were forced into the army; and I was told what they did about it. They chopped off a finger, or shot off a couple of toes; or better still, if they could manage it, they came to this country. And we understood that, and sympathized, and were glad to welcome them.

Now by present estimates four to six thousand Americans of draft age have left this country for Canada, another two or three thousand have gone to Europe, and it looks as though many more are preparing to emigrate.

A few months ago I received a letter from the Harvard Alumni Bulletin posing a series of questions that students might ask a professor involving what to do about the draft. I was asked to write what I would tell those students. All I had to say to those students was this: If any of them had decided to evade the draft and asked my help, I would help him in any way I could. I would feel as I suppose members of the underground railway felt in pre-Civil War days, helping runaway slaves to get to Canada. It wasn't altogether a popular position then; but what do you think of it now?

A bill to stop the draft was recently introduced in the Senate (S. 503), sponsored by a group of senators that ran the gamut from McGovern [3] and Hatfield [4] to Barry Goldwater.[5] I hope it goes through;

[3] George Stanley McGovern (1922–   ), teacher, author, Senator from South Dakota since 1963.
[4] Mark Hatfield (1922–   ), ex-professor, author, governor of Oregon (1959–1968), Senator since January 1, 1969.
[5] Barry Goldwater (1909–   ), merchant, author, politician, Senator from Arizona (1953–1964, 1969–   ).

but any time I find that Barry Goldwater and I are in agreement, that makes me take another look.

And indeed there are choices in getting rid of the draft. I think that when we get rid of the draft, we must also cut back the size of the armed forces. It seems to me that in peacetime a total of one million men is surely enough. If there is an argument for American military forces of more than one million men in peacetime, I should like to hear that argument debated.

There is another thing being said closely connected with this: that to keep an adequate volunteer army, one would have to raise the pay considerably. That's said so positively and often that people believe it. I don't think it is true.

The great bulk of our present armed forces are genuine volunteers. Among first-term enlistments, 49 percent are true volunteers. Another 30 percent are so-called "reluctant volunteers," persons who volunteer under pressure of the draft. Only 21 percent are draftees. All reenlistments, of course, are true volunteers.

So the great majority of our present armed forces are true volunteers. Whole services are composed entirely of volunteers: the Air Force for example, the Navy, almost all the Marines. That seems like proof to me that present pay rates are adequate. One must add that an Act of Congress in 1967 raised the base pay throughout the services in three installments, the third installment still to come, on April 1, 1969. So it is hard to understand why we are being told that to maintain adequate armed services on a volunteer basis will require large increases in pay; they will cost an extra $17 billion per year. It seems plain to me that we can get all the armed forces we need as volunteers, and at present rates of pay.

But there is something ever so much bigger and more important than the draft. That bigger thing, of course, is what ex-President Eisenhower warned us of, calling it the military-industrial complex. I am sad to say that we must begin to think of it now as the military-industrial-labor union complex. What happened under the plea of the Cold War was not alone that we built up the first big peacetime army in our history, but we institutionalized it. We built, I suppose, the biggest government building in our history to run it, and we institutionalized it.

I don't think we can live with the present military establishment and its $80 billion a year budget, and keep America anything like we have known it in the past. It is corrupting the life of the whole country. It is buying up everything in sight: industries, banks, investors, universities; and lately it seems also to have bought up the labor unions.

The Defense Department is always broke; but some of the things they do with that $80 billion a year would make Buck Rogers [6] envious. For example: the Rocky Mountain Arsenal on the outskirts of Denver

---

[6] Comic strip and comic book character equipped with fantastic weapons.

was manufacturing a deadly nerve poison on such a scale that there was a problem of waste disposal. Nothing daunted, they dug a tunnel two miles deep under Denver, into which they have injected so much poisoned water that beginning a couple of years ago Denver began to experience a series of earth tremors of increasing severity. Now there is a grave fear of a major earthquake. An interesting debate is in progress as to whether Denver will be safer if that lake of poisoned water is removed or left in place. (N.Y. Times, July 4, 1968; Science, Sept. 27, 1968).

Perhaps you have read also of those 6000 sheep that suddenly died in Skull Valley, Utah, killed by another nerve poison—a strange and, I believe, still unexplained accident, since the nearest testing seems to have been 30 miles away.

As for Vietnam, the expenditure of fire power has been frightening. Some of you may still remember Khe Sanh, a hamlet just south of the Demilitarized Zone, where a force of U.S. Marines was beleaguered for a time. During that period we dropped on the perimeter of Khe Sanh more explosives than fell on Japan throughout World War II, and more than fell on the whole of Europe during the years 1942 and 1943.

One of the officers there was quoted as having said afterward, "It looks like the world caught smallpox and died." (N.Y. *Times*, Mar. 28, 1968).

The only point of government is to safeguard and foster life. Our government has become preoccupied with death, with the business of killing and being killed. So-called Defense now absorbs 60 percent of the national budget, and about 12 percent of the Gross National Product.

A lively debate is beginning again on whether or not we should deploy antiballistic missiles, the ABM. I don't have to talk about them, everyone else here is doing that. But I should like to mention a curious circumstance. In September, 1967, or about 1½ years ago, we had a meeting of M.I.T.[7] and Harvard people, including experts on these matters, to talk about whether anything could be done to block the Sentinel system, the deployment of ABM's. Everyone present thought them undesirable; but a few of the most knowledgeable persons took what seemed to be the practical view, "Why fight about a dead issue? It has been decided, the funds have been appropriated. Let's go on from there."

Well, fortunately, it's not a dead issue.

An ABM is a nuclear weapon. It takes a nuclear weapon to stop a nuclear weapon. And our concern must be with the whole issue of nuclear weapons.

There is an entire semantics ready to deal with the sort of thing I am about to say. It involves such phrases as "those are the facts of life." No—they are the facts of death. I don't accept them, and I advise you not to accept them. We are under repeated pressures to accept things

[7] Massachusetts Institute of Technology, Cambridge.

that are presented to us as settled—decisions that have been made. Always there is the thought: let's go on from there! But this time we don't see how to go on. We will have to stick with those issues.

We are told that the United States and Russia between them have by now stockpiled in nuclear weapons approximately the explosive power of 15 tons of TNT for every man, woman and child on earth. And now it is suggested that we must make more. All very regrettable, of course; but those are "the facts of life." We really would like to disarm; but our new Secretary of Defense has made the ingenious proposal that now is the time to greatly increase our nuclear armaments so that we can disarm from a position of strength.

I think all of you know there is no adequate defense against massive nuclear attack. It is both easier and cheaper to circumvent any known nuclear defense system than to provide it. It's all pretty crazy. At the very moment we talk of deploying ABM's, we are also building the MIRV,[8] the weapon to circumvent ABM's.

So far as I know, the most conservative estimates of Americans killed in a major nuclear attack with everything working as well as can be hoped and all foreseeable precautions taken, run to about 50 millions. We have become callous to gruesome statistics, and this seems at first to be only another gruesome statistic. You think, Bang!—and next morning, if you're still there, you read in the newspapers that 50 million people were killed.

But that isn't the way it happens. When we killed close to 200,000 people with those first little, old-fashioned uranium bombs that we dropped on Hiroshima and Nagasaki, about the same number of persons was maimed, blinded, burned, poisoned and otherwise doomed. A lot of them took a long time to die.

That's the way it would be. Not a bang, and a certain number of corpses to bury; but a nation filled with millions of helpless, maimed, tortured and doomed persons, and the survivors huddled with their families in shelters, with guns ready to fight off their neighbors, trying to get some uncontaminated food and water.

A few months ago Sen. Richard Russell [9] of Georgia ended a speech in the Senate with the words: "If we have to start over again with another Adam and Eve, I want them to be Americans; and I want them on this continent and not in Europe." That was a United States senator holding a patriotic speech. Well, here is a Nobel Laureate who thinks that those words are criminally insane.

How real is the threat of full scale nuclear war? I have my own very inexpert idea, but realizing how little I know and fearful that I may be a little paranoid on this subject, I take every opportunity to ask reputed experts. I asked that question of a very distinguished professor of govern-

8 Multiple Independent-targeted Re-entry Vehicles.

9 (1897–   ), Senator since 1933.

ment at Harvard about a month ago. I asked him what sort of odds he would lay on the possibility of full-scale nuclear war within the foreseeable future. "Oh," he said comfortably, "I think I can give you a pretty good answer to that question. I estimate the probability of full-scale nuclear war, provided that the situation remains about as it is now, at 2 percent per year." Anybody can do the simple calculation that shows that 2 percent per year means that the chance of having that full-scale nuclear war by 1990 is about one in three, and by 2000 it is about 50-50.

I think I know what is bothering the students. I think that what we are up against is a generation that is by no means sure that it has a future.

I am growing old, and my future so to speak is already behind me. But there are those students of mine who are in my mind always; and there are my children, two of them now 7 and 9, whose future is infinitely more precious to me than my own. So it isn't just their generation; it's mine too. We're all in it together.

Are we to have a chance to live? We don't ask for prosperity, or security; only for a reasonable chance to live, to work out our destiny in peace and decency. Not to go down in history as the apocalyptic generation.

And it isn't only nuclear war. Another overwhelming threat is in the population explosion. That has not yet even begun to come under control. There is every indication that the world population will double before the year 2000; and there is a widespread expectation of famine on an unprecedented scale in many parts of the world. The experts tend to differ only in their estimates of when those famines will begin. Some think by 1980, others think they can be staved off until 1990, very few expect that they will not occur by the year 2000.

This is the problem. Unless we can be surer than we now are that this generation has a future, nothing else matters. It's not good enough to give it tender loving care, to supply it with breakfast foods, to buy it expensive educations. Those things don't mean anything unless this generation has a future. And we're not sure that it does.

I don't think that there are problems of youth, or student problems. All the real problems I know are grown-up problems.

Perhaps you will think me altogether absurd, or "academic", or hopelessly innocent—that is, until you think of the alternatives—if I say as I do to you now: we have to get rid of those nuclear weapons. There is nothing worth having that can be obtained by nuclear war: nothing material or ideological, no tradition that it can defend. It is utterly self-defeating. Those atom bombs represent an unusable weapon. The only use for an atom bomb is to keep somebody else from using it. It can give us no protection, but only the doubtful satisfaction of retaliation. Nuclear weapons offer us nothing but a balance of terror; and a balance of terror is still terror.

We have to get rid of those atomic weapons, here and everywhere. We cannot live with them.

I think we've reached a point of great decision, not just for our nation, not only for all humanity, but for life upon the Earth. I tell my students, with a feeling of pride that I hope they will share, that the carbon, nitrogen and oxygen that make up 99 percent of our living substance, were cooked in the deep interiors of earlier generations of dying stars. Gathered up from the ends of the universe, over billions of years, eventually they came to form in part the substance of our sun, its planets and ourselves. Three billion years ago life arose upon the Earth. It seems to be the only life in the solar system. Many a star has since been born and died.

About two million years ago, man appeared. He has become the dominant species on the Earth. All other living things, animal and plant, live by his sufferance. He is the custodian of life on Earth. It's a big responsibility.

The thought that we're in competition with Russians or with Chinese is all a mistake, and trivial. Only mutual destruction lies that way. We are one species, with a world to win. There's life all over this universe, but in all the universe we are the only men.

Our business is with life, not death. Our challenge is to give what account we can of what becomes of life in the solar system, this corner of the universe that is our home and, most of all, what becomes of men —all men of all nations, colors and creeds. It has become one world, a world for all men. It is only such a world that now can offer us life and the chance to go on.

Postscript

Probably the history of any present that brings itself up into the immediate Now must end tentatively, with questions rather than with confident assertions, without any ringing, all-inclusive conclusions at least, about the ultimate quality of the achievement, and certainly without any brisk forecasts. A few assessments, however, can be made.

Perhaps the most striking quality of literature in the United States in the past seventy years has been its critical character, its refusal to gloss over any of the limitations of the national experience, and with that, its aspiration to an expanded, an enriched, a more fulfilling experience. In a way, at least until quite recently, it has been the most positive literature of dissent in the modern world, and this has given it an international interest, stature, and respect. If many Americans are still provincial, philistine, conformist, and chauvinistic, its best writers are none of these. They say yes when they can, but do not hesitate, with Melville, to say, "No, in thunder," when they must, which seems to be most of the time.

A second quality, nearly as striking as the first, is the formal restlessness of this literature, its unwillingness to stay within established patterns of perception and statement, its constant need, through the exploratory powers of technique and of stylistic and structural innovation, to push farther the imaginative frontiers. When new developments in foreign literatures suggested paths in this endeavor, American literature did not hesitate to pursue those suggestions, but almost always for its own adventurous ends, almost never in behalf of a mere diffident imitativeness.

Those ends are directed at making the most comprehensive and the most exact estimate possible of the condition of the individual self within the rapidly changing conditions of its national circumstances. Those circumstances have been by no means congenial to the efforts of the creative spirit but, all too often, inimical to it. And yet one often feels that in the very opposition of his culture to his ends, the literary artist has found the means of strengthening himself and his purposes. The opposition of his culture to his ends forces the literary artist out of his innocence, including the innocent dependence on simplistic ideologies and dogmas, into a self-reliant maturity which may indeed often prove to be despairing and is almost inevitably lonely. Does not the great lesson of art lie in this, not only that you are necessarily alone, but further, that you alone are you? And is it not also the fact that only after one has been brought into a full imaginative awareness of this bittersweet truth that any meaningful relationship with others becomes possible and a meaningful, rather than a mechanical, community? American literature now, like other great literatures, helps us into such awareness.

We read much about—and many feel that they experience it daily—the deterioration of the quality of American life, its increasing mechanization, impersonalization, dehumanization. It is against exactly this quality that all our creative efforts pit themselves. Herman Hesse has said that "The true profession of man is to find his way to himself." This is only a variant on what was said earlier by the Dane Søren Kierkegaard: "The task of the human being is to become what he already is." Only man, among the animals, it sometimes seems, is determined to become what he is not. Literature, our own modern literature, and at its most intensely personal, tries to keep alive in us, against all the odds, this supremely important awareness, the sense of what we are.

MARK SCHORER

Index of Authors and Titles

Index of First Lines of Poetry